PRO FOOTBALL GUIDE

W9-AUB-321

1990 EDITION

Editor/Pro Football Guide
DAVE SLOAN

Contributing Editors/Pro Football Guide
HOWARD BALZER
BARRY SIEGEL

Publisher
THOMAS G. OSENTON

Editorial Director of Books and Periodicals
RON SMITH

Published by

The Sporting News

1212 North Lindbergh Boulevard
P.O. Box 56 — St. Louis, MO 63166

Copyright © 1990
The Sporting News Publishing Company

▼▼ A Times Mirror
◤ Company

ISBN 0-89204-363-6   ISSN 0732-1902

TABLE OF CONTENTS

ON THE COVER: San Francisco's Joe Montana had perhaps the best season of his 11-year National Football League career in 1989 as he led the 49ers to 17 victories in 19 games (including playoffs) and the team's fourth Super Bowl title in nine years.
Photograph by Paul Jasienski

THE NATIONAL FOOTBALL LEAGUE

WELLINGTON MARA	PAUL TAGLIABUE	LAMAR HUNT
President	Commissioner	President
National Football	National Football	American Football
Conference	League	Conference

COMMISSIONER'S OFFICE

PAUL TAGLIABUE, Commissioner
JAY MOYER, Executive V.P./Counsel to Commissioner
JOE BROWNE, V.P. of Communications & Development
VAL PINCHBECK, Jr., V.P. of Broadcasting & Production
JIM STEEG, Executive Director for Special Events
TOM SULLIVAN, Treasurer

★   ★   ★

PETE ABITANTE, AFC Director of Information
GREG AIELLO, Director of Communications
PHIL AYOUB, Comptroller
NANCY BEHAR, Asst. Dir. of Broadcasting & Production
JOEL BUSSERT, Director of Player Personnel
JOHN BUZZEO, Director of Administration
DAVE CORNWELL, Asst. Counsel/Dir. of Equal Employment
ROGER GOODELL, Dir. of Club Admin. & International Devel.
BILL GRANHOLM, Director of Special Projects
JIM HEFFERNAN, Director of Public Relations
LAMAR HUNT, President, American Football Conference
CHARLES JACKSON, Asst. Director of Security
WELLINGTON MARA, President, National Football Conference
DICK MAXWELL, Director of Broadcasting Services
SUSAN McCANN-MINOGUE, Asst. Dir. of Special Events
ART McNALLY, Director of Officiating
JAN VAN DUSER, Director of Game Operations
DON WEISS, Director of Planning
WARREN WELSH, Director of Security

LEAGUE OFFICES
410 Park Avenue
New York, New York 10022

TELEPHONE (Area Code 212)
Commissioner's Office: 758-1500

NATIONAL FOOTBALL LEAGUE

FINAL STANDINGS OF THE TEAMS—1989

AMERICAN CONFERENCE

EASTERN DIVISION

	W.	L.	T.	Pct.	Pts.	Opp.
*Buffalo	9	7	0	.563	409	317
Indianapolis	8	8	0	.500	298	301
Miami	8	8	0	.500	331	379
New England	5	11	0	.313	297	391
N.Y. Jets	4	12	0	.250	253	411

CENTRAL DIVISION

	W.	L.	T.	Pct.	Pts.	Opp.
*Cleveland	9	6	1	.594	334	254
†Houston	9	7	0	.563	365	412
†Pittsburgh	9	7	0	.563	265	326
Cincinnati	8	8	0	.500	404	285

WESTERN DIVISION

	W.	L.	T.	Pct.	Pts.	Opp.
*Denver	11	5	0	.688	362	226
Kansas City	8	7	1	.531	318	286
L.A. Raiders	8	8	0	.500	315	297
Seattle	7	9	0	.438	241	327
San Diego	6	10	0	.375	266	290

*Division champion.
†Wild-card team.

NATIONAL CONFERENCE

EASTERN DIVISION

	W.	L.	T.	Pct.	Pts.	Opp.
*N.Y. Giants	12	4	0	.750	348	252
†Philadelphia	11	5	0	.688	342	274
Washington	10	6	0	.625	386	308
Phoenix	5	11	0	.313	258	377
Dallas	1	15	0	.063	204	393

CENTRAL DIVISION

	W.	L.	T.	Pct.	Pts.	Opp.
*Minnesota	10	6	0	.625	351	275
Green Bay	10	6	0	.625	362	356
Detroit	7	9	0	.438	312	364
Chicago	6	10	0	.375	358	377
Tampa Bay	5	11	0	.313	320	419

WESTERN DIVISION

	W.	L.	T.	Pct.	Pts.	Opp.
*San Francisco	14	2	0	.875	442	253
†L.A. Rams	11	5	0	.688	426	344
New Orleans	9	7	0	.563	386	301
Atlanta	3	13	0	.188	279	437

*Division champion.
†Wild-card team.

AFC PLAYOFFS
WILD CARD
Pittsburgh 26, Houston 23 (OT)

SEMIFINALS
Cleveland 34, Buffalo 30
Denver 24, Pittsburgh 23

NFC PLAYOFFS
WILD CARD
L.A. Rams 21, Philadelphia 7

SEMIFINALS
San Francisco 41, Minnesota 13
L.A. Rams 19, N.Y. Giants 13 (OT)

AFC CHAMPIONSHIP
Denver 37, Cleveland 21

NFC CHAMPIONSHIP
San Francisco 30, L.A. Rams 3

NFL CHAMPIONSHIP
San Francisco 55, Denver 10

NATIONAL FOOTBALL LEAGUE CHAMPIONS

Year—Team	Coach
1921—Chicago Staleys†	George Halas
1922—Canton Bulldogs	Guy Chamberlin
1923—Canton Bulldogs	Guy Chamberlin
1924—Cleveland Bulldogs‡	Guy Chamberlin
1925—Chicago Cardinals	Norman Barry
1926—Frankford Yellowjackets	Guy Chamberlin
1927—New York Giants	Earl Potteiger
1928—Providence Steamrollers	Jim Conzelman
1929—Green Bay Packers	Curly Lambeau
1930—Green Bay Packers	Curly Lambeau
1931—Green Bay Packers	Curly Lambeau
1932—Chicago Bears	Ralph Jones
1933—Chicago Bears	George Halas
1934—New York Giants	Steve Owen
1935—Detroit Lions	Potsy Clark
1936—Green Bay Packers	Curly Lambeau
1937—Washington Redskins	Ray Flaherty
1938—New York Giants	Steve Owen
1939—Green Bay Packers	Curly Lambeau
1940—Chicago Bears	George Halas
1941—Chicago Bears	George Halas
1942—Washington Redskins	Ray Flaherty
1943—Chicago Bears	Luke Johnsos & Hunk Anderson
1944—Green Bay Packers	Curly Lambeau
1945—Cleveland Rams	Adam Walsh
1946—Chicago Bears	George Halas
1947—Chicago Cardinals	Jim Conzelman
1948—Philadelphia Eagles	Greasy Neale
1949—Philadelphia Eagles	Greasy Neale
1950—Cleveland Browns	Paul Brown
1951—Los Angeles Rams	Joe Stydahar
1952—Detroit Lions	Buddy Parker
1953—Detroit Lions	Buddy Parker
1954—Cleveland Browns	Paul Brown
1955—Cleveland Browns	Paul Brown
1956—New York Giants	Jim Lee Howell
1957—Detroit Lions	George Wilson
1958—Baltimore Colts	Weeb Ewbank
1959—Baltimore Colts	Weeb Ewbank
1960—Philadelphia Eagles	Buck Shaw
1961—Green Bay Packers	Vince Lombardi
1962—Green Bay Packers	Vince Lombardi
1963—Chicago Bears	George Halas
1964—Cleveland Browns	Blanton Collier
1965—Green Bay Packers	Vince Lombardi
1966—Green Bay Packers*	Vince Lombardi
1967—Green Bay Packers*	Vince Lombardi
1968—Baltimore Colts	Don Shula
1969—Minnesota Vikings	Bud Grant
1970—Baltimore Colts	Don McCafferty
1971—Dallas Cowboys	Tom Landry
1972—Miami Dolphins	Don Shula
1973—Miami Dolphins	Don Shula
1974—Pittsburgh Steelers	Chuck Noll
1975—Pittsburgh Steelers	Chuck Noll
1976—Oakland Raiders	John Madden
1977—Dallas Cowboys	Tom Landry
1978—Pittsburgh Steelers	Chuck Noll
1979—Pittsburgh Steelers	Chuck Noll
1980—Oakland Raiders	Tom Flores
1981—San Francisco 49ers	Bill Walsh
1982—Washington Redskins	Joe Gibbs
1983—Los Angeles Raiders	Tom Flores
1984—San Francisco 49ers	Bill Walsh
1985—Chicago Bears	Mike Ditka
1986—New York Giants	Bill Parcells
1987—Washington Redskins	Joe Gibbs
1988—San Francisco 49ers	Bill Walsh
1989—San Francisco 49ers	George Seifert

†Later called the Chicago Bears.

‡Franchise moved from Canton.

*Won AFL-NFL Championship Game.

ATLANTA FALCONS
(Western Division, National Conference)

Jerry Glanville

Chairman of the Board—Rankin M. Smith, Sr.
President—Taylor Smith
Vice President of Player Personnel—Ken Herock
Director of Pro Scouting—Chuck Connor
Head Coach—Jerry Glanville (5 years: 33-32)

Assistant Coaches:
Secondary—Jimmy Carr
Strength/Conditioning—Tim Jorgensen
Defensive Line—Bill Kollar
Offensive Line—Wayne McDuffie
Wide Receivers—Jimmy Robinson
Quarterbacks—Tom Rossley
Special Teams/Tight Ends—Keith Rowen
Asst. Head Coach/Offense—Ray Sherman
Asst. Head Coach/Defense—Doug Shively

Public Relations Director—Charlie Taylor
(Office Phone: 945-1111—Area Code 404)
Offices—I-85 & Suwanee Rd., Suwanee, Ga. 30174
Stadium—Atlanta-Fulton County Stadium (Capacity: 59,643)
Team Colors—Red, Black, Silver and White
Training Site—Atlanta Falcon Complex, Suwanee, Ga.

1990 SCHEDULE
(All times local.
All games Sunday unless noted otherwise.)

Sept. 9	HOUSTON	4:00
Sept. 16	at Detroit	1:00
Sept. 23	at San Francisco	1:00
Sept. 30	OPEN DATE	
Oct. 7	NEW ORLEANS	1:00
Oct. 14	SAN FRANCISCO	1:00
Oct. 21	at Los Angeles Rams	1:00
Oct. 28	CINCINNATI	8:00
Nov. 4	at Pittsburgh	1:00
Nov. 11	at Chicago	12:00
Nov. 18	PHILADELPHIA	1:00
Nov. 25	at New Orleans	12:00
Dec. 2	at Tampa Bay	1:00
Dec. 9	PHOENIX	1:00
Dec. 16	at Cleveland	1:00
Dec. 23	LOS ANGELES RAMS	1:00
Dec. 30	DALLAS	1:00

1989 RESULTS—(Won 3, Lost 13)

Falcons		Opp.		Att.
21	Los Angeles Rams	31	(H)	38,708
27	Dallas	21	(H)	55,285
9	Indianapolis	13	(A)	57,816
21	Green Bay	23	(A)	54,647
14	Los Angeles Rams	26	(A)	52,182
16	New England	15	(H)	39,697
20	Phoenix	34	(A)	33,894
13	New Orleans	20	(A)	65,153
30	Buffalo	28	(H)	45,267
3	San Francisco	45	(A)	59,914
17	New Orleans	26	(H)	53,173
7	New York Jets	27	(A)	40,429
10	San Francisco	23	(A)	43,128
17	Minnesota	43	(A)	58,116
30	Washington	31	(H)	37,501
24	Detroit	31	(H)	7,092

1989 GAMES STARTED

16 games: Tony Casillas, Shawn Collins, Jamie Dukes, Mike Gann, Houston Hoover, Jessie Tuggle.
15 games: Bill Fralic, Mike Kenn, Chris Miller, John Settle.
14 games: Tim Green, John Rade.
13 games: Aundray Bruce, Tim Gordon, Ron Heller, Ben Thomas.
12 games: Evan Cooper.
11 games: Bobby Butler, Michael Haynes.
10 games: Deion Sanders.
9 games: Stan Clayton, Keith Jones.
8 games: Scott Case.
7 games: Gene Lang.
6 games: Robert Moore.
5 games: Charles Dimry, Floyd Dixon.
4 games: Wayne Radloff, Tommy Robison.
3 games: Michael Reid, Joel Williams.
2 games: Brad Beckman, Rick Bryan.
1 game: Marcus Cotton, Kenny Flowers, Hugh Millen, Ralph Norwood, Gary Wilkins.

ATLANTA FALCONS 1990 VETERAN ROSTER

No.	Name	Pos.	Ht.	Wt.	NFL Exp.	Birth-date	College	Games in '89	How Acquired
82	†Bailey, Stacey	WR	6-1	163	9	2-10-60	San Jose State	15	D3, '82
62	Barrows, Scott	G/C	6-3	280	4	3-31-63	West Virginia	*0	FA, '90
65	†Bingham, Guy	C/G	6-3	260	11	2-25-58	Montana	16	FA, '89
70	Bowick, Tony	NT	6-2	265	2	10- 3-66	UT-Chattanooga	12	D12, '89
94	Brinson, Dana	WR	5-9	167	2	4-10-65	Nebraska	*10	FA, '90
93	Bruce, Aundray	LB	6-5	248	3	4-30-66	Auburn	16	D1, '88
77	Bryan, Rick	DE	6-4	265	7	3-20-62	Oklahoma	2	D1, '84
23	Butler, Bobby	CB	5-11	175	10	5-28-59	Florida State	16	D1, '81
10	Campbell, Scott	QB	6-0	195	5	4-15-62	Purdue	1	FA, '86
25	Case, Scott	CB	6-0	178	7	5-17-62	Oklahoma	14	D2, '84
75	†Casillas, Tony	NT	6-3	280	5	10-26-63	Oklahoma	16	D1, '86
74	†Clayton, Stan	G	6-3	265	3	1-31-65	Penn State	13	D10, '88
98	Cline, Jackie	DE/NT	6-5	280	4	3-13-60	Alabama	*15	UFA, '90
85	Collins, Shawn	WR	6-2	207	2	2-20-67	Northern Arizona	16	D1a, '89
51	Cotton, Marcus	LB	6-3	237	3	8-11-66	Southern California	16	D2, '88
5	Davis, Greg	K	5-11	197	4	10-29-65	The Citadel	6	FA, '89
22	Dimry, Charles	CB	6-0	175	3	1-31-66	Nevada-Las Vegas	16	D5, '88
86	Dixon, Floyd	WR	5-9	170	5	4- 9-64	Stephen F. Austin	16	D6, '86
90	Dixon, Titus	WR	5-6	152	2	6-15-66	Troy State	*4	FA, '90
64	†Dukes, Jamie	G	6-1	285	5	6-14-64	Florida State	16	OFA, '86
86	Floyd, Victor	RB	6-1	201	2	1-24-66	Florida State	*6	FA, '90
79	Fralic, Bill	G	6-5	280	6	10-31-62	Pittsburgh	15	D1, '85
17	†Fulhage, Scott	P	5-10	193	4	11-17-61	Kansas State	16	FA, '89
76	Gann, Mike	DE	6-5	270	6	10-19-63	Notre Dame	16	D2, '85
41	Gordon, Tim	S	6-0	188	4	5- 7-65	Tulsa	14	OFA, '87
99	†Green, Tim	LB	6-2	245	5	12-16-63	Syracuse	16	D1a, '86
	Guidry, Kevin	CB	6-0	176	3	5-16-64	Louisiana State	*3	FA, '90
81	Haynes, Michael	WR	6-0	180	3	12-24-65	Northern Arizona	13	D7, '88
91	Hinnant, Michael	TE	6-3	258	3	9- 8-66	Temple	*5	FA, '90
	Hinton, Chris	T	6-4	295	8	7-31-61	Northwestern	*14	T-Ind, '90
69	†Hoover, Houston	T/G	6-2	290	3	6- 2-65	Jackson State	16	D6a, '88
68	Hunter, John	T	6-8	296	2	8-16-65	Brigham Young	4	FA, '89
43	Johnson, Tracy	RB	6-0	280	2	3-13-60	Alabama	*16	UFA, '90
28	Johnson, Undra	RB	5-9	199	2	1- 8-66	West Virginia	1	FA, '89
38	Jones, Keith	RB	6-1	210	2	3-20-66	Illinois	14	D3, '89
40	Jordan, Brian	S	5-11	202	2	3-29-67	Richmond	4	FA, '89
78	Kenn, Mike	T	6-7	277	13	2- 9-56	Michigan	15	D1, '78
33	†Lang, Gene	RB	5-10	206	7	3-15-62	Louisiana State	15	FA, '88
	Lee, Gary	WR	6-1	201	3	2-12-65	Georgia Tech	*0	FA, '90
63	Lee, Ronnie	T	6-3	277	12	12-24-56	Baylor	*15	UFA, '90
6	McFadden, Paul	K	5-11	166	7	9-24-61	Youngstown State	9	UFA, '89
7	†Millen, Hugh	QB	6-5	216	4	11-22-63	Washington	5	FA, '88
12	Miller, Chris	QB	6-2	200	4	8- 9-65	Oregon	15	D1, '87
84	Milling, James	WR	5-9	156	2	2-14-65	Maryland	*0	FA, '90
39	Mitchell, Roland	CB	5-11	180	4	3-15-64	Texas Tech	*3	FA, '90
36	Paterra, Greg	RB	5-11	211	2	5-11-67	Slippery Rock	10	D11, '89
49	†Primus, James	RB	5-11	196	3	5-18-64	UCLA	5	D9, '88
59	†Rade, John	LB	6-1	240	8	8-31-60	Boise State	15	D8, '83
95	Reid, Michael	LB	6-2	235	4	6-25-64	Wisconsin	16	D7, '87
	Renfroe, Gilbert	QB	6-1	195	R	2-18-63	Tennessee State	*8	FA, '90
	Rison, Andre	WR	5-10	185	2	3-18-67	Michigan State	*16	T-Ind, '90
56	Ruether, Mike	C	6-4	275	5	9-20-62	Texas	*3	UFA, '90
21	Sanders, Deion	CB	6-0	187	2	8- 9-67	Florida State	15	D1, '89
	Scully, John	G	6-6	270	9	8- 2-58	Notre Dame	*0	D4, '81
44	Settle, John	RB	5-9	210	4	6- 2-65	Appalachian State	15	OFA, '87
37	†Shelley, Elbert	S	5-11	180	4	12-24-64	Arkansas State	10	D11, '87
67	Taylor, Malcolm	DE	6-6	280	7	6-20-60	Tennessee State	13	FA, '89
53	Thaxton, Galand	LB	6-1	242	2	10-23-64	Wyoming	16	FA, '89
72	Thomas, Ben	DE	6-3	275	5	7- 2-61	Auburn	16	FA, '89
89	†Thomas, George	WR	5-9	169	2	7-11-64	Nevada-Las Vegas	16	D6, '88
	Tippins, Ken	DE	6-1	240	2	7-22-66	Middle Tennessee State	*6	FA, '90
58	Tuggle, Jessie	LB	5-11	230	4	2-14-65	Valdosta State	16	FA, '87
66	Utt, Ben	G	6-6	293	9	6-13-59	Georgia Tech	*16	UFA, '90
	Watts, Randy	DE/NT	6-6	279	2	6-22-63	Catawba (N.C.)	*0	FA, '90
87	Wilkins, Gary	TE	6-2	235	3	11-23-63	Georgia Tech	13	FA, '89

*Barrows last active with Lions in '88; Brinson played 10 games with Chargers in '89; Cline played 15 games with Dolphins in '89; T. Dixon played 3 games with Jets, 1 with Colts in '89; Floyd played 6 games with Chargers in '89; Guidry played 3 games with Cardinals in '89; Hinnant played 5 games with

Steelers in '89; Hinton played 14 games with Colts in '89; T. Johnson played 16 games with Oilers in '89; G. Lee last active with Lions in '88; R. Lee played 15 games with Dolphins in '89; Milling last active with Falcons in '88; Mitchell played 3 games with Cardinals in '89; Renfroe played 8 games with Toronto-CFL in '89; Rison played 16 games with Colts in '89; Ruether played 3 games with Broncos in '89; Scully missed '89 season because of contract dispute; Tippins played 6 games with Cowboys in '89; Utt played 16 games with Colts in '89; Watts last active with Cowboys in '87.

†Unsigned; subject to developments.

Players lost through Plan B free agency: S Evan Cooper (16 games in '89; to T.B.); TE Ron Heller (15; to Sea.); G Wayne Radloff (11; to S.F.); G Tommy Robison (9; to Hou.); LB Tony Zackery (1; to N.E.).

Also played with Falcons in '89—TE Brad Beckman (15 games); RB Kenny Flowers (16); NT Curtis Maxey (2); S Robert Moore (16); T Ralph Norwood (11); LB Joel Williams (10).

D—Draft; T—Trade; FA—Free Agent; OFA—Original Free Agent; UFA—Unrestricted Free Agent.

ATLANTA FALCONS
1990 DRAFT CHOICES

(Number following name designates order of selection among 331 players drafted.)

Round and Player		Position	College
1. Choice to Indianapolis (a)			
1. BROUSSARD, Steve from Washington (b)	20	RB	Washington State
2. CONNER, Darion	27	LB	Jackson State
3. BARNETT, Oliver	55	DE	Kentucky
4. Choice to Indianapolis (a)			
5. Choice to Denver through Washington and New England (c)			
5. REDDING, Reggie from Indianapolis (a)	121	TE	Cal State-Fullerton
6. PRINGLE, Mike	139	RB	Cal State-Fullerton
7. Choice to New York Jets (d)			
8. EPPS, Tory	195	NT	Memphis State
9. JORDAN, Darrell	222	LB	Northern Arizona
10. SALUM, Donnie	250	LB	Arizona
11. ELLISON, Chris	278	DB	Houston
12. McCARTHY, Shawn	305	P	Purdue

(a) Traded pick and 4th-round pick for tackle Chris Hinton, wide receiver Andre Rison, 5th-round pick and 1st-round pick in 1991, April 20, 1990.

(b) Acquired pick and 2nd-round pick in 1989 for running back Gerald Riggs and 5th-round pick in 1990, April 23, 1989.

(c) Falcons traded pick to Redskins: see (b); Redskins traded pick and another 5th-round pick to Patriots for 4th-round pick, April 22, 1990; Patriots traded pick to Broncos for 4th-round pick in 1991, April 22, 1990.

(d) Traded pick for center Guy Bingham, September 4, 1989.

ATLANTA FALCONS
1990 ROOKIE AND FIRST-YEAR ROSTER

Name	Pos.	Hgt.	Wgt.	Birth-date	College	How Acquired
Adams, Scott	T	6-5	275	9-28-66	Georgia	*FA
Adleta, John	NT	6-4	280	3-21-66	North Carolina State	*FA
Barnett, Oliver	NT	6-3	288	4- 9-66	Kentucky	D3
Bergeson, Eric	DB	5-11	192	1- 1-66	Brigham Young	FA
Broussard, Steve	RB	5-7	201	2-22-67	Washington State	D1
Brown, David	DB	5-10	182	7- 7-66	Ohio State	FA
Conner, Darion	LB	6-2	256	9-28-67	Jackson State	D2
Ellison, Chris	S	5-10	200	12-20-67	Houston	D11
Epps, Tory	NT	6-0	280	5-28-67	Memphis State	D8
Evers, William	CB	5-10	175	9-24-68	Florida A&M	FA
Harris, Greg	WR	5-9	157	12-30-65	Troy State	*FA
Hopkins, Mark	TE	6-1	239	3- 9-67	Central Michigan	FA
Jordan, Darrell	LB	6-3	243	5-17-67	Northern Arizona	D9
Kuipers, Jason	C	6-2	275	2-16-66	Florida State	*FA
McCarthy, Shawn	P	6-6	227	2-22-68	Purdue	D12
Meerton, Joe	TE	6-4	245	3-15-67	Oregon	FA
Norris, Darron	RB	5-9	195	12- 5-66	Texas	*FA
Norwood, Johnny	S	6-2	200	5-16-65	Houston	FA
Parker, Chris	NT/DE	6-5	285	6- 9-66	West Virginia	*FA
Pringle, Mike	RB	5-8	186	10- 1-67	Cal State-Fullerton	D6
Redding, Reggie	G/T	6-3	281	9-22-68	Cal State-Fullerton	D5
Ross, Greg	DE/NT	6-3	268	1-11-67	Memphis State	*FA
Royal, Rickey	CB	5-9	187	7-26-66	Arizona	*FA
Sadowski, Troy	TE	6-5	243	12- 8-65	Georgia	*FA
Salum, Donnie	LB	6-1	233	7-18-66	Arizona	D10
Simien, Kevin	WR	6-4	202	8-25-66	Fort Hays State	*FA
Singer, Paul	QB	6-3	193	3-18-66	Western Illinois	*FA

*Adams: FA Dallas '89, released 9/5; Adleta: FA Tampa Bay '89, released 8/31; Harris: D11 N.Y. Giants '88, released 8/15, awarded on waivers to Tampa Bay 8/16, released 8/27, FA Atlanta '89, released 8/29; Kuipers: FA N.Y. Giants '89, released 8/29; Norris: D9 New England '89, released 8/30, DEV Atlanta 10/17, released 1/9/90; Parker: D8 Detroit '89, released 9/4; Ross: D10 Miami '89, injured reserve (knee), 8/29 through 10/10, released 10/11, DEV Seattle 10/18, released 10/24; Royal: D7 Phoenix '89, released 8/29; Sadowski: D6 Atlanta '89, released 8/30, DEV Atlanta 12/6, released 1/9/90; Simien: FA Atlanta '89, released 8/31, DEV Atlanta 9/6, released 1/9/90; Singer: D8 Atlanta '89, released 8/29, DEV Tampa Bay 9/6, released 11/7, DEV Atlanta 12/6, released 1/9/90.

BUFFALO BILLS
(Eastern Division, American Conference)

Marv Levy

President—Ralph C. Wilson, Jr.
General Manager/V.P., Administration—Bill Polian
Vice-President/Head Coach—Marv Levy (9 years: 61-65)
Asst. G.M./Director of Pro Personnel—Bob Ferguson
Director of Player Personnel—John Butler
Director of Public & Community Relations—Denny Lynch
Manager of Media Relations—Scott Berchtold
    (Office Phone: 648-1800—Area Code 716)
Assistant Coaches:
    Offensive Line—Tom Bresnahan
    Def. Coord./Linebackers—Walt Corey
    Defensive Assistant—Glenn Deadmond
    Special Teams—Bruce DeHaven
    Defensive Line—Chuck Dickerson
    Strength & Conditioning—Rusty Jones
    Off. Quality Control/Tight Ends—Don Lawrence
    Def. Quality Control/Admin. Asst.—Chuck Lester
    Offensive Coordinator—Ted Marchibroda
    Receivers—Nick Nicolau
    Running Backs—Elijah Pitts
    Defensive Backs—Dick Roach
Offices: One Bills Drive, Orchard Park, N. Y. 14127
Stadium—Rich Stadium (Capacity: 80,290)
Team Colors—Royal Blue, White and Scarlet
Training Site—Fredonia State University, Fredonia, N. Y.

1990 SCHEDULE
(All times local.
All games Sunday unless noted otherwise.)

Sept. 9	INDIANAPOLIS	4:00
Sept. 16	at Miami	1:00
Sept. 24	at New York Jets (Mon.)	9:00
Sept. 30	DENVER	1:00
Oct. 7	LOS ANGELES RAIDERS	7:30
Oct. 14	OPEN DATE	
Oct. 21	NEW YORK JETS	1:00
Oct. 28	at New England	1:00
Nov. 4	at Cleveland	1:00
Nov. 11	PHOENIX	1:00
Nov. 18	NEW ENGLAND	1:00
Nov. 26	at Houston (Mon.)	8:00
Dec. 2	PHILADELPHIA	1:00
Dec. 9	at Indianapolis	1:00
Dec. 15	at New York Giants (Sat.)	12:30
Dec. 23	MIAMI	1:00
Dec. 30	at Washington	1:00

1989 RESULTS—(Won 9, Lost 8)

Bills		Opp.		Att.
27	Miami	24	(A)	54,541
14	Denver	28	(H)	78,176
47	Houston (OT)	41	(A)	57,278
31	New England	10	(H)	78,921
14	Indianapolis	37	(A)	58,890
23	Los Angeles Rams	20	(H)	76,231
34	New York Jets	3	(H)	76,811
31	Miami	17	(H)	80,208
28	Atlanta	30	(A)	45,267
30	Indianapolis	7	(H)	79,256
24	New England	33	(A)	49,663
24	Cincinnati	7	(H)	80,074
16	Seattle	17	(A)	57,682
19	New Orleans	22	(H)	70,037
10	San Francisco	21	(A)	60,927
37	New York Jets	0	(A)	21,148

AFC SEMIFINAL GAME

30	Cleveland	34	(A)	77,706

1989 GAMES STARTED

16 games: Howard Ballard, Joe Devlin, Kent Hull, Mark Kelso, Pete Metzelaars, Nate Odomes, Andre Reed, Jim Richter, Fred Smerlas, Bruce Smith, Art Still, Darryl Talley, Thurman Thomas, Will Wolford.

15 games: Ray Bentley, Leonard Smith.

13 games: Kirby Jackson, Jim Kelly.

12 games: Cornelius Bennett, Scott Radecic.

10 games: Larry Kinnebrew.

9 games: Shane Conlan.

7 games: Keith McKeller.

5 games: Flip Johnson.

3 games: Derrick Burroughs, Jamie Mueller, Frank Reich.

2 games: Chris Burkett, Ronnie Harmon, James Lofton.

1 game: Dwight Drane, Butch Rolle.

BUFFALO BILLS 1990 VETERAN ROSTER

No.	Name	Pos.	Ht.	Wt.	NFL Exp.	Birth-date	College	Games in '89	How Acquired
	Adams, Michael	CB	5-10	195	4	4- 5-64	Arkansas State	*3	FA, '90
54	Bailey, Carlton	LB	6-2	237	3	12-15-64	North Carolina	16	D9, '88
75	Ballard, Howard	T	6-6	315	3	11- 3-63	Alabama A&M	16	D11, '87
	Banks, Roy	WR	5-10	190	2	2-19-65	Eastern Illinois	*0	FA, '90
24	Barnes, Lew	WR	5-8	170	3	12-27-62	Oregon	*2	FA, '90
55	Bennett, Cornelius	LB	6-2	235	4	8-25-66	Alabama	12	T-Ind, '87
50	Bentley, Ray	LB	6-2	235	5	11-25-60	Central Michigan	15	FA, '86
	Brady, Kerry	K	6-1	200	2	8-27-63	Hawaii	3	FA, '90
61	Burton, Leonard	T	6-3	277	5	6-18-64	South Carolina	16	D3, '86
90	Cofield, Timmy	LB	6-2	242	5	5-18-63	Elizabeth City State	5	W-NYJ, '89
58	Conlan, Shane	LB	6-3	235	4	4- 3-64	Penn State	10	D1, '87
79	Davis, John	T	6-4	310	4	8-22-65	Georgia Tech	16	UFA, '89
23	Davis, Kenneth	RB	5-10	209	5	4-10-62	Texas Christian	16	UFA, '89
45	†Drane, Dwight	S	6-2	205	5	5- 6-62	Oklahoma	16	SupD, '84
85	Franklin, Darryl	WR	5-11	185	2	2- 4-65	Washington	*0	FA, '89
59	Frerotte, Mitch	G	6-3	280	2	3-30-65	Penn State	*0	FA, '89
7	Gilbert, Gale	QB	6-3	210	3	12-20-61	California	*0	FA, '89
	Glover, Clyde	DE	6-6	280	2	7-16-60	Fresno State	*0	FA, '90
22	†Hagy, John	S	5-11	190	3	12- 9-65	Texas	9	D8, '88
	Hale, Chris	CB	5-7	161	2	1- 4-66	Southern California	16	D7a, '89
67	Hull, Kent	C	6-5	275	5	1-13-61	Mississippi State	16	FA, '86
47	†Jackson, Kirby	CB	5-10	180	4	2- 2-65	Mississippi State	14	FA, '87
	Jarvis, Ralph	DE	6-4	255	1	6- 1-65	Temple	*1	FA, '90
12	Kelly, Jim	QB	6-3	218	5	2-14-60	Miami (Fla.)	13	D1a, '83
38	Kelso, Mark	S	5-11	185	5	7-23-63	William & Mary	16	FA, '86
28	†Kinnebrew, Larry	RB	6-2	256	7	6-11-60	Tennessee State	15	FA, '89
63	†Lingner, Adam	C	6-4	268	8	11- 2-60	Illinois	16	UFA, '89
80	Lofton, James	WR	6-3	190	13	7- 5-56	Stanford	12	FA, '89
84	†McKeller, Keith	TE	6-4	245	3	7- 9-64	Jacksonville State	16	D9, '87
74	Mesner, Bruce	NT	6-5	280	4	3-21-64	Maryland	*0	D8, '87
88	†Metzelaars, Pete	TE	6-7	250	9	5-24-60	Wabash	16	T-Sea, '85
36	Mitchell, Devon	S	6-1	198	3	12-30-62	Iowa	*0	FA, '90
57	Monger, Matt	LB	6-1	240	5	11-15-61	Oklahoma State	9	FA, '89
39	†Mueller, Jamie	RB	6-1	230	4	10- 4-64	Benedictine	14	D3a, '87
11	Norwood, Scott	K	6-0	207	6	7-17-60	James Madison	16	FA, '85
37	Odomes, Nate	CB	5-10	188	4	8-25-65	Wisconsin	16	D2, '87
94	Pike, Mark	DE	6-4	272	4	12-27-63	Georgia Tech	16	D7a, '86
97	Radecic, Scott	LB	6-3	236	7	6-14-62	Penn State	16	W-KC, '87
83	Reed, Andre	WR	6-1	190	6	1-29-64	Kutztown State	16	D4, '85
14	Reich, Frank	QB	6-4	210	6	12- 4-61	Maryland	7	D3, '85
40	Riddick, Robb	RB	6-0	195	8	4-26-57	Millersville State	*0	D9, '81
51	Ritcher, Jim	G	6-3	273	11	5-21-58	North Carolina State	16	D1, '80
87	†Rolle, Butch	TE	6-4	245	5	8-19-64	Michigan State	16	D7b, '86
96	Seals, Leon	DE	6-5	267	4	1-30-64	Jackson State	16	D4, '87
78	Smith, Bruce	DE	6-4	280	6	6-18-63	Virginia Tech	16	D1, '85
30	Smith, Don	RB	5-11	200	3	10-30-63	Mississippi State	*11	UFA, '90
46	Smith, Leonard	S	5-11	202	8	9- 2-60	McNeese State	15	T-Phx, '88
20	Sutton, Mickey	CB/S/KR	5-9	172	5	8-28-60	Montana	*15	FA, '89
56	Talley, Darryl	LB	6-4	235	8	7-10-60	West Virginia	16	D2, '83
89	Tasker, Steve	WR	5-9	185	6	4-10-62	Northwestern	16	W-Hou, '86
34	Thomas, Thurman	RB	5-10	198	3	5-16-66	Oklahoma State	16	D2, '88
	Tuten, Rick	P	6-2	218	1	1- 5-65	Florida State	*2	UFA, '90
69	†Wolford, Will	T	6-5	290	5	5-18-64	Vanderbilt	16	D1a, '86
91	Wright, Jeff	NT	6-2	270	3	6-13-63	Central Missouri State	15	D8a, '88

*Adams played 3 games with Cardinals in '89; Banks last active with Colts in '88; Barnes played 2 games with Chiefs in '89; Franklin, Mesner and Riddick missed '89 season due to injury; Frerotte last active with Bills in '87 and missed '89 season due to injury; Gilbert last active with Seahawks in '86; Glover last active with 49ers in '87; Jarvis played 1 game with Calgary-CFL in '89; Mitchell last active with Lions in '88; D. Smith played 11 games with Buccaneers in '89; Sutton played 3 games with Packers and 12 with Bills in '89; Tuten played 2 games with Eagles in '89.

Players lost through Plan B free agency: RB Ronnie Harmon (15 games in '89; to S.D.); LB Richard Harvey (0; to N.E.); WR Flip Johnson (16; to G.B.); P John Kidd (16; to S.D.); NT Fred Smerlas (16; to S.F.).

Also played with Bills in '89: WR Chris Burkett (2 games), CB Derrick Burroughs (3); CB Wayne Davis (6), G Joe Devlin (16), DE Elston Ridgle (1), DE Art Still (16), KR-DB Erroll Tucker (4).

D—Draft; T—Trade; W—Waivers; FA—Free Agent; UFA—Unrestricted Free Agent; SupD—Supplemental Draft.

BUFFALO BILLS
1990 DRAFT CHOICES

(Number following name designates order of selection among 331 players drafted.)

Round and Player		Position	College
1. WILLIAMS, James	16	DB	Fresno State
2. GARDNER, Carwell	42	RB	Louisville
3. PARKER, Glenn	69	T	Arizona
4. FULLER, Eddie	100	RB	Louisiana State
5. Choice to Kansas City (a)			
6. NIES, John	154	P	Arizona
7. GRIFFITH, Brent from Dallas through New England (b)	166	G	Minnesota-Duluth
7. COLLINS, Brent from New England (c)	170	LB	Carson-Newman
7. DeRIGGI, Fred	181	NT	Syracuse
8. PATTON, Marvcus from Kansas City (a)	208	LB	UCLA
8. Choice exercised in 1989 Supplemental Draft for Brett Young, DB, Oregon			
9. HINES, Clarkston	238	WR	Duke
10. LODISH, Mike	265	DT	UCLA
11. EDWARDS, Al	292	WR	N.W. Louisiana
12. Choice to New England (c)			

(a) Traded 5th-round pick and 8th-round pick in 1989 for defensive end Art Still and 8th-round pick, June 23, 1988.

(b) Bills acquired pick and another 7th-round pick from Patriots for 12th-round pick and 4th-round pick in 1991, April 23, 1990; Patriots had acquired pick and 3rd- and 5th-round picks from Cowboys for 3rd-, 6th- and 8th-round picks, April 22, 1990.

(c) See first part of (b).

BUFFALO BILLS
1990 ROOKIE AND FIRST-YEAR ROSTER

Name	Pos.	Hgt.	Wgt.	Birth-date	College	How Acquired
Aguiar, Louie	P	6-3	210	6-30-66	Utah State	*FA
Collins, Brent	LB	6-1	238	4-27-68	Carson-Newman	D7a
DeRiggi, Fred	NT	6-2	268	1-15-67	Syracuse	D7b
Doctor, Sean	RB	6-1	235	7-10-66	Marshall	*FA
Doctor, Tom	LB	6-0	235	4- 1-65	Canisius	*FA, '89
Dominic, John	DL	6-2	250	7-20-65	Syracuse	*FA
Edwards, Al	WR	5-8	168	5-18-67	Northwestern (La.) State	D11
Finch, Lonnie	DB	6-0	188	10-12-66	Oklahoma	*FA
Franklin, Darryl	WR	5-11	185	2- 4-65	Washington	*FA, '89
Fuller, Eddie	RB	5-9	199	6-22-68	Louisiana State	D4
Gardner, Carwell	FB	6-2	232	11-27-66	Louisville	D2
Gerhart, Thomas	S	6-1	200	6- 4-65	Ohio University	*FA
Gicewicz, Rich	TE	6-4	248	12- 4-65	Michigan State	*FA
Glover, Deval	WR	5-11	184	9-12-66	Syracuse	*FA
Griffith, Brent	T	6-6	300	12-14-65	Minnesota-Duluth	D7
Hines, Clarkston	WR	5-11	163	3-21-67	Duke	D9
Hunter, Jeffrey	DE	6-5	285	4-12-66	Albany State	*FA
Jaworski, Matt	LB	6-1	227	10-23-67	Colgate	*FA
Kolesar, John	WR	5-10	187	4-14-67	Michigan	*D4, '89
Lodish, Mike	DT	6-3	260	8-11-67	UCLA	D10
Marshall, Derrell	T	6-4	305	6- 9-65	Southern California	*FA
Mims, Carl	CB	5-10	180	10-28-65	Sam Houston State	*FA, '89
Nelson, Todd	OL	6-5	290	3-23-66	Wisconsin	*FA
Nies, John	P/K	6-2	199	2-13-67	Arizona	D6
Parker, Glenn	T	6-6	301	4-22-66	Arizona	D3
Patton, Marvcus	LB	6-2	216	5- 1-67	UCLA	D8
Pritchett, Wes	LB	6-4	234	7- 7-66	Notre Dame	*FA
Schnell, Dave	QB	6-2	210	7-15-66	Indiana	FA
Smiley, Tim	S	6-0	190	5-11-66	Arkansas State	*FA
Southall, Cornelius	S	6-2	200	5-25-67	Notre Dame	*FA
Starr, Eric	RB	5-9	194	2- 2-66	North Carolina	*FA
Williams, James	CB	5-10	172	3-30-67	Fresno State	D1

*Aguiar: FA Buffalo '89, released 8/14; S. Doctor: D6 Buffalo '89, reserve/non-football illness (steroids) 8/29 through 9/25, reinstated 9/26, released 10/3; T. Doctor: FA Buffalo '89, reserve/non-football illness (steroids) 8/29 through 9/25, reinstated 9/26, injured reserve (knee) 9/26 through remainder of season; Dominic: FA Pittsburgh '88, released 8/30, FA Indianapolis '89, released 5/19, FA Buffalo 7/5, released 8/30; Finch: FA San Francisco '89, released 8/30, DEV San Francisco 9/28, released 10/18, DEV Cleveland 11/1, released 11/2; Franklin: D8 L.A. Rams '88, released 8/30, FA Buffalo '89, reserve/physically unable to perform (knee) 8/29 through entire season; Gerhart: FA Philadelphia '89, released 8/30; Gicewicz: FA Cincinnati '89, released 9/5, DEV Minnesota 9/19, released 10/18, released 1/29/90; Glover: D10 Miami '89, released 9/5, DEV Buffalo 9/6, released 1/29/90; Hunter: D11 Phoenix '89, released 8/29; Jaworski: FA Buffalo '89, reserve/non-football illness (steroids) 8/29 through 9/25, reinstated 9/26, released 10/3, DEV Buffalo 10/4, released 1/29/90; Kolesar: D4 Buffalo '89, injured reserve (knee) 8/29 through entire season; Marshall: D12 Buffalo '89, released 8/30, DEV Buffalo 9/6, released 1/29/90; Mims: D5 Washington '88, reserve/non-football injury (broken leg) 8/18 through entire season, injured reserve (ankle) 8/29/89 through 9/11, released 9/12, FA Buffalo 10/23, injured reserve (ankle) 10/25 through remainder of season; Nelson: D12 Phoenix '89, released 8/29; Pritchett: D6 Miami '89, released 9/5, DEV Buffalo 9/6, released 1/29/90; Smiley: D5 Washington '89, released 9/5, DEV Washington 9/6, released 9/27, DEV Buffalo 10/3, released 1/29/90; Southall: FA Indianapolis '89, released 8/25; Starr: FA Chicago '88, injured reserve (neck) 8/29 through entire season, unprotected free agent 2/1/89, UFA Miami 4/1, released 8/29.

CHICAGO BEARS
(Central Division, National Conference)

Mike Ditka

Chairman of the Board—Edward McCaskey
President and Chief Executive Officer—Michael McCaskey
Vice-President/Player Personnel—Bill Tobin
Director of Administration—Tim LeFevour
Director of Finance—Ted Phillips
Head Coach—Mike Ditka (8 years: 79-41)
Assistant Coaches:
    Special Teams/Tight Ends—Steve Kazor
    Offensive Coordinator—Greg Landry
    Research & Quality Control—Jim LaRue
    Defensive Line—John Levra
    Linebackers—Dave McGinnis
    Wide Receivers—Vic Rapp
    Running Backs—Johnny Roland
    Offensive Line—Dick Stanfel
    Defensive Coordinator—Vince Tobin
    Defensive Backs—Zaven Yaralian
Director of Public Relations—Bryan Harlan
    (Office Phone: 295-6600 Area Code 708)
Offices—250 N. Washington Rd., Lake Forest, Ill. 60045
Stadium—Soldier Field (Capacity: 66,949)
Team Colors—Orange, Navy Blue and White
Training Site—Halas Hall, Lake Forest, Ill.

1990 SCHEDULE
(All times local.
All games Sunday unless noted otherwise.)

Sept. 9	SEATTLE		12:00
Sept. 16	at Green Bay		12:00
Sept. 23	MINNESOTA		12:00
Sept. 30	at Los Angeles Raiders		1:00
Oct. 7	GREEN BAY		3:00
Oct. 14	LOS ANGELES RAMS		6:30
Oct. 21	OPEN DATE		
Oct. 28	at Phoenix		2:00
Nov. 4	at Tampa Bay		4:00
Nov. 11	ATLANTA		12:00
Nov. 18	at Denver		2:00
Nov. 25	at Minnesota		12:00
Dec. 2	DETROIT		12:00
Dec. 9	at Washington		4:00
Dec. 16	at Detroit		8:00
Dec. 23	TAMPA BAY		12:00
Dec. 29	KANSAS CITY (Sat.)		11:30

1989 RESULTS—(Won 6, Lost 10)

Bears		Opp.		Att.
17	Cincinnati	14	(H)	64,730
38	Minnesota	7	(H)	66,475
47	Detroit	27	(A)	71,418
27	Philadelphia	13	(H)	66,625
35	Tampa Bay	42	(A)	72,077
28	Houston	33	(A)	64,383
7	Cleveland	27	(A)	78,722
20	Los Angeles Rams	10	(H)	65,506
13	Green Bay	14	(A)	56,556
20	Pittsburgh	0	(A)	56,505
31	Tampa Bay	32	(H)	63,826
14	Washington	38	(A)	50,044
16	Minnesota	27	(A)	60,664
17	Detroit	27	(H)	52,650
28	Green Bay	40	(H)	44,781
0	San Francisco	26	(A)	65,675

1989 GAMES STARTED

16 games: Neal Anderson, Mark Bortz, Jay Hilgenberg, Steve McMichael, Brad Muster, Mike Singletary, Tom Thayer, James Thornton.

15 games: Jim Covert, Richard Dent, Vestee Jackson, Keith Van Horne.

14 games: Trace Armstrong, Shaun Gayle, Ron Rivera.

12 games: Dave Duerson.

11 games: Mike Tomczak, Donnell Woolford.

10 games: Dennis McKinnon, John Roper.

9 games: Ron Morris, William Perry.

7 games: Wendell Davis.

6 games: Dennis Gentry.

5 games: Jim Harbaugh.

4 games: Dan Hampton, Jim Morrissey, Lemuel Stinson, David Tate.

3 games: Dick Chapura, Markus Paul.

2 games: Lorenzo Lynch, Tony Woods.

1 game: Maurice Douglass, Chris Dyke, Dante Jones, Mickey Pruitt, John Shannon, John Wojciechowski.

CHICAGO BEARS 1990 VETERAN ROSTER

No.	Name	Pos.	Ht.	Wt.	NFL Exp.	Birth-date	College	Games in '89	How Acquired
35	Anderson, Neal	RB	5-11	210	5	8-14-64	Florida	16	D1, '86
93	Armstrong, Trace	DE	6-4	259	2	10- 5-65	Florida	15	D1a, '89
79	Becker, Kurt	G/T	6-5	280	9	12-22-58	Michigan	*2	UFA, '90
62	Bortz, Mark	G	6-6	272	8	2-12-61	Iowa	16	D8a, '83
86	Boso, Cap	TE	6-3	240	4	9-10-63	Illinois	16	W-StL, '87
8	Buford, Maury	P	6-0	198	9	2-18-60	Texas Tech	16	W-GB, '89
6	Butler, Kevin	K	6-1	204	6	7-24-62	Georgia	16	D4, '85
94	Chapura, Dick	DT	6-3	275	3	6-15-64	Missouri	16	D10, '87
74	†Covert, Jim	T	6-4	278	8	3-22-60	Pittsburgh	15	D1, '83
82	Davis, Wendell	WR	5-11	188	3	1- 3-66	Louisiana State	14	D1a, '88
95	Dent, Richard	DE	6-5	268	8	12-13-60	Tennessee State	15	D8, '83
37	†Douglass, Maurice	CB/S	5-11	200	5	2-12-64	Kentucky	10	D8, '86
22	Duerson, Dave	S	6-1	212	8	11-28-60	Notre Dame	12	D3, '83
68	Dyko, Chris	T	6-6	295	2	3-16-66	Washington State	8	D8a, '89
67	Fontenot, Jerry	C/G	6-3	272	2	11-21-66	Texas A&M	16	D3, '89
23	Gayle, Shaun	S	5-11	194	7	3- 8-62	Ohio State	14	D10, '84
29	Gentry, Dennis	WR	5-8	180	9	2-10-59	Baylor	16	D4, '82
31	Green, Mark	RB	5-11	184	2	3-22-67	Notre Dame	10	D5, '89
99	†Hampton, Dan	DT	6-5	274	12	9-19-57	Arkansas	4	D1, '79
4	Harbaugh, Jim	QB	6-3	204	4	12-23-63	Michigan	12	D1, '87
63	Hilgenberg, Jay	C	6-3	260	10	3-21-60	Iowa	16	OFA, '81
24	†Jackson, Vestee	CB/S	6-0	186	5	8-14-63	Washington	16	D2, '86
92	Johnson, Troy	LB	6-0	236	3	11-10-64	Oklahoma	7	D5, '88
53	Jones, Dante	LB	6-1	236	3	3-23-65	Oklahoma	10	D2, '88
88	Kozlowski, Glen	WR	6-1	205	4	12-31-62	Brigham Young	15	D11, '86
76	McMichael, Steve	DT	6-2	268	11	10-17-57	Texas	16	FA, '81
84	Morris, Ron	WR	6-1	195	4	11-14-64	Southern Methodist	16	D2, '87
51	Morrissey, Jim	LB	6-3	227	6	12-24-62	Michigan State	6	D11, '85
25	Muster, Brad	RB	6-3	231	3	4-11-65	Stanford	16	D1, '88
	Ortego, Keith	WR	6-0	180	4	8-30-63	McNeese State	*0	FA, '90
36	Paul, Markus	S	6-2	199	2	4- 1-66	Syracuse	16	D4, '89
72	Perry, William	DT	6-2	330	6	12-16-62	Clemson	13	D1, '85
52	†Pruitt, Mickey	LB	6-1	215	3	1-10-65	Colorado	14	OFA, '88
59	Rivera, Ron	LB	6-3	240	7	1- 7-62	California	16	D2, '84
55	Roper, John	LB	6-1	228	2	10- 4-65	Texas A&M	16	D2, '89
50	Singletary, Mike	LB	6-0	230	10	10- 9-58	Baylor	16	D2, '81
32	Stinson, Lemuel	CB/S	5-9	159	3	5-10-66	Texas Tech	12	D6, '88
49	Tate, David	S	6-0	177	3	11-22-64	Colorado	14	D8, '88
57	Thayer, Tom	G	6-4	270	4	8-16-61	Notre Dame	16	D4, '83
80	Thornton, Jim	TE	6-2	242	3	2- 8-65	Cal State Fullerton	16	D4, '88
18	†Tomczak, Mike	QB	6-1	198	6	10-23-62	Ohio State	16	FA, '85
78	Van Horne, Keith	T	6-6	283	10	11- 6-57	Southern California	15	D1, '81
	Williams, Scott	FB	6-2	234	4	7-21-62	Georgia	*0	FA, '90
73	†Wojciechowski, John	G/T	6-4	270	4	7-30-63	Michigan State	13	FA, '87
21	Woolford, Donnell	CB/S	5-9	187	2	1- 6-66	Clemson	11	D1, '89

*Becker played 2 games with Rams in '89; Ortego last active with Bears in '87; Williams last active with Lions in '88.

†Unsigned; subject to developments.

Players lost through Plan B free agency: CB/S Lorenzo Lynch (16 games in '89; to Phoe.); WR Dennis McKinnon (16; to Dall.); RB Thomas Sanders (16; to S.D.); DT John Shannon (12; to S.F.); CB/S George Streeter (4; to N.O.); DE Tony Woods (15; to N.O.); OT Dave Zawatson (4; to N.Y.J.).

Retired—Matt Suhey, 10-year running back, 16 games in '89.

Also played with Bears in '89—LB LaSalle Harper (3 games); LB Steve Hyche (6); RB Brian Taylor (5); WR Tom Waddle (3).

D—Draft; W—Waivers; FA—Free Agent; UFA—Unrestricted Free Agent.

CHICAGO BEARS
1990 DRAFT CHOICES

(Number following name designates order of selection among 331 players drafted.)

Round and Player		Position	College
1. CARRIER, Mark	6	DB	Southern Cal
2. WASHINGTON, Fred	32	DT	Texas Christian
2. COX, Ron from San Diego (a)	33	LB	Fresno State
3. RYAN, Tim	61	DT	Southern Cal
3. WILLIS, Peter Tom from Los Angeles Raiders (b)	63	QB	Florida State
4. MOSS, Tony	88	WR	Louisiana State
5. CHAFFEY, Pat	117	RB	Oregon State
6. MANGUM, John	144	DB	Alabama
7. Choice to L.A. Raiders (c)			
7. ANDERSON, Bill from Los Angeles Raiders (c)	176	C	Iowa
8. ROUSE, James	200	RB	Arkansas
9. BAILEY, Johnny	228	RB	Texas A&I
10. PRICE, Terry	255	DT	Texas A&M
11. WHITE, Brent	284	DE	Michigan
11. MATUSZ, Roman from Minnesota through L.A. Raiders (d)	298	T	Pittsburgh
12. COONEY, Anthony	310	DB	Arkansas

(a) Acquired pick for quarterback Jim McMahon, August 18, 1989.
(b) Acquired pick and 1st-round pick in 1989 for wide receiver Willie Gault, July 28, 1988.
(c) Traded 7th-round pick for 7th- and 11th-round picks, April 23, 1990.
(d) Bears acquired pick from Raiders: see (c); Raiders had acquired pick from Vikings for 12th-round pick in 1989, April 24, 1989.

CHICAGO BEARS
1990 ROOKIE AND FIRST-YEAR ROSTER

Name	Pos.	Hgt.	Wgt.	Birth-date	College	How Acquired
Anderson, Bill	C	6-3	267	10- 8-66	Iowa	D7
Armenteros, Alex	S	5-11	196	10-14-65	Bethune-Cookman	*FA
Bailey, Johnny	RB	5-9	180	3-17-67	Texas A&I	D9
Bero, Bryan	RB	6-0	235	5-21-66	Utah	*FA
Brineman, Bruce	G	6-6	287	10- 9-66	Purdue	FA
Carrier, Mark	S	6-1	180	4-28-68	Southern California	D1
Chaffey, Pat	RB	6-1	218	4-19-67	Oregon State	D5
Coley, James	TE	6-3	270	4-13-67	Clemson	*FA
Cooney, Anthony	CB/S	6-0	204	2- 8-67	Arkansas	D12
Cox, Ron	LB	6-2	242	2-27-68	Fresno State	D2a
Elmlinger, Steve	WR	6-0	207	4-30-67	Indiana State	FA
Fumi, Steve	TE	6-5	235	2-24-67	Miami (O.)	FA
Hennings, Ted	DT	6-3	265	12- 1-67	Northern Illinois	FA
Hood, Sloan	RB	5-11	239	1-17-66	Houston	FA
Koch, Allen	G	6-3	280	10- 5-67	Rice	FA
Lott, James	DB	5-9	181	1- 8-67	Clemson	FA
Mangum, John	CB/S	5-10	173	3-16-67	Alabama	D6
Manning, Rod	LB	6-1	224	5-15-67	North Texas	FA
Marconi, Tim	T	6-6	276	3- 4-67	Akron	FA
Matusz, Roman	T	6-4	270	5-10-67	Pittsburgh	D11a
Moses, James	DB	5-11	183	6- 9-67	Howard	FA
Moss, Tony	WR	5-7	169	....	Louisiana State	D4
Pontiflet, Keith	CB	5-11	168	1-19-67	Colorado	FA
Price, Terry	NT	6-4	270	4- 5-68	Texas A&M	D10
Ritchie, Thane	TE	6-3	232	12- 2-65	Wheaton	*FA
Roscoe, Chris	WR	6-1	205	2- 3-68	Hawaii	FA
Rouse, James	RB	6-1	220	12-18-66	Arkansas	D8
Ryan, Tim	NT	6-3	268	9- 8-67	Southern California	D3
Sanders, Glenell	LB	6-0	224	11- 4-66	Louisiana Tech	FA
Smith, Quintin	WR	5-10	172	8-17-68	Kansas	FA
Square, Lorenzo	LB	6-2	232	1- 8-67	Temple	FA
Sullivan, Kent	K	6-0	210	5-15-64	Cal-Lutheran	*FA
Tarasi, Ray	K	5-11	195	6- 8-67	Penn State	FA
Thompson, Steve	LB	6-4	245	12-13-67	Cal-Davis	FA
Tillman, Cedric	WR	5-11	168	4-22-68	Northern Colorado	FA
Tuten, Henry	WR	5-11	184	12- 9-66	Pittsburgh	FA
Washington, Fred	NT	6-2	277	7-11-67	Texas Christian	D2
Westbrooks, David	DE	6-4	252	3-23-68	Howard	FA
White, Brent	DE	6-4	254	2-28-67	Michigan	D11
Williams, Steve	WR	5-9	179	12-19-66	Western Illinois	FA
Willis, Peter Tom	QB	6-2	188	1- 4-67	Florida State	D3a

*Armenteros: FA Chicago '89, released 8/29; Bero: FA Chicago '89, released 9/5, DEV Chicago 9/6, released 1/4/90; Coley: FA Chicago '89, released 9/5, DEV Chicago 9/6, released 1/4/90; Ritchie: FA Pittsburgh '89, released 9/29; Sullivan: FA Chicago '89, released 8/29.

CINCINNATI BENGALS
(Central Division, American Conference)

Sam Wyche

Chairman of the Board—Austin E. Knowlton
President—John Sawyer
Vice-President, General Manager—Paul E. Brown
Assistant General Manager—Michael Brown
Director of Player Personnel—Pete Brown
Assistant Director of Player Personnel—Frank Smouse
Head Coach—Sam Wyche (6 years: 49-46)
Assistant Coaches:
    Offensive Backfield—Jim Anderson
    Quarterbacks—Dana Bible
    Special Teams—Marv Braden
    Tight Ends—Bill Johnson
    Defensive Coordinator—Dick LeBeau
    Offensive Line—Jim McNally
    Linebackers—Dick Selcer
    Receivers—Mike Stock
    Defensive Line—Chuck Studley
    Strength—Kim Wood
Director of Public Relations—Allan Heim
    (Office Phone: 621-3550 Area Code 513)
Offices—200 Riverfront Stadium, Cincinnati, O. 45202
Stadium—Riverfront Stadium (Capacity: 59,755)
Team Colors—Orange, Black and White
Training Site—Wilmington College, Wilmington, O.

1990 SCHEDULE
(All times local.
All games Sunday unless noted otherwise.)

Sept.	9	NEW YORK JETS	4:00
Sept.	16	at San Diego	1:00
Sept.	23	NEW ENGLAND	1:00
Oct.	1	at Seattle (Mon.)	6:00
Oct.	7	at Los Angeles Rams	1:00
Oct.	14	HOUSTON	1:00
Oct.	22	at Cleveland (Mon.)	9:00
Oct.	28	at Atlanta	8:00
Nov.	4	NEW ORLEANS	1:00
Nov.	11	OPEN DATE	
Nov.	18	PITTSBURGH	8:00
Nov.	25	INDIANAPOLIS	1:00
Dec.	2	at Pittsburgh	1:00
Dec.	9	SAN FRANCISCO	1:00
Dec.	16	at Los Angeles Raiders	1:00
Dec.	23	at Houston	12:00
Dec.	30	CLEVELAND	1:00

1989 RESULTS—(Won 8, Lost 8)

Bengals		Opp.		Att.
14	Chicago	17	(A)	64,730
41	Pittsburgh	10	(H)	53,855
21	Cleveland	14	(H)	55,996
21	Kansas City	17	(A)	60,165
26	Pittsburgh	16	(A)	52,785
13	Miami	20	(H)	58,184
12	Indianapolis	23	(H)	57,642
56	Tampa Bay	23	(H)	57,225
7	Los Angeles Raiders	28	(A)	51,080
24	Houston	26	(A)	60,694
42	Detroit	7	(H)	55,720
7	Buffalo	24	(A)	80,074
21	Cleveland	0	(A)	76,236
17	Seattle	24	(H)	54,744
61	Houston	7	(H)	47,510
21	Minnesota	29	(A)	58,829

1989 GAMES STARTED

16 games: Lewis Billups, Jason Buck, Rickey Dixon, David Fulcher, Joe Kelly, Tim Krumrie, Tim McGee, Anthony Munoz, Leon White, Reggie Williams, Carl Zander.

15 games: Eddie Brown, Boomer Esiason, Rodney Holman, Bruce Kozerski, Max Montoya, Bruce Reimers, Eric Thomas.

14 games: James Brooks.

11 games: Jim Skow.

10 games: Brian Blados.

9 games: Eric Ball.

7 games: Joe Walter.

6 games: Stanford Jennings.

5 games: Skip McClendon.

2 games: Paul Jetton, Ickey Woods.

1 game: Barney Bussey, Ira Hillary, Eric Kattus, Jim Riggs, Turk Schonert.

CINCINNATI BENGALS 1990 VETERAN ROSTER

No.	Name	Pos.	Ht.	Wt.	NFL Exp.	Birth-date	College	Games in '89	How Acquired
42	Ball, Eric	RB	6-2	211	2	7- 1-66	UCLA	15	D2, '89
35	Barber, Chris	S	6-0	187	3	11-15-64	North Carolina A&T	8	FA, '87
86	Barber, Mike	WR	5-10	172	2	6-19-67	Marshall	*8	UFA, '90
53	Barker, Leo	LB	6-2	227	7	11-7-59	New Mexico State	16	D7, '84
24	†Billups, Lewis	CB	5-11	179	5	10-10-63	North Alabama	16	D2, '86
74	Blados, Brian	G	6-5	296	7	1-11-62	North Carolina	13	D1b, '84
55	Brady, Ed	LB	6-2	236	7	6-17-60	Illinois	16	W-Ram, '86
3	Breech, Jim	K	5-6	161	12	4-11-56	California	12	FA, '89
21	Brooks, James	RB	5-10	180	10	12-28-58	Auburn	16	T-SD, '84
81	Brown, Eddie	WR	6-0	185	6	12-17-62	Miami (Fla.)	15	D1, '85
99	Buck, Jason	DE	6-5	258	4	7-27-63	Brigham Young	16	D1, '87
27	Bussey, Barney	S	6-0	206	5	5-20-62	South Carolina State	16	D5, '84
34	Carey, Richard	CB	5-9	185	2	5- 6-68	Idaho	7	OFA, '89
29	Dixon, Rickey	S	5-11	196	3	12-26-66	Oklahoma	16	D1, '88
7	Esiason, Boomer	QB	6-5	215	7	4-17-61	Maryland	16	D2, '84
33	†Fulcher, David	S	6-3	234	5	9-28-64	Arizona State	16	D3b, '86
48	Garrett, John	WR	5-11	180	2	3- 2-65	Princeton	1	FA, '89
16	Gelbaugh, Stan	QB	6-3	205	4	12- 4-62	Maryland	1	FA, '90
98	Grant, David	NT	6-4	288	4	9-17-65	West Virginia	16	D4, '88
71	Hammerstein, Mike	DE	6-4	272	4	3-29-63	Michigan	15	D3a, '86
40	Holifield, John	RB	6-0	202	2	7-14-64	West Virginia	3	FA, '88
82	Holman, Rodney	TE	6-3	238	9	4-20-60	Tulane	16	D3, '82
36	Jennings, Stanford	RB	6-1	209	7	3-12-62	Furman	16	D3, '84
68	Jetton, Paul	G	6-4	288	2	10- 6-64	Texas	5	D6, '88
11	Johnson, Lee	P/K	6-2	200	6	11-27-61	Brigham Young	16	FA, '88
77	Jones, Scott	T	6-5	278	2	3-20-66	Washington	15	D12, '89
84	Kattus, Eric	TE	6-5	241	5	3- 4-63	Michigan	16	D4, '86
58	†Kelly, Joe	LB	6-2	235	5	12-11-64	Washington	16	D1, '86
64	Kozerski, Bruce	C	6-4	287	7	4- 2-62	Holy Cross	15	D9, '84
69	Krumrie, Tim	NT	6-2	267	8	5-20-60	Wisconsin	16	D10, '83
88	Martin, Eric	WR	5-10	181	8	11-18-60	Illinois	12	D8, '83
72	McClendon, Skip	DE	6-7	283	4	4- 9-64	Arizona	16	D3a, '87
85	†McGee, Tim	WR	5-10	179	5	8- 7-64	Tennessee	16	D1a, '86
73	Moyer, Ken	T	6-6	292	2	11-19-66	Toledo	8	OFA, '89
78	†Munoz, Anthony	T	6-6	284	11	8-19-58	Southern California	16	D1, '80
	Murray, Dan	LB	6-1	240	1	10-20-66	East Stroudsburg State	*2	FA, '90
23	Palmer, Paul	RB	5-9	181	4	10-14-64	Temple	*14	UFA, '90
75	Reimers, Bruce	T	6-7	294	7	9-18-60	Iowa State	15	D8, '84
87	†Riggs, Jim	TE	6-5	245	4	9-29-63	Clemson	10	D4, '87
70	Skow, Jim	DE	6-3	243	5	6-29-63	Nebraska	11	D3, '86
83	Smith, Kendal	WR	5-9	189	2	11-23-65	Utah State	11	D7, '89
20	Taylor, Craig	RB	5-11	224	2	1- 3-66	West Virginia	12	D6, '89
22	†Thomas, Eric	CB	5-11	181	4	9-11-64	Tulane	16	D2, '87
96	Tuatagaloa, Natu	DE	6-4	265	2	5-25-66	California	14	D5, '89
59	Walker, Kevin	LB	6-3	233	3	12-24-65	Maryland	16	D3, '88
63	Walter, Joe	T	6-6	290	6	6-18-63	Texas Tech	10	D7a, '85
	Wells, Dana	NT	6-0	272	1	8- 5-66	Arizona	1	FA, '90
51	White, Leon	LB	6-3	237	5	10- 4-63	Brigham Young	16	D5, '86
	White, Todd	WR	6-0	195	1	9-15-65	Cal State-Fullerton	*3	FA, '90
41	Wilcots, Solomon	CB	5-11	190	4	10- 9-64	Colorado	16	D8, '87
4	Wilhelm, Erik	QB	6-3	210	2	11-19-65	Oregon State	6	D3, '89
30	Woods, Ickey	RB	6-2	232	2	2-28-66	Nevada-Las Vegas	2	D2, '88
91	Zander, Carl	LB	6-2	235	6	3-23-63	Tennessee	16	D2, '85

*M. Barber played 8 games with 49ers in '89; Murray played 2 games with Colts in '89; Palmer played 5 games with Lions, 9 with Cowboys in '89; T. White played 3 games with British Columbia-CFL in '89.

†Unsigned; subject to developments.

Players lost through Plan B free agency: WR Ira Hillary (16 games in '89; to Minn.); G Max Montoya (16; to L.A. Raid.); OT Rob Woods (0; to K.C.).

Retired—Reggie Williams, 14-year linebacker, 16 games in '89.

Also played with Bengals in '89—PK Jim Gallery (4 games); S Robert Jackson (14); WR Carl Parker (3); LB Rich Romer (5); QB Turk Schonert (7).

D—Draft; T—Trade; W—Waivers; FA—Free Agent; OFA—Original Free Agent; UFA—Unrestricted Free Agent.

CINCINNATI BENGALS
1990 DRAFT CHOICES

(Number following name designates order of selection among 331 players drafted.)

Round and Player		Position	College
1. FRANCIS, James	12	LB	Baylor
2. GREEN, Harold	38	RB	South Carolina
3. CLARK, Bernard	65	LB	Miami (Fla.)
4. BRENNAN, Mike	91	T	Notre Dame
5. JAMES, Lynn	122	WR	Arizona State
6. ODEGARD, Don	150	DB	Nevada-Las Vegas
7. OGLETREE, Craig	177	LB	Auburn
8. WELLSANDT, Doug	204	TE	Washington State
9. PRICE, Mitchell	234	DB	Tulane
10. CRIGLER, Eric	261	T	Murray State
11. O'CONNOR, Tim	288	T	Virginia
12. RILEY, Andre	314	WR	Washington

CINCINNATI BENGALS
1990 ROOKIE AND FIRST-YEAR ROSTER

Name	Pos.	Hgt.	Wgt.	Birth-date	College	How Acquired
Brennan, Mike	T	6-5	282	3-22-67	Notre Dame	D4
Browndyke, David	K	6-2	185	4-16-68	Louisiana State	FA
Chenault, Chris	LB	6-2	240	11-19-65	Kentucky	*FA
Clark, Bernard	LB	6-2	246	1-12-67	Miami (Fla.)	D3
Clark, David	RB	6-0	211	10- 5-68	Dartmouth	FA
Crigler, Eric	T	6-5	295	6- 3-67	Murray State	D10
Egerton, Tim	WR	5-11	165	1- 9-66	Delaware State	FA
Fitzpatrick, Greg	S	6-2	203	8- 7-65	Central State (O.)	FA
Foust, Mike	T	6-5	295	11-13-66	Fresno State	FA
Francis, James	LB	6-4	250	8- 4-68	Baylor	D1
Gaddis, Reggie	DE	6-0	268	7-23-66	Arizona	FA
Green, Anthony	WR	5-11	186	6-12-67	Western Kentucky	FA
Green, Harold	RB	6-2	218	1-29-68	South Carolina	D2
Herds, Tyreese	CB	5-11	195	5- 9-68	Kansas State	FA
Hargrove, Larry	CB/PR	5-8	169	11-18-67	Ohio University	FA
Hodge, David	TE	6-5	235	5-19-67	South Carolina	FA
James, Lynn	WR	6-0	191	1-25-67	Arizona State	D5
Milberg, Stuart	T	6-5	320	11-25-66	Connecticut	FA
Myers, Robert	P	6-1	205	9-11-68	Washington State	FA
Novacek, Jason	TE	6-3	231	5-13-66	Fresno State	FA
O'Connor, Tim	T	6-6	282	10-16-66	Virginia	D11
Patterson, Craig	NT	6-4	305	7-18-64	Brigham Young	FA
Odegard, Don	CB	5-11	177	11-22-66	Nevada-Las Vegas	D6
Ogletree, Craig	LB	6-1	231	4- 2-68	Auburn	D7
Philcox, Todd	QB	6-4	209	9-25-66	Syracuse	*FA
Price, Mitchell	CB	5-9	185	5-10-67	Tulane	D9
Riley, Andre	WR	5-8	174	12- 2-66	Washington	D12
Scrafford, Kirk	OL	6-6	255	3-16-67	Montana	FA
Segrist, Scott	PK	5-9	175	8- 8-66	Texas Tech	FA
Simpson, John	WR	6-0	172	2-24-66	Baylor	*FA
Varano, Rob	WR	6-1	187	7-18-66	Lehigh	FA
Wellsandt, Doug	TE	6-3	250	2- 9-67	Washington State	D8

*Chenault: D8 Cincinnati '89, released 9/5, DEV Cincinnati 9/6, released 1/29/90; Philcox: FA Cincinnati '89, released 9/5, DEV Cincinnati 9/6, released 1/29/90; Simpson: D10 Chicago '89, rights released after failed physical (knee) 5/26, FA Hamilton-CFL 6/3, released 6/22, DEV New England 11/30, released 1/29/90.

CLEVELAND BROWNS
(Central Division, American Conference)

Bud Carson

President—Arthur B. Modell
Executive Vice-President, Legal and Admin.—James Bailey
Executive Vice-President/Football Operations—Ernie Accorsi
Vice President/Asst. to President—David Modell
Treasurer—Mike Srsen
Director of Pro Personnel—Mike Lombardi
Vice President/Director of Public Relations—Kevin Byrne
  (Office Phone: 696-5555 Area Code 216)
Head Coach—Bud Carson (1 year: 9-6-1)
Assistant Coaches:
  Quarterbacks—Zeke Bratkowski
  Defensive Assistant—Mike Faulkiner
  Special Assistant—Hal Hunter
  Strength & Conditioning—Stan Jones
  Special Teams—Paul Lanham
  Receivers—Richard Mann
  Special Assistant—Joe Popp
  Off. Line/Asst. Head Coach—Dan Radakovich
  Running Backs—George Sefcik
  Offensive Coordinator—Jim Shofner
  Special Asst.-Offense/Tight Ends—Lionel Taylor
  Defensive Line—John Teerlinck
  Linebackers—Jim Vechiarella
  Asst. Strength & Conditioning—Gary Wroblewski
Offices—Cleveland Stadium, Cleveland, O. 44114
Stadium—Cleveland Stadium (Capacity: 80,098)
Team Colors—Brown, Orange and White
Training Site—Lakeland Community College, Mentor, O.

1990 SCHEDULE
(All times local.
All games Sunday unless noted otherwise.)

Sept. 9	PITTSBURGH	4:00
Sept. 16	at New York Jets	1:00
Sept. 23	SAN DIEGO	1:00
Sept. 30	at Kansas City	3:00
Oct. 8	at Denver (Mon.)	7:00
Oct. 14	at New Orleans	12:00
Oct. 22	CINCINNATI (Mon.)	9:00
Oct. 28	at San Francisco	1:00
Nov. 4	BUFFALO	1:00
Nov. 11	OPEN DATE	
Nov. 18	HOUSTON	1:00
Nov. 25	MIAMI	1:00
Dec. 2	LOS ANGELES RAMS	1:00
Dec. 9	at Houston	12:00
Dec. 16	ATLANTA	1:00
Dec. 23	at Pittsburgh	1:00
Dec. 30	at Cincinnati	1:00

1989 RESULTS—(Won 10, Lost 7, Tied 1)

Browns		Opp.		Att.
51	Pittsburgh	0	(A)	57,928
38	New York Jets	24	(H)	73,516
14	at Cincinnati	21	(A)	55,996
16	Denver	13	(H)	78,637
10	Miami (OT)	13	(A)	58,444
7	Pittsburgh	17	(H)	78,840
27	Chicago	7	(H)	78,722
28	Houston	17	(H)	78,765
42	Tampa Bay	31	(A)	69,162
17	Seattle	7	(A)	58,978
10	Kansas City (OT)	10	(H)	77,922
10	Detroit	13	(A)	65,624
0	Cincinnati	21	(H)	76,236
17	Indianapolis (OT)	23	(A)	58,550
23	Minnesota (OT)	17	(H)	70,777
24	Houston	20	(A)	58,342

AFC SEMIFINAL GAME

34	Buffalo	30	(H)	77,706

AFC CHAMPIONSHIP GAME

21	Denver	37	(A)	76,005

1989 GAMES STARTED

16 games: Al Baker, Ted Banker, Carl Hairston, Mike Johnson, Bernie Kosar, Clay Matthews, Frank Minnifield, Michael Dean Perry, Gregg Rakoczy, Cody Risien, Webster Slaughter, Felix Wright.

15 games: Robert Banks, Hanford Dixon, Thane Gash, Reggie Langhorne, Tim Manoa.

13 games: Paul Farren, Dan Fike, Ozzie Newsome.

11 games: Eric Metcalf.

10 games: Dave Grayson.

5 games: Van Waiters.

3 games: Rickey Bolden, Tony Jones, Derek Tennell.

2 games: Brian Brennan, Mark Harper, Keith Jones.

1 game: Anthony Blaylock, Tom Gibson, Kevin Mack, Barry Redden, Lawyer Tillman.

CLEVELAND BROWNS 1990 VETERAN ROSTER

No.	Name	Pos.	Ht.	Wt.	NFL Exp.	Birth-date	College	Games in '89	How Acquired
61	Baab, Mike	C	6-4	275	9	12- 6-59	Texas	*16	UFA, '90
9	Bahr, Matt	K	5-10	175	12	7- 6-56	Penn State	16	T-SF, '81
60	Baker, Al	DE	6-6	280	13	12- 9-56	Colorado State	16	UFA, '89
97	Banks, Robert	DE	6-5	255	4	12-10-63	Notre Dame	15	UFA, '89
64	Baugh, Tom	C	6-4	270	5	12- 1-63	Southern Illinois	16	UFA, '89
24	†Blaylock, Tony	CB	5-11	190	3	2-21-65	Winston-Salem	16	D4, '88
77	†Bolden, Rickey	T	6-6	300	7	9- 8-61	Southern Methodist	6	D4, '84
36	Braggs, Stephen	CB	5-9	180	4	8-29-65	Texas	7	D6, '87
86	Brennan, Brian	WR	5-10	185	7	2-15-62	Boston College	14	D4a, '84
	Buczkowski, Bob	DL	6-5	260	3	5- 5-64	Pittsburgh	*4	FA, '90
58	Charlton, Clifford	LB	6-3	240	3	2-16-65	Florida	15	D1, '88
43	Clack, Darryl	RB	5-11	225	5	10-29-63	Arizona State	*8	FA, ''90
26	Clayborn, Raymond	CB	6-1	190	14	1- 2-55	Texas	*14	UFA, '89
49	Dillahunt, Ellis	S	5-11	200	2	11-25-64	East Carolina	*0	FA, '90
	Faaola, Nuu	RB	5-11	220	5	1-15-64	Hawaii	*12	FA, '90
74	†Farren, Paul	T/G	6-6	270	8	12-24-60	Boston University	16	D12, '83
69	Fike, Dan	G	6-7	285	6	6-16-61	Florida	13	FA, '85
30	†Gash, Thane	S	6-0	200	3	9- 1-65	East Tennessee State	16	D7, '88
16	Gay, Everett	WR	6-2	210	2	10-23-64	Texas	*0	FA, '90
	Gibson, Tom	DE	6-8	275	2	12-20-63	Northern Arizona	16	UFA, '89
	Graybill, Mike	OL	6-7	275	2	10-14-66	Boston University	6	D7, '89
56	†Grayson, David	LB	6-3	235	4	2-27-64	Fresno State	16	FA, '87
	Hairston, Carl	DT	6-3	280	15	12-15-52	Maryland-Eastern Shore	16	T-Phi, '84
23	Harper, Mark	CB	5-9	185	5	11- 5-61	Alcorn State	16	FA, '86
51	Johnson, Eddie	LB	6-1	235	10	2- 3-59	Louisville	16	D7, '81
59	†Johnson, Mike	LB	6-1	230	5	11-26-62	Virginia Tech	16	SupD, '84
	Joines, Vernon	WR	6-2	210	2	6-20-65	Maryland	4	FA, '90
95	Jones, Marlon	DE	6-4	270	3	7- 1-64	Central State (O.)	8	FA, '87
66	†Jones, Tony	T	6-5	290	3	5-24-66	Western Carolina	9	FA, '88
	Kauric, Jerry	K	6-0	210	R	6-28-63	None	*18	FA, '90
19	Kosar, Bernie	QB	6-5	215	6	11-25-63	Miami (Fla.)	16	SupD, '85
40	Kramer, Kyle	S	6-3	190	2	1-12-67	Bowling Green State	14	D5, '89
88	Langhorne, Reggie	WR	6-2	205	6	4- 7-63	Elizabeth City State	16	D7, '85
	Lucas, Jeff	T	6-7	285	2	5-30-64	West Virginia	*0	FA, '90
34	Mack, Kevin	FB	6-0	230	6	8- 9-62	Clemson	4	SupD, '84
42	†Manoa, Tim	FB	6-1	245	4	9- 9-64	Penn State	16	D3, '87
57	†Matthews, Clay	LB	6-2	245	13	3-15-56	Southern California	16	D1, '78
53	McGrew, Lawrence	LB	6-6	250	10	7-23-57	Southern California	*16	UFA, '90
21	Metcalf, Eric	RB	5-10	185	2	1-23-68	Texas	16	D1, '89
31	†Minnifield, Frank	CB	5-9	180	7	1- 1-60	Louisville	16	FA, '84
82	Newsome, Ozzie	TE	6-3	225	13	3-16-56	Alabama	16	D1a, '78
89	Oliphant, Mike	WR/RS	5-9	171	2	5-19-63	Puget Sound	14	T-Was, '89
10	Pagel, Mike	QB	6-2	220	9	9-13-60	Arizona State	16	T-Ind, '86
92	Perry, Michael Dean	DE	6-1	285	3	8-27-65	Clemson	16	D2, '88
	Pike, Chris	DT	6-8	300	2	1-13-64	Tulsa	12	T-Phi, '88
73	†Rakoczy, Gregg	C	6-5	280	4	5-18-65	Miami (Fla.)	16	D2, '87
35	†Redden, Barry	FB	5-11	219	9	7-21-60	Richmond	16	T-SD, '89
	Robbins, Kevin	OL	6-6	300	1	12-12-67	Michigan State	1	FA, '89
52	Rose, Ken	LB	6-1	215	4	6- 9-62	Nevada-Las Vegas	*15	UFA, '90
	Simons, Kevin	T	6-4	335	1	4-25-67	Tennessee	1	FA, '89
84	Slaughter, Webster	WR	6-1	170	5	10-19-64	San Diego State	16	D2, '86
	Smith, Dave	T	6-8	290	2	12-12-64	Southern Illinois	*0	FA, '90
96	Stewart, Andrew	DE	6-5	265	2	11-20-65	Cincinnati	16	D4, '89
	Tamm, Ralph	OL	6-4	280	1	3-11-66	West Chester State	*0	UFA, '90
85	Tillman, Lawyer	WR	6-5	230	2	5-20-66	Auburn	14	D2, '89
15	Wagner, Bryan	P	6-1	200	4	3-28-62	Cal State-Northridge	16	UFA, '89
50	Waiters, Van	LB	6-4	250	3	2-27-65	Indiana	16	D3, '88
91	Weston, Rhondy	DL	6-5	280	2	6- 7-66	Florida	*12	UFA, '90
	Wright, Charlie	DB	5-9	175	3	4- 5-65	Tulsa	*0	FA, '90
22	†Wright, Felix	S	6-2	195	6	6-22-59	Drake	16	FA, '85

*Baab played 16 games with Patriots in '89; Buczkowski played 4 games with Cardinals in '89; Clack played 8 games with Cowboys in '89; Clayborn played 14 games with Patriots in '89; Dillahunt last active with Bengals in '88; Faaola played 2 games with Jets, 10 with Dolphins in '89; Gay active for 1 game with Buccaneers in '89, but did not play; Kauric played 18 games with Edmonton-CFL in '89; Lucas last active with Steelers in '87; McGrew played 16 games with Patriots in '89; Rose played 15 games with Jets in '89; Smith last active with Bengals in '89; Tamm inactive for 2 games with Redskins in '89; Weston played 12 games with Buccaneers in '89; C. Wright last active with Cowboys and Buccaneers in '88.

†Unsigned; subject to developments.

Players lost through Plan B free agency: CB Hanford Dixon (15 games in '89; to S.F.); RB Keith Jones (16; to Dall.); S Robert Lyons (9; to Minn.); RB Gerald McNeil (16; to Hou.); TE Ron Middleton (9; to Wash.).

Also played with Browns in '89—OL Ted Banker (16 games); CB Daryl Smith (4); TE Derek Tennell (14).

D—Draft; T—Trade; FA—Free Agent; UFA—Unrestricted Free Agent; SupD—Supplemental Draft.

CLEVELAND BROWNS
1990 DRAFT CHOICES

(Number following name designates order of selection among 331 players drafted.)

Round and Player		Position	College
1. Choice to Green Bay (a)			
2. HOARD, Leroy	45	RB	Michigan
3. PLEASANT, Anthony	73	DE	Tennessee State
4. BARNETT, Harlon	101	DB	Michigan State
5. BURNETT, Rob	129	DE	Syracuse
6. HILLIARD, Randy	157	DB	N.W. Louisiana
7. GALBRAITH, Scott from Miami (b)	178	TE	Southern Cal
7. Choice to San Diego (c)			
8. JONES, Jock	212	LB	Virginia Tech
9. ROWELL, Eugene	240	WR	So. Mississippi
10. WALLACE, Michael	268	DB	Jackson State
11. GORDON, Clemente	296	QB	Grambling
12. SIMIEN, Kerry	323	WR	Texas A&I

(a) Traded pick, running back Herman Fontenot and 3rd- and 5th-round picks in 1989 for 2nd- and 5th-round picks in 1989, April 23, 1989.
(b) Acquired pick for 5th-round pick in 1991, April 23, 1990.
(c) Traded pick for running back Barry Redden, September 4, 1989.

CLEVELAND BROWNS
1990 ROOKIE AND FIRST-YEAR ROSTER

Name	Pos.	Hgt.	Wgt.	Birth-date	College	How Acquired
Barnett, Harlon	S	5-11	195	1- 2-67	Michigan State	D4
Bolyard, Tom	P	6-1	195	1-24-67	Indiana	FA
Burnett, Rob	DT/NT	6-3	271	8-27-67	Syracuse	D5
Darrington, Charles	TE	6-3	245	6-26-66	Kentucky	*FA
Davis, Anthony	CB	5-10	180	1-10-67	Howard	FA
Florence, Anthony	CB	6-0	185	12-11-66	Bethune-Cookman	*FA
Gainer, Derrick	RB	5-10	220	8-15-66	Florida A&M	*FA
Galbraith, Scott	TE	6-2	257	1- 7-67	Southern California	D7
Gordon, Clemente	QB	6-2	222	8-14-67	Grambling State	D11
Graham, Jeff	QB	6-3	196	2- 5-66	Long Beach State	*FA
Hawthorne, George	T	6-6	250	11-23-67	Iowa	FA
Hilliard, Randy	CB	5-10	162	6- 2-67	N.W. Louisiana	D6
Hoard, Leroy	RB	5-10	227	5- 5-68	Michigan	D2
Jefferson, Ben	T	6-8	345	1-15-67	Maryland	*FA
Jones, Jock	LB	6-2	227	3-13-68	Virginia Tech	D8
Owens, Kerry	LB	6-1	233	7-16-66	Arkansas	*FA
Patchan, Matt	T	6-4	275	8-11-66	Miami (Fla.)	*FA
Pleasant, Anthony	DE	6-4	250	1-27-67	Tennessee State	D3
Rowell, Eugene	WR	6-0	184	6-12-68	Southern Mississippi	D9
Scott, Pete	G	6-4	276	1- 6-68	Missouri	FA
Simien, Kerry	WR/KR	5-9	181	12-14-66	Texas A&I	D12
Sprinkles, Kevin	TE	6-5	251	10- 8-67	Texas Tech	FA
Talley, John	TE	6-8	250	12-19-64	West Virginia	*FA
Tobey, Bryan	RB	6-1	250	4- 7-65	Grambling	*FA
Wallace, Mike	CB	6-0	182	8-28-68	Jackson State	D10

*Darrington: D9 Washington '89, released 8/30; Florence: D4 Tampa Bay '89, released 9/5, DEV Tampa Bay 9/6, released 1/29/90; Gainer: D8 Los Angeles Raiders '89, released 9/8, DEV Raiders 9/9, released 11/30, DEV Cleveland 12/12, released 1/29/90; Graham: D4 Green Bay '89, rights traded to Washington for rights to wide receiver Erik Affholter and 5th- and 8th-round picks in '89 draft, 4/23, released 8/30, DEV Cleveland 9/6, released 1/29/90; Jefferson: FA Indianapolis '89, released 9/5, DEV Indianapolis 9/6, released 10/19, DEV Cleveland 12/12, released 1/29/90; Owens: D4 Cincinnati '89, released 9/5, DEV Cleveland 9/7, released 1/29/90; Patchan: D3 Philadelphia '88, injured reserve (shoulder) 8/30 through entire season, released 9/5/89, DEV Miami 9/20, released 10/3; Talley: FA Phoenix '88, released 8/8, FA Cleveland '89, released 9/5, DEV Cleveland 9/6, released 9/21, DEV Miami 9/28, released 10/19, DEV Philadelphia 10/25, released 1/9/90; Tobey: D8 Kansas City '89, released 8/30.

DALLAS COWBOYS
(Eastern Division, National Conference)

Jimmy Johnson

President/General Manager—Jerry Jones
Head Coach—Jimmy Johnson (1 year: 1-15)
Director of Player Personnel—Bob Ackles
Assistant Coaches:
  Receivers—Hubbard Alexander
  Special Teams—Joe Avezzano
  Running Backs—Joe Brodsky
  Defensive Assistant—Dave Campo
  Defensive Line—Butch Davis
  Kickers/Quality Control—Steve Hoffman
  Tight Ends—Alan Lowry
  Defensive Backs—Dick Nolan
  Off. Coord./Quarterbacks—Dave Shula
  Def. Coordinator/Linebackers—Dave Wannstedt
  Offensive Line—Tony Wise
  Conditioning—Mike Woicik
Public Relations Director—Greg Aiello
  (Office Phone: 556-9900—Area Code 214)
Offices—One Cowboys Parkway, Irving, Tex. 75063
Stadium—Texas Stadium (Capacity: 65,024)
Team Colors—Royal Blue, Metallic Blue and White
Training Site—St. Edward's University, Austin, Tex.

1990 SCHEDULE
(All times local.
All games Sunday unless noted otherwise.)

Sept. 9	SAN DIEGO	3:00
Sept. 16	NEW YORK GIANTS	3:00
Sept. 23	at Washington	1:00
Sept. 30	at New York Giants	1:00
Oct. 7	TAMPA BAY	12:00
Oct. 14	at Phoenix	1:00
Oct. 21	at Tampa Bay	1:00
Oct. 28	PHILADELPHIA	12:00
Nov. 4	at New York Jets	1:00
Nov. 11	SAN FRANCISCO	7:00
Nov. 18	at Los Angeles Rams	1:00
Nov. 22	WASHINGTON (Thanksgiving)	3:00
Dec. 2	NEW ORLEANS	3:00
Dec. 9	OPEN DATE	
Dec. 16	PHOENIX	12:00
Dec. 23	at Philadelphia	1:00
Dec. 30	at Atlanta	1:00

1989 RESULTS—(Won 1, Lost 15)

Cowboys		Opp.		Att.
0	New Orleans	28	(A)	66,977
21	Atlanta	27	(A)	55,285
7	Washington	30	(H)	63,200
13	New York Giants	30	(H)	51,785
13	Green Bay	31	(A)	56,656
14	San Francisco	31	(H)	61,077
28	Kansas City	36	(A)	76,841
10	Phoenix	19	(H)	44,431
13	Washington	3	(A)	53,187
20	Phoenix	24	(A)	49,657
14	Miami	17	(H)	56,044
0	Philadelphia	27	(H)	54,444
31	Los Angeles Rams	35	(H)	46,100
10	Philadelphia	20	(A)	59,842
0	New York Giants	15	(A)	72,141
10	Green Bay	20	(H)	41,265

1989 GAMES STARTED

16 games: Vince Albritton, Steve Folsom, Ray Horton, Jim Jeffcoat, Crawford Ker, Eugene Lockhart, Nate Newton, Mark Tuinei.

14 games: Willie Broughton, Everson Walls.

13 games: Kevin Gogan, Dean Hamel, Ken Norton.

12 games: Jack Del Rio.

11 games: Troy Aikman, Kelvin Martin, Robert Williams.

10 games: Daryl Johnston, Ed Jones.

8 games: Paul Palmer, Tom Rafferty, Derrick Shepard.

7 games: James Dixon.

6 games: Michael Irvin.

5 games: Danny Noonan, Broderick Sargent, Tony Tolbert, Herschel Walker, Steve Walsh.

4 games: Ron Francis, Randy Shannon, Mark Stepnoski, Bob White.

3 games: Ron Burton, Manny Hendrix.

2 games: Dave Widell.

1 game: Cornell Burbage, Darryl Clack, Bernard Ford, Kevin Scott, Jesse Solomon, Jeff Zimmerman.

DALLAS COWBOYS 1990 VETERAN ROSTER

No.	Name	Pos.	Ht.	Wt.	NFL Exp.	Birth-date	College	Games in '89	How Acquired
32	Agee, Tommie	RB	6-0	218	3	2-22-64	Auburn	*9	UFA, '90
8	Aikman, Troy	QB	6-4	216	2	11-21-66	UCLA	11	D1, '89
36	Albritton, Vince	S	6-2	214	7	7-23-62	Washington	16	OFA, '84
31	Ankrom, Scott	S	6-1	194	2	1- 4-66	Texas Christian	10	D12, '89
40	Bates, Bill	S	6-1	199	8	6- 6-61	Tennessee	16	OFA, '83
79	Broughton, Willie	DT	6-5	275	4	9- 9-64	Miami (Fla.)	16	FA, '89
75	Carter, Jon	DT	6-4	273	2	3-12-65	Pittsburgh	13	FA, '89
	Cheek, Louis	T	6-6	295	3	10- 6-64	Texas A&M	*13	UFA, '90
58	Cooks, Terrence	LB	6-0	230	2	10-25-66	Nicholls State	*3	UFA, '90
	Delaney, Jarrod	WR	6-1	205	1	12- 1-66	Texas Christian	*1	FA, '90
55	Del Rio, Jack	LB	6-4	236	6	4- 4-63	Southern California	14	FA, '89
86	Dixon, James	WR	5-10	181	2	2- 2-67	Houston	16	W-Det, '89
	Flagler, Terrence	RB	6-0	200	4	9-24-64	Clemson	*15	T-SF, '90
85	Folsom, Steve	TE	6-5	240	5	3-21-58	Utah	16	FA, '87
38	Francis, Ron	CB	5-9	186	4	4- 7-64	Baylor	15	D2, '87
	Gibson, Antonio	S	6-3	204	5	7- 5-62	Cincinnati	*16	UFA, '90
66	Gogan, Kevin	T	6-7	309	4	11- 2-64	Washington	13	D8, '87
60	Hamel, Dean	DT	6-3	276	6	7- 7-61	Tulsa	16	T-Was., '89
	Harris, Rod	WR	5-10	183	2	11-14-66	Texas A&M	*11	UFA, '90
45	Hendrix, Manny	CB	5-10	186	5	10-20-64	Utah	16	OFA, '86
30	Holt, Issiac	CB	6-2	202	6	10- 4-62	Alcorn State	*14	T-Min., '89
20	Horton, Ray	S	5-11	187	8	4-12-60	Washington	16	UFA, '89
99	Howard, David	LB	6-2	230	6	12- 8-61	Long Beach State	*16	T-Min., '89
88	Irvin, Michael	WR	6-2	202	3	3- 5-66	Miami (Fla.)	6	D1, '88
77	Jeffcoat, Jim	DE	6-5	256	8	4- 1-61	Arizona State	16	D1, '83
84	Jennings, Keith	TE	6-4	251	2	5-19-66	Clemson	10	D5, '89
	Johnson, Greg	G	6-4	295	2	12-19-64	Oklahoma	*0	UFA, '90
	Johnson, Steve	TE	6-6	245	2	6-22-65	Virginia Tech	*0	FA, '90
91	Johnson, Walter	LB	6-0	240	4	11-13-63	Louisiana Tech	*15	UFA, '90
48	Johnston, Daryl	RB	6-2	234	2	2-10-66	Syracuse	16	D2a, '89
	Jones, Jimmie	RB	5-10	182	2	2- 5-66	Nebraska	*16	UFA, '90
68	Ker, Crawford	G	6-3	285	6	5- 5-62	Florida	16	D3, '85
15	Laufenberg, Babe	QB	6-3	203	5	12-5-59	Indiana	3	FA, '89
	Lee, Greg	CB/S	6-1	204	2	1-15-65	Arkansas State	*0	FA, '90
56	Lockhart, Eugene	LB	6-2	233	7	3- 8-61	Houston	16	D6, '84
83	Martin, Kelvin	WR	5-9	162	4	5-14-65	Boston College	11	D4, '87
81	McKinnon, Dennis	WR	6-1	185	7	8-22-61	Florida State	*16	UFA, '90
61	Newton, Nate	G	6-3	318	5	12-20-61	Florida A&M	16	FA, '86
73	Noonan, Danny	DT	6-4	270	4	7-14-65	Nebraska	7	D1, '87
51	Norton, Ken	LB	6-2	234	3	9-29-66	UCLA	13	D2, '88
89	Novacek, Jay	TE	6-4	235	6	10-24-62	Wyoming	*16	UFA, '90
	Robinson, Lybrant	DE	6-5	250	2	8-31-64	Delaware State	*5	UFA, '90
39	Sargent, Broderick	RB	5-11	220	4	9-16-62	Baylor	14	FA, '89
4	Saxon, Mike	P	6-3	198	6	7-10-62	San Diego State	16	FA, '85
35	Scott, Kevin	RB	5-9	177	3	10-24-63	Stanford	3	UFA, '89
94	Shannon, Randy	LB	6-1	221	2	2-24-66	Miami (Fla.)	16	D11, '89
87	Shepard, Derrick	WR	5-10	187	3	1-22-64	Oklahoma	*15	W-NO, '89
65	Slaton, Tony	C/G	6-3	280	7	4-12-61	Southern California	*15	UFA, '90
	Smith, Tim	RB	5-11	222	3	1-21-64	Texas Tech	*0	FA, '90
57	Smith, Vinson	LB	6-2	230	2	7- 3-65	East Carolina	*0	UFA, '90
54	†Solomon, Jesse	LB	6-0	235	5	11- 4-63	Florida State	*15	T-Min., '89
	Spears, Anthony	DT	6-5	285	1	11- 4-65	Portland State	*0	UFA, '90
70	Stepnoski, Mark	C/G	6-2	269	2	1-20-67	Pittsburgh	16	D3, '89
	Stubbs, Daniel	DE	6-4	260	3	1- 3-65	Miami (Fla.)	*16	T-SF, '90
25	Tautalatasi, Junior	RB	5-11	208	5	3-24-63	Washington State	13	FA, '89
92	Tolbert, Tony	DE	6-6	241	2	12-29-67	Texas-El Paso	16	D4, '89
71	Tuinei, Mark	T	6-5	286	8	3-31-60	Hawaii	16	OFA, '83
95	†Walen, Mark	DT	6-5	267	3	3-10-63	UCLA	*0	D3, '86
3	Walsh, Steve	QB	6-2	200	2	12- 1-66	Miami (Fla.)	8	SupD, '89
	Washington, James	S	6-1	196	3	1-10-65	UCLA	*9	UFA, '90
78	Widell, Dave	T	6-6	292	3	5-14-65	Boston College	15	D4, '88
	Williams, Mike	WR	5-10	177	1	10- 9-66	Northeastern	*1	UFA, '90
23	Williams, Robert	CB	5-10	184	4	10- 2-62	Baylor	13	FA, '87
98	Willis, Mitch	DT	6-8	285	5	3-16-62	Southern Methodist	*0	FA, '90
6	Zendejas, Luis	K	5-9	179	4	10-22-61	Arizona State	*15	FA, '89
76	Zimmerman, Jeff	G	6-3	313	3	1-10-65	Florida	16	D3, '87

*Agee played 9 games with Chiefs in '89; Cheek played 13 games with Dolphins in '89; Cooks played 3 games with Patriots in '89; Delaney active for 1 game with Vikings in '89, but did not play; Flagler played 15 games with 49ers in '89; Gibson played 16 games with Saints in '89; Harris played 11 games with Saints in '89; Holt played 5 games with Vikings, 9 with Cowboys in '89; Howard played 5 games with Vikings, 11 with Cowboys in '89; G. Johnson missed '89 season due to injury with Dolphins; S. Johnson last active with Patriots in '88; W. Johnson played 15 games with Saints in '89; K. Jones played 16 games with Browns in '89; Lee last active with Steelers in '88; McKinnon played 16 games with Bears in '89; Novacek played 16 games with Cardinals in '89; Robinson played 5 games with Redskins in '89; Shepard played 4 games with Saints, 11 with Cowboys in '89; Slaton played 15 games with Rams in '89; T. Smith last active with Redskins in '88; V. Smith missed '89 season due to injury with Steelers; Solomon played 4 games with Vikings, 11 with Cowboys in '89; Spears played 1 playoff game with Oilers in '89; Stubbs played 16 games with 49ers in '89; Walen missed '89 season due to injury; Washington played 9 games with Rams in '89; M. Williams played 1 game with Lions in '89; Willis last active with Raiders and Falcons in '88; Zendejas played 8 games with Eagles, 7 with Cowboys in '89.

†Unsigned; subject to developments.

Players lost through Plan B free agency: WR Cornell Burbage (10 games in '89; to Minn.); WR Bernard Ford (10; to Hou.); RB Paul Palmer (9; to Cin.); C Bob White (8; to N.E.).

Retired—Ed Jones, 15-year defensive end, 16 games in '89.

Also played with Cowboys in '89—WR Ray Alexander (2 games); CB/S Eric Brown (1); LB Ron Burton (6); TE Thornton Chandler (6); RB Darryl Clack (8); LB Garry Cobb (3); LB Onzy Elam (1); LB Steve Hendrickson (4); CB/S Tim Jackson (1); RB Undra Johnson (active for 1 game in '88; but did not play); NT Kevin Lilly (1); C Tom Rafferty (12); PK Roger Ruzek (9); OT Sean Smith (2); FB Curtis Stewart (2); LB Ken Tippins (6); RB Herschel Walker (5); CB Everson Walls (16).

D—Draft; T—Trade; W—Waivers; FA—Free Agent; OFA—Original Free Agent; UFA—Unrestricted Free Agent; SupD—Supplemental Draft.

DALLAS COWBOYS
1990 DRAFT CHOICES

(Number following name designates order of selection among 331 players drafted.)

Round and Player	Position	College
1. Choice exercised in 1989 Supplemental Draft for Steve Walsh, QB, Miami (Fla.)		
1. SMITH, Emmitt 17 from Pittsburgh (a)	RB	Florida
2. WRIGHT, Alexander 26	WR	Auburn
3. Choice to Minnesota (b)		
3. JONES, Jimmie 64 from Seattle through New England (c)	DT	Miami (Fla.)
4. Choice to Denver (d)		
5. Choice to New England through Washington (e)		
6. Choice to San Diego (f)		
7. Choice to Buffalo through New England (g)		
8. Choice to Detroit (h)		
9. GANT, Kenneth 221	DB	Albany State (Ga.)
10. Choice to Minnesota (b)		
11. HARPER, Dave 277	LB	Humboldt State
12. Choice exercised in 1989 Supplemental Draft for Mike Lowman, RB, Coffeyville (Kan.) JC		

(a) Acquired pick for 1st- and 3rd-round picks, April 22, 1990.

(b) Traded 3rd- and 10th-round picks and 3rd-round pick in 1991, February 2, 1990, completing deal of October 12, 1989, in which Cowboys traded running back Herschel Walker to Vikings for linebackers David Howard and Jesse Solomon, cornerback Issiac Holt, running back Darrin Nelson, defensive end Alex Stewart, 1st- and

2nd-round picks in 1990, 1st- and 2nd-round picks in 1991 and 1st-, 2nd- and 3rd-round picks in 1992. Nelson subsequently traded to Chargers with 6th-round pick in 1990 going from Vikings to Cowboys and 5th-round pick in 1990 going from Chargers to Vikings through Cowboys, October 17, 1989.

(c) Cowboys acquired pick and 6th- and 8th-round picks from Patriots for 3rd-, 5th- and 7th-round picks, April 22, 1990; Patriots had acquired pick, two 1st-round picks and 4th-round pick in 1991 from Seahawks for 1st-round pick, April 22, 1990.

(d) Traded pick and defensive end Kevin Brooks for 3rd-round pick, July 10, 1989.

(e) Cowboys traded pick to Redskins for defensive tackle Dean Hamel, August 28, 1989; Redskins traded pick and another 5th-round pick to Patriots for 4th-round pick, April 22, 1990.

(f) Traded pick and two other 6th-round picks for 3rd-round pick in 1991, April 22, 1990.

(g) Cowboys traded pick to Patriots: see first part of (c); Patriots traded pick and another 7th-round pick to Bills for 12th-round pick and 4th-round pick in 1991, April 23, 1990.

(h) Traded pick for running back Paul Palmer, October 17, 1989.

DALLAS COWBOYS
1990 ROOKIE AND FIRST-YEAR ROSTER

Name	Pos.	Hgt.	Wgt.	Birth-date	College	How Acquired
Brinkley, Lester	DE	6-6	270	5-13-65	Mississippi	*FA
Burnice, Karl	T	6-8	317	12-16-67	Oregon Tech	*FA
Crockett, Willis	LB	6-3	221	8-25-66	Georgia Tech	*D5a, '89
Ervin, Corris	CB/S	5-11	176	8-30-66	Central Florida	*FA
Franks, Dave	G	6-4	290	2- 7-66	Connecticut	*FA
Gant, Kenneth	CB	5-11	178	4-18-67	Albany State	D9
Harper, Dave	LB	6-1	220	5- 5-66	Humboldt State	D11
Henry, Charles	TE	6-4	230	4-18-64	Miami (Fla.)	*FA
Huebner, Tom	TE	6-6	250	10-17-66	Pittsburgh	FA
Jokisch, Paul	TE	6-7	248	1- 4-64	Michigan	*FA
Jones, Jimmie	NT	6-4	284	1- 9-66	Miami (Fla.)	D3
McNair, Fred	QB	6-1	220	12-11-68	Alcorn State	FA
Mull, Curt	T	6-5	282	9-17-67	Georgia	FA
Mullin, R.C.	T	6-6	300	6-28-65	Southwestern Louisiana	*FA
Smagala, Stan	CB	5-10	184	4- 6-68	Notre Dame	*T-Rai.
Smith, Emmitt	RB	5-9	199	5-15-69	Florida	D1
Warner, Mark	T	6-7	290	12-21-67	Canisius	FA
Willis, Ken	K	5-11	190	10- 6-66	Kentucky	FA
Wright, Alexander	WR	6-0	187	7-19-67	Auburn	D2

*Brinkley: FA Pittsburgh '89, released 9/5, DEV Pittsburgh 9/7, released 1/29/90; Burnice: FA Seattle '89, released 8/30, DEV Dallas 10/19, released 1/5/90; Crockett: D5 Dallas '89, injured reserve (knee) 8/28 through entire season; Ervin: D5 Denver '88, released 8/23, FA Denver '89, released 8/22, DEV San Francisco 9/14, released 9/28, DEV Dallas 11/22, released 1/5/90; Franks: D9 Seattle '89, released 8/22; Henry: FA Los Angeles Raiders '88, reserve/non-football injury 8/3 through entire season, released 9/5/89, DEV Raiders 9/6, released 9/26, DEV Dallas 10/5, released 1/5/90; Jokisch: D5 San Francisco '87, released 8/17, awarded on waivers to Houston 8/18, released 9/1, FA Los Angeles Rams '88, released 8/15, FA Minnesota '89, released 9/5, DEV Minnesota 9/13, released 1/8/90; Mullin: D10 Los Angeles Rams '88, injured reserve (back) 9/29 through entire season, injured reserve 8/29/89 through 9/4, released 9/5; Smagala: D5 Los Angeles Raiders '90, rights traded to Dallas for 6th-, 8th-, 9th-, 10th- and 11th-round picks in 1990 draft, 4/22.

DENVER BRONCOS
(Western Division, American Conference)

Dan Reeves

President and Chief Executive Officer—Patrick D. Bowlen
General Manager—John Beake
Vice-President/Head Coach—Dan Reeves (9 years: 85-50-1)
Assistant Coaches:
 Special Assistant—Marvin Bass
 Defensive Assistant—Barney Chavous
 Running Backs—Mo Forte
 Off. Coordinator/Wide Receivers—Chan Gailey
 Offensive Line—George Henshaw
 Defensive Line—Earl Leggett
 Tight Ends/Asst. Off. Line—Pete Mangurian
 Strength & Conditioning—Al Miller
 Linebackers—Mike Nolan
 Defensive Coordinator—Wade Phillips
 Special Teams—Harold Richardson
 Quarterbacks—Mike Shanahan
 Defensive Backs—Charlie Waters
Director of Media Relations—Jim Saccomano
 (Office Phone: 649-9000—Area Code 303)
Offices—13665 E. Dove Valley Pkwy, Englewood, Colo. 80112
Stadium—Mile High Stadium (Capacity: 76,273)
Team Colors—Orange, Blue and White
Training Site—University of Northern Colorado, Greeley, Colo.

1990 SCHEDULE
(All times local.
All games Sunday unless noted otherwise.)

Sept. 9	at Los Angeles Raiders	1:00
Sept. 17	KANSAS CITY (Mon.)	7:00
Sept. 23	SEATTLE	2:00
Sept. 30	at Buffalo	1:00
Oct. 8	CLEVELAND (Mon.)	7:00
Oct. 14	PITTSBURGH	2:00
Oct. 21	at Indianapolis	12:00
Oct. 28	OPEN DATE	
Nov. 4	at Minnesota	7:00
Nov. 11	at San Diego	1:00
Nov. 18	CHICAGO	2:00
Nov. 22	at Detroit (Thanksgiving)	12:30
Dec. 2	LOS ANGELES RAIDERS	2:00
Dec. 9	at Kansas City	3:00
Dec. 16	SAN DIEGO	2:00
Dec. 23	at Seattle	5:00
Dec. 30	GREEN BAY	2:00

1989 RESULTS—(Won 13, Lost 6)

Broncos		Opp.		Att.
34	Kansas City	20	(H)	74,284
28	Buffalo	14	(A)	78,176
31	Los Angeles Raiders	21	(H)	75,754
13	Cleveland	16	(A)	78,637
16	San Diego	10	(H)	75,222
14	Indianapolis	3	(H)	74,680
24	Seattle (OT)	21	(A)	62,353
24	Philadelphia	28	(H)	75,065
34	Pittsburgh	7	(H)	74,739
16	Kansas City	13	(A)	76,245
14	Washington	10	(A)	52,975
41	Seattle	14	(H)	75,117
13	L.A. Raiders (OT)	16	(A)	87,560
7	New York Giants	14	(H)	63,283
37	Phoenix	0	(A)	56,071
16	San Diego	19	(A)	50,524

AFC SEMIFINAL GAME

24	Pittsburgh	23	(H)	75,868

AFC CHAMPIONSHIP GAME

37	Cleveland	21	(H)	76,005

NFL CHAMPIONSHIP GAME

10	San Francisco	55	(*)	72,919

(*) Superdome, New Orleans, La.

1989 GAMES STARTED

16 games: Steve Atwater, Tyrone Braxton, Michael Brooks, Alphonso Carreker, Simon Fletcher, Mark Jackson, Vance Johnson, Jim Juriga, Keith Kartz, Clarence Kay, Ken Lanier.

15 games: John Elway, Wymon Henderson, Karl Mecklenburg, Gerald Perry.

14 games: Greg Kragen, Dennis Smith.

12 games: Bobby Humphrey.

11 games: Rick Dennison.

10 games: Andre Townsend, Doug Widell.

8 games: Ron Holmes.

7 games: Keith Bishop.

6 games: Jeff Alexander, Marc Munford.

5 games: Orson Mobley.

3 games: Melvin Bratton, Steve Sewell.

2 games: Randy Robbins, Sammy Winder.

1 game: Pat Kelly, Gary Kubiak, Warren Powers.

DENVER BRONCOS 1990 VETERAN ROSTER

No.	Name	Pos.	Ht.	Wt.	NFL Exp.	Birth-date	College	Games in '89	How Acquired
57	Allert, Ty	LB	6-2	238	5	7-23-63	Texas	*7	UFA, '90
40	Alexander, Jeff	RB	6-0	232	2	1-15-65	Southern University	14	FA, '89
27	Atwater, Steve	S	6-3	213	2	10-28-66	Arkansas	16	D1, '89
35	Bell, Ken	RB	5-10	190	5	11-16-64	Boston College	15	OFA, '86
54	Bishop, Keith	C/G	6-3	290	10	3-10-57	Baylor	14	D6, '80
32	Bratton, Melvin	RB	6-1	225	2	2- 2-65	Miami (Fla.)	16	D7, '89
34	Braxton, Tyrone	CB	5-11	185	4	12-17-64	North Dakota State	16	D12, '87
56	†Brooks, Michael	LB	6-1	235	4	10- 2-64	Louisiana State	16	D3, '87
92	Carreker, Alphonso	DE	6-6	272	5	5-25-62	Florida State	16	UFA, '89
29	Carrington, Darren	CB	6-1	189	2	10-10-66	Northern Arizona	16	D5, '89
25	†Corrington, Kip	S	6-0	175	2	4-12-65	Texas A&M	16	T-Det, '88
	Coyle, Eric	C	6-3	260	2	10-26-63	Colorado	*0	FA, '90
58	Curtis, Scott	LB	6-1	230	3	12-26-64	New Hampshire	16	UFA, '89
55	Dennison, Rick	LB	6-3	220	8	6-22-58	Colorado State	15	FA,'82
7	Elway, John	QB	6-3	215	8	6-28-60	Stanford	15	T-Bal, '83
85	Embree, Jon	TE	6-3	235	2	10-15-65	Colorado	*0	FA, '90
73	Fletcher, Simon	LB	6-5	240	6	2-18-62	Houston	16	D2b, '85
69	Hamilton, Darrell	T	6-5	298	2	5-11-65	North Carolina	*0	FA, '90
20	Hampton, Lorenzo	RB	5-11	208	6	3-12-62	Florida	*10	UFA, '90
36	Haynes, Mark	CB	5-11	195	11	11- 6-58	Colorado	14	T-NYG, '86
24	Henderson, Wymon	CB	5-9	186	4	12-15-61	Nevada-Las Vegas	16	UFA, '89
68	Henke, Brad	DE	6-3	275	2	4-10-66	Arizona	2	FA, '89
90	†Holmes, Ron	DE	6-4	265	6	8-26-63	Washington	15	T-TB, '89
2	Horan, Mike	P	5-11	190	7	2- 1-59	Long Beach State	16	FA, '86
26	Humphrey, Bobby	RB	6-1	201	2	10-11-66	Alabama	16	SupD, '89
80	Jackson, Mark	WR	5-9	180	4	7-23-63	Purdue	16	D6a, '86
81	Johnson, Jason	WR	5-10	178	3	11- 8-65	Illinois State	*14	UFA, '90
82	Johnson, Vance	WR	5-11	185	6	3-13-63	Arizona	16	D2, '85
66	†Juriga, Jim	G/T	6-6	275	4	9-12-64	Illinois	16	D4, '86
72	Kartz, Keith	C	6-4	270	4	5- 5-63	California	16	FA, '87
88	Kay, Clarence	TE	6-2	237	7	7-30-61	Georgia	16	D7, '84
71	†Kragen, Greg	NT	6-3	265	6	3- 4-62	Utah State	14	FA, '85
8	Kubiak, Gary	QB	6-0	192	8	8-15-61	Texas A&M	16	D8, '83
76	†Lanier, Ken	T	6-3	290	10	7- 8-59	Florida State	16	D5, '81
98	Little, David	TE	6-2	226	7	4-18-61	Middle Tenn. State	*16	UFA, '90
59	Lucas, Tim	LB	6-3	230	4	4- 3-61	California	16	FA, '87
96	McCullough, Jake	DE	6-5	270	2	7-23-65	Clemson	10	D4, '89
77	Mecklenburg, Karl	LB	6-3	240	8	9- 1-60	Minnesota	15	D12, '83
89	Mobley, Orson	TE	6-5	259	5	3- 4-63	Salem College	12	D6, '86
97	Mraz, Mark	DE	6-4	260	3	2- 9-65	Utah State	*11	UFA, '90
51	†Munford, Marc	LB	6-2	231	4	2-14-65	Nebraska	16	D4, '87
84	Nattiel, Ricky	WR	5-9	180	4	1-25-66	Florida	8	D1, '87
60	Perry, Gerald	T	6-6	305	3	11-12-64	Southern University	16	D2, '88
91	Powers, Warren	DE	6-6	287	2	2- 4-65	Maryland	15	D2a, '89
74	Provence, Andrew	NT	6-3	270	6	3- 8-61	South Carolina	*0	T-Atl, '88
48	Robbins, Randy	S	6-2	189	7	9-14-62	Arizona	16	D4, '84
30	Sewell, Steve	RB	6-3	210	6	4- 2-63	Oklahoma	16	D1, '85
49	Smith, Dennis	S	6-3	200	10	2- 3-59	Southern California	14	D1, '81
	Smith, Elliot	DB	6-2	192	1	8-14-67	Alcorn State	*2	UFA, '90
65	Smith, Monte	G	6-4	270	2	4-24-67	North Dakota	14	D9, '89
50	Stephens, Rod	LB	6-1	237	2	6-14-66	Georgia Tech	*10	UFA, '90
61	Townsend, Andre	DE/NT	6-3	265	7	10- 8-62	Mississippi	13	D2, '84
9	Treadwell, David	K	6-1	175	2	2-27-67	Clemson	16	T-Phx, '89
86	Verhulst, Chris	TE	6-2	249	3	5-16-66	Chico State	*16	UFA, '90
70	White, Robb	DE	6-4	270	3	5-26-65	South Dakota	*15	UFA, '90
67	Widell, Doug	G	6-4	287	2	9-23-66	Boston College	16	D2, '89
23	Winder, Sammy	RB	5-11	203	9	7-15-59	Southern Mississippi	16	D5, '82
83	Young, Mike	WR	6-1	183	6	2-21-62	UCLA	16	UFA, '89

*Allert played 7 games with Eagles in '89; Coyle last active with Redskins in '88; Embree last active with Rams in '88; Hamilton active for 3 games with Broncos in '89 but did not play; Hampton played 10 games with Dolphins in '89; J. Johnson played 14 games with Steelers in '89; Little played 16 games with Eagles in '89; Mraz played 11 games with Raiders in '89; Provence missed '89 season due to injury; E. Smith played 2 games with Chargers in '89; Stephens played 10 games with Seahawks in '89; Verhulst played 16 games with Oilers in '89; White played 15 games with Giants in '89.

†Unsigned; subject to developments.

Players lost through Plan B free agency: TE Pat Kelly (16 games in '89; to N.Y.J.), LB Bruce Klostermann (16; to L.A. Raid.); C Mike Ruether (3; to Atl.); LB Randy Thornton (0; to N.Y.G.).

Also played with Broncos in '89—CB Richard Shelton (3 games), WR Chris Woods (1).

D—Draft; T—Trade; FA—Free Agent; OFA—:Original Free Agent; UFA—Unrestricted Free Agent; SupD—Supplemental Draft.

DENVER BRONCOS
1990 DRAFT CHOICES

(Number following name designates order of selection among 331 players drafted.)

Round and Player		Position	College
1. Choice exercised in 1989 Supplemental Draft for Bobby Humphrey, RB, Alabama			
2. MONTGOMERY, Alton	52	DB	Houston
3. Choice to New England through Dallas (a)			
4. ROBINSON, Jeroy from Dallas (b)	82	LB	Texas A&M
4. Choice to Tampa Bay (c)			
5. DAVIDSON, Jeff from Atlanta through Washington and New England (d)	111	G	Ohio State
5. LANG, Le-Lo	136	DB	Washington
6. HALIBURTON, Ronnie	164	TE	Louisiana State
7. SHARPE, Shannon	192	WR	Savannah State
8. LEGGETT, Brad	219	C	Southern Cal
9. ELLIS, Todd	247	QB	South Carolina
10. SZYMANSKI, James from Indianapolis through Dallas and Los Angeles Raiders (e)	259	DE	Michigan State
10. THOMPSON, Anthony	275	LB	East Carolina
11. Choice to L.A. Raiders (f)			
12. Choice to Phoenix (g)			

(a) Broncos traded pick to Cowboys for defensive end Kevin Brooks and 4th-round pick, July 10, 1989; Cowboys traded pick and 5th- and 7th-round picks to Patriots for 3rd-, 6th- and 8th-round picks, April 22, 1990.

(b) See first part of (a).

(c) Traded pick for defensive end Ron Holmes, September 5, 1989.

(d) Broncos acquired pick from Patriots for 4th-round pick in 1991, April 22, 1990; Patriots had acquired pick and another 5th-round pick from Redskins for 4th-round pick, April 22, 1990; Redskins had acquired pick and running back Gerald Riggs from Falcons for 1st-round pick and 2nd-round pick in 1989, April 23, 1989.

(e) Broncos acquired pick from Raiders for 11th-round pick, April 23, 1990; Raiders had acquired pick and 6th-, 8th-, 9th- and 11th-round picks from Cowboys for rights to cornerback Stan Smagala, April 22, 1990; Cowboys had acquired pick from Colts for tackle Zefross Moss, August 22, 1989.

(f) See first part of (e).

(g) Traded pick for kicker David Treadwell, May 30, 1989.

DENVER BRONCOS
1990 ROOKIE AND FIRST-YEAR ROSTER

Name	Pos.	Hgt.	Wgt.	Birth-date	College	How Acquired
Allen, Chris	DL	6-5	274	7-10-68	Mesa (Colo.)	FA
Beavers, Scott	OL	6-4	277	2-17-67	Georgia Tech	FA
Brown, Karl	DB	6-2	185	5-26-67	Georgia Tech	FA
Calhoun, Paul	S/P	6-3	210	10-28-63	Kentucky	*FA
Davidson, Jeff	G	6-5	309	10- 3-67	Ohio State	D5
Ellis, Todd	QB	6-1	208	5-16-67	South Carolina	D9
Erney, Scott	QB	6-1	200	12-12-66	Rutgers	FA
Ezor, Blake	RB	5-8	181	10-11-66	Michigan State	FA
Goode, Pierre	WR	6-0	175	1-28-67	Alabama	FA
Haliburton, Ronnie	TE	6-4	230	4-14-68	Louisiana State	D6
Hegarty, Pat	QB	6-1	195	4-15-67	Texas-El Paso	*FA
Henderson, Joe	RB	5-8	178	11-23-67	Clemson	FA
Howfield, Ian	K	6-2	196	6- 6-66	Tennessee	*FA
Husby, John	OL	6-3	265	3-16-67	Washington State	FA
Jelks, Gene	DB	5-10	174	1-21-66	Alabama	FA
Jones, Tony	WR	5-11	178	1- 4-67	Florida	FA
Lang, Le-Lo	DB	5-11	185	1-23-67	Washington	D5a
Leggett, Brad	C	6-4	270	1-16-66	Southern California	D8
McCurdy, Paris	TE	..	..	....	Ball State	FA
McFadden, Wes	RB	5-11	203	1-25-67	Clemson	FA
McPhatter, Brian	DB	6-2	204	2-22-68	East Carolina	FA
Montgomery, Alton	DB	6-0	195	6-16-68	Houston	D2
Muilenburg, Darrin	OL	6-3	286	3-29-68	Colorado	FA
Parkinson, Brent	OL	6-5	267	5-26-67	Southern California	FA
Robinson, Jeroy	LB	6-1	241	6- 6-68	Texas A&M	D4
Sancho, Ron	LB	6-2	235	6-21-65	Louisiana State	*FA
Sharpe, Shannon	WR	6-2	225	6-26-68	Savannah State	D7
Smith, Greg	OL	6-7	275	10-18-67	Vanderbilt	FA
Szymanski, James	DE	6-5	268	9- 7-67	Michigan State	D10
Thompson, Anthony	LB	6-1	227	6-19-67	East Carolina	D10a
Turner, Vernon	RB	5-8	185	1- 6-67	Carson Newman	FA

*Calhoun: D5 Birmingham-USFL '85, FA St. Louis '85, released 8/19, FA St. Louis '86, released 7/18, FA Philadelphia 10/14/87 during strike, released 10/19; Hegarty: FA Denver '89, released 8/29, DEV Denver 9/7, released 1/29/90; Howfield: FA Miami '88, released 8/9, FA Seattle '89, released 8/30; Sancho: D7 Kansas City '89, released 9/5, DEV Denver 9/7, released 1/29/90.

DETROIT LIONS
(Central Division, National Conference)

Wayne Fontes

Owner and President—William Clay Ford
Executive Vice-President and CEO—Chuck Schmidt
Vice-President/Player Personnel—Jerry Vainisi
Head Coach—Wayne Fontes (2 years: 9-12)
Assistant Coaches:
   Administrative Asst.—Don Clemons
   Quarterbacks/Receivers—Darrel (Mouse) Davis
   Special Teams—Frank Gansz
   Quarterbacks/Receivers—June Jones
   Defensive Line—Lamar Leachman
   Administrative Assistant—Dave Levy
   Running Backs—Billie Matthews
   Inside Linebackers—Herb Paterra
   Slot Receivers—Charlie Sanders
   Offensive Line—Jerry Wampfler
   Def. Coord./Outside Linebackers—Woody Widenhofer
Public Relations Director—Bill Keenist
   (Office Phone: 335-4131—Area Code 313)
Offices—1200 Featherstone Road, Box 4200, Pontiac, Mich. 48057
Stadium—Pontiac Silverdome (Capacity: 80,500)
Team Colors—Honolulu Blue and Silver
Training Site—Pontiac Silverdome, Pontiac, Mich.

1990 SCHEDULE
(All times local.
All games Sunday unless noted otherwise.)

Sept. 9	TAMPA BAY	1:00
Sept. 16	ATLANTA	1:00
Sept. 23	at Tampa Bay	8:00
Sept. 30	GREEN BAY	1:00
Oct. 7	at Minnesota	12:00
Oct. 14	at Kansas City	12:00
Oct. 21	OPEN DATE	
Oct. 28	at New Orleans	12:00
Nov. 4	WASHINGTON	1:00
Nov. 11	MINNESOTA	1:00
Nov. 18	at New York Giants	1:00
Nov. 22	DENVER (Thanksgiving)	12:30
Dec. 2	at Chicago	12:00
Dec. 10	L.A. RAIDERS (Mon.)	9:00
Dec. 16	CHICAGO	8:00
Dec. 22	at Green Bay (Sat.)	11:30
Dec. 30	at Seattle	1:00

1989 RESULTS—(Won 7, Lost 9)

Lions		Opp.		Att.
13	Phoenix	16	(H)	36,735
14	New York Giants	24	(A)	76,021
27	Chicago	47	(H)	71,418
3	Pittsburgh	23	(H)	43,804
17	Minnesota	24	(A)	55,380
17	Tampa Bay	16	(A)	46,225
7	Minnesota	20	(H)	51,579
20	Green Bay (OT)	23	(A)	53,731
31	Houston	35	(A)	48,056
31	Green Bay	22	(H)	44,324
7	Cincinnati	42	(A)	55,720
13	Cleveland	10	(H)	65,624
21	New Orleans	14	(H)	38,550
27	Chicago	17	(A)	52,650
33	Tampa Bay	7	(H)	40,362
31	Atlanta	24	(A)	7,092

1989 GAMES STARTED

16 games: Eric Andolsek, Jerry Ball, Bennie Blades, Lomas Brown, Robert Clark, Kevin Glover, Jerry Holmes, Chris Spielman, Eric Williams, Jimmy Williams.

15 games: Kevin Brooks, Richard Johnson, Terry Taylor, William White.

13 games: Barry Sanders.

12 games: Walter Stanley.

11 games: Ken Dallafior.

9 games: Victor Jones.

8 games: Rodney Peete, Harvey Salem.

7 games: Mike Cofer, Bob Gagliano, Eric Sanders.

6 games: Dennis Gibson, George Jamison, Jason Phillips.

5 games: Stacey Mobley, Mike Utley.

4 games: Keith McDonald, Tony Paige.

3 games: Mark Brown.

2 games: Troy Johnson.

1 game: Bruce Alexander, Jeff Chadwick, Keith Ferguson, John Ford, Mel Gray, James Griffin, Eric Hipple, Joe Milinichik, Niko Noga.

DETROIT LIONS 1990 VETERAN ROSTER

No.	Name	Pos.	Ht.	Wt.	NFL Exp.	Birth-date	College	Games in '89	How Acquired
32	Alexander, Bruce	CB	5-9	169	2	9-17-65	Stephen F. Austin	8	OFA, '89
65	Andolsek, Eric	G	6-2	286	3	8-22-66	Louisiana State	16	D5, '88
6	Arnold, Jim	P	6-3	211	8	1-31-61	Vanderbilt	16	FA, '86
93	Ball, Jerry	NT	6-1	298	4	12-15-64	Southern Methodist	16	D3, '87
36	Blades, Bennie	S	6-1	221	3	9- 3-66	Miami (Fla.)	16	D1, '88
97	Brooks, Kevin	DE/NT	6-6	278	6	2- 9-63	Michigan	15	FA, '89
75	Brown, Lomas	T	6-4	287	6	3-30-63	Florida	16	D1, '85
95	†Brown, Mark	LB	6-2	240	8	7-18-61	Purdue	6	W-Mia, '89
50	Caston, Toby	LB	6-1	243	4	7-17-65	Louisiana State	16	UFA, '89
82	Clark, Robert	WR	5-11	173	3	8- 8-65	North Carolina Central	16	UFA, '89
30	Cocroft, Sherman	S	6-1	190	6	8-29-61	San Jose State	*10	UFA, '90
55	Cofer, Michael	LB	6-5	244	8	4- 7-60	Tennessee	15	D3, '83
	Collier, Steve	T	6-7	342	2	4-19-63	Bethune-Cookman	*0	FA, '90
39	Crockett, Ray	CB	5-9	181	2	1- 5-67	Baylor	16	D4, '89
67	†Dallafior, Ken	G/C	6-4	279	6	8-26-59	Minnesota	16	UFA, '89
79	Duckens, Mark	DE	6-4	270	2	3- 4-65	Arizona State	*15	UFA, '90
77	Ferguson, Keith	DE	6-5	276	10	4- 3-59	Ohio State	4	W-SD, '85
80	Ford, John	WR	6-2	204	2	7-31-66	Virginia	7	D2, '89
14	†Gagliano, Bob	QB	6-3	196	6	9- 5-58	Utah State	11	FA, '89
98	Gibson, Dennis	LB	6-2	243	4	2- 8-64	Iowa State	6	D8, '87
53	Glover, Kevin	C/G	6-2	282	6	6-17-63	Maryland	16	D2, '85
23	Gray, Mel	WR/KR	5-9	162	5	3-16-61	Purdue	10	UFA, '89
62	†Green, Curtis	DE/NT	6-3	273	10	6- 3-57	Alabama State	16	D2, '81
89	Greer, Terry	WR	6-1	192	4	9-27-57	Alabama State	*11	UFA, '90
58	Jamison, George	LB	6-1	228	4	9-30-62	Cincinnati	10	SupD, '84
84	Johnson, Richard	WR	5-6	184	2	10-19-61	Colorado	16	FA, '89
57	Jones, Victor	LB	6-2	240	3	10-19-66	Virginia Tech	11	UFA, '89
49	Judson, William	CB	6-1	192	9	3-26-59	South Carolina State	*14	UFA, '90
90	Karpinski, Keith	LB	6-3	225	2	10-12-66	Penn State	16	D11, '89
	Kramer, Erik	QB	6-1	195	2	11- 6-64	North Carolina State	*0	FA, '90
83	Matthews, Aubrey	WR	5-7	165	5	9-15-62	Delta State	*13	UFA, '90
29	McNorton, Bruce	CB	5-10	175	9	2-28-59	Georgetown (Ky.)	8	D4, '82
25	Miller, Chuck	CB/S	5-10	180	2	5- 9-65	UCLA	*0	FA, '90
44	Miller, John	S	6-1	195	2	6-22-66	Michigan State	9	OFA, '89
3	Murray, Eddie	K	5-10	180	11	8-29-56	Tulane	16	D7, '80
51	†Noga, Niko	LB	6-1	235	7	3- 2-62	Hawaii	14	FA, '89
26	Painter, Carl	RB	5-9	188	3	5-10-64	Hampton Institute (Va.)	15	D6, '88
9	Peete, Rodney	QB	6-0	193	2	3-16-66	Southern California	8	D6, '89
96	Pete, Lawrence	NT	6-0	282	2	1-18-66	Nebraska	16	D5, '89
24	Phillips, Jason	WR	5-7	168	2	10-11-66	Houston	16	D10, '89
31	Richard, Gary	CB	5-10	176	2	10- 9-65	Missouri	*0	FA, '90
73	Salem, Harvey	T/G	6-6	289	8	1-15-61	California	10	T-Hou, '86
20	Sanders, Barry	RB	5-8	203	2	7-16-68	Oklahoma State	15	D1, '89
64	†Sanders, Eric	T/G	6-7	286	10	10-22-58	Nevada-Reno	16	W-Atl, '86
54	Spielman, Chris	LB	6-0	244	3	10-11-65	Ohio State	16	D2, '88
21	†Taylor, Terry	CB	5-10	191	7	7-18-61	Southern Illinois	15	T-Sea, '89
60	Utley, Mike	G/T	6-6	279	2	12-20-65	Washington State	5	D3, '89
28	Welch, Herb	S	5-11	180	5	1-12-61	UCLA	*9	UFA, '90
35	White, William	CB/S	5-10	191	3	2-19-66	Ohio State	15	D4, '88
	Wilkerson, Eric	RB	5-9	185	1	12-19-66	Kent State	*1	UFA, '90
4	Williams, Byron	WR	6-2	185	4	10-31-60	Texas-Arlington	*10	FA, '90
76	†Williams, Eric	DE	6-4	286	7	2-24-62	Washington State	16	D3, '84
59	†Williams, Jimmy	LB	6-3	225	9	11-15-60	Nebraska	16	D1, '82

*Cocroft played 10 games with Buccaneers in '89; Collier last active with Packers in '88; Duckens played 15 games with Giants in '89; Greer played 11 games with 49ers in '89; Judson played 14 games with Dolphins in '89; Kramer last active with Falcons in '87; Matthews played 13 games with Packers in '89; C. Miller last active with Colts in '88; Richard last active with Packers in '88; Welch played 9 games with Redskins in '89; Wilkerson played 1 game with Steelers in '89; B. Williams played 10 games with Ottawa-CFL in '89.

†Unsigned; subject to developments.

Players lost through Plan B free agency: DE James Cribbs (7 games in '89; to G.B.); T Chris Gambol (6; to N.E.); S James Griffin (16; to K.C.); CB Jerry Holmes (16; to G.B.); C Trevor Matich (11; to N.Y.J.); G/T Joe Milinichik (15; to L.A. Rams); RB Tony Paige (16; to Mia.); WR Walter Stanley (14; to Was.); WR Mike Williams (1; to Hou.).

Also played with Lions in '89—CB Michael Brim (2 games); WR Jeff Chadwick (1); DE Byron Darby (1); QB Eric Hipple (1); WR Troy Johnson (9); QB Chuck Long (1); WR Keith McDonald (6); WR Stacey Mobley (10); RB Paul Palmer (5); CB Jerry Woods (2).

D—Draft; T—Trade; W—Waivers; FA—Free Agent; OFA—Original Free Agent; UFA—Unrestricted Free Agent; SupD—Supplemental Draft.

DETROIT LIONS
1990 DRAFT CHOICES

(Number following name designates order of selection among 331 players drafted.)

Round and Player		Position	College
1. WARE, Andre	7	QB	Houston
2. OWENS, Dan	35	DE	Southern Cal
3. SPINDLER, Marc	62	DE	Pittsburgh
4. HINCKLEY, Rob	90	LB	Stanford
4. OLDHAM, Chris from Los Angeles Rams (a)	105	DB	Oregon
5. CAMPBELL, Jeff	118	WR	Colorado
6. HENRY, Maurice	147	LB	Kansas State
7. HAYWORTH, Tracy	174	LB	Tennessee
8. GREEN, Willie from Dallas (b)	194	WR	Mississippi
8. FORTIN, Roman	203	G	San Diego State
9. LINN, Jack	229	T	West Virginia
10. MILLER, Bill	258	WR	Illinois State
11. WARNSLEY, Reginald	285	RB	So. Mississippi
12. CLAIBORNE, Robert	313	WR	San Diego State

(a) Acquired pick for tight end Pat Carter, August 18, 1989.
(b) Acquired pick for running back Paul Palmer, October 17, 1989.

DETROIT LIONS
1990 ROOKIE AND FIRST-YEAR ROSTER

Name	Pos.	Hgt.	Wgt.	Birth-date	College	How Acquired
Andrews, Robbie	CB	6-0	195	3-27-67	Eastern Kentucky	FA
Broady, Tim	CB/S	6-0	210	2-20-66	Murray State	*FA
Burks, Willie	DT	6-3	280	6-28-66	Georgia Tech	FA
Campbell, Jeff	WR	5-8	167	3-29-68	Colorado	D5
Chesley, Delmar	LB	6-2	235	1-13-66	Southern California	FA
Claiborne, Robert	WR	5-10	175	7-10-67	San Diego State	D12
Cole, Leon	DE	6-4	270	11- 8-65	Texas A&M	*FA
Dawson, Ken	RB	6-0	230	8-15-66	Appalachian State	FA
Dubose, Jim	LB	6-3	235	12- 4-66	Wake Forest	FA
Farr, Mike	WR	5-10	192	8- 8-67	UCLA	FA
Faunce, Troy	P	6-1	200	1-11-64	Kansas State	FA
Fortin, Roman	T	6-5	270	2-26-67	San Diego State	D8a
Grant, Eddie	C	6-2	270	8-16-67	Arizona State	FA
Green, Willie	WR	6-2	179	4- 2-66	Mississippi	D8
Hayworth, Tracy	LB/DE	6-3	250	12-18-67	Tennessee	D7
Henry, Maurice	RB	5-11	220	3-12-67	Kansas State	D6
Hinckley, Rob	LB	6-4	241	7-19-67	Stanford	D4
Hofland, Mark	T	6-7	285	6-16-67	Maryland	FA
Holmes, David	DB	6-2	192	7- 8-66	Syracuse	*FA
Hoyle, Wilson	K	..	..	....	Wake Forest	FA
Husko, Chris	G	6-3	270	1-28-67	Oregon	FA
Lewis, Kip	WR	5-10	170	2- 6-67	Arizona	FA
Linberger, George	OL	6-3	265	1-23-67	Toledo	FA
Linn, Jack	G	6-5	278	6-10-67	West Virginia	D9
Marlatt, Pat	DE	6-5	270	5- 3-66	West Virginia State	*FA
Miller, Bill	WR	5-10	180	6-28-67	Illinois State	D10
Nelson, M.J.	WR	5-9	155	1-27-68	Colorado	FA
Nua, Mark	T	..	..	....	Hawaii	FA
Oldham, Chris	CB	5-9	183	10-26-68	Oregon	D4a
Owens, Dan	DE	6-3	268	3-16-67	Southern California	D2
Parker, Scott	G	6-5	275	5- 2-67	West Virginia	FA
Robertson, Derrell	T	6-7	245	9-22-67	Mississippi State	FA
Smith, Davis	WR	5-4	150	3-27-67	Texas Southern	FA
Spindler, Marc	NT	6-5	277	11-28-69	Pittsburgh	D3
Towe, Eric	OL	6-5	275	3- 2-67	Eastern Michigan	FA
Ware, Andre	QB	6-2	205	7-31-68	Houston	D1
Warnsley, Reginald	RB	5-10	225	4- 5-68	Southern Mississippi	D11
Williams, Mike	LB	6-4	225	2-11-67	Southern California	FA
Wilson, Curtis	C	6-3	290	10-30-65	Missouri	*UFA

*Broady: FA Seattle '89, released 6/13; Cole: FA N.Y. Giants '89, released 9/5, DEV N.Y. Giants 9/6, released 11/16, DEV N.Y. Giants 11/20, released 1/29/90; Holmes: D4 Miami '89, released 8/30; Marlatt: D9 N.Y. Jets '89, released 9/1, DEV Washington 9/6, released 10/25, DEV Miami 10/31, released 11/10, DEV Washington 11/16, released 11/30; Wilson: D9 New England '89, injured reserve (knee) 8/22 through entire season, unprotected free agent 2/1/90.

GREEN BAY PACKERS
(Central Division, National Conference)

Lindy Infante

President and Chief Executive Officer—Bob Harlan
Vice President—John Fabry
Exec. Vice President/Football Operations—Tom Braatz
Head Coach—Lindy Infante (2 years: 14-18)
Assistant Coaches:
  Defensive Line—Greg Blache
  Defensive Coordinator—Hank Bullough
  Asst. Offensive Line—Joe Clark
  Offensive Line—Charlie Davis
  Receivers—Buddy Geis
  Defensive Backfield—Dick Jauron
  Stren./Cond./Tight Ends—Virgil Knight
  Outside Linebackers—Dick Moseley
  Offensive Backfield—Willie Peete
  Special Teams—Howard Tippett
Public Relations Director—Lee Remmel
  (Office Phone: 496-5700—Area Code 414)
Offices—1265 Lombardi Ave., Green Bay, Wis. 54304
Mailing Address—P.O. Box 10628, Green Bay, Wis. 54307-0628
Stadium—Lambeau Field, Green Bay (Capacity: 59,543); County Stadium, Milwaukee (Capacity: 56,051)
Team Colors—Green, Gold and White
Training Site—St. Norbert College, De Pere, Wis. (food and lodging only; workouts at Lambeau Field, Green Bay)

1990 SCHEDULE
(All times local.
All games Sunday unless noted otherwise.)

Sept.	9	LOS ANGELES RAMS	12:00
Sept.	16	CHICAGO	12:00
Sept.	23	KANSAS CITY	12:00
Sept.	30	at Detroit	1:00
Oct.	7	at Chicago	3:00
Oct.	14	at Tampa Bay	1:00
Oct.	21	OPEN DATE	
Oct.	28	MINNESOTA at Milwaukee	12:00
Nov.	4	SAN FRANCISCO	12:00
Nov.	11	at Los Angeles Raiders	1:00
Nov.	18	at Phoenix	2:00
Nov.	25	TAMPA BAY at Milwaukee	12:00
Dec.	2	at Minnesota	7:00
Dec.	9	SEATTLE at Milwaukee	12:00
Dec.	16	at Philadelphia	4:00
Dec.	22	DETROIT (Sat.)	11:30
Dec.	30	at Denver	2:00

1989 RESULTS—(Won 10, Lost 6)

Packers		Opp.		Att.
21	Tampa Bay	23	(H)	55,650
35	New Orleans	34	(H)	55,809
38	Los Angeles Rams	41	(A)	57,701
23	Atlanta	21	(H)	54,647
31	Dallas	13	(H)	56,656
14	Minnesota	26	(A)	62,075
20	Miami	23	(A)	56,624
23	Detroit (OT)	20	(H)	53,731
14	Chicago	13	(H)	56,556
22	Detroit	31	(A)	44,324
21	San Francisco	17	(A)	62,219
20	Minnesota	19	(H)	55,592
17	Tampa Bay	16	(A)	58,120
3	Kansas City	21	(H)	56,694
40	Chicago	28	(A)	44,781
20	Dallas	10	(A)	41,265

1989 GAMES STARTED

16 games: Dave Brown, Robert Brown, Ron Hallstrom, Tim Harris, Don Majkowski, Rich Moran, Mark Murphy, Bob Nelson, Brian Noble, Ken Ruettgers, Sterling Sharpe, Ken Stills, Alan Veingrad, Keith Woodside.

15 games: Blair Bush, Brent Fullwood, Johnny Holland.

14 games: John Anderson.

13 games: Perry Kemp.

12 games: Ed West.

10 games: Mark Lee, Blaise Winter.

6 games: Shawn Patterson.

4 games: Clint Didier, Van Jakes.

3 games: Aubrey Matthews.

2 games: Ron Pitts, Scott Stephen.

1 game: James Campen, Burnell Dent, Michael Haddix.

GREEN BAY PACKERS 1990 VETERAN ROSTER

No.	Name	Pos.	Ht.	Wt.	NFL Exp.	Birth-date	College	Games in '89	How Acquired
67	Ard, Billy	G	6-3	270	10	3-12-59	Wake Forest	15	UFA, '89
76	Ariey, Mike	T	6-5	285	2	3-12-64	San Diego State	1	UFA, '89
	Avery, Steve	RB	6-2	230	1	8-18-66	Northern Michigan	*1	FA, '90
83	Bland, Carl	WR	5-11	182	7	8-17-61	Virginia Union	16	UFA, '89
61	†Boyarsky, Jerry	NT	6-3	290	10	5-15-59	Pittsburgh	13	FA, '87
17	†Bracken, Don	P	6-1	211	6	2-16-62	Michigan	16	FA, '85
62	Brock, Matt	DE	6-4	267	2	1-14-66	Oregon	7	D3, '89
32	Brown, Dave	CB/S	6-1	197	16	1-16-53	Michigan	16	T-Sea, '87
93	†Brown, Robert	DE	6-2	267	9	5-21-60	Virginia Tech	16	D4, '82
51	Bush, Blair	C	6-3	272	13	11-25-56	Washington	16	UFA, '89
63	Campen, James	C/G	6-3	270	4	6-11-64	Tulane	15	UFA, '89
26	†Cecil, Chuck	S	6-0	184	3	11- 8-64	Arizona	9	D4a, '88
	Champion, Tony	WR	6-1	180	1	3-19-63	Tennessee-Martin	*17	FA, '90
55	Clark, Greg	LB	6-1	234	3	3- 5-65	Arizona State	*16	UFA, '90
92	Cribbs, James	DE	6-3	269	2	7-10-66	Memphis State	*7	UFA, '90
60	†Croston, David	T	6-5	280	2	11-10-63	Iowa	*0	D3, '87
49	Dee, Donnie	TE	6-4	252	3	3-17-65	Tulsa	*4	UFA, '90
56	Dent, Burnell	LB	6-1	236	5	3-16-63	Tulane	16	D6, '86
80	Didier, Clint	TE	6-5	240	9	4- 4-59	Portland State	16	FA, '88
8	Dilweg, Anthony	QB	6-3	215	2	3-28-65	Duke	1	D3a, '89
99	Dorsey, John	LB	6-2	243	6	8-31-60	Connecticut	*0	D4, '84
94	Fears, Willie	DE/NT	6-5	285	2	6- 4-64	Arkansas-Pine Bluff	*0	FA, '90
27	†Fontenot, Herman	RB	6-0	206	6	9-12-63	Louisiana State	16	T-Cle., '89
30	Frazier, Paul	RB	5-8	196	2	11-12-67	Northwestern (La.) St.	*15	UFA, '90
21	†Fullwood, Brent	RB	5-11	209	4	10-10-63	Auburn	15	D1, '87
23	†Greene, Tiger	S	6-0	194	6	2-15-62	Western Carolina	16	FA, '86
35	Haddix, Michael	RB	6-2	227	8	12-27-61	Mississippi State	16	UFA, '89
72	Hall, Mark	DE	6-4	285	2	8-21-65	S.W. Louisiana	7	D7, '89
65	†Hallstrom, Ron	G	6-6	290	9	6-11-59	Iowa	16	D1, '82
97	Harris, Tim	LB	6-5	235	5	9-10-64	Memphis State	16	D4, '86
48	Harris, William	TE	6-5	254	3	2-10-65	Bishop (Tex.)	*16	UFA, '90
5	Hatcher, Dale	P	6-3	240	6	4- 5-63	Clemson	*16	UFA, '90
50	Holland, Johnny	LB	6-2	221	4	3-11-65	Texas A&M	16	D2, '87
44	Holmes, Jerry	CB	6-2	175	9	12-22-57	West Virginia	*16	UFA, '90
13	Jacke, Chris	K	6-0	197	2	3-12-66	Texas-El Paso	16	D6, '89
24	Jakes, Van	CB	6-0	190	7	5-10-61	Kent State	16	UFA, '89
88	Johnson, Flip	WR	5-10	183	3	7-13-63	McNeese State	*16	UFA, '90
53	Johnson, M.L.	LB	6-3	229	4	1-26-64	Hawaii	*13	UFA, '90
	Keel, Mark	TE	6-4	245	2	10- 1-61	Arizona	*0	FA, '90
81	Kemp, Perry	WR	5-11	170	4	12-31-61	California State (Pa.)	14	FA, '88
10	†Kiel, Blair	QB	6-0	214	6	11-29-61	Notre Dame	*0	FA, '88
22	Lee, Mark	CB	5-11	189	11	3-20-58	Washington	12	D2, '80
7	†Majkowski, Don	QB	6-2	197	4	2-25-64	Virginia	16	D10, '87
77	Mandarich, Tony	T	6-5	300	2	9-23-66	Michigan State	14	D1, '89
47	Martin, Tracy	WR	6-2	205	2	12- 4-64	North Dakota	*0	FA, '90
98	Miller, Shawn	DE	6-4	255	7	3-14-61	Utah State	*16	UFA, '90
	Mobley, Stacey	WR	5-7	170	3	9-15-65	Jackson State	*10	FA, '90
57	†Moran, Rich	G	6-2	275	6	3-19-62	San Diego State	16	D3, '85
37	†Murphy, Mark	S	6-2	201	9	4-22-58	West Liberty	16	OFA, '80
79	†Nelson, Bob	NT	6-4	275	4	3- 3-59	Miami (Fla.)	16	FA, '88
91	†Noble, Brian	LB	6-3	252	6	9- 6-62	Arizona State	16	D5, '85
6	Norseth, Mike	QB	6-2	205	3	8-22-64	Kansas	*0	UFA, '90
96	Patterson, Shawn	DE	6-5	261	3	6-13-64	Arizona State	6	D2, '88
28	†Pitts, Ron	CB	5-10	175	5	10-14-62	UCLA	14	FA, '88
85	Query, Jeff	WR/KR	5-11	165	2	3- 7-67	Millikin	16	D5, '89
75	†Ruettgers, Ken	T	6-5	280	6	8-20-62	Southern California	16	D1, '85
84	Sharpe, Sterling	WR	5-11	202	3	4- 6-65	South Carolina	16	D1, '88
89	Spagnola, John	TE	6-4	242	11	8- 1-57	Yale	6	UFA, '89
54	Stephen, Scott	LB	6-2	232	4	6-18-64	Arizona State	16	D3a, '87
70	†Uecker, Keith	G/T	6-5	284	7	6-29-60	Auburn	*0	W-Den, '84
73	†Veingrad, Alan	T	6-5	277	4	7-24-63	East Texas State	16	FA, '86
87	Weathers, Clarence	WR	5-9	180	8	1-10-62	Delaware State	*15	UFA, '90
52	Weddington, Mike	LB	6-4	245	5	10- 9-60	Oklahoma	15	FA, '86
86	†West, Ed	TE	6-1	243	7	8- 2-61	Auburn	13	OFA, '84
68	†Winter, Blaise	DE/NT	6-3	275	6	1-31-62	Syracuse	16	T-SD, '88
33	†Woodside, Keith	RB	5-11	203	3	7-29-64	Texas A&M	16	D3, '88
46	Workman, Vince	RB	5-10	193	2	5- 9-68	Ohio State	15	D5a, '89
64	Yarno, George	C/G	6-2	270	10	8-12-57	Washington State	*11	UFA, '90

*Avery played 1 game with Oilers in '89; Champion played 17 games with Hamilton-CFL in '89; Clark played 16 games with Dolphins in '89; Cribbs played 7 games with Lions in '89; Croston, Dorsey and Uecker missed '89 season due to injury; Dee played 1 game with Colts, 3 games with Seahawks in '89; Fears last active with Bengals in '87; Frazier played 15 games with Saints in '89; W. Harris played 16 games with Buccaneers in '89; Hatcher played 16 games with Rams in '89; Holmes played 16 games with Lions in' 89; F. Johnson played 16 games with Bills in '89; M. Johnson played 13 games with Seahawks in '89; Keel last active with Chiefs in '87; Kiel active for 9 games with Packers in '89, but did not play; Martin last active with Jets in '87; Miller played 16 games with Rams in '89; Mobley played 10 games with Lions in '89; Norseth last active with Bengals in '88; Weathers played 4 games with Colts, 11 games with Chiefs in '89; Yarno played 11 games with Oilers in '89.

†Unsigned; subject to developments.

Players lost through Plan B free agency: WR Aubrey Matthews (13 games in '89; to Det.); CB/S Ken Stills (16; to Minn.).

Retired—John Anderson, 12-year linebacker, 14 games in '89.

Also played with Packers in '89—C Mark Cannon (1 game), CB/S Michael McGruder (2), CB Mickey Sutton (3).

D—Draft; T—Trade; W—Waivers; FA—Free Agent; OFA—Original Free Agent; UFA—Unrestricted Free Agent.

GREEN BAY PACKERS
1990 DRAFT CHOICES

(Number following name designates order of selection among 331 players drafted.)

Round and Player		Position	College
1. BENNETT, Tony from Cleveland (a)	18	LB	Mississippi
1. THOMPSON, Darrell	19	RB	Minnesota
2. BUTLER, LeRoy	48	DB	Florida State
3. HOUSTON, Bobby	75	LB	North Carolina State
4. HARRIS, Jackie	102	TE	N.E. Louisiana
5. WILSON, Charles	132	WR	Memphis State
6. PAUP, Bryce	159	LB	Northern Iowa
7. ARCHAMBEAU, Lester	186	DE	Stanford
8. BROWN, Roger	215	DB	Virginia Tech
9. BAUMGARTNER, Kirk	242	QB	Wis.-Stevens Point
10. MARTIN, Jerome	269	DB	Western Kentucky
11. JACKSON, Harry	299	RB	St. Cloud (Minn.)
12. MAGGIO, Kirk	325	P	UCLA

(a) Acquired pick, running back Herman Fontenot and 3rd- and 5th-round picks in 1989 for 2nd- and 5th-round picks in 1989, April 23, 1989.

GREEN BAY PACKERS
1990 ROOKIE AND FIRST-YEAR ROSTER

Name	Pos.	Hgt.	Wgt.	Birth-date	College	How Acquired
Aeilts, Rick	TE	6-3	235	12-13-65	S.E. Missouri State	*FA
Affholter, Erik	WR	5-11	181	4-10-66	Southern California	*D4, 89
Archambeau, Lester	DE	6-4	253	6-27-67	Stanford	D7
Baumgartner, Kirk	QB	6-2	203	11- 3-67	Wisconsin-Stevens Point	D9
Bennett, Tony	LB	6-1	234	7- 1-67	Mississippi	D1
Brown, Roger	CB	6-2	203	12-16-66	Virginia Tech	D8
Butler, LeRoy	CB	5-11	193	7-19-68	Florida State	D2
Chubb, Aaron	LB	6-5	235	8-17-66	Georgia	*UFA
Harris, Jackie	TE	6-3	231	1- 4-68	Northeast Louisiana	D4
Houston, Bobby	LB	6-1	230	10-26-67	North Carolina State	D3
Jackson, Harry	RB	5-10	223	3-15-68	St. Cloud State	D11
Kirby, Scott	T	6-6	284	8- 7-66	Arizona State	*FA
Maggio, Kirk	P	6-0	158	9-18-67	UCLA	D12
Martin, Jerome	S	6-0	210	2- 3-68	Western Kentucky	D10
Paup, Bryce	LB	6-4	238	2-29-68	Northern Iowa	D6
Perkins, Allen	S	6-0	209	3-27-67	Memphis State	*FA
Shiver, Stan	S	6-2	209	5-18-66	Florida State	*FA
Shulman, Brian	P	5-10	184	4-20-66	Auburn	*FA
Stell, Damon	RB	5-10	196	9- 8-66	Oklahoma	FA
Thompson, Darrell	RB	6-0	219	11-23-67	Minnesota	D1a
Wilson, Charles	WR	5-9	178	7- 1-68	Memphis State	D5
Wise, Deatrich	DT	6-4	268	5- 6-65	Jackson State	*FA
Wright, Charles	G	6-4	280	10-31-66	Florida	*FA

*Aeilts: D8 Cleveland '89, released 9/5, DEV Cleveland 9/6, released 10/18, DEV Green Bay 11/2, released 12/13; Affholter: D4 Washington '89, rights traded with 5th- and 8th-round picks in 1989 draft to Green Bay for rights to quarterback Jeff Graham 4/23, reserve/non-football injury (ankle) 8/28 through entire season; Chubb: D12 New England '89, injured reserve (hamstring) 8/29 through entire season, unprotected free agent 2/1/90; Kirby: D9 Green Bay '89, released 8/29, DEV Green Bay 11/15; Perkins: FA Pittsburgh '89, released 6/6; Shiver: D12 Green Bay '89, released 8/29; DEV Green Bay 9/6, released 12/27; Shulman: D8 Green Bay '89, released 8/29; Wise: D9 Seattle '88, released 8/24, FA New Orleans '89, released 9/5; Wright: Played with Helsinki Roosters of Scandinavian American Football League in '89.

HOUSTON OILERS
(Central Division, American Conference)

Jack Pardee

Owner-President—K. S. (Bud) Adams, Jr.
Executive Vice-President/General Manager—Mike Holovak
Director of College Scouting—Dick Corrick
Executive Administrator—Lewis Mangum
Director of Marketing & Broadcasting—Gregg Stengel
Director of Media Relations—Chip Namias
   (Office Phone: 797-9111—Area Code 713)
Head Coach—Jack Pardee (6 years: 44-46)

Assistant Coaches:
   Defensive Coordinator—Jim Eddy
   Offensive Coordinator—Kevin Gilbride
   Running Backs—Frank Novak
   Receivers—Chris Palmer
   Special Teams/Linebackers—Richard Smith
   Defensive Line—Jim Stanley
   Defensive Backs—Pat Thomas
   Strength/Rehabilitation—Steve Watterson
   Offensive Line—Bob Young

Offices—6910 Fannin, Houston, Tex. 77030
Mailing Address—P. O. Box 1516, Houston, Tex. 77251
Stadium—Astrodome (Capacity: 60,502)
Team Colors—Scarlet, Columbia Blue and White
Training Site—Southwest Texas State University, San Marcos, Tex.

1990 SCHEDULE
(All times local.
All games Sunday unless noted otherwise.)

Sept. 9	at Atlanta		4:00
Sept. 16	at Pittsburgh		8:00
Sept. 23	INDIANAPOLIS		12:00
Sept. 30	at San Diego		1:00
Oct. 7	SAN FRANCISCO		12:00
Oct. 14	at Cincinnati		1:00
Oct. 21	NEW ORLEANS		12:00
Oct. 28	NEW YORK JETS		12:00
Nov. 4	at Los Angeles Rams		1:00
Nov. 11	OPEN DATE		
Nov. 18	at Cleveland		1:00
Nov. 26	BUFFALO (Mon.)		8:00
Dec. 2	at Seattle		1:00
Dec. 9	CLEVELAND		12:00
Dec. 16	at Kansas City		12:00
Dec. 23	CINCINNATI		12:00
Dec. 30	PITTSBURGH		7:00

1989 RESULTS—(Won 9, Lost 8)

Oilers		Opp.		Att.
7	Minnesota	38	(A)	54,015
34	San Diego	27	(A)	42,013
41	Buffalo (OT)	47	(H)	57,278
39	Miami	7	(H)	51,426
13	New England	23	(A)	59,828
33	Chicago	28	(A)	64,383
27	Pittsburgh	0	(H)	59,091
17	Cleveland	28	(A)	78,765
35	Detroit	31	(H)	48,056
26	Cincinnati	24	(H)	60,694
23	Los Angeles Raiders	7	(H)	59,198
0	Kansas City	34	(A)	51,342
23	Pittsburgh	16	(A)	40,541
20	Tampa Bay	17	(H)	54,532
7	Cincinnati	61	(A)	47,510
20	Cleveland	24	(H)	58,342

AFC WILD-CARD GAME

23	Pittsburgh (OT)	26	(H)	58,306

1989 GAMES STARTED

16 games: Patrick Allen, Steve Brown, Bruce Davis, John Grimsley, Alonzo Highsmith, Bruce Matthews, Bubba McDowell, Johnny Meads, Warren Moon, Mike Munchak, Dean Steinkuhler.

15 games: Ernest Givins, Al Smith.

14 games: Ray Childress, Jeff Donaldson, Bob Mrosko.

13 games: Robert Lyles.

12 games: Drew Hill, Jay Pennison, Doug Smith.

10 games: Mike Rozier.

9 games: William Fuller.

8 games: Richard Byrd.

6 games: Allen Pinkett.

5 games: Sean Jones.

4 games: Haywood Jeffires.

3 games: Eric Fairs, George Yarno.

2 games: Tracey Eaton, Chris Verhulst.

1 game: Curtis Duncan, Don Maggs, Eugene Seale.

HOUSTON OILERS 1990 VETERAN ROSTER

No.	Name	Pos.	Ht.	Wt.	NFL Exp.	Birth-date	College	Games in '89	How Acquired
29	†Allen, Patrick	CB	5-10	182	7	8-26-61	Utah State	16	D4a, '84
31	Arnold, David	S	6-3	210	2	11-21-66	Michigan	*15	UFA, '90
33	Bell, Billy	CB	5-10	170	2	1-16-61	Lamar	4	FA, '89
58	Brantley, John	LB	6-2	240	2	10-23-65	Georgia	8	FA, '89
24	Brown, Steve	CB	5-11	187	8	3-20-60	Oregon	16	D3b, '83
71	Byrd, Richard	NT	6-4	273	6	3-20-62	Southern Mississippi	16	D2, '85
67	Camp, Reggie	DE	6-4	270	7	2-28-61	California	*6	FA, '90
14	†Carlson, Cody	QB	6-3	194	4	11- 5-63	Baylor	6	D3, '87
79	Childress, Ray	NT/DE	6-6	278	6	10-20-62	Texas A&M	14	D1, '85
	Courville, Vince	WR	5-10	165	1	12- 5-59	Rice	*0	FA, '90
	Crawford, Tim	LB	6-4	230	2	12-17-62	Texas Tech	*0	FA, '90
77	†Davis, Bruce	T	6-6	315	12	6-21-56	UCLA	16	T-Rai, '87
	Dawson, Doug	G	6-3	267	3	12-27-61	Texas	*0	FA, '90
	DiGiacomo, Curt	G	6-4	275	3	10-24-63	Arizona	*0	FA, '90
28	Dishman, Cris	CB	6-0	178	3	8-13-65	Purdue	16	D5, '88
80	Duncan, Curtis	WR	5-11	184	4	1-28-65	Northwestern	16	D10, '87
51	†Fairs, Eric	LB	6-3	238	5	2-17-64	Memphis State	16	FA, '86
88	Ford, Bernard	WR	5-10	171	2	5-13-66	Central Florida	*10	UFA, '90
95	Fuller, William	DE	6-3	269	5	3- 8-62	North Carolina	15	T-Ram, '86
97	Garalczyk, Mark	NT	6-5	272	3	8-12-64	Western Michigan	*0	UFA, '89
81	Givins, Ernest	WR	5-9	172	5	9- 3-64	Louisville	15	D2, '86
59	†Grimsley, John	LB	6-2	238	7	2-25-62	Kentucky	16	D6, '84
83	†Harris, Leonard	WR	5-8	162	5	11-27-60	Texas Tech	11	FA, '87
	Harry, Carl	WR	5-9	168	1	10-26-67	Utah	*1	UFA, '90
32	Highsmith, Alonzo	RB	6-1	234	4	2-28-65	Miami (Fla.)	16	D1, '87
85	Hill, Drew	WR	5-9	174	11	10- 5-56	Georgia Tech	14	T-Ram, '85
86	Jackson, Kenny	WR	6-0	183	7	2-15-62	Penn State	10	UFA, '89
84	Jeffires, Haywood	WR	6-2	201	4	12-12-64	North Carolina State	16	D1a, '87
90	Johnson, Ezra	DE	6-4	255	14	10- 2-55	Morris Brown	*16	UFA, '90
23	Johnson, Richard	CB	6-1	195	6	9-16-63	Wisconsin	14	D1a, '85
22	Jones, Quintin	S	5-11	194	2	7-28-66	Pittsburgh	*0	FA, '90
96	†Jones, Sean	DE	6-7	273	7	12-19-62	Northeastern	16	T-Rai, '88
27	Kinard, Terry	S	6-1	198	8	11-24-59	Clemson	*16	UFA, '90
21	Knight, Leander	CB/S	6-1	196	2	2-16-63	Montclair State	*13	UFA, '90
56	Kozak, Scott	LB	6-3	226	2	11-28-65	Oregon	16	D2, '89
93	Lyles, Robert	LB	6-1	230	7	3-21-61	Texas Christian	13	D5, '84
78	Maggs, Don	T/G	6-5	285	4	11- 1-61	Tulane	16	SupD, '84
74	Matthews, Bruce	G	6-5	288	8	8- 8-61	Southern California	16	D1, '83
25	McDowell, Bubba	S	6-1	195	2	11- 4-66	Miami (Fla.)	16	D3, '89
89	McNeil, Gerald	WR/KR	5-8	144	5	3-27-62	Baylor	*16	UFA, '90
91	Meads, Johnny	LB	6-2	232	7	6-25-61	Nicholls State	16	D3, '84
94	Montgomery, Glenn	NT	6-0	274	2	3-31-67	Houston	15	D5, '89
9	Montgomery, Greg	P	6-4	217	3	10-29-64	Michigan State	16	D3, '88
1	Moon, Warren	QB	6-3	210	7	11-18-56	Washington	16	FA, '84
63	Munchak, Mike	G	6-3	284	9	3- 5-60	Penn State	16	D1, '82
52	Pennison, Jay	C	6-1	282	5	9- 9-61	Nicholls State	12	FA, '86
20	†Pinkett, Allen	RB	5-9	192	5	1-25-64	Notre Dame	16	D3, '86
98	Reese, Jerry	NT/DE	6-2	275	2	7-11-64	Kentucky	*0	FA, '90
66	Robison, Tommy	G/T	6-4	295	3	11-17-61	Texas A&M	*9	UFA, '90
	Rosado, Dan	G	6-3	280	3	7- 6-59	Northern Illinois	*0	FA, '90
30	†Rozier, Mike	RB	5-10	213	6	3- 1-61	Nebraska	12	SupD, '84
53	Seale, Eugene	LB	5-10	250	4	6- 3-64	Lamar	15	FA, '87
54	Smith, Al	LB	6-1	240	4	11-26-64	Utah State	15	D6, '87
99	†Smith, Doug	NT	6-6	286	6	6-13-59	Auburn	15	D2, '84
70	Steinkuhler, Dean	T	6-3	287	7	1-27-61	Nebraska	16	D1, '84
44	White, Lorenzo	RB	5-11	218	3	4-12-66	Michigan State	16	D1, '88
69	Williams, Doug	G/T	6-6	295	3	10- 1-62	Texas A&M	*0	FA, '90
7	Zendejas, Tony	K	6-8	165	6	5-15-60	Nevada-Reno	16	T-Was, '85

*Arnold played 15 games with Steelers in '89; Camp last active with Falcons in '88; Courville active for one game with Oilers in '89 but did not play; Crawford last active with Browns in '87; Dawson last active with Cardinals in '86; DiGiacomo last active with Chiefs in '88; Ford played 10 games with Cowboys in '89; Garalczyk missed '89 season due to injury; Harry played 1 game with Redskins in '89; E. Johnson played 16 games with Colts in '89; Q. Jones last active with Oilers in '88; Kinard played 16 games with Giants in '89; Knight played 13 games with Jets in '89; McNeil played 16 games with Browns in '89; Reese last active with Steelers in '88; Robison played 9 games with Falcons in '89; Rosado last active with Chargers in '88; Williams last active with Oilers in '87.

†Unsigned; subject to developments.

Players lost through Plan B free agency: S Jeff Donaldson (14 games in '89; to K.C.); S Tracey Eaton (16; to Phoe.); RB Tracy Johnson (16; to Atl.); TE Bob Mrosko (15; to N.Y.G.); DE Anthony Spears (0; to Dall.); TE Chris Verhulst (16; to Den.); C George Yarno (11; to G.B.).

Also played with Oilers in '89—RB Steve Avery (1 game); S Kenny Johnson (16).

D—Draft; T—Trade; FA—Free Agent; UFA—Unrestricted Free Agent; SupD—Supplemental Draft.

HOUSTON OILERS
1990 DRAFT CHOICES

(Number following name designates order of selection among 331 players drafted.)

Round and Player		Position	College
1. LATHON, Lamar	15	LB	Houston
2. ALM, Jeff	41	DT	Notre Dame
3. PEGUESE, Willis	72	DE	Miami (Fla.)
4. STILL, Eric	99	G	Tennessee
5. NEWBILL, Richard	126	LB	Miami (Fla.)
6. JONES, Tony	153	WR	Texas
7. MURRAY, Andy	184	RB	Kentucky
8. TUCKER, Brett (a)	211	DB	Northern Illinois
9. COLEMAN, Pat	237	WR	Mississippi
10. THOMAS, Dee	264	DB	Nicholls State
11. BANES, Joey	295	T	Houston
12. SLACK, Reggie	321	QB	Auburn

(a) Tucker is expected to miss entire 1990 season because of knee injury.

HOUSTON OILERS
1990 ROOKIE AND FIRST-YEAR ROSTER

Name	Pos.	Hgt.	Wgt.	Birth-date	College	How Acquired
Alm, Jeff	NT	6-6	273	3-31-68	Notre Dame	D2
Banes, Joe	T	6-7	282	4- 7-67	Houston	D11
Canady, Bruce	DB	..	..	....	Washburn	FA
Coleman, Pat	WR	5-7	173	4- 8-67	Mississippi	D9
Dacus, David	QB	6-2	215	....	Houston	FA
Gordon, Cedric	WR	6-0	165	11- 6-66	Ferris State	*FA
Hartlieb, Chuck	QB	6-1	208	3-12-66	Iowa	*FA
Jackson, Mark	DB	..	..	....	Abilene Christian	FA
Jones, Max	LB	..	..	....	Massachusetts	FA
Jones, Tony	WR	5-7	142	12-30-65	Texas	D6
Jones, Victor	FB	5-9	205	....	Louisiana State	FA
Lathon, Lamar	LB	6-3	250	12-23-67	Houston	D1
Miotke, Frank	WR	6-0	175	12-22-65	Grand Valley State	*FA
Murray, Andy	RB	6-1	244	4-27-66	Kentucky	D7
Newbill, Richard	LB	6-1	240	2- 8-68	Miami (Fla.)	D5
Norgard, Erik	C/G	6-1	285	11- 4-65	Colorado	*FA
Orlando, Bo	S	5-10	180	4- 3-66	West Virginia	*FA
Owens, Al	WR	5-9	166	3-26-66	New Mexico	*FA
Peguese, Willis	DE	6-4	267	12-18-66	Miami (Fla.)	D3
Perez, Mike	QB	6-1	210	3- 7-65	San Jose State	*FA
Slack, Reggie	QB	6-1	217	5- 2-68	Auburn	D12
Stewart, Alex	DE	6-3	263	8-24-64	Fullerton State	*FA
Still, Eric	G/T	6-3	279	6-28-67	Tennessee	D4
Thomas, Dee	CB/S	5-10	176	11- 7-67	Nicholls State	D10
Tucker, Brett	CB/S	5-11	194	9- 6-67	Northern Illinois	*D8

*Gordon: FA Washington '89, released 7/25, DEV Green Bay 9/12, released 12/27; Hartlieb: D12 Houston '89, released 9/5, DEV Houston 9/8, released 1/2/90; Miotke: FA New York Giants '89, released 9/5, DEV New York Giants 9/6, released 1/29/90; Norgard: FA Houston '89, released 8/30, DEV Houston 9/6, released 1/2/90; Orlando: D6 Houston '89, released 9/5, DEV Houston 9/8, released 1/2/90; Owens: FA New Orleans '89, released 7/25; Perez: D7 New York Giants '88, injured reserve (pulled stomach muscle) 9/19 through entire season, released 8/23/89; Stewart: D8 Minnesota '89, injured reserve (hand) 9/5 through 10/11, traded to Dallas in Herschel Walker deal 10/12, remained on injured reserve through 11/9, released 11/10; Tucker: Expected to miss entire 1990 season with knee injury.

INDIANAPOLIS COLTS
(Eastern Division, American Conference)

Ron Meyer

President and Treasurer—Robert Irsay
General Manager—Jim Irsay
Assistant General Manager—Bob Terpening
Player Personnel Director—Jack Bushofsky
Head Coach—Ron Meyer (7 years: 47-37)

Assistant Coaches:
  Running Backs—Leon Burtnett
  Secondary—George Catavolos
  Receivers—Milt Jackson
  Offensive Coordinator—Larry Kennan
  Defensive Line—Bill Muir
  Offensive Line—Dante Scarnecchia
  Special Teams—Brad Seely
  Linebackers—Rick Venturi
  Strength & Conditioning—Tom Zupancic

Public Relations Director—Craig Kelley
  (Office Phone: 297-2658—Area Code 317)

Mailing Address—P. O. Box 535000 Indianapolis, Ind. 46253
Stadium—Hoosier Dome (Capacity: 60,127)
Team Colors—Royal Blue and White
Training Site—Anderson University, Anderson, Ind.

1990 SCHEDULE
(All times local.
All games Sunday unless noted otherwise.)

Sept. 9	at Buffalo	4:00
Sept. 16	NEW ENGLAND	12:00
Sept. 23	at Houston	12:00
Sept. 30	at Philadelphia	1:00
Oct. 7	KANSAS CITY	12:00
Oct. 14	OPEN DATE	
Oct. 21	DENVER	12:00
Oct. 28	MIAMI	1:00
Nov. 5	NEW YORK GIANTS (Mon.)	9:00
Nov. 11	at New England	1:00
Nov. 18	NEW YORK JETS	4:00
Nov. 25	at Cincinnati	1:00
Dec. 2	at Phoenix	2:00
Dec. 9	BUFFALO	1:00
Dec. 16	at New York Jets	1:00
Dec. 22	WASHINGTON (Sat.)	8:00
Dec. 30	at Miami	1:00

1989 RESULTS—(Won 8, Lost 8)

Colts		Opp.		Att.
24	San Francisco	30	(H)	60,111
17	Los Angeles Rams	31	(A)	63,995
13	Atlanta	9	(H)	57,816
17	New York Jets	10	(A)	65,542
37	Buffalo	14	(H)	58,890
3	Denver	14	(A)	74,680
23	Cincinnati	12	(A)	57,642
20	New England (OT)	23	(H)	59,256
13	Miami	19	(A)	52,680
7	Buffalo	30	(A)	79,256
27	New York Jets	10	(H)	58,236
10	San Diego	6	(H)	58,822
16	New England	22	(A)	32,234
23	Cleveland (OT)	17	(H)	58,550
42	Miami	13	(H)	55,665
6	New Orleans	41	(A)	49,009

1989 GAMES STARTED

16 games: Harvey Armstrong, Michael Ball, Duane Bickett, Bill Brooks, Randy Dixon, Ray Donaldson, Mike Prior, Donnell Thompson, Ben Utt.

15 games: Kevin Call, Jon Hand, Fredd Young.

14 games: Eugene Daniel, Eric Dickerson, Jeff Herrod, Chris Hinton.

13 games: Pat Beach, Andre Rison.

12 games: Jack Trudeau.

10 games: Chip Banks.

8 games: John Baylor, Albert Bentley, Chris Goode.

7 games: Clarence Verdin.

5 games: Mark Boyer.

4 games: O'Brien Alston.

3 games: Brian Baldinger, Chris Chandler, Cliff Odom, James Pruitt.

2 games: Quintus McDonald, Bruce Plummer.

1 game: Ivy Joe Hunter, Ezra Johnson, Tom Ramsey.

INDIANAPOLIS COLTS 1990 VETERAN ROSTER

No.	Name	Pos.	Ht.	Wt.	NFL Exp.	Birth-date	College	Games in '89	How Acquired
97	†Alston, O'Brien	LB	6-6	241	3	12-21-65	Maryland	4	D10, '88
79	Armstrong, Harvey	NT	6-3	282	7	12-29-59	Southern Methodist	16	FA, '86
62	Baldinger, Brian	G	6-4	272	8	1- 7-59	Duke	16	FA, '88
	Baldinger, Gary	DE	6-2	271	4	10- 4-63	Wake Forest	*0	FA, '90
31	Ball, Michael	CB/S	6-0	217	3	8- 5-64	Southern University	18	D4, '88
51	Banks, Chip	LB	6-4	245	8	9-18-59	Southern California	10	T-SD, '89
36	†Baylor, John	CB/S	6-0	203	2	3- 5-65	Southern Mississippi	16	D5, '88
81	Beach, Pat	TE	6-4	252	8	12-28-59	Washington State	16	D6, '82
95	Benson, Mitchell	NT	6-3	302	2	5-30-67	Texas Christian	16	D3, '89
20	Bentley, Albert	RB	5-11	214	6	8-15-60	Miami (Fla.)	16	SupD, '84
4	†Biasucci, Dean	K	6-0	189	6	7-25-62	Western Carolina	16	FA, '86
50	Bickett, Duane	LB	6-5	251	6	12- 1-62	Southern California	16	D1, '85
80	Brooks, Bill	WR	6-0	185	5	4- 6-64	Boston University	16	D4, '86
71	Call, Kevin	T	6-7	308	7	11-13-61	Colorado State	15	D5a, '84
17	Chandler, Chris	QB	6-4	218	3	10-12-65	Washington	3	D3, '88
91	Clancy, Sam	DE	6-7	264	7	5-29-58	Pittsburgh	16	UFA, '89
	Conlin, Chris	T	6-4	288	2	6- 7-65	Penn State	*0	FA, '90
38	Daniel, Eugene	CB	5-11	188	7	5- 4-61	Louisiana State	15	D8, '84
	Dean, Kevin	LB	6-1	241	2	2- 5-65	Texas Christian	*0	FA, '90
29	Dickerson, Eric	RB	6-3	224	8	9- 2-60	Southern Methodist	15	T-Ram, '87
69	†Dixon, Randy	G	6-3	302	4	3-12-65	Pittsburgh	16	D4, '87
53	Donaldson, Ray	C	6-3	292	11	5-17-58	Georgia	16	D2, '80
67	Eisenhooth, Stan	T/G	6-5	290	3	7- 8-63	Towson State	16	UFA, '89
37	†Goode, Chris	CB	6-0	195	4	9-17-63	Alabama	15	D10, '87
78	†Hand, Jon	DE	6-7	301	5	11-13-63	Alabama	16	D1, '86
54	†Herrod, Jeff	LB	6-0	246	3	7-29-66	Mississippi	15	D9, '88
	Hester, Jessie	WR	5-11	172	5	1-21-63	Florida State	*0	FA, '90
63	Knight, Steve	T	6-4	326	2	3-13-62	Tennessee	*0	FA, '89
	Kolic, Larry	LB	6-1	229	2	8-31-63	Ohio State	*0	FA, '90
59	Larson, Kurt	LB	6-4	236	2	2-25-66	Michigan State	13	D8, '89
96	McDonald, Quintus	LB	6-3	240	2	12-14-66	Penn State	15	D6, '89
	McNanie, Sean	DE	6-5	268	6	9- 9-61	San Diego State	*0	FA, '90
73	Moss, Zefross	T	6-6	315	2	8-17-66	Alabama State	16	T-Dal, '89
39	Prior, Mike	CB/S	6-10	210	5	11-14-63	Illinois State	16	FA, '87
49	†Pruitt, James	WR	6-3	201	5	1-29-64	Cal State-Fullerton	16	W-Mia, '88
	Rentie, Caesar	T	6-3	304	2	11-10-64	Oklahoma	*0	FA, '90
3	Stark, Rohn	P	6-3	203	9	5- 4-59	Florida State	16	D2a, '82
27	Taylor, Keith	CB/S	5-11	206	3	12-21-64	Illinois	16	FA, '88
99	Thompson, Donnell	DE	6-4	280	10	10-27-58	North Carolina	16	D1a, '81
10	Trudeau, Jack	QB	6-3	219	5	9- 9-62	Illinois	13	D2, '86
83	Verdin, Clarence	WR	5-8	170	5	6-14-63	Southwestern Louisiana	16	T-Was, '88
56	Young, Fredd	LB	6-1	235	7	11-14-61	New Mexico State	15	T-Sea, '88

*G. Baldinger last active with Chiefs in '88; Conlin last active with Dolphins in '87; Dean last active with 49ers in '87; Hester last active with Falcons in '88; Knight missed '89 season due to injury; Kolic last active with Dolphins in '87; McNanie last active with Bills in '88; Rentie last active with Bears in '88.

†Unsigned; subject to developments.

Players lost through Plan B free agency: TE Mark Boyer (16 games in '89; to N.Y.J.); TE John Brandes (16; to Wash.); DE Ezra Johnson (16; to Hou.); LB Cliff Odom (16; to Mia.); CB/S Anthony Parker (1; to N.Y.J.); DB Bruce Plummer (16; to S.D.); G Ben Utt (16; to Atl); CB/S Charles Washington (16; to K.C.).

Also played with Colts in '89—WR Matt Bouza (2 games); TE Donnie Dee (1); WR Titus Dixon (1); T Chris Hinton (14); QB Wayne Johnson (active for 4 games but did not play); LB Orlando Lowery (9); LB Dan Murray (2); LB Eric Naposki (1); QB Tom Ramsey (7); WR Andre Rison (16); QB Don Strock (active for 9 games in '89, but did not play); LB Ronnie Washington (2); WR Clarence Weathers (4).

D—Draft; T—Trade; W—Waivers; FA—Free Agent; UFA—Unrestricted Free Agent; SupD—Supplemental Draft.

INDIANAPOLIS COLTS
1990 DRAFT CHOICES

(Number following name designates order of selection among 331 players drafted.)

Round and Player	Position		College
1. GEORGE, Jeff from Atlanta (a)	1	QB	Illinois
1. Choice to New England through Seattle (b)			
2. JOHNSON, Anthony	36	RB	Notre Dame
3. Choice to San Diego (c)			
4. SIMMONS, Stacey from Atlanta (a)	83	WR	Florida
4. SCHULTZ, Bill	94	G	Southern Cal
4. GRANT, Alan from Washington (d)	103	DB	Stanford
4. CUNNINGHAM, Pat from Philadelphia (e)	106	T	Texas A&M
5. Choice to Atlanta (a)			
6. WALKER, Tony	148	LB	S.E. Missouri
7. SINGLETARY, James	179	LB	East Carolina
8. CLARK, Ken	206	RB	Nebraska
8. WILSON, Harvey from Washington (d)	213	DB	Southern U.
9. HUFFMAN, Darvell	232	WR	Boston University
10. Choice to Denver through Dallas and Los Angeles Raiders (f)			
11. SMITH, Carnel	290	DE	Pittsburgh
12. BENHART, Gene from San Diego (g)	311	QB	Western Illinois
12. BROWN, Dean	316	G	Notre Dame

(a) Acquired 1st- and 4th-round picks for tackle Chris Hinton, wide receiver Andre Rison, 5th-round pick and 1st-round pick in 1991, April 20, 1990.

(b) Colts traded pick and 1st-round pick in 1989 to Seahawks for linebacker Fredd Young, September 9, 1988; Seahawks traded pick, another 1st-round pick, 3rd-round pick and 4th-round pick in 1991 to Patriots for 1st- and 2nd-round picks, April 22, 1990.

(c) Traded pick for linebacker Chip Banks, October 17, 1989.

(d) Acquired 4th- and 8th-round picks for 5th-round pick in 1989, April 23, 1989.

(e) Acquired pick and 1st-round pick in 1989 for guard Ron Solt, October 4, 1988.

(f) Colts traded pick to Cowboys for tackle Zefross Moss, August 22, 1989; Cowboys traded pick and 6th-, 8th-, 9th- and 11th-round picks to Raiders for rights to cornerback Stan Smagala, April 22, 1990; Raiders traded pick to Broncos for 11th-round pick, April 23, 1990.

(g) Acquired pick for defensive back Leonard Coleman, July 8, 1988.

INDIANAPOLIS COLTS
1990 ROOKIE AND FIRST-YEAR ROSTER

Name	Pos.	Hgt.	Wgt.	Birth-date	College	How Acquired
Ames, Bill	TE	6-5	254	6-24-67	Washington	FA
Amos, Dale	WR	6-0	178	9-25-66	Franklin & Marshall	FA
Barnes, Reggie	RB	5-11	196	2-13-67	NE Oklahoma State	FA
Bell, Jim	RB	6-0	210	6-24-65	Boston College	*FA
Benhart, Gene	QB	6-4	220	1- 4-67	Western Illinois	D12
Brown, Dean	G/T	6-3	292	9- 7-68	Notre Dame	D12a
Clark, Ken	RB	5-9	201	6-11-66	Nebraska	D8
Cunningham, Pat	T	6-6	295	1- 4-69	Texas A&M	D4c
Davis, Pat	TE	6-3	284	6-13-66	Syracuse	*FA
Finkelston, Tim	WR	5-10	182	7-25-67	Virginia	FA
Fortune, Chad	TE	6-5	238	12- 1-66	Louisville	FA
Freeman, Tim	T	6-4	292	12-16-66	Penn State	FA
George, Jeff	QB	6-4	221	12- 8-67	Illinois	D1
Grant, Alan	CB/S	5-10	187	10- 1-66	Stanford	D4b
Henderson, Joe	RB	6-0	212	4- 9-66	Iowa State	*FA
Holloway, Cornell	CB/S	5-11	185	1-30-66	Pittsburgh	*FA
Huffman, Darvell	WR	5-7	158	5- 5-67	Boston University	D9
Jackson, Orsorio	CB/S	6-0	194	9-15-68	Tennessee State	FA
Johnson, Anthony	RB	6-0	222	10-25-67	Notre Dame	D2
Johnson, Ricky	RB	6-0	200	3- 7-60	Maryland	FA
Lowery, Doug	DE	6-5	267	4-23-68	DePauw	FA
O'Connor, Dwayne	TE	6-3	239	12-17-67	Purdue	FA
Rawls, Alfred	RB	5-9	201	12-20-66	Kentucky	FA
Rider, David	CB/S	6-2	201	9-15-66	New Mexico State	FA
Riley, Eugene	TE	6-2	227	10- 9-66	Ball State	FA
Robinson, Ron	CB/S	6-0	185	5-26-67	Kentucky	FA
Schultz, William	T	6-5	293	5- 1-67	Southern California	D4a
Simmons, Stacey	WR	5-9	183	8- 5-68	Florida	D4
Singletary, James	LB	6-2	231	8-17-66	East Carolina	D7
Siragusa, Tony	NT	6-3	296	5-14-67	Pittsburgh	FA
Smith, Carnel	DE	6-2	263	11-13-66	Pittsburgh	D11
Teeter, Mike	NT	6-2	255	10-14-67	Michigan	FA
Tomberlin, Pat	T	6-2	320	1-29-66	Florida State	D4
Vanderbeek, Matt	DE	6-3	241	8-16-67	Michigan State	FA
Vargo, Ron	C	6-1	283	2- 9-67	Indiana	FA
Walker, Tony	LB	6-3	235	4- 2-68	Southeast Missouri State	D6
Williams, Reggie	WR	6-1	190	2- 8-66	Pittsburgh	FA
Wilson, Harvey	CB/S	6-1	191	12-13-68	Southern University	D8a
Wright, Bo	RB	5-10	221	9-19-65	Alabama	*FA

*Bell: D11 San Francisco '89, released 8/23, DEV San Francisco 9/6, released 1/19/90; Davis: D9 San Diego '89, released 8/30, DEV Indianapolis 9/13, released 12/26; Henderson: D10 New Orleans '89, released 8/30, DEV Indianapolis 9/7, released 12/26; Holloway: D10 Cincinnati '89, released 9/5, DEV Indianapolis 9/7, released 12/26; Wright: D7 Buffalo '88, injured reserve 8/29 through entire season, released 8/30/89.

KANSAS CITY CHIEFS
(Western Division, American Conference)

Marty Schottenheimer

Owner—Lamar Hunt
Chairman of the Board—Jack Steadman
President/G.M. & Chief Operating Officer—Carl Peterson
Director of Player Personnel—Whitey Dovell
Head Coach—Marty Schottenheimer (6 years: 52-34-1)
Assistant Coaches:
    Running Backs—Bruce Arians
    Asst. Strength & Conditioning—Russ Ball
    Def. Coordinator/Linebackers—Bill Cowher
    Defensive Backs—Tony Dungy
    Offensive Line/Tight Ends—Jim Erkenbeck
    Offensive Line—Howard Mudd
    Off. Coordinator/Quarterbacks—Joe Pendry
    Defensive Line—Tom Pratt
    Strength & Conditioning—Dave Redding
    Receivers—Al Saunders
    Special Teams—Kurt Schottenheimer
    Quality Control—Darvin Wallis
Public Relations Director—Robert Moore
    (Office Phone: 924-9300—Area Code 816)
Offices—One Arrowhead Drive, Kansas City, Mo. 64129
Stadium—Arrowhead Stadium (Capacity: 78,067)
Team Colors—Red, Gold and White
Training Site—William Jewell College, Liberty, Mo.

1990 SCHEDULE
(All times local.
All games Sunday unless noted otherwise.)

Sept. 9	MINNESOTA	12:00
Sept. 17	at Denver (Mon.)	7:00
Sept. 23	at Green Bay	12:00
Sept. 30	CLEVELAND	3:00
Oct. 7	at Indianapolis	12:00
Oct. 14	DETROIT	12:00
Oct. 21	at Seattle	1:00
Oct. 28	OPEN DATE	
Nov. 4	LOS ANGELES RAIDERS	12:00
Nov. 11	SEATTLE	12:00
Nov. 18	SAN DIEGO	12:00
Nov. 25	at Los Angeles Raiders	1:00
Dec. 2	at New England	1:00
Dec. 9	DENVER	3:00
Dec. 16	HOUSTON	12:00
Dec. 23	at San Diego	1:00
Dec. 29	at Chicago (Sat.)	11:30

1989 RESULTS—(Won 8, Lost 7, Tied 1)

Chiefs		Opp.		Att.
20	Denver	34	(A)	74,284
24	Los Angeles Raiders	19	(H)	71,741
6	San Diego	21	(A)	40,128
17	Cincinnati	21	(H)	60,165
20	Seattle	16	(A)	60,715
14	Los Angeles Rams	20	(A)	40,453
36	Dallas	28	(H)	76,841
17	Pittsburgh	23	(A)	54,194
20	Seattle	10	(H)	54,488
13	Denver	16	(H)	76,245
10	Cleveland (OT)	10	(A)	77,922
34	Houston	0	(H)	51,342
26	Miami	21	(H)	54,610
21	Green Bay	3	(A)	56,694
13	San Diego	20	(H)	40,623
27	Miami	24	(A)	43,612

1989 GAMES STARTED

16 games: John Alt, Jonathan Hayes, Albert Lewis, David Lutz, Chris Martin, Kevin Porter, Derrick Thomas, Mike Webster.

15 games: Walker Lee Ashley, Deron Cherry, Neil Smith.

14 games: Christian Okoye.

13 games: Irv Eatman, Dino Hackett, Kevin Ross.

12 games: Pete Mandley, Stephone Paige.

11 games: Mark Adickes, Leonard Griffin.

10 games: Steve DeBerg, Herman Heard, Bill Maas.

8 games: Rich Baldinger, Dan Saleaumua.

6 games: Mike Bell, Emile Harry.

3 games: Carlos Carson, Ron Jaworski, J.C. Pearson, Steve Pelluer.

2 games: Rob McGovern, Alfredo Roberts, James Saxon.

1 game: Lloyd Burruss, Paul Ott Carruth, Robb Thomas, Naz Worthen.

KANSAS CITY CHIEFS 1990 VETERAN ROSTER

No.	Name	Pos.	Ht.	Wt.	NFL Exp.	Birth-date	College	Games in '89	How Acquired
76	Alt, John	T	6-7	300	7	5-30-62	Iowa	16	D1a, '84
54	Ashley, Walker Lee	LB	6-0	231	7	7-28-60	Penn State	16	UFA, '89
77	Baldinger, Rich	G/T	6-4	292	9	12-31-59	Wake Forest	16	FA, '83
99	Bell, Mike	DE	6-4	262	10	8-30-57	Colorado State	15	D1, '79
34	Burruss, Lloyd	S	6-0	205	10	10-31-57	Maryland	9	D3b, '81
70	Cannon, Mark	C	6-3	258	7	6-14-62	Texas-Arlington	11	FA, '89
20	Cherry, Deron	S	5-11	202	10	9-12-59	Rutgers	15	OFA, '81
62	Chilton, Gene	C/G	6-3	286	4	3-27-64	Texas	16	FA, '89
55	†Cooper, Louis	LB	6-2	238	6	8- 5-63	Western Carolina	16	FA, '85
25	Copeland, Danny	S/KR	6-2	210	2	1-24-66	Eastern Kentucky	16	UFA, '89
17	DeBerg, Steve	QB	6-3	214	14	1- 9-54	San Jose State	12	T-TB, '88
42	Donaldson, Jeff	S	6-0	190	7	4-19-62	Colorado	*14	UFA, '90
75	†Eatman, Irv	T	6-7	298	5	1- 1-61	UCLA	13	D8, '83
10	Elkins, Mike	QB	6-3	225	2	7-20-66	Wake Forest	1	D2, '89
22	Gamble, Kenny	RB/KR	5-10	204	2	3- 8-65	Colgate	2	D10, '88
2	Goodburn, Kelly	P	6-2	201	4	4-14-62	Emporia State	16	FA, '87
49	Griffin, James	S	6-2	203	8	9- 7-61	Middle Tennessee St.	*16	UFA, '90
98	†Griffin, Leonard	DE	6-4	272	5	9-22-62	Grambling State	16	D3, '86
56	†Hackett, Dino	LB	6-3	228	5	6-28-64	Appalachian State	13	D2, '86
26	Harmon, Kevin	RB	6-0	190	3	10-26-65	Iowa	*4	UFA, '90
73	Harris, Michael	G/C	6-4	306	2	8-30-66	Grambling State	3	OFA, '89
86	Harry, Emile	WR	5-11	178	4	4- 5-63	Stanford	16	FA, '86
85	Hayes, Jonathan	TE	6-5	254	6	8-11-62	Iowa	16	D2, '85
44	†Heard, Herman	RB	5-10	194	7	11-24-61	Southern Colorado	16	D3, '84
41	Hill, Will	S	6-0	200	2	3- 5-63	Bishop	*0	FA, '90
7	Jaworski, Ron	QB	6-1	202	16	3-23-51	Youngstown State	6	UFA, '89
	Johnson, Sidney	CB	5-9	175	2	3- 7-65	California	*0	FA, '90
91	Jones, Rod	TE	6-4	245	4	3- 3-64	Washington	*4	UFA, '90
3	Karcher, Ken	QB	6-3	205	3	7- 1-63	Tulane	*0	FA, '90
29	Lewis, Albert	CB	6-2	198	8	10- 6-60	Grambling	16	D3, '83
8	Lowery, Nick	K	6-4	189	11	5-27-56	Dartmouth	16	FA, '80
72	†Lutz, David	G/T	6-6	303	8	12-30-59	Georgia Tech	16	D2, '83
63	Maas, Bill	NT/DE	6-5	277	7	12-19-60	Pittsburgh	10	D1, '84
89	†Mandley, Pete	WR	5-10	195	7	7-29-61	Northern Arizona	13	FA, '89
57	Martin, Chris	LB	6-2	232	8	12-19-60	Auburn	16	FA, '88
92	McCabe, Jerry	LB	6-2	225	3	1-25-65	Holy Cross	*0	FA, '90
50	McGovern, Rob	LB	6-2	223	2	10- 1-66	Holy Cross	16	D10, '89
48	McNair, Todd	RB/KR	6-1	185	2	10- 7-65	Temple	14	D8a, '89
69	Meisner, Greg	DE/NT	6-3	271	10	4-23-59	Pittsburgh	12	UFA, '89
68	Morris, Michael	C	6-5	275	3	2-22-61	Northeast Missouri St.	*16	UFA, '90
64	Neville, Tom	G	6-5	300	3	9- 4-61	Fresno State	*0	FA, '90
9	Nittmo, Bjorn	K	5-11	179	2	7-26-66	Appalachian State	*6	UFA, '90
35	Okoye, Christian	RB	6-1	260	4	8-16-61	Azusa Pacific	15	D2, '87
83	Paige, Stephone	WR	6-2	185	8	10-15-61	Fresno State	14	OFA, '83
24	Pearson, Jayice	CB	5-11	185	5	8-17-63	Washington	16	FA, '86
11	Pelluer, Steve	QB	6-4	212	7	7-29-62	Washington	5	T-Dal, '89
45	Petry, Stan	CB	5-11	175	2	8-14-66	Texas Christian	16	D4, '89
27	Porter, Kevin	S	5-10	219	3	4-11-66	Auburn	16	D3, '88
87	Roberts, Alfredo	TE	6-3	246	3	3- 1-65	Miami (Fla.)	16	D8, '88
31	†Ross, Kevin	CB	5-9	182	7	1-16-62	Temple	15	D7, '84
97	Saleaumua, Dan	NT	6-0	289	4	11-11-65	Arizona State	16	UFA, '89
21	†Saxon, James	RB	5-11	215	3	3-23-66	San Jose State	16	D6, '88
	Shorts, Peter	DE	6-8	278	1	7-12-66	Illinois State	*1	UFA, '90
90	Smith, Neil	DE	6-4	271	3	4-10-66	Nebraska	15	D1, '88
52	Snipes, Angelo	LB	6-0	228	4	1-11-63	West Georgia	2	FA, '87
58	Thomas, Derrick	LB	6-3	234	2	1- 1-67	Alabama	16	D1, '89
47	Thomas, Johnny	CB/S	5-9	185	3	8- 3-64	Baylor	*13	FA, '90
81	Thomas, Robb	WR	5-11	171	2	3-29-66	Oregon State	8	D6, '89
94	Ward, David	LB	6-2	232	3	3-10-64	Southern Arkansas	*16	UFA, '90
19	Ware, Timmie	WR	5-10	175	2	4- 2-63	Southern California	*13	UFA, '90
46	Washington, Charles	CB/S	6-1	208	2	10- 8-66	Cameron	*16	UFA, '90
53	Webster, Mike	C	6-2	260	17	3-18-52	Wisconsin	16	UFA, '89
65	Winters, Frank	C/G	6-3	280	4	1-23-64	Western Illinois	*15	UFA, '90
	Word, Barry	RB	6-2	220	2	7-17-64	Virginia	*0	FA, '90
84	Worthen, Naz	WR	5-8	177	2	3-27-66	North Carolina State	10	D3, '89

*Donaldson played 14 games with Oilers in '89; J. Griffin played 16 games with Lions in '89; Harmon played 4 games with Seahawks in '89; Hill last active with Browns in '88; Johnson last active with Chiefs in '88; Jones played 4 games with Seahawks in '89; Karcher last active with Broncos in '88; McCabe missed '89 season due to injury; Morris played 11 games with Patriots, 5 with Chiefs in '89; Neville last active with Packers in '88; Nittmo played 6 games with Giants in '89; Shorts played 1 game with Patriots in '89; J. Thomas played 13 games with Chargers in '89; Ward played 16 games with Patriots in '89; Ware played 13 games with Raiders in '89; Washington played 16 games with Colts in '89; Winters played 15 games with Giants in '89; Word last active with Saints in '88.

†Unsigned; subject to developments.

Players lost through Plan B free agency: G Mark Adickes (16 games in 89; to Wash.); RB Tommie Agee (9; to Dall.); LB Stacy Harvey (9; to Mia.); WR Clarence Weathers (11; to G.B.).

Also played with Chiefs in '89—WR/KR Lew Barnes (2 games); RB Paul Ott Carruth (2); WR Carlos Carson (7); DE Bruce Clark (11); TE Chris Dressel (7); S Kenny Hill (8); LB Mike Junkin (5).

D—Draft; T—Trade; FA—Free Agent; OFA—Original Free Agent; UFA—Unrestricted Free Agent.

KANSAS CITY CHIEFS
1990 DRAFT CHOICES

(Number following name designates order of selection among 331 players drafted.)

Round and Player		Position	College
1. SNOW, Percy	13	LB	Michigan State
2. GRUNHARD, Tim	40	C	Notre Dame
3. Choice to San Francisco through Dallas (a)			
4. JONES, Fred	96	WR	Grambling
5. GRAHAM, Derrick	124	T	Appalachian State
5. HACKEMACK, Ken from Buffalo (b)	127	T	Texas
6. SIMS, Tom	152	DT	Pittsburgh
7. SZOTT, Dave	180	G	Penn State
8. Choice to Buffalo (b)			
9. OWENS, Michael	235	RB	Syracuse
10. HUDSON, Craig	263	TE	Wisconsin
11. THOMPSON, Ernest	291	RB	Georgia Southern
12. JEFFERY, Tony	318	WR	San Jose State

(a) Chiefs traded pick and conditional 1991 pick to Cowboys for quarterback Steve Pelluer, October 17, 1989; Cowboys traded pick and 2nd-round pick to 49ers for running back Terrence Flagler, defensive end Dan Stubbs and 3rd- and 11th-round picks, April 19, 1990.

(b) Acquired 5th-round pick and 8th-round pick in 1989 for defensive end Art Still and 8th-round pick, June 23, 1988.

KANSAS CITY CHIEFS
1990 ROOKIE AND FIRST-YEAR ROSTER

Name	Pos.	Hgt.	Wgt.	Birth-date	College	How Acquired
Barker, Bryan	P	6-1	187	6-28-64	Santa Clara	*FA
Birden, J.J.	WR	5-9	160	6-16-65	Oregon	*FA
Davis, Willie	WR	6-0	159	10-10-67	Central Arkansas	FA
Floyd, Norman	CB	6-1	205	2-10-64	South Carolina	*FA
Graham, Derrick	T	6-4	305	3-18-67	Appalachian State	D5
Grunhard, Tim	C-G	6-2	292	5-17-68	Notre Dame	D2
Hackemack, Ken	DT	6-8	298	9-20-67	Texas	D5a
Huckaby, Howard	WR-K	5-9	180	8-22-68	Florida A&M	FA
Hudson, Craig	LB	6-3	245	5- 7-67	Wisconsin	D10
Jeffery, Tony	WR	5-10	173	1-11-67	San Jose State	D12
Johnson, Lee	NT	6-0	266	6- 9-67	Missouri	FA
Jones, Bill	RB	5-11	222	9-10-66	S.W. Texas State	*FA
Jones, Fred	WR	5-9	175	3- 6-67	Grambling State	D4
Kiselak, Mike	G	6-3	279	3- 9-67	Maryland	FA
Lowery, Bren	RB	5-10	197	5-29-67	Maryland	FA
Marts, Lonnie	LB	6-1	225	11-10-68	Tulane	FA
Owens, Michael	RB	5-11	218	4- 7-68	Syracuse	D9
Rainge, Sherrod	S	6-0	203	7-13-67	Penn State	FA
Rogers, Tracy	LB	6-2	235	8-13-67	Fresno State	*FA
Schonewolf, Rich	DT	6-4	278	12-19-66	Penn State	FA
Sims, Tom	DT	6-2	273	4-18-87	Pittsburgh	D6
Snow, Percy	LB	6-2	244	11- 5-67	Michigan State	D1
Szott, David	G	6-4	273	12-12-67	Penn State	D7
Thomas, Eric	LB	6-0	225	6-19-68	Georgia Tech	FA
Thompson, Ernest	RB	6-2	236	3-25-67	Georgia Southern	D11
Whitaker, Danta	TE	6-4	243	3-14-64	Mississippi Valley State	*FA
Wolkow, Troy	G	6-4	280	6-25-66	Minnesota	*FA
Woods, Rob	T	6-5	275	10- 3-65	Arizona	*UFA

*Barker: FA Denver '88, released 7/19, FA Seattle '89, released 8/30; Birden: D8 Cleveland '88, physically unable to perform (knee) 8/23 through entire season, released 9/5/89, DEV Dallas 11/1, released 1/5/90; Floyd: D11 Minnesota '88, injured reserve (shoulder) 8/23 through entire season, unprotected free agent 2/1/89, UFA Atlanta 3/13, released 8/8; B. Jones: D12 Kansas City '89, released 8/30, DEV Kansas City 10/26, released 1/18/90; Rogers: D7 Houston '89, released 9/5, DEV Houston 9/8, released 1/2/90; Whitaker: D7 New York Giants '88, injured reserve (ankle) 8/23 through entire season, unprotected free agent 2/1/89, UFA Atlanta 3/29, released 9/5, DEV Kansas City 11/1, released 1/18/90; Wolkow: D5 New England '88, injured reserve (dislocated shoulder) 8/23 through entire season, unprotected free agent 2/1/89, UFA Kansas City 3/20, released 8/30; Woods: D4 Cincinnati '89, injured reserve 9/5 through entire season, unprotected free agent 2/1/90.

LOS ANGELES RAIDERS
(Western Division, American Conference)

Art Shell

President of the Managing General Partners—Al Davis
Executive Assistant—Al LoCasale
Personnel Operations—Ron Wolf
Pro Football Scout—George Karras
Senior Executive—John Herrera
Senior Administrators—Irv Kaze, Morris Bradshaw
Head Coach—Art Shell (1 year: 7-5)
Assistant Coaches:
   Defense—Dave Adolph
   Receivers—Fred Biletnikoff
   Linebackers—Sam Gruneisen
   Offensive Line—Kim Helton
   Special Projects—Odis McKinney
   Football Oper./Special Teams—Steve Ortmayer
   Tight Ends—Terry Robiskie
   Offensive Backfield—Joe Scannella
   Strength & Conditioning—Todd Sperber
   Defensive Backfield—Jack Stanton
   Defensive Line—Bill Urbanik
   Offense—Tom Walsh
   Quarterbacks—Mike White
   (Office Phone: 322-3451—Area Code 213)
Offices—332 Center St., El Segundo, Calif. 90245
Stadium—Los Angeles Memorial Coliseum (Capacity: 92,488)
Team Colors—Silver and Black
Training Site—Oxnard, Calif.

1990 SCHEDULE
(All times local.
All games Sunday unless noted otherwise.)

Sept. 9	DENVER	1:00
Sept. 16	at Seattle	1:00
Sept. 23	PITTSBURGH	1:00
Sept. 30	CHICAGO	1:00
Oct. 7	at Buffalo	7:30
Oct. 14	SEATTLE	1:00
Oct. 21	at San Diego	1:00
Oct. 28	OPEN DATE	
Nov. 4	at Kansas City	12:00
Nov. 11	GREEN BAY	1:00
Nov. 19	at Miami (Mon.)	9:00
Nov. 25	KANSAS CITY	1:00
Dec. 2	at Denver	2:00
Dec. 10	at Detroit (Mon.)	9:00
Dec. 16	CINCINNATI	1:00
Dec. 22	at Minnesota (Sat.)	3:00
Dec. 30	SAN DIEGO	1:00

1989 RESULTS—(Won 8, Lost 8)

Raiders		Opp.		Att.
40	San Diego	14	(H)	40,237
19	Kansas City	24	(A)	71,741
21	Denver	31	(A)	75,754
20	Seattle	24	(H)	44,319
14	New York Jets	7	(A)	68,040
20	Kansas City	14	(H)	40,453
7	Philadelphia	10	(A)	64,019
37	Washington	24	(H)	52,781
28	Cincinnati	7	(H)	51,080
12	San Diego	14	(A)	59,151
7	Houston	23	(A)	59,198
24	New England	21	(H)	38,747
16	Denver (OT)	13	(H)	87,560
16	Phoenix	14	(H)	41,785
17	Seattle	23	(A)	61,076
17	New York Giants	34	(A)	70,306

1989 GAMES STARTED

16 games: Thomas Benson, Mike Dyal, Willie Gault, John Gesek, Bob Golic, Steve Smith, Lionel Washington, Bruce Wilkerson.

15 games: Rory Graves, Terry McDaniel, Steve Wisniewski.

13 games: Scott Davis, Mervyn Fernandez, Linden King.

12 games: Mike Harden, Greg Townsend.

11 games: Howie Long, Don Mosebar, Jerry Robinson.

10 games: Eddie Anderson.

9 games: Bo Jackson, Jay Schroeder, Mike Wise.

7 games: Steve Beuerlein.

6 games: Zeph Lee.

5 games: Marcus Allen, Dan Turk.

4 games: Vann McElroy.

3 games: Emanuel King, Bill Pickel, Jackie Shipp, Steve Wright.

2 games: Vance Mueller.

1 game: Tim Brown, Mike Haynes, Ethan Horton, Ricky Hunley, Otis Wilson.

LOS ANGELES RAIDERS 1990 VETERAN ROSTER

No.	Name	Pos.	Ht.	Wt.	NFL Exp.	Birth-date	College	Games in '89	How Acquired
44	†Adams, Stefon	WR	5-10	185	5	8-11-63	East Carolina	14	D3a, '85
89	†Alexander, Mike	WR	6-3	195	2	3-19-65	Penn State	16	D8, '88
32	†Allen, Marcus	RB	6-2	205	9	3-26-60	Southern California	8	D1, '82
	Alzado, Lyle	DE	6-3	260	15	4- 3-49	Yankton	*0	FA, '90
33	Anderson, Eddie	CB	6-1	200	5	7-22-63	Fort Valley State	15	FA, '87
	Barksdale, Rod	WR	6-1	193	3	9- 8-62	Arizona	*0	FA, '90
54	Benson, Tom	LB	6-2	240	7	9- 6-61	Oklahoma	16	UFA, '89
7	†Beuerlein, Steve	QB	6-2	210	3	3- 7-65	Notre Dame	10	D4, '87
24	Brown, Ron	CB	5-11	185	7	3-31-61	Arizona State	*16	UFA, '90
81	Brown, Tim	WR	6-0	195	2	7-22-66	Notre Dame	1	D1, '88
50	Burton, Ron	LB	6-1	245	4	5- 2-64	North Carolina	*16	UFA, '90
99	Campbell, Joe	DE	6-3	240	3	12-28-66	New Mexico State	*9	UFA, '90
29	Carter, Russell	S	6-2	200	7	2-10-62	Southern Methodist	9	T-NYJ, '88
	Charles, Mike	NT	6-4	296	8	9-23-62	Syracuse	*6	FA, '90
	Cormier, Joe	LB	6-6	245	2	5- 3-63	Southern California	*0	FA, '90
23	Crudup, Derrick	RB	6-2	210	2	2-15-65	Oklahoma	4	FA, '90
70	Davis, Scott	DE	6-7	275	3	8- 7-65	Illinois	14	D1b, '88
84	†Dyal, Mike	TE	6-2	240	2	5-20-66	Texas A&I	16	FA, '88
	Ellison, Riki	LB	6-2	225	7	8-15-60	Southern California	*0	FA, '90
	Evans, Vince	QB	6-2	210	10	6-14-55	Southern California	1	FA, '90
86	Fernandez, Mervyn	WR	6-3	200	4	12-29-59	San Jose State	16	D10, '83
73	FitzPatrick, James	T	6-7	300	5	2- 1-64	Southern California	*13	UFA, '90
83	Gault, Willie	WR	6-1	180	8	9-15-60	Tennessee	16	T-Chi, '88
63	Gesek, John	G	6-5	280	4	2-18-63	Cal State-Sacramento	16	D10a, '87
79	Golic, Bob	DT	6-2	275	11	10-26-57	Notre Dame	16	UFA, '89
6	Gossett, Jeff	P	6-2	195	9	1-25-57	Eastern Illinois	16	T-Hou, '88
85	Graddy, Sam	WR	5-10	175	3	2-10-64	Tennessee	*0	UFA, '90
60	Graves, Rory	T	6-6	290	3	7-21-63	Ohio State	15	FA, '88
45	Harden, Mike	S	6-1	195	11	2-16-59	Michigan	15	FA, '89
22	†Haynes, Mike	CB	6-2	195	15	7- 1-53	Arizona State	13	T-NE, '83
61	Hellestrae, Dale	G	6-5	285	4	7-11-62	Southern Methodist	*0	UFA, '89
	Holland, Jamie	WR	6-1	195	4	2- 1-64	Ohio State	*16	T-SD, '90
88	†Horton, Ethan	TE	6-4	240	4	12-19-62	North Carolina	16	FA, '89
98	†Hunley, Ricky	LB	6-2	250	7	1-11-61	Arizona	12	FA, '89
34	Jackson, Bo	RB	6-1	230	4	11-30-62	Auburn	11	D7, '87
18	Jaeger, Jeff	K	5-11	195	3	11-26-64	Washington	16	UFA, '89
53	Jordan, Darin	LB	6-1	235	2	12- 4-64	Northeastern	*0	FA, '90
87	Junkin, Trey	TE	6-2	240	8	1-23-61	Louisiana Tech	16	FA, '85
92	King, Emanuel	LB	6-4	250	6	8-15-63	Alabama	16	UFA, '89
52	†King, Linden	LB	6-4	250	13	6-28-55	Colorado State	14	FA, '86
97	Klostermann, Bruce	LB	6-4	230	4	4-17-63	South Dakota State	*16	UFA, '90
25	Land, Dan	CB	6-0	190	2	7- 3-65	Albany State	10	FA, '89
75	Long, Howie	DE	6-5	270	10	1- 6-60	Villanova	14	D2, '81
	McCallum, Napoleon	RB	6-2	215	2	10- 6-63	Navy	*0	T-SD, '90
36	McDaniel, Terry	CB	5-10	175	2	2- 8-65	Tennessee	16	D1a, '88
26	†McElroy, Vann	S	6-2	195	9	1-13-60	Baylor	7	D3, '82
65	Montoya, Max	G	6-5	280	13	5-12-56	UCLA	*16	UFA, '90
72	Mosebar, Don	C	6-6	280	8	9-11-61	Southern California	12	D1, '83
42	†Mueller, Vance	RB	6-0	215	5	5- 5-64	Occidental	16	D4a, '86
43	Patterson, Elvis	CB	5-11	195	7	10-21-60	Kansas	*16	UFA, '90
74	Peat, Todd	T	6-2	310	4	5-20-64	Northern Illinois	*4	FA, '90
71	Pickel, Bill	DT	6-5	260	8	11- 5-59	Rutgers	16	D2, '83
31	†Porter, Kerry	RB	6-1	215	3	9-23-64	Washington State	16	FA, '89
20	†Price, Dennis	CB	6-1	175	3	6-14-65	UCLA	5	D5, '88
57	Robinson, Jerry	LB	6-2	225	12	12-18-56	UCLA	11	T-Phi, '85
78	Rother, Tim	T	6-7	275	2	9-28-65	Nebraska	16	D4, '88
13	†Schroeder, Jay	QB	6-4	215	7	6-28-61	UCLA	11	T-Was, '88
35	†Smith, Steve	RB	6-1	235	4	8-30-64	Penn State	16	D3, '87
39	†Strachan, Steve	RB	6-1	225	6	3-22-63	Boston College	16	D11, '85
27	Streeter, George	S	6-1	205	2	8-28-67	Notre Dame	*4	UFA, '90
93	‖Townsend, Greg	DE	6-3	260	8	11- 3-61	Texas Christian	16	D4, '83
67	Turk, Dan	C	6-4	270	5	6-25-62	Wisconsin	16	FA, '89
48	Washington, Lionel	CB	6-0	185	8	10-21-60	Tulane	16	T-StL, '87
68	Wilkerson, Bruce	T	6-5	285	4	7-28-64	Tennessee	16	D2, '87
90	Wise, Mike	DE	6-7	270	4	6- 5-64	California-Davis	16	D4, '86
76	Wisniewski, Steve	G	6-4	280	2	4- 7-67	Penn State	15	T-Dal, '89
66	Wright, Steve	T	6-6	280	8	4- 8-59	Northern Illinois	16	FA, '87

*Alzado last active with Raiders in '85; Barksdale last active with Cowboys in '87; R. Brown played

16 games with Rams in '89; Burton played 6 games with Cowboys, 10 with Cardinals in '89; Campbell played 9 games with Chargers in '89; Charles played 6 games with Chargers in '89; Cormier last active with Raiders in '87; Ellison missed '89 season due to injury with 49ers; FitzPatrick played 13 games with Chargers in '89; Graddy and Hellestrae missed '89 season due to injury; Holland played 16 games with Chargers in '89; Jordan last active with Steelers in '88; Klostermann played 16 games with Broncos in '89; McCallum last active with Raiders in '86; Montoya played 16 games with Bengals in '89; Patterson played 16 games with Chargers in '89; Peat played 4 games with Cardinals in '89; Streeter played 4 games with Bears in '89.

†Unsigned; subject to developments.

Players lost through Plan B free agency: WR Bobby Joe Edmonds (7 games in '89; to Sea.); C Bill Lewis (0; to Phx.); DE Mark Mraz (11; to Den.); WR Timmie Ware (13; to K.C.).

Also played with Raiders in '89—LB Joe Costello (2 games); DE Pete Koch (4); S Zeph Lee (13); LB Jackie Shipp (3); LB Otis Wilson (1).

D—Draft; T—Trade; FA—Free Agent; UFA—Unrestricted Free Agent.

LOS ANGELES RAIDERS
1990 DRAFT CHOICES

(Number following name designates order of selection among 331 players drafted.)

Round and Player		Position	College
1. SMITH, Anthony	11	DE	Arizona
2. WALLACE, Aaron	37	LB	Texas A & M
3. Choice to Chicago (a)			
4. DORN, Torin	95	DB	North Carolina
5. SMAGALA, Stan (b)	123	DB	Notre Dame
6. WILSON, Marcus	149	RB	Virginia
7. LEWIS, Garry from Chicago (c)	173	DB	Alcorn State
7. Choice to Chicago (c)			
8. JIMERSON, Arthur from New England through Dallas (d)	197	LB	Norfolk State
8. Choice to New Orleans (e)			
9. PERRY, Leon from Seattle through Dallas (f)	230	RB	Oklahoma
9. Choice to New Orleans (e)			
10. Choice to New Orleans (e)			
11. Choice to New Orleans (e)			
11. LEWIS, Ron from Denver (g)	303	WR	Jackson State
11. JONES, Myron from San Francisco through Dallas (h)	304	RB	Fresno State
12. HARRIS, Major (i)	317	QB	West Virginia
12. DAVIS, Demetrius from San Francisco (j)	331	TE	Nevada-Reno

(a) Traded pick and 1st-round pick in 1989 for wide receiver Willie Gault, July 28, 1988.
(b) Rights to Smagala traded to Cowboys for 6th-, 8th-, 9th-, 10th- and 11th-round picks, April 22, 1990.
(c) Acquired 7th-round pick for 7th- and 11th-round picks, April 23, 1990.
(d) Raiders acquired pick from Cowboys: see (b); Cowboys had acquired pick and 3rd- and 6th-round picks from Patriots for 3rd-, 5th- and 7th-round picks, April 22, 1990.
(e) Traded 6th-, 8th-, 9th-, 10th- and 11th-round picks for 4th-round pick in 1991, April 22, 1990.

(f) Raiders acquired pick from Cowboys: see (b); Cowboys had acquired pick from Seahawks for tackle Daryle Smith, July 24, 1989.

(g) Acquired pick for 10th-round pick, April 23, 1990.

(h) Raiders acquired pick from Cowboys: see (b); Cowboys had acquired pick, 3rd-round pick, running back Terrence Flagler and defensive end Dan Stubbs from 49ers for 2nd- and 3rd-round picks, April 19, 1990.

(i) Harris signed to play for the British Columbia Lions of the Canadian Football League.

(j) Acquired pick and 12th-round pick in 1989 for 11th-round pick in 1989, April 24, 1989.

LOS ANGELES RAIDERS
1990 ROOKIE AND FIRST-YEAR ROSTER

Name	Pos.	Hgt.	Wgt.	Birth-date	College	How Acquired
Bartlewski, Rich	TE	6-5	250	8-15-67	Fresno State	FA
Davis, Demetrius	TE	6-5	225	1- 3-67	Nevada-Reno	D12a
Dorn, Torin	CB	6-0	195	2-29-68	North Carolina	D4
Francis, Jeff	QB	6-4	220	7- 7-66	Tennessee	*FA
Gilbert, Greg	LB	6-1	220	6-20-67	Alabama	*FA
Harrell, Newt	G	6-5	295	9-17-64	West Texas State	*D10, '88
Jimerson, Art	LB	6-3	225	5-12-68	Norfolk State	D8
Jones, Myron	RB	5-9	195	2-21-68	Fresno State	D11a
Layfield, John	T	6-5	275	11-29-66	Abilene Christian	FA
Lewis, Garry	CB	5-11	180	8-25-67	Alcorn State	D7
Lewis, Ron	WR	6-1	200	7-31-66	Jackson State	D11
Lloyd, Doug	RB	6-1	220	8-31-65	North Dakota State	*FA
Mitchel, Eric	S	5-11	205	2-13-67	Oklahoma	*FA
Perry, Leon	RB	6-1	230	10-16-66	Oklahoma	D9
Smith, Anthony	DE	6-3	260	6-28-67	Arizona	D1
Walker, Arthur	DE	6-4	275	3-21-68	Colorado	FA
Wallace, Aaron	LB	6-3	240	4-17-67	Texas A&M	D2
Wilson, Marcus	RB	6-1	205	4-16-68	Virginia	D6

*Francis: D6 Los Angeles Raiders '89, released 9/5, DEV Raiders 9/6, released 1/29/90; Gilbert: D5 Chicago '89, released 8/28, awarded on waivers to Dallas 8/29, released 9/5, DEV Dallas 9/6, released 9/8, DEV Indianapolis 10/11, released 12/26; Harrell: D10 Los Angeles Raiders '88, injured reserve (neck) 8/22 through entire season, injured reserve (neck) 9/9/89 through entire season; Lloyd: D7 Los Angeles Raiders '89, released 9/5, DEV Raiders 9/6, released 1/29/90; Mitchel: D6 New England '89, released 9/5, DEV New England 9/6, released 9/14.

LOS ANGELES RAMS
(Western Division, National Conference)

John Robinson

President—Georgia Frontiere
Executive Vice-President—John Shaw
Vice President & General Counsel—Jay Zygmunt
V.P.-Media & Community Relations—Marshall Klein
Administrator of Football Operations—Jack Faulkner
Director of Operations—Dick Beam
Director of Player Personnel—John Math
Head Coach—John Robinson (7 years: 67-44)
Assistant Coaches:
    Asst. Defensive Line—Larry Brooks
    Quarterbacks—Dick Coury
    Assistant Linebackers—Artie Gigantino
    Defensive Line—Marv Goux
    Running Backs—Gil Haskell
    Offensive Line—Hudson Houck
    Special Teams—Jairo Penaranda
    Defensive Backfield—Steve Shafer
    Defensive Coordinator—Fritz Shurmur
    Wide Receivers/Tight Ends—Norval Turner
    Linebackers—Fred Whittingham
    Offensive Coordinator—Ernie Zampese
Director of Public Relations—John Oswald
    (Office Phone: 535-7267—Area Code 714)
Offices—2327 W. Lincoln Ave., Anaheim, Calif. 92801
Stadium—Anaheim Stadium (Capacity: 69,008)
Team Colors—Royal Blue, Gold and White
Training Site—University of California at Irvine.

1990 SCHEDULE
(All times local.
All games Sunday unless noted otherwise.)

Sept. 9	at Green Bay	12:00
Sept. 16	at Tampa Bay	1:00
Sept. 23	PHILADELPHIA	1:00
Sept. 30	OPEN DATE	
Oct. 7	CINCINNATI	1:00
Oct. 14	at Chicago	6:30
Oct. 21	ATLANTA	1:00
Oct. 29	at Pittsburgh (Mon.)	9:00
Nov. 4	HOUSTON	1:00
Nov. 11	NEW YORK GIANTS	1:00
Nov. 18	DALLAS	1:00
Nov. 25	at San Francisco	1:00
Dec. 2	at Cleveland	1:00
Dec. 9	NEW ORLEANS	1:00
Dec. 17	SAN FRANCISCO (Mon.)	6:00
Dec. 23	at Atlanta	1:00
Dec. 31	at New Orleans (Mon.)	7:00

1989 RESULTS—(Won 13, Lost 6)

Rams		Opp.		Att.
31	Atlanta	21	(A)	38,708
31	Indianapolis	17	(H)	63,995
41	Green Bay	38	(H)	57,701
13	San Francisco	12	(A)	64,250
26	Atlanta	14	(H)	52,182
20	Buffalo	23	(A)	76,231
21	New Orleans	40	(H)	57,567
10	Chicago	20	(A)	65,506
21	Minnesota (OT)	23	(A)	59,600
31	New York Giants	10	(H)	65,127
37	Phoenix	14	(H)	53,176
20	New Orleans (OT)	17	(A)	68,274
35	Dallas	31	(A)	46,100
27	San Francisco	30	(H)	67,959
38	New York Jets	14	(H)	53,063
24	New England	20	(A)	27,940

NFC WILD-CARD GAME

21	Philadelphia	7	(A)	57,869

NFC SEMIFINAL GAME

19	New York Giants (OT)	13	(A)	76,325

NFC CHAMPIONSHIP GAME

3	San Francisco	30	(A)	64,769

1989 GAMES STARTED

16 games: Jim Everett, Jerry Gray, Kevin Greene, Damone Johnson, Tom Newberry, Vince Newsome, Jackie Slater, Doug Smith, Mike Wilcher, Alvin Wright.

15 games: Greg Bell, Tony Slaton, Michael Stewart.

14 games: Irv Pankey.

13 games: Willie Anderson, Buford McGee.

12 games: Henry Ellard, Fred Strickland.

11 games: Shawn Miller, Mel Owens, Doug Reed.

10 games: LeRoy Irvin.

6 games: Cliff Hicks, Pete Holohan, Larry Kelm, Mike Piel.

3 games: Aaron Cox, Frank Stams.

2 games: Richard Brown, Robert Cox.

1 game: Robert Delpino, Gaston Green, Bill Hawkins, Duval Love, Anthony Newman, Sean Smith.

LOS ANGELES RAMS 1990 VETERAN ROSTER

No.	Name	Pos.	Ht.	Wt.	NFL Exp.	Birth-date	College	Games in '89	How Acquired
83	Anderson, Willie	WR	6-0	172	3	3- 7-65	UCLA	16	D2a, '88
42	Bell, Greg	RB	5-10	210	7	8- 1-62	Notre Dame	16	T-Buf, '87
57	Bethune, George	LB	6-4	240	2	3-30-67	Alabama	16	D7, '89
88	Carter, Pat	TE	6-4	250	3	8- 1-66	Florida State	16	T-Det., '89
84	Cox, Aaron	WR	5-9	178	3	3-13-65	Arizona State	16	D1a, '88
72	Cox, Robert	T	6-5	285	5	12-30-63	UCLA	16	D6, '86
14	Craig, Paco	WR	5-10	170	2	2- 2-65	UCLA	*0	FA, '90
39	Delpino, Robert	RB	6-0	205	3	11- 2-65	Missouri	16	D5, '88
80	Ellard, Henry	WR	5-11	182	8	7-21-61	Fresno State	14	D2, '83
11	Everett, Jim	QB	6-5	212	5	1- 3-63	Purdue	16	T-Hou., '86
	Farr, Mel	RB	6-0	223	1	8-12-66	UCLA	1	FA, '89
51	†Faryniarz, Brett	LB	6-3	235	3	7-23-65	San Diego State	16	FA, '88
43	Gary, Cleveland	RB	6-0	226	2	5- 4-66	Miami (Fla.)	10	D1a, '89
25	Gray, Jerry	CB	6-0	185	6	12- 2-62	Texas	16	D1, '85
30	Green, Gaston	RB	5-11	192	3	8- 1-66	UCLA	6	D1, '88
91	†Greene, Kevin	LB	6-3	250	6	7-31-62	Auburn	16	D5, '85
70	Hawkins, Bill	DT	6-6	268	2	5- 9-66	Miami (Fla.)	13	D1, '89
20	Henley, Darryl	CB	5-9	170	2	10-30-66	UCLA	15	D2b, '89
9	†Herrmann, Mark	QB	6-4	202	10	1- 9-59	Purdue	3	FA, '88
28	†Hicks, Clifford	CB	5-10	188	4	8-18-64	Oregon	15	D3, '87
81	†Holohan, Pete	TE	6-4	232	10	7-25-59	Notre Dame	16	T-SD, '88
	Humphery, Bobby	CB	5-10	180	7	8-23-61	New Mexico State	*16	T-NYJ, '90
8	Ilesic, Hank	P	6-1	210	2	9- 7-59	None	*14	UFA, '90
31	Jackson, Alfred	CB	6-0	177	2	7-10-67	San Diego State	7	D5, '89
86	†Johnson, Damone	TE	6-4	250	5	3- 2-62	Cal Poly-SLO	16	D6, '85
	Johnson, Rick	QB	6-2	205	R	1-21-61	Southern Illinois	*6	FA, '90
52	Kelm, Larry	LB	6-4	240	4	11-29-64	Texas A&M	7	D4a, '87
1	Lansford, Mike	K	6-0	190	9	7-20-58	Washington	16	FA, '82
	Long, Chuck	QB	6-4	221	5	2-18-63	Iowa	*1	T-Det, '90
	Lossow, Rodney	C	6-3	273	1	8-28-65	Wisconsin	*0	FA, '90
67	Love, Duval	G	6-3	287	6	6-24-63	UCLA	15	D10, '85
90	†McDonald, Mike	LB	6-1	235	6	6-22-58	Southern California	16	FA, '87
24	McGee, Buford	RB	6-0	210	7	8-16-60	Mississippi	16	T-SD, '87
	†Messner, Mark	LB	6-2	256	2	12-19-65	Michigan	4	D6a, '89
71	Milinichik, Joe	G	6-5	275	4	3-30-63	North Carolina State	*15	UFA, '90
66	Newberry, Tom	G	6-2	285	5	12-20-62	Wisconsin-LaCrosse	16	D2, '86
26	Newman, Anthony	S	6-0	199	3	11-25-65	Oregon	15	D2, '88
22	Newsome, Vince	S	6-1	185	8	1-22-61	Washington	16	D4a, '83
58	Owens, Mel	LB	6-2	240	10	12- 7-58	Michigan	16	D1, '81
75	Pankey, Irv	T	6-5	295	11	2-15-58	Penn State	14	D2, '80
95	Piel, Mike	DT	6-4	263	2	9-21-65	Illinois	13	D3, '88
93	†Reed, Doug	DE	6-3	265	7	7-16-60	San Diego State	11	D4, '83
	Sanchez, Lupe	CB	5-10	190	4	10-28-61	UCLA	*0	FA, '90
	Sanders, Chuck	RB	6-2	235	3	4-24-64	Slippery Rock	*0	FA, '90
78	Slater, Jackie	T	6-4	285	15	5-27-54	Jackson State	16	D3, '76
96	Smith, Brian	LB/DT	6-6	242	2	4-23-66	Auburn	3	D2a, '89
56	Smith, Doug	C	6-3	272	13	11-25-56	Bowling Green State	16	OFA, '78
97	Smith, Sean	DT	6-4	275	4	3-27-65	Grambling State	2	FA, '89
50	Stams, Frank	LB	6-2	240	2	7-17-65	Notre Dame	16	D2, '89
23	†Stewart, Michael	S	6-0	195	4	7-12-65	Fresno State	16	D8, '87
53	Strickland, Fred	LB	6-2	250	3	8-15-66	Purdue	12	D2b, '88
	Taylor, Gene	WR	6-3	192	3	11-12-62	Fresno State	*3	FA, '90
21	Warner, Curt	RB	5-11	205	8	3-18-61	Penn State	*16	UFA, '90
54	Wilcher, Mike	LB	6-3	245	8	3-20-60	North Carolina	16	D2a, '83
99	†Wright, Alvin	NT	6-2	285	5	2- 5-61	Jacksonville State	16	FA, '86

*Craig played 1 game with Toronto-CFL in '89; Humphery played 16 games with Jets in '89; Ilesic played 14 games with Chargers in '89; R. Johnson played 6 games with Toronto-CFL in '89; Long played 1 game with Lions in '89; Lossow last active with Calgary-CFL in '88; Milinichik played 15 games with Lions in '89; Sanchez last active with Steelers in '88; Sanders last active with Steelers in '87; Taylor played 3 games with Saskatchewan-CFL in '89; Warner played 16 games with Seahawks in '89.

†Unsigned; subject to developments.

Players lost through Plan B free agency: G Kurt Becker (2 games in '89; to Chi.); DB Ron Brown (16; to L.A. Raid.); P Dale Hatcher (16; to G.B.); DT Shawn Miller (16; to G.B.); G Tony Slaton (15; to Dall.); S James Washington (9; to Dall.).

Also played with Rams in '89—LB Richard Brown (13 games); CB LeRoy Irvin (13); LB Mark Jerue (6); QB Steve Dils (active for 1 game, but did not play).

D—Draft; T—Trade; FA—Free Agent; OFA—Original Free Agent; UFA—Unrestricted Free Agent.

LOS ANGELES RAMS
1990 DRAFT CHOICES

(Number following name designates order of selection among 331 players drafted.)

Round and Player		Position	College
1. BROSTEK, Bern	23	C	Washington
2. TERRELL, Pat	49	DB	Notre Dame
3. BERRY, Latin	78	RB	Oregon
4. Choice to Detroit (a)			
5. Choice to New York Jets (b)			
6. STALLWORTH, Tim	161	WR	Washington State
7. ELMORE, Kent	190	P	Tennessee
8. SAVAGE, Ray (c)	198	LB	Virginia
from Tampa Bay (d)			
8. CRAWFORD, Elbert	216	C	Arkansas
9. LOMACK, Tony	245	WR	Florida
10. BATES, Steve	272	DE	James Madison
11. GOLDBERG, Bill	301	DT	Georgia
12. LANG, David	328	RB	Northern Arizona

(a) Traded pick for tight end Pat Carter, August 18, 1989.
(b) Traded pick for cornerback Bobby Humphery, April 22, 1990.
(c) Rights released June 11, 1990.
(d) Acquired pick for two 11th-round picks in 1989 and 12th-round pick in 1989, April 24, 1989.

LOS ANGELES RAMS
1990 ROOKIE AND FIRST-YEAR ROSTER

Name	Pos.	Hgt.	Wgt.	Birth-date	College	How Acquired
Adams, Theo	T	6-5	265	4-24-66	Hawaii	FA
Ashe, Richard	TE	6-4	260	3-14-67	Humboldt State	*FA
Bates, Stephen	DE	6-4	249	6-28-66	James Madison	D10
Berry, Latin	CB	5-10	196	1-13-67	Oregon	D3
Brostek, Bern	C	6-3	300	9-11-66	Washington	D1
Brown, General	DT	6-4	270	8-15-67	Savannah State	FA
Bruno, Anthony	DE	6-5	278	11-24-65	Cal State-Hayward	FA
Caylor, David	K	..	..	....	Long Beach State	*FA
Crawford, Elbert	C	6-3	280	6-20-66	Arkansas	D8a
Eldridge, David	RB	6-0	212	4-25-66	Arizona	FA
Elmore, Kent	P	6-2	180	4-27-67	Tennessee	D7
Faison, Derrick	WR	6-4	200	8-24-67	Howard	FA
Fienold, Bobby	CB	5-10	178	8-17-67	Long Beach State	FA
Gilbreath, Monty	WR	5-8	175	10-24-68	San Diego State	FA
Goldberg, Bill	NT	6-3	266	12-27-68	Georgia	D11
Gray, Terry	T	6-2	280	6-25-68	Baylor	FA
Hord, Randall	DT	6-4	253	12-20-67	Southern California	FA
Johnson, Damon	DT	6-4	290	6-28-67	Savannah State	FA
Jones, Dewayne	S	6-1	195	1-22-67	California	FA
Kane, Michael	RB	5-10	195	8-28-65	Cal State-Northridge	FA
Knudson, Gary	TE	6-4	242	5- 6-66	Arizona State	*FA
Lang, David	RB	5-11	201	3-28-67	Northern Arizona	D12
Leggett, Jerry	LB	6-4	266	8-23-65	Cal State-Fullerton	*FA
Lomack, Tony	WR	5-8	180	4-27-68	Florida	D9
Manu, Tony	LB	6-0	245	2- 5-68	Idaho State	FA
Mickel, Jeff	G	6-6	300	8- 4-68	Eastern Washington	*FA
Mitchell, Mario	DB	5-10	180	12-23-66	San Diego State	*FA
Ortega, David	LB	6-1	238	12-20-66	California	FA
Pellum, William	WR	5-10	170	10-31-66	Washington State	FA
Price, Jim	TE	6-4	247	10- 2-66	Stanford	DA
Sargent, Anthony	WR	5-9	172	12- 1-66	Wyoming	*FA
Stallworth, Tim	WR	5-10	180	8-26-66	Washington State	D6
Terrell, Pat	S	6-0	195	3-18-68	Notre Dame	D2
Whittingham, Fred	RB	5-10	200	3-16-67	Brigham Young	FA
Yniguez, Paul	C	6-3	275	11-21-67	Kansas State	FA

*Ashe: FA Los Angeles Rams '89, released 9/5, DEV Rams 9/6, released 1/29/90; Caylor: FA Dallas '88, released 8/9; Knudson: FA Los Angeles Rams '89, released 8/30; Leggett: D9 New Orleans '89, released 8/30, DEV San Francisco 9/12, released 10/16, DEV Philadelphia 10/19, released 10/20, DEV Los Angeles Rams 12/21, released 1/29/90; Mickel: D6 Minnesota '89, released 9/5, DEV Denver 9/7, released 1/29/90; Mitchell: FA San Diego '89, released 7/31; Sargent: FA Los Angeles Rams '89, released 8/30, DEV Rams 9/20, released 1/29/90.

MIAMI DOLPHINS
(Eastern Division, American Conference)

Don Shula

President—Timothy J. Robbie
Executive Vice-President and G.M.—Eddie J. Jones
Head Coach—Don Shula (27 years: 269-119-6)
Director of Player Personnel—Charley Winner
Director of Pro Personnel—Monte Clark
Director of College Scouting—Tom Heckert
Assistant Coaches:
    Linebackers—George Hill
    Defense—Tom Olivadotti
    Defensive Backfield—Mel Phillips
    Asst. Head Coach/Offensive Line—John Sandusky
    Receivers—Larry Seiple
    Defensive Line—Dan Sekanovich
    Quarterbacks/Pass Offense—Gary Stevens
    Offensive Backfield—Carl Taseff
    Strength & Conditioning—Junior Wade
    Special Teams—Mike Westhoff
Director of Publicity—Harvey Greene
    (Office Phone: 620-5000—Area Code 305)
Offices—Joe Robbie Stadium, 2269 NW 199 Street, Miami, Fla. 33056
Stadium—Joe Robbie Stadium (Capacity: 75,000)
Team Colors—Aqua and Orange
Training Site—St. Thomas University, Miami, Fla.

1990 SCHEDULE
(All times local.
All games Sunday unless noted otherwise.)

Sept. 9	at New England	4:00
Sept. 16	BUFFALO	1:00
Sept. 23	at New York Giants	1:00
Sept. 30	at Pittsburgh	1:00
Oct. 7	NEW YORK JETS	1:00
Oct. 14	OPEN DATE	
Oct. 18	NEW ENGLAND (Thurs.)	8:00
Oct. 28	at Indianapolis	1:00
Nov. 4	PHOENIX	1:00
Nov. 11	at New York Jets	1:00
Nov. 19	L.A. RAIDERS (Mon.)	9:00
Nov. 25	at Cleveland	1:00
Dec. 2	at Washington	1:00
Dec. 9	PHILADELPHIA	8:00
Dec. 16	SEATTLE	1:00
Dec. 23	at Buffalo	1:00
Dec. 30	INDIANAPOLIS	1:00

1989 RESULTS—(Won 8, Lost 8)

Dolphins		Opp.		Att.
24	Buffalo	27	(H)	54,541
24	New England	10	(A)	57,043
33	New York Jets	40	(H)	65,908
7	Houston	39	(A)	51,426
13	Cleveland (OT)	10	(A)	58,444
20	Cincinnati	13	(A)	58,184
23	Green Bay	20	(H)	56,624
17	Buffalo	31	(A)	80,208
19	Indianapolis	13	(H)	52,680
31	New York Jets	23	(A)	65,923
17	Dallas	14	(A)	56,044
14	Pittsburgh	34	(H)	59,936
21	Kansas City	26	(A)	54,610
31	New England	10	(H)	62,127
13	Indianapolis	42	(A)	55,665
24	Kansas City	27	(H)	43,612

1989 GAMES STARTED

16 games: Jeff Cross, Jeff Dellenbach, Ferrell Edmunds, Roy Foster, Hugh Green, Paul Lankford, Dan Marino, Brian Sochia, Jarvis Williams.

15 games: Mark Clayton, Ronnie Lee, Jeff Uhlenhake.

14 games: Mark Duper, Harry Galbreath, William Judson.

13 games: Louis Oliver.

12 games: E.J. Junior, Barry Krauss, Sammie Smith.

11 games: T.J. Turner.

8 games: Dave Ahrens, John Offerdahl.

7 games: Tom Brown.

4 games: Greg Clark, Rick Graf, Marc Logan, Troy Stradford.

3 games: Fred Banks, John Bosa, Ron Davenport, Liffort Hobley.

2 games: Jackie Cline, Rodney Thomas, Tom Toth.

1 game: Louis Cheek, Mark Dennis, Nuu Faaola, Jim Jensen.

MIAMI DOLPHINS 1990 VETERAN ROSTER

No.	Name	Pos.	Ht.	Wt.	NFL Exp.	Birth-date	College	Games in '89	How Acquired
86	Banks, Fred	WR	5-10	180	5	5-26-62	Liberty (Va.)	15	FA, '87
	Baty, Greg	TE	6-5	240	3	8-28-64	Stanford	*0	FA, '90
	Bone, Warren	TE	6-4	255	1	11- 4-64	Texas Southern	*0	FA, '90
97	Bosa, John	DE	6-4	270	4	1-10-64	Boston College	13	D1, '87
82	Brown, Andre	WR	6-3	210	2	8-21-66	Miami (Fla.)	16	OFA, '89
37	Brown, J.B.	CB	6-0	192	2	1- 5-67	Maryland	16	D12, '89
	Brown, Tony	T	6-5	280	1	7-11-64	Pittsburgh	*0	FA, '90
83	Clayton, Mark	WR	5-9	184	8	4- 8-61	Louisville	15	D8, '83
91	Cross, Jeff	DE	6-4	270	3	3-25-66	Missouri	16	D9, '88
65	†Dellenbach, Jeff	T/C	6-6	282	6	2-14-63	Wisconsin	16	D4a, '85
74	†Dennis, Mark	T	6-6	290	4	4-15-65	Illinois	8	D8a, '87
85	Duper, Mark	WR	5-9	190	9	1-25-59	Northwestern (La.) St.	15	D2, '82
80	Edmunds, Ferrell	TE	6-6	252	3	4-16-65	Maryland	16	D3, '88
	Elder, Donnie	CB	5-9	175	5	12-13-63	Memphis State	*16	UFA, '90
	Faulkner, Jeff	DE	6-3	280	2	4- 4-64	Southern	*0	FA, '90
61	†Foster, Roy	G	6-4	277	9	5-24-60	Southern California	16	D1, '82
62	Galbreath, Harry	G/C	6-1	275	3	1- 1-65	Tennessee	14	D8, '88
	Glenn, Kerry	CB	5-9	175	4	1- 3-62	Minnesota	*14	UFA, '90
99	†Graf, Rick	LB	6-5	249	4	8-29-63	Wisconsin	4	D2, '87
55	†Green, Hugh	LB	6-2	228	10	7-27-59	Pittsburgh	16	T-TB, '85
92	Griggs, David	LB	6-3	239	2	2- 5-67	Virginia	5	FA, '89
	Harvey, Stacy	LB	6-4	245	2	3- 8-65	Arizona State	*9	UFA, '90
	Higgs, Mark	RB	5-7	188	3	4-11-66	Kentucky	*15	UFA, '90
29	Hobley, Liffort	S	6-0	202	5	5-12-62	Louisiana State	16	FA, '87
11	†Jensen, Jim	WR/RB	6-4	224	10	11-14-58	Boston University	16	D11, '81
54	Junior, E.J.	LB	6-3	242	10	12- 8-59	Alabama	16	UFA, '89
88	†Kinchen, Brian	TE	6-2	232	3	8- 6-65	Louisiana State	16	D12, '88
58	Krauss, Barry	LB	6-3	260	12	3-17-57	Alabama	16	W-Cle, '89
90	Kumerow, Eric	DE	6-7	268	3	4-17-65	Ohio State	12	D1, '88
44	Lankford, Paul	CB	6-1	190	9	6-15-58	Penn State	16	D3, '82
20	Logan, Marc	RB	5-11	220	4	5- 9-65	Kentucky	10	UFA, '89
13	Marino, Dan	QB	6-4	224	8	9-15-61	Pittsburgh	16	D1, '83
	McGruder, Michael	CB	5-11	190	1	5- 6-62	Kent State	*2	FA, '90
	McKyer, Tim	CB	6-1	177	5	9- 5-63	Texas-Arlington	*7	T-SF, '90
	Odom, Cliff	LB	6-2	251	10	8-15-58	Texas-Arlington	*16	UFA, '90
56	Offerdahl, John	LB	6-3	240	5	8-17-64	Western Michigan	10	D2, '86
25	Oliver, Louis	S	6-2	226	2	3- 9-66	Florida	15	D1a, '89
	Paige, Tony	RB	5-10	235	7	10-14-62	Virginia Tech	*16	UFA, '90
	Pettyjohn, Barry	T	6-5	280	1	3-29-64	Pittsburgh	*0	FA, '90
	Reichenbach, Mike	LB	6-2	235	7	9-14-61	East Stroudsburg	*16	UFA, '90
4	Roby, Reggie	P	6-2	246	8	7-30-61	Iowa	16	D6, '83
81	†Schwedes, Scott	WR/KR	6-0	182	4	6-30-65	Syracuse	9	D2a, '87
9	Secules, Scott	QB	6-3	219	3	11- 8-64	Virginia	15	T-Dal, '89
33	Smith, Sammie	RB	6-2	226	2	5-16-67	Florida State	13	D1, '89
70	Sochia, Brian	NT	6-3	278	8	7-21-61	Northwestern Okla.	16	FA, '86
18	†Stoudt, Cliff	QB	6-4	218	12	3-27-55	Youngstown State	16	FA, '89
10	Stoyanovich, Pete	K	5-10	180	2	4-28-67	Indiana	16	D8, '89
23	†Stradford, Troy	RB	5-9	192	4	9-11-64	Boston College	7	D4, '87
	Swarn, George	RB	5-11	222	1	2-15-64	Miami (O.)	*0	FA, '90
24	Thomas, Rodney	CB	5-10	190	3	12-21-65	Brigham Young	16	D5, '88
95	Turner, T.J.	DE	6-4	280	5	5-16-63	Houston	14	D3, '86
63	Uhlenhake, Jeff	C	6-3	282	2	1-28-66	Ohio State	16	D5, '89
26	Williams, Jarvis	S	5-11	198	3	5-16-65	Florida	16	D2, '88
	Wilson, Karl	DE	6-4	275	4	3-10-64	Louisiana State	*15	UFA, '90

*Baty last active with Cardinals in '88; Bone last active with Packers in '87; T. Brown last active with Bills in '87; Elder played 16 games with Buccaneers in '89; Faulkner last active with Chiefs in '87; Glenn played 14 games with Jets in '89; Harvey played 9 games with Chiefs in '89; Higgs played 15 games with Eagles in '89; McGruder played 2 games with Packers in '89; McKyer played 7 games with 49ers in '89; Odom played 16 games with Colts in '89; Paige played 16 games with Lions in '89; Pettyjohn last active with Oilers in '87; Reichenbach played 16 games with Eagles in '89; Swarn last active with Browns in '87; Wilson played 15 games with Cardinals in '89.

†Unsigned; subject to developments.

Players lost through Plan B free agency: LB Dave Ahrens (11 games in '89; to Sea.); RB Tom Brown (9; to Wash.); T Louis Cheek (13; to Dall.); LB Greg Clark (16; to G.B.); DE Jackie Cline (15; to Atl.); CB Ernest Gibson (5; to N.E.); RB Lorenzo Hampton (10; to Den.); G Greg Johnson (0; to Dall.); CB Wiliam Judson (14; to Det.); T Ronnie Lee (15; to Atl.); G Tom Toth (16; to S.D.).

Retired—Bob Brudzinski, 14-year linebacker, 10 games in '89.

Also played with Dolphins in '89—RB Ron Davenport (9 games); RB Nuu Faaola (10); LB David Frye (11); RB Kerry Goode (1); TE Bruce Hardy (1); NT Mike Lambrecht (6); CB Don McNeal (12); G Alvin Powell (2); RB Willard Reeves (2).

D—Draft; T—Trade; W—Waivers; FA—Free Agent; OFA—Original Free Agent; UFA—Unrestricted Free Agent.

MIAMI DOLPHINS
1990 DRAFT CHOICES

(Number following name designates order of selection among 331 players drafted.)

Round and Player		Position	College
1. WEBB, Richmond	9	T	Texas A & M
2. SIMS, Keith	39	G	Iowa State
3. OGLESBY, Alfred	66	DT	Houston
4. MITCHELL, Scott	93	QB	Utah
5. Choice to New England through Dallas (a)			
5. HOLT, Leroy from San Francisco through Los Angeles Raiders and Washington (b)	137	RB	Southern Cal
6. VANHORSE, Sean	151	DB	Howard
7. Choice to Cleveland (c)			
8. WOODS, Thomas	205	WR	Tennessee
9. ROSS, Phil	231	TE	Oregon State
10. Choice to Washington (d)			
11. Choice to San Francisco (e)			
12. HARDEN, Bobby	315	DB	Miami (Fla.)

(a) Dolphins traded pick to Cowboys for quarterback Scott Secules, August 6, 1989; Cowboys traded pick and 3rd- and 7th-round picks to Patriots for 3rd-, 6th- and 8th-round picks, April 22, 1990.

(b) Dolphins acquired pick from Redskins for 10th-round pick and 4th-round pick in 1991, April 22, 1990; Redskins had acquired pick and 4th-round pick, tackle Jim Lachey and 2nd-, 4th- and 5th-round picks in 1989 from Raiders for quarterback Jay Schroeder and 2nd-round pick in 1989, September 9, 1988; to get into position to send last pick of round to Redskins, Raiders acquired pick and 4th-round picks from 49ers for 4th-round pick, April 20, 1990.

(c) Traded pick for 5th-round pick in 1991, April 23, 1990.

(d) See first part of (b).

(e) Traded pick and 2nd-round pick in 1991 for cornerback Tim McKyer, April 23, 1990.

MIAMI DOLPHINS
1990 ROOKIE AND FIRST-YEAR ROSTER

Name	Pos.	Hgt.	Wgt.	Birth-date	College	How Acquired
Berg, Steve	DE	6-4	275	3-15-66	Gustavus Adolphus	*FA
Cartwright, Ricardo	WR	5-10	175	5-27-65	Florida A&M	*FA
Cockrell, Randy	LB	6-1	240	6-13-67	Virginia Tech	FA
Davis, Darryl	LB	6-3	235	12-18-66	Florida A&M	FA
Flores, Sam	K	..	..	....	C.W. Post	*FA
Grant, African	S	6-0	200	8- 2-65	Illinois	*FA, '89
Harden, Bobby	S	6-0	192	2- 8-67	Miami (Fla.)	D12
Haering, Chris	LB	6-2	232	6-10-67	West Virginia	FA
Healy, Tim	RB	6-0	226	2- 6-67	Delaware	*FA
Highsmith, Fred	RB	6-2	220	12- 7-67	Miami (Fla.)	*FA
Holley, Bret	P	6-1	185	6-29-66	Arizona	*FA
Holt, Leroy	RB	5-10	236	2- 7-67	Southern California	D5
Johnson, Andre	WR	5-8	170	12- 8-67	Ferris State	FA
Jones, Clarence	RB	6-1	205	3-24-65	Army	FA
Jurkovic, John	NT	6-2	278	8-18-67	Eastern Illinois	FA
Limbrick, Garrett	RB	6-2	235	11-16-65	Oklahoma State	*FA
Martin, Tony	WR	6-0	174	9- 5-65	Mesa (Colo.)	*FA, '89
Mitchell, Scott	QB	6-6	231	1- 2-68	Utah	D4
Moore, Stevon	CB	5-11	205	2- 9-67	Mississippi	*UFA
Oglesby, Alfred	NT	6-3	271	1-27-67	Houston	D3
Pacitti, Dave	T	6-5	288	2-15-66	Villanova	FA
Popp, Dave	T	6-5	285	10-30-66	Eastern Illinois	*FA
Redman, Sean	RB	5-9	196	4-24-67	Penn State	FA
Ross, Phil	TE	6-4	221	6-14-67	Oregon State	D9
Rosson, Mike	DE	6-6	270	8-15-67	Tulsa	FA
Roth, Jeff	NT	6-3	258	4-21-66	Florida	*FA
Schneider, Craig	T	6-4	285	9-11-68	Illinois	FA
Searels, Stacy	G-C	6-5	280	5-19-65	Auburn	*FA
Sims, Keith	G	6-2	310	6-17-67	Iowa State	D2
Smith, Dee	RB	5-11	190	11-21-67	Louisville	FA
Smith, Pee Wee	WR	6-1	175	1- 3-68	Miami (Fla.)	FA
Soltis, Paul	LB	6-3	240	10- 1-66	Youngstown State	FA
Vanhorse, Sean	CB	5-10	178	7-22-68	Howard University	D6
Webb, Richmond	T	6-6	291	1-11-67	Texas A&M	D1
Weidner, Bert	WT	6-3	275	1-20-66	Kent State	*FA
Woods, Thomas	WR	5-10	174	2-21-65	Tennessee	D8
Zdelar, Jim	T	6-5	290	5-24-66	Youngstown State	*D7, '89

*Berg: FA San Francisco '89, released 8/22; Cartwright: FA Miami '89, released 8/22; Flores: FA San Diego '88, released 7/28; Grant: FA Washington '88, released 8/24, FA Miami '89, injured reserve (thumb) 9/6 through entire season: Healy: FA New York Jets '89, released 8/29; Highsmith: FA Pittsburgh '89, released 8/29; Holley: FA Kansas City '89, released 7/26; Limbrick: FA Chicago '89, released 8/29, DEV Philadelphia 9/6, released 9/22; Martin: D5 New York Jets '89, released 9/5, DEV Miami 9/6, activated 12/23 (on inactive list for 1 game); Moore: D7 New York Jets '89, injured reserve (knee) 8/28 through entire season, unprotected free agent 2/1/90; Popp: D7 New York Giants '89, released 9/5, DEV New York Giants 9/6, released 1/29/90; Roth: D5 Dallas '89, released 9/5, DEV San Francisco 12/18, released 1/22/90; Searels: D4 San Diego '89, injured reserve (hand) 8/20 through entire season, released 9/5/89, DEV San Diego 9/7, released 1/29/90; Weidner: D11 Miami '89, released 9/5, DEV Miami 9/6, released 1/29/90; Zdelar: D7 Miami '89, reserve/left squad 8/1 through entire season, reinstated 4/3/90.

MINNESOTA VIKINGS
(Central Division, National Conference)

Jerry Burns

President—Wheelock Whitney
Executive Vice-President and General Manager—Mike Lynn
Asst. G.M./Administration—Jeff Diamond
Asst. G.M./Football—Bob Hollway
Director of Football Operations—Jerry Reichow
Player Personnel Director—Frank Gilliam
Head Coach—Jerry Burns (4 years: 38-25)
Assistant Coaches:
    Tight Ends/Special Teams—Tom Batta
    Linebackers—Maxie Baughan
    Secondary—Jerry Brown
    Running Backs—John Brunner
    Offensive Line—John Michels
    Asst. Head Coach/Offense—Tom Moore
    Defensive Coordinator—Floyd Peters
    Receivers—Dick Rehbein
    Offensive Coordinator—Bob Schnelker
    Admin. Asst. to Head Coach—Marc Trestman
    Defensive Line—Paul Wiggin
Public Relations Director—Merrill Swanson
    (Office Phone: 828-6500—Area Code 612)
Offices—9520 Viking Drive, Eden Prairie, Minn. 55344
Stadium—Metrodome, Minneapolis, Minn. (Capacity: 63,000)
Team Colors—Purple, Gold and White
Training Site—Mankato State University, Mankato, Minn.

1990 SCHEDULE
(All times local.
All games Sunday unless noted otherwise.)

Sept. 9	at Kansas City	12:00
Sept. 16	NEW ORLEANS	3:00
Sept. 23	at Chicago	12:00
Sept. 30	TAMPA BAY	12:00
Oct. 7	DETROIT	12:00
Oct. 15	at Philadelphia (Mon.)	9:00
Oct. 21	OPEN DATE	
Oct. 28	Green Bay at Milwaukee	12:00
Nov. 4	DENVER	7:00
Nov. 11	at Detroit	1:00
Nov. 18	at Seattle	1:00
Nov. 25	CHICAGO	12:00
Dec. 2	GREEN BAY	7:00
Dec. 9	at New York Giants	1:00
Dec. 16	at Tampa Bay	1:00
Dec. 22	LOS ANGELES RAIDERS (Sat.)	3:00
Dec. 30	SAN FRANCISCO	12:00

1989 RESULTS—(Won 10, Lost 7)

Vikings		Opp.		Att.
38 Houston		7	(H)	54,015
7 Chicago		38	(A)	66,475
14 Pittsburgh		27	(A)	50,744
17 Tampa Bay		3	(H)	54,817
24 Detroit		17	(H)	55,380
26 Green Bay		14	(H)	62,075
20 Detroit		7	(A)	51,579
14 New York Giants		24	(A)	76,041
23 Los Angeles Rams (OT)		21	(H)	59,600
24 Tampa Bay		10	(A)	56,271
9 Philadelphia		10	(A)	65,944
19 Green Bay		20	(A)	55,592
27 Chicago		16	(H)	60,664
43 Atlanta		17	(H)	58,116
17 Cleveland (OT)		23	(A)	70,777
29 Cincinnati		21	(H)	58,829

NFC SEMIFINAL GAME

13 San Francisco		41	(A)	64,585

1989 GAMES STARTED

16 games: Joey Browner, Anthony Carter, Chris Doleman, Tim Irwin, Todd Kalis, Carl Lee, Kirk Lowdermilk, Keith Millard, Reggie Rutland, Scott Studwell, Gary Zimmerman.

15 games: Steve Jordan, Mike Merriweather, Al Noga.

14 games: Henry Thomas.

13 games: Hassan Jones, Randall McDaniel.

12 games: Wade Wilson.

11 games: Travis Curtis.

10 games: Ray Berry.

9 games: Herschel Walker.

8 games: Alfred Anderson, Rick Fenney.

6 games: D.J. Dozier.

4 games: Tommy Kramer.

3 games: David Howard, Dave Huffman, Brent Novoselsky.

2 games: Darrell Fullington, Darryl Ingram, Audrey McMillian, Tim Newton.

1 game: Mark Dusbabek, Brad Edwards, Issiac Holt, Doug Martin, Daryl Smith, Jesse Solomon.

MINNESOTA VIKINGS 1990 VETERAN ROSTER

No.	Name	Pos.	Ht.	Wt.	NFL Exp.	Birth-date	College	Games in '89	How Acquired
46	Anderson, Alfred	RB	6-1	219	6	8- 4-61	Baylor	11	D3, '84
50	Berry, Ray	LB	6-2	230	4	10-28-63	Baylor	16	D2, '87
68	Blair, Paul	T	6-4	280	3	8- 3-63	Oklahoma State	*0	FA, '90
53	Braxton, David	LB	6-1	232	2	5-26-65	Wake Forest	3	D2, '89
44	†Brim, Michael	CB	6-0	186	3	1-23-66	Virginia Union	7	FA, '89
47	Browner, Jocy	CB/S	6-2	212	8	5-15-60	Southern California	16	D1, '83
19	Burbage, Cornell	WR	5-10	189	4	2-22-65	Kentucky	*10	UFA, '90
81	†Carter, Anthony	WR	5-11	166	6	9-17-60	Michigan	16	T-Mia, '85
33	†Clark, Jessie	RB	6-0	223	8	1- 3-60	Arkansas	3	FA, '89
71	†Clarke, Ken	DT	6-2	281	12	8-28-56	Syracuse	11	FA, '89
56	Doleman, Chris	DE	6-5	250	6	10-16-61	Pittsburgh	16	D1, '85
42	†Dozier, D.J.	RB	6-0	198	4	9-21-65	Penn State	14	D1, '87
59	Dusbabek, Mark	LB	6-3	230	2	6-23-64	Minnesota	16	FA, '89
31	Fenney, Rick	RB	6-1	240	4	12- 7-64	Washington	16	D8, '87
62	†Foote, Chris	C	6-4	265	8	12- 2-56	Southern California	16	T-NYG, '87
29	Fullington, Darrell	S	6-1	183	3	4-17-64	Miami (Fla.)	16	D5, '88
	Gallery, Jim	K	6-0	190	3	9-15-61	Minnesota	*4	FA, '90
51	†Galvin, John	LB	6-3	226	2	7-9-65	Boston College	11	UFA, '89
16	†Gannon, Rich	QB	6-3	197	4	12-20-65	Delaware	*0	T-NE, '87
80	†Gustafson, Jim	WR	6-1	181	5	3-16-61	St. Thomas (Minn.)	16	FA, '85
74	Habib, Brian	T	6-7	282	2	12- 2-64	Washington	16	D10, '88
89	Hillary, Ira	WR	5-11	190	4	11-13-62	South Carolina	*16	UFA, '90
72	†Huffman, David	G	6-6	283	10	4- 4-57	Notre Dame	16	D2, '79
76	Ingram, Darryl	TE	6-2	230	2	5- 2-66	California	16	D4, '89
76	Irwin, Tim	T	6-6	289	10	12-13-58	Tennessee	16	D3, '81
	Johnson, Kenneth	S	6-2	197	1	9-14-66	Florida A&M	1	FA, '90
84	Jones, Hassan	WR	6-0	195	5	7- 2-64	Florida State	16	D5, '86
83	Jordan, Steve	TE	6-3	236	9	1-10-61	Brown	16	D7, '82
69	Kalis, Todd	G	6-5	269	3	6-10-65	Arizona State	16	D4, '88
30	†Karlis, Rich	K	6-0	180	9	5-23-59	Cincinnati	13	FA, '89
77	Knight, Shawn	DT/DE	6-6	280	4	6- 4-64	Brigham Young	*7	UFA, '90
39	Lee, Carl	CB	5-11	184	8	4- 6-61	Marshall	16	D7, '83
87	†Lewis, Leo	WR	5-8	171	9	9-17-56	Missouri	16	FA, '81
63	†Lowdermilk, Kirk	C	6-3	263	6	4-10-63	Ohio State	16	D3, '85
49	Lyons, Robert	S	6-1	195	2	5-16-66	Akron	*9	UFA, '90
78	Marrone, Doug	C/G	6-5	295	3	7-25-64	Syracuse	*1	UFA, '90
64	McDaniel, Randall	G	6-3	268	3	12-19-64	Arizona State	14	D1, '88
26	McMillian, Audrey	CB	6-0	190	5	8-13-62	Houston	16	UFA, '89
57	Merriweather, Mike	LB	6-2	221	8	11-26-60	Pacific	15	T-Pit, '89
75	Millard, Keith	DT	6-6	260	6	3-18-62	Washington State	16	D1, '84
18	Newsome, Harry	P	6-0	188	6	1-25-63	Wake Forest	*16	UFA, '90
85	Novoselsky, Brent	TE	6-2	238	3	1- 8-66	Pennsylvania	15	FA, '89
99	Noga, Al	DT	6-1	245	3	9-16-66	Hawaii	16	D3, '88
36	Rice, Allen	RB	5-10	203	7	4-5-62	Baylor	4	D5, '84
48	†Rutland, Reggie	S	6-1	195	4	6-20-64	Georgia Tech	16	D4, '87
12	Salisbury, Sean	QB	6-5	215	3	3- 9-63	Southern California	*17	FA, '90
17	Schillinger, Andy	WR	5-11	186	2	11-22-64	Miami (O.)	*0	UFA, '90
60	Schreiber, Adam	C/G	6-4	285	7	2-20-62	Texas	*16	UFA, '90
13	†Scribner, Bucky	P	6-0	205	5	7-11-60	Kansas	16	FA, '87
27	Stills, Ken	S	5-10	196	6	9- 6-63	Wisconsin	*16	UFA, '90
94	Strauthers, Thomas	DE	6-4	265	7	4- 6-61	Jackson State	12	UFA, '89
55	Studwell, Scott	LB	6-2	228	14	8-27-54	Illinois	16	D9, '77
97	Thomas, Henry	NT	6-2	268	4	1-12-65	Louisiana State	14	D3, '87
34	Walker, Herschel	RB	6-1	226	5	3- 3-62	Georgia	*16	T-Dal, '89
11	Wilson, Wade	QB	6-3	208	10	2- 1-59	East Texas State	14	D8, '81
73	Wolfley, Craig	G/T	6-1	270	11	5-19-58	Syracuse	*15	UFA, '89
	Woodson, Shawn	LB	6-2	226	1	8-12-66	James Madison	*1	FA, '90
65	Zimmerman, Gary	T	6-6	277	5	12-13-61	Oregon	16	T-NYG, '86

*Blair last active with Bears in '87; Burbage played 10 games with Cowboys in '89; Gallery played 4 games with Bengals in '89; Gannon active for 13 games in '89, but did not play; Hillary played 16 games with Bengals in '89; Knight played 7 games with Cardinals in '89; Lyons played 9 games with Browns in '89; Marrone played 1 game with Saints in '89; Newsome played 16 games with Steelers in '89; Salisbury last active with Colts in '87 and played 17 games with Winnipeg-CFL in '89; Schillinger missed '89 season due to injury with Cardinals; Schreiber played 16 games with Jets in '89; Stills played 16 games with Packers in '89; Walker played 5 games with Cowboys, 11 games with Vikings in '89; Wolfley played 15 games with Steelers in '89; Woodson played 1 game with Toronto-CFL in '89.

†Unsigned; subject to developments.

Players lost through Plan B free agency: S Travis Curtis (16 games in '89; to N.Y.J.); S Brad Edwards (9; to Wash.); C Mark Rodenhauser (16; to S.D.).

Also played with Vikings in '89—C John Adickes (1 game); RB Rick Bayless (1); WR Jarrod Delaney (active for 1 game in '89, but did not play); K Teddy Garcia (3); TE Carl Hilton (1); CB Issiac Holt (5); QB Tommy Kramer (8); DE Doug Martin (7); RB Darrin Nelson (5); DT Tim Newton (9); CB Daryl Smith (5); LB Jesse Solomon (4).

D—Draft; T—Trade; FA—Free Agent; UFA—Unrestricted Free Agent.

MINNESOTA VIKINGS
1990 DRAFT CHOICES

(Number following name designates order of selection among 331 players drafted.)

Round and Player		Position	College
1. Choice to Pittsburgh through Dallas (a)			
2. Choice to San Francisco through Dallas (b)			
3. JONES, Mike from Dallas (c)	54	TE	Texas A&M
3. HOBBY, Marion	74	DE	Tennessee
4. HAMPTON, Alonzo	104	DB	Pittsburgh
5. THORNTON, Reggie from San Diego through Dallas (d)	116	WR	Bowling Green State
5. SMITH, Cedric	131	RB	Florida
6. Choice to New Orleans through Dallas and Los Angeles Raiders (e)			
7. LEVELIS, John	188	LB	C.W. Post (N.Y.)
8. SCHLICHTING, Craig	214	DE	Wyoming
9. ALLEN, Terry	241	RB	Clemson
10. NEWMAN, Pat from Dallas (c)	249	WR	Utah State
10. SMITH, Donald	271	DB	Liberty (Va.)
11. Choice to Chicago through Los Angeles Raiders (f)			
12. GOETZ, Ron	324	LB	Minnesota

(a) Vikings traded 1st-round pick, linebackers David Howard and Jesse Solomon, cornerback Issiac Holt, running back Darrin Nelson, defensive end Alex Stewart, 1st-round picks in 1991 and 1992, 2nd-round picks in 1990, 1991 and 1992 and 3rd-round pick in 1992 to Cowboys for running back Herschel Walker, October 12, 1989. Nelson subsequently traded to Chargers with 6th-round pick going from Vikings to Cowboys and 5th-round pick going from Chargers to Vikings through Cowboys, October 17, 1989. Deal completed February 2, 1990, with Cowboys sending 3rd- and 10th-round picks in 1990 and 3rd-round pick in 1991 to Vikings; Cowboys traded 1st-round pick in 1990 and 3rd-round pick to Steelers for 1st-round pick, April 22, 1990.

(b) Vikings traded pick to Cowboys: see first part of (a); Cowboys traded pick and 3rd-round pick to 49ers for running back Terrence Flagler, defensive end Dan Stubbs and 3rd- and 11th-round picks, April 19, 1990.

(c) See first part of (a).

(d) Vikings acquired pick from Cowboys and Cowboys had acquired pick from Chargers: see first part of (a).

(e) Vikings traded pick to Cowboys: see first part of (a); Cowboys traded pick and 8th-,

9th-, 10th- and 11th-round picks to Raiders for rights to cornerback Stan Smagala, April 22, 1990; Raiders traded pick and 6th-, 9th-, 10th- and 11th-round picks to Saints for 4th-round pick in 1991, April 22, 1990.

(f) Vikings traded pick to Raiders for 12th-round pick in 1989, April 24, 1989; Raiders traded pick and 7th-round pick to Bears for 7th-round pick, April 23, 1990.

MINNESOTA VIKINGS
1990 ROOKIE AND FIRST-YEAR ROSTER

Name	Pos.	Hgt.	Wgt.	Birth-date	College	How Acquired
Allen, Terry	RB	5-10	210	2-21-68	Clemson	D9
Becker, Chris	P	6-1	192	9- 6-66	Texas Christian	*FA
Campbell, Jim	K	6-3	220	5-17-67	Eastern Kentucky	FA
Eilers, Pat	S	5-11	193	9- 3-66	Notre Dame	FA
Florence, Phil	WR	5-11	175	12-12-67	The Citadel	FA
Gaiters, Chris	WR	5-11	187	12-12-67	Minnesota	FA
Goetz, Ron	LB	6-3	236	2- 8-68	Minnesota	D12
Hampton, Alonzo	CB	5-10	197	1-19-67	Pittsburgh	D4
Harper, James	T	6-2	282	9- 6-66	Alcorn State	FA
Hobby, Marion	DE	6-4	277	11- 7-66	Tennessee	D3a
Jones, Mike	TE	6-3	255	11-10-66	Texas A&M	D3
Levelis, John	LB	6-1	235	4-19-67	C.W. Post	D7
Newman, Pat	WR	5-11	189	9-10-68	Utah State	D10
Peterson, Tim	QB	6-3	214	12-28-67	Wisconsin-Stout	FA
Randle, John	DE	6-1	244	12-12-67	Texas A&I	FA
Schlichting, Craig	DE	6-5	257	2-20-67	Wyoming	D8
Smith, Cedric	RB	5-10	223	5-27-68	Florida	D5a
Smith, Donald	CB	5-11	186	2-21-68	Liberty (Va.)	D10a
Thornton, Reggie	WR	5-11	165	9-26-67	Bowling Green State	D5
Williams, Wayne	RB	5-10	197	8-13-67	Florida	*FA

*Becker: D10 Phoenix '89, released 8/28, awarded on waivers to Minnesota 8/29, released 9/5, DEV Minnesota 9/6, released 10/26; Williams: D9 Denver '89, released 9/5, DEV Denver 9/6, released 11/7, DEV Dallas 11/8, released 12/2, DEV Denver 12/20, released 1/29/90.

NEW ENGLAND PATRIOTS
(Eastern Division, American Conference)

Rod Rust

Chairman—Victor K. Kiam II
Vice Chairman—Francis W. Murray
President—William H. Sullivan, Jr.
Vice-President—Francis (Bucko) Kilroy
General Manager—Patrick Sullivan
Director of Player Operations—Joe Mendes
Vice-President/Administration—Robert L. Durkin
Head Coach—Rod Rust (First Year)
Assistant Coaches:
    Outside Linebackers—Don Blackmon
    Special Teams/Tight Ends—Steve Crosby
    Offensive Backs—Bobby Grier
    Offensive Line—Rod Humenuik
    Defensive Line—Dale Lindsey
    Inside Linebackers—Steve Nelson
    Special Assistant—John Polonchek
    Off. Coord./Quarterbacks—Jimmy Raye
    Strength & Conditioning—Jerry Simmons
    Def. Coord./Defensive Backs—Charlie Sumner
    Receivers—Richard Wood
Director of Media Relations—Jim Oldham
    (Office Phone: 543-8200—Area Code 508)
Offices—Foxboro Stadium, Route 1, Foxboro, Mass. 02035
Stadium—Sullivan Stadium, Foxboro, Mass. (Capacity: 60,794)
Team Colors—Red, White and Blue
Training Site—Bryant College, Smithfield, R. I.

1990 SCHEDULE
(All times local.
All games Sunday unless noted otherwise.)

Sept. 9	MIAMI	4:00
Sept. 16	at Indianapolis	12:00
Sept. 23	at Cincinnati	1:00
Sept. 30	NEW YORK JETS	4:00
Oct. 7	SEATTLE	1:00
Oct. 14	OPEN DATE	
Oct. 18	at Miami (Thurs.)	8:00
Oct. 28	BUFFALO	1:00
Nov. 4	at Philadelphia	1:00
Nov. 11	INDIANAPOLIS	1:00
Nov. 18	at Buffalo	1:00
Nov. 25	at Phoenix	2:00
Dec. 2	KANSAS CITY	1:00
Dec. 9	at Pittsburgh	1:00
Dec. 15	WASHINGTON (Sat.)	4:00
Dec. 23	at New York Jets	1:00
Dec. 30	NEW YORK GIANTS	1:00

1989 RESULTS—(Won 5, Lost 11)

Patriots		Opp.		Att.
27	New York Jets	24	(A)	64,541
10	Miami	24	(H)	57,043
3	Seattle	24	(H)	48,025
10	Buffalo	31	(A)	78,921
23	Houston	13	(H)	59,828
15	Atlanta	16	(A)	39,697
20	San Francisco	37	(A)	70,000
23	Indianapolis (OT)	20	(A)	59,256
26	New York Jets	27	(H)	53,366
24	New Orleans	28	(H)	47,680
33	Buffalo	24	(H)	49,663
21	Los Angeles Raiders	24	(A)	38,747
22	Indianapolis	16	(H)	32,234
10	Miami	31	(A)	62,127
10	Pittsburgh	28	(A)	26,594
20	Los Angeles Rams	24	(H)	27,940

1989 GAMES STARTED

16 games: Bruce Armstrong, Mike Baab, Tim Goad, Fred Marion, Larry McGrew, Johnny Rembert, Ed Reynolds, Brent Williams.

15 games: Kenneth Sims, Danny Villa.

14 games: Raymond Clayborn, Paul Fairchild, Sean Farrell, Maurice Hurst, Roland James, Bob Perryman.

13 games: Lin Dawson.

12 games: Cedric Jones, John Stephens.

10 games: Vincent Brown, Stanley Morgan.

6 games: Hart Lee Dykes, Steve Grogan.

5 games: Irving Fryar, Eric Sievers.

4 games: Tim Jordan, Rod McSwain, Dave Viaene, Marc Wilson.

3 games: Tony Eason, Doug Flutie.

2 games: Jim Bowman, Reggie Dupard, Bruce Scholtz.

1 game: David Douglas, Milford Hodge, Sammy Martin.

NEW ENGLAND PATRIOTS 1990 VETERAN ROSTER

No.	Name	Pos.	Ht.	Wt.	NFL Exp.	Birth-date	College	Games in '89	How Acquired
	Adams, George	RB	6-1	225	5	12-22-62	Kentucky	*14	UFA, '90
39	†Allen, Marvin	RB	5-10	208	3	11-23-65	Tulane	3	D11, '88
78	Armstrong, Bruce	T	6-4	284	4	9- 7-65	Louisville	16	D1, '87
28	Bowman, Jim	S	6-2	215	6	10-26-63	Central Michigan	13	D2a, '85
59	Brown, Vincent	LB	6-2	245	3	1- 9-65	Mississippi Valley State	14	D2, '88
22	Coleman, Eric	CB	6-0	190	2	12-27-66	Wyoming	8	D2, '89
46	Cook, Marv	TE	6-4	234	2	2-24-66	Iowa	16	D3a, '89
87	Dawson, Lin	TE	6-3	240	9	6-24-59	North Carolina State	16	D8a, '81
67	Douglas, David	G/C	6-4	280	5	3-20-63	Tennessee	5	UFA, '89
88	Dykes, Hart Lee	WR	6-4	218	2	9- 2-66	Oklahoma State	16	D1, '89
66	Fairchild, Paul	G	6-4	270	7	9-14-61	Kansas	14	D5, '84
62	Farrell, Sean	G	6-3	260	9	5-25-60	Penn State	14	T-TB, '87
63	Feehery, Gerry	C	6-2	270	8	3- 9-60	Syracuse	*0	FA, '89
80	Fryar, Irving	WR/KR	6-0	200	7	9-28-62	Nebraska	11	D1, '84
	Gambol, Chris	T	6-6	303	3	9- 4-64	Iowa	*6	UFA, '90
	Gannon, Chris	DE	6-6	265	2	1-20-66	Southw'tern Louisiana	*10	UFA, '90
	Gibson, Ernest	CB	5-10	185	7	10- 3-61	Furman	*5	UFA, '90
72	Goad, Tim	NT	6-3	280	3	2-28-66	North Carolina	16	D4, '88
14	Grogan, Steve	QB	6-4	210	16	7-24-53	Kansas State	7	D5, '75
	Hansen, Brian	P	6-3	209	6	10-18-60	Sioux Falls	*0	FA, '90
37	Hurst, Maurice	CB	5-10	185	2	9-17-67	Southern University	16	D4a, '89
38	James, Roland	S	6-2	191	11	2-18-58	Tennessee	14	D1, '80
	Jarostchuk, Ilia	LB	6-3	236	4	8- 1-64	New Hampshire	*16	UFA, '90
99	Jeter, Gary	DE	6-4	260	14	1-24-55	Southern California	14	UFA, '89
	Johnson, Damian	T	6-5	290	5	12-18-62	Kansas State	*4	UFA, '90
83	Jones, Cedric	WR	6-1	184	9	6- 1-60	Duke	15	D3, '82
93	†Jordan, Tim	LB	6-3	226	4	4-26-64	Wisconsin	9	D4b, '87
42	Lippett, Ronnie	CB	5-11	180	7	12-10-60	Miami (Fla.)	*0	D8, '83
91	†Lowry, Orlando	LB	6-4	236	7	8-14-61	Ohio State	2	FA, '89
31	Marion, Fred	S	6-2	191	9	1- 2-59	Miami (Fla.)	16	D5, '82
82	Martin, Sammy	WR/KR	5-11	175	3	8-21-65	Louisiana State	10	D4a, '88
23	†McSwain, Rod	CB	6-1	198	7	1-28-62	Clemson	9	T-Atl, '84
	Morris, Jamie	RB	5-7	188	3	6- 6-65	Michigan	*12	UFA, '90
	Mowatt, Zeke	TE	6-3	240	7	3- 5-61	Florida State	*16	UFA, '90
34	†Perryman, Robert	RB	6-1	233	4	10-16-64	Michigan	16	D3, '87
52	Rembert, Johnny	LB	6-3	234	8	1-19-61	Clemson	16	D4, '83
95	Reynolds, Ed	LB	6-5	242	8	9-23-61	Virginia	16	OFA, '83
51	Scholtz, Bruce	LB	6-6	244	9	9-26-58	Texas	8	FA, '89
85	Sievers, Eric	TE	6-4	238	10	11- 9-57	Maryland	16	UFA, '89
77	Sims, Kenneth	DE	6-5	271	8	10-31-59	Texas	15	D1, '82
4	Staurovsky, Jason	K	5-9	170	3	3-23-63	Tulsa	7	FA, '88
44	Stephens, John	RB	6-1	215	3	2-23-66	Northwestern (La.) St.	14	D1, '88
30	Tatupu, Mosi	RB	6-0	227	13	4-26-55	Southern California	14	D8a, '78
49	Taylor, Kitrick	WR/KR	5-11	190	3	7-22-64	Washington State	4	FA, '89
56	Tippett, Andre	LB	6-3	241	8	12-27-59	Iowa	*0	D2a, '82
21	Tucker, Erroll	CB/KR	5-8	170	3	7- 6-64	Utah	5	FA, '89
60	Veris, Garin	DE	6-4	255	5	2-27-63	Stanford	*0	D2, '85
70	Viaene, David	T	6-5	300	2	7-14-65	Minnesota-Duluth	16	UFA, '90
75	Villa, Danny	T	6-5	305	4	9-21-64	Arizona State	15	D5, '87
	White, Bob	C	6-5	273	4	4- 9-63	Rhode Island	*8	UFA, '90
96	Williams, Brent	DE	6-4	275	5	10-23-64	Toledo	16	D7a, '86
54	Williams, Ed	LB	6-4	244	6	9- 8-61	Texas	*0	D2, '84
15	Wilson, Marc	QB	6-5	205	10	2-15-57	Brigham Young	14	FA, '89
35	Wonsley, George	RB	5-10	219	7	11-23-60	Mississippi State	5	FA, '89
	Zackery, Tony	S	6-2	195	1	11-20-66	Washington	*1	UFA, '90

*Adams played 14 games with Giants in '89; Feehery active for 3 games with Patriots in '89, but did not play; Gambol played 6 games with Lions in '89; Gannon played 10 games with Chargers in '89; Gibson played 5 games with Dolphins in '89; Hansen last active with Saints in '88; Jarostchuk played 16 games with Cardinals in '89; Johnson played 4 games with Giants in '89; Lippett, Tippett, Veris and E. Williams missed '89 season due to injury; Morris played 12 games with Redskins in '89; Mowatt played 16 games with Giants in '89; White played 8 games with Cowboys in '89; Zackery played 1 game with Falcons in '89.

†Unsigned; subject to developments.

Players lost through Plan B free agency: WR Glenn Antrum (1 game in '89; to N.Y.J.); C Mike Baab (16; to Clev.); LB Aaron Chubb (0; to G.B.); CB Raymond Clayborn (14; to Clev.); LB Terrence Cooks (3; to Dall.); RB Patrick Egu (7; to N.Y.J.); CB Howard Feggins (11; to N.Y.G.); NT Milford Hodge (16; to Wash.); S Darryl Holmes (13; to Pitt.); LB Lawrence McGrew (16; to Clev.); NT Emanuel McNeil (1; to

K.C.); C Mike Morris (11; to K.C.); T Tom Rehder (16; to N.Y.J.); CB Rodney Rice (10; to T.B.); DE Peter Shorts (1; to K.C.); LB David Ward (16; to K.C.); C Curtis Wilson (0; to Det.).

Also played with Patriots in '89—K Greg Davis (9 games); RB Reggie Dupard (7); QB Tony Eason (3); P Jeff Feagles (16); QB Doug Flutie (5); WR Stanley Morgan (10); LB Eric Naposki (1).

D—Draft; T—Trade; FA—Free Agent; OFA—Original Free Agent; UFA—Unrestricted Free Agent.

NEW ENGLAND PATRIOTS
1990 DRAFT CHOICES

(Number following name designates order of selection among 331 players drafted.)

Round and Player		Position	College
1. Choice to Seattle (a)			
1. SINGLETON, Chris from Seattle (a)	8	LB	Arizona
1. AGNEW, Ray from Indianapolis through Seattle (b)	10	DE	North Carolina State
2. Choice to Seattle (a)			
3. HODSON, Tommy	59	QB	Louisiana State
3. McMURTRY, Greg from Denver through Dallas (c)	80	WR	Michigan
4. Choice to Washington (d)			
5. ROBINSON, Junior from Dallas through Washington (e)	110	DB	East Carolina
5. MELANDER, Jon	113	T	Minnesota
5. GRAY, James from Miami through Dallas (f)	120	RB	Texas Tech
6. Choice to San Diego through Dallas (g)			
7. Choice to Buffalo (h)			
8. Choice to L.A. Raiders through Dallas (i)			
9. BOUWENS, Shawn	226	G	Nebraska Wesleyan
10. LANDRY, Anthony	253	RB	Stephen F. Austin
11. SMITH, Sean	280	DE	Georgia Tech
12. DONELSON, Ventson	309	DB	Michigan State
12. ROSE, Blaine from Buffalo (h)	322	G	Maryland

(a) Traded 1st- and 2nd-round picks for two 1st-round picks, 3rd-round pick and 4th-round pick in 1991, April 22, 1990.

(b) Patriots acquired pick from Seahawks: see (a); Seahawks had acquired pick and 1st-round pick in 1989 from Colts for linebacker Fredd Young, September 9, 1988.

(c) Patriots acquired pick and 5th- and 7th-round picks from Cowboys for 3rd-, 6th- and 8th-round picks, April 22, 1990; Cowboys had acquired pick from Broncos for defensive end Kevin Brooks and 4th-round pick, July 10, 1989.

(d) Traded pick for two 5th-round picks, April 22, 1990.

(e) Patriots acquired pick from Redskins: see (d); Redskins acquired pick from Cowboys for defensive tackle Dean Hamel, August 28, 1989.

(f) Patriots acquired pick from Cowboys: see first part of (c); Cowboys acquired pick from Dolphins for quarterback Scott Secules, August 6, 1989.

(g) Patriots traded pick to Cowboys: see first part of (c); Cowboys traded pick and two other 6th-round picks to Chargers for 3rd-round pick in 1991, April 22, 1990.

(h) Traded pick and another 7th-round pick for 12th-round pick and 4th-round pick in 1991, April 23, 1990.

(i) Patriots traded pick to Cowboys: see first part of (c); Cowboys traded pick and 6th-, 9th-, 10th- and 11th-round picks to Raiders for rights to cornerback Stan Smagala, April 22, 1990.

NEW ENGLAND PATRIOTS
1990 ROOKIE AND FIRST-YEAR ROSTER

Name	Pos.	Hgt.	Wgt.	Birth-date	College	How Acquired
Agnew, Ray	DE	6-3	272	12- 9-67	North Carolina State	D1a
Bouwens, Shawn	G	6-4	280	5-26-68	Nebraska Wesleyan	D9
Crowley, Pat	G	6-2	284	8-29-67	North Carolina	FA
Donelson, Ventson	CB	5-11	180	2- 2-68	Michigan State	D12
Gray, James	RB	5-11	200	3- 2-67	Texas Tech	D5b
Gregory, Morgan	WR	5-11	185	4- 8-68	Nebraska	FA
Harvey, Richard	LB	6-1	227	11-11-66	Tulane	*UFA
Hauk, Tim	S	5-11	185	12-20-66	Montana	FA
Hodson, Tom	QB	6-3	195	1-28-67	Louisiana State	D3
Hutson, Brian	S	6-1	198	2-20-65	Mississippi State	*FA
Jackson, Charles	DE	6-4	280	8- 4-66	Jackson State	*FA
Landry, Anthony	RB	5-9	200	10-28-66	Stephen F. Austin	D10
McMurtry, Greg	WR	6-2	207	10-15-67	Michigan	D3a
Melander, Jon	T	6-7	280	12-27-66	Minnesota	D5a
Murphy, Mike	WR	..	..	......	SW Texas State	FA
Overton, Don	RB	..	..	......	Fairmont State	FA
Proctor, Michael	QB	..	..	......	Murray State	FA
Robinson, Junior	CB	5-9	181	2- 3-68	East Carolina	D5
Rose, Blaine	G	6-5	271	6-13-66	Maryland	D12a
Singleton, Chris	LB	6-2	247	2-20-67	Arizona	D1
Smith, Sean	DE	6-7	280	5-29-67	Georgia Tech	D11
Stephens, Mac	LB	6-3	217	1-21-68	Minnesota	FA
Tardits, Richard	LB	6-2	218	7-30-65	Georgia	*FA
Warner, Kirk	TE	6-4	225	11-24-67	Georgia	FA
Williams, Chris	NT	6-3	309	11-23-68	American International	FA

*Harvey: D11 Buffalo '89, injured reserve (shoulder) 9/4 through entire season, unprotected free agent 2/1/90; Hutson: FA Los Angeles Raiders '87, injured reserve (broken foot) 8/27 through entire season, released 8/23/88; Jackson: D10 Los Angeles Raiders '89, released 7/31; Tardits: D5 Phoenix '89, released 9/5, DEV Phoenix 9/6, released 11/8, DEV Phoenix 11/10, released 1/3/90.

NEW ORLEANS SAINTS
(Western Division, National Conference)

Jim Mora

Managing General Partner—Tom Benson
President/General Manager—Jim Finks
Director of Player Personnel—Bill Kuharich
Vice-President/Administration—Jim Miller
Head Coach—Jim Mora (4 years: 38-25)
Assistant Coaches:
    Offensive Line—Paul Boudreau
    Secondary—Dom Capers
    Linebackers—Vic Fangio
    Tight Ends/Special Teams—Joe Marciano
    Strength & Conditioning—Russell Paternostro
    Defensive Line—John Pease
    Defensive Coordinator—Steve Sidwell
    Running Backs—Jim Skipper
    Offensive Coordinator—Carl Smith
    Receivers—Steve Walters
Director of Media Relations—Rusty Kasmiersky
    (Office Phone: 733-6147—Area Code 504)
Offices—6928 Saints Dr., Metairie, La. 70003
Stadium—Louisiana Superdome (Capacity: 69,065)
Team Colors—Old Gold, Black and White
Training Site—University of Wisconsin at LaCrosse.

1990 SCHEDULE
(All times local.
All games Sunday unless noted otherwise.)

Sept. 10	SAN FRANCISCO (Mon.)	8:00
Sept. 16	at Minnesota	3:00
Sept. 23	PHOENIX	12:00
Sept. 30	OPEN DATE	
Oct. 7	at Atlanta	1:00
Oct. 14	CLEVELAND	12:00
Oct. 21	at Houston	12:00
Oct. 28	DETROIT	12:00
Nov. 4	at Cincinnati	1:00
Nov. 11	TAMPA BAY	12:00
Nov. 18	at Washington	1:00
Nov. 25	ATLANTA	12:00
Dec. 2	at Dallas	3:00
Dec. 9	at Los Angeles Rams	1:00
Dec. 16	PITTSBURGH	12:00
Dec. 23	at San Francisco	1:00
Dec. 31	LOS ANGELES RAMS (Mon.)	7:00

1989 RESULTS—(Won 9, Lost 7)

Saints		Opp.		Att.
28	Dallas	0	(H)	66,977
34	Green Bay	35	(A)	55,809
10	Tampa Bay	20	(A)	44,053
14	Washington	16	(H)	64,358
20	San Francisco	24	(H)	60,488
29	New York Jets	14	(H)	59,521
40	Los Angeles Rams	21	(A)	57,567
20	Atlanta	13	(H)	65,153
13	San Francisco	31	(A)	60,667
28	New England	24	(A)	47,680
26	Atlanta	17	(A)	53,173
17	Los Angeles Rams (OT)	20	(H)	68,274
14	Detroit	21	(A)	38,550
22	Buffalo	19	(A)	70,037
30	Philadelphia	20	(H)	68,561
41	Indianapolis	6	(H)	49,009

1989 GAMES STARTED

16 games: Hoby Brenner, Stan Brock, Jim Dombrowski, Dalton Hilliard, Vaughn Johnson, Eric Martin, Robert Massey, Steve Trapilo, Frank Warren, Dave Waymer.

15 games: James Geathers, Sam Mills, Pat Swilling, Jim Wilks.

14 games: Toi Cook, Rickey Jackson.

13 games: Bobby Hebert, Joel Hilgenberg.

12 games: Gene Atkins, Lonzell Hill.

8 games: Brad Edelman.

7 games: Kevin Haverdink, Buford Jordan.

6 games: Craig Heyward.

4 games: Steve Korte, Milton Mack, Greg Scales.

3 games: John Fourcade, Antonio Gibson.

2 games: James Haynes, Brett Maxie, John Tice.

1 game: Brian Forde, Brett Perriman.

NEW ORLEANS SAINTS 1990 VETERAN ROSTER

No.	Name	Pos.	Ht.	Wt.	NFL Exp.	Birth-date	College	Games in '89	How Acquired
	Alphin, Gerald	WR	6-3	220	1	5-21-64	Kansas State	*17	FA, '90
7	Andersen, Morten	K	6-2	221	9	8-19-60	Michigan State	16	D4, '82
28	†Atkins, Gene	S	6-1	200	4	11-22-64	Florida A&M	14	D7, '87
6	Barnhardt, Tommy	P	6-2	207	4	6-11-63	North Carolina	11	FA, '89
85	Brenner, Hoby	TE	6-5	245	10	6- 2-59	Southern California	16	D3a, '81
67	†Brock, Stan	T	6 6	292	11	6- 8-58	Colorado	16	D1, '80
41	†Cook, Toi	CB	5-11	188	4	12- 3-64	Stanford	16	D8, '87
79	Derby, Glenn	T	6-6	290	2	6-27-64	Wisconsin	3	D8, '88
72	†Dombrowski, Jim	T	6-5	298	5	10-19-63	Virginia	16	D1, '86
63	Edelman, Brad	G	6-6	270	9	9- 3-60	Missouri	8	D2, '82
	Fenerty, Gill	RB	6-0	205	R	8-24-63	Holy Cross	*16	D7, '86
52	†Forde, Brian	LB	6-3	225	3	11- 1-63	Washington State	16	D7, '88
11	Fourcade, John	QB	6-1	215	4	10-11-60	Mississippi	13	FA, '87
74	Haverdink, Kevin	T	6-5	285	2	10-20-65	Western Michigan	16	D5, '89
3	†Hebert, Bobby	QB	6-4	215	6	8-19-60	Northwestern (La.) St.	14	FA, '85
34	Heyward, Craig	RB	5-11	260	3	9-26-66	Pittsburgh	16	D1, '88
61	Hilgenberg, Joel	C/G	6-2	252	7	7-10-62	Iowa	16	D4, '84
87	†Hill, Lonzell	WR	5-11	189	4	9-25-65	Washington	16	D2, '87
21	Hilliard, Dalton	RB	5-8	204	5	1-21-64	Louisiana State	16	D2, '86
57	†Jackson, Rickey	LB	6-2	243	10	3-20-58	Pittsburgh	14	D2, '81
53	Johnson, Vaughan	LB	6-3	235	5	3-24-62	North Carolina State	16	SupD, '84
23	Jordan, Buford	RB	6-0	223	5	6-26-62	McNeese State	11	FA, '86
60	Korte, Steve	C	6-2	271	8	1-15-60	Arkansas	5	D2, '83
24	Mack, Milton	CB	5-11	182	4	9-20-63	Alcorn State	16	D5, '87
84	Martin, Eric	WR	6-1	207	6	11- 8-61	Louisiana State	16	D7, '85
93	Martin, Wayne	DE	6-5	275	2	10-26-65	Arkansas	16	D1, '89
40	Massey, Robert	CB	5-10	182	2	2-17-67	North Carolina Central	16	D2, '89
39	†Maxie, Brett	S	6-2	194	6	1-13-62	Texas Southern	16	OFA, '85
36	Mayes, Rueben	RB	5-11	200	4	6- 6-63	Washington State	*0	D3, '86
51	Mills, Sam	LB	5-9	225	5	6- 3-59	Montclair State	16	FA, '86
35	Morse, Bobby	RB	5-10	213	3	10- 3-65	Michigan State	11	T-Phi, '89
	Nicholson, Calvin	CB	5-9	183	1	7- 9-67	Oregon State	1	FA, '89
80	Perriman, Brett	WR	5-9	180	3	10-10-65	Miami (Fla.)	14	D2, '88
43	Phillips, Kim	CB	5-9	188	2	10-28-66	North Texas	5	D3, '89
83	Scales, Greg	TE	6-4	253	3	5- 9-66	Wake Forest	14	D5, '88
	Simien, Tracy	LB	6-1	245	1	5-21-67	Texas Christian	*0	UFA, '90
	Simmons, Michael	DE	6-4	269	1	11-14-65	Mississippi State	1	FA, '89
56	†Swilling, Pat	LB	6-3	242	5	10-25-64	Georgia Tech	16	D3a, '86
	Thompson, Bennie	S	6-0	200	1	2-10-63	Grambling	2	FA, '89
82	Tice, John	TE	6-5	249	8	6-22-60	Maryland	15	D3, '83
54	Toles, Alvin	LB	6-1	234	5	3-23-63	Tennessee	*0	D1, '85
65	†Trapilo, Steve	G	6-5	281	4	9-20-64	Boston College	16	D4, '87
88	Turner, Floyd	WR	5-11	188	2	5-29-66	Northwestern (La.) St.	13	D6, '89
94	Wilks, Jim	NT	6-5	275	10	3-12-58	San Diego State	16	D12, '81
18	Wilson, Dave	QB	6-3	206	9	4-27-59	Illinois	*0	SupD, '81
69	Woods, Tony	DE	6-4	274	2	3-14-66	Oklahoma	*15	UFA, '90

*Alphin played 17 games with Ottawa-CFL in '89; Fenerty played 16 games with Toronto-CFL in '89; Mayes and Toles missed '89 season due to injury; Simien played 1 playoff game with Steelers in '89; Wilson active for 15 games in '89, but did not play; Woods played 15 games with Bears in '89.

†Unsigned; subject to developments.

Players lost through Plan B free agency: RB Paul Frazier (15 games in '89; to G.B.); DE James Geathers (15; to Wash.); S Antonio Gibson (16; to Dall.) WR Rod Harris (11; to Dall.); LB Walter Johnson (15; to Dall.); LB Joe Kohlbrand (16; to N.Y.J.); G Doug Marrone (1; to Minn.); NT Pat Swoopes (15; to Wash.); G Jeff Walker (13; to Phoe.); S Dave Waymer (16; to S.F.).

Also played with Saints in '89—LB James Haynes (3 games); RB Undra Johnson (5); WR Mike Jones (3); CB Michael Mayes (2); WR Derrick Shepard (4); DE Frank Warren (16); P George Winslow (5).

D—Draft; FA—Free Agent; OFA—Original Free Agent; UFA—Unrestricted Free Agent; SupD—Supplemental Draft.

NEW ORLEANS SAINTS
1990 DRAFT CHOICES

(Number following name designates order of selection among 331 players drafted.)

Round and Player		Position	College
1. TURNBULL, Renaldo	14	DE	West Virginia
2. BUCK, Vince	44	DB	Central State (O.)
3. SMEENGE, Joel	71	DE	Western Michigan
4. WINSTON, DeMond	98	LB	Vanderbilt
5. ARBUCKLE, Charles	125	TE	UCLA
6. BUCK, Mike	156	QB	Maine
6. WILLIAMS, James from Minnesota through Dallas and Los Angeles Raiders (a)	158	LB	Mississippi State
7. HOUGH, Scott	183	G	Maine
8. GDOWSKI, Gerry from Los Angeles Raiders (b)	207	QB	Nebraska
8. CARR, Derrick	210	DE	Bowling Green State
9. GRAVES, Broderick from Los Angeles Raiders (b)	233	RB	Winston-Salem
9. BROCKMAN, Lonnie	236	LB	West Virginia
10. COOPER, Gary from Los Angeles Raiders (b)	260	WR	Clemson
10. SPEARS, Ernest	267	DB	Southern Cal
11. BURNETT, Webbie from Los Angeles Raiders (b)	287	NT	Western Kentucky
11. Choice to Philadelphia (c)			
12. PORT, Chris	320	G	Duke

(a) Saints acquired pick and 8th-, 9th-, 10th- and 11th-round picks from Raiders for 4th-round pick in 1991, April 22, 1990; Raiders had acquired pick and 8th-, 9th-, 10th- and 11th-round picks from Cowboys for rights to cornerback Stan Smagala, April 22, 1990; Cowboys had acquired pick from Vikings in Herschel Walker trade, October 12, 1989.

(b) See first part of (a).

(c) Traded pick for fullback Bobby Morse, April 24, 1989.

NEW ORLEANS SAINTS
1990 ROOKIE AND FIRST-YEAR ROSTER

Name	Pos.	Hgt.	Wgt.	Birth-date	College	How Acquired
Arbuckle, Charles...............	TE	6-2	238	9-13-68	UCLA	D5
Brady, Robert......................	WR	6-0	189	....	Villanova	FA
Brockman, Lonnie	LB	6-3	230	3-14-68	West Virginia	D9a
Buck, Mike	QB	6-3	227	4-22-67	Maine	D6
Buck, Vince......................	CB	6-0	198	1-12-68	Central State (O.)	D2
Burnett, Webbie.................	NT	6-2	277	11- 7-67	Western Kentucky	D11
Carr, Derrick....................	DE	6-5	259	1-30-67	Bowling Green State	D8a
Cooper, Gary......................	WR	6-1	190	12-14-66	Clemson	D10a
Cooper, Richard	T	6-4	285	11- 1-64	Tennessee	*FA
Davis, Richard	NT	6-0	271	11-29-65	Arizona State	FA
DeShazer, Steven...............	LB	6-3	240	10-27-66	Nebraska Wesleyan	FA
Fisher, Randy.....................	WR	5-10	168	3- 1-67	Valdosta State	FA
Ford, Michael.....................	WR	6-2	212	6-11-68	California	FA
Garrett, Jason	QB	6-0	196	3-28-66	Princeton	*FA
Gdowski, Gerry..................	QB	6-0	192	8- 9-67	Nebraska	D8
Graves, Broderick.............	RB	5-11	194	4- 7-68	Winston-Salem State	D9
Griffin, Willie....................	NT	6-3	280	3-24-66	Nebraska	*FA
Hough, Scott......................	G-T	6-4	282	5-14-66	Maine	D7
King, Buddy	T	6-6	270	9-11-67	Southern Mississippi	FA
King, Thomas.....................	S	6-1	190	3-31-66	Southwestern Louisiana	*FA
Ledbetter, Mark	LB	6-2	230	12-14-66	Washington State	FA
Liimatta, Daniel	T	6-6	289	9- 4-66	Minnesota	FA
Lindstrom, Eric	LB	6-3	235	5-27-66	Boston College	*FA
McIntosh, Jerome	WR	6-0	183	10-27-67	Tulane	FA
Port, Chris..........................	T	6-5	290	11- 2-67	Duke	D12
Sanders, Aaron...................	LB	6-3	240	2- 9-67	Connecticut	FA
Smeenge, Joel	DE	6-5	250	4- 1-68	Western Michigan	D3
Spears, Ernest	S	5-11	192	11- 6-67	Southern California	D10b
Turnbull, Renaldo	DE	6-4	248	1- 5-66	West Virginia	D1
Washington, Derek	WR	6-1	178	7- 8-67	Long Beach State	FA
Wheeler, Todd...................	C	6-4	269	7-25-67	Georgia	*FA
Whitney, Kenny.................	G	6-4	290	7- 1-65	Cal Lutheran	FA
Williams, James.................	LB	6-0	230	10-10-68	Mississippi State	D6a
Winston, DeMond.............	LB	6-2	239	9-14-68	Vanderbilt	D4

*R. Cooper: FA Seattle '88, released 8/1, FA New Orleans '89, released 9/5, DEV New Orleans 9/6, released 12/29; Garrett: FA New Orleans '89, released 8/30, DEV New Orleans 9/6, released 12/29; Griffin: D11 Tampa Bay '89, released 8/30; T. King: D8 Green Bay '89, released 8/29; Lindstrom: D7 New England '89, released 8/30, DEV Minnesota 11/9, released 12/12; Wheeler: FA New Orleans '89, released 8/30, DEV New Orleans 11/22, released 12/29.

NEW YORK GIANTS
(Eastern Division, National Conference)

Bill Parcells

President—Wellington T. Mara
Vice-President and Treasurer—Timothy J. Mara
Vice-President and Secretary—Raymond J. Walsh
Vice-President and General Manager—George Young
Assistant General Manager—Harry Hulmes
Director of Player Personnel—Tom Boisture
Director of Pro Personnel—Tim Rooney
Head Coach—Bill Parcells (7 years: 64-46-1)
Assistant Coaches:
  Defensive Coordinator/Defensive Backs—Bill Belichick
  Receivers—Tom Coughlin
  Offensive Coordinator—Ron Erhardt
  Linebackers—Al Groh
  Running Backs—Ray Handley
  Offensive Line—Fred Hoaglin
  Strength & Conditioning—Johnny Parker
  Tight Ends—Mike Pope
  Special Teams—Mike Sweatman
  Defensive Assistant—Charlie Weis
Director of Media Services—Ed Croke
  (Office Phone: 935-8111—Area Code 201)
Offices—Giants Stadium, East Rutherford, N. J. 07073
Stadium—Giants Stadium (Capacity: 77,311)
Team Colors—Royal Blue, Red and White
Training Site—Fairleigh-Dickinson University (Madison),
  Florham Park, N.J.

1990 SCHEDULE
(All times local.)
All games Sunday unless noted otherwise.)

Sept. 9	PHILADELPHIA	8:00
Sept. 16	at Dallas	3:00
Sept. 23	MIAMI	1:00
Sept. 30	DALLAS	1:00
Oct. 7	OPEN DATE	
Oct. 14	at Washington	4:00
Oct. 21	PHOENIX	4:00
Oct. 28	WASHINGTON	4:00
Nov. 5	at Indianapolis (Mon.)	9:00
Nov. 11	at Los Angeles Rams	1:00
Nov. 18	DETROIT	1:00
Nov. 25	at Philadelphia	1:00
Dec. 3	at San Francisco (Mon.)	6:00
Dec. 9	MINNESOTA	1:00
Dec. 15	BUFFALO (Sat.)	12:30
Dec. 23	at Phoenix	2:00
Dec. 30	at New England	1:00

1989 RESULTS—(Won 12, Lost 5)

Giants		Opp.		Att.
27	Washington	24	(A)	54,160
24	Detroit	14	(H)	76,021
35	Phoenix	7	(H)	75,742
30	Dallas	13	(A)	51,785
19	Philadelphia	21	(A)	65,688
20	Washington	17	(H)	76,245
20	San Diego	13	(A)	48,566
24	Minnesota	14	(H)	76,041
20	Phoenix	13	(A)	46,588
10	Los Angeles Rams	31	(A)	65,127
15	Seattle	3	(H)	75,014
24	San Francisco	34	(A)	63,461
17	Philadelphia	24	(H)	74,809
14	Denver	7	(A)	63,283
15	Dallas	0	(H)	72,141
34	Los Angeles Raiders	17	(H)	70,306

NFC SEMIFINAL GAME
13 Los Angeles Rams (OT) ...... 19 (H) 76,325

1989 GAMES STARTED

16 games: Ottis Anderson, Carl Banks, Mark Collins, Erik Howard, Terry Kinard, Leonard Marshall, Bart Oates, Doug Riesenberg, William Roberts, Perry Williams.

15 games: Myron Guyton, Phil Simms, Lawrence Taylor.

14 games: John Washington.

13 games: Johnie Cooks, Eric Moore.

12 games: Lionel Manuel, Gary Reasons.

11 games: John Elliott, Zeke Mowatt.

10 games: Maurice Carthon, Odessa Turner.

7 games: Mark Bavaro.

4 games: Stephen Baker, Howard Cross, Damian Johnson, Pepper Johnson, Brian Williams.

3 games: Steve DeOssie, Mark Ingram.

2 games: Eric Dorsey, Dave Meggett.

1 game: Jeff Hostetler, Greg Jackson, Bob Kratch, Sheldon White.

NEW YORK GIANTS 1990 VETERAN ROSTER

No.	Name	Pos.	Ht.	Wt.	NFL Exp.	Birth-date	College	Games in '89	How Acquired
2	Allegre, Raul	K	5-10	167	8	6-15-59	Texas	10	FA, '86
24	Anderson, Ottis	RB	6-2	225	12	11-19-57	Miami (Fla.)	16	T-StL, '86
85	Baker, Stephen	WR	5-8	160	4	8-30-64	Fresno State	15	D3, '87
58	Banks, Carl	LB	6-4	235	7	8-29-62	Michigan State	16	D1, '84
89	Bavaro, Mark	TE	6-4	245	6	4-28-63	Notre Dame	7	D4, '85
44	†Carthon, Maurice	RB	6-1	225	6	4-24-61	Arkansas State	16	FA, '85
	Chandler, Thornton	TE	6-5	240	5	11-27-63	Alabama	*6	FA, '90
25	†Collins, Mark	CB	5-10	190	5	1-16-64	Cal State-Fullerton	16	D2, '86
98	Cooks, Johnie	LB	6-4	251	9	11-23-58	Mississippi State	16	W-Ind, '88
87	Cross, Howard	TE	6-5	245	2	8- 8-67	Alabama	16	D6, '89
99	DeOssie, Steve	LB	6-2	248	7	11-22-62	Boston College	9	T-Dal, '89
77	†Dorsey, Eric	DE	6-5	280	5	8- 5-64	Notre Dame	2	D1, '86
76	Elliott, John	T	6-7	305	3	4- 1-65	Michigan	13	D2, '88
	Feggins, Howard	CB	5-10	190	2	5- 6-65	UNC-Charlotte	*11	UFA, '90
29	Guyton, Myron	CB/S	6-1	205	2	8-26-67	Eastern Kentucky	16	D8, '89
	Harper, LaSalle	LB	6-1	241	2	5-16-67	Arkansas	*4	FA, '90
15	Hostetler, Jeff	QB	6-3	212	6	4-22-61	West Virginia	16	D3, '84
74	†Howard, Erik	NT	6-4	268	5	11-12-64	Washington State	16	D2a, '86
82	Ingram, Mark	WR	5-10	188	4	8-23-65	Michigan State	16	D1, '87
47	Jackson, Greg	S	6-1	200	2	8-20-66	Louisiana State	16	D3a, '89
54	Jiles, Dwayne	LB	6-4	245	6	11-23-61	Texas Tech	9	FA, '89
52	Johnson, Pepper	LB	6-3	248	5	6-29-64	Ohio State	14	D2b, '86
61	Kratch, Bob	G	6-3	288	2	1- 6-66	Iowa	4	D3, '89
5	†Landeta, Sean	P	6-0	200	5	1- 6-62	Towson State	16	FA, '85
86	Manuel, Lionel	WR	5-11	180	7	4-13-62	Pacific	16	D7, '84
70	Marshall, Leonard	DE	6-3	285	8	10-22-61	Louisiana State	16	D2, '83
30	Meggett, David	RB	5-7	180	2	4- 3-66	Towson State	16	D5, '89
60	Moore, Eric	T	6-5	290	3	1-21-65	Indiana	16	D1, '88
20	Morris, Joe	RB	5-7	195	9	9-15-60	Syracuse	*0	D2, '82
	Mrosko, Robert	TE	6-5	270	2	11-13-65	Penn State	*15	UFA, '90
65	Oates, Bart	C	6-3	265	6	12-16-58	Brigham Young	16	FA, '85
55	†Reasons, Gary	LB	6-4	234	7	2-18-62	Northwestern (La.) St.	16	D4a, '84
72	Riesenberg, Doug	T	6-5	275	4	7-22-65	California	16	D6a, '87
66	Roberts, William	T	6-5	280	6	8- 5-62	Ohio State	16	D1a, '84
81	†Robinson, Stacy	WR	5-11	186	6	2-19-62	North Dakota State	6	D2, '85
22	†Rouson, Lee	RB	6-1	222	6	10-18-62	Colorado	16	D8, '85
11	Simms, Phil	QB	6-3	214	11	11- 3-56	Morehead State	15	D1, '79
56	Taylor, Lawrence	LB	6-3	243	10	2- 4-59	North Carolina	16	D1, '81
21	Thompson, Reyna	CB	6-0	193	5	8-28-63	Baylor	16	UFA, '89
34	Tillman, Lewis	RB	6-0	195	2	4-16-66	Jackson State	16	D4, '89
83	Turner, Odessa	WR	6-3	205	4	10-12-64	Northwestern (La.) St.	13	D4, '87
	Walls, Everson	DB	6-1	194	10	12-28-59	Grambling State	*16	FA, '90
73	Washington, John	DE	6-4	275	5	2-20-63	Oklahoma State	16	D3, '86
36	†White, Adrian	S	6-0	200	4	4- 6-64	Florida	15	D2, '87
39	White, Sheldon	CB/S	5-11	188	3	3- 1-65	Miami (O.)	16	D3, '88
59	Williams, Brian	C/G	6-5	300	2	6- 8-66	Minnesota	14	D1, '89
23	Williams, Perry	CB	6-2	203	7	5-12-61	North Carolina State	16	D7, '83

*Chandler played 6 games with Cowboys in '89; Feggins played 11 games with Patriots in '89; Harper played 1 game with Giants and 3 games with Bears in '89; Morris missed '89 season due to injury; Mrosko played 15 games with Oilers in '89; Walls played 16 games with Cowboys in '89.

†Unsigned; subject to developments.

Players lost through Plan B free agency: RB George Adams (14 games in '89; to N.E.); S Greg Cox (16; to S.F.); DE Mark Duckens (15; to Det.); G Damian Johnson (4; to N.E.); S Terry Kinard (16; to Hou.); TE Zeke Mowatt (16; to N.E.); K Bjorn Nittmo (6; to K.C.); QB Jeff Rutledge (1; to Wash.); DE Robb White (15; to Den.); C Frank Winters (15; to K.C.).

Also played with Giants in '89—LB Ricky Shaw (7 games).

D—Draft; T—Trade; W—Waivers; FA—Free Agent; UFA—Unrestricted Free Agent.

NEW YORK GIANTS
1990 DRAFT CHOICES

(Number following name designates order of selection among 331 players drafted.)

Round and Player		Position	College
1. HAMPTON, Rodney	24	RB	Georgia
2. FOX, Mike	51	DT	West Virginia
3. MARK, Greg	79	DE	Miami (Fla.)
4. WHITMORE, David	107	DB	Stephen F. Austin
5. KUPP, Craig	135	QB	Pacific Lutheran
6. Choice to San Diego through Dallas (a)			
7. EMANUEL, Aaron	191	RB	Southern Cal
8. VOORHEES, Barry	218	T	Cal State-Northridge
9. JAMES, Clint	246	DE	Louisiana State
10. MOORE, Otis	274	DT	Clemson
11. DOWNING, Tim	302	DE	Washington State
12. STOVER, Matt	329	K	Louisiana Tech

(a) Giants traded pick to Cowboys for linebacker Steve DeOssie, June 2, 1989; Cowboys traded pick to Chargers in Herschel Walker trade involving Darrin Nelson, October 17, 1989.

NEW YORK GIANTS
1990 ROOKIE AND FIRST-YEAR ROSTER

Name	Pos.	Hgt.	Wgt.	Birth-date	College	How Acquired
Abrams, Bobby	LB	6-3	230	4-12-67	Michigan	FA
Apolskis, Rich	G	6-3	288	1- 6-67	Arkansas	FA
Barlow, Gary	G	6-4	281	3-26-67	Pacific	FA
Baur, Frank	QB	6-1	220	7- 5-66	Lafayette	FA
Boysaw, Greg	CB/S	6-1	207	12-11-66	Illinois	FA
Brown, Roy	G	6-4	270	10-27-67	Virginia	FA
Bryant, Winfred	DT	6-3	274	11- 7-66	Nicholls State	FA
Cunningham, Ed	T	6-8	295	5-10-66	Texas	FA
Dennis, Mark	LB	6-1	238	10-25-67	Central Michigan	FA
Downing, Tim	DE	6-5	260	4- 9-67	Washington State	D11
Doyen, William	T	6-8	328	12-19-64	West Virginia Tech	FA
Emanuel, Aaron	RB	6-2	225	1-10-67	Southern California	D7
Fishback, Joe	CB/S	5-11	198	11-29-67	Carson-Newman	FA
Fox, Mike	DE	6-6	275	8- 5-67	West Virginia	D2
Gravely, Tracy	DB	...	...	....	Concord	FA
Greene, Terrance	CB/S	6-3	210	4-26-67	DePauw	FA
Grider, David	NT	6-3	290	1- 7-67	Northeast Oklahoma	FA
Hampton, Rodney	RB	5-11	215	4- 3-69	Georgia	D1
Holmes, Jeffrey	CB/S	6-2	212	8- 8-67	Azusa Pacific	FA
Hooten, Mike	LB	6-4	240	11- 1-65	Wake Forest	*FA, '89
James, Clint	DE	6-6	270	4-17-67	Louisiana State	D9
Kupp, Craig	QB	6-4	215	4-14-67	Pacific Lutheran	D5
Kyles, Troy	WR	6-0	180	8-13-68	Howard	FA
Lang, Bruce	WR	6-0	184	1-25-66	Fairmont State	FA
Lindsey, Michael	LB	6-1	240	1-30-66	Southern	FA
Lock, Andy	T	6-3	275	9-16-67	Missouri	FA
Mark, Greg	DE	6-2	252	7- 7-67	Miami (Fla.)	D3
Millington, Sean	RB	6-2	225	2- 1-68	Simon Fraser	FA
Molander, Scooter	QB	6-2	200	10-26-66	Colorado State	*FA
Moore, Otis	NT	6-4	270	4-26-67	Clemson	D10
Ng, Philip	WR	6-0	185	7- 7-66	Lafayette	FA
Riddick, Michael	WR	6-3	195	1- 7-68	Delaware State	FA
Robinson, Chad	LB	6-3	230	6-18-67	Brigham Young	FA
Sanders, Terry	DE	6-6	330	8-18-67	Grambling State	FA
Seay, Clarence	WR	5-9	170	8-11-67	Texas-El Paso	FA
Smith, Billy	P	5-11	190	9-30-66	UT-Chattanooga	*FA
Stover, Matt	K	5-11	178	1-27-68	Louisiana Tech	D12
Thornton, Randy	LB	6-4	240	12-23-64	Houston	*UFA
Thorson, Chad	LB	6-2	243	7- 6-67	Wheaton	FA
Vines, Kenneth	C	6-4	285	5- 3-67	Central State	FA
Voorhees, Barry	G	6-5	290	12- 7-63	Cal State-Northridge	D8
Whitmore, David	S	6-0	235	7- 6-67	Stephen F. Austin	D4

*Hooten: FA New York Giants '89, injured reserve 8/14 through entire season; Molander: FA Cleveland '89, released 8/30, DEV Kansas City 9/7, released 10/17; Smith: FA New York Giants '89, released 9/5; Thornton: FA Denver '88, injured reserve (finger) 8/29 through entire season, injured reserve (knee) 8/28/89 through entire season, unprotected free agent 2/1/90.

NEW YORK JETS
(Eastern Division, American Conference)

Bruce Coslet

Chairman of the Board—Leon Hess
President—Steve Gutman
Vice President & General Manager—Dick Steinberg
Director of Pro Personnel—Jim Royer
Head Coach—Bruce Coslet (First Year)
Assistant Coaches:
    Offensive Line—Larry Beightol
    Running Backs—Kippy Brown
    Defensive Coordinator—Pete Carroll
    Def. Asst./Secondary—Ed Donatell
    Special Teams Coord.—Foge Fazio
    Linebackers—Monte Kiffin
    Receivers—Chip Myers
    Defensive Line—Greg Robinson
    Off. Asst./Tight Ends—Bob Wylie
Director of Public Relations—Frank Ramos
    (Office Phone: 538-6600—Area Code 516)
Offices—1000 Fulton Ave., Hempstead, N.Y. 11550
Stadium—Giants Stadium (Capacity: 76,891)
Team Colors—Kelly Green and White
Training Site—Hofstra University, Hempstead, N.Y.

1990 SCHEDULE
(All times local.
All games Sunday unless noted otherwise.)

Sept. 9	at Cincinnati	4:00
Sept. 16	CLEVELAND	1:00
Sept. 24	BUFFALO (Mon.)	9:00
Sept. 30	at New England	4:00
Oct. 7	at Miami	1:00
Oct. 14	SAN DIEGO	1:00
Oct. 21	at Buffalo	1:00
Oct. 28	at Houston	12:00
Nov. 4	DALLAS	1:00
Nov. 11	MIAMI	1:00
Nov. 18	at Indianapolis	4:00
Nov. 25	PITTSBURGH	4:00
Dec. 2	at San Diego	1:00
Dec. 9	OPEN DATE	
Dec. 16	INDIANAPOLIS	1:00
Dec. 23	NEW ENGLAND	1:00
Dec. 30	at Tampa Bay	4:00

1989 RESULTS—(Won 4, Lost 12)

Jets	Opp.		Att.
24 New England	27	(H)	64,541
24 Cleveland	38	(A)	73,516
40 Miami	33	(A)	65,908
10 Indianapolis	17	(H)	65,542
7 Los Angeles Raiders	14	(H)	68,040
14 New Orleans	29	(A)	59,521
3 Buffalo	34	(A)	76,811
10 San Francisco	23	(H)	62,805
27 New England	26	(A)	53,366
23 Miami	31	(H)	65,923
10 Indianapolis	27	(A)	58,236
27 Atlanta	7	(H)	40,429
20 San Diego	17	(A)	38,954
0 Pittsburgh	13	(H)	41,037
14 Los Angeles Rams	38	(A)	53,063
0 Buffalo	37	(H)	21,148

1989 GAMES STARTED

16 games: Kyle Clifton, Jeff Criswell, James Hasty, Bobby Humphery, Erik McMillan, Jim Sweeney.

15 games: Troy Benson, Alex Gordon, Jeff Lageman, Reggie McElroy, Scott Mersereau.

14 games: Dan Alexander, Paul Frase.

13 games: Mike Haight.

12 games: Keith Neubert, Ken O'Brien, George Radachowsky.

10 games: Marty Lyons, Al Toon, Roger Vick.

9 games: Johnny Hector, Ron Stallworth.

7 games: Freeman McNeil, Mickey Shuler.

6 games: JoJo Townsell.

4 games: Dave Cadigan, Michael Harper, Greg Werner.

3 games: Chris Burkett, Billy Griggs, Wesley Walker.

2 games: Tim Cofield, Tony Eason, Rich Miano.

1 game: John Booty, Chris Dressel, K.D. Dunn, Kyle Mackey, Kevin McArthur, Ken Rose, Pat Ryan, Curt Singer, Mike Withycombe.

NEW YORK JETS 1990 VETERAN ROSTER

No.	Name	Pos.	Ht.	Wt.	NFL Exp.	Birth-date	College	Games in '89	How Acquired
	Adams, Curtis	RB	6-1	185	4	4-30-62	Central Michigan	*0	FA, '90
	Antrum, Glenn	WR	5-11	175	1	2- 3-66	Connecticut	*1	UFA, '90
	Baxter, Brad	RB	6-1	231	1	5- 5-67	Alabama State	1	FA, '89
54	Benson, Troy	LB	6-2	235	5	7-30-63	Pittsburgh	16	D5a, '85
42	†Booty, John	CB/S	6-0	179	3	10- 9-65	Texas Christian	9	D10, '88
80	Boyer, Mark	TE	6-4	252	6	9-16-62	Southern California	*16	UFA, '90
29	Brown, A.B.	RB	5-9	212	2	12- 4-65	West Virginia	16	D8, '89
87	Burkett, Chris	WR	6-4	210	6	8-21-62	Jackson State	*15	FA, '89
90	Byrd, Dennis	DE	6-5	270	2	10- 5-66	Tulsa	16	D2, '89
31	Byrum, Carl	RB	6-0	237	4	6-29-62	Mississippi Valley State	*0	FA, '90
66	Cadigan, Dave	G/T	6-4	280	3	4- 6-65	Southern California	13	D1, '88
59	Clifton, Kyle	LB	6-4	236	7	8-23-62	Texas Christian	16	D3, '84
61	Criswell, Jeff	T	6-7	290	4	3- 7-64	Graceland (Ia.)	16	FA, '88
49	Curtis, Travis	S	5-10	180	4	9-27-65	West Virginia	*16	UFA, '90
84	†Dressel, Chris	TE	6-4	245	6	2- 7-61	Stanford	*15	W-KC, '89
11	Eason, Tony	QB	6-4	212	8	10- 8-59	Illinois	*5	W-NE, '89
45	Egu, Patrick	RB	5-11	205	2	2-20-67	Nevada-Reno	*7	UFA, '90
91	Frase, Paul	DE/DT	6-5	267	3	5- 5-65	Syracuse	16	D6, '88
55	Gordon, Alex	LB	6-5	246	4	9-14-64	Cincinnati	16	De, '87
79	†Haight, Mike	G	6-4	281	5	10- 6-62	Iowa	13	D1, '86
40	Hasty, James	CB	6-0	197	3	5-23-65	Washington State	16	D3a, '88
34	†Hector, Johnny	RB	5-11	202	8	11-26-60	Texas A&M	15	D2, '83
28	Howard, Carl	CB/S	6-2	190	7	9-20-61	Rutgers	15	FA, '85
81	Kelly, Pat	TE	6-6	252	3	10-29-65	Syracuse	*16	UFA, '90
57	Kohlbrand, Joe	LB	6-4	242	6	3-18-63	Miami (Fla.)	*16	UFA, '90
56	Lageman, Jeff	LB	6-5	250	2	7-18-67	Virginia	16	D1, '89
5	Leahy, Pat	K	6-0	196	17	3-19-51	St. Louis	16	FA, '74
93	Lyons, Marty	DE/DT	6-5	269	12	1-15-57	Alabama	10	D1, '79
64	Matich, Trevor	C/G/T	6-4	270	6	10- 9-61	Brigham Young	*11	UFA, '90
	Mayes, Michael	CB	5-10	182	1	8-17-66	Louisiana State	*2	FA, '90
68	McElroy, Reggie	T	6-6	276	8	3- 4-60	West Texas State	15	D2, '82
22	McMillan, Erik	S	6-2	197	3	5- 3-65	Missouri	16	D3, '88
	McNeil, Emanuel	DT	6-3	285	1	6- 9-67	Tennessee-Martin	*1	UFA, '90
24	McNeil, Freeman	RB	5-11	212	10	4-22-59	UCLA	11	D1, '81
94	Mersereau, Scott	DT/DE	6-3	280	4	4- 8-65	Southern Connecticut	16	FA, '87
36	Miano, Rich	S	6-0	200	5	9- 3-62	Hawaii	2	D6a, '85
72	Miller, Brett	T	6-7	300	9	10- 2-58	Iowa	*14	UFA, '90
51	Mott, Joe	LB	6-4	253	2	10- 6-65	Iowa	16	D3, '89
95	Naposki, Eric	LB	6-2	230	2	12-20-66	Connecticut	*2	FA, '90
86	Neubert, Keith	TE	6-6	248	2	9-13-64	Nebraska	16	D8, '88
77	†Nichols, Gerald	DT/DE	6-2	267	4	2-10-64	Florida State	16	D7, '87
7	O'Brien, Ken	QB	6-4	206	8	11-27-60	California-Davis	15	D1, '83
	Oliver, Jeff	OL	6-4	292	2	7-28-65	Boston College	1	FA, '89
	Parker, Anthony	CB	5-10	181	1	2-11-66	Arizona State	*1	FA, '90
17	Parker, Carl	WR	6-2	201	3	2- 5-65	Vanderbilt	*3	FA, '90
6	Prokop, Joe	P	6-2	224	5	7- 7-60	Cal Poly-Pomona	16	FA, '88
	Radachowsky, George	S	5-11	195	6	9- 7-62	Boston College	16	FA, '87
71	Rehder, Tom	T/G	6-7	280	3	1-27-65	Notre Dame	*16	UFA, '90
82	Shuler, Mickey	TE	6-3	231	13	8-21-56	Penn State	7	D3, '78
74	†Singer, Curt	T	6-5	279	4	11- 4-61	Tennessee	6	FA, '89
96	Stallworth, Ron	DE	6-5	262	2	2-25-66	Auburn	16	D4, '89
53	†Sweeney, Jim	C	6-4	270	7	8- 8-62	Pittsburgh	16	D2, '84
88	Toon, Al	WR	6-4	205	6	4-30-63	Wisconsin	11	D1, '85
83	Townsell, JoJo	WR/KR	5-9	180	6	11- 4-60	UCLA	16	D3, '83
43	Vick, Roger	RB	6-3	235	4	8-11-64	Texas A&M	16	D1, '87
21	Washington, Brian	S	6-1	220	2	9-10-65	Nebraska	*0	W-Cle, '89
97	Washington, Marvin	DT/DE	6-6	260	2	10-22-65	Idaho	16	D6, '89
76	Withycombe, Mike	T/G	6-5	300	3	11-18-64	Fresno State	5	D5, '88
63	Zawatson, Dave	G/T	6-5	275	2	4-13-66	California	*4	UFA, '90

*Adams last active with Chargers in '88; Antrum played 1 game with Patriots in '89; Boyer played 16 games with Colts in '89; Burkett played 2 games with Bills, 13 with Jets in '89; Byrum last active with Bills in '88; Curtis played 16 games with Vikings in '89; Dressel played 7 games with Chiefs, 8 with Jets in '89; Eason played 3 games with Patriots, 2 with Jets in '89; Egu played 7 games with Patriots in '89; Kelly played 16 games with Broncos in '89; Kohlbrand played 16 games with Saints in '89; Match played 11 games with Lions in '89; Mayes played 2 games with Saints in '89; E. McNeil played 1 game with Patriots in '89; Miller played 14 games with Chargers in '89; Naposki played 1 game with Patriots, 1 with Colts in '89; A. Parker played 1 game with Colts in '89; C. Parker played 3 games with Bengals in '89; Rehder played 16 games with Patriots in '89; B. Washington last active with Browns in '88; Zawatson played 4 games with Bears in '89.

†Unsigned; subject to developments.

Players lost through Plan B free agency: LB Adam Bob (5 games in '89; to Clev.); CB Kerry Glenn (14; to Mia.); TE Billy Griggs (5; to Pitt.); CB/S Leander Knight (13; to Hou.); LB Kevin McArthur (9; to Wash.); CB/S Stevon Moore (0; to Mia.); LB Ken Rose (15; to Clev.); C/G Adam Schreiber (16; to G.B.); TE Greg Werner (10; to Phil.).

Retired—Wesley Walker, 13-year wide receiver, 6 games in '89.

Also played with Jets in '89—G Dan Alexander (14 games); WR Sanjay Beach (1); LB Tim Cofield (6); WR/KR Titus Dixon (3); TE K.D. Dunn (1); WR/KR Phillip Epps (10); RB Nuu Faaola (2); WR/KR Michael Harper (6); CB Bobby Humphery (16); QB Kyle Mackey (4); QB Mark Malone (1); CB Michael Mitchell (5); QB Pat Ryan (7).

D—Draft; W—Waivers; FA—Free Agent; UFA—Unrestricted Free Agent.

NEW YORK JETS
1990 DRAFT CHOICES

(Number following name designates order of selection among 331 players drafted.)

Round and Player		Position	College
1. THOMAS, Blair	2	RB	Penn State
2. REMBERT, Reggie	28	WR	West Virginia
3. STARGELL, Tony	56	DB	Tennessee State
4. TAYLOR, Troy	84	QB	California
5. SAVAGE, Tony	112	DT	Washington State
5. McWRIGHT, Robert from Los Angeles Rams (a)	134	DB	Texas Christian
6. MATHIS, Terance	140	WR	New Mexico
7. WHITE, Dwayne from Atlanta (b)	167	G	Alcorn State
7. PROCTOR, Basil	168	LB	West Virginia
8. DUFFY, Roger	196	C	Penn State
9. DAWKINS, Dale	223	WR	Miami (Fla.)
10. QUAST, Brad	251	LB	Iowa
11. KELSON, Derrick	279	DB	Purdue
12. DAVIS, Darrell	306	LB	Texas Christian

(a) Acquired pick for cornerback Bobby Humphery, April 22, 1990.
(b) Acquired pick for center Guy Bingham, September 4, 1989.

NEW YORK JETS
1990 ROOKIE AND FIRST-YEAR ROSTER

Name	Pos.	Hgt.	Wgt.	Birth-date	College	How Acquired
Allen, Donnie	WR	6-0	155	5-10-67	Georgia Southern	FA
Bell, Grantis	WR-KR	5-9	150	8-11-66	West Virginia	*FA
Boone, Randell	S	6-3	196	2-14-68	Georgia Southern	FA
Burman, Jon	T	6-8	300	6- 7-66	Illinois	*FA
Davis, Darrell	LB	6-2	255	3-10-66	Texas Christian	D12
Dawkins, Dale	WR	6-1	190	10-30-66	Miami (Fla.)	D9
Douglas, Demetrious	LB	6-2	221	6- 8-67	Georgia	FA
Duffy, Roger	C	6-3	285	7-16-67	Penn State	D8
Ebubedike, Victor	RB	6-0	214	1- 2-66	Vauxhall, England	FA
Greene, Kevin	K	..	..	....	Syracuse	FA
Hall, Michael	CB	6-1	193	1-14-65	New Mexico State	FA
Kelson, Derrick	CB	6-0	190	5-14-68	Purdue	D11
Mathis, Terance	WR-KR	5-10	170	6- 7-67	New Mexico	D6
McWright, Robert	CB	5-9	185	11-10-65	Texas Christian	D5a
Moore, James	WR	5-11	170	5-31-66	Hofstra	FA
Proctor, Basil	LB	6-4	230	10- 6-66	West Virginia	D7a
Quast, Brad	LB	6-1	245	6- 5-68	Iowa	D10
Rembert, Reggie	WR	6-4	200	12-25-66	West Virginia	D2
Rudison, Phil	P	..	..	....	Akron	FA
Savage, Tony	NT	6-3	295	7- 7-67	Washington State	D5
Smith, Irvin	CB-S	5-10	181	3-12-67	Maryland	*FA
Snyder, Brent	QB	6-3	230	6- 4-66	Utah State	*FA
Stargell, Tony	CB	5-11	190	8- 7-66	Tennessee State	D3
Taylor, Troy	QB	6-4	205	4- 5-68	California	D4
Thomas, Blair	RB	5-10	195	10- 7-67	Penn State	D1
Vinson, Phil	WR	6-3	190	1-28-67	New Mexico State	FA
Weaver, Neil	K	5-7	170	9-27-68	Panhandle State	FA
White, Dwayne	G	6-2	315	2-10-67	Alcorn State	D7
Williams, Patrick	S	6-2	196	12-17-66	Arkansas	FA
Wulff, Paul	G	..	..	....	Washington State	FA

*Bell: FA Washington '89, released 8/30, DEV Washington 9/6, released 12/29; Burman: FA San Francisco '89, released 8/28, DEV Miami 10/3, released 10/13, DEV New York Jets 11/1, released 1/29/90; Smith: FA New York Jets '89, reserve/left squad 8/28 through entire season, reinstated 3/20/90; Snyder: D7 Chicago '89, released 9/5, DEV Chicago 9/6, released 1/4/90.

PHILADELPHIA EAGLES
(Eastern Division, National Conference)

Buddy Ryan

Owner—Norman Braman

President—Harry T. Gamble

Head Coach—Buddy Ryan (4 years: 33-29-1)

Director of Player Personnel—Joe Woolley

Assistant Coaches:
Offensive Backfield—Dave Atkins
Defensive Backs—Tom Bettis
Receivers—Lew Carpenter
Def. Coordinator/Linebackers—Jeff Fisher
Defensive Line—Dale Haupt
Strength & Conditioning—Ronnie Jones
Off. Coord./Quarterbacks—Rich Kotite
Offensive Line—Dan Neal
Special Teams—Al Roberts
Offensive Line—Bill Walsh

Director of Public Relations—Ron Howard
(Office Phone: 463-2500—Area Code 215)

Offices—Veterans Stadium, Philadelphia, Pa. 19148

Stadium—Veterans Stadium (Capacity: 65,356)

Team Colors—Kelly Green, White and Silver

Training Site—West Chester University, West Chester, Pa.

1990 SCHEDULE
**(All times local.
All games Sunday unless noted otherwise.)**

Sept. 9	at New York Giants	8:00
Sept. 16	PHOENIX	1:00
Sept. 23	at Los Angeles Rams	1:00
Sept. 30	INDIANAPOLIS	1:00
Oct. 7	OPEN DATE	
Oct. 15	MINNESOTA (Mon.)	9:00
Oct. 21	at Washington	1:00
Oct. 28	at Dallas	12:00
Nov. 4	NEW ENGLAND	1:00
Nov. 12	WASHINGTON (Mon.)	9:00
Nov. 18	at Atlanta	1:00
Nov. 25	NEW YORK GIANTS	1:00
Dec. 2	at Buffalo	1:00
Dec. 9	at Miami	8:00
Dec. 16	GREEN BAY	4:00
Dec. 23	DALLAS	1:00
Dec. 29	at Phoenix (Sat.)	2:00

1989 RESULTS—(Won 11, Lost 6)

Eagles		Opp.		Att.
31	Seattle	7	(H)	64,287
42	Washington	37	(A)	53,493
28	San Francisco	38	(H)	66,042
13	Chicago	27	(A)	66,625
21	New York Giants	19	(H)	65,688
17	Phoenix	5	(A)	42,620
10	Los Angeles Raiders	7	(H)	64,019
28	Denver	24	(A)	75,065
17	San Diego	20	(A)	47,019
3	Washington	10	(H)	65,443
10	Minnesota	9	(H)	65,944
27	Dallas	0	(A)	54,444
24	New York Giants	17	(A)	74,809
20	Dallas	10	(H)	59,842
20	New Orleans	30	(A)	68,561
31	Phoenix	14	(H)	43,287

NFC WILD-CARD GAME

7	Los Angeles Rams	21	(H)	57,869

1989 GAMES STARTED

16 games: David Alexander, Jerome Brown, Randall Cunningham, Byron Evans, Al Harris, Ron Heller, Mike Pitts, Mike Schad, Clyde Simmons, Reggie White.

15 games: Eric Allen, Keith Byars, Cris Carter, Wes Hopkins.

14 games: Seth Joyner, Anthony Toney.

13 games: Izel Jenkins, Andre Waters.

12 games: Matt Darwin, Keith Jackson, Ron Solt.

9 games: Ron Johnson.

5 games: Jimmie Giles, Mike Quick.

4 games: Todd Bell, Mike Reichenbach, Ben Tamburello.

3 games: Ken Reeves.

1 game: Carlos Carson, Robert Drummond, Eric Everett, Mark Higgs, David Little, Dave Rimington, Heath Sherman, Jessie Small.

PHILADELPHIA EAGLES 1990 VETERAN ROSTER

No.	Name	Pos.	Ht.	Wt.	NFL Exp.	Birth-date	College	Games in '89	How Acquired
72	†Alexander, David	C/T	6-3	282	4	7-28-64	Tulsa	16	D5, '87
21	Allen, Eric	CB	5-10	188	3	11-22-65	Arizona State	15	D2, '88
49	Bell, Todd	S	6-1	215	9	11-28-58	Ohio State	4	FA, '88
99	Brown, Jerome	DT	6-2	295	4	2- 4-65	Miami (Fla.)	16	D1, '87
41	†Byars, Keith	RB	6-1	238	5	10-14-63	Ohio State	16	D1, '86
80	Carter, Cris	WR	6-3	198	4	11-25-65	Ohio State	16	SupD, '87
6	Cavanaugh, Matt	QB	6-2	210	13	10-27-56	Pittsburgh	9	T-SF, '86
12	Cunningham, Randall	QB	6-4	203	6	3-27-63	Nevada-Las Vegas	16	D2, '85
78	Darwin, Matt	T	6-4	275	5	3-11-63	Texas A&M	15	D4, '86
	Dial, Alan	S	6-1	188	1	2- 2-65	UCLA	1	FA, '90
36	Drummond, Robert	RB	6-1	205	2	6-21-67	Syracuse	16	D3, '89
84	Edwards, Anthony	WR/KR	5-11	195	2	5-26-66	New Mexico Highlands	9	FA, '89
56	†Evans, Byron	LB	6-2	235	4	2-23-64	Arizona	16	D4, '87
	Feagles, Jeff	P	6-0	198	3	3- 7-66	Miami (Fla.)	*16	W-NE, '90
33	Frizzell, William	CB/S	6-3	206	7	9- 8-62	North Carolina Central	16	FA, '89
	Gabbard, Steve	T	6-4	275	1	7-19-66	Florida State	*0	FA, '89
86	†Garrity, Gregg	WR	5-10	175	8	11-24-60	Penn State	9	W-Pit, '84
90	Golic, Mike	DT	6-5	275	5	12-12-62	Notre Dame	16	FA, '87
54	Hager, Britt	LB	6-1	222	2	2-20-66	Texas	16	D3a, '89
95	Harris, Al	LB	6-5	265	11	12-31-56	Arizona State	16	UFA, '89
73	†Heller, Ron	T	6-6	280	7	8-25-62	Penn State	16	T-Sea, '88
34	†Hoage, Terry	S	6-3	201	7	4-11-62	Georgia	6	FA, '86
48	†Hopkins, Wes	S	6-1	215	7	9-26-61	Southern Methodist	16	D2, '83
88	Jackson, Keith	TE	6-2	250	3	4-19-65	Oklahoma	14	D1, '88
46	†Jenkins, Izel	CB	5-10	191	3	5-27-64	North Carolina State	16	D11, '88
85	Johnson, Ron	WR	6-3	190	6	9-21-58	Long Beach State	14	FA, '88
31	Jones, Tyrone	S	6-4	223	2	11- 9-66	Arkansas State	3	OFA, '89
59	Joyner, Seth	LB	6-2	248	5	11-18-64	Texas-El Paso	14	D8, '86
94	†Kaufusi, Steve	DE/DT	6-4	274	2	10-17-63	Brigham Young	16	D12, '88
87	Le Bel, Harper	TE	6-4	251	2	7-14-63	Colorado State	*16	UFA, '90
37	Lilly, Sammy	CB	5-9	178	2	2-12-65	Georgia Tech	15	UFA, '89
	†McPherson, Don	QB	6-1	193	1	10- 4-60	Syracuse	*0	D6, '88
74	Pitts, Mike	DT	6-5	277	8	9-25-60	Alabama	16	T-Atl, '87
82	Quick, Mike	WR	6-2	195	9	5-14-59	North Carolina State	6	D1, '82
66	Reeves, Ken	T/G	6-5	270	6	10- 4-61	Texas A&M	14	D6, '85
50	†Rimington, Dave	C/G	6-3	285	8	5-22-60	Nebraska	6	FA, '88
7	†Ruzek, Roger	K	6-1	195	4	12-17-60	Weber State	*14	FA, '89
79	Schad, Mike	G	6-5	290	3	10- 2-63	Queens College (Can.)	16	UFA, '89
51	Shaw, Ricky	LB	6-4	240	3	7-28-65	Oklahoma State	*15	FA, '89
23	Sherman, Heath	RB/KR	6-0	190	2	3-27-67	Texas A&I	15	D6, '89
96	Simmons, Clyde	DE	6-6	275	5	8- 4-64	Western Carolina	16	D9, '86
68	Singletary, Reggie	G/T	6-3	285	4	1-17-64	North Carolina State	1	D12, '86
52	Small, Jessie	LB	6-3	239	2	11-30-66	Eastern Kentucky	16	D2, '89
	Smith, Daryle	T	6-5	278	4	1-18-64	Tennessee	*4	FA, '90
65	Solt, Ron	G	6-3	288	6	5-19-62	Maryland	13	T-Ind, '88
61	†Tamburello, Ben	G/C	6-3	278	3	9- 9-64	Auburn	16	D3, '87
10	†Teltschik, John	P	6-2	210	5	3- 8-64	Texas	10	FA, '86
25	†Toney, Anthony	RB	6-0	227	5	9-23-62	Texas A&M	14	D2, '86
20	Waters, Andre	S	5-11	199	7	3-10-62	Cheyney State	16	OFA, '84
47	Werner, Greg	TE	6-4	236	2	10-21-66	DePauw	*10	UFA, '90
92	White, Reggie	DE	6-5	285	6	12-19-61	Tennessee	16	SupD, '84

*Feagles played 16 games with Patriots in '89; Gabbard active for 1 game with Eagles in '89, but did not play; Le Bel played 16 games with Seahawks in '89; McPherson active for 1 game with Eagles in '89, but did not play; Ruzek played 9 games with Cowboys, 5 with Eagles in '89; Shaw played 7 games with Giants, 8 with Eagles in '89; Smith played 4 games with Browns in '89; Werner played 10 games with Jets in '89.

†Unsigned; subject to developments.

Players lost through Plan B free agency: LB Ty Allert (7 games in '89; to Den.); CB Eric Everett (16; to T.B.); RB Mark Higgs (15; to Mia.); TE David Little (16; to Den.); LB Mike Reichenbach (16; to Mia.); P Rick Tuten (2; to Buff.).

Also played with Eagles in '89—WR Carlos Carson (6 games); K Steve DeLine (3); TE Jimmie Giles (16); LB Dwayne Jiles (1); P Max Runager (4); WR Henry Williams (13); K Luis Zendejas (8).

D—Draft; T—Trade; W—Waivers; FA—Free Agent; OFA—Original Free Agent; UFA—Unrestricted Free Agent; SupD—Supplemental Draft.

PHILADELPHIA EAGLES
1990 DRAFT CHOICES

(Number following name designates order of selection among 331 players drafted.)

Round and Player		Position	College
1. SMITH, Ben	22	DB	Georgia
2. BELLAMY, Mike	50	WR	Illinois
3. BARNETT, Fred	77	WR	Arkansas State
4. Choice to Indianapolis (a)			
5. WILLIAMS, Calvin	133	WR	Purdue
6. THOMPSON, Kevin	162	DB	Oklahoma
7. STROUF, Terry	189	T	Wisconsin-LaCrosse
8. DYKES, Curt	217	T	Oregon
9. GRAY, Cecil	244	DT	North Carolina
10. ADAMS, Orlando	273	DT	Jacksonville State
11. HUDSON, John from New Orleans (b)	294	C	Auburn
11. WATSON, Tyrone	300	WR	Tennessee State
12. GARRETT, Judd	327	RB	Princeton

(a) Traded pick and 1st-round pick in 1989 for guard Ron Solt, October 4, 1988.
(b) Acquired pick for fullback Bobby Morse, April 24, 1989.

PHILADELPHIA EAGLES
1990 ROOKIE AND FIRST-YEAR ROSTER

Name	Pos.	Hgt.	Wgt.	Birth-date	College	How Acquired
Adams, Orlando	DT	6-0	303	8- 6-67	Jacksonville State	D10
Bailey, David	DE	6-4	240	9- 3-65	Oklahoma State	*FA
Baldwin, Damon	OL	6-5	275	4-16-67	San Diego State	FA
Barnett, Fred	WR	6-0	203	6-17-66	Arkansas State	D3
Beaune, Tony	DT	6-3	260	5-24-67	Wayne State	FA
Bellamy, Mike	WR	6-0	195	6-28-66	Illinois	D2
Brown, Ben	QB	6-3	220	5-26-68	Tennessee State	FA
Dawson, Carl	DE	6-5	271	7-28-67	Alabama A&M	FA
Dawson, Kenneth	RB	5-9	175	.....	Wyoming	FA
Dykes, Curt	T	6-3	274	12-27-67	Oregon	D8
Farris, Ervin	RB	5-10	223	6-28-66	Texas Tech	*W-Dal.
Form, Norman	FB	5-9	190	11- 5-68	New Hampshire	FA
Frantz, Matt	K	5-8	170	5-17-65	Ohio State	FA
Garrett, Judd	RB	6-1	205	6-25-67	Princeton	D12
Gray, Cecil	DT	6-4	264	2-16-68	North Carolina	D9
Grisby, Kevin	DB	6-3	200	5-24-68	Bethune-Cookman	FA
Harrison, Demetrius	LB	6-2	210	4-11-68	North Carolina A&T	FA
Hudson, John	C	6-2	265	1-29-68	Auburn	D11
Johnson, Maurice	TE	6-2	242	1- 9-67	Temple	FA
Kinne, Gary	LB	6-0	230	6-12-67	Baylor	FA
McDonald, John	DE	6-4	240	11-16-66	Duke	FA
Mitchell, Bennie	WR	..	..	.....	....	FA
Moronta, Horacio	DE	..	..	.....	Wagner	FA
Nash, DeWayne	DB	..	..	.....	Savannah State	FA
Porter, Mark	K	6-0	190	12- 3-65	Kansas State	*FA
Renna, Michael	DE	6-4	270	7-26-67	Delaware	FA
Salmon, David	P	6-4	220	5-16-65	North Carolina State	*FA
Sherman, Paul	OL	6-5	315	9- 5-67	East Tennessee State	FA
Smith, Ben	FS	5-11	183	5-14-67	Georgia	D1
Smith, Otis	CB	5-11	185	10-22-65	Missouri	FA
Strouf, Terry	T	6-2	285	10- 1-66	Wisconsin-La Crosse	D7
Thompson, Kevin	S	6-0	190	4-17-66	Oklahoma	D6
Vaughn, Willie	WR	5-11	205	6- 7-67	Kansas	FA
Wainwright, Eric	LB	5-11	231	11- 6-66	Delaware State	FA
Walker, Adam	RB	6-3	200	6- 7-68	Pittsburgh	FA
Walsh, Dan	RB	6-0	220	2-14-66	Montclair State	FA
Watson, Mickey	LB	6-3	240	4-23-68	Villanova	FA
Watson, Tyrone	WR	6-4	210	2-10-67	Tennessee State	D11a
Williams, Calvin	WR	5-11	181	3- 3-67	Purdue	D5
Williams, Dante	DE	6-2	265	9-11-66	Oklahoma	FA

*Bailey: FA Philadelphia '89, released 9/5, DEV Philadelphia 9/6, released 1/9/90; Farris: FA Dallas '89, released 7/13, FA Dallas '90, released 5/10, awarded on waivers to Philadelphia 5/22; Porter: FA Kansas City '89, released 9/1; Salmon: FA Minnesota '88, released 8/18.

PHOENIX CARDINALS
(Eastern Division, National Conference)

Joe Bugel

President—William V. Bidwill
General Manager—Larry Wilson
Exec. Vice President—Joe Rhein
Vice President of Administration—Curt Mosher
Vice President of Communications—Terry Bledsoe
Director of Player Personnel—George Boone
Director of Pro Personnel—Erik Widmark
Head Coach—Joe Bugel (First Year)
Assistant Coaches:
    Defensive Line—Ted Cottrell
    Running Backs—Bobby Hammond
    Defensive Backs—Jim Johnson
    Offensive Line—Tom Lovat
    Def. Asst./Quality Control—Mike Murphy
    Defensive Coordinator—Joe Pascale
    Receivers—Ted Plumb
    Offensive Coordinator—Jerry Rhome
    Special Teams—Pete Rodriguez
    Strength & Conditioning—Bob Rogucki
Director of Public Relations—Paul Jensen
    (Office Phone: 967-1010—Area Code 602)
Offices—8701 Hardy Drive, Tempe, Ariz. 85281
Stadium—Sun Devil Stadium (Capacity: 74,724)
Team Colors—Cardinal Red, Black and White
Training Site—Northern Arizona University, Flagstaff, Ariz.

1990 SCHEDULE
(All times local.
All games Sunday unless noted otherwise.)

Sept. 9	at Washington	1:00
Sept. 16	at Philadelphia	1:00
Sept. 23	at New Orleans	12:00
Sept. 30	WASHINGTON	5:00
Oct. 7	OPEN DATE	
Oct. 14	DALLAS	1:00
Oct. 21	at New York Giants	4:00
Oct. 28	CHICAGO	2:00
Nov. 4	at Miami	1:00
Nov. 11	at Buffalo	1:00
Nov. 18	GREEN BAY	2:00
Nov. 25	NEW ENGLAND	2:00
Dec. 2	INDIANAPOLIS	2:00
Dec. 9	at Atlanta	1:00
Dec. 16	at Dallas	12:00
Dec. 23	NEW YORK GIANTS	2:00
Dec. 29	PHILADELPHIA (Sat.)	2:00

1989 RESULTS—(Won 5, Lost 11)

Cardinals		Opp.		Att.
16	Detroit	13	(A)	36,735
34	Seattle	24	(A)	60,444
7	New York Giants	35	(A)	75,742
13	San Diego	24	(H)	44,201
28	Washington	30	(A)	53,335
5	Philadelphia	17	(H)	42,620
34	Atlanta	20	(H)	33,894
19	Dallas	10	(A)	44,431
13	New York Giants	20	(H)	46,588
24	Dallas	20	(H)	49,657
14	Los Angeles Rams	37	(A)	53,176
13	Tampa Bay	14	(H)	33,297
10	Washington	29	(H)	38,870
14	Los Angeles Raiders	16	(H)	41,785
0	Denver	37	(H)	56,071
14	Philadelphia	31	(A)	43,287

1989 GAMES STARTED

16 games: Ken Harvey, Cedric Mack, Tim McDonald, Lance Smith.

15 games: Robert Awalt, Anthony Bell, Carl Carter, Earl Ferrell, Rod Saddler, Joe Wolf.

14 games: Eric Hill, Derek Kennard, Luis Sharpe.

13 games: Gary Hogeboom.

12 games: Roy Green, Freddie Joe Nunn.

11 games: David Galloway, Jim Wahler.

9 games: Ernie Jones, Tootie Robbins, Lonnie Young.

8 games: Tony Jordan, J.T. Smith.

7 games: Mike Zordich.

6 games: Karl Wilson, Mike Zandofsky.

4 games: Bob Clasby, Gary Hadd, Todd Peat.

3 games: Stump Mitchell, Walter Reeves.

2 games: Tony Baker, Kani Kauahi, Vai Sikahema, Jay Taylor, Tom Tupa.

1 game: Don Holmes, Ilia Jarostchuk, Shawn Knight, Roland Mitchell, Jay Novacek, Timm Rosenbach, Ron Wolfley.

PHOENIX CARDINALS 1990 VETERAN ROSTER

No.	Name	Pos.	Ht.	Wt.	NFL Exp.	Birth-date	College	Games in '89	How Acquired
80	†Awalt, Robert	TE	6-5	244	4	4- 9-64	San Diego State	16	D3, '87
44	†Baker, Tony	RB	5-10	190	4	6-11-64	East Carolina	10	FA, '89
55	†Bell, Anthony	LB	6-3	235	5	7- 2-64	Michigan State	16	D1, '86
	Blair, Stanley	CB	6-0	190	R	7- 4-64	Southeastern Okla. St.	*18	FA, '90
71	Bostic, Joe	G	6-3	276	11	4-20-57	Clemson	*0	D3, '79
16	†Camarillo, Rich	P	5-11	185	10	11-29-59	Washington	15	FA, '89
45	Carr, Lydell	RB	6-1	228	2	5-27-65	Oklahoma	5	UFA, '89
41	Carter, Carl	CB	5-11	189	5	3- 7-64	Texas Tech	15	D4, '86
79	†Clasby, Bob	DT	6-5	276	5	9-28-60	Notre Dame	4	FA, '86
17	Del Greco, Al	K	5-10	198	7	3- 2-62	Auburn	16	FA, '87
21	Eaton, Tracey	S	6-1	190	2	7-19-65	Portland State	*16	UFA, '90
	Flutie, Darren	WR	5-10	184	2	11-18-66	Boston College	*0	FA, '90
65	Galloway, David	DE	6-3	259	9	2-16-59	Florida	12	D2, '82
81	†Green, Roy	WR	6-0	194	12	6-30-57	Henderson State	12	D4, '79
73	Hadd, Gary	DT	6-4	278	3	10-19-65	Minnesota	10	UFA, '89
56	Harvey, Ken	LB	6-2	230	3	5- 6-65	California	16	D1, '88
5	Hogeboom, Gary	QB	6-4	207	11	8-21-58	Central Michigan	14	UFA, '89
83	Holmes, Don	WR	5-10	177	5	4- 1-61	Mesa (Colo.)	15	W-Ind, '86
53	Jax, Garth	LB	6-2	229	5	9-16-63	Florida State	16	UFA, '89
86	Jones, Ernie	WR	5-11	191	3	12-15-64	Indiana	15	D7, '88
32	†Jordan, Tony	RB	6-2	220	3	5- 5-65	Kansas State	13	D5a, '88
57	†Kauahi, Kani	C	6-2	270	8	9- 6-59	Hawaii	16	UFA, '89
70	†Kennard, Derek	C/G	6-3	309	5	9- 9-62	Nevada-Reno	14	SupD, '84
52	Kirk, Randy	LB	6-2	231	4	12-27-64	San Diego State	6	UFA, '89
51	Lewis, Bill	C	6-7	275	5	7-12-63	Nebraska	*0	UFA, '90
29	Lynch, Lorenzo	CB	5-9	199	3	4- 6-63	Cal State-Sacramento	*16	UFA, '90
47	†Mack, Cedric	CB	6-0	185	8	9-14-60	Baylor	16	D2, '83
	Maxwell, Vernon	LB	6-2	225	7	10-25-61	Arizona State	*9	FA, '90
46	†McDonald, Tim	CB/S	6-2	209	4	1- 6-65	Southern California	16	D2, '87
54	McKenzie, Reggie	LB	6-1	242	5	2- 8-63	Tennessee	*0	UFA, '89
30	†Mitchell, Stump	RB	5-9	194	10	3-15-59	The Citadel	3	D9, '81
78	†Nunn, Freddie Joe	DE	6-4	250	6	4- 9-62	Mississippi	12	D1, '85
89	Reeves, Walter	TE	6-3	249	2	12-15-65	Auburn	16	D2, '89
63	Robbins, Tootie	T	6-5	307	9	6- 2-58	East Carolina	9	D4, '82
3	Rosenbach, Timm	QB	6-2	210	2	10-27-66	Washington State	2	SupD, '89
72	†Saddler, Rod	DE	6-5	280	4	9-26-65	Texas A&M	15	D4, '87
67	Sharpe, Luis	T	6-4	260	9	6-16-60	UCLA	14	D1, '82
36	†Sikahema, Vai	RB/KR	5-9	184	5	8-29-62	Brigham Young	16	D10, '86
84	Smith, J.T.	WR	6-2	187	13	10-29-55	North Texas	9	FA, '85
61	Smith, Lance	T/G	6-2	278	6	11- 1-63	Louisiana State	16	D3, '85
27	Taylor, Jay	CB	5-9	170	2	11- 8-67	San Jose State	16	D6, '89
19	Tupa, Tom	QB/P	6-4	220	3	9- 6-66	Ohio State	14	D3, '88
23	Turner, Marcus	CB/S	6-0	191	2	1-13-66	UCLA	13	W-Den, '89
66	Wahler, Jim	DT	6-3	268	2	7-29-66	UCLA	13	D4, '89
60	Walker, Jeff	T	6-4	295	4	1-22-63	Memphis State	*13	UFA, '90
68	Wolf, Joe	T/G	6-5	279	2	12-28-66	Boston College	16	D1a, '89
24	†Wolfley, Ron	RB	6-0	222	6	10-14-62	West Virginia	16	D4, '85
43	Young, Lonnie	CB/S	6-1	191	6	7-18-63	Michigan State	10	D12, '85
38	Zordich, Mike	CB/S	5-11	197	4	10-12-63	Penn State	16	UFA, '89

*Blair played 8 games with Edmonton-CFL in '89; Bostic and McKenzie missed '89 season due to injury; Eaton played 16 games with Oilers in '89; Flutie last active with Chargers in '88; Lewis active for 8 games with Raiders in '89, but did not play; Lynch played 16 games with Bears in '89; Maxwell played 9 games with Seahawks in '89; Walker played 13 games with Saints in '89.

†Unsigned; subject to developments.

Players lost through Plan B free agency: WR Mike Barber (0 games in '89; to Cin.); LB Ron Burton (10; to L.A. Raid.); T Scott Dill (16; to T.B.); LB Ilia Jarostchuk (16; to N.E.); DT Shawn Knight (7; to Minn.); TE Jay Novacek (16; to Dall.); WR Andy Schillinger (0; to Minn.); DE Karl Wilson (15; to Mia.).

Also played with Cardinals in '89—CB Michael Adams (3 games); DE Bob Buczkowski (4); RB Jessie Clark (11); RB Earl Ferrell (15); DE Freddie Gilbert (2); CB Kevin Guidry (3); WR Phil McConkey (6); CB Roland Mitchell (3); G Todd Peat (4); T Mark Traynowicz (2); WR Daryl Usher (7).

D—Draft; W—Waivers; FA—Free Agent; UFA—Unrestricted Free Agent; SupD—Supplemental Draft.

PHOENIX CARDINALS
1990 DRAFT CHOICES

(Number following name designates order of selection among 331 players drafted.)

Round and Player		Position	College
1. Choice exercised in 1989 Supplemental Draft for Timm Rosenbach, QB, Washington State			
2. THOMPSON, Anthony	31	RB	Indiana
3. PROEHL, Ricky	58	WR	Wake Forest
4. DAVIS, Travis	85	DT	Michigan State
5. CENTERS, Larry	115	RB	Stephen F. Austin
6. SHAVERS, Tyrone	142	WR	Lamar
7. JOHNSON, Johnny	169	RB	San Jose State
8. WASHINGTON, Mickey	199	DB	Texas A & M
9. BAVARO, David	225	LB	Syracuse
10. ELLE, Dave	252	TE	South Dakota
11. NORMAN, Dempsey	282	WR	St. Francis (Ill.)
12. RILEY, Donnie	308	RB	Central Michigan
12. McMICHEL, Ken from Denver (a)	330	DB	Oklahoma

(a) Acquired pick for kicker David Treadwell, May 30, 1989.

PHOENIX CARDINALS
1990 ROOKIE AND FIRST-YEAR ROSTER

Name	Pos.	Hgt.	Wgt.	Birth-date	College	How Acquired
Applewhite, Mike	DE-DT	6-2	256	4- 7-66	East Carolina	FA
Bavaro, David	LB	6-0	231	3-27-67	Syracuse	D9
Brandom, John	G	6-2	273	8- 4-66	Arizona	FA
Burch, John	RB	5-10	200	4- 4-66	Tennessee-Martin	*FA
Centers, Larry	RB	5-10	203	6- 1-68	Stephen F. Austin	D5
Davis, Bob	LB	6-0	236	1-25-69	Brigham Young	FA
Davis, Travis	DT	6-1	274	5-10-66	Michigan State	D4
Elle, David	TE	6-4	241	10-14-66	South Dakota	D10
Field, Amod	WR	5-11	181	10-11-67	Montclair State	FA
Hess, Bill	WR	5-9	172	2- 6-66	Utah	*FA
Jackson, James	DE-DT	6-1	280	10-30-65	Northern Arizona	FA
Jackson, John	WR	5-10	170	1- 2-67	Southern California	FA
Johnson, Johnny	RB	6-2	212	6-11-68	San Jose State	D7
Johnson, Mike	QB	6-1	185	5- 2-67	Akron	FA
Jones, DeWaine	FB	5-10	200	12-14-67	Wyoming	FA
Jorden, Tim	TE	6-3	233	10-30-66	Indiana	*FA
Lawrence, Oliver	LB	6-1	243	11- 9-67	Louisiana State	FA
Lyle, Win	K	5-9	170	3-13-68	Auburn	FA
Mathis, Jeff	DT-DE	6-1	279	5-18-67	Georgia Tech	FA
McMichel, Ken	LB	6-0	208	6- 4-67	Oklahoma	D12a
Nicholl, Kevin	K	5-10	184	8- 1-68	Central Michigan	FA
Norman, Dempsey	WR	5-7	175	2- 7-66	St. Francis	D11
Osborne, Eldonta	LB	6-0	215	8-12-67	Louisiana Tech	FA
Pfeifer, Mike	T	6-6	318	8- 9-66	Kentucky	FA
Proehl, Ricky	WR	5-10	181	3- 7-68	Wake Forest	D3
Prouty, Lance	T-G	6-5	292	11-23-66	South Dakota State	FA
Riley, Donnie	CB	5-9	205	10- 2-66	Central Michigan	D12
Shavers, Tyrone	WR	6-2	205	7-14-67	Lamar	D6
Smith, Dennis	TE	6-0	224	2-14-67	Utah	FA
Smith, Vernice	G-T	6-2	280	10-24-65	Florida A&M	*FA
Thompson, Anthony	RB	5-11	207	4- 8-67	Indiana	D2
Washington, Mickey	CB	5-9	187	7- 8-68	Texas A&M	D8
Waters, Preston	CB	5-9	185	8- 8-68	West Virginia	FA

*Burch: D8 Phoenix '89, released 9/5, DEV Phoenix 9/6, released 1/3/90; Hess: FA Philadelphia '89, released 8/30, DEV Philadelphia 12/26, released 12/27; Jorden: FA Phoenix '89, released 9/5, DEV Phoenix 9/6, released 1/3/90; V. Smith: FA Miami '87, released 9/7, FA Dallas '88, released 8/30, FA Cleveland '89, released 8/30, DEV Phoenix 9/14, released 11/1, DEV Phoenix 11/8, released 1/3/90.

PITTSBURGH STEELERS
(Central Division, American Conference)

Chuck Noll

President—Daniel M. Rooney
Vice-President—John R. McGinley
Vice-President—Arthur J. Rooney, Jr.
Director of Player Personnel—Dick Haley
Director of Pro Personnel—Tom Donahoe
Head Coach—Chuck Noll (21 years: 177-132-1)
Assistant Coaches:
  Offensive Line—Ron Blackledge
  Defensive Coordinator—Dave Brazil
  Defensive Backs—John Fox
  Defensive Line—Joe Greene
  Offensive Backfield—Dick Hoak
  Tight Ends & Conditioning—Jon Kolb
  Receivers—Dwain Painter
  Special Teams—George Stewart
  Linebackers—Bob Valesente
  Offensive Coordinator—Joe Walton
Public Relations Director—Dan Edwards
  (Office Phone: 323-1200—Area Code 412)
Offices—Three Rivers Stadium, 300 Stadium Circle, Pittsburgh, Pa. 15212
Stadium—Three Rivers Stadium (Capacity: 59,000)
Colors—Black and Gold
Training Site—St. Vincent College, Latrobe, Pa.

1990 SCHEDULE
(All times local.
All games Sunday unless noted otherwise.)

Sept. 9	at Cleveland	4:00
Sept. 16	HOUSTON	8:00
Sept. 23	at Los Angeles Raiders	1:00
Sept. 30	MIAMI	1:00
Oct. 7	SAN DIEGO	1:00
Oct. 14	at Denver	2:00
Oct. 21	at San Francisco	1:00
Oct. 29	LOS ANGELES RAMS (Mon.)	9:00
Nov. 4	ATLANTA	1:00
Nov. 11	OPEN DATE	
Nov. 18	at Cincinnati	8:00
Nov. 25	at New York Jets	4:00
Dec. 2	CINCINNATI	1:00
Dec. 9	NEW ENGLAND	1:00
Dec. 16	at New Orleans	12:00
Dec. 23	CLEVELAND	1:00
Dec. 30	at Houston	7:00

1989 RESULTS—(Won 10, Lost 8)

Steelers		Opp.		Att.
0	Cleveland	51	(H)	57,928
10	Cincinnati	41	(A)	53,855
27	Minnesota	14	(H)	50,744
23	Detroit	3	(A)	43,804
16	Cincinnati	26	(H)	52,785
17	Cleveland	7	(A)	78,840
0	Houston	27	(A)	59,091
23	Kansas City	17	(A)	54,194
7	Denver	34	(A)	74,739
0	Chicago	20	(H)	56,505
20	San Diego	17	(A)	44,203
34	Miami	14	(A)	59,936
16	Houston	23	(H)	40,541
13	New York Jets	0	(A)	41,037
28	New England	10	(H)	26,594
31	Tampa Bay	22	(A)	29,690

AFC WILD-CARD GAME
26	Houston (OT)	23	(A)	58,306

AFC SEMIFINAL GAME
23	Denver	24	(A)	75,868

1989 GAMES STARTED

16 games: Dermontti Dawson, Thomas Everett, Merril Hoge, Tunch Ilkin, Louis Lipps, David Little, Greg Lloyd, Gerald Williams, Keith Willis, Dwayne Woodruff.

15 games: Carnell Lake.

14 games: Bubby Brister, Tim Johnson, Mike Mularkey, John Rienstra, Rod Woodson, Tim Worley.

13 games: Bryan Hinkle.

12 games: John Jackson.

9 games: Terry Long.

8 games: Derek Hill, Hardy Nickerson, Jerry Olsavsky, Dwight Stone.

7 games: Brian Blankenship.

4 games: Craig Wolfley.

3 games: Jerrol Williams.

2 games: Todd Blackledge, Delton Hall, Aaron Jones, Terry O'Shea, Tom Ricketts, Warren Williams.

1 game: Larry Griffin.

PITTSBURGH STEELERS 1990 VETERAN ROSTER

No.	Name	Pos.	Ht.	Wt.	NFL Exp.	Birth-date	College	Games in '89	How Acquired
1	Anderson, Gary	K	5-11	180	9	7-16-59	Syracuse	16	W-Buf, '82
60	Blankenship, Brian	G/C	6-1	275	4	4- 7-63	Nebraska	16	FA, '87
6	Brister, Bubby	QB	6-3	210	5	8-15-62	Northeast Louisiana	14	D3, '86
24	Carter, Rodney	RB	6-0	210	4	10-30-64	Purdue	15	D7, '86
63	Dawson, Dermontti	C/G	6-2	275	3	6-17-65	Kentucky	16	D2, '88
	Evans, Donald	DE	6-2	265	2	3-14-64	Winston-Salem State	*0	FA, '90
27	Everett, Thomas	S	5-9	184	4	11-21-64	Baylor	16	D4, '87
68	Freeman, Lorenzo	NT	6-5	298	4	5-23-64	Pittsburgh	16	FA, '87
22	Griffin, Larry	S	6-0	200	5	1-11-63	North Carolina	16	FA, '87
81	Griggs, Billy	TE	6-3	230	6	8- 4-62	Virginia	*5	UFA, '90
35	Hall, Delton	CB	6-1	207	4	1-16-65	Clemson	16	D2, '87
82	Hill, Derek	WR	6-1	193	2	11- 4-67	Arizona	16	D3, '89
53	Hinkle, Bryan	LB	6-2	225	9	6- 4-59	Oregon	13	D6, '81
33	Hoge, Merril	RB	6-2	230	4	1-26-65	Idaho State	16	D10, '87
41	Holmes, Darryl	CB/S	6-2	190	4	9- 6-64	Fort Valley State	*13	UFA, '90
62	Ilkin, Tunch	T	6-3	266	11	9-23-57	Indiana State	16	D6, '80
65	Jackson, John	T	6-6	288	3	1- 4-65	Eastern Kentucky	14	D10, '88
99	Jenkins, A.J.	LB/DE	6-2	237	2	4-12-66	Cal State-Fullerton	16	D9, '89
44	Johnson, David	CB	6-0	185	2	2-14-66	Kentucky	16	D7, '89
78	†Johnson, Tim	DE/NT	6-3	269	4	1-29-65	Penn State	14	D6, '87
97	Jones, Aaron	DE	6-5	257	3	12-18-66	Eastern Kentucky	16	D1, '88
37	Lake, Carnell	S	6-1	205	2	7-15-67	UCLA	15	D2, '89
51	Lanza, Chuck	C	6-2	260	3	9-20-64	Notre Dame	11	D3, '88
83	Lipps, Louis	WR	5-10	190	7	8- 9-62	Southern Mississippi	16	D1, '84
50	Little, David	LB	6-1	233	10	1- 3-59	Florida	16	D7, '81
95	Lloyd, Greg	LB	6-2	222	3	5-26-65	Fort Valley State	16	D6, '87
74	Long, Terry	G	5-11	275	7	7-21-59	East Carolina	13	D4a, '84
84	Mularkey, Mike	TE	6-4	237	8	11-19-61	Florida	14	UFA, '89
54	Nickerson, Hardy	LB	6-2	231	4	9- 1-65	California	10	D5, '87
92	Olsavsky, Jerry	LB	6-1	222	2	3-29-67	Pittsburgh	16	D10, '89
85	O'Shea, Terry	TE	6-4	236	2	12- 3-66	California (Pa.)	16	OFA, '89
28	Owens, Billy	CB	6-0	198	2	12- 2-65	Pittsburgh	*0	FA, '90
71	Ricketts, Tom	T	6-5	298	2	11-21-65	Pittsburgh	12	D1a, '89
79	Rienstra, John	G	6-5	264	5	3-22-63	Temple	15	D1, '86
94	Romer, Rich	LB	6-3	214	3	2-27-66	Union College	*5	FA, '90
47	Roundtree, Ray	WR	6-0	182	2	4-19-66	Penn State	*0	FA, '90
40	Shelton, Richard	CB	5-11	186	2	1- 2-66	Liberty (Va.)	*3	FA, '90
80	Stock, Mark	WR	5-11	177	2	4-27-66	Virginia Military	8	D6, '89
20	Stone, Dwight	WR/RB	6-0	190	4	1-28-64	Middle Tennessee St.	16	OFA, '87
90	Stowe, Tyronne	LB	6-1	236	4	5-30-65	Rutgers	16	FA, '88
11	Strom, Rick	QB	6-2	210	2	3-11-65	Georgia Tech	3	FA, '89
87	†Thompson, Weegie	WR	6-6	215	7	3-21-61	Florida State	16	D4a, '84
23	Tyrrell, Tim	RB	6-2	215	7	2-19-61	Northern Illinois	7	FA, '89
43	Wallace, Ray	RB	6-0	233	4	12- 3-63	Purdue	9	UFA, '89
98	†Williams, Gerald	NT	6-3	279	5	9- 8-63	Auburn	16	D2, '86
57	Williams, Jerrol	LB	6-5	242	2	7- 5-67	Purdue	16	D4, '89
42	Williams, Warren	RB	6-0	204	3	7-29-65	Miami (Fla.)	5	D6, '88
93	Willis, Keith	DE	6-1	263	8	7-29-59	Northeastern	16	OFA, '82
49	Woodruff, Dwayne	CB	6-0	195	11	2-18-57	Louisville	16	D6a, '79
26	Woodson, Rod	CB/KR	6-0	196	4	3-10-65	Purdue	15	D1, '87
38	Worley, Tim	RB	6-2	228	2	9-24-66	Georgia	15	D1, '89
9	Wright, Randy	QB	6-2	203	6	1-21-61	Wisconsin	*0	FA, '90

*Evans last active with Eagles in '88; Griggs played 5 games with Jets in '89; Holmes played 13 games with Patriots in '89; Owens last active with Cowboys in '88; Romer played 5 games with Bengals in '89; Roundtree last active with Lions in '88; Shelton played 3 games with Broncos in '89; Wright last active with Packers in '88.

†Unsigned; subject to developments.

Players lost through Plan B free agency: CB David Arnold (15 games in '89; to Hou.); WR Jason Johnson (14; to Den.); P Harry Newsome (16; to Minn.); LB Tracy Simien (0; to N.O.); LB Vinson Smith (0; to Dall.); WR Eric Wilkerson (0; to Det.); G/T Craig Wolfley (15; to Minn.).

Also played with Steelers in '89—QB Todd Blackledge (3 games); TE Mike Hinnant (5).

D—Draft; W—Waivers; FA—Free Agent; OFA—Original Free Agent; UFA—Unrestricted Free Agent.

PITTSBURGH STEELERS
1990 DRAFT CHOICES

(Number following name designates order of selection among 331 players drafted.)

Round and Player		Position	College
1. Choice to Dallas (a)			
1. GREEN, Eric from Minnesota through Dallas (b)	21	TE	Liberty (Va.)
2. DAVIDSON, Kenny	43	DE	Louisiana State
3. O'DONNELL, Neil	70	QB	Maryland
3. VEASEY, Craig from San Francisco through Dallas (c)	81	DT	Houston
4. CALLOWAY, Chris	97	WR	Michigan
5. FOSTER, Barry	128	RB	Arkansas
6. HEARD, Ronald	155	WR	Bowling Green State
7. GRAYSON, Dan	182	LB	Washington State
8. DUNBAR, Karl	209	DT	Louisiana State
9. JONES, Gary	239	DB	Texas A & M
10. MILES, Eddie	266	LB	Minnesota
11. STRZELCZYK, Justin	293	T	Maine
12. BELL, Richard	319	RB	Nebraska

(a) Traded pick for 1st- and 3rd-round picks, April 22, 1990.

(b) Steelers acquired pick from Cowboys: see (a); Cowboys acquired pick from Vikings in Herschel Walker trade, October 12, 1989.

(c) Steelers acquired pick from Cowboys: see (a); Cowboys acquired pick, 11th-round pick, running back Terrence Flagler and defensive end Dan Stubbs from 49ers for 2nd- and 3rd-round picks, April 19, 1990.

PITTSBURGH STEELERS
1990 ROOKIE AND FIRST-YEAR ROSTER

Name	Pos.	Hgt.	Wgt.	Birth-date	College	How Acquired
Anders, Kimble	RB	5-11	210	9-10-66	Houston	FA
Bell, Richard	RB	6-0	196	5- 3-67	Nebraska	D12
Buddenberg, John	T	6-5	275	10- 9-65	Akron	*FA
Calloway, Chris	WR	5-10	181	3-29-68	Michigan	D4
Cullinane, Gene	C-G	6-4	278	11-10-66	Washburn	*FA
Davidson, Ken	DE	6-5	274	8-17-67	Louisiana State	D2
Davis, Lorenzo	WR	5-11	185	2-12-68	Youngstown State	FA
Dunbar, Karl	DE	6-4	273	5-18-67	Louisiana State	D8
Fair, Ron	WR	5-11	190	10-28-66	Arizona State	FA
Foster, Barry	RB	5-10	222	12- 8-68	Arkansas	D5
Fryar, Jeff	T	6-6	290	12- 7-64	Indiana	*FA
Gordon, Robert	WR	5-10	180	7- 9-68	Nebraska-Omaha	FA
Gouldsby, Mace	DT	6-2	290	8-24-65	San Jose State	*FA
Grayson, Dan	LB	6-2	239	7-27-67	Washington State	D7
Green, Eric	TE	6-5	274	6-22-67	Liberty (Va.)	D1
Haselrig, Carlton	G	6-1	273	1-22-66	Pittsburgh-Johnstown	*D12
Heard, Ron	WR	5-10	177	8-20-67	Bowling Green State	D6
Jones, Adrian	CB	6-0	180	1-18-69	Missouri	FA
Jones, Gary	CB	6-1	203	11-30-67	Texas A&M	D9
Kirk, Vernon	TE	6-2	245	10-14-66	Pittsburgh	*FA
Lee, Mitch	LB	6-1	225	12-16-68	Cornell	FA
Miles, Eddie	LB	6-1	233	9-13-68	Minnesota	D10
Ober, Mike	DT	6-4	270	1-25-67	Sam Houston State	FA
O'Donnell, Neil	QB	6-2	217	7- 3-66	Maryland	D3
Pavlik, Michael	G	6-3	285	12-10-66	Virginia Tech	FA
Rutter, Pete	P	6-2	214	11-23-67	Baylor	FA
Stryzinski, Dan	P	6-1	195	5-15-65	Indiana	*FA
Strzelczyk, Justin	T	6-5	272	8-18-68	Maine	D11
Veasey, Craig	DT	6-2	270	12-25-65	Houston	D3a
Williams, Marlin	DE	6-3	270	4-12-65	Western Illinois	*FA

*Buddenberg: D10 Cleveland '89, released 8/30, DEV Cleveland 9/28, released 11/8, DEV Minnesota 11/28, released 1/8/90; Cullinane: FA Pittsburgh '89, released 8/29; Fryar: FA New York Giants '89, released 8/23; Gouldsby: FA San Francisco '89, released 9/5, DEV San Francisco 9/6, released 9/20, DEV Pittsburgh 12/1, released 1/29/90; Haselrig: D12 Pittsburgh '89, released 9/5, DEV Pittsburgh 9/6, released 1/29/90; Kirk: D9 Los Angeles Rams '89, reserve/non-football illness (steroids) 8/29 through 9/19, released 9/20; Stryzinski: FA Indianapolis '88, released 8/23, FA Cleveland 8/25, released 8/30, FA Cleveland '89, released 8/30, DEV New Orleans 10/11, released 10/18; Williams: D8 Seattle '89, released 8/30.

SAN DIEGO CHARGERS
(Western Division, American Conference)

Dan Henning

Chairman of the Board/President—Alex G. Spanos
Vice-Chairman—Dean A. Spanos
General Manager—Bobby Beathard
Asst. General Manager—Dick Daniels
Director of Administration—Jack Teele
Assistant to Chairman—Warren Jones
Head Coach—Dan Henning (5 years: 28-51-1)
Assistant Coaches:
   Defensive Line—Gunther Cunningham
   Strength—John Dunn
   Offensive Line—Alex Gibbs
   Linebackers—Mike Haluchak
   Offensive Backs—Bobby Jackson
   Receivers—Charlie Joiner
   Defensive Coordinator—Ron Lynn
   Special Teams Assistant—LeCharls McDaniel
   Secondary—Jim Mora, Jr.
   Special Teams Coordinator—Larry Pasquale
   Offensive Assistant—Jack Reilly
   Asst. Head Coach—Ted Tollner
   Tight Ends—Ed White
Director of Public Relations—Bill Johnston
   (Office Phone: 280-2111—Area Code 619)
Offices—San Diego Jack Murphy Stadium, P. O. Box 20666, San Diego, Calif. 92160
Stadium—San Diego Jack Murphy Stadium (Capacity: 60,750)
Team Colors—Navy Blue, White and Gold
Training Site—University of California, at San Diego

1990 SCHEDULE
(All times local.
All games Sunday unless noted otherwise.)

Sept. 9	at Dallas	3:00
Sept. 16	CINCINNATI	1:00
Sept. 23	at Cleveland	1:00
Sept. 30	HOUSTON	1:00
Oct. 7	at Pittsburgh	1:00
Oct. 14	at New York Jets	1:00
Oct. 21	LOS ANGELES RAIDERS	1:00
Oct. 28	TAMPA BAY	1:00
Nov. 4	at Seattle	1:00
Nov. 11	DENVER	1:00
Nov. 18	at Kansas City	12:00
Nov. 25	SEATTLE	5:00
Dec. 2	NEW YORK JETS	1:00
Dec. 9	OPEN DATE	
Dec. 16	at Denver	2:00
Dec. 23	KANSAS CITY	1:00
Dec. 30	at Los Angeles Raiders	1:00

1989 RESULTS—(Won 6, Lost 10)

Chargers		Opp.		Att.
14	Los Angeles Raiders	40	(A)	40,237
27	Houston	34	(H)	42,013
21	Kansas City	6	(H)	40,128
24	Phoenix	13	(A)	44,201
10	Denver	16	(A)	75,222
16	Seattle	17	(H)	50,079
13	New York Giants	20	(H)	48,566
7	Seattle	10	(A)	59,691
20	Philadelphia	17	(H)	47,019
14	Los Angeles Raiders	12	(H)	59,151
17	Pittsburgh	20	(A)	44,203
6	Indianapolis	10	(A)	58,822
17	New York Jets	20	(H)	38,954
21	Washington	26	(A)	47,693
20	Kansas City	13	(A)	40,623
19	Denver	16	(H)	50,524

1989 GAMES STARTED

16 games: Martin Bayless, Gill Byrd, Arthur Cox, Vencie Glenn, Burt Grossman, Courtney Hall, Anthony Miller, Leslie O'Neal, Gary Plummer, David Richards, Billy Ray Smith, Broderick Thompson, Lee Williams.

15 games: Joe Phillips.

14 games: Cedric Figaro, Joel Patten.

12 games: Sam Seale.

11 games: Jim McMahon, Brett Miller, Tim Spencer.

9 games: Joe Caravello.

6 games: Jamie Holland, Andy Parker.

5 games: Marion Butts, James FitzPatrick, Billy Joe Tolliver.

4 games: Wayne Walker.

3 games: Quinn Early, Craig McEwen, Elvis Patterson.

2 games: Jim Collins, Joey Howard.

1 game: Mike Charles, Chris Gannon, Lester Lyles.

SAN DIEGO CHARGERS 1990 VETERAN ROSTER

No.	Name	Pos.	Ht.	Wt.	NFL Exp.	Birth-date	College	Games in '89	How Acquired
15	†Archer, David	QB	6-2	208	7	2-15-62	Iowa State	16	FA, '89
44	Bayless, Martin	S	6-2	212	7	10-11-62	Bowling Green	16	T-Buf, '87
82	Bernstine, Rod	RB	6-3	238	4	2- 8-65	Texas A&M	5	D1, '87
58	†Brandon, David	LB	6-4	230	4	2- 9-65	Memphis State	13	T-Buf, '87
	Brooks, Michael	S	6-0	195	1	3-12-67	North Carolina State	1	FA, '89
	Brown, Richard	LB	6-3	240	3	9-21-65	San Diego State	*13	FA, '90
35	Butts, Marion	RB	6-1	248	2	8- 1-66	Florida State	15	D7, '89
22	†Byrd, Gill	CB	5-11	198	8	2-20-61	San Jose State	16	D1b, '83
46	Caravello, Joe	RB	6-3	270	4	6- 6-63	Tulane	12	UFA, '89
	Carney, John	K	5-11	160	2	4-20-64	Notre Dame	*1	UFA, '90
88	†Cox, Arthur	TE	6-2	277	8	2- 5-61	Texas Southern	16	FA, '88
87	Early, Quinn	WR	6-0	190	3	4-13-65	Iowa	6	D3, '88
51	†Figaro, Cedric	LB	6-2	250	3	8-17-66	Notre Dame	16	D6, '88
	Fuller, Joe	CB	5-11	180	1	9-25-64	Northern Iowa	*0	FA, '90
25	†Glenn, Vencie	S	6-0	192	5	10-26-64	Indiana State	16	T-NE, '86
92	Grossman, Burt	DE	6-6	270	2	4-10-67	Pittsburgh	16	D1, '89
53	Hall, Courtney	C	6-1	269	2	8-26-68	Rice	16	D2, '89
	Harmon, Ronnie	RB	5-11	200	5	5- 7-64	Iowa	*15	UFA, '90
	Hill, Nate	DE	6-4	275	2	2-21-66	Auburn	*0	FA, '90
97	†Hinkle, George	DE	6-5	269	3	3-17-65	Arizona	14	D11a, '88
79	Howard, Joey	T	6-5	305	2	9-14-65	Tennessee	9	D9, '88
	Jackson, Tim	CB	5-11	192	1	11- 7-65	Nebraska	*1	FA, '90
	Kidd, John	P	6-3	208	7	8-22-61	Northwestern	*16	UFA, '90
24	Lyles, Lester	S	6-3	200	6	12-27-62	Virginia	16	UFA, '89
31	†McEwen, Craig	RB	6-1	220	4	12-16-65	Utah	4	FA, '89
60	†McKnight, Dennis	C/G	6-3	280	8	9-12-59	Drake	*0	FA, '82
	Mickles, Joe	RB	5-10	221	2	12-25-65	Mississippi	*9	UFA, '90
83	Miller, Anthony	WR	5-11	185	3	4-15-65	Tennessee	16	D1, '88
69	Miller, Les	NT	6-7	293	4	3- 1-65	Fort Hays State	14	FA, '87
20	Nelson, Darrin	RB	5-9	185	9	1- 2-59	Stanford	*14	T-Dal, '89
91	†O'Neal, Leslie	LB	6-4	259	4	5- 7-64	Oklahoma State	16	D1, '86
85	Parker, Andy	TE	6-5	245	7	9- 8-61	Utah	10	UFA, '89
78	Patten, Joel	T	6-7	307	6	2- 7-58	Duke	14	UFA, '89
75	Phillips, Joe	NT	6-5	275	5	7-15-63	Southern Methodist	16	FA, '87
	Plummer, Bruce	S	6-1	203	4	9- 1-64	Mississippi State	*16	UFA, '90
50	Plummer, Gary	LB	6-2	240	5	1-26-60	California	16	FA, '86
7	Reveiz, Fuad	K	5-11	216	5	2-24-63	Tennessee	*0	FA, '90
65	†Richards, David	G/T	6-4	310	3	4-11-66	UCLA	16	D4b, '88
98	Robinson, Gerald	DE	6-3	262	3	5- 4-63	Auburn	2	FA, '89
	Rodenhauser, Mark	C	6-5	263	3	6- 1-61	Illinois State	*16	UFA, '90
	Rolling, Henry	LB	6-2	225	3	9- 8-65	Nevada-Reno	*6	FA, '90
	Sanders, Thomas	RB	5-11	203	6	1- 4-62	Texas A&M	*16	UFA, '90
30	†Seale, Sam	CB	5-9	185	7	10- 6-62	Western State (Colo.)	13	FA, '88
	Simmonds, Mike	G	6-4	285	2	8-12-64	Indiana State	*5	UFA, '90
54	Smith, Billy Ray	LB	6-3	236	8	8-10-61	Arkansas	16	D1, '83
43	†Spencer, Tim	RB	6-1	223	6	12-10-60	Ohio State	16	D11a, '83
76	†Thompson, Broderick	G/T	6-4	295	5	8-14-60	Kansas	16	FA, '87
11	Tolliver, Billy Joe	QB	6-1	218	2	2- 7-66	Texas Tech	5	D2a, '89
	Toth, Tom	G	6-5	282	5	5-23-62	Western Michigan	*16	UFA, '90
13	Vlasic, Mark	QB	6-3	206	3	10-25-63	Iowa	*0	D4, '87
80	Walker, Wayne	WR	5-8	162	2	12-27-66	Texas Tech	13	OFA, '89
67	Williams, Larry	G	6-5	290	4	7- 3-63	Notre Dame	*0	UFA, '90
99	Williams, Lee	DE	6-5	271	7	10-15-62	Bethune-Cookman	16	SupD, '84
59	†Woodard, Ken	LB	6-1	220	9	1-22-60	Tuskegee Institute	16	FA, '88
80	Yarber, Eric	WR	5-8	152	2	9-22-63	Idaho	*0	FA, '90

*Brown played 13 games with Rams in '89; Carney played 1 game with Buccaneers in '89; Fuller last active with Saskatchewan-CFL in '88; Harmon played 15 games with Bills in '89; Hill last active with Packers and Dolphins in '88; Jackson played 1 game with Cowboys in '89; Kidd played 16 games with Bills in '89; McKnight and Vlasic missed '89 season due to injury; Mickles played 9 games with Redskins in '89; Nelson played 5 games with Vikings, 9 with Chargers in '89; B. Plummer played 16 games with Colts in '89; Reveiz last active with Dolphins in '88; Rodenhauser played 16 games with Vikings in '89; Rolling played 6 games with Buccaneers in '89; Sanders played 16 games with Bears in '89; Simmonds played 5 games with Buccaneers in '89; Toth played 16 games with Dolphins in '89; La. Williams last active with Browns in '88; Yarber last active with Redskins in '87.

†Unsigned; subject to developments.

Players lost through Plan B free agency: LB Joe Campbell (9 games in '89; to L.A. Raid.); T James FitzPatrick (13; to L.A. Raid.); TE Chris Gannon (10; to N.E.); P Hank Ilesic (14; to L.A. Rams); T Brett

Miller (14; to N.Y.J.); CB Elvis Patterson (16; to L.A. Raid.); CB/S Elliot Smith (2; to Den.).

Retired—Don Macek, 14-year center, 2 games in '89.

Also played with Chargers in '89—WR Anthony Allen (7 games); K Chris Bahr (16); CB Roy Bennett (16); RB Dana Brinson (10); NT Mike Charles (6); P Lewis Colbert (2); S Leonard Coleman (1); LB Jim Collins (13); RB Victor Floyd (6); WR Jamie Holland (16); WR Phil McConkey (5); QB Jim McMahon (12); CB Johnny Thomas (13); WR Darryl Usher (6); TE Mark Walczak (6).

D—Draft; T—Trade; FA—Free Agent; OFA—Original Free Agent; UFA—Unrestricted Free Agent; SupD—Supplemental Draft.

SAN DIEGO CHARGERS
1990 DRAFT CHOICES

(Number following name designates order of selection among 331 players drafted.)

Round and Player		Position	College
1. SEAU, Junior	5	LB	Southern Cal
2. Choice to Chicago (a)			
3. MILLS, Jeff from Tampa Bay (b)	57	LB	Nebraska
3. GOEAS, Leo	60	G	Hawaii
3. WILSON, Walter from Indianapolis (c)	67	WR	East Carolina
4. Choice to San Francisco through Los Angeles Raiders (d)			
5. Choice to Minnesota through Dallas (e)			
6. FRIESZ, John from Dallas (e)	138	QB	Idaho
6. CORNISH, Frank from New England through Dallas (f)	143	C	UCLA
6. POOL, David	145	DB	Carson-Newman
6. WALKER, Derrick from New York Giants through Dallas (g)	163	TE	Michigan
7. NOVAK, Jeff	172	G	S.W. Texas State
7. STAYSNIAK, Joe from Cleveland (h)	185	T	Ohio State
7. LEWIS, Nate from Washington (i)	187	WR	Oregon Tech
7. COLLINS, Keith from San Francisco (j)	193	DB	Appalachian State
8. FLANNIGAN, J.J.	201	RB	Colorado
9. GOETZ, Chris	227	G	Pittsburgh
10. BERRY, Kenny	256	DB	Miami (Fla.)
11. STOWERS, Tommie	283	TE	Missouri
12. Choice to Indianapolis (k)			
12. SEARCY, Elliott from Washington (m)	326	WR	Southern U.

(a) Traded pick for quarterback Jim McMahon, August 18, 1989.

(b) Acquired pick and conditional pick in 1991 for running back Gary Anderson, April 21, 1990.

(c) Acquired pick for linebacker Chip Banks, October 17, 1989.

(d) Chargers traded pick and 3rd-round pick in 1989 to Raiders for running back Napoleon McCallum, October 11, 1988; Raiders traded pick to 49ers for 4th- and 5th-round picks, April 20, 1990.

(e) Chargers traded 5th-round pick to Cowboys, Cowboys traded pick to Vikings and Chargers acquired 6th-round pick from Cowboys in Herschel Walker/Darrin Nelson trade, October 17, 1989.

(f) Chargers acquired pick and two other 6th-round picks from Cowboys for 3rd-round pick in 1991, April 22, 1990; Cowboys had acquired pick and 3rd- and 8th-round picks from Patriots for 3rd-, 5th- and 7th-round picks, April 22, 1990.

(g) Chargers acquired pick from Cowboys: see first part of (f); Cowboys had acquired pick from Giants for linebacker Steve DeOssie, June 2, 1989.

(h) Acquired pick for running back Barry Redden, September 4, 1989.

(i) Acquired pick for punter Ralf Mojsiejenko, August 29, 1989.

(j) Acquired pick, center Fred Quillan and 7th-round pick in 1989 for wide receiver Wes Chandler, June 2, 1988.

(k) Traded pick for defensive back Leonard Coleman, July 8, 1988.

(m) Acquired pick for 12th-round pick in 1989, April 24, 1989.

SAN DIEGO CHARGERS
1990 ROOKIE AND FIRST-YEAR ROSTER

Name	Pos.	Hgt.	Wgt.	Birth-date	College	How Acquired
Allen, Lee	WR	5-10	165	10- 9-67	Idaho	FA
Bankston, Bobby	WR	5-7	170	1-20-63	East Texas State	*FA
Belli, Barry	K	5-10	167	8- 7-65	Fresno State	*FA
Berry, Ken	CB	6-2	185	10-12-66	Miami (Fla.)	D10
Cleveland, Terence	WR	5-8	166	11- 6-66	Tennessee	FA
Collins, Keith	CB	5-11	183	2- 6-68	Appalachian State	D7c
Colonna, Dave	TE	6-5	235	11-15-67	Duke	FA
Cornish, Frank	C/G	6-4	281	9-24-67	UCLA	D6a
Davis, Willie	CB	5-10	185	1- 6-67	Southern Illinois	FA
Debnam, Derick	DE	6-2	255	4-18-68	North Carolina	FA
Dickson, Wayne	LB	6-3	253	11-27-67	Oklahoma	FA
English, Keith	P	6-3	220	3-10-66	Colorado	*FA
Estes, Mike	DE	6-5	270	4-17-65	Central Washington	FA
Flannigan, J.J.	RB	5-10	195	9-16-68	Colorado	D8
Floyd, Eric	T	6-5	300	10-28-65	Auburn	*FA
Frank, Donald	CB/S	6-0	200	10-24-65	Winston-Salem State	FA
Friesz, John	QB	6-4	209	5-19-67	Idaho	D6
Goeas, Leo	T	6-3	280	8-15-66	Hawaii	D3a
Goetz, Chris	G	6-2	272	3-13-67	Pittsburgh	D9
Gunn, Tony	NT	6-5	310	4- 5-65	Nevada-Las Vegas	FA
Jones, Mike	LB	6-0	224	7-14-67	Colorado	FA
Lewis, Nate	WR	5-11	197	10-19-66	Oregon Tech	D7b
Mays, Jerry	RB	5-7	173	12- 8-67	Georgia Tech	FA
Mills, Jeff	LB	6-3	238	10- 8-68	Nebraska	D3
Moorer, Pat	LB	6-1	225	6-20-68	Florida	FA
Novak, Jeff	G	6-5	279	7-27-67	S.W. Texas State	D7
Pool, David	CB	5-9	188	12-20-66	Carson-Newman	D6b
Sale, Ken	LB	6-2	245	5- 3-68	Texas-El Paso	FA
Searcy, Elliott	WR	5-7	173	9-18-67	Southern University	D12
Seau, Junior	LB	6-3	243	1-19-69	Southern California	D1
Shahbo, Khaled	TE	..	..	....	Cal St.-Santa Barbara	FA
Shelley, Stephen	WR	6-0	180	7- 7-67	Fresno State	FA
Staysniak, Joe	T	6-4	244	8-23-67	Ohio State	D7a
Stowers, Tommie	TE	6-3	225	11-18-66	Missouri	D11
Walker, Derrick	TE	6-0	244	6-23-67	Michigan	D6c
Whelihan, Thomas	K	5-10	198	8-15-66	Missouri	*FA
Wilson, Walter	WR	5-10	185	10- 6-66	East Carolina	D3b
Wise, Dartangian	NT	6-4	275	8- 8-67	Nevada-Las Vegas	FA

*Bankston: FA Tampa Bay '87, injured reserve (wrist) 9/3 through 11/2, released 11/3, FA San Francisco '88, released 8/8, FA Cleveland '89, released 5/8, FA Houston 7/18, released 8/4, awarded on waivers to Tampa Bay 8/7, released 8/22; Belli: FA Minnesota '88, released 8/18, FA New England '89, released 6/13; English: FA Los Angeles Raiders '89, released 8/29, awarded on waivers to Atlanta 8/30, released 9/5; Floyd: FA San Diego '88, released 8/25, FA San Diego '89, released 8/30, DEV San Diego 9/7, released 12/7; Whelihan: FA Detroit '89, released 7/20.

SAN FRANCISCO 49ers
(Western Division, National Conference)

George Seifert

Owner-President—Edward J. DeBartolo, Jr.
Exec. V.P., Front Office & League Relations—Carmen Policy
V.P., Football Administration—John McVay
Director of College Scouting—Tony Razzano
Director of Pro Personnel—Allan Webb
Head Coach—George Seifert (1 year: 14-2)
Assistant Coaches:
    Strength & Conditioning—Jerry Attaway
    Defensive Line—Tommy Hart
    Quarterbacks—Mike Holmgren
    Running Backs—Al Lavan
    Wide Receivers—Sherman Lewis
    Defensive Line—John Marshall
    Offensive Line—Bobb McKittrick
    Defensive Coordinator—Bill McPherson
    Secondary—Ray Rhodes
    Tight Ends—Lynn Stiles
    Linebackers—Bob Zeman
Public Relations Director—Jerry Walker
    (Office Phone: 562-4949—Area Code 408)
Offices—4949 Centennial Blvd., Santa Clara, Calif. 95054
Stadium—Candlestick Park (Capacity: 66,390)
Team Colors—49er Gold and Scarlet
Training Site—Sierra College, Rocklin, Calif.

1990 SCHEDULE
(All times local.
All games Sunday unless noted otherwise.)

Sept. 10	at New Orleans (Mon.)	8:00
Sept. 16	WASHINGTON	1:00
Sept. 23	ATLANTA	1:00
Sept. 30	OPEN DATE	
Oct. 7	at Houston	12:00
Oct. 14	at Atlanta	1:00
Oct. 21	PITTSBURGH	1:00
Oct. 28	CLEVELAND	1:00
Nov. 4	at Green Bay	12:00
Nov. 11	at Dallas	7:00
Nov. 18	TAMPA BAY	1:00
Nov. 25	LOS ANGELES RAMS	1:00
Dec. 3	NEW YORK GIANTS (Mon.)	6:00
Dec. 9	at Cincinnati	1:00
Dec. 17	at Los Angeles Rams (Mon.)	6:00
Dec. 23	NEW ORLEANS	1:00
Dec. 30	at Minnesota	12:00

1989 RESULTS—(Won 17, Lost 2)

49ers	Opp.		Att.
30 Indianapolis	24	(A)	60,111
20 Tampa Bay	16	(A)	64,087
38 Philadelphia	28	(A)	66,042
12 Los Angeles Rams	13	(H)	64,250
24 New Orleans	20	(A)	60,488
31 Dallas	14	(A)	61,077
37 New England	20	(H)	70,000
23 New York Jets	10	(A)	62,805
31 New Orleans	13	(H)	60,667
45 Atlanta	3	(H)	59,914
17 Green Bay	21	(H)	62,219
34 New York Giants	24	(H)	63,461
23 Atlanta	10	(A)	43,128
30 Los Angeles Rams	27	(A)	67,959
21 Buffalo	10	(H)	60,927
26 Chicago	0	(H)	65,675
NFC SEMIFINAL GAME			
41 Minnesota	13	(H)	64,585
NFC CHAMPIONSHIP GAME			
30 Los Angeles Rams	3	(H)	64,769
NFL CHAMPIONSHIP GAME			
55 Denver	10	(*)	72,919

(*)Superdome, New Orleans, La.

1989 GAMES STARTED

16 games: Harris Barton, Roger Craig, Don Griffin, Charles Haley, Brent Jones, Bubba Paris, Tom Rathman, Jerry Rice, Jesse Sapolu, Mike Walter.

15 games: Chet Brooks, Bruce Collie, Kevin Fagan, John Taylor.

14 games: Darryl Pollard.

13 games: Guy McIntyre, Joe Montana.

12 games: Keena Turner.

11 games: Pierce Holt, Ronnie Lott.

9 games: Matt Millen.

8 games: Michael Carter.

7 games: Jim Fahnhorst.

6 games: Pete Kugler.

5 games: Larry Roberts.

4 games: Jeff Fuller, Bill Romanowski.

3 games: Jeff Bregel, Jim Burt, Steve Young.

2 games: Johnny Jackson.

1 game: Tim McKyer, Steve Wallace, Mike Wilson, Eric Wright.

SAN FRANCISCO 49ers 1990 VETERAN ROSTER

No.	Name	Pos.	Ht.	Wt.	NFL Exp.	Birth-date	College	Games in '89	How Acquired
67	Aronson, Doug	G	6-4	278	2	8-14-64	San Diego State	*0	FA, '90
79	†Barton, Harris	T	6-4	280	4	4-19-64	North Carolina	16	D1, '87
	Beach, Sanjay	WR	6-1	190	1	2-21-66	Colorado State	*1	FA, '90
13	Bono, Steve	QB	6-4	215	6	5-11-62	UCLA	1	FA, '89
65	†Bregel, Jeff	G	6-4	280	4	5- 1-64	Southern California	3	D2, '87
31	†Brooks, Chet	S	5-11	191	3	1- 1-66	Texas A&M	15	D11, '88
64	†Burt, Jim	NT	6-1	270	10	6- 7-59	Miami (Fla.)	8	FA, '89
	Bynum, Reggie	WR	6-1	190	1	2-10-64	Oregon State	*1	FA, '90
95	Carter, Michael	NT	6-2	285	7	10-29-60	Southern Methodist	8	D5, '84
6	Cofer, Mike	K	6-1	190	3	2-19-62	North Carolina State	16	FA, '88
69	Collie, Bruce	G/T	6-6	275	6	6-27-62	Texas-Arlington	16	D5, '85
38	Cox, Greg	S	6-0	217	3	1- 6-65	San Jose State	*16	UFA, '90
33	Craig, Roger	RB	6-0	224	8	7-10-60	Nebraska	16	D2, '83
68	Cullity, Dave	T	6-7	275	2	6-15-64	Utah	2	FA, '89
59	DeLong, Keith	LB	6-2	235	2	8-14-67	Tennessee	15	D1, '89
28	Dixon, Hanford	CB	6-0	185	10	12-25-58	Southern Mississippi	*15	UFA, '90
75	†Fagan, Kevin	DE	6-4	265	4	4-25-63	Miami (Fla.)	16	D4c, '86
55	†Fahnhorst, Jim	LB	6-4	230	7	11- 8-58	Minnesota	7	FA, '84
98	Goss, Antonio	LB	6-4	228	2	8-11-66	North Carolina	8	D12, '89
29	Griffin, Don	CB	6-0	176	5	3-17-64	Middle Tennessee State	16	D6, '86
94	†Haley, Charles	LB/DE	6-5	230	5	1- 6-64	James Madison	16	D4, '86
65	Hamilton, Steve	DE	6-4	275	5	9-29-61	East Carolina	*0	FA, '90
9	Helton, Barry	P	6-3	205	3	1- 2-66	Colorado	16	D4, '88
30	Henderson, Keith	RB	6-1	220	2	8- 4-66	Georgia	6	D3, '89
56	Hendrickson, Steve	LB	6-0	245	2	8-30-66	California	11	D6, '89
78	Holt, Pierce	DE	6-4	280	3	1- 1-62	Angelo State	16	D2a, '88
4	Horne, Greg	P	6-0	190	3	11-22-64	Arkansas	*0	FA, '90
40	Jackson, Johnny	S	6-1	204	2	1-11-67	Houston	16	D5, '89
	Jeffery, Tony	RB	5-11	208	2	7- 8-64	Texas Christian	*0	FA, '90
84	Jones, Brent	TE	6-4	230	4	2-12-63	Santa Clara	16	FA, '87
57	Kennedy, Sam	LB	6-3	235	2	7-10-64	San Jose State	*0	FA, '88
60	Lockett, Danny	LB	6-2	250	3	7-11-64	Arizona	*0	FA, '90
42	Lott, Ronnie	S	6-0	200	10	5- 8-59	Southern California	11	D1, '81
62	McIntyre, Guy	G	6-3	265	7	2-17-61	Georgia	16	D3, '84
54	†Millen, Matt	LB	6-2	245	11	3-12-58	Penn State	15	FA, '89
16	Montana, Joe	QB	6-2	195	12	6-11-56	Notre Dame	13	D3, '79
77	Paris, Bubba	T	6-6	306	8	10- 6-60	Michigan	16	D2, '82
26	Pollard, Darryl	CB	5-11	187	4	5-11-65	Weber State	16	FA, '88
76	Putzier, Rollin	NT	6-4	279	3	12-10-65	Oregon	11	FA, '89
57	Radloff, Wayne	C	6-5	277	6	5-17-61	Georgia	*11	UFA, '90
44	Rathman, Tom	RB	6-1	232	5	10- 7-62	Nebraska	16	D3, '86
80	Rice, Jerry	WR	6-2	200	6	10-13-62	Mississippi Valley State	16	D1, '85
91	Roberts, Larry	DE	6-3	275	5	6- 2-63	Alabama	15	D2, '86
53	Romanowski, Bill	LB	6-4	231	3	4- 2-66	Boston College	16	D3, '88
61	Sapolu, Jessie	C	6-4	260	5	3-10-61	Hawaii	16	D11, '83
71	Shannon, John	DE	6-3	270	3	1-18-65	Kentucky	*12	UFA, '90
88	Sherrard, Mike	WR	6-2	187	2	6-21-63	UCLA	*0	UFA, '89
72	Smerlas, Fred	NT	6-4	291	12	4- 8-57	Boston College	*16	UFA, '90
32	Swoope, Craig	S	6-2	210	4	2- 3-64	Illinois	*0	FA, '90
24	Sydney, Harry	RB	6-0	217	4	6-26-59	Kansas	7	FA, '87
66	Tausch, Terry	G	6-4	278	9	2- 5-59	Texas	9	UFA, '89
82	Taylor, John	WR	6-1	185	4	3-31-62	Delaware State	15	D3c, '86
47	Tennell, Derek	TE	6-5	248	4	2-12-64	UCLA	*14	FA, '90
60	†Thomas, Chuck	C	6-3	280	5	12-24-60	Oklahoma	16	FA, '87
23	Tillman, Spencer	RB	5-11	206	4	4-21-64	Oklahoma	15	UFA, '89
58	Turner, Keena	LB	6-2	222	11	10-22-58	Purdue	13	D2, '80
74	Wallace, Steve	T	6-5	276	5	12-27-64	Auburn	16	D4a, '86
89	Walls, Wesley	TE	6-5	246	2	2-26-66	Mississippi	16	D2, '89
99	Walter, Michael	LB	6-3	238	8	11-30-60	Oregon	16	W-Dal, '84
51	Washington, Chris	LB	6-4	240	6	3- 6-62	Iowa State	*0	UFA, '89
43	Waymer, Dave	S	6-1	188	11	7- 1-58	Notre Dame	*16	UFA, '90
	Weir, Robert	NT	6-3	270	1	2- 4-61	Southern Methodist	*18	FA, '90
81	Williams, Jamie	TE	6-4	245	8	2-25-60	Nebraska	3	UFA, '89
85	Wilson, Mike	WR	6-3	215	10	12-19-58	Washington State	16	FA, '81
21	Wright, Eric	CB	6-1	185	9	4-18-59	Missouri	11	D2a, '81
8	Young, Steve	QB	6-2	200	6	10-11-61	Brigham Young	10	T-TB, '87

*Aronson last active with Bengals in '87; Beach played 1 game with Jets in '89; Bynum played 1 game with Hamilton-CFL in '89; Cox played 16 games with Giants in '89; Dixon played 15 games with

Browns in '89; Hamilton last active with Redskins in '88; Horne last active with Cardinals in '88; Jeffery last active with Cardinals in '88; Kennedy last active with 49ers in '88; Lockett last active with Lions in '88; Radloff played 11 games with Falcons in '89; Shannon played 12 games with Bears in '89; Sherrard and Washington missed '89 season due to injury; Smerlas played 16 games with Bills in '89; Swoope last active with Colts in '88; Tennell played 14 games with Browns in '89; Waymer played 16 games with Saints in '89; Weir played 18 games with Ottawa-CFL in '89.

†Unsigned; subject to developments.

Players lost through Plan B free agency: WR Terry Greer (11 games in '89; to Det.).

Also played with 49ers in '89—WR Mike Barber (8 games); RB Terrence Flagler (15); S Jeff Fuller (6); S Tom Holmoe (7); DE Pete Kugler (14); NT Kevin Lilly (1); CB Tim McKyer (7); CB Mike Richardson (3); DE Daniel Stubbs (16).

D—Draft; T—Trade; W—Waivers; FA—Free Agent; OFA—Original Free Agent; UFA—Unrestricted Free Agent.

SAN FRANCISCO 49ers
1990 DRAFT CHOICES

(Number following name designates order of selection among 331 players drafted.)

Round and Player		Position	College
1. CARTER, Dexter	25	RB	Florida State
2. BROWN, Dennis from Minnesota through Dallas (a)	47	DT	Washington
2. DAVIS, Eric	53	DB	Jacksonville State
3. LEWIS, Ron from Kansas City through Dallas (b)	68	WR	Florida State
3. Choice to Pittsburgh through Dallas (c)			
4. CALIGUIRE, Dean from San Diego through L.A. Raiders (d)	92	C	Pittsburgh
4. Choice to Washington through Los Angeles Raiders (e)			
5. Choice to Miami through L.A. Raiders and Washington (f)			
6. POLLACK, Frank	165	T	Northern Arizona
7. Choice to San Diego (g)			
8. PICKENS, Dwight	220	WR	Fresno State
9. HAGGINS, Odell	248	DT	Florida State
10. HARRISON, Martin	276	DE	Washington
11. SHELTON, Anthony from Miami (h)	289	DB	Tennessee State
11. Choice to L.A. Raiders through Dallas (i)			
12. Choice to L.A. Raiders (j)			

(a) 49ers acquired pick and 3rd-round pick from Cowboys for running back Terrence Flagler, defensive end Dan Stubbs and 3rd- and 11th-round picks, April 19, 1990; Cowboys had acquired pick from Vikings in Herschel Walker trade, October 12, 1989.

(b) 49ers acquired pick from Cowboys: see first part of (a); Cowboys had acquired pick and conditional pick in 1991 from Chiefs for quarterback Steve Pelluer, October 17, 1989.

(c) 49ers traded pick to Cowboys: see first part of (a); Cowboys traded pick and 1st-round pick to Steelers for 1st-round pick, April 22, 1990.

(d) 49ers acquired pick from Raiders for 4th- and 5th-round picks, April 20, 1990;

Raiders had acquired pick and 3rd-round pick in 1989 from Chargers for running back Napoleon McCallum, October 11, 1988.

(e) 49ers traded pick to Raiders: see first part of (d); Raiders traded pick and 5th-round pick to Redskins as part of September 8, 1988, deal in which Raiders acquired quarterback Jay Schroeder and 2nd-round pick in 1989 for tackle Jim Lachey and 2nd-, 4th- and 5th-round picks in 1989.

(f) 49ers traded pick to Raiders and Raiders traded pick to Redskins: see (e); Redskins traded pick to Dolphins for 10th-round pick and 4th-round pick in 1991, April 22, 1990.

(g) Traded pick, center Fred Quillan and 7th-round pick in 1989 for wide receiver Wes Chandler, June 2, 1988.

(h) Acquired pick and 2nd-round pick in 1991 for cornerback Tim McKyer, April 23, 1990.

(i) 49ers traded pick to Cowboys: see first part of (a); Cowboys traded pick and 6th-, 8th-, 9th- and 10th-round picks to Raiders for rights to cornerback Stan Smagala, April 22, 1990.

(j) Traded pick and 12th-round pick in 1989 for 11th-round pick in 1989, April 24, 1989.

SAN FRANCISCO 49ers
1990 ROOKIE AND FIRST-YEAR ROSTER

Name	Pos.	Hgt.	Wgt.	Birth-date	College	How Acquired
Brown, Dennis	DE	6-4	290	11- 6-67	Washington	D2
Caliguire, Dean	C	6-2	282	3- 2-67	Pittsburgh	D4
Carter, Dexter	RB	5-9	170	9-15-67	Florida State	D1
Davis, Eric	WR	5-11	178	1-28-68	Jacksonville State	D2a
Dillard, Rodney	LB	6-3	230	6-30-65	Arizona State	FA
Edeen, David	DE	6-4	280	5-23-66	Wyoming	*FA
Haggins, Odell	NT	6-2	255	2-27-67	Florida State	D9
Harrison, Martin	LB/DE	6-5	240	9-20-67	Washington	D10
Knox, Tyreese	RB	6-0	212	7- 3-65	Nebraska	*FA
Lewis, Kevin	CB	5-10	180	11-14-66	Northwestern (La.) State	*FA
Lewis, Ronald	WR	5-11	173	3-25-68	Florida State	D3
Nedved, Jeff	WR	5-8	167	11- 2-64	Cal State-Hayward	*FA, '89
Pickens, Dwight	WR	5-10	170	5-18-66	Fresno State	D8
Pollack, Frank	T	6-4	277	5-18-66	Northern Arizona	D6
Shelton, Anthony	S	5-11	195	9- 4-67	Tennessee State	D11
Shepherd, Mark	DE	6-4	272	9-23-67	Arkansas	FA
Siglar, Ricky	T	6-7	296	6-14-66	San Jose State	*FA, '89
Slater, Brian	WR	6-4	200	5-15-66	Washington	*FA
Stephenson, Jeff	LB	6-4	240	12-14-65	St. Cloud State	*FA, '89
Turner, Lafayette	S	6-1	206	9-24-66	Texas A&M	FA
Wiese, Brett	G/C	6-4	280	8- 8-66	Washington	*FA
Wyatt, Greg	QB	6-3	195	2-15-67	Northern Arizona	FA
Young, Todd	TE	6-5	257	2- 2-67	Penn State	FA

*Edeen: D5 Phoenix '89, released 9/5, DEV Phoenix 9/6, released 9/14, DEV New York Giants 10/5, released 10/18, DEV Giants 10/23, released 12/29; Knox: FA Atlanta '89, released 8/22; K. Lewis: FA Phoenix '89, released 7/28; Nedved: FA San Francisco '89, released 9/1, DEV San Francisco 11/21, released 1/29/90; Siglar: FA Dallas '89, released 9/5, DEV San Francisco 9/20, released 1/29/90; Slater: D11 Pittsburgh '89, released 8/29; Stephenson: FA Seattle '89, released 9/5, DEV Los Angeles Raiders 9/26, released 10/4, DEV San Francisco 11/29, released 1/29/90; Wiese: FA New England '89, released 8/30.

SEATTLE SEAHAWKS
(Western Division, American Conference)

Chuck Knox

Owner—Ken Behring
President/General Manager—Tom Flores
V.P./Asst. General Manager—Chuck Allen
Director of Player Personnel—Mike Allman
V.P./Public Relations—Gary Wright
   (Office Phone: 827-9777—Area Code 206)
Head Coach—Chuck Knox (17 years: 155-98-1)
Assistant Coaches:
   Offensive Coordinator/Receivers—John Becker
   Asst. Head Coach/Def. Coord./Linebackers—Tom Catlin
   Defensive Line—George Dyer
   Offensive Backs—Chick Harris
   Quarterbacks—Ken Meyer
   Defensive Backs—Rod Perry
   Tight Ends/Asst. Special Teams—Russ Purnell
   Strength & Conditioning—Frank Raines
   Offensive Line—Kent Stephenson
   Linebackers/Special Teams—Rusty Tillman
   Special Assignments—Joe Vitt
Offices—11220 N.E. 53rd St., Kirkland, Wash. 98033
Stadium—The Kingdome (Capacity: 64,984)
Team Colors—Blue, Green and Silver
Training Site—Seahawks Complex, Kirkland, Wash.

1990 SCHEDULE
(All times local.
All games Sunday unless noted otherwise.)

Sept. 9	at Chicago	12:00
Sept. 16	LOS ANGELES RAIDERS	1:00
Sept. 23	at Denver	2:00
Oct. 1	CINCINNATI (Mon.)	6:00
Oct. 7	at New England	1:00
Oct. 14	at Los Angeles Raiders	1:00
Oct. 21	KANSAS CITY	1:00
Oct. 28	OPEN DATE	
Nov. 4	SAN DIEGO	1:00
Nov. 11	at Kansas City	12:00
Nov. 18	MINNESOTA	1:00
Nov. 25	at San Diego	5:00
Dec. 2	HOUSTON	1:00
Dec. 9	Green Bay at Milwaukee	12:00
Dec. 16	at Miami	1:00
Dec. 23	DENVER	5:00
Dec. 30	DETROIT	1:00

1989 RESULTS—(Won 7, Lost 9)

Seahawks		Opp.		Att.
7	Philadelphia	31	(A)	64,287
24	Phoenix	34	(H)	60,444
24	New England	3	(A)	48,025
24	Los Angeles Raiders	20	(A)	44,319
16	Kansas City	20	(H)	60,715
17	San Diego	16	(A)	50,079
21	Denver (OT)	24	(H)	62,353
10	San Diego	7	(H)	59,691
10	Kansas City	20	(A)	54,488
7	Cleveland	17	(H)	58,978
3	New York Giants	15	(A)	75,014
14	Denver	41	(A)	75,117
17	Buffalo	16	(H)	57,682
24	Cincinnati	17	(A)	54,744
23	Los Angeles Raiders	17	(H)	61,076
0	Washington	29	(H)	60,294

1989 GAMES STARTED

16 games: Edwin Bailey, Grant Feasel, Nesby Glasgow, Bryan Millard, Joe Nash, Mike Wilson, Dave Wyman.

15 games: Jeff Bryant, Curt Warner, John L. Williams.

14 games: Brian Blades, Jacob Green, Patrick Hunter, Dave Krieg, Eugene Robinson.

13 games: Darren Comeaux, Dwayne Harper.

12 games: Tony Woods.

9 games: Andy Heck, Steve Largent, Robert Tyler.

8 games: M.L. Johnson, Ron Mattes.

7 games: Vernon Maxwell.

6 games: Louis Clark, Travis McNeal.

3 games: Donnie Dee, Melvin Jenkins, Alonzo Mitz, Paul Moyer, Rufus Porter.

2 games: Brian Bosworth, Kelly Stouffer.

1 game: Derrick Fenner, Jethro Franklin, Roy Hart, James Jefferson, Johnnie Johnson, Paul Skansi.

SEATTLE SEAHAWKS 1990 VETERAN ROSTER

No.	Name	Pos.	Ht.	Wt.	NFL Exp.	Birth-date	College	Games in '89	How Acquired
50	Ahrens, Dave	LB	6-4	245	10	12- 5-58	Wisconsin	*11	UFA, '90
	Alvord, Steve	DT	6-4	272	3	10- 2-64	Washington	*0	FA, '90
65	Bailey, Edwin	G	6-4	273	10	5-15-59	South Carolina State	16	D5, '81
	Bellini, Mark	WR	5-11	185	3	1-19-64	Brigham Young	*0	FA, '90
89	Blades, Brian	WR	5-11	184	3	7-24-65	Miami (Fla.)	16	D2, '88
55	Bosworth, Brian	LB	6-2	236	3	3- 9-65	Oklahoma	2	SupD, '87
8	Bouyer, Willie	WR	6-3	200	2	9-24-66	Michigan State	1	FA, '90
64	Brilz, Darrick	G	6-3	270	4	2-14-64	Oregon State	14	FA, '89
77	†Bryant, Jeff	DE	6-5	277	9	5-22-60	Clemson	15	D1, '82
59	Cain, Joe	LB	6-1	228	2	6-11-65	Oregon Tech	9	FA, '89
88	Chadwick, Jeff	WR	6-3	190	8	12-16-60	Grand Valley State	11	FA, '89
84	Clark, Louis	WR	6-0	199	4	7- 3-64	Mississippi State	16	D10, '87
53	†Comeaux, Darren	LB	6-1	239	9	4-15-60	Arizona State	16	W-SF, '88
3	Donnelly, Rick	P	6-0	190	5	2-17-62	Wyoming	*0	UFA, '90
31	Edmonds, Bobby Joe	RB	5-11	186	5	9-26-64	Arkansas	*7	UFA, '90
54	Feasel, Grant	C	6-7	279	6	6-28-60	Abilene Christian	16	FA, '87
44	Fenner, Derrick	RB	6-3	229	2	4- 6-67	North Carolina	5	D10, '89
90	Franklin, Jethro	DE	6-1	258	2	10-25-65	Fresno State	7	FA, '89
	Garcia, Teddy	K	5-10	187	3	6- 4-64	Northeast Louisiana	*3	FA, '90
22	†Glasgow, Nesby	S	5-10	187	12	4-15-57	Washington	16	FA, '88
79	Green, Jacob	DE	6-3	254	11	1-21-57	Texas A&M	15	D1, '80
29	†Harper, Dwayne	CB	5-11	174	3	3-29-66	South Carolina State	16	D11a, '88
33	Harris, Elroy	RB	5-9	218	2	8-18-66	Eastern Kentucky	14	D3, '89
63	Hart, Roy	NT	6-1	279	2	7-10-65	South Carolina	16	D6, '88
66	Heck, Andy	T	6-6	291	2	1- 1-67	Notre Dame	16	D1, '89
85	Heller, Ron	TE	6-3	236	4	9-18-63	Oregon State	*15	UFA, '90
23	†Hunter, Patrick	CB	5-11	186	5	10-24-64	Nevada-Reno	16	D3, '86
26	Jefferson, James	CB	6-1	199	2	11-18-63	Texas A&I	16	FA, '89
24	Jenkins, Melvin	CB	5-10	182	4	3-16-62	Cincinnati	16	FA, '87
9	Johnson, Norm	K	6-2	197	9	5-31-60	UCLA	16	OFA, '82
30	Jones, James	RB	6-2	229	8	3-21-61	Florida	2	T-Det, '89
81	Kane, Tommy	WR	5-11	176	3	1-14-64	Syracuse	5	D3, '88
	Kaumeyer, Thom	S	5-11	187	1	3-17-67	Oregon	1	FA, '89
15	†Kemp, Jeff	QB	6-0	201	10	7-11-59	Dartmouth	9	T-SF, '87
58	Kimmel, Jamie	LB	6-3	235	3	3-28-62	Syracuse	*0	FA, '90
17	†Krieg, Dave	QB	6-1	192	11	10-20-58	Milton	15	OFA, '80
70	Mattes, Ron	T	6-6	302	5	8- 8-63	Virginia	16	D7, '85
40	McLemore, Chris	RB	6-1	230	3	12-31-63	Arizona	*0	FA, '90
86	McNeal, Travis	TE	6-3	248	2	1-10-67	UT-Chattanooga	16	D4, '89
71	Millard, Bryan	G	6-5	281	7	12- 2-60	Texas	16	FA, '84
91	Miller, Darrin	LB	6-1	236	3	3-24-65	Tennessee	16	FA, '88
72	Nash, Joe	NT	6-2	269	9	10-11-60	Boston College	16	OFA, '82
97	Porter, Rufus	LB	6-1	221	3	5-18-65	Southern University	16	OFA, '88
98	Ridgle, Elston	DE	6-5	270	2	8-24-63	Nevada-Reno	2	FA, '89
41	Robinson, Eugene	S	6-0	186	6	5-28-63	Colgate	16	OFA, '85
5	†Rodriguez, Ruben	P	6-2	217	4	3- 3-65	Arizona	16	D5a, '87
	Sandusky, Jim	WR	5-10	182	1	9- 1-61	San Diego State	*0	FA, '89
82	Skansi, Paul	WR	5-11	186	8	1-11-61	Washington	16	FA, '85
11	Stouffer, Kelly	QB	6-3	207	3	7- 6-64	Colorado State	3	T-Phx, '88
56	Tofflemire, Joe	C	6-2	274	2	7- 7-65	Arizona	*0	D2, '89
87	Tyler, Robert	TE	6-5	257	2	10-12-65	South Carolina State	9	D8, '88
	Wheat, Warren	G	6-6	274	1	5-13-67	Brigham Young	2	W-Ram, '89
	Williams, Dokie	WR	5-11	180	6	8-25-60	UCLA	*0	FA, '90
32	Williams, John L.	RB	5-11	228	5	11-23-64	Florida	15	D1, '86
57	Woods, Tony	LB	6-4	259	4	9-11-65	Pittsburgh	16	D1, '87
92	†Wyman, David	LB	6-2	242	4	3-31-64	Stanford	16	D2, '87

*Ahrens played 11 games with Dolphins in '89; Alvord last active with Cardinals in '88; Bellini last active with Colts in '88; Donnelly missed '89 season due to injury with Falcons; Edmonds played 7 games with Raiders in '89; Garcia played 3 games with Vikings in '89; Heller played 15 games with Falcons in '89; Kimmel last active with Raiders in '87; McLemore last active with Raiders in '88; Sandusky missed '89 season due to injury; Tofflemire active for 16 games with Seahawks in '89, but did not play; D. Williams last active with Raiders in '87.

†Unsigned; subject to developments.

Retired—Steve Largent, 14-year wide receiver, 10 games in '89; Mike Wilson, 12-year offensive tackle, 16 games in '89.

Players lost through Plan B free agency: TE Donnie Dee (3 games in '89; to G.B.); RB Kevin

Harmon (4; to K.C.); LB M.L. Johnson (13; to G.B.); TE Rod Jones (4; to K.C.); TE Harper LeBel (16; to Phi.); LB Rod Stephens (10; to Den.); RB Curt Warner (16; to L.A. Rams).

Also played with Seahawks in '89—S David Hollis (10 games); S Johnnie Johnson (3); LB Vernon Maxwell (9); S Paul Moyer (11).

D—Draft; T—Trade; W—Waivers; FA—Free Agent; OFA—Original Free Agent; UFA—Unrestricted Free Agent; SupD—Supplemental Draft.

SEATTLE SEAHAWKS
1990 DRAFT CHOICES

(Number following name designates order of selection among 331 players drafted.)

Round and Player		Position	College
1. KENNEDY, Cortez from New England (a)	3	DT	Miami (Fla.)
1. Choice to New England (a)			
2. WOODEN, Terry from New England (a)	29	LB	Syracuse
2. BLACKMON, Robert	34	DB	Baylor
3. Choice to Dallas through New England (b)			
4. WARREN, Chris	89	RB	Ferrum (Va.)
5. HAYES, Eric	119	DT	Florida State
6. BOLCAR, Ned	146	LB	Notre Dame
7. KULA, Bob	175	T	Michigan State
8. HITCHCOCK, Bill	202	T	Purdue
9. Choice to L.A. Raiders through Dallas (c)			
10. MORRIS, Robert	257	DE	Valdosta State
11. REED, Daryl	286	DB	Oregon
12. GROMOS, John	312	QB	Vanderbilt

(a) Acquired 1st- and 2nd-round picks for two 1st-round picks, 3rd-round pick and 4th-round pick in 1991, April 22, 1990.

(b) Seahawks traded pick to Patriots: see (a); Patriots traded pick and 6th- and 8th-round picks to Cowboys for 3rd-, 5th- and 7th-round picks, April 22, 1990.

(c) Seahawks traded pick to Cowboys for tackle Daryle Smith, July 24, 1989; Cowboys traded pick and 6th-, 8th-, 10th- and 11th-round picks to Raiders for rights to cornerback Stan Smagala, April 22, 1990.

SEATTLE SEAHAWKS
1990 ROOKIE AND FIRST-YEAR ROSTER

Name	Pos.	Hgt.	Wgt.	Birth-date	College	How Acquired
Andrews, Ricky	LB	6-2	236	4-14-66	Washington	*FA
Baumann, Charlie	K	6-1	203	8-25-67	West Virginia	*FA
Bednarz, Blake	G	6-3	303	9-17-68	Syracuse	FA
Blackmon, Robert	S	6-0	198	5-12-67	Baylor	D2a
Blaylock, Lavent	CB	5-10	180	7-28-66	Indiana State	FA
Bolcar, Ned	LB	6-1	235	1-12-67	Notre Dame	D6
Brown, Jerry	G	6-4	277	10- 8-65	Utah State	*FA
Dodge, Dedrick	S	6-2	180	6-14-67	Florida State	FA
Fletcher, Dewayne	CB	6-2	191	9- 2-67	Toledo	FA
Garcia, Bobby	G	6-3	253	5- 3-67	Miami (Fla.)	FA
Gray, Randy	NT	6-6	270	4- 3-67	Washington State	FA
Gromos, John	QB	6-5	210	12- 9-66	Vanderbilt	D12
Hayes, Eric	NT	6-3	285	1-12-67	Florida State	D5
Hitchcock, Bill	T	6-8	308	8-26-65	Purdue	D8
Horton, Derek	CB	5-11	184	11- 8-67	Oregon	FA
Hunter, Art	DB	..	..	....	Central State (O.)	FA
Jordan, Xavier	LB	6-1	236	8-18-67	Western Kentucky	FA
Kennedy, Cortez	NT	6-3	293	8-23-68	Miami (Fla.)	D1
Kors, R.J.	S	6-0	195	6-27-66	Long Beach State	*FA
Kula, Bob	T	6-3	282	8-24-67	Michigan State	D7
Lee, Alvin	WR	5-10	188	12- 6-67	Louisiana State	FA
Lindsay, Mike	T	6-7	290	10-20-66	Gardner-Webb	FA
Loville, Derek	RB	5-10	198	7- 4-68	Oregon	FA
McJulian, Paul	P	5-10	190	2-24-65	Jackson State	*FA
Miller, Donald	LB	6-2	223	4- 9-64	Idaho State	FA
Morris, Robert	DE	6-6	265	5-12-68	Valdosta State	D10
Murphy, Dave	S	6-0	190	2-16-68	Holy Cross	FA
Obee, Terry	WR	5-10	182	6-15-68	Oregon	FA
Oberdorf, Todd	T	6-6	290	1-21-67	Indiana	FA
Olson, Rodd	TE	6-4	224	11-27-66	Washington State	FA
Parquet, Felton	RB	6-0	228	11-12-66	Louisiana State	FA
Reed, Daryl	CB	6-1	186	10-27-67	Oregon	D11
Tanks, Michael	C	6-1	254	8- 4-67	Florida State	FA
Walker, Willie	LB	6-1	243	4- 8-67	North Carolina	FA
Warren, Chris	RB	6-2	225	1-24-67	Ferrum (Va.)	D4
Wooden, Terry	LB	6-3	232	1-14-67	Syracuse	D2

*Andrews: D10 San Diego '89, released 9/5, DEV San Diego 9/7, released 11/8; Baumann: FA Buffalo '89, released 8/30, DEV Minnesota 9/6, released 9/12; Brown: FA Miami '89, released 8/24; Kors: D12 Seattle '89, released 8/30; McJulian: FA San Diego '88, released 8/2.

TAMPA BAY BUCCANEERS
(Central Division, National Conference)

Ray Perkins

Owner/President—Hugh F. Culverhouse
Vice President/Head Coach—Ray Perkins (7 years: 37-67)
Vice-President—Joy Culverhouse
Assistant to the President—Phil Krueger
Director of Player Personnel—Jerry Angelo
Assistant Coaches:
    Offensive Line—John Bobo
    Defensive Line—Tommy Brasher
    Def. Coord./Secondary—Fred Bruney
    Running Backs—Sylvester Croom
    Defensive Assistant—Jeff Fitzgerald
    Strength & Conditioning—Kent Johnston
    Linebackers—Joe Kines
    Special Teams—Rodney Stokes
    Receivers—Richard Williamson
Director of Public Relations—Rick Odioso
    (Office Phone: 870-2700—Area Code 813)
Offices—One Buccaneer Place, Tampa, Fla. 33607
Stadium—Tampa Stadium (Capacity: 74,296)
Team Colors—Florida Orange, White and Red
Training Site—University of Tampa, Tampa, Fla.

1990 SCHEDULE
(All times local.)
All games Sunday unless noted otherwise.

Sept. 9	at Detroit	1:00
Sept. 16	LOS ANGELES RAMS	1:00
Sept. 23	DETROIT	8:00
Sept. 30	at Minnesota	12:00
Oct. 7	at Dallas	12:00
Oct. 14	GREEN BAY	1:00
Oct. 21	DALLAS	1:00
Oct. 28	at San Diego	1:00
Nov. 4	CHICAGO	4:00
Nov. 11	at New Orleans	12:00
Nov. 18	at San Francisco	1:00
Nov. 25	Green Bay at Milwaukee	12:00
Dec. 2	ATLANTA	1:00
Dec. 9	OPEN DATE	
Dec. 16	MINNESOTA	1:00
Dec. 23	at Chicago	12:00
Dec. 30	NEW YORK JETS	4:00

1989 RESULTS—(Won 5, Lost 11)

Buccaneers		Opp.		Att.
23	Green Bay	21	(A)	55,650
16	San Francisco	20	(H)	64,087
20	New Orleans	10	(H)	44,053
3	Minnesota	17	(A)	54,817
42	Chicago	35	(H)	72,077
16	Detroit	17	(H)	46,225
28	Washington	32	(A)	52,862
23	Cincinnati	56	(A)	57,225
31	Cleveland	42	(H)	69,162
10	Minnesota	24	(H)	56,271
32	Chicago	31	(A)	63,826
14	Phoenix	13	(A)	33,297
16	Green Bay	17	(A)	58,120
17	Houston	20	(A)	54,532
7	Detroit	33	(A)	40,362
22	Pittsburgh	31	(H)	29,690

1989 GAMES STARTED

16 games: Randy Grimes, Paul Gruber, Bruce Hill, Rod Jones, Eugene Marve, Winston Moss, Kevin Murphy, Ervin Randle, Rob Taylor.

15 games: Mark Carrier, Reuben Davis, Ron Hall, Ricky Reynolds, Mark Robinson.

14 games: Lars Tate, Vinny Testaverde.

13 games: Harry Hamilton.

12 games: Robert Goff, William Howard, Curt Jarvis.

10 games: Tom McHale.

8 games: John Bruhin.

5 games: Mark Cooper, Mike Simmonds.

4 games: Carl Bax, James Wilder.

3 games: John Cannon, Shawn Lee.

2 games: Sherman Cocroft, Joe Ferguson, Odie Harris, William Harris, Rhondy Weston.

1 game: Bobby Futrell, Danny Peebles, Sean Smith, Sylvester Stamps.

TAMPA BAY BUCCANEERS 1990 VETERAN ROSTER

No.	Name	Pos.	Ht.	Wt.	NFL Exp.	Birth-date	College	Games in '89	How Acquired
	Anderson, Gary	RB	6-0	181	5	4-18-61	Arkansas	*0	T-SD, '90
56	Anno, Sam	LB	6-2	235	4	1-26-65	Southern California	16	UFA, '89
	Bailey, Eric	TE	6-5	245	2	5-12-63	Kansas State	*0	FA, '90
75	Bax, Carl	G	6-4	290	2	1- 5-66	Missouri	6	D8, '89
55	Bob, Adam	LB	6-3	255	2	10-30-67	Texas A&M	*5	UFA, '90
69	Bruhln, John	G	6-3	285	3	12- 9-64	Tennessee	9	D4a, '88
78	Cannon, John	DE	6-5	265	9	7-30-60	William & Mary	16	D3a, '82
88	†Carrier, Mark	WR	6-0	185	4	10-28-65	Nicholls State	16	D3, '87
53	Coleman, Sidney	LB	6-2	250	3	1-14-64	Southern Mississippi	4	FA, '88
23	Cooper, Evan	CB/S	5-11	195	7	6-28-62	Michigan	*16	UFA, '90
71	Cooper, Mark	T	6-5	280	8	2-14-60	Miami (Fla.)	6	FA, '87
79	†Davis, Reuben	DE	6-4	285	3	5- 7-65	North Carolina	16	D9, '88
76	Dill, Scott	T	6-5	285	3	4- 5-66	Memphis State	*16	UFA, '90
87	Drewrey, Willie	WR	5-7	170	6	4-28-63	West Virginia	16	UFA, '89
42	Everett, Eric	CB/S	5-10	170	3	7-13-66	Texas Tech	*16	UFA, '90
36	†Futrell, Bobby	CB/S	5-11	190	5	8- 4-62	Elizabeth City State	16	FA, '86
94	Goff, Robert	DE	6-3	270	3	10- 2-65	Auburn	12	D4, '88
65	Graham, Dan	C	6-2	270	2	5-10-65	Northern Illinois	*0	FA, '88
60	Grimes, Randy	C	6-4	275	8	7-20-60	Baylor	16	D2, '83
74	Gruber, Paul	T	6-5	290	3	2-24-65	Wisconsin	16	D1, '88
45	Haddix, Wayne	RB	6-1	205	3	7-23-65	Liberty (Va.)	*0	FA, '90
82	Hall, Ron	TE	6-4	245	4	3-15-64	Hawaii	16	D4a, '87
39	Hamilton, Harry	CB/S	6-0	195	7	11-29-62	Penn State	13	FA, '88
20	Harris, Odie	CB/S	6-0	190	3	4- 1-66	Sam Houston State	16	FA, '88
84	†Hill, Bruce	WR	6-0	180	4	2-29-64	Arizona State	16	D4b, '87
43	Howard, William	RB	6-0	240	3	6- 2-64	Tennessee	16	D5, '88
1	Igwebuike, Donald	K	5-9	190	6	12-27-60	Clemson	16	D10, '85
95	Jarvis, Curt	NT	6-2	270	3	1-28-65	Alabama	14	D7, '87
22	†Jones, Rod	CB/S	6-0	185	5	3-31-64	Southern Methodist	16	D1a, '86
38	Lawson, Jamie	RB	5-10	240	2	10- 2-65	Nicholls State	5	D5, '89
97	†Lee, Shawn	NT	6-2	285	3	10-24-66	North Alabama	15	D6, '88
99	†Marve, Eugene	LB	6-2	240	9	8-14-60	Saginaw Valley State	16	T-Buf, '88
73	McHale, Tom	G	6-4	280	4	2-25-63	Cornell	15	OFA, '87
41	Mitchell, Alvin	RB	6-0	235	2	8-20-64	Auburn	5	OFA, '89
5	Mohr, Chris	P	6-4	220	2	5-11-66	Alabama	16	D6, '89
58	†Moss, Winston	LB	6-3	235	4	12-24-65	Miami (Fla.)	16	D2a, '87
59	†Murphy, Kevin	LB	6-2	235	5	9- 8-63	Oklahoma	16	D2a, '86
57	†Najarian, Pete	LB	6-2	235	3	12-22-63	Minnesota	12	FA, '88
96	Newton, Tim	NT	6-0	275	6	3-23-63	Florida	*9	FA, '90
86	Parks, Jeff	TE	6-4	245	4	9-14-64	Auburn	*0	FA, '88
83	Peebles, Danny	WR	5-11	180	2	4-30-66	North Carolina State	13	D2, '89
80	†Pillow, Frank	WR	5-10	170	3	3-11-65	Tennessee State	3	D11, '88
54	Randle, Ervin	LB	6-1	250	6	10-12-62	Baylor	16	D3, '85
29	†Reynolds, Ricky	CB/S	5-11	190	4	1-19-65	Washington State	16	D2, '87
31	Rice, Rodney	CB/S	5-8	180	2	6-18-66	Brigham Young	*10	UFA, '90
30	Robinson, Mark	CB/S	5-11	200	7	9-13-62	Penn State	15	T-KC, '88
	Royals, Mark	P	6-5	213	1	6-22-63	Appalachian State	*0	FA, '90
	Seals, Ray	DE	6-3	245	1	6-17-65	None	2	FA, '88
24	Stamps, Sylvester	RB	5-7	80	6	2-24-61	Jackson State	10	UFA, '89
70	†Swayne, Harry	T	6-5	270	4	2- 2-65	Rutgers	16	D7a, '87
34	Tate, Lars	RB	6-2	215	3	2- 2-66	Georgia	15	D2, '88
72	†Taylor, Rob	T	6-6	290	5	11-14-60	Northwestern	16	FA, '86
14	Testaverde, Vinny	QB	6-5	215	4	11-13-63	Miami (Fla.)	14	D1, '87
51	Thomas, Broderick	LB	6-4	245	2	2-20-67	Nebraska	16	D1, '89

*Anderson last active with Chargers in '88; Bailey last active with Eagles in '87; Bob played 5 games with Jets in '89; E. Cooper played 16 games with Falcons in '89; Dill played 16 games with Cardinals in '89; Everett played 16 games with Eagles in '89; Graham active for 16 games with Buccaneers in '89, but did not play; Haddix last active with Giants in '88; Newton played 9 games with Vikings in '89; Parks last active with Buccaneers in '88; Rice played 10 games with Patriots in '89; Royals last active with Eagles in '87.

†Unsigned; subject to developments.

Players lost through Plan B free agency: PK John Carney (1 game in '89; to S.D.); S Sherman Cocroft (10; to Det.); S/CB Donnie Elder (16; to Mia.); TE William Harris (16; to G.B.); G Mike Simmonds (5; to S.D.); RB Don Smith (11; to Buff.); DE Rhondy Weston (12; to Clev.); RB James Wilder (15; to Wash.).

Also played with Buccaneers in '89—QB Kerwin Bell (active for 4 games in '89, but did not play); QB Joe Ferguson (5 games); WR Everett Gay (1); DE Sean Smith (3); TE Jackie Walker (14).

D—Draft; T—Trade; FA—Free Agent; OFA—Original Free Agent; UFA—Unrestricted Free Agent.

TAMPA BAY BUCCANEERS
1990 DRAFT CHOICES

(Number following name designates order of selection among 331 players drafted.)

Round and Player		Position	College
1. McCANTS, Keith	4	LB	Alabama
2. COBB, Reggie	30	RB	Tennessee
3. Choice to San Diego (a)			
4. ANDERSON, Jesse	87	TE	Mississippi State
4. MAYBERRY, Tony from Denver (b)	108	C	Wake Forest
5. BECKLES, Ian	114	G	Indiana
6. DOUGLAS, Derrick	141	RB	Louisiana Tech
7. GARDNER, Donnie	171	DE	Kentucky
8. Choice to L.A. Rams (c)			
9. COOK, Terry	224	DE	Fresno State
10. BUSCH, Mike	254	TE	Iowa State
11. ANTHONY, Terry	281	WR	Florida State
12. HAMMEL, Todd	307	QB	Stephen F. Austin

(a) Traded pick and conditional pick in 1991 for running back Gary Anderson, April 21, 1990.

(b) Acquired pick for defensive end Ron Holmes, September 5, 1989.

(c) Traded pick for two 11th-round picks in 1989 and 12th-round pick in 1989, April 24, 1989.

TAMPA BAY BUCCANEERS
1990 ROOKIE AND FIRST-YEAR ROSTER

Name	Pos.	Hgt.	Wgt.	Birth-date	College	How Acquired
Anderson, Jesse	TE	6-2	245	5- 8-67	Mississippi State	D4
Anthony, Terry	WR	6-0	200	3- 9-68	Florida State	D11
Beckles, Ian	G	6-1	295	7-20-67	Indiana	D5
Blackmon, Terry	CB/S	5-9	170	12-21-65	Texas A&I	FA
Busch, Mike	TE	6-4	250	7- 7-68	Iowa State	D10
Carlson, Jeff	QB	6-3	215	5-23-66	Weber State	*FA
Cheattom, Carlo	CB/S	5-11	190	3-18-67	Auburn	*FA
Christie, Steve	K	6-0	185	.....	William & Mary	FA
Citizen, Tony	RB	5-9	210	5-25-66	McNeese State	FA
Cobb, Reggie	RB	6-0	225	7- 7-68	Tennessee	D2
Cook, Terry	DE	6-3	270	4-29-64	Fresno State	D9
DeWitt, Ken	RB	5-9	180	12-20-66	Northwestern (La.) State	FA
Douglas, Derrick	RB	5-10	205	8-10-68	Louisiana Tech	D6
Duncan, Herb	WR	6-0	185	12-18-65	Northern Arizona	*FA
Fleming, Terry	LB	6-1	230	12-10-66	Mississippi College	FA
Ford, Chris	WR	6-1	185	5-20-67	Lamar	FA
Gardner, Donnie	DE	6-4	265	2-17-68	Kentucky	D7
Goods, Bennie	LB	6-3	255	2-20-68	Alcorn State	FA
Greene, A.J.	CB/S	5-9	175	6-24-66	Wake Forest	*FA
Hammel, Todd	QB	6-1	205	12- 7-66	Stephen F. Austin	D12
Harvey, John	RB	5-11	185	12-28-66	Texas-El Paso	*FA
Lucas, Sean	DB	6-2	217	9- 1-67	Virginia Tech	FA
Massaro, Chuck	C	6-2	270	6- 6-66	North Carolina State	*FA, '89
Mayberry, Tony	C	6-4	285	12- 8-67	Wake Forest	D4a
McCants, Keith	LB	6-3	255	11-19-68	Alabama	D1
Oliver, Maurice	LB	6-3	230	6-15-67	Southern Mississippi	*FA
Perkins, Bruce	RB	6-2	230	8-14-67	Arizona State	FA
Roland, Benji	NT	6-4	270	4- 4-67	Auburn	*FA
Royals, Mark	P	6-5	215	6-22-64	Appalachian State	FA
Seals, Ray	NT	6-3	270	6-17-65	None	FA, '88
Smith, David	QB	6-0	185	4-30-65	Alabama	FA
Thomas, Stevie	WR	6-1	195	7-24-67	Bethune-Cookman	FA
Thompson, Shelton	DE	6-3	280	1- 9-67	Florida State	FA
Watts, Carl	G	6-3	260	5-30-67	North Carolina	FA
Wyatt, Willie	DE	6-0	266	9-27-67	Alabama	FA

*Carlson: D4 Los Angeles Rams '89, released 9/5, DEV Rams 9/6, released 1/29/90; Cheattom: D10 Buffalo '89, released 8/30, DEV Buffalo 9/6, released 10/3; Duncan: D11 Tampa Bay '89, released 9/5, DEV Tampa Bay 9/6, released 1/29/90; Greene: D9 New York Giants '89, released 9/5, DEV Giants 9/6, released 1/29/90; Harvey: FA Tampa Bay '89, released 9/5, DEV Tampa Bay 9/6, released 11/22; Massaro: FA Tampa Bay '89, injured reserve 8/28 through entire season; Oliver: FA Tampa Bay '89, released 9/5, DEV Tampa Bay 9/28, released 1/29/90; Roland: D7 Minnesota '89, released 9/5, DEV Atlanta 9/6, released 1/9/90.

WASHINGTON REDSKINS
(Eastern Division, National Conference)

Joe Gibbs

Chairman, Chief Operating Officer—Jack Kent Cooke
Executive Vice President—John Kent Cooke
General Manager—Charley Casserly
Director of Pro Personnel—Kirk Mee
Director of Pro Scouting—Joe Mack
Head Coach—Joe Gibbs (9 years: 91-45)
Assistant Coaches:
   Running Backs—Don Breaux
   Quarterbacks—Jack Burns
   Administrative Asst.—Bobby DePaul
   Offensive Asst./Passing Game—Rod Dowhower
   Offensive Line—Jim Hanifan
   Defensive Coordinator—Larry Peccatiello
   Assistant Head Coach-Defense—Richie Petitbon
   Strength Coach—Dan Riley
   Special Teams—Wayne Sevier
   Tight Ends—Warren Simmons
   Off. Asst./Receivers—Charley Taylor
   Defensive Backs—Emmitt Thomas
   Defensive Line—Torgy Torgeson
   Assistant Strength Coach—Steve Wetzel
Vice President of Communications—Charlie Dayton
   (Office Phone: 471-9100—Area Code 703)
Offices—Redskin Park, 13832 Redskin Drive, Herndon, Va., 22071; Mailing Address: P. O. Box 17247, Dulles International Airport, Washington, D. C. 20041
Stadium—RFK Memorial Stadium (Capacity: 55,750)
Team Colors—Burgundy and Gold
Training Site—Dickinson College, Carlisle, Pa.

1990 SCHEDULE
(All times local. All games Sunday unless noted otherwise.)

Sept. 9	PHOENIX	1:00
Sept. 16	at San Francisco	1:00
Sept. 23	DALLAS	1:00
Sept. 30	at Phoenix	5:00
Oct. 7	OPEN DATE	
Oct. 14	NEW YORK GIANTS	4:00
Oct. 21	PHILADELPHIA	1:00
Oct. 28	at New York Giants	4:00
Nov. 4	at Detroit	1:00
Nov. 12	at Philadelphia (Mon.)	9:00
Nov. 18	NEW ORLEANS	1:00
Nov. 22	at Dallas (Thanksgiving)	3:00
Dec. 2	MIAMI	1:00
Dec. 9	CHICAGO	4:00
Dec. 15	at New England	4:00
Dec. 22	at Indianapolis	8:00
Dec. 30	BUFFALO	1:00

1989 RESULTS—(Won 10, Lost 6)

Redskins		Opp.		Att.
24	New York Giants	27	(H)	54,160
37	Philadelphia	42	(H)	53,493
30	Dallas	7	(A)	63,200
16	New Orleans	14	(A)	64,358
30	Phoenix	28	(H)	53,335
17	New York Giants	20	(A)	76,245
32	Tampa Bay	28	(H)	52,862
24	Los Angeles Raiders	37	(A)	52,781
3	Dallas	13	(H)	53,187
10	Philadelphia	3	(A)	65,443
10	Denver	14	(H)	52,975
38	Chicago	14	(H)	50,044
29	Phoenix	10	(A)	38,870
26	San Diego	21	(H)	47,693
31	Atlanta	30	(A)	37,501
29	Seattle	0	(A)	60,294

1989 GAMES STARTED

16 games: Jeff Bostic, Todd Bowles, Darryl Grant, Charles Mann, Wilber Marshall.
15 games: Don Warren.
14 games: Jim Lachey, Mark Rypien.
13 games: Earnest Byner, Ravin Caldwell.
12 games: Gary Clark, Art Monk, Ricky Sanders, Alvin Walton.
10 games: Joe Jacoby, Dexter Manley, Tracy Rocker.
9 games: Brian Davis, Russ Grimm, Mark May.
8 games: A.J. Johnson, Raleigh McKenzie, Neal Olkewicz, Ed Simmons.
7 games: Darrell Green, Markus Koch, Greg Manusky, Martin Mayhew, Gerald Riggs.
6 games: Mark Schlereth.
5 games: Fred Stokes, Mike Tice.
4 games: Clarence Vaughn.
3 games: Monte Coleman, Jamie Morris.
2 games: Doug Williams.
1 game: Kurt Gouveia, Terry Orr, Barry Wilburn.

WASHINGTON REDSKINS 1990 VETERAN ROSTER

No.	Name	Pos.	Ht.	Wt.	NFL Exp.	Birth-date	College	Games in '89	How Acquired
61	Adickes, Mark	G	6-4	275	5	4-22-61	Baylor	*16	UFA, '90
	Andrews, Romel	DL	6-4	262	R	7- 4-63	Tennessee-Martin	*18	FA, '90
	Bennett, Roy	CB	6-2	195	3	7- 5-61	Jackson State	*16	FA, '90
56	†Bonner, Brian	LB	6-2	225	2	10- 9-65	Minnesota	6	W-SF, '88
53	†Bostic, Jeff	C	6-2	260	11	9-18-58	Clemson	16	FA, '80
23	†Bowles, Todd	S	6-2	203	5	11-18-63	Temple	16	OFA, '86
29	Branch, Reggie	RB	5-11	235	6	10-22-62	East Carolina	10	FA, '86
46	Brandes, John	TE	6-2	250	4	4- 2-64	Cameron	*16	UFA, '90
67	Brown, Ray	T	6-5	280	5	12-12-62	Arkansas State	7	UFA, '89
38	Brown, Tom	RB	6-1	228	2	11-20-64	Pittsburgh	*9	UFA, '90
24	Bryant, Kelvin	RB	6-2	195	4	9-26-60	North Carolina	*0	D7, '83
21	Byner, Earnest	RB	5-10	215	7	9-15-62	East Carolina	16	T-Cle, '89
50	†Caldwell, Ravin	LB	6-3	229	4	8- 4-63	Arkansas	15	D5, '86
84	Clark, Gary	WR	5-9	173	6	5- 1-62	James Madison	15	SupD, '84
51	†Coleman, Monte	LB	6-2	230	12	11- 4-57	Central Arkansas	15	D11, '79
34	Davis, Brian	CB	6-2	190	4	8-31-63	Nebraska	15	D2, '87
26	†Davis, Wayne	CB	5-11	180	6	7-17-63	Indiana State	8	FA, '89
25	†Dupard, Reggie	RB	5-11	205	5	10-30-63	Southern Methodist	*7	FA, '89
27	Edwards, Brad	S	6-2	196	3	3-22-66	South Carolina	*9	UFA, '90
97	Geathers, James	DE	6-7	290	6	6-26-60	Wichita State	*15	UFA, '90
54	Gouveia, Kurt	LB	6-1	227	4	9-14-64	Brigham Young	15	D8, '86
77	†Grant, Darryl	DT	6-1	275	10	11-22-59	Rice	16	D9, '81
28	Green, Darrell	CB	5-8	170	8	2-15-60	Texas A&I	7	D1, '83
68	Grimm, Russ	G	6-3	275	10	5- 2-59	Pittsburgh	12	D3, '81
59	Harbour, Dave	C	6-4	265	3	10-23-65	Illinois	16	OFA, '88
75	Hodge, Milford	DT	6-3	278	5	3-11-61	Washington State	*16	UFA, '90
80	†Howard, Joe	WR	5-8	170	3	12-21-62	Notre Dame	15	FA, '89
16	Humphries, Stan	QB	6-2	223	2	4-14-65	Northwestern (La.) St.	2	D6, '88
66	Jacoby, Joe	T	6-7	310	10	7- 6-59	Louisville	10	OFA, '81
47	Johnson, A.J.	CB	5-8	176	2	6-22-67	Southwest Texas State	16	D6, '89
88	Johnson, Jimmie	TE	6-2	246	2	10- 6-66	Howard	16	D12, '89
74	†Koch, Markus	DE	6-5	275	5	2-13-63	Boise State	10	D2, '86
79	Lachey, Jim	T	6-6	290	6	6- 4-63	Ohio State	14	T-Rai, '88
22	Lockett, Charles	WR	6-0	185	3	10- 1-65	Long Beach State	*0	FA, '90
8	Lohmiller, Chip	K	6-3	213	3	7-16-66	Minnesota	16	D2, '88
71	Mann, Charles	DE	6-6	270	8	4-12-61	Nevada-Reno	16	D3, '83
91	†Manusky, Greg	LB	6-1	242	3	8-12-66	Colgate	16	OFA, '88
58	Marshall, Wilber	LB	6-1	230	7	4-18-62	Florida	16	VFA, '88
73	May, Mark	G/T	6-6	295	10	11-2-59	Pittsburgh	9	D1, '81
35	Mayhew, Martin	CB	5-8	172	2	10-8-65	Florida State	16	UFA, '89
57	McArthur, Kevin	LB	6-2	250	5	5-11-63	Lamar	*9	UFA, '90
63	McKenzie, Raleigh	C/G	6-2	270	6	2-8-63	Tennessee	15	D11, '85
48	Middleton, Ron	TE	6-2	255	5	7-17-65	Auburn	*9	UFA, '90
62	Mitz, Alonzo	DE	6-3	275	5	6-5-63	Florida	*12	FA, '90
2	Mojsiejenko, Ralf	P	6-2	212	6	1-28-63	Michigan State	16	T-Was, '89
81	Monk, Art	WR	6-3	209	11	12- 5-57	Syracuse	16	D1, '80
87	Orr, Terry	TE	6-3	227	5	9-27-61	Texas	16	D10, '85
35	Profit, Eugene	CB	5-10	175	3	11-11-64	Yale	*0	UFA, '89
37	†Riggs, Gerald	RB	6-1	232	9	11-6-60	Arizona State	12	T-Atl, '89
99	Rocker, Tracy	DT	6-3	288	2	4-9-66	Auburn	16	D3, '89
10	Rutledge, Jeff	QB	6-1	195	12	1-22-57	Alabama	*1	UFA, '90
11	Rypien, Mark	QB	6-4	234	4	10-2-62	Washington State	14	D6, '86
83	Sanders, Ricky	WR	5-11	180	5	8-30-62	Southwest Texas State	16	T-NE, '86
69	Schlereth, Mark	G	6-3	285	2	1-25-66	Idaho	6	D10, '89
76	Simmons, Ed	T	6-5	300	4	12-31-63	Eastern Washington	16	D6a, '87
89	Stanley, Walter	WR	5-9	180	6	11- 5-62	Mesa (Colo.)	*14	UFA, '89
60	Stokes, Fred	DE	6-3	262	4	3-14-64	Georgia Southern	16	UFA, '89
64	Swoopes, Pat	DT	6-3	280	3	3-4-64	Mississippi State	*15	UFA, '90
86	Tice, Mike	TE	6-7	247	10	2-2-59	Maryland	16	UFA, '89
31	Vaughn, Clarence	S	6-0	202	4	7-17-64	Northern Illinois	16	D8, '87
40	Walton, Alvin	S	8-0	180	5	3-14-64	Kansas	13	D3, '86
85	†Warren, Don	TE	6-4	242	12	5-5-56	San Diego State	15	D4, '79
82	Whisenhunt, Ken	TE	6-3	240	5	2-28-62	Georgia Tech	*0	UFA, '89
32	Wilder, James	RB	6-3	225	10	5-12-58	Missouri	*15	UFA, '90
	Wolfolk, Kevin	LB	6-1	225	R	2- 6-67	Portland State	*3	FA, '90

*Adickes played 16 games with Chiefs in '89; Andrews played 18 games with Winnipeg-CFL in '89; Bennett played 16 games with Chargers in '89; Brandes played 16 games with Colts in '89; T. Brown played 9 games with Dolphins in '89; Bryant, Profit and Whisenhunt missed '89 season due to injury;

Dupard played 7 games with Patriots, 7 with Redskins in '89; Edwards played 9 games with Vikings in '89; Geathers played 15 games with Saints in '89; Hodge played 16 games with Patriots in '89; Lockett last active with Steelers in '88; McArthur played 9 games with Jets in '89; Middleton played 9 games with Browns in '89; Mitz played 12 games with Seahawks in '89; Rutledge played 1 game with Giants in '89; Stanley played 14 games with Lions in '89; Swoopes played 15 games with Saints in '89; Wilder played 15 games with Buccaneers in '89; Wolfolk played 3 games with Toronto-CFL in '89.

†Unsigned; subject to developments.

Players lost through Plan B free agency: WR Carl Harry (1 game in '89; to Hou.); RB Joe Mickles (9; to S.D.); RB Jamie Morris (12; to N.E.); DE Lybrant Robinson (5; to Dall.); G Ralph Tamm (0; to Cle.); S Herb Welch (9; to Det.).

Retired—Neal Olkewicz, 11-year linebacker, 9 games in '89.

Also played with Redskins in '89—LB Don Graham (1 game); S Chris Mandeville (1); DE Dexter Manley (10); RB Willard Reaves (1); DT Mike Stensrud (8); CB Barry Wilburn (8); QB Doug Williams (4).

D—Draft; T—Trade; W—Waivers; FA—Free Agent; OFA—Original Free Agent; UFA—Unrestricted Free Agent; VFA—Veteran Free Agent; SupD—Supplemental Draft.

WASHINGTON REDSKINS
1990 DRAFT CHOICES

(Number following name designates order of selection among 331 players drafted.)

Round and Player		Position	College
1. Choice to Atlanta (a)			
2. COLLINS, Andre	46	LB	Penn State
3. ELEWONIBI, Mohammed	76	G	Brigham Young
4. CONKLIN, Cary from New England (b)	86	QB	Washington
4. Choice to Indianapolis (c)			
4. LABBE, Rico from San Francisco through L.A. Raiders (d)	109	DB	Boston College
5. MITCHELL, Brian	130	RB	S.W. Louisiana
6. WELLS, Kent	160	DT	Nebraska
7. Choice to San Diego (e)			
8. Choice to Indianapolis (c)			
9. MOXLEY, Tim	243	G	Ohio State
10. FRANCISCO, D'Juan from Miami (f)	262	DB	Notre Dame
10. RAYAM, Thomas	270	DT	Alabama
11. LEVERENZ, Jon	297	LB	Minnesota
12. Choice to San Diego (g)			

(a) Traded pick and 2nd-round pick in 1989 for running back Gerald Riggs and 5th-round pick in 1990, April 23, 1989.

(b) Acquired pick for two 5th-round picks, April 22, 1990.

(c) Traded picks for 5th-round pick in 1989, April 23, 1989.

(d) Redskins acquired pick and 5th-round pick from Raiders as part of deal of September 8, 1988, in which Redskins acquired tackle Jim Lachey and 2nd-, 4th- and 5th-round picks in 1989 for quarterback Jay Schroeder and 2nd-round pick in 1989; Raiders got into position for pick by trading 4th-round pick to 49ers for 4th- and 5th-round picks, April 20, 1990.

(e) Traded pick for punter Ralf Mojsiejenko, August 29, 1989.

(f) Acquired pick and 4th-round pick in 1991 for 5th-round pick, April 22, 1990.

(g) Traded pick for 12th-round pick in 1989, April 24, 1989.

WASHINGTON REDSKINS
1990 ROOKIE AND FIRST-YEAR ROSTER

Name	Pos.	Hgt.	Wgt.	Birth-date	College	How Acquired
Adams, Tim	DL	6-4	280	3-16-66	Brigham Young	FA
Cherry, Marcus	WR	5-9	183	2-14-67	Boston College	FA
Collins, Andre	LB	6-1	230	5- 4-68	Penn State	D2
Conklin, Cary	QB	6-4	215	2-29-68	Washington	D4
Crossman, Dan	DB	6-0	198	1-17-67	Pittsburgh	FA
Dunn, Chris	LB	6-3	235	2- 1-66	Cal Poly-SLO	*FA
Durden, John	T	6-6	294	8- 2-67	Florida	FA
Elewonibi, Mohammed	G	6-4	282	12-16-65	Brigham Young	D3
Fagan, Jay	G	6-3	280	4-15-67	Montana	FA
Forsythe, Byron	C	6-3	270	12-27-66	Houston	FA
Francisco, D'Juan	CB	5-10	185	2- 5-67	Notre Dame	D10
Glaser, Doug	T	6-6	295	5-24-68	Nebraska	FA
Hobbs, Steve	WR	5-11	195	11-14-65	North Alabama	*UFA, '89
Labbe, Rico	S	6-0	210	6-16-67	Boston College	D4a
Leverenz, Jon	LB	6-2	230	8-29-67	Minnesota	D11
Mays, Alvoid	CB	5-9	170	7-10-66	West Virginia	*FA
Mitchell, Brian	RB	5-10	195	8-18-68	Southwestern Louisiana	D5
Moxley, Tim	G	6-7	320	3- 6-67	Ohio State	D9
Rayam, Thomas	DE	6-6	285	1- 3-68	Alabama	D10a
Ritchie, Derrick	CB	5-10	180	3-16-67	Texas A&M	FA
Searcy, George	RB	5-11	210	11-22-68	East Tennessee State	FA
Smith, Paul	WR	5-8	185	5-21-67	Houston	FA
Vladic, Larry	DB	6-0	192	6-28-68	Oregon State	FA
Waddle, Percy	WR	6-0	180	9-13-67	Texas A&M	FA
Wells, Kent	DT	6-4	295	7-25-67	Nebraska	D6

*Dunn: D9 Atlanta '89, released 8/29; Hobbs: FA Kansas City '88, injured reserve (knee) 8/22 through entire season, unprotected free agent 2/1/89, UFA Washington 3/7, injured reserve 9/6 through entire season; Mays: D8 Houston '89, released 8/30.

Historic Changes Mark 1989

By VITO STELLINO

The San Francisco 49ers' continued dominance of the National Football League provided a stark contrast to a 1989 season marked by a pair of historic changes.

While the 49ers were storming to their fourth Super Bowl championship in the last nine years, NFL owners were searching for a replacement for Commissioner Pete Rozelle, who had announced at the league meetings in March 1989 that he was ready to retire. Rozelle had served as the league's chief executive since 1960, when the owners arrived on the "Boy Commissioner" as a compromise choice.

Perhaps even more notable was the Los Angeles Raiders' hiring of Art Shell as head coach on October 3. For the first time in more than six decades, the NFL had a black head coach.

And for the first time in one decade, the NFL had a repeat Super Bowl winner. The 49ers charged through the regular season with only two losses, then won their two National Football Conference playoff games by a combined score of 71-16 and destroyed the Denver Broncos, 55-10, in Super Bowl XXIV in New Orleans. The 49ers thus became the first team since the 1978-79 Pittsburgh Steelers to win back-to-back Super Bowls and the second (after Pittsburgh) to win four overall. They were the undisputed team of the '80s.

The star of the show again was quarterback Joe Montana, who directed the 49ers to all four Super Bowl titles and was named the game's Most Valuable Player for the third time. Montana, who was the league's top-ranked passer in the regular season, also virtually rewrote the Super Bowl record book while throwing five touchdown passes against the Broncos. He has completed more passes (83) for more yards (1,142) and more touchdowns (11) than any quarterback in Super Bowl history.

"You can talk about Gordie Howe," said veteran linebacker Matt Millen, who joined the 49ers in 1989. "You can talk about (Wayne) Gretzky. You can talk about (Joe) DiMaggio, (Babe) Ruth. You can talk about (John) Havlicek, Wilt Chamberlain. You can talk about anybody from the National Football League. In my short time, 32 years, I've never seen anyone who can dominate not only each game, but the season (like Montana). It was the greatest season I've ever seen anybody play. It was unbelievable."

The 49ers managed to stay on top despite changing coaches after their Super Bowl XXIII championship. When Bill Walsh moved from the sidelines to the TV booth and was replaced as head coach by former assistant George Seifert, the team didn't miss a beat. There even was some speculation that Walsh's resignation

Jerry Rice (above) and John Taylor are two reasons why the 49ers are pro football's best team.

Newly named NFL Commissioner Paul Tagliabue (left) and outgoing boss Pete Rozelle share the spotlight following the announcement of Tagliabue's election October 26 in Cleveland.

inspired the 49ers to show they could win without him. John McVay assumed Walsh's player personnel responsibilities and was named The Sporting News' NFL Executive of the Year.

The presentation of the Vince Lombardi Trophy in the 49ers' joyful locker room has come to be a familiar sight for football fans, but the presenter at the 1990 ceremony was not so familiar. It was Paul Tagliabue, who had been elected as Rozelle's successor just three months earlier after a bitter fight among the 28 club owners.

Tagliabue beat out New Orleans Saints General Manager Jim Finks, who had originally been recommended for the job by a selection committee. Finks needed votes from 19 owners to be elected commissioner, but he fell three short in a July 6 meeting in Chicago when a group of 11 owners—promptly dubbed the new guard—banded together to block his election.

The issue wasn't really Finks himself, but the feeling among the league's newer owners that they had been left out of the selection process. After a second selection committee was named, the new-guard owners supported Tagliabue, an attorney who had worked on the league account for 20 years with the firm of Covington and Burling in Washington, D.C. Thus began a power struggle between two fac-

tions of owners that had little to do with the respective merits of the two candidates.

The owners met again on October 10 and 11 in Dallas, but their vote was split down the middle. A frustrated Rozelle then appointed a five-man committee to recommend a candidate who could win the election. The committee was chaired by Pittsburgh's Dan Rooney, a former Finks supporter who had switched to Tagliabue; two members of the old guard (Wellington Mara of the New York Giants and Cleveland's Art Modell), and two from the new guard (Minnesota's Mike Lynn and Denver's Pat Bowlen). Rooney persuaded Modell and Mara to support Tagliabue—the alternative was starting over with a new search committee and going outside the league for a commissioner—and the committee unanimously recommended Tagliabue, paving the way for his October 26 election in Cleveland.

Finks, who never sought the job in the first place, accepted his defeat without bitterness. "They've picked a hell of a guy who's going to be a fine commissioner and make a contribution to this league for 20 years," he said.

Tagliabue, who turned 49 a month after his election, said he would have no problems working with all factions within the league. "I feel I have a very good relationship with all 28

Tale of two rookies: Detroit's Barry Sanders (above) and Dallas' Troy Aikman both spent most of the 1989 season on the run.

clubs," he said.

Tagliabue got off to a good start when he helped negotiate a four-year, $3.64 billion television contract that boosted the annual TV revenue for each team from $17 million to an average of $32 million. As a concession to the various TV networks, however, the league's schedule and playoff format were substantially altered.

In 1990 and 1991, each team will play 16 games over 17 weeks, with one bye. That gives the networks an extra week to televise regular-season games. Then in 1992 and 1993, each team will play 16 games over 18 weeks, with two byes. The league also agreed to provide more postseason games by increasing the number of wild-card teams in each conference from two to three. The third wild-card team will play the division champion with the worst record, while the other two division champions will get a bye.

Tagliabue also seemed ready to move forward on expansion. The NFL has added only two teams since it merged with the American Football League in 1970, but Tagliabue predicted the league will expand, "possibly by 1992, certainly by 1993."

Tagliabue's election as commissioner came less than a month after another historic event in NFL history—the Raiders' naming of Shell as head coach.

From a football standpoint, the move meant that Al Davis, the team's managing general partner, was going back into the Raider family for a coach. He had hired former Denver assistant Mike Shanahan at the start of the 1988 season when he thought the club needed an infusion of new ideas. It turned out Davis didn't like new ideas, especially when the team went 7-9 in 1988 and started out 1-3 in 1989. He wanted things done the old Raider way—and nobody knew that way better than Shell, an offensive tackle who played in eight Pro Bowls and two Super Bowls for the Raiders and was inducted into the Hall of Fame in August 1989.

Shell also became the NFL's first black head coach since Fritz Pollard was a player/coach for the Hammond Pros from 1923-25.

"It's a historic event," Shell said, "and I understand the significance of it. But I'm also a Raider, and I don't believe the color of my skin entered into this decision. If you know Al Davis and you know this organization, you'll understand that."

Said Davis: "If this is a historic occasion—and I realize who he is and what's happening here; I'm not lost on that—it's only meaningful and historic if he's a great success."

Shell won his first two games and had the Raiders in playoff contention at 8-6 before they lost their last two games. It was the fourth straight year the Raiders missed the playoffs.

After the '89 season, Davis announced plans to move the team back to Oakland in 1992,

Art Shell of the Los Angeles Raiders in 1989 became the National Football League's first black head coach in more than half a century.

pending the Oakland City Council's approval of a $660 million deal. When community opposition surfaced in Oakland, Davis agreed to cut some of the ticket guarantees to scale the deal back to $428 million. But many angry taxpayers still opposed the plan, and Oakland Mayor Lionel Wilson recommended that the council kill the deal. It did so in April 1990, although it left open the possibility of resuming negotiations with the Raiders.

Los Angeles was one of six teams to change coaches during and after the '89 season. Following the Raiders were the Phoenix Cardinals, who fired Gene Stallings with a 5-6 record at the 11-game mark. The action was taken after Stallings, who was frustrated because he hadn't been offered a new contract, announced that he wouldn't seek a renewal at the end of the season. Hank Kuhlmann finished up as interim coach for the final five games, all Phoenix losses. The Cardinals then named Washington Redskins offensive line coach Joe Bugel as their new coach.

The week after Stallings departed, Marion Campbell retired as coach of the Atlanta Falcons amid rumors of his imminent dismissal. The Falcons were 3-9 at that point, and they lost their four remaining games under interim coach Jim Hanifan. But the Falcons suffered two more tragic losses in the last month of the season when two players were killed in separate car accidents—rookie tackle Ralph Norwood on November 24 and tight end Brad Beckman on December 18.

After the season, the Falcons hired Jerry Glanville, a former Atlanta assistant who had recently resigned under pressure as the Houston Oilers' head coach. Glanville took the Oilers to the playoffs in 1987, '88 and '89, but his overall record was 35-35. The Falcons are hoping the flamboyant, controversial Glanville is the right man to revive a franchise that drew only 7,092 fans to its final 1989 home game.

To replace Glanville, the Oilers hired Jack Pardee, the former Chicago and Washington coach who made a cross-town move from the University of Houston.

When Coach Raymond Berry refused to go outside his staff for offensive and defensive coordinators after New England's 5-11 season, the Patriots fired him. He was replaced by Rod Rust, a former Patriots assistant who was Pittsburgh's defensive coordinator in 1989.

The New York Jets got not only a new coach, but also a new front office when Dick Steinberg was brought in from New England as the team's general manager. Out went Coach Joe Walton and his entire staff, plus player personnel director Mike Hickey. Walton was replaced by Bruce Coslet, previously the Cincinnati Bengals' offensive coordinator.

Another team with new front-office leadership is San Diego, which fired Steve Ortmayer, the Chargers' director of football operations, and hired Bobby Beathard to run the team. Beathard, who had resigned as Washington's general manager in May 1989, spent the '89 season appearing on NBC's "NFL Live" pregame show before signing on with the Chargers. He retained Dan Henning, hired the previous year by Ortmayer, as head coach.

Although there were no changes in ownership during the season, Wayne Huizenga, chairman of Blockbuster Entertainment Corp., bought 15 percent of the Miami Dolphins and 50 percent of Joe Robbie Stadium Corp. from the Robbie family in March 1990. The sale was made two months after the January 7 death of Joe Robbie, the founding father of the Dolphins who built the stadium with private funds. His son, Tim, became the team president and quickly signed Coach Don Shula to a new three-year contract.

A few days after the sale of the Dolphins, the club owners met in Orlando, Fla., where they approved the league's new TV deal, discussed expansion and divisional realignment and amended several minor rules. They voted to keep the instant-replay rule, but only after a lengthy debate and a 21-7 vote that barely produced the required three-fourths majority. Many had predicted an end to the use of the instant replay in officiating because Rozelle and Tex Schramm, the former Dallas Cowboys president and general manager who had moved on to the NFL's new international league, were no longer around to lobby for it. In a concession to replay opponents, however, the league decided that the replay official will have only two minutes to make a decision or else the call will stand.

The effect instant replay can have on the outcome of a game was never more evident than during a November 5 contest between Green Bay and Chicago. After Packers quarterback Don Majkowski threw a 14-yard, fourth-down pass to Sterling Sharpe in the end zone with 32 seconds left in the fourth quarter, a field official ruled that Majkowski had crossed the line of scrimmage before he threw the ball. But the call was overturned by the instant-replay official and Green Bay was awarded the touchdown to tie the game, 13-13. Chris Jacke then kicked the winning extra point.

That game was like many for the 1989 Packers. They went 7-3 in games decided by four points or less and set an NFL record by winning four one-point games. Five contests came down to an extra point or a field-goal attempt by Jacke in the final two minutes or overtime, and he made all five kicks.

The result was that the Packers went from 4-12 in 1988 to 10-6 last year. The turnaround earned Lindy Infante Coach of the Year honors in his second season, but it didn't help the Packers make the playoffs. Despite posting the same 10-6 record as Minnesota, Green Bay lost the NFC Central Division championship to the Vikings on a tiebreaker and came up short for an NFC wild-card bid.

The race for playoff spots was heated through the final weekend of the season. Only three teams (the 49ers, Broncos and Giants) had clinched playoff spots going into Week 16, and 14 teams were vying for the other seven spots. Four teams won division titles in the final weekend: the Cleveland Browns in the AFC Central, the Buffalo Bills in the AFC East, the Giants in the NFC East and the Vikings in the NFC Central. Pittsburgh, Houston, Philadelphia and the Los Angeles Rams won wild-card spots in their regular-season finales.

The American Football Conference playoffs featured three close contests leading up to the championship game. Pittsburgh defeated Houston in overtime in the wild-card matchup and then lost a one-point decision to Denver in the divisional playoffs. Cleveland registered a four-point victory over Buffalo to advance to the AFC title game against Denver. It was the third such matchup for the Browns and Broncos, and for the third time the Browns failed to reach the Super Bowl. The Broncos won, 37-21.

The Broncos' subsequent drubbing by the 49ers—they joined the Vikings as the only four-time Super Bowl losers—obscured the fact that they had a successful season. Two rookies, safety Steve Atwater and running back Bobby Humphrey, helped revitalize the Broncos as they bounced back from a disappointing 8-8 season in 1988 to start off 10-2 en route to an 11-5 finish.

The Steelers had the league's most improbable finish. They scraped themselves off the floor after losing their first two games by a combined 92-10 score to post a 9-7 record and make the playoffs for the first time since 1984. That hushed the critics of Coach Chuck Noll, who had come under fire during a lackluster decade in which the Steelers fielded four fewer Super Bowl teams (none) than the decade before. Noll's ability to turn the team around in 1989 may have been his finest coaching job ever.

Led by quarterback Jim Everett, the wild-card Rams advanced to the NFC championship game by knocking off both the Eagles and Giants on the road in their first two playoff games. They then were routed by the 49ers, 30-3.

San Francisco's 41-13 whipping of Minnesota in the NFC divisional playoffs underscored the Vikings' 1989 disappointment. They won their division, but the Vikings clearly were shooting for Super Bowl XXIV when they traded a slew

Pittsburgh's Chuck Noll may have done his best coaching job in his 21st season with the Steelers.

of players and high draft picks to Dallas for running back Herschel Walker on October 12. They not only failed to make the Super Bowl, but also failed to improve with Walker aboard, going 3-2 before the trade and 7-4 after it. After rushing for 148 yards against Green Bay in his first game in Viking purple, Walker dropped to 89 yards in his second game and never got more than 76 in any game thereafter.

The Cowboys, meanwhile, struggled through a 1-15 season in their first year under new Coach Jimmy Johnson, the successor to the legendary Tom Landry. The Cowboys showed they'll need lots of help from their numerous draft picks if Johnson's second season is to be any easier.

The most disappointing team was probably Chicago, which had won the NFC Central with a 12-4 record in 1988. After getting off to a 4-0 start, the Bears lost defensive tackle Dan Hampton for the season with knee surgery. The team collapsed, staggering to a 6-10 finish. Coach Mike Ditka ranted and raved on the sidelines and in the newspapers, but to no avail. After criticizing his team severely during the season, Ditka was more upbeat when it was over. "We can win in the future," he said. "The nucleus is still there."

The runaway choice for NFL Rookie of the Year was Detroit's Barry Sanders, the 1988 Heisman Trophy winner who gained 1,470 yards rushing for the Lions after passing up his

senior year at Oklahoma State to turn pro. Sanders' instant success made the NFL that much more attractive to underclassmen, and the league decided to open its draft to juniors who applied. Thirty-eight of them opted for the 1990 draft, although only 18 were selected.

Sanders lost the league rushing title by only 10 yards to Kansas City's Christian Okoye, who led the Chiefs to an 8-7-1 mark in the first year of Coach Marty Schottenheimer's rebuilding program.

Indianapolis' Eric Dickerson reached 10,000 rushing yards faster than any player in history when he gained 106 yards in the Colts' 1989 opener. He finished the game—his 91st—with 10,021 yards. The 29-year-old running back rushed for 1,311 yards in 1989 to boost his career total to 11,226, putting him within reach of Walter Payton's career mark of 16,726 yards. But Dickerson said he was unhappy in Indianapolis and threatened to retire before the '90 season if the Colts refused to trade him.

The Redskins managed the rare feat of having three players (Gary Clark, Art Monk and Ricky Sanders) each tally more than 1,000 receiving yards in the same season. The only previous trio of season-long teammates to do it were Kellen Winslow, John Jefferson and Charlie Joiner with the 1980 Chargers. At the time, Redskins Coach Joe Gibbs was San Diego's offensive coordinator.

Two likely Hall of Famers, Seattle wide receiver Steve Largent and Denver running back Tony Dorsett, announced their retirement after the '89 season. Largent was limited to 28 catches in 1989 when he fractured an elbow in the Seahawks' season opener, but he finished his career with NFL records for most catches (819), receiving yards (13,089), touchdown catches (100) and consecutive games with a reception (177), among others. Dorsett, a longtime Cowboy, spent his second season in Denver on the injured reserve list after blowing out a knee in training camp. But he left the game as the league's No. 2 all-time rusher behind Payton with 12,739 yards.

The league played a third straight season without a collective bargaining agreement with the NFL Players Association, which continued its efforts to obtain unfettered free agency by announcing that it had decertified. The reasoning was that if the union didn't exist, the league no longer was entitled to an exemption from antitrust laws. In April 1990, eight players filed individual suits charging the league with antitrust violations regarding free agency. The league, meanwhile, sought legal recognition of the NFLPA as the players' bargaining agent.

The league set a paid attendance record of 13,626,672, with an average attendance of 60,833. Those figures surpassed the previous records, both set in 1981, of 13,606,990 and 60,745.

'89 REGULAR SEASON GAMES
FIRST WEEK

RESULTS OF WEEK 1
Sunday, September 10

Buffalo 27, Miami 24 at Mia.
Chicago 17, Cincinnati 14 at Chi.
Cleveland 51, Pittsburgh 0 at Pitts.
Denver 34, Kansas City 20 at Den.
L.A. Raiders 40, San Diego 14 at L.A.
L.A. Rams 31, Atlanta 21 at Atl.
Minnesota 38, Houston 7 at Minn.
New England 27, N.Y. Jets 24 at N.Y.
New Orleans 28, Dallas 0 at N.O.
Philadelphia 31, Seattle 7 at Phila.
Phoenix 16, Detroit 13 at Det.
San Francisco 30, Indianapolis 24 at Ind.
Tampa Bay 23, Green Bay 21 at G.B.

Monday, September 11

N.Y. Giants 27, Washington 24 at Wash.

The National Football League's 70th season opened September 10 with one of pro football's most stable franchises ever, the Dallas Cowboys, revamped through drastic off-season changes.

The Cowboys were the NFL's model team of the 1970s and early 1980s under the direction of founding Owner Clint Murchison, personnel director Gil Brandt, General Manager Tex Schramm and Coach Tom Landry. From 1970 through 1985, Dallas appeared in 10 National Football Conference championship games (winning five) and annexed nine NFC Eastern Division titles.

Entering their 30th NFL season, however, the 1989 Cowboys resembled the Cowboys of old in name only.

After Dallas' disastrous 3-13 finish in 1988, Arkansas oil man Jerry Jones stepped forward to purchase the club for a reported $140 million from fifth-year Owner H.R. (Bum) Bright. In a shocking first move, Jones replaced Landry, the franchise's first and only head coach, with Jimmy Johnson, a colorful, well-coiffed Texas native who had led the University of Miami (Fla.) to 52 victories over the previous five seasons and the 1987 national championship.

Jones and Johnson had been football teammates at Arkansas in the early 1960s, when they helped the Razorbacks to a 10-1 record in 1964 and a share of college football's national championship. "I wouldn't have bought the Dallas Cowboys," Jones insisted, "if Jimmy Johnson couldn't be my coach."

By the time training camp opened in July, the two former college roommates had overhauled the organization from top to bottom. Besides Landry, Schramm and Brandt, seven other key front-office employees were dismissed or quit. Johnson retained only four of the 11 assistant coaches he inherited from Landry.

"He (Jones) might as well change the uniforms and change the (team) name," said one worker who survived the purge. "I don't recognize anything around here."

But while the Cowboys were a different team off the field in 1989, memories of 1988 flooded back whenever they suited up on game day. They opened the season with a 28-0 loss in New Orleans, becoming the first Cowboy team ever shut out on opening day. They managed only 20 yards rushing (the fewest in club history) and totaled just 41 yards on offense in a first half that ended with the Saints ahead, 21-0.

And for those loyalists who were still smarting over the unceremonious dismissal of Landry back in February, there was this: the Landry-coached Cowboys were not shut out until their 10th season (a 31-0 loss to Los Angeles in the meeting between the losers of the 1969 conference championship games). What's more, Dallas had been blanked just four times in 457 games under Landry.

"It would have been nice to start off better than we did, because I know we have a better football team than we showed," said Johnson, who had no previous NFL coaching experience. "We just did not play as well as we are capable of playing."

Dallas had the ball in New Orleans territory on only two possessions, once after the Saints botched a punt and the other during a late-game drive against reserve players. Cowboy quarterback Troy Aikman, the first overall pick in the 1989 draft, experienced a rough pro debut. He was sacked twice, threw two interceptions, had three third-down passes dropped and saw a touchdown pass wiped out by a holding penalty.

Tailback Herschel Walker, the Cowboys' main running threat, carried just eight times—for 10 yards. A 13-yard scramble in the final quarter by Aikman made the rookie the team's rushing leader.

"We never really did get the running game started," Walker said in a huge understatement. "When you fall behind 21-0, what you have to do is come out and pass the ball."

The Saints, on the other hand, had little trouble solving the Dallas defense. New Orleans controlled the football for more than 44 minutes and had scoring drives of 74, 73 and 89 yards. Three running backs—Dalton Hilliard, Paul Frazier and Craig Heyward—scored touchdowns for the Saints.

The spotlight after the game, however, was on the losers, not the winners.

"There's no need for a re-evaluation," said

Dallas' Jimmy Johnson (left) and San Francisco's George Seifert (right) made their NFL head coaching debuts in Week 1 with different results.

Johnson, who acknowledged that expectations for his team had been boosted by a 3-1 preseason record. "We knew a long time ago we had a long way to go. We still know that. I told the players it's not how they start, it's how they finish."

Despite a coaching change of their own, the defending Super Bowl champion San Francisco 49ers opened defense of their NFL title with a 30-24 victory over the Indianapolis Colts. George Seifert, who had served as the 49ers' defensive coordinator since 1983, took over the team after Bill Walsh resigned as coach in January 1989.

Scoring on five of their first seven possessions, the 49ers appeared as sharp as they had in a 20-16 victory over Cincinnati in Super Bowl XXIII. Wide receiver Jerry Rice (the Super Bowl MVP) caught six passes for 163 yards, including a 58-yard scoring reception after Indianapolis had pulled to within 23-17 early in the final quarter. The touchdown was the 50th of Rice's five-year NFL career.

The lone bright spot for the Colts (who lost their sixth straight season-opener) was running back Eric Dickerson. Carrying 19 times for 106 yards, Dickerson became only the seventh player to surpass the 10,000-yard rushing plateau, finishing the game with 10,021 career yards. He reached the mark in his 91st game, seven games fewer than former Cleveland great Jim Brown and faster than any player in NFL history.

Another successful coaching debut was made in Pittsburgh, where the visiting Cleveland Browns made new Coach Bud Carson's inaugural an overwhelming success by routing the Steelers, 51-0. It was the most lopsided victory in the 79-game series between the longtime AFC Central Division rivals and the Steelers' worst loss ever.

Carson had served as the Steelers' defensive coordinator under Coach Chuck Noll when the club won its first two Super Bowls, after the 1974 and 1975 seasons. Fittingly, it was his Browns' defense that was most responsible for the team's seventh straight triumph over Pittsburgh. The Cleveland defense scored three touchdowns, forced eight turnovers and had six sacks.

Yet another impressive debut occurred in Detroit, where Lions rookie running back Barry Sanders provided a hint of things to come in a 16-13 loss to the Phoenix Cardinals.

Sanders, who had practiced just twice with the Lions due to a lengthy contract holdout, rushed for 71 yards on nine carries after entering the game 9:26 into the second half.

The 1988 Heisman Trophy winner carried the ball on his first four plays, the last of which was a three-yard touchdown that lifted Detroit to a 10-6 lead. Phoenix rallied to win, however, when Al Del Greco's third field goal (from 33 yards out) broke a 13-13 tie with 13 seconds left.

In Atlanta, another rookie named Sanders made his presence felt in a big way. But, like the Lions' Barry, he saw his team come up short on the scoreboard.

Former Florida State cornerback Deion Sanders, the fifth player selected in the 1989 draft, played only three downs on defense for the Atlanta Falcons but returned a punt 68 yards for a touchdown in a 31-21 loss to the Los Angeles Rams. Sanders initially fumbled the punt before embarking on a spinning, electrifying return that pushed the Falcons ahead, 7-0, after 5:31 of the first quarter.

A versatile athlete who is dabbling in two sports ala Bo Jackson, Sanders scored the touchdown just five days after he homered, smacked two doubles and drove in four runs for the New York Yankees in a 12-2 victory over the Seattle Mariners. Sanders abruptly ended his baseball season when he signed a four-year, $4.5 million contract with Atlanta only three days before the season-opener.

The Rams, who had beaten the Falcons in their last three meetings by a combined 88-7 score, prevailed behind the efforts of running back Greg Bell and quarterback Jim Everett. Bell ran for touchdowns from two and eight yards out, while Everett carried 13 yards for another score and made good on a 46-yard "Hail Mary" pass to Henry Ellard that put Los Angeles in front, 17-14, on the final play of the first half.

Drama was at its peak in Miami, however, where the visiting Buffalo Bills scored two touchdowns in the final three minutes to overtake the Dolphins, 27-24. Buffalo quarterback Jim Kelly ran two yards up the middle as time expired to cap a 51-yard scoring drive, thus cinching the Bills' fifth straight win over Miami.

The Dolphins appeared to have the game in hand when quarterback Dan Marino tossed an eight-yard scoring strike to rookie Andre Brown with 4:17 to play. The Miami lead stood at 11, but Kelly led the Bills back with a 26-yard touchdown pass to Flip Johnson with 2:50 left. On the ensuing Miami possession, cornerback Nate Odomes intercepted a Marino pass at midfield with 1:44 left, setting up the game-winning drive.

It was the second Marino pass picked off by Odomes, whose first interception at the Buffalo 15-yard line halted a Dolphins scoring threat. Odomes also forced a fumble by Troy Strad-

ford on the Miami 6-yard line to set up the Bills' first touchdown.

The loss was the Dolphins' fifth straight on opening day.

Green Bay also dropped its fifth successive opener, losing a 23-21 decision at home to Tampa Bay. Packers quarterback Don Majkowski threw three costly interceptions, the first two leading to Buccaneer touchdowns. Safety Mark Robinson's second interception halted a Green Bay drive at the Tampa Bay 16-yard line with 5:32 to play.

Ironically, Bucs quarterback Vinny Testaverde, who had thrown a league-high 35 interceptions in 1988, did not have a pass picked off. He completed 22 of 27 attempts, helping the Bucs push their winning streak against the division-rival Pack to four games.

Two teams, the Chicago Bears and New England Patriots, won their season-opening games for the sixth year in succession.

The Bears used a 14-play, 95-yard touchdown drive in the fourth quarter to edge the Cincinnati Bengals, 17-14. Chicago quarterback Mike Tomczak, who completed just six of his first 17 passes, connected on four of seven attempts for 79 yards during the game-winning drive. Tomczak's final toss covered 20 yards to tight end James Thornton for the score.

Veteran tackle Dan Hampton enjoyed a big day for the Chicago defense. Starting his 11th NFL season, Hampton blocked a field-goal attempt, had two sacks, knocked down two passes and stopped Bengals running back Ickey Woods on a fourth-and-one play at the Bears' 18-yard line in the second quarter.

The Patriots, meanwhile, pulled out a 27-24 victory over the New York Jets when running back Reggie Dupard scampered four yards for a touchdown with 1:55 to play. Dupard was given a chance to save face after being stopped on a fourth-down play from the Jets' 4-yard line with 3:28 left.

The New England defense held up well playing its first game without linebacker Andre Tippett, cornerback Ronnie Lippett and end Garin Veris, all of whom would sit out the 1989 season because of injuries. The Patriots held the Jets scoreless in the first half, allowing only 52 yards on eight plays.

New York scored its first touchdown—a one-yard pass from Ken O'Brien to Roger Vick—after Erik McMillan blocked a punt out of bounds inside the New England 1-yard line.

A blocked punt also set the tone for the Philadelphia Eagles in their 31-7 victory over Seattle. On the Seahawks' first possession, Andre Waters leaped in front of a Ruben Rodriguez punt, setting up a one-yard scoring run by Anthony Toney just three minutes into the game. Waters' block came after a 70-yard punt by Rodriguez was nullified by a penalty.

The block was the first against the Seahawks since the Oakland Raiders did it on November 17, 1980.

Although his team eventually lost the game, Atlanta rookie Deion Sanders returned a punt 68 yards for a touchdown to give the Falcons a 7-0, first-quarter lead against the Los Angeles Rams.

Seattle's lone touchdown was scored by veteran receiver Steve Largent, who caught a game-tying 23-yard pass from Dave Krieg late in the first period. It would be Largent's only catch for the next seven weeks, however. In the second quarter, he suffered a fractured right elbow, an injury that would keep him sidelined until Week 8.

In Los Angeles, Raiders quarterback Jay Schroeder suffered a separated collarbone on the first play from scrimmage, but replacement Steve Beuerlein passed for 206 yards and two touchdowns to key a 40-14 romp over San Diego. Schroeder did, however, remain in the game long enough to throw a 26-yard scoring strike to running back Vance Mueller.

Los Angeles, an 0-4 team during the preseason schedule, rolled up 518 yards on offense to ruin the Charger debuts of Coach Dan Henning, Atlanta's field boss from 1983 through 1986, and quarterback Jim McMahon, late of the Bears. The flamboyant McMahon left the game midway through the third quarter after completing just seven of 18 passes for 91 yards.

In addition to Schroeder, the Raiders lost 1988 rookie sensation Tim Brown, who suffered torn ligaments in his left knee while returning a kickoff. The injury sidelined Brown for the remainder of the season.

The Denver Broncos converted four turnovers into 24 points en route to a 34-20 AFC Western Division victory over the Kansas City Chiefs. The loss spoiled the Kansas City coaching debut of Marty Schottenheimer, the former Cleveland coach who left the Browns after the 1988 season due to a disagreement with Owner Art Modell.

Schottenheimer watched his new team play catch-up all afternoon. After a 41-yard field goal by rookie David Treadwell put Denver ahead, 3-0, Broncos safety Tyrone Braxton intercepted a Steve DeBerg pass and returned it 34 yards for a score. On the Chiefs' next play from scrimmage, Denver recovered a DeBerg fumble on the Kansas City 8-yard line. Four plays later, running back Sammy Winder made it a 17-0 game.

After vowing publicly that "I won't put my best foot forward" due to a contract dispute with management, Minnesota wide receiver Anthony Carter put aside his differences and caught seven passes for 123 yards in the Vikings' 38-7 rout of Houston.

On Minnesota's first possession, Carter had receptions of 14 and 13 yards before catching a 32-yard touchdown pass from Wade Wilson.

The Vikes dominated the game both offensively and defensively. After Houston opened the scoring with a 13-play, 61-yard drive, Minnesota yielded just 43 total yards over the remainder of the game. Oilers quarterback Warren Moon was sacked seven times and completed just eight of 20 passes.

The season's first Monday night game featured a rematch of the 1988 Monday night opener—with similar results. The New York Giants, 27-20 victors over Washington a year before, toppled the Redskins, 27-24, on a 52-yard field goal by Raul Allegre as time expired. Allegre's 32-yarder had tied the game, 24-24, with 2:17 left.

New York had led, 21-10, early in the fourth quarter, but the Redskins struck for two touchdowns in less than a minute to take a 24-21 advantage. The Giants' victory was their eighth against Washington in their last 10 non-strike meetings.

Rams-Falcons
SUNDAY, SEPTEMBER 10
SCORE BY PERIODS

Los Angeles Rams	3	14	7	7—31
Atlanta	7	7	0	7—21

SCORING
Atlanta—Sanders 68 punt return (McFadden kick), 5:31 1st.
Los Angeles—Field goal Lansford 23, 10:18 1st.
Los Angeles—Bell 2 run (Lansford kick), 1:35 2nd.
Atlanta—Dixon 53 pass from Miller (McFadden kick), 14:11 2nd.
Los Angeles—Ellard 46 pass from Everett (Lansford kick), 15:00 2nd.
Los Angeles—Everett 13 run (Lansford kick), 5:53 3rd.
Los Angeles—Bell 8 run (Lansford kick), 0:58 4th.
Atlanta—Haynes 33 pass from Miller (McFadden kick), 5:36 4th.

TEAM STATISTICS

	Los Angeles	Atlanta
First downs	19	16
Rushes-Yards	36-169	15-46
Sacked-Yards lost	1-11	5-26
Passing yards	195	271
Passes	14-25-0	23-37-0
Punts	5-42	6-41
Fumbles-Lost	1-1	0-0
Penalties-Yards	4-10	5-39
Time of possession	36:13	23:47
Attendance—38,708.		

INDIVIDUAL STATISTICS
Rushing—Los Angeles, Bell 26-128, Everett 3-18, Ron Brown 1-12, Green 4-7, Delpino 1-2, McGee 1-2; Atlanta, Settle 8-27, Lang 6-19, Flowers 1-0.
Passing—Los Angeles, Everett 14-25-0—206; Atlanta, Miller 23-37-0—299.
Receiving—Los Angeles, Ellard 5-99, Holohan 5-76, Johnson 1-22, Bell 1-10, Delpino 1-4, Green 1-minus 51; Atlanta, Collins 6-76, Haynes 4-62, Lang 4-29, Settle 4-28, Heller 3-44, Dixon 1-53, Bailey 1-7.
Kickoff Returns—Los Angeles, Ron Brown 3-81, Delpino 1-30; Atlanta, G. Thomas 5-98.
Punt Returns—Los Angeles, Henley 2-41; Atlanta, Sanders 2-83.
Interceptions—
Punting—Los Angeles, Hatcher 5-41.6; Atlanta, Fulhage 6-41.2.
Field Goals—Los Angeles, Lansford 1-2 (missed: 43); Atlanta, McFadden 0-1 (missed: 43).
Sacks—Los Angeles, Greene 3, Reed, Wright; Atlanta, Bryan.

Patriots-Jets
SUNDAY, SEPTEMBER 10
SCORE BY PERIODS

New England	7	14	0	6—27
New York Jets	0	0	17	7—24

SCORING
New England—Fryar 20 pass from Eason (Davis kick), 10:49 1st.
New England—Morgan 30 pass from Eason (Davis kick), 1:05 2nd.
New England—Stephens 1 run (Davis kick), 9:27 2nd.
New York—Vick 1 pass from O'Brien (Leahy kick), 3:37 3rd.
New York—Field goal Leahy 40, 8:47 3rd.
New York—Prokop 17 run (Leahy kick), 13:34 3rd.
New York—Townsell 48 pass from O'Brien (Leahy kick), 7:32 4th.
New England—Dupard 4 run (kick failed), 13:05 4th.

TEAM STATISTICS

	New England	New York
First downs	26	14
Rushes-Yards	48-154	16-49
Sacked-Yards lost	0-0	1-6
Passing yards	273	255
Passes	15-23-2	18-31-1
Punts	3-25.0	6-38.3
Fumbles-Lost	2-1	1-0
Penalties-Yards	2-17	4-35
Time of possession	37:11	22:49
Attendance—64,541.		

INDIVIDUAL STATISTICS
Rushing—New England, Stephens 28-89, Dupard 7-24, Perryman 7-24, Allen 4-19, Eason 2-minus 2; New York, NcNeil 9-17, Prokop 1-17, Vick 4-9, O'Brien 2-6.
Passing—New England, Eason 15-23-2—273; New York, O'Brien 18-31-1—261.
Receiving—New England, Jones 8-148, Morgan 4-74, Fryar 2-48, Dykes 1-3; New York, McNeil 6-65, Townsell 5-97, Shuler 4-38, Harper 2-60, Vick 1-1.
Kickoff Returns—New England, Martin 3-76, Rice 1-46, Allen 1-19; New York, Townsell 2-34, Dixon 2-36.
Punt Returns—New England, Fryar 5-34; New York, Townsell 1-9.
Interceptions—New England, McSwain 1-18; New York, McMillan 2-0.
Punting—New England, Feagles 2-37.5; New York, Prokop 6-38.3.
Field Goals—New England, none attempted; New York, Leahy 1-1.
Sacks—New England, McGrew.

Seahawks-Eagles
SUNDAY, SEPTEMBER 10
SCORE BY PERIODS

Seattle	7	0	0	0— 7
Philadelphia	7	10	7	7—31

SCORING
Philadelphia—Toney 1 run (Zendejas kick), 3:11 1st.
Seattle—Largent 23 pass from Krieg (Johnson kick), 13:04 1st.
Philadelphia—Field goal Zendejas 23, 3:33 2nd.
Philadelphia—Carter 8 pass from Cunningham (Zendejas kick), 10:09 2nd.
Philadelphia—Quick 8 pass from Cunningham (Zendejas kick), 5:11 3rd.
Philadelphia—Everett 30 interception return (Zendejas kick), 12:24 4th.

TEAM STATISTICS

	Seattle	Philadelphia
First downs	17	18
Rushes-Yards	19-77	37-131
Sacked-Yards lost	4-29	1-6
Passing yards	193	234
Passes	18-41-3	13-27-0
Punts	8-36	6-45
Fumbles-Lost	1-0	0-0
Penalties-Yards	11-95	6-52
Time of possession	28:54	31:06
Attendance—64,287.		

INDIVIDUAL STATISTICS

Rushing—Seattle, Warner 12-47, Williams 6-24, Harris 1-6; Philadelphia, Higgs 13-44, Sherman 6-37, Toney 10-30, Byars 4-8, Cunningham 2-6, Drummond 2-6.

Passing—Seattle, Krieg 15-34-2—210, Stouffer 2-6-1—8, Rodriguez 1-1-0—4; Philadelphia, Cunningham 13-27-0—240.

Receiving—Seattle, Williams 4-30, Clark 3-63, Tyler 3-61, Skansi 3-24, Blades 2-15, Largent 1-23, Glasgow 1-4, Warner 1-2; Philadelphia, Quick 6-140, Carter 3-63, Byars 1-16, Williams 1-8, Jackson 1-8, Toney 1-5.

Kickoff Returns—Seattle, Jefferson 3-83; Philadelphia, Higgs 1-30.

Punt Returns—Seattle, Jefferson 2-8; Philadelphia, Williams 4-25.

Interceptions—Philadelphia, Jenkins 1-18, Bell 1-13, Everett 1-30.

Punting—Seattle, Rodriguez 7-43.4; Philadelphia, Teltschik 6-45.3.

Field Goals—Seattle, none attempted; Philadelphia, Zendejas 1-2 (missed: 33).

Sacks—Seattle, Bryant; Philadelphia, Simmons 3, Hopkins.

Chiefs-Broncos
SUNDAY, SEPTEMBER 10
SCORE BY PERIODS

Kansas City	0	10	3	7—20
Denver	17	0	7	10—34

SCORING

Denver—Field goal Treadwell 41, 6:11 1st.
Denver—Braxton 34 interception return (Treadwell kick), 6:29 1st.
Denver—Winder 2 run (Treadwell kick), 8:30 1st.
Kansas City—Field goal Lowery 41, 0:53 2nd.
Kansas City—Gamble 1 run (Lowery kick), 14:34 2nd.
Kansas City—Field goal Lowery 23, 8:17 3rd.
Denver—Sewell 9 pass from Elway (Treadwell kick), 13:13 3rd.
Denver—Field goal Treadwell 29, 2:58 4th.
Kansas City—Carson 5 pass from DeBerg (Lowery kick), 7:07 4th.
Denver—Robbins 18 interception return (Treadwell kick), 11:49 4th.

TEAM STATISTICS

	Kansas City	Denver
First downs	14	14
Rushes-Yards	19-56	32-100
Sacked-Yards lost	3-19	0-0
Passing yards	231	150
Passes	21-34-2	16-28-2
Punts	3-46.7	3-43.7
Fumbles-Lost	3-2	0-0
Penalties-Yards	5-31	2-15
Time of possession	29:37	30:23
Attendance—74,284.		

INDIVIDUAL STATISTICS

Rushing—Kansas City, Heard 9-27, Okoye 5-23, Gamble 4-4, Saxon 1-2; Denver, Winder 11-38, Alexander 8-35, Bratton 2-16, Humphrey 6-15, Elway 5-minus 4.

Passing—Kansas City, DeBerg 21-34-2—250; Denver, Elway 16-28-2—150.

Receiving—Kansas City, Harry 4-69, Carson 4-68, Worthen 4-57, Heard 3-22, Gamble 2-2, Dressel 1-21, Hayes 1-7, Saxon 1-2, R. Thomas 1-2; Denver, Alexander 3-35, Johnson 3-30, Kay 3-26, Winder 2-13, Kelly 2-11, Jackson 1-13, Bratton 1-11, Sewell 1-9.

Kickoff Returns—Kansas City, Copeland 3-58, Gamble 1-18; Denver, Bell 2-53, Humphrey 2-33.

Punt Returns—Kansas City, Barnes 2-41; Denver, Bell 2-23.

Interceptions—Kansas City, Snipes 1-16, Lewis 1-0; Denver, Braxton 1-34, Robbins 1-18.

Punting—Kansas City, Goodburn 3-46.7; Denver, Horan 3-43.7.

Field Goals—Kansas City, Lowery 2-3 (missed: 54); Denver, Treadwell 2-2.

Sacks—Denver, Munford, Townsend, Fletcher.

Oilers-Vikings
SUNDAY, SEPTEMBER 10
SCORE BY PERIODS

Houston	7	0	0	0—7
Minnesota	14	10	7	7—38

SCORING

Houston—Highsmith 1 run (Zendejas kick), 7:46 1st.
Minnesota—Carter 32 pass from Wilson (Garcia kick), 10:26 1st.
Minnesota—Jordan 2 pass from Wilson (Garcia kick), 14:36 1st.
Minnesota—Fenney 1 run (Garcia kick), 9:28 2nd.
Minnesota—Field goal Garcia 35, 12:19 2nd.
Minnesota—Fenney 3 run (Garcia kick), 12:06 3rd.
Minnesota—Anderson 2 run (Garcia kick), 11:05 4th.

TEAM STATISTICS

	Houston	Minnesota
First downs	11	29
Rushes-Yards	23-70	37-145
Passing yards	34	198
Passes	10-24-1	16-25-0
Sacked-Yards lost	7-44	2-20
Punts	7-46.7	3-43.3
Fumbles-Lost	2-2	1-0
Penalties-Yards	13-98	8-56
Time of possession	25:48	34:12
Attendance—54,015.		

INDIVIDUAL STATISTICS

Rushing—Houston, Pinkett 5-37, Highsmith 6-18, White 10-10, Moon 1-5, Montgomery 1-0; Minnesota, Dozier 7-41, Fenney 9-37, Anderson 6-20, Nelson 7-30, Carter 1-13, Wilson 4-10, Rice 3-minus 6.

Passing—Houston, Moon 8-20-1—69, Carlson 2-4-0—9; Minnesota, Wilson 16-25-0—216.

Receiving—Houston, Givins 4-33, Hill 2-26, Duncan 1-6, Verhulst 1-5, Jeffires 1-3, Jackson 1-3; Minnesota, Carter 7-123, Ingram 4-45, Jones 1-20, Dozier 1-12, Nelson 1-10, Fenney 1-6, Jordan 1-2.

Kickoff Returns—Houston, Harris 6-142, K. Johnson 1-26; Minnesota, Dozier 1-15.

Punt Returns—Houston, K. Johnson 2-22; Minnesota, Lewis 4-36.

Interceptions—Minnesota, Merriweather 1-3.

Punting—Houston, Montgomery 7-46.7; Minnesota, Scribner 3-43.3.

Field Goals—Houston, none attempted; Minnesota, Garcia 1-2 (missed: 51).

Sacks—Houston, Childress 2; Minnesota, Millard 3, Thomas 1½, Doleman 1½, Noga.

Bills-Dolphins
SUNDAY, SEPTEMBER 10
SCORE BY PERIODS

Buffalo	3	0	10	14—27
Miami	0	10	7	7—24

SCORING

Buffalo—Field goal Norwood 34, 12:26 1st.
Miami—Stradford 1 run (Stoyanovich kick), 9:12 2nd.
Miami—Field goal Stoyanovich 29, 14:57 2nd.
Buffalo—Kinnebrew 2 run (Norwood kick), 3:02 3rd.
Miami—Logan 2 blocked punt return (Stoyanovich kick), 7:57 3rd.
Buffalo—Field goal Norwood 37, 12:49 3rd.
Miami—A.B. Brown 8 pass from Marino (Stoyanovich kick), 10:43 4th.
Buffalo—Johnson 26 pass from Kelly (Norwood kick), 12:10 4th.
Buffalo—Kelly 2 run (Norwood kick), 15:00 4th.

TEAM STATISTICS

	Buffalo	Miami
First downs	27	21
Rushes-Yards	27-141	23-68
Sacked-Yards lost	4-39	0-0
Passing yards	226	255
Passes	25-40-0	25-38-2
Punts	4-48.0	4-39.0
Fumbles-Lost	2-2	3-2
Penalties-Yards	7-65	8-67
Time of possession	29:18	30:42

Attendance—54,541.

INDIVIDUAL STATISTICS

Rushing—Buffalo, Thomas 13-94, Mueller 5-18, Harmon 4-17, Kinnebrew 4-10, Kelly 1-2; Miami, Stradford 12-43, Hampton 6-19, Davenport 2-4, T. Brown 2-2, Marino 1-0.

Passing—Buffalo, Kelly 25-40-0—265; Miami, Marino 25-38-2—255.

Receiving—Buffalo, Thomas 8-65, Reed 6-58, Harmon 4-55, Johnson 3-60, Burkett 2-14, Mueller 1-8, Metzelaars 1-5; Miami, Edmunds 5-58, T. Brown 5-57, A.B. Brown 4-58, Hampton 3-5, Duper 2-30, Jensen 2-27, Stradford 2-7, Banks 1-11, Hardy 1-2.

Kickoff Returns—Buffalo, Tucker 3-48, Mueller 1-19, Harmon 1-25; Miami, Logan 3-77, Hampton 2-37.

Punt Returns—Buffalo, Tucker 1-14; Miami, Stradford 2-21.

Interceptions—Buffalo, Odomes 2-7.

Punting—Buffalo, Kidd 4-48.0; Miami, Roby 4-39.0.

Field Goals—Buffalo, Norwood 2-2; Miami, Stoyanovich 1-1.

Sacks—Miami, Graf, Cline, Cross, Sochia.

Browns-Steelers
SUNDAY, SEPTEMBER 10
SCORE BY PERIODS

Cleveland	17	13	14	7—51
Pittsburgh	0	0	0	0— 0

SCORING

Cleveland—Matthews 3 fumble return (Bahr kick), 9:18 1st.
Cleveland—Field goal Bahr 27, 12:07 1st.
Cleveland—Grayson 28 fumble return (Bahr kick), 12:29 1st.
Cleveland—Field goal Bahr 20, 6:06 2nd.
Cleveland—Manoa 3 run (Bahr kick), 11:32 2nd.
Cleveland—Field goal Bahr 27, 14:21 2nd.
Cleveland—Manoa 2 run (Bahr kick), 2:34 3rd.
Cleveland—Grayson 14 interception return (Bahr kick), 3:46 3rd.
Cleveland—Oliphant 21 run (Bahr kick), 3:26 4th.

TEAM STATISTICS

	Cleveland	Pittsburgh
First downs	19	5
Rushes-Yards	44-152	17-36
Sacked-Yards lost	1-2	6-67
Passing yards	205	17
Passes	16-25-0	10-22-3
Punts	5-38.0	6-45.2
Fumbles-Lost	0-0	6-5
Penalties-Yards	8-70	6-38
Time of possession	40:50	19:10

Attendance—57,928.

INDIVIDUAL STATISTICS

Rushing—Cleveland, Oliphant 6-48, K. Jones 11-31, Redden 7-30, Metcalf 10-28, Manoa 9-20, Pagel 1-minus 5; Pittsburgh, Worley 10-36, Hoge 4-5, Lipps 1-3, Brister 2-minus 8.

Passing—Cleveland, Kosar 15-25-0—207; Pittsburgh, Brister 10-22-3—84.

Receiving—Cleveland, Slaughter 4-75, Metcalf 4-9, Langhorne 3-32, Brennan 2-52, Manoa 2-31, Newsome 1-8; Pittsburgh, Carter 3-13, Hill 2-28, Hoge 2-25,

Thompson 1-21, Lipps 1-7, Brister 1-minus 10.

Kickoff Returns—Pittsburgh, Woodson 5-102, J. Johnson 3-43.

Punt Returns—Cleveland, McNeil 5-47; Pittsburgh, Woodson 1-6, J. Johnson 2-22.

Interceptions—Cleveland, Harper 2-0, Grayson 1-14.

Punting—Cleveland, Wagner 5-38.0; Pittsburgh, Newsome 6-45.2.

Field Goals—Cleveland, Bahr 3-3; Pittsburgh, none attempted.

Sacks—Cleveland, Hairston 2, Banks, Blaylock, Charlton, Stewart; Pittsburgh, Lloyd.

Cowboys-Saints
SUNDAY, SEPTEMBER 10
SCORE BY PERIODS

Dallas	0	0	0	0— 0
New Orleans	7	14	0	7—28

SCORING

New Orleans—Hilliard 4 run (Andersen kick), 10:55 1st.
New Orleans—Heyward 1 run (Andersen kick), 12:56 2nd.
New Orleans—Shepard 56 punt return (Andersen kick), 14:09 2nd.
New Orleans—Frazier 1 run (Andersen kick), 7:18 4th.

TEAM STATISTICS

	Dallas	New Orleans
First downs	10	26
Rushes-Yards	10-20	45-190
Sacked-Yards lost	2-30	1-8
Passing yards	154	145
Passes	18-36-2	16-19-0
Punts	6-45.2	3-30.0
Fumbles-Lost	2-0	3-1
Penalties-Yards	10-91	7-40
Time of possession	15:58	44:02

Attendance—66,977.

INDIVIDUAL STATISTICS

Rushing—Dallas, Walker 8-10, Aikman 1-13, Scott 1-minus 3; New Orleans, Hilliard 22-83, Frazier 12-74, Heyward 7-26, Hebert 2-11, Jordan 1-3, Hill 1-minus 7.

Passing—Dallas, Aikman 18-36-2—180, Saxon 1-1-0—4; New Orleans, Hebert 16-19-0—153.

Receiving—Dallas, Irvin 4-53, Martin 4-47, Walker 4-36, Scott 4-30, Folsom 1-4, Ruzek 1-4; New Orleans, Hill 5-47, Martin 5-46, Turner 2-23, Shepard 1-13, Brenner 1-10, Hilliard 1-9, Scales 1-5.

Kickoff Returns—Dallas, Burbage 3-55; New Orleans, Frazier 1-4.

Punt Returns—Dallas, Martin 1-9; New Orleans, Shepard 3-67, Hill 3-11.

Interceptions—New Orleans, Waymer 1-0, Maxie 1-8.

Punting—Dallas, Saxon 6-45.2; New Orleans, Winslow 3-30.0.

Field Goals—None attempted.

Sacks—Dallas, Jeffcoat; New Orleans, Cook, W. Martin.

Buccaneers-Packers
SUNDAY, SEPTEMBER 10
SCORE BY PERIODS

Tampa Bay	0	20	3	0—23
Green Bay	7	0	7	7—21

SCORING

Green Bay—Fullwood 3 run (Jacke kick), 6:10 1st.
Tampa Bay—Tate 2 run (Igwebuike kick), :09 2nd.
Tampa Bay—Tate 1 run (Igwebuike kick), 6:44 2nd.
Tampa Bay—Howard 9 pass from Testaverde (kick failed), 14:35 2nd.
Green Bay—West 11 pass from Majkowski (Jacke kick), 0:08 3rd.
Tampa Bay—Field goal Igwebuike 52, 13:20 3rd.
Green Bay—Bland recovered fumble in end zone (Jacke kick), 0:55 4th.

TEAM STATISTICS

	Tampa Bay	Green Bay
First downs	26	17
Rushes-Yards	40-142	17-103
Sacked-Yards lost	0-0	2-2
Passing yards	205	218
Passes	22-27-0	17-27-3
Punts	3-34.3	1-44.0
Fumbles-Lost	0-0	2-0
Penalties-Yards	6-55	6-62
Time of possession	37:54	22:06

Attendance—55,650.

INDIVIDUAL STATISTICS

Rushing—Tampa Bay, Howard 17-67, Tate 14-38, Stamps 3-15, Testaverde 2-14, Wilder 4-8; Green Bay, Fullwood 8-54, Haddix 4-21, Woodside 2-12, Majkowski 1-7, Fontenot 1-5, Kemp 1-4.

Passing—Tampa Bay, Testaverde 22-27-0—205; Green Bay, Majkowski 17-27-3—220.

Receiving—Tampa Bay, Howard 7-59, Carrier 6-73, Harris 3-24, Tate 2-15, Hall 2-15, Wilder 1-13, Hill 1-6; Green Bay, Woodside 6-49, Sharpe 3-25, Query 2-65, West 2-37, Kemp 2-12, Haddix 1-23, Fontenot 1-9.

Kickoff Returns—Tampa Bay, Elder 2-39, Stamps 1-16; Green Bay, Fullwood 4-97.

Punt Returns—Green Bay, Sutton 1-0.

Interceptions—Tampa Bay, Robinson 2-22, Hamilton 1-24.

Punting—Tampa Bay, Mohr 3-34.3; Green Bay, Bracken 1-44.0.

Field Goals—Tampa Bay, Igwebuike 1-1; Green Bay, none attempted.

Sacks—Tampa Bay, Seals, Davis.

Chargers-Raiders
SUNDAY, SEPTEMBER 10
SCORE BY PERIODS

San Diego	7	0	7	0—14
Los Angeles Raiders	7	14	7	12—40

SCORING

Los Angeles—Mueller 26 pass from Schroeder (Jaeger kick), 2:50 1st.
San Diego—Butts 50 run (Bahr kick), 8:15 1st.
Los Angeles—Fernandez 4 pass from Beuerlein (Jaeger kick), 6:25 2nd.
Los Angeles—Allen 1 run (Jaeger kick), 12:50 2nd.
Los Angeles—Gault 39 pass from Beuerlein (Jaeger kick), 2:14 3rd.
San Diego—Butts 1 run (Bahr kick), 4:54 3rd.
Los Angeles—Field goal Jaeger 22, 4:33 4th.
Los Angeles—Safety, Floyd tackled in end zone, 4:43 4th.
Los Angeles—Mueller 1 run (Jaeger kick), 9:47 4th.

TEAM STATISTICS

	San Diego	Los Angeles
First downs	16	23
Rushes-Yards	25-171	40-260
Sacked-Yards lost	3-19	3-27
Passing yards	134	258
Passes	12-29-1	17-25-0
Punts	6-34.3	2-45.0
Fumbles-Lost	0-0	2-1
Penalties-Yards	3-13	4-17
Time of possession	21:59	38:01

Attendance—40,237.

INDIVIDUAL STATISTICS

Rushing—San Diego, Butts 9-64, McMahon 5-22, Bernstine 2-22, Early 1-19, Brinson 2-17, Archer 1-14, Spencer 3-10, Floyd 1-3, Caravello 1-0; Los Angeles, Allen 13-51, Smith 12-42, Mueller 10-29, Porter 2-23, Fernandez 2-16, Beuerlein 1-minus 1.

Passing—San Diego, McMahon 7-18-0—91, Archer 5-11-1—62; Los Angeles, Schroeder 2-3-0—79, Beuerlein 15-22-0—206.

Receiving—San Diego, A. Miller 3-58, Bernstine 3-34,

Holland 2-11, Spencer 1-23, Caravello 1-11, Brinson 1-10, Early 1-6; Los Angeles, Gault 4-131, Fernandez 4-65, Mueller 2-36, Smith 2-19, Allen 2-minus 1, Dyal 1-17, Horton 1-10, T. Brown 1-8.

Kickoff Returns—San Diego, Holland 4-44, Floyd 3-12; Los Angeles, T. Brown 3-63.

Punt Returns—San Diego, Walker 2-6; Los Angeles, T. Brown 4-43.

Interceptions—Los Angeles, McElroy 1-0.

Punting—San Diego, Colbert 6-34.3; Los Angeles, Gossett 2-45.0.

Field Goals—San Diego, none attempted; Los Angeles, Jaeger 1-2 (missed: 38).

Sacks—San Diego, O'Neal, Williams 2; Los Angeles, Benson, Pickel, Wise.

Cardinals-Lions
SUNDAY, SEPTEMBER 10
SCORE BY PERIODS

Phoenix	0	6	0	10—16
Detroit	3	0	7	3—13

SCORING

Detroit—Field goal Murray 30, 8:03 1st.
Phoenix—Field goal Del Greco 29, 9:15 2nd.
Phoenix—Field goal Del Greco 23, 14:27 2nd.
Detroit—B. Sanders 3 run (Murray kick), 11:59 3rd.
Phoenix—Green 15 pass from Hogeboom (Del Greco kick), 2:27 4th.
Detroit—Field goal Murray 23, 6:46 4th.
Phoenix—Field goal Del Greco 33, 14:47 4th.

TEAM STATISTICS

	Phoenix	Detroit
First downs	19	13
Rushes-Yards	25-65	27-159
Sacked-Yards lost	0-0	2-17
Passing yards	264	99
Passes	21-35-1	7-20-0
Punts	4-40.8	5-49.0
Fumbles-Lost	0-0	1-0
Penalties-Yards	6-67	10-87
Time of possession	32:28	27:32

Attendance—36,735.

INDIVIDUAL STATISTICS

Rushing—Phoenix, Mitchell 18-52, Wolfley 3-7, Ferrell 2-6, Jordan 1-2, Hogeboom 1-minus 2; Detroit, B. Sanders 9-71, Gagliano 4-28, Paige 7-26, Painter 5-26, Gray 2-8.

Passing—Phoenix, Hogeboom 21-35-1—264; Detroit, Gagliano 7-20-0—116.

Receiving—Phoenix, J.T. Smith 10-121, Awalt 4-65, Wolfley 3-35, Green 2-34, Ferrell 1-5, Novacek 1-4; Detroit, Mobley 2-44, Gray 1-30, R. Johnson 1-15, Clark 1-11, Chadwick 1-9, Phillips 1-7.

Kickoff Returns—Phoenix, Sikahema 4-83; Detroit, Gray 3-66, Woods 2-28.

Punt Returns—Phoenix, Sikahema 2-23; Detroit, Gray 2-18.

Interceptions—Detroit, White 1-0.

Punting—Phoenix, Camarillo 4-40.8; Detroit, Arnold 5-49.0.

Field Goals—Phoenix, Del Greco 3-3; Detroit, Murray 2-2.

Sacks—Phoenix, Harvey, Nunn.

49ers-Colts
SUNDAY, SEPTEMBER 10
SCORE BY PERIODS

San Francisco	3	10	10	7—30
Indianapolis	3	7	0	14—24

SCORING

San Francisco—Field goal Cofer 38, 8:15 1st.
Indianapolis—Field goal Biasucci 31, 12:33 1st.
San Francisco—Craig 1 run (Cofer kick), 2:19 2nd.

Indianapolis—Brooks 22 pass from Chandler (Biasucci kick), 6:54 2nd.
San Francisco—Field goal Cofer 26, 15:00 2nd.
San Francisco—Craig 4 run (Cofer kick), 4:27 3rd.
San Francisco—Field goal Cofer 31, 13:25 3rd.
Indianapolis—Chandler 1 run (Biasucci kick), 6:21 4th.
San Francisco—Rice 58 pass from Montana (Cofer kick), 9:39 4th.
Indianapolis—Bentley recovered blocked punt in end zone (Biasucci kick), 13:32 4th.

TEAM STATISTICS

	San Francisco	Indianapolis
First downs	24	22
Rushes-Yards	37-200	27-154
Sacked-Yards lost	3-29	1-10
Passing yards	204	190
Passes	15-26-0	14-32-1
Punts	3-42.3	3-44.7
Fumbles-Lost	0-0	1-0
Penalties-Yards	8-60	7-48
Time of possession	31:27	28:33

Attendance—60,111.

INDIVIDUAL STATISTICS

Rushing—San Francisco, Craig 24-131, Montana 4-21, Flagler 3-18, Rice 1-17, Rathman 4-10, Sydney 1-3; Indianapolis, Dickerson 19-106, Bentley 3-22, Chandler 4-21, Verdin 1-5.

Passing—San Francisco, Montana 15-26-0—233; Indianapolis, Chandler 14-32-1—200.

Receiving—San Francisco, Rice 6-163, J. Taylor 4-49, Rathman 2-6, Sydney 1-11, Walls 1-4, Craig 1-0; Indianapolis, Brooks 4-80, Rison 3-62, Weathers 2-29, Verdin 2-21, Bentley 2-9, Dickerson 1-minus 1.

Kickoff Returns—San Francisco, Flagler 3-91, Jackson 1-0; Indianapolis, Hunter 4-58, Bentley 2-34.

Punt Returns—San Francisco, J. Taylor 2-15; Indianapolis, Verdin 1-12.

Interceptions—San Francisco, McKyer 1-18.

Punting—San Francisco, Helton 3-42.3; Indianapolis, Stark 3-44.7.

Field Goals—San Francisco, Cofer 3-3; Indianapolis, Biasucci 1-3 (missed: 50, 52).

Sacks—San Francisco, Walter; Indianapolis, Bickett, Johnson 2.

Bengals-Bears
SUNDAY, SEPTEMBER 10
SCORE BY PERIODS

Cincinnati	7	0	7	0—14
Chicago	0	7	3	7—17

SCORING

Cincinnati—Brooks 4 pass from Esiason (Gallery kick), 5:08 1st.
Chicago—Tomczak 11 run (Butler kick), 14:50 2nd.
Cincinnati—Woods 5 run (Gallery kick), 6:32 3rd.
Chicago—Field goal Butler 29, 3:20 3rd.
Chicago—Thornton 20 pass from Tomczak (Butler kick), 4:54 4th.

TEAM STATISTICS

	Cincinnati	Chicago
First downs	23	19
Rushes-Yards	41-179	38-212
Sacked-Yards lost	3-33	1-6
Passing yards	151	153
Passes	18-36-0	10-24-2
Punts	4-41.3	2-41.0
Fumbles-Lost	2-0	1-1
Penalties-Yards	4-21	6-39
Time of possession	31:50	28:10

Attendance—64,730.

INDIVIDUAL STATISTICS

Rushing—Cincinnati, Brooks 13-88, Woods 20-62, Esiason 5-20, Ball 2-4, Jennings 1-5; Chicago, Anderson 21-

146, Muster 4-11, Sanders 5-23, Buford 1-6, Tomczak 5-14, Gentry 2-12.

Passing—Cincinnati, Esiason 18-36-0—184; Chicago, Tomczak 10-24-2—159.

Receiving—Cincinnati, Brooks 5-46, Kattus 5-40, McGee 2-38, Smith 2-19, Martin 2-23, Hillary 1-10, Holman 1-8; Chicago, Thornton 4-86, Gentry 3-39, Morris 1-21, Boso 1-9, Muster 1-4.

Kickoff Returns—Cincinnati, Ball 1-19, Jennings 3-61; Chicago, Gentry 3-93.

Punt Returns—Cincinnati, Hillary 1-0; Chicago, Green 2-33.

Interceptions—Cincinnati, Dixon 2-47.

Punting—Cincinnati, L. Johnson 4-41.3; Chicago, Buford 2-41.0.

Field Goals—Cincinnati, Gallery 0-1 (missed: 45); Chicago, Butler 1-1.

Sacks—Cincinnati, Skow; Chicago, Hampton 2, Rivera.

Giants-Redskins
MONDAY, SEPTEMBER 11
SCORE BY PERIODS

New York Giants	7	7	0	13—27
Washington	0	3	7	14—24

SCORING

New York—Turner 30 pass from Simms (Allegre kick), 14:13 1st.
New York—Meggett 62 pass from Simms (Allegre kick), 5:58 2nd.
Washington—Field goal Lohmiller 24, 13:32 2nd.
Washington—Sanders 48 pass from Rypien (Lohmiller kick), 13:04 3rd.
New York—Anderson 14 run (Allegre kick), 1:34 4th.
Washington—Monk 6 pass from Rypien (Lohmiller kick), 6:45 4th.
Washington—Coleman 24 interception return (Lohmiller kick), 7:39 4th.
New York—Field goal Allegre 32, 12:43 4th.
New York—Field goal Allegre 52, 15:00 4th.

TEAM STATISTICS

	New York	Washington
First downs	19	19
Rushes-Yards	37-159	25-112
Sacked-Yards lost	4-24	1-4
Passing yards	231	345
Passes	11-19-2	22-32-1
Punts	4-51.0	4-41.8
Fumbles-Lost	1-1	3-2
Penalties-Yards	4-31	7-38
Time of possession	31:49	28:11

Attendance—54,160.

INDIVIDUAL STATISTICS

Rushing—New York, Anderson 23-93, Carthon 8-19, Simms 2-22, Meggett 2-17, Rouson 2-8; Washington, Riggs 24-111, Monk 1-1.

Passing—New York, Simms 11-19-2-255; Washington, Rypien 22-32-1—349.

Receiving—New York, Turner 3-99, Bavaro 3-48, Meggett 1-62, Mowatt 1-31, Ingram 1-6, Rouson 1-5, Anderson 1-4; Washington, Sanders 6-143, Clark 6-101, Monk 4-38, Warren 2-31, Riggs 2-22, J. Johnson 1-13, Byner 1-1.

Kickoff Returns—New York, Meggett 4-85; Washington, A.J. Johnson 5-103.

Punt Returns—New York, Meggett 3-41; Washington, Howard 2-19.

Interceptions—New York, White 1-18; Washington, Walton 1-20, Coleman 1-24.

Punting—New York, Landeta 4-51.0; Washington, Mojsiejenko 4-41.8.

Field Goals—New York, Allegre 2-3 (missed: 42); Washington, Lohmiller 1-2 (missed: 49).

Sacks—New York, Taylor; Washington, Coleman, Mann, Grant 1½, Manley ½.

SECOND WEEK

RESULTS OF WEEK 2
Sunday, September 17

Atlanta 27, Dallas 21 at Atl.
Chicago 38, Minnesota 7 at Chi.
Cincinnati 41, Pittsburgh 10 at Cin.
Cleveland 38, N.Y. Jets 24 at Cleve.
Green Bay 35, New Orleans 34 at G.B.
Houston 34, San Diego 27 at S.D.
Kansas City 24, L.A. Raiders 19 at K.C.
L.A. Rams 31, Indianapolis 17 at L.A.
Miami 24, New England 10 at N.E.
N.Y. Giants 24, Detroit 14 at N.Y.
Philadelphia 42, Washington 37 at Wash.
Phoenix 34, Seattle 24 at Sea.
San Francisco 20, Tampa Bay 16 at T.B.

Monday, September 18

Denver 28, Buffalo 14 at Buff.

"I thought last week was bad," muttered Washington guard Russ Grimm, still smarting over the Redskins' season-opening loss to the New York Giants on a last-second, 52-yard field goal. "I couldn't remember ever getting beat in the closing seconds on a field goal, let alone have something like this happen."

What happened against the Philadelphia Eagles in Week 2 were six Washington turnovers, the last being the costliest of all.

With just 1:16 remaining, the Redskins had the lead, 37-35, and the ball at the Philadelphia 22-yard line. On a third-and-10 play, however, running back Gerald Riggs ran into offensive lineman Raleigh McKenzie and dropped the football. Eagles linebacker Al Harris scooped up the fumble and lateraled to safety Wes Hopkins, who dashed 77 yards to the Washington 4-yard line.

"They (teammates) told me to give up the football, so I did," Harris said, laughing.

On the next play, quarterback Randall Cunningham, who set a club record with 447 yards passing, threw his fifth touchdown pass of the game—and third to Keith Jackson—to lift the Eagles to a stunning 42-37 victory, their first in Washington since 1985.

The Redskins had led 20-0 after 10 minutes, 30-14 at halftime and 37-28 with three minutes to play.

The fumble marred an otherwise fabulous day for Riggs, who rushed for 221 yards, a career high and Redskins record. The fumble was the third of the young season for Riggs, who in 1985 never fumbled while carrying a league-high 397 times for the Atlanta Falcons.

"Gerald's big day is basically null and void, right?" mused teammate Earnest Byner, the former Brown whose fumble inside the 5-yard line with 1:05 left proved critical in Cleveland's 38-33 loss to Denver in the 1987 American Football Conference championship. "Same as my situation in Denver. I kicked their butt all day long and one play erased the whole day for me. Same for Gerald. You know, that stuff shouldn't happen."

But it did. And the Redskins, who had defeated Philadelphia in six of their seven previous meetings, dropped to 0-2 for the year. The Eagles' last two touchdowns were scored in the final 1:48.

"It's probably one of the low points since I've been here," said Washington Coach Joe Gibbs, who took over the team in 1981. "It was one of the toughest losses I've ever been associated with."

The New Orleans Saints also fell victim to a comeback in Week 2, losing a 35-34 decision to Green Bay after leading at halftime, 24-7. The Saints scored touchdowns on their first three possessions only to have the Packers counter with four touchdowns on four possessions in the second half.

Despite running only three plays from scrimmage in the third quarter, New Orleans appeared to regain command when Morten Andersen kicked a 32-yard field goal with 2:21 to play. The Packers were down, 34-28, but not out. They drove 80 yards in 55 seconds to score the game-winning touchdown on a three-yard pass from Don Majkowski to Sterling Sharpe.

The key play in the drive was a controversial 23-yard reception by rookie Jeff Query on a fourth-and-17 situation from the Green Bay 48-yard line. Query appeared to step out of bounds after the catch, and the side judge, Doyle Jackson, ruled accordingly. Head linesman Tom Barnes overruled Jackson, however, and the instant replay was deemed inconclusive.

Majkowski, who connected on 25 of 32 passes for 354 yards, completed 18 straight attempts in the second half to set a club record.

In Los Angeles, quarterback Jim Everett threw 14 consecutive completions to establish a Rams individual record, leading Los Angeles to a 31-17 victory over Indianapolis. Everett, good on 28 of 35 passes for 368 yards overall, threw three scoring strikes to Henry Ellard, the Rams' leading receiver with 12 catches for 230 yards.

Everett was eight-of-eight on a game-tying 90-yard drive late in the first half, then four-of-four on a 77-yard, go-ahead drive early in the third quarter.

The heroics of the Everett-Ellard connection overshadowed the homecoming of Colts running back Eric Dickerson, the former Rams star who played his first game at Anaheim Stadium since the October 1987 trade that sent him to Indianapolis. Dickerson, greeted by boos from the 63,995 fans, was thrown for a three-yard loss on his first carry.

He finished the game with 116 yards rushing, tying Lydell Mitchell's club record of 16 100-

yard performances.

Another homecoming took place in Atlanta, where Dallas Cowboys running back Herschel Walker made his first pro appearance in Georgia in a 27-21 Cowboys loss. Walker, the 1982 Heisman Trophy winner while at the University of Georgia, last played in his home state in a 38-18 victory over Georgia Tech on November 27, 1982.

Walker's 85 yards rushing and two touchdowns weren't enough to prevent Dallas from starting a season 0-2 for the first time since 1963. The Falcons, who trailed 21-10 at halftime, put together scoring marches of 49, 75 and 79 yards after the intermission. On the two drives that resulted in touchdowns, quarterback Chris Miller completed 10 of 12 for 120 yards.

Walker's return attracted 55,285 fans, the Falcons' largest home crowd since 1986, but an even larger gathering, 71,741, turned out at Kansas City's Arrowhead Stadium to welcome new Coach Marty Schottenheimer. The Chiefs rewarded Schottenheimer with his first victory at their helm, a 24-19 decision over the Los Angeles Raiders.

The Raiders were generous guests. They were flagged for 60 yards in penalties on the Chiefs' game-winning 87-yard touchdown drive midway through the fourth quarter. Cornerback Terry McDaniel was whistled for two pass interference penalties that covered 60 yards.

Kansas City fullback Christian Okoye, who missed the entire preseason with a neck injury, rushed for 95 yards and two touchdowns on 27 carries, the most rushing attempts by a Chiefs player since 1981.

Okoye's one-yard touchdown plunge in the final quarter proved to be decisive, but rookie linebacker Derrick Thomas ensured the victory by sacking quarterback Jay Schroeder on consecutive plays on the Raiders' ensuing possession.

The best team defense in the first two weeks was being played by the Cleveland Browns, whose defensive unit scored its fourth touchdown of the year in a 38-24 triumph over the New York Jets. Safety Thane Gash's 36-yard interception return for a touchdown staked the Browns to a 14-7 lead at halftime.

Jets quarterback Ken O'Brien threw a career-high four interceptions, but New York managed to cut Cleveland's lead to 28-24 early in the fourth quarter on Freeman McNeil's one-yard touchdown run. Browns rookie Eric Metcalf returned the ensuing kickoff 47 yards, however, setting up a 41-yard drive for the game's final touchdown.

The Browns hadn't won their first two games since 1979.

One team that would have liked to start the season anew was Pittsburgh, whose 41-10 thrashing at the hands of Cincinnati added to

Doug Reed gave former teammate Eric Dickerson a rude welcome home on his first carry in the Rams' 31-17 victory over the Colts.

the humiliation of a 51-0 loss to Cleveland on opening weekend.

The Bengals amassed 520 yards on offense, just 39 fewer than the 559 yards they accumulated against the Steelers a year earlier (an all-time high against Pittsburgh). Through the first two weeks, the Steelers had surrendered 877 total yards, yielded 12 sacks and committed eight turnovers.

This game was a mismatch from the start. Cincinnati scored on every possession except one: when a fumble by running back Ickey Woods at the Pittsburgh 11 killed a 60-yard drive. Quarterback Boomer Esiason completed 16 of 27 passes for 328 yards, paving the way for the Bengals' 11th straight win at home.

The Miami Dolphins snapped an 11-game losing streak against AFC Eastern Division competition with a 24-10 victory at New England. The Dolphins scored all their points in the first half en route to their first victory over the Patriots since 1985.

Miami struck quickly, scoring 17 points on its first three possessions. The last two drives came after New England twice botched fake punts deep in its own territory. On both occasions, with the Patriots facing fourth-and-16 sit-

Sterling Sharpe caught eight passes for 107 yards and scored the winning touchdown with 1:26 left in Green Bay's 35-34 victory over New Orleans.

uations, punter Jeff Feagles' passes to wideout Sammy Martin fell incomplete, giving Miami possession inside the Pats' 30-yard line.

Dolphins quarterback Dan Marino threw three touchdown passes to increase his career total to 200, a plateau he reached faster than any other quarterback in NFL history. Marino's 200th scoring strike came in his 89th game; former Colts great Johnny Unitas, now the runner-up, achieved the mark in his 121st contest.

San Diego quarterback Jim McMahon passed for a career-high 389 yards in Week 2, but his arm wasn't enough to prevent the Chargers' second straight defeat, a 34-27 loss to Houston. It was the Oilers' first regular-season victory in San Diego since 1962, when both teams played in the old American Football League.

McMahon's 300-yard passing performance was just the second of his eight-year career. Both have come in losing efforts, the first back in 1987 when McMahon threw for 311 yards in the Chicago Bears' 31-29 loss to Denver.

The bigger story of this game, however, was Houston quarterback Warren Moon, who passed for two touchdowns and ran for a third. The Oilers, who scored 31 straight points in one stretch, converted five San Diego turnovers into 24 points.

Turnovers also proved pivotal in Chicago, where the Bears took advantage of four interceptions thrown by Minnesota quarterback Wade Wilson to record a 38-7 victory. The Bears intercepted three passes in the fourth quarter and exploded for 28 points, tying a club scoring record for one period.

Shaun Gayle, Ron Rivera and Lemuel Stinson picked off Wilson in the final period, with Stinson returning his interception 29 yards for a touchdown. Rookie Donnell Woolford's interception at the Bears' 3-yard line late in the first half preserved a 10-7 Chicago lead.

Running back Neal Anderson scored three touchdowns for the Bears, who avenged a Vikings' sweep of their 1988 season series.

The Detroit Lions entered their Week 2 game against the New York Giants also looking to exact revenge for a sweep suffered the previous year. Detroit wasn't up to the task, however, losing again, 24-14.

The Lions appeared headed for the upset when they took a 14-3 lead on rookie Barry Sanders' four-yard touchdown run early in the second half. They turned the ball over on four of their next six possessions, however, and managed just 90 yards on offense the rest of the game.

The Giants scored on three straight possessions following Sanders' touchdown, the first coming on an 11-yard touchdown run by Ottis Anderson. Giants quarterback Phil Simms connected on 12 of 14 passes in the second half.

San Francisco's Joe Montana completed four of seven passes for 53 yards on a game-winning drive that was capped by the quarter-

Tight end Keith Jackson caught three touchdown passes in Philadelphia's 42-37 win at Washington.

back's four-yard scoring run, lifting the 49ers to a 20-16 victory over Tampa Bay. Montana's touchdown, with just 40 seconds remaining, overcame a 16-13 Buccaneers lead assumed three minutes earlier on an 18-yard scoring pass from Vinny Testaverde to Mark Carrier.

The 49ers' game-winning drive was helped by three holding penalties against Tampa Bay, including one against defensive back Donnie Elder two plays prior to the touchdown.

The Bucs probably deserved a better fate. They sacked Montana four times and held the San Francisco running game to 63 yards on 30 attempts. Ricky Reynolds intercepted two Montana passes and forced a Roger Craig fumble that Tampa Bay recovered at its 1-yard line early in the fourth quarter.

It took the Phoenix Cardinals just five plays to move 90 yards for a touchdown that set the tone for a 34-24 victory over the Seattle Seahawks. The Cardinals followed up with successive touchdown drives of 96, 41, 74 and 78 yards on their way to 469 yards in total offense. Quarterback Gary Hogeboom completed 18 of 24 passes for 298 yards.

Hogeboom, who took over the Phoenix starting job when veteran Neil Lomax elected to sit out the year with an arthritic hip condition, threw four touchdown passes, including three to wide receiver Roy Green. Green and team-mate J.T. Smith caught a combined 15 passes for 270 yards and four touchdowns.

It was the Cardinals' second straight road win of the season.

The Denver Broncos snapped an eight-game losing streak on artificial turf with a 28-14 victory at Buffalo in the Monday night game. The Broncos, who hadn't won on carpet since Week 3 of the 1986 season, handed the Bills their first loss at Rich Stadium since 1987.

The Broncos scored the game's first 21 points before Buffalo cut the deficit to 21-14 with touchdown drives of 77 and 66 yards in the third and fourth quarters, respectively. Late in the game, however, Denver quarterback John Elway passed to Vance Johnson for a 25-yard gain, then ran 31 yards to the Bills' 5-yard line to set up rookie Bobby Humphrey's scoring run.

Cardinals-Seahawks
SUNDAY, SEPTEMBER 17
SCORE BY PERIODS

Phoenix	13	0	7	14—34
Seattle	0	7	7	10—24

SCORING
Phoenix—Green 51 pass from Hogeboom (kick failed), 2:40 1st.
Phoenix—Jordan 1 run (Del Greco kick), 12:44 1st.
Seattle—Skansi 3 pass from Krieg (N. Johnson kick), 6:37 2nd.

Phoenix—J.T. Smith 25 pass from Hogeboom (Del Greco kick), 3:10 3rd.

Seattle—Skansi 17 pass from Krieg (N. Johnson kick), 7:01 3rd.

Phoenix—Green 6 pass from Hogeboom (Del Greco kick), 0:08 4th.

Seattle—Field goal N. Johnson 39, 7:05 4th.

Phoenix—Green 59 pass from Hogeboom (Del Greco kick), 10:44 4th.

Seattle—Blades 5 pass from Krieg (N. Johnson kick), 13:15 4th.

TEAM STATISTICS

	Phoenix	Seattle
First downs	25	23
Rushes-Yards	42-171	20-77
Sacked-Yards lost	0-0	3-10
Passing yards	298	269
Passes	18-24-1	25-43-1
Punts	1-46.0	4-39.5
Fumbles-Lost	3-2	2-0
Penalties-Yards	13-90	7-64
Time of possession	32:07	27:53

Attendance—60,444.

INDIVIDUAL STATISTICS

Rushing—Phoenix, Mitchell 18-95, Clark 10-42, Wolfley 4-15, Jordan 7-11, Hogeboom 3-8; Seattle, Williams 9-36, Krieg 3-21, Warner 8-20.

Passing—Phoenix, Hogeboom 18-24-1—298; Seattle, Krieg 25-43-1—279.

Receiving—Phoenix, Green 8-166, J.T. Smith 7-104, Jones 1-14, Mitchell 1-10, Awalt 1-4; Seattle, Blades 9-146, Skansi 6-80, Williams 3-4, Kane 2-31, Tyler 2-8, Warner 2-1, Bouyer 1-9.

Kickoff Returns—Phoenix, Sikahema 3-59, Jones 1-17; Seattle, Harris 3-49, Jefferson 3-58.

Punt Returns—Phoenix, Sikahema 2-4.

Interceptions—Phoenix, McDonald 1-0; Seattle, J. Johnson 1-18.

Punting—Phoenix, Camarillo 1-46.0; Seattle, Rodriguez 4-39.5.

Field Goals—Phoenix, none attempted; Seattle, N. Johnson 1-2 (missed: 48).

Sacks—Phoenix, Harvey, Clasby, Saddler.

Steelers-Bengals

SUNDAY, SEPTEMBER 17
SCORE BY PERIODS

Pittsburgh	3	0	7	0—10
Cincinnati	3	17	7	14—41

SCORING

Cincinnati—Field goal Gallery 26, 9:57 1st.

Pittsburgh—Field goal Anderson 38, 13:09 1st.

Cincinnati—Brown 27 pass from Esiason (Gallery kick), 1:08 2nd.

Cincinnati—Field goal Gallery 47, 8:39 2nd.

Cincinnati—Woods 1 run (Gallery kick), 11:02 2nd.

Pittsburgh—Hill 7 pass from Brister (Anderson kick), 5:03 3rd.

Cincinnati—Jennings 1 run (Gallery kick), 11:29 3rd.

Cincinnati—Brooks 2 run (Gallery kick), 0:59 4th.

Cincinnati—Jennings 43 pass from Esiason (Gallery kick), 11:07 4th.

TEAM STATISTICS

	Pittsburgh	Cincinnati
First downs	18	30
Rushes-Yards	25-86	37-192
Sacked-Yards lost	6-56	0-0
Passing yards	188	328
Passes	19-35-0	16-27-0
Punts	5-39.6	0-00.0
Fumbles-Lost	0-0	2-1
Penalties-Yards	12-144	7-50
Time of possession	31:57	28:03

Attendance—53,855.

INDIVIDUAL STATISTICS

Rushing—Pittsburgh, Worley 10-37, Hoge 13-33, Brister 1-15, Carter 1-1; Cincinnati, Brooks 20-113, Woods 9-32, Esiason 2-26, Jennings 3-17, Ball 2-6, Hillary 1-minus 2.

Passing—Pittsburgh, Brister 19-35-0—244; Cincinnati, Esiason 16-27-0—328.

Receiving—Pittsburgh, Lipps 5-122, Mularkey 4-56, Carter 3-20, Stone 2-26, Hoge 2-7, O'Shea 1-8, Hill 1-7, Worley 1-minus 2; Cincinnati, McGee 6-100, Brown 2-66, Holman 2-30, Parker 1-45, Jennings 1-43, Brooks 1-17, Smith 1-12, Hillary 1-11, Kattus 1-4.

Kickoff Returns—Pittsburgh, Woodson 4-165, G. Williams 1-22, Stone 1-12; Cincinnati, Jennings 3-64.

Punt Returns—Cincinnati, Hillary 2-7.

Interceptions—

Punting—Pittsburgh, Newsome 5-39.6; Cincinnati, none attempted.

Field Goals—Pittsburgh, Anderson 1-1; Cincinnati, Gallery 2-2.

Sacks—Cincinnati, Tuatagaloa, Skow, Zander, Bussey, Hammerstein, McClendon ½, Grant ½.

Jets-Browns

SUNDAY, SEPTEMBER 17
SCORE BY PERIODS

New York Jets	0	7	10	7—24
Cleveland	0	14	14	10—38

SCORING

New York—Vick 39 run (Leahy kick), 3:14 2nd.

Cleveland—Slaughter 35 pass from Kosar (Bahr kick), 8:59 2nd.

Cleveland—Gash 36 interception return (Bahr kick), 10:06 2nd.

New York—Townsell 49 pass from O'Brien (Leahy kick), 3:35 3rd.

Cleveland—Manoa 6 pass from Kosar (Bahr kick), 6:33 3rd.

New York—Field goal Leahy 36, 7:42 3rd.

Cleveland—K. Jones 9 run (Bahr kick), 10:51 3rd.

New York—McNeil 1 run (Leahy kick), 2:54 4th.

Cleveland—Newsome 4 pass from Kosar (Bahr kick), 7:07 4th.

Cleveland—Field goal Bahr 21, 12:48 4th.

TEAM STATISTICS

	New York	Cleveland
First downs	21	18
Rushes-Yards	31-136	23-85
Sacked-Yards lost	3-24	1-4
Passing yards	246	192
Passes	24-43-4	15-30-0
Punts	3-41.3	6-40.3
Fumbles-Lost	2-0	1-1
Penalties-Yards	7-70	11-64
Time of possession	33:08	26:52

Attendance—73,516.

INDIVIDUAL STATISTICS

Rushing—New York, Vick 12-80, McNeil 16-50, Hector 3-6; Cleveland, K. Jones 9-49, Manoa 8-15, Langhorne 1-14, Kosar 3-4, Metcalf 2-3.

Passing—New York, O'Brien 24-43-4—270; Cleveland, Kosar 15-30-0—196.

Receiving—New York, Shuler 6-69, McNeil 6-40, Toon 5-66, Vick 3-24, Townsell 2-57, Griggs 1-9, Hector 1-5; Cleveland, Newsome 4-31, Slaughter 3-69, K. Jones 3-55, Langhorne 3-28, Metcalf 1-7, Manoa 1-6.

Kickoff Returns—New York, Townsell 3-113, Humphery 1-20, Dixon 1-10; Cleveland, Metcalf 3-102, K. Jones 1-25.

Punt Returns—New York, Townsell 3-49; Cleveland, McNeil 3-7.

Interceptions—Cleveland, Gash 1-36, Wright 2-13, M. Johnson 1-23.

Punting—New York, Prokop 3-41.3; Cleveland, Wagner 6-40.3.

Field Goals—New York, Leahy 1-3 (missed: 43, 32); Cleveland, Bahr 1-1.

Sacks—New York, Washington; Cleveland, Baker, Perry, Stewart.

49ers-Buccaneers
SUNDAY, SEPTEMBER 17
SCORE BY PERIODS

San Francisco	0	6	0	14—20
Tampa Bay	3	0	6	7—16

SCORING

Tampa Bay—Field goal Igwebuike 23, 8:24 1st.
San Francisco—Field goal Cofer 47, 2:23 2nd.
San Francisco—Field goal Cofer 32, 14:51 2nd.
Tampa Bay—Field goal Igwebuike 44, 5:28 3rd.
Tampa Bay—Field goal Igwebuike 37, 10:00 3rd.
San Francisco—Rice 2 pass from Montana (Cofer kick), 6:29 4th.
Tampa Bay—Carrier 18 pass from Testaverde (Igwebuike kick), 11:35 4th.
San Francisco—Montana 4 run (Cofer kick), 14:20 4th.

TEAM STATISTICS

	San Francisco	Tampa Bay
First downs	22	13
Rushes-Yards	30-63	26-91
Sacked-Yards lost	4-22	2-20
Passing yards	244	126
Passes	25-39-2	14-35-2
Punts	6-44.3	8-42.9
Fumbles-Lost	1-1	3-1
Penalties-Yards	6-60	4-24
Time of possession	31:43	28:17
Attendance—64,087.		

INDIVIDUAL STATISTICS

Rushing—San Francisco, Craig 16-36, Montana 9-21, Rice 1-11, Rathman 2-1, Sydney 1-0, Flagler 1-minus 6; Tampa Bay, Howard 12-41, Testaverde 5-28, Tate 7-16, Stamps 2-6.

Passing—San Francisco, Montana 25-39-2—266; Tampa Bay, Testaverde 14-35-2—146.

Receiving—San Francisco, Rice 8-122, Rathman 7-43, Craig 3-30, Jones 3-26, J. Taylor 2-27, Wilson 1-15, Sydney 1-3; Tampa Bay, Carrier 5-86, Hall 4-44, Hill 1-7, Tate 1-6, Howard 1-4, Smith 1-3, Stamps 1-minus 4.

Kickoff Returns—San Francisco, Flagler 2-47; Tampa Bay, Elder 3-42.

Punt Returns—San Francisco, J. Taylor 5-55; Tampa Bay, Futrell 6-42.

Interceptions—San Francisco, Lott 2-0; Tampa Bay, Reynolds 2-6.

Punting—San Francisco, Helton 6-44.3; Tampa Bay, Mohr 8-42.9.

Field Goals—San Francisco, Cofer 2-2; Tampa Bay, Igwebuike 3-3.

Sacks—San Francisco, Brooks, Haley; Tampa Bay, Murphy 2, Moss, Jarvis.

Dolphins-Patriots
SUNDAY, SEPTEMBER 17
SCORE BY PERIODS

Miami	17	7	0	0—24
New England	0	0	3	7—10

SCORING

Miami—Clayton 15 pass from Marino (Stoyanovich kick), 3:29 1st.
Miami—Jensen 16 pass from Marino (Stoyanovich kick), 7:15 1st.
Miami—Field goal Stoyanovich 31, 10:56 1st.
Miami—Jensen 10 pass from Marino (Stoyanovich kick), 7:15 2nd.

New England—Field goal Davis 28, 3:49 3rd.
New England—Dykes 10 pass from Eason (Davis kick), 15:00 4th.

TEAM STATISTICS

	Miami	New England
First downs	18	19
Rushes-Yards	30-103	13-43
Sacked-Yards lost	0-0	7-59
Passing yards	226	282
Passes	17-28-3	25-51-1
Punts	3-46.7	3-37.3
Fumbles-Lost	1-1	1-0
Penalties-Yards	7-63	4-47
Time of possession	33:03	26:57
Attendance—57,043.		

INDIVIDUAL STATISTICS

Rushing—Miami, Smith 7-40, Logan 8-31, Stradford 7-28, T. Brown 3-4, Hampton 3-3, Marino 2-minus 3; New England, Stephens 9-31, Perryman 3-8, Dupard 1-4.

Passing—Miami, Marino 17-28-3—226; New England, Eason 25-49-1—341, Feagles 0-2-0—0.

Receiving—Miami, Clayton 6-79, Edmunds 3-57, Jensen 3-34, Duper 2-27, A. Brown 1-15, T. Brown 1-10, Hampton 1-4; New England, Sievers 9-70, Morgan 6-88, Dupard 4-64, Fryar 3-80, Jones 2-29, Dykes 1-10.

Kickoff Returns—Miami, Hampton 1-26, Logan 1-17; New England, Martin 3-83, Rice 1-19.

Punt Returns—Miami, Stradford 3-22; New England, Fryar 1-10.

Interceptions—Miami, Lankford 1-0; New England, James 1-28, Rembert 1-0, McGrew 1-minus 4.

Punting—Miami, Roby 3-46.7; New England, Feagles 3-37.3.

Field Goals—Miami, Stoyanovich 1-1; New England, Davis 1-2 (missed: 40).

Sacks—Miami, Krauss 3, Kumerow 2, Sochia, Frye.

Colts-Rams
SUNDAY, SEPTEMBER 17
SCORE BY PERIODS

Indianapolis	3	14	0	0—17
Los Angeles Rams	10	7	7	7—31

SCORING

Los Angeles—Field goal Lansford 40, 8:58 1st.
Indianapolis—Field goal Biasucci 19, 12:54 1st.
Los Angeles—Ellard 29 pass from Everett (Lansford kick), 14:50 1st.
Indianapolis—Verdin 82 pass from Chandler (Biasucci kick), 0:10 2nd.
Indianapolis—Dickerson 2 run (Biasucci kick), 7:08 2nd.
Los Angeles—Ellard 17 pass from Everett (Lansford kick), 13:30 2nd.
Los Angeles—Ellard 6 pass from Everett (Lansford kick), 6:16 3rd.
Los Angeles—Bell 2 run (Lansford kick), 13:26 4th.

TEAM STATISTICS

	Indianapolis	Los Angeles
First downs	20	27
Rushes-Yards	22-120	28-97
Sacked-Yards lost	0-0	3-16
Passing yards	266	352
Passes	20-33-1	28-35-1
Punts	3-45.3	2-33.5
Fumbles-Lost	2-1	3-0
Penalties-Yards	8-38	6-50
Time of possession	25:12	34:48
Attendance—63,995.		

INDIVIDUAL STATISTICS

Rushing—Indianapolis, Dickerson 21-116, Chandler 1-4; Los Angeles, Bell 22-68, Delpino 4-21, Ron Brown 1-5, Everett 1-3.

Passing—Indianapolis, Chandler 20-33-1—266; Los Angeles, Everett 28-35-1—368.

Receiving—Indianapolis, Brooks 5-64, Dickerson 5-45, Weathers 4-33, Verdin 2-83, Rison 2-16, Bentley 1-13, Beach 1-12; Los Angeles, Ellard 12-230, Bell 5-13, Holohan 4-25, McGee 4-21, Anderson 3-79.

Kickoff Returns—Indianapolis, Verdin 5-108, Bentley 1-minus 1; Los Angeles, Ron Brown 4-59.

Punt Returns—None.

Interceptions—Indianapolis, Ball 1-5; Los Angeles, Gray 1-0.

Punting—Indianapolis, Stark 3-45.3; Los Angeles, Hatcher 2-33.5.

Field Goals—Indianapolis, Biasucci 1-1; Los Angeles, Lansford 1-1.

Sacks—Indianapolis, Hand, Johnson, Alston.

Cowboys-Falcons
SUNDAY, SEPTEMBER 17
SCORE BY PERIODS

Dallas	14	7	0	0—21
Atlanta	7	3	10	7—27

SCORING

Dallas—Irvin 65 pass from Aikman (Ruzek kick), 1:11 1st.
Atlanta—Butler 29 fumble return (McFadden kick), 8:09 1st.
Dallas—Walker 4 run (Ruzek kick), 14:04 1st.
Atlanta—Field goal McFadden 28, 11:51 2nd.
Dallas—Walker 20 run (Ruzek kick), 14:21 2nd.
Atlanta—Field goal McFadden 38, 4:00 3rd.
Atlanta—Flowers 1 run (McFadden kick), 12:43 3rd.
Atlanta—Settle 4 run (McFadden kick), 7:32 4th.

TEAM STATISTICS

	Dallas	Atlanta
First downs	18	23
Rushes-Yards	30-108	30-90
Sacked-Yards lost	0-0	2-12
Passing yards	241	243
Passes	13-23-2	21-29-0
Punts	4-44.3	4-34.5
Fumbles-Lost	2-1	0-0
Penalties-Yards	8-85	3-17
Time of possession	28:51	31:09
Attendance—55,285.		

INDIVIDUAL STATISTICS

Rushing—Dallas, Walker 23-85, Aikman 5-13, Irvin 1-6, Sargent 1-4; Atlanta, Settle 23-82, Lang 3-8, Flowers 1-1, Haynes 1-0, Miller 2-minus 1.

Passing—Dallas, Aikman 13-23-2—241; Atlanta, Miller 21-29-0—255.

Receiving—Dallas, Irvin 5-115, Walker 2-60, Folsom 2-26, Scott 2-17, Martin 1-19, Johnston 1-4; Atlanta, Collins 5-95, Haynes 5-57, Heller 5-51, Lang 3-27, Beckman 2-15, Settle 1-10.

Kickoff Returns—Dallas, Dixon 3-62, Ankrom 1-1; Atlanta, Jones 4-69.

Punt Returns—Dallas, Martin 1-10; Atlanta, Sanders 2-19.

Interceptions—Atlanta, Case 1-13, Sanders 1-0.

Punting—Dallas, Saxon 4-44.3; Atlanta, Fulhage 4-34.5.

Field Goals—Dallas, none attempted; Atlanta, McFadden 2-3 (missed: 48).

Sacks—Dallas, Norton 2.

Oilers-Chargers
SUNDAY, SEPTEMBER 17
SCORE BY PERIODS

Houston	3	17	14	0—34
San Diego	7	7	0	13—27

SCORING

Houston—Field goal Zendejas 24, 6:01 1st.
San Diego—A. Miller 63 pass from McMahon (Bahr kick), 9:56 1st.

San Diego—Butts 1 run (Bahr kick), 0:16 2nd.
Houston—Givins 14 pass from Moon (Zendejas kick), 3:42 2nd.
Houston—Moon 1 run (Zendejas kick), 11:19 2nd.
Houston—Field goal Zendejas 32, 15:00 2nd.
Houston—Hill 5 pass from Moon (Zendejas kick), 3:39 3rd.
Houston—Highsmith 16 run (Zendejas kick), 14:44 3rd.
San Diego—Butts 1 run (pass failed), 5:56 4th.
San Diego—A. Miller 10 pass from McMahon (Bahr kick), 14:05 4th.

TEAM STATISTICS

	Houston	San Diego
First downs	26	24
Rushes-Yards	35-132	17-41
Sacked-Yards lost	0-0	3-17
Passing yards	235	372
Passes	21-35-0	27-45-3
Punts	3-28.7	2-30.0
Fumbles-Lost	0-0	2-2
Penalties-Yards	8-70	13-117
Time of possession	35:26	24:34
Attendance—42,013.		

INDIVIDUAL STATISTICS

Rushing—Houston, Highsmith 8-50, Pinkett 12-46, White 8-16, Moon 5-15, Rozier 2-5; San Diego, Bernstine 2-24, Floyd 6-10, Butts 5-10, McMahon 1-10, Spencer 2-4, A. Miller 1-minus 17.

Passing—Houston, Moon 21-35-0—235; San Diego, McMahon 27-45-3—389.

Receiving—Houston, Pinkett 7-55, Hill 6-69, Jeffires 4-66, Duncan 2-25, Givins 2-20; San Diego, Bernstine 8-78, A. Miller 7-162, Cox 4-45, Early 3-46, Holland 2-33, Brinson 1-11, Butts 1-8, Spencer 1-6.

Kickoff Returns—Houston, Harris 1-63, K. Johnson 1-25, T. Johnson 1-16; San Diego, Usher 4-59.

Punt Returns—San Diego, Usher 1-4.

Interceptions—Houston, Brown 1-0, Eaton 1-20, Lyles 1-18.

Punting—Houston, Montgomery 2-43.0; San Diego, Colbert 2-30.0.

Field Goals—Houston, Zendejas 2-5 (missed: 47, 24, 44); San Diego, none attempted.

Sacks—Houston, Fairs 1½, McDowell, Childress ½.

Raiders-Chiefs
SUNDAY, SEPTEMBER 17
SCORE BY PERIODS

Los Angeles Raiders	6	10	3	0—19
Kansas City	7	10	0	7—24

SCORING

Los Angeles—Fernandez 25 pass from Schroeder (kick failed), 7:46 1st.
Kansas City—Dressel 49 pass from DeBerg (Lowery kick), 10:56 1st.
Los Angeles—Junkin 3 pass from Schroeder (Jaeger kick), 1:32 2nd.
Kansas City—Field goal Lowery 47, 4:58 2nd.
Los Angeles—Field goal Jaeger 39, 10:02 2nd.
Kansas City—Okoye 8 run (Lowery kick), 14:01 2nd.
Los Angeles—Field goal Jaeger 40, 4:57 3rd.
Kansas City—Okoye 1 run (Lowery kick), 7:09 4th.

TEAM STATISTICS

	Los Angeles	Kansas City
First downs	18	23
Rushes-Yards	29-115	42-152
Sacked-Yards lost	4-39	0-0
Passing yards	153	171
Passes	14-21-1	12-18-1
Punts	2-29.0	1-41.0
Fumbles-Lost	1-0	1-0
Penalties-Yards	11-125	10-93
Time of possession	28:03	31:57
Attendance—71,741.		

INDIVIDUAL STATISTICS

Rushing—Los Angeles, Allen 18-58, S. Smith 8-38, Schroeder 1-12, Porter 2-7; Kansas City, Okoye 27-95, Saxon 3-25, Gamble 2-20, Heard 7-18, DeBerg 3-minus 6.

Passing—Los Angeles, Schroeder 14-21-1—192; Kansas City, DeBerg 12-18-1—171.

Receiving—Los Angeles, Allen 3-44, Mueller 3-38, Fernandez 2-44, Junkin 2-31, S. Smith 2-15, Gault 1-10, Dyal 1-10; Kansas City, Dressel 3-65, Harry 3-37, R. Thomas 2-15, Saxon 1-18, Carson 1-15, Hayes 1-12, Heard 1-9.

Kickoff Returns—Los Angeles, Edmonds 3-80; Kansas City, Gamble 2-37, Copeland 1-17.

Punt Returns—Los Angeles, Edmonds 1-12.

Interceptions—Los Angeles, McElroy 1-0; Kansas City, Ross 1-0.

Punting—Los Angeles, Gossett 2-29.0; Kansas City, Goodburn 1-41.0.

Field Goals—Los Angeles, Jaeger 2-2; Kansas City, Lowery 1-2 (missed: 57).

Sacks—Kansas City, D. Thomas 2½, Saleaumua, Smith ½.

Eagles-Redskins
SUNDAY, SEPTEMBER 17
SCORE BY PERIODS

Philadelphia	7	7	7	21—42
Washington	20	10	0	7—37

SCORING

Washington—Clark 80 pass from Rypien (kick failed), 0:15 1st.

Washington—Riggs 41 run (Lohmiller kick), 2:26 1st.

Washington—Byner 11 pass from Rypien (Lohmiller kick), 9:54 1st.

Philadelphia—Jackson 17 pass from Cunningham (Zendejas kick), 13:24 1st.

Washington—Clark 5 pass from Rypien (Lohmiller kick), 2:17 2nd.

Philadelphia—Toney 3 run (Zendejas kick), 8:00 2nd.

Washington—Field goal Lohmiller 25, 13:40 2nd.

Philadelphia—Jackson 5 pass from Cunningham (Zendejas kick), 10:26 3rd.

Philadelphia—Carter 5 pass from Cunningham (Zendejas kick), 2:21 4th.

Washington—Monk 43 pass from Rypien (Lohmiller kick), 11:54 4th.

Philadelphia—Quick 2 pass from Cunningham (Zendejas kick), 13:12 4th.

Philadelphia—Jackson 4 pass from Cunningham (Zendejas kick), 14:08 4th.

TEAM STATISTICS

	Philadelphia	Washington
First downs	32	16
Rushes-Yards	28-65	32-220
Sacked-Yards lost	4-38	2-16
Passing yards	409	272
Passes	34-46-1	12-23-2
Punts	3-29.0	2-51.0
Fumbles-Lost	3-2	4-4
Penalties-Yards	8-61	5-49
Time of possession	31:57	28:03

Attendance—53,493.

INDIVIDUAL STATISTICS

Rushing—Philadelphia, Toney 9-24, Higgs 5-16, Sherman 3-11, Byars 4-8, Cunningham 7-6; Washington, Riggs 29-221, Morris 2-0, Reaves 1-minus 1.

Passing—Philadelphia, Cunningham 34-46-1—447; Washington, Rypien 12-23-2—288.

Receiving—Philadelphia, Jackson 12-126, Byars 8-130, Carter 5-79, Toney 3-25, Garrity 2-41, Quick 2-23, Sherman 1-15, Higgs 1-8; Washington, Clark 4-153, Monk 4-87, Sanders 2-27, Byner 1-11, Warren 1-10.

Kickoff Returns—Philadelphia, Sherman 4-76, Williams 2-42, Higgs 1-20; Washington, A. Johnson 2-49, Howard 1-23.

Punt Returns—Philadelphia, Williams 1-11.

Lions-Giants
SUNDAY, SEPTEMBER 17
SCORE BY PERIODS

Detroit	0	7	7	0—14
New York Giants	3	0	14	7—24

SCORING

New York—Field goal Allegre 49, 8:14 1st.

Detroit—R. Johnson 71 pass from Gagliano (Murray kick), 6:57 2nd.

Detroit—B. Sanders 4 run (Murray kick), 5:05 3rd.

New York—Anderson 11 run (Allegre kick), 9:50 3rd.

New York—Turner 9 pass from Simms (Allegre kick), 14:17 3rd.

New York—Bavaro 24 pass from Simms (Allegre kick), 5:18 4th.

TEAM STATISTICS

	Detroit	New York
First downs	19	21
Rushes-Yards	19-95	39-129
Sacked-Yards lost	4-29	1-2
Passing yards	315	216
Passes	21-31-3	20-26-0
Punts	5-41.0	5-38.2
Fumbles-Lost	3-2	2-1
Penalties-Yards	7-40	1-10
Time of possession	23:52	36:08

Attendance—76,021.

INDIVIDUAL STATISTICS

Rushing—Detroit, B. Sanders 12-57, Gagliano 7-38; New York, Anderson 25-85, Carthon 3-15, Adams 3-14, Simms 5-11, Rouson 1-5, Meggett 1-2, Turner 1-minus 3.

Passing—Detroit, Gagliano 21-31-3—344; New York, Simms 20-26-0—218.

Receiving—Detroit, R. Johnson 9-172, B. Sanders 6-96, Mobley 3-23, Phillips 2-31, T. Johnson 1-22; New York, Turner 5-67, Bavaro 5-64, Carthon 4-28, Manuel 2-29, Mowatt 2-11, Anderson 1-13, Ingram 1-6.

Kickoff Returns—Detroit, Gray 1-22, Palmer 1-18, Crockett 1-8, T. Johnson 1-16; New York, Ingram 2-33, Meggett 1-16.

Punt Returns—Detroit, Gray 1-0; New York, Meggett 3-41.

Interceptions—New York, Guyton 1-13, DeOssie 1-10, Collins 1-0.

Punting—Detroit, Arnold 5-41.0; New York, Landeta 5-28.2.

Field Goals—Detroit, none attempted; New York, Allegre 1-2 (missed: 49).

Sacks—Detroit, Ball ½, Griffin ½; New York, Taylor 2½, Marshall ½, Banks ½, Howard ½.

Vikings-Bears
SUNDAY, SEPTEMBER 17
SCORE BY PERIODS

Minnesota	0	7	0	0— 7
Chicago	7	3	0	28—38

SCORING

Chicago—Anderson 24 pass from Tomczak (Butler kick), 9:50 1st.

Minnesota—Gustafson 4 pass from Wilson (Garcia kick), 6:58 2nd.

Chicago—Field goal Butler 40, 13:20 2nd.

Chicago—Anderson 2 run (Butler kick), 4:38 4th.

Chicago—Anderson 13 run (Butler kick), 10:04 4th.

Chicago—Stinson 29 interception return (Butler kick), 10:21 4th.
Chicago—Green 37 run (Butler kick), 12:37 4th.

TEAM STATISTICS

	Minnesota	Chicago
First downs	18	20
Rushes-Yards	21-67	39-164
Sacked-Yards lost	0-0	0-0
Passing yards	253	142
Passes	24-42-4	10-26-1
Punts	5-34.6	5-49.8
Fumbles-Lost	2-0	0-0
Penalties-Yards	6-45	5-22
Time of possession	25:12	34:48

Attendance—66,475.

INDIVIDUAL STATISTICS

Rushing—Minnesota, Anderson 5-25, Rice 3-19, Fenney 3-12, Dozier 4-7, Wilson 2-3, Nelson 4-1; Chicago, Anderson 23-97, Green 1-37, Sanders 8-31, Thornton 1-4, Tomczak 2-1, Harbaugh 1-minus 1, Muster 3-minus 5.

Passing—Minnesota, Wilson 24-42-4—253; Chicago, Tomczak 10-26-1—142.

Receiving—Minnesota, Carter 6-80, Anderson 4-22, Dozier 3-37, Jordan 2-37, Jones 2-27, Fenney 2-22, Gustafson 2-13, Rice 2-5, Nelson 1-10; Chicago, McKinnon 4-46, Anderson 3-58, Suhey 1-22, Morris 1-15, Muster 1-1.

Kickoff Returns—Minnesota, Nelson 5-108, Rice 1-13, Fenney 1-12; Chicago, Gentry 1-28, Green 1-23.

Punt Returns—Minnesota, Lewis 3-11; Chicago, Green 3-26.

Interceptions—Minnesota, Browner 1-0; Chicago, Stinson 1-29, Woolford 1-0, Gayle 1-0, Rivera 1-0.

Punting—Minnesota, Scribner 5-34.6; Chicago, Buford 5-49.8.

Field Goals—Minnesota, Garcia 0-2 (missed: 33, 34); Chicago, Butler 1-1.

Saints-Packers
SUNDAY, SEPTEMBER 17
SCORE BY PERIODS

New Orleans	14	10	0	10—	34
Green Bay	0	7	14	14—	35

SCORING

New Orleans—Hill 32 pass from Hebert (Andersen kick), 4:35 1st.
New Orleans—Hilliard 3 run (Andersen kick), 9:52 1st.
New Orleans—Brenner 1 pass from Hebert (Andersen kick), 0:46 2nd.
Green Bay—Fullwood 1 run (Jacke kick), 10:02 2nd.
New Orleans—Field goal Andersen 38, 14:48 2nd.
Green Bay—Fullwood 4 run (Jacke kick), 8:57 3rd.
Green Bay—West 3 pass from Majkowski (Jacke kick), 14:02 3rd.
New Orleans—Hill 24 pass from Hebert (Andersen kick), 1:36 4th.
Green Bay—West 17 pass from Majkowski (Jacke kick), 4:25 4th.
New Orleans—Field goal Andersen 32, 12:39 4th.
Green Bay—Sharpe 3 pass from Majkowski (Jacke kick), 13:34 4th.

TEAM STATISTICS

	New Orleans	Green Bay
First downs	21	29
Rushes-Yards	24-85	27-149
Sacked-Yards lost	0-0	2-13
Passing yards	282	341
Passes	23-32-1	25-32-1
Punts	2-35.5	2-34.0
Fumbles-Lost	1-1	4-1
Penalties-Yards	3-20	4-33
Time of possession	31:08	28:52

Attendance—55,809.

INDIVIDUAL STATISTICS

Rushing—New Orleans, Hilliard 13-43, Heyward 4-25, Frazier 6-11, Turner 1-6; Green Bay, Fullwood 18-125, Majkowski 7-28, Sharpe 1-minus 1, Woodside 1-minus 3.

Passing—New Orleans, Hebert 23-32-1—282; Green Bay, Majkowski 25-32-1—354.

Receiving—New Orleans, Hill 6-90, Brenner 5-43, Turner 3-31, Scales 3-30, E. Martin 2-41, Heyward 2-16, Shepard 1-23, Cook 1-8; Green Bay, Sharpe 8-107, West 6-87, Query 4-84, Kemp 3-41, Woodside 3-27, Fontenot 1-8.

Kickoff Returns—New Orleans, Frazier 3-66; Shepard 1-24, Phillips 1-24; Green Bay, Bland 3-54, Fullwood 1-0.

Punt Returns—New Orleans, Shepard 1-2; Green Bay, Sutton 1-11.

Interceptions—New Orleans, Waymer 1-22; Green Bay, Jakes 1-0.

Punting—New Orleans, Winslow 2-35.5; Green Bay, Bracken 2-34.0.

Field Goals—New Orleans, Andersen 2-2; Green Bay, none attempted.

Sacks—New Orleans, Wilks, Mack.

Broncos-Bills
MONDAY, SEPTEMBER 18
SCORE BY PERIODS

Denver	5	13	3	7—	28
Buffalo	0	0	7	7—	14

SCORING

Denver—Safety, Mueller tackled in end zone, 8:31 1st.
Denver—Field goal Treadwell 22, 12:45 1st.
Denver—Field goal Treadwell 33, 1:24 2nd.
Denver—Johnson 9 pass from Elway (Treadwell kick), 6:54 2nd.
Denver—Field goal Treadwell 46, 15:00 2nd.
Denver—Field goal Treadwell 24, 8:00 3rd.
Buffalo—Kinnebrew 1 run (Norwood kick), 11:37 3rd.
Buffalo—Harmon 20 pass from Kelly (Norwood kick), 0:37 4th.
Denver—Humphrey 5 run (Treadwell kick), 11:05 4th.

TEAM STATISTICS

	Denver	Buffalo
First downs	26	29
Rushes-Yards	43-201	22-94
Sacked-Yards lost	2-26	3-21
Passing yards	181	319
Passes	15-29-2	28-46-3
Punts	5-38.0	3-35.0
Fumbles-Lost	2-0	2-1
Penalties-Yards	10-71	8-66
Time of possession	33:58	26:02

Attendance—78,176.

INDIVIDUAL STATISTICS

Rushing—Denver, Humphrey 10-76, Winder 23-65, Elway 3-33, Jackson 3-15, Alexander 4-12; Buffalo, Kelly 5-51, Thomas 11-38, Mueller 3-6, Kinnebrew 2-0, Harmon 1-minus 1.

Passing—Denver, Elway 15-28-2—207, Johnson 0-1-0—0; Buffalo, Kelly 26-44-3—298, Reich 2-2-0—42.

Receiving—Denver, Johnson 5-51, Alexander 4-40, Sewell 2-66, Jackson 2-18, Young 1-26, Winder 1-6; Buffalo, Reed 13-157, K. Davis 3-55, Harmon 3-47, Thomas 3-30, Johnson 3-23, Kinnebrew 1-14, Metzelaars 1-8, Burkett 1-6.

Kickoff Returns—Denver, Bell 3-52, Humphrey 1-24; Buffalo, Harmon 2-24, Tucker 3-55, K. Davis 1-15.

Punt Returns—Buffalo, Johnson 1-7.

Interceptions—Denver, Braxton 1-26, Henderson 2-36; Buffalo, Odomes 1-0, Kelso 1-4.

Punting—Denver, Horan 5-38.0; Buffalo, Kidd 3-35.0.

Field Goals—Denver, Treadwell 4-4; Buffalo, Norwood 0-1 (missed: 43).

Sacks—Denver, Fletcher, Powers 1½, Townsend ½; Buffalo, Burroughs, B. Smith ½, Bennett ½.

THIRD WEEK

RESULTS OF WEEK 3
Sunday, September 24

Buffalo 47, Houston 41 (OT) at Hous.
Chicago 47, Detroit 27 at Det.
Denver 31, L.A. Raiders 21 at Den.
Indianapolis 13, Atlanta 9 at Ind.
L.A. Rams 41, Green Bay 38 at L.A.
N.Y. Giants 35, Phoenix 7 at N.Y.
N.Y. Jets 40, Miami 33 at Mia.
Pittsburgh 27, Minnesota 14 at Pitts.
San Diego 21, Kansas City 6 at S.D.
San Francisco 38, Philadelphia 28 at Phila.
Seattle 24, New England 3 at N.E.
Tampa Bay 20, New Orleans 10 at T.B.
Washington 30, Dallas 7 at Dall.

Monday, September 25

Cincinnati 21, Cleveland 14 at Cin.

The 1988 National Football League season was untypically disappointing for the Denver Broncos. Coming off back-to-back Super Bowl appearances, Denver finished out of the playoffs with an 8-8 record.

One memory that stayed with the team was borne in Week 4, when the Broncos squandered a 24-0 halftime lead at home and lost, 30-27, in overtime to the Los Angeles Raiders.

When the two longtime AFC Western Division rivals met again at Mile High Stadium in the third week of the 1989 season, that same script was nearly played out again. The Broncos raced to a 28-0 halftime lead, scored only three points in the second half but narrowly escaped with a 31-21 victory. The outcome remained in doubt until rookie free safety Steve Atwater intercepted a Raider pass with 3:20 to play, setting up a David Treadwell field goal with 27 seconds remaining.

Were the Broncos thinking about 1988 as the Raiders mounted their second-half comeback?

"Heck, everybody in this stadium was," Broncos quarterback John Elway said.

Denver Coach Dan Reeves was even more blunt: "You've got to be dumb not to let it enter your mind."

Elway led Denver's first-half salvo with two touchdown passes to Mark Jackson and a 29-yard run for another score. In the second half, however, the veteran quarterback let Los Angeles back in the game with two turnovers, both of them leading to Raider touchdowns.

Cornerback Lionel Washington intercepted a poorly thrown Elway pass early in the third quarter and returned it 32 yards for the Raiders' first touchdown. After Jay Schroeder and Mervyn Fernandez combined for a 75-yard touchdown to cut the deficit to 28-14, Elway fumbled on the Broncos' next possession while being sacked by Greg Townsend. Linden King scooped up the ball and ran 15 yards for another score, cutting the Bronco lead to seven with 4:51 to play.

"We just didn't adjust to the way their defense was playing in the second half," Elway said. "They were playing like a team with nothing to lose, gambling on every down. That caused us a lot of problems."

What ultimately saved the Broncos, however, was a subpar performance by Schroeder. He accounted for all six Raider turnovers, including three first-half fumbles that resulted in Bronco touchdowns. The most critical turnover in Denver's mind was the pass Atwater picked off just as it left Schroeder's hand.

"Our defense continues to make the big plays," Reeves said. "None was any bigger than Atwater's interception at the line of scrimmage. It takes great athletic ability to intercept one that close to the quarterback."

The Los Angeles Rams also built a huge lead in Week 3 only to narrowly pull out a 41-38 victory over Green Bay. The Packers, who rallied from a 24-7 halftime deficit to defeat New Orleans, 35-34, in Week 2, just missed another miracle comeback after trailing the Rams, 38-7, at intermission.

Led by running back Greg Bell, the Rams scored on five of their first six possessions. Bell, who rushed for a career-high 221 yards, had touchdown runs of 1 and 45 yards in the first two periods. Quarterback Jim Everett put up a pair of four-yard scoring passes, to Buford McGee and Damone Johnson, while safety Vince Newsome returned an interception 81 yards for another score.

The second half, however, belonged to the Packers. They scored touchdowns on drives of 61, 22 and 79 yards in the third quarter before Chris Jacke's 43-yard field goal cut the Rams' lead to 38-31 one minute into the final period. Green Bay then lost a golden opportunity to tie when fullback Brent Fullwood fumbled into the end zone on a play from the Rams' 1-yard line. Los Angeles recovered for a touchback.

Fullwood's fumble proved critical. The Rams extended their lead to 41-31 on the ensuing possession when Mike Lansford booted a 45-yard field goal with 5:17 left.

After losing their starting quarterback and star running back to injuries, the Indianapolis Colts rallied from a 9-0 deficit to defeat Atlanta, 13-9, in an interconference matchup. Quarterback Chris Chandler (left knee) and running back Eric Dickerson (hamstring) both were injured on a third-quarter drive that led to a Colts field goal. Chandler would miss the remainder of the season.

Quarterback Jack Trudeau and running back Albert Bentley filled in admirably. Bentley rushed for 28 yards and caught two passes for 32 yards in Dickerson's stead, but the catalyst was Trudeau, a former starter who lost

Greg Bell rushed for a career-high 221 yards in the Rams' 41-38 triumph over Green Bay.

that status to Chandler in training camp. On the first play of the fourth quarter, Trudeau scored the game-winning touchdown on a one-yard run, a score he set up with a 16-yard pass to rookie Andre Rison two plays earlier.

The Falcons, who have never beaten the Colts in 10 meetings, saw their own starting quarterback, Chris Miller, forced out of the game due to a rib injury in the third period. Replacement Hugh Millen threw an end-zone interception and fumbled on Atlanta's final two possessions.

In Tampa Bay, the New Orleans Saints had both quarterbacks on their active roster banged up in a 20-10 loss to the Buccaneers. It was the Bucs' first victory over the Saints since 1982.

On New Orleans' first possession, starter Bobby Hebert suffered a slight concussion just one play before Dalton Hilliard scored the Saints' lone touchdown. Hebert was replaced by John Fourcade, who completed four of 11 passes before he was forced to depart late in the first half with stretched ligaments in his knee and ankle.

A groggy Hebert returned in the second half but failed to lead the Saints to another score. The Bucs' scoring resulted from an 11-yard pass from Vinny Testaverde to Ron Hall, a five-yard run by Lars Tate and two Donald Igwebuike field goals.

The week's high-scoring shootout was staged in the Houston Astrodome, where the Oilers and Buffalo Bills combined for 88 points in an overtime bout won by the Bills, 47-41. After Houston placekicker Tony Zendejas missed field-goal attempts of 47 and 37 yards in the extra period, Buffalo pulled out the victory on a 28-yard touchdown pass from Jim Kelly to Andre Reed.

Kelly's fifth touchdown pass, a career high, climaxed a wild affair that saw both clubs' special teams score touchdowns. Mark Kelso's 76-yard return of a blocked field goal put the Bills ahead, 20-10, on the final play of the first half, while a seven-yard blocked-punt return by the Oilers' Cris Dishman cut Buffalo's lead to 27-24 late in the third quarter.

Zendejas, who kicked a 52-yard field goal with three seconds remaining in regulation to force overtime, was destined to crack at crunch time. His 47-yard field-goal attempt was blocked by the Bills' Ray Bentley in the extra period, but an offside penalty allowed the kicker a second chance. This attempt, from 37 yards, sailed wide to the left.

Kelly's five touchdown passes were matched by San Francisco's Joe Montana, who completed 25 of 34 attempts for 428 yards in the 49ers' 38-28 victory at Philadelphia. Montana led San Francisco back from an 11-point deficit with three scoring passes in the game's final 6:03.

Wide receiver Jerry Rice had two touchdown receptions, including a 68-yarder on San Francisco's sixth play from scrimmage. With 2:02 to play, he gathered in a 33-yard pass for the game's final points. Rice finished with six catches for 164 yards but wasn't the lone receiving threat. Teammate John Taylor had six receptions for 136 yards, including a 70-yard scoring catch.

Eagles kicker Luis Zendejas, cousin of the Oilers' Tony, kicked four field goals in the losing effort.

The New York Jets also put together an impressive fourth-quarter rally to defeat Miami, 40-33, in an AFC Eastern Division game. The Jets outscored the Dolphins, 21-3, in the final 15 minutes and drove for touchdowns on all four of their second-half possessions. An 11-yard pass from Ken O'Brien to Roger Vick with 1:29 remaining broke a 33-33 tie.

The Jets' game-winning drive was set up by cornerback James Hasty, who picked off a Dan Marino pass and returned the ball 15 yards to the Miami 41. It was Hasty's second interception of the game.

The Dolphins, beaten by New York for the third straight time, threatened on their final possession, but wide receiver Mark Clayton dropped passes at the Jets' 13- and 20-yard lines in the last 20 seconds.

The upset of the week was played in Pittsburgh, where the Steelers stunned Minnesota, 27-14, after scoring only 10 points to their opponents' 92 to open the season. The Vikings, despite a 38-7 loss at Chicago in Week 2, were picked by many to contend for a Super Bowl berth. The Steelers, as evidenced in the first two weeks, weren't given much chance to make the playoffs, which they hadn't done anyway since 1984.

The Pittsburgh offense marched 81 yards for a touchdown on its first possession, but the upset was made possible by the defense, which entered the game ranked last in the league. The Steelers, who had recorded just two sacks in their last six regular-season games, sacked Vikings quarterbacks Wade Wilson and Tommy Kramer five times and intercepted two passes.

The San Diego Chargers picked off five passes, their highest single-game total in eight years, en route to a 21-6 AFC Western Division victory over Kansas City. Gill Byrd intercepted two passes, while Vencie Glenn, Martin Bayless and Lester Lyles had one each in Coach Dan Henning's first win at the Chargers' helm.

The San Diego offense had its moments as well. Although the Chargers scored only three touchdowns, they rushed for 200 yards and did not commit a turnover. Tight end Rod Bernstine scored on a one-yard pass from Jim McMahon in the third quarter and again on a 32-yard run in the final period.

The Chicago Bears displayed a potent offense in Detroit, rolling up 542 yards in a 47-27 rout of the Lions. The Bears scored on their first four possessions and seven of their first eight.

Chicago quarterback Mike Tomczak passed for a career-high 302 yards with no interceptions, Neal Anderson rushed for 116 yards on 16 carries and Kevin Butler kicked four field goals. It was the Bears' 10th consecutive win over the division-rival Lions, who lost for the third straight week.

Detroit running back Barry Sanders ran for 126 yards before a hip pointer forced the rookie to the sidelines early in the second half.

The Dallas Cowboys remained the only other NFL team without a victory through three weeks, losing a 30-7 decision to Washington in their home opener at Texas Stadium. The Redskins used a ball-control offense to gain the upper hand in the battle of 0-2 clubs.

Washington received a big lift from second-year running back Jamie Morris, who replaced an injured Gerald Riggs (bruised chest) in the second period and carried 26 times for 100 yards and a touchdown. Earnest Byner, acquired from Cleveland in the off-season, ran 12 yards for a touchdown on his first carry as a Redskin.

The Seattle Seahawks also rebounded from two season-opening losses with a 24-3 victory at New England. It marked the first time in 24 games that the Seahawks had held an opponent without a touchdown.

Seattle scored the only points it would need when Dave Krieg found Louis Clark with a 27-yard scoring pass midway through the second period. That touchdown gave Seattle its first lead of the 1989 season and came four plays after linebacker Vernon Maxwell recovered a fumble by the Pats' Reggie Dupard at the Seahawks' 41-yard line.

After Clark's touchdown, Seattle scored points on its next three possessions to take command. Krieg hit Paul Skansi and John L. Williams with touchdown passes before Norm Johnson kicked a 23-yard field goal. Melvin Jenkins set up the Seahawks' final touchdown by recovering a fumble on the kickoff following Skansi's scoring catch.

The New York Giants forced six Phoenix turnovers, all in the first half, and cruised to a 35-7 NFC Eastern Division decision over the Cardinals. The victory, the Giants' sixth straight over the Big Red at Giants Stadium, gave New York its first 3-0 start since 1968.

The Giants picked off four of the first eight passes thrown by Cardinals quarterback Gary Hogeboom. Safety Terry Kinard returned an interception 58 yards for a score, just two minutes after Phil Simms hit Stephen Baker with a 39-yard scoring pass on the Giants' first possession.

Phoenix, which had not allowed a sack while winning its first two games, surrendered five

John Taylor scored the first of four San Francisco touchdowns in the final 13½ minutes in the 49ers' 38-28 comeback win at Philadelphia.

sacks in this contest. Former Cardinals running back Ottis Anderson ran for one touchdown and 98 yards overall, his best rushing day since joining the Giants in 1986.

The Cincinnati Bengals twice stopped the Cleveland Browns inside the 10-yard line in the final eight minutes to preserve a 21-14 victory in the Monday night game.

With 7:52 to play, Bengals defensive end Jim Skow tackled Tim Manoa for no gain on a fourth-and-1 play at the 9 line. With 1:41 remaining, cornerback Eric Thomas batted down a fourth-down Bernie Kosar pass intended for Reggie Langhorne at the 3-yard line. The Browns had a first down at the 7 on the latter drive.

Cincinnati quarterback Boomer Esiason, who had thrown just three touchdown passes against Cleveland in nine previous games, equaled that output with scoring strikes of eight and 16 yards to tight end Rodney Holman and 19 yards to running back James Brooks.

Chiefs-Chargers
SUNDAY, SEPTEMBER 24

SCORE BY PERIODS

Kansas City	3	3	0	0— 6
San Diego	7	0	7	7—21

SCORING

San Diego—Spencer 9 run (Bahr kick), 11:23 1st.
Kansas City—Field goal Lowery 23, 14:37 1st.
Kansas City—Field goal Lowery 31, 13:56 2nd.
San Diego—Bernstine 1 pass from McMahon (Bahr kick), 6:55 3rd.
San Diego—Bernstine 32 run (Bahr kick), 11:29 4th.

TEAM STATISTICS

	Kansas City	San Diego
First downs	13	18
Rushes-Yards	22-118	37-200
Sacked-Yards lost	3-23	0-0
Passing yards	154	96
Passes	16-28-5	11-18-0
Punts	2-41.5	5-44.8
Fumbles-Lost	0-0	1-0
Penalties-Yards	7-38	5-36
Time of possession	29:19	30:41

Attendance—40,128.

INDIVIDUAL STATISTICS

Rushing—Kansas City, Okoye 16-112, Saxon 2-6, Heard 4-0; San Diego, Bernstine 5-73, Butts 15-62, Spencer 13-57, Brinson 1-5, McMahon 3-3.

Passing—Kansas City, DeBerg 16-28-5—177; San Diego, McMahon 11-18-0—96.

Receiving—Kansas City, McNair 7-83, Harry 3-31, Dressel 3-23, Paige 1-30, R. Thomas 1-7, Carruth 1-3; San Diego, Bernstine 3-14, A. Miller 2-55, Spencer 2-11, Brinson 2-5, Cox 1-6, Caravello 1-5.

Kickoff Returns—Kansas City, Copeland 3-41; San Diego, Usher 2-29, Holland 1-15.

Punt Returns—Kansas City, Harry 2-6, Worthen 1-17; San Diego, Usher 1-11.

Interceptions—San Diego, Glenn 1-31, Byrd 2-12, Bayless 1-0, Lyles 1-28.

Punting—Kansas City, Goodburn 2-41.5; San Diego, Ilesic 5-44.8.

Field Goals—Kansas City, Lowery 2-3 (missed: 40); San Diego, none attempted.

Sacks—San Diego, Smith ½, O'Neal 1½, Grossman.

Vikings-Steelers
SUNDAY, SEPTEMBER 24
SCORE BY PERIODS

Minnesota	7	7	0	0—14
Pittsburgh	7	14	0	6—27

SCORING

Pittsburgh—Mularkey 15 pass from Brister (Anderson kick), 5:23 1st.
Minnesota—Wilson 1 run (Garcia kick), 9:57 1st.
Pittsburgh—Worley 8 run (Anderson kick), 2:53 2nd.
Minnesota—Thomas 27 fumble return (Garcia kick), 8:21 2nd.
Pittsburgh—Hoge 2 run (Anderson kick), 13:50 2nd.
Pittsburgh—Field goal Anderson 38, 2:54 4th.
Pittsburgh—Field goal Anderson 44, 12:47 4th.

TEAM STATISTICS

	Minnesota	Pittsburgh
First downs	17	23
Rushes-Yards	25-112	42-159
Sacked-Yards lost	5-20	4-38
Passing yards	146	119
Passes	15-30-2	16-22-0
Punts	6-38.7	3-41.0
Fumbles-Lost	0-0	1-1
Penalties-Yards	8-95	4-35
Time of possession	24:56	35:04
Attendance—50,744.		

INDIVIDUAL STATISTICS

Rushing—Minnesota, Jones 1-37, Fenney 5-35, Anderson 7-25, Dozier 6-12, Wilson 3-19, Nelson 2-4, Carter 1-minus 12; Pittsburgh, Hoge 17-64, Worley 16-52, Lipps 2-36, W. Williams 1-11, Carter 2-6, Brister 4-minus 10.

Passing—Minnesota, Wilson 12-22-1—118, Kramer 3-8-1—48; Pittsburgh, Brister 16-22-0—157.

Receiving—Minnesota, Carter 5-56, Jones 4-44, Rice 2-24, Fenney 1-22, Gustafson 1-12, Jordan 1-7, Nelson 1-1; Pittsburgh, Carter 5-37, Worley 4-45, Mularkey 3-26, Lipps 2-26, W. Williams 1-16, Hoge 1-7.

Kickoff Returns—Minnesota, Nelson 5-117; Pittsburgh, Woodson 2-42.

Punt Returns—Minnesota, Lewis 1-13; Pittsburgh, Woodson 3-43.

Interceptions—Pittsburgh, Little 1-4, Everett 1-4.

Punting—Minnesota, Scribner 6-38.7; Pittsburgh, Newsome 3-41.0.

Field Goals—Minnesota, Garcia 0-1 (missed: 37); Pittsburgh, Anderson 2-3 (missed: 43).

Sacks—Minnesota, Thomas, Millard, Doleman 2; Pittsburgh, T. Johnson 2, J. Williams 2, Nickerson.

Seahawks-Patriots
SUNDAY, SEPTEMBER 24
SCORE BY PERIODS

Seattle	0	21	3	0—24
New England	3	0	0	0— 3

SCORING

New England—Field goal Davis 35, 11:24 1st.
Seattle—Clark 27 pass from Krieg (N. Johnson kick), 6:45 2nd.
Seattle—Skansi 19 pass from Krieg (N. Johnson kick), 13:17 2nd.
Seattle—Williams 10 pass from Krieg (N. Johnson kick), 14:25 2nd.
Seattle—Field goal N. Johnson 23, 6:57 3rd.

TEAM STATISTICS

	Seattle	New England
First downs	17	15
Rushes-Yards	37-157	23-91
Sacked-Yards lost	2-18	3-19
Passing yards	159	128
Passes	14-24-0	17-33-1
Punts	6-42.3	4-41.0
Fumbles-Lost	1-0	3-2
Penalties-Yards	5-49	2-10
Time of possession	33:07	26:53
Attendance—48,025.		

INDIVIDUAL STATISTICS

Rushing—Seattle, Warner 16-65, Williams 17-64, Krieg 4-28; New England, Perryman 11-46, Dupard 8-26, Tatupu 4-19.

Passing—Seattle, Krieg 14-24-0—177; New England, Eason 17-33-1—147.

Receiving—Seattle, Williams 5-71, Clark 3-51, Warner 2-7, Skansi 1-19, Blades 1-14, Kane 1-12, Tyler 1-3; New England, Perryman 5-44, Sievers 4-43, Jones 2-22, Martin 2-16, Dawson 2-13, Cook 2-9.

Kickoff Returns—Seattle, Jefferson 1-16; New England, Martin 2-56, Rice 1-12.

Punt Returns—Seattle, Jefferson 2-20; New England, Fryar 3-38.

Interceptions—Seattle, Harper 1-15.

Punting—Seattle, Rodriguez 6-42.3; New England, Feagles 4-41.0.

Field Goals—Seattle, N. Johnson 1-1; New England, Davis 1-1.

Sacks—Seattle, Nash, Green, Porter; New England, McGrew, Jeter.

Falcons-Colts
SUNDAY, SEPTEMBER 24
SCORE BY PERIODS

Atlanta	3	3	3	0— 9
Indianapolis	0	0	6	7—13

SCORING

Atlanta—Field goal McFadden 19, 12:30 1st.
Atlanta—Field goal McFadden 34, 11:10 2nd.
Atlanta—Field goal McFadden 27, 2:45 3rd.
Indianapolis—Field goal Biasucci 25, 9:27 3rd.
Indianapolis—Field goal Biasucci 29, 13:28 3rd.
Indianapolis—Trudeau 1 run (Biasucci kick), 0:01 4th.

TEAM STATISTICS

	Atlanta	Indianapolis
First downs	11	15
Rushes-Yards	24-105	39-130
Sacked-Yards lost	4-30	2-7
Passing yards	103	84
Passes	13-28-1	7-21-1
Punts	5-42.6	5-43.8
Fumbles-Lost	3-2	0-0
Penalties-Yards	8-70	3-31
Time of possession	28:41	31:19
Attendance—57,816.		

INDIVIDUAL STATISTICS

Rushing—Atlanta, Settle 18-71, Haynes 1-21, Lang 2-5, Miller 2-5, Flowers 1-3; Indianapolis, Dickerson 22-80, Chandler 2-32, Bentley 10-28, Rison 1-1, Trudeau 3-0, Stark 1-minus 11.

Passing—Atlanta, Miller 10-21-0—100, Millen 3-7-1—33; Indianapolis, Chandler 5-15-1—71, Trudeau 2-6-0—20.

Receiving—Atlanta, Lang 5-74, Settle 4-19, Beckman 2-25, Haynes 1-10, Collins 1-5; Indianapolis, Rison 2-36, Bentley 2-32, Verdin 2-18, Dickerson 1-5.

Kickoff Returns—Atlanta, G. Thomas 2-44, Jones 2-43; Indianapolis, Rison 3-59.

Punt Returns—Atlanta, Sanders 3-15; Indianapolis, Verdin 3-33.

Interceptions—Atlanta, Cooper 1-38; Indianapolis, Taylor 1-27.

Punting—Atlanta, Fulhage 5-42.6; Indianapolis, Stark 5-43.8.

Field Goals—Atlanta, McFadden 3-3; Indianapolis, Biasucci 2-2.

Sacks—Atlanta, Cotton, B. Thomas ½, Casillas ½; Indianapolis, Johnson 2, Armstrong, Hand.

Saints-Buccaneers
SUNDAY, SEPTEMBER 24
SCORE BY PERIODS

New Orleans	7	3	0	0—10
Tampa Bay	0	10	7	3—20

SCORING

New Orleans—Hilliard 1 run (Andersen kick), 8:25 1st.
Tampa Bay—Field goal Igwebuike 34, 1:06 2nd.
Tampa Bay—Hall 11 pass from Testaverde (Igwebuike kick), 12:07 2nd.
New Orleans—Field goal Andersen 33, 14:52 2nd.
Tampa Bay—Tate 5 run (Igwebuike kick), 7:13 3rd.
Tampa Bay—Field goal Igwebuike 37, 2:29 4th.

TEAM STATISTICS

	New Orleans	Tampa Bay
First downs	25	20
Rushes-Yards	29-125	29-118
Sacked-Yards lost	3-30	1-9
Passing yards	200	218
Passes	19-34-2	15-26-1
Punts	2-40.5	1-58.0
Fumbles-Lost	0-0	4-2
Penalties-Yards	10-77	10-95
Time of possession	32:52	27:08
Attendance—44,053.		

INDIVIDUAL STATISTICS

Rushing—New Orleans, Hilliard 20-80, Hebert 2-18, Fourcade 2-9, Frazier 2-6, E. Martin 1-11, Heyward 1-1, Jordan 1-0; Tampa Bay, Tate 12-52, Howard 12-52, Smith 1-17, Testaverde 4-minus 3.

Passing—New Orleans, Hebert 15-23-1—169, Fourcade 4-11-1—61; Tampa Bay, Testaverde 15-26-1—227.

Receiving—New Orleans, E. Martin 6-85, Hilliard 5-42, Hill 2-32, Perriman 2-26, Turner 2-14, Brenner 1-17, Jordan 1-14; Tampa Bay, Carrier 5-120, Hall 4-43, Howard 3-18, Hill 2-24, Peebles 1-22.

Kickoff Returns—New Orleans, Shepard 4-66; Tampa Bay, Elder 1-19, Futrell 1-15.

Punt Returns—Tampa Bay, Futrell 1-0.

Interceptions—New Orleans, Massey 1-0; Tampa Bay, Robinson 1-16, Hamilton 1-0.

Punting—New Orleans, Winslow 2-40.5; Tampa Bay, Mohr 1-58.0.

Field Goals—New Orleans, Andersen 1-3 (missed: 54, 47); Tampa Bay, Igwebuike 2-2.

Sacks—New Orleans, Mills; Tampa Bay, Murphy 2, Lee.

Redskins-Cowboys
SUNDAY, SEPTEMBER 24
SCORE BY PERIODS

Washington	14	3	3	10—30
Dallas	7	0	0	0— 7

SCORING

Washington—Walton 29 interception return (Lohmiller kick), 6:00 1st.
Dallas—Jeffcoat 77 fumble return (Ruzek kick), 8:53 1st.
Washington—Byner 12 run (Lohmiller kick), 14:37 1st.
Washington—Field goal Lohmiller 26, 5:09 2nd.
Washington—Field goal Lohmiller 37, 11:49 3rd.
Washington—Morris 12 run (Lohmiller kick), 4:16 4th.
Washington—Field goal Lohmiller 33, 10:52 4th.

TEAM STATISTICS

	Washington	Dallas
First downs	21	10
Rushes-Yards	40-165	15-34
Sacked-Yards lost	1-8	4-27
Passing yards	208	156
Passes	15-37-0	15-39-4
Punts	7-38.5	7-42.1
Fumbles-Lost	1-1	0-0
Penalties-Yards	6-40	9-52
Time of possession	39:13	20:47
Attendance—63,200.		

INDIVIDUAL STATISTICS

Rushing—Washington, Morris 26-100, Byner 3-30, Riggs 10-26, Rypien 1-9; Dallas, Walker 11-33, Aikman 1-3, Saxon 1-1, Scott 1-minus 1, Sargent 1-minus 2.

Passing—Washington, Rypien 15-37-0—216; Dallas, Aikman 6-21-2—83, Walsh 9-18-2—100.

Receiving—Washington, Monk 6-114, Sanders 4-35, Clark 2-40, Morris 2-16, Byner 1-11; Dallas, Irvin 5-78, Walker 3-35, Scott 3-16, Martin 2-30, Alexander 1-16, Sargent 1-8.

Kickoff Returns—Washington, Howard 2-44; Dallas, Dixon 6-142.

Punt Returns—Washington, Howard 2-14; Dallas, Martin 2-13.

Interceptions—Washington, Walton 1-29, Bowles 1-0, Grant 1-0, Marshall 1-18.

Punting—Washington, Mojsiejenko 7-38.5; Dallas, Saxon 6-44.5, Ruzek 1-28.0.

Field Goals—Washington, Lohmiller 3-3; Dallas, none attempted.

Sacks—Washington, Bowles, Marshall, Mann, Caldwell; Dallas, Horton.

Jets-Dolphins
SUNDAY, SEPTEMBER 24
SCORE BY PERIODS

New York Jets	3	9	7	21—40
Miami	7	13	10	3—33

SCORING

New York—Field goal Leahy 32, 11:50 1st.
Miami—Edmunds 8 pass from Marino (Stoyanovich kick), 14:31 1st.
Miami—Edmunds 19 pass from Jensen (kick failed), 4:09 2nd.
New York—Radachowsky 78 blocked field goal return (Leahy kick), 10:25 2nd.
New York—Safety, punt snapped out of end zone, 11:03 2nd.
Miami—Banks 43 pass from Marino (Stoyanovich kick), 15:00 2nd.
Miami—Field goal Stoyanovich 21, 5:39 3rd.
New York—Toon 37 pass from O'Brien (Leahy kick), 9:48 3rd.
Miami—Clayton 14 pass from Marino (Stoyanovich kick), 14:31 3rd.

New York—Hector 23 pass from O'Brien (Leahy kick), 1:41 4th.
Miami—Field goal Stoyanovich 20, 6:48 4th.
New York—Hector 1 run (Leahy kick), 11:38 4th.
New York—Vick 11 pass from O'Brien (Leahy kick), 13:31 4th.

TEAM STATISTICS

	New York	Miami
First downs	24	31
Rushes-Yards	25-102	20-78
Sacked-Yards lost	4-20	0-0
Passing yards	309	446
Passes	27-37-1	34-56-2
Punts	3-35.0	1-52.0
Fumbles-Lost	1-1	1-0
Penalties-Yards	8-64	3-25
Time of possession	30:23	29:37
Attendance—65,908.		

INDIVIDUAL STATISTICS

Rushing—New York, McNeil 12-64, Vick 7-26, Hector 5-9, Harper 1-3; Miami, Logan 10-52, Stradford 9-26, Roby 1-0.

Passing—New York, O'Brien 27-37-1—329; Miami, Marino 33-55-2—427, Jensen 1-1-0—19.

Receiving—New York, Toon 10-159, Shuler 4-43, Vick 4-31, NcNeil 3-31, Harper 3-27, Hector 2-29, Griggs 1-9; Miami, Stradford 8-96, Jensen 7-66, Duper 6-113, Clayton 6-54, Edmunds 5-60, Banks 1-43, T. Brown 1-14.

Kickoff Returns—New York, Humphery 4-89, Townsell 1-22, Dixon 1-21; Miami, Logan 5-141.

Punt Returns—None.

Interceptions—New York, Hasty 2-16, Miami, Thomas 1-0.

Punting—New York, Prokop 3-35.0; Miami, Roby 1-52.0.

Field Goals—New York, Leahy 1-1; Miami, Stoyanovich 2-3 (missed: 41).

Sacks—Miami, Lankford, Green, Sochia, Williams.

Bears-Lions
SUNDAY, SEPTEMBER 24
SCORE BY PERIODS

Chicago	10	10	13	14—47
Detroit	0	13	7	7—27

SCORING

Chicago—Field goal Butler 21, 8:19 1st.
Chicago—Muster 6 run (Butler kick), 13:47 1st.
Detroit—B. Sanders 3 run (Murray kick), 1:08 2nd.
Chicago—McKinnon 40 pass from Tomczak (Butler kick), 5:47 2nd.
Detroit—Field goal Murray 40, 8:33 2nd.
Chicago—Field goal Butler 22, 13:02 2nd.
Detroit—Field goal Murray 48, 14:33 2nd.
Chicago—Anderson 53 run (Butler kick), 2:29 3rd.
Detroit—Gagliano 1 run (Murray kick), 4:59 3rd.
Chicago—Field goal Butler 25, 10:45 3rd.
Chicago—Field goal Butler 32, 14:06 3rd.
Chicago—Muster 3 pass from Tomczak (Butler kick), 9:00 4th.
Chicago—Harbaugh 1 run (Butler kick), 11:14 4th.
Detroit—Gagliano 1 run (Murray kick), 13:01 4th.

TEAM STATISTICS

	Chicago	Detroit
First downs	23	20
Rushes-Yards	37-219	29-198
Sacked-Yards lost	0-0	4-19
Passing yards	323	107
Passes	18-26-0	9-19-3
Punts	1-42.0	1-40.0
Fumbles-Lost	0-0	2-2
Penalties-Yards	7-79	2-45
Time of possession	36:46	23:14
Attendance—71,418.		

INDIVIDUAL STATISTICS

Rushing—Chicago, Anderson 16-116, Muster 10-73, Tomczak 2-19, Sanders 2-7, Suhey 2-3, Harbaugh 3-3, Green 2-minus 2; Detroit, B. Sanders 18-126, Paige 4-31, Gagliano 4-20, Gray 1-14, Painter 2-7.

Passing—Chicago, Tomczak 17-25-0—302, Harbaugh 1-1-0—21; Detroit, Gagliano 9-19-3—126.

Receiving—Chicago, McKinnon 3-62, Anderson 3-18, Muster 3-11, Boso 2-60, Morris 2-49, Gentry 2-19, Kozlowski 1-55, Thornton 1-28, Green 1-21; Detroit, R. Johnson 4-62, Clark 1-25, Stanley 1-14, B. Sanders 1-10, Painter 1-8, T. Johnson 1-7.

Kickoff Returns—Chicago, Green 3-62, Gentry 1-20, Kozlowski 1-12; Detroit, Gray 6-165, Palmer 2-89, Dallafior 1-13, Stanley 1-8.

Punt Returns—Detroit, Stanley 1-5.

Interceptions—Chicago, Lynch 2-14, Roper 1-43.

Punting—Chicago, Buford 1-42.0; Detroit, Arnold 1-40.0.

Field Goals—Chicago, Butler 4-4; Detroit, Murray 2-2.

Sacks—Chicago, Roper, Perry, Armstrong, Dent.

Bills-Oilers
SUNDAY, SEPTEMBER 24
SCORE BY PERIODS

Buffalo	10	10	7	14	6—47
Houston	7	3	14	17	0—41

SCORING

Buffalo—Field goal Norwood 43, 3:01 1st.
Houston—Moon 1 run (Zendejas kick), 7:48 1st.
Buffalo—Thomas 6 pass from Kelly (Norwood kick), 14:50' 1st.
Buffalo—Field goal Norwood 26, 3:47 2nd.
Houston—Field goal Zendejas 26, 14:03 2nd.
Buffalo—Kelso 76 blocked field goal return (Norwood kick), 15:00 2nd.
Buffalo—Beebe 63 pass from Kelly (Norwood kick), 6:12 3rd.
Houston—Highsmith 4 run (Zendejas kick), 11:01 3rd.
Houston—Dishman 7 blocked punt return (Zendejas kick), 14:33 3rd.
Buffalo—Reed 78 pass from Kelly (Norwood kick), 0:10 4th.
Houston—Givins 26 pass from Moon (Zendejas kick), 5:28 4th.
Houston—White 1 run (Zendejas kick), 10:20 4th.
Buffalo—Thomas 26 pass from Kelly (Norwood kick), 13:08 4th.
Houston—Field goal Zendejas 52, 14:57 4th.
Buffalo—Reed 28 pass from Kelly (no kick), 8:42 OT.

TEAM STATISTICS

	Buffalo	Houston
First downs	23	33
Rushes-Yards	24-112	39-128
Sacked-Yards lost	3-26	3-27
Passing yards	337	311
Passes	17-29-1	28-42-2
Punts	3-28.3	1-55.0
Fumbles-Lost	1-0	1-0
Penalties-Yards	13-84	10-59
Time of possession	25:31	43:11
Attendance—57,278.		

INDIVIDUAL STATISTICS

Rushing—Buffalo, Thomas 12-58, Kelly 3-43, Kinnebrew 9-11; Houston, Highsmith 14-55, Moon 5-36, Pinkett 12-26, White 8-11.

Passing—Buffalo, Kelly 17-29-1—363; Houston, Moon 28-42-2—338.

Receiving—Buffalo, Reed 5-135, Johnson 5-86, Thomas 3-37, Metzelaars 2-36, Beebe 1-63, McKeller 1-6; Houston, Duncan 6-69, Jeffires 6-57, Givins 4-65, Highsmith 4-47, Hill 3-58, Pinkett 2-13, Harris 1-13, White 1-11, Mrosko 1-5.

Kickoff Returns—Buffalo, Rolle 1-6, Tucker 1-15; Houston, T. Johnson 5-71, Harris 3-49.

Punt Returns—Buffalo, Tucker 1-14; Houston, K. Johnson 1-14.

Interceptions—Buffalo, L. Smith 1-22, Kelso 1-43; Houston, Brown 1-41.

Punting—Buffalo, Kidd 2-42.5; Houston, Greg Montgomery 1-55.0.

Field Goals—Buffalo, Norwood 2-2; Houston, Zendejas 2-4 (missed: 47, 37).

Sacks—Buffalo, B. Smith, Seals, Wright; Houston, Fuller 2½, Jones ½.

49ers-Eagles
SUNDAY, SEPTEMBER 24
SCORE BY PERIODS

San Francisco	7	3	0	28—38
Philadelphia	9	3	6	10—28

SCORING

San Francisco—Rice 68 pass from Montana (Cofer kick), 2:56 1st.

Philadelphia—Sherman 2 run (Zendejas kick), 13:12 1st.

Philadelphia—Safety, Montana tackled in end zone by Harris, 14:27 1st.

Philadelphia—Field goal Zendejas 35, 3:00 2nd.

San Francisco—Field goal Cofer 32, 12:49 2nd.

Philadelphia—Field goal Zendejas 35, 6:41 3rd.

Philadelphia—Field goal Zendejas 44, 11:45 3rd.

Philadelphia—Field goal Zendejas 20, 0:10 4th.

San Francisco—Taylor 70 pass from Montana (Cofer kick), 1:28 4th.

Philadelphia—Giles 3 pass from Cunningham (Zendejas kick), 6:36 4th.

San Francisco—Rathman 8 pass from Montana (Cofer kick), 8:57 4th.

San Francisco—Jones 25 pass from Montana (Cofer kick), 11:43 4th.

San Francisco—Rice 33 pass from Montana (Cofer kick), 12:58 4th.

TEAM STATISTICS

	San Francisco	Philadelphia
First downs	19	22
Rushes-Yards	19-46	37-154
Sacked-Yards lost	8-43	4-31
Passing yards	385	161
Passes	25-34-1	19-38-1
Punts	4-44.3	7-39.9
Fumbles-Lost	5-2	4-2
Penalties-Yards	10-70	4-35
Time of possession	27:03	32:57
Attendance—66,042.		

INDIVIDUAL STATISTICS

Rushing—San Francisco, Sydney 4-30, Craig 8-14, Montana 4-14, Rice 1-3, Rathman 1-minus 2, Helton 1-minus 13; Philadelphia, Cunningham 8-52, Sherman 16-43, Higgs 6-29, Teltschik 1-23, Byars 6-7.

Passing—San Francisco, Montana 25-34-1—428; Philadelphia, Cunningham 19-38-1—192.

Receiving—San Francisco, Rice 6-164, J. Taylor 6-136, Craig 4-20, Rathman 3-19, Jones 3-65, Sydney 2-22, Walls 1-2; Philadelphia, Sherman 4-53, Byars 3-29, Jackson 3-25, Giles 2-34, Garrity 2-14, Quick 2-13, Carter 2-13, Johnson 1-11.

Kickoff Returns—San Francisco, Flagler 5-98; Philadelphia, Higgs 3-58, Williams 1-18.

Punt Returns—San Francisco, J. Taylor 4-21, Romanowski 1-0; Philadelphia, Williams 4-50.

Interceptions—San Francisco, Lott 1-6; Philadelphia, Harris 1-11.

Punting—San Francisco, Helton 4-44.3; Philadelphia, Teltschik 7-39.9.

Field Goals—San Francisco, Cofer 1-1; Philadelphia, Zendejas 4-4.

Sacks—San Francisco, Haley 1½, Fagan, Kugler, Holt ½; Philadelphia, White 3, Pitts 2, Simmons 2, Harris.

Cardinals-Giants
SUNDAY, SEPTEMBER 24
SCORE BY PERIODS

Phoenix	0	0	0	7— 7
New York Giants	14	6	5	10—35

SCORING

New York—Baker 39 pass from Simms (Allegre kick), 5:58 1st.

New York—Kinard 58 interception return (Allegre kick), 8:20 1st.

New York—Field goal Allegre 22, 3:11 2nd.

New York—Field goal Allegre 38, 14:58 2nd.

New York—Field goal Allegre 32, 2:37 3rd.

New York—Safety, Hogeboom tackled in end zone by Reasons, 9:19 3rd.

New York—Anderson 36 run (Allegre kick), 2:00 4th.

New York—Field goal Allegre 32, 10:27 4th.

Phoenix—J.T. Smith 21 pass from Hogeboom (Del Greco kick), 13:13 4th.

TEAM STATISTICS

	Phoenix	New York
First downs	16	16
Rushes-Yards	25-65	38-162
Sacked-Yards lost	5-39	1-6
Passing yards	183	204
Passes	19-32-4	12-22-0
Punts	4-46.3	4-46.3
Fumbles-Lost	4-2	1-1
Penalties-Yards	7-54	6-48
Time of possession	30:23	29:37
Attendance—75,742.		

INDIVIDUAL STATISTICS

Rushing—Phoenix, Jordan 6-23, Ferrell 11-22, S. Mitchell 7-18, Wolfley 1-2; New York, Anderson 21-98, Tillman 6-34, Adams 5-15, Carthon 2-6, Simms 1-5, Rouson 2-4, Meggett 1-0.

Passing—Phoenix, Hogeboom 19-32-4—222; New York, Simms 11-21-0—202, Hostetler 1-1-0—8.

Receiving—Phoenix, J.T. Smith 8-87, Green 4-50, Novacek 3-29, Jones 2-31, Awalt 2-25; New York, Manuel 3-69, Turner 2-34, Meggett 2-17, Anderson 2-15, Baker 1-39, Rouson 1-25, Mowatt 1-11.

Kickoff Returns—Phoenix, Sikahema 1-29, Jones 6-107, Clark 1-0; New York, Meggett 1-14.

Punt Returns—Phoenix, Sikahema 2-13; New York, Meggett 4-49.

Interceptions—New York, Kinard 1-58, S. White 2-8, P. Williams 1-0.

Punting—Phoenix, Camarillo 4-46.3; New York, Landeta 4-46.3.

Field Goals—Phoenix, Del Greco 0-1 (missed: 47); New York, Allegre 4-5 (missed: 50).

Sacks—Phoenix, Zordich; New York, Marshall 2, Reasons, Taylor, Howard.

Raiders-Broncos
SUNDAY, SEPTEMBER 24
SCORE BY PERIODS

Los Angeles Raiders	0	0	7	14—21
Denver	21	7	0	3—31

SCORING

Denver—Elway 29 run (Treadwell kick), 8:08 1st.

Denver—Alexander 1 run (Treadwell kick), 11:14 1st.

Denver—Jackson 46 pass from Elway (Treadwell kick), 13:17 1st.

Denver—Jackson 11 pass from Elway (Treadwell kick), 14:24 2nd.

Los Angeles—Washington 32 interception return (Jaeger kick), 1:41 3rd.

Los Angeles—Fernandez 75 pass from Schroeder (Jaeger kick), 6:16 4th.

Los Angeles—L. King 15 fumble return (Jaeger kick), 10:09 4th.

Denver—Field goal Treadwell 38, 14:33 4th.

TEAM STATISTICS

	Los Angeles	Denver
First downs	15	18
Rushes-Yards	22-90	41-170
Sacked-Yards lost	3-20	1-18
Passing yards	270	113
Passes	15-28-3	11-23-1
Punts	3-46.0	6-46.7
Fumbles-Lost	6-3	2-2
Penalties-Yards	12-101	6-45
Time of possession	25:50	34:10

Attendance—75,754.

INDIVIDUAL STATISTICS

Rushing—Los Angeles, Allen 10-45, Smith 7-26, Schroeder 4-18, Mueller 1-1; Denver, Humphrey 19-57, Winder 11-48, Elway 2-35, Alexander 8-23, Bratton 1-7.

Passing—Los Angeles, Schroeder 15-28-3—290; Denver, Elway 11-23-1—131.

Receiving—Los Angeles, Allen 6-63, Fernandez 4-124, Smith 2-24, Alexander 1-61, Mueller 1-9, Dyal 1-9; Denver, Humphrey 3-22, Jackson 2-57, Sewell 1-19, Bratton 1-14, Winder 1-7, Kay 1-5, Johnson 1-5, Kelly 1-2.

Kickoff Returns—Los Angeles, Edmonds 3-67, Adams 1-13; Denver, Bell 1-16.

Punt Returns—Los Angeles, Edmonds 3-27; Denver, Bell 2-7.

Interceptions—Los Angeles, Washington 1-32; Denver, Atwater 2-34, Braxton 1-24.

Punting—Los Angeles, Gossett 3-46.0; Denver, Horan 6-46.7.

Field Goals—Los Angeles, none attempted; Denver, Treadwell 1-1.

Sacks—Los Angeles, Townsend; Denver, Fletcher 2, Brooks.

Packers-Rams
SUNDAY, SEPTEMBER 24
SCORE BY PERIODS

Green Bay	0	7	21	10—38	
Los Angeles Rams	10	28	0	3—41	

SCORING

Los Angeles—Field goal Lansford 39, 7:27 1st.

Los Angeles—Bell 1 run (Lansford kick), 11:31 1st.

Green Bay—Majkowski 8 run (Jacke kick), 0:48 2nd.

Los Angeles—McGee 4 pass from Everett (Lansford kick), 4:00 2nd.

Los Angeles—Newsome 81 interception return (Lansford kick), 8:07 2nd.

Los Angeles—Bell 45 run (Lansford kick), 10:41 2nd.

Los Angeles—Johnson 4 pass from Everett (Lansford kick), 14:41 2nd.

Green Bay—Sharpe 18 pass from Majkowski (Jacke kick), 5:25 3rd.

Green Bay—Fullwood 11 run (Jacke kick), 8:16 3rd.

Green Bay—West 1 pass from Majkowski (Jacke kick), 12:26 3rd.

Green Bay—Field goal Jacke 43, 1:03 4th.

Los Angeles—Field goal Lansford 45, 9:43 4th.

Green Bay—Fullwood 1 run (Jacke kick), 12:39 4th.

TEAM STATISTICS

	Green Bay	Los Angeles
First downs	29	21
Rushes-Yards	23-116	33-217
Sacked-Yards lost	3-9	2-15
Passing yards	326	223
Passes	25-43-3	19-31-2
Punts	2-37.5	4-39.0
Fumbles-Lost	3-2	1-0
Penalties-Yards	3-20	10-87
Time of possession	28:34	31:26

Attendance—57,701.

INDIVIDUAL STATISTICS

Rushing—Green Bay, Fullwood 14-52, Woodside 5-23, Majkowski 3-22, Fontenot 1-19; Los Angeles, Bell 28-221, McGee 1-2, Ron Brown 1-0, Everett 3-minus 6.

Passing—Green Bay, Majkowski 25-43-3—335; Los Angeles, Everett 19-31-2—238.

Receiving—Green Bay, Sharpe 8-164, Woodside 6-75, Kemp 4-22, West 3-33, Query 1-14, Haddix 1-10, Bland 1-10, Fullwood 1-7; Los Angeles, Ellard 5-79, Holohan 4-22, McGee 3-12, Anderson 2-95, Johnson 2-9, Cox 1-11, Delpino 1-6, Bell 1-4.

Kickoff Returns—Green Bay, Query 3-67, Workman 1-46, Fontenot 1-20, Stephen 2-0; Los Angeles, Delpino 1-15, Ron Brown 5-119.

Punt Returns—Green Bay, Sutton 3-31; Los Angeles, Henley 1-15.

Interceptions—Green Bay, Noble 1-10, Stills 1-8; Los Angeles, Hicks 1-27, Newsome 1-81, Wilcher 1-4.

Punting—Green Bay, Bracken 2-37.5; Los Angeles, Hatcher 4-39.0.

Field Goals—Green Bay, Jacke 1-1; Los Angeles, Lansford 2-2.

Sacks—Green Bay, Harris 1½, Patterson ½; Los Angeles, Miller, Greene, Piel.

Browns-Bengals
MONDAY, SEPTEMBER 25
SCORE BY PERIODS

Cleveland	0	14	0	0—14	
Cincinnati	0	14	7	0—21	

SCORING

Cincinnati—Holman 8 pass from Esiason (Gallery kick), 2:09 2nd.

Cleveland—Metcalf 5 pass from Kosar (Bahr kick), 5:05 2nd.

Cincinnati—Holman 16 pass from Esiason (Gallery kick), 10:17 2nd.

Cleveland—Manoa 6 pass from Kosar (Bahr kick), 14:01 2nd.

Cincinnati—Brooks 19 pass from Esiason (Gallery kick), 5:05 3rd.

TEAM STATISTICS

	Cleveland	Cincinnati
First downs	16	21
Rushes-Yards	21-92	40-187
Sacked-Yards lost	6-28	0-0
Passing yards	175	184
Passes	15-23-0	14-20-1
Punts	5-42.8	2-42.5
Fumbles-Lost	1-0	2-0
Penalties-Yards	2-15	9-61
Time of possession	24:22	35:38

Attendance—55,996.

INDIVIDUAL STATISTICS

Rushing—Cleveland, Metcalf 8-34, McNeil 2-32, K. Jones 6-14, Manoa 4-11, Kosar 1-1; Cincinnati, Ball 18-78, Brooks 13-67, Esiason 9-42.

Passing—Cleveland, Kosar 15-23-0—203; Cincinnati, Esiason 14-20-1—184.

Receiving—Cleveland, Slaughter 4-85, Manoa 4-28, Newsome 2-32, K. Jones 2-11, McNeil 1-32, Langhorne 1-10, Metcalf 1-5; Cincinnati, Holman 6-50, Brooks 2-44, McGee 2-38, Martin 2-27, Brown 1-20, Kattus 1-5.

Kickoff Returns—Cleveland, Metcalf 3-56; Cincinnati, Jennings 1-20, Hillary 1-15.

Punt Returns—Cincinnati, Martin 3-21.

Interceptions—Cleveland, M. Johnson 1-0.

Punting—Cleveland, Wagner 5-42.8; Cincinnati, Johnson 2-42.5.

Field Goals—Cleveland, none attempted; Cincinnati, Gallery 0-2 (missed: 48, 44).

Sacks—Cincinnati, Krumrie, Williams ½, Skow 2½, Buck 2.

FOURTH WEEK

RESULTS OF WEEK 4
Sunday, October 1

Buffalo 31, New England 10 at Buff.
Cincinnati 21, Kansas City 17 at K.C.
Cleveland 16, Denver 13 at Clevc.
Green Bay 23, Atlanta 21 at Milw.
Houston 39, Miami 7 at Hous.
Indianapolis 17, N.Y. Jets 10 at N.Y.
L.A. Rams 13, San Francisco 12 at S.F.
Minnesota 17, Tampa Bay 3 at Minn.
N.Y. Giants 30, Dallas 13 at Dall.
Pittsburgh 23, Detroit 3 at Det.
San Diego 24, Phoenix 13 at Phoe.
Seattle 24, L.A. Raiders 20 at L.A.
Washington 16, New Orleans 14 at N.O.

Monday, October 2

Chicago 27, Philadelphia 13 at Chi.

Through the first four weeks of the 1989 National Football League season, the Green Bay Packers were strictly a second-half football team—which wasn't necessarily that bad.

Green Bay trailed at halftime in each of its first four games only to rally in the second half, sometimes successfully, sometimes not. Overall, the Pack took as much as it gave, scoring 117 points to the opposition's 119 en route to a 2-2 record.

A scoring breakdown by halves showed a team with two separate identities, however. Over their first four games, the Packers were outgunned in the first half, 96-27, but owned a 90-23 scoring advantage after intermission. In Week 1, they trailed Tampa Bay, 20-7, at halftime before losing, 23-21. The next week, they were down, 24-7, at the half against New Orleans but rallied for a 35-34 victory. In Week 3, the Pack fell behind the Rams, 38-7, but lost by three points, 41-38.

What gives?

"I don't know, but my heart can't stand it," Green Bay safety Mark Murphy said. "We know we have to get a better start. You talk about it preparing for the game and you say that you can't have another slow start like we did last week.

"If you could put your finger on it, you could do something to correct it."

The Packers were true to form in Week 4, however, defeating the Atlanta Falcons, 23-21, after trailing at halftime, 14-6. Green Bay prevailed on the strength of 17 unanswered fourth-quarter points, the last coming on Chris Jacke's 22-yard field goal with 1:42 to play. The winning kick capped a 13-play, 67-yard drive that began shortly after a 96-yard kickoff return for an apparent score by Atlanta's Deion Sanders was nullified by a holding penalty. Had Sanders' touchdown counted, the Falcons would have led, 28-20, with less than 10 minutes to play, making another Green Bay comeback much more difficult.

"That killed us," Atlanta Coach Marion Campbell said. "We do an outstanding individual job on the run and the hold brings it back."

With 13:53 to play, the Packers scored their first points of the second half when Sterling Sharpe picked up a fumble by fellow receiver Jeff Query and returned it five yards for a touchdown. Four minutes later, a 37-yard scoring pass from Don Majkowski to Herman Fontenot cut the Falcons' lead to 21-20. That set the stage for Sanders' wiped out touchdown and Jacke's winning field goal.

"One of these days we'll learn not to get so far behind," Packers Coach Lindy Infante said. "We seem to do things to get behind and have people boo us before we start to play."

But the Packers' latest comeback had the 54,647 fans at Milwaukee's County Stadium cheering by game's end. Green Bay's 2-2 start was its best since 1983.

"Since I've been here, we've never been 2-2," said fourth-year linebacker Tim Harris. "We're all feeling really good about the team."

The Los Angeles Rams were decidedly upbeat after improving to 4-0 with a 13-12 victory over NFC Western Division nemesis San Francisco. The Rams matched their perfect start of 1988, when they finished 10-6 but lost the division title to the 10-6 49ers due to the league's tie-breaker procedure.

The Rams' offense struggled for most of the game but drove 72 yards in the final minutes to overcome a 12-10 deficit. Quarterback Jim Everett led the march by completing six of seven passes, setting up Mike Lansford's game-winning field goal from the 26 with two seconds left.

The 49ers, losers of their home opener after winning three straight on the road, scored their points on four field goals by Mike Cofer. They failed to score touchdowns on two possessions at the Rams' 1-yard line, then set up the Rams' game-winning drive by fumbling at the Los Angeles 19 with 2:59 to play.

The New York Giants also remained unbeaten through four weeks, claiming a 30-13 victory over Dallas to post their best start since 1968. The Cowboys' 0-4 mark was their poorest since 1963.

Dallas picked off three passes and recovered two New York fumbles but converted none of the five turnovers into a score. Roger Ruzek kicked two field goals for the Cowboys before Steve Walsh passed 27 yards to Herschel Walker for a touchdown with 2:03 remaining. It was the Cowboys' first offensive touchdown after a drought of nine consecutive quarters.

Walsh, a rookie from the University of Miami, entered the game in the first quarter when the Cowboys' other rookie quarterback, Troy Aikman, suffered a broken left index finger.

Vikings quarterback Wade Wilson also went to the sidelines with a broken finger in Minnesota, but 13-year veteran Tommy Kramer came off the bench to throw two touchdown passes and key a 17-3 victory over the Tampa Bay Buccaneers.

Kramer took over just six minutes into the game and led the Vikes on an 11-play, 88-yard touchdown drive on their next possession. He completed his first six passes, throwing 12 yards to Anthony Carter for Minnesota's first points.

Tampa Bay quarterback Vinny Testaverde completed only six passes all game in the face of a Viking defense that held the Bucs to under seven yards on nine of their 12 offensive possessions. Testaverde had a string of 11 straight incompletions at one point.

In Cleveland, Denver quarterback John Elway also completed just six passes, his lowest output since his 1983 rookie season, as the Broncos dropped a 16-13 decision to the Browns. One of those completions, however, was a seven-yard touchdown pass to Vance Johnson that tied the game, 13-13, with 3:58 to play.

The Broncos appeared poised to take the lead until running back Sammy Winder fumbled at the Cleveland 16-yard line with 1:42 remaining. Frank Minnifield recovered for the Browns, who marched 62 yards behind quarterback Bernie Kosar to set up a game-winning 48-yard field goal by Matt Bahr as time expired.

Bahr's kick was surrounded by postgame controversy, however. Due to referee Tom Dooley's decision to switch end zones 2:29 into the final quarter, the Browns wound up driving toward a goal line they should have been defending. Fans in Cleveland Stadium's end-zone bleachers, a raucous area known as the "Dawg Pound," had begun pelting the Broncos with dog biscuits, eggs and other debris as Denver prepared for a play at its own 4-yard line. Rather than wait for the fans to stop, Dooley elected to continue the game at the opposite end of the field.

The switch gave the Browns a slight wind advantage, which paid dividends when Bahr's winning kick barely cleared the crossbar.

There was more controversy in Kansas City, where the Cincinnati Bengals pulled out a 21-17 victory over the Chiefs on linebacker Leon White's 22-yard fumble return for a touchdown early in the fourth quarter.

With Kansas City facing second down at its own 19-yard line, running back Christian Okoye carried around right end and was buried in a pile of bodies. Players on both teams appeared to ease up, apparently assuming the play was whistled dead. White, howev-

Mike Lansford celebrates after his 26-yard field goal with two seconds left gave the Rams a 13-12 victory at San Francisco.

er, snatched the ball from Okoye's hands and ran untouched into the Kansas City end zone.

Confusion reigned before the on-field officials ruled that White had stolen the ball before Okoye's knee touched the ground. The call stood when the replay officials declared the video inconclusive.

The Chiefs were livid, but they ultimately decided their own fate. Five of Kansas City's eight possessions in the second half ended in turnovers, including two inside the Bengals' 10-yard line. Veteran quarterback Ron Jaworski, making his first NFL start since 1986, threw four interceptions.

Bengals safety David Fulcher picked off three passes and recovered one fumble.

Turnovers also proved to be the bane of the Detroit Lions, who gave away the ball four times in a 23-3 loss to Pittsburgh. The Steelers converted all four turnovers into points to win their second consecutive game.

The most critical turnover was committed by rookie running back Barry Sanders, who fumbled at the Pittsburgh 1-yard line on a first-and-goal play in the second quarter. The Lions, who led, 3-0, then allowed Pittsburgh to drive the length of the field in eight plays to take a 7-3 lead.

Sanders, bothered by a hip pointer suffered the previous week against Chicago, carried just five times in the first half for one yard before exiting the game. The Lions managed only 18 yards rushing.

The Pittsburgh offense was sparked by quarterback Bubby Brister, who threw for 267 yards and completed a club-record 15 consecutive passes over one stretch. He was sacked seven times but none came at a critical time.

The San Diego Chargers took advantage of numerous Phoenix mistakes to spoil the Cardinals' home opener, 24-13. The game drew only 44,201 fans, the smallest turnout since the team moved from St. Louis to Phoenix in 1988.

Those on hand were dismayed by what they witnessed. The Cards led, 13-7, entering the fourth quarter but surrendered 17 unanswered points. Marion Butts started the San Diego comeback with a two-yard touchdown run, one play after Phoenix was penalized for holding on a Charger field-goal attempt. San Diego was awarded a first down at the Phoenix 2 and scored on the next play.

On the Cardinals' next possession, Earl Ferrell's fumble was picked up by linebacker Billy Ray Smith, who raced 15 yards for the first touchdown of his seven-year NFL career. Smith then recovered a fumble by Ernie Jones at the Cards' 25-yard line, setting up a 37-yard Chris Bahr field goal.

In an AFC Western Division matchup, the Seattle Seahawks scored 17 points in the final period to overcome a 10-point deficit and defeat the Los Angeles Raiders, 24-20. Norm Johnson's 48-yard field goal with 1:15 remaining gave Seattle a four-point cushion after the Raiders had pulled to within one on a Jeff Jaeger field goal.

Trailing 17-7, the Seahawks drove 80 yards to cut the Raiders' lead to three points on a six-yard scoring run by Curt Warner just 58 seconds into the fourth quarter. They took a 21-17 lead four minutes later on a 19-yard Dave Krieg touchdown pass to Brian Blades.

In New Orleans, the Saints held a decisive edge over Washington in total yardage and first downs, but the Redskins hung on for a 16-14 victory after New Orleans' Morten Andersen missed a 36-yard field-goal attempt with 2:34 to play. The usually reliable Andersen, who entered the game as the NFL's all-time leader in field-goal accuracy, also missed a 52-yard attempt in the third quarter.

That the Saints were even in position to win was a break in itself. The Redskins, whose only touchdown came on a nine-yard run by Gerald Riggs, had 10 chances inside the New Orleans' 7-yard line but couldn't cross the goal line.

Chip Lohmiller booted three Washington field goals, two after the Saints turned the ball over deep in their own territory.

In Houston, the Oilers followed through on every offensive opportunity, rolling up 448 total yards en route to a 39-7 romp over Miami. Oilers quarterback Warren Moon led the onslaught by completing 19 of 23 passes for 254 yards and two touchdowns.

Dolphins quarterback Dan Marino, meanwhile, suffered through one of the worst games

Thurman Thomas put on a one-man show in Buffalo's 31-10 triumph over Miami.

of his seven-year NFL career. One week after throwing for 427 yards against the Jets, Marino was held to 103 yards, a career low as a starter. The Dolphins managed just nine first downs and 43 yards rushing, never once advancing inside the Houston 20. Their lone score came on Marc Logan's 97-yard kickoff return in the fourth quarter.

In a game decided by defense and special teams, the Indianapolis Colts overcame a 10-0 halftime deficit to claim a 17-10 AFC Eastern Division victory over the New York Jets.

Neither team had as many as 75 yards rushing, and the lone offensive touchdown came on a 55-yard pass from Colts quarterback Jack Trudeau to Bill Brooks. Indianapolis notched the winning score when Clarence Verdin returned a punt 49 yards for a touchdown with 9:18 to play.

The Jets scored their only touchdown on a 92-yard interception return by Erik McMillan. Prior to the turnover, on both first and second downs, the Colts had apparent touchdowns called back by an instant-replay decision and illegal motion, respectively.

In another AFC Eastern Division matchup, Buffalo running back Thurman Thomas was a one-man wrecking crew in the Bills' 31-10 victory over New England. Thomas, a second-year player from Oklahoma State, scored two touchdowns, rushed for 105 yards and caught four passes for 99 yards, including a 74-yard reception for the Bills' final score. It was Buffalo quarterback Jim Kelly's third scoring pass of the game.

Patriots quarterback Doug Flutie had a game to forget, completing just 15 of 41 attempts.

The Chicago Bears remained one of the NFL's three unbeaten teams following a 27-13 victory over Philadelphia in the Monday night game. Mike Tomczak led the Bears' attack with three touchdown passes, including a 36-yarder to tight end James Thornton with 6:09 left.

That touchdown afforded the Bears some breathing room after the Eagles scored 10 points in the opening five minutes of the fourth quarter, cutting Chicago's lead to 20-13. Philadelphia quarterback Randall Cunningham passed for 348 yards in the second half and 401 in the game. His 62 attempts set a club record.

The loss was the Eagles' 13th straight in Chicago, dating back to 1939.

Broncos-Browns
SUNDAY, OCTOBER 1
SCORE BY PERIODS

Denver	0	3	3	7—13
Cleveland	7	3	3	3—16

SCORING
Cleveland—Slaughter 9 pass from Kosar (Bahr kick), 13:28 1st.
Denver—Field goal Treadwell 21, 6.06 2nd.
Cleveland—Field goal Bahr 36, 15:00 2nd.
Cleveland—Field goal Bahr 48, 9:43 3rd.
Denver—Field goal Treadwell 26, 12:51 3rd.
Denver—Johnson 7 pass from Elway (Treadwell kick), 11:02 4th.
Cleveland—Field goal Bahr 48, 15:00 4th.

TEAM STATISTICS
	Denver	Cleveland
First downs	10	16
Rushes-Yards	25-80	26-95
Passing yards	161	201
Passes	6-19-1	25-38-1
Sacked-Yards lost	4-37	3-15
Punts	6-40.0	6-27.3
Fumbles-Lost	4-2	0-0
Penalties-Yards	3-20	10-81
Time of possession	23:10	36:50
Attendance—78,637.		

INDIVIDUAL STATISTICS
Rushing—Denver, Humphrey 10-44, Alexander 5-17, Winder 8-16, Elway 1-2, Jackson 1-1; Cleveland, Kosar 4-33, Metcalf 9-26, Manoa 4-21, K. Jones 7-21, Redden 1-4, Langhorne 1-minus 10.
Passing—Denver, Elway 6-19-1—198; Cleveland, Kosar 25-38-1—216.
Receiving—Denver, Johnson 5-145, Sewell 1-53; Cleveland, Langhorne 7-67, Slaughter 5-67, Metcalf 5-24, Newsome 3-21, Brennan 2-20, Manoa 1-7, K. Jones 1-5, Tillman 1-5.
Kickoff Returns—Denver, Bell 3-68; Cleveland, Metcalf 3-72, Joines 1-12.
Punt Returns—Denver, Bell 2-10; Cleveland, McNeil 3-78.
Interceptions—Denver, Munford 1-10; Cleveland, Grayson 1-11.
Punting—Denver, Horan 6-40.8; Cleveland, Wagner 6-27.3.
Field Goals—Denver, Treadwell 2-2; Cleveland, Bahr 3-5 (missed: 47, 42).

Sacks—Denver, Fletcher 2½, Townsend ½; Cleveland, Grayson, Matthews, Perry, Baker ½, Hairston ½.

Chargers-Cardinals
SUNDAY, OCTOBER 1
SCORE BY PERIODS

San Diego	0	0	7	17—24
Phoenix	0	3	10	0—13

SCORING
Phoenix—Field goal Del Greco 36, 14:45 2nd.
Phoenix—Field goal Del Greco 33, 6:27 3rd.
San Diego—A. Miller 16 pass from McMahon (Bahr kick), 8:24 3rd.
Phoenix—Green 59 pass from Hogeboom (Del Greco kick), 9:31 3rd.
San Diego—Butts 2 run (Bahr kick), 1:07 4th.
San Diego—Smith 15 fumble return (Bahr kick), 2:10 4th.
San Diego—Field goal Bahr 37, 10:43 4th.

TEAM STATISTICS
	San Diego	Phoenix
First downs	13	17
Rushes-Yards	31-103	22-69
Passing yards	165	232
Passes	15-23-0	22-43-2
Sacked-Yards lost	4-23	4-29
Punts	9-41.0	5-43.0
Fumbles-Lost	0-0	3-2
Penalties-Yards	8-66	3-12
Time of possession	31:49	28:11
Attendance—44,201.		

INDIVIDUAL STATISTICS
Rushing—San Diego, Butts 9-26, McMahon 4-22, Brinson 5-19, Spencer 8-18, Bernstine 5-18; Phoenix, Ferrell 10-38, Hogeboom 4-13, J.T. Smith 1-10, Jordan 7-8.
Passing—San Diego, McMahon 15-23-0—188; Phoenix, Hogeboom 22-43-2—261.
Receiving—San Diego, Bernstine 5-51, A. Miller 3-66, Early 3-36, Spencer 2-15, Holland 1-20, Butts 1-0; Phoenix, J.T. Smith 11-123, Awalt 3-23, Green 2-61, Ferrell 2-minus 8, Holmes 1-35, Jones 1-12, Jordan 1-8, Novacek 1-7.
Kickoff Returns—San Diego, Usher 2-43, A. Miller 1-23, Holland 1-15; Phoenix, Sikahema 3-52, Baker 2-45.
Punt Returns—San Diego, Brinson 4-43; Phoenix, Sikahema 6-84.
Interceptions—San Diego, Bennett 1-0, Byrd 1-22.
Punting—San Diego, Ilesic 9-41.0; Phoenix, Camarillo 5-43.0.
Field Goals—San Diego, Bahr 1-1; Phoenix, Del Greco 2-2.
Sacks—San Diego, Bayless, Williams 2, Hinkle; Phoenix, Harvey, Galloway, Clasby, Wilson.

Giants-Cowboys
SUNDAY, OCTOBER 1
SCORE BY PERIODS

New York Giants	3	17	7	3—30
Dallas	0	6	0	7—13

SCORING
New York—Field goal Allegre 37, 6:26 1st.
Dallas—Field goal Ruzek 19, 0:03 2nd.
New York—Anderson 1 run (Allegre kick), 6:19 2nd.
Dallas—Field goal Ruzek 33, 11:14 2nd.
New York—Meggett 33 pass from Simms (Allegre kick), 13:48 2nd.
New York—Field goal Allegre 32, 14:57 2nd.
New York—Bavaro 13 pass from Simms (Allegre kick), 6:50 3rd.
New York—Field goal Allegre 27, 0:25 4th.
Dallas—Walker 27 pass from Walsh (Ruzek kick), 12:57 4th.

TEAM STATISTICS

	New York	Dallas
First downs	20	12
Rushes-Yards	36-137	31-87
Passing yards	205	201
Passes	14-19-3	14-30-2
Sacked-Yards lost	1-6	0-0
Punts	1-38.0	5-45.4
Fumbles-Lost	2-2	0-0
Penalties-Yards	1-15	8-47
Time of possession	29:08	30:52

Attendance—51,785.

INDIVIDUAL STATISTICS

Rushing—New York, Anderson 16-45, Tillman 6-31, Simms 2-29, Carthon 7-27, Rouson 2-6, Adams 1-0, Hostetler 1-0, Meggett 1-minus 1; Dallas, Walker 27-74, Aikman 2-9, Sargent 2-4.

Passing—New York, Simms 14-19-3—211; Dallas, Walsh 13-24-2—190, Aikman 1-6-0—11.

Receiving—New York, Bavaro 4-60, Anderson 3-59, Turner 3-30, Meggett 2-38, Manuel 2-24; Dallas, Walker 9-85, Martin 4-86, Dixon 1-30.

Kickoff Returns—New York, Meggett 1-34, Collins 1-0; Dallas, Dixon 4-36, Clack 2-38, Tautalatasi 1-9.

Punt Returns—New York, Meggett 2-16.

Interceptions—New York, P. Williams 1-0, Reasons 1-40; Dallas, Burton 1-0, Lockhart 1-2, Francis 1-2.

Punting—New York, Landeta 1-38.0; Dallas, Saxon 5-45.4.

Field Goals—New York, Allegre 3-3; Dallas, Ruzek 2-3 (missed: 53).

Sacks—Dallas, Jeffcoat ½, Lockhart ½.

Patriots-Bills
SUNDAY, OCTOBER 1
SCORE BY PERIODS

New England	3	0	7	0—10
Buffalo	7	17	0	7—31

SCORING

New England—Field goal Davis 35, 10:26 1st.
Buffalo—Thomas 4 run (Norwood kick), 14:29 1st.
Buffalo—McKeller 39 pass from Kelly (Norwood kick), 6:40 2nd.
Buffalo—Metzelaars 8 pass from Kelly (Norwood kick), 10:08 2nd.
Buffalo—Field goal Norwood 36, 14:59 2nd.
New England—Jones 20 pass from Flutie (Davis kick), 13:14 3rd.
Buffalo—Thomas 74 pass from Kelly (Norwood kick), 0:10 4th.

TEAM STATISTICS

	New England	Buffalo
First downs	17	16
Rushes-Yards	30-124	31-115
Passing yards	155	256
Passes	15-41-1	12-17-0
Sacked-Yards lost	2-21	3-22
Punts	6-41.2	6-42.2
Fumbles-Lost	0-0	2-1
Penalties-Yards	5-68	7-55
Time of possession	33:24	26:36

Attendance—78,921.

INDIVIDUAL STATISTICS

Rushing—New England, Perryman 15-68, Flutie 7-43, Dupard 7-11, Allen 1-2; Buffalo, Thomas 21-105, K. Davis 3-7, Harmon 2-2, Mueller 1-2, Kelly 4-minus 1.

Passing—New England, Flutie 15-41-1—176; Buffalo, Kelly 12-17-0—278.

Receiving—New England, Jones 4-48, Dawson 3-28, Morgan 2-27, Perryman 2-13, Dykes 1-29, Martin 1-19, Sievers 1-9, Dupard 1-3; Buffalo, Reed 4-114, Thomas 4-99, Metzelaars 3-26, McKeller 1-39.

Kickoff Returns—New England, Allen 3-63, Martin 1-25, Tatupu 1-2; Buffalo, Tucker 3-48.

Punt Returns—New England, Martin 2-33; Buffalo, Tucker 4-35.

Interceptions—Buffalo, L. Smith 1-24.

Punting—New England, Feagles 6-41.2; Buffalo, Kidd 6-42.2.

Field Goals—New England, Davis 1-2 (missed: 37); Buffalo, Norwood 1-1.

Sacks—New England, Williams 2, Rembert; Buffalo, B. Smith, Odomes.

Redskins-Saints
SUNDAY, OCTOBER 1
SCORE BY PERIODS

Washington	3	0	10	3—16
New Orleans	7	7	0	0—14

SCORING

Washington—Field goal Lohmiller 48, 1:58 1st.
New Orleans—Hill 11 pass from Hebert (Andersen kick), 3:47 1st.
New Orleans—Hilliard 3 run (Andersen kick), 2:35 2nd.
Washington—Field goal Lohmiller 19, 5:27 3rd.
Washington—Riggs 9 run (Lohmiller kick), 13:42 3rd.
Washington—Field goal Lohmiller 18, 4:49 4th.

TEAM STATISTICS

	Washington	New Orleans
First downs	13	20
Rushes-Yards	33-92	28-136
Passing yards	216	245
Passes	15-28-1	16-25-1
Sacked-Yards lost	0-0	2-14
Punts	4-55.5	2-49.0
Fumbles-Lost	0-0	3-3
Penalties-Yards	10-75	6-50
Time of possession	28:56	31:04

Attendance—64,358.

INDIVIDUAL STATISTICS

Rushing—Washington, Riggs 18-50, Morris 9-26, Byner 2-18, Sanders 1-0, Rypien 3-minus 2; New Orleans, Hilliard 19-52, Morse 1-39, Jordan 1-32, Heyward 7-13.

Passing—Washington, Rypien 15-28-1—216; New Orleans, Hebert 16-25-1—259.

Receiving—Washington, Monk 5-94, Sanders 4-51, Riggs 2-16, Byner 2-11, Orr 1-48, Morris 1-minus 1; New Orleans, Hill 4-79, E. Martin 3-30, Heyward 3-24, Brenner 2-42, Perriman 1-47, Turner 1-20, Hilliard 1-12, Tice 1-5.

Kickoff Returns—Washington, A. Johnson 2-46, Howard 1-20; New Orleans, Shepard 3-45, Atkins 2-44.

Punt Returns—Washington, Howard 1-7; New Orleans, Shepard 3-22.

Interceptions—Washington, Bowles 1-0; New Orleans, Waymer 1-2.

Punting—Washington, Mojsiejenko 4-55.5; New Orleans, Winslow 2-49.0.

Field Goals—Washington, Lohmiller 3-3; New Orleans, Andersen 0-2 (missed: 52, 36).

Sacks—Washington, Manley, Mann.

Colts-Jets
SUNDAY, OCTOBER 1
SCORE BY PERIODS

Indianapolis	0	0	7	10—17
New York Jets	7	3	0	0—10

SCORING

New York—McMillan 92 interception return (Leahy kick), 9:36 1st.
New York—Field goal Leahy 26, 15:00 2nd.
Indianapolis—Brooks 55 pass from Trudeau (Biasucci kick), 2:10 3rd.
Indianapolis—Field goal Biasucci 38, 4:24 4th.
Indianapolis—Verdin 49 punt return (Biasucci kick), 5:42 4th.

TEAM STATISTICS

	Indianapolis	New York
First downs	17	18
Rushes-Yards	32-74	23-63
Passing yards	242	182
Passes	17-31-1	20-32-1
Sacked-Yards lost	2-4	5-40
Punts	4-48.3	7-40.4
Fumbles-Lost	4-1	2-1
Penalties-Yards	7-45	6-59
Time of possession	30:28	29:32
Attendance—65,542.		

INDIVIDUAL STATISTICS

Rushing—Indianapolis, Dickerson 18-52, Bentley 9-25, Brooks 1-0, Trudeau 4-minus 3; New York, Hector 11-30, McNeil 5-22, Vick 7-11.

Passing—Indianapolis, Trudeau 17-30-1—246, Bentley 0-1-0—0; New York, O'Brien 20-31-1—222, Mackey 0-1-0—0.

Receiving—Indianapolis, Brooks 7-159, Bentley 6-58, Beach 1-17, Boyer 1-6, Rison 1-3, Verdin 1-3; New York, Shuler 5-60, Townsell 4-46, Harper 2-40, Toon 2-26, Griggs 2-18, Hector 2-14, Vick 2-12, McNeil 1-6.

Kickoff Returns—Indianapolis, Rison 2-37; New York, Townsell 3-59, Humphery 1-6.

Punt Returns—Indianapolis, Verdin 4-79; New York, Townsell 2-25.

Interceptions—Indianapolis, Daniel 1-34; New York, McMillan 1-92.

Punting—Indianapolis, Stark 4-48.3; New York, Prokop 7-40.4.

Field Goals—Indianapolis, Biasucci 1-1; New York, Leahy 1-1.

Sacks—Indianapolis, E. Johnson ½, Plummer, McDonald 2, Hand ½; New York, Lageman, Nichols.

Falcons-Packers
SUNDAY, OCTOBER 1
SCORE BY PERIODS

Atlanta	7	7	7	0—	21
Green Bay	0	6	0	17—	23

SCORING

Atlanta—Beckman 3 pass from Millen (McFadden kick), 7:25 1st.

Green Bay—Field goal Jacke 35, 0:07 2nd.

Atlanta—Settle 1 run (McFadden kick), 13:03 2nd.

Green Bay—Field goal Jacke 52, 15:00 2nd.

Atlanta—Lang 10 run (McFadden kick), 7:53 3rd.

Green Bay—Sharpe 5 fumble return (Jacke kick), 1:07 4th.

Green Bay—Fontenot 37 pass from Majkowski (Jacke kick), 5:16 4th.

Green Bay—Field goal Jacke 22, 13:18 4th.

TEAM STATISTICS

	Atlanta	Green Bay
First downs	17	27
Rushes-Yards	23-75	35-153
Passing yards	258	295
Passes	20-28-1	19-35-2
Sacked-Yards lost	5-36	0-0
Punts	6-39.8	3-35.0
Fumbles-Lost	1-0	2-0
Penalties-Yards	8-45	3-24
Time of possession	27:22	32:38
Attendance—54,647.		

INDIVIDUAL STATISTICS

Rushing—Atlanta, Settle 15-49, Lang 4-17, Jones 1-5, Flowers 2-4, Millen 1-0; Green Bay, Fullwood 19-84, Majkowski 9-39, Kemp 1-14, Woodside 3-8, Fontenot 1-5, Haddix 2-3.

Passing—Atlanta, Millen 20-28-1—294; Green Bay, Majkowski 19-35-2—295.

Receiving—Atlanta, Collins 5-126, Settle 5-53, Beckman 5-46, Jones 2-26, Haynes 2-25, Bailey 1-18; Green Bay, Kemp 5-80, Sharpe 4-78, Fontenot 3-60, Woodside 3-43, Fullwood 3-17, Query 1-17.

Kickoff Returns—Atlanta, Sanders 3-55; Green Bay, Fullwood 1-23, Workman 1-14, Fontenot 1-10.

Punt Returns—Atlanta, Sanders 1-8; Green Bay, Query 2-12.

Interceptions—Atlanta, Case 1-0, Cooper 1-0; Green Bay, D. Brown 1-0.

Punting—Atlanta, Fulhage 6-39.8; Green Bay, Bracken 3-35.0.

Field Goals—Atlanta, none attempted; Green Bay, Jacke 3-3.

Sacks—Green Bay, Harris 4, Greene.

Rams-49ers
SUNDAY, OCTOBER 1
SCORE BY PERIODS

Los Angeles Rams	3	7	0	3—	13
San Francisco	6	3	0	3—	12

SCORING

San Francisco—Field goal Cofer 26, 6:18 1st.

Los Angeles—Field goal Lansford 40, 10:06 1st.

San Francisco—Field goal Cofer 32, 14:41 1st.

Los Angeles—Anderson 65 pass from Everett (Lansford kick), 1:28 2nd.

San Francisco—Field goal Cofer 41, 14:48 2nd.

San Francisco—Field goal Cofer 17, 6:07 4th.

Los Angeles—Field goal Lansford 26, 14:58 4th.

TEAM STATISTICS

	Los Angeles	San Francisco
First downs	11	22
Rushes-Yards	20-37	33-152
Passing yards	250	215
Passes	16-25-0	25-35-0
Sacked-Yards lost	0-0	2-12
Punts	5-36.8	3-46.0
Fumbles-Lost	0-0	3-1
Penalties-Yards	7-55	3-25
Time of possession	21:20	38:40
Attendance—64,250.		

INDIVIDUAL STATISTICS

Rushing—Los Angeles, Bell 14-33, Gary 2-5, Ellard 1-4, McGee 1-minus 1, Everett 2-minus 4; San Francisco, Craig 18-67, Rathman 7-42, Montana 4-29, Sydney 2-24, Flagler 1-1, Rice 1-minus 11.

Passing—Los Angeles, Everett 16-25-0—250; San Francisco, Montana 25-35-0—227.

Receiving—Los Angeles, Ellard 5-63, Anderson 4-112, Holohan 3-56, Delpino 1-10, Johnson 1-6, McGee 1-2, Bell 1-1; San Francisco, Jones 5-51, Flagler 5-40, Sydney 4-22, Taylor 3-33, Rathman 3-26, Rice 2-36, Craig 2-10, Walls 1-9.

Kickoff Returns—Los Angeles, Ron Brown 4-87, Delpino 1-21; San Francisco, Sydney 2-0, Flagler 1-14, Tillman 1-16.

Punt Returns—Los Angeles, Henley 2-33; San Francisco, Taylor 2-20.

Interceptions—None.

Punting—Los Angeles, Hatcher 5-36.8; San Francisco, Helton 3-46.0.

Field Goals—Los Angeles, Lansford 2-3 (missed: 50); San Francisco, Cofer 4-5 (missed: 42).

Sacks—Los Angeles, Wilcher, Reed.

Dolphins-Oilers
SUNDAY, OCTOBER 1
SCORE BY PERIODS

Miami	0	0	0	7—	7
Houston	2	17	6	14—	39

SCORING

Houston—Safety, Roby fumbled out of end zone, 6:43 1st.

Houston—Field goal Zendejas 32, 5:18 2nd.

Houston—Highsmith 3 run (Zendejas kick), 10:10 2nd.
Houston—Pinkett 2 pass from Moon (Zendejas kick), 14:29 2nd.
Houston—Field goal Zendejas 40, 8:24 3rd.
Houston—Field goal Zendejas 32, 14:36 3rd.
Houston—Duncan 25 pass from Moon (Zendejas kick), 3:25 4th.
Houston—Pinkett 10 run (Zendejas kick), 12:02 4th.
Miami—Logan 97 kickoff return (Stoyanovich kick), 12:20 4th.

TEAM STATISTICS

	Miami	Houston
First downs	9	23
Rushes-Yards	11-43	41-197
Passing yards	117	251
Passes	12-32-2	20-25-1
Sacked-Yards lost	0-0	2-13
Punts	5-37.6	3-45.7
Fumbles-Lost	2-1	2-0
Penalties-Yards	5-30	8-60
Time of possession	16:32	43:28

Attendance—51,426.

INDIVIDUAL STATISTICS

Rushing—Miami, Smith 6-18, Jensen 1-11, Stradford 1-7, Logan 2-4, Secules 1-3; Houston, White 17-97, Highsmith 11-53, Pinkett 10-42, Moon 2-6, T. Johnson 1-minus-1.

Passing—Miami, Marino 11-29-2—103, Secules 1-3-0—14; Houston, Moon 19-23-0—254, Carlson 1-1-0—10, Zendejas 0-1-1—0.

Receiving—Miami, Jensen 4-40, Stradford 3-21, Duper 2-16, Clayton 1-24, A. Brown 1-14, Edmunds 1-2; Houston, Hill 5-56, Givins 4-95, Pinkett 4-20, Jeffires 3-34, Duncan 2-34, Highsmith 2-25.

Kickoff Returns—Miami, Logan 3-138, Williams 1-21, Kinchen 1-9; Houston, K. Johnson 1-15, Harris 1-18, Verhulst 1-0.

Punt Returns—Miami, Stradford 1-7; Houston, K. Johnson 1-0.

Interceptions—Miami, Oliver 1-0; Houston, R. Johnson 1-0, Lyles 1-48.

Punting—Miami, Roby 5-37.6; Houston, Greg Montgomery 3-45.7.

Field Goals—Miami, none attempted; Houston, Zendejas 3-3.

Sacks—Miami, Green 2.

Bengals-Chiefs
SUNDAY, OCTOBER 1
SCORE BY PERIODS

Cincinnati	0	14	0	7—21
Kansas City	3	14	0	0—17

SCORING

Kansas City—Field goal Lowery 23, 7:28 1st.
Kansas City—Okoye 11 run (Lowery kick), 1:43 2nd.
Cincinnati—McGee 40 pass from Esiason (Gallery kick), 4:21 2nd.
Kansas City—R. Thomas 5 pass from Jaworski (Lowery kick), 11:23 2nd.
Cincinnati—Ball 2 run (Gallery kick), 13:58 2nd.
Cincinnati—White 22 fumble return (Gallery kick), 1:49 4th.

TEAM STATISTICS

	Cincinnati	Kansas City
First downs	14	16
Rushes-Yards	39-163	34-139
Passing yards	114	153
Passes	6-16-1	14-28-4
Sacked-Yards lost	4-38	1-10
Punts	7-41.3	4-40.0
Fumbles-Lost	2-2	2-2
Penalties-Yards	6-55	6-54
Time of possession	29:40	30:20

Attendance—60,165.

INDIVIDUAL STATISTICS

Rushing—Cincinnati, Ball 16-71, Jennings 10-35, Brooks 7-34, Esiason 6-23; Kansas City, Okoye 25-101, Heard 2-14, Mandley 1-8, Saxon 3-6, McNair 2-6, Jaworski 1-4.

Passing—Cincinnati, Esiason 6-14-1—152, Schonert 0-2-0—0; Kansas City, Jaworski 14-28-4-163.

Receiving—Cincinnati, Holman 2-45, Brown 1-42, McGee 1-40, Hillary 1-17, Ball 1-8; Kansas City, Mandley 4-51, Paige 3-56, R. Thomas 3-23, Harry 2-24, Dressel 1-6, Heard 1-3.

Kickoff Returns—Cincinnati, Jennings 3-79; Kansas City, Copeland 1-36, Saxon 1-14.

Punt Returns—Cincinnati, Martin 2-9; Kansas City, Mandley 2-20, Ross 1-0.

Interceptions—Cincinnati, Fulcher 3-38, Billups 1-0; Kansas City, Ross 1-0.

Punting—Cincinnati, Johnson 7-41.3; Kansas City, Goodburn 4-40.0.

Field Goals—Cincinnati, Gallery 0-1 (missed: 31); Kansas City, Lowery 1-1.

Sacks—Cincinnati, White; Kansas City, Griffin 2, Martin, D. Thomas.

Seahawks-Raiders
SUNDAY, OCTOBER 1
SCORE BY PERIODS

Seattle	7	0	0	17—24
Los Angeles Raiders	0	10	7	3—20

SCORING

Seattle—Williams 4 pass from Krieg (N. Johnson kick), 8:29 1st.
Los Angeles—Field goal Jaeger 45, 6:12 2nd.
Los Angeles—Washington 37 fumble return (Jaeger kick), 8:42 2nd.
Los Angeles—Fernandez 36 pass from Schroeder (Jaeger kick), 5:21 3rd.
Seattle—Warner 6 run (N. Johnson kick), 0:58 4th.
Seattle—Blades 19 pass from Krieg (N. Johnson kick), 5:02 4th.
Los Angeles—Field goal Jaeger 28, 9:02 4th.
Seattle—Field goal N. Johnson 48, 13:45 4th.

TEAM STATISTICS

	Seattle	Los Angeles
First downs	25	16
Rushes-Yards	40-160	18-114
Passing yards	194	197
Passes	22-31-0	16-30-1
Sacked-Yards lost	4-33	2-16
Punts	3-38.3	4-34.3
Fumbles-Lost	3-2	2-1
Penalties-Yards	3-49	8-64
Time of possession	36:02	23:58

Attendance—44,319.

INDIVIDUAL STATISTICS

Rushing—Seattle, Warner 21-102, Williams 14-43, Krieg 5-15; Los Angeles, Allen 11-65, Smith 4-31, Schroeder 1-10, Mueller 2-8.

Passing—Seattle, Krieg 22-31-0—227; Los Angeles, Schroeder 16-30-1—213.

Receiving—Seattle, Blades 7-113, Williams 6-34, Clark 4-20, Tyler 3-36, Kane 1-19, Warner 1-5; Los Angeles, Fernandez 7-113, Allen 3-31, Dyal 2-35, Alexander 2-20, Mueller 1-9, Gault 1-5.

Kickoff Returns—Seattle, Jefferson 2-43, Hollis 2-14; Los Angeles, Edmonds 4-58.

Punt Returns—Seattle, Jefferson 2-0.

Interceptions—Seattle, Robinson 1-0.

Punting—Seattle, Rodriguez 3-38.3; Los Angeles, Gossett 4-34.3.

Field Goals—Seattle, N. Johnson 1-2 (missed: 24); Los Angeles, Jaeger 2-3 (missed: 23).

Sacks—Seattle, Mitz, Nash; Los Angeles, Townsend 2, Davis, Pickel ½, Wise ½.

Steelers-Lions
SUNDAY, OCTOBER 1
SCORE BY PERIODS

Pittsburgh	0	10	7	6—23
Detroit	3	0	0	0— 3

SCORING
Detroit—Field goal Murray 37, 5:14 1st.
Pittsburgh—Lipps 48 pass from Brister (Anderson kick), 12:45 2nd.
Pittsburgh—Field goal Anderson 20, 14:37 2nd.
Pittsburgh—Carter 1 run (Anderson kick), 12:08 3rd.
Pittsburgh—Wallace 2 run (pass failed), 6:30 4th.

TEAM STATISTICS

	Pittsburgh	Detroit
First downs	20	13
Rushes-Yards	38-102	10-18
Passing yards	213	222
Passes	21-27-0	19-46-2
Sacked-Yards lost	7-54	3-13
Punts	9-45.1	6-49.8
Fumbles-Lost	0-0	2-2
Penalties-Yards	7-71	7-50
Time of possession	38:50	21:10
Attendance—43,804.		

INDIVIDUAL STATISTICS
Rushing—Pittsburgh, W. Williams 12-47, Brister 5-22, Lipps 2-15, Hoge 12-15, Wallace 1-2, Carter 1-1, Worley 5-0; Detroit, R. Johnson 1-8, Paige 2-5, Brown 1-3, Gagliano 1-1, B. Sanders 5-1.

Passing—Pittsburgh, Brister 21-27-0—267; Detroit, Peete 15-30-1—160, Gagliano 4-16-1—75.

Receiving—Pittsburgh, Lipps 7-126, Carter 6-52, Hill 4-62, Hoge 2-9, Thompson 1-10, Mularkey 1-8; Detroit, Clark 6-124, Mobley 3-44, Stanley 3-21, R. Johnson 3-17, B. Sanders 2-11, Paige 1-15, Phillips 1-3.

Kickoff Returns—Pittsburgh, Stone 2-46; Detroit, Gray 2-73, Dallafior 1-0.

Punt Returns—Pittsburgh, Lipps 4-27; Detroit, Gray 4-40, Stanley 1-17.

Interceptions—Pittsburgh, Griffin 1-15, Woodruff 1-8.

Punting—Pittsburgh, Newsome 9-45.1; Detroit, Arnold 6-49.8.

Field Goals—Pittsburgh, Anderson 1-1; Detroit, Murray 1-1.

Sacks—Pittsburgh, J. Williams, G. Williams, Willis; Detroit, E. Williams 3, Cofer 2, Spielman, McNorton.

Buccaneers-Vikings
SUNDAY, OCTOBER 1
SCORE BY PERIODS

Tampa Bay	0	3	0	0— 3
Minnesota	0	10	7	0—17

SCORING
Minnesota—Carter 12 pass from Kramer (Karlis kick), 2:16 2nd.
Minnesota—Field goal Karlis 20, 9:22 2nd.
Tampa Bay—Field goal Igwebuike 44, 15:00 2nd.
Minnesota—Lewis 28 pass from Kramer (Karlis kick), 11:48 3rd.

TEAM STATISTICS

	Tampa Bay	Minnesota
First downs	7	23
Rushes-Yards	25-94	41-162
Passing yards	64	203
Passes	6-23-0	21-35-2
Punts	9-40.6	4-40.0
Sacked-Yards lost	2-18	2-27
Fumbles-Lost	2-1	1-1
Penalties-Yards	3-20	7-50
Time of possession	23:56	36:04
Attendance—54,817.		

INDIVIDUAL STATISTICS
Rushing—Tampa Bay, Tate 13-64, Howard 8-13, Smith 2-9, Testaverde 1-6, Wilder 1-2; Minnesota, Nelson 11-67, Fenney 14-38, Dozier 6-33, Anderson 7-19, Kramer 2-3, Rice 1-2.

Passing—Tampa Bay, Testaverde 6-23-0—82; Minnesota, Wilson 3-3-0—40, Kramer 18-32-2—190.

Receiving—Tampa Bay, Hill 3-48, Smith 1-19, W. Harris 1-9, Carrier 1-6; Minnesota, Carter 6-87, Anderson 4-48, Jones 3-38, Lewis 3-32, Nelson 2-12, Fenney 2-6, Jordan 1-7.

Kickoff Returns—Tampa Bay, Elder 4-89; Minnesota, Nelson 1-30.

Punt Returns—Minnesota, Lewis 6-101.

Interceptions—Tampa Bay, Hamilton 2-30.

Punting—Tampa Bay, Mohr 9-40.6; Minnesota, Scribner 4-40.0.

Field Goals—Tampa Bay, Igwebuike 1-2 (missed: 46); Minnesota, Karlis 1-2 (missed: 44).

Sacks—Tampa Bay, Jarvis, Murphy; Minnesota, Doleman, Millard.

Eagles-Bears
MONDAY, OCTOBER 2
SCORE BY PERIODS

Philadelphia	0	0	3	10—13
Chicago	0	13	7	7—27

SCORING
Chicago—McKinnon 14 pass from Tomczak (Butler kick), 0:52 2nd.
Chicago—Suhey 1 pass from Tomczak (kick failed), 4:28 2nd.
Philadelphia—Field goal Zendejas 47, 4:58 3rd.
Chicago—Anderson 2 run (Butler kick), 11:47 3rd.
Philadelphia—Garrity 24 pass from Cunningham (Zendejas kick), 2:54 4th.
Philadelphia—Field goal Zendejas 19, 4:59 4th.
Chicago—Thornton 36 pass from Tomczak (Butler kick), 8:51 4th.

TEAM STATISTICS

	Philadelphia	Chicago
First downs	23	21
Rushes-Yards	15-67	35-108
Passing yards	368	266
Passes	32-62-4	24-38-1
Sacked-Yards lost	4-33	0-0
Punts	5-41.4	8-38.0
Fumbles-Lost	2-2	2-2
Penalties-Yards	9-70	6-35
Time of possession	22:25	37:35
Attendance—66,625.		

INDIVIDUAL STATISTICS
Rushing—Philadelphia, Cunningham 5-41, Toney 8-20, Higgs 1-5, Byars 1-1; Chicago, Anderson 23-85, Sanders 8-23, McKinnon 1-2, Muster 1-1, Tomczak 2-minus 3.

Passing—Philadelphia, Cunningham 32-62-4—401; Chicago, Tomczak 24-38-1—266.

Receiving—Philadelphia, Byars 10-87, Carter 8-113, Jackson 6-78, Garrity 4-83, Williams 2-18, Toney 1-15, Quick 1-7; Chicago, Thornton 5-94, Gentry 5-48, Suhey 4-18, McKinnon 3-36, Boso 3-34, Morris 1-9, Davis 1-9, Sanders 1-5, Anderson 1-3.

Kickoff Returns—Philadelphia, Williams 3-52, Little 1-12, Higgs 1-19; Chicago, Gentry 2-24, Green 1-21, Suhey 1-9.

Punt Returns—Philadelphia, Williams 3-17; Chicago, McKinnon 2-1.

Interceptions—Philadelphia, Allen 1-3; Chicago, Gayle 1-19, Roper 1-3, Tate 1-0, Stinson 1-0.

Punting—Philadelphia, Teltschik 2-37.5, Cunningham 3-44.0; Chicago, Buford 8-38.0.

Field Goals—Philadelphia, Zendejas 2-3 (missed: 45); Chicago, none attempted.

Sacks—Chicago, Roper 1½, Dent 2½.

FIFTH WEEK

RESULTS OF WEEK 5
Sunday, October 8

Cincinnati 26, Pittsburgh 16 at Pitts.
Denver 16, San Diego 10 at Den.
Green Bay 31, Dallas 13 at G.B.
Indianapolis 37, Buffalo 14 at Ind.
Kansas City 20, Seattle 16 at Sea.
L.A. Rams 26, Atlanta 14 at L.A.
Miami 13, Cleveland 10 (OT) at Mia.
Minnesota 24, Detroit 17 at Minn.
New England 23, Houston 13 at N.E.
Philadelphia 21, N.Y. Giants 19 at Phila.
San Francisco 24, New Orleans 20 at N.O.
Tampa Bay 42, Chicago 35 at T.B.
Washington 30, Phoenix 28 at Wash.

Monday, October 9

L.A. Raiders 14, N.Y. Jets 7 at N.Y.

Call it an act of great defiance. The Tampa Bay Buccaneers, used and abused by the Chicago Bears for years, weren't going to take it anymore.

Dating back to their first-ever meeting in 1977, the Bucs had lost 18 of 22 games to their NFC Central Division rivals. Since 1983, Chicago had squeezed Tampa Bay for two victories a year for six straight seasons, winning by an average margin of 17 points.

In the fifth week of the 1989 National Football League season, the Buccaneers exacted some long-awaited revenge. Scoring touchdowns on three of their first four possessions, they dealt the previously unbeaten Bears a particularly painful loss, 42-35. Tampa Bay's 42 points (second-most in club history) were the most scored against Chicago since 1981.

"I'm not surprised with this," said Bucs quarterback Vinny Testaverde, who completed his first seven attempts and threw three touchdown passes. "I knew if we could get up on them, we'd stay up the whole game."

Indeed, the Buccaneers scored three touchdowns in the first 16 minutes to take a 21-0 lead. And while the Bears pulled to within 28-21 after three periods, two scoring runs by Lars Tate in the fourth quarter restored the Bucs' 21-point lead. Tate finished with a career-high 112 yards rushing.

"We're not going to be intimidated by Chicago anymore," linebacker Kevin Murphy said. "Things have a funny way of working out. Times change. People change."

The Bucs' victory came one week after a distressing 17-3 loss to Minnesota, a game in which Testaverde completed only six of 23 passes for 82 yards. He surpassed that yardage total on Tampa Bay's first drive against the Bears.

"This is the kind of win we've been looking for, the kind of win to get us over the hump,"

Bucs Coach Ray Perkins said. His team improved to 3-2.

Were the Bears simply looking past a .500 team they had beaten so many times before?

"I was worried more about this football game than other people were," Chicago Coach Mike Ditka said. "Those people (the Buccaneers) were tired of getting beaten by the Bears. They deserve all the credit in the world. They just whipped us."

A whipping also took place in Indianapolis, where the Colts converted seven Buffalo turnovers into 23 points en route to a 37-14 AFC Eastern Division victory. Colts safety Keith Taylor intercepted two passes, returning one 80 yards for the game's final touchdown.

The Bills were plagued by turnovers from the start. After Indianapolis drove 80 yards for a touchdown to begin the game, Buffalo quarterback Jim Kelly was stripped of the football on the ensuing possession. Donnell Thompson recovered at the Bills' 36 for the Colts, who crossed the goal line five plays later on Jack Trudeau's one-yard run.

Indianapolis' Eric Dickerson, who didn't start the game because of a sore hamstring, finished with 92 yards rushing and two touchdowns. Kelly, meanwhile, suffered a separated left shoulder on a hard hit by Jon Hand as he completed a 16-yard scoring pass to Andre Reed in the third quarter. The injury would sideline the quarterback for three weeks.

In Los Angeles, the Rams remained the league's lone unbeaten team after parlaying two Jim Everett touchdown passes and four Mike Lansford field goals into a 26-14 victory over Atlanta. The Rams' Henry Ellard had 165 receiving yards on eight catches, though none went for a touchdown.

Falcons quarterback Chris Miller threw for a career-high 340 yards but couldn't prevent his club's fourth loss in five games. Atlanta failed to convert on two key plays: In the second period, John Settle was stopped on fourth-and-goal at the Rams' 1-yard line; in the fourth quarter, Gene Lang was bottled up on a fourth-and-three play at the Rams' 10.

The Denver Broncos, meanwhile, converted two important plays into first downs on their final possession to pull out a 16-10 AFC Western Division victory over San Diego.

On a game-winning 74-yard drive, Broncos quarterback John Elway found tight end Orson Mobley for a 17-yard gain on third-and-11, then Steve Sewell picked up seven yards on a fourth-and-one play to set up Bobby Humphrey's 17-yard scoring run with 1:03 left. Humphrey, selected from Alabama in the 1989 supplemental draft, finished with 102 yards rushing in his first NFL start.

Denver had trailed, 10-6, entering the fourth quarter, but the Chargers committed a costly

Vinny Testaverde guided the Tampa Bay Buccaneers to a 42-35 victory over Chicago in Week 5.

turnover when Tim Spencer fumbled midway through the period. Denver's Tyrone Braxton recovered at San Diego's 23, setting up a 27-yard David Treadwell field goal with 7:41 to play.

The biggest field goal of Week 5 was kicked in Miami, where Dolphins rookie Pete Stoyanovich solidified his job status and clinched a 13-10 victory over Cleveland with a 35-yard kick at 6:28 of overtime. Stoyanovich had missed 46- and 45-yard attempts in regulation, the latter with just eight seconds left.

The winning field goal capped a 55-yard drive that included a 20-yard pass play from Dan Marino to Fred Banks and a 26-yard pass interference penalty against Browns cornerback Stephen Braggs.

Marino threw for 234 yards to become the Dolphins' all-time passing leader and the 25th quarterback in NFL history to surpass the 25,000-yard plateau. His 25,101 career yards eclipsed the previous Miami record of 25,092 yards set by Hall of Famer Bob Griese.

Dallas rookie Steve Walsh made his first

NFL start but couldn't prevent the Cowboys' fifth straight loss, a 31-13 drubbing in Green Bay. The Cowboys' 0-5 start was their worst since 1960, the team's inaugural season.

Things looked up briefly. James Dixon returned the opening kickoff 90 yards to the Green Bay 6-yard line to set up a Walsh-to-Michael Irvin touchdown pass in the first minute. It turned out to be the only touchdown scored by the Dallas offense all day.

Packers quarterback Don Majkowski, meanwhile, guided the Packers to 502 total yards, passing for 313 yards and four touchdowns. His 79-yard strike to Sterling Sharpe in the final minute of the first half wiped out a 13-10 Dallas advantage and gave the Pack its first halftime lead of the season.

In Washington, the Redskins and Phoenix Cardinals combined for 889 yards in an NFC Eastern Division matchup won by the Redskins, 30-28. It was the Cardinals' 11th straight loss at RFK Stadium and the Redskins' first victory there after five consecutive defeats.

Washington trailed late in the third period,

Defensive tackle Keith Millard was the focal point of a relentless Minnesota defense in the Vikings' 24-17 victory over Detroit.

21-13, but took command with a 17-point run in the final quarter. After Chip Lohmiller's 37-yard field goal reduced the Phoenix lead to 21-16, the Redskins put together a 92-yard scoring drive climaxed by a Mark Rypien-to-Art Monk touchdown pass.

Barry Wilburn intercepted a Gary Hogeboom pass on the Cards' next possession, setting up a 63-yard drive that ended on Rypien's 23-yard scoring pass to Gary Clark with 1:54 left.

In an AFC Western Division matchup, the Kansas City Chiefs rallied from a 16-3 halftime deficit with 17 unanswered points to defeat Seattle, 20-16. Consequently, Seattle lost its first two home games for the first time in nine years, allowing the Chiefs to escape with their first victory at the Kingdome since 1981.

Kansas City's offensive star was running back Christian Okoye, who rushed 30 times for a career-high 156 yards. He scored the Chiefs' first touchdown by breaking four tackles on a 13-yard run midway through the third period.

Safety Deron Cherry was the Chiefs' defen-sive hero, intercepting two passes in the fourth quarter. He returned his first interception 27 yards to the Seahawks' 11-yard line to set up Kansas City's game-winning touchdown, then picked off a throw on the game's final play to thwart a Seattle threat.

The paramount defensive performance of Week 5 was turned in by Minnesota tackle Keith Millard, who recorded three sacks, forced one interception and returned another 48 yards in the Vikings' 24-17 victory over the Detroit Lions.

Millard was the focal point of a relentless defense that had eight sacks, forced four turnovers and held Detroit to 84 net yards passing. He pressured Lions quarterback Eric Hipple on a second-quarter pass that Mike Merriweather picked off and returned 15 yards for a touchdown, giving the Vikings a lead (10-7) they never relinquished.

Five minutes later, the defense scored again on cornerback Issiac Holt's 90-yard interception return. Minnesota sealed the victory by sacking Bob Gagliano on three straight plays after D.J. Dozier's fumble gave Detroit one final chance at the Vikings' 41-yard line.

At New England, Patriots running back John Stephens returned to the lineup after a two-game absence to spark the Pats to a 23-13 triumph over Houston. The victory snapped a three-game New England losing streak.

Stephens, who had been sidelined with an ankle injury, scored on an 11-yard run in the third quarter after Pats linebacker Vincent Brown recovered a fumbled punt by the Oilers' Kenny Johnson. Marvin Allen scored New England's first touchdown on a one-yard run, only six plays after he recovered a fumble by Houston's Leonard Harris on a kickoff.

Philadelphia quarterback Randall Cunningham overcame a horrid start by completing three key passes in the final minutes to rally the Eagles to a 21-19 victory over the New York Giants. Cunningham had connected on just seven of 19 passes for 47 yards before leading an 81-yard drive that culminated with Anthony Toney's two-yard touchdown run with 2:18 to play.

Cunningham, who scrambled for seven yards on the play before Toney's touchdown, threw a 23-yard pass to Cris Carter, a 21-yarder to Mike Quick and a 15-yard completion to Gregg Garrity on the game-winning drive. The pass to Carter was his first completion of the second half.

The Giants struggled all day on offense and suffered their first loss of the season. They managed just 84 yards rushing, allowed four sacks and failed to score a touchdown. New York's lone touchdown came on a 22-yard pass from Jeff Hostetler to Carl Banks on a fake field-goal attempt.

The Cincinnati Bengals took advantage of James Brooks' 127 yards rushing to topple the Pittsburgh Steelers, 26-16. The win was the Bengals' fourth straight over the Steelers and second in four weeks. It was Pittsburgh's 10th loss in its last 11 AFC Central Division games.

Thirteen was not an unlucky number for the Bengals on this day. Brooks snapped a 13-13 tie with a 13-yard touchdown run 13 seconds into the fourth quarter. Pittsburgh's Gary Anderson cut the Bengals' lead to 19-16 with a 34-yard field goal, but Brooks ran 65 yards for another score with 1:49 remaining. His touchdown came on a third-and-27 play.

Joe Montana capped three second-half drives with touchdown passes to lead the San Francisco 49ers to a 24-20 victory at New Orleans. The victory gave Montana a perfect 7-0 career record (as a starter) against the Saints in the Superdome.

Trailing 10-3 at halftime, the 49ers rallied to post their fourth come-from-behind victory on the road. Montana threw touchdown passes of 60 yards to Jerry Rice and 21 and 32 yards to John Taylor after the intermission. The Saints

Kansas City's Christian Okoye (above) and Washington's Art Monk each scored one touchdown in their teams' Week 5 victories.

suffered their fourth straight loss, the team's longest losing streak since Jim Mora became coach in 1986.

In the Monday night game, Art Shell made a historic coaching debut with the Los Angeles Raiders, who had dismissed former coach Mike Shanahan in the wake of the team's 1-3 start. Shell, a Hall of Fame offensive tackle for 15 seasons with the Raiders, became only the second black head coach in NFL history next to Fritz Pollard, a player-coach in the league's formative years. Shell started the season as the Raiders' offensive line coach.

On the field, Los Angeles reversed a three-game losing streak by scoring touchdowns on two long plays to defeat the New York Jets, 14-7. An 87-yard interception return by Eddie Anderson and a 73-yard pass reception by Mervyn Fernandez improved the Raiders record in Monday night games to 27-6-1, best in the NFL.

Bills-Colts
SUNDAY, OCTOBER 8
SCORE BY PERIODS

Buffalo	0	0	7	7—14
Indianapolis	14	6	3	14—37

SCORING
Indianapolis—Dickerson 1 run (Biasucci kick), 7:16 1st.
Indianapolis—Trudeau 1 run (Biasucci kick), 12:07 1st.
Indianapolis—Field goal Biasucci 32, 12:48 2nd.
Indianapolis—Field goal Biasucci 46, 14:34 2nd.
Indianapolis—Field goal Biasucci 25, 2:47 3rd.
Buffalo—Reed 16 pass from Kelly (Norwood kick), 11:16 3rd.
Indianapolis—Dickerson 4 run (Biasucci kick), 3:46 4th.
Buffalo—K. Davis 17 pass from Reich (Norwood kick), 9:54 4th.
Indianapolis—Taylor 80 interception return (Biasucci kick), 12:22 4th.

TEAM STATISTICS

	Buffalo	Indianapolis
First downs	25	20
Rushes-Yards	17-71	39-153
Passing yards	353	177
Passes	31-51-4	13-24-1
Sacked-Yards lost	4-40	3-16
Punts	2-51.0	4-38.5
Fumbles-Lost	5-3	2-0
Penalties-Yards	4-34	1-10
Time of possession	23:13	36:47
Attendance—58,890.		

INDIVIDUAL STATISTICS
Rushing—Buffalo, Thomas 12-53, Harmon 1-14, Kelly 2-6, K. Davis 2-minius 2; Indianapolis, Dickerson 22-92, Bentley 10-56, Trudeau 6-4, Verdin 1-1.

Passing—Buffalo, Kelly 20-32-3—216, Reich 11-19-1—177; Indianapolis, Trudeau 13-24-1—193.

Receiving—Buffalo, Harmon 8-75, Reed 7-75, Thomas 6-81, Johnson 4-67, Beebe 4-67, K. Davis 1-17, McKeller 1-11; Indianapolis, Brooks 5-111, Rison 4-47, Verdin 2-22, Bentley 1-7, Beach 1-6.

Kickoff Returns—Buffalo, Harmon 4-91, Tasker 1-19; Indianapolis, Pruitt 1-22.

Punt Returns—Buffalo, Sutton 2-17; Indianapolis, Verdin 1-6.

Interceptions—Buffalo, Drane 1-25; Indianapolis, Taylor 2-82, Bickett 1-6, Plummer 1-18.

Punting—Buffalo, Kidd 2-51.0; Indianapolis, Stark 4-38.5.

Field Goals—Buffalo, Norwood 0-1 (missed: 40); Indianapolis, Biasucci 3-3.

Sacks—Buffalo, Talley, Smerlas, Wright; Indianapolis, E. Johnson 2, Young, Thompson.

Oilers-Patriots
SUNDAY, OCTOBER 8
SCORE BY PERIODS

Houston	0	3	0	10—13
New England	10	0	10	3—23

SCORING
New England—Field goal Davis 30, 11:18 1st.
New England—Allen 1 run (Davis kick), 13:52 1st.
Houston—Field goal Zendejas 46, 15:00 2nd.
New England—Field goal Davis 34, 3:13 3rd.
New England—Stephens 11 run (Davis kick), 9:02 3rd.
Houston—Field goal Zendejas 22, 2:36 4th.
New England—Field goal Davis 43, 8:11 4th.
Houston—Hill 20 pass from Moon (Zendejas kick), 9:49 4th.

TEAM STATISTICS

	Houston	New England
First downs	14	19
Rushes-Yards	24-105	43-144
Passing yards	202	138
Passes	14-29-2	9-18-0
Sacked-Yards lost	3-25	1-7
Punts	5-44.6	3-32.0
Fumbles-Lost	2-1	1-1
Penalties-Yards	10-102	4-30
Time of possession	24:49	35:11
Attendance—59,828.		

INDIVIDUAL STATISTICS
Rushing—Houston, Moon 4-28, Pinkett 6-28, White 7-22, Highsmith 6-16, Greg Montgomery 1-11; New England, Stephens 21-59, Perryman 10-31, Allen 6-30, Flutie 6-24.

Passing—Houston, Moon 14-29-2—227; New England, Flutie 9-18-0—145.

Receiving—Houston, Givins 5-128, Hill 4-49, Jeffires 3-19, Duncan 1-18, Highsmith 1-13; New England, Fryar 3-42, Sievers 1-36, Perryman 1-16, Martin 1-16, Stephens 1-15, Jones 1-13, Morgan 1-7.

Kickoff Returns—Houston, Harris 2-37, White 4-66; New England, Allen 2-42.

Punt Returns—Houston, K. Johnson 2-8; New England, Fryar 2-11, Martin 1-28.

Interceptions—New England, Hurst 1-13, Coleman 1-1.

Punting—Houston, Greg Montgomery 5-44.6; New England, Feagles 3-32.0.

Field Goals—Houston, Zendejas 2-2; New England, Davis 3-4 (missed: 45).

Sacks—Houston, Lyles; New England, Williams, McGrew, Sims.

Cowboys-Packers
SUNDAY, OCTOBER 8
SCORE BY PERIODS

Dallas	6	7	0	0—13
Green Bay	10	7	7	7—31

SCORING
Dallas—Irvin 5 pass from Walsh (kick blocked), 0:58 1st.
Green Bay—Field goal Jacke 26, 5:54 1st.
Green Bay—Fontenot 7 pass from Majkowski (Jacke kick), 7:41 1st.
Dallas—Lockhart 40 fumble return (Ruzek kick), 6:29 2nd.
Green Bay—Sharpe 79 pass from Majkowski (Jacke kick), 14:01 2nd.
Green Bay—Fontenot 38 pass from Majkowski (Jacke kick), 14:20 3rd.
Green Bay—Kemp 4 pass from Majkowski (Jacke kick), 12:27 4th.

TEAM STATISTICS

	Dallas	Green Bay
First downs	12	28
Rushes-Yards	13-45	45-189
Passing yards	168	313
Passes	18-29-1	21-32-0
Sacked-Yards lost	3-25	0-0
Punts	7-39.7	3-36.3
Fumbles-Lost	2-1	2-1
Penalties-Yards	2-20	4-25
Time of possession	20:02	39:58

Attendance—56,656.

INDIVIDUAL STATISTICS

Rushing—Dallas, Walker 12-44, Johnston 1-1; Green Bay, Fullwood 28-119, Majkowski 9-32, Haddix 6-23, Kemp 1-8, Woodside 1-7.

Passing—Dallas, Walsh 18-29-1—193; Green Bay, Majkowski 21-32-0—313.

Receiving—Dallas, Irvin 6-72, Walker 4-45, Sargent 3-27, Martin 3-23, Dixon 1-18, Johnston 1-8; Green Bay, Sharpe 6-132, Kemp 6-56, Woodside 4-42, Fontenot 2-45, Fullwood 1-14, Query 1-13, Didier 1-11.

Kickoff Returns—Dallas, Dixon 5-186, Clark 1-18; Green Bay, Fullwood 1-19, Workman 2-38.

Punt Returns—Dallas, Shepard 1-6; Green Bay, Query 2-12.

Interceptions—Green Bay, Greene 1-0.

Punting—Dallas, Saxon 7-39.9; Green Bay, Bracken 3-36.3.

Field Goals—Dallas, Ruzek 0-1 (missed: 46); Green Bay, Jacke 1-3 (missed: 46, 37).

Sacks—Green Bay, Harris 2, Nelson.

Bengals-Steelers
SUNDAY, OCTOBER 8
SCORE BY PERIODS

Cincinnati	0	13	0	13—26
Pittsburgh	7	3	3	3—16

SCORING

Pittsburgh—Carter 22 pass from Brister (Anderson kick), 9:06 1st.

Cincinnati—Field goal Breech 24, 0:07 2nd.

Cincinnati—Field goal Breech 27, 7:09 2nd.

Pittsburgh—Field goal Anderson 24, 12:23 2nd.

Cincinnati—Martin 7 pass from Esiason (Breech kick), 14:52 2nd.

Pittsburgh—Field goal Anderson 40, 11:13 3rd.

Cincinnati—Brooks 13 run (kick failed), 0:13 4th.

Pittsburgh—Field goal Anderson 34, 7:42 4th.

Cincinnati—Brooks 65 run (Breech kick), 13:11 4th.

TEAM STATISTICS

	Cincinnati	Pittsburgh
First downs	21	24
Rushes-Yards	28-190	36-172
Passing yards	192	168
Passes	17-32-0	21-36-0
Sacked-Yards lost	3-27	3-35
Punts	4-40.3	3-43.3
Fumbles-Lost	1-1	2-1
Penalties-Yards	3-50	7-40
Time of possession	23:31	36:29

Attendance—52,785.

INDIVIDUAL STATISTICS

Rushing—Cincinnati, Brooks 17-127, Esiason 4-38, Ball 7-25; Pittsburgh, Worley 15-74, Hoge 16-68, Brister 4-20, Lipps 1-10.

Passing—Cincinnati, Esiason 17-32-0—219; Pittsburgh, Brister 19-31-0—169, Blackledge 2-5-0—34.

Receiving—Cincinnati, Brown 5-80, McGee 4-49, Martin 3-29, Holman 2-35, Brooks 2-12, Ball 1-14; Pittsburgh, Lipps 8-99, Carter 5-39, Mularkey 3-33, Hill 2-23, Stone 1-16, Hoge 1-minus 1, Worley 1-minus 6.

Kickoff Returns—Cincinnati, Jennings 2-38, Hillary 1-19; Pittsburgh, Woodson 5-136, Hinnant 1-13.

Punt Returns—Cincinnati, Martin 2-19; Pittsburgh, Woodson 4-17.

Interceptions—None.

Punting—Cincinnati, Johnson 4-40.3; Pittsburgh, Newsome 3-43.3.

Field Goals—Cincinnati, Breech 2-2; Pittsburgh, Anderson 3-4 (missed: 46).

Sacks—Cincinnati, Buck, Wilcots, Zander ½, Hammerstein ½; Pittsburgh, Willis, T. Johnson, Lloyd.

Falcons-Rams
SUNDAY, OCTOBER 8
SCORE BY PERIODS

Atlanta	7	0	7	0—14
Los Angeles Rams	10	10	6	0—26

SCORING

Los Angeles—Holohan 13 pass from Everett (Lansford kick), 5:01 1st.

Atlanta—Collins 9 pass from Miller (McFadden kick), 9:18 1st.

Los Angeles—Field goal Lansford 48, 12:38 1st.

Los Angeles—Delpino 9 pass from Everett (Lansford kick), 3:35 2nd.

Los Angeles—Field goal Lansford 35, 12:50 2nd.

Los Angeles—Field goal Lansford 27, 3:40 3rd.

Atlanta—Jones 3 run (McFadden kick), 7:56 3rd.

Los Angeles—Field goal Lansford 42, 10:24 3rd.

TEAM STATISTICS

	Atlanta	Los Angeles
First downs	19	21
Rushes-Yards	15-38	33-165
Passing yards	315	273
Passes	28-39-1	16-28-1
Sacked-Yards lost	2-25	2-17
Punts	3-43.7	1-40.0
Fumbles-Lost	2-0	0-0
Penalties-Yards	2-19	4-45
Time of possession	28:10	31:50

Attendance—52,182.

INDIVIDUAL STATISTICS

Rushing—Atlanta, Settle 7-26, Jones 3-7, Lang 3-3, Miller 2-2; Los Angeles, Bell 10-62, Delpino 4-48, Green 9-36, Gary 7-25, Everett 3-minus 6.

Passing—Atlanta, Miller 28-39-1—340; Los Angeles, Everett 16-28-1—290.

Receiving—Atlanta, Collins 6-62, Jones 4-61, Lang 4-47, Heller 4-28, Settle 4-8, Haynes 2-55, Dixon 2-31, Bailey 1-37, G. Thomas 1-11; Los Angeles, Ellard 8-165, Holohan 3-49, Anderson 2-54, Johnson 1-10, Delpino 1-7, Gary 1-5.

Kickoff Returns—Atlanta, Sanders 3-37, Jones 3-46, Primus 1-16; Los Angeles, Ron Brown 2-96, Delpino 1-22.

Punt Returns—Atlanta, Sanders 1-1; Los Angeles, Henley 1-21.

Interceptions—Atlanta, Sanders 1-8; Los Angeles, Irvin 1-12.

Punting—Atlanta, Fulhage 3-43.7; Los Angeles, Hatcher 1-40.0.

Field Goals—Atlanta, none attempted; Los Angeles, Lansford 4-4.

Sacks—Atlanta, Green, Bruce; Los Angeles, Greene 2.

Chargers-Broncos
SUNDAY, OCTOBER 8
SCORE BY PERIODS

San Diego	3	0	7	0—10
Denver	0	6	0	10—16

SCORING

San Diego—Field goal Bahr 39, 8:07 1st.

Denver—Field goal Treadwell 46, 1:35 2nd.

Denver—Field goal Treadwell 18, 13:03 2nd.
San Diego—Butts 2 run (Bahr kick), 4:42 3rd.
Denver—Field goal Treadwell 27, 7:19 4th.
Denver—Humphrey 17 run (Treadwell kick), 13:57 4th.

TEAM STATISTICS

	San Diego	Denver
First downs	12	24
Rushes-Yards	26-118	35-156
Passing yards	93	179
Passes	10-19-1	19-35-1
Sacked-Yards lost	3-23	3-20
Punts	5-49.8	3-43.7
Fumbles-Lost	1-1	0-0
Penalties-Yards	10-57	3-25
Time of possession	26:51	33:09
Attendance—75,222.		

INDIVIDUAL STATISTICS

Rushing—San Diego, Spencer 15-78, Butts 6-18, Holland 1-9, Brinson 1-7, McMahon 2-6, Bernstine 1-0; Denver, Humphrey 23-102, Elway 7-30, Winder 3-15, Sewell 1-7, Alexander 1-2.

Passing—San Diego, McMahon 10-19-1—116; Denver, Elway 19-35-1—199.

Receiving—San Diego, Brinson 3-23, Bernstine 2-45, A. Miller 2-29, Cox 2-13, Spencer 1-6; Denver, Johnson 6-65, Jackson 4-53, Mobley 3-27, Young 2-34, Winder 1-6, Kay 1-6, Sewell 1-5, Humphrey 1-3.

Kickoff Returns—San Diego, Holland 4-96; Denver, Bell 2-43.

Punt Returns—San Diego, Brinson 1-52; Denver, Bell 3-41.

Interceptions—San Diego, Byrd 1-0; Denver, Corrington 1-8.

Punting—San Diego, Ilesic 5-49.8; Denver, Horan 3-43.7.

Field Goals—San Diego, Bahr 1-1; Denver, Treadwell 3-4 (missed: 54).

Sacks—San Diego, Hinkle, O'Neal, Phillips; Denver, Mecklenburg, Townsend, Carreker.

Lions-Vikings
SUNDAY, OCTOBER 8
SCORE BY PERIODS

Detroit	7	3	0	7—17
Minnesota	0	24	0	0—24

SCORING

Detroit—Hipple 1 run (Murray kick), 12:37 1st.
Minnesota—Field goal Karlis 22, 2:15 2nd.
Minnesota—Merriweather 15 interception return (Karlis kick), 3:18 2nd.
Minnesota—Holt 90 interception return (Karlis kick), 8:37 2nd.
Minnesota—Novoselsky 2 pass from Kramer (Karlis kick), 14:06 2nd.
Detroit—Field goal Murray 50, 15:00 2nd.
Detroit—Gagliano 1 run (Murray kick), 10:35 4th.

TEAM STATISTICS

	Detroit	Minnesota
First downs	20	14
Rushes-Yards	34-153	32-91
Passing yards	84	138
Passes	11-27-3	11-18-0
Sacked-Yards lost	8-46	2-8
Punts	6-40.0	4-35.3
Fumbles-Lost	1-1	3-3
Penalties-Yards	13-106	10-69
Time of possession	32:38	27:22
Attendance—55,380.		

INDIVIDUAL STATISTICS

Rushing—Detroit, B. Sanders 23-99, Gagliano 4-23, R. Johnson 3-20, Hipple 2-11, Paige 2-0; Minnesota, Fenney 9-35, Nelson 7-22, Anderson 7-19, Dozier 6-12, Kramer 3-3.

Passing—Detroit, Hipple 7-18-3—90, Gagliano 4-9-0—40; Minnesota, Kramer 11-18-0—146.

Receiving—Detroit, R. Johnson 3-38, Mobley 2-30, B. Sanders 2-30, Phillips 2-17, Clark 2-15; Minnesota, Jones 2-44, Jordan 2-23, Nelson 2-19, Carter 1-19, Anderson 1-18, Gustafson 1-12, Fenney 1-9, Novoselsky 1-2.

Kickoff Returns—Detroit, Palmer 4-64; Minnesota, Nelson 3-62.

Punt Returns—Detroit, Stanley 2-43; Minnesota, Lewis 3-9.

Interceptions—Minnesota, Merriweather 1-15, Holt 1-90, Millard 1-48.

Punting—Detroit, Arnold 6-40.0; Minnesota, Scribner 4-35.3.

Field Goals—Detroit, Murray 1-1; Minnesota, Karlis 1-2 (missed: 29).

Sacks—Detroit, J. Williams 1½, Ball ½; Minnesota, Millard 3, Noga 2½, Berry, Clark, Merriweather ½.

Bears-Buccaneers
SUNDAY, OCTOBER 8
SCORE BY PERIODS

Chicago	0	14	7	14—35
Tampa Bay	14	14	0	14—42

SCORING

Tampa Bay—Carrier 11 pass from Testaverde (Igwebuike kick), 4:34 1st.
Tampa Bay—Howard 1 run (Igwebuike kick), 9:36 1st.
Tampa Bay—Harris 3 pass from Testaverde (Igwebuike kick), 0:52 2nd.
Chicago—Anderson 5 run (Butler kick), 8:08 2nd.
Tampa Bay—Hill 22 pass from Testaverde (Igwebuike kick), 10:55 2nd.
Chicago—Anderson 1 run (Butler kick), 13:09 2nd.
Chicago—Sanders 16 pass from Tomczak (Butler kick), 5:29 3rd.
Tampa Bay—Tate 16 run (Igwebuike kick), 3:52 4th.
Tampa Bay—Tate 4 run (Mohr run), 8:14 4th.
Chicago—Harbaugh 26 run (Butler kick), 10:04 4th.
Chicago—Anderson 1 run (Butler kick), 13:12 4th.

TEAM STATISTICS

	Chicago	Tampa Bay
First downs	21	26
Rushes-Yards	26-136	31-147
Passing yards	229	268
Passes	22-37-1	22-36-2
Sacked-Yards lost	2-13	1-1
Punts	6-40.2	5-41.6
Fumbles-Lost	3-2	0-0
Penalties-Yards	5-22	5-22
Time of possession	27:04	32:56
Attendance—72,077.		

INDIVIDUAL STATISTICS

Rushing—Chicago, Anderson 17-86, Harbaugh 3-34, Sanders 2-7, Suhey 2-5, Tomczak 2-4; Tampa Bay, Tate 18-112, Testaverde 3-18, Howard 7-12, Wilder 2-7, Ferguson 1-minus 2.

Passing—Chicago, Tomczak 16-29-1—162, Harbaugh 6-8-0—80; Tampa Bay, Testaverde 22-36-2—269.

Receiving—Chicago, Anderson 6-30, Gentry 4-38, Morris 3-54, Thornton 2-38, Green 2-19, Muster 2-8, McKinnon 1-32, Sanders 1-16, Suhey 1-7; Tampa Bay, Hill 6-107, Carrier 6-105, W. Harris 4-24, Howard 3-7, Drewrey 1-18, Wilder 1-5, Tate 1-3.

Kickoff Returns—Chicago, Gentry 3-91, Tate 1-12, Green 1-20, Suhey 1-21; Tampa Bay, Elder 2-17.

Punt Returns—Chicago, McKinnon 1-0, Green 2-31; Tampa Bay, Futrell 2-13.

Interceptions—Chicago, Morrissey 2-0; Tampa Bay, Robinson 1-0.

Punting—Chicago, Buford 6-40.2; Tampa Bay, Mohr 5-41.6.

Field Goals—None attempted.

Sacks—Chicago, McMichael; Tampa Bay, Goff, Murphy.

Giants-Eagles
SUNDAY, OCTOBER 8
SCORE BY PERIODS

New York Giants	3	10	0	6—19
Philadelphia	0	7	0	14—21

SCORING
New York—Field goal Allegre 25, 11:10 1st.
New York—Banks 22 pass from Hostetler (Allegre kick), 1:37 2nd.
Philadelphia—Cunningham 5 run (Zendejas kick), 12:59 2nd.
New York—Field goal Allegre 41, 14:55 2nd.
New York—Field goal Allegre 45, 0:05 4th.
Philadelphia—Cunningham 1 run (Zendejas kick), 3:11 4th.
New York—Field goal Allegre 24, 9:07 4th.
Philadelphia—Toney 2 run (Zendejas kick), 12:42 4th.

TEAM STATISTICS

	New York	Philadelphia
First downs	20	18
Rushes-Yards	26-84	36-158
Passing yards	245	85
Passes	22-40-1	10-24-0
Sacked-Yards lost	4-18	2-21
Punts	4-44.0	7-36.6
Fumbles-Lost	2-0	4-0
Penalties-Yards	6-56	2-25
Time of possession	31:05	28:55
Attendance—65,688.		

INDIVIDUAL STATISTICS
Rushing—New York, Meggett 7-29, Simms 5-29, Anderson 13-25, Carthon 1-1; Philadelphia, Toney 12-68, Cunningham 10-44, Byars 11-41, Higgs 3-5.

Passing—New York, Simms 21-39-1—241, Hostetler 1-1-0—22; Philadelphia, Cunningham 10-24-0—106.

Receiving—New York, Meggett 6-89, Bavaro 4-32, Ingram 2-26, Anderson 2-11, Banks 1-22, Baker 1-20, Carthon 1-18, Rouson 1-17, Manuel 1-12, Mowatt 1-7, Cross 1-6, Turner 1-3; Philadelphia, Byars 3-16, Carter 2-27, Giles 2-25, Quick 1-21, Garrity 1-15, Toney 1-2.

Kickoff Returns—New York, Ingram 1-19, Meggett 1-19; Philadelphia, Sherman 3-68, Little 1-2, Higgs 2-30.

Punt Returns—New York, Meggett 4-29; Philadelphia, Williams 2-29.

Interceptions—Philadelphia, Frizzell 1-8.

Punting—New York, Landeta 4-44.0; Philadelphia, Teltschik 7-36.6.

Field Goals—New York, Allegre 4-5 (missed: 39); Philadelphia, none attempted.

Sacks—New York, Taylor 2; Philadelphia, White 2, Simmons, Joyner.

Cardinals-Redskins
SUNDAY, OCTOBER 8
SCORE BY PERIODS

Phoenix	0	14	7	7—28
Washington	10	3	0	17—30

SCORING
Washington—Field goal Lohmiller 22, 5:44 1st.
Washington—Byner 2 pass from Rypien (Lohmiller kick), 12:43 1st.
Washington—Field goal Lohmiller 32, 0:58 2nd.
Phoenix—J.T. Smith 7 pass from Hogeboom (Del Greco kick), 7:44 2nd.
Phoenix—J.T. Smith 20 pass from Hogeboom (Del Greco kick), 13:51 2nd.
Phoenix—Ferrell 44 run (Del Greco kick), 12:27 3rd.
Washington—Field goal Lohmiller 37, 1:43 4th.
Washington—Monk 12 pass from Rypien (Lohmiller kick), 7:13 4th.
Washington—Clark 23 pass from Rypien (Lohmiller kick), 13:06 4th.
Phoenix—J.T. Smith 17 pass from Hogeboom (Del Greco kick), 14:46 4th.

TEAM STATISTICS

	Phoenix	Washington
First downs	19	28
Rushes-Yards	20-90	42-175
Passing yards	291	333
Passes	20-36-4	23-42-1
Sacked-Yards lost	1-5	0-0
Punts	5-41.0	5-40.0
Fumbles-Lost	0-0	0-0
Penalties-Yards	12-76	5-40
Time of possession	22:27	37:33
Attendance—53,335.		

INDIVIDUAL STATISTICS
Rushing—Phoenix, Ferrell 7-53, Sikahema 1-28, Baker 7-8, Hogeboom 3-6, Jordan 2-minus 5; Washington, Byner 14-100, Riggs 27-60, Rypien 1-15.

Passing—Phoenix, Hogeboom 20-35-3—296, Awalt 0-1-1—0; Washington, Rypien 23-42-1—333.

Receiving—Phoenix, J.T. Smith 8-114, Novacek 4-39, Holmes 3-63, Green 2-36, Awalt 1-20, Sikahema 1-16, Jones 1-8; Washington, Monk 8-102, Sanders 6-87, Byner 5-71, Clark 4-73.

Kickoff Returns—Phoenix, Sikahema 5-88, Baker 2-44; Washington, Howard 1-42, A.J. Johnson 3-74.

Punt Returns—Phoenix, Sikahema 2-62; Washington, Howard 1-11.

Interceptions—Phoenix, Wahler 1-5; Washington, Green 2-0, Walton 1-0, Wilburn 1-13.

Punting—Phoenix, Camarillo 5-41.0; Washington, Mojsiejenko 5-40.0.

Field Goals—Phoenix, none attempted; Washington, Lohmiller 3-4 (missed: 42).

Sacks—Washington, Mann.

49ers-Saints
SUNDAY, OCTOBER 8
SCORE BY PERIODS

San Francisco	0	3	7	14—24
New Orleans	0	10	7	3—20

SCORING
San Francisco—Field goal Cofer 41, 5:11 2nd.
New Orleans—Brenner 2 pass from Hebert (Andersen kick), 13:48 2nd.
New Orleans—Field goal Andersen 49, 14:55 2nd.
New Orleans—Hilliard 19 pass from Hebert (Andersen kick), 7:31 3rd.
San Francisco—Rice 60 pass from Montana (Cofer kick), 8:00 3rd.
San Francisco—Taylor 21 pass from Montana (Cofer kick), 0:10 4th.
New Orleans—Field goal Andersen 39, 4:40 4th.
San Francisco—Taylor 32 pass from Montana (Cofer kick), 6:56 4th.

TEAM STATISTICS

	San Francisco	New Orleans
First downs	18	18
Rushes-Yards	23-76	16-35
Passing yards	282	299
Passes	21-29-0	31-49-0
Sacked-Yards lost	2-9	1-9
Punts	6-40.7	7-36.4
Fumbles-Lost	3-1	2-0
Penalties-Yards	6-38	4-25
Time of possession	25:58	34:02
Attendance—60,488.		

INDIVIDUAL STATISTICS
Rushing—San Francisco, Craig 18-70, Montana 1-11, Sydney 1-minus 1, Young 3-minus 4; New Orleans, Heyward 4-21, Hilliard 10-9, Hebert 1-5, Winslow 1-0.

Passing—San Francisco, Montana 21-29-0—291; New Orleans, Hebert 31-49-0—308.

Receiving—San Francisco, Rice 7-149, Rathman 5-34, Craig 4-37, Taylor 2-53, Jones 2-16, Wilson 1-2; New Orleans, Hilliard 9-77, Hill 8-88, Martin 5-86, Heyward 3-13, Brenner 3-13, Tice 1-16, Turner 1-11, Perriman 1-4.

Kickoff Returns—San Francisco, Flagler 3-54, Sydney 1-16; New Orleans, Atkins 3-55, Frazier 1-21.

Punt Returns—San Francisco, Taylor 3-43; New Orleans, Hill 3-20, Turner 1-7.

Interceptions—None.

Punting—San Francisco, Helton 6-40.7; New Orleans, Winslow 7-36.4.

Field Goals—San Francisco, Cofer 1-2 (missed: 44); New Orleans, Andersen 2-2.

Sacks—San Francisco, Haley; New Orleans, Swilling, Wilks.

Browns-Dolphins
SUNDAY, OCTOBER 8
SCORE BY PERIODS

Cleveland	0	3	7	0	0—10
Miami	3	7	0	0	3—13

SCORING

Miami—Field goal Stoyanovich 43, 6:25 1st.

Miami—Duper 35 pass from Marino (Stoyanovich kick), 8:14 2nd.

Cleveland—Field goal Bahr 50, 12:28 2nd.

Cleveland—Metcalf 8 run (Bahr kick), 6:35 3rd.

Miami—Field goal Stoyanovich 35, 6:28 OT.

TEAM STATISTICS

	Cleveland	Miami
First downs	19	18
Rushes-Yards	27-141	29-70
Passing yards	189	234
Passes	22-35-2	19-33-1
Sacked-Yards lost	3-21	0-0
Punts	4-41.0	4-45.7
Fumbles-Lost	1-0	0-0
Penalties-Yards	8-86	3-30
Time of possession	33:30	32:58
Attendance—58,444.		

INDIVIDUAL STATISTICS

Rushing—Cleveland, Metcalf 16-78, K. Jones 5-33, Manoa 4-28, Redden 1-3, Kosar 1-minus 1; Miami, Stradford 11-37, Smith 16-23, Logan 2-10.

Passing—Cleveland, Kosar 22-35-2—210; Miami, Marino 19-33-1—234.

Receiving—Cleveland, Brennan 5-51, Langhorne 5-47, Slaughter 4-39, Newsome 3-40, Metcalf 3-28, K. Jones 1-4, Redden 1-1; Miami, Duper 5-83, Jensen 5-46, Stradford 3-21, Banks 2-36, Clayton 2-20, Edmunds 1-15, Smith 1-13.

Kickoff Returns—Cleveland, Oliphant 1-28, Metcalf 1-20; Miami, Logan 1-21.

Punt Returns—Cleveland, McNeil 3-17; Miami, Stradford 3-34.

Interceptions—Cleveland, Wright 1-17; Miami, McNeal 1-minus 6, Oliver 1-23.

Punting—Cleveland, Wagner 4-41.0; Miami, Roby 4-45.7.

Field Goals—Cleveland, Bahr 1-2 (missed: 44); Miami, Stoyanovich 2-4 (missed: 46, 45).

Sacks—Miami, Sochia 2, Cross.

Chiefs-Seahawks
SUNDAY, OCTOBER 8
SCORE BY PERIODS

Kansas City	3	0	7	10—20	
Seattle	7	9	0	0—16	

SCORING

Seattle—Jefferson 97 kickoff return (N. Johnson kick), 0:17 1st.

Kansas City—Field goal Lowery 39, 10:31 1st.

Seattle—Field goal N. Johnson 37, 9:57 2nd.

Seattle—Field goal N. Johnson 26, 13:11 2nd.

Seattle—Field goal N. Johnson 37, 14:56 2nd.

Kansas City—Okoye 13 run (Lowery kick), 7:07 3rd.

Kansas City—Field goal Lowery 25, 3:08 4th.

Kansas City—Roberts 2 pass from Jaworski (Lowery kick), 5:33 4th.

TEAM STATISTICS

	Kansas City	Seattle
First downs	17	16
Rushes-Yards	40-199	19-52
Passing yards	104	236
Passes	12-18-0	20-36-2
Sacked-Yards lost	0-0	2-16
Punts	5-42.2	5-37.0
Fumbles-Lost	2-1	1-0
Penalties-Yards	4-34	5-40
TIme of possession	34:18	25:42
Attendance—60,715.		

INDIVIDUAL STATISTICS

Rushing—Kansas City, Okoye 30-156, Heard 4-28, Saxon 4-15, McNair 1-0, Jaworski 1-0; Seattle, Krieg 3-29, Williams 9-22, Warner 7-1.

Passing—Kansas City, Jaworski 12-18-0—104; Seattle, Krieg 20-36-2—252.

Receiving—Kansas City, Harry 3-41, Saxon 2-13, McNair 2-11, Dressel 1-21, Paige 1-7, Mandley 1-5, Heard 1-4, Roberts 1-2; Seattle, Skansi 5-79, Williams 5-32, Blades 4-86, Kane 3-32, Clark 2-14, Tyler 1-9.

Kickoff Returns—Kansas City, Copeland 4-62, Saleaumua 1-8; Seattle, Jefferson 5-168.

Punt Returns—Kansas City, Mandley 3-18; Seattle, Hollis 4-33.

Interceptions—Kansas City, Cherry 2-27.

Punting—Kansas City, Goodburn 5-42.2; Seattle, Rodriguez 5-37.0.

Field Goals—Kansas City, Lowery 2-2; Seattle, N. Johnson 3-3.

Sacks—Kansas City, Smith, D. Thomas.

Raiders-Jets
MONDAY, OCTOBER 9
SCORE BY PERIODS

Los Angeles Raiders	0	0	7	7—14	
New York Jets	0	0	7	0— 7	

SCORING

Los Angeles—Fernandez 73 pass from Schroeder (Jaeger kick), 0:09 3rd.

New York—Vick 1 run (Leahy kick), 5:28 3rd.

Los Angeles—Anderson 87 interception return (Jaeger kick), 4:55 4th.

TEAM STATISTICS

	Los Angeles	New York
First downs	14	20
Rushes-Yards	27-130	25-80
Passing yards	185	312
Passes	11-24-1	25-49-2
Sacked-Yards lost	3-12	3-36
Punts	7-37.0	7-30.7
Fumbles-Lost	1-0	3-0
Penalties-Yards	8-57	7-65
Time of possession	26:11	33:49
Attendance—68,040.		

INDIVIDUAL STATISTICS

Rushing—Los Angeles, Allen 10-43, Smith 8-42, Mueller 6-30, Porter 3-15; New York, McNeil 10-39, Hector 8-38, Vick 7-3.

Passing—Los Angeles, Schroeder 11-24-1—197; New York, O'Brien 25-49-2—348.

Receiving—Los Angeles, Allen 4-34, Gault 3-47, Alexander 2-26, Fernandez 1-73, Mueller 1-17; New York, Burkett 6-95, Townsell 6-93, Griggs 4-60, McNeil 4-42, Toon 3-25, Hector 1-22, Vick 1-11.

Kickoff Returns—Los Angeles, Ware 2-29; New York, Townsell 1-24, Humphery 2-3.

Punt Returns—New York, Townsell 5-20.

Interceptions—Los Angeles, Anderson 1-87, McDaniel 1-20; New York, McMillan 1-41.

Punting—Los Angeles, Gossett 7-37.0; New York, Prokop 7-30.7.

Field Goals—Los Angeles, Jaeger 0-1 (missed: 52); New York, none attempted.

Sacks—Los Angeles, Davis, Golic, Long ½, Wise ½; New York, Clifton ½, Nichols ½, Byrd, Frase.

SIXTH WEEK

RESULTS OF WEEK 6
Sunday, October 15

Atlanta 16, New England 15 at Atl.
Denver 14, Indianapolis 3 at Den.
Detroit 17, Tampa Bay 16 at T.B.
Houston 33, Chicago 28 at Chi.
L.A. Raiders 20, Kansas City 14 at L.A.
Miami 20, Cincinnati 13 at Cin.
Minnesota 26, Green Bay 14 at Minn.
New Orleans 29, N.Y. Jets 14 at N.O.
N.Y. Giants 20, Washington 17 at N.Y.
Philadelphia 17, Phoenix 5 at Phoe.
Pittsburgh 17, Cleveland 7 at Cleve.
San Francisco 31, Dallas 14 at Dall.
Seattle 17, San Diego 16 at S.D.

Monday, October 16

Buffalo 23, L.A. Rams 20 at Buff.

In many circles, the Minnesota Vikings entered the 1989 National Football League season favored to advance to Super Bowl XXIV. This was a team loaded with individual talent, having placed a league-high nine players in the previous Pro Bowl game.

Through the first five weeks of the 1989 schedule, however, the Vikings owned only a 3-2 record. They had been blown out, 38-7, by division rival Chicago, and lost, 27-14, to a down Pittsburgh team.

Minnesota's most glaring problem was a weak running attack. The team had averaged just 117 yards rushing per game, giving opponents the luxury of overplaying the pass. The Vikes' had netted only four touchdowns on the ground, one more touchdown than the defense had managed.

On October 12, in one bold stroke designed to relieve this pressing problem, General Manager Mike Lynn surrendered five players, a 1992 first-round draft choice and six conditional draft picks to the Dallas Cowboys for running back Herschel Walker, a player of immense talent who was languishing in a new pass-oriented offense installed by Cowboys Coach Jimmy Johnson.

Walker had led the National Conference with 1,514 yards rushing in 1988, but this season he had gained only 246 yards in Dallas' first five games. The trade rocked the pro football establishment, but Walker was a player the rebuilding Cowboys could afford to give up and someone the Vikings felt they desperately needed.

"If we don't win the (NFC) Central Division and if we don't win the Super Bowl while Herschel Walker is here, then we have not made a good trade," said Lynn, placing more than a little burden on the broad shoulders of his newest player.

If his debut with Minnesota was any indica-

tion, Walker was up to the task. Playing before a near-record crowd of 62,075 in the Metrodome, the big running back rushed for 148 yards on 18 carries to lead the Vikings to a 26-14 victory over Green Bay.

"He did all the things you'd expect of him," said Packers safety Ken Stills. "He's behind a good offensive line now and he made them a better team."

Walker was devastating against Green Bay, a team that had held him to 44 yards rushing one week earlier in his Dallas finale. Vikings Coach Jerry Burns had planned to use Walker sparingly to allow him time to learn the Minnesota offense. But after Walker ripped off 98 yards the first two times he touched the ball (51 yards on a kickoff return nullified by a penalty and 47 on a run from scrimmage), those plans went out the window.

"I'm not the smartest guy, but I'm not a complete idiot either," Burns said. "When I saw what he was doing, I said, 'Keep him in and keep feeding him the ball.'"

Walker averaged 8.2 yards a carry leading a Vikings ground attack that netted 238 yards.

"I've learned systems overnight before," said Walker, who had practiced twice with his new team. "I kept telling the coaches that I stayed up nights with the playbook."

Burns was excited about his team's future with Walker on board, but he was a bit more restrained than his boss, Lynn.

"He's not responsible for getting us to the Super Bowl," the coach said, "but I have to say I'm happy he's here."

Walker's former team, the Cowboys, managed to do some things just as easily without him—namely, lose. Dallas dropped to 0-6 following a 31-14 loss to San Francisco.

The Cowboys were able to tie the game, 14-14, late in the third quarter, but the 49ers exploded for 17 unanswered points to improve to 5-1. Early in the fourth quarter, safety Tom Holmoe intercepted a pass by Dallas rookie Steve Walsh and returned it 23 yards to the Cowboys' 20-yard line. Three plays later, Steve Young (subbing for the injured Joe Montana) threw an eight-yard strike to Jerry Rice for the go-ahead points.

San Francisco rookie Johnny Jackson scored his first NFL touchdown on a 68-yard return of a blocked field goal in the third quarter.

In San Diego, the Seattle Seahawks blocked extra-point and field-goal attempts in the final five minutes to preserve a 17-16 AFC Western Division victory over the Chargers. The victory was the Seahawks' ninth in their last 10 games against the Chargers.

With 4:14 to play, Jeff Bryant blocked Chris Bahr's extra-point try after a two-yard touchdown run by San Diego's Marion Butts had nar-

Vikings Coach Jerry Burns and Herschel Walker are all smiles after a block-buster trade on October 12 sent the running back from Dallas to Minnesota.

rowed Seattle's lead to one point. Then, after the Seahawks' James Jefferson fumbled away the ensuing kickoff, Joe Nash recorded his eighth career block by batting down Bahr's 51-yard field-goal attempt.

Seattle had capitalized on a fumbled punt by San Diego to take a 17-10 lead in the third quarter. Three plays after Nesby Glasgow recovered the loose ball at the Chargers' 16, Dave Krieg hit John L. Williams with a six-yard touchdown pass.

Another one-point game was played at Tampa Bay, where the Detroit Lions handed the Buccaneers a 17-16 defeat on rookie quarterback Rodney Peete's five-yard touchdown run with 23 seconds to play. Peete's fourth-down scramble climaxed a 76-yard drive he orchestrated with pass completions of 21, 24 and 19 yards to wide receiver Robert Clark.

Peete's late heroics made amends for his two costly interceptions and a critical fumble earlier in the game. Ricky Reynolds returned one interception 68 yards for the Bucs' only touchdown and later recovered a Peete fumble at the Tampa Bay 4-yard line. The Lions entered the game with a league-leading 19 turnovers.

The Buccaneers were forced to play without regular quarterback Vinny Testaverde, who was sidelined by a bruised right knee. Joe Ferguson, the NFL's oldest player at age 39, started in his place and completed 16 of 29 passes for 128 yards.

The victory was Detroit's first in 1989 after four preseason losses and five regular-season setbacks.

In Atlanta, the Falcons claimed only their second victory of the season, posting a 16-15 interconference win over New England. Paul McFadden kicked the decisive field goal, his third of the game, from 22 yards away with five seconds left. About three minutes earlier, he had missed a 39-yard attempt. The Falcons' game-winning drive included a 20-yard completion from Chris Miller to rookie Shawn Collins on a fourth-and-10 play with 1:47 left.

McFadden's three field goals were matched by the Patriots' Greg Davis, who was the Falcons' regular placekicker in 1988 before going to New England as a Plan B free agent. Davis, however, missed a pivotal extra-point kick following the Patriots' only touchdown.

At Soldier Field in Chicago, the Houston Oilers rallied from a nine-point deficit in the final four minutes to upset the Bears, 33-28. Coming on the heels of a 42-35 loss at Tampa Bay, it marked the first time since the 1987 season that Chicago had lost two successive games.

The Bears led, 28-19, before a one-yard sneak by Oilers quarterback Warren Moon narrowed the score to 28-26 with 3:38 left. On Houston's next possession, Allen Pinkett sprinted 60 yards to the Bears' 20-yard line to set up a 12-yard touchdown run by Lorenzo White with 1:46 to play.

Moon passed for 317 yards against a Chicago defense that was missing injured starting linemen Dan Hampton and Trace Armstrong. Another starter, end Richard Dent, was hampered by a deep thigh bruise and played sparingly.

At Denver, the Broncos' defense yielded just 128 total yards to key a 14-3 victory over the Indianapolis Colts. Through six weeks, the Broncos had surrendered 84 points, the fewest in the NFL.

With the victory, Denver avenged a 55-23 setback in Indianapolis one year earlier. In that game, the Colts amassed 464 total yards, including 159 yards rushing and four touchdowns by running back Eric Dickerson. Dickerson was held to 35 yards in the rematch, and the Colts failed to score on four plays from the Denver 3-yard line in the third period.

The Pittsburgh Steelers also settled a score in Week 6, rebounding from a 51-0 loss to Cleveland in Week 1 with a 17-7 victory over the Browns in the rematch. It was the Steelers' first victory against their AFC Central Division rivals since 1985.

Pittsburgh turned the ball over eight times on opening weekend but forced seven Cleveland turnovers on this day, including a career-high four interceptions of quarterback Bernie Kosar. The Browns squandered scoring opportunities when running back Mike Oliphant fumbled at the Pittsburgh 9-yard line and Carnell Lake intercepted Kosar at the Steelers' 15.

The Cincinnati Bengals had a 12-game winning streak at home snapped when the Miami Dolphins reeled off 17 straight points in the second half en route to a 20-13 victory. It was the Dolphins' fifth straight win over the Bengals.

The Bengals led at halftime, 13-3, although the lead probably should have been greater. They were forced to settle for field goals on two possessions inside the Miami 10-yard line.

Dolphins quarterback Dan Marino, who had only 59 yards passing in the first half, went airborne for 207 yards in the second. He led a 92-yard drive at the start of the third quarter, capping it with a one-yard touchdown run that cut the Bengals' lead to 13-10. Miami converted seven of nine third-down plays after the intermission.

Like Marino, Philadelphia Eagles quarterback Randall Cunningham rebounded from a poor first half to lead his team to a 17-5 victory over the Phoenix Cardinals. Cunningham completed just four passes for 33 yards in the opening 30 minutes but threw two touchdown passes to wide receiver Cris Carter in the third quarter.

Cunningham's second-half surge magnified the problems of Cardinals starter Tom Tupa, a second-year player who was making his first NFL start after veteran Gary Hogeboom was sidelined by a sore elbow. Tupa passed for 266 yards but completed only 16 of 41 attempts and was intercepted six times.

Tupa also was the victim of six sacks, with tackle Jerome Brown recording 2½ sacks. Brown finished the game with eight tackles, one fumble recovery, one forced fumble and one pass deflection.

In another NFC Eastern Division matchup, the New York Giants trailed 10-6 after three quarters but scored two touchdowns in the fourth period to defeat the Washington Redskins, 20-17. The Giants had played eight consecutive quarters without an offensive touchdown before drives of 77 and 49 yards netted those two scores.

Phil Simms threw scoring passes of 12 and 25 yards to Mark Bavaro and Odessa Turner, respectively, after Ottis Anderson kept both drives alive with key fourth-down runs. Anderson, who became the Giants' starting tailback after a season-ending injury to Joe Morris, carried the ball 25 times for 101 yards, his first 100-yard game since 1985.

Kansas City running back Christian Okoye, who led the AFC with 487 yards rushing coming into Week 6, was held to just 52 yards by the Los Angeles Raiders in a 20-14 Chiefs loss. The Raiders' defense, which had allowed an average of 147 yards rushing per game, limited the Chiefs to only 78 yards on 28 carries.

The Raiders' running game, meanwhile, was helped by the addition of Bo Jackson, who played in his first game of 1989 after completing his major league baseball season. The Kansas City Royals' star outfielder burned that city's pro football team with 85 yards rushing and one touchdown. He keyed what proved to be a game-winning, 70-yard drive in the second half with runs of 45 and 11 yards.

In New Orleans, quarterback Bobby Hebert passed for three touchdowns to lead the Saints to a 29-14 victory over the New York Jets. The win, the Saints' ninth straight against AFC competition, snapped a four-game New Orleans losing streak.

The Saints rolled up 418 yards against a team that had little offense of its own. The Jets committed four turnovers, were held to 52 yards rushing and didn't cross the New Orleans 37-yard line until their final possession. Their touchdowns came on a 34-yard interception return by James Hasty and a 74-yard fumble return by Erik McMillan.

The loss dropped the Jets' record to 1-5, their worst start since 1980.

The Los Angeles Rams lost for the first time in 1989 when the Buffalo Bills orchestrated a miraculous comeback in the final minute for a 23-20 victory in the Monday night game. Three of the game's four touchdowns were scored in the final 2½ minutes.

The impetus for the Bills' upset came from an unexpected source: quarterback Frank Reich, who was making his first pro start after

Jim Kelly suffered a separated shoulder one week earlier. When he relieved Kelly in Week 5 against Indianapolis, Reich had attempted only 20 passes in four NFL seasons.

Against the Rams, Reich completed only five of 15 passes for 33 yards in the first half, but he found his mark 16 of 22 times for 181 yards after the intermission. He tossed six straight completions for 56 yards before throwing an eight-yard strike to Andre Reed with 16 seconds remaining for the game-winning touchdown.

That score capped three wild minutes of football. After catching a one-yard touchdown pass from Reich to give the Bills a 16-13 lead with 2:23 to play, Thurman Thomas fumbled on Buffalo's next possession. The Rams recovered on their own 22-yard line, and on the next play from scrimmage, Jim Everett passed 78 yards to Willie Anderson for a score. That put Los Angeles back in front, 20-16, setting the stage for Reich's last-minute heroics.

Dolphins-Bengals

SUNDAY, OCTOBER 15

SCORE BY PERIODS

Miami	0	3	7	10—20
Cincinnati	10	3	0	0—13

SCORING

Cincinnati—Field goal Breech 20, 4:34 1st.
Cincinnati—Holman 38 pass from Esiason (Breech kick), 13:24 1st.
Miami—Field goal Stoyanovich 29, 5:55 2nd.
Cincinnati—Field goal Breech 22, 14:56 2nd.
Miami—Marino 1 run (Stoyanovich kick), 6:42 3rd.
Miami—Field goal Stoyanovich 33, 4:13 4th.
Miami—Davenport 5 run (Stoyanovich kick), 10:29 4th.

TEAM STATISTICS

	Miami	Cincinnati
First downs	19	14
Rushes-Yards	34-107	32-146
Passing yards	266	168
Passes	16-33-1	16-24-0
Sacked-Yards lost	0-0	3-26
Punts	5-39.4	8-31.6
Fumbles-Lost	0-0	0-0
Penalties-Yards	2-12	4-29
Time of possession	29:46	30:14
Attendance—58,184.		

INDIVIDUAL STATISTICS

Rushing—Miami, Smith 15-50, Stradford 11-46, Davenport 2-7, Logan 2-4, Jensen 1-4, Marino 3-minus 4; Cincinnati, Brooks 20-95, Esiason 4-25, Jennings 6-19, Ball 2-7.

Passing—Miami, Marino 16-33-1—266; Cincinnati, Esiason 16-24-0—194.

Receiving—Miami, Duper 5-129, Stradford 5-37, Clayton 3-51, Edmunds 1-22, Banks 1-18, Davenport 1-9; Cincinnati, Holman 7-93, Brooks 4-45, Hillary 2-22, Martin 1-16, Brown 1-9, McGee 1-9.

Kickoff Returns—Miami, Logan 2-41; Cincinnati, Jennings 1-14, Hillary 1-18, Smith 2-33.

Punt Returns—Miami, Stradford 2-15; Cincinnati, Martin 3-41.

Interceptions—Cincinnati, Fulcher 1-10.

Punting—Miami, Roby 5-39.4; Cincinnati, Breech 1-32.0, Johnson 7-31.6.

Field Goals—Miami, Stoyanovich 2-2; Cincinnati, Breech 2-2.

Sacks—Miami, Cross, Ahrens, Green.

Chiefs-Raiders

SUNDAY, OCTOBER 15

SCORE BY PERIODS

Kansas City	7	0	0	7—14
Los Angeles Raiders	3	7	3	7—20

SCORING

Kansas City—Okoye 2 run (Lowery kick), 6:01 1st.
Los Angeles—Field goal Jaeger 24, 12:39 1st.
Los Angeles—Jackson 2 run (Jaeger kick), 14:04 2nd.
Los Angeles—Field goal Jaeger 50, 4:47 3rd.
Los Angeles—Mueller 6 run (Jaeger kick), 3:42 4th.
Kansas City—R. Thomas 11 pass from DeBerg (Lowery kick), 14:41 4th.

TEAM STATISTICS

	Kansas City	Los Angeles
First downs	17	13
Rushes-Yards	28-78	35-157
Passing yards	227	89
Passes	23-33-1	6-21-2
Sacked-Yards lost	0-0	1-13
Punts	4-47.8	4-49.5
Fumbles-Lost	4-3	1-0
Penalties-Yards	7-56	5-35
Time of possession	29:53	30:07
Attendance—40,453.		

INDIVIDUAL STATISTICS

Rushing—Kansas City, Okoye 18-52, McNair 2-20, Saxon 3-5, Jaworski 2-1, Heard 3-0; Los Angeles, Jackson 11-85, Mueller 10-38, Smith 9-27, Porter 3-5, Schroeder 1-3, Beuerlein 1-minus 1.

Passing—Kansas City, Jaworski 10-15-1—118, DeBerg 13-18-0—109; Los Angeles, Schroeder 5-16-1—87, Beuerlein 1-5-1—15.

Receiving—Kansas City, Heard 9-90, Mandley 5-74, Weathers 2-21, McNair 2-10, Roberts 2-5, R. Thomas 1-11, Paige 1-8, Okoye 1-8; Los Angeles, Dyal 2-50, Mueller 2-24, Fernandez 1-15, Horton 1-13.

Kickoff Returns—Kansas City, Copeland 2-23, McNair 2-38; Los Angeles, Edmonds 2-30.

Punt Returns—Kansas City, Mandley 3-28; Los Angeles, Edmonds 4-54.

Interceptions—Kansas City, Ross 1-23, Hill 1-3; Los Angeles, Anderson 1-23.

Punting—Kansas City, Goodburn 4-47.8; Los Angeles, Gossett 4-49.5.

Field Goals—Kansas City, Lowery 0-1 (missed: 35); Los Angeles, Jaeger 2-2.

Sacks—Kansas City, D. Thomas.

Steelers-Browns

SUNDAY, OCTOBER 15

SCORE BY PERIODS

Pittsburgh	3	0	7	7—17
Cleveland	0	0	0	7— 7

SCORING

Pittsburgh—Field goal Anderson 49, 5:22 1st.
Pittsburgh—Carter 14 pass from Blackledge (Anderson kick), 6:09 3rd.
Cleveland—Metcalf 2 run (Bahr kick), 7:00 4th.
Pittsburgh—W. Williams 1 run (Anderson kick), 13:04 4th.

TEAM STATISTICS

	Pittsburgh	Cleveland
First downs	16	17
Rushes-Yards	35-93	23-107
Passing yards	138	153
Passes	10-29-1	15-41-4
Sacked-Yards lost	3-20	2-9
Punts	8-40.9	6-40.7
Fumbles-Lost	2-1	3-3
Penalties-Yards	10-121	10-86
Time of possession	35:20	24:40
Attendance—78,840.		

INDIVIDUAL STATISTICS

Rushing—Pittsburgh, W. Williams 15-47, Hoge 9-35, Blackledge 6-7, Wallace 2-3, Carter 1-2, Worley 2-minus 1; Cleveland, Metcalf 13-57, Oliphant 5-30, Manoa 4-11, Kosar 1-9.

Passing—Pittsburgh, Blackledge 9-28-1—143, Carter 1-1-0—15; Cleveland, Kosar 15-41-4—162.

Receiving—Pittsburgh, Carter 3-30, Thompson 2-43, Mularkey 1-30, Lipps 1-20, Hoge 1-15, Hill 1-12, W. Williams 1-8; Cleveland, Slaughter 7-106, Newsome 2-28, Metcalf 2-13, McNeil 1-9, Brennan 1-8, K. Jones 1-5, Kosar 1-minus 7.

Kickoff Returns—Pittsburgh, Stone 1-73; Cleveland, Metcalf 1-42, Braggs 2-20.

Punt Returns—Pittsburgh, Hill 3-20; Cleveland, McNeil 6-67.

Interceptions—Pittsburgh, Woodruff 1-5, Everett 1-32, Hall 1-6, Lake 1-0; Cleveland, Gash 1-14.

Punting—Pittsburgh, Newsome 8-40.9; Cleveland, Wagner 6-40.7.

Field Goals—Pittsburgh, Anderson 1-2 (missed: 45); Cleveland, none attempted.

Sacks—Pittsburgh, G. Williams, T. Johnson ½, Willis ½; Cleveland, Blaylock, Baker, Gibson.

Oilers-Bears
SUNDAY, OCTOBER 15
SCORE BY PERIODS

Houston	0	10	9	14—33	
Chicago	0	14	7	7—28	

SCORING

Chicago—Anderson 6 pass from Tomczak (Butler kick), 1:37 2nd.

Houston—Field goal Zendejas 27, 8:34 2nd.

Houston—Hill 42 pass from Moon (Zendejas kick), 11:11 2nd.

Chicago—Anderson 1 run (Butler kick), 14:23 2nd.

Houston—Field goal Zendejas 19, 3:15 3rd.

Chicago—Gentry 79 pass from Tomczak (Butler kick), 6:27 3rd.

Houston—Jeffires 45 pass from Moon (pass failed), 14:36 3rd.

Chicago—Thornton 7 pass from Tomczak (Butler kick), 10:05 4th.

Houston—Moon 1 run (Zendejas kick), 11:22 4th.

Houston—White 12 run (Zendejas kick), 13:14 4th.

TEAM STATISTICS

	Houston	Chicago
First downs	20	22
Rushes-Yards	32-140	36-93
Passing yards	317	239
Passes	16-26-2	20-29-4
Sacked-Yards lost	0-0	1-8
Punts	3-37.7	2-35.0
Fumbles-Lost	1-0	2-2
Penalties-Yards	7-65	5-65
Time of possession	27:25	32:35
Attendance—64,383.		

INDIVIDUAL STATISTICS

Rushing—Houston, Pinkett 6-70, Highsmith 9-21, Moon 10-20, White 4-19, Greg Montgomery 1-6, Rozier 2-4; Chicago, Anderson 23-69, Muster 2-5, Gentry 2-5, Suhey 1-3, Tomczak 3-1, McKinnon 1-0, Sanders 2-minus 1.

Passing—Houston, Moon 16-26-2—317; Chicago, Tomczak 20-29-4—247.

Receiving—Houston, Hill 5-128, Jeffires 3-72, Givins 3-71, Pinkett 3-23, Duncan 1-14, Jackson 1-9; Chicago, Gentry 6-110, Anderson 6-51, Thornton 4-41, Morris 2-23, McKinnon 1-15, Davis 1-7.

Kickoff Returns—Houston, White 2-38, T. Johnson 1-20, K. Johnson 1-39; Chicago, Green 4-98.

Punt Returns—Chicago, Green 1-4.

Interceptions—Houston, Brown 1-0, Lyles 2-0, Dishman 1-0; Chicago, Lynch 1-41, Woolford 1-0.

Punting—Houston, Greg Montgomery 3-37.7; Chicago, Buford 2-35.0.

Field Goals—Houston, Zendejas 2-3 (missed: 42); Chicago, none attempted.

Sacks—Houston, Childress.

49ers-Cowboys
SUNDAY, OCTOBER 15
SCORE BY PERIODS

San Francisco	0	7	7	17—31
Dallas	0	7	7	0—14

SCORING

San Francisco—Jones 36 pass from Young (Cofer kick), 1:35 2nd.

Dallas—Martin 32 pass from Walsh (Ruzek kick), 14:39 2nd.

San Francisco—Jackson 75 blocked field goal return (Cofer kick), 6:37 3rd.

Dallas—Clack 1 run (Ruzek kick), 12:10 3rd.

San Francisco—Rice 8 pass from Young (Cofer kick), 3:21 4th.

San Francisco—Field goal Cofer 31, 10:03 4th.

San Francisco—Craig 1 run (Cofer kick), 13:03 4th.

TEAM STATISTICS

	San Francisco	Dallas
First downs	17	19
Rushes-Yards	31-146	19-46
Passing yards	172	261
Passes	13-18-1	22-36-2
Sacked-Yards lost	1-2	4-24
Punts	2-40.0	2-37.5
Fumbles-Lost	1-0	4-1
Penalties-Yards	8-48	3-25
Time of possession	30:40	29:20
Attendance—61,077.		

INDIVIDUAL STATISTICS

Rushing—San Francisco, Young 11-79, Craig 18-61, Rathman 2-6; Dallas, Clack 12-32, Dixon 1-11, Johnston 3-3, Walsh 3-0.

Passing—San Francisco, Young 13-18-1—174; Dallas, Walsh 22-36-2—285.

Receiving—San Francisco, Rathman 5-64, Craig 3-23, Rice 2-28, Jones 1-36, Sydney 1-13, Taylor 1-10; Dallas, Irvin 6-60, Folsom 5-59, Martin 4-72, Clack 3-60, Shepard 2-21, Johnston 2-13.

Kickoff Returns—San Francisco, Flagler 3-45; Dallas, Shepard 3-65, Dixon 2-47, Chandler 1-8.

Punt Returns—San Francisco, Taylor 1-15.

Interceptions—San Francisco, Holmoe 1-23, Turner 1-42; Dallas, Lockhart 1-12.

Punting—San Francisco, Helton 2-40.0; Dallas, Saxon 2-37.5.

Field Goals—San Francisco, Cofer 1-1; Dallas, Ruzek 0-2 (missed: 43, 48).

Sacks—San Francisco, Kugler 2, Holt, Haley; Dallas, Lockhart.

Lions-Buccaneers
SUNDAY, OCTOBER 15
SCORE BY PERIODS

Detroit	3	0	7	7—17
Tampa Bay	0	10	3	3—16

SCORING

Detroit—Field goal Murray 28, 4:32 1st.

Tampa Bay—Reynolds 68 interception return (Igwebuike kick), 2:37 2nd.

Tampa Bay—Field goal Igwebuike 27, 11:32 2nd.

Detroit—Clark 33 pass from Peete (Murray kick), 7:04 3rd.

Tampa Bay—Field goal Igwebuike 34, 9:55 3rd.

Tampa Bay—Field goal Igwebuike 33, 13:15 4th.

Detroit—Peete 5 run (Murray kick), 14:37 4th.

TEAM STATISTICS

	Detroit	Tampa Bay
First downs	20	14
Rushes-Yards	27-139	30-88
Passing yards	237	103
Passes	17-31-2	16-29-1
Sacked-Yards lost	4-31	3-25
Punts	4-48.5	6-37.0
Fumbles-Lost	3-2	0-0
Penalties-Yards	13-110	7-75
Time of possession	26:23	33:37

Attendance—46,225.

INDIVIDUAL STATISTICS

Rushing—Detroit, Peete 10-78, Paige 9-33, R. Johnson 4-20, Painter 4-8; Tampa Bay, Tate 20-45, Wilder 4-24, Howard 4-11, Ferguson 1-7, Smith 1-1.

Passing—Detroit, Peete 17-31-2—268; Tampa Bay, Ferguson 16-29-1—128.

Receiving—Detroit, Stanley 5-86, Clark 4-97, R. Johnson 3-29, Mobley 3-17, Painter 1-27, Paige 1-12; Tampa Bay, Hill 6-49, Howard 4-12, Carrier 3-27, Drewrey 1-13, Wilder 1-10, W. Harris 1-7.

Kickoff Returns—Detroit, Palmer 4-84; Tampa Bay, Elder 3-59, Futrell 1-7.

Punt Returns—Detroit, Stanley 4-26; Tampa Bay, Futrell 3-21.

Interceptions—Detroit, J. Williams 1-9; Tampa Bay, Hamilton 1-16, Reynolds 1-68.

Punting—Detroit, Arnold 4-48.5; Tampa Bay, Mohr 6-37.0.

Field Goals—Detroit, Murray 1-1; Tampa Bay, Igwebuike 3-3.

Sacks—Detroit, Cofer 2, Ball; Tampa Bay, Goff 2, Moss, Randle.

Jets-Saints
SUNDAY, OCTOBER 15
SCORE BY PERIODS

New York Jets	0	7	0	7—	14
New Orleans	6	7	7	9—	29

SCORING

New Orleans—Field goal Andersen 42, 4:20 1st.

New Orleans—Field goal Andersen 29, 6:27 1st.

New York—Hasty 34 interception return (Leahy kick), 12:00 2nd.

New Orleans—Hill 3 pass from Hebert (Andersen kick), 14:37 2nd.

New Orleans—Martin 4 pass from Hebert (Andersen kick), 12:34 3rd.

New Orleans—Safety, Schreiber holding penalty in end zone, 3:02 4th.

New Orleans—E. Martin 53 pass from Hebert (Andersen kick), 3:21 4th.

New York—McMillan 74 fumble return (Leahy kick), 10:34 4th.

TEAM STATISTICS

	New York	New Orleans
First downs	15	20
Rushes-Yards	21-52	36-152
Passing yards	199	266
Passes	21-34-1	18-30-1
Sacked-Yards lost	5-32	3-15
Punts	6-39.7	4-36.5
Fumbles-Lost	4-3	4-3
Penalties-Yards	8-60	4-29
Time of possession	25:28	34:32

Attendance—59,521.

INDIVIDUAL STATISTICS

Rushing—New York, Hector 8-31, McNeil 7-22, Mackey 2-3, Vick 3-0, Burkett 1-minus 4; New Orleans, Hilliard 22-89, Heyward 10-47, Hebert 2-13, Frazier 2-3.

Passing—New York, Mackey 7-14-1—74, O'Brien 14-20-0—157; New Orleans, Hebert 18-29-1—281, Fourcade 0-1-0—0.

Receiving—New York, McNeil 5-56, Shuler 5-54, Hector 4-49, Townsell 3-36, Burkett 2-11, Griggs 1-16, Vick 1-9; New Orleans, E. Martin 5-131, Hill 5-83, Brenner 2-31, Turner 2-20, Hilliard 2-14, Tice 1-3, Heyward 1-minus 1.

Kickoff Returns—New York, Humphery 2-35, Townsell 1-18; New Orleans, Harris 3-67, Cook 1-0.

Punt Returns—New York, Townsell 3-8; New Orleans, Harris 3-38.

Interceptions—New York, Hasty 1-34; New Orleans, Mack 1-0.

Punting—New York, Prokop 6-37.3; New Orleans, Barnhardt 4-36.5.

Field Goals—New York, none attempted; New Orleans, Andersen 2-2.

Sacks—New York, Gordon, Frase, Clifton; New Orleans, Warren, Jackson 2, W. Martin, Swilling.

Redskins-Giants
SUNDAY, OCTOBER 15
SCORE BY PERIODS

Washington	0	3	7	7—	17
New York Giants	3	0	3	14—	20

SCORING

New York—Field goal Allegre 33, 6:50 1st.

Washington—Field goal Lohmiller 37, 13:05 2nd.

New York—Field goal Allegre 49, 8:54 3rd.

Washington—Sanders 29 pass from Rypien (Lohmiller kick), 13:45 3rd.

New York—Bavaro 12 pass from Simms (Allegre kick), 3:45 4th.

New York—Turner 25 pass from Simms (Allegre kick), 9:44 4th.

Washington—Monk 5 pass from Rypien (Lohmiller kick), 11:50 4th.

TEAM STATISTICS

	Washington	New York
First downs	18	19
Rushes-Yards	23-122	38-133
Passing yards	194	173
Passes	19-30-0	16-32-1
Sacked-Yards lost	1-11	3-28
Punts	4-45.8	4-48.8
Fumbles-Lost	4-2	1-0
Penalties-Yards	6-47	3-20
Time of possession	24:43	35:17

Attendance—76,245.

INDIVIDUAL STATISTICS

Rushing—Washington, Riggs 18-91, Byner 4-24, Rypien 1-7; New York, Anderson 25-101, Tillman 8-21, Simms 4-11, Carthon 1-0.

Passing—Washington, Rypien 19-30-0—205; New York, Simms 16-32-1—201.

Receiving—Washington, Clark 5-60, Byner 5-45, Monk 3-25, Sanders 2-44, Riggs 2-18, Warren 2-13; New York, Bavaro 4-30, Turner 3-39, Manuel 2-39, Ingram 2-30, Meggett 2-29, Baker 1-18, Carthon 1-9, Mowatt 1-7.

Kickoff Returns—Washington, A. Johnson 3-74, Howard 1-30, Mandeville 1-10; New York, Meggett 3-62.

Punt Returns—Washington, Green 1-11, Howard 1-5; New York, Meggett 2-26.

Interceptions—Washington, Walton 1-0.

Punting—Washington, Mojsiejenko 4-45.8; New York, Landeta 4-48.8.

Field Goals—Washington, Lohmiller 1-1; New York, Allegre 2-2.

Sacks—Washington, Manley 2, Caldwell; New York, Marshall.

Packers-Vikings
SUNDAY, OCTOBER 15
SCORE BY PERIODS

Green Bay	7	0	0	7—	14
Minnesota	0	17	9	0—	26

SCORING

Green Bay—Fontenot 1 run (Jacke kick), 8:33 1st.
Minnesota—Field goal Karlis 28, 3:51 2nd.
Minnesota—Fenney 8 run (Karlis kick), 7:10 2nd.
Minnesota—Gustafson 6 pass from Kramer (Karlis kick), 14:17 2nd.
Minnesota—Fenney 8 pass from Kramer (Karlis kick), 11:28 3rd.
Minnesota—Safety, Majkowski tackled in end zone, 11:52 3rd.
Green Bay—Bland 46 pass from Majkowski (Jacke kick), 11:45 4th.

TEAM STATISTICS

	Green Bay	Minnesota
First downs	11	21
Rushes-Yards	18-68	43-238
Passing yards	151	160
Passes	9-24-2	14-24-1
Sacked-Yards lost	8-47	1-12
Punts	5-46.2	3-50.7
Fumbles-Lost	3-1	1-1
Penalties-Yards	11-77	9-64
Time of possession	23:54	36:06

Attendance—62,075.

INDIVIDUAL STATISTICS

Rushing—Green Bay, Woodside 3-36, Fullwood 7-14, Majkowski 3-8, Kemp 1-5, Fontenot 2-5, Haddix 2-0; Minnesota, Walker 18-148, Anderson 7-34, Dozier 8-31, Fenney 6-25, Kramer 4-0.
Passing—Green Bay, Majkowski 9-24-2—198; Minnesota, Kramer 14-24-1—172.
Receiving—Green Bay, Woodside 3-23, Sharpe 2-82, Kemp 2-35, Bland 1-46, Fullwood 1-12; Minnesota, Jones 4-68, Carter 4-47, Carter 1-15, Anderson 1-15, Fenney 1-8, Walker 1-7, Gustafson 1-6, Jordan 1-6.
Kickoff Returns—Green Bay, Workman 5-83; Minnesota, Walker 2-40, Lewis 1-15.
Punt Returns—Green Bay, Query 3-30; Minnesota, Lewis 3-37.
Interceptions—Green Bay, Stills 1-0; Minnesota, Rutland 2-7.
Punting—Green Bay, Bracken 5-46.2; Minnesota, Scribner 3-50.7.
Field Goals—Green Bay, none attempted; Minnesota, Karlis 1-3 (missed: 51, 47).
Sacks—Green Bay, R. Brown; Minnesota, Millard 4, Doleman 2, Berry, Thomas.

Eagles-Cardinals
SUNDAY, OCTOBER 15
SCORE BY PERIODS

Philadelphia	0	0	14	3—17
Phoenix	0	5	0	0— 5

SCORING

Phoenix—Safety, Toney tackled by Wilson in end zone, 2:06 2nd.
Phoenix—Field goal Del Greco 41, 13:07 2nd.
Philadelphia—Carter 2 pass from Cunningham (Zendejas kick), 2:57 3rd.
Philadelphia—Carter 40 pass from Cunningham (Zendejas kick), 7:26 3rd.
Philadelphia—Field goal Zendejas 42, 9:13 4th.

TEAM STATISTICS

	Philadelphia	Phoenix
First downs	18	20
Rushes-Yards	39-167	30-114
Passing yards	186	223
Passes	16-29-3	16-41-6
Sacked-Yards lost	1-6	6-43
Punts	5-43.4	6-42.5
Fumbles-Lost	1-1	3-2
Penalties-Yards	7-70	7-95
Time of possession	28:04	31:56

Attendance—42,620.

INDIVIDUAL STATISTICS

Rushing—Philadelphia, Cunningham 7-70, Toney 19-52, Higgs 10-34, Byars 1-6, Carter 1-5, Sherman 1-0; Phoenix, Ferrell 13-54, Tupa 4-30, Jordan 11-28, Sikahema 2-2.
Passing—Philadelphia, Cunningham 16-29-3—192; Phoenix, Tupa 16-41-6—266.
Receiving—Philadelphia, Giles 4-38, Carter 2-42, Garrity 2-31, Jackson 2-18, Byars 1-25, Quick 1-24, Little 1-7, Drummond 1-5, Higgs 1-2, Toney 1-0; Phoenix, Jones 8-144, J.T. Smith 3-54, Ferrell 2-30, Holmes 1-18, Sikahema 1-17, Novacek 1-3.
Kickoff Returns—Philadelphia, Williams 1-28, Sherman 1-21; Phoenix, Sikahema 2-29, Baker 2-41.
Punt Returns—Philadelphia, Williams 5-33; Phoenix, Sikahema 4-42, McConkey 1-13.
Interceptions—Philadelphia, Jenkins 1-0, Harris 1-7, Waters 1-20, Joyner 1-0, Frizzell 1-27, Allen 1-0; Phoenix, Carter 1-0, Downs 1-37, Mack 1-0.
Punting—Philadelphia, Teltschik, 5-43.4; Phoenix, Camarillo 6-42.5.
Field Goals—Philadelphia, Zendejas 1-2 (missed: 40); Phoenix, Del Greco 1-1.
Sacks—Philadelphia, Golic, Waters ½, Evans, Simmons ½, Brown 2½, Frizzell ½; Phoenix, Galloway.

Seahawks-Chargers
SUNDAY, OCTOBER 15
SCORE BY PERIODS

Seattle	10	0	7	0—17
San Diego	7	3	0	6—16

SCORING

San Diego—Cox 3 pass from McMahon (Bahr kick), 4:35 1st.
Seattle—Warner 1 run (N. Johnson kick), 9:12 1st.
Seattle—Field goal N. Johnson 50, 14:56 1st.
San Diego—Field goal Bahr 29, 6:16 2nd.
Seattle—Williams 6 pass from Krieg (N. Johnson kick), 5:25 3rd.
San Diego—Butts 2 run (kick failed), 10:46 4th.

TEAM STATISTICS

	Seattle	San Diego
First downs	14	26
Rushes-Yards	27-85	31-94
Passing yards	139	268
Passes	14-24-2	25-39-2
Sacked-Yards lost	0-0	3-18
Punts	5-39.0	3-40.3
Fumbles-Lost	3-1	4-2
Penalties-Yards	8-82	7-42
Time of possession	25:58	34:02

Attendance—50,079.

INDIVIDUAL STATISTICS

Rushing—Seattle, Williams 11-54, Warner 13-30, Krieg 3-1; San Diego, Spencer 16-49, Butts 6-19, McMahon 3-11, Brinson 3-9, Plummer 1-6, Floyd 1-2, Holland 1-minus 2.
Passing—Seattle, Krieg 14-24-2—139; San Diego, McMahon 25-39-2—286.
Receiving—Seattle, Williams 6-53, Blades 3-37, Skansi 2-23, Tyler 2-7, Chadwick 1-19; San Diego, A. Miller 7-116, Caravello 5-38, Walker 3-71, Holland 3-23, Brinson 3-15, Spencer 1-11, Floyd 1-6, Cox 1-3, Butts 1-3.
Kickoff Returns—Seattle, Jefferson 2-39, Harris 2-25; San Diego, Holland 3-40.
Punt Returns—Seattle, Jefferson 1-19; San Diego, Brinson 3-8, Usher 1-0.
Interceptions—Seattle, Comeaux 1-0, Robinson 1-20; San Diego, Byrd 1-0, Glenn 1-3.
Punting—Seattle, Rodriguez 5-39.0; San Diego, Ilesic 3-40.3.
Field Goals—Seattle, N. Johnson 1-1; San Diego, Bahr 1-2 (missed: 51).
Sacks—Seattle, Green 2, Porter.

Patriots-Falcons
SCORE BY PERIODS

New England	6	9	0	0—15
Atlanta	3	10	0	3—16

SCORING
New England—Field goal Davis 52, 3:43 1st.
Atlanta—Field goal McFadden 30, 7:14 1st.
New England—Field goal Davis 32, 13:40 1st.
New England—Field goal Davis 32, 3:01 2nd.
Atlanta—Field goal McFadden 30, 9:31 2nd.
New England—Jones 15 pass from Flutie (kick failed), 12:25 2nd.
Atlanta—Jones 1 run (McFadden kick), 13:55 2nd.
Atlanta—Field goal McFadden 22, 14:55 4th.

TEAM STATISTICS

	New England	Atlanta
First downs	13	14
Rushes-Yards	33-93	21-72
Passing yards	148	240
Passes	12-30-3	19-34-1
Sacked-Yards lost	3-24	4-25
Punts	6-43.8	7-49.1
Fumbles-Lost	0-0	1-1
Penalties-Yards	3-10	5-35
Time of possession	32:34	27:26
Attendance—39,697.		

INDIVIDUAL STATISTICS
Rushing—New England, Stephens 19-64, Perryman 10-20, Flutie 2-11, Dupard 2-minus 2; Atlanta, Lang 9-48, Flowers 8-18, Jones 4-6.

Passing—New England, Flutie 12-30-3—172; Atlanta, Miller 19-34-1—265.

Receiving—New England, Martin 3-60, Jones 3-53, Dykes 3-41, Morgan 1-16, Perryman 1-5, Stephens 1-minus 3; Atlanta, Lang 5-66, Jones 3-66, Heller 3-26, Dixon 3-24, Collins 2-30, Wilkins 1-36, Haynes 1-13, Beckman 1-4.

Kickoff Returns—New England, Martin 4-91, Rice 1-0; Atlanta, Sanders 2-83, Jones 3-77.

Punt Returns—New England, Martin 5-46; Atlanta, Sanders 3-28.

Interceptions—New England, Clayborn 1-0; Atlanta, Cooper 2-16, Gordon 1-0.

Punting—New England, Feagles 6-43.8; Atlanta, Fulhage 7-49.1.

Field Goals—New England, Davis 3-3; Atlanta, McFadden 3-4 (missed: 39).

Sacks—New England, Williams 2, McGrew 1½, Rembert ½; Atlanta, Bruce 2, Case.

Colts-Broncos
SCORE BY PERIODS

Indianapolis	3	0	0	0— 3
Denver	0	7	0	7—14

SCORING
Indianapolis—Field goal Biasucci 55, 8:45 1st.
Denver—Humphrey 2 run (Treadwell kick), 1:27 2nd.
Denver—Winder 1 run (Treadwell kick), 13:04 4th.

TEAM STATISTICS

	Indianapolis	Denver
First downs	7	20
Rushes-Yards	17-44	43-169
Passing yards	84	150
Passes	12-28-1	13-25-1
Sacked-Yards lost	2-16	0-0
Punts	6-47.8	5-42.6
Fumbles-Lost	3-0	4-1
Penalties-Yards	3-19	3-20
Time of possession	22:11	37:49
Attendance—74,680.		

INDIVIDUAL STATISTICS
Rushing—Indianapolis, Dickerson 13-35, Trudeau 4-9; Denver, Winder 21-92, Humphrey 11-37, Alexander 5-25, Elway 5-8, Bratton 1-7.

Passing—Indianapolis, Trudeau 12-28-1—100; Denver, Elway 13-25-1—150.

Receiving—Indianapolis, Bentley 4-40, Rison 2-18, Dickerson 2-8, Brooks 1-21, Pruitt 1-8, Beach 1-5, Boyer 1-0; Denver, Johnson 7-80, Winder 1-19, Mobley 1-15, Young 1-12, Sewell 1-11, Kay 1-9, Jackson 1-4.

Kickoff Returns—Indianapolis, Verdin 2-32; Denver, Humphrey 1-29.

Punt Returns—Indianapolis, Verdin 2-37; Denver, Bell 4-26.

Interceptions—Indianapolis, Young 1-minus 4; Denver, D. Smith 1-50.

Punting—Indianapolis, Stark 6-47.8; Denver, Horan 5-42.6.

Field Goals—Indianapolis, Biasucci 1-2 (missed: 49); Denver, none attempted.

Sacks—Denver, Fletcher, Dennison.

Rams-Bills
SCORE BY PERIODS

Los Angeles Rams	7	0	3	10—20
Buffalo	0	6	0	17—23

SCORING
Los Angeles—McGee 3 pass from Everett (Lansford kick), 9:58 1st.
Buffalo—Field goal Norwood 38, 10:50 2nd.
Buffalo—Field goal Norwood 47, 10:04 2nd.
Los Angeles—Field goal Lansford 34, 12:04 3rd.
Buffalo—Field goal Norwood 40, 0:51 4th.
Los Angeles—Field goal Lansford 36, 5:59 4th.
Buffalo—Thomas 1 pass from Reich (Norwood kick), 12:37 4th.
Los Angeles—Anderson 78 pass from Everett (Lansford kick), 13:38 4th.
Buffalo—Reed 8 pass from Reich (Norwood kick), 14:44 4th.

TEAM STATISTICS

	Los Angeles	Buffalo
First downs	15	17
Rushes-Yards	30-59	31-134
Passing yards	207	214
Passes	15-36-1	21-37-1
Sacked-Yards lost	2-12	0-0
Punts	7-37.3	6-36.0
Fumbles-Lost	5-1	4-3
Penalties-Yards	4.30	7-69
Time of possession	30:29	29:31
Attendance—76,231.		

INDIVIDUAL STATISTICS
Rushing—Los Angeles, Bell 21-44, Delpino 4-6, Ron Brown 2-5, Everett 3-4; Buffalo, Thomas 24-105, Kinnebrew 4-16, Harmon 2-12, Reich 1-1.

Passing—Los Angeles, Everett 15-36-1—219; Buffalo, Reich 21-37-1—214.

Receiving—Los Angeles, Ellard 4-70, Holohan 3-19, Anderson 2-87, A. Cox 2-20, McGee 2-13, Johnson 1-6, Delpino 1-4; Buffalo, Thomas 9-67, Reed 8-106, McKeller 2-21, Harmon 1-14, Metzelaars 1-6.

Kickoff Returns—Los Angeles, Ron Brown 5-56, McDonald 1-12; Buffalo, Harmon 5-94.

Punt Returns—Los Angeles, Henley 1-18; Buffalo, Sutton 3-8.

Interceptions—Los Angeles, Gray 1-10; Buffalo, Kelso 1-33.

Punting—Los Angeles, Hatcher 7-37.3; Buffalo, Kidd 6-36.0.

Field Goals—Los Angeles, Lansford 2-2; Buffalo, Norwood 3-3.

Sacks—Buffalo, B. Smith 2.

SEVENTH WEEK

RESULTS OF WEEK 7
Sunday, October 22

Buffalo 34, N.Y. Jets 3 at Buff.
Denver 24, Seattle 21 (OT) at Sea.
Houston 27, Pittsburgh 0 at Hous.
Indianapolis 23, Cincinnati 12 at Cin.
Kansas City 36, Dallas 28 at K.C.
Miami 23, Green Bay 20 at Mia.
Minnesota 20, Detroit 7 at Det.
New Orleans 40, L.A. Rams 21 at L.A.
N.Y. Giants 20, San Diego 13 at S.D.
Philadelphia 10, L.A. Raiders 7 at Phila.
Phoenix 34, Atlanta 20 at Phoe.
San Francisco 37, New England 20 at S.F.
Washington 32, Tampa Bay 28 at Wash.

Monday, October 23

Cleveland 27, Chicago 7 at Cleve.

It's a good thing the San Francisco 49ers were so successful playing away from Candlestick Park. Heading into Week 7 of the 1989 National Football League season, they weren't getting many chances to play on their home turf.

At this juncture of the decade of the 1980s, the 49ers had compiled a 55-23-1 record (including playoffs) in games away from Candlestick. That was the best road record of any NFL team during the '80s and included victories in Super Bowls XVI, XIX and XXIII.

The 49ers were scheduled to play three of their first seven games of the 1989 season at Candlestick but, after seven weeks, had played there only once. They lost, 13-12, to the Rams in Week 4 at Candlestick before an October 8 game with the New Orleans Saints was moved from San Francisco to New Orleans to allow the San Francisco Giants to host a National League baseball playoff game. The 49ers' Week 7 game with the New England Patriots would be moved from Candlestick for a more serious reason.

On October 17, an earthquake measuring 7.1 on the Richter scale rocked the San Francisco Bay Area just as a Giants-Oakland Athletics World Series game was ready to begin. It was the area's worst quake since 1906, killing more than 60 people, injuring scores of others and leaving the area with damages estimated into the billions of dollars.

Structural damage to Candlestick Park forced a 10-day postponement of the World Series and the relocation of the 49ers-Patriots game (scheduled for October 22) to Stanford Stadium in Palo Alto.

Technically, it would be considered a home game for the 49ers but, in reality, it was a 35-mile trip south of San Francisco. It marked the first time in NFL history that a game site was changed because of a natural disaster.

Although none of the 49ers or their families suffered earthquake-related injuries, getting ready to play football was probably not the athletes' top priority in the five days between the quake and the game. But the players seemed to realize that playing the game was the best way for the area to begin its long road back to recovery.

"We felt like we had to give people something to be happy about, some kind of joy," 49ers nose tackle Michael Carter said. "If football is it, that's OK with us."

The 49ers did their part by beating the Patriots, 37-20, before a crowd estimated at 70,000. Steve Young replaced an injured Joe Montana at quarterback late in the first half and threw three touchdown passes, including a one-yarder to Wesley Walls on the final play of the half to give San Francisco a 17-10 lead.

The 49ers, however, paid a heavy price for the victory. In addition to Montana (sprained knee), linebacker Jim Fahnhorst (stress fracture in his right foot), running back Harry Sydney (broken arm) and defensive back Jeff Fuller (fractured vertebrae in his neck) were injured in the game.

"It's a bittersweet type of situation, no question about it," San Francisco Coach George Seifert said. "We had so many players hurt, I looked around and it was like a battlefield."

Fuller's injury was the most serious. The sixth-year safety suffered a career-ending nerve injury to his neck when he attempted to tackle Patriots running back John Stephens on the second play of the game. Fuller briefly lost consciousness and went into a seizure before paramedics removed him from the field.

"I never saw a man's face look like that," said San Francisco linebacker Michael Walter. "It looked like he was in shock. His eyes looked . . . huge. You just wanted to look at him and go, 'Oh, God.'

"I've had too many reality checks this week."

The 49ers' victory improved their record to 6-1 and gave them a one-game lead in the NFC West over the Los Angeles Rams, who dropped a 40-21 decision at home to division rival New Orleans. It marked the third straight season in which the Saints had beaten the Rams at Anaheim Stadium.

Dalton Hilliard led the Saints' attack by running for two touchdowns and catching a 20-yard pass from Bobby Hebert for a third. Hebert threw for three touchdowns altogether, including passes of 54 and 37 yards to Floyd Turner and Eric Martin, respectively, early in the second half. The touchdowns gave the Saints a commanding 33-7 lead.

Rams quarterback Jim Everett also threw three touchdown passes but was sacked five times and intercepted twice. He was replaced

Dalton Hilliard scored three touchdowns to lead New Orleans to its third straight win over the Rams at Anaheim Stadium.

late in the game by Mark Herrmann, who threw one interception and was sacked once.

The most lopsided game of Week 7 was played in Buffalo, where the Bills used a flawless offense and a stingy defense to whip the New York Jets, 34-3, in an AFC Eastern Division game.

The final statistics revealed just how one-sided this game was, with the Bills enjoying huge advantages in time of possession (42 minutes, 53 seconds to 17:07), total yards (343 to 154), offensive plays (73 to 48) and first downs (22 to nine). The Buffalo offense didn't commit a turnover and quarterback Frank Reich, subbing for the injured Jim Kelly for the second straight week, threw three touchdown passes.

The Bills' defense recorded five sacks, forced three turnovers and held New York to just three yards rushing in the first half.

The Houston Oilers posted their first shutout victory in nine years when they defeated the Pittsburgh Steelers, 27-0, in an AFC Central Division game. The Oilers' last shutout had been a 6-0 triumph over the Steelers on December 4,

1980. In the first six weeks of the '89 season, the Oilers had allowed more points (170) than any other NFL team except Dallas.

Houston dominated from the outset, scoring on four of its five first-half possessions to take a 24-0 lead. Warren Moon threw three touchdown passes in the half, including two to running back Alonzo Highsmith.

The Steelers' offense, on the other hand, was pathetic for most of the game. Pittsburgh managed only 42 yards through the first three quarters and finished with 132. The closest the Steelers came to scoring was a drive that ended on downs at the Houston 5-yard line with 10 minutes left.

There was no lack of offense in Washington, where the Redskins withstood a furious fourth-quarter comeback by the Tampa Bay Buccaneers and held on for a 32-28 victory. The Redskins led, 29-7, entering the final period before the Bucs scored three touchdowns to make the game close.

The Bucs' three scoring drives took a combined 4:03 as quarterback Vinny Testaverde passed for 197 yards in the quarter. Tampa Bay had only four first downs in the game before getting nine in the fourth quarter.

Prior to their fourth-quarter rally, the Bucs had notched their only touchdown on a 33-yard blocked-punt return by Ricky Reynolds, the first such TD in Tampa Bay history. The Bucs' offense ran 11 plays from scrimmage in the second quarter for minus 26 yards.

The Redskins, who outscored the Bucs 29-0 in the second and third periods, took the steam out of Tampa Bay's late rally with a 12-play drive that set up a 29-yard field goal by Chip Lohmiller with 3:04 left.

A 33-yard field goal by rookie Pete Stoyanovich with six seconds to play gave the Miami Dolphins a 23-20 interconference triumph over Green Bay. Stoyanovich's third field goal of the game capped a five-play, 53-yard drive on which Dan Marino hit on pass completions of 24 yards to Fred Banks and 20 and 14 yards to Mark Clayton.

The Packers, who have never beaten the Dolphins in six tries, tied the score at 20-20 with 53 seconds left on a 10-yard touchdown pass from Don Majkowski to Sterling Sharpe. The pair had combined on a 22-yard touchdown play earlier in the quarter to cut a 20-6 Miami lead to seven points.

The best comeback of Week 7 came in Seattle, where the Denver Broncos rallied from a 14-0 halftime deficit to upend the Seahawks, 24-21, in overtime, in an AFC Western Division game. David Treadwell kicked a 27-yard field goal 7:46 into the extra period after Dennis Smith intercepted a pass by Seattle quarterback Dave Krieg and returned it 28 yards to the Seahawks' 10.

Treadwell had missed three field-goal attempts in regulation time, including a 27-yarder in the closing seconds. He had made 12 of 13 field-goal attempts in Denver's first six games.

Two touchdowns by running back John L. Williams had given the Seahawks their halftime lead before a one-yard touchdown run by Denver's Bobby Humphrey in the third quarter cut the lead in half. Broncos quarterback John Elway then threw two touchdown passes in the fourth quarter, including a 54-yarder to Vance Johnson with 2:19 left to force the overtime.

Elway, who wasn't sacked in the second half after going down four times before the intermission, completed 18 of 35 passes for 344 yards without an interception.

The Broncos' sixth victory gave them a three-game lead in the AFC West, the largest edge enjoyed by any NFL division leader after seven games. One of their pursuers, the Kansas City Chiefs, kept pace with a 36-28 victory over the winless Dallas Cowboys.

The Chiefs-Cowboys game was not as close as the final score might indicate. The Cowboys scored two touchdowns in the fourth quarter

after the Chiefs had built a 22-point lead. Dallas finished with 14 first downs, but only four came in the first three quarters. One of Dallas' scores came on the Cowboys' first kickoff-return touchdown since 1975, a 97-yard sprint by James Dixon.

The Chiefs' offense had little difficulty moving the ball. Kansas City compiled 423 total yards and scored four touchdowns rushing in one game for the first time in 13 years. Christian Okoye led the ground attack with 170 yards on 33 carries, including touchdown bursts of two and 13 yards. James Saxon and Steve Pelluer also ran for TDs against a defense that was yielding an average of 153 yards rushing per game.

The Phoenix Cardinals scored four rushing touchdowns for the first time since 1984 in their 34-20 victory over the Atlanta Falcons. Fullback Earl Ferrell scored a career-high three touchdowns on runs of one, six and three yards.

The Cardinals, who snapped a four-game losing streak, had only two rushing touchdowns in their first six games.

The NFL's No. 1-rated defense after seven weeks resided in Minnesota. The Vikings intercepted two passes, recovered three fumbles and had eight sacks in their latest outing, a 20-7 defeat of Detroit. Linebacker Mike Merriweather, acquired in an off-season trade with Pittsburgh, had two sacks, one interception, forced two fumbles and recovered one—by Lions quarterback Rodney Peete on the Vikings' 1 at the end of the first half.

The Vikings scored two touchdowns in the game and both came after Detroit turnovers. Herschel Walker scored on a one-yard run six plays after Chris Doleman recovered a fumble by Lions running back Barry Sanders at the Detroit 17.

The victory was Minnesota's second over Detroit in three weeks and seventh straight in the NFC Central Division series.

The Indianapolis Colts held the Cincinnati Bengals to their lowest total-yardage output in four years en route to a 23-12 triumph. The Bengals' offense mustered just 218 yards—95 rushing—and failed to score a touchdown despite four drives that carried to the Colts' 10 or closer. Four field goals by Jim Breech accounted for Cincinnati's points.

Despite Cincinnati's offensive woes, it took two touchdowns in the final minutes for the Colts to pull out the victory. A three-yard scoring pass from Jack Trudeau to Albert Bentley with 2:07 left gave Indianapolis its first lead at 16-12. After Keith Taylor intercepted a Boomer Esiason pass on the Bengals' next possession, Eric Dickerson scored on a 21-yard run with 1:22 remaining to increase the Colts' lead to 11 points.

Dickerson, who had been held under 100 yards rushing four straight weeks largely be-

Cleveland rookie Eric Metcalf splits the Chicago defense for a seven-yard touchdown run in the third quarter of the Browns' 27-7 victory.

cause of a strained hamstring, finished with 152 yards on 31 attempts to set a Colts team record with his 17th career 100-yard rushing game.

The New York Giants were off to their best start in 30 years following a 20-13 interconference conquest of the San Diego Chargers. The Giants' 6-1 ledger tied the New Yorkers with Denver and San Francisco for the NFL's best record and marked the first time since 1959 that New York had won six of its first seven games.

Veteran running back Ottis Anderson scored two touchdowns against the Chargers, but the key to the Giants' victory was their defense, which held San Diego to nine first downs, 179 total yards and one-of-11 success on third-down conversions. The Chargers' only touchdown came on a club-record 81-yard fumble return by Vencie Glenn with 2:27 left in the game.

The Philadelphia Eagles remained one game behind the Giants in the NFC Eastern Division following a 10-7 triumph over the Los Angeles Raiders. The Eagles struggled on offense for most of the game before scoring twice in the last two minutes of the third quarter after Raider turnovers.

After Izel Jenkins intercepted a Jay Schroeder pass, returning it 22 yards to the Los Angeles 24, Randall Cunningham hit Ron Johnson for a 12-yard gain on Philadelphia's first play from scrimmage. Anthony Toney then carried on consecutive plays for 11 yards before Cunningham ran the final yard for the touchdown.

On the Raiders' next possession, Byron Evans intercepted a pass by Steve Beuerlein and returned it 15 yards to Los Angeles' 17. Eagles place-kicker Luis Zendejas hit the left upright on a 39-yard field-goal attempt but, after an offside penalty against the Raiders gave him a second chance, he connected from 34 yards for what proved to be the game-winning points.

The Raiders put together an eight-play, 80-yard touchdown drive in the fourth quarter but missed a chance to tie when Jeff Jaeger was wide right on a 42-yard field-goal attempt with 1:59 left.

Cleveland quarterback Bernie Kosar rebounded from a poor performance in Week 6 against Pittsburgh by completing 22 of 29 passes for 281 yards to lead the Browns to a 27-7 victory over Chicago in the Monday night game. Kosar, who yielded a career-high four interceptions against the Steelers, completed seven of his first eight passes against the Bears, including a three-yard touchdown pass to rookie Eric Metcalf on the Browns' first possession.

Kosar and wide receiver Webster Slaughter later hooked up on a 97-yard touchdown pass play in the fourth period for the longest play from scrimmage in Cleveland history.

The Bears, meanwhile, lost their third straight game for the first time since 1981. Their only points came on a five-yard touchdown pass from Jim Harbaugh to Wendell Davis with 3:47 remaining in the game.

The loss dropped Chicago's record to 4-3 and marked the first time since the end of the 1983 season that the Bears did not at least share first place in the NFC Central Division.

Broncos-Seahawks
SUNDAY, OCTOBER 22
SCORE BY PERIODS

Denver	0	0	7	14	3—24
Seattle	7	7	0	7	0—21

SCORING
Seattle—Williams 4 run (N. Johnson kick), 7:23 1st.
Seattle—Williams 6 pass from Krieg (N. Johnson kick), 2:50 2nd.
Denver—Humphrey 1 run (Treadwell kick), 12:49 3rd.
Denver—Kay 2 pass from Elway (Treadwell kick), 4:37 4th.
Seattle—Skansi 24 pass from Krieg (N. Johnson kick), 9:27 4th.
Denver—Johnson 54 pass from Elway (Treadwell kick), 12:41 4th.
Denver—Field goal Treadwell 27, 7:46 OT.

TEAM STATISTICS

	Denver	Seattle
First downs	15	23
Rushes-Yards	23-55	43-139
Passing yards	316	224
Passes	18-35-0	22-38-2
Sacked-Yards lost	4-28	2-13
Punts	9-35.3	7-31.7
Fumbles-Lost	2-1	4-2
Penalties-Yards	13-84	4-35
Time of possession	27:25	40:21
Attendance—62,353.		

INDIVIDUAL STATISTICS
Rushing—Denver, Humphrey 17-50, Elway 3-3, Alexander 1-2, Winder 2-0; Seattle, Warner 22-74, Williams 18-62, Krieg 2-3, Kemp 1-0.
Passing—Denver, Elway 18-35-0—344; Seattle, Krieg 22-38-2—237.
Receiving—Denver, Young 6-137, Jackson 3-74, Johnson 3-67, Mobley 2-38, Kay 2-9, Winder 1-13, Sewell 1-6; Seattle, Blades 6-61, Skansi 5-81, Williams 5-28, Clark 3-25, Warner 2-30, Tyler 1-12.
Kickoff Returns—Denver, Bell 3-60; Seattle, Jefferson 5-88.
Punt Returns—Denver, Bell 4-24.
Interceptions—Denver, D. Smith 1-28, Braxton 1-19.
Punting—Denver, Horan 9-35.3; Seattle, Rodriquez 7-31.7.
Field Goals—Denver, Treadwell 1-4 (missed: 46, 46, 27); Seattle, N. Johnson 0-1 (missed: 40).
Sacks—Denver, Holmes, Mecklenburg; Seattle, Porter 2, Bryant, Nash.

Packers-Dolphins
SUNDAY, OCTOBER 22
SCORE BY PERIODS

Green Bay	3	3	0	14—20
Miami	7	3	7	6—23

SCORING
Miami—Jensen 7 pass from Marino (Stoyanovich kick), 6:43 1st.
Green Bay—Field goal Jacke 44, 11:30 1st.
Green Bay—Field goal Jacke 21, 7:40 2nd.
Miami—Field goal Stoyanovich 36, 14:19 2nd.

Miami—Clayton 24 pass from Marino (Stoyanovich kick), 8:15 3rd.
Miami—Field goal Stoyanovich 21, 0:08 4th.
Green Bay—Sharpe 22 pass from Majkowski (Jacke kick), 9:06 4th.
Green Bay—Sharpe 10 pass from Majkowski (Jacke kick), 14:07 4th.
Miami—Field goal Stoyanovich 33, 14:54 4th.

TEAM STATISTICS

	Green Bay	Miami
First downs	21	25
Rushes-Yards	21-81	28-105
Passing yards	215	333
Passes	26-42-0	24-37-2
Sacked-Yards lost	2-6	0-0
Punts	4-45.0	2-41.5
Fumbles-Lost	1-0	3-1
Penalties-Yards	6-40	7-45
Time of possession	30:39	29:21
Attendance—56,624.		

INDIVIDUAL STATISTICS
Rushing—Green Bay, Fullwood 11-45, Haddix 4-19, Majkowski 3-12, Woodside 1-3, Fontenot 2-2; Miami, Stradford 15-53, Logan 9-33, Clayton 1-11, Jensen 1-5, Davenport 1-3, Marino 1-0.
Passing—Green Bay, Majkowski 26-42-0—221; Miami, Marino 24-37-2—333.
Receiving—Green Bay, Sharpe 7-81, Kemp 6-62, Woodside 5-34, Fontenot 4-21, Matthews 1-9, Haddix 1-6, Query 1-5, Didier 1-3; Miami, Clayton 7-89, Duper 4-53, Stradford 4-51, Jensen 4-30, Banks 2-85, Edmunds 2-13, Kinchen 1-12.
Kickoff Returns—Green Bay, Workman 4-60, Query 2-40; Miami, Logan 3-75, Davenport 1-19.
Punt Returns—Green Bay, Query 1-14; Miami, Stradford 3-30.
Interceptions—Green Bay, Pitts 1-37, Murphy 1-8.
Punting—Green Bay, Bracken 4-45.0; Miami, Roby 2-41.5.
Field Goals—Green Bay, Jacke 2-2; Miami, Stoyanovich 3-3.
Sacks—Miami, Green, Bosa.

Raiders-Eagles
SUNDAY, OCTOBER 22
SCORE BY PERIODS

Los Angeles Raiders	0	0	0	7— 7
Philadelphia	0	0	10	0—10

SCORING
Philadelphia—Cunningham 1 run (Zendejas kick), 13:04 3rd.
Philadelphia—Field goal Zendejas 34, 14:59 3rd.
Los Angeles—Gault 24 pass from Beuerlein (Jaeger kick), 3:47 4th.

TEAM STATISTICS

	Los Angeles	Philadelphia
First downs	20	13
Rushes-Yards	34-128	32-132
Passing yards	140	63
Passes	12-30-2	8-20-0
Sacked-Yards lost	4-22	1-1
Punts	4-39.0	6-41.0
Fumbles-Lost	1-0	1-0
Penalties-Yards	8-60	6-40
Time of possession	34:36	25:24
Attendance—64,019.		

INDIVIDUAL STATISTICS
Rushing—Los Angeles, Jackson 20-79, Smith 10-36, Beuerlein 1-8, Mueller 1-3, Schroeder 2-2; Philadelphia, Toney 15-61, Cunningham 9-57, Byars 7-16, Higgs 1-minus 2.
Passing—Los Angeles, Schroeder 7-22-1—87, Beuerlein 5-8-1—75; Philadelphia, Cunningham 8-20-0—64.

Receiving—Los Angeles, Dyal 2-48, Fernandez 2-25, Mueller 2-25, Smith 2-11, Gault 1-24, Horton 1-20, Alexander 1-12, Jackson 1-minus 3; Philadelphia, Jackson 3-22, Johnson 2-24, Byars 2-15, Toney 1-3.

Kickoff Returns—Los Angeles, Edmonds 1-16, Junkin 1-0.

Punt Returns—Los Angeles, Edmonds 4-40; Philadelphia, Williams 2-9.

Interceptions—Philadelphia, Jenkins 1-22, Evans 1-15.

Punting—Los Angeles, Gossett 4-39.0; Philadelphia, Teltschik 6-41.0.

Field Goals—Los Angeles, Jaeger 0-2 (missed: 28, 42); Philadelphia, Zendejas 1-2 (missed: 41).

Sacks—Los Angeles, Golic ½, Wise ½; Philadelphia, Pitts 2, Joyner 2.

Vikings-Lions
SUNDAY, OCTOBER 22
SCORE BY PERIODS

Minnesota	3	10	7	0—20
Detroit	0	0	0	7— 7

SCORING

Minnesota—Field goal Karlis 40, 7:36 1st.
Minnesota—Field goal Karlis 40, 0:05 2nd.
Minnesota—Walker 1 run (Karlis kick), 4:41 2nd.
Minnesota—Anderson 4 run (Karlis kick), 5:22 3rd.
Detroit—Peete 2 run (Murray kick), 9:53 4th.

TEAM STATISTICS

	Minnesota	Detroit
First downs	12	21
Rushes-Yards	32-117	23-84
Passing yards	147	198
Passes	17-24-0	19-36-2
Sacked-Yards lost	3-13	8-42
Punts	5-41.2	5-41.2
Fumbles-Lost	2-1	3-3
Penalties-Yards	10-122	6-38
Time of possession	33:29	26:31
Attendance—51,579.		

INDIVIDUAL STATISTICS

Rushing—Minnesota, Walker 20-89, Fenney 5-19, Anderson 3-7, Kramer 3-3, Wilson 1-minus 1; Detroit, B. Sanders 15-59, Peete 8-25.

Passing—Minnesota, Kramer 15-20-0—143, Wilson 2-4-0—17; Detroit, Peete 19-36-2—240.

Receiving—Minnesota, Anderson 4-35, Walker 3-7, Gustafson 2-32, Fenney 2-18, Jones 2-4, Jordan 1-27, Lewis 1-19, Carter 1-16, Dozier 1-2; Detroit, Stanley 6-60, R. Johnson 5-47, Clark 4-84, McDonald 3-40, B. Sanders 1-9.

Kickoff Returns—Minnesota, Curtis 1-18; Detroit, B. Sanders 1-18, Painter 1-14, Stanley 1-minus 5.

Punt Returns—Minnesota, Lewis 2-13.

Interceptions—Minnesota, Browner 1-27, Merriweather 1-11.

Punting—Minnesota, Scribner 5-41.2; Detroit, Arnold 5-41.2.

Field Goals—Minnesota, Karlis 2-2; Detroit, none attempted.

Sacks—Minnesota, Merriweather 2, Noga 2, Studwell, Thomas, Clarke, Strauthers; Detroit, Jamison, Ball 2.

Cowboys-Chiefs
SUNDAY, OCTOBER 22
SCORE BY PERIODS

Dallas	7	7	0	14—28
Kansas City	14	13	9	0—36

SCORING

Kansas City—Okoye 2 run (Lowery kick), 6:43 1st.
Dallas—Palmer 63 run (Ruzek kick), 8:40 1st.
Kansas City—Okoye 13 run (Lowery kick), 14:24 1st.
Kansas City—Saxon 4 run (Lowery kick), 4:47 2nd.

Dallas—Dixon 97 kickoff return (Ruzek kick), 5:03 2nd.
Kansas City—Field goal Lowery 43, 13:04 2nd.
Kansas City—Field goal Lowery 27, 14:57 2nd.
Kansas City—Safety, McGovern blocked punt out of end zone, 4:08 3rd.
Kansas City—Pelluer 5 run (Lowery kick), 12:39 3rd.
Dallas—Clack 1 run (Ruzek kick), 4:45 4th.
Dallas—Folsom 4 pass from Walsh (Ruzek kick), 11:12 4th.

TEAM STATISTICS

	Dallas	Kansas City
First downs	14	26
Rushes-Yards	17-116	43-202
Passing yards	166	221
Passes	14-29-0	17-25-0
Sacked-Yards lost	0-0	2-16
Punts	5-35.2	4.43.3
Fumbles-Lost	1-1	2-0
Penalties-Yards	13-88	7-50
Time of possession	21:27	38:33
Attendance—76,841.		

INDIVIDUAL STATISTICS

Rushing—Dallas, Palmer 9-85, Shepard 1-12, Clack 2-8, Johnston 3-5, Sargent 1-5, Walsh 1-1; Kansas City, Okoye 33-170, McNair 2-18, Pelluer 2-13, Saxon 3-11, Heard 1-minus 1, DeBerg 1-minus 2, Mandley 1-minus 7.

Passing—Dallas, Walsh 14-29-0—166; Kansas City, DeBerg 17-22-0—237, Pelluer 0-3-0—0.

Receiving—Dallas, Palmer 5-30, Martin 4-52, Dixon 1-36, Johnston 1-28, Shepard 1-9, Ford 1-7, Folsom 1-4; Kansas City, Weathers 5-60, Harry 3-64, McNair 3-29, Hayes 2-41, Paige 2-33, Roberts 1-6, Heard 1-4.

Kickoff Returns—Dallas, Dixon 4-164, Shepard 2-40, Sargent 1-0; Kansas City, Copeland 2-35, Mandley 1-0.

Punt Returns—Dallas, Shepard 3-8; Kansas City, Mandley 4-39.

Interceptions—None.

Punting—Dallas, Saxon 4-44.0; Kansas City, Goodburn 4-43.3.

Field Goals—Dallas, none attempted; Kansas City, Lowery 2-2.

Sacks—Dallas, Jones.

Giants-Chargers
SUNDAY, OCTOBER 22
SCORE BY PERIODS

New York Giants	3	3	7	7—20
San Diego	0	3	3	7—13

SCORING

New York—Field goal Allegre 21, 6:08 1st.
San Diego—Field goal Bahr 26, 10:59 2nd.
New York—Field goal Allegre 40, 15:00 2nd.
New York—Anderson 4 run (Allegre kick), 8:29 3rd.
San Diego—Field goal Bahr 30, 11:53 3rd.
New York—Anderson 4 run (Allegre kick), 8:30 4th.
San Diego—Glenn 81 fumble return (Bahr kick), 12:33 4th.

TEAM STATISTICS

	New York	San Diego
First downs	24	9
Rushes-Yards	38-109	19-51
Passing yards	218	128
Passes	22-33-1	12-27-1
Sacked-Yards lost	2-14	1-5
Punts	3-41.7	3-22.3
Fumbles-Lost	2-1	1-0
Penalties-Yards	6-44	4-26
Time of possession	37:25	22:35
Attendance—48,566.		

INDIVIDUAL STATISTICS

Rushing—New York, Anderson 27-96, Carthon 4-6, Tillman 2-4, Meggett 1-3, Simms 4-0; San Diego, Spencer 11-34, McMahon 2-18, Butts 2-2, Nelson 2-minus 1, Holland 2-minus 2.

Passing—New York, Simms 22-33-1—232; San Diego, McMahon 12-27-1—133.

Receiving—New York, Turner 5-47, Manuel 4-36, Mowatt 4-24, Bavaro 2-44, Ingram 2-28, Rouson 2-28, Anderson 2-14, Meggett 1-11; San Diego, Nelson 3-38, A. Miller 3-24, Holland 3-32, Cox 2-30, Caravello 1-minus 1.

Kickoff Returns—New York, Meggett 2-37, Ingram 1-10; San Diego, Usher 2-28, A. Miller 2-57.

Punt Returns—San Diego, Walker 2-22.

Interceptions—New York, S. White 1-0; San Diego, Seale 1-0.

Punting—New York, Landeta 3-41.7; San Diego, Ilesic 3-22.3.

Field Goals—New York, Allegre 2-3 (missed: 43); San Diego, Bahr 2-3 (missed: 52).

Sacks—New York, Howard; San Diego, Williams 2.

Patriots-49ers
SUNDAY, OCTOBER 22
SCORE BY PERIODS

New England	0	10	7	3—20	
San Francisco	0	17	7	13—37	

SCORING

New England—Morgan 55 pass from Grogan (Davis kick), 0:09 2nd.

San Francisco—Rice 3 pass from Montana (Cofer kick), 6:32 2nd.

San Francisco—Field goal Cofer 23, 12:18 2nd.

New England—Field goal Davis 49, 13:59 2nd.

San Francisco—Walls 1 pass from Young (Cofer kick), 15:00 2nd.

New England—Morgan 19 pass from Grogan (Davis kick), 7:06 3rd.

San Francisco—Rice 50 pass from Young (Cofer kick), 9:53 3rd.

New England—Field goal Davis 21, 7:31 4th.

San Francisco—Taylor 43 pass from Young (Cofer kick), 11:45 4th.

San Francisco—Craig 3 run (kick failed), 14:06 4th.

TEAM STATISTICS

	New England	San Francisco
First downs	19	27
Rushes-Yards	28-94	31-141
Passing yards	231	353
Passes	15-29-2	27-34-0
Sacked-Yards lost	1-9	2-13
Punts	1-35.0	1-43.0
Fumbles-Lost	0-0	0-0
Penalties-Yards	4-55	9-95
Time of possession	26:18	33:42
Attendance—70,000 (est.).		

INDIVIDUAL STATISTICS

Rushing—New England, Stephens 21-63, Perryman 5-24, Morgan 1-7, Tatupu 1-0; San Francisco, Craig 22-66, Montana 3-40, Young 3-17, Rathman 2-12, Taylor 1-6.

Passing—New England, Grogan 15-29-2—240; San Francisco, Montana 16-22-0—178, Young 11-12-0—188.

Receiving—New England, Fryar 5-102, Morgan 3-83, C. Jones 3-19, Dykes 1-19, Sievers 1-7, Stephens 1-7, Dupard 1-3; San Francisco, Rathman 11-103, Rice 6-112, Taylor 5-78, Craig 3-55, B. Jones 1-17, Walls 1-1.

Kickoff Returns—New England, Martin 3-96, Rice 1-19; San Francisco, Flagler 2-49, Tillman 1-19.

Punt Returns—New England, Martin 1-14; San Francisco, Taylor 1-12.

Interceptions—San Francisco, Pollard 1-12, Griffin 1-3.

Punting—New England, Feagles 1-35.0; San Francisco, Helton 1-43.0.

Field Goals—New England, Davis 2-2; San Francisco, Cofer 1-3 (missed: 33, 45).

Sacks—New England, Rembert, Jeter; San Francisco, Roberts.

Buccaneers-Redskins
SUNDAY, OCTOBER 22
SCORE BY PERIODS

Tampa Bay	7	0	0	21—28	
Washington	0	12	17	3—32	

SCORING

Tampa Bay—Reynolds 33 blocked punt return (Igwebuike kick), 9:56 1st.

Washington—Field goal Lohmiller 33, 2:15 2nd.

Washington—Safety, Testaverde tackled by Manley in end zone, 4:26 2nd.

Washington—Clark 7 pass from Rypien (Lohmiller kick), 14:47 2nd.

Washington—Clark 10 pass from Rypien (Lohmiller kick), 4:30 3rd.

Washington—Field goal Lohmiller 42, 8:40 3rd.

Washington—Riggs 6 run (Lohmiller kick), 13:40 3rd.

Tampa Bay—Tate 10 pass from Testaverde (Igwebuike kick), 0:24 4th.

Tampa Bay—Hill 20 pass from Testaverde (Igwebuike kick), 0:50 4th.

Washington—Field goal Lohmiller 29, 11:56 4th.

Tampa Bay—Carrier 4 pass from Testaverde (Igwebuike kick), 13:49 4th.

TEAM STATISTICS

	Tampa Bay	Washington
First downs	13	24
Rushes-Yards	10-1	41-179
Passing yards	296	209
Passes	19-38-2	24-36-1
Sacked-Yards lost	2-15	2-12
Punts	5-37.4	4-33.5
Fumbles-Lost	0-0	3-1
Penalties-Yards	6-62	3-28
Time of possession	18:54	41:06
Attendance—52,862.		

INDIVIDUAL STATISTICS

Rushing—Tampa Bay, Tate 6-7, Howard 1-3, Wilder 3-minus 9; Washington, Riggs 28-99, Byner 5-43, Monk 1-14, Clark 1-11, Rypien 5-9, Morris 1-3.

Passing—Tampa Bay, Testaverde 19-38-2—311; Washington, Rypien 24-36-1—221.

Receiving—Tampa Bay, Carrier 8-106, Hill 3-42, Peebles 2-63, Wilder 2-25, Smith 1-44, Drewrey 1-13, Tate 1-10, Howard 1-8; Washington, Clark 10-73, Monk 8-97, Sanders 4-39, J. Johnson 1-8, Byner 1-4.

Kickoff Returns—Tampa Bay, Elder 4-82, Wilder 1-23; Washington, Howard 1-12, Branch 1-6, A.J. Johnson 2-41.

Punt Returns—Tampa Bay, Drewrey 2-14; Washington, Howard 3-38, Davis 1-3.

Interceptions—Tampa Bay, Robinson 1-0; Washington, Wilburn 1-0, Bowles 1-25.

Punting—Tampa Bay, Mohr 5-37.4; Washington, Mojsiejenko 3-44.7.

Field Goals—Tampa Bay, Igwebuike 0-1 (missed: 41); Washington, Lohmiller 3-3.

Sacks—Tampa Bay, Thomas, Robinson; Washington, Grant, Manley.

Jets-Bills
SUNDAY, OCTOBER 22
SCORE BY PERIODS

New York Jets	0	0	3	0— 3	
Buffalo	3	10	7	14—34	

SCORING

Buffalo—Field goal Norwood 38, 9:05 1st.

Buffalo—Thomas 3 run (Norwood kick), 1:43 2nd.

Buffalo—Field goal Norwood 27, 12:26 2nd.

Buffalo—Reed 20 pass from Reich (Norwood kick), 7:08 3rd.

New York—Field goal Leahy 41, 14:44 3rd.

Buffalo—Harmon 12 pass from Reich (Norwood kick), 6:18 4th.

Buffalo—K. Davis 7 pass from Reich (Norwood kick), 9:38 4th.

TEAM STATISTICS

	New York	Buffalo
First downs	9	22
Rushes-Yards	12-39	52-204
Passing yards	115	139
Passes	13-31-1	13-20-0
Sacked-Yards lost	5-38	1-6
Punts	6-26.7	3-41.3
Fumbles-Lost	2-2	0-0
Penalties-Yards	9-65	5-40
Time of possession	17:07	42:53

Attendance—76,811.

INDIVIDUAL STATISTICS

Rushing—New York, McNeil 5-22, Hector 5-15, Vick 1-2, Malone 1.0; Buffalo, Kinnebrew 17-77, Thomas 20-49, Reich 5-32, K. Davis 7-31, Harmon 1-13, Mueller 1-5, Gelbaugh 1-minus 3.

Passing—New York, O'Brien 11-29-1—140, Malone 2-2-0—13; Buffalo, Reich 13-20-0—145.

Receiving—New York, Burkett 3-42, Shuler 3-34, Townsell 2-33, Hector 2-21, McNeil 2-18, Vick 1-5; Buffalo, Reed 5-58, Metzelaars 4-41, McKeller 1-20, Harmon 1-12, K. Davis 1-7, Johnson 1-7.

Kickoff Returns—New York, Townsell 5-81, Epps 1-23; Buffalo, Tasker 1-20.

Punt Returns—Buffalo, Sutton 1-19.

Interceptions—Buffalo, Sutton 1-3.

Punting—New York, Prokop 6-26.7; Buffalo, Kidd 3-41.3.

Field Goals—New York, Leahy 1-2 (missed: 52); Buffalo, Norwood 2-3 (missed: 37).

Sacks—New York, Lageman ½, Frase ½; Buffalo, B. Smith 3, Talley, Bennett.

Falcons-Cardinals
SUNDAY, OCTOBER 22
SCORE BY PERIODS

Atlanta	0	6	7	7	20
Phoenix	14	7	3	10	34

SCORING

Phoenix—Ferrell 1 run (Del Greco kick), 8:43 1st.
Phoenix—Ferrell 6 run (Del Greco kick), 13:46 1st.
Atlanta—Field goal McFadden 37, 3:06 2nd.
Phoenix—Wolfley 5 run (Del Greco kick), 13:12 2nd.
Atlanta—Field goal McFadden 37, 14:53 2nd.
Phoenix—Field goal Del Greco 50, 6:29 3rd.
Atlanta—Jones 14 run (McFadden kick), 13:33 3rd.
Phoenix—Ferrell 3 run (Del Greco kick), 2:29 4th.
Atlanta—Settle 16 pass from Miller (McFadden kick), 5:44 4th.
Phoenix—Field goal Del Greco 22, 9:34 4th.

TEAM STATISTICS

	Atlanta	Phoenix
First downs	22	21
Rushes-Yards	20-111	37-125
Passing yards	240	174
Passes	24-44-0	17-25-1
Sacked-Yards lost	2-9	2-7
Punts	2-42.5	2-43.0
Fumbles-Lost	2-2	0-0
Penalties-Yards	3-30	2-36
Time of possession	23:39	36:21

Attendance—33,894.

INDIVIDUAL STATISTICS

Rushing—Atlanta, Settle 14-87, Jones 5-22, Haynes 1-2; Phoenix, Jordan 12-49, Ferrell 15-46, Hogeboom 5-11, J.T. Smith 1-11, Wolfley 1-5, Sikahema 1-2, Baker 2-1.

Passing—Atlanta, Miller 24-44-0—249; Phoenix, Hogeboom 17-25-1—181.

Receiving—Atlanta, Jones 8-57, Settle 5-46, Haynes 4-66, Collins 2-34, Thomas 2-27, Heller 2-8, Bailey 1-11;

Phoenix, J.T. Smith 7-96, Awalt 3-35, Jones 2-10, Ferrell 2-9, Sikahema 1-23, McConkey 1-8, Jordan 1-0.

Kickoff Returns—Atlanta, Jones 1-22, Sanders 4-80, Paterra 2-40; Phoenix, Sikahema 4-112, Baker 1-29.

Punt Returns—Phoenix, Sikahema 1-1.

Interceptions—Atlanta, Sanders 1-1.

Punting—Atlanta, Fulhage 2-42.5; Phoenix, Camarillo 2-43.0.

Field Goals—Atlanta, McFadden 2-3 (missed: 43); Phoenix, Del Greco 2-2.

Sacks—Atlanta, Casillas, Cotton; Phoenix, Bell, Galloway.

Colts-Bengals
SUNDAY, OCTOBER 22
SCORE BY PERIODS

Indianapolis	0	3	6	14	23
Cincinnati	6	3	0	3	12

SCORING

Cincinnati—Field goal Breech 30, 9:04 1st.
Cincinnati—Field goal Breech 29, 13:27 1st.
Cincinnati—Field goal Breech 23, 5:28 2nd.
Indianapolis—Field goal Biasucci 27, 14:46 2nd.
Indianapolis—Brooks 2 pass from Trudeau (kick failed), 8:46 3rd.
Cincinnati—Field goal Breech 21, 5:38 4th.
Indianapolis—Bentley 3 pass from Trudeau (Biasucci kick), 12:53 4th.
Indianapolis—Dickerson 21 run (Biasucci kick), 13:38 4th.

TEAM STATISTICS

	Indianapolis	Cincinnati
First downs	18	15
Rushes-Yards	36-168	28-95
Passing yards	168	123
Passes	14-27-1	14-31-2
Sacked-Yards lost	0-0	5-46
Punts	4-38.7	3-49.0
Fumbles-Lost	2-2	1-1
Penalties-Yards	7-95	1-5
Time of possession	27:44	32:16

Attendance—57,642.

INDIVIDUAL STATISTICS

Rushing—Indianapolis, Dickerson 31-152, Bentley 4-10, Trudeau 1-6; Cincinnati, Brooks 11-37, Ball 11-24, Esiason 5-31, Jennings 1-3.

Passing—Indianapolis, Trudeau 14-27-1—168; Cincinnati, Esiason 14-31-2—169.

Receiving—Indianapolis, Rison 5-42, Verdin 3-63, Brooks 3-44, Bentley 3-19; Cincinnati, Brown 4-62, Brooks 4-29, Holman 3-51, Martin 1-10, Kattus 1-9, McGee 1-8.

Kickoff Returns—Indianapolis, Verdin 3-59; Cincinnati, Hillary 3-45, Jennings 2-57.

Punt Returns—Indianapolis, Verdin 3-34; Cincinnati, Martin 2-12.

Interceptions—Indianapolis, Taylor 2-37; Cincinnati, Dixon 1-0.

Punting—Indianapolis, Stark 4-38.7; Cincinnati, Johnson 3-49.0.

Field Goals—Indianapolis, Biasucci 1-1; Cincinnati, Breech 4-4.

Sacks—Indianapolis, Hand 1½, Bickett 1½, Thompson 1½, E. Johnson ½.

Steelers-Oilers
SUNDAY, OCTOBER 22
SCORE BY PERIODS

Pittsburgh	0	0	0	0	0
Houston	7	17	3	0	27

SCORING

Houston—Highsmith 3 pass from Moon (Zendejas kick), 14:36 1st.

Houston—Field goal Zendejas 41, 2:15 2nd.
Houston—Duncan 51 pass from Moon (Zendejas kick), 11:10 2nd.
Houston—Highsmith 5 pass from Moon (Zendejas kick), 14:48 2nd.
Houston—Field goal Zendejas 51, 13:05 3rd.

TEAM STATISTICS

	Pittsburgh	Houston
First downs	10	22
Rushes-Yards	17-32	41-132
Passing yards	100	229
Passes	11-27-2	17-30-0
Sacked-Yards lost	1-5	0-0
Punts	6-38.3	3-45.3
Fumbles-Lost	2-2	6-1
Penalties-Yards	8-70	9-70
Time of possession	20:28	39:32
Attendance—59,091.		

INDIVIDUAL STATISTICS

Rushing—Pittsburgh, Blackledge 3-13, Hoge 2-8, Worley 11-6, Wallace 1-5; Houston, Rozier 17-50, Highsmith 7-43, Moon 4-15, White 8-13, Pinkett 4-12, Carlson 1-minus 1.

Passing—Pittsburgh, Blackledge 11-27-2—105; Houston, Moon 17-29-0—229, Carlson 0-1-0—0.

Receiving—Pittsburgh, Stone 2-27, Lipps 2-23, Worley 2-23, Carter 2-11, Hill 1-17, Hoge 1-4, W. Williams 1-0; Houston, Duncan 3-86, Hill 3-58, Givins 3-29, Jeffires 2-20, Highsmith 2-8, White 2-5, Mrosko 1-14, Pinkett 1-9.

Kickoff Returns—Pittsburgh, Thompson 2-23, J. Williams 1-2, Griffin 1-21, Woodson 1-24, Stone 1-0; Houston, K. Johnson 1-24.

Punt Returns—Houston, K. Johnson 1-0.

Interceptions—Houston, McDowell 2-39.

Punting—Pittsburgh, Newsome 6-38.3; Houston, Greg Montgomery 3-45.3.

Field Goals—Pittsburgh, none attempted; Houston, Zendejas 2-4 (missed: 31, 41).

Sacks—Houston, Jones.

Saints-Rams
SUNDAY, OCTOBER 22
SCORE BY PERIODS

New Orleans	10	9	14	7—40
Los Angeles Rams	7	0	7	7—21

SCORING

New Orleans—Hilliard 20 pass from Hebert (Andersen kick), 2:08 1st.
New Orleans—Field goal Andersen 39, 5:43 1st.
Los Angeles—Ellard 3 pass from Everett (Lansford kick), 14:45 1st.
New Orleans—Hilliard 2 run (kick failed), 8:07 2nd.
New Orleans—Field goal Andersen 27, 14:21 2nd.
New Orleans—Turner 54 pass from Hebert (Andersen kick), 2:33 3rd.
New Orleans—E. Martin 37 pass from Hebert (Andersen kick), 4:16 3rd.
Los Angeles—Johnson 1 pass from Everett (Lansford kick), 9:35 3rd.
New Orleans—Hilliard 7 run (Andersen kick), 4:12 4th.
Los Angeles—Johnson 3 pass from Everett (Lansford kick), 8:13 4th.

TEAM STATISTICS

	New Orleans	Los Angeles
First downs	16	22
Rushes-Yards	31-106	18-53
Passing yards	267	260
Passes	15-22-1	27-46-3
Sacked-Yards lost	1-9	6-50
Punts	4-30.0	6-36.2
Fumbles-Lost	2-0	2-0
Penalties-Yards	5-35	4-25
Time of possession	29:36	30:24
Attendance—57,567.		

INDIVIDUAL STATISTICS

Rushing—New Orleans, Hilliard 20-87, Hebert 5-7, Heyward 4-6, Morse 1-4, Frazier 1-2; Los Angeles, Bell 14-53, Delpino 2-1, Green 1-1, Everett 1-minus 2.

Passing—New Orleans, Hebert 15-22-1—276; Los Angeles, Everett 24-42-2—263, Herrmann 3-4-1—47.

Receiving—New Orleans, E. Martin 5-116, Turner 3-73, Hill 2-27, Hilliard 2-24, Frazier 1-22, Tice 1-9, Heyward 1-5; Los Angeles, Ellard 7-95, McGee 5-44, Holohan 4-30, Johnson 4-28, A. Cox 3-51, Anderson 2-49, Gary 1-8, Delpino 1-5.

Kickoff Returns—New Orleans, Harris 3-65, Scales 1-0; Los Angeles, Ron Brown 5-76, Delpino 2-22.

Punt Returns—New Orleans, Harris 5-48; Los Angeles, Henley 1-minus 4.

Interceptions—New Orleans, Waymer 1-42, Mack 1-0, Cook 1-10; Los Angeles, Stams 1-20.

Punting—New Orleans, Barnhardt 4-30.0; Los Angeles, Hatcher 6-36.2.

Field Goals—New Orleans, Andersen 2-2; Los Angeles, none attempted.

Sacks—New Orleans, Swilling 2, Warren 2, Wilks, Jackson; Los Angeles, Jerue ½, Green ½.

Bears-Browns
MONDAY, OCTOBER 23
SCORE BY PERIODS

Chicago	0	0	0	7— 7
Cleveland	7	0	10	10—27

SCORING

Cleveland—Metcalf 3 pass from Kosar (Bahr kick), 14:32 1st.
Cleveland—Field goal Bahr 31, 6:24 3rd.
Cleveland—Metcalf 7 run (Bahr kick), 10:25 3rd.
Cleveland—Slaughter 97 pass from Kosar (Bahr kick), 8:04 4th.
Chicago—Davis 5 pass from Harbaugh (Butler kick), 11:13 4th.
Cleveland—Field goal Bahr 35, 13:52 4th.

TEAM STATISTICS

	Chicago	Cleveland
First downs	17	16
Rushes-Yards	31-149	24-53
Passing yards	152	273
Passes	13-30-1	22-29-0
Sacked-Yards lost	3-17	2-8
Punts	7-40.7	6-43.3
Fumbles-Lost	0-0	0-0
Penalties-Yards	6-55	6-33
Time of possession	31:29	28:31
Attendance—78,722.		

INDIVIDUAL STATISTICS

Rushing—Chicago, Anderson 15-69, Muster 10-48, Gentry 2-22, Harbaugh 3-7, Sanders 1-3; Cleveland, Metcalf 12-16, Oliphant 2-10, Manoa 4-10, K. Jones 2-8, Pagel 1-4, Redden 2-4, Kosar 1-1.

Passing—Chicago, Tomczak 4-14-1—76, Harbaugh 9-16-0—93; Cleveland, Kosar 22-29-0—281.

Receiving—Chicago, McKinnon 3-40, Davis 3-37, Gentry 2-24, Muster 2-12, Anderson 1-31, Thornton 1-23, Green 1-2; Cleveland, Slaughter 8-186, Metcalf 4-8, Langhorne 3-27, Manoa 3-19, Newsome 2-26, Brennan 2-15.

Kickoff Returns—Chicago, Gentry 3-66, Sanders 3-60; Cleveland, Metcalf 1-25.

Punt Returns—Chicago, Green 3-24; Cleveland, McNeil 4-52.

Interceptions—Cleveland, Minnifield 1-2.

Punting—Chicago, Buford 7-40.7; Cleveland, Wagner 6-43.3.

Field Goals—Chicago, none attempted; Cleveland, Bahr 2-2.

Sacks—Chicago, Rivera, Woods; Cleveland, Gibson, Banks, Hairston ½, Perry ½.

EIGHTH WEEK

RESULTS OF WEEK 8
Sunday, October 29

Buffalo 31, Miami 17 at Buff.
Chicago 20, L.A. Rams 10 at Chi.
Cincinnati 56, Tampa Bay 23 at Cin.
Cleveland 28, Houston 17 at Cleve.
Green Bay 23, Detroit 20 (OT) at Milw.
L.A. Raiders 37, Washington 24 at L.A.
New England 23, Indianapolis 20 (OT) at Ind.
New Orleans 20, Atlanta 13 at N.O.
Philadelphia 28, Denver 24 at Den.
Phoenix 19, Dallas 10 at Dall.
Pittsburgh 23, Kansas City 17 at Pitts.
San Francisco 23, N.Y. Jets 10 at N.Y.
Seattle 10, San Diego 7 at Sea.

Monday, October 30

N.Y. Giants 24, Minnesota 14 at N.Y.

Although any decision a National Football League coach makes can be second-guessed, few decisions create as much controversy or are as important as the changing of quarterbacks.

When the Chicago Bears traded veteran quarterback Jim McMahon to San Diego in August 1989, Coach Mike Ditka gave the starting job to Mike Tomczak, a former free agent who had spent four years as McMahon's primary backup. Although he entered the '89 season with nearly twice as many interceptions (26) as touchdown passes (14) in his pro career, Tomczak saw more action than a typical NFL backup because of McMahon's numerous injuries. He was in line to inherit the No. 1 job.

But just as important to Ditka, the Bears were 16-3 in games Tomczak had started through 1988, a statistic that was difficult to ignore.

Entering their game against the Los Angeles Rams in Week 8, though, the Bears were 4-3 with Tomczak starting and had lost three consecutive games. It was Chicago's longest losing streak in Ditka's eight years as coach. So when the Bears fell behind the Rams, 3-0, midway through the second quarter, Ditka had seen enough. He replaced Tomczak—who had completed just four of 16 passes for 29 yards—with seldom-used Jim Harbaugh.

"You live in life on gut instincts," Ditka said.

The move paid off. A Chicago offense that had mustered just 39 yards with Tomczak at the controls got the same amount on its first possession under Harbaugh. That drive resulted in a 35-yard field goal by Kevin Butler that tied the score at 3-3 shortly before halftime.

In the third quarter, Harbaugh completed a 14-yard pass to Brad Muster to set up Chicago's first touchdown. He later directed a seven-play, 70-yard drive that culminated with his own one-yard touchdown run with 11:11 left.

All told, 279 of the Bears' 318 total yards in their 20-10 victory were gained after the switch. Harbaugh finished the game with 10 completions in 13 attempts for 157 yards.

"It wasn't me," said Harbaugh, a 1987 first-round draft choice from Michigan. "We made some adjustments at halftime to pick up their blitzing. If Mike had been in there, he could have done the same thing."

Chicago linebacker Ron Rivera said the victory was crucial—"so big you can't measure it"—to the Bears' hopes of qualifying for postseason play.

Another big victory was achieved by the Cincinnati Bengals, who scored a team-record eight touchdowns in a 56-23 rout of the Tampa Bay Buccaneers. The Bengals scored touchdowns on seven of their first nine possessions. Boomer Esiason tied his own club record with five touchdown passes. And five Cincinnati players scored at least one touchdown.

Amazingly, the Bengals entered this game without having scored an offensive touchdown in seven quarters.

The 56 points represented the second-highest total ever scored by the Bengals.

The Cleveland Browns kept pace with Cincinnati atop the AFC Central Division standings with a come-from-behind 28-17 victory over the Houston Oilers. The Browns trailed, 10-0, at halftime before scoring touchdowns on their first four second-half possessions to take command.

Quarterback Bernie Kosar led the assault by throwing for two touchdowns and running for another in the third period. Kosar capped a 13-play, 71-yard drive with a five-yard touchdown run to open the second half before burning the Oilers with scoring passes of 80 and 77 yards to wide receiver Webster Slaughter. The 80-yard touchdown came on a flea-flicker, with running back Eric Metcalf taking a handoff and flipping the ball back to Kosar, who hit Slaughter 10 yards behind the Houston secondary.

The Browns had 326 yards in total offense in the second half after being held to just 57 in a scoreless first half.

Kosar completed 14 of 19 passes in the game —including all eight in the second half—but none to tight end Ozzie Newsome, who had a string of consecutive games with at least one pass reception snapped at 150. It marked the first time the 12-year veteran from Alabama had failed to catch a pass since an October 14, 1979, game against Washington.

Another streak ending in Week 8 involved Miami quarterback Dan Marino, who was sacked for the first time in 20 games in the Dolphins' 31-17 loss at Buffalo. The Bills' defense actually got to the Dolphins' star twice in the game, with nose tackle Jeff Wright and

Rookie placekicker Chris Jacke's 38-yard field goal at 2:14 of overtime gave the Green Bay Packers a 23-20 triumph over Detroit.

linebacker Cornelius Bennett getting credit for the sacks. Wright's second-quarter tackle of Marino snapped a streak of 759 pass attempts by Miami quarterbacks without being sacked.

In contrast to a Miami running game that mustered only 65 yards, the Bills' running attack was relentless. Thurman Thomas ran for a career-high 148 yards and Larry Kinnebrew added 121. Both players scored touchdowns as the Bills rolled up 280 yards rushing on 51 attempts. Buffalo quarterback Frank Reich attempted only nine passes.

The week's top rushing performance came from Detroit rookie Barry Sanders, who carried the ball 30 times for 184 yards in the Lions' 23-20 overtime loss to the Green Bay Packers. The 1988 Heisman Trophy winner from Oklahoma State also had a seven-yard touchdown run nullified by an illegal block.

Unfortunately for the Lions, that was not the only mistake they made in their seventh loss in eight weeks. Packers safety Mark Murphy intercepted a pass by rookie quarterback Rodney Peete on Detroit's first play from scrimmage in overtime, setting up a 38-yard field goal by Green Bay's Chris Jacke for the game-winning points.

Jacke had missed a 50-yard attempt on the final play in regulation after linebacker Tim Harris recovered a Peete fumble at the Green Bay 36.

Turnovers also proved to be the downfall of

the Washington Redskins, who gave away the ball eight times and also suffered seven sacks in a 37-24 interconference loss to the Los Angeles Raiders. Redskins quarterback Mark Rypien threw three interceptions and lost two fumbles. Rypien did throw for 364 yards before being replaced midway through the third period by Stan Humphries, who had his second pass intercepted and returned 45 yards for a touchdown by Raiders safety Eddie Anderson.

Anderson's touchdown gave Los Angeles a 37-10 lead, with a 99-yard kickoff return by Joe Howard accounting for Washington's touchdown.

The Raiders' offense had little problem moving the ball. Los Angeles rolled up 166 yards and 10 first downs in the first period alone as quarterback Steve Beuerlein and wide receiver Mervyn Fernandez hooked up for touchdowns on the team's first two possessions.

Running back Bo Jackson carried the ball 19 times for 144 yards for the Raiders' first 100-yard rushing performance of 1989. Jackson ran 73 yards for a touchdown early in the third quarter and had a 45-yard scoring run called back on a penalty.

Two touchdown runs by Keith Byars and two touchdown passes by Randall Cunningham helped the Philadelphia Eagles to a 28-24 triumph over the Denver Broncos. Byars' one-yard run with 5:25 left proved to be the game-winner and came six plays after William Friz-

Neal Anderson rushed for 80 yards in Chicago's 20-10 win over the Los Angeles Rams.

zell recovered a fumbled punt by Broncos rookie Darren Carrington at the Denver 24.

The Eagles used an effective running game in winning for the fourth straight week. They ran on all 13 plays of a 96-yard march on their first possession, and Byars capped the drive with a 16-yard touchdown run. Cunningham's five-yard touchdown pass to Cris Carter later in the first quarter increased the Philadelphia lead to 14-0.

The Broncos, however, fought back with two touchdown passes and a 10-yard scoring run by John Elway. The Denver quarterback's four-yard touchdown pass to Melvin Bratton gave the Broncos a 24-21 lead in the fourth quarter before Byars scored four minutes later to win it for the Eagles.

Dalton Hilliard's second touchdown of the game—a one-yard run with 2:12 remaining—gave the New Orleans Saints a 20-13 NFC Western Division victory over Atlanta. The touchdown capped a six-play, 74-yard drive that included a 50-yard pass from Bobby Hebert to Eric Martin.

Hilliard, who accounted for 190 of the Saints' 392 yards in total offense, also caught a 21-yard pass from Hebert for New Orleans' first touchdown.

The Saints' defense was outstanding. It yielded only 11 first downs, held the Falcons to fewer than 100 yards both running and passing and recovered three fumbles. Linebacker Pat Swilling recovered two Atlanta fumbles deep in New Orleans territory to end scoring threats. Swilling also was credited with three of the Saints' six quarterback sacks.

The Falcons' offense had just four yards in the first half.

The Pittsburgh Steelers jumped to a 16-0

lead against Kansas City in Week 8 before weathering a late Chiefs rally for a 23-17 triumph. Steelers quarterback Bubby Brister, who had missed two games because of a sprained knee, threw two touchdown passes to wide receiver Louis Lipps, including one of 64 yards late in the third period for the winning points.

It didn't appear the Steelers would need that touchdown or any more points after they scored on their first four possessions to take their 16-0 lead. But the Chiefs battled back, eventually taking a 17-16 edge on a four-yard fumble-return touchdown by nose tackle Bill Maas. It was the fifth touchdown scored by the opposition on a Pittsburgh turnover in eight games.

After the Steelers regained the lead on Lipps' second touchdown, Kansas City failed on two other scoring chances. The Chiefs drove to the Pittsburgh 2 on their next possession before fullback Christian Okoye was stopped short of the goal line on consecutive plays. A disputed delay-of-game penalty cost the Chiefs a play before a fourth-down lob pass by quarterback Steve DeBerg was intercepted by Rod Woodson in the end zone.

Kansas City's last possession ended when a DeBerg pass went through the hands of wide receiver Stephone Paige in the Pittsburgh end zone with eight seconds left.

It also came down to the wire in Seattle, where the Seahawks edged the San Diego Chargers, 10-7, on Dave Krieg's 21-yard touchdown pass to Brian Blades with 40 seconds to go. The touchdown came at the end of an eight-play, 71-yard drive that took just 1:02. It was the Seahawks' first victory at the Kingdome in four games.

New England would have been forced to punt from its 8.

That controversy overshadowed a fine performance by Grogan, who completed 28 of 46 passes for 355 yards, including 20 of 26 for 248 yards in the second half. He completed 13 straight passes at one point after connecting on just two of his first nine attempts.

There were no doubts about the outcome in New York, where the San Francisco 49ers beat the Jets, 23-10, in an interconference game. It was the defending Super Bowl champions' seventh victory in eight games and their sixth straight triumph on the road. It was the 1-7 Jets' fifth straight loss and fourth at home.

With Joe Montana sidelined because of a knee injury, Steve Young and Steve Bono shared the quarterbacking duties and each threw one touchdown pass while combining for 240 yards passing.

The New York offense, on the other hand, was held to just one field goal. The Jets' only touchdown came on a 45-yard fumble return by safety Erik McMillan.

The Phoenix Cardinals also did not score an offensive touchdown in Week 8 but won anyway, 19-10, over the Dallas Cowboys. Four field goals by Al Del Greco and a 16-yard interception return by Mike Zordich accounted for all the scoring Phoenix needed. It marked the first time since 1963-1964 that the Cardinals—who won 16-10 at Texas Stadium in 1988—had won at Dallas in successive seasons.

It helped, of course, that the Cards were playing against the NFL's only winless team. The Cowboys' loss was their eighth straight and their 19th in their last 20 games. They had a good shot at winning after cutting the Cardinals' lead to 16-10 on quarterback Steve Walsh's 37-yard touchdown pass to Derrick Shepard with 4:27 left. Shepard, however, fumbled a punt at his own 31 in the final two minutes. Marcus Turner recovered for Phoenix.

Fumbles on consecutive kickoffs proved to be the undoing of the Minnesota Vikings in their 24-14 loss to the New York Giants in the Monday night game. Alfred Anderson was the guilty party both times as the Giants converted both of his third-quarter miscues into touchdowns.

After Raul Allegre put the Giants ahead, 10-7, with a 39-yard field goal late in the third quarter, Anderson fumbled the ensuing kickoff after being hit by the Giants' Lewis Tillman. Dwayne Jiles recovered at the Minnesota 9 and, three plays later, Jeff Hostetler threw an 11-yard touchdown pass to Lionel Manuel.

Anderson then mishandled the next kickoff on a hit by Greg Jackson, with Myron Guyton recovering for the Giants at the Vikings' 19. Ottis Anderson's two-yard touchdown run early in the fourth quarter increased the Giants' lead to 24-7.

The Giants improved their record to 7-1 de-

Bo Jackson carried 19 times for 144 yards in the Los Angeles Raiders' 37-24 victory over Washington.

The only two touchdowns in this game between AFC Western Division rivals were scored in the last two minutes. After Chargers rookie quarterback Billy Joe Tolliver completed just six of 17 passes for 41 yards in his first pro start, he was replaced by veteran Jim McMahon, who led the team 55 yards in 10 plays for a touchdown on his second possession. McMahon's 14-yard touchdown pass to tight end Arthur Cox gave the Chargers a short-lived 7-3 lead with 1:53 left.

The New England Patriots beat the Indianapolis Colts in overtime, 23-20, on a 51-yard field goal by Greg Davis 9:57 into the extra period. Davis' third field goal of the game ended a drive that the Patriots began at their 12. The drive included a controversial 28-yard pass from Steve Grogan to Sammy Martin at the New England 36.

The field officials ruled that Martin was in-bounds when he made the catch but the Colts contended he was out of bounds. The instant-replay officials could not determine conclusively that Martin was out, so they allowed the play to stand. Had the catch been disallowed,

spite losing quarterback Phil Simms (ankle injury) on the first series of the game. Their first points came via a 39-yard interception return for a touchdown by linebacker Pepper Johnson four minutes into the second half.

The Vikings, who had a four-game winning streak snapped, had not allowed any points in the third quarter all season before the Giants blitzed them for 17 points in that period.

Cardinals-Cowboys
SUNDAY, OCTOBER 29
SCORE BY PERIODS

Phoenix	6	0	7	6	19
Dallas	0	3	0	7	10

SCORING

Phoenix—Field goal Del Greco 40, 3:37 1st.
Phoenix—Field goal Del Greco 25, 7:26 1st.
Dallas—Field goal Ruzek 37, 14:41 2nd.
Phoenix—Zordich 16 interception return (Del Greco kick), 10:53 3rd.
Phoenix—Field goal Del Greco 31, 8:20 4th.
Dallas—Shepard 37 pass from Walsh (Ruzek kick), 10:33 4th.
Phoenix—Field goal Del Greco 42, 13:37 4th.

TEAM STATISTICS

	Phoenix	Dallas
First downs	17	18
Rushes-Yards	44-158	14-33
Passing yards	142	264
Passes	17-31-0	21-49-2
Sacked-Yards lost	4-22	0-0
Punts	8-43.2	6-42.3
Fumbles-Lost	0-0	1-1
Penalties-Yards	7-47	3-30
Time of possession	39:25	20:35

Attendance—44,431.

INDIVIDUAL STATISTICS

Rushing—Phoenix, Ferrell 18-71, Jordan 18-68, Hogeboom 3-9, Baker 3-5, Sikahema 1-3, Wolfley 1-2; Dallas, Palmer 14-33.

Passing—Phoenix, Hogeboom 17-31-0—164; Dallas, Walsh 21-49-2—264.

Receiving—Phoenix, J.T. Smith 6-60, Jones 3-50, Awalt 3-18, Novacek 1-12, Sikahema 1-12, Baker 1-9, Ferrell 1-3, Jordan 1-0; Dallas, Martin 7-78, Shepard 4-92, Dixon 3-33, Tautalatasi 2-35, Folsom 2-12, Palmer 2-8, Johnston 1-6.

Kickoff Returns—Phoenix, Sikahema 3-59; Dallas, Shepard 2-44, Dixon 2-58.

Punt Returns—Phoenix, Sikahema 2-19; Dallas, Shepard 5-38.

Interceptions—Phoenix, Zordich 1-16, McDonald 1-0.

Punting—Phoenix, Camarillo 8-43.2; Dallas, Saxon 6-42.3.

Field Goals—Phoenix, Del Greco 4-4; Dallas, Ruzek 1-2 (missed: 31).

Sacks—Dallas, Broughton 2, Jeffcoat 2.

Chiefs-Steelers
SUNDAY, OCTOBER 29
SCORE BY PERIODS

Kansas City	0	3	14	0	17
Pittsburgh	10	6	7	0	23

SCORING

Pittsburgh—Field goal Anderson 41, 4:24 1st.
Pittsburgh—Lipps 16 pass from Brister (Anderson kick), 10:19 1st.
Pittsburgh—Field goal Anderson 47, 7:53 2nd.
Pittsburgh—Field goal Anderson 29, 14:36 2nd.
Kansas City—Field goal Lowery 50, 15:00 2nd.

Kansas City—Mandley 8 pass from DeBerg (Lowery kick), 3:59 3rd.
Kansas City—Maas 4 fumble return (Lowery kick), 11:09 3rd.
Pittsburgh—Lipps 64 pass from Brister (Anderson kick), 14:50 3rd.

TEAM STATISTICS

	Kansas City	Pittsburgh
First downs	23	19
Rushes-Yards	28-120	31-80
Passing yards	318	232
Passes	24-36-2	17-27-0
Sacked-Yards lost	2-20	2-21
Punts	4-41.8	3-39.3
Fumbles-Lost	2-0	1-1
Penalties-Yards	10-79	7-50
Time of possession	35:05	24:55

Attendance—54,194.

INDIVIDUAL STATISTICS

Rushing—Kansas City, Okoye 23-101, Saxon 2-10, Heard 1-6, DeBerg 2-3; Pittsburgh, Hoge 15-65, W. Williams 9-26, Carter 3-7, Wallace 1-0, Brister 2-minus 2, Stone 1-minus 16.

Passing—Kansas City, DeBerg 24-36-2—338; Pittsburgh, Brister 17-27-0—253.

Receiving—Kansas City, Paige 7-163, McNair 4-73, Mandley 4-35, Harry 2-15, Heard 2-8, Saxon 2-8, Roberts 1-25, Carson 1-7, Okoye 1-4; Pittsburgh, Lipps 7-130, Hoge 3-32, W. Williams 3-24, Hill 2-48, Stone 1-5, Carter 1-4.

Kickoff Returns—Kansas City, McNair 2-38, Copeland 2-45; Pittsburgh, Woodson 1-16.

Punt Returns—Kansas City, Mandley 2-28; Pittsburgh, Woodson 1-1.

Interceptions—Pittsburgh, Little 1-6, Woodson 1-0.

Punting—Kansas City, Goodburn 4-41.8; Pittsburgh, Newsome 3-39.3.

Field Goals—Kansas City, Lowery 1-1; Pittsburgh, Anderson 3-4 (missed: 41).

Sacks—Kansas City, Thomas, Smith; Pittsburgh, Willis 2.

Rams-Bears
SUNDAY, OCTOBER 29
SCORE BY PERIODS

Los Angeles Rams	0	3	0	7	10
Chicago	0	3	7	10	20

SCORING

Los Angeles—Field goal Lansford 45, 8:57 2nd.
Chicago—Field goal Butler 35, 13:09 2nd.
Chicago—Muster 1 run (Butler kick), 14:21 3rd.
Chicago—Harbaugh 1 run (Butler kick), 3:49 4th.
Los Angeles—Bell 1 run (Lansford kick), 8:57 4th.
Chicago—Field goal Butler 46, 12:13 4th.

TEAM STATISTICS

	Los Angeles	Chicago
First downs	18	21
Rushes-Yards	24-84	39-148
Passing yards	168	170
Passes	13-35-2	14-29-0
Sacked-Yards lost	3-17	3-16
Punts	7-44.4	8-45.1
Fumbles-Lost	1-1	1-0
Penalties-Yards	7-53	6-59
Time of possession	24:26	35:34

Attendance—65,506.

INDIVIDUAL STATISTICS

Rushing—Los Angeles, Bell 12-32, Delpino 4-25, Green 5-14, Gary 3-13; Chicago, Anderson 22-80, Muster 9-33, Harbaugh 5-31, McKinnon 1-3, Gentry 1-1, Sanders 1-0.

Passing—Los Angeles, Everett 13-35-2—185, Chicago, Tomczak 4-16-0—29, Harbaugh 10-13-0—157.

Receiving—Los Angeles, Ellard 5-100, McGee 3-29,

Delpino 2-26, Holohan 1-13, Johnson 1-9, Bell 1-8; Chicago, Muster 4-44, Davis 2-49, McKinnon 2-46, Thornton 2-19, Morris 2-11, Anderson 1-11, Boso 1-6.

Kickoff Returns—Los Angeles, Ron Brown 4-84; Chicago, Gentry 2-48, Sanders 1-21.

Punt Returns—Los Angeles, Hicks 4-39, Ellard 2-20; Chicago, Green 1-0.

Interceptions—Chicago, Paul 1-20, Woolford 1-0.

Punting—Los Angeles, Hatcher 7-44.4; Chicago, Buford 8-45.1.

Field Goals—Los Angeles, Lansford 1-1; Chicago, Butler 2-2.

Sacks—Los Angeles, Wilcher 2, Greene; Chicago, McMichael, Armstrong, Dent.

Eagles - Broncos
SUNDAY, OCTOBER 29
SCORE BY PERIODS

Philadelphia	14	0	7	7—28
Denver	0	7	10	7—24

SCORING

Philadelphia—Byars 16 run (Zendejas kick), 6:29 1st.
Philadelphia—Carter 5 pass from Cunningham (Zendejas kick), 12:00 1st.
Denver—Elway 10 run (Treadwell kick), 11:16 2nd.
Philadelphia—Giles 66 pass from Cunningham (Zendejas kick), 4:36 3rd.
Denver—Johnson 13 pass from Elway (Treadwell kick), 8:45 3rd.
Denver—Field goal Treadwell 18, 13:56 3rd.
Denver—Bratton 4 pass from Elway (Treadwell kick), 5:42 4th.
Philadelphia—Byars 1 run (Zendejas kick), 9:35 4th.

TEAM STATISTICS

	Philadelphia	Denver
First downs	17	22
Rushes-Yards	45-215	20-104
Passing yards	98	216
Passes	11-21-1	19-39-3
Sacked-Yards lost	4-28	7-62
Punts	8-41.0	5-47.0
Fumbles-Lost	4-1	6-3
Penalties-Yards	8-67	4-35
Time of possession	32.57	27:03
Attendance—75,065.		

INDIVIDUAL STATISTICS

Rushing—Philadelphia, Byars 23-93, Cunningham 6-57, Toney 8-38, Higgs 4-17, Sherman 2-4, Drummond 1-3, Johnson 1-3; Denver, Elway 4-45, Humphrey 12-44, Bratton 3-10, Sewell 1-5.

Passing—Philadelphia, Cunningham 11-20-0—126, Cavanaugh 0-1-1—0; Denver, Elway 19-39-3—278.

Receiving—Philadelphia, Byars 3-22, Carter 2-9, Sherman 2-8, Giles 1-66, Garrity 1-21, Toney 1-1, Higgs 1-minus 1; Denver, Johnson 9-148, Jackson 4-71, Sewell 3-26, Young 1-18, Mobley 1-11, Bratton 1-4.

Kickoff Returns—Philadelphia, Sherman 3-33, Williams 1-24; Denver, Bell 4-101.

Punt Returns—Philadelphia, Williams 3-45; Denver, Bell 4-12, Corrington 1-0.

Interceptions—Philadelphia, Jenkins 1-18, Allen 1-3, Everett 1-17; Denver, Dennison 1-1.

Punting—Philadelphia, Teltschik 8-41.0; Denver, Horan 5-47.0.

Field Goals—Philadelphia, Zendejas 0-1 (missed: 41); Denver, Treadwell 1-1.

Sacks—Philadelphia, Pitts, White 1½, Simmons 3½, Brown; Denver, Fletcher, Carreker, Holmes 2.

Dolphins - Bills
SUNDAY, OCTOBER 29
SCORE BY PERIODS

Miami	3	0	7	7—17
Buffalo	0	21	0	10—31

SCORING

Miami—Field goal Stoyanovich 45, 6:27 1st.
Buffalo—Kinnebrew 1 run (Norwood kick), 0:02 2nd.
Buffalo—Thomas 30 run (Norwood kick), 5:55 2nd.
Buffalo—Beebe 63 pass from Reich (Norwood kick), 13:21 2nd.
Miami—Clayton 44 pass from Marino (Stoyanovich kick), 7:41 3rd.
Buffalo—Field goal Norwood 45, 4:38 4th.
Buffalo—Jackson 40 interception return (Norwood kick), 12:00 4th.
Miami—A. Brown 44 pass from Secules (Stoyanovich kick), 13:10 4th.

TEAM STATISTICS

	Miami	Buffalo
First downs	19	18
Rushes-Yards	18-65	51-280
Passing yards	348	114
Passes	26-47-3	6-9-0
Sacked-Yards lost	2-16	2-9
Punts	4-45.3	5-35.2
Fumbles-Lost	0-0	1-1
Penalties-Yards	5-29	8-70
Time of possession	25:19	34:41
Attendance—80,208.		

INDIVIDUAL STATISTICS

Rushing—Miami, Smith 15-36, Davenport 2-12, Secules 1-17; Buffalo, Thomas 27-148, Kinnebrew 21-121, K. Davis 2-9, Harmon 1-2.

Passing—Miami, Marino 20-36-3—255, Secules 6-11-0—109; Buffalo, Reich 6-9-0—123.

Receiving—Miami, Clayton 7-122, A. Brown 5-105, Banks 4-39, Duper 4-30, Jensen 3-19, Edmunds 1-30, Smith 1-12, Davenport 1-7; Buffalo, McKeller 2-36, Thomas 2-21, Beebe 1-63, Johnson 1-3.

Kickoff Returns—Miami, Reaves 4-66, A. Brown 1-0, Goode 1-8; Buffalo, Beebe 1-21, K. Davis 1-20.

Punt Returns—Buffalo, Sutton 2-20.

Interceptions—Buffalo, Jackson 2-43, Bennett 1-6.

Punting—Miami, Roby 4-45.3; Buffalo, Kidd 5-35.2.

Field Goals—Miami, Stoyanovich 1-1; Buffalo, Norwood 1-2 (missed: 43).

Sacks—Miami, Cross; Buffalo, Bennett, Wright.

Patriots - Colts
SUNDAY, OCTOBER 29
SCORE BY PERIODS

New England	3	0	7	10	3—23
Indianapolis	10	0	0	10	0—20

SCORING

New England—Field goal Davis 47, 2:02 1st.
Indianapolis—Rison 22 pass from Trudeau (Biasucci kick), 6:39 1st.
Indianapolis—Field goal Biasucci 32, 13:56 1st.
New England—Jones 8 pass from Grogan (Davis kick), 12:35 3rd.
New England—Field goal Davis 48, 2:35 4th.
Indianapolis—Boyer 7 pass from Trudeau (Biasucci kick), 7:12 4th.
New England—Stephens 1 run (Davis kick), 12:38 4th.
Indianapolis—Field goal Biasucci 39, 14:09 4th.
New England—Field goal Davis 51, 9:57 OT.

TEAM STATISTICS

	New England	Indianapolis
First downs	30	19
Rushes-Yards	39-120	27-130
Passing yards	328	227
Passes	28-46-2	16-33-0
Sacked-Yards lost	3-27	3-20
Punts	5-45.8	6-43.5
Fumbles-Lost	2-0	4-2
Penalties-Yards	5-45	9-61
Time of possession	43:05	26:52
Attendance—59,256.		

INDIVIDUAL STATISTICS

Rushing—New England, Stephens 23-68, Perryman 12-50, Grogan 3-6, Tatupu 1-minus 4; Indianapolis, Dickerson 14-60, Bentley 6-39, Hunter 3-18, Trudeau 4-13.

Passing—New England, Grogan 28-46-2—355; Indianapolis, Trudeau 16-33-0—247.

Receiving—New England, Sievers 7-113, Perryman 6-27, Jones 5-46, Martin 4-64, Dykes 2-28, Stephens 2-18, Morgan 1-50, Tatupu 1-9; Indianapolis, Rison 6-129, Bentley 4-28, Brooks 2-52, Verdin 2-26, Boyer 1-7, Beach 1-5.

Kickoff Returns—New England, Martin 3-55, Rice 3-73; Indianapolis, Pruitt 4-117, Verdin 1-13.

Punt Returns—New England, Martin 4-15; Indianapolis, Verdin 3-24.

Interceptions—Indianapolis, Prior 2-6.

Punting—New England, Feagles 5-45.8; Indianapolis, Stark 6-43.5.

Field Goals—New England, Davis 3-5 (missed: 38, 46); Indianapolis, Biasucci 2-2.

Sacks—New England, Williams, Jeter, Brown; Indianapolis, Thompson, Bickett, Hand.

Buccaneers-Bengals
SUNDAY, OCTOBER 29
SCORE BY PERIODS

Tampa Bay	7	9	0	7—23
Cincinnati	7	14	21	14—56

SCORING

Tampa Bay—Hill 3 pass from Testaverde (Igwebuike kick), 4:30 1st.

Cincinnati—Holman 1 pass from Esiason (Breech kick), 8:49 1st.

Cincinnati—Ball 1 run (Breech kick), 0:57 2nd.

Tampa Bay—Safety, Esiason ran out of end zone, 6:23 2nd.

Tampa Bay—Carrier 17 pass from Testaverde (Igwebuike kick), 10:23 2nd.

Cincinnati—Brown 8 pass from Esiason (Breech kick), 14:43 2nd.

Cincinnati—Brooks 4 run (Breech kick), 2:02 3rd.

Cincinnati—McGee 14 pass from Esiason (Breech kick), 6:17 3rd.

Cincinnati—Holman 9 pass from Esiason (Breech kick), 13:18 3rd.

Cincinnati—Brown 18 pass from Esiason (Breech kick), 2:47 4th.

Cincinnati—McGee 46 pass from Wilhelm (Breech kick), 7:32 4th.

Tampa Bay—Hill 2 pass from Testaverde (Igwebuike kick), 10:08 4th.

TEAM STATISTICS

	Tampa Bay	Cincinnati
First downs	21	30
Rushes-Yards	27-139	33-188
Passing yards	336	294
Passes	23-39-3	22-34-0
Sacked-Yards lost	0-0	1-1
Punts	3-35.7	1-37.0
Fumbles-Lost	1-1	2-2
Penalties-Yards	5-106	2-10
Time of possession	28:56	31:04
Attendance—57,225.		

INDIVIDUAL STATISTICS

Rushing—Tampa Bay, Tate 17-84, Wilder 9-54, Testaverde 1-1; Cincinnati, Brooks 17-131, Ball 9-23, Taylor 3-18, McGee 1-25, Jennings 3-minus 9.

Passing—Tampa Bay, Testaverde 23-39-3—336; Cincinnati, Esiason 17-28-0—197, Wilhelm 5-6-0—98.

Receiving—Tampa Bay, Carrier 7-100, Hill 7-125, Wilder 6-48, Peebles 2-38, Hall 1-25; Cincinnati, McGee 5-127, Holman 5-56, Brown 4-49, Brooks 3-17, Martin 2-19, Taylor 1-13, Jennings 1-9, Riggs 1-5.

Kickoff Returns—Tampa Bay, Elder 3-59, Futrell 1-14, Howard 1-19; Cincinnati, Hillary 2-17.

Punt Returns—Tampa Bay, Drewrey 1-9; Cincinnati, Martin 2-1.

Interceptions—Cincinnati, Kelly 1-25, Bussey 1-0, Thomas 1-0.

Punting—Tampa Bay, Mohr 3-35.7; Cincinnati, Johnson 1-37.0.

Field Goals—None attempted.

Sacks—Tampa Bay, S. Smith.

Lions-Packers
SUNDAY, OCTOBER 29
SCORE BY PERIODS

Detroit	7	3	0	10	0—20
Green Bay	3	7	10	0	3—23

SCORING

Green Bay—Field goal Jacke 49, 7:02 1st.

Detroit—R. Johnson 6 pass from Peete (Murray kick), 14:10 1st.

Detroit—Field goal Murray 42, 4:21 2nd.

Green Bay—Query 4 pass from Majkowski (Jacke kick), 14:45 2nd.

Green Bay—Field goal Jacke 21, 4:14 3rd.

Green Bay—Sharpe 2 pass from Majkowski (Jacke kick), 10:52 3rd.

Detroit—Field goal Murray 46, 3:24 4th.

Detroit—Peete 14 run (Murray kick), 11:01 4th.

Green Bay—Field goal Jacke 38, 2:14 OT.

TEAM STATISTICS

	Detroit	Green Bay
First downs	21	24
Rushes-Yards	34-210	20-76
Passing yards	192	345
Passes	14-28-1	29-45-1
Sacked-Yards lost	1-9	4-22
Punts	4-40.0	4-45.5
Fumbles-Lost	3-1	1-1
Penalties-Yards	9-89	4-30
Time of possession	30:48	31:26
Attendance—53,731.		

INDIVIDUAL STATISTICS

Rushing—Detroit, B. Sanders 30-184, Peete 4-26; Green Bay, Fullwood 12-35, Majkowski 3-25, Woodside 2-10, Haddix 3-6.

Passing—Detroit, Peete 14-28-1—201; Green Bay, Majkowski 29-45-1—367.

Receiving—Detroit, R. Johnson 5-85, McDonald 4-57, Clark 4-42, Stanley 1-17; Green Bay, Sharpe 7-105, Fontenot 7-76, Woodside 5-59, West 3-37, Kemp 2-56, Query 2-18, Fullwood 2-7, Matthews 1-9.

Kickoff Returns—Detroit, B. Sanders 2-41, Stanley 1-14; Green Bay, Workman 4-57.

Punt Returns—Detroit, Stanley 4-56; Green Bay, Query 1-10.

Interceptions—Detroit, Holmes 1-16; Green Bay, Murphy 1-3.

Punting—Detroit, Arnold 4-40.0; Green Bay, Bracken 4-45.5.

Field Goals—Detroit, Murray 2-3 (missed: 34); Green Bay, Jacke 3-4 (missed: 50).

Sacks—Detroit, Spielman, Brooks, E. Williams, Cofer; Green Bay, Noble.

Chargers-Seahawks
SUNDAY, OCTOBER 29
SCORE BY PERIODS

San Diego	0	0	0	7— 7
Seattle	3	0	0	7—10

SCORING

Seattle—Field goal N. Johnson 27, 12:57 1st.

San Diego—Cox 14 pass from McMahon (Bahr kick), 13:07 4th.

Seattle—Blades 21 pass from Krieg (N. Johnson kick), 14:20 4th.

TEAM STATISTICS

	San Diego	Seattle
First downs	11	23
Rushes-Yards	17-92	27-70
Passing yards	103	269
Passes	15-29-1	27-49-2
Sacked-Yards lost	2-20	5-42
Punts	37.6	4-42.3
Fumbles-Lost	2-0	1-0
Penalties-Yards	13-76	3-25
Time of possession	23:38	36:22

Attendance—59,691.

INDIVIDUAL STATISTICS

Rushing—San Diego, Butts 7-44, Nelson 3-31, Spencer 6-17, Tolliver 1-0; Seattle, Warner 15-40, Williams 11-27, Blades 1-3.

Passing—San Diego, McMahon 9-12-0—82, Tolliver 6-17-1—41; Seattle, Krieg 27-49-2—311.

Receiving—San Diego, Walker 3-36, Holland 2-20, Cox 2-15, Butts 2-11, Spencer 2-8, Nelson 2-7, A. Miller 1-22, McMahon 1-4; Seattle, Blades 10-117, Williams 6-53, Largent 2-32, Skansi 2-32, Clark 2-31, Tyler 1-12, Chadwick 1-11, Harris 1-11, Jones 1-8, Warner 1-4.

Kickoff Returns—San Diego, A. Miller 1-26; Seattle, Jefferson 1-16, Harris 1-14.

Punt Returns—Seattle, Jefferson 3-28.

Interceptions—San Diego, Patterson 1-10, Smith 1-9; Seattle, Robinson 1-0.

Punting—San Diego, Ilesic 8-37.6; Seattle, Rodriguez 4-42.3.

Field Goals—San Diego, none attempted; Seattle, N. Johnson 1-4 (missed: 53, 49, 52).

Sacks—San Diego, Grossman 2, Williams, O'Neal 2; Seattle, Porter, Green.

Falcons-Saints
SUNDAY, OCTOBER 29
SCORE BY PERIODS

Atlanta	0	0	10	3	—13
New Orleans	7	3	3	7	—20

SCORING

New Orleans—Hilliard 21 pass from Hebert (Andersen kick), 7:19 1st.

New Orleans—Field goal Andersen 32, 7:57 2nd.

Atlanta—Collins 18 pass from Miller (McFadden kick), 6:19 3rd.

New Orleans—Field goal Andersen 44, 11:41 3rd.

Atlanta—Field goal McFadden 41, 13:07 3rd.

Atlanta—Field goal McFadden 48, 10:54 4th.

New Orleans—Hilliard 1 run (Andersen kick), 12:48 4th.

TEAM STATISTICS

	Atlanta	New Orleans
First downs	11	17
Rushes-Yards	19-57	34-131
Passing yards	91	261
Passes	15-32-0	18-30-1
Sacked-Yards lost	6-44	2-11
Punts	6-39.3	5-33.4
Fumbles-Lost	3-3	2-1
Penalties-Yards	4-22	8-55
Time of possession	24:21	35:39

Attendance—65,153.

INDIVIDUAL STATISTICS

Rushing—Atlanta, Settle 12-34, Jones 6-23, Lang 1-0; New Orleans, Hilliard 25-93, Heyward 4-22, Hebert 4-14, Frazier 1-2.

Passing—Atlanta, Miller 15-32-0—135; New Orleans, Hebert 18-30-1—272.

Receiving—Atlanta, Dixon 4-37, Settle 4-23, Collins 2-29, Heller 2-20, Jones 2-9, Lang 1-17; New Orleans, Hilliard 7-97, Hill 4-54, E. Martin 2-89, Turner 2-23, Scales 1-4, Heyward 1-4, Frazier 1-1.

Kickoff Returns—Atlanta, Sanders 3-96, Paterra 1-17; New Orleans, Atkins 3-54, Johnson 1-15.

Punt Returns—Atlanta, Sanders 2-10; New Orleans, Harris 3-8, Hill 1-10.

Interceptions—Atlanta, Dimry 1-40.

Punting—Atlanta, Fulhage 6-39.3; New Orleans, Barnhardt 5-33.4.

Field Goals—Atlanta, McFadden 2-2; New Orleans, Andersen 2-3 (missed: 23).

Sacks—Atlanta, Cotton, Green; New Orleans, Swilling 3, Warren 1½, Wilks, Jackson ½.

Oilers-Browns
SUNDAY, OCTOBER 29
SCORE BY PERIODS

Houston	7	3	7	0	—17
Cleveland	0	0	21	7	—28

SCORING

Houston—Jeffires 13 pass from Moon (Zendejas kick), 8:48 1st.

Houston—Field goal Zendejas 23, 10:43 2nd.

Cleveland—Kosar 5 run (Bahr kick), 6:33 3rd.

Cleveland—Slaughter 80 pass from Kosar (Bahr kick), 9:49 3rd.

Houston—Rozier 1 run (Zendejas kick), 12:56 3rd.

Cleveland—Slaughter 77 pass from Kosar (Bahr kick), 13:51 3rd.

Cleveland—Langhorne 32 pass from Metcalf (Bahr kick), 1:33 4th.

TEAM STATISTICS

	Houston	Cleveland
First downs	16	18
Rushes-Yards	25-89	31-103
Passing yards	210	280
Passes	15-25-0	15-20-2
Sacked-Yards lost	3-31	2-14
Punts	6-44.0	2-46.5
Fumbles-Lost	2-0	0-0
Penalties-Yards	9-66	5-45
Time of possession	30:19	29:41

Attendance—78,765.

INDIVIDUAL STATISTICS

Rushing—Houston, Highsmith 12-58, Rozier 6-13, Pinkett 5-12, Moon 2-6; Cleveland, Metcalf 17-48, Manoa 7-27, Langhorne 1-18, Redden 2-10, Kosar 4-0.

Passing—Houston, Moon 15-25-0—241; Cleveland, Kosar 14-19-2—262, Metcalf 1-1-0—32.

Receiving—Houston, Hill 3-67, Givins 3-42, Jeffires 3-30, Duncan 2-61, Pinkett 2-29, Rozier 1-6, Highsmith 1-6; Cleveland, Metcalf 6-46, Slaughter 4-184, Langhorne 4-59, Manoa 1-5.

Kickoff Returns—Houston, T. Johnson 1-25, White 3-59, K. Johnson 1-0; Cleveland, E. Johnson 1-8, K. Jones 3-17.

Punt Returns—None.

Interceptions—Houston, McDowell 1-13, Brown 1-13.

Punting—Houston, Greg Montgomery 6-44.0; Cleveland, Wagner 2-46.5.

Field Goals—Houston, Zendejas 1-1; Cleveland, none attempted.

Sacks—Houston, Childress, D. Smith; Cleveland, Stewart, Gash 2.

49ers-Jets
SUNDAY, OCTOBER 29
SCORE BY PERIODS

San Francisco	7	13	3	0	—23
New York Jets	0	7	3	0	—10

SCORING

San Francisco—Jones 10 pass from Young (Cofer kick), 13:05 1st.

New York—McMillan 45 fumble return (Leahy kick), 4:15 2nd.

San Francisco—Rice 45 pass from Bono (Cofer kick), 6:43 2nd.

San Francisco—Field goal Cofer 25, 11:46 2nd.
San Francisco—Field goal Cofer 41, 15:00 2nd.
New York—Field goal Leahy 24, 3:39 3rd.
San Francisco—Field goal Cofer 40, 10:34 3rd.

TEAM STATISTICS

	San Francisco	New York
First downs	20	19
Rushes-Yards	35-159	22-130
Passing yards	240	121
Passes	17-25-0	25-36-0
Sacked-Yards lost	1-4	9-82
Punts	3-40.3	5-43.8
Fumbles-Lost	5-1	3-2
Penalties-Yards	8-49	7-60
Time of possession	29:46	30:14
Attendance—62,805.		

INDIVIDUAL STATISTICS

Rushing—San Francisco, Craig 17-78, Rathman 9-46, Flagler 4-23, Young 5-12; New York, Hector 13-77, McNeil 4-38, Vick 3-11, O'Brien 2-4.

Passing—San Francisco, Young 13-20-0—182, Bono 4-5-0—62; New York, O'Brien 25-36-0—203.

Receiving—San Francisco, Craig 6-85, Rice 5-95, Jones 2-24, Taylor 2-16, Rathman 1-13, Wilson 1-11; New York, Neubert 4-40, Walker 4-25, Burkett 3-38, Townsell 3-23, Hector 3-21, Shuler 2-24, Dunn 2-13, Vick 2-11, McNeil 2-8.

Kickoff Returns—San Francisco, Tillman 1-22, Flagler 1-18; New York, Townsell 3-48.

Punt Returns—San Francisco, Taylor 3-10.

Interceptions—None.

Punting—San Francisco, Helton 3-40.3; New York, Prokop 5-43.8.

Field Goals—San Francisco, Cofer 3-3; New York, Leahy 1-1.

Sacks—San Francisco, Fagan 2, Holt, Roberts 2, Haley 3, Stubbs; New York, Lyons.

Redskins-Raiders
SUNDAY, OCTOBER 29
SCORE BY PERIODS

Washington	7	3	7	7—24
Los Angeles Raiders	14	3	20	0—37

SCORING

Los Angeles—Fernandez 18 pass from Beuerlein (Jaeger kick), 5:32 1st.
Los Angeles—Fernandez 8 pass from Beuerlein (Jaeger kick), 8:41 1st.
Washington—Howard 99 kickoff return (Lohmiller kick), 8:58 1st.
Los Angeles—Field goal Jaeger 26, 0:57 2nd.
Washington—Field goal Lohmiller 43, 15:00 2nd.
Los Angeles—Jackson 73 run (Jaeger kick), 1:02 3rd.
Los Angeles—Field goal Jaeger 29, 3:52 3rd.
Los Angeles—Field goal Jaeger 37, 7:18 3rd.
Los Angeles—Anderson 45 interception return (Jaeger kick), 8:48 3rd.
Washington—Clark 27 pass from Rypien (Lohmiller kick), 11:57 3rd.
Washington—Sanders 14 pass from Humphries (Lohmiller kick), 12:54 4th.

TEAM STATISTICS

	Washington	Los Angeles
First downs	23	18
Rushes-Yards	14-21	38-187
Passing yards	420	155
Passes	32-63-4	12-31-2
Sacked-Yards lost	7-35	0-0
Punts	4-47.5	5-40.8
Fumbles-Lost	8-4	3-2
Penalties-Yards	12-135	7-75
Time of possession	27:29	32:31
Attendance—52,781.		

INDIVIDUAL STATISTICS

Rushing—Washington, Byner 6-9, Humphries 1-9, Rypien 1-4, Morris 6-minus 1; Los Angeles, Jackson 19-144, Smith 7-28, Mueller 6-14, Beuerlein 1-6, Porter 3-4, Schroeder 2-minus 9.

Passing—Washington, Rypien 27-53-3—364, Humphries 5-10-1—91; Los Angeles, Beuerlein 11-22-1—154, Schroeder 1-8-1—1, Gossett 0-1-0—0.

Receiving—Washington, Sanders 12-158, Clark 8-145, Byner 5-43, Warren 3-32, Monk 2-29, J. Johnson 1-39, Morris 1-9; Los Angeles, Fernandez 4-58, Gault 3-63, Smith 3-15, Alexander 1-14, Dyal 1-5.

Kickoff Returns—Washington, Howard 4-130, A. Johnson 2-30; Los Angeles, Edmonds 1-20, Lee 1-0.

Punt Returns—Washington, Howard 3-9; Los Angeles, Edmonds 3-35.

Interceptions—Washington, Wilburn 1-0, Davis 1-15; Los Angeles, Anderson 2-68, Robinson 1-25, Benson 1-19.

Punting—Washington, Mojsiejenko 4-47.5; Los Angeles, Gossett 5-40.8.

Field Goals—Washington, Lohmiller 1-1; Los Angeles, Jaeger 3-4 (missed: 46).

Sacks—Los Angeles, Pickel 2, Townsend 3, Long 1½, Wise ½.

Vikings-Giants
MONDAY, OCTOBER 30
SCORE BY PERIODS

Minnesota	7	0	0	7—14
New York Giants	0	0	17	7—24

SCORING

Minnesota—Walker 8 pass from Kramer (Karlis kick), 9:15 1st.
New York—Johnson 39 interception return (Allegre kick), 3:56 3rd.
New York—Field goal Allegre 39, 12:47 3rd.
New York—Manuel 11 pass from Hostetler (Allegre kick), 13:49 3rd.
New York—Anderson 2 run (Allegre kick), 0:12 4th.
Minnesota—Fenney 1 run (Karlis kick), 10:57 4th.

TEAM STATISTICS

	Minnesota	New York
First downs	20	13
Rushes-Yards	24-110	42-119
Passing yards	140	55
Passes	18-34-2	6-14-0
Sacked-Yards lost	6-46	5-32
Punts	5-43.2	8-40.8
Fumbles-Lost	3-2	2-0
Penalties-Yards	9-50	9-75
Time of possession	28:32	31:28
Attendance—76,041.		

INDIVIDUAL STATISTICS

Rushing—Minnesota, Walker 12-68, Fenney 7-24, Anderson 3-16, Dozier 2-2; New York, Anderson 29-66, Hostetler 4-21, Rouson 2-15, Tillman 5-13, Meggett 1-5, Carthon 1-minus 1.

Passing—Minnesota, Kramer 10-18-2—127, Wilson 8-16-0—59; New York, Simms 0-1-0—0, Hostetler 6-13-0—87.

Receiving—Minnesota, Jordan 5-73, Walker 4-26, Carter 3-30, Fenney 3-23, Jones 2-23, Anderson 1-11; New York, Manuel 4-47, Meggett 1-23, Anderson 1-17.

Kickoff Returns—Minnesota, Dozier 2-76, Anderson 3-36; New York, Meggett 1-17.

Punt Returns—Minnesota, Lewis 2-8; New York, Meggett 4-8.

Interceptions—New York, Kinard 1-16, Johnson 1-39.

Punting—Minnesota, Scribner 5-43.2; New York, Landeta 8-40.8.

Field Goals—Minnesota, Karlis 0-1 (missed: 49); New York, Allegre 1-1.

Sacks—Minnesota, Noga 2, Millard, Thomas, Berry; New York, Taylor 2½, Marshall 2, Banks 1½.

NINTH WEEK

RESULTS OF WEEK 9
Sunday, November 5

Atlanta 30, Buffalo 28 at Atl.
Cleveland 42, Tampa Bay 31 at T.B.
Dallas 13, Washington 3 at Wash.
Denver 34, Pittsburgh 7 at Den.
Green Bay 14, Chicago 13 at G.B.
Houston 35, Detroit 31 at Hous.
Kansas City 20, Seattle 10 at K.C.
L.A. Raiders 28, Cincinnati 7 at L.A.
Miami 19, Indianapolis 13 at Mia.
Minnesota 23, L.A. Rams 21 (OT) at Minn.
N.Y. Giants 20, Phoenix 13 at Phoe.
N.Y. Jets 27, New England 26 at N.E.
San Diego 20, Philadelphia 17 at S.D.

Monday, November 6

San Francisco 31, New Orleans 13 at S.F.

Few things upset National Football League coaches more than penalties, which inevitably seem to stall a drive, end a possession or keep an opponent's offensive march alive.

It is rare, however, when such infractions actually work to the benefit of the team that commits them.

That was the case, however, for the San Diego Chargers in their Week 9 interconference game against the Philadelphia Eagles.

The game was tied, 17-17, when San Diego kicker Chris Bahr's 44-yard field-goal attempt sailed wide left with four seconds to play. But Chargers offensive lineman James FitzPatrick moved before the snap, resulting in a dead-ball foul against the Chargers.

After the obligatory five-yard markoff, Bahr made good on a second chance, splitting the uprights from 49 yards to give San Diego a 20-17 victory.

"That's the first time I can ever remember a penalty helping me," said Chargers Coach Dan Henning, whose team snapped a four-game losing streak.

"When I looked up and saw the ball hook (on the first attempt), I knew it would be a dead-ball foul," FitzPatrick said. "I just hoped for the best on our second chance."

The Chargers should not have needed a late field goal to win. They led, 17-7, after three periods before giving up 10 points early in the fourth. The Eagles' tying touchdown—a three-yard run by Keith Byars with 10:11 left—came three plays after Philadelphia cornerback Eric Allen intercepted a Jim McMahon pass, returning it 18 yards to the San Diego 23.

Then, on their final possession, the Chargers got into field-goal position with the help of a 49-yard completion from Jim McMahon to Wayne Walker that took San Diego from its 24-yard line to the Eagles' 27.

"I had messed up earlier in the game and I

needed to do something," said Walker, a rookie from Texas Tech who had fumbled a punt in the second quarter. "I just outran the guy (cornerback Izel Jenkins) and was able to make the catch. It was a perfect throw."

Which led to a less-than-perfect ending.

"I saw my whole life flash in front of my face," said FitzPatrick, who knew he had moved before the snap on Bahr's first attempt. "The first thing that goes through your mind is, 'Gee, I hope nobody saw it.'"

Since Bahr missed the kick, though, the Chargers were fortunate that the officials did see the infraction. Was the 36-year-old Bahr, San Diego's oldest player, nervous about getting a reprieve?

"Sure, I was nervous," he said. "Anybody who says they aren't in that situation is a liar. But I wasn't scared. And there's a difference."

Bahr's game-winning kick was pivotal, of course, but the place-kicker who grabbed the most headlines in Week 9 was Minnesota's Rich Karlis, who booted seven field goals in the Vikings' 23-21 overtime victory against the Los Angeles Rams. Karlis' seven field goals tied the NFL single-game record set by Jim Bakken of the St. Louis Cardinals on September 24, 1967.

As it turned out, Karlis tied the record in an overtime game that was decided by a safety—not a field goal or touchdown. The game-winning points came at 2:14 of the extra period when Minnesota's Mike Merriweather blocked a punt by Dale Hatcher through the back of the Rams' end zone. It marked the first time since the NFL instituted overtime play in 1974 that a game decided in an extra session had been won via a safety.

Karlis' big day was made possible, in large part, by his teammates' inability to score touchdowns. His first six field goals came after Viking drives stalled at the Rams' 3-, 7-, 5-, 8-, 12- and 19-yard lines. His longest was a 40-yarder with eight seconds left in regulation time that sent the game into overtime.

The Rams, who blew a 21-18 lead in the final minute of regulation time, suffered their fourth consecutive loss after starting the season with five straight victories.

Another team struggling to turn around its fortunes was the New York Jets, who snapped a five-game losing streak with a 27-26 AFC Eastern Division victory over New England. The Jets' winning points came on Pat Leahy's 23-yard field goal as time expired. Quarterback Ken O'Brien completed four consecutive passes for 72 yards in the final minute to set it up.

The Patriots appeared headed to their fifth straight victory in the division series when quarterback Marc Wilson's 11-yard touchdown pass to rookie Hart Lee Dykes gave them a

Minnesota's Rich Karlis kicks his record-tying seventh field goal against the Los Angeles Rams.

26-24 advantage with 1:03 left.

It was the second touchdown pass of the fourth quarter for Wilson, a former Los Angeles Raider who was playing in his first NFL game in almost two years. Wilson, who last played in the league in December 1987, replaced Steve Grogan early in the second half after Grogan was knocked out of the game on a late hit by the Jets' Ron Stallworth.

The Patriots scored three touchdowns and one field goal on their five possessions with Wilson at the helm.

Wilson, however, was no match for O'Brien, who snapped out of a slump by completing 22 of 29 passes for 386 yards without an interception. O'Brien, who had not thrown a touchdown pass in the Jets' losing streak, fired two scoring passes against New England, including a 35-yarder to JoJo Townsell to give New York a 14-3 halftime lead.

A 50-yard field goal by Paul McFadden with two seconds left capped a wild final two minutes and gave the Atlanta Falcons a 30-28 victory over the Buffalo Bills. McFadden's winning kick was his second field goal of 50 yards

or more in the game and came one play after Chris Miller and Stacey Bailey had combined on a 41-yard pass play to the Buffalo 33-yard line.

The Falcons appeared to be in control after taking a 27-21 lead on a three-yard touchdown run by rookie Keith Jones with 1:22 to play. But Bills rookie Don Beebe returned the ensuing kickoff 85 yards to the Atlanta 8, setting up Larry Kinnebrew's one-yard touchdown run with 29 seconds left.

The Falcons, who trailed by one point after Kinnebrew's touchdown and the conversion kick, began their game-winning drive at their 26 with 24 seconds left.

Another wild finish took place in Green Bay, where the Packers edged the Bears, 14-13, on a disputed 14-yard touchdown pass from Don Majkowski to Sterling Sharpe on fourth down with 32 seconds left. Line judge Jim Quirk ruled that Majkowski had illegally crossed the line of scrimmage before releasing the football. However, after an instant-replay review that lasted nearly five minutes, replay official Bill Parkinson overruled Quirk's call, saying that regardless of where the Packers' quarterback was at the time of his release, the ball itself was behind the line.

That touchdown capped a 73-yard drive and helped turn Majkowski from goat to hero. The third-year player from Virginia threw an interception and fumbled to kill two Green Bay possessions deep in Chicago territory early in the fourth quarter. Bears linebacker Ron Rivera was credited with the takeaways in both instances.

The Kansas City Chiefs swept their AFC Western Division series with Seattle for the first time since 1981 with a 20-10 victory over the Seahawks at Arrowhead Stadium. The Chiefs had beaten the Seahawks, 20-16, four weeks earlier in Seattle.

Just as in the first game between the teams, the key player was Chiefs running back Christian Okoye, who rushed a team-record 37 times for 126 yards and one touchdown. His eight-yard touchdown run in the first period capped an 81-yard drive to tie the game at 7-7.

The Seahawks' only touchdown came on Nesby Glasgow's 38-yard fumble return 70 seconds into the game.

Okoye, who had rushed for 156 yards against Seattle a month earlier, set a Kansas City record with his sixth 100-yard rushing game of the season. Okoye was the NFL's rushing leader with 936 yards after nine weeks.

After failing to win a game in the first half of the season, the Dallas Cowboys started the second half with a surprising 13-3 victory over the Washington Redskins at RFK Stadium. The site of the Cowboys' last victory? RFK Stadium, Week 15 of the 1988 season.

The Cowboys' star was running back Paul Palmer, a former No. 1 draft choice of Kansas

Rookie Sammie Smith rushed for 123 yards in Miami's 19-13 victory over Indianapolis.

City who had been acquired by Dallas earlier in the season on waivers from Detroit. Palmer rushed for 110 yards and scored the game's only touchdown on a two-yard run in the third quarter. The touchdown broke a 3-3 tie and came two plays after Palmer had run 47 yards to the Washington 6-yard line.

For the first time in four seasons, the Miami Dolphins compiled more yards rushing than passing en route to a 19-13 AFC Eastern Division victory over Indianapolis. Rookie Sammie Smith rushed for 123 yards to lead a running game that rolled up 159 yards on 37 attempts. Dolphins quarterback Dan Marino attempted only 26 passes, completing 14 for 149 yards.

Smith, a first-round draft pick from Florida State, had rushed for just 240 yards in the Dolphins' first eight games. He became the first Miami player since 1987 to rush for 100 yards.

The Dolphins, who entered the game with the league's second-worst rushing attack, used their ground game to put together touchdown drives of 70 and 80 yards in the second and third quarters that consumed more than six minutes each. Marino capped the first drive with a 13-yard pass to Mark Clayton and the second with a 10-yard pitch to Andre Brown.

The best rushing performance of Week 9 came from the Raiders' Bo Jackson, who compiled 159 yards on only 13 attempts in leading the Raiders to a 28-7 victory over Cincinnati. All but 67 of the yards came on a team-record 92-yard touchdown run late in the first period that gave Los Angeles a 14-0 advantage. Jackson earlier had scored the Raiders' first touchdown on a seven-yard run.

Jackson's 92-yarder was one of three big plays that accounted for 239 of the Raiders' 429 total yards. Jay Schroeder hit Willie Gault for a 63-yard gain on the team's first play from scrimmage to set up Jackson's first touchdown. The duo later hooked up on an 84-yard touchdown pass to increase Los Angeles' lead to 28-0 after three quarters.

The Bengals, who scored a team-record eight touchdowns in a victory over Tampa Bay one week earlier, scored their only points on a 34-yard touchdown pass from rookie quarter-

Don Majkowski threw two touchdown passes in Green Bay's 14-13 win over Chicago.

back Erik Wilhelm to Tim McGee in the fourth quarter.

Because of injuries, the Bengals were forced to play most of the game without starting quarterback Boomer Esiason (bruised lung) and starting running backs James Brooks (bruised ribs) and Eric Ball (bruised hip). All three players were injured in the first half.

No team, however, had been decimated by injuries as much as the Phoenix Cardinals, who began the 1989 season without their No. 1 quarterback, Neil Lomax, and then lost 11 more starters due to injury in their first nine games.

Wide receiver J.T. Smith, tackle Luis Sharpe, fullback Ron Wolfley, defensive tackle David Galloway and running backs Tony Baker and Tony Jordan all were injured in a 20-13 loss to the New York Giants in Week 9.

The loss of Smith, who suffered a fractured fibula, was the most serious. The 12-year veteran, who caught two passes against New York to increase his league-leading reception total to 62, would be sidelined for the remainder of the season.

The Giants were able to overcome an injury of their own to win their eighth game in nine weeks. Jeff Hostetler made his second career

start at quarterback after veteran Phil Simms was forced to miss the game because of an ankle sprain.

And Hostetler didn't disappoint. Although he passed for only 177 yards, he ran for the first two touchdowns of his six-year career and beat a safety blitz to complete a 35-yard scoring pass to Stephen Baker in the second quarter. Hostetler's 19-yard touchdown run in the first period capped a nine-play, 71-yard drive to give New York a 7-0 lead.

The Houston Oilers rallied from a 24-14 deficit early in the second half by scoring three straight touchdowns to win, 35-31, in an interconference game against Detroit. Oilers quarterback Warren Moon, who finished with 30 completions in 38 attempts for 345 yards, threw two touchdown passes in the third quarter before scoring the game-winning touchdown on a two-yard run with 3:15 left.

Houston compiled 30 first downs and 455 total yards in the victory and did not punt in a game for the first time in 27 years.

The Denver Broncos rolled up 414 yards in offense and rookie Bobby Humphrey scored two touchdowns in their 34-7 victory over Pittsburgh. The Broncos scored 10 points in the first quarter of this game after being shut out in the first period of their five previous games.

The Pittsburgh offense, on the other hand, never got going. The Steelers had only seven first downs, 170 total yards and scored their only touchdown after linebacker Bryan Hinkle intercepted a John Elway pass at the Denver 22 in the second quarter.

The Cleveland Browns intercepted four Vinny Testaverde passes and returned two of them for touchdowns in a 42-31 interconference victory over the Tampa Bay Buccaneers. Safeties Felix Wright (27 yards) and Thane Gash (15) returned interceptions for touchdowns in a 19-second span of the second quarter to increase Cleveland's lead to 28-7. Frank Minnifield returned an interception 25 yards to set up another Browns touchdown.

Bernie Kosar threw three touchdown passes, including a 24-yarder to rookie Eric Metcalf for Cleveland's first touchdown.

Metcalf, whose father Terry was one of the NFL's best multi-purpose players in the 1970s, had a fabulous game against the Buccaneers. Cleveland's 1989 first-round draft choice from Texas caught seven passes for 52 yards, rushed 17 times for 87 yards and returned three kickoffs for 94 yards.

San Francisco quarterback Joe Montana returned to the lineup after sitting out a week and didn't appear to miss a beat in leading his team to a 31-13 victory over New Orleans in the Monday night game. Montana, who missed the 49ers' Week 8 game against the Jets due to a knee injury, threw three touchdown passes and ran for another to account for all four San Francisco touchdowns against the Saints.

Montana, who completed 22 of 31 passes for 302 yards and no interceptions, threw a 13-yard pass to John Taylor on the 49ers' first play from scrimmage and ended the 78-yard drive with a 32-yard touchdown pass to Jerry Rice. He later threw a two-yard touchdown pass to Rice, a 46-yarder to Taylor and completed San Francisco's scoring with a three-yard touchdown run with 6:43 left.

The 49ers' victory tied them with the Giants for the league's best record at 8-1 and increased their lead in the NFC Western Division to three games over the Los Angeles Rams.

Seahawks-Chiefs
SUNDAY, NOVEMBER 5
SCORE BY PERIODS

Seattle	7	3	0	0—10
Kansas City	7	10	0	3—20

SCORING

Seattle—Glasgow 38 fumble return (N. Johnson kick), 1:10 1st.
Kansas City—Okoye 8 run (Lowery kick), 6:09 1st.
Kansas City—Pelluer 10 run (Lowery kick), 3:11 2nd.
Kansas City—Field goal Lowery 34, 10:27 2nd.
Seattle—Field goal N. Johnson 18, 14:45 2nd.
Kansas City—Field goal Lowery 33, 9:23 4th.

TEAM STATISTICS

	Seattle	Kansas City
First downs	10	18
Rushes-Yards	14-39	57-246
Passing yards	90	69
Passes	14-32-0	7-13-0
Sacked-Yards lost	5-36	1-11
Punts	6-42.3	4-34.8
Fumbles-Lost	8-4	3-2
Penalties-Yards	2-10	8-59
Time of possession	18:44	41:16
Attendance—54,488.		

INDIVIDUAL STATISTICS

Rushing—Seattle, Williams 6-28, Warner 5-11, Krieg 3-0; Kansas City, Okoye 37-126, Pelluer 8-69, Heard 9-43, Saxon 3-8.
Passing—Seattle, Krieg 14-32-0—126; Kansas City, Pelluer 7-13-0—80.
Receiving—Seattle, Blades 4-34, Largent 3-47, Skansi 3-26, Williams 2-12, Feasel 1-5, Warner 1-2; Kansas City, Mandley 2-15, Hayes 1-20, Paige 1-17, McNair 1-12, Harry 1-11, Carson 1-5.
Kickoff Returns—Seattle, Harris 2-36; Kansas City, Copeland 1-18, McNair 1-13.
Punt Returns—Seattle, Jefferson 2-12; Kansas City, Mandley 2-7.
Interceptions—None.
Punting—Seattle, Rodriguez 6-42.3; Kansas City, Goodburn 4-34.8.
Field Goals—Seattle, N. Johnson 1-1; Kansas City, Lowery 2-3 (missed: 32).
Sacks—Seattle, Porter; Kansas City, Cherry, D. Thomas, Smith, Cooper.

Bears-Packers
SUNDAY, NOVEMBER 5
SCORE BY PERIODS

Chicago	3	0	10	0—13
Green Bay	7	0	0	7—14

SCORING

Green Bay—Didier 24 pass from Majkowski (Jacke kick), 3:30 1st.
Chicago—Field goal Butler 25, 11:28 1st.
Chicago—Field goal Butler 37, 5:28 3rd.
Chicago—Muster 2 run (Butler kick), 11:57 3rd.
Green Bay—Sharpe 14 pass from Majkowski (Jacke kick), 14:28 4th.

TEAM STATISTICS

	Chicago	Green Bay
First downs	19	19
Rushes-Yards	34-133	15-69
Passing yards	188	270
Passes	16-30-0	23-40-1
Sacked-Yards lost	2-15	5-29
Punts	6-35.0	6-48.3
Fumbles-Lost	0-0	2-1
Penalties-Yards	7-60	5-45
Time of possession	34:26	25:34
Attendance—56,556.		

INDIVIDUAL STATISTICS

Rushing—Chicago, Anderson 15-58, Harbaugh 3-29, Suhey 4-19, Muster 8-16, Sanders 2-8, Gentry 2-3; Green Bay, Fullwood 10-38, Majkowski 1-14, Woodside 2-11, Haddix 1-3, Workman 1-3.
Passing—Chicago, Harbaugh 16-30-0—203; Green Bay, Majkowski 23-40-1—299.
Receiving—Chicago, Muster 6-68, Boso 3-1, Suhey 2-21, Gentry 1-46, Thornton 1-22, McKinnon 1-19, Davis 1-17, Morris 1-9; Green Bay, Kemp 4-55, Woodside 4-41, West 3-31, Query 3-17, Fullwood 2-76, Sharpe 2-19, Fontenot 2-15, Didier 1-24, Matthews 1-11, Haddix 1-10.
Kickoff Returns—Chicago, Gentry 1-23, Sanders 1-14; Green Bay, Fullwood 1-28, Workman 2-27, Query 1-18.
Punt Returns—Chicago, McKinnon 3-34; Green Bay, Query 1-11.
Interceptions—Chicago, Rivera 1-0.
Punting—Chicago, Buford 6-35.0; Green Bay, Bracken 6-48.3.
Field Goals—Chicago, Butler 2-2; Green Bay, none attempted.
Sacks—Chicago, Roper 2, Dent, Chapura, Armstrong ½, McMichael ½; Green Bay, Harris 2.

Steelers-Broncos
SUNDAY, NOVEMBER 5
SCORE BY PERIODS

Pittsburgh	0	7	0	0— 7
Denver	10	3	7	14—34

SCORING

Denver—Humphrey 22 run (Treadwell kick), 5:57 1st.
Denver—Field goal Treadwell 26, 8:09 1st.
Pittsburgh—Carter 15 pass from Brister (Anderson kick), 4:37 2nd.
Denver—Field goal Treadwell 26, 15:00 2nd.
Denver—Johnson 44 pass from Elway (Treadwell kick), 10:38 3rd.
Denver—Elway 2 run (Treadwell kick), 6:07 4th.
Denver—Humphrey 12 run (Treadwell kick), 12:00 4th.

TEAM STATISTICS

	Pittsburgh	Denver
First downs	7	22
Rushes-Yards	25-93	44-153
Passing yards	77	261
Passes	11-26-0	16-23-2
Sacked-Yards lost	2-24	3-30
Punts	8-44.4	4-40.0
Fumbles-Lost	3-1	0-0
Penalties-Yards	5-31	5-29
Time of possession	23:08	36:52
Attendance—74,739.		

INDIVIDUAL STATISTICS

Rushing—Pittsburgh, Worley 12-75, Hoge 11-17, Carter 1-1, Newsome 1-0; Denver, Humphrey 25-105, Elway 7-34, Bratton 3-8, Winder 4-4, Sewell 1-4, Kubiak 3-1, Jackson 1-minus 3.

Passing—Pittsburgh, Brister 11-26-0—101; Denver, Elway 14-21-2—261, Kubiak 2-2-0—30.

Receiving—Pittsburgh, Hoge 5-30, Hill 2-31, Carter 1-15, Mularkey 1-10, Lipps 1-9, Worley 1-6; Denver, Humphrey 4-30, Johnson 3-96, Sewell 3-72, Nattiel 3-68, Kay 2-13, Jackson 1-12.

Kickoff Returns—Pittsburgh, Woodson 5-109; Denver, Bratton 1-10.

Punt Returns—Pittsburgh, Woodson 1-minus 4; Denver, Johnson 4-54.

Interceptions—Pittsburgh, Woodson 1-0, Hinkle 1-4.

Punting—Pittsburgh, Newsome 8-44.4; Denver, Horan 3-42.0, Elway 1-34.0.

Field Goals—Pittsburgh, none attempted; Denver, Treadwell 2-2.

Sacks—Pittsburgh, Lloyd, Little, Lake; Denver, Holmes, Fletcher.

Eagles-Chargers
SUNDAY, NOVEMBER 5
SCORE BY PERIODS

Philadelphia	0	7	0	10—	17
San Diego	7	0	10	3—	20

SCORING

San Diego—A. Miller 6 pass from McMahon (Bahr kick), 6:07 1st.

Philadelphia—Garrity 4 pass from Cunningham (DeLine kick), 12:36 2nd.

San Diego—Field goal Bahr 23, 9:21 3rd.

San Diego—A. Miller 69 pass from McMahon (Bahr kick), 11:27 3rd.

Philadelphia—Field goal DeLine 43, 1:34 4th.

Philadelphia—Byars 3 run (DeLine kick), 4:49 4th.

San Diego—Field goal Bahr 49, 14:56 4th.

TEAM STATISTICS

	Philadelphia	San Diego
First downs	24	17
Rushes-Yards	33-178	26-104
Passing yards	195	254
Passes	19-29-1	14-29-1
Sacked-Yards lost	5-41	2-10
Punts	5-35.8	4-38.0
Fumbles-Lost	2-2	2-2
Penalties-Yards	8-80	5-30
Time of possession	34:11	25:49
Attendance—47,019.		

INDIVIDUAL STATISTICS

Rushing—Philadelphia, Drummond 14-77, Byars 13-57, Cunningham 6-44; San Diego, Butts 16-72, Spencer 3-19, Brinson 5-7, McMahon 2-6.

Passing—Philadelphia, Cunningham 19-29-1—236; San Diego, McMahon 14-29-1—264.

Receiving—Philadelphia, Drummond 5-74, Jackson 4-34, Carter 3-47, Johnson 3-37, Byars 2-33, Giles 1-7, Garrity 1-4; San Diego, A. Miller 5-129, Walker 2-65, Caravello 2-42, Holland 2-22, Brinson 2-7, Cox 1-minus 1.

Kickoff Returns—Philadelphia, Edwards 2-12, Williams 2-20, Byars 1-27; San Diego, Holland 1-22, A. Miller 3-73.

Punt Returns—Philadelphia, Williams 1-7; San Diego, Walker 1-0.

Interceptions—Philadelphia, Allen 1-18; San Diego, Seale 1-22.

Punting—Philadelphia, Teltschik 5-35.8; San Diego, Ilesic 4-38.0.

Field Goals—Philadelphia, DeLine 1-2 (missed: 48); San Diego, Bahr 2-3 (missed: 33).

Sacks—Philadelphia, Pitts, White; San Diego, O'Neal 3½, Grossman 1½.

Giants-Cardinals
SUNDAY, NOVEMBER 5
SCORE BY PERIODS

New York Giants	7	7	6	0—	20
Phoenix	3	0	7	3—	13

SCORING

New York—Hostetler 19 run (Allegre kick), 5:29 1st.

Phoenix—Field goal Del Greco 37, 11:56 1st.

New York—Baker 35 pass from Hostetler (Allegre kick), 0:54 2nd.

Phoenix—Hogeboom 5 run (Del Greco kick), 2:53 3rd.

New York—Hostetler 3 run (kick failed), 5:55 3rd.

Phoenix—Field goal Del Greco 46, 9:17 4th.

TEAM STATISTICS

	New York	Phoenix
First downs	22	14
Rushes-Yards	48-210	17-75
Passing yards	174	111
Passes	12-24-2	13-31-1
Sacked-Yards lost	1-3	7-46
Punts	5-41.8	6-46.3
Fumbles-Lost	0-0	1-0
Penalties-Yards	8-86	5-37
Time of possession	38:10	21:50
Attendance—46,588.		

INDIVIDUAL STATISTICS

Rushing—New York, Anderson 27-89, Hostetler 5-47, Tillman 11-45, Meggett 4-22, Rouson 1-7; Phoenix, Sikahema 8-42, Jones 1-18, Ferrell 4-7, Hogeboom 1-5, Jordan 2-3, Baker 1-0.

Passing—New York, Hostetler 12-24-2—177; Phoenix, Hogeboom 13-31-1—157.

Receiving—New York, Turner 5-45, Manuel 2-36, Anderson 2-29, Baker 1-35, Mowatt 1-16, Meggett 1-16; Phoenix, Jones 3-42, Sikahema 2-34, Holmes 2-26, Novacek 2-24, J.T. Smith 2-19, Ferrell 1-9, Wolfley 1-3.

Kickoff Returns—New York, Meggett 3-63, Ingram 1-29; Phoenix, Baker 3-74, McConkey 1-19.

Punt Returns—New York, Meggett 5-46; Phoenix, Sikahema 2-26.

Interceptions—New York, Johnson 1-7; Phoenix, McDonald 2-58.

Punting—New York, Landeta 5-41.8; Phoenix, Camarillo 6-46.3.

Field Goals—New York, Allegre 0-1 (missed: 47); Phoenix, Del Greco 2-3 (missed: 42).

Sacks—New York, Taylor 3, Collins, Banks, Marshall, Johnson; Phoenix, Saddler ½, Nunn ½.

Bengals-Raiders
SUNDAY, NOVEMBER 5
SCORE BY PERIODS

Cincinnati	0	0	0	7—	7
Los Angeles Raiders	14	7	7	0—	28

SCORING

Los Angeles—Jackson 7 run (Jaeger kick), 3:38 1st.

Los Angeles—Jackson 92 run (Jaeger kick), 12:29 1st.

Los Angeles—Mueller 25 pass from Schroeder (Jaeger kick), 7:58 2nd.

Los Angeles—Gault 84 pass from Schroeder (Jaeger kick), 14:13 3rd.

Cincinnati—McGee 34 pass from Wilhelm (Breech kick), 2:51 4th.

TEAM STATISTICS

	Cincinnati	Los Angeles
First downs	20	12
Rushes-Yards	30-145	28-206
Passing yards	196	223
Passes	17-40-1	8-17-1
Sacked-Yards lost	3-22	2-8
Punts	5-42.4	5-42.8
Fumbles-Lost	3-2	0-0
Penalties-Yards	4-20	14-120
Time of possession	31:44	28:16
Attendance—51,080.		

INDIVIDUAL STATISTICS

Rushing—Cincinnati, Jennings 19-92, Brooks 7-29, Wilhelm 3-18, Ball 1-6; Los Angeles, Jackson 13-159, Smith 9-33, Mueller 3-14, Schroeder 3-0.

Passing—Cincinnati, Esiason 2-4-0—18, Wilhelm 15-36-1—200; Los Angeles, Schroeder 8-17-1—231.

Receiving—Cincinnati, Brown 5-74, McGee 3-60, Holman 3-29, Smith 2-31, Kattus 2-14, Brooks 1-6, Hillary 1-4; Los Angeles, Gault 2-147, Mueller 2-40, Dyal 2-26, Fernandez 2-18.

Kickoff Returns—Cincinnati, Hillary 2-33, Jennings 1-20, Smith 1-1; Los Angeles, Gault 1-16.

Punt Returns—Cincinnati, Martin 1-5, Smith 1-9; Los Angeles, Adams 1-5.

Interceptions—Cincinnati, Billups 1-0; Los Angeles, McDaniel 1-1.

Punting—Cincinnati, Johnson 4-53.0; Los Angeles, Gossett 5-42.8.

Field Goals—Cincinnati, Breech 0-1 (missed: 34); Los Angeles, Jaeger 0-1 (missed: 46).

Sacks—Cincinnati, Bussey, White; Los Angeles, Long, Townsend 2.

Rams-Vikings
SUNDAY, NOVEMBER 5
SCORE BY PERIODS

Los Angeles Rams	7	0	0	14	0—21
Minnesota	3	9	6	3	2—23

SCORING

Minnesota—Field goal Karlis 20, 9:48 1st.
Los Angeles—Bell 1 run (Lansford kick), 14:19 1st.
Minnesota—Field goal Karlis 24, 5:51 2nd.
Minnesota—Field goal Karlis 22, 11:10 2nd.
Minnesota—Field goal Karlis 25, 15:00 2nd.
Minnesota—Field goal Karlis 29, 6:13 3rd.
Minnesota—Field goal Karlis 36, 11:40 3rd.
Los Angeles—Ellard 6 pass from Everett (Lansford kick), 7:40 4th.
Los Angeles—Bell 1 run (Lansford kick), 14:32 4th.
Minnesota—Field goal Karlis 40, 14:52 4th.
Minnesota—Safety, Merriweather blocked punt out of end zone, 2:14 OT.

TEAM STATISTICS

	Los Angeles	Minnesota
First downs	14	23
Rushes-Yards	27-119	33-100
Passing yards	185	276
Passes	18-30-1	20-39-1
Sacked-Yards lost	1-15	1-5
Punts	6-32.2	4-44.3
Fumbles-Lost	1-1	1-0
Penalties-Yards	11-101	6-45
Time of possession	28:34	33:40

Attendance—59,600.

INDIVIDUAL STATISTICS

Rushing—Los Angeles, Bell 19-73, Delpino 5-36, Ellard 1-6, Everett 2-4; Minnesota, Walker 24-76, Anderson 3-10, Wilson 2-7, Fenney 4-7.

Passing—Los Angeles, Everett 18-30-1—200; Minnesota, Wilson 20-39-1—281.

Receiving—Los Angeles, Johnson 5-23, Ellard 4-82, McGee 3-26, Delpino 3-32, Anderson 1-39, Holohan 1-7, Bell 1-1; Minnesota, Jones 4-88, Carter 4-76, Walker 4-52, Anderson 4-37, Jordan 2-21, Fenney 2-7.

Kickoff Returns—Los Angeles, Delpino 3-59, McDonald 1-10, Ron Brown 3-85; Minnesota, Walker 2-78, Dozier 1-3.

Punt Returns—Los Angeles, Henley 4-37; Minnesota, Lewis 1-7, Carter 1-2.

Interceptions—Los Angeles, Owens 1-4; Minnesota, Browner 1-0.

Punting—Los Angeles, Hatcher 5-38.6; Minnesota, Scribner 4-44.3.

Field Goals—Los Angeles, Lansford 0-1 (missed: 47); Minnesota, Karlis 7-7.

Sacks—Los Angeles, Reed; Minnesota, Doleman.

Bills-Falcons
SUNDAY, NOVEMBER 5
SCORE BY PERIODS

Buffalo	7	0	14	7—28
Atlanta	0	3	17	10—30

SCORING

Buffalo—Lofton 6 pass from Kelly (Norwood kick), 13:18 1st.
Atlanta—Field goal McFadden 54, 10:13 2nd.
Atlanta—Jones 1 run (McFadden kick), 2:43 3rd.
Buffalo—McKeller 11 pass from Kelly (Norwood kick), 5:06 3rd.
Atlanta—Dixon 26 pass from Miller (McFadden kick), 6:14 3rd.
Atlanta—Field goal McFadden 26, 7:52 3rd.
Buffalo—Thomas 2 run (Norwood kick), 12:44 3rd.
Atlanta—Jones 3 run (McFadden kick), 13:38 4th.
Buffalo—Kinnebrew 1 run (Norwood kick), 14:31 4th.
Atlanta—Field goal McFadden 50, 14:58 4th.

TEAM STATISTICS

	Buffalo	Atlanta
First downs	19	20
Rushes-Yards	31-118	37-127
Passing yards	211	213
Passes	17-22-1	10-23-0
Sacked-Yards lost	4-20	2-7
Punts	5-44.6	5-44.4
Fumbles-Lost	2-1	0-0
Penalties-Yards	9-81	6-44
Time of possession	30:55	29:05

Attendance—45,267.

INDIVIDUAL STATISTICS

Rushing—Buffalo, Thomas 21-95, Kinnebrew 8-24, Kelly 2-minus 1; Atlanta, Settle 22-83, Jones 11-32, Miller 1-7, Lang 3-5.

Passing—Buffalo, Kelly 17-22-1—231; Atlanta, Miller 10-23-0—220.

Receiving—Buffalo, Reed 5-100, Johnson 4-29, McKeller 3-55, Lofton 2-16, Kinnebrew 1-17, Thomas 1-9, Beebe 1-5; Atlanta, Bailey 3-93, Dixon 3-60, Jones 3-50, Settle 1-17.

Kickoff Returns—Buffalo, Beebe 4-125, K. Davis 1-17; Atlanta, Jones 1-23, Sanders 3-43.

Punt Returns—Buffalo, Sutton 1-0; Atlanta, Sanders 3-39.

Interceptions—Atlanta, Shelley 1-31.

Punting—Buffalo, Kidd 5-44.6; Atlanta, Fulhage 5-44.4.

Field Goals—Buffalo, none attempted; Atlanta, McFadden 3-4 (missed: 45).

Sacks—Buffalo, Talley 2; Atlanta, Green, Dimry, Taylor, B. Thomas.

Lions-Oilers
SUNDAY, NOVEMBER 5
SCORE BY PERIODS

Detroit	7	10	7	7—31
Houston	7	7	14	7—35

SCORING

Detroit—B. Sanders 1 run (Murray kick), 4:01 1st.
Houston—White 1 run (Zendejas kick), 9:50 1st.
Detroit—Clark 16 pass from Peete (Murray kick), 5:35 2nd.
Houston—Rozier 1 run (Zendejas kick), 11:59 2nd.
Detroit—Field goal Murray 47, 14:58 2nd.
Detroit—White 20 fumble return (Murray kick), 0:19 3rd.
Houston—Givins 6 pass from Moon (Zendejas kick), 4:29 3rd.
Houston—Hill 7 pass from Moon (Zendejas kick), 14:04 3rd.
Houston—Moon 2 run (Zendejas kick), 11:45 4th.
Detroit—B. Sanders 14 run (Murray kick), 13:09 4th.

TEAM STATISTICS

	Detroit	Houston
First downs	19	30
Rushes-Yards	20-94	38-110
Passing yards	257	345
Passes	18-29-1	30-38-1
Sacked-Yards lost	3-16	0-0
Punts	3-39.0	0-0.0
Fumbles-Lost	2-1	4-3
Penalties-Yards	7-50	10-85
Time of possession	20:21	39:39

Attendance—48,056.

INDIVIDUAL STATISTICS

Rushing—Detroit, B. Sanders 19-91, Peete 1-3; Houston, Pinkett 8-40, Highsmith 9-23, Rozier 10-23, Moon 8-22, White 3-2.

Passing—Detroit, Peete 18-29-1—273; Houston, Moon 30-38-1—345.

Receiving—Detroit, Clark 6-141, R. Johnson 6-77, McDonald 3-29, Stanley 2-29, B. Sanders 1-minus 3; Houston, Hill 9-101, Givins 6-77, Duncan 6-66, Jeffires 4-49, Pinkett 2-29, Highsmith 2-16, White 1-7.

Kickoff Returns—Detroit, Stanley 6-78; Houston, K. Johnson 4-58, Williams 1-0, Lyles 1-0.

Punt Returns—Houston, K. Johnson 1-6.

Interceptions—Detroit, J. Williams 1-3; Houston, Eaton 1-0.

Punting—Detroit, Arnold 3-39.0; Houston, none attempted.

Field Goals—Detroit, Murray 1-1; Houston, none attempted.

Sacks—Houston, Childress 2½, Jones ½.

Colts-Dolphins
SUNDAY, NOVEMBER 5
SCORE BY PERIODS

Indianapolis	3	0	0	10	13
Miami	3	9	7	0	19

SCORING

Miami—Field goal Stoyanovich 18, 7:18 1st.

Indianapolis—Field goal Biasucci 36, 12:41 1st.

Miami—Clayton 13 pass from Marino (Stoyanovich kick), 10:24 2nd.

Miami—Safety, ball snapped out of end zone, 12:04 2nd.

Miami—A. Brown 10 pass from Marino (Stoyanovich kick), 6:19 3rd.

Indianapolis—Field goal Biasucci 33, 2:48 4th.

Indianapolis—Rison 7 pass from Trudeau (Biasucci kick), 13:18 4th.

TEAM STATISTICS

	Indianapolis	Miami
First downs	17	19
Rushes-Yards	23-85	37-159
Passing yards	214	149
Passes	21-41-2	14-26-0
Sacked-Yards lost	1-8	0-0
Punts	3-43.0	4-45.3
Fumbles-Lost	1-1	5-3
Penalties-Yards	6-60	6-40
Time of possession	28:00	32:00

Attendance—52,680.

INDIVIDUAL STATISTICS

Rushing—Indianapolis, Bentley 21-73, Trudeau 2-12; Miami, Smith 25-123, Davenport 6-26, Jensen 3-13, Clayton 1-minus 1, Marino 2-minus 2.

Passing—Indianapolis, Trudeau 20-38-2—215, Ramsey 1-3-0—7; Miami, Marino 14-26-0—149.

Receiving—Indianapolis, Bentley 6-86, Brooks 5-36, Rison 4-55, Boyer 3-28, Beach 3-17; Miami, Banks 4-41, Jensen 3-39, Edmunds 2-13, Schwedes 1-21, Clayton 1-13, A. Brown 1-10, Duper 1-9, Davenport 1-3.

Kickoff Returns—Indianapolis, Pruitt 2-40, Verdin 1-29; Miami, Reaves 2-18, Schwedes 2-24.

Punt Returns—Indianapolis, Washington 1-6, Verdin 1-

17; Miami, Schwedes 2-18.

Interceptions—Miami, Williams 2-43.

Punting—Indianapolis, Stark 3-43.0; Miami, Roby 4-45.3.

Field Goals—Indianapolis, Biasucci 2-3 (missed: 48); Miami, Stoyanovich 1-1.

Sacks—Miami, Cross.

Jets-Patriots
SUNDAY, NOVEMBER 5
SCORE BY PERIODS

New York Jets	7	7	3	10	27
New England	3	0	6	17	26

SCORING

New York—McNeil 19 run (Leahy kick), 6:16 1st.

New England—Field goal Davis 47, 9:38 1st.

New York—Townsell 35 pass from O'Brien (Leahy kick), 4:02 2nd.

New England—Stephens 35 run (kick failed), 3:33 3rd.

New York—Field goal Leahy 18, 11:52 3rd.

New England—Field goal Davis 26, 0:07 4th.

New York—Burkett 29 pass from O'Brien (Leahy kick), 2:36 4th.

New England—Jones 65 pass from Wilson (Davis kick), 3:01 4th.

New England—Dykes 11 pass from Wilson (Davis kick), 13:57 4th.

New York—Field goal Leahy 23, 15:00 4th.

TEAM STATISTICS

	New York	New England
First downs	19	27
Rushes-Yards	33-112	29-135
Passing yards	374	318
Passes	22-29-0	25-44-1
Sacked-Yards lost	2-12	2-19
Punts	6-46.6	3-39.0
Fumbles-Lost	0-0	2-0
Penalties-Yards	9-81	5-24
Time of possession	31:12	28:48

Attendance—53,366.

INDIVIDUAL STATISTICS

Rushing—New York, Hector 21-72, McNeil 3-27, Vick 6-14, O'Brien 2-4, Lageman 1-minus 5; New England, Stephens 18-86, Perryman 9-37, Grogan 1-7, Wilson 1-5.

Passing—New York, O'Brien 22-29-0—386; New England, Grogan 13-26-1—160, Wilson 12-18-0—177.

Receiving—New York, Neubert 5-66, Hector 4-32, Werner 3-61, Townsell 2-92, Dressel 2-47, Walker 2-25, Burkett 1-29, McNeil 1-16, Epps 1-11, Vick 1-7; New England, Sievers 7-50, Jones 6-127, Morgan 5-72, Perryman 2-23, Dawson 2-11, Martin 1-37, Dykes 1-11, Stephens 1-6.

Kickoff Returns—New York, Epps 3-44, Townsell 2-23; New England, Martin 2-37, Timpson 1-13, Rice 2-47.

Punt Returns—New York, Townsell 1-8; New England, Martin 3-16.

Interceptions—New York, McMillan 1-7.

Punting—New York, Prokop 6-46.6; New England, Feagles 3-39.0.

Field Goals—New York, Leahy 2-2; New England, Davis 2-4 (missed: 43, 39).

Sacks—New York, Nichols, Byrd; New England, Sims, Jeter.

Browns-Buccaneers
SUNDAY, NOVEMBER 5
SCORE BY PERIODS

Cleveland	7	28	0	7	42
Tampa Bay	7	10	7	7	31

SCORING

Tampa Bay—Tate 1 run (Igwebuike kick), 6:42 1st.

Cleveland—Metcalf 24 pass from Kosar (Bahr kick), 12:24 1st.

Cleveland—Tillman 7 pass from Kosar (Bahr kick), 0:53 2nd.

Cleveland—Wright 27 interception return (Bahr kick), 7:18 2nd.

Cleveland—Gash 15 interception return (Bahr kick), 7:37 2nd.

Tampa Bay—Wilder 9 pass from Testaverde (Igwebuike kick), 11:06 2nd.

Cleveland—Tennell 4 pass from Kosar (Bahr kick), 12:34 2nd.

Tampa Bay—Field goal Igwebuike 53, 13:43 2nd.

Tampa Bay—Wilder 9 pass from Testaverde (Igwebuike kick), 11:07 3rd.

Cleveland—Metcalf 43 run (Bahr kick), 0:57 4th.

Tampa Bay—Tate 1 run (Igwebuike kick), 5:25 4th.

TEAM STATISTICS

	Cleveland	Tampa Bay
First downs	18	24
Rushes-Yards	29-114	16-49
Passing yards	157	349
Passes	18-22-0	27-50-4
Sacked-Yards lost	1-7	2-21
Punts	5-37.6	2-40.0
Fumbles-Lost	2-0	1-0
Penalties-Yards	6-57	7-56
Time of possession	32:02	27:58
Attendance—69,162.		

INDIVIDUAL STATISTICS

Rushing—Cleveland, Metcalf 17-87, Manoa 4-15, Oliphant 1-14, Redden 2-4, Kosar 5-minus 6; Tampa Bay, Wilder 6-23, Tate 6-15, Howard 1-6, D. Smith 1-6, Stamps 1-6, Peebles 1-minus 7.

Passing—Cleveland, Kosar 18-22-0—164; Tampa Bay, Testaverde 27-50-4—370.

Receiving—Cleveland, Metcalf 7-52, Langhorne 3-53, Manoa 2-17, K. Jones 2-7, Slaughter 1-15, Oliphant 1-9, Tennell 1-4, Tillman 1-7; Tampa Bay, Wilder 8-107, Hill 4-58, Hall 3-57, Drewrey 3-31, Carrier 2-33, D. Smith 2-30, Stamps 2-4, Tate 1-15, W. Harris 1-21, Howard 1-14.

Kickoff Returns—Cleveland, Metcalf 3-94, Oliphant 1-11; Tampa Bay, Elder 5-70, Stamps 1-24.

Punt Returns—Cleveland, McNeil 1-minus 1; Tampa Bay, Drewrey 2-14.

Interceptions—Cleveland, Minnifield 1-25, Wright 1-27, Gash 1-15, Lyons 1-0.

Punting—Cleveland, Wagner 5-37.6; Tampa Bay, Mohr 2-40.0.

Field Goals—Cleveland, none attempted; Tampa Bay, Igwebuike 1-2 (missed: 47).

Sacks—Cleveland, Baker, Pike; Tampa Bay, Weston.

Cowboys-Redskins
SUNDAY, NOVEMBER 5
SCORE BY PERIODS

Dallas	0	3	7	3—13
Washington	0	0	3	0— 3

SCORING

Dallas—Field goal Ruzek 20, 14:58 2nd.

Washington—Field goal Lohmiller 35, 10:02 3rd.

Dallas—Palmer 2 run (Ruzek kick), 12:43 3rd.

Dallas—Field goal Ruzek 43, 10:55 4th.

TEAM STATISTICS

	Dallas	Washington
First downs	17	20
Rushes-Yards	29-148	21-50
Passing yards	114	296
Passes	10-30-0	28-52-2
Sacked-Yards lost	3-28	0-0
Punts	6-42.8	5-44.8
Fumbles-Lost	1-0	0-0
Penalties-Yards	0-0	8-65
Time of possession	27:44	32:16
Attendance—53,187.		

INDIVIDUAL STATISTICS

Rushing—Dallas, Palmer 18-110, Dixon 2-19, Shepard 1-7, Johnston 3-5, Tautalatasi 3-4, Sargent 1-2, Walsh 1-1; Washington, Morris 11-36, Riggs 6-11, Byner 3-10, Monk 1-minus 7.

Passing—Dallas, Walsh 10-30-0—142; Washington, Williams 28-52-2—296.

Receiving—Dallas, Martin 5-93, Folsom 3-36, Johnston 1-7, Palmer 1-6; Washington, Byner 9-75, Monk 8-98, Sanders 6-46, Clark 3-46, Warren 2-31.

Kickoff Returns—Dallas, Dixon 2-60; Washington, Sanders 4-70.

Punt Returns—Dallas, Shepard 4-31; Washington, Howard 2-15.

Interceptions—Dallas, Albritton 1-3, Bates 1-18.

Punting—Dallas, Saxon 6-42.8; Washington, Mojsiejenko 5-44.8.

Field Goals—Dallas, Ruzek 2-3 (missed: 35); Washington, Lohmiller 1-2 (missed: 45).

Sacks—Washington, Mann, Caldwell, Coleman ½, Manley ½.

Saints-49ers
MONDAY, NOVEMBER 6
SCORE BY PERIODS

New Orleans	7	3	3	0—13
San Francisco	7	14	3	7—31

SCORING

San Francisco—Rice 32 pass from Montana (Cofer kick), 9:30 1st.

New Orleans—Hilliard 1 run (Andersen kick), 13:45 1st.

San Francisco—Rice 2 pass from Montana (Cofer kick), 4:29 2nd.

New Orleans—Field goal Andersen 39, 10:35 2nd.

San Francisco—Taylor 46 pass from Montana (Cofer kick), 14:33 2nd.

New Orleans—Field goal Andersen 23, 4:50 3rd.

San Francisco—Field goal Cofer 44, 13:53 3rd.

San Francisco—Montana 3 run (Cofer kick), 8:17 4th.

TEAM STATISTICS

	New Orleans	San Francisco
First downs	16	21
Rushes-Yards	20-83	30-95
Passing yards	160	302
Passes	20-33-2	22-31-0
Sacked-Yards lost	3-23	0-0
Punts	4-30.5	4-39.5
Fumbles-Lost	0-0	1-0
Penalties-Yards	2-10	5-55
Time of possession	28:16	31:44
Attendance—60,667.		

INDIVIDUAL STATISTICS

Rushing—New Orleans, Hilliard 18-80, Jordan 1-2, Hebert 1-1; San Francisco, Craig 17-51, Rathman 5-21, Montana 5-17, Flagler 3-6.

Passing—New Orleans, Hebert 20-33-2—183; San Francisco, Montana 22-31-0—302.

Receiving—New Orleans, Hilliard 5-31, Turner 3-42, Brenner 3-34, Hill 2-35, Jordan 2-24, Perriman 2-10, E. Martin 2-6, Heyward 1-1; San Francisco, Rathman 7-64, Rice 6-93, Taylor 4-78, Craig 3-24, Greer 1-26, Jones 1-17.

Kickoff Returns—New Orleans, Harris 3-57, Morse 1-25, Frazier 1-23; San Francisco, Flagler 2-34, Tillman 1-13.

Punt Returns—New Orleans, Harris 4-51; San Francisco, Taylor 1-5.

Interceptions—San Francisco, Wright 1-23, Brooks 1-19.

Punting—New Orleans, Barnhardt 4-30.5; San Francisco, Helton 4-39.5.

Field Goals—New Orleans, Andersen 2-2; San Francisco, Cofer 1-1.

Sacks—San Francisco, Fagan, Holt 2.

TENTH WEEK

RESULTS OF WEEK 10

Sunday, November 12

Buffalo 30, Indianapolis 7 at Buff.
Chicago 20, Pittsburgh 0 at Pitts.
Cleveland 17, Seattle 7 at Sea.
Denver 16, Kansas City 13 at K.C.
Detroit 31, Green Bay 22 at Det.
L.A. Rams 31, N.Y. Giants 10 at L.A.
Miami 31, N.Y. Jets 23 at N.Y.
Minnesota 24, Tampa Bay 10 at T.B.
New Orleans 28, New England 24 at N.E.
Phoenix 24, Dallas 20 at Phoe.
San Diego 14, L.A. Raiders 12 at S.D.
San Francisco 45, Atlanta 3 at S.F.
Washington 10, Philadelphia 3 at Phila.

Monday, November 13

Houston 26, Cincinnati 24 at Hous.

Although many of the statistics kept in professional sports can be interpreted in more ways than one, perhaps the most important statistic used by the National Football League is the takeaway/giveaway ratio.

The ratio, which is the difference between the number of turnovers a team commits and the number it forces, usually has a direct correlation to a team's won-lost record. For example, the 1983 Washington Redskins intercepted a franchise-record 34 passes and recovered 27 fumbles (also a team mark) for a total of 61 takeaways. The Redskins' offense, meanwhile, turned the ball over just 18 times (11 interceptions and seven fumbles). Washington's plus-43 takeaway/giveaway ratio that season set an NFL record that still stands.

Not surprisingly, the '83 Redskins compiled a league-best 14-2 record and advanced to that season's Super Bowl game.

Five years later, the Redskins had an NFL-worst ratio of minus-24 (22 takeaways against 46 giveaways) and ended the 1988 season with a 7-9 record. They did not make the playoffs.

Turnovers are very important, and if the New England Patriots did not already know it, they learned it the hard way in Week 10.

The visiting New Orleans Saints converted two Patriot fumbles and one interception into 21 points on the way to a 28-24 interconference victory. All three touchdowns came in the second quarter to help New Orleans build a 28-0 bulge.

"This may be the middle of November, but it was Christmas today," Patriots Coach Raymond Berry said. "We gave them three gifts."

The Pats' gift-giving began shortly after the Saints took a 7-0 lead on Dalton Hilliard's three-yard touchdown run with 1:43 left in the first period. Three plays after Hilliard's touchdown, Saints rookie Wayne Martin recovered a fumble by the Pats' Bob Perryman at the New England 27-yard line. Four plays after taking possession, New Orleans quarterback Bobby Hebert hit tight end Hoby Brenner with a one-yard touchdown pass for a 14-0 Saints lead.

On the Patriots' next possession, Saints safety Brett Maxie intercepted a Steve Grogan pass intended for Perryman and returned it 26 yards for another New Orleans touchdown. On the ensuing kickoff, the Saints' Brian Forde recovered a fumble by the Pats' Michael Timpson at the New England 28. Hilliard scored on a 10-yard run six plays later for a 28-0 New Orleans lead.

It took the Saints less than seven minutes to score four touchdowns.

"Before you knew it, they had 28 points and we were climbing uphill," Patriots defensive end Gary Jeter said.

"The turnovers were the key," understated Saints Coach Jim Mora, whose team won its 10th straight game against an AFC opponent. "They got us quick points and, most importantly, it took them out of their running game."

The Patriots, who have a mediocre ground game under the best of circumstances, almost abandoned their running game completely after New Orleans took its big lead. Grogan attempted a whopping 44 passes in the second half after throwing just 15 in the first two quarters. He completed 11 of 17 passes on the Patriots' last two possessions—both of which resulted in touchdowns—but it was a case of too little, too late.

"It was a crazy game," Mora said. "I was just pleased to get out of here with a win."

Another visiting team happy to escape town with a victory in Week 10 was the Denver Broncos, who edged AFC Western Division rival Kansas City, 16-13, on rookie kicker David Treadwell's 26-yard field goal with one second left. Treadwell's kick capped a 10-play, 71-yard drive that included a 30-yard gain by running back Steve Sewell to the Kansas City 9 with four seconds to play.

It was the third time in the game that the Broncos had successfully executed the shovel-pass play from quarterback John Elway to Sewell. Chiefs nose tackle Bill Maas broke his arm on the play and would be forced to miss the remainder of the season.

Kansas City, which had to play without league-leading rusher Christian Okoye (who was suffering from a deep thigh bruise), tied the game at 13-13 with 5:36 left on Steve Pelluer's three-yard touchdown pass to Emile Harry.

That set the stage for the Broncos and Elway, who had thrown for just 71 yards in the game before completing all four of his attempts for 62 yards in the game-winning drive.

The Broncos' triumph improved their record to 8-2 and increased their lead in the AFC West to three games over the Los Angeles Raiders, who dropped to 5-5 following a 14-12 loss at San Diego. The Raiders led, 12-0, late in the third quarter before the Chargers fought back. Anthony Miller scored San Diego's first touchdown on a 91-yard kickoff return with 5:10 left in the third quarter.

Running back Tim Spencer, who cost the Chargers a touchdown by fumbling at the Raiders' goal line early in the fourth quarter, made amends by scoring what proved to be the game-winning touchdown on a five-yard run with 8:48 left. Spencer's touchdown came four plays after the Chargers took possession at the Los Angeles 23 following a partially blocked punt. Spencer caught a pass for eight yards on first down before running three times for the remaining 15 yards.

Another late-game comeback occurred at Phoenix, where the Cardinals edged the Dallas Cowboys, 24-20, on quarterback Tom Tupa's 72-yard touchdown pass to wide receiver Ernie Jones with 58 seconds left. The touchdown was the second of the fourth quarter for Jones, who caught a 38-yard scoring pass from Tupa with 6:25 left. The Cowboys answered that score with a 75-yard touchdown pass from Troy Aikman to James Dixon with 1:43 remaining.

Aikman, the first player selected in the 1989 draft, completed 21 of 40 passes for 379 yards in his first game back after breaking the index finger on his left hand in a game six weeks earlier. He left this game with a mild concussion after being hit by Phoenix linebacker Anthony Bell while completing the touchdown pass to Dixon.

The Cardinals, who had defeated the Cowboys, 19-10, two weeks earlier at Dallas, swept the teams' NFC Eastern Division series for the first time since 1970.

For the sixth straight season, the AFC Eastern Division series between the Buffalo Bills and Indianapolis Colts would end in a split. That was assured by the Bills' 30-7 triumph in Week 10 that avenged a 37-14 loss at Indianapolis five weeks earlier.

The tone for the game was set on the opening kickoff, when the Bills' Mark Pike ripped the ball out of James Pruitt's hands and Mickey Sutton recovered for Buffalo at the Colts' 22. Jim Kelly threw an eight-yard touchdown pass to Thurman Thomas four plays later for the game's first points.

Then, on each of Indianapolis' next two possessions, running back Eric Dickerson fumbled without being hit, leading to two Scott Norwood field goals and a 13-0 Buffalo lead.

The Colts, who didn't cross midfield until they trailed 30-0, were so fumble-prone that their only points also were scored on a fumble. Offensive tackle Randy Dixon recovered a Dickerson bobble in the Buffalo end zone with 8:47 to play for Indianapolis' only touchdown.

The NFL's No. 1-rated defense through 10

Roger Craig carried the ball 17 times for 109 yards in San Francisco's 45-3 victory over Atlanta.

weeks belonged to the Minnesota Vikings, who did nothing to weaken that ranking in a 24-10 triumph at Tampa Bay. The Vikings sacked Buccaneers quarterback Vinny Testaverde seven times, held Tampa Bay to 13 first downs and 201 total yards and scored their first touchdown when Reggie Rutland scooped up a fumble by Bucs wide receiver Bruce Hill and rambled 27 yards for a score.

The loss was Tampa Bay's fifth in a row.

The Cleveland Browns won for the fourth straight week after intercepting three second-half passes by Seattle Seahawks quarterback Dave Krieg in a 17-7 victory at Seattle. Safety Felix Wright intercepted Krieg at the Cleveland 13 early in the third period and the Browns proceeded to drive 87 yards in 12 plays to break a 7-7 tie on Bernie Kosar's 17-yard touchdown pass to rookie Lawyer Tillman.

The victory was the Browns' first over the Seahawks since 1982 after four defeats.

Los Angeles Rams quarterback Jim Everett completed 23 of 33 passes for 295 yards and two touchdowns to lead the Rams to their first victory in five weeks, a 31-10 triumph over the New York Giants. The Giants, who had won their previous four games to lead the NFC East with an 8-1 record, were held to just six yards rushing on 10 attempts.

Everett's two touchdown passes came in a 14-second span in the final minute of the first half to help the Rams take command. After the Rams' quarterback connected with wide receiver Aaron Cox for a 51-yard touchdown before the intermission, Rams rookie George Bethune recovered a fumbled kickoff by Giants rookie Dave Meggett at the New York 21. Everett then hit Willie Anderson for a touchdown on the next play to increase the L.A. lead to 24-3.

Everett, who was not sacked, set a Rams record with 18 consecutive completions during the game.

San Francisco quarterback Joe Montana, who completed an NFL-record 22 straight passes over two games during the 1987 season, was nearly as flawless in Week 10 of the 1989 season. The 11-year veteran and future Hall of Famer completed 16 of 19 passes for 270 yards and three touchdowns in leading the 49ers to their sixth straight triumph, a 45-3 thrashing of division rival Atlanta.

San Francisco Coach George Seifert replaced his star signal-caller with backup Steve Young in the third quarter.

The Falcons, who were outgained 515-192 in total yards, would have been shut out had it not been for Chris Miller's 25-yard field goal in the second period. Miller, Atlanta's starting quarterback, found himself kicking in a game for the first time since high school after regular place-kicker Paul McFadden sprained a thigh in pregame warmups.

The Washington Redskins, who were forced to play without five injured starters, came up with enough reserve firepower to upend Philadelphia, 10-3, in an NFC Eastern Division game. The Redskins, who were without offensive tackles Jim Lachey and Mark May, cornerbacks Darrell Green and Barry Wilburn and running back Gerald Riggs, scored the game's only touchdown on Earnest Byner's one-yard run with 4:45 left in the first half.

The touchdown climaxed a seven-play, 42-yard drive that included a 24-yard completion from Doug Williams to rookie tight end Jimmie Johnson on a fourth down-and-inches play at the Eagles' 32.

The Philadelphia offense, which crossed midfield only four times, was held to 204 total yards and one field goal. Randall Cunningham completed 17 of 39 passes for 177 yards but had at least 10 passes dropped.

The Chicago Bears converted six Pittsburgh Steelers turnovers into 17 points en route to a 20-0 victory in an interconference game. The Bears' triumph snapped a three-game road losing streak and was a homecoming of sorts for Chicago Coach Mike Ditka, a former University of Pittsburgh star who was coaching in his home area for the first time since becoming the Bears' coach in 1982.

Three of the turnovers were interceptions of Steelers quarterback Bubby Brister, who had not been intercepted since the first week of the season. Lemuel Stinson, who started in place of injured rookie Donnell Woolford, picked off Brister's first pass attempt of the game and later killed a Steelers' drive at the Chicago 5 with another interception.

Pittsburgh's six possessions in the first half ended with two fumbles, two missed field goals, an interception and a punt.

The Bears' offense, meanwhile, rolled up 337 yards behind quarterback Jim Harbaugh, who was starting his second game in place of an ineffective Mike Tomczak. Harbaugh completed only 13 passes for 125 yards and one touchdown but rushed for 56 yards on seven carries.

The Miami Dolphins beat the New York Jets on the Jets' home field for the first time since 1984 as quarterback Dan Marino led a quick-strike Miami offense with three touchdown passes in a 31-23 victory. Marino threw scoring passes of 78 and 65 yards to Mark Clayton and Scott Schwedes, respectively, in the third period to give the Dolphins an 11-point lead after three quarters.

Miami's five scoring drives in the game covered a combined 266 yards in less than five minutes.

The Dolphins got a 59-yard field goal by rookie place-kicker Pete Stoyanovich in the second quarter. Stoyanovich's kick, which was aided by a stiff wind, tied for the third-longest field goal in NFL history. The only other 59-yarder had been kicked exactly 10 years to the day earlier—by Philadelphia's Tony Franklin against Dallas on November 12, 1979.

The Detroit Lions won for only the second time in 1989 by scoring 21 points in the second quarter for a 31-22 NFC Central Division victory over the Green Bay Packers. It was a classic case of one team dominating another in almost every statistical category except the one that matters: points scored.

The Packers finished the game with huge advantages in first downs (31-8), total yards (432-128) and time of possession (39:25 to 20:35). But Green Bay also led in turnovers, 4-2, and the Lions pounced on every opportunity.

Quarterback Don Majkowski's fumble at Green Bay's 36 in the first period led to a 45-yard field goal by the Lions' Eddie Murray, and Jerry Holmes' 23-yard interception return of a Majkowski pass for a touchdown in the second quarter helped Detroit take a 24-3 halftime lead.

The Houston Oilers improved their record to 6-4 and dropped defending AFC champion Cincinnati to 5-5 with a come-from-behind 26-24 victory over the Bengals in the Monday night game. The Oilers' winning points came on Tony Zendejas' fourth field goal of the night, a 28-yard kick as time expired.

Zendejas' game-winner capped a 15-play, 80-yard drive that began at the Houston 20 with 4:48 left. Oilers quarterback Warren Moon kept the drive alive by barely making a first down on a third-and-10 scramble at the Cincinnati 47.

Packers-Lions
SUNDAY, NOVEMBER 12
SCORE BY PERIODS

Green Bay	0	3	14	5—22
Detroit	3	21	0	7—31

SCORING
Detroit—Field goal Murray 45, 11:12 1st.
Detroit—Johnson 17 pass from Peete (Murray kick), 0:47 2nd.
Detroit—Johnson 8 pass from Peete (Murray kick), 6:02 2nd.
Green Bay—Field goal Jacke 34, 9:24 2nd.
Detroit—Holmes 23 interception return (Murray kick), 13:14 2nd.
Green Bay—Haddix 6 pass from Majkowski (Jacke kick), 7:37 3rd.
Green Bay—Workman 1 run (Jacke kick), 10:05 3rd.
Green Bay—Field goal Jacke 40, 1:35 4th.
Detroit—B. Sanders 1 run (Murray kick), 6:26 4th.
Green Bay—Safety, Peete runs out of end zone, 14:54 4th.

TEAM STATISTICS

	Green Bay	Detroit
First downs	31	8
Rushes-Yards	27-104	23-74
Passing yards	328	54
Passes	35-60-2	7-15-1
Sacked-Yards lost	5-36	4-23
Punts	4-36.7	6-48.3
Fumbles-Lost	3-2	2-1
Penalties-Yards	5-45	8-61
Time of possession	39:25	20:35
Attendance—44,324.		

INDIVIDUAL STATISTICS
Rushing—Green Bay, Majkowski 8-46, Haddix 12-42, Woodside 4-11, Workman 3-5; Detroit, B. Sanders 16-69, Johnson 1-5, Peete 6-0.
Passing—Green Bay, Majkowski 34-59-2—357, Dilweg 1-1-0—7; Detroit, Peete 7-15-1—77.
Receiving—Green Bay, Sharpe 6-74, Woodside 5-35, Haddix 5-27, Query 4-52, Matthews 4-49, Bland 3-43, West 3-30, Fontenot 2-10, Didier 1-15, Kemp 1-19, Murphy 1-10; Detroit, Johnson 5-53, B. Sanders 1-20, Phillips 1-4.
Kickoff Returns—Green Bay, Bland 3-62, Workman 3-34; Detroit, Gray 4-120.
Punt Returns—Green Bay, Query 5-37; Detroit, Stanley 2-104.
Interceptions—Green Bay, Murphy 1-20; Detroit,

Holmes 1-23, J. Williams 1-3.
Punting—Green Bay, Bracken 4-36.7; Detroit, Arnold 6-48.3.
Field Goals—Green Bay, Jacke 2-3 (missed: 52); Detroit, Murray 1-1.
Sacks—Green Bay, Harris 3, Stephen; Detroit, White, Jamison, Ball 2, E. Williams ½, J. Williams ½.

Raiders-Chargers
SUNDAY, NOVEMBER 12
SCORE BY PERIODS

Los Angeles Raiders	3	6	3	0—12
San Diego	0	0	7	7—14

SCORING
Los Angeles—Field goal Jaeger 23, 6:50 1st.
Los Angeles—Field goal Jaeger 36, 1:57 2nd.
Los Angeles—Field goal Jaeger 33, 14:45 2nd.
Los Angeles—Field goal Jaeger 32, 9:34 3rd.
San Diego—A. Miller 91 kickoff return (Bahr kick), 9:50 3rd.
San Diego—Spencer 5 run (Bahr kick), 6:12 4th.

TEAM STATISTICS

	Los Angeles	San Diego
First downs	15	12
Rushes-Yards	33-134	27-136
Passing yards	151	66
Passes	12-25-3	9-20-1
Sacked-Yards lost	3-22	3-22
Punts	4-34.8	4-41.0
Fumbles-Lost	0-0	2-1
Penalties-Yards	6-42	10-66
Time of possession	33:50	26:10
Attendance—59,151.		

INDIVIDUAL STATISTICS
Rushing—Los Angeles, Jackson 21-103, Smith 6-18, Mueller 5-11, Schroeder 1-2; San Diego, Spencer 10-59, Butts 11-56, McMahon 5-21, Archer 1-0.
Passing—Los Angeles, Schroeder 12-25-3—173; San Diego, McMahon 9-20-1—88.
Receiving—Los Angeles, Gault 5-88, Fernandez 3-49, Jackson 2-18, Dyal 1-14, Smith 1-4; San Diego, A. Miller 5-54, Nelson 2-15, Allen 1-11, Spencer 1-8.
Kickoff Returns—Los Angeles, Adams 1-25, Mueller 2-30; San Diego, Holland 1-14, A. Miller 2-106.
Punt Returns—Los Angeles, Adams 3-15, Harden 1-11; San Diego, Brinson 2-9, Figaro 1-0.
Interceptions—Los Angeles, Harden 1-0; San Diego, Patterson 1-34, Bennett 1-4, Seale 1-25.
Punting—Los Angeles, Gossett 4-34.8; San Diego, Ilesic 4-41.0.
Field Goals—Los Angeles, Jaeger 4-4; San Diego, none attempted.
Sacks—Los Angeles, Davis, Golic, Townsend; San Diego, Smith, O'Neal, Hinkle.

Cowboys-Cardinals
SUNDAY, NOVEMBER 12
SCORE BY PERIODS

Dallas	3	10	0	7—20
Phoenix	0	7	0	17—24

SCORING
Dallas—Field goal Zendejas 32, 13:08 1st.
Dallas—Field goal Zendejas 29, 6:25 2nd.
Phoenix—McDonald 53 interception return (Del Greco kick), 10:55 2nd.
Dallas—Martin 5 pass from Aikman (Zendejas kick), 14:35 2nd.
Phoenix—Field goal Del Greco 45, 5:46 4th.
Phoenix—Jones 38 pass from Tupa (Del Greco kick), 8:35 4th.
Dallas—Dixon 75 pass from Aikman (Zendejas kick), 13:17 4th.

Phoenix—Jones 72 pass from Tupa (Del Greco kick), 14:02 4th.

TEAM STATISTICS

	Dallas	Phoenix
First downs	21	15
Rushes-Yards	25-77	24-69
Passing yards	367	316
Passes	21-40-2	21-35-0
Sacked-Yards lost	1-12	3-20
Punts	6-42.5	6-42.3
Fumbles-Lost	2-2	0-0
Penalties-Yards	4-35	8-50
Time of possession	32:15	27:45
Attendance—49,657.		

INDIVIDUAL STATISTICS

Rushing—Dallas, Palmer 22-66, Sargent 1-5, Johnston 1-4, Tautalatasi 1-2; Phoenix, Ferrell 13-44, Tupa 5-14, Sikahema 5-6, Hogeboom 1-5.

Passing—Dallas, Aikman 21-40-2—379; Phoenix, Tupa 14-22-0—245, Hogeboom 7-13-0—91.

Receiving—Dallas, Dixon 6-203, Martin 5-62, Shepard 4-76, Palmer 3-8, Folsom 1-16, Johnston 1-8, Tautalatasi 1-6; Phoenix, Awalt 6-105, Green 4-39, Sikahema 4-22, Jones 3-139, Ferrell 3-26, Reeves 1-5.

Kickoff Returns—Dallas, Shepard 3-80, Dixon 2-24; Phoenix, Usher 3-80, McConkey 1-21, Sikahema 1-21.

Punt Returns—Dallas, Shepard 3-16; Phoenix, Usher 1-10, Sikahema 2-36.

Interceptions—Phoenix, McDonald 2-95.

Punting—Dallas, Saxon 6-42.5; Phoenix, Camarillo 6-42.3.

Field Goals—Dallas, Zendejas 2-2; Phoenix, Del Greco 1-3 (missed: 44, 41).

Sacks—Dallas, Hamel, Jeffcoat, Tolbert; Phoenix, Harvey.

Falcons-49ers
SUNDAY, NOVEMBER 12
SCORE BY PERIODS

Atlanta	0	3	0	0— 3
San Francisco	7	21	10	7—45

SCORING

San Francisco—Montana 1 run (Cofer kick), 6:59 1st.
Atlanta—Field goal Miller 25, 4:26 2nd.
San Francisco—Rice 39 pass from Montana (Cofer kick), 10:26 2nd.
San Francisco—Haley 3 fumble return (Cofer kick), 10:53 2nd.
San Francisco—Taylor 2 pass from Montana (Cofer kick), 14:07 2nd.
San Francisco—Rice 11 pass from Montana (Cofer kick), 2:31 3rd.
San Francisco—Field goal Cofer 18, 10:12 3rd.
San Francisco—Henderson 11 run (Cofer kick), 0:36 4th.

TEAM STATISTICS

	Atlanta	San Francisco
First downs	11	30
Rushes-Yards	17-73	48-234
Passing yards	119	281
Passes	17-32-0	17-20-0
Sacked-Yards lost	3-30	1-5
Punts	8-38.6	1-38.0
Fumbles-Lost	3-1	4-2
Penalties-Yards	6-36	3-24
Time of possession	23:57	36:03
Attendance—59,914.		

INDIVIDUAL STATISTICS

Rushing—Atlanta, Settle 8-31, Lang 4-29, Jones 4-12, Paterra 1-1; San Francisco, Craig 17-109, Rathman 16-77, Flagler 5-23, Montana 5-12, Henderson 2-11, Young 3-2.

Passing—Atlanta, Miller 17-32-0—149; San Francisco, Montana 16-19-0—270, Young 1-1-0—16.

Receiving—Atlanta, Dixon 4-48, Collins 3-37, Lang 3-13, Wilkins 2-29, Heller 2-17, Jones 2-6, Settle 1-minus 1; San Francisco, Rathman 6-43, Rice 3-81, B. Jones 2-47, Craig 2-15, Taylor 2-6, Henderson 1-78, Wilson 1-16.

Kickoff Returns—Atlanta, Sanders 3-49, Jones 2-31, Paterra 1-21, Beckman 1-0; San Francisco, Flagler 1-20.

Punt Returns—San Francisco, Taylor 6-104, Greer 1-3.

Interceptions—None.

Punting—Atlanta, Fulhage 8-38.6; San Francisco, Helton 1-38.0.

Field Goals—Atlanta, Miller 1-1; San Francisco, Cofer 1-1.

Sacks—Atlanta, Bruce; San Francisco, Holt, Stubbs.

Bears-Steelers
SUNDAY, NOVEMBER 12
SCORE BY PERIODS

Chicago	7	13	0	0—20
Pittsburgh	0	0	0	0— 0

SCORING

Chicago—Anderson 2 run (Butler kick), 6:01 1st.
Chicago—Field goal Butler 39, 12:53 2nd.
Chicago—Muster 20 pass from Harbaugh (Butler kick), 13:47 2nd.
Chicago—Field goal Butler 35, 14:54 2nd.

TEAM STATISTICS

	Chicago	Pittsburgh
First downs	20	10
Rushes-Yards	44-203	16-54
Passing yards	134	162
Passes	14-28-1	14-26-3
Sacked-Yards lost	2-1	4-35
Punts	4-43.5	3-33.7
Fumbles-Lost	4-3	4-3
Penalties-Yards	5-40	5-45
Time of possession	37:32	22:28
Attendance—56,505.		

INDIVIDUAL STATISTICS

Rushing—Chicago, Anderson 17-64, Harbaugh 7-56, Gentry 1-29, Muster 8-25, Sanders 5-18, Suhey 2-7, Taylor 2-7, Tomczak 2-minus 3; Pittsburgh, Stone 1-32, Worley 10-21, Hoge 4-1, Lipps 1-0.

Passing—Chicago, Harbaugh 13-25-1—125, Tomczak 1-3-0—10; Pittsburgh, Brister 14-26-3—197.

Receiving—Chicago, Davis 4-38, Muster 3-31, Morris 2-37, Anderson 2-7, McKinnon 1-7, Sanders 1-7, Gentry 1-6; Pittsburgh, Lipps 4-112, Carter 4-23, Hoge 3-39, Mularkey 1-10, Hill 1-9, Worley 1-4.

Kickoff Returns—Chicago, Gentry 1-20; Pittsburgh, Woodson 3-61, Stone 1-24.

Punt Returns—Chicago, McKinnon 2-9; Pittsburgh, Woodson 2-9.

Interceptions—Chicago, Stinson 2-30, Douglass 1-0; Pittsburgh, Lloyd 1-2.

Punting—Chicago, Buford 4-43.5; Pittsburgh, Newsome 3-33.7.

Field Goals—Chicago, Butler 2-2; Pittsburgh, Anderson 0-2 (missed: 39, 45).

Sacks—Chicago, McMichael, Perry 2, Chapura; Pittsburgh, Willis, G. Williams.

Browns-Seahawks
SUNDAY, NOVEMBER 12
SCORE BY PERIODS

Cleveland	0	7	7	3—17
Seattle	7	0	0	0— 7

SCORING

Seattle—Blades 8 pass from Krieg (N. Johnson kick), 8:40 1st.
Cleveland—Manoa 1 run (Bahr kick), 14:37 2nd.
Cleveland—Tillman 17 pass from Kosar (Bahr kick), 1:34 3rd.
Cleveland—Field goal Bahr 29, 11:35 4th.

TEAM STATISTICS

	Cleveland	Seattle
First downs	20	14
Rushes-Yards	34-139	22-46
Passing yards	138	134
Passes	16-27-0	17-30-3
Sacked-Yards lost	4-35	1-7
Punts	5-41.4	4-47.0
Fumbles-Lost	0-0	2-0
Penalties-Yards	11-80	4-40
Time of possession	33:15	26:45

Attendance—58,978.

INDIVIDUAL STATISTICS

Rushing—Cleveland, Metcalf 19-75, Manoa 14-65, Kosar 1-minus 1; Seattle, Warner 13-29, Williams 7-11, Krieg 2-6.

Passing—Cleveland, Kosar 16-27-0—173; Seattle, Krieg 17-30-3—141.

Receiving—Cleveland, Manoa 4-35, Langhorne 3-49, Brennan 2-14, Tillman 1-17, McNeil 1-15, Slaughter 1-15, K. Jones 1-7, Metcalf 1-7, Newsome 1-7, Redden 1-7; Seattle, Blades 4-57, Largent 4-33, Williams 4-20, Skansi 3-22, Clark 2-9.

Kickoff Returns—Cleveland, Metcalf 2-53; Seattle, Harris 2-43, Hollis 1-20, McNeal 1-17.

Punt Returns—Cleveland, McNeil 1-1; Seattle, Hollis 4-53.

Interceptions—Cleveland, Matthews 1-25, Dixon 1-2, Wright 1-0.

Punting—Cleveland, Wagner 5-41.4; Seattle, Rodriguez 4-47.0.

Field Goals—Cleveland, Bahr 1-1; Seattle, none attempted.

Sacks—Cleveland, Perry; Seattle, Porter 2, Hart 2.

Redskins-Eagles
SUNDAY, NOVEMBER 12
SCORE BY PERIODS

Washington	3	7	0	0—10	
Philadelphia	0	3	0	0— 3	

SCORING

Washington—Field goal Lohmiller 34, 3:17 1st.
Washington—Byner 1 run (Lohmiller kick), 10:15 2nd.
Philadelphia—Field goal DeLine 49, 14:59 2nd.

TEAM STATISTICS

	Washington	Philadelphia
First downs	14	10
Rushes-Yards	42-103	19-47
Passing yards	151	157
Passes	14-24-0	17-39-1
Sacked-Yards lost	2-10	3-20
Punts	8-45.0	8-38.4
Fumbles-Lost	1-1	5-1
Penalties-Yards	9-85	3-20
Time of possession	37:10	22:50

Attendance—65,443.

INDIVIDUAL STATISTICS

Rushing—Washington, Morris 38-88, Byner 4-15; Philadelphia, Byars 7-36, Toney 7-11, Drummond 1-0, Cunningham 4-0.

Passing—Washington, Williams 14-24-0—161; Philadelphia, Cunningham 17-39-1—177.

Receiving—Washington, Sanders 5-48, Morris 3-34, Clark 2-28, Byner 2-19, J. Johnson 1-24, Monk 1-8; Philadelphia, Giles 4-29, Johnson 3-52, Byars 3-30, Carter 3-29, Drummond 2-23, Toney 1-8, Williams 1-6.

Kickoff Returns—Philadelphia, Williams 2-27.

Punt Returns—Washington, Howard 1-9; Philadelphia, Williams 1-7.

Interceptions—Washington, Gouveia 1-1.

Punting—Washington, Mojsiejenko 8-45.0; Philadelphia, Teltschik 8-38.4.

Field Goals—Washington, Lohmiller 1-2 (missed: 35); Philadelphia, DeLine 1-1.

Sacks—Washington, Manley 3; Philadelphia, Hopkins, White.

Dolphins-Jets
SUNDAY, NOVEMBER 12
SCORE BY PERIODS

Miami	0	10	21	0—31	
New York Jets	3	17	0	3—23	

SCORING

New York—Field goal Leahy 38, 13:41 1st.
New York—Field goal Leahy 20, 6:39 2nd.
New York—Vick 26 run (Leahy kick), 8:06 2nd.
Miami—Field goal Stoyanovich 59, 10:17 2nd.
New York—McNeil 25 pass from O'Brien (Leahy kick), 13:32 2nd.
Miami—A. Brown 8 pass from Marino (Stoyanovich kick), 14:16 2nd.
Miami—Clayton 78 pass from Marino (Stoyanovich kick), 3:07 3rd.
Miami—Schwedes 65 pass from Marino (Stoyanovich kick), 12:14 3rd.
Miami—Smith 2 run (Stoyanovich kick), 12:48 3rd.
New York—Field goal Leahy 22, 4:58 4th.

TEAM STATISTICS

	Miami	New York
First downs	19	23
Rushes-Yards	27-103	32-136
Passing yards	344	274
Passes	18-34-2	22-35-3
Sacked-Yards lost	2-15	2-15
Punts	3-44.0	4-44.3
Fumbles-Lost	3-1	0-0
Penalties-Yards	6-50	6-50
Time of possession	26:38	33:22

Attendance—65,923.

INDIVIDUAL STATISTICS

Rushing—Miami, Smith 19-61, Hampton 4-19, Jensen 1-14, Faaola 1-5, Davenport 1-4, Marino 1-0; New York, Hector 20-60, McNeil 8-41, Vick 2-31, O'Brien 2-4.

Passing—Miami, Marino 18-34-2—359; New York, O'Brien 22-35-3—289.

Receiving—Miami, Clayton 4-125, Banks 4-79, Schwedes 3-107, Jensen 3-21, Hampton 1-12, Faaola 1-8, A. Brown 1-7, Smith 1-0; New York, Townsell 5-82, Neubert 4-53, Werner 4-41, Toon 4-40, Vick 2-35, McNeil 1-25, Burkett 1-10, Hector 1-3.

Kickoff Returns—Miami, Schwedes 1-0, Ahrens 1-10, Kinchen 1-17, Hampton 1-17; New York, Townsell 2-45, Epps 2-26, Humphery 1-12.

Punt Returns—Miami, Schwedes 3-6; New York, Townsell 1-12.

Interceptions—Miami, Thomas 1-4, Judson 1-3, McNeal 1-0; New York, Glenn 1-0, Booty 1-13.

Punting—Miami, Roby 3-44.0; New York, Prokop 4-44.3.

Field Goals—Miami, Stoyanovich 1-3 (missed: 34, 52); New York, Leahy 3-3.

Sacks—Miami, Green, Offerdahl ½, Cross ½; New York, McMillan, Clifton ½, Washington ½.

Broncos-Chiefs
SUNDAY, NOVEMBER 12
SCORE BY PERIODS

Denver	3	7	3	3—16	
Kansas City	0	6	0	7—13	

SCORING

Denver—Field goal Treadwell 18, 5:07 1st.
Kansas City—Field goal Lowery 39, 0:35 2nd.
Denver—Kragen 17 fumble return (Treadwell kick), 3:15 2nd.
Kansas City—Field goal Lowery 46, 14:48 2nd.
Denver—Field goal Treadwell 27, 8:13 3rd.

Kansas City—Harry 5 pass from Pelluer (Lowery kick), 9:24 4th.
Denver—Field goal Treadwell 26, 14:59 4th.

TEAM STATISTICS

	Denver	Kansas City
First downs	12	20
Rushes-Yards	29-101	35-141
Passing yards	112	171
Passes	11-22-1	17-27-0
Sacked-Yards lost	2-21	4-34
Punts	4-43.3	4-36.3
Fumbles-Lost	0-0	4-2
Penalties-Yards	2-10	12-90
Time of possession	29:33	30:27

Attendance—76,245.

INDIVIDUAL STATISTICS

Rushing—Denver, Humphrey 21-77, Sewell 2-16, Winder 3-7, Alexander 2-3, Elway 1-minus 2; Kansas City, Saxon 18-57, Pelluer 6-43, Heard 9-33, McNair 2-8.

Passing—Denver, Elway 11-22-1—133; Kansas City, Pelluer 17-27-0—205.

Receiving—Denver, Sewell 5-84, Kay 3-21, Jackson 2-29, Humphrey 1-minus 1; Kansas City, Mandley 4-44, McNair 3-41, Paige 2-48, Heard 2-31, Harry 2-10, Hayes 2-10, Worthen 1-12, Weathers 1-9.

Kickoff Returns—Denver, Carrington 1-68, Bratton 1-9, Woods 1-17; Kansas City, Copeland 2-55, McNair 2-35, Saxon 1-0.

Punt Returns—Denver, Woods 2-6; Kansas City, Worthen 3-16.

Interceptions—Kansas City, Saleaumua 1-21.

Punting—Denver, Horan 4-43.3; Kansas City, Goodburn 4-36.3.

Field Goals—Denver, Treadwell 3-3; Kansas City, Lowery 2-2.

Sacks—Denver, Mecklenburg 2, Kragen, Carreker; Kansas City, D. Thomas.

Vikings-Buccaneers
SUNDAY, NOVEMBER 12
SCORE BY PERIODS

Minnesota	17	0	0	7—24
Tampa Bay	0	3	0	7—10

SCORING

Minnesota—Field goal Karlis 41, 8:40 1st.
Minnesota—Rutland 27 fumble return (Karlis kick), 10:27 1st.
Minnesota—Jordan 3 pass from Wilson (Karlis kick), 12:36 1st.
Tampa Bay—Field goal Igwebuike 22, 2:54 2nd.
Tampa Bay—Wilder 5 pass from Testaverde (Igwebuike kick), 1:34 4th.
Minnesota—Walker 1 run (Karlis kick), 9:20 4th.

TEAM STATISTICS

	Minnesota	Tampa Bay
First downs	18	13
Rushes-Yards	39-158	27-90
Passing yards	145	111
Passes	13-21-0	18-30-1
Sacked-Yards lost	1-1	7-54
Punts	4-38.5	5-45.6
Fumbles-Lost	1-1	3-1
Penalties-Yards	5-42	6-31
Time of possession	30:44	29:16

Attendance—56,271.

INDIVIDUAL STATISTICS

Rushing—Minnesota, Fenney 13-55, Wilson 8-55, Walker 18-48; Tampa Bay, Wilder 8-30, Tate 13-27, Testaverde 2-20, Stamps 2-8, Howard 1-3, Ferguson 1-2.

Passing—Minnesota, Wilson 13-21-0—146; Tampa Bay, Testaverde 18-28-0—165, Ferguson 0-2-1—0.

Receiving—Minnesota, Jordan 4-25, Carter 2-49, Gustafson 2-22, Dozier 1-16, Jones 1-13, Walker 1-8, Fenney

1-7, Lewis 1-6; Tampa Bay, Hill 4-55, Wilder 4-42, Stamps 4-23, Carrier 2-31, Drewrey 2-10, Hall 1-2, Tate 1-2.

Kickoff Returns—Minnesota, Dozier 3-69; Tampa Bay, Elder 1-14, Stamps 1-0.

Punt Returns—Minnesota, Lewis 4-28; Tampa Bay, Drewrey 2-27.

Interceptions—Minnesota, Brim 1-0.

Punting—Minnesota, Scribner 4-38.5; Tampa Bay, Mohr 5-45.6.

Field Goals—Minnesota, Karlis 1-1; Tampa Bay, Igwebuike 1-1.

Sacks—Minnesota, Doleman 3, Millard 2, Noga 2; Tampa Bay, Moss.

Colts-Bills
SUNDAY, NOVEMBER 12
SCORE BY PERIODS

Indianapolis	0	0	0	7— 7
Buffalo	13	14	0	3—30

SCORING

Buffalo—Thomas 8 pass from Kelly (Norwood kick), 2:12 1st.
Buffalo—Field goal Norwood 42, 7:28 1st.
Buffalo—Field goal Norwood 40, 10:34 1st.
Buffalo—Reed 32 pass from Kelly (Norwood kick), 5:54 2nd.
Buffalo—Reed 3 pass from Kelly (Norwood kick), 14:52 2nd.
Buffalo—Field goal Norwood 32, 3:58 4th.
Indianapolis—Dixon fumble recovery in end zone (Biasucci kick), 6:13 4th.

TEAM STATISTICS

	Indianapolis	Buffalo
First downs	13	26
Rushes-Yards	20-86	51-232
Passing yards	103	161
Passes	12-27-0	14-30-0
Sacked-Yards lost	3-22	2-11
Punts	6-38.3	4-41.5
Fumbles-Lost	4-3	1-0
Penalties-Yards	3-15	5-30
Time of possession	18:46	41:14

Attendance—79,256.

INDIVIDUAL STATISTICS

Rushing—Indianapolis, Dickerson 19-79, Verdin 1-7; Buffalo, Thomas 29-127, K. Davis 7-59, Kinnebrew 9-38, Mueller 4-9, Kelly 2-minus 1.

Passing—Indianapolis, Ramsey 12-27-0—125; Buffalo, Kelly 14-30-0—172.

Receiving—Indianapolis, Rison 4-81, Brooks 2-15, Dickerson 2-8, Boyer 2-7, Beach 1-7, Bentley 1-7; Buffalo, Reed 6-76, McKeller 3-41, Thomas 2-21, Johnson 1-14, Beebe 1-12, Kinnebrew 1-8.

Kickoff Returns—Indianapolis, Pruitt 4-53, Verdin 2-38; Buffalo, Jackson 1-0.

Punt Returns—Buffalo, Sutton 4-34.

Interceptions—None.

Punting—Indianapolis, Stark 6-38.3; Buffalo, Kidd 4-41.5.

Field Goals—Indianapolis, none attempted; Buffalo, Norwood 3-4 (missed: 42).

Sacks—Indianapolis, Hand, Thompson; Buffalo, Seals, Bennett, B. Smith.

Saints-Patriots
SUNDAY, NOVEMBER 12
SCORE BY PERIODS

New Orleans	7	21	0	0—28
New England	0	10	0	14—24

SCORING

New Orleans—Hilliard 3 run (Andersen kick), 13:17 1st.

New Orleans—Brenner 1 pass from Hebert (Andersen kick), 1:25 2nd.
New Orleans—Maxie 26 interception return (Andersen kick), 1:53 2nd.
New Orleans—Hilliard 10 run (Andersen kick), 5:06 2nd.
New England—Perryman 1 run (Staurovsky kick), 6:28 2nd.
New England—Field goal Staurovsky 44, 14:52 2nd.
New England—Dykes 13 pass from Grogan (Staurovsky kick), 11:43 4th.
New England—Perryman 3 run (Staurovsky kick), 13:46 4th.

TEAM STATISTICS

	New Orleans	New England
First downs	14	28
Rushes-Yards	39-129	23-82
Passing yards	82	272
Passes	9-17-1	27-59-1
Sacked-Yards lost	2-19	2-11
Punts	6-37.3	4-27.5
Fumbles-Lost	0-0	3-3
Penalties-Yards	11-76	2-15
Time of possession	32:20	27:40

Attendance—47,680.

INDIVIDUAL STATISTICS

Rushing—New Orleans, Hilliard 28-106, Jordan 7-22, Hebert 4-1; New England, Perryman 9-40, Stephens 8-21, Martin 1-13, Grogan 2-5, Tatupu 3-3.

Passing—New Orleans, Hebert 9-16-1—101, Fourcade 0-1-0—0; New England, Grogan 27-59-1—283.

Receiving—New Orleans, E. Martin 3-25, Hill 2-18, Brenner 2-9, Scales 1-26, Hilliard 1-23; New England, Tatupu 8-34, Dykes 5-105, Morgan 5-69, Sievers 5-40, Perryman 3-18, Martin 1-17.

Kickoff Returns—New Orleans, Harris 2-45, Atkins 1-21; New England, Martin 3-65, Rice 1-26, Timpson 1-0.

Punt Returns—New Orleans, Harris 1-8; New England, Martin 3-12, Hurst 1-6.

Interceptions—New Orleans, Maxie 1-26; New England, Marion 1-1.

Punting—New Orleans, Barnhardt 6-37.3; New England, Feagles 4-27.5.

Field Goals—New Orleans, none attempted; New England, Staurovsky 1-1.

Sacks—New Orleans, Swilling 2; New England, Brown, Jeter.

Giants-Rams
SUNDAY, NOVEMBER 12
SCORE BY PERIODS

New York Giants	0	3	0	7—10
Los Angeles Rams	10	14	7	0—31

SCORING

Los Angeles—Field goal Lansford 44, 7:16 1st.
Los Angeles—Bell 1 run (Lansford kick), 13:02 1st.
New York—Field goal Allegre 22, 13:10 2nd.
Los Angeles—A. Cox 51 pass from Everett (Lansford kick), 14:15 2nd.
Los Angeles—Anderson 21 pass from Everett (Lansford kick), 14:29 2nd.
Los Angeles—Bell 2 run (Lansford kick), 7:22 3rd.
New York—Anderson 1 run (Allegre kick), 3:30 4th.

TEAM STATISTICS

	New York	Los Angeles
First downs	13	29
Rushes-Yards	10-6	40-150
Passing yards	201	295
Passes	25-38-1	23-33-2
Sacked-Yards lost	4-36	0-0
Punts	7-47.1	4-34.8
Fumbles-Lost	3-1	2-0
Penalties-Yards	7-52	4-38
Time of possession	22:24	37:36

Attendance—65,127.

INDIVIDUAL STATISTICS

Rushing—New York, Anderson 9-7, Simms 1-minus 1; Los Angeles, Gary 8-45, Bell 14-42, Delpino 11-34, McGee 5-17, Everett 2-12.

Passing—New York, Simms 25-38-1—237; Los Angeles, Everett 23-33-2—295.

Receiving—New York, Meggett 5-51, Anderson 5-32, Turner 4-27, Ingram 3-58, Manuel 2-21, Mowatt 2-12, Baker 1-19, Carthon 1-13, Rouson 1-7, Adams 1-minus 3; Los Angeles, Holohan 6-44, Bell 5-42, Delpino 4-70, McGee 3-16, A. Cox 2-66, Ellard 1-30, Anderson 1-21, Johnson 1-6.

Kickoff Returns—New York, Ingram 5-78, Meggett 1-10; Los Angeles, Delpino 2-38.

Punt Returns—New York, Meggett 2-10; Los Angeles, Henley 5-24.

Interceptions—New York, Kinard 1-37, Guyton 1-14; Los Angeles, Henley 1-10.

Punting—New York, Landeta 7-47.1; Los Angeles, Hatcher 4-34.8.

Field Goals—New York, Allegre 1-1; Los Angeles, Lansford 1-1.

Sacks—Los Angeles, Piel 2, Greene 2.

Bengals-Oilers
MONDAY, NOVEMBER 13
SCORE BY PERIODS

Cincinnati	0	14	0	10—24
Houston	0	7	6	13—26

SCORING

Cincinnati—Brooks 58 run (Breech kick), 0:48 2nd.
Houston—Seale recovered blocked punt in end zone (Zendejas kick), 12:00 2nd.
Cincinnati—Taylor 1 run (Breech kick), 14:47 2nd.
Houston—Field goal Zendejas 32, 11:32 3rd.
Houston—Field goal Zendejas 42, 1:34 3rd.
Houston—Field goal Zendejas 37, 0:42 4th.
Cincinnati—Holman 73 pass from Esiason (Breech kick), 1:49 4th.
Houston—Harris 23 pass from Moon (Zendejas kick), 3:11 4th.
Cincinnati—Field goal Breech 38, 7:27 4th.
Houston—Field goal Zendejas 28, 15:00 4th.

TEAM STATISTICS

	Cincinnati	Houston
First downs	16	20
Rushes-Yards	31-162	32-136
Passing yards	175	175
Passes	11-19-0	17-33-1
Sacked-Yards lost	4-34	2-23
Punts	5-35.2	3-41.7
Fumbles-Lost	1-1	0-0
Penalties-Yards	5-39	8-73
Time of possession	27:57	32:03

Attendance—60,694.

INDIVIDUAL STATISTICS

Rushing—Cincinnati, Brooks 19-141, Jennings 9-16, Esiason 1-11, Taylor 1-1, Johnson 1-minus 7; Houston, Highsmith 15-63, Rozier 10-39, Moon 4-23, Pinkett 3-11.

Passing—Cincinnati, Esiason 11-19-0—209; Houston, Moon 17-33-1—198.

Receiving—Cincinnati, Brown 4-45, McGee 3-53, Holman 2-93, Jennings 2-18; Houston, Givins 5-44, Hill 4-33, Harris 3-77, Jeffires 3-41, White 1-8, Pinkett 1-minus 5.

Kickoff Returns—Cincinnati, Hillary 3-62, Smith 1-12, Jennings 2-28; Houston, White 1-18, K. Johnson 1-13.

Punt Returns—Houston, K. Johnson 2-29.

Interceptions—Cincinnati, Thomas 1-0.

Punting—Cincinnati, Johnson 4-44.0; Houston, Greg Montgomery 3-41.7.

Field Goals—Cincinnati, Breech 1-1; Houston, Zendejas 4-4.

Sacks—Cincinnati, Thomas 2; Houston, Fuller 2, Childress, Glenn Montgomery.

ELEVENTH WEEK

RESULTS OF WEEK 11
Sunday, November 19

Cincinnati 42, Detroit 7 at Cin.
Cleveland 10, Kansas City 10 (OT) at Cleve.
Green Bay 21, San Francisco 17 at S.F.
Houston 23, L.A. Raiders 7 at Hous.
Indianapolis 27, N.Y. Jets 10 at Ind.
L.A. Rams 37, Phoenix 14 at L.A.
Miami 17, Dallas 14 at Dall.
New England 33, Buffalo 24 at N.E.
New Orleans 26, Atlanta 17 at Atl.
N.Y. Giants 15, Seattle 3 at N.Y.
Philadelphia 10, Minnesota 9 at Phila.
Pittsburgh 20, San Diego 17 at Pitts.
Tampa Bay 32, Chicago 31 at Chi.

Monday, November 20

Denver 14, Washington 10 at Wash.

The game was billed as The Return of Marty Schottenheimer. The postgame talk centered more on The Agony of Nick Lowery.

Schottenheimer, who resigned as coach of the Cleveland Browns after the 1988 season following a well-publicized falling-out with Browns Owner Art Modell, returned to Cleveland in Week 11 of the 1989 season with his new team, the Kansas City Chiefs. But Schottenheimer, who became the Chiefs' coach one month after leaving the Browns, was not able to exact complete revenge against his former team.

He got half, though.

The Chiefs and Browns played to a 10-10 tie at Cleveland Stadium, the only tie game of the '89 NFL season and the first for the Browns since 1973. The game ended deadlocked largely because of Lowery, the veteran Kansas City place-kicker who missed two field goals in the final seconds of regulation time and another in the waning seconds of overtime.

Lowery, who entered the 1989 season in second place on the National Football League's all-time field-goal accuracy list (201 of 258 for 77.9 percent), missed attempts of 45 and 39 yards in the final 10 seconds of regulation. The second try came after the Browns were penalized for being offside. And then he failed on a 47-yarder with seven seconds left in overtime.

"It's just frustrating," said Lowery, who trailed only Morten Andersen of the New Orleans Saints (151 of 193, 78.2 percent) heading into '89. "I let the guys down when I had my chance.

"The toughest thing about being a kicker is, you're out there by yourself and you've got to be able to handle the fact that sooner or later there are going to be ups and downs. Until today, I felt like I was kicking as well as ever."

The Browns, too, were disappointed in the outcome. Lowery tied the game at 10-10 by hit-

ting a line-drive 41-yard field goal with 3:48 left in the fourth quarter, a score that was set up by Cleveland rookie Eric Metcalf's fumble at his 38.

"It was a tough game to lose, obviously," said Browns Coach Bud Carson, a longtime NFL assistant who succeeded Schottenheimer. "A tough game to tie, excuse me. Most of our players feel like we lost."

In truth, neither team did enough on offense to deserve to win. The Chiefs threw three interceptions and punted 11 times. The Kansas City offense did not get inside the Cleveland 38 until late in the fourth quarter. And Christian Okoye, the NFL's rushing leader, had only 40 yards on 21 carries.

The Browns lost four fumbles and one interception and equaled their club record by punting 12 times. Mike Oliphant fumbled twice—Neil Smith returned one bobble for a Kansas City touchdown—and Tim Manoa fumbled to kill another Cleveland drive at the Chiefs' 14.

But because of the way the game ended, it was Lowery—not Okoye, Metcalf, Oliphant or Manoa—who was singled out for most of the blame.

"You can't fault Nick that he missed those field goals," Smith said. "He can't be the hero every game. It just wasn't his day. We all have those days."

Another player to suffer through a final few minutes he'd just as soon forget was Buffalo quarterback Jim Kelly, who turned the ball over two times in the final three minutes of the Bills' 33-24 loss to the New England Patriots.

The Bills were ahead with three minutes left before Patriots rookie cornerback Maurice Hurst stepped in front of a Kelly pass intended for James Lofton and returned the interception 16 yards for a New England touchdown. Kelly then fumbled at the Patriots' 31 to kill the Bills' last possession.

Hurst's first pro touchdown came on Buffalo's first play from scrimmage after Jason Staurovsky's 34-yard field goal with 3:06 left had cut the Bills' lead to 24-23.

The team that scored the most points in Week 11 was the Cincinnati Bengals, who took advantage of five Detroit turnovers and blasted the Lions, 42-7, in an interconference clash. The Bengals exploded for four touchdowns in the second quarter, two of them coming after Detroit fumbles and another when Barney Bussey recovered a blocked punt in the Lions' end zone. It marked the first time Cincinnati had scored a touchdown off a blocked punt since 1978.

The Lions, who entered the game with an NFL-high 34 turnovers, converted just two of 13 third-down opportunities while losing for the ninth time in 11 games.

The Bengals, on the other hand, had little

difficulty scoring points or moving the football. Quarterback Boomer Esiason completed 30 of 39 passes for 399 yards and wide receiver Tim McGee established a Bengals regular-season record with 11 receptions (for a career-high 194 yards). Eleven players caught passes for Cincinnati as the Bengals set a team record with 447 net passing yards.

There also was no shortage of offense in Week 11 for the Indianapolis Colts, who scored on five of their first six possessions en route to a 27-10 AFC Eastern Division conquest of the New York Jets. The Colts rolled up a season-high 424 yards in total offense and quarterback Jack Trudeau completed 17 of 28 passes for 255 yards. Indianapolis had lost its last three games.

After being shut down on offense for most of the game, the Pittsburgh Steelers put together a 91-yard scoring drive in the fourth quarter to upend the San Diego Chargers, 20-17. The Steelers, held to minus four yards of total offense in the second half prior to the long march, scored what proved to be the game-winning touchdown on Merril Hoge's one-yard run with 6:17 left.

Hoge's touchdown came on fourth down after the Chargers' defense had held the Steelers on three straight plays inside the San Diego 2. It was the first touchdown scored by the Pittsburgh offense in 10 quarters.

The Philadelphia Eagles didn't score an offensive touchdown until the final three minutes but it proved to be enough in a 10-9 victory over the Minnesota Vikings. Cris Carter's juggling catch of a three-yard pass from Randall Cunningham with 2:32 remaining gave the Eagles their only touchdown despite five earlier drives inside the Minnesota 25. Carter's touchdown came seven plays after a fumble by the Vikings' Herschel Walker.

Walker, who had scored the game's only touchdown to that point on a 93-yard return of the opening kickoff, fumbled after being hit by the Eagles' Clyde Simmons on a first-down play at the Philadelphia 46 with 4:54 to go. Byron Evans picked up the loose ball and rambled 17 yards before lateraling to teammate Eric Allen, who carried the ball another seven yards to the Minnesota 20.

Another one-point game was played in Chicago, where the Bears lost to NFC Central Division rival Tampa Bay, 32-31, on Donald Igwebuike's 28-yard field goal as time expired. Igwebuike's kick capped a wild final five minutes in which the two teams combined for 33 points.

Igwebuike's fourth field goal of the game was made necessary by the late-game heroics of Chicago quarterback Mike Tomczak, who came off the bench with 4:27 left in the fourth quarter and nearly guided the Bears to victory. Tomczak, who had lost his starting job to Jim Harbaugh two weeks earlier, threw three

Jim Everett passed for 308 yards in the Rams' 37-14 victory over the Phoenix Cardinals.

touchdown passes in 2:41 after replacing Harbaugh with the Bears trailing 23-10. Tomczak's 52-yard scoring pass to Wendell Davis with 1:46 left gave Chicago a 31-29 lead before Igwebuike's game-winner.

The Bucs, who had not won since a 42-35 victory over the Bears in Week 5, snapped a five-game losing streak and swept their season series with Chicago for the first time ever.

The New Orleans Saints defeated NFC Western Division rival Atlanta for the sixth straight time with a 26-17 triumph over the Falcons in Week 11. Dalton Hilliard rushed for a career-high 158 yards on 29 attempts and scored on a 22-yard run midway through the third period. Hilliard carried the ball eight times for 71 yards on the nine-play, 75-yard scoring drive.

Hilliard's touchdown tied the score at 10-10 and may have been the game's turning point. Falcons rookie Deion Sanders shoved the Saints running back out of the end zone on the play and was assessed a personal-foul penalty. Sanders' roughhouse play fired up the Saints and, on Atlanta's next possession, Brian Forde blocked a Scott Fulhage punt out of the Falcons' end zone for a safety to give New Orleans a 12-10 lead.

It was easy to discern the turning point in the Miami Dolphins' 17-14 interconference victory over the Dallas Cowboys at Texas Stadium.

The Cowboys led, 14-3, with one second left in the first half when the Dolphins' offense lined up at the Dallas 48 for the final play. Dan Marino heaved a "Hail Mary" pass near the Cowboys' goal line and rookie Andre Brown, seemingly well-covered, outjumped five Dallas defenders before catching the ball on the 1 and falling into the end zone for a Miami touchdown.

The stunned Cowboys didn't score a point in the second half.

The Dolphins, meanwhile, took their first lead of the game on rookie Sammie Smith's one-yard touchdown run with 11:05 left. The touchdown came after Marino completed four passes for 62 yards on a drive that began with a 22-yard interception return by safety Liffort Hobley.

This game was a disaster for proponents of the NFL's instant-replay system, which had often been blasted by critics for being time-consuming and too often inconclusive. Fourteen plays were reviewed by the replay officials but no on-field rulings were overturned.

The biggest upset of the week and one of the biggest of the '89 season was registered by the Green Bay Packers, who forced four turnovers and had six quarterback sacks in a 21-17 victory over the San Francisco 49ers. It was the Packers' first triumph in San Francisco since 1963 and snapped a six-game winning streak for the defending Super Bowl champions.

Quarterback Don Majkowski, who ran two yards for one Green Bay touchdown before passing four yards to Sterling Sharpe for another, scored the game-winning TD on an eight-yard run with 11:55 left.

The 49ers, however, were as much responsible for their loss as the Packers were. Besides having their highest turnover total in 21 games, the 49ers were penalized 10 times for 72 yards—and often were whistled for infractions at the worst times. San Francisco was penalized three times for 35 yards on the Packers' game-winning drive and lineman Daniel Stubbs was ruled offside on a play that wiped out a 94-yard interception return for an apparent touchdown by Chet Brooks.

After the 49ers drove to the Green Bay 28 in the last three minutes of play, two more penalties and a sack of quarterback Joe Montana killed San Francisco's final scoring threat.

The 49ers' loss dropped their record to 9-2 and cut their lead in the NFC Western Division to two games over the Los Angeles Rams, who built up a 24-0 halftime lead over the Phoenix Cardinals on the way to a 37-14 victory. The Rams got off to a fast start when safety Michael Stewart returned an interception 41 yards for a touchdown on the Cards' third play from scrimmage.

Stewart's interception was the first of four by a Rams defense that also had five sacks and didn't allow a point until late in the third quarter. The Cards used three quarterbacks—veterans Gary Hogeboom and Tom Tupa and rookie Timm Rosenbach—but all proved ineffective at moving the team.

The Rams' offense, however, compiled 436 total yards and Jim Everett completed 15 of 24 passes for 308 yards and two touchdowns. Both of the fourth-year quarterback's scoring passes were caught by Henry Ellard, who finished with five receptions for 163 yards.

Houston quarterback Warren Moon threw two touchdown passes and Tony Zendejas kicked three field goals to lead the Oilers to a 23-7 victory over the Los Angeles Raiders. Houston's third straight victory gave the team its longest winning streak since 1985.

The Oilers' defense played havoc with the Raiders all afternoon, recording four sacks and forcing five turnovers that led to 13 Houston points. The Oilers held running back Bo Jackson—who had more than 100 yards rushing in the Raiders' three previous games—to only 54 yards on 11 carries. Jackson rushed for just four yards in the second half as Los Angeles tried to rebound from a 17-7 halftime deficit.

The New York Giants took the opening kickoff and drove 68 yards in 12 plays for a touchdown and then made it hold up in a 15-3 decision over Seattle. The Giants later added two field goals by rookie Bjorn Nittmo and a safety to improve their record to 9-2 and maintain a two-game lead over Philadelphia in the NFC Eastern Division race.

The Seahawks started second-year player Kelly Stouffer in place of veteran quarterback Dave Krieg in an effort to revitalize a sluggish offense but the move didn't work. The Seattle offense managed just 195 yards and 12 first downs and did not score until Norm Johnson booted a 42-yard field goal with 9:08 to play.

The Seahawks, who dropped to 4-7 with the loss, crossed midfield only twice in the game.

The biggest lead any division leader enjoyed after 11 weeks belonged to the Denver Broncos, who increased their edge in the AFC Western Division to four games with a 14-10 victory at Washington in the Monday night game. The Broncos, whose closest pursuers in the AFC West were the 5-6 Raiders, were tied with San Francisco and the New York Giants for the league's best overall record at 9-2.

This game marked the first meeting between the Broncos and Redskins since Washington's 42-10 victory over Denver in Super Bowl XXII in January 1988. Neither of the starting quarterbacks in that showcase game started in this one. Washington's Doug Williams, the Most Valuable Player in Super Bowl XXII, missed the game because of a bad back and Denver's John Elway was sidelined by a stomach virus.

Elway's replacement, however, was more than up to the task. Gary Kubiak, who had attempted only two passes previously in 1989 and was making his first NFL start in five years, threw touchdown passes to Melvin Bratton and Ricky Nattiel.

Although Kubiak fumbled on Denver's third play of the game to set up Washington's only touchdown, the seven-year veteran demonstrated coolness under fire. He punted two times and directed a 14-play drive that kept the ball away from the Redskins and allowed the Broncos to use up the remaining 6:45 on the clock.

Cardinals-Rams
SUNDAY, NOVEMBER 19
SCORE BY PERIODS

Phoenix	0	0	7	7—14
Los Angeles Rams	14	10	3	10—37

SCORING
Los Angeles—Stewart 41 interception return (Lansford kick), 1:46 1st.
Los Angeles—Ellard 49 pass from Everett (Lansford kick), 10:19 1st.
Los Angeles—Delpino 32 run (Lansford kick), 2:37 2nd.
Los Angeles—Field goal Lansford 27, 14:10 2nd.
Los Angeles—Field goal Lansford 23, 8:46 3rd.
Phoenix—Holmes 77 pass from Tupa (Del Greco kick), 10:17 3rd.
Los Angeles—Field goal Lansford 40, 0:04 4th.
Los Angeles—Ellard 42 pass from Everett (Lansford kick), 5:11 4th.
Phoenix—Jordan 1 run (Del Greco kick), 11:42 4th.

TEAM STATISTICS

	Phoenix	Los Angeles
First downs	13	16
Rushes-Yards	21-76	35-135
Passing yards	216	301
Passes	20-36-4	15-24-0
Sacked-Yards lost	5-27	1-7
Punts	7-48.6	5-42.8
Fumbles-Lost	2-0	1-1
Penalties-Yards	8-60	11-75
Time of possession	29:34	30:26
Attendance—53,176.		

INDIVIDUAL STATISTICS
Rushing—Phoenix, Jordan 7-18, Rosenbach 4-18, Sikahema 3-14, Ferrell 4-12, Tupa 2-11, Hogeboom 1-3; Los Angeles, Delpino 11-68, Bell 11-32, Gary 6-16, McGee 2-11, Green 3-9, Herrmann 2-minus 1.

Passing—Phoenix, Hogeboom 6-10-2—48, Tupa 7-12-1—114, Rosenbach 7-14-1—81; Los Angeles, Everett 15-24-0—308.

Receiving—Phoenix, Sikahema 5-37, Jones 4-72, Green 4-38, Awalt 2-6, Holmes 1-77, McConkey 1-10, Novacek 1-5, Jordan 1-1, Ferrell 1-minus 3; Los Angeles, Ellard 5-163, Delpino 3-46, Anderson 2-48, Ron Brown 2-33, Holohan 2-13, McGee 1-5.

Kickoff Returns—Phoenix, Usher 7-145; Los Angeles, Delpino 1-20, Ron Brown 1-16.

Punt Returns—Phoenix, Sikahema 3-32; Los Angeles, Henley 4-30.

Interceptions—Los Angeles, Stewart 1-41, Gray 2-11, Hicks 1-0.

Punting—Phoenix, Camarillo 7-48.6; Los Angeles, Hatcher 5-42.8.

Field Goals—Phoenix, none attempted; Los Angeles, Lansford 3-3.

Sacks—Phoenix, Bell; Los Angeles, Wilcher, Bethune, Strickland, Greene 2.

Chiefs-Browns
SUNDAY, NOVEMBER 19
SCORE BY PERIODS

Kansas City	0	0	7	3 0—10
Cleveland	0	3	7	0 0—10

SCORING
Cleveland—Field goal Bahr 40, 15:00 2nd.
Kansas City—Smith 3 fumble return (Lowery kick), 0:21 3rd.
Cleveland—Metcalf 1 run (Bahr kick), 13:36 3rd.
Kansas City—Field goal Lowery 41, 11:12 4th.

TEAM STATISTICS

	Kansas City	Cleveland
First downs	17	17
Rushes-Yards	33-119	37-78
Passing yards	188	183
Passes	19-45-3	21-42-1
Sacked-Yards lost	5-37	3-15
Punts	11-37.0	12-38.6
Fumbles-Lost	0-0	4-4
Penalties-Yards	10-80	12-98
Time of possession	38:10	36:50
Attendance—77,922.		

INDIVIDUAL STATISTICS
Rushing—Kansas City, Okoye 21-40, Heard 7-35, Pelluer 1-18, DeBerg 1-15, McNair 3-11; Cleveland, Metcalf 23-49, Manoa 13-34, Oliphant 1-minus 5.

Passing—Kansas City, DeBerg 17-40-2—209, Pelluer 2-4-0—16, Saxon 0-1-1—0; Cleveland, Kosar 21-42-1—198.

Receiving—Kansas City, McNair 5-33, Mandley 4-56, Harry 3-47, Heard 3-40, Weathers 3-35, Paige 1-14; Cleveland, Slaughter 6-67, Metcalf 4-27, Manoa 3-41, Langhorne 3-19, Brennan 2-20, Oliphant 2-13, Tillman 1-11.

Kickoff Returns—Kansas City, Worthen 1-19, Copeland 1-14; Cleveland, Metcalf 3-38.

Punt Returns—Kansas City, Worthen 6-36; Cleveland, McNeil 7-53.

Interceptions—Kansas City, Lewis 1-0; Cleveland, Harper 1-8, M. Johnson 1-20, Wright 1-8.

Punting—Kansas City, Goodburn 11-37.0; Cleveland, Wagner 12-38.6.

Field Goals—Kansas City, Lowery 1-3 (missed: 39, 47); Cleveland, Bahr 1-1.

Sacks—Kansas City, Smith, Griffin, Bell; Cleveland, Baker 2, Blaylock, Stewart, Perry ½, Banks ½.

Bills-Patriots
SUNDAY, NOVEMBER 19
SCORE BY PERIODS

Buffalo	7	3	0	14—24
New England	0	6	7	20—33

SCORING
Buffalo—Thomas 3 run (Norwood kick), 9:52 1st.
New England—Field goal Staurovsky 34, 4:28 2nd.
New England—Field goal Staurovsky 24, 7:56 2nd.
Buffalo—Field goal Norwood 31, 14:25 2nd.
New England—Egu 15 run (Staurovsky kick), 9:23 3rd.
Buffalo—Kinnebrew 1 run (Norwood kick), 0:02 4th.
Buffalo—Thomas 25 pass from Kelly (Norwood kick), 6:14 4th.
New England—Dykes 14 pass from Grogan (Staurovsky kick), 7:15 4th.
New England—Field goal Staurovsky 34, 11:54 4th.
New England—Hurst 16 interception return (Staurovsky kick), 12:11 4th.
New England—Field goal Staurovsky 38, 14:47 4th.

TEAM STATISTICS

	Buffalo	New England
First downs	24	20
Rushes-Yards	28-84	38-192
Passing yards	340	167
Passes	21-41-2	12-26-3
Sacked-Yards lost	3-16	0-0
Punts	4-34.0	4-33.2
Fumbles-Lost	4-4	3-1
Penalties-Yards	8-89	6-33
Time of possession	30:50	29:10

Attendance—49,663.

INDIVIDUAL STATISTICS

Rushing—Buffalo, Thomas 22-73, Kinnebrew 5-10, Kelly 1-1; New England, Stephens 23-126, Perryman 13-48, Egu 2-18.

Passing—Buffalo, Kelly 21-41-2—356; New England, Grogan 12-26-3—167.

Receiving—Buffalo, Reed 6-107, Thomas 6-98, Beebe 4-49, Lofton 2-58, Harmon 1-22, McKeller 1-15, Metzelaars 1-7; New England, Stephens 4-76, Dykes 3-53, Jones 3-25, Sievers 2-13.

Kickoff Returns—Buffalo, Beebe 5-83, Harmon 2-38, Rolle 1-14; New England, Tucker 1-17, Taylor 1-22.

Punt Returns—Buffalo, Sutton 1-14; New England, Tucker 3-29.

Interceptions—Buffalo, Kelso 1-21, Bailey 1-16, Wright 1-0; New England, James 1-22, Hurst 1-16.

Punting—Buffalo, Kidd 4-34.0; New England, Feagles 4-33.2.

Field Goals—Buffalo, Norwood 1-2 (missed: 24); New England, Staurovsky 4-4.

Sacks—New England, Williams 2, Jeter.

Dolphins-Cowboys
SUNDAY, NOVEMBER 19
SCORE BY PERIODS

Miami	0	10	0	7—17
Dallas	7	7	0	0—14

SCORING

Dallas—Sargent 1 run (Zendejas kick), 6:41 1st.
Miami—Field goal Stoyanovich 23, 6:05 2nd.
Dallas—Johnston 6 pass from Aikman (Zendejas kick), 14:25 2nd.
Miami—A. Brown 48 pass from Marino (Stoyanovich kick), 15:00 2nd.
Miami—Smith 1 run (Stoyanovich kick), 3:55 4th.

TEAM STATISTICS

	Miami	Dallas
First downs	18	28
Rushes-Yards	19-65	35-167
Passing yards	238	261
Passes	21-36-0	25-33-1
Sacked-Yards lost	2-17	0-0
Punts	5-38.1	2-31.0
Fumbles-Lost	1-1	3-1
Penalties-Yards	4-35	7-49
Time of possession	26:12	33:48

Attendance—56,044.

INDIVIDUAL STATISTICS

Rushing—Miami, Smith 14-45, T. Brown 4-15, Faaola 1-5; Dallas, Aikman 8-71, Johnston 11-50, Palmer 12-43, Tautalatasi 1-6, Sargent 2-4, Shepard 1-minus 7.

Passing—Miami, Marino 21-36-0—255; Dallas, Aikman 25-33-1—261.

Receiving—Miami, Duper 7-90, Jensen 5-46, T. Brown 3-21, Edmunds 3-17, A. Brown 2-72, Clayton 1-9; Dallas, Martin 7-82, Tautalatasi 4-45, Johnston 3-21, Palmer 3-15, Folsom 2-34, Dixon 2-28, Burbage 2-18, Shepard 1-9, Sargent 1-9.

Kickoff Returns—Miami, Hampton 2-33, Faaola 1-13; Dallas, Dixon 3-73.

Punt Returns—Miami, Schwedes 1-4; Dallas, Shepard 2-12.

Interceptions—Miami, Hobley 1-22.
Punting—Miami, Roby 5-38.1; Dallas, Saxon 2-31.0.
Field Goals—Miami, Stoyanovich 1-1; Dallas, Zendejas 0-2 (missed: 52, 53).
Sacks—Dallas, Jeffcoat 1½, Hamel ½.

Jets-Colts
SUNDAY, NOVEMBER 19
SCORE BY PERIODS

New York Jets	0	3	0	7—10
Indianapolis	3	17	7	0—27

SCORING

Indianapolis—Field goal Biasucci 45, 2:09 1st.
Indianapolis—Bentley 1 run (Biasucci kick), 3:01 2nd.
New York—Field goal Leahy 46, 4:03 2nd.
Indianapolis—Beach 1 pass from Trudeau (Biasucci kick), 11:48 2nd.
Indianapolis—Field goal Biasucci 31, 14:46 2nd.
Indianapolis—Dickerson 1 run (Biasucci kick), 7:03 3rd.
New York—Townsell 23 pass from Ryan (Leahy kick), 15:00 4th.

TEAM STATISTICS

	New York	Indianapolis
First downs	22	23
Rushes-Yards	22-110	40-185
Passing yards	244	239
Passes	27-43-3	17-28-0
Sacked-Yards lost	5-39	2-16
Punts	3-39.3	4-35.3
Fumbles-Lost	0-0	3-0
Penalties-Yards	9-70	8-85
Time of possession	27:17	32:43

Attendance—58,236.

INDIVIDUAL STATISTICS

Rushing—New York, Hector 18-88, Vick 3-15, Brown 1-7; Indianapolis, Dickerson 31-131, Bentley 7-27, Verdin 1-26, Ramsey 1-1.

Passing—New York, O'Brien 19-33-2—215, Ryan 8-10-1—68; Indianapolis, Trudeau 17-28-0—255.

Receiving—New York, Toon 11-89, Hector 6-70, Townsell 3-45, Neubert 2-20, Vick 2-9, Walker 1-31, McNeil 1-13, Brown 1-6; Indianapolis, Rison 5-108, Brooks 5-63, Verdin 2-62, Beach 2-7, Bentley 1-9, Boyer 1-8, Dickerson 1-minus 2.

Kickoff Returns—New York, Humphery 3-67, Townsell 2-60, Epps 1-12; Indianapolis, Pruitt 1-25, Bentley 1-16.

Punt Returns—New York, Townsell 2-16; Indianapolis, Verdin 1-16.

Interceptions—Indianapolis, Banks 1-11, Taylor 1-2, Prior 1-0.

Punting—New York, Prokop 3-39.3; Indianapolis, Stark 4-35.3.

Field Goals—New York, Leahy 1-2 (missed: 45); Indianapolis, Biasucci 2-3 (missed: 37).

Sacks—New York, Nichols, Lageman; Indianapolis, Banks, Thompson 1½, Johnson ½, Herrod, Larson.

Chargers-Steelers
SUNDAY, NOVEMBER 19
SCORE BY PERIODS

San Diego	0	7	10	0—17
Pittsburgh	3	3	7	7—20

SCORING

Pittsburgh—Field goal Anderson 49, 5:35 1st.
San Diego—A. Miller 20 pass from McMahon (Bahr kick), 3:07 2nd.
Pittsburgh—Field goal Anderson 28, 14:10 2nd.
San Diego—Field goal Bahr 27, 7:29 3rd.
Pittsburgh—Woodson 84 kickoff return (Anderson kick), 7:46 3rd.
San Diego—A. Miller 19 pass from McMahon (Bahr kick), 12:28 3rd.
Pittsburgh—Hoge 1 run (Anderson kick), 8:43 4th.

TEAM STATISTICS

	San Diego	Pittsburgh
First downs	20	14
Rushes-Yards	29-134	30-88
Passing yards	225	103
Passes	19-36-1	12-27-0
Sacked-Yards lost	2-1	4-39
Punts	4-39.0	6-38.5
Fumbles-Lost	2-2	2-1
Penalties-Yards	6-46	6-59
Time of possession	33:34	26:26

Attendance—44,203.

INDIVIDUAL STATISTICS

Rushing—San Diego, Spencer 22-87, Nelson 4-43, Butts 2-4, McMahon 1-0; Pittsburgh, Worley 17-53, Hoge 11-40, Brister 2-minus 5.

Passing—San Diego, McMahon 19-36-1—226; Pittsburgh, Brister 12-27-0—142.

Receiving—San Diego, A. Miller 7-104, Holland 3-69, Walker 3-20, Spencer 3-11, Cox 1-11, Allen 1-8, Nelson 1-3; Pittsburgh, Hoge 3-24, Mularkey 2-34, Lipps 2-25, Hill 2-21, Worley 1-19, Stock 1-13, Carter 1-6.

Kickoff Returns—San Diego, Holland 4-92, A. Miller 1-24; Pittsburgh, Woodson 3-125, Thompson 1-8.

Punt Returns—San Diego, Walker 1-3, Brinson 1-0, Allen 2-3, Lyles 1-0; Pittsburgh, Woodson 1-3, Hill 2-2.

Interceptions—Pittsburgh, Little 1-13.

Punting—San Diego, Ilesic 4-39.0; Pittsburgh, Newsome 6-38.5.

Field Goals—San Diego, Bahr 1-2 (missed: 38); Pittsburgh, Anderson 2-2.

Sacks—San Diego, Williams 2, Grossman, Smith; Pittsburgh, Willis, Jones.

Seahawks-Giants
SUNDAY, NOVEMBER 19
SCORE BY PERIODS

Seattle	0	0	0	3—	3
New York Giants	7	0	8	0—	15

SCORING

New York—Cross 16 pass from Simms (Nittmo kick), 6:45 1st.

New York—Field goal Nittmo 32, 3:28 3rd.

New York—Safety, Stouffer fumbled ball out of end zone, 4:20 3rd.

New York—Field goal Nittmo 32, 14:28 3rd.

Seattle—Field goal N. Johnson 42, 5:52 4th.

TEAM STATISTICS

	Seattle	New York
First downs	12	21
Rushes-Yards	20-63	45-162
Passing yards	132	187
Passes	16-29-2	17-26-0
Sacked-Yards lost	2-23	1-7
Punts	4-44.3	2-37.0
Fumbles-Lost	1-0	2-1
Penalties-Yards	4-35	5-40
Time of possession	24:26	35:34

Attendance—75,014.

INDIVIDUAL STATISTICS

Rushing—Seattle, Willliams 3-23, Warner 10-22, Fenner 3-13, Harris 3-3, Stouffer 1-2; New York, Tillman 13-68, Anderson 23-65, Turner 1-14, Carthon 4-9, Meggett 1-5, Hostetler 1-3, Simms 2-minus 2.

Passing—Seattle, Stouffer 16-29-2—155; New York, Simms 17-26-0—194.

Receiving—Seattle, Largent 4-39, Blades 3-36, McNeal 2-22, Fenner 2-17, Skansi 1-13, Chadwick 1-10, Harris 1-7, Clark 1-6, Warner 1-5; New York, Mowatt 5-32, Cross 3-52, Baker 3-41, Turner 2-21, Meggett 2-14, Manuel 1-18, Carthon 1-16.

Kickoff Returns—Seattle, Hollis 2-28, Harris 1-20; New York, Meggett 3-58.

Punt Returns—New York, Meggett 3-98.

Interceptions—New York, Banks 1-6, Collins 1-12.

Punting—Seattle, Rodriguez 4-44.3; New York, Landeta 2-37.0.

Field Goals—Seattle, N. Johnson 1-2 (missed: 35); New York, Nittmo 2-3 (missed: 27).

Sacks—Seattle, Woods; New York, Marshall 2.

Buccaneers-Bears
SUNDAY, NOVEMBER 19
SCORE BY PERIODS

Tampa Bay	10	0	3	19—32	
Chicago	0	3	7	21—31	

SCORING

Tampa Bay—Field goal Igwebuike 26, 7:19 1st.

Tampa Bay—Davis 13 interception return (Igwebuike kick), 7:31 1st.

Chicago—Field goal Butler 40, 6:22 2nd.

Tampa Bay—Field goal Igwebuike 22, 5:27 3rd.

Chicago—Anderson 59 run (Butler kick), 5:44 3rd.

Tampa Bay—Tate 15 run (Igwebuike kick), 4:13 4th.

Tampa Bay—Field goal Igwebuike 29, 10:10 4th.

Chicago—Morris 58 pass from Tomczak (Butler kick), 10:33 4th.

Tampa Bay—Carrier 78 pass from Testaverde (kick failed), 11:39 4th.

Chicago—Davis 26 pass from Tomczak (Butler kick), 12:24 4th.

Chicago—Davis 52 pass from Tomczak (Butler kick), 13:14 4th.

Tampa Bay—Field goal Igwebuike 28, 15:00 4th.

TEAM STATISTICS

	Tampa Bay	Chicago
First downs	21	14
Rushes-Yards	31-127	24-111
Passing yards	263	266
Passes	19-42-0	18-31-3
Sacked-Yards lost	4-25	3-16
Punts	7-34.4	4-33.0
Fumbles-Lost	0-0	1-1
Penalties-Yards	11-123	10-74
Time of possession	33:52	26:08

Attendance—63,826.

INDIVIDUAL STATISTICS

Rushing—Tampa Bay, Wilder 16-62, Tate 10-40, Stamps 2-20, Smith 2-4, Peebles 1-1; Chicago, Anderson 15-100, Muster 4-18, Harbaugh 3-6, Suhey 1-1, Morris 1-minus 14.

Passing—Tampa Bay, Testaverde 19-42-0—288; Chicago, Harbaugh 12-24-3—126, Tomczak 6-7-0—156.

Receiving—Tampa Bay, Carrier 6-164, Hill 3-30, Peebles 3-29, Hall 2-26, Smith 2-14, Wilder 1-14, Drewrey 1-14, Tate 1-minus 3; Chicago, Anderson 6-48, Morris 3-96, Davis 2-78, Muster 2-27, Gentry 2-15, McKinnon 1-7, Boso 1-6, Thornton 1-5.

Kickoff Returns—Tampa Bay, Elder 3-57, Howard 3-49; Chicago, Gentry 1-25, Suhey 1-14, Pruitt 1-11, Sanders 2-39, Chapura 1-8.

Punt Returns—Tampa Bay, Drewrey 1-11; Chicago, Kozlowski 4-minus 2.

Interceptions—Tampa Bay, Davis 1-13, Hamilton 1-0, Robinson 1-6.

Punting—Tampa Bay, Mohr 7-34.4; Chicago, Buford 4-33.0.

Field Goals—Tampa Bay, Igwebuike 4-5 (missed: 52); Chicago, Butler 1-1.

Sacks—Tampa Bay, Davis 2, Goff; Chicago, Armstrong, Singletary, McMichael, Dent.

Saints-Falcons
SUNDAY, NOVEMBER 19
SCORE BY PERIODS

New Orleans	3	0	9	14—26	
Atlanta	3	7	7	0—17	

SCORING

Atlanta—Field goal Davis 45, 3:29 1st.

New Orleans—Field goal Andersen 33, 10:15 1st.

Atlanta—Settle 27 pass from Miller (Davis kick), 10:02 2nd.

New Orleans—Hilliard 22 run (Andersen kick), 7:30 3rd.

New Orleans—Safety, Forde blocked punt out of end zone, 9:51 3rd.

Atlanta—Wilkins 19 pass from Miller (Davis kick), 14:05 3rd.

New Orleans—Jordan 2 run (Andersen kick), 5:40 4th.

New Orleans—Jordan 1 run (Andersen kick), 12:22 4th.

TEAM STATISTICS

	New Orleans	Atlanta
First downs	20	15
Rushes-Yards	41-206	16-77
Passing yards	148	190
Passes	13-24-4	18-38-1
Sacked-Yards lost	0-0	4-42
Punts	1-30.0	3-29.0
Fumbles-Lost	2-0	1-0
Penalties-Yards	4-20	8-82
Time of possession	39:29	20:31
Attendance—53,173.		

INDIVIDUAL STATISTICS

Rushing—New Orleans, Hilliard 29-158, Jordan 8-33, Heyward 3-13, Turner 1-2; Atlanta, Settle 12-74, Lang 3-3, Miller 1-0.

Passing—New Orleans, Hebert 13-24-4—148; Atlanta, Miller 18-38-1—232.

Receiving—New Orleans, Hilliard 3-22, E. Martin 3-13, Perriman 2-54, Brenner 2-20, Tice 1-23, Hill 1-11, Turner 1-5; Atlanta, Dixon 5-74, Settle 4-71, Collins 3-48, Lang 3-23, Wilkins 1-19, Heller 1-5, Sanders 1-minus 8.

Kickoff Returns—New Orleans, Atkins 3-71, Harris 1-19, Hill 1-13; Atlanta, Sanders 3-57.

Punt Returns—New Orleans, Harris 3-7; Atlanta, Sanders 1-10.

Interceptions—New Orleans, Massey 1-4; Atlanta, Gordon 2-26, Dimry 1-32, Sanders 1-21.

Punting—New Orleans, Barnhardt 1-30.0; Atlanta, Fulhage 3-29.0.

Field Goals—New Orleans, Andersen 1-1; Atlanta, Davis 1-2 (missed: 37).

Sacks—New Orleans, Swilling 3½, W. Martin ½.

Raiders-Oilers
SUNDAY, NOVEMBER 19
SCORE BY PERIODS

Los Angeles Raiders	0	7	0	0— 7
Houston	7	10	3	3—23

SCORING

Houston—Duncan 25 pass from Moon (Zendejas kick), 4:21 1st.

Los Angeles—Dyal 22 pass from Beuerlein (Jaeger kick), 2:39 2nd.

Houston—Field goal Zendejas 20, 10:39 2nd.

Houston—Harris 11 pass from Moon (Zendejas kick), 14:35 2nd.

Houston—Field goal Zendejas 20, 3:46 3rd.

Houston—Field goal Zendejas 46, 4:34 4th.

TEAM STATISTICS

	Los Angeles	Houston
First downs	12	23
Rushes-Yards	15-74	41-170
Passing yards	169	249
Passes	12-27-3	20-30-1
Sacked-Yards lost	4-30	0-0
Punts	4-42.3	3-42.7
Fumbles-Lost	2-2	2-1
Penalties-Yards	12-119	8-49
Time of possession	20:12	39:48
Attendance—59,198.		

INDIVIDUAL STATISTICS

Rushing—Los Angeles, Jackson 11-54, Evans 1-16, Smith 1-3, Beuerlein 2-1; Houston, Rozier 15-59, Pinkett 8-45, Highsmith 7-37, White 6-20, Moon 4-11, Carlson 1-minus 2.

Passing—Los Angeles, Beuerlein 10-25-3—149, Evans 2-2-0—50; Houston, Moon 20-30-1—249.

Receiving—Los Angeles, Fernandez 5-102, Gault 2-48, Jackson 2-5, Dyal 1-22, Mueller 1-12, Alexander 1-10; Houston, Duncan 5-60, Harris 4-54, Jeffires 3-79, Givins 3-24, Pinkett 3-11, Highsmith 1-13, T. Johnson 1-8.

Kickoff Returns—Los Angeles, Adams 4-86, Ware 2-52; Houston, T. Johnson 1-10, White 1-11.

Punt Returns—Los Angeles, Adams 2-11.

Interceptions—Los Angeles, Harden 1-1; Houston, Eaton 1-13, Brown 1-0, Dishman 1-0.

Punting—Los Angeles, Gossett 4-42.3; Houston, Greg Montgomery 3-42.7.

Field Goals—Los Angeles, none attempted; Houston, Zendejas 3-3.

Sacks—Houston, Fuller, Fairs, Glenn Montgomery, Meads.

Vikings-Eagles
SUNDAY, NOVEMBER 19
SCORE BY PERIODS

Minnesota	6	0	3	0— 9
Philadelphia	3	0	0	7—10

SCORING

Minnesota—Walker 93 kickoff return (kick failed), 0:15 1st.

Philadelphia—Field goal DeLine 34, 10:37 1st.

Minnesota—Field goal Karlis 49, 13:05 3rd.

Philadelphia—Carter 3 pass from Cunningham (DeLine kick), 12:28 4th.

TEAM STATISTICS

	Minnesota	Philadelphia
First downs	18	22
Rushes-Yards	25-83	32-101
Passing yards	136	169
Passes	14-34-2	26-43-0
Sacked-Yards lost	2-21	5-38
Punts	3-44.3	5-32.6
Fumbles-Lost	3-3	1-1
Penalties-Yards	10-74	5-50
Time of possession	23:47	36:13
Attendance—65,944.		

INDIVIDUAL STATISTICS

Rushing—Minnesota, Walker 13-48, Fenney 11-36, Wilson 1-minus 1; Philadelphia, Byars 12-41, Toney 8-28, Cunningham 8-18, Carter 1-11, Drummond 3-3.

Passing—Minnesota, Wilson 14-34-2—157; Philadelphia, Cunningham 26-43-0—207.

Receiving—Minnesota, Carter 6-73, Fenney 3-28, Lewis 2-17, Walker 1-24, Jones 1-8, Jordan 1-7; Philadelphia, Jackson 12-87, Byars 6-48, Carter 4-27, Drummond 3-28, Johnson 1-17.

Kickoff Returns—Minnesota, Walker 1-93, Dozier 1-25; Philadelphia, Williams 2-38, Sherman 1-17.

Punt Returns—Minnesota, Lewis 2-7; Philadelphia, Williams 2-8.

Interceptions—Philadelphia, Allen 1-0, Frizzell 1-0.

Punting—Minnesota, Scribner 3-44.3; Philadelphia, Runager 5-32.6.

Field Goals—Minnesota, Karlis 1-2 (missed: 37); Philadelphia, DeLine 1-4 (missed: 45, 32, 46).

Sacks—Minnesota, Doleman 2, Thomas, Merriweather, Browner; Philadelphia, Joyner, Brown.

Packers-49ers
SUNDAY, NOVEMBER 19
SCORE BY PERIODS

Green Bay	7	7	0	7—21
San Francisco	7	7	0	3—17

SCORING

Green Bay—Majkowski 2 run (Jacke kick), 6:46 1st.

San Francisco—Craig 4 pass from Montana (Cofer kick), 10:49 1st.

Green Bay—Sharpe 4 pass from Majkowski (Jacke kick), 5:06 2nd.

San Francisco—Rice 9 pass from Montana (Cofer kick), 14:51 2nd.

Green Bay—Majkowski 8 run (Jacke kick), 3:05 4th.

San Francisco—Field goal Cofer 44, 7:17 4th.

TEAM STATISTICS

	Green Bay	San Francisco
First downs	21	22
Rushes-Yards	31-109	16-71
Passing yards	139	289
Passes	18-30-0	30-42-1
Sacked-Yards lost	2-14	6-36
Punts	5-35.4	2-45.5
Fumbles-Lost	1-1	3-3
Penalties-Yards	3-25	10-72
Time of possession	32:05	27:55
Attendance—62,219.		

INDIVIDUAL STATISTICS

Rushing—Green Bay, Fullwood 16-76, Haddix 5-15, Majkowski 6-15, Fontenot 2-3, Woodside 2-0; San Francisco, Craig 8-41, Rathman 6-17, Montana 2-13.

Passing—Green Bay, Majkowski 18-30-0—153; San Francisco, Montana 30-42-1—325.

Receiving—Green Bay, Sharpe 6-59, Matthews 3-30, Fullwood 3-18, Bland 2-21, Haddix 2-3, Woodside 1-13, Didier 1-9; San Francisco, Rice 9-106, Taylor 7-71, Rathman 6-43, Craig 5-76, Jones 2-16, Wilson 1-13.

Kickoff Returns—Green Bay, Bland 2-40, Workman 1-14; San Francisco, Taylor 2-51, Greer 1-17.

Punt Returns—Green Bay, Query 1-14; San Francisco, Taylor 1-8.

Interceptions—Green Bay, Cecil 1-16.

Punting—Green Bay, Bracken 5-35.4; San Francisco, Helton 2-45.5.

Field Goals—Green Bay, Jacke 0-1 (missed: 38); San Francisco, Cofer 1-2 (missed: 45).

Sacks—Green Bay, Harris, R. Brown, Greene, Murphy, Winter, Noble; San Francisco, Haley, Stubbs.

Lions-Bengals
SUNDAY, NOVEMBER 19
SCORE BY PERIODS

Detroit	7	0	0	0— 7
Cincinnati	0	28	7	7—42

SCORING

Detroit—B. Sanders 2 run (Murray kick), 1:07 1st.

Cincinnati—McGee 17 pass from Esiason (Breech kick), 1:31 2nd.

Cincinnati—Taylor 3 run (Breech kick), 10:21 2nd.

Cincinnati—Taylor 1 pass from Esiason (Breech kick), 11:34 2nd.

Cincinnati—Bussey recovered blocked punt in end zone (Breech kick), 12:51 2nd.

Cincinnati—Martin 15 pass from Esiason (Breech kick), 7:32 3rd.

Cincinnati—Smith 41 pass from Wilhelm (Breech kick), 10:28 4th.

TEAM STATISTICS

	Detroit	Cincinnati
First downs	10	27
Rushes-Yards	28-122	31-99
Passing yards	156	447
Passes	13-27-2	33-45-2
Sacked-Yards lost	2-15	1-3
Punts	9-35.2	4-39.5
Fumbles-Lost	6-3	2-1
Penalties-Yards	8-61	7-65
Time of possession	24:24	35:36
Attendance—55,720.		

INDIVIDUAL STATISTICS

Rushing—Detroit, B. Sanders 18-114, Gagliano 2-12, Painter 2-8, Johnson 2-minus 7, Peete 1-minus 1, Paige 2-minus 2, McDonald 1-minus 2; Cincinnati, Brooks 11-51, Jennings 9-19, Taylor 6-21, Ball 2-5, Wilhelm 2-2, Esiason 1-1.

Passing—Detroit, Peete 5-8-0—83, Gagliano 8-19-2—88; Cincinnati, Esiason 30-39-1—399, Wilhelm 3-6-1—51.

Receiving—Detroit, Phillips 3-41, Clark 2-78, Ford 2-15, McDonald 2-12, Gray 1-17, Painter 1-6, B. Sanders 1-6, Stanley 1-minus 4; Cincinnati, McGee 11-194, Holman 5-76, Brown 5-72, Martin 4-36, Jennings 2-11, Smith 1-41, Hillary 1-7, Kattus 1-5, Ball 1-4, Riggs 1-3, Taylor 1-1.

Kickoff Returns—Detroit, Alexander 1-25, Gray 1-19; Cincinnati, Jennings 2-37.

Punt Returns—Detroit, Stanley 3-20; Cincinnati, Martin 2-11.

Interceptions—Detroit, Holmes 1-0, Noga 1-0; Cincinnati, Thomas 1-0, Carey 1-5.

Punting—Detroit, Arnold 8-39.6; Cincinnati, Johnson 4-39.5.

Field Goals—Detroit, none attempted; Cincinnati, Breech 0-1 (missed: 49).

Sacks—Detroit, Spielman; Cincinnati, Krumrie, Buck.

Broncos-Redskins
MONDAY, NOVEMBER 20
SCORE BY PERIODS

Denver	7	7	0	0—14
Washington	7	0	3	0—10

SCORING

Washington—Morris 8 run (Lohmiller kick), 1:07 1st.

Denver—Bratton 1 pass from Kubiak (Treadwell kick), 6:12 1st.

Denver—Nattiel 5 pass from Kubiak (Treadwell kick), 5:35 2nd.

Washington—Field goal Lohmiller 32, 8:03 3rd.

TEAM STATISTICS

	Denver	Washington
First downs	19	14
Rushes-Yards	43-131	25-77
Passing yards	101	146
Passes	13-27-1	15-29-0
Sacked-Yards lost	3-22	0-0
Punts	6-30.0	3-32.0
Fumbles-Lost	1-1	2-2
Penalties-Yards	4-25	2-20
Time of possession	36:59	23:01
Attendance—52,975.		

INDIVIDUAL STATISTICS

Rushing—Denver, Humphrey 31-110, Kubiak 5-16, Bratton 4-6, Alexander 1-3, Winder 2-minus 4; Washington, Morris 15-51, Byner 6-15, Clark 1-8, Rypien 2-4, Coleman 1-minus 1.

Passing—Denver, Kubiak 13-27-1—123; Washington, Rypien 15-29-0—146.

Receiving—Denver, Johnson 4-37, Jackson 2-30, Young 2-27, Winder 2-5, Mobley 1-18, Nattiel 1-5, Bratton 1-1; Washington, Sanders 6-53, Clark 4-61, Byner 3-16, Monk 2-16.

Kickoff Returns—Denver, Carrington 1-11, Bell 1-16; Washington, Howard 1-24, Gouveia 1-0, Sanders 1-0.

Punt Returns—Denver, Johnson 1-12, Nattiel 1-minus 1; Washington, Howard 1-0.

Interceptions—Washington, A. Johnson 1-28.

Punting—Denver, Horan 4-34.3, Kubiak 2-21.5; Washington, Mojsiejenko 3-32.0.

Field Goals—Denver, none attempted; Washington, Lohmiller 1-2 (missed: 38).

Sacks—Washington, Stokes, Koch, Rocker.

TWELFTH WEEK

RESULTS OF WEEK 12

Thursday, November 23

Detroit 13, Cleveland 10 at Det.
Philadelphia 27, Dallas 0 at Dall.

Sunday, November 26

Buffalo 24, Cincinnati 7 at Buff.
Denver 41, Seattle 14 at Den.
Green Bay 20, Minnesota 19 at Milw.
Indianapolis 10, San Diego 6 at Ind.
Kansas City 34, Houston 0 at K.C.
L.A. Raiders 24, New England 21 at L.A.
L.A. Rams 20, New Orleans 17 (OT) at N.O.
N.Y. Jets 27, Atlanta 7 at N.Y.
Pittsburgh 34, Miami 14 at Mia.
Tampa Bay 14, Phoenix 13 at Phoe.
Washington 38, Chicago 14 at Wash.

Monday, November 27

San Francisco 34, N.Y. Giants 24 at S.F.

Thanksgiving Day is a time when Americans give thanks for their good fortune. Traditionally, they note the occasion with an all-the-trimmings turkey feast.

On Thanksgiving Day 1989, the Philadelphia Eagles had good reason to be thankful—the NFC Eastern Division contenders were matched against a Dallas Cowboys team that had managed only one victory all season long. Another kind of feast seemed imminent for Coach Buddy Ryan's Eagles.

By day's end, Philadelphia had indeed kicked the stuffing out of Dallas—to the tune of 27-0—and Cowboys Coach Jimmy Johnson was irate over the way his club had been carved up on a not-so-pleasant "turkey day."

Talk after the game at Texas Stadium had little to do with football. Johnson, who had just tasted defeat for the 11th time in 12 games as a rookie National Football League coach, accused Ryan of placing a "bounty" on two of his players: quarterback Troy Aikman and place-kicker Luis Zendejas. Ryan denied the charge, but Johnson's comments overshadowed anything that happened in the game itself.

"I have no respect for the way Philadelphia played the game," Johnson said. "An (Eagles) assistant coach told us last night and it was verified by two players today that there was a $200 bounty on Luis Zendejas and $500 on Troy Aikman. I will file a protest to the league office.

"I didn't think a head football coach would stoop this low...I wanted to say something to Buddy (after the game), but he put his rear end into the dressing room."

Johnson cited two plays to support his charges. Eagles rookie linebacker Jessie Small hit Zendejas—a former Eagle cut by Ryan two weeks earlier—in the back of the head on the second-half kickoff. Small ran past three Dallas players, including standout special-teams performer Bill Bates, and made a beeline for Zendejas.

"All I could do was duck because he was going for my legs and he just came straight at me," Zendejas said. Ironically, Zendejas was called for a penalty on the play for hitting Small below the waist.

On the other play, Aikman—the NFL's 1989 No. 1 draft choice—was hit by the Eagles' Britt Hager after the whistle had stopped play.

Ryan, a veteran of more than 20 NFL seasons as an assistant or head coach, laughed at Johnson's allegations.

"I've heard that stuff since I've been in this league," he said. "People saying they're going to take shots. That's all talk. That's that macho stuff that goes on in the NFL. It's been going around for years."

Ryan thought Johnson was using the "bounty" charge as a way to deflect attention away from his 1-11 team. The loss was the Cowboys' worst in 22 Thanksgiving Day home games.

It also was the Eagles' fourth straight victory over Dallas in a division series the Cowboys once dominated.

"The Cowboys are just trying to take everybody's mind off the fact they got whipped," Eagles safety Wes Hopkins said. "It's the cry of losers."

"Winning and losing concerns me," said Johnson, who already had lost more games in his first year at Dallas than he had in five seasons (1984-88) at the University of Miami (nine). "But what concerns me more is when you take away from the integrity of the game. That's not the way the game is supposed to be played."

Zendejas said he had been told by several Eagles players, as well as by Philadelphia special-teams coach Al Roberts, that there was a bounty on him. Roberts denied it.

Ryan and Johnson, who shook hands and chatted at midfield before the game, did not partake in the customary postgame handshake.

"Our day will come," vowed Johnson, citing a rematch between the teams in Philadelphia in 2½ weeks.

The other Thanksgiving Day game was much closer and more subdued. The Detroit Lions, behind a 145-yard rushing performance by rookie Barry Sanders, defeated the Cleveland Browns, 13-10, in an interconference game. Sanders, who won the 1988 Heisman Trophy as a junior at Oklahoma State, became the first player to rush for 100 yards against the Browns in 1989 and the first NFL player to reach the 1,000-yard mark for the season. His total stood at 1,016.

Sanders carried the ball six times for 43

Coaches Jimmy Johnson of Dallas (left) and Buddy Ryan of Philadelphia enjoy a few laughs before their teams met on Thanksgiving Day at Texas Stadium. Johnson was not smiling after the Cowboys lost, 27-0.

yards on Detroit's 10-play, 63-yard drive that ended with Eddie Murray's 35-yard field goal for the game-winning points late in the third quarter.

The first team to clinch a division title in 1989 was the Denver Broncos, who scored 38 unanswered points in the first half en route to a 41-14 thumping of the Seattle Seahawks. The triumph improved the Broncos' record to 10-2, gave them a four-game lead over the Los Angeles Raiders in the AFC Western Division with four games remaining and left Denver with an insurmountable edge in the league's tiebreaker system.

Denver became only the second team to wrap up a division title after just 12 games since the NFL adopted a 16-game regular-season schedule in 1978. The Buffalo Bills accomplished the feat in 1988.

John Elway threw four touchdown passes in the first half to give the Broncos their big lead before sitting out the second half. Denver scored on its first three possessions, with its first two touchdowns coming on drives of 80 and 84 yards. Vance Johnson caught two of Elway's scoring passes and finished with six

receptions for 154 yards before he, too, went to the bench for the final two periods.

The only bright spot for Seattle, which lost its fourth straight game, was wide receiver Steve Largent, who caught a 31-yard pass from Dave Krieg late in the game for the Seahawks' second touchdown. The touchdown reception was the 99th of Largent's 14-year NFL career, tying the league record set by former Green Bay Packer great Don Hutson from 1935-45.

The NFL record for single-game receiving yardage was smashed in Week 12 by Willie (Flipper) Anderson of the Los Angeles Rams, who caught 15 passes for 336 yards in the Rams' 20-17 overtime victory against the New Orleans Saints.

One of Anderson's biggest catches was his last—a 26-yarder from Jim Everett that set up Mike Lansford's 31-yard field goal at 6:38 of overtime for the game-deciding points.

Anderson, a second-year pro from UCLA, broke the one-game record of 309 yards set by Kansas City's Stephone Paige in 1985. Anderson's record-setting total was three times greater than his previous career-best effort of 112 yards in a Week 4 game against San Francisco. The Rams were playing without their leading pass-catcher, Henry Ellard, and the veteran receiver's absence forced Anderson to carry a heavier workload than usual. Ellard strained his right calf muscle in practice two days before this game.

The Saints appeared headed to victory before the Rams scored two touchdowns in the final 2:46 to erase a 17-3 New Orleans lead. Anderson set up the first touchdown with a 46-yard reception to the Saints' 4 (Buford McGee scored the touchdown) before scoring the second TD himself on a 15-yard pass from Everett with 1:02 left. Everett completed 29 of 51 passes for a career-high 454 yards.

Washington's Mark Rypien threw for a career-high 401 yards and four touchdowns to lead the Redskins to a 38-14 trouncing of the Chicago Bears. The game was tied, 14-14, at halftime before the Redskins scored 24 consecutive points in the second half.

Chip Lohmiller broke the tie by kicking a 28-yard field goal with 4:35 left in the third quarter. On the ensuing kickoff, the Redskins surprised the Bears with an onside kick, with Joe Howard recovering the ball for Washington at midfield. Four plays after the recovery, Rypien threw an 18-yard touchdown pass to Art Monk for a 24-14 Redskins lead.

Monk caught two touchdown passes from Rypien and finished the game with nine catches for 152 yards. Monk's receptions increased his career total to 636 and enabled him to leapfrog Raymond Berry, Ozzie Newsome and Don Maynard and move into fourth place on the league's all-time pass-receiving list.

The most lopsided game of Week 12 was played in Kansas City, where the Chiefs took advantage of a team-record 16 Houston penalties for a 34-0 victory over the Oilers. The shutout was the Chiefs' first since 1981 and the 34-point margin of victory was their largest in 21 years.

The Oilers, who had won five of their last six games, were their own worst enemy in their first shutout loss since 1986. Their 16 penalties cost them 115 yards, with 50 of those yards coming in the first quarter alone. Quarterback Warren Moon, who completed just eight of 20 passes for 99 yards before being lifted in the final period, got into a sideline brawl with Chiefs linebacker Derrick Thomas early in the first quarter. Moon was penalized for starting the fight, and Oilers Coach Jerry Glanville was slapped with another penalty for arguing the one called against Moon.

The two infractions cost Houston 24 yards and gave the Chiefs a first down at the Oilers' 8. After another Houston penalty—this one for grabbing a face mask—James Saxon ran four yards for Kansas City's first touchdown.

In a game between teams that had combined to win just five of their first 22 games,

the New York Jets beat the Atlanta Falcons, 27-7, on the strength of two touchdown runs by fullback Johnny Hector. The Jets, who entered the contest with a 2-9 record, won their first game at home in 1989 after five losses. The 3-9 Falcons lost their ninth straight road game over two seasons.

Even though Denver's Week 12 victory over Seattle ended the Raiders' slim hopes of capturing the AFC Western Division title, Los Angeles beat New England, 24-21, to remain in the hunt for an AFC wild-card playoff berth. Jeff Jaeger's 32-yard field goal with 5:57 left capped a 13-play, 53-yard drive to improve L.A.'s record to .500.

Steve Grogan threw three touchdown passes in a losing effort for the Patriots.

Buffalo's Jim Kelly fired three scoring passes, leading the Bills to a 24-7 triumph over the Cincinnati Bengals. It was a particularly sweet victory for the Bills, who had lost to Cincinnati in the AFC championship game following the 1988 season.

Cincinnati blew a good scoring opportunity late in the first half and then committed a costly turnover early in the second half. The Bengals failed to score after driving to the Bills' 9 with 58 seconds left in the first half and two timeouts remaining. James Brooks was thrown for a four-yard loss on first down and the Bengals failed to call a timeout until the clock ticked below 20 seconds. Bills defensive back Nate Odomes then picked off a Boomer Esiason pass in the end zone on Cincinnati's next play, but a face-mask penalty on Bruce Smith nullified the turnover.

Jim Breech kicked a 26-yard field goal for the Bengals after the penalty, but an illegal-procedure call against Cincinnati wiped out the play.

Brooks then fumbled on the third play of the third period, with Mark Kelso recovering for Buffalo at the Cincinnati 44. Two plays after the recovery, Kelly hit Ronnie Harmon with a 42-yard scoring pass to build the Bills' lead to 17-0.

Buffalo's eighth victory in 12 games moved the Bills into sole possession of first place in the AFC Eastern Division, one game in front of the Miami Dolphins, who committed five turnovers in a 34-14 loss to the Pittsburgh Steelers. The Dolphins, who had won their three previous games to tie the Bills for the division lead, led 14-0 after one quarter before yielding 34 consecutive Pittsburgh points in the second and third periods.

The Steelers did not commit a turnover despite torrential rain that fell for most of the afternoon. An estimated 2½ inches of rain fell in less than one hour, most of it after the Dolphins had scored their two touchdowns. Running back Merril Hoge ran for three Pittsburgh touchdowns.

Despite doing very little on offense for most

Pittsburgh's Tim Worley rushed for 95 yards in the Steelers' 34-14 triumph at Miami.

of the game, the Indianapolis Colts put together a six-play, 87-yard touchdown drive in the final minutes to edge San Diego, 10-6. Jack Trudeau's 25-yard touchdown pass to Bill Brooks with 1:54 remaining capped a drive the Colts began at their 13 with 3:32 to play.

The Colts compiled just 11 first downs and crossed midfield only three times. They finished with 59 yards rushing and mustered 11 total yards on 11 first-down rushing attempts.

The Green Bay Packers tied Minnesota for the top spot in the NFC Central Division, edging the Vikings by a 20-19 score at Milwaukee's County Stadium. The result left both teams at 7-5 with four games left to play.

The Packers' hero was quarterback Don Majkowski, who completed 26 of 35 passes for 276 yards despite not practicing because of knee and rib injuries. Majkowski completed his first 14 passes and hit on 17 of 19 attempts for 177 yards in the first half to help Green Bay to a 10-6 lead. Sterling Sharpe caught 10 passes overall for 157 yards and two touchdowns, the second one a nine-yard reception with 11 minutes left to give the Packers a 20-16 advantage.

The Vikings' offense was held to one touchdown and four field goals on five possessions inside the Green Bay 20. Rich Karlis' fourth field goal with 6:07 to play cut the Packers' lead to 20-19 after Minnesota Coach Jerry Burns opted to go for a field goal instead of a touchdown on a fourth-and-goal play at the 1.

Vinny Testaverde's five-yard touchdown pass to Mark Carrier with 43 seconds left gave the Tampa Bay Buccaneers a 14-13 victory over the Phoenix Cardinals. The touchdown capped a 14-play, 82-yard drive that took just 2:10. Testaverde rallied the Bucs after Phoenix safety Tim McDonald had intercepted one of his passes at the Cardinals' 19 with 4:02 to go.

It marked the first time since 1984 that the Buccaneers had won back-to-back games and the first time in 10 years they had won consecutive games away from home.

The Cardinals' loss was their seventh in 10 weeks and first under interim Coach Hank Kuhlmann, who had taken over the team six days earlier after Gene Stallings was fired. Kuhlmann, who had been the team's running-backs coach, saw his hopes for a first-game victory vanish on two costly fourth-quarter turnovers—a fumble by Tony Jordan at the Bucs' 20 and another by Roy Green at Tampa Bay's 31.

The crowd of 33,297 at Sun Devil Stadium was the smallest for a Cardinals home game since the team moved to Phoenix from St. Louis after the 1987 season.

The two teams with the best records in the National Conference—the San Francisco 49ers and New York Giants (both 9-2)—squared off on Monday night and played a game that lived up to its billing. The 49ers won, 34-24, to take a one-game lead over the Giants in the battle for home-field advantage in the NFC playoffs.

The game was tied until the final minutes. San Francisco quarterback Joe Montana, who threw three touchdown passes to stake his team to a 24-7 halftime lead, moved the 49ers into position for a 50-yard field-goal attempt by Mike Cofer with 4:12 left. Cofer missed the kick, but a penalty against the Giants for lining up in the neutral zone gave him another chance. Cofer's kick—from 45 yards out this time—was good, and San Francisco took a 27-24 lead.

On New York's next possession, the 49ers' Eric Wright intercepted a Phil Simms pass at the Giants' 31 and returned it to the New York 17. That set up the game's final touchdown, a one-yard run by Tom Rathman with 1:08 remaining.

The Giants turned the ball over five times in the game, including three times on their last four possessions.

Eagles-Cowboys
THURSDAY, NOVEMBER 23
SCORE BY PERIODS

Philadelphia	0	10	14	3—27
Dallas	0	0	0	0— 0

SCORING

Philadelphia—Carter 6 pass from Cunningham (Ruzek kick), 1:23 2nd.
Philadelphia—Field goal Ruzek 36, 12:14 2nd.
Philadelphia—Carter 18 pass from Cunningham (Ruzek kick), 3:33 3rd.
Philadelphia—Byars 1 run (Ruzek kick), 8:08 3rd.
Philadelphia—Field goal Ruzek 38, 0:04 4th.

TEAM STATISTICS

	Philadelphia	Dallas
First downs	22	10
Rushes-Yards	34-138	19-123
Passing yards	243	68
Passes	22-35-0	9-25.3
Sacked-Yards lost	0-0	2-8
Punts	4-36.5	4-43.8
Fumbles-Lost	3-1	3-2
Penalties-Yards	13-95	7-55
Time of possession	37:57	22:03
Attendance—54,444.		

INDIVIDUAL STATISTICS

Rushing—Philadelphia, Cunningham 5-46, Toney 11-44, Higgs 3-18, Sherman 3-16, Drummond 2-11, Byars 8-6, Cavanaugh 2-minus 3; Dallas, Sargent 3-44, Johnston 6-39, Aikman 4-25, Palmer 6-15.

Passing—Philadelphia, Cunningham 21-33-0—234, Cavanaugh 1-2-0—9; Dallas, Aikman 7-21-3—54, Walsh 2-4-0—22.

Receiving—Philadelphia, Byars 8-90, Jackson 5-45, Carter 3-53, Johnson 2-26, Toney 2-11, Drummond 1-9, Sherman 1-9; Dallas, Folsom 4-24, Shepard 3-25, Tautalatasi 1-15, Dixon 1-12.

Kickoff Returns—Philadelphia, Edwards 1-11; Dallas, Shepard 2-30, Dixon 3-79.

Punt Returns—Philadelphia, Williams 2-16; Dallas, Shepard 2-13.

Interceptions—Philadelphia, Golic 1-23, Allen 1-0, Evans 1-8.

Punting—Philadelphia, Runager 4-36.5; Dallas, Saxon 4-43.8.

Field Goals—Philadelphia, Ruzek 2-2; Dallas, Zendejas 0-1 (missed: 45).

Sacks—Philadelphia, Waters, White.

Browns-Lions
THURSDAY, NOVEMBER 23
SCORE BY PERIODS

Cleveland	0	10	0	0—10
Detroit	0	10	3	0—13

SCORING

Detroit—Field goal Murray 39, 2:29 2nd.
Cleveland—Field goal Bahr 35, 7:27 2nd.
Detroit—Johnson 27 pass from Gagliano (Murray kick), 11:39 2nd.
Cleveland—Redden 38 run (Bahr kick), 13:53 2nd.
Detroit—Field goal Murray 35, 11:17 3rd.

TEAM STATISTICS

	Cleveland	Detroit
First downs	14	15
Rushes-Yards	18-70	29-146
Passing yards	289	125
Passes	29-39-1	9-19-0
Sacked-Yards lost	1-7	4-18
Punts	5-41.2	6-44.3
Fumbles-Lost	2-1	2-1
Penalties-Yards	10-90	8-55
Time of possession	32:13	27:47
Attendance—65,624.		

INDIVIDUAL STATISTICS

Rushing—Cleveland, Redden 1-38, Metcalf 11-19, Kosar 1-5, Manoa 2-4, Jones 3-4; Detroit, B. Sanders 28-145, Gagliano 1-1.

Passing—Cleveland, Kosar 28-38-1—296; Metcalf 0-1-0—0; Detroit, Gagliano 9-19-0—143.

Receiving—Cleveland, Langhorne 5-72, Slaughter 5-60, Newsome 4-53, Jones 4-32, Manoa 3-17, Metcalf 2-18, McNeil 2-17, Redden 2-16, Tillman 1-11; Detroit, Phillips 4-42, Johnson 3-57, B. Sanders 2-44.

Kickoff Returns—Cleveland, Oliphant 2-11, Metcalf 1-11; Detroit, Alexander 2-38, Gray 1-36.

Punt Returns—Cleveland, McNeil 4-34; Detroit, Stanley 3-44.

Interceptions—Detroit, Holmes 1-36.

Punting—Cleveland, Wagner 5-41.2; Detroit, Arnold 6-44.3.

Field Goals—Cleveland, Bahr 1-2 (missed: 44); Detroit, Murray 2-2.

Sacks—Cleveland, Hairston 3, Matthews; Detroit, Ball.

Oilers-Chiefs
SUNDAY, NOVEMBER 26
SCORE BY PERIODS

Houston	0	0	0	0— 0
Kansas City	10	10	7	7—34

SCORING

Kansas City—Field goal Lowery 31, 3:08 1st.
Kansas City—Saxon 4 run (Lowery kick), 13:54 1st.
Kansas City—Field goal Lowery 34, 8:51 2nd.
Kansas City—Pearson 1 blocked punt return (Lowery kick), 10:44 2nd.
Kansas City—Hayes 7 pass from DeBerg (Lowery kick), 8:17 3rd.
Kansas City—Okoye 17 run (Lowery kick), 0:53 4th.

TEAM STATISTICS

	Houston	Kansas City
First downs	12	20
Rushes-Yards	27-103	31-87
Passing yards	112	226
Passes	13-31-1	16-27-1
Sacked-Yards lost	5-38	1-3
Punts	7-34.3	3-47.3
Fumbles-Lost	3-0	0-0
Penalties-Yards	16-115	2-15
Time of possession	28:51	31:09
Attendance—51,342.		

INDIVIDUAL STATISTICS

Rushing—Houston, Moon 4-35, Highsmith 8-24, Pinkett 3-17, White 5-15, Rozier 6-12, Carlson 1-0; Kansas City, Okoye 21-67, McNair 6-16, Saxon 1-4, Agee 1-3, Heard 2- minus 3.

Passing—Houston, Moon 8-20-1—99, Carlson 5-11-0 —51; Kansas City, DeBerg 15-25-0—224, Elkins 1-2-1— 5.

Receiving—Houston, Harris 4-49, Jeffires 3-26, Jackson 2-19, Highsmith 1-26, Duncan 1-16, Rozier 1-8, White 1-6; Kansas City, Paige 7-114, Mandley 3-70, McNair 2-26, Hayes 2-15, Saxon 1-10, Roberts 1-minus 6.

Kickoff Returns—Houston, K. Johnson 3-50, White 1-22, Harris 1-22; Kansas City, Worthen 1-21.

Punt Returns—Houston, K. Johnson 2-31; Kansas City, Worthen 3-28.

Interceptions—Houston, McDowell 1-13; Kansas City, Ashley 1-0.

Punting—Houston, Greg Montgomery 6-40.0; Kansas City, Goodburn 3-47.3.

Field Goals—Houston, Zendejas 0-1 (missed: 39); Kansas City, Lowery 2-3 (missed: 39).

Sacks—Houston, Meads; Kansas City, Griffin 2½, Martin, Pearson, Meisner ½.

Steelers-Dolphins
SUNDAY, NOVEMBER 26
SCORE BY PERIODS

Pittsburgh	0	17	17	0—34
Miami	14	0	0	0—14

SCORING

Miami—Smith 1 run (Stoyanovich kick), 6:47 1st.
Miami—Clayton 66 pass from Marino (Stoyanovich kick), 11:56 1st.
Pittsburgh—Hoge 1 run (Anderson kick), 6:45 2nd.
Pittsburgh—Woodruff 21 run with lateral after Lake 2 fumble return (Anderson kick), 8:16 2nd.
Pittsburgh—Field goal Anderson 27, 15:00 2nd.
Pittsburgh—Hoge 5 run (Anderson kick), 5:36 3rd.
Pittsburgh—Field goal Anderson 42, 6:51 3rd.
Pittsburgh—Hoge 1 run (Anderson kick), 14:49 3rd.

TEAM STATISTICS

	Pittsburgh	Miami
First downs	13	15
Rushes-Yards	45-125	28-80
Passing yards	167	222
Passes	8-18-0	15-35-2
Sacked-Yards lost	0-0	0-0
Punts	5-43.4	5-39.8
Fumbles-Lost	0-0	6-3
Penalties-Yards	9-55	4-30
Time of possession	33:12	26:48
Attendance—59,936.		

INDIVIDUAL STATISTICS

Rushing—Pittsburgh, Worley 22-95, Hoge 14-37, Stone 4-8, Brister 2-minus 7, Carter 3-minus 8; Miami, Smith 22-72, T. Brown 3-7, Hampton 1-1, Roby 1-0, Marino 1-0.

Passing—Pittsburgh, Brister 8-18-0—167; Miami, Marino 8-16-0—128, Secules 7-19-2—94.

Receiving—Pittsburgh, Hill 3-93, Hoge 2-17, Mularkey 1-34, Worley 1-15, Stone 1-8; Miami, Clayton 4-87, A. Brown 4-73, Duper 3-34, Edmunds 2-20, Hampton 1-5, T. Brown 1-3.

Kickoff Returns—Pittsburgh, Woodson 1-24, Thompson 1-10, Stone 1-18; Miami, Faaola 1-17, Hampton 5-89.

Punt Returns—Pittsburgh, Woodson 5-61; Miami, Schwedes 4-26.

Interceptions—Pittsburgh, Lloyd 1-31, Everett 1-32.

Punting—Pittsburgh, Newsome 5-43.4; Miami, Roby 5-39.8.

Field Goals—Pittsburgh, Anderson 2-4 (missed: 39, 39); Miami, none attempted.

Sacks—None.

Chargers-Colts
SUNDAY, NOVEMBER 26
SCORE BY PERIODS

San Diego	0	3	0	3— 6
Indianapolis	0	3	0	7—10

SCORING

San Diego—Field goal Bahr 33, 4:21 2nd.
Indianapolis—Field goal Biasucci 22, 14:06 2nd.
San Diego—Field goal Bahr 38, 11:19 4th.
Indianapolis—Brooks 25 pass from Trudeau (Biasucci kick), 13:06 4th.

TEAM STATISTICS

	San Diego	Indianapolis
First downs	14	11
Rushes-Yards	33-177	24-59
Passing yards	137	205
Passes	18-33-0	16-30-1
Sacked-Yards lost	5-36	2-11
Punts	7-45.3	9-40.7
Fumbles-Lost	1-1	1-1
Penalties-Yards	13-97	4-45
Time of possession	37:34	22:26
Attendance—58,822.		

INDIVIDUAL STATISTICS

Rushing—San Diego, Spencer 20-78, Nelson 9-41, Holland 2-41, McMahon 2-17; Indianapolis, Dickerson 17-30, Rison 1-18, Bentley 2-11, Ramsey 1-3, Trudeau 3-minus 3.

Passing—San Diego, McMahon 18-32-0—173, Archer 0-1-0—0; Indianapolis, Trudeau 14-24-1—153, Ramsey 2-6-0—63.

Receiving—San Diego, A. Miller 5-55, Holland 4-58, Walker 3-35, Spencer 3-5, Nelson 2-12, Cox 1-8; Indianapolis, Brooks 8-101, Bentley 4-62, Rison 2-23, Verdin 1-29, Dickerson 1-1.

Kickoff Returns—San Diego, A. Miller 2-41, Holland 1-21; Indianapolis, Verdin 3-61.

Punt Returns—San Diego, McConkey 8-75; Indianapolis, Verdin 1-14.

Interceptions—San Diego, Glenn 1-0.

Punting—San Diego, Ilesic 7-45.3; Indianapolis, Stark 9-40.7.

Field Goals—San Diego, Bahr 2-3 (missed: 44); Indianapolis, Biasucci 1-1.

Sacks—San Diego, Grossman, Williams; Indianapolis, Hand 2, Herrod, Thompson, Bickett.

Falcons-Jets
SUNDAY, NOVEMBER 26
SCORE BY PERIODS

Atlanta	0	0	7	0— 7
New York Jets	3	14	10	0—27

SCORING

New York—Field goal Leahy 28, 7:19 1st.
New York—Hector 1 run (Leahy kick), 7:01 2nd.
New York—Toon 12 pass from O'Brien (Leahy kick), 13:18 2nd.
New York—Field goal Leahy 46, 5:47 3rd.
Atlanta—Wilkins 16 pass from Miller (Davis kick), 10:02 3rd.
New York—Hector 1 run (Leahy kick), 14:42 3rd.

TEAM STATISTICS

	Atlanta	New York
First downs	12	24
Rushes-Yards	18-66	43-180
Passing yards	147	138
Passes	13-41-1	20-34-0
Sacked-Yards lost	2-11	1-3
Punts	8-39.1	6-44.8
Fumbles-Lost	3-1	3-2
Penalties-Yards	4-51	8-76
Time of possession	19:54	40:06
Attendance—40,429.		

INDIVIDUAL STATISTICS

Rushing—Atlanta, Settle 13-46, Jones 2-15, Lang 1-5, Fulhage 1-0, Dixon 1-0; New York, Hector 18-71, Vick 16-54, Brown 8-41, Epps 1-14.

Passing—Atlanta, Miller 13-41-1—158; New York, O'Brien 17-29-0—117, Ryan 3-5-0—24.

Receiving—Atlanta, Collins 5-69, Wilkins 2-34, Lang 2-29, Settle 2-19, Dixon 1-6, Jones 1-1; New York, Toon 8-66, Vick 3-9, Hector 3-9, Townsell 2-15, Neubert 2-13, Walker 1-8, Brown 1-1.

Kickoff Returns—Atlanta, Jones 2-40, Beckman 1-15, Sanders 1-15; New York, Humphery 2-19.

Punt Returns—Atlanta, Sanders 4-14; New York, Townsell 4-42.

Interceptions—New York, Mersereau 1-4.

Punting—Atlanta, Fulhage 8-39.1; New York, Prokop 6-44.8.

Field Goals—Atlanta, none attempted; New York, Leahy 2-2.

Sacks—Atlanta, Cotton; New York, Byrd, Stallworth.

Vikings-Packers
SUNDAY, NOVEMBER 26
SCORE BY PERIODS

Minnesota	3	3	10	3—19
Green Bay	3	7	3	7—20

SCORING

Green Bay—Field goal Jacke 36, 6:41 1st.
Minnesota—Field goal Karlis 19, 13:17 1st.
Green Bay—Sharpe 34 pass from Majkowski (Jacke kick), 1:59 2nd.
Minnesota—Field goal Karlis 34, 6:00 2nd.
Minnesota—Field goal Karlis 27, 4:08 3rd.
Minnesota—Walker 6 run (Karlis kick), 7:47 3rd.
Green Bay—Field goal Jacke 42, 12:15 3rd.
Green Bay—Sharpe 9 pass from Majkowski (Jacke kick), 4:00 4th.
Minnesota—Field goal Karlis 19, 8:53 4th.

TEAM STATISTICS

	Minnesota	Green Bay
First downs	22	16
Rushes-Yards	27-76	23-84
Passing yards	301	248
Passes	23-38-2	26-35-1
Sacked-Yards lost	2-8	4-28
Punts	5-36.2	6-44.0
Fumbles-Lost	2-0	2-0
Penalties-Yards	3-35	4-31
Time of possession	29:45	30:15
Attendance—55,592.		

INDIVIDUAL STATISTICS

Rushing—Minnesota, Walker 14-42, Fenney 8-21, Lewis 1-11, Dozier 1-2, Wilson 3-0; Green Bay, Fullwood 13-57, Woodside 3-15, Fontenot 3-9, Majkowski 4-3.

Passing—Minnesota, Wilson 23-38-2—309; Green Bay, Majkowski 26-35-1—276.

Receiving—Minnesota, Carter 6-103, Lewis 3-50, Jones 3-42, Dozier 3-29, Jordan 2-42, Gustafson 2-15, Fenney 2-11, Walker 1-11, Novoselsky 1-6; Green Bay, Sharpe 10-157, Fontenot 8-58, Woodside 3-8, Matthews 2-15, Bland 2-14, Fullwood 1-3.

Kickoff Returns—Minnesota, Walker 2-21, Dozier 2-44; Green Bay, Woodside 2-38, Fullwood 1-35, Bland 1-16, Workman 1-30.

Punt Returns—Minnesota, Lewis 1-12; Green Bay, Query 2-22.

Interceptions—Minnesota, Browner 1-34; Green Bay, D. Brown 2-0.

Punting—Minnesota, Scribner 5-36.2; Green Bay, Bracken 6-44.0.

Field Goals—Minnesota, Karlis 4-4; Green Bay, Jacke 2-3 (missed: 40).

Sacks—Minnesota, Thomas 2, Doleman 2; Green Bay, Weddington, Harris.

Bengals-Bills
SUNDAY, NOVEMBER 26
SCORE BY PERIODS

Cincinnati	0	0	7	0— 7
Buffalo	3	7	7	7—24

SCORING

Buffalo—Field goal Norwood 24, 10:31 1st.
Buffalo—Reed 19 pass from Kelly (Norwood kick), 7:56 2nd.
Buffalo—Harmon 42 pass from Kelly (Norwood kick), 1:31 3rd.
Cincinnati—Jennings 5 run (Breech kick), 11:05 3rd.
Buffalo—Rolle 1 pass from Kelly (Norwood kick), 4:05 4th.

TEAM STATISTICS

	Cincinnati	Buffalo
First downs	16	18
Rushes-Yards	30-165	47-228
Passing yards	133	117
Passes	11-26-1	10-15-0
Sacked-Yards lost	1-3	1-6
Punts	4-36.0	4-35.0
Fumbles-Lost	3-2	3-2
Penalties-Yards	3-15	5-35
Time of possession	25:21	34:39
Attendance—80,074.		

INDIVIDUAL STATISTICS

Rushing—Cincinnati, Brooks 20-105, Taylor 2-22, Esiason 4-18, Jennings 3-9, McGee 1-11; Buffalo, Thomas 26-100, Kinnebrew 15-66, Reed 1-23, Kelly 1-15, Harmon 2-12, K. Davis 2-12.

Passing—Cincinnati, Esiason 11-26-1—136; Buffalo, Kelly 10-15-0—123.

Receiving—Cincinnati, McGee 5-89, Riggs 2-16, Jennings 1-14, Holman 1-11, Hillary 1-6, Brown 1-0; Buffalo, Thomas 3-30, Johnson 2-8, Harmon 1-42, Reed 1-19, K. Davis 1-13, Beebe 1-10, Rolle 1-1.

Kickoff Returns—Cincinnati, Jennings 2-26, Hillary 1-14; Buffalo, Harmon 1-40, Beebe 1-30.

Punt Returns—Cincinnati, Hillary 1-0, Smith 1-0; Buffalo, Sutton 2-12.

Interceptions—Buffalo, Conlan 1-0.

Punting—Cincinnati, Johnson 4-36.0; Buffalo, Kidd 4-35.0.

Field Goals—Cincinnati, none attempted; Buffalo, Norwood 1-1.

Sacks—Cincinnati, Williams; Buffalo, Cofield.

Buccaneers-Cardinals
SUNDAY, NOVEMBER 26
SCORE BY PERIODS

Tampa Bay	0	7	0	7—14
Phoenix	0	10	3	0—13

SCORING

Tampa Bay—Hill 5 pass from Testaverde (Igwebuike kick), 8:59 2nd.
Phoenix—Ferrell 1 run (Del Greco kick), 13:51 2nd.
Phoenix—Field goal Del Greco 21, 14:42 2nd.
Phoenix—Field goal Del Greco 28, 12:31 3rd.
Tampa Bay—Carrier 5 pass from Testaverde (Igwebuike kick), 14:17 4th.

TEAM STATISTICS

	Tampa Bay	Phoenix
First downs	23	12
Rushes-Yards	35-121	22-43
Passing yards	139	194
Passes	19-42-1	17-38-0
Sacked-Yards lost	5-61	2-13
Punts	8-36.1	6-44.0
Fumbles-Lost	1-1	2-2
Penalties-Yards	7-64	8-55
Time of possession	38:05	21:55
Attendance—33,297.		

INDIVIDUAL STATISTICS

Rushing—Tampa Bay, Howard 21-83, Tate 6-15, Stamps 5-12, Testaverde 3-11; Phoenix, Tupa 3-22, Ferrell 10-14, Jordan 8-6, Sikahema 1-1.

Passing—Tampa Bay, Testaverde 19-42-1—200; Phoenix, Tupa 17-38-0—207.

Receiving—Tampa Bay, Carrier 8-90, Hill 6-64, Howard 2-20, Mitchell 1-11, Drewrey 1-10, Peebles 1-5; Phoenix, Green 4-62, Novacek 4-33, Jones 3-50, Awalt 2-26, Holmes 2-26, Ferrell 1-6, Jordan 1-4.

Kickoff Returns—Tampa Bay, Elder 3-65, Pillow 1-17; Phoenix, Sikahema 2-45, Carr 1-15.

Punt Returns—Tampa Bay, Drewrey 4-22; Phoenix, Sikahema 5-85.

Interceptions—Phoenix, McDonald 1-17.

Punting—Tampa Bay, Mohr 7-41.3; Phoenix, Camarillo 6-44.0.

Field Goals—Tampa Bay, none attempted; Phoenix, Del Greco 2-3 (missed: 47).

Sacks—Tampa Bay, Jarvis, Weston; Phoenix, Nunn 2, Harvey, Galloway, Saddler.

Patriots-Raiders

SUNDAY, NOVEMBER 26
SCORE BY PERIODS

New England	0	14	7	0—21
Los Angeles Raiders	7	7	7	3—24

SCORING

Los Angeles—Alexander 12 pass from Beuerlein (Jaeger kick), 11:08 1st.

New England—C. Jones 1 pass from Grogan (Staurovsky kick), 6:55 2nd.

New England—Fryar 49 pass from Grogan (Staurovsky kick), 10:33 2nd.

Los Angeles—Fernandez 13 pass from Beuerlein (Jaeger kick), 14:36 2nd.

Los Angeles—Smith 11 run (Jaeger kick), 2:59 3rd.

New England—Dykes 34 pass from Grogan (Staurovsky kick), 8:08 3rd.

Los Angeles—Field goal Jaeger 32, 9:03 4th.

TEAM STATISTICS

	New England	Los Angeles
First downs	13	19
Rushes-Yards	19-30	37-132
Passing yards	194	136
Passes	14-31-3	15-25-0
Sacked-Yards lost	0-0	4-33
Punts	6-38.2	7-38.0
Fumbles-Lost	0-0	1-0
Penalties-Yards	5-40	7-69
Time of possession	24:42	35:18
Attendance—38,747.		

INDIVIDUAL STATISTICS

Rushing—New England, Perryman 8-20, Stephens 8-6, C. Jones 1-3, Egu 1-2, Grogan 1-minus 1; Los Angeles, Jackson 20-64, Smith 11-49, Mueller 4-13, Beuerlein 2-6.

Passing—New England, Grogan 13-29-3—179, Tatupu 1-1-0—15, Flutie 0-1-0—0; Los Angeles, Beuerlein 15-25-0—169.

Receiving—New England, Dykes 4-75, C. Jones 3-28, Stephens 3-22, Perryman 2-13, Fryar 1-49, Dawson 1-7; Los Angeles, Smith 4-33, Mueller 3-20, Alexander 2-40, Jackson 2-35, Fernandez 2-16, Dyal 2-15.

Kickoff Returns—New England, Tucker 3-69, Taylor 1-18; Los Angeles, Adams 4-79.

Punt Returns—New England, Tucker 5-32; Los Angeles, Adams 4-41.

Interceptions—Los Angeles, Anderson 1-55, Benson 1-17, McDaniel 1-0.

Punting—New England, Feagles 6-38.2; Los Angeles, Gossett 7-38.0.

Field Goals—New England, none attempted; Los Angeles, Jaeger 1-2 (missed: 45).

Sacks—New England, Brown 2, Sims, Jeter.

Seahawks-Broncos

SUNDAY, NOVEMBER 26
SCORE BY PERIODS

Seattle	0	0	7	7—14
Denver	14	24	0	3—41

SCORING

Denver—Johnson 4 pass from Elway (Treadwell kick), 9:21 1st.

Denver—Humphrey 4 run (Treadwell kick), 13:37 1st.

Denver—Field goal Treadwell 30, 2:13 2nd.

Denver—Johnson 10 pass from Elway (Treadwell kick), 9:42 2nd.

Denver—Sewell 32 pass from Elway (Treadwell kick), 10:00 2nd.

Denver—Young 9 pass from Elway (Treadwell kick), 13:57 2nd.

Seattle—Fenner 5 run (N. Johnson kick), 13:22 3rd.

Denver—Field goal Treadwell 25, 3:55 4th.

Seattle—Largent 31 pass from Krieg (N. Johnson kick), 13:50 4th.

TEAM STATISTICS

	Seattle	Denver
First downs	21	18
Rushes-Yards	21-133	37-137
Passing yards	192	216
Passes	22-46-2	11-24-0
Sacked-Yards lost	8-86	2-14
Punts	4-45.0	6-44.2
Fumbles-Lost	5-2	0-0
Penalties-Yards	6-58	2-20
Time of possession	28:53	31:07
Attendance—75,117.		

INDIVIDUAL STATISTICS

Rushing—Seattle, Warner 6-51, Fenner 8-28, Harmon 1-24, Harris 4-14, Stouffer 1-9, Krieg 1-7; Denver, Humphrey 25-86, Elway 2-17, Winder 3-10, Alexander 2-10, Sewell 1-10, Kubiak 3-3, Bratton 1-1.

Passing—Seattle, Stouffer 11-24-0—107, Krieg 11-22-2—171; Denver, Elway 10-19-0—217, Kubiak 1-5-0—13.

Receiving—Seattle, Blades 8-122, Largent 5-83, Warner 4-24, McNeal 1-21, Skansi 1-8, Harris 1-8, Chadwick 1-6, Fenner 1-6; Denver, Johnson 6-154, Sewell 2-37, Nattiel 1-17, Mobley 1-13, Young 1-9.

Kickoff Returns—Seattle, Harmon 3-33, Hollis 3-68, Woods 1-13, Comeaux 1-9; Denver, Bell 2-28.

Punt Returns—Seattle, Hollis 2-19; Denver, Johnson 2-16, Nattiel 1-7.

Interceptions—Denver, Braxton 1-0, Munford 1-6.

Punting—Seattle, Rodriguez 4-45.0; Denver, Horan 6-44.2.

Field Goals—Seattle, none attempted; Denver, Treadwell 2-2.

Sacks—Seattle, Nash, Woods; Denver, Holmes 2, Carreker, Powers ½, Mecklenburg 2½, Lucas.

Bears-Redskins

SUNDAY, NOVEMBER 26
SCORE BY PERIODS

Chicago	0	14	0	0—14
Washington	0	14	10	14—38

SCORING

Washington—Warren 3 pass from Rypien (Lohmiller kick), 0:38 2nd.

Washington—Clark 5 pass from Rypien (Lohmiller kick), 4:06 2nd.

Chicago—Sanders 96 kickoff return (Butler kick), 4:26 2nd.

Chicago—McKinnon 12 pass from Tomczak (Butler kick), 8:44 2nd.

Washington—Field goal Lohmiller 28, 10:25 3rd.

Washington—Monk 18 pass from Rypien (Lohmiller kick), 12:27 3rd.

Washington—Monk 9 pass from Rypien (Lohmiller kick), 4:48 4th.

Washington—Byner 4 run (Lohmiller kick), 9:24 4th.

TEAM STATISTICS

	Chicago	Washington
First downs	13	35
Rushes-Yards	19-59	37-102
Passing yards	132	390
Passes	13-24-2	30-47-1
Sacked-Yards lost	1-5	2-11
Punts	5-37.2	1-55.0
Fumbles-Lost	1-1	2-1
Penalties-Yards	9-108	5-51
Time of possession	21:08	38:52

Attendance—50,044.

INDIVIDUAL STATISTICS

Rushing—Chicago, Anderson 13-27, Gentry 1-13, Tomczak 2-10, Muster 3-9; Washington, Byner 20-82, Morris 12-20, Dupard 1-7, Rypien 3-minus 3, Sanders 1-minus 4.

Passing—Chicago, Tomczak 13-24-2—137; Washington, Rypien 30-47-1—401.

Receiving—Chicago, McKinnon 3-48, Gentry 3-28, Morris 2-26, Anderson 2-13, Boso 1-9, Davis 1-7, Muster 1-6; Washington, Monk 9-152, Clark 8-124, Sanders 6-67, Byner 5-45, Morris 1-10, Warren 1-3.

Kickoff Returns—Chicago, Sanders 3-124, Gentry 2-38, Suhey 1-18; Washington, Sanders 2-29, Howard 1-14.

Punt Returns—Chicago, Woolford 1-12; Washington, Howard 1-19.

Interceptions—Chicago, Duerson 1-2; Washington, Coleman 1-0, B. Davis 1-0.

Punting—Chicago, Buford 5-37.2; Washington, Mojsiejenko 1-55.0.

Field Goals—Chicago, none attempted; Washington, Lohmiller 1-3 (missed: 40, 55).

Sacks—Chicago, Armstrong, McMichael; Washington, Coleman.

Rams-Saints
SUNDAY, NOVEMBER 26
SCORE BY PERIODS

Los Angeles Rams	0	3	0	14	3—20
New Orleans	7	3	7	0	0—17

SCORING

New Orleans—E. Martin 19 pass from Hebert (Andersen kick), 13:32 1st.

New Orleans—Field goal Andersen 36, 4:29 2nd.

Los Angeles—Field goal Lansford 32, 8:37 2nd.

New Orleans—E. Martin 35 pass from Hilliard (Andersen kick), 12:59 3rd.

Los Angeles—McGee 5 run (Lansford kick), 12:14 4th.

Los Angeles—Anderson 15 pass from Everett (Lansford kick), 13:58 4th.

Los Angeles—Field goal Lansford 31, 6:38 OT.

TEAM STATISTICS

	Los Angeles	New Orleans
First downs	23	14
Rushes-Yards	22-57	31-138
Passing yards	415	163
Passes	29-51-2	13-27-1
Sacked-Yards lost	6-39	4-27
Punts	5-35.2	10-41.5
Fumbles-Lost	1-1	1-1
Penalties-Yards	10-77	8-99
Time of possession	33:24	33:14

Attendance—68,274.

INDIVIDUAL STATISTICS

Rushing—Los Angeles, Delpino 7-28, Bell 11-17, McGee 2-9, Brown 1-5, Everett 1-minus 2; New Orleans, Hilliard 24-112, Jordan 4-21, Hebert 2-8, Heyward 1-minus 3.

Passing—Los Angeles, Everett 29-51-2—454; New Orleans, Hebert 12-26-1—155, Hilliard 1-1-0—35.

Receiving—Los Angeles, Anderson 15-336, Delpino 5-33, A. Cox 4-55, Holohan 2-15, Johnson 2-4, McGee 1-11; New Orleans, E. Martin 5-107, Turner 2-17, Hilliard 2-12, Scales 1-17, Brenner 1-16, Jordan 1-15, Hill 1-6.

Kickoff Returns—Los Angeles, Ron Brown 1-19; New Orleans, Harris 3-63, Hilliard 1-20, V. Johnson 1-19.

Punt Returns—Los Angeles, Henley 3-13; New Orleans, Harris 3-14.

Interceptions—Los Angeles, Miller 1-3; New Orleans, Massey 2-0.

Punting—Los Angeles, Hatcher 5-35.2; New Orleans, Barnhardt 10-41.5.

Field Goals—Los Angeles, Lansford 2-4 (missed: 22, 52); New Orleans, Andersen 1-1.

Sacks—Los Angeles, Wilcher, Green 2, Piel; New Orleans, Jackson, Warren 2, Mills, V. Johnson, Swilling.

Giants-49ers
MONDAY, NOVEMBER 27
SCORE BY PERIODS

New York Giants	7	3	7	7—24
San Francisco	14	10	0	10—34

SCORING

San Francisco—Taylor 4 pass from Montana (Cofer kick), 4:13 1st.

New York—Anderson 2 run (Nittmo kick), 12:39 1st.

San Francisco—Rice 4 pass from Montana (Cofer kick), 13:42 1st.

San Francisco—Field goal Cofer 44, 7:59 2nd.

San Francisco—Jones 17 pass from Montana (Cofer kick), 9:31 2nd.

New York—Field goal Nittmo 39, 14:50 2nd.

New York—Meggett 53 pass from Simms (Nittmo kick), 1:51 3rd.

New York—Turner 7 pass from Simms (Nittmo kick), 7:54 4th.

San Francisco—Field goal Cofer 45, 10:48 4th.

San Francisco—Rathman 1 run (Cofer kick), 13:52 4th.

TEAM STATISTICS

	New York	San Francisco
First downs	23	24
Rushes-Yards	14-52	32-96
Passing yards	290	285
Passes	25-48-3	27-34-0
Sacked-Yards lost	7-36	2-7
Punts	3-44.3	3-42.0
Fumbles-Lost	3-2	3-3
Penalties-Yards	9-74	10-80
Time of possession	26:38	33:22

Attendance—63,461.

INDIVIDUAL STATISTICS

Rushing—New York, Meggett 5-29, Simms 2-11, Anderson 5-8, Carthon 1-3, Tillman 1-1; San Francisco, Craig 20-49, Rathman 7-18, Montana 3-15, Rice 1-13, Young 1-1.

Passing—New York, Simms 25-48-3—326; San Francisco, Montana 27-33-0—292, Young 0-1-0—0.

Receiving—New York, Mowatt 5-62, Turner 5-55, Meggett 4-72, Manuel 4-62, Anderson 4-31, Ingram 1-21, Baker 1-18, Carthon 1-5; San Francisco, Rice 7-117, Jones 5-53, Rathman 5-47, Taylor 4-42, Craig 4-13, Wilson 2-20.

Kickoff Returns—New York, Ingram 4-66, Meggett 2-43, Rouson 1-17; San Francisco, Flagler 3-51, Tillman 1-60.

Punt Returns—New York, Meggett 2-27; San Francisco, Taylor 1-16.

Interceptions—San Francisco, Millen 1-10, Brooks 1-12, Wright 1-14.

Punting—New York, Landeta 3-44.3; San Francisco, Helton 3-42.0.

Field Goals—New York, Nittmo 1-1; San Francisco, Cofer 2-2.

Sacks—New York, Cox, Banks; San Francisco, Holt 4, Romanowski, Fagan, Roberts ½, Stubbs ½.

THIRTEENTH WEEK

RESULTS OF WEEK 13

Sunday, December 3

Cincinnati 21, Cleveland 0 at Cleve.
Detroit 21, New Orleans 14 at Det.
Green Bay 17, Tampa Bay 16 at T.B.
Houston 23, Pittsburgh 16 at Pitts.
Kansas City 26, Miami 21 at K.C.
L.A. Raiders 16, Denver 13 (OT) at L.A.
L.A. Rams 35, Dallas 31 at Dall.
Minnesota 27, Chicago 16 at Minn.
New England 22, Indianapolis 16 at N.E.
N.Y. Jets 20, San Diego 17 at S.D.
Philadelphia 24, N.Y. Giants 17 at N.Y.
San Francisco 23, Atlanta 10 at Atl.
Washington 29, Phoenix 10 at Phoe.

Monday, December 4

Seattle 17, Buffalo 16 at Sea.

Heading into the final four weeks of the National Football League's 1989 regular season, the time had come for teams with a legitimate shot at making the playoffs to get their act together. Only 10 playoff spots were available for the league's 28 teams, and one of those berths already belonged to the Denver Broncos.

One team on the bubble for postseason play at this juncture of the season was the New Orleans Saints, a team that had qualified for the playoffs only once (1987) in 22 previous NFL seasons. The Saints, clearly in need of a late-season surge, entered their Week 13 game at Detroit with a record of 6-6.

In their biggest game of the season against a very beatable opponent (Detroit was 3-9), Coach Jim Mora's Saints fell flat and lost to the Lions, 21-14. It was a crippling blow to New Orleans' postseason hopes.

The defeat was the Saints' second straight and third in five games, hardly the kind of stretch-run performance that Mora had hoped for.

"Our postgame discussion lasted a little longer than usual," said Mora, who kept the team's dressing room closed to reporters for half an hour after the game. "I'm always upset when we lose."

No loss is acceptable, but for Mora, the Saints and their fans, this one was particularly galling. Detroit, coming off a victory over Cleveland, entered the game as the last-place team in the NFC Central Division and had not won games in consecutive weeks since 1986. Its starting quarterback, rookie Rodney Peete, was forced to leave the game with a knee injury early in the second half. Peete's replacement, Bob Gagliano, was a longtime NFL journeyman quarterback.

Gagliano stepped in and threw for 166 yards, 75 of them coming on his first completion. On the receiving end of that initial strike was

Richard Johnson, a former United States Football League player who finished the day with eight catches for 248 yards (the second-highest yardage total by a receiver in Detroit history).

"It seemed like a dream," said Johnson, whose NFL experience before 1989 had consisted of one game with the Washington Redskins in 1987. "I'm just so excited. I knew I had the ability to play in this league. I just had to get the opportunity."

While Johnson and his teammates were rolling up 401 yards in total offense, the New Orleans offense was stagnant most of the day. The Saints had fewer than 100 yards both rushing and passing and made only 11 first downs.

One New Orleans touchdown came on a 99-yard kickoff return by Bobby Morse in the second quarter.

"A team we should've beat, beat us," Saints linebacker Rickey Jackson said. "This team (New Orleans) isn't as close as it should be. The coaches are not close to the players. It has to be more of a family thing."

The Rams, second in the NFC Western Division, boosted their postseason hopes by notching their fourth consecutive victory, a 35-31 decision over the Dallas Cowboys. The triumph improved the Rams' record to 9-4.

Jim Everett threw four touchdown passes for Los Angeles, including two in the last four minutes to erase a 31-21 Dallas lead. Everett's 39-yard touchdown pass to Ron Brown with 3:58 left and his 23-yarder to Aaron Cox with 1:50 to play overcame a run of 21 consecutive points by the Cowboys.

Dallas rookie Troy Aikman also unloaded four touchdown passes. The loss was the Cowboys' 12th of the season and 13th straight at Texas Stadium.

In contrast to the Cowboys' woes at home, the Minnesota Vikings won their 10th straight regular-season game at the Metrodome in Week 13, a 27-16 triumph over the Chicago Bears. The Vikings' victory snapped a two-game losing streak and handed the Bears their third straight defeat.

After the Bears took an early 3-0 lead on Kevin Butler's 33-yard field goal, the Vikings responded with a seven-play, 66-yard touchdown drive on their next possession. Herschel Walker's one-yard scoring run with 4:29 left in the opening period put Minnesota ahead—to stay.

Butler's field goal was about the only bright spot for the Bears, whose record dropped below .500 (6-7) for the first time in six years. The field goal was Butler's 24th in a row, snapping the NFL record of 23 straight set by Washington's Mark Moseley in 1981-82. Butler's streak ended when Brad Edwards blocked a 44-yard attempt in the second quarter.

The most important field goal of Week 13,

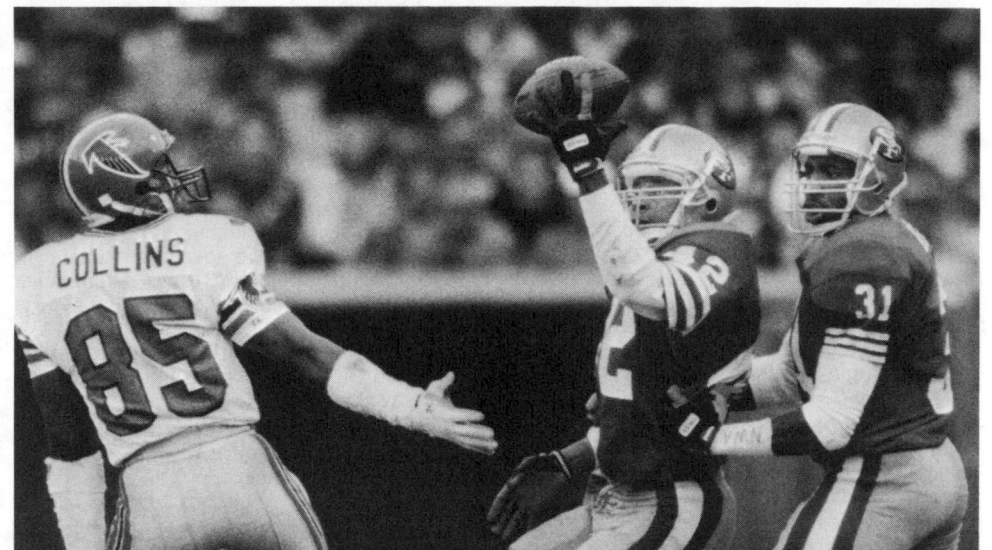

San Francisco free safety Ronnie Lott intercepts a pass intended for wide receiver Shawn Collins in the 49ers' 23-10 win at Atlanta.

however, was kicked by Green Bay rookie Chris Jacke, who booted a 47-yarder with no time left to enable the Packers to slip past Tampa Bay, 17-16. It was Green Bay's fourth one-point victory of the season and marked the fourth straight game between the Packers and Buccaneers decided by three or fewer points.

Jacke's winning kick climaxed a 12-play, 52-yard drive that was kept alive by a critical hands-to-the-face penalty against Bucs lineman Shawn Lee. The penalty gave the Packers a first down after Don Majkowski's fourth-down pass fell incomplete on a play that originated from the Green Bay 39 with 47 seconds left.

The Bucs, whose record dropped to 5-8, had taken a 16-14 lead on Donald Igwebuike's 36-yard field goal with 1:35 remaining.

Another important field goal was kicked at the Los Angeles Coliseum, where Jeff Jaeger's 26-yarder at 7:02 of overtime gave the Raiders a 16-13 victory over Denver. Jaeger's winning kick came at the end of a six-play, 62-yard drive highlighted by Steve Beuerlein's 26- and 15-yard passes to Mike Dyal and a 16-yard run by Steve Smith.

Dyal, a rookie from Texas A&I who missed the entire 1988 season because of injuries, caught four passes for 134 yards. Among his receptions was a 67-yarder for a touchdown with seven minutes left that forced the overtime.

Los Angeles' victory meant that the Raiders and Broncos had split their season series for the first time since 1977. Amazingly, each year in the 11-season span from 1978 through 1988, one club or the other had swept the series. (Only one game was played between the teams in the strike-shortened 1982 season.)

The Cincinnati Bengals swept their AFC Central Division series from cross-state rival Cleveland for the first time since 1984 with a 21-0 triumph in Week 13. It was Cincinnati's first shutout victory since 1980.

The Bengals, who scored two touchdowns after Cleveland turnovers and had another touchdown drive aided by a personal-foul penalty, never allowed the Browns' offense to cross the Cincinnati 22. Cleveland quarterback Bernie Kosar was benched by Coach Bud Carson after three periods, the first time he had been replaced in a game due to ineffectiveness since his 1985 rookie season.

The Browns had now scored just 20 points in three games (two losses and one tie)—the lowest output of any three-game stretch in club history.

One team not having offensive problems was the San Francisco 49ers, who increased their league-leading point total to 365 with a 23-10 victory at Atlanta. The 49ers, who were only four points shy of their total for the entire 1988 regular season, took control of this game by scoring 17 consecutive points against the Falcons in the second half.

Steve Young, who replaced Joe Montana late in the second quarter after the 49ers' starter suffered a rib injury, completed his first 10 passes in the second half—including a 38-yard touchdown throw to wide receiver John Taylor. Young finished with 11 completions in 12 attempts, and Taylor caught five passes for 162 yards.

The Falcons lost for the 10th time in 13 games in their first outing under interim Coach Jim Hanifan, who took over following Marion Campbell's abrupt resignation five days earlier. Hanifan coached the then-St. Louis Cardinals from 1980-85 before joining the Falcons as an assistant in 1987.

The NFC West's Falcons, who earlier had lost two games each to the Rams and Saints and another to the 49ers, failed to win a game in their division for the first time since 1974.

The NFL's best-balanced division was the AFC Central, where only two games separated first-place Houston (8-5) and last-place Pittsburgh (6-7) following the Oilers' 23-16 victory over the Steelers in Week 13. Houston moved into the top spot for the first time all season, claiming a half-game lead over Cleveland (7-5-1) with three games left. Cincinnati (7-6) was right there, too.

The Houston-Pittsburgh game was played in brutal conditions, with blowing snow and a wind-chill factor of minus-25 degrees making it difficult for both offenses to move the ball, particularly the Steelers. Pittsburgh finished with just 43 net yards passing as Bubby Brister completed only nine of 21 pass attempts.

Two Steeler drives broke down at the Houston 1, resulting in a pair of 18-yard field goals by Gary Anderson.

The Oilers were able to move the ball when they had to. Warren Moon passed for 171 yards, including a 37-yard completion to Haywood Jeffires on the game-winning drive. Jeffires' reception carried to the Pittsburgh 27, and three consecutive runs by Lorenzo White —including a one-yard touchdown burst with 21 seconds left—gave Houston the victory.

Another division race that figured to come down to the final week was the NFC East, where the Philadelphia Eagles and New York Giants were tied for first place at 9-4 after the Eagles edged the Giants, 24-17, in East Rutherford, N.J. It was the Giants' first home loss of 1989.

It also was the Eagles' fourth straight victory over New York, one that was aided by Giant mistakes. The Giants turned the ball over five times, with quarterback Phil Simms accounting for four of the misplays with two fumbles and two interceptions. All 24 Philadelphia points were scored after turnovers by the New York quarterback.

Simms' first turnover came on the Giants' third play from scrimmage, when he fumbled the ball while being sacked by Reggie White. William Frizzell picked up the loose ball at the New York 16 and ran 13 yards to the 3 before lateraling to teammate Andre Waters, who ran the rest of the way for the game's first touchdown.

Philadelphia's game-winning touchdown also came after a Simms fumble. After Eagles quarterback Randall Cunningham launched a team-record 91-yard punt (aided by a stiff wind) to get his team out of a fourth-down jam at its own 1, Mike Golic sacked Simms on the Giants' ensuing possession. Mike Pitts recov-

ered for the Eagles at the 7, setting up a two-yard touchdown run by Keith Byars three plays later.

A turnover also played a pivotal role in another NFC East game as the Washington Redskins won at Phoenix, 29-10, to keep their hopes alive for a wild-card playoff berth. The victory improved the Redskins' record to 7-6.

The game was tied, 10-10, at halftime before Washington took the second-half kickoff 61 yards in 11 plays for the go-ahead touchdown, a one-yard run by Gerald Riggs six minutes into the third quarter. On the Cardinals' next possession, Redskins rookie cornerback A.J. Johnson stepped in front of a pass intended for Roy Green and raced 59 yards for a touchdown to give Washington a 24-10 lead.

The Cardinals rushed for a season-low 29 yards in losing for the third straight week.

Johnny Hector rushed for 106 yards on 20 carries and Roger Vick ran for two touchdowns in the final period, leading the New York Jets past the San Diego Chargers, 20-17. Hector, who also caught a nine-yard pass from Ken O'Brien for New York's first touchdown, became the first Jets player to rush for 100 yards in 1989.

Vick scored his second touchdown two plays after Erik McMillan returned an interception of a Billy Joe Tolliver pass 40 yards to the Chargers' 16. Tolliver, a rookie from Texas Tech, was sacked five times and intercepted twice in his second NFL game.

The Chargers' Chris Bahr missed a 37-yard field goal with 10 seconds left that would have sent the game into overtime.

The New England Patriots capitalized on a mistake late in the game to upend Indianapolis, 22-16, in an AFC Eastern Division game. Colts lineman Ezra Johnson was penalized for being offside after Pats quarterback Marc Wilson threw an incomplete pass on third-and-26 from the New England 21 with a minute left. Wilson completed a 30-yard pass to tight end Eric Sievers on the next play to put the ball at the Colts' 44.

Wilson then hit Irving Fryar for 17 yards to the Indianapolis 27 before John Stephens scored the game-winning touchdown on a 10-yard run two plays later.

The Colts had taken a 16-15 lead with 1:59 left on an eight-yard pass from Jack Trudeau to Eric Dickerson.

Dickerson, who has led the league in rushing four times, ran 24 times for 80 yards to increase his season total to 1,013. Dickerson became the first player in NFL history to rush for more than 1,000 yards in seven consecutive seasons.

The league's leading ground-gainer in 1989, however, was Kansas City's Christian Okoye, who increased his season total to a club-record 1,191 in the Chiefs' 26-21 victory over Miami. Okoye ran for 148 yards on 32 carries to help the Chiefs post their first victory over Miami in Kansas City since 1969.

Kansas City's winning touchdown came on an eight-yard pass from Steve DeBerg to Herman Heard with five minutes left.

The Seattle Seahawks broke a four-game losing streak and handed Buffalo its fourth straight road loss with a 17-16 victory over the Bills in the Monday night game. Dave Krieg and John L. Williams hooked up on a 51-yard pass play with 5:32 left for the game-winning touchdown. It was the Seahawks' longest play from scrimmage in 1989.

Despite the loss, Buffalo maintained a one-game lead in the AFC Eastern Division with three weeks left.

Dolphins-Chiefs
SUNDAY, DECEMBER 3
SCORE BY PERIODS

Miami	0	0	7	14—21
Kansas City	13	3	3	7—26

SCORING
Kansas City—Okoye 3 run (kick failed), 6:54 1st.
Kansas City—Paige 38 pass from DeBerg (Lowery kick), 11:59 1st.
Kansas City—Field goal Lowery 34, 14:45 2nd.
Miami—Jensen 8 pass from Marino (Stoyanovich kick), 5:29 3rd.
Kansas City—Field goal Lowery 28, 11:53 3rd.
Miami—Clayton 15 pass from Marino (Stoyanovich kick), 4:23 4th.
Kansas City—Heard 8 pass from DeBerg (Lowery kick), 10:00 4th.
Miami—Jensen 9 pass from Marino (Stoyanovich kick), 14:07 4th.

TEAM STATISTICS

	Miami	Kansas City
First downs	16	25
Rushes-Yards	19-74	42-199
Passing yards	218	239
Passes	18-37-1	15-25-1
Sacked-Yards lost	0-0	0-0
Punts	4-42.3	2-44.5
Fumbles-Lost	2-2	2-2
Penalties-Yards	3-20	8-55
Time of possession	23:12	36:48
Attendance—54,610.		

INDIVIDUAL STATISTICS
Rushing—Miami, Smith 14-49, Secules 1-17, Hampton 3-6, Marino 1-2; Kansas City, Okoye 32-148, Saxon 6-51, Heard 2-2, DeBerg 2-minus 2.

Passing—Miami, Marino 18-37-1—218; Kansas City, DeBerg 15-25-1—239.

Receiving—Miami, Clayton 9-128, Jensen 2-17, Banks 2-14, Edmunds 1-25, Duper 1-18, A. Brown 1-15, Smith 1-5, Hampton 1-minus 4; Kansas City, Paige 7-133, Mandley 3-43, Saxon 2-20, Weathers 1-27, Roberts 1-8, Heard 1-8.

Kickoff Returns—Miami, A. Brown 1-9, Brudzinski 1-6, Hampton 1-17; Kansas City, Copeland 2-37, Worthen 1-27.

Punt Returns—Miami, Schwedes 2-23.

Interceptions—Miami, Judson 1-28; Kansas City, Lewis 1-22.

Punting—Miami, Roby 4-42.3; Kansas City, Goodburn 2-44.5.

Field Goals—Miami, none attempted; Kansas City, Lowery 2-2.

Sacks—None.

Bengals-Browns
SUNDAY, DECEMBER 3
SCORE BY PERIODS

Cincinnati	0	7	14	0—21
Cleveland	0	0	0	0— 0

SCORING
Cincinnati—Brooks 1 run (Breech kick), 4:49 2nd.
Cincinnati—McGee 38 pass from Esiason (Breech kick), 5:47 3rd.
Cincinnati—Holman 9 pass from Esiason (Breech kick), 11:34 3rd.

TEAM STATISTICS

	Cincinnati	Cleveland
First downs	16	15
Rushes-Yards	34-101	23-88
Passing yards	197	176
Passes	14-32-2	19-43-2
Sacked-Yards lost	0-0	0-0
Punts	6-35.7	8-38.5
Fumbles-Lost	1-1	2-1
Penalties-Yards	10-65	6-37
Time of possession	30:43	29:17
Attendance—76,236.		

INDIVIDUAL STATISTICS
Rushing—Cincinnati, Brooks 15-47, Esiason 2-19, Taylor 9-15, Ball 4-14, Jennings 3-5, Wilhelm 1-1; Cleveland, Metcalf 13-56, Redden 5-21, Manoa 3-14, Kosar 1-0, Mack 1-minus 3.

Passing—Cincinnati, Esiason 14-32-2—197; Cleveland, Kosar 15-30-1—130, Pagel 4-13-1—46.

Receiving—Cincinnati, McGee 4-94, Brown 3-43, Hillary 2-19, Holman 2-17, Brooks 2-12, Smith 1-12; Cleveland, Langhorne 7-78, Slaughter 3-33, Metcalf 3-5, Brennan 2-22, Newsome 2-16, McNeil 1-18, Redden 1-4.

Kickoff Returns—Cincinnati, Smith 1-19; Cleveland, Metcalf 3-52.

Punt Returns—Cincinnati, Smith 5-31; Cleveland, McNeil 2-14.

Interceptions—Cincinnati, White 1-22, Fulcher 1-17; Cleveland, Wright 1-0, Minnifield 1-2.

Punting—Cincinnati, Johnson 6-35.7; Cleveland, Wagner 8-38.5.

Field Goals—Cincinnati, none attempted; Cleveland, Bahr 0-2 (missed: 51, 48).

Sacks—None.

Jets-Chargers
SUNDAY, DECEMBER 3
SCORE BY PERIODS

New York Jets	7	0	0	13—20
San Diego	0	7	3	7—17

SCORING
New York—Hector 9 pass from O'Brien (Leahy kick), 12:40 1st.
San Diego—Butts 40 run (Bahr kick), 9:59 2nd.
San Diego—Field goal Bahr 39, 12:53 3rd.
New York—Vick 1 run (Leahy kick), 5:41 4th.
New York—Vick 14 run (kick failed), 7:05 4th.
San Diego—A. Miller 8 pass from Tolliver (Bahr kick), 11:35 4th.

TEAM STATISTICS

	New York	San Diego
First downs	19	14
Rushes-Yards	37-181	15-71
Passing yards	68	187
Passes	12-31-3	24-51-2
Sacked-Yards lost	5-49	5-43
Punts	9-39.4	9-42.3
Fumbles-Lost	1-1	0-0
Penalties-Yards	9-82	4-34
Time of possession	33:47	26:13
Attendance—38,954.		

INDIVIDUAL STATISTICS

Rushing—New York, Hector 20-106, Vick 16-76, Ryan 1-minus 1; San Diego, Butts 5-42, Nelson 6-23, Spencer 3-9, Tolliver 1-minus 3.

Passing—New York, O'Brien 9-20-1—81, Ryan 3-11-2—36; San Diego, Tolliver 24-51-2—230.

Receiving—New York, Toon 7-57, Hector 3-21, Vick 1-20, Townsell 1-19; San Diego, A. Miller 7-70, Nelson 6-54, Holland 4-48, Walker 2-39, Cox 2-11, Spencer 1-8, Parker 1-4, Butts 1-minus 4.

Kickoff Returns—New York, Humphery 1-53, Townsell 3-46; San Diego, A. Miller 2-41, Holland 2-41.

Punt Returns—New York, Townsell 7-85; San Diego, McConkey 1-10.

Interceptions—New York, Hasty 1-12, McMillan 1-40; San Diego, Seale 1-0, Byrd 1-4, Lyles 1-0.

Punting—New York, Prokop 9-39.4; San Diego, Ilesic 9-42.3.

Field Goals—New York, none attempted; San Diego, Bahr 1-2 (missed: 37).

Sacks—New York, Glenn, Lageman, Stallworth, Byrd 2; San Diego, Glenn, Grossman ½, L. Miller 1½, Williams 2.

Redskins-Cardinals
SUNDAY, DECEMBER 3
SCORE BY PERIODS

Washington	3	7	14	5	29
Phoenix	0	10	0	0	10

SCORING

Washington—Field goal Lohmiller 29, 9:26 1st.
Washington—Byner 1 run (Lohmiller kick), 3:31 2nd.
Phoenix—Field goal Del Greco 27, 7:57 2nd.
Phoenix—Ferrell 1 run (Del Greco kick), 13:36 2nd.
Washington—Riggs 1 run (Lohmiller kick), 6:07 3rd.
Washington—Johnson 59 interception return (Lohmiller kick), 9:33 3rd.
Washington—Field goal Lohmiller 23, 13:22 4th.
Washington—Safety, Tupa intentional grounding penalty in end zone, 14:07 4th.

TEAM STATISTICS

	Washington	Phoenix
First downs	23	15
Rushes-Yards	37-135	16-29
Passing yards	168	234
Passes	18-28-1	18-32-3
Sacked-Yards lost	1-7	2-21
Punts	3-48.7	2-45.0
Fumbles-Lost	1-0	0-0
Penalties-Yards	7-61	10-79
Time of possession	33:31	26:29
Attendance—38,870.		

INDIVIDUAL STATISTICS

Rushing—Washington, Byner 20-86, Riggs 12-39, Morris 4-13, Rypien 1-minus 1; Phoenix, Ferrell 8-14, Baker 4-12, Sikahema 2-7, Hogeboom 1-minus 2, Tupa 1-minus 2.

Passing—Washington, Rypien 16-22-0—153, Williams 2-5-1—22, Byner 0-1-0—0; Phoenix, Hogeboom 8-11-1—131, Tupa 10-20-2—124, Sikahema 0-1-0—0.

Receiving—Washington, Monk 6-45, Byner 4-54, Sanders 3-38, Clark 3-25, Riggs 1-11, Tice 1-2; Phoenix, Green 8-116, Jones 4-78, Holmes 2-22, Sikahema 2-22, Baker 1-9, Ferrell 1-8.

Kickoff Returns—Washington, Howard 4-76; Phoenix, Sikahema 5-105.

Punt Returns—Washington, Howard 1-5; Phoenix, Sikahema 2-19.

Interceptions—Washington, A. Johnson 2-66, W. Davis 1-11; Phoenix, Mack 1-9.

Punting—Washington, Mojsiejenko 3-48.7; Phoenix, Camarillo 2-45.0.

Field Goals—Washington, Lohmiller 2-2; Phoenix, Del Greco 1-2 (missed: 50).

Sacks—Washington, Marshall, Stokes; Phoenix, Harvey.

Rams-Cowboys
SUNDAY, DECEMBER 3
SCORE BY PERIODS

Los Angeles Rams	14	0	7	14	35
Dallas	0	10	7	14	31

SCORING

Los Angeles—Johnson 1 pass from Everett (Lansford kick), 8:05 1st.
Los Angeles—Bell 1 run (Lansford kick), 10:30 1st.
Dallas—Johnston 9 pass from Aikman (Zendejas kick), 7:26 2nd.
Dallas—Field goal Zendejas 47, 15:00 2nd.
Los Angeles—A. Cox 18 pass from Everett (Lansford kick), 8:46 3rd.
Dallas—Dixon 35 pass from Aikman (Zendejas kick), 13:58 3rd.
Dallas—Folsom 5 pass from Aikman (Zendejas kick), 3:37 4th.
Dallas—Ford 10 pass from Aikman (Zendejas kick), 5:26 4th.
Los Angeles—Ron Brown 39 pass from Everett (Lansford kick), 11:02 4th.
Los Angeles—A. Cox 23 pass from Everett (Lansford kick), 13:10 4th.

TEAM STATISTICS

	Los Angeles	Dallas
First downs	20	20
Rushes-Yards	28-78	31-138
Passing yards	325	165
Passes	27-37-1	19-34-1
Sacked-Yards lost	2-16	2-14
Punts	5-38.8	5-36.8
Fumbles-Lost	2-0	5-3
Penalties-Yards	8-77	3-15
Time of possession	32:21	27:39
Attendance—46,100.		

INDIVIDUAL STATISTICS

Rushing—Los Angeles, Delpino 11-45, Bell 15-22, McGee 1-11, Hatcher 1-0; Dallas, Aikman 4-57, Palmer 12-51, Johnson 15-30.

Passing—Los Angeles, Everett 27-37-1—341; Dallas, Aikman 19-34-1—179.

Receiving—Los Angeles, A. Cox 5-103, Holohan 5-33, Anderson 4-77, McGee 4-53, Delpino 4-36, Johnson 2-5, Bell 2-minus 5, Ron Brown 1-39; Dallas, Burbage 7-64, Ford 3-28, Tautalatasi 3-15, Dixon 2-43, Johnston 2-15, Folsom 2-14.

Kickoff Returns—Los Angeles, Ron Brown 4-74, Delpino 1-23; Dallas, Dixon 3-92, Shepard 3-62.

Punt Returns—Los Angeles, Henley 1-1; Dallas, Shepard 2-22, Burbage 1-0.

Interceptions—Los Angeles, Irvin 1-13; Dallas, Horton 1-0.

Punting—Los Angeles, Hatcher 5-38.8; Dallas, Saxon 5-36.8.

Field Goals—Los Angeles, none attempted; Dallas, Zendejas 1-1.

Sacks—Los Angeles, Strickland, Greene; Dallas, Jeffcoat, Hamel.

Broncos-Raiders
SUNDAY, DECEMBER 3
SCORE BY PERIODS

Denver	0	10	0	3	0	13
L.A. Raiders	3	0	3	7	3	16

SCORING

Los Angeles—Field goal Jaeger 37, 7:24 1st.
Denver—Field goal Treadwell 34, 4:22 2nd.
Denver—Bratton 5 run (Treadwell kick), 14:23 2nd.
Los Angeles—Field goal Jaeger 46, 8:11 3rd.
Denver—Field goal Treadwell 35, 1:56 4th.
Los Angeles—Dyal 67 pass from Beuerlein (Jaeger kick), 7:55 4th.
Los Angeles—Field goal Jaeger 26, 7:02 OT.

— 232 —

TEAM STATISTICS

	Denver	Los Angeles
First downs	26	11
Rushes-Yards	38-156	21-79
Passing yards	176	178
Passes	23-37-2	9-23-0
Sacked-Yards lost	3-21	2-22
Punts	4-32.8	5-47.2
Fumbles-Lost	0-0	1-1
Penalties-Yards	9-64	4-29
Time of possession	44:03	22:59

Attendance—87,560.

INDIVIDUAL STATISTICS

Rushing—Denver, Humphrey 31-125, Elway 2-16, Bratton 2-10, Alexander 2-5, Winder 1-0; Los Angeles, Jackson 14-44, Smith 5-30, Beuerlein 2-5.

Passing—Denver, Elway 23-36-2—197, Humphrey 0-1-0—0; Los Angeles, Beuerlein 9-23-0—200.

Receiving—Denver, Mobley 5-51, Humphrey 5-45, Johnson 4-29, Winder 4-16, Nattiel 3-42, Young 1-9, Bratton 1-5; Los Angeles, Dyal 4-134, Fernandez 3-50, Smith 2-16.

Kickoff Returns—Denver, Bell 4-63, Carrington 1-7; Los Angeles, Adams 2-42, Mueller 2-41.

Punt Returns—Denver, Nattiel 2-39, Johnson 1-6.

Interceptions—Los Angeles, Washington 2-14.

Punting—Denver, Horan 4-32.8; Los Angeles, Gossett 5-47.2.

Field Goals—Denver, Treadwell 2-3 (missed: 42); Los Angeles, Jaeger 3-3.

Sacks—Denver, Mecklenburg, Holmes; Los Angeles, Benson, Davis, Long.

49ers-Falcons
SUNDAY, DECEMBER 3
SCORE BY PERIODS

San Francisco	6	0	7	10	23
Atlanta	0	10	0	0	10

SCORING

San Francisco—Field goal Cofer 35, 5:42 1st.
San Francisco—Field goal Cofer 23, 15:00 1st.
Atlanta—Field goal Davis 46, 5:00 2nd.
Atlanta—Heller 28 pass from Miller (Davis kick), 13:05 2nd.
San Francisco—Taylor 38 pass from Young (Cofer kick), 8:00 3rd.
San Francisco—Young 1 run (Cofer kick), 0:12 4th.
San Francisco—Field goal Cofer 27, 7:00 4th.

TEAM STATISTICS

	San Francisco	Atlanta
First downs	23	13
Rushes-Yards	33-129	14-37
Passing yards	296	226
Passes	20-25-1	18-34-2
Sacked-Yards lost	3-24	2-17
Punts	3-39.7	4-40.3
Fumbles-Lost	1-0	4-0
Penalties-Yards	7-56	5-40
Time of possession	34:58	25:02

Attendance—43,128.

INDIVIDUAL STATISTICS

Rushing—San Francisco, Craig 17-97, Rathman 10-19, Young 5-8, Montana 1-5; Atlanta, Settle 10-15, Jones 1-13, Lang 2-9, Miller 1-0.

Passing—San Francisco, Montana 9-13-1—145, Young 11-12-0—175; Atlanta, Miller 17-32-2—231, Fulhage 1-1-0—12, Jones 0-1-0—0.

Receiving—San Francisco, Taylor 5-162, Rathman 5-43, Rice 3-32, Jones 3-32, Craig 3-32, Wilson 1-19; Atlanta, Collins 5-71, Haynes 4-53, Heller 3-57, Jones 2-23, Lang 2-19, Beckman 1-12, G. Thomas 1-8.

Kickoff Returns—San Francisco, Tillman 2-20, Flagler 1-8; Atlanta, Sanders 2-50, Bruce 1-15, Jones 1-4.

Punt Returns—San Francisco, Taylor 1-28; Atlanta, Sanders 2-25.

Interceptions—San Francisco, Lott 1-0, Jackson 1-19; Atlanta, Sanders 1-22.

Punting—San Francisco, Helton 3-39.7; Atlanta, Fulhage 4-40.3.

Field Goals—San Francisco, Cofer 3-3; Atlanta, Davis 1-2 (missed: 47).

Sacks—San Francisco, Haley, Stubbs; Atlanta, Green, Bruce, Cotton.

Packers-Buccaneers
SUNDAY, DECEMBER 3
SCORE BY PERIODS

Green Bay	7	0	0	10	17
Tampa Bay	0	3	3	10	16

SCORING

Green Bay—Sharpe 21 pass from Majkowski (Jacke kick), 12:20 1st.
Tampa Bay—Field goal Igwebuike 49, 2:25 2nd.
Tampa Bay—Field goal Igwebuike 40, 4:37 3rd.
Tampa Bay—Stamps 21 run (Igwebuike kick), 2:30 4th.
Green Bay—Sharpe 55 pass from Majkowski (Jacke kick), 5:05 4th.
Tampa Bay—Field goal Igwebuike 36, 13:25 4th.
Green Bay—Field goal Jacke 47, 15:00 4th.

TEAM STATISTICS

	Green Bay	Tampa Bay
First downs	19	18
Rushes-Yards	20-61	27-88
Passing yards	315	170
Passes	25-53-2	19-39-5
Sacked-Yards lost	2-16	4-18
Punts	9-38.2	6-43.2
Fumbles-Lost	2-1	1-0
Penalties-Yards	10-94	6-35
Time of possession	30:26	29:34

Attendance—58,120.

INDIVIDUAL STATISTICS

Rushing—Green Bay, Fullwood 13-37, Woodside 3-16, Majkowski 3-8, Fontenot 1-0; Tampa Bay, Howard 17-49, Stamps 7-33, Wilder 3-6.

Passing—Green Bay, Majkowski 25-53-2—331; Tampa Bay, Testaverde 19-39-5—188.

Receiving—Green Bay, Sharpe 8-169, Fontenot 5-34, Fullwood 3-24, Query 2-40, Woodside 2-17, Kemp 2-14, Bland 1-17, Didier 1-9, Matthews 1-7; Tampa Bay, Carrier 7-104, Howard 6-21, Hall 3-19, Hill 2-40, Stamps 1-4.

Kickoff Returns—Green Bay, Workman 4-64, Bland 1-12; Tampa Bay, Stamps 1-36, Howard 1-14, Elder 1-4.

Punt Returns—Green Bay, Query 4-37; Tampa Bay, Drewrey 3-63.

Interceptions—Green Bay, Noble 1-0, Lee 1-0, Stephen 1-8, D. Brown 2-12; Tampa Bay, Reynolds 1-8, O. Harris 1-19.

Punting—Green Bay, Bracken 9-38.2; Tampa Bay, Mohr 6-43.2.

Field Goals—Green Bay, Jacke 1-1; Tampa Bay, Igwebuike 3-4 (missed: 49).

Sacks—Green Bay, Harris 2, R. Brown, Winter; Tampa Bay, Moss, Cannon.

Saints-Lions
SUNDAY, DECEMBER 3
SCORE BY PERIODS

New Orleans	0	14	0	0	14
Detroit	7	7	7	0	21

SCORING

Detroit—Peete 6 run (Murray kick), 7:30 1st.
New Orleans—Hilliard 1 run (Andersen kick), 0:40 2nd.
Detroit—B. Sanders 3 run (Murray kick), 3:53 2nd.
New Orleans—Morse 99 kickoff return (Andersen kick), 4:14 2nd.
Detroit—Johnson 75 pass from Gagliano (Murray kick), 8:13 3rd.

TEAM STATISTICS

	New Orleans	Detroit
First downs	11	17
Rushes-Yards	24-70	26-85
Passing yards	99	316
Passes	18-29-1	14-31-1
Sacked-Yards lost	3-29	4-27
Punts	9-44.4	8-41.5
Fumbles-Lost	2-1	1-1
Penalties-Yards	3-30	10-75
Time of possession	33:47	26:13

Attendance—38,550.

INDIVIDUAL STATISTICS

Rushing—New Orleans, Hilliard 18-67, Hebert 2-9, Jordan 3-4, Perriman 1-minus 10; Detroit, B. Sanders 20-72, Peete 3-17, Gagliano 3-minus 4.

Passing—New Orleans, Hebert 16-26-1—99; Fourcade 2-3-0—29; Detroit, Peete 8-18-1—177, Gagliano 6-13-0—166.

Receiving—New Orleans, Hilliard 6-31, Brenner 4-48, E. Martin 3-19, Hill 2-17, Perriman 2-6, Scales 1-7; Detroit, Johnson 8-248, Phillips 3-49, B. Sanders 2-9, Stanley 1-37.

Kickoff Returns—New Orleans, Morse 2-112, Harris 1-8; Detroit, Gray 2-48.

Punt Returns—New Orleans, Harris 6-38, Perriman 1-10; Detroit, Stanley 7-53.

Interceptions—New Orleans, Massey 1-22; Detroit, Holmes 1-0.

Punting—New Orleans, Barnhardt 9-44.4; Detroit, Arnold 8-41.5.

Field Goals—New Orleans, Andersen 0-1 (missed: 48); Detroit, none attempted.

Sacks—New Orleans, Mills, Jackson 2, Geathers; Detroit, Spielman, Cofer, E. Williams.

Oilers-Steelers
SUNDAY, DECEMBER 3
SCORE BY PERIODS

Houston	0	14	2	7—23
Pittsburgh	3	7	3	3—16

SCORING

Pittsburgh—Field goal Anderson 18, 6:29 1st.
Pittsburgh—Hoge 4 run (Anderson kick), 5:00 2nd.
Houston—Duncan 18 pass from Moon (Zendejas kick), 13:06 2nd.
Houston—Hill 27 pass from Moon (Zendejas kick), 14:40 2nd.
Pittsburgh—Field goal Anderson 37, 3:10 3rd.
Houston—Safety, McDowell tackled Newsome in end zone, 9:45 3rd.
Pittsburgh—Field goal Anderson 18, 9:17 4th.
Houston—White 1 run (Zendejas kick), 14:39 4th.

TEAM STATISTICS

	Houston	Pittsburgh
First downs	19	15
Rushes-Yards	34-140	36-169
Passing yards	144	43
Passes	12-20-0	9-21-1
Sacked-Yards lost	3-27	3-30
Punts	3-37.7	4-39.5
Fumbles-Lost	7-3	4-0
Penalties-Yards	3-30	8-89
Time of possession	29:39	30:21

Attendance—40,541.

INDIVIDUAL STATISTICS

Rushing—Houston, White 23-115, Moon 5-21, Rozier 2-5, Highsmith 1-3, Pinkett 3-minus 4; Pittsburgh, Worley 18-103, Lipps 4-38, Hoge 11-37, Brister 1-0, Strom 1-minus 1, Newsome 1-minus 8.

Passing—Houston, Moon 12-20-0—171; Pittsburgh, Brister 9-21-1—73.

Receiving—Houston, Hill 4-56, Jeffires 3-50, Duncan 3-42, Givins 1-12, Pinkett 1-11; Pittsburgh, Hoge 3-22, Hill 2-22, Carter 2-13, Mularkey 1-11, Worley 1-5.

Kickoff Returns—Houston, K. Johnson 3-72, T. Johnson 1-27, Mrosko 1-17; Pittsburgh, Woodson 2-43, J. Williams 2-7.

Punt Returns—Houston, K. Johnson 2-minus 3; Pittsburgh, Woodson 2-5.

Interceptions—Houston, Dishman 1-0.

Punting—Houston, Greg Montgomery 3-37.7; Pittsburgh, Newsome 4-39.5.

Field Goals—Houston, Zendejas 0-1 (missed: 37); Pittsburgh, Anderson 3-3.

Sacks—Houston, Meads 3; Pittsburgh, Olsavsky, Lloyd 2.

Eagles-Giants
SUNDAY, DECEMBER 3
SCORE BY PERIODS

Philadelphia	14	3	0	7—24
New York Giants	7	0	10	0—17

SCORING

Philadelphia—Waters 3 fumble return (Ruzek kick), 1:35 1st.
Philadelphia—Simmons 60 interception return (Ruzek kick), 9:45 1st.
New York—Ingram 41 pass from Simms (Nittmo kick), 12:52 1st.
Philadelphia—Field goal Ruzek 35, 7:31 2nd.
New York—Field goal Nittmo 38, 2:21 3rd.
New York—Anderson 1 run (Nittmo kick), 13:39 3rd.
Philadelphia—Byars 2 run (Ruzek kick), 4:10 4th.

TEAM STATISTICS

	Philadelphia	New York
First downs	13	17
Rushes-Yards	45-149	25-58
Passing yards	130	236
Passes	9-16-1	11-37-2
Sacked-Yards lost	1-10	5-29
Punts	4-43.5	3-50.0
Fumbles-Lost	5-1	4-3
Penalties-Yards	16-111	6-35
Time of possession	32:29	27:31

Attendance—74,809.

INDIVIDUAL STATISTICS

Rushing—Philadelphia, Toney 22-68, Byars 14-66, Cunningham 5-10, Runager 2-5, Drummond 2-0; New York, Anderson 16-46, Tillman 8-11, Meggett 1-1.

Passing—Philadelphia, Cunningham 9-16-1—140; New York, Simms 11-37-2—265.

Receiving—Philadelphia, Jackson 5-97, Byars 3-12, Johnson 1-31; New York, Manuel 4-126, Ingram 3-83, Meggett 2-18, Mowatt 1-29, Tillman 1-9.

Kickoff Returns—Philadelphia, Higgs 3-54; New York, Meggett 3-74, Ingram 2-35.

Punt Returns—New York, Meggett 2-19.

Interceptions—Philadelphia, Simmons 1-60, Allen 1-11; New York, Johnson 1-14.

Punting—Philadelphia, Runager 3-27.7, Cunningham 1-91.0; New York, Landeta 3-50.0.

Field Goals—Philadelphia, Ruzek 1-1; New York, Nittmo 1-2 (missed: 47).

Sacks—Philadelphia, Golic, White, Pitts, Hopkins, Simmons; New York, Howard.

Colts-Patriots
SUNDAY, DECEMBER 3
SCORE BY PERIODS

Indianapolis	0	3	7	6—16
New England	6	0	3	13—22

SCORING

New England—Field goal Staurovsky 44, 12:39 1st.
New England—Field goal Staurovsky 37, 15:00 1st.
Indianapolis—Field goal Biasucci 18, 0:03 2nd.

New England—Field goal Staurovsky 24, 9:26 3rd.
Indianapolis—Bentley 9 pass from Trudeau (Biasucci kick), 14:58 3rd.
New England—Field goal Staurovsky 50, 4:47 4th.
New England—Field goal Staurovsky 23, 11:01 4th.
Indianapolis—Dickerson 8 pass from Trudeau (kick failed), 13:01 4th.
New England—Stephens 10 run (Staurovsky kick), 14:35 4th.

TEAM STATISTICS

	Indianapolis	New England
First downs	14	23
Rushes-Yards	29-88	41-187
Passing yards	207	239
Passes	12-30-3	17-32-1
Sacked-Yards lost	0-0	1-16
Punts	6-46.5	2-20.0
Fumbles-Lost	1-0	3-1
Penalties-Yards	7-42	5-33
Time of possession	24:16	35:44
Attendance—32,234.		

INDIVIDUAL STATISTICS

Rushing—Indianapolis, Dickerson 24-80, Hunter 3-4, Trudeau 1-2, Bentley 1-2; New England, Stephens 27-124, Perryman 9-32, Tatupu 1-20, Flutie 1-9, Wilson 2-4, Wonsley 1-minus 2.

Passing—Indianapolis, Trudeau 12-30-3—207; New England, Wilson 17-31-1—255, Flutie 0-1-0—0.

Receiving—Indianapolis, Bentley 3-77, Dickerson 3-31, Verdin 2-41, Brooks 2-30, Rison 2-28; New England, Dykes 6-114, Sievers 3-44, Perryman 3-10, Jones 2-43, Stephens 2-27, Fryar 1-17.

Kickoff Returns—Indianapolis, Rison 3-54, Verdin 2-31; New England, Tucker 2-42, Rehder 1-14, Taylor 1-12.

Punt Returns—Indianapolis, Verdin 1-6; New England, Tucker 4-30.

Interceptions—Indianapolis, Banks 1-2; New England, Feggins 1-4, Hurst 1-0, Brown 1-minus 1.

Punting—Indianapolis, Stark 6-46.5; New England, Feagles 2-20.0.

Field Goals—Indianapolis, Biasucci 1-1; New England, Staurovsky 5-7 (missed: 40, 34).

Sacks—Indianapolis, Hand.

Bears-Vikings
SUNDAY, DECEMBER 3
SCORE BY PERIODS

Chicago	3	0	7	6—16
Minnesota	7	10	7	3—27

SCORING

Chicago—Field goal Butler 33, 3:28 1st.
Minnesota—Walker 1 run (Karlis kick), 11:31 1st.
Minnesota—Jones 46 pass from Wilson (Karlis kick), 11:42 2nd.
Minnesota—Field goal Karlis 51, 15:00 2nd.
Chicago—Boso 3 pass from Tomczak (Butler kick), 3:31 3rd.
Minnesota—Carter 24 pass from Wilson (Karlis kick), 4:44 3rd.
Chicago—Suhey 1 run (kick blocked), 0:03 4th.
Minnesota—Field goal Karlis 45, 6:35 4th.

TEAM STATISTICS

	Chicago	Minnesota
First downs	18	24
Rushes-Yards	34-137	35-136
Passing yards	178	251
Passes	13-33-2	15-26-1
Sacked-Yards lost	1-2	2-9
Punts	5-42.8	4-42.5
Fumbles-Lost	0-0	2-1
Penalties-Yards	8-85	6-40
Time of possession	30:55	29:05
Attendance—60,664.		

INDIVIDUAL STATISTICS

Rushing—Chicago, Anderson 17-76, Muster 3-23, Gentry 1-16, Suhey 7-12, Sanders 3-8, Tomczak 3-2; Minnesota, Fenney 12-53, Walker 18-36, Wilson 4-34, Dozier 1-13.

Passing—Chicago, Tomczak 13-33-2—180; Minnesota, Wilson 15-26-1—260.

Receiving—Chicago, Davis 4-87, Gentry 3-19, Boso 2-15, Anderson 2-12, Morris 1-42, Suhey 1-5; Minnesota, Jones 4-97, Carter 3-66, Jordan 2-39, Walker 2-22, Gustafson 2-21, Fenney 2-15.

Kickoff Returns—Chicago, Gentry 4-111, Sanders 1-23; Minnesota, Walker 4-87.

Punt Returns—Chicago, McKinnon 1-11; Minnesota, Lewis 1-8.

Interceptions—Chicago, Jackson 1-0; Minnesota, Lee 1-0, Edwards 1-18.

Punting—Chicago, Buford 5-42.8; Minnesota, Scribner 4-42.5.

Field Goals—Chicago, Butler 1-2 (missed: 44); Minnesota, Karlis 2-2.

Sacks—Chicago, McMichael ½, Armstrong ½, Dent; Minnesota, Millard.

Bills-Seahawks
MONDAY, DECEMBER 4
SCORE BY PERIODS

Buffalo	0	10	6	0—16
Seattle	10	0	0	7—17

SCORING

Seattle—Field goal N. Johnson 29, 3:56 1st.
Seattle—Warner 1 run (Largent run), 8:04 1st.
Buffalo—Reed 61 pass from Kelly (Norwood kick), 2:08 2nd.
Buffalo—Field goal Norwood 32, 13:52 2nd.
Buffalo—Field goal Norwood 40, 2:47 3rd.
Buffalo—Field goal Norwood 43, 8:20 3rd.
Seattle—Williams 51 pass from Krieg (N. Johnson kick), 9:28 4th.

TEAM STATISTICS

	Buffalo	Seattle
First downs	11	22
Rushes-Yards	29-97	29-78
Passing yards	135	277
Passes	10-23-1	20-40-2
Sacked-Yards lost	1-9	2-21
Punts	6-41.3	5-38.8
Fumbles-Lost	1-1	2-0
Penalties-Yards	6-36	2-15
Time of possession	26:16	33:44
Attendance—57,682.		

INDIVIDUAL STATISTICS

Rushing—Buffalo, Thomas 21-79, Kinnebrew 6-14, Kelly 2-4; Seattle, Warner 16-57, Williams 10-23, Rodriguez 1-0, Krieg 2-minus 2.

Passing—Buffalo, Kelly 10-23-1—144; Seattle, Krieg 20-40-2—298.

Receiving—Buffalo, Reed 2-77, McKeller 2-26, Kinnebrew 2-21, Lofton 1-10, Harmon 1-6, Metzelaars 1-6, Thomas 1-minus 2; Seattle, Williams 5-80, Blades 5-66, Warner 5-55, Clark 2-14, McNeal 1-48, Largent 1-24, Skansi 1-11.

Kickoff Returns—Seattle, Harmon 3-51, Hollis 2-44.

Punt Returns—Buffalo, Sutton 4-56; Seattle, Hollis 3-27.

Interceptions—Buffalo, Still 1-10, Odomes 1-0; Seattle, Robinson 1-4.

Punting—Buffalo, Kidd 6-41.3; Seattle, Rodriguez 5-38.8.

Field Goals—Buffalo, Norwood 3-4 (missed: 48); Seattle, N. Johnson 1-3 (missed: 50, 53).

Sacks—Buffalo, Seals, Talley; Seattle, Nash.

FOURTEENTH WEEK

RESULTS OF WEEK 14
Sunday, December 10

Detroit 27, Chicago 17 at Chi.
Houston 20, Tampa Bay 17 at Hous.
Indianapolis 23, Cleveland 17 (OT) at Ind.
Kansas City 21, Green Bay 3 at G.B.
L.A. Raiders 16, Phoenix 14 at L.A.
Miami 31, New England 10 at Mia.
Minnesota 43, Atlanta 17 at Minn.
New Orleans 22, Buffalo 19 at Buff.
N.Y. Giants 14, Denver 7 at Den.
Philadelphia 20, Dallas 10 at Phila.
Pittsburgh 13, N.Y. Jets 0 at N.Y.
Seattle 24, Cincinnati 17 at Cin.
Washington 26, San Diego 21 at Wash.

Monday, December 11

San Francisco 30, L.A. Rams 27 at L.A.

After coming within five points of a Super Bowl title the previous January, the Cincinnati Bengals entered the 1989 season hoping to carry their quest one step beyond. In other words, nothing less than a championship ring would do this time around.

But it was not to be. The Bengals were on their way to an 8-8 record, becoming only the third Super Bowl loser in history to miss the playoffs the following season. Their disappointing year started on an ominous note—star running back Ickey Woods suffered a season-ending knee injury in Cincinnati's second game—and never improved.

Despite resounding victories by scores of 41-10, 56-23, 42-7 and 61-7, the Bengals also lost games they should have won—to Miami, Indianapolis and the Los Angeles Raiders. Cincinnati did not win two games in a row after Week 5.

The Bengals' most perplexing loss of the season was a 24-17 setback to Seattle in Week 14. After leading 10-0 late in the second quarter, Cincinnati lost the game in the last four minutes on a touchdown pass from Dave Krieg to Curt Warner. The Bengals appeared to have stopped Warner for a yard loss on a third-and-goal situation at the 1, only to have officials call it a dead play when they couldn't agree on a false-start call. After considerable confusion, the down was played over and this time the Seahawks scored, with Warner catching a one-yard toss from Krieg with 3:51 remaining to break a 17-17 tie.

It was the Bengals' third loss in 1989 at Riverfront Stadium, a place where they were undefeated a year earlier.

"I've never seen anything quite like that in my life," Cincinnati Coach Sam Wyche said. "I'm sure it will be reviewed and I'm sure explanations will be given to you (reporters) later . . . I feel so sorry for them (the Bengals) that they had to lose this way."

Wyche was so incensed that he kept the Cincinnati locker room closed to reporters after the game. He also put a gag order on his players.

"I told them not to say anything," the coach said. "It's kind of like officiating—sometimes things aren't fair."

Wyche's antics earned him a reported $3,000 fine from the NFL, but his anger was undoubtedly fueled by the entire season and not just one game. The loss dropped the Bengals' record to 7-7, two games behind AFC Central Division leader Houston with only two games left.

"I thought we made too many mistakes to win," said defensive coordinator Dick LeBeau, the only Cincinnati coach or player to talk with the media afterward. "We gave up too many big plays."

One of the biggest plays his defense yielded was a 10-yard touchdown pass to Steve Largent in the final minute of the first half. It capped a 12-play, 78-yard drive to cut Cincinnati's lead to 10-7 at halftime. It also was Largent's 100th career touchdown reception, eclipsing Don Hutson's NFL record of 99 that had stood since 1945.

"That gave us some momentum," said Krieg, who completed 22 of 33 passes for 258 yards and two touchdowns on a snowy afternoon.

Cincinnati's Boomer Esiason, meanwhile, completed 21 of 42 passes for 246 yards and one touchdown. But he failed to complete a possible game-tying fourth-down pass to Rodney Holman at the back of the Seattle end zone with 53 seconds left.

The Bengals' loss dropped them into a third-place tie in the AFC Central with the Pittsburgh Steelers, who kept their playoff hopes alive with a 13-0 defeat of the New York Jets. It was the Steelers' first shutout victory since 1985 and the 10th time they had beaten the Jets in 11 meetings.

The Steelers scored the only points they needed on rookie Tim Worley's 35-yard touchdown run five minutes into the game. Gary Anderson rounded out the scoring with two field goals in the final period as the Steelers handed the Jets their first shutout at home since 1977.

The Detroit Lions had their first three-game winning streak since 1978 following their 27-17 victory at Chicago in Week 14. It was the Lions' first victory over the Bears in 11 games and officially eliminated Chicago (6-8) from winning a sixth straight NFC Central Division crown.

Rookie Barry Sanders, who entered the game as the NFC's rushing leader, picked up 120 yards on 26 carries and scored two touchdowns. He ran for 71 yards in Detroit's 17-point second period.

Marcus Allen's one-yard touchdown run with

Barry Sanders blitzed the Bears for 120 yards on 26 carries in Detroit's 27-17 victory at Chicago in Week 14.

40 seconds left helped the Los Angeles Raiders to a 16-14 interconference victory over the Phoenix Cardinals. The touchdown capped a 13-play, 46-yard drive that was set up by a 49-yard kickoff return by Vance Mueller. Allen kept the drive alive with a three-yard run on fourth-and-two to put the ball at the Cardinals' 1.

Phoenix had taken a 14-9 lead on Gary Hogeboom's two-yard touchdown pass to Jay Novacek with 5:10 to play. Novacek's touchdown ended a 15-play, 90-yard drive.

The Cardinals' fourth straight loss dropped their record to 5-9 and assured them of a losing record for the fifth straight year.

Losing seasons also were becoming old hat for the Atlanta Falcons, whose record dropped to 3-11 after a 43-17 loss at Minnesota. The Falcons failed to win a game on the road for the first time in 22 years.

Atlanta's last winning record in a non-strike year was 1980, when the Falcons went 12-4 in winning the NFC Western Division title.

That also was the last season the Vikings won the NFC Central Division crown, something they appeared ready to do again with the victory over Atlanta. The win improved Minnesota's record to 9-5 and broke a tie with Green Bay atop the Central Division standings.

The Vikings' defense was outstanding against the Falcons, particularly end Chris Doleman. The fifth-year pro had four sacks, two of which caused fumbles that were returned by teammates for touchdowns. Keith Millard (31 yards) and Tim Newton (five yards) returned Chris Miller fumbles for Minnesota touchdowns in a 17-point third quarter.

It was the first time the Vikings had returned two fumbles for touchdowns in the same game.

The Packers lost their share of the division lead with a 21-3 interconference loss to Kansas City. The Packers' offense was held to a season-low 208 total yards (166 below its average) and failed to score a touchdown for the first time in 17 games.

Green Bay quarterback Don Majkowski threw one interception and was sacked four times. His fumble at his own 15 late in the first half was recovered by the Chiefs' Neil Smith, setting up a 12-yard touchdown pass from Steve DeBerg to Emile Harry. The touchdown was the Chiefs' second in 54 seconds en route to an 18-point halftime lead.

DeBerg was superb in leading Kansas City to its third straight victory, completing 15 of 19 passes for 203 yards and two touchdowns. Two of his four incompletions were catchable passes dropped by receivers.

The only overtime game in Week 14 was played at Indianapolis, where the Colts intercepted two Bernie Kosar passes in a 23-17 victory over the Cleveland Browns. The first interception sent the game into overtime and the second won the game for Indianapolis.

The Browns led, 17-10, before Keith Taylor intercepted a Kosar pass two yards deep in the end zone and returned it 77 yards to the Cleveland 25. That led to a one-yard touchdown pass from Tom Ramsey to Pat Beach with 1:56 left to tie the game.

In the overtime, Mike Prior picked off a Kosar pass and returned it 58 yards for the game-winning touchdown.

The overtime game was the Browns' third of 1989 without a victory (0-2-1). Veteran place-kicker Matt Bahr missed two possible game-winning field goals: a 39-yarder with 25 seconds left in regulation time and a 35-yard attempt in the extra period.

The triumph improved the Colts' record to 7-7 and kept them one game behind co-AFC Eastern Division leaders Buffalo and Miami.

The Bills, who were trying to repeat as division champs, saw their chances dimmed by a 22-19 loss at home to the New Orleans Saints. The Bills committed turnovers on their first two possessions and the Saints took advantage, scoring touchdowns after each to take a 13-0 lead. Both touchdowns came on passes by John Fourcade, a 29-year-old veteran of four professional football leagues who was making his first NFL start in a non-strike game.

Buffalo's most critical turnovers, however, occurred late in the game. Jim Kelly had a pass intercepted by Toi Cook at the Saints' goal line in the fourth quarter, leading to an 81-yard New Orleans drive that set up the game-winning points: a 22-yard field goal by Morten Andersen with 1:53 remaining.

Brett Maxie then intercepted Kelly to end the Bills' final possession.

The Miami Dolphins moved into a tie with Buffalo atop the AFC East with a 31-10 victory over New England, giving the Dolphins their first series sweep over the Patriots since 1984.

Rookie Sammie Smith scored three touchdowns for Miami and Dan Marino, who completed 21 of 32 passes for 300 yards, notched the other.

The Dallas-Philadelphia game in Week 14 at Veterans Stadium was dubbed the "Bounty Bowl" after Cowboys Coach Jimmy Johnson had accused the Eagles' Buddy Ryan of offering payments to his players for making injury-causing hits against Cowboys quarterback Troy Aikman and place-kicker Tony Zendejas when the teams played in Dallas on Thanksgiving Day. NFL Commissioner Paul Tagliabue investigated Johnson's charges before dismissing the protest.

Tagliabue attended the teams' rematch 17 days later in Philadelphia. Although there were no obvious attempts to injure in the Eagles' 20-10 victory, the teams played a very physical game that resulted in a total of 21 penalties for 177 yards. That figure did not include five offsetting unnecessary-roughness penalties.

The Eagles, who were playing one day after the death of quarterbacks coach Doug Scovil, took control early by marching 75 yards for a touchdown on their first possession. Randall Cunningham capped the 14-play drive with a four-yard touchdown pass to Cris Carter.

The New York Giants kept pace with the Eagles atop the NFC East standings with a 14-7 interconference victory at Denver. Like the Eagles, the Giants took command with a long scoring march on their first possession, driving 85 yards in 15 plays to take a 7-0 lead on a three-yard run by Ottis Anderson.

New York's second touchdown was a one-man effort by rookie Dave Meggett. Meggett returned a punt 26 yards to the Denver 36 before a penalty and a sack put the Giants back at their 43. Then the fifth-round draft choice from Towson State hauled in a short screen pass from Phil Simms and bolted 57 yards for the game-winning touchdown.

Another NFC East team, the Washington Redskins, kept their own slim playoff hopes alive with a 26-21 decision over the San Diego Chargers. Mark Rypien threw two touchdown passes and Chip Lohmiller kicked four field goals as Washington improved its record to 8-6 and gave Coach Joe Gibbs his 100th NFL coaching victory.

Gibbs, who succeeded Jack Pardee as the Redskins' coach in 1981, became only the 19th coach in league history to win 100 games.

After the Chargers scored touchdowns on their first two possessions to take a 14-0 lead, the Redskins scored 16 straight points to seize a 16-14 edge after three quarters. A 10-yard run by rookie Marion Butts put San Diego ahead again, 21-16, before Rypien threw a 33-yard touchdown pass to Gary Clark with 7:27 to play for the game-winning score.

Rookie quarterback Billy Joe Tolliver fumbled on the Chargers' next possession to set up a 28-yard field goal by Lohmiller with 3:22 left for the game's final points.

The Houston Oilers kept their grip on first place in the AFC Central with a 20-17 interconference victory over the Tampa Bay Buccaneers.

Defense and special teams were the keys for Houston, with the Oilers blocking two punts, intercepting one pass and recovering one fumble. Rookie safety Bubba McDowell made the fumble recovery, pouncing on James Wilder's bobble at the Houston 21 with 1:18 remaining and thereby killing a Tampa Bay scoring threat.

Cris Dishman's interception of Vinny Testaverde set up an Oilers touchdown, while one of the two blocked punts led to a field goal.

Quarterback Warren Moon completed 13 of 18 passes in Houston's 20-point first half, including touchdown passes of 12 yards to Drew Hill and 16 yards to Curtis Duncan.

The San Francisco 49ers clinched their sixth NFC Western Division title in seven seasons with a 30-27 victory over the Los Angeles Rams on Monday night. The win lifted the 49ers' record to 12-2 and assured them home-field advantage throughout the NFC playoffs.

San Francisco pulled out the victory despite trailing by 17 points on two occasions and committing 10 penalties for 145 yards. The Rams led 17-0 after 12 minutes on a three-yard touchdown run by Greg Bell, a four-yard Jim Everett scoring pass to Damone Johnson and a 25-yard Mike Lansford field goal.

The 49ers used the big play to come back.

Joe Montana and John Taylor hooked up on a 92-yard pass in the second quarter for San Francisco's first touchdown and then connected on a 95-yarder in the fourth to cut the Rams' lead to 27-23. The second Montana-to-Taylor touchdown came one play after Matt Millen recovered a fumble by Everett at the San Francisco 5.

Montana completed 30 of 42 passes for 458 yards; Taylor finished with 11 catches for 286 yards. Both of Taylor's figures set San Francisco team records.

The 49ers' winning touchdown—a one-yard run by Roger Craig with 3:42 left—came six plays after Keith Henderson recovered a fumbled kickoff by the Rams' Ron Brown at the L.A. 27. The score capped a 20-point fourth quarter for San Francisco.

Browns-Colts
SUNDAY, DECEMBER 10
SCORE BY PERIODS

Cleveland	0	10	7	0	0—17
Indianapolis	7	0	3	7	6—23

SCORING
Indianapolis—Rison 51 pass from Trudeau (Biasucci kick), 2:03 1st.
Cleveland—Metcalf 12 run (Bahr kick), 2:27 2nd.
Cleveland—Field goal Bahr 48, 15:00 2nd.
Cleveland—Tillman recovered blocked punt in end zone (Bahr kick), 1:42 3rd.
Indianapolis—Field goal Biasucci 35, 7:23 3rd.
Indianapolis—Beach 1 pass from Ramsey (Biasucci kick), 13:04 4th.
Indianapolis—Prior 58 interception return (no kick), 10:54 OT.

TEAM STATISTICS

	Cleveland	Indianapolis
First downs	24	19
Rushes-Yards	33-123	30-145
Passing yards	347	251
Passes	26-40-2	23-44-1
Sacked-Yards lost	1-6	4-20
Punts	6-42.7	8-38.5
Fumbles-Lost	4-2	3-0
Penalties-Yards	9-50	10-70
Time of possession	35:55	34:59
Attendance—58,550.		

INDIVIDUAL STATISTICS
Rushing—Cleveland, Redden 10-42, Metcalf 11-39, Mack 6-16, Manoa 5-14, Kosar 1-12; Indianapolis, Dickerson 26-137, Trudeau 2-7, Ramsey 2-1.
Passing—Cleveland, Kosar 26-40-2—353; Indianapolis, Trudeau 15-32-1—200, Ramsey 8-12-0—71.
Receiving—Cleveland, Metcalf 7-58, Slaughter 6-152, Newsome 3-43, Manoa 3-35, McNeil 3-17, Langhorne 2-30, Brennan 2-18; Indianapolis, Brooks 6-42, Bentley 6-13, Rison 5-135, Dickerson 3-34, Beach 2-7, Pruitt 1-40.
Kickoff Returns—Cleveland, Metcalf 4-68; Indianapolis, Bentley 3-67.
Punt Returns—Cleveland, McNeil 5-103; Indianapolis, Verdin 1-11, Rison 2-20.
Interceptions—Cleveland, Wright 1-4; Indianapolis, Taylor 1-77, Prior 1-58.
Punting—Cleveland, Wagner 6-42.7; Indianapolis, Stark 7-44.0.
Field Goals—Cleveland, Bahr 1-3 (missed: 39, 35); Indianapolis, Biasucci 1-2 (missed: 53).
Sacks—Cleveland, Perry 2, M. Johnson, Hairston; Indianapolis, Young.

Giants-Broncos
SUNDAY, DECEMBER 10
SCORE BY PERIODS

New York Giants	0	14	0	0—14
Denver	0	0	0	7— 7

SCORING
New York—Anderson 3 run (Nittmo kick), 0:46 2nd.
New York—Meggett 57 pass from Simms (Nittmo kick), 7:49 2nd
Denver—Young 32 pass from Elway (Treadwell kick), 0:31 4th.

TEAM STATISTICS

	New York	Denver
First downs	16	18
Rushes-Yards	37-113	24-83
Passing yards	148	284
Passes	13-22-0	23-47-0
Sacked-Yards lost	3-23	1-8
Punts	7-41.0	5-37.4
Fumbles-Lost	1-0	0-0
Penalties-Yards	2-21	8-62
Time of possession	30:58	29:02
Attendance—63,283.		

INDIVIDUAL STATISTICS
Rushing—New York, Carthon 11-43, Anderson 18-34, Simms 3-19, Meggett 1-8, Rouson 1-6, Reasons 1-2, Tillman 2-1; Denver, Humphrey 15-44, Elway 4-26, Bratton 3-7, Winder 2-6.
Passing—New York, Simms 13-22-0—171; Denver, Elway 23-47-0—292.
Receiving—New York, Carthon 5-34, Meggett 2-66, Baker 2-24, Ingram 1-21, Adams 1-10, Mowatt 1-9, Anderson 1-7; Denver, Johnson 6-98, Humphrey 5-36, Young 4-79, Kay 3-30, Jackson 2-35, Bratton 2-6, Nattiel 1-8.
Kickoff Returns—New York, Ingram 2-20; Denver, Bell 2-47, Carrington 1-11.
Punt Returns—New York, Meggett 2-36; Denver, Nattiel 3-21.
Interceptions—None.
Punting—New York, Landeta 7-41.0; Denver, Horan 5-37.4.
Field Goals—New York, Nittmo 0-1 (missed: 47); Denver, none attempted.
Sacks—New York, Marshall; Denver, Carreker 1½, Fletcher ½, Holmes.

Chiefs-Packers
SUNDAY, DECEMBER 10
SCORE BY PERIODS

Kansas City	0	21	0	0—21
Green Bay	0	3	0	0— 3

SCORING
Kansas City—Hayes 11 pass from DeBerg (Lowery kick), 0:05 2nd.
Green Bay—Field goal Jacke 25, 11:03 2nd.
Kansas City—Okoye 3 run (Lowery kick), 13:59 2nd.
Kansas City—Harry 12 pass from DeBerg (Lowery kick), 14:53 2nd.

TEAM STATISTICS

	Kansas City	Green Bay
First downs	21	11
Rushes-Yards	48-178	17-110
Passing yards	203	98
Passes	15-19-0	14-34-1
Sacked-Yards lost	0-0	4-25
Punts	5-42.0	8-36.1
Fumbles-Lost	4-3	3-1
Penalties-Yards	5-50	3-25
Time of possession	37:03	22:57
Attendance—56,694.		

INDIVIDUAL STATISTICS

Rushing—Kansas City, Okoye 38-131, Saxon 7-26, Heard 2-13, McNair 1-8; Green Bay, Fullwood 10-39, Majkowski 4-33, Sharpe 1-26, Fontenot 2-12.

Passing—Kansas City, DeBerg 15-19-0—203; Green Bay, Majkowski 14-34-1—123.

Receiving—Kansas City, Hayes 4-53, Paige 4-51, Harry 3-40, Heard 1-27, Roberts 1-15, Saxon 1-9, McNair 1-8; Green Bay, Kemp 3-29, Fontenot 3-20, Matthews 2-22, Fullwood 2-15, Spagnola 1-14, Bland 1-13, Haddix 1-5, Sharpe 1-5.

Kickoff Returns—Kansas City, Worthen 2-46; Green Bay, Workman 2-19, Didier 1-0, Fullwood 1-23.

Punt Returns—Kansas City, Mandley 2-11, Worthen 2-16; Green Bay, Query 5-33.

Interceptions—Kansas City, Burruss 1-0.

Punting—Kansas City, Goodburn 5-42.0; Green Bay, Bracken 8-36.1.

Field Goals—Kansas City, Lowery 0-1 (missed: 34); Green Bay, Jacke 1-1.

Sacks—Kansas City, Saleaumua 1½, Smith 1½, Lewis.

Saints-Bills
SUNDAY, DECEMBER 10
SCORE BY PERIODS

New Orleans	13	3	3	3—22
Buffalo	0	12	7	0—19

SCORING

New Orleans—Tice 12 pass from Fourcade (kick failed), 2:18 1st.

New Orleans—Hilliard 54 pass from Fourcade (Andersen kick), 9:00 1st.

Buffalo—Lofton 42 pass from Kelly (kick failed), 0:05 2nd.

New Orleans—Field goal Andersen 31, 4:18 2nd.

Buffalo—Field goal Norwood 43, 7:30 2nd.

Buffalo—Field goal Norwood 48, 14:52 2nd.

Buffalo—Metzelaars 2 pass from Kelly (Norwood kick), 0:47 3rd.

New Orleans—Field goal Andersen 26, 4:58 3rd.

New Orleans—Field goal Andersen 22, 13:07 4th.

TEAM STATISTICS

	New Orleans	Buffalo
First downs	21	16
Rushes-Yards	41-149	25-75
Passing yards	287	204
Passes	15-27-1	17-35-3
Sacked-Yards lost	2-15	2-7
Punts	2-39.6	4-33.0
Fumbles-Lost	2-1	1-1
Penalties-Yards	4-25	2-15
Time of possession	34:13	25:47
Attendance—70,037.		

INDIVIDUAL STATISTICS

Rushing—New Orleans, Hilliard 32-97, Jordan 4-34, Fourcade 4-14, Heyward 1-4; Buffalo, Thomas 16-40, Kinnebrew 7-27, Kelly 1-8, K. Davis 1-0.

Passing—New Orleans, Fourcade 15-27-1—302; Buffalo, Kelly 17-35-3—211.

Receiving—New Orleans, E. Martin 4-100, Perriman 4-96, Hilliard 3-55, Tice 2-20, Hill 1-23, Brenner 1-8; Buffalo, Thomas 4-51, Reed 4-35, McKeller 2-40, Harmon 2-15, Metzelaars 2-14, Lofton 1-42, Beebe 1-8, Johnson 1-6.

Kickoff Returns—New Orleans, Morse 2-40, Harris 2-36; Buffalo, Beebe 4-62.

Punt Returns—New Orleans, Morse 3-0; Buffalo, Sutton 2-9.

Interceptions—New Orleans, Swilling 1-14, Cook 1-8, Maxie 1-7; Buffalo, Odomes 1-13.

Punting—New Orleans, Barnhardt 2-39.5; Buffalo, Kidd 4-33.0.

Field Goals—New Orleans, Andersen 3-5 (missed: 41, 50); Buffalo, Norwood 2-2.

Sacks—New Orleans, Jackson, Warren; Buffalo, Conlan, B. Smith.

Steelers-Jets
SUNDAY, DECEMBER 10
SCORE BY PERIODS

Pittsburgh	7	0	0	6—13
New York Jets	0	0	0	0— 0

SCORING

Pittsburgh—Worley 35 run (Anderson kick), 5:18 1st.

Pittsburgh—Field goal Anderson 42, 3:45 4th.

Pittsburgh—Field goal Anderson 45, 9:55 4th.

TEAM STATISTICS

	Pittsburgh	New York
First downs	17	19
Rushes-Yards	32-157	23-70
Passing yards	160	243
Passes	15-30-1	27-42-2
Sacked-Yards lost	2-15	1-8
Punts	4-44.8	4-41.3
Fumbles-Lost	2-0	3-1
Penalties-Yards	6-35	5-20
Time of possession	32:19	27:41
Attendance—41,037.		

INDIVIDUAL STATISTICS

Rushing—Pittsburgh, Worley 10-64, Hoge 14-43, Stone 4-29, Lipps 1-20, Brister 1-2, Strom 2-minus 1; New York, Vick 7-28, Hector 12-27, Brown 3-15, O'Brien 1-0.

Passing—Pittsburgh, Brister 15-29-1—175, Strom 0-1-0—0; New York, Ryan 1-4-0—25, O'Brien 26-38-2—226.

Receiving—Pittsburgh, Lipps 4-75, Hill 3-36, Hoge 3-12, Stock 2-34, Carter 1-8, Mularkey 1-7, Worley 1-3; New York, Epps 6-79, Neubert 6-40, Townsell 4-51, Vick 4-18, Burkett 3-21, Toon 1-25, Warner 1-13, Hector 1-3, Brown 1-1.

Kickoff Returns—New York, Townsell 1-22, Humphery 3-55.

Punt Returns—Pittsburgh, Woodson 1-4; New York, Townsell 2-8.

Interceptions—Pittsburgh, Lloyd 1-16, Woodruff 1-9; New York, Hasty 1-0.

Punting—Pittsburgh, Newsome 4-44.8; New York, Prokop 4-41.3.

Field Goals—Pittsburgh, Anderson 2-3 (missed: 48); Leahy 0-2 (missed: 47, 41).

Sacks—Pittsburgh, Lloyd; New York, McMillan, Byrd.

Lions-Bears
SUNDAY, DECEMBER 10
SCORE BY PERIODS

Detroit	0	17	7	3—27
Chicago	3	7	0	7—17

SCORING

Chicago—Field goal Butler 22, 5:38 1st.

Detroit—Gagliano 14 run (Murray kick), 0:50 2nd.

Detroit—B. Sanders 18 run (Murray kick), 7:35 2nd.

Chicago—Muster 11 run (Butler kick), 12:17 2nd.

Detroit—Field goal Murray 45, 14:16 2nd.

Detroit—B. Sanders 3 run (Murray kick), 7:05 3rd.

Detroit—Field goal Murray 28, 2:14 4th.

Chicago—Anderson 1 run (Butler kick), 9:26 4th.

TEAM STATISTICS

	Detroit	Chicago
First downs	17	21
Rushes-Yards	31-127	27-130
Passing yards	168	172
Passes	13-23-1	25-37-1
Sacked-Yards lost	0-0	5-52
Punts	5-29.4	5-36.4
Fumbles-Lost	2-1	3-1
Penalties-Yards	7-65	4-25
Time of possession	28:15	31:45
Attendance—52,650.		

INDIVIDUAL STATISTICS

Rushing—Detroit, B. Sanders 26-120, Gagliano 4-15, Johnson 1-minus 8; Chicago, Harbaugh 8-61, Anderson 12-42, Muster 3-17, Gentry 3-8, Sanders 1-2.

Passing—Detroit, Gagliano 13-23-1—168; Chicago, Tomczak 4-8-0—45, Harbaugh 21-29-1—179.

Receiving—Detroit, Johnson 4-30, Phillips 3-47, B. Sanders 3-39, Stanley 2-28, Clark 1-24; Chicago, Anderson 9-58, Morris 5-40, Muster 3-31, Gentry 2-26, Davis 2-23, McKinnon 1-22, Kozlowski 1-13, Thornton 1-6, Boso 1-5.

Kickoff Returns—Detroit, Alexander 2-37, B. Sanders 2-59; Chicago, Suhey 1-11, Sanders 4-49, Gentry 1-19.

Punt Returns—Detroit, Stanley 2-32; Chicago, McKinnon 1-12, Waddle 1-2.

Interceptions—Detroit, J. Williams 1-0; Chicago, Jackson 1-16.

Punting—Detroit, Arnold 5-29.4; Chicago, Buford 5-36.4.

Field Goals—Detroit, Murray 2-2; Chicago, Butler 1-3 (missed: 43, 37).

Sacks—Detroit, Spielman, Cofer, J. Williams, Ball 2.

Seahawks-Bengals
SUNDAY, DECEMBER 10
SCORE BY PERIODS

Seattle	0	7	10	7—24
Cincinnati	7	3	0	7—17

SCORING

Cincinnati—McGee 21 pass from Esiason (Breech kick), 9:42 1st.

Cincinnati—Field goal Breech 24, 4:23 2nd.

Seattle—Largent 10 pass from Krieg (N. Johnson kick), 14:18 2nd.

Seattle—Field goal N. Johnson 48, 2:02 3rd.

Seattle—Blades 60 pass from Krieg (N. Johnson kick), 4:46 3rd.

Cincinnati—Thomas 18 interception return (Breech kick), 5:21 4th.

Seattle—Warner 1 pass from Krieg (N. Johnson kick), 11:09 4th.

TEAM STATISTICS

	Seattle	Cincinnati
First downs	15	23
Rushes-Yards	25-109	29-150
Passing yards	252	215
Passes	22-33-1	21-42-0
Sacked-Yards lost	1-6	4-31
Punts	6-35.3	6-33.3
Fumbles-Lost	1-0	2-1
Penalties-Yards	8-69	6-38
Time of possession	29:34	30:26
Attendance—54,744.		

INDIVIDUAL STATISTICS

Rushing—Seattle, Warner 14-51, Williams 7-35, Krieg 4-23; Cincinnati, Brooks 11-52, Jennings 8-41, Ball 6-35, Esiason 1-15, Taylor 3-7.

Passing—Seattle, Krieg 22-33-1—258; Cincinnati, Esiason 21-42-0—246.

Receiving—Seattle, Williams 7-46, Blades 6-107, Largent 5-68, McNeal 2-28, Skansi 1-8, Warner 1-1; Cincinnati, McGee 7-109, Hillary 5-49, Brown 4-36, Smith 2-15, Ball 1-15, Holman 1-14, Jennings 1-8.

Kickoff Returns—Seattle, Harris 3-65; Cincinnati, Jennings 4-81.

Punt Returns—Seattle, Hollis 2-17; Cincinnati, Smith 5-14.

Interceptions—Cincinnati, Thomas 1-18.

Punting—Seattle, Rodriguez 6-35.3; Cincinnati, Johnson 5-34.8, Breech 1-26.0.

Field Goals—Seattle, N. Johnson 1-2 (missed: 41); Cincinnati, Breech 1-1.

Sacks—Seattle, Nash, Hunter, Porter, Wyman; Cincinnati, Kelly.

Buccaneers-Oilers
SUNDAY, DECEMBER 10
SCORE BY PERIODS

Tampa Bay	3	0	7	7—17
Houston	3	17	0	0—20

SCORING

Houston—Field goal Zendejas 30, 4:57 1st.

Tampa Bay—Field goal Igwebuike 21, 9:52 1st.

Houston—Hill 12 pass from Moon (Zendejas kick), 1:26 2nd.

Houston—Field goal Zendejas 37, 4:46 2nd.

Houston—Duncan 16 pass from Moon (Zendejas kick), 13:31 2nd.

Tampa Bay—Drewrey 6 pass from Testaverde (Igwebuike kick), 7:37 3rd.

Tampa Bay—Hall 24 pass from Testaverde (Igwebuike kick), 8:48 4th.

TEAM STATISTICS

	Tampa Bay	Houston
First downs	23	16
Rushes-Yards	19-66	30-135
Passing yards	287	149
Passes	31-48-1	14-23-0
Sacked-Yards lost	4-41	0-0
Punts	4-20.8	3-45.0
Fumbles-Lost	2-1	3-2
Penalties-Yards	4-23	6-50
Time of possession	33:12	26:48
Attendance—54,532.		

INDIVIDUAL STATISTICS

Rushing—Tampa Bay, Testaverde 3-28, Tate 7-18, Wilder 6-13, Stamps 3-7; Houston, Rozier 13-82, Highsmith 7-44, Moon 7-5, Pinkett 1-4, White 1-0, Duncan 1-0.

Passing—Tampa Bay, Testaverde 31-48-1—328; Houston, Moon 14-23-0—149.

Receiving—Tampa Bay, Carrier 10-135, Hall 6-61, Wilder 6-50, Stamps 4-21, Drewrey 2-24, Hill 2-18, Peebles 1-19; Houston, Givins 5-56, Hill 2-17, Rozier 2-14, Jeffires 1-23; Duncan 1-16, Mrosko 1-9, Pinkett 1-8, Verhulst 1-6.

Kickoff Returns—Tampa Bay, Futrell 1-22; Houston, White 3-50, Mrosko 1-19.

Punt Returns—Tampa Bay, Drewrey 1-6; Houston, K. Johnson 1-1.

Interceptions—Houston, Dishman 1-31.

Punting—Tampa Bay, Mohr 3-27.7; Houston, Greg Montgomery 3-45.0.

Field Goals—Tampa Bay, Igwebuike 1-2 (missed: 48); Houston, Zendejas 2-2.

Sacks—Houston, Jones 2, Brown 2.

Falcons-Vikings
SUNDAY, DECEMBER 10
SCORE BY PERIODS

Atlanta	3	7	7	0—17
Minnesota	7	13	17	6—43

SCORING

Minnesota—Ingram 2 pass from Wilson (Karlis kick), 9:17 1st.

Atlanta—Field goal Davis 26, 12:21 1st.

Minnesota—Field goal Karlis 21, 1:21 2nd.

Atlanta—Wilkins 26 pass from Miller (Davis kick), 6:23 2nd.

Minnesota—Carter 19 pass from Dozier (Karlis kick), 7:22 2nd.

Minnesota—Field goal Karlis 39, 14:01 2nd.

Atlanta—Collins 17 pass from Miller (Davis kick), 2:14 3rd.

Minnesota—Millard 31 fumble return (Karlis kick), 6:54 3rd.

Minnesota—Field goal Karlis 26, 12:44 3rd.

Minnesota—Newton 5 fumble return (Karlis kick), 13:43 3rd.

Minnesota—Field goal Karlis 29, 2:45 4th.
Minnesota—Field goal Karlis 19, 12:34 4th.

TEAM STATISTICS

	Atlanta	Minnesota
First downs	15	23
Rushes-Yards	18-90	37-220
Passing yards	165	237
Passes	15-28-1	15-26-1
Sacked-Yards lost	5-61	4-23
Punts	5-39.8	1-55.0
Fumbles-Lost	2-2	0-0
Penalties-Yards	1-10	7-51
Time of possession	23:08	36:52
Attendance—58,116.		

INDIVIDUAL STATISTICS

Rushing—Atlanta, Settle 9-43, Jones 4-21, Haynes 1-12, Miller 1-7, Lang 3-7; Minnesota, Fenney 17-89, Clark 10-57, Dozier 5-54, Walker 4-14, Wilson 1-6.

Passing—Atlanta, Miller 11-23-1—182, Millen 4-5-0—44; Minnesota, Wilson 14-25-1—241, Dozier 1-1-0—19.

Receiving—Atlanta, Haynes 5-88, Jones 5-37, Collins 2-58, Wilkins 1-26, Paterra 1-13, Settle 1-4; Minnesota, Carter 3-78, Jordan 3-71, Jones 3-64, Fenney 1-18, Lewis 1-15, Dozier 1-5, Walker 1-5, Clark 1-2, Ingram 1-2.

Kickoff Returns—Atlanta, Jones 4-65, Sanders 2-31, Paterra 1-8; Minnesota, Dozier 2-26, Lewis 1-15.

Punt Returns—Atlanta, Sanders 1-7; Minnesota, Lewis 3-49.

Interceptions—Atlanta, Bruce 1-0; Minnesota, Browner 1-9.

Punting—Atlanta, Fulhage 5-39.8; Minnesota, Scribner 1-55.0.

Field Goals—Atlanta, Davis 1-1; Minnesota, Karlis 5-5.

Sacks—Atlanta, Cotton 2, Bruce, Green; Minnesota, Doleman 4, Noga.

Cardinals-Raiders
SUNDAY, DECEMBER 10
SCORE BY PERIODS

Phoenix	0	7	0	7—14
Los Angeles Raiders	0	6	3	7—16

SCORING
Los Angeles—Field goal Jaeger 25, 2:37 2nd.
Phoenix—Jones 35 pass from Hogeboom (Del Greco kick), 12:44 2nd.
Los Angeles—Field goal Jaeger 30, 14:39 2nd.
Los Angeles—Field goal Jaeger 48, 8:36 3rd.
Phoenix—Novacek 2 pass from Hogeboom (Del Greco kick), 9:50 4th.
Los Angeles—Allen 1 run (Jaeger kick), 14:20 4th.

TEAM STATISTICS

	Phoenix	Los Angeles
First downs	18	19
Rushes-Yards	30-122	34-154
Passing yards	126	230
Passes	12-24-0	13-30-0
Sacked-Yards lost	5-34	4-25
Punts	6-46.7	3-39.7
Fumbles-Lost	3-2	2-1
Penalties-Yards	6-33	8-61
Time of possession	31:04	28:56
Attendance—41,785.		

INDIVIDUAL STATISTICS

Rushing—Phoenix, Ferrell 15-57, Hogeboom 4-33, Sikahema 7-26, Baker 3-5, Wolfley 1-1; Los Angeles, Jackson 22-114, Smith 8-30, Allen 4-10.

Passing—Phoenix, Hogeboom 12-24-0—160; Los Angeles, Beuerlein 13-30-0—255.

Receiving—Phoenix, Jones 4-97, Ferrell 2-20, Novacek 2-13, Awalt 2-12, Holmes 1-9, Sikahema 1-9; Los Angeles, Fernandez 5-119, Dyal 5-71, Gault 2-56, Allen 1-9.

Kickoff Returns—Phoenix, Sikahema 2-42, Usher 2-39, Reeves 1-5; Los Angeles, Mueller 1-49, Adams 1-23.

Punt Returns—Phoenix, Sikahema 2-1; Los Angeles, Adams 4-41.

Interceptions—None.

Punting—Phoenix, Tupa 6-46.7; Los Angeles, Gossett 3-39.7.

Field Goals—Phoenix, none attempted; Los Angeles, Jaeger 3-6 (missed: 42, 49, 42).

Sacks—Phoenix, Hill, Saddler, Galloway, Nunn; Los Angeles, Davis, Long, Townsend, Golic ½, Wise ½, Robinson ½, Mraz ½.

Cowboys-Eagles
SUNDAY, DECEMBER 10
SCORE BY PERIODS

Dallas	0	3	7	0—10
Philadelphia	0	17	3	0—20

SCORING
Philadelphia—Carter 4 pass from Cunningham (Ruzek kick), 0:52 2nd.
Philadelphia—Carter 13 pass from Cavanaugh (Ruzek kick), 7:00 2nd.
Dallas—Field goal Zendejas 47, 12:28 2nd.
Philadelphia—Field goal Ruzek 29, 14:58 2nd.
Philadelphia—Field goal Ruzek 46, 3:11 3rd.
Dallas—Johnston 18 pass from Aikman (Zendejas kick), 8:58 3rd.

TEAM STATISTICS

	Dallas	Philadelphia
First downs	14	19
Rushes-Yards	23-87	35-122
Passing yards	107	158
Passes	17-30-0	18-32-0
Sacked-Yards lost	5-45	4-25
Punts	8-35.0	7-38.9
Fumbles-Lost	2-1	3-0
Penalties-Yards	12-107	9-70
Time of possession	30:21	29:39
Attendance—59,842.		

INDIVIDUAL STATISTICS

Rushing—Dallas, Aikman 6-60, Palmer 9-19, Sargent 3-5, Tautalatasi 1-3, Johnston 4-0; Philadelphia, Toney 17-49, Cunningham 6-47, Byars 11-35, Carson 1-minus 9.

Passing—Dallas, Aikman 17-30-0—152; Philadelphia, Cunningham 17-31-0—170, Cavanaugh 1-1-0—13.

Receiving—Dallas, Dixon 6-69, Johnston 3-23, Ford 2-35, Folsom 2-9, Tautalatasi 2-minus 3, Palmer 1-13, Burbage 1-6; Philadelphia, Byars 6-42, Carter 4-44, Jackson 3-57, Johnson 3-34, Toney 2-6.

Kickoff Returns—Dallas, Dixon 4-84; Philadelphia, Higgs 3-60.

Punt Returns—Dallas, Burbage 1-0; Philadelphia, Edwards 3-12.

Interceptions—None.

Punting—Dallas, Saxon 8-35.0; Philadelphia, Runager 5-35.2, Cunningham 2-48.0.

Field Goals—Dallas, Zendejas 1-2 (missed: 42); Philadelphia, Ruzek 2-3 (missed: 30).

Sacks—Dallas, Jeffcoat 2, Noonan, Tolbert; Philadelphia, White, Golic, Pitts, Hopkins, Simmons.

Chargers-Redskins
SUNDAY, DECEMBER 10
SCORE BY PERIODS

San Diego	14	0	0	7—21
Washington	0	7	9	10—26

SCORING
San Diego—A. Miller 25 pass from Tolliver (Bahr kick), 3:26 1st.
San Diego—Walker 5 pass from Tolliver (Bahr kick), 12:06 1st.

Washington—Sanders 45 pass from Rypien (Lohmiller kick), 14:45 2nd.
Washington—Field goal Lohmiller 38, 3:56 3rd.
Washington—Field goal Lohmiller 31, 8:31 3rd.
Washington—Field goal Lohmiller 32, 12:53 3rd.
San Diego—Butts 10 run (Bahr kick), 6:56 4th.
Washington—Clark 33 pass from Rypien (Lohmiller kick), 7:33 4th.
Washington—Field goal Lohmiller 28, 11:38 4th.

TEAM STATISTICS

	San Diego	Washington
First downs	21	20
Rushes-Yards	27-77	24-87
Passing yards	350	302
Passes	24-39-0	23-39-1
Sacked-Yards lost	0-0	0-0
Punts	6-35.6	4-36.5
Fumbles-Lost	1-1	0-0
Penalties-Yards	5-25	9-60
Time of possession	31:48	28:12

Attendance—47,693.

INDIVIDUAL STATISTICS

Rushing—San Diego, Butts 22-72, Tolliver 2-3, Nelson 3-2; Washington, Byner 16-60, Riggs 4-20, Rypien 4-7.

Passing—San Diego, Tolliver 24-39-0—350; Washington, Rypien 23-39-1—302.

Receiving—San Diego, A. Miller 8-152, Walker 7-105, Nelson 6-78, Cox 1-7, McEwen 1-5, Butts 1-3; Washington, Monk 9-81, Clark 7-92, Sanders 4-98, Byner 2-12, Warren 1-19.

Kickoff Returns—San Diego, Holland 4-70, Figaro 1-21, A. Miller 2-45; Washington, Howard 2-71, Sanders 1-27.

Punt Returns—San Diego, McConkey 2-13; Washington, Howard 2-49.

Interceptions—San Diego, Byrd 1-0.

Punting—San Diego, Ilesic 6-35.6; Washington, Mojsiejenko 4-36.5.

Field Goals—San Diego, none attempted; Washington, Lohmiller 4-4.

Sacks—None.

Patriots-Dolphins
SUNDAY, DECEMBER 10
SCORE BY PERIODS

New England	3	0	7	0—10
Miami	7	14	0	10—31

SCORING
Miami—Smith 1 run (Stoyanovich kick), 7:37 1st.
New England—Field goal Staurovsky 36, 11:34 1st.
Miami—Smith 7 run (Stoyanovich kick), 8:52 2nd.
Miami—Marino 1 run (Stoyanovich kick), 14:50 2nd.
New England—Stephens 1 run (Staurovsky kick), 7:52 3rd.
Miami—Smith 2 run (Stoyanovich kick), 0:59 4th.
Miami—Field goal Stoyanovich 23, 3:02 4th.

TEAM STATISTICS

	New England	Miami
First downs	17	24
Rushes-Yards	19-66	41-108
Passing yards	231	300
Passes	17-37-1	21-32-1
Sacked-Yards lost	5-30	0-0
Punts	5-37.2	4-38.7
Fumbles-Lost	2-1	1-0
Penalties-Yards	5-32	5-43
Time of possession	24:18	35:42

Attendance—62,127.

INDIVIDUAL STATISTICS
Rushing—New England, Perryman 8-37, Stephens 10-20, Wilson 1-9; Miami, Smith 21-62, Logan 16-45, Jensen 1-3, Marino 2-0, T. Brown 1-minus 2.

Passing—New England, Wilson 17-37-1—261; Miami, Marino 21-32-1—300.

Receiving—New England, Sievers 6-117, Stephens 4-26, Dykes 3-69, Fryar 3-38, Perryman 1-11; Miami, Banks 6-119, Clayton 6-102, Jensen 6-45, Logan 2-21, Edmunds 1-13.

Kickoff Returns—New England, Tucker 6-118; Miami, Logan 2-21.

Punt Returns—New England, Tucker 1-11; Miami, Schwedes 4-46.

Interceptions—New England, Hurst 1-0; Miami, McNeal 1-0.

Punting—New England, Feagles 5-37.2; Miami, Roby 4-38.7.

Field Goals—New England, Staurovsky 1-1; Miami, Stoyanovich 1-1.

Sacks—Miami, Thomas, Hobley, Green ½, Cross 1½, Bosa.

49ers-Rams
MONDAY, DECEMBER 11
SCORE BY PERIODS

San Francisco	0	10	0	20—30
Los Angeles Rams	17	0	7	3—27

SCORING
Los Angeles—Bell 3 run (Lansford kick), 3:43 1st.
Los Angeles—Johnson 4 pass from Everett (Lansford kick), 10:13 1st.
Los Angeles—Field goal Lansford 25, 12:04 1st.
San Francisco—Field goal Cofer 19, 0:49 2nd.
San Francisco—Taylor 92 pass from Montana (Cofer kick), 12:33 2nd.
Los Angeles—McGee 13 pass from Everett (Lansford kick), 4:32 3rd.
Los Angeles—Field goal Lansford 22, 1:26 4th.
San Francisco—Wilson 7 pass from Montana (Cofer kick), 4:56 4th.
San Francisco—Taylor 95 pass from Montana (kick failed), 8:33 4th.
San Francisco—Craig 1 run (Cofer kick), 11:18 4th.

TEAM STATISTICS

	San Francisco	Los Angeles
First downs	25	24
Rushes-Yards	25-63	31-106
Passing yards	439	231
Passes	30-42-2	18-31-0
Sacked-Yards lost	2-19	1-8
Punts	4-34.8	4-40.3
Fumbles-Lost	2-0	2-2
Penalties-Yards	10-145	6-41
Time of possession	28:49	31:11

Attendance—67,959.

INDIVIDUAL STATISTICS
Rushing—San Francisco, Craig 16-48, Montana 7-12, Rathman 2-3; Los Angeles, Bell 14-48, Delpino 8-23, McGee 5-24, Everett 2-9, Holohan 1-3, Anderson 1-minus 1.

Passing—San Francisco, Montana 30-42-2—458; Los Angeles, Everett 18-31-0—239.

Receiving—San Francisco, Taylor 11-286, Jones 7-85, Rice 5-38, Craig 4-31, Rathman 2-11, Wilson 1-7; Los Angeles, A. Cox 3-34, Holohan 3-31, McGee 3-25, Anderson 2-72, Ellard 2-38, Bell 2-11, Ron Brown 1-27, Johnson 1-4, Delpino 1-minus 3.

Kickoff Returns—San Francisco, Flagler 3-76, Henderson 1-8, Tillman 2-39; Los Angeles, Delpino 1-20, Ron Brown 4-75.

Punt Returns—San Francisco, Taylor 3-35; Los Angeles, Henley 1-17.

Interceptions—Los Angeles, Irvin 1-18, Stewart 1-35.

Punting—San Francisco, Helton 4-34.8; Los Angeles, Hatcher 4-40.3.

Field Goals—San Francisco, Cofer 1-2 (missed: 54); Los Angeles, Lansford 2-2.

Sacks—San Francisco, Holt; Los Angeles, Greene, Wright.

FIFTEENTH WEEK

RESULTS OF WEEK 15

Saturday, December 16

Denver 37, Phoenix 0 at Phoe.
N.Y. Giants 15, Dallas 0 at N.Y.

Sunday, December 17

Cincinnati 61, Houston 7 at Cin.
Cleveland 23, Minnnesota 17 (OT) at Cleve.
Detroit 33, Tampa Bay 7 at Det.
Green Bay 40, Chicago 28 at Chi.
Indianapolis 42, Miami 13 at Ind.
L.A. Rams 38, N.Y. Jets 14 at L.A.
Pittsburgh 28, New England 10 at Pitts.
San Diego 20, Kansas City 13 at K.C.
San Francisco 21, Buffalo 10 at S.F.
Seattle 23, L.A. Raiders 17 at Sea.
Washington 31, Atlanta 30 at Atl.

Monday, December 18

New Orleans 30, Philadelphia 20 at N.O.

The 1989 National Football League regular season was almost over, and if a booby prize had been awarded to the league's most disappointing team, it would have gone to the Chicago Bears.

The Bears entered the '89 season as winners of five consecutive NFC Central Division championships and were heavily favored to make it six straight. But a 40-28 loss to division rival Green Bay in Week 15 dropped their record to 6-9, assuring the franchise its first sub-.500 finish since 1982.

With their playoff hopes long gone and pride their only motivating factor, the Bears came up with a sorry performance against the Packers.

"Take all your hurts and put them together and you can't even imagine how much I hurt," Chicago Coach Mike Ditka said after his team's fifth straight loss. "It's no fun. It's embarrassing, it's humiliating."

Although there was plenty of blame to pass around, the Bears' main problem was their defense, which in recent seasons had been the team's backbone. Because of injuries, only tackle Steve McMichael and middle linebacker Mike Singletary started each of Chicago's first 15 games, with rookies accounting for 38 starts.

The biggest loss was veteran tackle Dan Hampton, who was sidelined for the season because of knee problems after just four games (the Bears were undefeated at the time). The defense was never able to overcome his absence.

"We went into the game with a lot of respect for the Bears' defense. I was shocked we were able to do as much as we did," said Green Bay Coach Lindy Infante, whose team swept the season series from Chicago for the first time in eight years.

The Packers wasted little time in laying the Bears' defense to waste, with Keith Woodside running 68 yards for a touchdown on the game's fourth play. Although the Bears tied the score at 7-7 with a touchdown three minutes later, Green Bay regained the lead on a 27-yard scoring pass from Don Majkowski to Perry Kemp on its next possession.

The Packers' offense rolled up 456 yards and never punted. Green Bay's only two non-scoring drives ended on an interception and with the halftime gun.

"Any time a team doesn't punt the ball once on you, you've got a problem," Ditka said.

That problem, however, was only one of many that the Chicago front office would have to deal with once the long season ended. There were a lot of theories as to why the Bears went bad in 1989, ranging from a lack of leadership on the field to Ditka's rantings off it.

"What does it matter?" center Jay Hilgenberg said. "We're not going to be in the playoffs, and there are no consolation prizes."

There also would be no consolation prize for the Los Angeles Raiders, who saw their slim playoff hopes become even slimmer in a 23-17 loss to the Seattle Seahawks. The Raiders, who were shooting for their fourth straight victory, would have clinched an AFC wild-card berth had they won.

Los Angeles scored two touchdowns in the first six minutes of the second half to take a 17-13 lead. But the Seahawks, who put together an 83-yard touchdown drive on their first possession, marched 76 yards in 14 plays to regain the lead on a 13-yard pass from Dave Krieg to John L. Williams.

Krieg completed 25 of 34 passes for 270 yards and two touchdowns with no interceptions.

Another team to have its playoff hopes damaged in Week 15 was the Kansas City Chiefs, who blew a 13-0 lead and fell to AFC Western Division rival San Diego, 20-13. The Chiefs, who had not lost in four weeks, suffered their fifth straight defeat at the hands of the Chargers.

The Chargers were led by rookies Billy Joe Tolliver and Marion Butts, who helped the San Diego offense compile 376 total yards against the AFC's No. 1-ranked defense. Tolliver, a second-round draft choice from Texas Tech, threw two touchdown passes while Butts, a seventh-round pick from Florida State, rushed for 176 yards on a team-record 39 attempts. The Chargers' 219 yards rushing were the most yielded by the Chiefs all season.

The Los Angeles Rams exploded for 21 unanswered points in the second quarter to defeat the New York Jets, 38-14, in an interconference game. Jim Everett threw for two touchdowns and Greg Bell ran for two others to fuel a Rams offense that rolled up 422 total yards.

Boomer Esiason threw four touchdown passes in Cincinnati's 61-7 rout of AFC Central Division rival Houston in Week 15.

The Rams' defense was outstanding, with linebacker Brett Faryniarz leading the way with three sacks, two fumble recoveries and six tackles. Overall, the L.A. defense had seven sacks, including four of Tony Eason, the former No. 1 draft pick of the New England Patriots who was making his first start after joining the Jets seven weeks earlier.

Phoenix rookie Timm Rosenbach made the first start of his NFL career one to forget as the Cardinals absorbed a 37-0 pounding from the Denver Broncos. The victory clinched home-field advantage for the Broncos throughout the AFC playoffs.

Rosenbach, who was selected in the June supplemental draft, completed just two of eight passes for 14 yards in six series before being lifted for veteran Gary Hogeboom. Rosenbach also was sacked once, had a pass batted down at the line of scrimmage and lost a fumble that Karl Mecklenburg returned 23 yards for the game's first touchdown.

The Cardinals, who lost for the fifth straight week, were down 17-0 at the time of the quarterback switch and finished the game with 101 yards in total offense, their lowest total in 34 years.

The Broncos, on the other hand, compiled 475 yards of offense. Bobby Humphrey rushed for 128 yards to become the first Denver player ever to run for 1,000 yards in his rookie season.

Another rookie running back, Detroit's Barry Sanders, rushed for 104 yards on 21 carries to lead the Lions to their fourth straight triumph, a 33-7 decision over Tampa Bay.

Detroit seized control early, moving 67 yards

in six plays after the opening kickoff and scoring on Bob Gagliano's two-yard pass to Richard Johnson. Gagliano later threw a 55-yard pass to rookie Jason Phillips for another touchdown before the first of Eddie Murray's four field goals increased the Lions' lead to 17-0.

The Buccaneers were forced to play most of the day without No. 1 quarterback Vinny Testaverde, who suffered an ankle sprain early in the second quarter. Tampa Bay didn't score until backup quarterback Joe Ferguson and Mark Carrier combined on a 69-yard touchdown strike on the last play of the game and finished with just six first downs and 62 yards rushing.

There was certainly no shortage of offense in Cincinnati, where the Bengals tied a team record for points scored in a 61-7 thrashing of the Houston Oilers. It was the Bengals' most lopsided victory ever and the Oilers' worst defeat.

Three plays after the Bengals recovered a fumble at the Oilers' 26 on Houston's first play from scrimmage, Boomer Esiason tossed a 22-yard scoring pass to Eddie Brown. The Bengals then increased their lead to 14-0 on a 14-yard touchdown run by James Brooks before the game was five minutes old.

The Oilers, who would have nailed down their first AFC Central Division title with a victory, committed five turnovers—all in the first half—as the Bengals built a 31-0 halftime bulge.

Esiason, who completed 20 of 27 passes for 326 yards, threw four touchdown passes in the game, including two to Brown, who caught six passes for 107 yards. Tim McGee had six receptions for 147 yards.

The Oilers' failure to clinch the AFC Central left the door ajar for the Cleveland Browns, who improved their record to 8-6-1 with a 23-17 overtime victory against the Minnesota Vikings. The Browns' win and the Oilers' loss meant that the division title would be decided when Cleveland and Houston met at the Astrodome the following week.

The Browns beat the Vikings on a trick play. The winning touchdown came on a 14-yard pass from Mike Pagel to Van Waiters after Cleveland's Matt Bahr—who kicked a game-tying, 32-yard field goal with 24 seconds left in regulation—lined up for an apparent field-goal attempt on third down. A wide-open Waiters caught Pagel's pass at the Minnesota 10 and raced in for the touchdown with 5:30 left in overtime.

Although they were officially eliminated from the playoffs when the Rams beat the Jets earlier in the day, the Washington Redskins rallied from a 17-point halftime deficit and edged the Atlanta Falcons, 31-30. The Redskins' fourth straight victory improved their record to 9-6, while the Falcons' sixth straight setback dropped their slate to 3-12.

Quarterback Mark Rypien sparked the Redskins' comeback by figuring in all three of Washington's third-quarter touchdowns. He threw a 60-yard touchdown pass to Art Monk to cut Atlanta's 27-10 halftime lead to 10 points before completing a 68-yard pass to Ricky Sanders to the Atlanta 1 to set up an Earnest Byner touchdown run. He then scrambled nine yards for another touchdown three minutes later to put the Redskins ahead, 31-27.

Sanders finished the game with seven receptions for 167 yards; Monk caught six passes for 131. Both players passed the 1,000-yard mark in receiving yardage for the season, giving the Redskins three players (Gary Clark was the other) who achieved that plateau in 1989. The only other team in NFL history with three 1,000-yard receivers was the 1980 San Diego Chargers, who featured John Jefferson (1,340), Kellen Winslow (1,290) and Charlie Joiner (1,132).

A player not known for his receiving ability —Indianapolis running back Eric Dickerson— caught a career-high nine passes for 63 yards and paced the Colts to a 42-13 romp over the Miami Dolphins. Dickerson also rushed 21 times for 107 yards to help the 8-7 Colts pull into a first-place tie with Miami and Buffalo in the AFC Eastern Division.

Jack Trudeau threw a career-high four touchdown passes for Indianapolis, the first a six-yard pass to rookie Andre Rison after Miami had jumped out to a 10-0 lead. After the Dolphins increased their lead to 13-7 on a Pete Stoyanovich field goal, the Colts scored 35 straight points to take control of the game.

Buffalo missed a chance to clinch the AFC East crown when the Bills were dealt a 21-10 loss at San Francisco. The defeat was the Bills' fourth in five weeks and fifth straight away from home.

The Bills were their own worst enemy, committing five second-half turnovers that wiped out a 3-0 halftime lead. Three of the turnovers came on consecutive possessions deep in Buffalo territory, with the 49ers converting each of them into touchdowns.

Steve Young replaced an injured Joe Montana at quarterback for the 49ers and threw for one touchdown and ran for another.

In contrast to Buffalo's late-season slide, the Pittsburgh Steelers were winners for the fourth time in five weeks, the latest success being a 28-10 triumph over the New England Patriots. The victory improved the Steelers' record to 8-7 and kept alive their hopes for the franchise's first playoff berth since 1984.

Merril Hoge scored twice for Pittsburgh, but the Steelers' most important touchdown probably was a 58-yard run by Louis Lipps late in the third quarter. That TD increased Pittsburgh's lead to 21-3 and came one play after linebacker Greg Lloyd recovered a fumble by New England's Bob Perryman.

The New York Giants clinched their first playoff berth since 1986 with a 15-0 victory over the NFL's worst team, the Dallas Cowboys. The Giants' defense held the Cowboys to just 108 total yards in registering its first shutout since a 17-0 victory over Washington in the '86 NFC championship game.

Bjorn Nittmo kicked three field goals for the Giants, who ran their record to 11-4. The Cowboys, whose record fell to 1-14, failed to score on four straight plays from the New York 1 early in the fourth quarter.

The Giants' victory gave them a one-game lead in the NFC Eastern Division over the Philadelphia Eagles, who lost a share of the top spot following a 30-20 loss at New Orleans on Monday night. The Eagles outgained the Saints in total yards, 408-291, but committed four turnovers that led to three New Orleans touchdowns.

John Fourcade threw three touchdown passes for the Saints, including two to wide receiver Eric Martin. Martin's 17-yard reception for the game's first touchdown came five plays after Brett Maxie recovered a Randall Cunningham fumble at the Eagles' 35.

Broncos-Cardinals
SATURDAY, DECEMBER 16
SCORE BY PERIODS

Denver	7	13	14	3—37
Phoenix	0	0	0	0— 0

SCORING
Denver—Mecklenburg 23 fumble return (Treadwell kick), 11:47 1st.

Denver—Field goal Treadwell 38, 1:43 2nd.

Denver—Sewell 14 pass from Elway (Treadwell kick), 9:16 2nd.

Denver—Field goal Treadwell 33, 14:17 2nd.

Denver—Bratton 17 pass from Humphrey (Treadwell kick), 6:14 3rd.
Denver—Kay 20 pass from Elway (Treadwell kick), 11:20 3rd.
Denver—Field goal Treadwell 35, 7:42 4th.

TEAM STATISTICS

	Denver	Phoenix
First downs	28	7
Rushes-Yards	47-204	12-22
Passing yards	271	79
Passes	25-34-2	15-31-1
Sacked-Yards lost	2-14	6-41
Punts	2-39.0	8-41.5
Fumbles-Lost	3-0	2-2
Penalties-Yards	7-54	3-30
Time of possession	40:31	19:29

Attendance—56,071.

INDIVIDUAL STATISTICS

Rushing—Denver, Humphrey 23-128, Winder 13-46, Bratton 4-17, Alexander 4-8, Kubiak 1-4, Elway 2-1; Phoenix, Ferrell 3-9, Rosenbach 2-8, Wolfley 2-4, Sikahema 3-1, Jordan 2-0.

Passing—Denver, Elway 20-29-2—247, Kubiak 4-4-0-21, Humphrey 1-1-0—17; Phoenix, Rosenbach 2-8-0—14, Hogeboom 12-22-1—106, Camarillo 1-1-0—0.

Receiving—Denver, Johnson 9-52, Kay 4-64, Jackson 3-35, Sewell 3-23, Young 2-40, Bratton 2-22, Nattiel 1-43, Humphrey 1-6; Phoenix, Awalt 4-21, Green 3-38, Sikahema 3-18, Novacek 2-26, Holmes 1-10, Jordan 1-7, Wolfley 1-0.

Kickoff Returns—Denver, Bell 1-13; Phoenix, Sikahema 5-89, Usher 2-31, Baker 1-12.

Punt Returns—Denver, Nattiel 2-11, V. Johnson 2-8; Phoenix, Sikahema 1-minus 1.

Interceptions—Denver, Braxton 1-0; Phoenix, Mack 2-6.

Punting—Denver, Horan 2-39.0; Phoenix, Camarillo 8-41.5.

Field Goals—Denver, Treadwell 3-3; Phoenix, none attempted.

Sacks—Denver, Fletcher 2, Holmes, Kragen, Lucas, Powers; Phoenix, Harvey, Nunn.

Cowboys-Giants
SATURDAY, DECEMBER 16
SCORE BY PERIODS

Dallas	0	0	0	0—	0
New York Giants	6	3	6	0—	15

SCORING

New York—Field goal Nittmo 33, 11:39 1st.
New York—Field goal Nittmo 22, 14:19 1st.
New York—Field goal Nittmo 26, 13:09 2nd.
New York—Anderson 1 run (kick blocked), 11:42 3rd.

TEAM STATISTICS

	Dallas	New York
First downs	7	14
Rushes-Yards	18-41	46-140
Passing yards	67	133
Passes	11-22-1	9-19-0
Sacked-Yards lost	2-17	2-6
Punts	6-29.0	5-38.0
Fumbles-Lost	0-0	0-0
Penalties-Yards	3-17	6-36
Time of possession	18:01	41-59

Attendance—72,141.

INDIVIDUAL STATISTICS

Rushing—Dallas, Johnston 4-15, Aikman 3-14, Palmer 9-12, Bates 1-0, Sargent 1-0; New York, Anderson 25-91, Tillman 9-40, Carthon 8-7, Simms 1-4, Ingram 1-1, Meggett 2-minus 3.

Passing—Dallas, Aikman 11-22-1—84; New York, Simms 9-19-0—139.

Receiving—Dallas, Tautalatasi 2-26, Burbage 2-22, Palmer 2-13, Jennings 2-10, Folsom 2-5, Ford 1-8; New York, Robinson 3-36, Anderson 2-20, Rouson 1-39, Baker 1-24, Ingram 1-11, Manuel 1-9.

Kickoff Returns—Dallas, Shepard 2-25, Dixon 2-32; New York, Ingram 1-9.

Punt Returns—Dallas, Burbage 1-5; New York, Meggett 3-22.

Interceptions—New York, Kinard 1-7.

Punting—Dallas, Saxon 5-34.8; New York, Landeta 5-38.0.

Field Goals—Dallas, none attempted; New York, Nittmo 3-3.

Sacks—Dallas, Hamel, Broughton ½, Norton ½; New York, Howard, Taylor.

Bills-49ers
SUNDAY, DECEMBER 17
SCORE BY PERIODS

Buffalo	3	0	0	7—	10
San Francisco	0	0	7	14—	21

SCORING

Buffalo—Field goal Norwood 23, 4:23 1st.
San Francisco—Craig 1 run (Cofer kick), 12:07 3rd.
San Francisco—Young 2 run (Cofer kick), 1:30 4th.
San Francisco—Rice 8 pass from Young (Cofer kick), 2:47 4th.
Buffalo—Kelly 1 run (Norwood kick), 7:11 4th.

TEAM STATISTICS

	Buffalo	San Francisco
First downs	16	18
Rushes-Yards	18-46	43-149
Passing yards	255	134
Passes	26-42-3	9-19-2
Sacked-Yards lost	2-10	3-32
Punts	5-34.6	5-37.0
Fumbles-Lost	2-2	0-0
Penalties-Yards	4-28	3-25
Time of possession	24:21	35:39

Attendance—60,927.

INDIVIDUAL STATISTICS

Rushing—Buffalo, Kinnebrew 8-29, Kelly 4-10, Thomas 6-7; San Francisco, Craig 25-105, Flagler 8-23, Rathman 2-13, Henderson 3-10, Young 5-minus 2.

Passing—Buffalo, Kelly 26-42-3—265; San Francisco, Young 9-19-2—166.

Receiving—Buffalo, Reed 10-115, Thomas 8-62, Harmon 4-33, Beebe 3-40, Lofton 1-15; San Francisco, Rice 3-46, Rathman 2-38, Taylor 2-30, Henderson 1-40, Craig 1-12.

Kickoff Returns—Buffalo, Harmon 2-48, Beebe 1-32; San Francisco, Flagler 1-17, Tillman 1-17, Henderson 1-13.

Punt Returns—Buffalo, Sutton 3-26; San Francisco, Taylor 3-30.

Interceptions—Buffalo, Kelso 2-0; San Francisco, Lott 1-28, Romanowski 1-13, Brooks 1-0.

Punting—Buffalo, Kidd 5-34.6; San Francisco, Helton 5-37.0.

Field Goals—Buffalo, Norwood 1-1; San Francisco, Cofer 0-1 (missed: 44).

Sacks—Buffalo, Radecic 1½, Talley, B. Smith ½; San Francisco, Fagan 2.

Patriots-Steelers
SUNDAY, DECEMBER 17
SCORE BY PERIODS

New England	3	0	0	7—	10
Pittsburgh	7	7	7	7—	28

SCORING

Pittsburgh—Worley 8 run (Anderson kick), 5:15 1st.
New England—Field goal Staurovsky 20, 13:01 1st.
Pittsburgh—Hoge 1 run (Anderson kick), 2:41 2nd.
Pittsburgh—Lipps 58 run (Anderson kick), 10:24 3rd.
Pittsburgh—Hoge 2 run (Anderson kick), 9:34 4th.

New England—Jones 12 pass from Wilson (Staurovsky kick), 13:44 4th.

TEAM STATISTICS

	New England	Pittsburgh
First downs	26	18
Rushes-Yards	35-121	39-219
Passing yards	282	128
Passes	27-56-2	9-17-0
Sacked-Yards lost	3-15	2-30
Punts	5-40.6	5-34.4
Fumbles-Lost	2-1	2-2
Penalties-Yards	4-25	6-40
Time of possession	38:28	24:22

Attendance—26,594.

INDIVIDUAL STATISTICS

Rushing—New England, Perryman 16-58, Stephens 14-35, Wilson 3-24, Fryar 1-4, Wonsley 1-0; Pittsburgh, Worley 19-104, Hoge 15-63, Lipps 1-58, Tyrrell 1-3, Strom 1-minus 1, Brister 2-minus 8.

Passing—New England, Wilson 27-56-2—297; Pittsburgh, Brister 9-17-0—158.

Receiving—New England, Dykes 10-130, Fryar 5-62, Sievers 5-41, Dawson 4-42, Jones 2-18, Cook 1-4; Pittsburgh, Mularkey 2-40, Lipps 2-33, Hoge 2-19, Hill 1-33, Stock 1-27, Carter 1-minus 4.

Kickoff Returns—New England, Egu 2-26, Tucker 1-24, Wonsley 1-18; Pittsburgh, Woodson 2-49.

Punt Returns—New England, Fryar 1-14; Pittsburgh, Woodson 5-46.

Interceptions—Pittsburgh, Woodruff 1-35, D. Johnson 1-0.

Punting—New England, Feagles 5-40.6; Pittsburgh, Newsome 5-34.4.

Field Goals—New England, Staurovsky 1-2 (missed: 37); Pittsburgh, none attempted.

Sacks—New England, Goad; Pittsburgh, Jones, T. Johnson, Little.

Vikings-Browns
SUNDAY, DECEMBER 17
SCORE BY PERIODS

Minnesota	0	3	7	7	0—17
Cleveland	0	0	14	3	6—23

SCORING

Minnesota—Field goal Karlis 44, 14:33 2nd.
Cleveland—Middleton 5 pass from Kosar (Bahr kick), 5:57 3rd.
Minnesota—Walker 26 run (Karlis kick), 14:00 3rd.
Cleveland—Langhorne 62 pass from Kosar (Bahr kick), 14:25 3rd.
Minnesota—Jordan 2 pass from Kramer (Karlis kick), 11:23 4th.
Cleveland—Field goal Bahr 32, 14:36 4th.
Cleveland—Waiters 14 pass from Pagel (no kick), 9:30 OT.

TEAM STATISTICS

	Minnesota	Cleveland
First downs	19	16
Rushes-Yards	30-122	29-64
Passing yards	194	256
Passes	17-48-1	18-39-0
Sacked-Yards lost	2-27	3-12
Punts	11-34.4	10-35.3
Fumbles-Lost	3-0	2-2
Penalties-Yards	8-81	7-40
Time of possession	35:53	33:37

Attendance—70,777.

INDIVIDUAL STATISTICS

Rushing—Minnesota, Walker 16-57, Fenney 11-40, Carter 1-17, Anderson 1-5, Wilson 1-3; Cleveland, Mack 18-55, Kosar 3-6, Metcalf 2-4, Manoa 1-1, Redden 3-1, Langhorne 2-minus 3.

Passing—Minnesota, Wilson 11-32-0—141, Kramer 6-16-1—80; Cleveland, Kosar 17-38-0—254, Pagel 1-1-0—14.

Receiving—Minnesota, Jordan 6-87, Carter 4-77, Jones 2-24, Clark 1-12, Lewis 1-9, Anderson 1-7, Fenney 1-3, Novoselsky 1-2; Cleveland, Langhorne 6-140, Brennan 4-35, Metcalf 2-16, Tillman 1-19, Newsome 1-18, Slaughter 1-17, Waiters 1-14, Middleton 1-5, Mack 1-4.

Kickoff Returns—Minnesota, Anderson 2-39, Walker 1-16, Clarke 1-6; Cleveland, Metcalf 2-64, Redden 2-2, Oliphant 1-19.

Punt Returns—Minnesota, Lewis 3-19; Cleveland, McNeil 3-16.

Interceptions—Cleveland, Kramer 1-12.

Punting—Minnesota, Scribner 11-34.4; Cleveland, Wagner 10-35.3.

Field Goals—Minnesota, Karlis 1-2 (missed: 40); Cleveland, Bahr 1-1.

Sacks—Minnesota, Millard 2, Noga; Cleveland, Matthews, Baker ½, Perry ½.

Packers-Bears
SUNDAY, DECEMBER 17
SCORE BY PERIODS

Green Bay	14	10	6	10—40
Chicago	7	7	14	0—28

SCORING

Green Bay—Woodside 68 run (Jacke kick), 2:41 1st.
Chicago—Muster 3 pass from Harbaugh (Butler kick), 5:39 1st.
Green Bay—Kemp 27 pass from Majkowski (Jacke kick), 11:43 1st.
Chicago—Anderson 21 pass from Harbaugh (Butler kick), 0:56 2nd.
Green Bay—Field goal Jacke 19, 7:45 2nd.
Green Bay—Majkowski 17 run (Jacke kick), 13:07 2nd.
Green Bay—Field goal Jacke 44, 1:04 3rd.
Chicago—Anderson 49 pass from Harbaugh (Butler kick), 4:04 3rd.
Green Bay—Field goal Jacke 23, 10:41 3rd.
Chicago—Muster 4 run (Butler kick), 14:28 3rd.
Green Bay—Majkowski 1 run (Jacke kick), 9:39 4th.
Green Bay—Field goal Jacke 21, 13:32 4th.

TEAM STATISTICS

	Green Bay	Chicago
First downs	24	19
Rushes-Yards	36-217	23-158
Passing yards	239	197
Passes	21-36-1	20-28-3
Sacked-Yards lost	1-5	2-8
Punts	0-00.0	1-44.0
Fumbles-Lost	2-0	3-2
Penalties-Yards	8-75	4-73
Time of possession	37:12	22:48

Attendance—44,781.

INDIVIDUAL STATISTICS

Rushing—Green Bay, Woodside 10-116, Majkowski 6-59, Fullwood 13-30, Fontenot 2-9, Haddix 5-3; Chicago, Anderson 12-119, Muster 8-35, Harbaugh 2-6, Sanders 1-minus 2.

Passing—Green Bay, Majkowski 21-36-1—244; Chicago, Harbaugh 20-28-3—205.

Receiving—Green Bay, Sharpe 7-94, Woodside 5-43, Haddix 3-27, Kemp 2-45, Matthews 2-33, Fontenot 1-3, Spagnola 1-minus 1; Chicago, Anderson 6-90, Gentry 4-37, Davis 3-26, Muster 2-11, Boso 1-11, Thornton 1-10, McKinnon 1-8, Kozlowski 1-6, Green 1-6.

Kickoff Returns—Green Bay, Bland 2-44, Fullwood 1-18, Workman 1-8, Mandarich 1-0; Chicago, Sanders 5-109, Suhey 1-20, Pruitt 1-6.

Punt Returns—Green Bay, Query 1-9.

Interceptions—Green Bay, Dent 1-53, Lee 1-10, Stephen 1-8; Chicago, Dent 1-30.

Punting—Green Bay, none attempted; Chicago, Buford 1-44.0.

Field Goals—Green Bay, Jacke 4-4; Chicago, none attempted.

Sacks—Green Bay, Harris 2; Chicago, Roper.

Jets-Rams

SUNDAY, DECEMBER 17

SCORE BY PERIODS

New York Jets	7	0	0	7—14	
Los Angeles Rams	7	21	0	10—38	

SCORING

Los Angeles—Holohan 25 pass from Everett (Lansford kick), 9:33 1st.

New York—Townsell 63 pass from Eason (Leahy kick), 12:04 1st.

Los Angeles—Bell 1 run (Lansford kick), 6:52 2nd.

Los Angeles—Anderson 43 pass from Everett (Lansford kick), 10:21 2nd.

Los Angeles—Bell 5 run (Lansford kick), 14:22 2nd.

Los Angeles—Field goal Lansford 37, 0:51 4th.

Los Angeles—Gary 5 run (Lansford kick), 11:57 4th.

New York—Neubert 35 pass from O'Brien (Leahy kick), 13:01 4th.

TEAM STATISTICS

	New York	Los Angeles
First downs	14	21
Rushes-Yards	20-92	35-150
Passing yards	199	272
Passes	20-32-1	17-27-0
Sacked-Yards lost	7-43	2-13
Punts	5-41.8	5-34.4
Fumbles-Lost	5-3	2-1
Penalties-Yards	8-59	5-40
Time of possession	28:11	31:49
Attendance—53,063.		

INDIVIDUAL STATISTICS

Rushing—New York, Vick 12-47, Hector 8-45; Los Angeles, Bell 15-52, Gary 8-49, Delpino 5-24, McGee 2-17, Green 4-7, Everett 1-1.

Passing—New York, Eason 10-14-1—130, O'Brien 10-18-0—112; Los Angeles, Everett 16-26-0—273, Herrmann 1-1-0—12.

Receiving—New York, Toon 6-53, Neubert 4-63, Vick 4-26, Hector 4-20, Townsell 1-63, Burkett 1-17; Los Angeles, Holohan 4-70, Ellard 3-57, Delpino 3-47, McGee 3-39, Johnson 2-15, Anderson 1-43, Brown 1-14.

Kickoff Returns—New York, Humphery 4-56, Epps 1-43, Nichols 2-9; Los Angeles, Delpino 2-40, Gary 1-4.

Punt Returns—New York, Townsell 1-2; Los Angeles, Henley 1-8.

Interceptions—Los Angeles, Gray 1-0.

Punting—New York, Prokop 5-41.8; Los Angeles, Hatcher 5-34.4.

Field Goals—New York, none attempted; Los Angeles, Lansford 1-1.

Sacks—New York, Lageman, Byrd; Los Angeles, Faryniarz 3, B. Smith 2, Bethune, Wright.

Dolphins-Colts

SUNDAY, DECEMBER 17

SCORE BY PERIODS

Miami	10	3	0	0—13	
Indianapolis	7	7	14	14—42	

SCORING

Miami—Field goal Stoyanovich 43, 6:05 1st.

Miami—Schwedes 70 punt return (Stoyanovich kick), 8:02 1st.

Indianapolis—Rison 6 pass from Trudeau (Biasucci kick), 11:57 1st.

Miami—Field goal Stoyanovich 47, 7:09 2nd.

Indianapolis—Boyer 1 pass from Trudeau (Biasucci kick), 13:54 2nd.

Indianapolis—Dickerson 1 run (Biasucci kick), 2:28 3rd.

Indianapolis—Pruitt 5 pass from Trudeau (Biasucci kick), 15:00 3rd.

Indianapolis—Bentley 6 pass from Trudeau (Biasucci kick), 5:32 4th.

Indianapolis—Dickerson 2 run (Biasucci kick), 8:12 4th.

TEAM STATISTICS

	Miami	Indianapolis
First downs	16	25
Rushes-Yards	17-41	29-121
Passing yards	201	184
Passes	23-50-2	23-35-1
Sacked-Yards lost	2-18	2-11
Punts	4-38.0	3-40.7
Fumbles-Lost	1-1	1-0
Penalties-Yards	10-70	3-15
Time of possession	27:23	32:37
Attendance—55,665.		

INDIVIDUAL STATISTICS

Rushing—Miami, Smith 12-35, Logan 3-5, Secules 1-2, Clayton 1-minus 1; Indianapolis, Dickerson 21-107, Hunter 4-11, Trudeau 2-6, Bentley 1-0, Brooks 1-minus 3.

Passing—Miami, Marino 15-33-1—150, Secules 8-17-1—69; Indianapolis, Trudeau 23-35-1—195.

Receiving—Miami, Jensen 7-62, Schwedes 3-46, A. Brown 3-31, Banks 2-26, Smith 2-17, T. Brown 2-12, Edmunds 1-10, Clayton 1-6, Logan 1-6, Hampton 1-3; Indianapolis, Dickerson 9-63, Brooks 4-60, Bentley 4-38, Pruitt 3-23, Rison 1-6, Beach 1-4, Boyer 1-1.

Kickoff Returns—Miami, Logan 4-82, Hampton 2-40; Indianapolis, Bentley 4-102.

Punt Returns—Miami, Schwedes 1-70; Indianapolis, Verdin 1-11.

Interceptions—Miami, Oliver 1-9; Indianapolis, Young 1-6, Prior 1-0.

Punting—Miami, Roby 3-50.7; Indianapolis, Stark 3-40.7.

Field Goals—Miami, Stoyanovich 2-3 (missed: 44); Indianapolis, none attempted.

Sacks—Miami, Junior, Offerdahl; Indianapolis, Bickett, Hand.

Buccaneers-Lions

SUNDAY, DECEMBER 17

SCORE BY PERIODS

Tampa Bay	0	0	0	7— 7	
Detroit	14	10	3	6—33	

SCORING

Detroit—Johnson 2 pass from Gagliano (Murray kick), 3:37 1st.

Detroit—Phillips 55 pass from Gagliano (Murray kick), 10:03 1st.

Detroit—Field goal Murray 33, 1:42 2nd.

Detroit—B. Sanders 4 run (Murray kick), 12:06 2nd.

Detroit—Field goal Murray 43, 5:51 3rd.

Detroit—Field goal Murray 35, 12:02 4th.

Detroit—Field goal Murray 36, 14:40 4th.

Tampa Bay—Carrier 69 pass from Ferguson (Igwebuike kick), 15:00 4th.

TEAM STATISTICS

	Tampa Bay	Detroit
First downs	6	24
Rushes-Yards	15-62	35-170
Passing yards	163	212
Passes	11-26-4	21-38-1
Sacked-Yards lost	4-16	3-22
Punts	8-44	5-51
Fumbles-Lost	3-1	2-1
Penalties-Yards	10-80	4-25
Time of possession	21:46	38:14
Attendance—40,362.		

INDIVIDUAL STATISTICS

Rushing—Tampa Bay, Tate 7-18, Stamps 2-16, Testaverde 2-16, Wilder 1-11, Howard 2-2, Ferguson 1-minus 1; Detroit, B. Sanders 21-104, Gagliano 5-37, Painter 2-15, Paige 4-12, Long 3-2.

Passing—Tampa Bay, Ferguson 7-18-3—161, Testaverde 4-8-1—18; Detroit, Gagliano 19-33-1—192, Long 2-5-0—42.

Receiving—Tampa Bay, Carrier 4-131, Wilder 4-17,

Howard 1-18, Tate 1-7, Hall 1-6; Detroit, Phillips 10-115, Johnson 4-26, Clark 3-33, Ford 2-37, Stanley 1-15, B. Sanders 1-8.

Kickoff Returns—Tampa Bay, Elder 3-31, Stamps 3-30, Wilder 1-19; Detroit, Gray 1-37.

Punt Returns—Tampa Bay, Drewrey 3-45; Detroit, Stanley 5-66, Gray 2-11.

Interceptions—Tampa Bay, Elder 1-0; Detroit, Crockett 1-5, Holmes 1-2, Taylor 1-0, J. Williams 1-0.

Punting—Tampa Bay, Mohr 8-44.3; Detroit, Arnold 5-51.0.

Field Goals—Tampa Bay, none attempted; Detroit, Murray 4-4.

Sacks—Tampa Bay, Moss 1½, Robinson 1½; Detroit, Cofer, J. Williams, Pete, Brooks.

Chargers-Chiefs
SUNDAY, DECEMBER 17
SCORE BY PERIODS

San Diego	0	7	3	10—20	
Kansas City	0	13	0	0—13	

SCORING
Kansas City—Field goal Lowery 36, 4:40 2nd.
Kansas City—Field goal Lowery 30, 9:20 2nd.
Kansas City—McNair 11 pass from DeBerg (Lowery kick), 13:15 2nd.
San Diego—Parker 1 pass from Tolliver (Bahr kick), 14:43 2nd.
San Diego—Field goal Bahr 43, 8:34 3rd.
San Diego—A. Miller 5 pass from Tolliver (Bahr kick), 0:04 4th.
San Diego—Field goal Bahr 20, 6:19 4th.

TEAM STATISTICS

	San Diego	Kansas City
First downs	23	11
Rushes-Yards	43-219	23-90
Passing yards	157	124
Passes	13-30-1	14-33-2
Sacked-Yards lost	3-14	2-18
Punts	5-31.6	8-33.9
Fumbles-Lost	3-3	2-1
Penalties-Yards	6-55	5-30
Time of possession	34:45	25:15
Attendance—40,623.		

INDIVIDUAL STATISTICS
Rushing—San Diego, Butts 39-176, Nelson 2-35, Walker 1-9, Tolliver 1-minus 1; Kansas City, Okoye 18-60, McNair 3-30, Saxon 1-1, DeBerg 1-minus 1.

Passing—San Diego, Tolliver 13-30-1—171; Kansas City, DeBerg 14-33-2—142.

Receiving—San Diego, A. Miller 5-93, Cox 3-32, Nelson 3-29, McEwen 1-16, Parker 1-1; Kansas City, Weathers 5-40, Paige 4-42, McNair 3-31, Mandley 1-20, Hayes 1-9.

Kickoff Returns—San Diego, Holland 2-27, A. Miller 2-42; Kansas City, McNair 5-112.

Punt Returns—Kansas City, Worthen 2-10, Ross 1-0.

Interceptions—San Diego, Figaro 1-2, Bennett 1-0; Kansas City, Ross 1-6.

Punting—San Diego, Ilesic 5-31.6; Kansas City, Goodburn 8-33.9.

Field Goals—San Diego, Bahr 2-3 (missed: 42); Kansas City, Lowery 2-2.

Sacks—San Diego, Grossman, Lyles; Kansas City, Griffin, Martin, Smith.

Oilers-Bengals
SUNDAY, DECEMBER 17
SCORE BY PERIODS

Houston	0	0	0	7— 7	
Cincinnati	21	10	21	9—61	

SCORING
Cincinnati—Brown 22 pass from Esiason (Breech kick), 1:01 1st.

Cincinnati—Brooks 14 run (Breech kick), 4:48 1st.
Cincinnati—Brown 35 pass from Esiason (Breech kick), 10:15 1st.
Cincinnati—Holman 5 pass from Esiason (Breech kick), 3:51 2nd.
Cincinnati—Field goal Breech 27, 14:50 2nd.
Cincinnati—Taylor 5 run (Breech kick), 5:26 3rd.
Cincinnati—McGee 74 pass from Esiason (Breech kick), 7:12 3rd.
Cincinnati—Ball 5 run (Breech kick), 10:39 3rd.
Houston—White 1 run (Zendejas kick), 2:36 4th.
Cincinnati—Hillary 10 pass from Wilhelm (kick failed), 7:48 4th.
Cincinnati—Field goal Breech 30, 14:39 4th.

TEAM STATISTICS

	Houston	Cincinnati
First downs	14	35
Rushes-Yards	14-39	43-192
Passing yards	147	392
Passes	16-34-3	27-35-0
Sacked-Yards lost	4-26	3-10
Punts	4-42.2	1-45.0
Fumbles-Lost	2-2	2-2
Penalties-Yards	9-60	3-30
Time of possession	19:19	40:41
Attendance—47,510.		

INDIVIDUAL STATISTICS
Rushing—Houston, T. Johnson 3-17, Highsmith 4-9, White 4-9, Rozier 2-4, Pennison 1-0; Cincinnati, Ball 13-86, Jennings 6-30, Brooks 5-29, Holifield 11-20, Taylor 5-18, Esiason 3-9.

Passing—Houston, Moon 9-20-2—96, Carlson 7-14-1—85; Cincinnati, Esiason 20-27-0—326, Wilhelm 7-8-0—76.

Receiving—Houston, Hill 6-77, Jeffires 5-50, Duncan 2-15, Givins 1-23, Highsmith 1-7, Harris 1-1; Cincinnati, McGee 6-147, Brown 6-107, Holman 5-44, Garrett 2-29, Holifield 2-18, Hillary 2-17, Brooks 1-12, Taylor 1-12, Jennings 1-11, Riggs 1-5.

Kickoff Returns—Houston, White 1-16, Williams 1-8, Glenn Montgomery 1-0, Fairs 1-1, T. Johnson 2-44, K. Johnson 3-49, Mrosko 1-10; Cincinnati, Carey 1-23, Taylor 1-5.

Punt Returns—Houston, K. Johnson 1-10; Cincinnati, Carey 3-29.

Interceptions—Cincinnati, Fulcher 3-22.

Punting—Houston, Greg Montgomery 4-42.2; Cincinnati, Johnson 1-45.0.

Field Goals—Houston, Zendejas 0-1 (missed: 32); Cincinnati, Breech 2-2.

Sacks—Houston, Brown, Fuller, Jones; Cincinnati, Buck 2, Krumrie, Bussey ½, Tuatagaloa ½.

Redskins-Falcons
SUNDAY, DECEMBER 17
SCORE BY PERIODS

Washington	3	7	21	0—31	
Atlanta	3	24	3	0—30	

SCORING
Atlanta—Field goal Davis 33, 1:11 1st.
Washington—Field goal Lohmiller 37, 10:02 1st.
Washington—Monk 34 pass from Williams (Lohmiller kick), 0:57 2nd.
Atlanta—Haynes 72 pass from Miller (Davis kick), 1:15 2nd.
Atlanta—Haynes 17 pass from Miller (Davis kick), 4:57 2nd.
Atlanta—Field goal Davis 24, 7:45 2nd.
Atlanta—Settle 3 run (Davis kick), 9:42 2nd.
Washington—Monk 60 pass from Rypien (Lohmiller kick), 2:17 3rd.
Washington—Byner 1 run (Lohmiller kick), 2:55 3rd.
Washington—Rypien 9 run (Lohmiller kick), 5:55 3rd.

Atlanta—Field goal Davis 32, 12:22 3rd.

TEAM STATISTICS

	Washington	Atlanta
First downs	24	17
Rushes-Yards	37-131	9-28
Passing yards	376	346
Passes	24-39-1	21-44-2
Sacked-Yards lost	2-14	3-25
Punts	3-39.3	5-43.6
Fumbles-Lost	3-2	0-0
Penalties-Yards	6-53	8-81
Time of possession	37:52	22:08
Attendance—37,501.		

INDIVIDUAL STATISTICS

Rushing—Washington, Riggs 20-84, Byner 12-25, Sanders 1-13, Rypien 4-9; Atlanta, Settle 5-19, Jones 4-9.

Passing—Washington, Rypien 17-27-1—284, Williams 7-12-0—106; Atlanta, Miller 17-35-2—310, Millen 4-9-0—61.

Receiving—Washington, Sanders 7-167, Monk 6-131, Clark 4-59, Byner 4-5, Warren 2-18, Orr 1-10; Atlanta, Haynes 6-190, Collins 5-64, Jones 2-22, Settle 2-16, Heller 2-15, Wilkins 1-35, Lang 1-8, Dixon 1-8, Paterra 1-2.

Kickoff Returns—Washington, A. Johnson 4-61, Howard 2-36, Orr 1-0; Atlanta, Sanders 5-109, Jones 1-20.

Punt Returns—Washington, Sanders 1-5, Mayhew 1-0; Atlanta, Sanders 3-48.

Interceptions—Washington, Grant 1-0, A. Johnson 1-0; Atlanta, Gordon 1-34.

Punting—Washington, Mojsiejenko 3-39.3; Atlanta, Fulhage 5-43.6.

Field Goals—Washington, Lohmiller 1-4 (missed: 47, 43, 43); Atlanta, Davis 3-4 (missed: 40).

Sacks—Washington, Mann, Marshall, Caldwell ½, Coleman ½; Atlanta, Gann 2.

Raiders-Seahawks
SUNDAY, DECEMBER 17
SCORE BY PERIODS

Los Angeles Raiders	3	0	14	0—17
Seattle	7	6	7	3—23

SCORING

Seattle—Skansi 5 pass from Krieg (N. Johnson kick), 5:37 1st.

Los Angeles—Field goal Jaeger 19, 13:34 1st.

Seattle—Field goal N. Johnson 29, 4:22 2nd.

Seattle—Field goal N. Johnson 25, 13:03 2nd.

Los Angeles—Gault 36 pass from Beuerlein (Jaeger kick), 1:53 3rd.

Los Angeles—Junkin 1 pass from Beuerlein (Jaeger kick), 5:34 3rd.

Seattle—Williams 13 pass from Krieg (N. Johnson kick), 13:49 3rd.

Seattle—Field goal N. Johnson 43, 8:16 4th.

TEAM STATISTICS

	Los Angeles	Seattle
First downs	15	22
Rushes-Yards	19-98	33-82
Passing yards	175	268
Passes	13-23-1	25-34-0
Sacked-Yards lost	2-13	1-2
Punts	3-41.3	2-34.0
Fumbles-Lost	1-0	1-0
Penalties-Yards	9-49	4-61
Time of possession	21:55	38:05
Attendance—61,076.		

INDIVIDUAL STATISTICS

Rushing—Los Angeles, Jackson 12-69, Smith 5-14, Allen 1-8, Beuerlein 1-7; Seattle, Williams 14-38, Warner 13-23, Krieg 6-21.

Passing—Los Angeles, Beuerlein 13-23-1—188; Seattle, Krieg 25-34-0—270.

Receiving—Los Angeles, Fernandez 6-73, Gault 2-54, Dyal 2-43, Alexander 1-14, Smith 1-3, Junkin 1-1; Seattle, Williams 12-129, Skansi 4-44, McNeal 3-28, Chadwick 2-28, Warner 2-17, Largent 1-13, Clark 1-11.

Kickoff Returns—Los Angeles, Adams 5-101; Seattle, Hollis 4-60.

Punt Returns—Los Angeles, Adams 1-11; Seattle, Hollis 2-7.

Interceptions—Seattle, Harper 1-0.

Punting—Los Angeles, Gossett 3-41.3; Seattle, Rodriguez 2-34.0.

Field Goals—Los Angeles, Jaeger 1-1; Seattle, N. Johnson 3-3.

Sacks—Los Angeles, McDaniel; Seattle, Bryant, Woods.

Eagles-Saints
MONDAY, DECEMBER 18
SCORE BY PERIODS

Philadelphia	0	10	10	0—20
New Orleans	7	9	0	14—30

SCORING

New Orleans—Martin 17 pass from Fourcade (Andersen kick), 11:38 1st.

New Orleans—Hilliard 35 pass from Fourcade (Andersen kick), 0:10 2nd.

Philadelphia—Johnson 13 pass from Cunningham (Ruzek kick), 2:46 2nd.

Philadelphia—Field goal Ruzek 21, 6:40 2nd.

New Orleans—Safety, Warren tackled Cunningham in end zone, 14:32 2nd.

Philadelphia—Little 1 pass from Cunningham (Ruzek kick), 5:51 3rd.

Philadelphia—Field goal Ruzek 19, 14:44 3rd.

New Orleans—Martin 20 pass from Fourcade (Andersen kick), 2:39 4th.

New Orleans—Jordan 1 run (Andersen kick), 8:48 4th.

TEAM STATISTICS

	Philadelphia	New Orleans
First downs	23	21
Rushes-Yards	27-127	31-86
Passing yards	281	205
Passes	20-40-2	18-35-1
Sacked-Yards lost	4-36	5-31
Punts	3-35.7	8-46.6
Fumbles-Lost	4-2	3-0
Penalties-Yards	7-62	6-50
Time of possession	28:07	31:53
Attendance—68,561.		

INDIVIDUAL STATISTICS

Rushing—Philadelphia, Cunningham 8-92, Byars 10-28, Toney 9-7; New Orleans, Hilliard 24-45, Fourcade 4-37, Jordan 3-4.

Passing—Philadelphia, Cunningham 19-39-2—306, Cavanaugh 1-1-0—11; New Orleans, Fourcade 18-35-1—236.

Receiving—Philadelphia, Byars 6-109, Jackson 5-45, Johnson 4-63, Edwards 2-74, Giles 1-17, Carter 1-8, Little 1-1; New Orleans, Martin 9-120, Hilliard 3-52, Brenner 3-21, Perriman 1-26, Tice 1-15, Frazier 1-2.

Kickoff Returns—Philadelphia, Higgs 1-6; New Orleans, Morse 3-65, Frazier 2-33, Harris 1-18.

Punt Returns—Philadelphia, Edwards 4-52; New Orleans, Morse 1-1.

Interceptions—Philadelphia, Everett 1-17; New Orleans, Atkins 1-minus 2, Waymer 1-0.

Punting—Philadelphia, Tuten 3-35.7; New Orleans, Barnhart 8-46.6.

Field Goals—Philadelphia, Ruzek 2-3 (missed: 20); New Orleans, Anderson 0-1 (missed: 55).

Sacks—Philadelphia, Brown 2, Simmons, Frizzell, Harris ½, Joyner ½; New Orleans, Warren 3, Swilling.

SIXTEENTH WEEK

RESULTS OF WEEK 16

Saturday, December 23

Buffalo 37, N.Y. Jets 0 at N.Y.
Cleveland 24, Houston 20 at Hous.
Washington 29, Seattle 0 at Sea.

Sunday, December 24

Detroit 31, Atlanta 24 at Atl.
Green Bay 20, Dallas 10 at Dall.
Kansas City 27, Miami 24 at Mia.
L.A. Rams 24, New England 20 at N.E.
New Orleans 41, Indianapolis 6 at N.O.
N.Y. Giants 34, L.A. Raiders 17 at N.Y.
Philadelphia 31, Phoenix 14 at Phila.
Pittsburgh 31, Tampa Bay 22 at T.B.
San Diego 19, Denver 16 at S.D.
San Francisco 26, Chicago 0 at S.F.

Monday, December 25

Minnesota 29, Cincinnati 21 at Minn.

When the National Football League's powers-that-be sit down in the spring to put together a schedule for the upcoming season, they attempt to arrange late-season matchups that might have a bearing on the division races.

In 1989, they hit a bull's-eye by scheduling Cleveland at Houston in Week 16.

The Oilers and Browns entered the final week of regular-season play separated by only a half game in the AFC Central Division standings. Houston was 9-6; Cleveland stood at 8-6-1. The winner would be division champion.

In the final few weeks of the season, however, it didn't appear either team was interested in claiming the crown. The Browns, who had won three straight division titles beginning in 1985, were winless in four straight games before squeaking out a 23-17 overtime victory against Minnesota in Week 15. The Oilers, who had yet to win a division championship since the NFL-AFL merger was implemented in 1970, were trying to regroup after suffering a 61-7 embarrassment at Cincinnati the previous week.

With the division crown hanging in the balance, Cleveland beat Houston, 24-20, on Kevin Mack's four-yard touchdown run with 39 seconds left. The touchdown capped a 58-yard drive the Browns began with no timeouts and 2:30 left on the clock.

The Browns, who held a 17-0 lead at one point in the first half, had only 68 total yards in the second half prior to their game-winning drive.

Mack was playing in just his fourth game all year after serving a 30-day jail sentence for cocaine possession and later undergoing arthroscopic knee surgery.

"I guess when all the trouble started, it was hard to see ahead to the good times coming back again," said Mack, who rushed for 27 yards on the final drive. "But a lot of people believed in me and now I am back."

"We were in a rough slump for a while and I'm so happy for this team," Browns Owner Art Modell said. "And I'm happy for Kevin Mack. He erased some of the past.

"He had the sentence, the knee surgery, but he came back and did well."

Cleveland seemed in command after it took a 17-point lead on a 40-yard touchdown pass from Bernie Kosar to Webster Slaughter with 1:45 left in the first half. The Oilers, however, rebounded for 20 straight points. Houston's go-ahead touchdown—a 27-yard pass from Warren Moon to Drew Hill with 4:46 remaining in the game—came one play after Cleveland's Clay Matthews recovered a fumble by Moon, only to give it back on an ill-advised lateral. Ernest Givins recovered the ball for the Oilers.

"If we had lost, I would have hung Clay from the propeller of the plane," cracked Cleveland Coach Bud Carson.

The Browns, however, held on to capture their fourth division title in five years. The Oilers, on the other hand, would need help from other teams to make the playoffs as a wild-card qualifier. Houston lost its last two games when a victory in either contest would have given the Oilers the AFC Central title.

"We kept thinking when we were 9-5 that all we had to do was win one game," Moon said. "But we played bad in Cincinnati and we didn't get it done (against Cleveland).

"If we get in, it will only be because someone is watching over us."

The football gods smiled on the Oilers the next day. Houston got an AFC wild-card berth when the Indianapolis Colts lost at New Orleans, 41-6. The Colts, who ended their season at 8-8, would have nailed down the wild-card spot had they won.

The Saints' standout was quarterback John Fourcade, who passed for two touchdowns and ran for a third. He completed 21 of 28 passes for 291 yards and guided a New Orleans offense that rolled up 389 total yards.

Dalton Hilliard's seven-yard touchdown run in the third quarter for New Orleans was his league-leading 18th TD of the season. His 108 points—the NFL high among non-kickers—enabled him to become the first non-kicker in Saints history to score more than 100 points.

The Los Angeles Raiders joined the Colts on the outside looking in as the playoff puzzle began to come together. The Raiders lost their finale, 34-17, to the New York Giants. The Raiders led 14-7 early in the second period before the NFC East champions took control by scoring 27 of the game's next 30 points.

New York snapped a 17-17 halftime tie with

a 10-play scoring drive early in the third quarter. Veteran running back Ottis Anderson, who finished with 74 yards rushing to surpass the 1,000-yard mark (1,023) for the sixth time in his career, ran the ball seven straight plays on the go-ahead drive. He capped the possession with his second one-yard touchdown run of the game.

The Raiders finished the '89 season at 8-8 and missed the playoffs for the fourth straight year.

The beneficiary of the Colt and Raider downfalls was Pittsburgh, which took the inside track for a possible wild-card berth by winning, 31-22, at Tampa Bay. The Steelers' fifth victory in six weeks put them in position for their first playoff appearance in five years, depending on the outcome of the Cincinnati-Minnesota game the next night.

Pittsburgh took the momentum against Tampa Bay when Rod Woodson returned the opening kickoff 72 yards, setting up a one-yard touchdown run by Tim Worley before three minutes had elapsed. Bubby Brister and Louis Lipps later hooked up on touchdown pass plays of 79 and 12 yards to help the Steelers take a 24-10 halftime lead.

The Buccaneers lost nine of their last 11 games to finish with a losing record (5-11) for the seventh straight year.

Despite losses in five of their previous seven games, the Buffalo Bills routed the New York Jets, 37-0, in Week 16 to clinch their second straight AFC Eastern Division crown. Running backs Larry Kinnebrew, Thurman Thomas and Kenneth Davis scored touchdowns to pace a Bills running game that rolled up 233 yards on 48 attempts.

Although the Bills' 9-7 record was the poorest of any division champion in 1989, it looked terrific compared with New York's 4-12 mark, the Jets' worst performance since they posted the same record in 1980. The team's sorry season led to the dismissal of Coach Joe Walton and his entire staff three days after the Buffalo game—and one day after Christmas.

Walton, who succeeded Walt Michaels prior to the 1983 season, compiled a record of 54-59-1 (including two playoff appearances) in seven seasons with the Jets.

One coach who had to be elated that the 1989 regular season was finally over was Dallas' Jimmy Johnson, who saw the last game of his rookie NFL season end like so many others—with a defeat. The Cowboys finished the year with the league's worst record (1-15) after losing yet another game at Texas Stadium, 20-10, to the Green Bay Packers. The Cowboys' 14th straight home loss set a league record and their 15th loss of the season tied an NFL mark set in 1980 by New Orleans.

In contrast with the Cowboys' season, Green Bay's 10-6 record was its best since the Packers went 10-4 while winning the NFC Central

Ottis Anderson had two one-yard touchdown runs in the Giants' 34-17 win over the Raiders.

Division title in 1972. Although they did not duplicate the franchise's division-winning effort of 17 years earlier, the '89 Packers played well enough to provide some genuine optimism for their long-suffering fans.

Green Bay lost its chance at an NFC wild-card berth when the Los Angeles Rams upended New England, 24-20, to earn a spot with an 11-5 record. It marked the fifth time in Coach John Robinson's seven-year tenure that the Rams had qualified for postseason play as a wild card. (The Rams made the playoffs six times overall in that span, once qualifying as the divisional champions.)

Los Angeles had to hold on to beat a New England team that was finishing its first losing season (5-11) since 1981. After Greg Bell scored on a three-yard run with 1:55 left to give the Rams the lead, the Patriots drove to a first down at the L.A. 4 with nine seconds remaining. However, Steve Grogan overthrew Irving Fryar with five seconds left, missed connections with Eric Sievers with one second to play and failed to hit rookie Hart Lee Dykes at the back of the Rams' end zone as time expired.

Grogan, who threw for 313 yards after replacing Marc Wilson in the second quarter, had completed five of seven passes before missing his last three.

Being relegated to wild-card status comes naturally to a team that finds itself in the same division as the powerful San Francisco 49ers. San Francisco compiled the NFL's best record in 1989, winning 14 of 16 games, and the 49ers captured their sixth NFC Western Division crown in seven seasons.

San Francisco ended the season on a five-game winning streak, applying a 26-0 whitewash to the Chicago Bears in the finale. The 49ers took command by scoring 10 points in the final 29 seconds of the first half. Rookie Johnny Jackson intercepted a pass by Chicago quarterback Mike Tomczak to set up a 36-yard Mike Cofer field goal, which came just 25 seconds after Jerry Rice caught a 29-yard touchdown pass from Joe Montana.

Montana completed 10 of 21 passes for 106 yards on the way to establishing an NFL season record for quarterback rating points. Montana, who also is the NFL's career leader in that department, finished the '89 season with a 112.4 mark to eclipse the record of 110.4 achieved by Cleveland's Milt Plum in 1960.

Cofer kicked four field goals against Chicago to finish as the league's top scorer in 1989 with 136 points (29 field goals, 49 extra points).

The NFL's rushing leader for 1989 was Kansas City's Christian Okoye, who carried 26 times for 98 yards in leading the Chiefs to a season-ending 27-24 victory at Miami. Okoye finished his third NFL campaign with 1,480 yards on 370 attempts to edge Detroit's Barry Sanders by 10 yards.

The Chiefs drove 44 yards on nine plays to set up Nick Lowery's 41-yard field goal with 1:31 left for the game-winning points. The Dolphins, who trailed 24-14 entering the final period, had tied the game at 24-24 on Dan Marino's seven-yard touchdown pass to Mark Clayton with 4:24 remaining.

Kansas City posted a record of 8-7-1 in Marty Schottenheimer's first season as the Chiefs' coach, but his team missed out on a wild-card berth when Pittsburgh beat Tampa Bay. Don Shula's 20th Miami club finished 8-8 after losing four of its final five games and failed to make the playoffs for the fourth straight season.

The Lions' Sanders finished with 1,470 yards rushing after ending his rookie season with a 158-yard performance against the Atlanta Falcons. Sanders burned Atlanta with touchdown runs of 25, 17 and 18 yards to help Detroit win its fifth straight game, 31-24, and finish with a 7-9 record. The Lions' five-game winning streak was their longest in 19 years.

The Falcons, on the other hand, ended their seventh straight losing season with seven consecutive losses and finished 3-13.

There also would be few regrets that the

Christian Okoye rushed for 98 yards in Kansas City's season finale and finished the '89 season with a league-leading 1,470 yards.

season was over among the Phoenix Cardinals, who closed out a 5-11 year with their sixth straight loss, a 31-14 defeat at Philadelphia. The Cardinals failed to win in five games under interim Coach Hank Kuhlmann, who replaced the fired Gene Stallings late in the year.

Philadelphia, meanwhile, nailed down a wild-card playoff berth by finishing with a record of 11-5, one game behind the New York Giants in the NFC East. The Eagles, who rushed for a season-high 267 yards, tied the game at 7-7 with a 72-yard first-quarter drive culminated by Randall Cunningham's 14-yard touchdown run. Philadelphia took the lead for good in the second quarter when Roger Ruzek threw a 22-yard touchdown pass to Cris Carter off a fake field-goal attempt.

The San Diego Chargers finished at 6-10 for the second successive year after a 19-16 AFC Western Division win over Denver. Chris Bahr's 45-yard field goal as time expired put San Diego in front after Denver's Jeff Alexander had gone one yard for a touchdown with 35 seconds left to tie the score at 16-16.

The Broncos, who had clinched the AFC

Mark Rypien completed 22 of 31 passes for 290 yards in Washington's 29-0 victory at Seattle.

West title four weeks earlier, ended the regular season with an AFC-best record of 11-5 despite losing three of their last four games.

The Washington Redskins completed a 10-6 season with their fifth straight triumph, a 29-0 interconference victory at Seattle. Mark Rypien completed 22 of 31 passes for 290 yards, including a 44-yard touchdown pass to Gary Clark in the third quarter. Clark, one of three Redskins receivers with more than 1,000 yards in pass receptions during the '89 season, caught nine passes for 149 yards against the Seahawks.

The NFL's all-time leading pass receiver, Steve Largent, had two receptions for 41 yards in the final game of his illustrious 14-year career. Largent, who was drafted by Houston in the fourth round of the 1976 draft before being traded to Seattle, caught 819 passes in his NFL career for 13,089 yards and 100 touchdowns—all three ranking as NFL records.

The Seahawks' 7-9 record represented the team's first losing season in Chuck Knox's seven seasons as the Seattle coach.

The 1989 regular season came to a close and the playoff field was finally completed following Minnesota's 29-21 triumph over Cincinnati on Monday night. The Vikings' victory gave them the NFC Central title and denied division rival Green Bay the crown and accompanying playoff berth.

The Bengals' loss kept them out—and put Pittsburgh in—as the final wild-card team from the AFC.

Minnesota used five Rich Karlis field goals and a stiff defense to secure its first division title in nine years. The Vikings scored on their first five possessions—four ending on Karlis field goals—to take a 19-0 lead before the Bengals finally scored on a 34-yard pass from Boomer Esiason to Eddie Brown.

After another Karlis field goal increased Minnesota's lead to 22-7 at the half, the Bengals responded by scoring two touchdowns to cut the deficit to 22-21 midway through the fourth quarter.

The Vikings, however, then put together a 67-yard drive—27 yards coming on Cincinnati penalties—to score the game's final touchdown on Wade Wilson's one-yard pass to tight end Brent Novoselsky with 4:17 left.

The Vikings finished the season at 10-6 and posted the league's only undefeated record at home (8-0).

Browns-Oilers
SATURDAY, DECEMBER 23
SCORE BY PERIODS

Cleveland	10	7	0	7—24
Houston	0	3	7	10—20

SCORING

Cleveland—Field goal Bahr 32, 5:01 1st.
Cleveland—Metcalf 68 pass from Kosar (Bahr kick), 11:56 1st.
Cleveland—Slaughter 40 pass from Kosar (Bahr kick), 13:15 2nd.
Houston—Field goal Zendejas 30, 14:36 2nd.
Houston—Hill 9 pass from Moon (Zendejas kick), 4:37 3rd.
Houston—Field goal Zendejas 37, 1:48 4th.
Houston—Hill 27 pass from Moon (Zendejas kick), 10:14 4th.
Cleveland—Mack 4 run (Bahr kick), 14:21 4th.

TEAM STATISTICS

	Cleveland	Houston
First downs	21	28
Rushes-Yards	26-105	19-102
Passing yards	219	381
Passes	18-36-0	32-51-1
Sacked-Yards lost	1-9	5-33
Punts	6-44.2	4-43.0
Fumbles-Lost	1-1	2-1
Penalties-Yards	7-41	12-77
Time of possession	29:46	30:14
Attendance—58,342.		

INDIVIDUAL STATISTICS

Rushing—Cleveland, Mack 12-62, Redden 6-23, Metcalf 4-14, Kosar 3-7, Manoa 1-minus 1; Houston, Pinkett 8-63, Moon 4-20, Highsmith 4-14, Rozier 3-5.

Passing—Cleveland, Kosar 18-36-0—228; Houston, Moon 32-51-1—414.

Receiving—Cleveland, Langhorne 5-38, Brennan 4-34, Slaughter 3-66, Metcalf 2-74, McNeil 1-6, Redden 1-6, Mack 1-3, Newsome 1-1; Houston, Hill 10-141, Duncan 7-85, Givins 6-75, Pinkett 4-36, Highsmith 3-40, Verhulst 2-37.

Kickoff Returns—Cleveland, Metcalf 1-21, McNeil 4-61; Houston, T. Johnson 1-11, White 1-29, K. Johnson 1-1.

Punt Returns—Cleveland, NcNeil 2-8; Houston, K. Johnson 3-4.

Interceptions—Cleveland, Wright 1-22.

Punting—Cleveland, Wagner 6-44.2; Houston, Greg Montgomery 4-43.0.

Field Goals—Cleveland, Bahr 1-1; Houston, Zendejas 2-3 (missed: 48).

Sacks—Cleveland, Banks 1½, Baker 1½, Matthews, Harper; Houston, Lyles.

Bills-Jets
SATURDAY, DECEMBER 23
SCORE BY PERIODS

Buffalo	3	7	20	7—37
New York Jets	0	0	0	0— 0

SCORING

Buffalo—Field goal Norwood 26, 10:34 1st.
Buffalo—Kinnebrew 1 run (Norwood kick), 13:53 2nd.
Buffalo—Lofton 18 pass from Kelly (kick failed), 4:11 3rd.
Buffalo—Harmon 25 pass from Kelly (Norwood kick), 10:21 3rd.
Buffalo—Thomas 3 run (Norwood kick), 14:24 3rd.
Buffalo—K. Davis 17 run (Norwood kick), 12:16 4th.

TEAM STATISTICS

	Buffalo	New York
First downs	28	11
Rushes-Yards	48-233	14-54
Passing yards	208	146

	Buffalo	New York
Passes	13-21-1	16-32-1
Sacked-Yards lost	0-0	4-30
Punts	2-40.5	7-39.9
Fumbles-Lost	0-0	2-1
Penalties-Yards	4-30	6-40
Time of possession	35:53	24:07
Attendance—21,148.		

INDIVIDUAL STATISTICS

Rushing—Buffalo, Kinnebrew 17-91, Thomas 17-73, K. Davis 5-33, Harmon 3-28, Reed 1-8, Mueller 1-3, Kelly 1-0, Reich 3-minus 3; New York, Hector 7-27, Vick 6-27, Eason 1-0.

Passing—Buffalo, Kelly 13-21-1—208; New York, Eason 12-22-1—125, Mackey 4-10-0—51.

Receiving—Buffalo, Reed 6-80, Harmon 3-42, Metzelaars 2-30, McKeller 1-31, Lofton 1-25; New York, Toon 6-67, Townsell 2-35, Vick 2-13, Epps 1-18, Burkett 1-15, Hector 1-11, Dressel 1-8, Neubert 1-7, Brown 1-2.

Kickoff Returns—Buffalo, Harmon 1-49; New York, Townsell 5-58, Epps 1-16, Byrd 1-1.

Punt Returns—Buffalo, Sutton 1-16; New York, Townsell 1-10.

Interceptions—Buffalo, Bennett 1-minus 1; New York, Gordon 1-2.

Punting—Buffalo, Kidd 2-40.5; New York, Prokop 7-39.9.

Field Goals—Buffalo, Norwood 1-1; New York, Leahy 0-1 (missed: 29).

Sacks—Buffalo, B. Smith 2, Bennett 2.

Redskins-Seahawks
SATURDAY, DECEMBER 23
SCORE BY PERIODS

Washington	10	3	16	0—29
Seattle	0	0	0	0— 0

SCORING

Washington—Field goal Lohmiller 29, 11:24 1st.
Washington—Byner 2 run (Lohmiller kick), 12:59 1st.
Washington—Field goal Lohmiller 27, 7:35 2nd.
Washington—Clark 44 pass from Rypien (Lohmiller kick), 1:38 3rd.
Washington—Safety, Krieg tackled by Stokes in end zone, 1:53 3rd.
Washington—Byner 8 run (Lohmiller kick), 5:33 3rd.

TEAM STATISTICS

	Washington	Seattle
First downs	26	12
Rushes-Yards	40-137	8-26
Passing yards	319	176
Passes	23-32-1	18-29-1
Sacked-Yards lost	1-3	4-37
Punts	2-33.5	3-40.0
Fumbles-Lost	0-0	4-3
Penalties-Yards	4-30	2-16
Time of possession	41:17	18:43
Attendance—60,294.		

INDIVIDUAL STATISTICS

Rushing—Washington, Byner 19-63, Dupard 11-41, Riggs 5-22, Sanders 1-10, Humphries 4-1; Seattle, Krieg 1-9, Williams 4-9, Warner 3-8.

Passing—Washington, Rypien 22-31-1—290, Sanders 1-1-0—32; Seattle, Krieg 18-29-1—213.

Receiving—Washington, Clark 9-149, Monk 5-69, Byner 4-35, Sanders 3-37, Orr 1-22, Warren 1-10; Seattle, Williams 6-65, Blades 5-52, Largent 2-41, Chadwick 2-21, Clark 2-16, Skansi 1-18.

Kickoff Returns—Washington, A. Johnson 1-26, Sanders 1-8; Seattle, Harris 4-82, Hollis 1-13.

Punt Returns—Washington, Sanders 1-7; Seattle, Hollis 1-8.

Interceptions—Washington, B. Davis 1-12; Seattle, Robinson 1-0.

Punting—Washington, Mojsiejenko 2-32.5; Seattle, Rodriguez 3-40.0.

Field Goals—Washington, Lohmiller 2-3 (missed: 42); Seattle, none attempted.

Sacks—Washington, Mann 2, Coleman, Stokes; Seattle, Nash.

Broncos-Chargers
SUNDAY, DECEMBER 24
SCORE BY PERIODS

Denver	0	7	3	6—16
San Diego	0	6	3	10—19

SCORING

San Diego—Field goal Bahr 22, 6:31 2nd.
Denver—Humphrey 12 pass from Elway (Treadway kick), 9:04 2nd.
San Diego—Field goal Bahr 41, 14:35 2nd.
San Diego—Field goal Bahr 53, 2:17 3rd.
Denver—Field goal Treadway 24, 8:45 3rd.
San Diego—Spencer 1 run (Bahr kick), 7:26 4th.
Denver—Alexander 1 run (kick failed), 14:25 4th.
San Diego—Field goal Bahr 45, 15:00 4th.

TEAM STATISTICS

	Denver	San Diego
First downs	16	18
Rushes-Yards	29-97	29-82
Passing yards	109	305
Passes	17-27-1	22-48-4
Sacked-Yards lost	7-35	0-0
Punts	7-38.4	4-44.0
Fumbles-Lost	2-2	2-2
Penalties-Yards	2-10	8-97
Time of possession	29:16	30:44
Attendance—50,524.		

INDIVIDUAL STATISTICS

Rushing—Denver, Humphrey 15-51, Bratton 6-19, Kubiak 2-16, Winder 3-8, Sewell 1-2, Alexander 2-1; San Diego, A. Miller 3-38, Nelson 7-23, Butts 16-16, Tolliver 1-3, Spencer 2-2.

Passing—Denver, Elway 5-10-0—47, Kubiak 12-17-1—97; San Diego, Tolliver 22-48-4—305.

Receiving—Denver, Johnson 5-38, Mobley 3-27, Humphrey 2-15, Jackson 1-15, Kay 1-14, Young 1-11, Alexander 1-9, Bratton 1-6, Sewell 1-5, Winder 1-4; San Diego, Nelson 6-92, McEwen 5-78, A. Miller 5-53, Early 4-38, Walker 1-24, Cox 1-20.

Kickoff Returns—Denver, Bell 2-55, Carrington 2-55; San Diego, A. Miller 3-55, Holland 1-13.

Punt Returns—Denver, Johnson 2-22; San Diego, McConkey 3-13.

Interceptions—Denver, Henderson 1-22, Carrington 1-2, Robbins 1-0, Atwater 1-0; San Diego, Glenn 1-0.

Punting—Denver, Horan 7-38.4; San Diego, Ilesic 4-44.0.

Field Goals—Denver, Treadwell 1-2 (missed: 43); San Diego, Bahr 4-5 (missed: 52).

Sacks—San Diego, L. Miller, O'Neal 2, Grossman 2, Williams 2.

Packers-Cowboys
SUNDAY, DECEMBER 24
SCORE BY PERIODS

Green Bay	3	7	7	3—20
Dallas	3	0	7	0—10

SCORING

Green Bay—Field goal Jacke 28, 5:41 1st.
Dallas—Field goal Zendejas 41, 12:12 1st.
Green Bay—Query 14 pass from Majkowski (Jacke kick), 14:29 2nd.
Dallas—Del Rio 57 fumble return (Zendejas kick), 8:09 3rd.
Green Bay—West 5 pass from Majkowski (Jacke kick), 12:07 3rd.
Green Bay—Field goal Jacke 24, 11:36 4th.

TEAM STATISTICS

	Green Bay	Dallas
First downs	16	16
Rushes-Yards	22-43	24-113
Passing yards	207	116
Passes	21-32-0	18-27-4
Sacked-Yards lost	4-25	2-9
Punts	4-44.2	3-38.6
Fumbles-Lost	2-1	1-1
Penalties-Yards	2-15	6-35
Time of possession	30:44	29:16
Attendance—41,265.		

INDIVIDUAL STATISTICS

Rushing—Green Bay, Fullwood 12-16, Kemp 1-12, Woodside 4-8, Majkowski 5-7; Dallas, Johnston 16-60, Aikman 4-37, Sargent 4-16.

Passing—Green Bay, Majkowski 21-32-0—232; Dallas, Aikman 18-27-4—125.

Receiving—Green Bay, Kemp 6-85, Sharpe 5-72, Woodside 4-18, Query 2-25, West 2-14, Matthews 1-15, Fontenot 1-3; Dallas, Burbage 5-24, Jennings 4-37, Shepard 3-36, Tautalatasi 2-18, Folsom 1-12, Sargent 1-6, Dixon 1-5, Aikman 1-minus 13.

Kickoff Returns—Green Bay, Workman 2-53, Bland 1-28; Dallas, Shepard 2-51, Ankrom 1-5, Dixon 2-42.

Punt Returns—Green Bay, Query 2-6; Dallas, Shepard 2-14.

Interceptions—Green Bay, Holland 1-26, Stills 1-12, Anderson 1-1, D. Brown 1-0.

Punting—Green Bay, Bracken 4-44.2; Dallas, Saxon 3-38.6.

Field Goals—Green Bay, Jacke 2-2; Dallas, Zendejas 1-1.

Sacks—Green Bay, Harris, Hall; Dallas, Jeffcoat 3, Broughton.

Lions-Falcons
SUNDAY, DECEMBER 24
SCORE BY PERIODS

Detroit	7	7	10	7—31
Atlanta	0	10	0	14—24

SCORING

Detroit—Johnson 34 pass from Gagliano (Murray kick), 4:22 1st.
Atlanta—Field goal Davis 25, 1:03 2nd.
Detroit—B. Sanders 25 run (Murray kick), 4:22 2nd.
Atlanta—Lang 9 pass from Miller (Davis kick), 14:41 2nd.
Detroit—Field goal Murray 39, 3:28 3rd.
Detroit—B. Sanders 17 run (Murray kick), 8:50 3rd.
Detroit—B. Sanders 18 run (Murray kick), 0:52 4th.
Atlanta—Jones 1 run (Davis kick), 11:23 4th.
Atlanta—Haynes 6 pass from Miller (Davis kick), 14:09 4th.

TEAM STATISTICS

	Detroit	Atlanta
First downs	17	27
Rushes-Yards	26-179	21-89
Passing yards	197	324
Passes	17-30-1	37-66-1
Sacked-Yards lost	3-16	1-10
Punts	5-45.0	7-41.9
Fumbles-Lost	2-1	1-0
Penalties-Yards	1-15	5-45
Time of possession	22:50	37:10
Attendance—7,092.		

INDIVIDUAL STATISTICS

Rushing—Detroit, B. Sanders 20-158, Gagliano 6-21; Atlanta, Jones 7-37, Paterra 8-31, Lang 3-18, Settle 3-3.

Passing—Detroit, Gagliano 17-30-1—213; Atlanta, Miller 37-66-1—334.

Receiving—Detroit, Johnson 7-135, Clark 6-67, Ford 1-4, Phillips 1-3, B. Sanders 1-3, Stanley 1-1; Atlanta, Jones 7-38, Lang 6-73, Haynes 6-62, Collins 6-58, Heller

6-53, Paterra 3-27, Dixon 1-16, Bailey 1-4, Settle 1-3.

Kickoff Returns—Detroit, Gray 2-38, Griffin 1-1; Atlanta, Paterra 3-43, Jordan 3-47.

Punt Returns—Detroit, Stanley 3-35, Gray 1-15; Atlanta, Jordan 4-34.

Interceptions—Detroit, Gibson 1-10; Atlanta, Zackery 1-3.

Punting—Detroit, Arnold 5-45.0; Atlanta, Fulhage 7-41.9.

Field Goals—Detroit, Murray 1-1; Atlanta, Davis 1-2 (missed: 42).

Sacks—Detroit, Cofer; Atlanta, Cotton 2, Tuggle.

Steelers-Buccaneers
SUNDAY, DECEMBER 24
SCORE BY PERIODS

Pittsburgh	7	17	7	0—31
Tampa Bay	7	3	3	9—22

SCORING

Pittsburgh—Worley 1 run (Anderson kick), 2:49 1st.

Tampa Bay—Carrier 7 pass from Ferguson (Igwebuike kick), 8:15 1st.

Pittsburgh—Lipps 79 pass from Brister (Anderson kick), 1:06 2nd.

Tampa Bay—Field goal Igwebuike 45, 8:27 2nd.

Pittsburgh—Lipps 12 pass from Brister (Anderson kick), 13:59 2nd.

Pittsburgh—Field goal Anderson 32, 15:00 2nd.

Tampa Bay—Field goal Igwebuike 24, 10:04 3rd.

Pittsburgh—Worley 1 run (Anderson kick), 14:55 3rd.

Tampa Bay—Safety, Cocroft blocked punt out of end zone, 11:08 4th.

Tampa Bay—Carrier 39 pass from Ferguson (Igwebuike kick), 11:58 4th.

TEAM STATISTICS

	Pittsburgh	Tampa Bay
First downs	14	19
Rushes-Yards	37-147	25-84
Passing yards	169	237
Passes	7-15-2	21-41-1
Sacked-Yards lost	1-9	1-7
Punts	5-30.4	6-30.7
Fumbles-Lost	2-1	0-0
Penalties-Yards	8-53	2-10
Time of possession	26:45	33:15
Attendance—29,690.		

INDIVIDUAL STATISTICS

Rushing—Pittsburgh, Hoge 18-90, Worley 18-51, Brister 1-6; Tampa Bay, Tate 11-38, Stamps 2-18, Howard 5-15, Wilder 7-13.

Passing—Pittsburgh, Brister 7-15-2—178; Tampa Bay, Ferguson 21-41-1—244.

Receiving—Pittsburgh, Lipps 4-137, Mularkey 1-27, Hill 1-13, Worley 1-1; Tampa Bay, Carrier 6-101, Stamps 3-34, Hall 3-33, Drewrey 2-24, Tate 2-20, Wilder 2-4, W. Harris 1-17, Howard 1-7, Peebles 1-4.

Kickoff Returns—Pittsburgh, Woodson 2-86; Tampa Bay, Stamps 2-39, Elder 2-38, Drewrey 1-26.

Punt Returns—Pittsburgh, Woodson 3-12; Tampa Bay, Drewrey 1-9.

Interceptions—Pittsburgh, Woodson 1-39; Tampa Bay, Futrell 1-1, Reynolds 1-5.

Punting—Pittsburgh, Newsome 4-38.0; Tampa Bay, Mohr 6-30.7.

Field Goals—Pittsburgh, Anderson 1-1; Tampa Bay, Igwebuike 2-2.

Sacks—Pittsburgh, Lloyd; Tampa Bay, Thomas.

Cardinals-Eagles
SUNDAY, DECEMBER 24
SCORE BY PERIODS

Phoenix	7	7	0	0—14
Philadelphia	7	14	3	7—31

SCORING

Phoenix—Green 6 pass from Hogeboom (Del Greco kick), 7:08 1st.

Philadelphia—Cunningham 14 run (Ruzek kick), 12:02 1st.

Philadelphia—Carter 22 pass from Ruzek (Ruzek kick), 7:48 2nd.

Philadelphia—Drummond 4 pass from Cunningham (Ruzek kick), 14:51 2nd.

Phoenix—Green 36 pass from Hogeboom (Del Greco kick), 14:51 2nd.

Philadelphia—Field goal Ruzek 39, 11:07 3rd.

Philadelphia—Sherman 7 run (Ruzek kick), 9:51 4th.

TEAM STATISTICS

	Phoenix	Philadelphia
First downs	14	26
Rushes-Yards	20-68	46-267
Passing yards	197	165
Passes	13-29-2	20-37-1
Sacked-Yards lost	4-32	2-19
Punts	6-39.8	4-37.3
Fumbles-Lost	2-1	0-0
Penalties-Yards	4-20	4-35
Time of possession	23:41	36:19
Attendance—43,287.		

INDIVIDUAL STATISTICS

Rushing—Phoenix, Ferrell 16-55, Sikahema 4-13; Philadelphia, Toney 17-82, Sherman 9-66, Cunningham 8-41, Reichenbach 1-30, Drummond 7-27, Higgs 3-18, Byars 1-3.

Passing—Phoenix, Hogeboom 12-28-2—212, Tupa 1-1-0—17; Philadelphia, Cunningham 19-36-1—162, Ruzek 1-1-0—22.

Receiving—Phoenix, Jones 5-76, Green 3-63, Sikahema 2-35, Novacek 1-30, Ferrell 1-17, Usher 1-8; Philadelphia, Toney 5-48, Drummond 5-41, Carter 3-51, Byars 3-17, Jackson 2-6, Carson 1-12, Giles 1-9.

Kickoff Returns—Phoenix, Usher 3-52, Sikahema 3-61; Philadelphia, Higgs 1-16, Sherman 1-7.

Punt Returns—None.

Interceptions—Phoenix, Young 1-32; Philadelphia, Evans 1-0, Everett 1-0.

Punting—Phoenix, Camarillo 6-39.8; Philadelphia, Tuten 4-37.3.

Field Goals—Phoenix, Del Greco 0-2 (missed: 39, 45); Philadelphia, Ruzek 1-2 (missed: 34).

Sacks—Phoenix, Mack, Wahler; Philadelphia, Joyner, Simmons, Harris, White.

Bears-49ers
SUNDAY, DECEMBER 24
SCORE BY PERIODS

Chicago	0	0	0	0— 0
San Francisco	3	13	3	7—26

SCORING

San Francisco—Field goal Cofer 29, 3:38 1st.

San Francisco—Field goal Cofer 24, 7:27 2nd.

San Francisco—Rice 29 pass from Montana (Cofer kick), 14:31 2nd.

San Francisco—Field goal Cofer 36, 14:56 2nd.

San Francisco—Field goal Cofer 47, 9:43 3rd.

San Francisco—Flagler 29 run (Cofer kick), 9:16 4th.

TEAM STATISTICS

	Chicago	San Francisco
First downs	15	17
Rushes-Yards	31-122	29-130
Passing yards	167	184
Passes	17-34-3	16-30-1
Sacked-Yards lost	1-10	3-22
Punts	3-35.7	5-34.8
Fumbles-Lost	2-2	0-0
Penalties-Yards	1-5	2-20
Time of possession	29:50	30:10
Attendance—65,675.		

INDIVIDUAL STATISTICS

Rushing—Chicago, Harbaugh 7-44, Anderson 13-41, Tomczak 2-21, Green 2-11, Muster 4-7, Suhey 1-1, Gentry 2-minus 3; San Francisco, Flagler 8-41, Craig 10-31, Rathman 4-22, Montana 2-16, Young 3-11, Henderson 2-9.

Passing—Chicago, Harbaugh 3-4-1—30, Tomczak 14-30-2—147; San Francisco, Montana 10-21-1—106, Young 6-9-0—100.

Receiving—Chicago, McKinnon 3-43, Morris 3-36, Davis 3-27, Muster 2-5, Anderson 2-4, Boso 1-26, Thornton 1-20, Gentry 1-8, Waddle 1-8; San Francisco, Rice 4-101, Williams 3-38, Rathman 3-19, Jones 3-15, Henderson 1-12, Flagler 1-11, Craig 1-10.

Kickoff Returns—Chicago, Sanders 3-52, Gentry 3-61, Green 1-15; San Francisco, Flagler 1-21.

Punt Returns—Chicago, Green 4-23; San Francisco, Griffin 1-9.

Interceptions—Chicago, Gayle 1-20; San Francisco, Jackson 1-16, Griffin 1-3, DeLong 1-1.

Punting—Chicago, Buford 3-35.7; San Francisco, Helton 5-34.8.

Field Goals—Chicago, Butler 0-1 (missed: 50); San Francisco, Cofer 4-4.

Sacks—Chicago, McMichael, Chapura, Dent; San Francisco, Haley.

Rams-Patriots
SUNDAY, DECEMBER 24
SCORE BY PERIODS

Los Angeles Rams	3	7	7	7—24
New England	0	3	7	10—20

SCORING

Los Angeles—Field goal Lansford 19, 9:25 1st.
Los Angeles—Gray 27 interception return (Lansford kick), 14:20 2nd.
New England—Field goal Staurovsky 44, 15:00 2nd.
Los Angeles—McGee 7 pass from Everett (Lansford kick), 5:36 3rd.
New England—Fryar 47 pass from Grogan (Staurovsky kick), 8:21 3rd.
New England—Stephens 4 run (Staurovsky kick), 3:19 4th.
New England—Field goal Staurovsky 48, 9:32 4th.
Los Angeles—Bell 3 run (Lansford kick), 13:05 4th.

TEAM STATISTICS

	Los Angeles	New England
First downs	22	26
Rushes-Yards	32-234	24-73
Passing yards	181	321
Passes	13-29-2	27-54-3
Sacked-Yards lost	0-0	1-8
Punts	3-47.0	4-36.8
Fumbles-Lost	2-0	1-0
Penalties-Yards	3-25	2-14
Time of possession	27:40	32:20

Attendance—27,940.

INDIVIDUAL STATISTICS

Rushing—Los Angeles, Bell 26-210, Gary 3-10, McGee 1-7, Delpino 1-7, Everett 1-0; New England, Stephens 15-41, Perryman 5-19, Fryar 1-11, Grogan 2-2, Tatupu 1-0.

Passing—Los Angeles, Everett 13-29-2—181; New England, Grogan 25-46-2—313, Wilson 2-8-1—16.

Receiving—Los Angeles, Ellard 4-111, Anderson 3-34, Delpino 3-21, McGee 1-7, Holohan 1-7; New England, Dykes 8-108, Fryar 6-99, Jones 4-51, Sievers 3-32, Perryman 3-15, Stephens 2-13, Tatupu 1-11.

Kickoff Returns—Los Angeles, R. Brown 2-41, Delpino 1-24; New England, Wonsley 2-51, Hodge 2-19, Fryar 1-47.

Punt Returns—Los Angeles, Henley 1-12, Irvin 1-7.

Interceptions—Los Angeles, Strickland 2-56, Gray 1-27; New England, Marion 1-18, Hurst 1-2.

Punting—Los Angeles, Hatcher 3-47.0; New England, Feagles 4-36.8.

Field Goals—Los Angeles, Lansford 1-3 (missed: 50, 50); New England, Staurovsky 2-2.

Sacks—Los Angeles, Greene.

Colts-Saints
SUNDAY, DECEMBER 24
SCORE BY PERIODS

Indianapolis	0	6	0	0— 6
New Orleans	3	7	7	24—41

SCORING

New Orleans—Field goal Andersen 21, 7:17 1st.
Indianapolis—Field goal Biasucci 41, 3:37 2nd.
New Orleans—Martin 3 pass from Fourcade (Andersen kick), 10:39 2nd.
Indianapolis—Field goal Biasucci 24, 15:00 2nd.
New Orleans—Hilliard 7 run (Andersen kick), 8:22 3rd.
New Orleans—Brenner 30 pass from Fourcade (Andersen kick), 0:55 4th.
New Orleans—Fourcade 2 run (Andersen kick), 7:32 4th.
New Orleans—Field goal Andersen 29, 11:57 4th.
New Orleans—Cook 63 interception return (Andersen kick), 13:23 4th.

TEAM STATISTICS

	Indianapolis	New Orleans
First downs	13	23
Rushes-Yards	24-111	34-128
Passing yards	119	261
Passes	16-29-2	21-28-1
Sacked-Yards lost	1-13	3-30
Punts	6-45.2	2-45.5
Fumbles-Lost	1-0	1-0
Penalties-Yards	4-30	5-35
Time of possession	22:57	37:03

Attendance—49,009.

INDIVIDUAL STATISTICS

Rushing—Indianapolis, Dickerson 16-54, Trudeau 3-38, Hunter 3-14, Bentley 1-6, Rison 1-minus 1; New Orleans, Hilliard 20-61, Fourcade 5-30, Jordan 5-24, Heyward 3-8, Frazier 1-5.

Passing—Indianapolis, Trudeau 15-27-1—118, Ramsey 1-2-1—14; New Orleans, Fourcade 21-28-1—291.

Receiving—Indianapolis, Brooks 4-41; Rison 4-31, Bentley 4-27, Dickerson 2-19, Verdin 1-13, Boyer 1-1; New Orleans, Perriman 5-87, E. Martin 5-65, Brenner 4-86, Hill 3-26, Hilliard 2-13, Tice 1-7, Heyward 1-7.

Kickoff Returns—Indianapolis, Bentley 6-110; New Orleans, Morse 2-36.

Punt Returns—New Orleans, Morse 6-28, Massey 0-54.

Interceptions—Indianapolis, Prior 1-0; New Orleans, Waymer 1-0, Cook 1-63.

Punting—Indianapolis, Stark 6-45.2; New Orleans, Barnhardt 2-45.5.

Field Goals—Indianapolis, Biasucci 2-2; New Orleans, Andersen 2-2.

Sacks—Indianapolis, Bickett 2, Thompson; New Orleans, Swilling.

Chiefs-Dolphins
SUNDAY, DECEMBER 24
SCORE BY PERIODS

Kansas City	0	21	3	3—27
Miami	7	7	0	10—24

SCORING

Miami—Jensen 4 pass from Marino (Stoyanovich kick), 10:47 1st.
Kansas City—Paige 20 pass from DeBerg (Lowery kick), 0:05 2nd.
Miami—Edmunds 3 pass from Marino (Stoyanovich kick), 4:55 2nd.
Kansas City—Saxon 6 run (Lowery kick), 9:08 2nd.
Kansas City—Okoye 1 run (Lowery kick), 13:21 2nd.
Kansas City—Field goal Lowery 19, 13:15 3rd.

Miami—Field goal Stoyanovich 22, 4:16 4th.
Miami—Clayton 7 pass from Marino (Stoyanovich kick), 10:36 4th.
Kansas City—Field goal Lowery 41, 13:29 4th.

TEAM STATISTICS

	Kansas City	Miami
First downs	23	27
Rushes-Yards	32-117	19-62
Passing yards	225	319
Passes	17-26-1	28-47-1
Sacked-Yards lost	1-5	2-20
Punts	3-36.3	2-40.0
Fumbles-Lost	1-0	1-0
Penalties-Yards	8-44	4-20
Time of possession	30:13	29:47

Attendance—43,612.

INDIVIDUAL STATISTICS

Rushing—Kansas City, Okoye 26-98, Harry 1-9, Saxon 1-6, McNair 1-4, Heard 1-1, DeBerg 2-minus 1; Miami, Smith 14-45, Logan 5-17.

Passing—Kansas City, DeBerg 17-26-1—230; Miami, Marino 28-47-1—339.

Receiving—Kansas City, Mandley 4-63, Hayes 4-62, Harry 4-41, Paige 3-43, McNair 1-15, Saxon 1-6; Miami, Duper 7-85, Jensen 7-65, Clayton 6-102, Edmunds 3-27, Logan 2-7, Smith 1-34, A. Brown 1-10, Banks 1-9.

Kickoff Returns—Kansas City, Saxon 1-2, McNair 1-21, Copeland 2-23; Miami, Hampton 3-44.

Punt Returns—Kansas City, Worthen 2-10; Miami, Schwedes 1-17, Gibson 1-minus 1.

Interceptions—Kansas City, Lewis 1-15; Miami, Oliver 1-0.

Punting—Kansas City, Goodburn 3-36.3; Miami, Roby 2-40.0.

Field Goals—Kansas City, Lowery 2-2; Miami, Stoyanovich 1-2 (missed: 56).

Sacks—Kansas City, Petry ½, Bell ½, Martin; Miami, Green.

Raiders-Giants
SUNDAY, DECEMBER 24
SCORE BY PERIODS

Los Angeles Raiders	7	10	0	0—17
New York Giants	7	10	10	7—34

SCORING

New York—Meggett 76 punt return (Nittmo kick), 2:20 1st.
Los Angeles—Horton 1 pass from Beuerlein (Jaeger kick), 9:25 1st.
Los Angeles—Fernandez 30 pass from Beuerlein (Jaeger kick), 2:10 2nd.
New York—Anderson 1 run (Nittmo kick), 8:52 2nd.
Los Angeles—Field goal Jaeger 42, 13:58 2nd.
New York—Field goal Nittmo 28, 14:58 2nd.
New York—Anderson 1 run (Nittmo kick), 7:56 3rd.
New York—Field goal Nittmo 21, 11:31 3rd.
New York—Simms 3 run (Nittmo kick), 5:02 4th.

TEAM STATISTICS

	Los Angeles	New York
First downs	19	20
Rushes-Yards	23-82	38-116
Passing yards	230	164
Passes	16-34-2	13-25-0
Sacked-Yards lost	4-36	1-5
Punts	5-40.8	5-41.2
Fumbles-Lost	4-1	4-1
Penalties-Yards	9-82	3-28
Time of possession	27:01	32:59

Attendance—70,306.

INDIVIDUAL STATISTICS

Rushing—Los Angeles, Jackson 10-35, Smith 7-24, Allen 2-13, Beuerlein 4-10; New York, Anderson 23-74, Tillman 8-21, Carthon 6-18, Simms 1-3.

Passing—Los Angeles, Beuerlein 16-34-2—266, New York, Simms 13-25-0—169.

Receiving—Los Angeles, Fernandez 6-125, Alexander 4-98, Gault 2-17, Jackson 2-14, Allen 1-11, Horton 1-1; New York, Meggett 3-25, Cross 2-19, Mowatt 2-37, Anderson 2-16, Baker 1-17, Manuel 1-11, Carthon 1-9, Robinson 1-5.

Kickoff Returns—Los Angeles, Adams 3-29, Smith 2-19, Turk 1-2; New York, Meggett 1-43, Ingram 3-33.

Punt Returns—Los Angeles, Adams 4-37; New York, Meggett 5-114.

Interceptions—New York, P. Williams 1-14, Kinard 1-17.

Punting—Los Angeles, Gossett 5-40.8; New York, Landeta 5-41.2.

Field Goals—Los Angeles, Jaeger 1-1; New York, Nittmo 2-2.

Sacks—Los Angeles, Davis; New York, Taylor 2, Howard, Cooks.

Bengals-Vikings
MONDAY, DECEMBER 25
SCORE BY PERIODS

Cincinnati	0	7	7	7—21
Minnesota	6	16	0	7—29

SCORING

Minnesota—Field goal Karlis 31, 5:30 1st.
Minnesota—Field goal Karlis 37, 11:13 1st.
Minnesota—Field goal Karlis 22, 3:19 2nd.
Minnesota—Fenney 11 pass from Wilson (Karlis kick), 4:54 2nd.
Minnesota—Field goal Karlis 42, 8:18 2nd.
Cincinnati—Brown 34 pass from Esiason (Breech kick), 11:29 2nd.
Minnesota—Field goal Karlis 24, 15:00 2nd.
Cincinnati—Holman 65 pass from Esiason (Breech kick), 0:25 3rd.
Cincinnati—Taylor 18 pass from Esiason (Breech kick), 6:11 4th.
Minnesota—Novoselsky 1 pass from Wilson (Karlis kick), 10:43 4th.

TEAM STATISTICS

	Cincinnati	Minnesota
First downs	26	24
Rushes-Yards	23-120	34-119
Passing yards	309	274
Passes	31-54-3	19-35-0
Sacked-Yards lost	6-58	4-29
Punts	5-43.6	5-41.4
Fumbles-Lost	3-2	3-1
Penalties-Yards	10-84	7-55
Time of possession	28:58	31:02

Attendance—58,829.

INDIVIDUAL STATISTICS

Rushing—Cincinnati, Brooks 15-93, Jennings 2-11, Taylor 1-9, Ball 5-7; Minnesota, Fenney 17-62, Walker 12-43, A. Anderson 3-9, Wilson 2-5.

Passing—Cincinnati, Esiason 31-54-3—367; Minnesota, Wilson 19-35-0—303.

Receiving—Cincinnati, Brooks 12-66, Brown 6-109, McGee 4-56, Holman 3-84, Ball 2-3, Taylor 1-18, Kattus 1-16, Smith 1-10; Minnesota, Carter 7-118, Fenney 5-51, H. Jones 4-90, Jordan 1-32, Gustafson 1-11, Novoselsky 1-1.

Kickoff Returns—Cincinnati, Carey 5-81, Holifield 1-0; Minnesota, Walker 1-39, Carter 1-19.

Punt Returns—Minnesota, Lewis 5-88.

Interceptions—Minnesota, Fullington 1-0, Studwell 1-0, Dusbabek 1-2.

Punting—Cincinnati, Johnson 5-43.6; Minnesota, Scribner 5-41.4.

Field Goals—Cincinnati, none attempted; Minnesota, Karlis 5-6 (missed: 52).

Sacks—Cincinnati, Williams 2, McClendon, Tuatagaloa; Minnesota, Doleman 4, Thomas 2.

WILD-CARD GAMES

RAMS 21, EAGLES 7

PHILADELPHIA—"We expected to win, and we did."

Los Angeles Rams Coach John Robinson made that statement shortly after his team had defeated the Philadelphia Eagles, 21-7, in the National Football Conference wild-card game. Robinson may not have had any doubt that his team would win, but even he had to be a little shocked that his game plan worked so well.

The Rams ended the 1989 regular season with the league's poorest defense against the pass and were preparing to face one of the NFL's top pass/run threats in Philadelphia quarterback Randall Cunningham. Figuring that speed would fare better against the Eagles' star than strength, L.A. defensive coordinator Fritz Shurmur installed a five-linebacker, six-defensive back alignment for this game. Except for obvious running situations, the Rams' down linemen stayed pretty well glued to the bench.

The strategy worked. Cunningham completed 24 of 40 passes for 238 yards, with most of that yardage coming on short flare passes and screens. Fifteen of Cunningham's passes were caught by running backs; tight ends and wide receivers caught only nine.

The Eagles had 15 possessions and nine ended with a punt. Three other possessions ended with turnovers and Philadelphia didn't score until 11 minutes were left on the clock.

"I thought we'd play a ton of zone," said Shurmur, whose defense didn't play a single down of man-to-man. "We thought that was the best way. With five linebackers, we'd have as much speed as we could on the field. And in our zone, our backs would never be turned to Cunningham."

A defense turning its back to Cunningham is usually a dangerous thing. He led the Eagles in rushing (621 yards) for the third straight season and probably ranks as the league's best improvising quarterback. He was held to 39 yards on six rushing attempts by the Rams.

"There were a couple of times early when I'd step up in the pocket and be ready to throw, but so many defenders would be there," Cunningham said.

"... I have to tip my hat to their defensive coordinator."

"Their defense should get a game ball," Philadelphia Coach Buddy Ryan said. "We couldn't catch. We couldn't run. We couldn't do anything."

The Los Angeles offense, on the other hand, had little difficulty solving the Eagles' defense. Jim Everett threw a 39-yard touchdown pass to Henry Ellard on the Rams' first possession and a four-yarder to Damone Johnson five minutes later.

The Rams led, 14-0, after just 12 plays from scrimmage.

"I don't know what they'll do with their game plan for the 49ers," said Everett, who was one of many Rams upset by comments Philadelphia players made indicating that they were looking past their first postseason game.

Instead, Philadelphia suffered a first-round playoff loss for the second year in a row.

The Rams' victory marked the first time since the franchise moved from Cleveland to Los Angeles in 1946 that the team had won a playoff game held in an outdoor stadium in a northern city. The Rams had lost nine other such games.

Robinson, however, was not much interested in oddities like that.

"Stats in a game like this mean nothing," he said. "I think it's the will of a football team that ultimately decides the game.

"On this day, our will was stronger."

Rams-Eagles

SUNDAY, DECEMBER 31

SCORE BY PERIODS

Los Angeles Rams	14	0	0	7	21
Philadelphia	0	0	0	7	7

SCORING

Los Angeles—Ellard 39 pass from Everett (Lansford kick), 2:25 1st. Drive: 83 yards, 5 plays.

Los Angeles—Johnson 4 pass from Everett (Lansford kick), 7:20 1st. Drive: 46 yards, 7 plays.

Philadelphia—Toney 1 run (Ruzek kick), 4:02 4th. Drive: 80 yards, 11 plays.

Los Angeles—Bell 7 run (Lansford kick), 12:46 4th. Drive: 84 yards, 7 plays.

TEAM STATISTICS

	Los Angeles	Philadelphia
FIRST DOWNS	19	14
By rushing	6	6
By passing	12	8
By penalty	1	0
THIRD DOWN EFFICIENCY	5-16	6-16
TOTAL NET YARDS	409	306
Offensive plays	71	62
Average gain per play	5.8	4.9
NET YARDS RUSHING	144	95
Total rushes	36	20
Average gain per rush	4.0	4.8
NET YARDS PASSING	265	211
Sacked-Yards lost	2-16	2-27
Gross yards passing	281	238
PASSES	18-33-2	24-40-1
Average gain per pass	7.8	5.0
PUNTS	7-37.0	9-36.3
Had blocked	0	0

A key to the Rams' victory was their ability to contain Randall Cunningham. Linebacker Kevin Greene sacked the Eagles' quarterback twice.

	Los Angeles	Philadelphia
TOTAL RETURN YARDAGE	29	91
Punt returns............................	15	5
Kickoff returns......................	14	52
Interception returns	0	34
PENALTIES-YARDS	1-5	4-35
FUMBLES-LOST	1-1	6-2
TIME OF POSSESSION............	33:38	26:22
Attendance—57,869.		

INDIVIDUAL STATISTICS

Rushing—Los Angeles, Bell 27-124, Everett 7-2, McGee 2-18; Philadelphia, Sherman 9-44, Cunningham 6-39, Toney 5-12.

Passing—Los Angeles, Everett 18-33-2—281; Philadelphia, Cunningham 24-40-1—238.

Receiving—Los Angeles, Ellard 4-87, Holohan 4-37, Delpino 3-31, McGee 3-22, Anderson 2-77, Bell 1-23, D. Johnson 1-4; Philadelphia, Byars 9-68, Toney 4-35, Jackson 3-47, R. Johnson 2-38, Sherman 2-18, Carter 2-16, Garrity 2-16.

Kickoff Returns—Los Angeles, Delpino 1-0, Brown 1-14; Philadelphia, Edwards 3-37, Higgs 1-15.

Punt Returns—Los Angeles, Henley 3-15; Philadelphia, Edwards 2-5.

Interceptions—Los Angeles, Irvin 1-0; Philadelphia, Jenkins 1-33, Joyner 1-1.

Punting—Los Angeles, Hatcher 7-37.0; Philadelphia, Tuten 8-38.4, Cunningham 1-20.0.

Field Goals—Los Angeles, Lansford 0-1 (missed: 47); Philadelphia, Ruzek 0-1 (missed: 40).

Sacks—Los Angeles, Greene 2; Philadelphia, Brown, White.

STEELERS 26, OILERS 23 (OT)

HOUSTON—The Houston Oilers like to call the Astrodome the "House of Pain" because of the way they physically abuse visiting teams. But the last two home games of 1989 brought nothing but pain to the Oilers themselves.

In their final regular-season game at the Astrodome in Week 16, the Oilers lost to the Cleveland Browns, 24-20, when a victory would

have given them their first-ever American Football Conference Central Division title. One week later, playing host to the Pittsburgh Steelers in the AFC wild-card game, the Oilers lost again, this time in overtime, 26-23.

The loss to Pittsburgh was especially hard to swallow because the Oilers had swept the teams' two regular-season games, including a 27-0 rout at the Astrodome on October 22.

"It's hard to fool a team three times," Houston quarterback Warren Moon said. "A lot of positive things happened, but we had higher expectations. We thought we were better than a wild-card team, and we thought we should have advanced further than one game, even if we were a wild card."

The Oilers' season was abruptly ended by a Pittsburgh team that had been given up for dead by many people just two weeks into the 1989 campaign. The Steelers, who lost their first two games by a cumulative score of 92-10, rebounded to win five of their last six games to clinch their first playoff berth since 1984.

"It was very emotional for our football team just to make the playoffs," said Steelers Coach Chuck Noll, whose team finished the regular season with a 9-7 record.

Pittsburgh beat Houston in dramatic fashion, with Gary Anderson kicking a season-best 50-yard field goal 3:26 into overtime. The veteran place-kicker's fourth field goal of the game set a Steeler playoff record.

"I felt real good going into that situation," said Anderson, whose longest field goal in the regular season was 49 yards. "It's not really any different than any other kick.

"What makes it doubly sweet is that nobody

Bubby Brister guided the Steelers to their upset win over the Oilers in the AFC wild-card game.

has given us much hope or credit all season."

Anderson's game-winner came four plays after Rod Woodson stripped the ball from Oilers running back Lorenzo White and then recovered it at the Houston 46-yard line. It was the Oilers' first and only play from scrimmage in the overtime period.

"I tried to cover up the ball, but somebody hit me, and it came free," White said. "I was hoping it would go out of bounds. I want to be in the game in pressure situations . . . I had my chance, and I messed it up."

"We talked all week about protecting the football because (the Steelers) are good at stripping it," Houston Coach Jerry Glanville said.

The Oilers, who had a 380-289 edge in total yards, seemed to be in contol after Moon threw two touchdown passes to Ernest Givins in the fourth quarter. Moon's nine-yard pass to Givins with six minutes left put Houston ahead, 23-16.

But the Steelers fought back, driving 82 yards on 11 plays to tie the score on Merril Hoge's two-yard touchdown run with 46 seconds remaining.

"This game was a gut-check," Noll said. "There's no question the big play was when Woodson knocked the ball loose.

"Any time you get to the playoffs and win, it's a big thing," added Noll, who had the Steelers in the playoffs for the 12th time in his 21 seasons as coach.

"That's what you work for. The third time (against Houston) was a charm. We like charms."

Steelers-Oilers
SUNDAY, DECEMBER 31
SCORE BY PERIODS

Pittsburgh	7	3	3	10	3—26
Houston	0	6	3	14	0—23

SCORING

Pittsburgh—Worley 9 run (Anderson kick), 12:07 1st. Drive: 32 yards, 5 plays.

Houston—Field goal Zendejas 26, 5:53 2nd. Drive: 87 yards, 18 plays.

Houston—Field goal Zendejas 35, 8:50 2nd. Drive: 24 yards, 5 plays.

Pittsburgh—Field goal Anderson 25, 13:03 2nd. Drive: 78 yards, 8 plays.

Houston—Field goal Zendejas 26, 3:30 3rd. Drive: 6 yards, 4 plays.

Pittsburgh—Field goal Anderson 30, 11:55 3rd. Drive: 30 yards, 7 plays.

Pittsburgh—Field goal Anderson 48, 0:30 4th. Drive: 33 yards, 9 plays.

Houston—Givins 18 pass from Moon (Zendejas kick), 5:46 4th. Drive: 80 yards, 10 plays.

Houston—Givins 9 pass from Moon (Zendejas kick), 8:58 4th. Drive: 38 yards, 5 plays.

Pittsburgh—Hoge 2 run (Anderson kick), 14:14 4th. Drive: 82 yards, 11 plays.

Pittsburgh—Field goal Anderson 50, 3:26 OT. Drive: 14 yards, 5 plays.

TEAM STATISTICS

	Pittsburgh	Houston
FIRST DOWNS	17	22
By rushing	8	2
By passing	9	18
By penalty	0	2
THIRD DOWN EFFICIENCY	3-14	8-18
TOTAL NET YARDS	289	380
Offensive plays	64	73
Average gain per play	4.5	5.2
NET YARDS RUSHING	177	65
Total rushes	30	25
Average gain per rush	5.9	2.6
NET YARDS PASSING	112	315
Sacked-Yards lost	1-15	0-0
Gross yards passing	127	315
PASSES	15-33-0	29-48-0
Average gain per pass	3.2	6.5
PUNTS	6-25.3	4-33.0
Had blocked	1	1
TOTAL RETURN YARDAGE	119	27
Punt returns	20	0
Kickoff returns	99	27
Interception returns	0	0
PENALTIES-YARDS	5-40	8-45
FUMBLES-LOST	1-1	3-2
TIME OF POSSESSION	27:42	35:44

Attendance—58,306.

INDIVIDUAL STATISTICS

Rushing—Pittsburgh, Hoge 17-100, Worley 11-54, Stone 1-22, Brister 1-1; Houston, Pinkett 8-26, White 7-13, Moon 3-12, Rozier 5-12, Highsmith 2-2.

Passing—Pittsburgh, Brister 15-33-0—177; Houston, Moon 29-48-0—315.

Receiving—Pittsburgh, Worley 4-23, Mularkey 3-40, Hoge 3-26, Lipps 3-24, Stock 1-7, Hill 1-7; Houston, Givins 11-136, Hill 6-98, Pinkett 3-24, Highsmith 3-21, Jeffires 3-16, Duncan 2-15, Rozier 1-5.

Kickoff Returns—Pittsburgh, Woodson 4-74, Stone 1-14, Thompson 1-11; Houston, K. Johnson 1-18, White 1-9.

Punt Returns—Pittsburgh, Woodson 2-20; Houston, K. Johnson 1-0.

Punting—Pittsburgh, Newsome 5-30.4; Houston, Greg Montgomery 3-44.0.

Field Goals—Pittsburgh, Anderson 4-4; Houston, Zendejas 3-4 (missed: 55).

Sacks—Houston, Jones.

DIVISIONAL PLAYOFF GAMES

BROWNS 34, BILLS 30

CLEVELAND—For the Cleveland Browns, it was almost a case of deja vu. Almost.

They were leading the Buffalo Bills, 34-30, late in the teams' American Football Conference playoff game at Cleveland Stadium. The Bills, who needed to score a touchdown after place-kicker Scott Norwood's missed extra-point attempt four minutes earlier, were methodically being driven downfield by quarterback Jim Kelly, who would finish the game with a career-high 405 yards passing.

In the 1986 AFC championship game against Denver in the same stadium, Broncos quarterback John Elway drove his team 98 yards for a touchdown in the final minutes of regulation to send the game into overtime. The Broncos eventually won, 23-20, on a field goal.

In this game, Kelly marched the Bills from their own 26-yard line to the Cleveland 11 in the final minutes. It didn't seem to be a question of whether the Bills would score a touchdown, but how?

It never happened. A wide-open Ronnie Harmon dropped a Kelly pass in the rear left corner of the Cleveland end zone with nine seconds left. Then, on the next play, Browns linebacker Clay Matthews stepped in front of a Kelly pass intended for Thurman Thomas. Matthews' interception with three seconds left sealed Cleveland's victory and sent the Bills back to Buffalo to start a long off-season.

Were the Browns thinking about their loss to Denver three years earlier?

"The thought went through my mind once or twice," cornerback Hanford Dixon admitted. "You can't help but think about that."

In a game with many big plays, none were bigger than Harmon's drop and Matthews' interception.

"I thought it was a touchdown," Buffalo wide receiver Don Beebe said. "The ball hit (Harmon) right in the hands, but those things happen."

"I'd say Ronnie Harmon catches that ball 50 times out of 50," Browns defensive end Bubba Baker said.

Despite Harmon's drop, Buffalo still had another chance. But Matthews promptly killed it by grabbing Kelly's pass at the goal line. Thomas had caught 13 passes from Kelly for 150 yards, so it didn't surprise the Browns defense when Kelly went to the same well once again.

"Thurman Thomas had been having a great day," Matthews said. "They had been going to him all day, and I had a feeling they'd try it again."

"I was not the primary receiver on that last play, but I thought Jim read the coverage at the line of scrimmage," Thomas said. "I was

Clay Matthews celebrates after his interception with three seconds left preserved Cleveland's 34-30 victory.

only open for a split second."

The two big plays in the final seconds took some of the spotlight away from what had been the game's biggest play—Cleveland rookie Eric Metcalf's 90-yard kickoff return for a touchdown in the third quarter. That touchdown increased the Browns' lead to 31-21 and came right after Thomas had caught a six-yard scoring pass from Kelly that cut Cleveland's lead to three points.

"It was probably the big play of a game where there were many big plays," Buffalo Coach Marv Levy said. "We just scored and they turn around and take that touchdown away from us."

Metcalf's touchdown was the first ever scored by a Cleveland player on a kickoff return in a playoff game.

The Browns' victory sent them into the AFC title game for the third time in four years and denied the Eastern Division-champion Bills a return trip to the conference title game.

"It's awful to lose this way," Thomas said. "I would have rather lost 34-0. We certainly had our chances in this game."

Bills - Browns
SATURDAY, JANUARY 6
SCORE BY PERIODS

Buffalo	7	7	7	9—30
Cleveland	3	14	14	3—34

SCORING
Buffalo—Reed 72 pass from Kelly (Norwood kick), 9:56 1st. Drive: 72 yards, 2 plays.

Cleveland—Field goal Bahr 45, 14:12 1st. Drive: 39 yards, 10 plays.

Cleveland—Slaughter 52 pass from Kosar (Bahr kick), 4:33 2nd. Drive: 79 yards, 7 plays.

Buffalo—Lofton 33 pass from Kelly (Norwood kick), 7:12 2nd. Drive: 66 yards, 5 plays.

Cleveland—Middleton 3 pass from Kosar (Bahr kick), 13:54 2nd. Drive: 55 yards, 8 plays.

Cleveland—Slaughter 44 pass from Kosar (Bahr kick), 4:21 3rd. Drive: 46 yards, 3 plays.

Buffalo—Thomas 6 pass from Kelly (Norwood kick), 10:22 3rd. Drive: 21 yards, 6 plays.

Cleveland—Metcalf 90 kickoff return (Bahr kick), 10:37 3rd.

Buffalo—Field goal Norwood 30, 1:08 4th. Drive: 68 yards, 11 plays.

Cleveland—Field goal Bahr 47, 8:10 4th. Drive: 38 yards, 11 plays.

Buffalo—Thomas 3 pass from Kelly (kick failed), 11:00 4th. Drive: 77 yards, 8 plays.

TEAM STATISTICS

	Buffalo	Cleveland
FIRST DOWNS	24	18
By rushing	2	10
By passing	20	8
By penalty	2	0
THIRD DOWN EFFICIENCY	6-15	6-13
TOTAL NET YARDS	453	325
Offensive plays	73	61
Average gain per play	6.2	5.3
NET YARDS RUSHING	49	90
Total rushes	18	30
Average gain per rush	2.7	3.0
NET YARDS PASSING	404	235
Sacked-Yards lost	1-1	2-16
Gross yards passing	405	251
PASSES	28-54-2	20-29-0
Average gain per pass	7.3	7.6
PUNTS	3-41.3	3-37.7
Had blocked	0	0
TOTAL RETURN YARDAGE	109	180
Punt returns	4	0
Kickoff returns	105	180
Interception returns	0	0
PENALTIES-YARDS	6-35	5-30
FUMBLES-LOST	2-1	1-1
TIME OF POSSESSION	25:44	34:16

Attendance—77,706.

INDIVIDUAL STATISTICS
Rushing—Buffalo, Thomas 10-27, Kinnebrew 7-17, Kelly 1-5; Cleveland, Mack 12-62, Tillman 1-8, Manoa 3-6, Metcalf 4-2, Langhorne 1-0, Kosar 3-minus 1.

Passing—Buffalo, Kelly 28-54-2—405; Cleveland, Kosar 20-29-0—251.

Receiving—Buffalo, Thomas 13-150, Reed 6-115, Harmon 4-50, Lofton 3-33, Beebe 1-17, Kinnebrew 1-7; Cleveland, Langhorne 6-48, Newsome 4-35, Slaughter 3-114, Middleton 3-12, Mack 2-19, Brennan 1-15, Metcalf 1-8.

Kickoff Returns—Buffalo, Harmon 3-52, Beebe 2-53; Cleveland, Metcalf 4-159, Oliphant 2-21.

Punt Returns—Buffalo, Sutton 1-4; Cleveland, McNeil 1-0.

Interceptions—Cleveland, Matthews 1-0, Harper 1-0.

Punting—Buffalo, Kidd 3-41.3; Cleveland, Wagner 3-37.7.

Field Goals—Buffalo, Norwood 1-1; Cleveland, Bahr 2-3 (missed: 45).

Sacks—Buffalo, Talley, Radecic ½, B. Smith ½; Cleveland, Hairston.

49ers 41, VIKINGS 13
SAN FRANCISCO—Even though they were an important part of the best team in the National Football League, members of San Francisco's offensive line didn't feel they got much respect during the 1989 season.

The defending Super Bowl champions compiled a league-best 14-2 record in '89, but the only offensive players who received much acclaim were quarterback Joe Montana, running back Roger Craig and wide receivers Jerry Rice and John Taylor, all of whom made the Pro Bowl. Guard Guy McIntyre was the only offensive lineman to receive that honor.

"It's been insinuated that we're the worst offensive line in the league," guard Bruce Collie said.

Collie was exaggerating, but there was no doubt the San Francisco offensive line played its best game of the season in a 41-13 victory over the Minnesota Vikings in a first-round NFC playoff game. The 49ers' line dominated a Vikings' defensive front four that included Pro Bowlers Keith Millard and Chris Doleman.

"Our offensive line just had a great day," said Montana, who completed 13 of 16 passes for 210 yards and four touchdowns in the first half alone. "When you get the time I had, and with the guys I have to throw to, good things are going to happen."

Nothing but good things happened to the San Francisco offense in this game. It rolled up 403 yards against a defense that had been ranked No. 1 in the NFL throughout the 16-week regular season. The 49ers' offense was on cruise control in the second half after amassing 320 yards on 32 plays (a 10-yard average) en route to a 27-3 halftime lead.

"Our line just exploded. They were aggressive. They took control," said Craig, who rushed for 125 yards on 18 carries to become the first player to rush for more than 100 yards against Minnesota all season.

"It's fun for any running back to be in a situation like that."

The Minnesota defense came into the game having allowed the fewest average yards per game (261) while recording the most sacks (71) during the regular season. Doleman led the NFL with 21 sacks while Millard (18 sacks) was the league's consensus Defensive Player of the Year.

It almost was assumed that the Vikings' defensive front four would run roughshod against the 49ers. But that storyline never played out. Doleman and Millard had just two tackles each and Montana was not sacked—and rarely even touched. Most of his 17 completions were short but effective.

Chris Doleman (left) and other Minnesota defenders had a rough time against San Francisco's offensive line in the 49ers' 41-13 win.

"Even if we didn't have people open, I wanted him to throw the ball away," 49ers offensive coordinator Mike Holmgren said. "I didn't want him holding it, holding it, bang, taking a sack."

One of Montana's biggest completions was to Rice in the first quarter. The fleet receiver caught the ball seven yards beyond the line of scrimmage before evading the Minnesota defense to score a 72-yard touchdown. The touchdown came just 23 seconds after a 38-yard field goal by Rich Karlis had given the visitors a 3-0 lead. Rice's touchdown seemed to take something out of the Vikings.

"After that, we just started going into a big shell," said Minnesota defensive coordinator Floyd Peters, whose defense yielded 20 straight points in the second period. "We didn't play with any fight or aggressiveness."

"(The 49ers) had a good game plan and we couldn't stay with them," Millard said.

The 49ers' triumph propelled them into the NFC championship game for the fifth time in nine years and kept alive their hopes for a second straight Super Bowl title.

"All during the week, for six days, (the Vikings' defense) won the battle as far as what

was written (in the newspapers)," 49ers center Jesse Sapolu said. "Today was the only day we won, but it's the only day that counts."

Vikings-49ers
SATURDAY, JANUARY 6
SCORE BY PERIODS

Minnesota	3	0	3	7—13
San Francisco	7	20	0	14—41

SCORING

Minnesota—Field goal Karlis 38, 9:39 1st. Drive: 70 yards, 14 plays.

San Francisco—Rice 72 pass from Montana (Cofer kick), 10:02 1st. Drive: 72 yards, 1 play.

San Francisco—Jones 8 pass from Montana (Cofer kick), 1:59 2nd. Drive: 74 yards, 7 plays.

San Francisco—Taylor 8 pass from Montana (kick failed), 8:42 2nd. Drive: 21 yards, 3 plays.

San Francisco—Rice 13 pass from Montana (Cofer kick), 13:57 2nd. Drive: 51 yards, 9 plays.

Minnesota—Field goal Karlis 44, 1:46 3rd. Drive: 44 yards, 7 plays.

San Francisco—Lott 58 interception return (Cofer kick), 1:43 4th.

San Francisco—Craig 4 run (Cofer kick), 6:04 4th. Drive: 4 yards, 1 play.

Minnesota—Fenney 3 run (Karlis kick), 9:13 4th. Drive: 77 yards, 10 plays.

	Minnesota	San Francisco
FIRST DOWNS	25	22
By rushing	7	10
By passing	17	11
By penalty	1	1
THIRD DOWN EFFICIENCY	2-10	3-9
TOTAL NET YARDS	385	403
Offensive plays	79	57
Average gain per play	4.9	7.1
NET YARDS RUSHING	86	162
Total rushes	21	32
Average gain per rush	4.1	5.1
NET YARDS PASSING	299	241
Sacked-Yards lost	4-39	0-0
Gross yards passing	338	241
PASSES	31-54-4	17-25-0
Average gain per pass	5.2	9.6
PUNTS	5-25.6	4-30.8
Had blocked	1	0
TOTAL RETURN YARDAGE	148	217
Punt returns	18	6
Kickoff returns	130	84
Interception returns	0	127
PENALTIES-YARDS	4-31	9-65
FUMBLES-LOST	1-1	1-1
TIME OF POSSESSION	31:20	28:40

Attendance—64,585.

INDIVIDUAL STATISTICS

Rushing—Minnesota, Wilson 3-29, Walker 9-29, Dozier 3-13, Fenney 4-8, Gannon 2-7; San Francisco, Craig 18-125, Rathman 7-24, Flagler 5-13, Montana 2-0.

Passing—Minnesota, Wilson 9-17-2—84, Kramer 9-19-1—110, Gannon 13-18-1—144; San Francisco, Montana 17-24-0—241, Young 0-1-0—0.

Receiving—Minnesota, Jordan 9-149, Carter 4-44, Fenney 4-15, Anderson 3-18, Dozier 3-15, Gustafson 2-46, Lewis 2-19, Jones 2-18, Walker 2-14; San Francisco, Rice 6-114, Taylor 3-50, Rathman 3-29, Jones 3-24, Henderson 2-24.

Kickoff Returns—Minnesota, Walker 5-97, Dozier 1-19, Lewis 1-14; San Francisco, Tillman 2-26, Flagler 1-58, Rathman 1-0.

Punt Returns—Minnesota, Lewis 2-18; San Francisco, Taylor 2-6.

Interceptions—San Francisco, Lott 1-58, McKyer 1-41, Brooks 1-28, Griffin 1-0.

Punting—Minnesota, Scribner 4-32.0; San Francisco, Helton 4-30.8.

Field Goals—Minnesota, Karlis 2-2; San Francisco, Cofer 0-2 (missed: 31, 32).

Sacks—San Francisco, Fagan 2, Haley, Stubbs.

RAMS 19, GIANTS 13 (OT)

EAST RUTHERFORD, N.J.—After Los Angeles had defeated Philadelphia, 21-7, in the National Football Conference wild-card game, Rams linebacker Kevin Greene was asked about his team's chances against its next opponent, the New York Giants.

"We'll win," he said. "I'm positive we'll win."

That was a big prediction, considering that the Giants posted a 12-4 record in 1989 while winning the Eastern Division championship. And because they were a wild-card team, the Rams would once again have to play on the road, marking the third straight week the Rams would have to cross the country to play an Eastern team (at Foxboro, Mass., Philadelphia and New York).

But the frequent-flier miles didn't bother the Rams. They had to play overtime, but they beat the Giants, 19-13, on a 30-yard touchdown

pass from Jim Everett to Willie Anderson just 66 seconds into the extra period. It was the fastest overtime score ever in an NFL playoff game and put the Rams into the NFC championship game the following week.

"It was an all-out blitz," said Giants cornerback Mark Collins, who was beaten by Anderson on the play. "It was me and the wide receiver. We had to do something. The ball was already close to the end zone. They were already in good position for a field goal."

The Rams, however, didn't need a field goal after a mistake by the Giants gave them a huge break. New York's Sheldon White was flagged for pass interference against Anderson two plays before the touchdown. The 27-yard penalty put the ball at the Giants' 25-yard line and, after a five-yard penalty against Los Angeles, Everett hit a streaking Anderson down the right sideline for the game-winning score.

"The ball wasn't catchable," White said in his own defense. "It wasn't even close. We were both going for the ball and the ball was way out, five yards wide. Superman couldn't have caught that ball."

Anderson, who also caught a 20-yard pass from Everett in the second quarter for the Rams' other touchdown, begged to differ.

"(White) got me. As soon as I reached for the ball, he touched me and you're not allowed to do that downfield. It's a penalty."

"The defensive man did not play the ball, he played the man," said field judge Bernie Kukar, who made the call. "The ball was still in the air. He wrapped up the receiver while the ball was still catchable. That is pass interference."

The Giants were incensed by Kukar's call, but they probably should never have let the game go into overtime in the first place. They led, 13-7, after three periods before the Rams put together drives of 69 and 75 yards that resulted in two Mike Lansford field goals that forced overtime.

In the first half, the Giants badly outplayed the Rams but trailed, 7-6, at the intermission. A pass by New York quarterback Phil Simms in the final minute was tipped by Jerry Gray and intercepted by Michael Stewart, who returned the ball 29 yards to the Giants' 20. Everett hit Anderson for a touchdown on the following play to give Los Angeles a one-point lead.

"We were being outplayed most of the half and we went in with a lead," said Everett, who completed 25 of 44 passes for 315 yards. "That kind of told us we might have some breaks."

The Giants regained the lead at 13-7 on Ottis Anderson's two-yard touchdown run late in the third period. But that 14-play, 82-yard march turned out to be New York's only touchdown drive of the game. The Giants' offense never solved a Rams defense that finished 21st overall—last against the pass—during the regular season.

New York didn't have a possession in the overtime.

"I'm sorry we had to lose this way," Giants Coach Bill Parcells said, "but I think it was more than just one play."

Rams-Giants
SUNDAY, JANUARY 7
SCORE BY PERIODS

Los Angeles Rams	0	7	0	6	6—19
New York Giants	6	0	7	0	0—13

SCORING

New York—Field goal Allegre 35, 4:33 1st. Drive: 57 yards, 8 plays.

New York—Field goal Allegre 41, 14:05 1st. Drive: 65 yards, 13 plays.

Los Angeles—Anderson 20 pass from Everett (Lansford kick), 14:43 2nd. Drive: 20 yards, 1 play.

New York—Anderson 2 run (Allegre kick), 13:03 3rd. Drive: 82 yards, 14 plays.

Los Angeles—Field goal Lansford 31, 2:09 4th. Drive: 69 yards, 10 plays.

Los Angeles—Field goal Lansford 22, 11:59 4th. Drive: 75 yards, 13 plays.

Los Angeles—Anderson 30 pass from Everett (no kick), 1:06 OT. Drive: 77 yards, 4 plays.

TEAM STATISTICS

	Los Angeles	New York
FIRST DOWNS	26	20
By rushing	6	11
By passing	18	8
By penalty	2	1
THIRD DOWN EFFICIENCY	7-14	9-16
TOTAL NET YARDS	448	344
Offensive plays	70	67
Average gain per play	6.4	5.1
NET YARDS RUSHING	146	171
Total rushes	24	36
Average gain per rush	6.1	4.8
NET YARDS PASSING	302	173
Sacked-Yards lost	2-13	1-7
Gross yards passing	315	180
PASSES	25-44-1	14-30-1
Average gain per pass	6.6	5.6
PUNTS	4-30.3	5-37.2
Had blocked	0	0
TOTAL RETURN YARDAGE	126	75
Punt returns	—1	0
Kickoff returns	98	75
Interception returns	29	0
PENALTIES-YARDS	5-35	4-59
FUMBLES-LOST	1-1	3-0
TIME OF POSSESSION	28:19	32:47

Attendance—76,325.

INDIVIDUAL STATISTICS

Rushing—Los Angeles, Bell 19-87, McGee 3-34, Everett 2-25; New York, Anderson 24-120, Tillman 7-25, Simms 3-16, Meggett 1-7, Carthon 1-3.

Passing—Los Angeles, Everett 25-44-1—315; New York, Simms 14-29-1—180, Meggett 0-1-0—0.

Receiving—Los Angeles, Ellard 8-125, Holohan 5-48, Brown 3-35, Johnson 3-15, Anderson 2-50, McGee 2-31, Bell 2-11; New York, Meggett 4-52, Mowatt 3-52, Anderson 3-minus 2, Baker 2-46, Manuel 1-24, Carthon 1-8.

Kickoff Returns—Los Angeles, Brown 1-38, Delpino 4-60; New York, Meggett 1-25, Ingram 2-41, Cross 1-9.

Punt Returns—Los Angeles, Irvin 1-3, Henley 2-(minus 4); New York, Meggett 1-0.

Interceptions—Los Angeles, Stewart 1-29; New York, Collins 1-0.

Punting—Los Angeles, Hatcher 4-30.3; New York, Landeta 5-37.2.

Field Goals—Los Angeles, Lansford 2-2; New York, Allegre 2-2.

Sacks—Los Angeles, Greene; New York, Taylor 2.

Willie Anderson makes the game-winning catch in overtime to give the Rams a 19-13 victory over the Giants.

BRONCOS 24, STEELERS 23

DENVER—On paper, this American Football Conference playoff game figured to be a mismatch. It turned out to be anything but.

When Pittsburgh met Denver at Mile High Stadium in Week 9 of the regular season, the Broncos pounded the Steelers, 34-7, and held the Pittsburgh offense to just seven first downs and 170 total yards. Denver's offense, by comparison, had 22 first downs and 414 yards.

By the time the teams met again nine weeks later, the Steelers looked like a completely different offensive team. They scored on five of their first seven possessions, rolled up 404 total yards and led at various times by scores of 10-0, 17-7 and 23-17. Pittsburgh averaged an NFL-low 250 offensive yards during the regular season but had that many in the first half alone against the Broncos.

"We were down all day, but we had confidence we could come back," Denver running back Bobby Humphrey said. "When you have guys with experience like we do, you always know you're in the game."

The Broncos finally did come back, putting together a nine-play, 71-yard touchdown drive in the final seven minutes to pull out a 24-23 victory. Melvin Bratton's one-yard run with 2:27 left gave the Broncos their first lead of the game.

"The bottom line is, we never give up," said Broncos quarterback John Elway, who completed an 18-yard pass to Mark Jackson and a 36-yard flea flicker to Vance Johnson on the game-winning drive. "That's been a trademark of this team all year. It's the reason we are where we are."

The Broncos had the AFC's best record during the regular season but certainly didn't play like an 11-5 team in the first 3½ quarters against Pittsburgh. The Steelers used an effective running game to build their leads, including 13 runs for 65 yards on their first possession that resulted in a Gary Anderson field goal.

Running back Merril Hoge, who finished with 120 yards rushing on 16 attempts, had 100 before halftime and 75 on five carries in the first period alone.

"We knew they were going to try to run the ball," Denver defensive coordinator Wade Phillips said. "They didn't do much we didn't expect. They just executed well, and we didn't tackle well at times."

Phillips received a lot of credit in 1989 for taking a defense that finished 22nd in the league in 1988 and molding it into the NFL's third-best unit a year later. The Broncos allowed fewer points (226) than any other team in 1989.

"I never thought we would steamroll (the Steelers)," Denver Coach Dan Reeves said. "They were playing too well and had a lot of confidence."

Pittsburgh came into the game as one of the hottest teams in the NFL. It had won five of its last six regular-season games to qualify for the playoffs and then edged Houston, 26-23, in overtime in the AFC wild-card game.

The Steelers committed two turnovers and one of them proved to be a killer. Rookie running back Tim Worley fumbled after being hit by linebacker Greg Kragen early in the second half, with Tyrone Braxton recovering the ball for Denver at the Steelers' 37-yard line. On the next play, Elway threw a touchdown pass to Johnson to tie the game at 17-17.

"He (Worley) tried to turn upfield," Kragen said. "He's a big guy. I didn't think he'd try to juke me. I thought he'd try to run over me. I just tried to hit him as hard as I could."

Kragen knocked the ball out of Worley's hands and the Broncos knocked the Steelers out of their first playoff since 1984.

"You can't say we played well enough to win," Pittsburgh quarterback Bubby Brister said, "because that's not true. We didn't win."

Steelers-Broncos
SUNDAY, JANUARY 7
SCORE BY PERIODS

Pittsburgh	3	14	3	3—23
Denver	0	10	7	7—24

SCORING
Pittsburgh—Field goal Anderson 32, 7:47 1st. Drive: 65 yards, 13 plays.
Pittsburgh—Hoge 7 run (Anderson kick), 1:38 2nd. Drive: 93 yards, 5 plays.
Denver—Bratton 1 run (Treadwell kick), 8:38 2nd. Drive: 75 yards, 12 plays.
Pittsburgh—Lipps 9 pass from Brister (Anderson kick), 14:34 2nd. Drive: 77 yards, 12 plays.
Denver—Field goal Treadwell 43, 15:00 2nd. Drive: 41 yards, 3 plays.
Denver—Johnson 37 pass from Elway (Treadwell kick), 1:58 3rd. Drive: 37 yards, 1 play.
Pittsburgh—Field goal Anderson 35, 7:26 3rd. Drive: 62 yards, 10 plays.
Pittsburgh—Field goal Anderson 32, 0:07 4th. Drive: 34 yards, 10 plays.
Denver—Bratton 1 run (Treadwell kick), 12:33 4th. Drive: 71 yards, 9 plays.

TEAM STATISTICS
	Pittsburgh	Denver
FIRST DOWNS	19	19
By rushing	7	8
By passing	12	9
By penalty	0	2
THIRD DOWN EFFICIENCY	9-15	6-10
TOTAL NET YARDS	404	364
Offensive plays	61	52
Average gain per play	6.6	7.0
NET YARDS RUSHING	175	138
Total rushes	32	31
Average gain per rush	5.5	4.5
NET YARDS PASSING	229	226
Sacked-Yards lost	0-0	1-13
Gross yards passing	229	239
PASSES	19-29-0	12-20-1
Average gain per pass	7.9	10.8
PUNTS	2-43.0	4-37.5
Had blocked	0	0
TOTAL RETURN YARDAGE	59	125
Punt returns	0	6
Kickoff returns	33	119
Interception returns	26	0
PENALTIES-YARDS	8-50	2-19
FUMBLES-LOST	2-2	1-0
TIME OF POSSESSION	34:14	25:46
Attendance—75,868.		

INDIVIDUAL STATISTICS
Rushing—Pittsburgh, Hoge 16-120, Worley 13-50, Brister 2-4, Lipps 1-1; Denver, Humphrey 18-85, Elway 7-44, Bratton 4-3, Sewell 1-6, Winder 1-0.

Passing—Pittsburgh, Brister 19-29-0—229; Denver, Elway 12-20-1—239.

Receiving—Pittsburgh, Hoge 8-60, Lipps 3-29, Stone 3-18, Mularkey 2-36, Worley 1-33, Stock 1-30, Thompson 1-23; Denver, Jackson 5-111, Johnson 3-85, Young 2-22, Nattiel 1-15, Humphrey 1-6.

Kickoff Returns—Pittsburgh, Woodson 2-33; Denver, Bell 2-62, Carrington 2-51, Bratton 1-6.

Punt Returns—Denver, Johnson 1-6.

Interceptions—Pittsburgh, Everett 1-26.

Punting—Pittsburgh, Newsome 2-43.0; Denver, Horan 3-44.3, Elway 1-17.0.

Field Goals—Pittsburgh, Anderson 3-3; Denver, Treadwell 1-1.

Sacks—Pittsburgh, Jones.

AFC CHAMPIONSHIP GAME

BRONCOS 37, BROWNS 21

DENVER—The Denver Broncos have developed a reputation over the past few years of a National Football League team unable to win the "Big Game."

Blowout losses to the New York Giants (39-20) and Washington Redskins (42-10) in Super Bowls XXI and XXII, respectively, have earned the Broncos their rep, but what does that make the Cleveland Browns? Denver beat Cleveland in the American Football Conference championship game both times they advanced to the Super Bowl, but—because the scores of those games were close (23-20 in overtime and 38-33)—the Browns' reputation has been largely untarnished.

That may change following the Broncos' 37-21 win over the Browns in the 1989 conference title game. The Browns, regular-season AFC Central Division champions, played one of their worst games of the season with a trip to the Super Bowl on the line.

"I never felt we were in sync," Cleveland offensive tackle Rickey Bolden said. "We just didn't go get 'em."

The Browns were certainly out of sync on offense. Quarterback Bernie Kosar, who was nursing shoulder, elbow and finger injuries, completed just 19 of 44 pass attempts and was intercepted three times. His ailments forced him to throw more sidearm than usual, resulting in six of his passes being batted down by defensive linemen.

"I've had physical problems that are well documented, but I haven't used that as an excuse in the past and I don't plan to start now," said Kosar, who also was sacked four times.

Denver quarterback John Elway, on the other hand, was spectacular. He completed 20 of 36 passes for 385 yards and three touchdowns without throwing an interception. Including his team-high 39 yards rushing, Elway accounted for a whopping 424 of Denver's 497 yards in total offense.

Broncos Coach Dan Reeves was among the impressed.

"The biggest thing we saw today was what a great athlete John Elway is," Reeves said. "I think he showed everyone today how talented he is. He made some outstanding athletic plays, running and throwing the ball, and never quit. He did a tremendous job."

Elway saved his best plays for third downs, just when it appeared the Cleveland defense would be forcing a Denver punt. The Broncos converted nine of 18 third-down attempts, with most of those third-down plays setting up or resulting in Denver touchdowns.

"This was the best we played all year," Elway said. "We handled the lead better than any game I can remember."

Denver's Michael Young eludes Browns cornerback Frank Minnifield to score the game's first touchdown.

The Broncos' four touchdown drives covered 82, 80, 60 and 80 yards.

"We just gave Denver too many big plays, the kind of big plays you shouldn't give anybody," Browns Coach Bud Carson said. "Our cornerbacks kept falling down...."

Cleveland cornerbacks Frank Minnifield and Hanford Dixon, each of whom had been voted to the previous three Pro Bowls, played as though the field was one large oil slick. Minnifield fell down trying to cover wide receiver Michael Young on a 70-yard pass play on Denver's first touchdown and Dixon fell on a 53-yard Elway-to-Young pass on the Broncos' second touchdown drive.

Later in the game, after the Browns had narrowed a 24-7 Denver lead to 24-21, Dixon fell down again on Denver's next possession while trying to cover Vance Johnson on a 23-yard pass from Elway.

"There's a CB (cornerback) after my name in the lineup, not an HC (head coach)," said Minnifield, who was beaten later in the game on a 39-yard Elway touchdown pass to Sammy Winder. "I'm not paid to make evaluations like that."

Minnifield need not have felt that he was the only Cleveland player to play poorly on this day. Kosar, who completed just seven of 23

The Broncos' John Elway beat Cleveland in the AFC title game with both his legs and his arm.

Cleveland	0	0	21	0—21
Denver	3	7	14	13—37

SCORING

Denver Field goal Treadwell 29, 12:59 1st. Drive: 20 yards, 5 plays.

Denver—Young 70 pass from Elway (Treadwell kick), 9:03 2nd. Drive: 82 yards, 4 plays.

Cleveland—Brennan 27 pass from Kosar (Bahr kick), 3:19 3rd. Drive: 71 yards, 8 plays.

Denver—Mobley 5 pass from Elway (Treadwell kick), 7:00 3rd. Drive: 80 yards, 6 plays.

Denver—Winder 7 run (Treadwell kick), 10:41 3rd. Drive: 60 yards, 6 plays.

Cleveland—Brennan 10 pass from Kosar (Bahr kick), 12:48 3rd. Drive: 72 yards, 6 plays.

Cleveland—Manoa 2 run (Bahr kick), 14:59 3rd. Drive: 2 yards, 2 plays.

Denver—Winder 39 pass from Elway (Treadwell kick), 2:25 4th. Drive: 80 yards, 6 plays.

Denver—Field goal Treadwell 34, 6:38 4th. Drive: 22 yards, 7 plays.

Denver—Field goal Treadwell 31, 13:00 4th. Drive: 34 yards, 10 plays.

TEAM STATISTICS

	Cleveland	Denver
FIRST DOWNS	14	22
By rushing	3	6
By passing	11	14
By penalty	0	2
THIRD DOWN EFFICIENCY	3-13	9-18
TOTAL NET YARDS	256	497
Offensive plays	62	76
Average gain per play	4.1	6.5
NET YARDS RUSHING	66	120
Total rushes	14	39
Average gain per rush	4.7	3.1
NET YARDS PASSING	190	377
Sacked-Yards lost	4-20	1-8
Gross yards passing	210	385
PASSES	19-44-3	20-36-0
Average gain per pass	4.0	10.2
PUNTS	8-42.3	5-46.4
Had blocked	0	0
TOTAL RETURN YARDAGE	137	50
Punt returns	7	36
Kickoff returns	130	0
Interception returns	0	14
PENALTIES-YARDS	8-55	1-5
FUMBLES-LOST	3-0	2-2
TIME OF POSSESSION	23:07	36:53
Attendance—76,005.		

INDIVIDUAL STATISTICS

Rushing—Cleveland, Mack 6-36, Kosar 2-22, Manoa 2-5, Metcalf 3-4, Langhorne 1-minus 1; Denver, Elway 5-39, Winder 21-37, Humphrey 8-23, Sewell 4-17, Bratton 1-4.

Passing—Cleveland, Kosar 19-44-3—210; Denver, Elway 20-36-0—385.

Receiving—Cleveland, Langhorne 5-78, Brennan 5-58, Slaughter 3-36, Mack 2-8, Metcalf 2-7, Tillman 1-15, Manoa 1-8; Denver, Johnson 7-91, Sewell 3-55, Young 2-123, Winder 2-39, Jackson 2-25, Mobley 2-22, Humphrey 1-23, Bratton 1-7.

Kickoff Returns—Cleveland, Metcalf 6-118, K. Jones 1-12.

Punt Returns—Cleveland, McNeil 1-7; Denver, Johnson 4-36.

Interceptions—Denver, D. Smith 2-13, Corrington 1-1.

Punting—Cleveland, Wagner 8-42.3; Denver, Horan 5-46.4.

Field Goals—Cleveland, none attempted; Denver, Treadwell 3-4 (54-yard attempt blocked).

Sacks—Cleveland, Hairston; Denver, Townsend, Carreker, Fletcher 2.

passes in the first half, momentarily came out of his doldrums by directing the Browns on an eight-play, 71-yard scoring drive on their first possession of the second half, completing the march with a 27-yard touchdown pass to Brian Brennan to cut the Broncos' lead to 10-7.

But the Broncos responded immediately, driving 80 yards in six plays on their next possession to regain a 10-point lead (17-7) on a five-yard Elway touchdown pass to tight end Orson Mobley. Later, Elway directed a 60-yard drive for another Denver touchdown, which came on a seven-yard run by Winder. Elway kept that drive alive with a 25-yard scramble on a third-down play before Dixon aided the Denver cause by holding the Broncos' Steve Sewell on an unsuccessful pass play at the Cleveland 12-yard line.

The Broncos' victory put them into the Super Bowl for the third time in four years, where their opponent would be the defending league-champion San Francisco 49ers.

This is precisely the step at which the 1986 and 1987 Denver teams had stumbled.

"I know it's great to win the AFC championship," Elway said, "but if we don't win the (Super Bowl), it won't mean a hell of a lot.

"I'm thrilled to death that I get to go to (the Super Bowl) again. We're a better team this time."

NFC CHAMPIONSHIP GAME

49ers 30, RAMS 3

SAN FRANCISCO—The only things that appear certain in life are death, taxes and the excellence of San Francisco 49ers quarterback Joe Montana.

Montana has been as good—but never better—than he was in leading the 49ers to a 30-3 rout of the Los Angeles Rams in the National Football Conference championship game. He completed 26 of 30 pass attempts for 262 yards and his 86.7 completion percentage set an NFC title-game record. Montana completed 18 of 21 passes to stake San Francisco to a 21-3 halftime lead before spending most of the second half handing the ball off to running backs Roger Craig and Tom Rathman.

"The poise that Joe shows in these kind of games is just amazing," said San Francisco's George Seifert, who was trying to guide the 49ers to their second straight Super Bowl championship in his rookie season as coach.

The last team to win back-to-back Super Bowl titles was the Pittsburgh Steelers in 1978-79.

Seifert's team was within one victory of accomplishing that feat after completely destroying a Rams team that had split with the 49ers in two regular season games. The Rams, who felt they should have won both of those matchups (the 49ers had to rally from two 17-point deficits to win the second game), did not lack for confidence coming into the conference title game.

"We are the road warriors," Rams quarterback Jim Everett proclaimed, citing his team's 21-7 and 19-13 (in overtime) victories at Philadelphia and New York, respectively, that put Los Angeles into the NFC championship game. "We are going for the jugular."

Unfortunately for Everett, all the blood spilled in this game belonged to the Rams. The 49ers methodically carved them to pieces with an offensive and defensive display that was shocking in its simplicity and awesome in its finality. The final score could have been much worse.

"I don't think (the Rams) have much to say now," 49ers wide receiver Jerry Rice said.

The Rams actually scored first, taking a 3-0 lead 5:22 into the game on a 23-yard field goal by Mike Lansford. They probably should have gotten more, but the Los Angeles offense bogged down and the Rams failed to score a touchdown on three plays from the San Francisco 9-yard line.

The key play of the game, however, came on the Rams' next possession. On a second-and-three play from the San Francisco 40, wide receiver Willie (Flipper) Anderson ran a streak pattern down the right sideline while the offense faked an end-around, hoping 49ers free safety Ronnie Lott would fall for the running play. The San Francisco secondary changed responsibilities at the last moment and no one moved to cover Anderson, who was left wide open.

Everett lofted a pass to Anderson that appeared to be a certain Los Angeles touchdown, but Lott—who had to run nearly the width of the field to get near the play—tipped the ball away at the last moment.

Instead of taking a 10-0 advantage, the Rams' lead remained at three.

"Ronnie saw the guy and made a heckuva break. He saved us," 49ers cornerback Eric Wright said. "If those guys would've scored then, the momentum would've swung the other way."

"It was the play of the game," Rams Coach John Robinson conceded. "After that, we didn't get much going."

The play inspired the 49ers as much as it deflated the Rams. On San Francisco's next possession, Montana directed an 89-yard drive that ended with a 20-yard touchdown pass to tight end Brent Jones. After cornerback Tim McKyer intercepted an Everett pass on the Rams' next possession, the 49ers were at it again, with a one-yard touchdown run by Craig five plays later increasing the 49ers' lead to 14-3.

The rout was on. An 18-yard touchdown pass from Montana to John Taylor and three Mike Cofer field goals rounded out the San Francisco scoring while the Rams never put another point on the scoreboard.

"We just couldn't do enough on offense to make the game competitive," said Robinson, whose offense mustered just 156 total yards after getting a combined 857 in the victories over the Eagles and Giants. In the second half, the Rams managed just 33 yards on 20 plays from scrimmage.

Everett was intercepted three times and completed just 16 of his 36 passes for a season-low 141 yards. The L.A. running game produced just 26 yards on 10 attempts, none resulting in a first down. It was the first time in 1989 that the Rams had failed to score at least 10 points in a game. It also was the Rams' fourth straight appearance without a touchdown in an NFC title game (1978, '79 and '85 were the others).

The victory was San Francisco's 16th in 18 games and perhaps its most impressive. The 49ers were at the top of their game and ready to challenge for the franchise's fourth Super Bowl title in nine years.

"This is just as exciting, maybe more so, than the other Super Bowls," Montana said. "That's because we have a chance to repeat, and that hasn't been done for a long time."

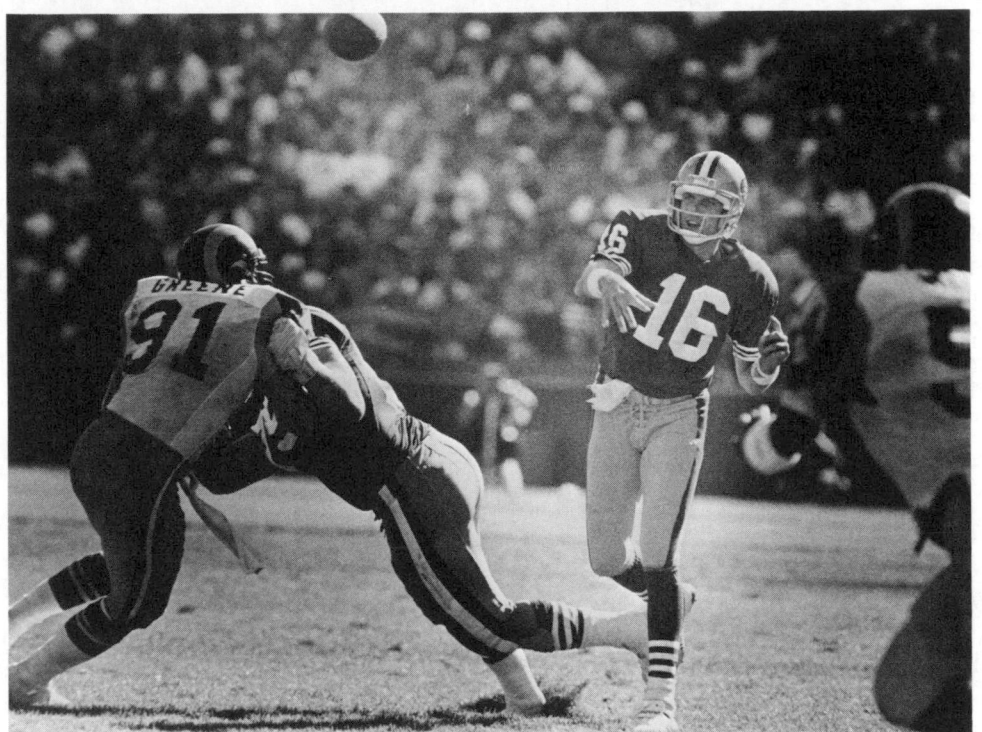

Joe Montana completed 26 of 30 passes for 262 yards and two touchdowns in San Francisco's 30-3 victory over the Rams in the NFC championship game.

Rams-49ers

SUNDAY, JANUARY 14

SCORE BY PERIODS

Los Angeles Rams	3	0	0	0— 3
San Francisco	0	21	3	6—30

SCORING

Los Angeles—Field goal Lansford 23, 5:22 1st. Drive: 44 yards, 10 plays.

San Francisco—Jones 20 pass from Montana (Cofer kick), 3:33 2nd. Drive: 89 yards, 13 plays.

San Francisco—Craig 1 run (Cofer kick), 7:49 2nd. Drive: 27 yards, 5 plays.

San Francisco—Taylor 18 pass from Montana (Cofer kick), 14:51 2nd. Drive: 87 yards, 14 plays.

San Francisco—Field goal Cofer 28, 7:16 3rd. Drive: 61 yards, 12 plays.

San Francisco—Field goal Cofer 36, 0:04 4th. Drive: 33 yards, 7 plays.

San Francisco—Field goal Cofer 25, 9:22 4th. Drive: 73 yards, 14 plays.

TEAM STATISTICS

	Los Angeles	San Francisco
FIRST DOWNS	9	29
By rushing	0	12
By passing	9	16
By penalty	0	1
THIRD DOWN EFFICIENCY	3-12	7-13
TOTAL NET YARDS	156	442
Offensive plays	47	76
Average gain per play	3.3	5.8
NET YARDS RUSHING	26	179
Total rushes	10	44
Average gain per rush	2.6	4.1
NET YARDS PASSING	130	263
Sacked-Yards lost	1-11	1-5

	Los Angeles	San Francisco
Gross yards passing	141	268
PASSES	16-36-3	27-31-0
Average gain per pass	3.5	8.2
PUNTS	7-31.4	2-31.0
Had blocked	0	0
TOTAL RETURN YARDAGE	156	93
Punt returns	10	2
Kickoff returns	146	35
Interception returns	0	56
PENALTIES-YARDS	1-10	4-40
FUMBLES-LOST	1-0	3-2
TIME OF POSSESSION	20:12	39:48

Attendance—64,769.

INDIVIDUAL STATISTICS

Rushing—Los Angeles, Bell 8-20, Gary 1-3, Delpino 1-3; San Francisco, Craig 23-93, Rathman 10-63, Flagler 8-19, Montana 1-4, Henderson 1-1, Young 1-minus 1.

Passing—Los Angeles, Everett 16-36-3—141; San Francisco, Montana 26-30-0—262, Young 1-1-0—6.

Receiving—Los Angeles, McGee 7-53, Holohan 3-26, Bell 2-23, Ellard 2-18, Anderson 1-14, Johnson 1-7; San Francisco, Rice 6-55, Rathman 6-48, Jones 4-46, Taylor 4-45, Craig 3-40, Sherrard 2-21, Wilson 1-7, Williams 1-6.

Kickoff Returns—Los Angeles, Delpino 4-91, Brown 2-51; San Francisco, Flagler 1-19, Tillman 1-16.

Punt Returns—Los Angeles, Irvin 1-0; San Francisco, Taylor 1-4.

Interceptions—San Francisco, McKyer 1-27, Turner 1-15, Lott 1-14.

Punting—Los Angeles, Hatcher 7-31.4; San Francisco, Helton 2-31.0.

Field Goals—Los Angeles, Lansford 1-1; San Francisco, Cofer 3-4 (missed: 38).

Sacks—Los Angeles, Kelm; San Francisco, Roberts.

Team of the '80s Does It Again

By PAUL ATTNER
National Correspondent

NEW ORLEANS—This one was over early. But for the Denver Broncos, it seemed to take forever to end.

The San Francisco 49ers, pro football's Team of the 1980s, entered Super Bowl XXIV at the Louisiana Superdome January 28 needing a victory over the American Football Conference champion Broncos to become the first National Football League team since the 1978-79 Pittsburgh Steelers to win back-to-back Super Bowl titles.

They ended up with a 55-10 victory in the most lopsided game in Super Bowl history.

"Each Super Bowl becomes more precious," said 49ers quarterback Joe Montana, the architect of San Francisco's four Super Bowl championships in the 1980s. "The more, the merrier. They are all sweet, and this was the sweetest yet."

The 49ers' latest title was their most impressive. They were nearly flawless in destroying a Denver team that was outclassed, outmanned and overmatched.

"This is one of the fine teams ever to play," 49ers Coach George Seifert said. "I think our '84 team was a great team, but obviously there have been other great football teams."

San Francisco marched 66 yards in 10 plays for a touchdown the first time it had the football and never looked back.

"We saw fear in (the Broncos') eyes when we scored on our first possession," running back Roger Craig said. "We set the tempo of the game. We went right after them, attacking them."

"I knew we were great, but I didn't think we were going to be this great," said veteran safety Ronnie Lott, who played on all four championship teams. "No question, this is the most talented 49er team I've been on."

The Broncos provided little resistance—despite their bold words in the days preceding the game. "This could be the second-greatest upset in sports history," Broncos Coach Dan Reeves had predicted. "We could do what the American hockey team did against the Russians."

Instead, the Broncos suffered their third embarrassing Super Bowl defeat in four years and their fourth overall, tying the Minnesota Vikings for Super Bowl ineptitude. And every beating was worse than the one before: a 27-10 loss to Dallas in Super Bowl XII, a 39-20 loss to the New York Giants in Super Bowl XXI, a 42-10 loss to Washington in Super Bowl XXII and, finally, this 45-point trouncing. The latest busting of the Broncos produced Super Bowl records for the largest margin of victory and for

The 49ers hurried and harrassed Denver quarterback John Elway throughout Super Bowl XXIV.

points scored by the winner.

If any team was to match the achievement of the great Steeler clubs, it had to be one led by Montana, perhaps the greatest quarterback ever. Montana was the trigger of an incredibly versatile offense that had Denver reeling midway through the second quarter. And what was supposed to be the redemption of Broncos quarterback John Elway turned into his most horrid nightmare. The 49er defense confused and stifled him, rendering him virtually useless at a time when Denver needed him to be Superman.

Montana rightfully was named the game's Most Valuable Player—his record third such honor in four Super Bowl appearances—after demonstrating his magnificence under pressure once again. He completed 22 of 29 attempts for 297 yards and a Super Bowl-record five touchdowns. Montana set another record with 13 straight completions at one point. He also took sole possession of all the major career Super Bowl passing marks, including completions (83), attempts (122), yards (1,142), touchdowns (11) and completion percentage

Joe Montana and Guy McIntyre celebrate after one of the San Francisco quarterback's five touchdown passes.

(.680, improving the record he already held). And in four Super Bowls, Montana was never intercepted.

"Joe is getting better and better all the time," said wide receiver Jerry Rice, who caught three touchdown passes. "He's like a little kid out there. He loves playing the game, and that's a big part of his success. No doubt—he's the best."

Against Denver, Montana put the finishing touches on a remarkable postseason in which he threw 83 passes without an interception. He completed 65 of them for 800 yards and 11 touchdowns in the 49ers' three playoff games. The 49ers won those contests by a total of 100 points (126-26), something no other club had ever done. That was evidence enough of the gap San Francisco had opened between itself and the rest of the league.

Denver discovered the futility of trying to stop this offensive juggernaut. The 49ers had carved up the Vikings (41-13) and Los Angeles Rams (30-3) in their two prior playoff games. The Bronco defense had not allowed more than 28 points in a game all season before this one. San Francisco had 27 by halftime.

"Man-to-man, zone, two-deep zone, three-deep zone, everything you could have played," Broncos defensive coordinator Wade Phillips said about his game plan. "They could have lined up in a single wing and we could have put

nine men on the line, and we still couldn't have stopped them."

But this was one time Montana and the San Francisco offense couldn't hog the whole spotlight. The 49er defense was a significant force over the club's last five games of the year. It held Buffalo to 10 points and shut out Chicago in San Francisco's final two regular-season games, and the Rams' offense managed only 156 yards in the National Football Conference championship game. Then in the Super Bowl, the 49er defense limited the Broncos to 167 yards and Elway to a woeful 10-for-26, 108-yard, two-interception performance—his lowest full-game passing production in more than two years. He was confused, harried and frustrated by the 49ers' quickness, depth and finely tuned schemes, which took away his wide receivers and plugged his scrambling avenues. Elway completed just two passes to wide receivers.

"The 49ers combined good coverages with good pressure and I couldn't throw the ball to them (his receivers) or get it completed," Elway said. "I'm definitely disappointed by the way I played.

"It seems like every time you come to a Super Bowl, there is too much emphasis placed on the quarterback," Elway said. "I guess it comes with the territory. But I don't want to put any more pressure on myself. There's already enough there."

Whereas Elway was worried about pressure, Montana's only worry was becoming overconfident. He probably wanted this Super Bowl victory more than he had the previous three. He wanted to show that a team could repeat. He wanted to cap off what already had been the most impressive season of his wonderful career. He set a single-season NFL record with a 112.4 quarterback rating in 1989.

"I expect a lot from myself," he said.

Montana kept the 49ers' opening Super Bowl drive alive with a 10-yard, third-down scramble to the Broncos' 22-yard line. Two plays later, he waited patiently in the pocket, looked off a couple of receivers and then connected with Rice at the 8-yard line. Denver rookie free safety Steve Atwater smacked into him but bounced off, and Rice stepped into the end zone for the touchdown and, following Mike Cofer's extra-point kick, a 7-0 lead with 10:06 left in the quarter.

The Broncos answered with a 42-yard field goal by David Treadwell after stalling at the San Francisco 25. But Denver's game plan, which was designed to control the ball and keep Montana off the field, already was showing cracks. Elway had completed only one of his first seven passes, and that had been a two-yard shovel pass to rookie running back Bobby Humphrey, who turned it into a 27-yard gain. On Elway's first power throw, a long sideline pattern, the ball had bounced two yards short. The strong-armed Elway normally delivered such passes on a line.

"When I saw that," Lott said, "I knew something wasn't right with him. He never bounces that pass."

Things soon got worse for Denver. After forcing the 49ers to punt on their next possession, the Broncos took over at their own 49. But on the first play from scrimmage, Humphrey, who was playing despite cracked ribs, was stripped of the ball and 49ers safety Chet Brooks recovered. If there was any crucial play in a 45-point blowout, this was it. It drained the Broncos and gave the 49ers great field position at their own 46.

Following an offensive holding penalty, Montana quickly found Rice for 20 yards over the middle—the Broncos never would shore up that spot—and then again later for 21 to the Denver 10-yard line. In between, Seifert had his first difficult decision of the game when the 49ers faced a fourth-and-one play at the 35. He didn't hesitate. The 49ers went for it and fullback Tom Rathman bulled for four yards. Five plays later, Montana connected from seven yards out with tight end Brent Jones, who broke through two tackles and scored. Cofer missed the extra point and San Francisco led, 13-3.

On Denver's next possession, the Broncos again had three downs and a punt as Elway threw two more incompletions, giving him

Jerry Rice is ecstatic after catching a 20-yard touchdown pass from Joe Montana in the first quarter.

eight misfires in 10 tries. He could only watch helplessly as Montana proceeded to drive the 49ers 69 yards in a 14-play drive that consumed more than seven minutes and ended with a one-yard TD run by Rathman. Cofer's kick made it 20-3.

Denver, meanwhile, could establish nothing on offense. A combination of a fierce pass rush and a lot of bumping on the Broncos' receivers kept Elway out of sync and running for his life. He finished the half with only six completions in 20 attempts for 64 yards, and he didn't complete a pass downfield until two minutes before intermission.

That was hardly good enough to offset Montana, who wrapped up a wonderful opening half by finding Rice wide open down the middle of the field with 34 seconds left. Rice pulled in the 38-yard toss, and the 49ers went into the locker room with a 27-3 advantage.

If anything, the second half was even worse for the Broncos. Elway's first pass landed in linebacker Michael Walter's stomach, and Montana used first down to throw 28 yards to Rice for another score. This time, Atwater had moved to help out on John Taylor over the middle, leaving Rice one-on-one with cornerback Tyrone Braxton.

"We thought we had a slight advantage with our receivers against their corners," 49ers offensive coordinator Mike Holmgren said diplomatically.

On the next series, Elway tossed a lame duck that was picked off by Brooks. On second down, Montana exploited the deep middle of the Denver defense again, this time to Taylor for 35 yards and a 41-3 lead. Later, following an 11-play San Francisco drive that was capped by Rathman's three-yard TD run, Elway would fumble and end Daniel Stubbs would return it to the Bronco 1. Craig took it in from there.

Four Denver turnovers, four San Francisco touchdowns. The 49ers had no turnovers.

Elway scored Denver's only touchdown on a three-yard keeper midway through the third quarter. But there was no celebration on the Broncos' sideline. The score took little sting out of the whipping they were receiving. Besides seeing their own defense decimated by Montana, Rice, Taylor, Craig, Rathman and, eventually, a cast of substitutes, the Broncos also had to watch San Francisco's defense play so well that Elway couldn't even scramble. The 49ers had completed a total shutdown of one of the league's best players.

"I'm just trying to figure out how we can win one of these one of these days, or at least be in one," Elway said. Indeed, the Broncos hadn't just lost their fourth Super Bowl. They had failed for the third time with Elway to even make a game of it. The aggregate score of Denver's three most recent Super Bowl losses was 136-40.

"I think the 49ers are playing as well as anybody ever has," said Reeves, whose Super Bowl record as either a player, assistant coach or head coach dropped to 2-6. "They are playing at a level that is incredible. We've got a long way to go to get to that level."

"I knew they were good," Atwater said, "but by the fourth quarter, I felt we had been up against one of the best teams that ever was."

SUPERDOME, NEW ORLEANS, LA.
SUNDAY, JANUARY 28

SCORE BY PERIODS

San Francisco	13	14	14	14	55
Denver	3	0	7	0	10

SCORING

San Francisco—Rice 20 pass from Montana (Cofer kick), 4:54 1st. Drive: 66 yards, 10 plays.

Denver—Field goal Treadwell 42, 8:13 1st. Drive: 49 yards, 10 plays.

San Francisco—Jones 7 pass from Montana (kick failed), 14:57 1st. Drive: 54 yards, 10 plays.

San Francisco—Rathman 1 run (Cofer kick), 7:45 2nd. Drive: 69 yards, 14 plays.

San Francisco—Rice 38 pass from Montana (Cofer kick), 14:26 2nd. Drive: 59 yards, 5 plays.

San Francisco—Rice 28 pass from Montana (Cofer kick), 2:12 3rd. Drive: 28 yards, 1 play.

San Francisco—Taylor 35 pass from Montana (Cofer kick), 5:16 3rd. Drive: 37 yards, 2 plays.

Denver—Elway 3 run (Treadwell kick), 8:07 3rd. Drive: 61 yards, 5 plays.

San Francisco—Rathman 4 run (Cofer kick), 0:03 4th. Drive: 75 yards, 11 plays.

San Francisco—Craig 1 run (Cofer kick), 1:13 4th. Drive: 1 yard, 1 play.

TEAM STATISTICS

	San Francisco	Denver
FIRST DOWNS	28	12
By rushing	14	5
By passing	14	6
By penalty	0	1
THIRD DOWN EFFICIENCY	8-15	3-11
TOTAL NET YARDS	461	167
Offensive plays	77	52
Average gain per play	6.0	3.2
NET YARDS RUSHING	144	64
Total rushes	44	17
Average gain per rush	3.3	3.8

	San Francisco	Denver
NET YARDS PASSING	317	103
Sacked-Yards lost	1-0	6-33
Gross yards passing	317	136
PASSES	24-32-0	11-29-2
Average gain per pass	9.6	2.9
PUNTS	4-39.5	6-38.5
Had blocked	0	0
TOTAL RETURN YARDAGE	129	207
Punt returns	38	11
Kickoff returns	49	196
Interception returns	42	0
PENALTIES-YARDS	4-38	0-0
FUMBLES-LOST	0-0	3-2
TIME OF POSSESSION	39:31	20:29
Attendance—72,919.		

INDIVIDUAL STATISTICS

Rushing—San Francisco, Craig 20-69, Rathman 11-38, Montana 2-15, Flagler 6-14, Young 4-6, Sydney 1-2; Denver, Humphrey 12-61, Elway 4-8, Winder 1-minus 5.

Passing—San Francisco, Montana 22-29-0—297, Young 2-3-0—20; Denver, Elway 10-26-2—108, Kubiak 1-3-0—28.

Receiving—San Francisco, Rice 7-148, Craig 5-34, Rathman 4-43, Taylor 3-49, Sherrard 1-13, Walls 1-9, Jones 1-7, Williams 1-7, Sydney 1-7; Denver, Humphrey 3-38, Sewell 2-22, Johnson 2-21, Nattiel 1-28, Bratton 1-14, Winder 1-7, Kay 1-6.

Kickoff Returns—San Francisco, Flagler 3-49; Denver, Carrington 6-146, Bell 2-41, Bratton 1-9.

Punt Returns—San Francisco, Taylor 3-28; Denver, Johnson 2-11.

Interceptions—San Francisco, Brooks 1-38, Walter 1-4.

Punting—San Francisco, Helton 4-39.5; Denver, Horan 6-38.5.

Field Goals—San Francisco, none attempted; Denver, Treadwell 1-1.

Sacks—San Francisco, Stubbs 2, Roberts, Griffin, Fagan, Kugler; Denver, Braxton.

SUPER BOWL SUMMARIES

SUPER BOWL I

January 15, 1967 at Los Angeles
Attendance—61,946

Kansas City (AFL) ...	0	10	0	0 —	10
Green Bay (NFL)	7	7	14	7 —	35

Winning coach—Vince Lombardi.
Most Valuable Player—Bart Starr.

SUPER BOWL II

January 14, 1968 at Miami
Attendance—75,546

Green Bay (NFL)	3	13	10	7 —	33
Oakland (AFL)	0	7	0	7 —	14

Winning coach—Vince Lombardi.
Most Valuable Player—Bart Starr.

SUPER BOWL III

January 12, 1969 at Miami
Attendance—75,389

New York (AFL).......	0	7	6	3 —	16
Baltimore (NFL)	0	0	0	7 —	7

Winning coach—Weeb Ewbank.
Most Valuable Player—Joe Namath.

SUPER BOWL IV

January 11, 1970 at New Orleans
Attendance—80,562

Minnesota (NFL)	0	0	7	0 —	7
Kansas City (AFL) ...	3	13	7	0 —	23

Winning coach—Hank Stram.
Most Valuable Player—Len Dawson.

SUPER BOWL V

January 17, 1971 at Miami
Attendance—79,204

Baltimore (AFC)......	0	6	0	10 —	16
Dallas (NFC)	3	10	0	0 —	13

Winning coach—Don McCafferty.
Most Valuable Player—Chuck Howley.

SUPER BOWL VI

January 16, 1972 at New Orleans
Attendance—81,023

Dallas (NFC)	3	7	7	7 —	24
Miami (AFC)	0	3	0	0 —	3

Winning coach—Tom Landry.
Most Valuable Player—Roger Staubach.

SUPER BOWL VII

January 14, 1973 at Los Angeles
Attendance—90,182

Miami (AFC)	7	7	0	0 —	14
Washington (NFC) ...	0	0	0	7 —	7

Winning coach—Don Shula.
Most Valuable Player—Jake Scott.

SUPER BOWL VIII

January 13, 1974 at Houston
Attendance—71,882

Minnesota (NFC).....	0	0	0	7 —	7
Miami (AFC)	14	3	7	0 —	24

Winning coach—Don Shula.
Most Valuable Player—Larry Csonka.

SUPER BOWL IX

January 12, 1975 at New Orleans
Attendance—80,997

Pittsburgh (AFC)	0	2	7	7 —	16
Minnesota (NFC).....	0	0	0	6 —	6

Winning coach—Chuck Noll.
Most Valuable Player—Franco Harris.

SUPER BOWL X

January 18, 1976 at Miami
Attendance—80,187

Dallas (NFC)	7	3	0	7 —	17
Pittsburgh (AFC)	7	0	0	14 —	21

Winning coach—Chuck Noll.
Most Valuable Player—Lynn Swann.

SUPER BOWL XI

January 9, 1977 at Pasadena
Attendance—103,428

Oakland (AFC)	0	16	3	13 —	32
Minnesota (NFC).....	0	0	7	7 —	14

Winning coach—John Madden.
Most Valuable Player—Fred Biletnikoff.

SUPER BOWL XII

January 15, 1978 at New Orleans
Attendance—75,804

Dallas (NFC)	10	3	7	7 —	27
Denver (AFC)...........	0	0	10	0 —	10

Winning coach—Tom Landry.
Most Valuable Players—Harvey Martin and Randy White.

SUPER BOWL XIII

January 21, 1979 at Miami
Attendance—78,656

Pittsburgh (AFC)	7	14	0	14 —	35
Dallas (NFC)	7	7	3	14 —	31

Winning coach—Chuck Noll.
Most Valuable Player—Terry Bradshaw.

SUPER BOWL XIV

January 20, 1980 at Pasadena
Attendance—103,985

Los Angeles (NFC) ..	7	6	6	0 — 19
Pittsburgh (AFC)	3	7	7	14 — 31

Winning coach—Chuck Noll.
Most Valuable Player—Terry Bradshaw.

SUPER BOWL XV

January 25, 1981 at New Orleans
Attendance—75,500

Oakland (AFC)	14	0	10	3 — 27
Philadelphia (NFC) ..	0	3	0	7 — 10

Winning coach—Tom Flores.
Most Valuable Player—Jim Plunkett.

SUPER BOWL XVI

January 24, 1982 at Pontiac
Attendance—81,270

San Fran. (NFC)	7	13	0	6 — 26
Cincinnati (AFC)	0	0	7	14 — 21

Winning coach—Bill Walsh.
Most Valuable Player—Joe Montana.

SUPER BOWL XVII

January 30, 1983 at Pasadena
Attendance—103,667

Miami (AFC)	7	10	0	0 — 17
Washington (NFC) ...	0	10	3	14 — 27

Winning coach—Joe Gibbs.
Most Valuable Player—John Riggins.

SUPER BOWL XVIII

January 22, 1984 at Tampa
Attendance—72,920

Washington (NFC) ...	0	3	6	0 — 9
Los Angeles (AFC) ..	7	14	14	3 — 38

Winning coach—Tom Flores.
Most Valuable Player—Marcus Allen.

SUPER BOWL XIX

January 20, 1985 at Palo Alto
Attendance—84,059

Miami (AFC)	10	6	0	0 — 16
San Fran. (NFC)	7	21	10	0 — 38

Winning coach—Bill Walsh.
Most Valuable Player—Joe Montana.

SUPER BOWL XX

January 26, 1986 at New Orleans
Attendance—73,818

Chicago (NFC)	13	10	21	2 — 46
New England (AFC)	3	0	0	7 — 10

Winning coach—Mike Ditka.
Most Valuable Player—Richard Dent.

SUPER BOWL XXI

January 25, 1987 at Pasadena
Attendance—101,063

Denver (AFC)	10	0	0	10 — 20
N.Y. Giants (NFC)	7	2	17	13 — 39

Winning coach—Bill Parcells.
Most Valuable Player—Phil Simms.

SUPER BOWL XXII

January 31, 1988 at San Diego
Attendance—73,302

Washington (NFC) ...	0	35	0	7 — 42
Denver (AFC)	10	0	0	0 — 10

Winning coach—Joe Gibbs.
Most Valuable Player—Doug Williams.

SUPER BOWL XXIII

January 22, 1989 at Miami
Attendance—75,179

Cincinnati (AFC)	0	3	10	3 — 16
San Fran. (NFC)	3	0	3	14 — 20

Winning coach—Bill Walsh.
Most Valuable Player—Jerry Rice.

SUPER BOWL XXIV

January 28, 1990 at New Orleans
Attendance—72,919

San Fran. (NFC)	13	14	14	14 — 55
Denver (AFC)	3	0	7	0 — 10

Winning coach—George Seifert.
Most Valuable Player—Joe Montana.

1989 NFL Statistics
1989 RUSHING

MOST YARDS, SEASON
AFC: 1480—Christian Okoye, Kansas City.
NFC: 1470—Barry Sanders, Detroit.

MOST YARDS, GAME
NFC: 221—Gerald Riggs, Washington vs. Philadelphia, September 17.
Greg Bell, L.A. Rams vs. Green Bay, September 24.
AFC: 176—Marion Butts, San Diego at Kansas City, December 17.

LONGEST GAIN
AFC: 92—Bo Jackson, L.A. Raiders vs. Cincinnati, November 5 (TD).
NFC: 73—Neal Anderson, Chicago vs. Green Bay, December 17.

MOST ATTEMPTS, SEASON
AFC: 370—Christian Okoye, Kansas City.
NFC: 344—Dalton Hilliard, New Orleans.

MOST ATTEMPTS, GAME
AFC: 39—Marion Butts, San Diego at Kansas City, December 17 (176 yards).
NFC: 38—Jamie Morris, Washington at Philadelphia, November 12 (88 yards).

AVERAGE YARDS PER ATTEMPT
NFC: 6.0—Randall Cunningham, Philadelphia.
AFC: 5.6—James Brooks, Cincinnati.

MOST TOUCHDOWNS
NFC: 15—Greg Bell, L.A. Rams.
AFC: 12—Christian Okoye, Kansas City.

TEAM LEADERS
AFC: BUFFALO: 1244, Thurman Thomas; CINCINNATI: 1239, James Brooks; CLEVELAND: 633, Eric Metcalf; DENVER: 1151, Bobby Humphrey; HOUSTON: 531, Alonzo Highsmith; INDIANAPOLIS: 1311, Eric Dickerson; KANSAS CITY: 1480, Christian Okoye; L.A. RAIDERS: 950, Bo Jackson; MIAMI: 659, Sammie Smith; NEW ENGLAND: 833, John Stephens; N.Y. JETS: 702, Johnny Hector; PITTSBURGH: 770, Tim Worley; SAN DIEGO: 683, Marion Butts; SEATTLE: 631, Curt Warner.
NFC: ATLANTA: 689, John Settle; CHICAGO: 1275, Neal Anderson; DALLAS: 446, Paul Palmer; DETROIT: 1470, Barry Sanders; GREEN BAY: 821, Brent Fullwood; L.A. RAMS: 1137, Greg Bell; MINNESOTA: 669, Herschel Walker; NEW ORLEANS: 1262, Dalton Hilliard; N.Y. GIANTS: 1023, Ottis Anderson; PHILADELPHIA: 621, Randall Cunningham; PHOENIX: 502, Earl Ferrell; SAN FRANCISCO: 1054, Roger Craig; TAMPA BAY: 589, Lars Tate; WASHINGTON: 834, Gerald Riggs.

TEAM CHAMPION
AFC: 2483—Cincinnati.
NFC: 2287—Chicago.

RUSHING—TEAM

AMERICAN FOOTBALL CONFERENCE

	Att.	Yards	Avg.	Long	TDs.
Cincinnati	529	2483	4.7	t65	17
Buffalo	532	2264	4.3	38	15
Kansas City	559	2227	4.0	59	18
Denver	554	2092	3.8	40	15
L.A. Raiders	454	2038	4.5	t92	9
Houston	495	1928	3.9	60	16
San Diego	432	1873	4.3	t50	13
Indianapolis	458	1853	4.0	26	11
Pittsburgh	500	1818	3.6	t58	17
New England	485	1749	3.6	t35	12
Cleveland	448	1609	3.6	t43	14
N.Y. Jets	400	1596	4.0	t39	11
Seattle	405	1392	3.4	34	5
Miami	400	1330	3.3	25	10
Conference Total	6651	26252	....	t92	183
Conference Average	475.1	1875.1	3.9	....	13.1

NATIONAL FOOTBALL CONFERENCE

	Att.	Yards	Avg.	Long	TDs.
Chicago	516	2287	4.4	73	22
Philadelphia	540	2208	4.1	51	14
Minnesota	514	2066	4.0	47	12
Detroit	421	2053	4.9	34	23
San Francisco	493	1966	4.0	t29	14
New Orleans	502	1948	3.9	40	19
L.A. Rams	472	1909	4.0	47	19
Washington	514	1904	3.7	58	14
N.Y. Giants	556	1889	3.4	t36	17
Green Bay	397	1732	4.4	t68	13
Tampa Bay	412	1507	3.7	48	10
Dallas	355	1409	4.0	t63	7
Phoenix	407	1361	3.3	t44	10
Atlanta	318	1155	3.6	22	11
Conference Total	6417	25394	....	73	205
Conference Average	458.4	1813.9	4.0	....	14.6
League Total	13068	51646	....	t92	388
League Average	446.7	1844.5	4.0	....	13.9

TOP TEN RUSHERS

	Att.	Yards	Avg.	Long	TDs.
OKOYE, CHRISTIAN, Kansas City	370	1480	4.0	59	12
Sanders, Barry, Detroit	280	1470	5.3	34	14
Dickerson, Eric, Indianapolis	314	1311	4.2	t21	7
Anderson, Neal, Chicago	274	1275	4.7	73	11
Hilliard, Dalton, New Orleans	344	1262	3.7	40	13
Thomas, Thurman, Buffalo	298	1244	4.2	38	6
Brooks, James, Cincinnati	221	1239	5.6	t65	7
Humphrey, Bobby, Denver	294	1151	3.9	40	7
Bell, Greg, L.A. Rams	272	1137	4.2	47	15
Craig, Roger, San Francisco	271	1054	3.9	27	6

AFC—INDIVIDUALS

Player—Team	Att.	Yds.	Avg.	Lng.	TD	Player—Team	Att.	Yds.	Avg.	Lng.	TD
OKOYE, K.C.	370	1480	4.0	59	12	Ball, Cin.	98	391	4.0	27	3
Dickerson, Ind.	314	1311	4.2	t21	7	McNeil, Jets	80	352	4.4	t19	2
Thomas, Buff.	298	1244	4.2	38	6	Winder, Den.	110	351	3.2	16	2
Brooks, Cin.	221	1239	5.6	t65	7	White, Hou.	104	349	3.4	33	5
Humphrey, Den.	294	1151	3.9	40	7	Nelson, Minn.-S.D.	67	321	4.8	28	0
Jackson, Raiders	173	950	5.5	t92	4	Rozier, Hou.	88	301	3.4	17	2
Stephens, N.E.	244	833	3.4	t35	7	Bentley, Ind.	75	299	4.0	22	1
Worley, Pitt.	195	770	3.9	38	5	Allen, Raiders	69	293	4.2	15	2
Hector, Jets	177	702	4.0	24	3	Jennings, Cin.	83	293	3.5	17	2
Butts, S.D.	170	683	4.0	t50	9	Manoa, Cin.	87	289	3.3	22	3
Smith, Mia.	200	659	3.3	25	6	Esiason, Cin.	47	278	5.9	24	0
Metcalf, Clev.	187	633	3.4	t43	6	Moon, Hou.	70	268	3.8	19	4
Warner, Sea.	194	631	3.3	34	3	Elway, Den.	48	244	5.1	31	3
Hoge, Pitt.	186	621	3.3	31	8	Stradford, Mia.	66	240	3.6	13	1
Perryman, N.E.	150	562	3.7	18	2	Saxon, K.C.	58	233	4.0	19	3
Kinnebrew, Buff.	131	533	4.1	25	6	Heard, K.C.	63	216	3.4	28	0
Highsmith, Hou.	128	531	4.1	25	4	Logan, Mia.	57	201	3.5	14	0
Spencer, S.D.	134	521	3.9	15	3	Lipps, Pitt.	13	180	13.8	t58	1
Williams, Sea.	146	499	3.4	21	1	Redden, Clev.	40	180	4.5	t38	1
Smith, Raiders	117	471	4.0	21	1	Mueller, Raiders	48	161	3.4	19	2
Pinkett, Hou.	94	449	4.8	60	1	K. Jones, Clev.	43	160	3.7	15	1
Vick, Jets	112	434	3.9	t39	5	Krieg, Sea.	40	160	4.0	18	0

Player—Team	Att.	Yds.	Avg.	Lng.	TD
K. Davis, Buff.	29	149	5.1	21	1
Alexander, Den.	45	146	3.2	11	2
Pelluer, K.C.	17	143	8.4	27	2
McMahon, S.D.	29	141	4.9	15	0
Bernstine, S.D.	15	137	9.1	t32	1
Kelly, Buff.	29	137	4.7	19	2
W. Williams, Pitt.	37	131	3.5	13	1
Mack, Clev.	37	130	3.5	12	1
McNair, K.C.	23	121	5.3	25	0
Taylor, Cin.	30	111	3.7	16	3
Bratton, Den.	30	108	3.6	9	1
Harmon, Buff.	17	99	5.8	24	0
Oliphant, Clev.	15	97	6.5	t21	1
Woods, Cin.	29	94	3.2	12	2
Trudeau, Ind.	35	91	2.6	17	2
Flutie, N.E.	16	87	5.4	22	0
Kosar, Clev.	30	70	2.3	23	1
Brinson, S.D.	17	64	3.8	9	0
Brown, Jets	12	63	5.3	17	0
Chandler, Ind.	7	57	8.1	23	1
Davenport, Mia.	14	56	4.0	9	1
Porter, Raiders	13	54	4.2	23	0
Stone, Pitt.	10	53	5.3	32	0
Allen, N.E.	11	51	4.6	18	1
Jensen, Mia.	8	50	6.3	14	0
Hampton, Mia.	17	47	2.8	9	0
Hunter, Ind.	13	47	3.6	11	0
Holland, S.D.	6	46	7.7	24	0
Mueller, Buff.	16	44	2.8	9	0
Sewell, Den.	7	44	6.3	10	0
Wilson, N.E.	7	42	6.0	11	0
Fenner, Sea.	11	41	3.7	9	1
Beuerlein, Raiders	16	39	2.4	10	0
Secules, Mia.	4	39	9.8	17	0
Verdin, Ind.	4	39	9.8	26	0
Schroeder, Raiders	15	38	2.5	19	0
Tatupu, N.E.	11	38	3.5	20	0
McGee, Cin.	2	36	18.0	25	0
Kubiak, Den.	15	35	2.3	10	0
McNeil, Clev.	2	32	16.0	18	0
Reed, Buff.	2	31	15.5	23	0
Reich, Buff.	9	30	3.3	9	0
Wilhelm, Cin.	6	30	5.0	14	0
T. Brown, Mia.	13	26	2.0	6	0
Brister, Pitt.	27	25	0.9	15	0
Gamble, K.C.	6	24	4.0	20	1
Harmon, Sea.	1	24	24.0	24	0
Harris, Sea.	8	23	2.9	8	0
A. Miller, S.D.	4	21	5.3	24	0
Blackledge, Pitt.	9	20	2.2	11	0
Egu, N.E.	3	20	6.7	t15	1
Holifield, Cin.	11	20	1.8	11	0
Martin, N.E.	2	20	10.0	13	0
Early, S.D.	1	19	19.0	19	0
Grogan, N.E.	9	19	2.1	7	0
Langhorne, Clev.	5	19	3.8	18	0
O'Brien, Jets	9	18	2.0	5	0
Rison, Ind.	3	18	6.0	18	0
Gr. Montgomery, Hou.	3	17	5.7	11	0
Prokop, Jets	1	17	17.0	t17	1
Carter, Pitt.	11	16	1.5	7	1
Evans, Raiders	1	16	16.0	16	0
Fernandez, Raiders	2	16	8.0	12	0
T. Johnson, Hou.	4	16	4.0	8	0
Floyd, S.D.	8	15	1.9	5	0
Fryar, N.E.	2	15	7.5	11	0
Archer, S.D.	2	14	7.0	14	0
Epps, Jets	1	14	14.0	14	0
Jackson, Den.	5	13	2.6	8	0
Stouffer, Sea.	2	11	5.5	9	0
Faaola, Mia.	2	10	5.0	5	0
Wallace, Pitt.	5	10	2.0	5	1
Clayton, Mia.	3	9	3.0	11	0
Harry, K.C.	1	9	9.0	9	0
Walker, S.D.	1	9	9.0	9	0
Plummer, S.D.	1	6	6.0	6	0
Jaworski, K.C.	4	5	1.3	4	0
Ramsey, Ind.	4	5	1.3	3	0
Agee, K.C.	1	3	3.0	3	0
Blades, Sea.	1	3	3.0	3	0
Harper, Jets	1	3	3.0	3	0
C. Jones, N.E.	1	3	3.0	3	0
Mackey, Jets	2	3	1.5	5	0
Tyrrell, Pitt.	1	3	3.0	3	0
Mandley, K.C.	2	1	0.5	8	0
Caravello, S.D.	1	0	0.0	0	0
Duncan, Hou.	1	0	0.0	0	0
Kemp, Sea.	1	0	0.0	0	0
Malone, Jets	1	0	0.0	0	0
Roby, Mia.	2	0	0.0	0	0
Rodriguez, Sea.	1	0	0.0	0	0
Tolliver, S.D.	7	0	0.0	3	0
Pagel, Clev.	2	−1	−0.5	4	0
Ryan, Jets	1	−1	−1.0	−1	0
Eason, N.E.-Jets	3	−2	−0.7	0	0
Hillary, Cin.	1	−2	−2.0	−2	0
Wonsley, N.E.	2	−2	−1.0	0	0
Brooks, Ind.	2	−3	−1.5	0	0
Carlson, Hou.	3	−3	−1.0	0	0
Gelbaugh, Buff.	1	−3	−3.0	−3	0
Strom, Pitt.	4	−3	−0.8	0	0
Burkett, Jets	1	−4	−4.0	−4	0
Lageman, Jets	1	−5	−5.0	−5	0
Johnson, Cin.	1	−7	−7.0	−7	0
Marino, Mia.	14	−7	−0.5	2	2
DeBerg, K.C.	14	−8	−0.6	15	0
Newsome, Pitt.	2	−8	−4.0	0	0
Stark, Ind.	1	−11	−11.0	−11	0

NFC—INDIVIDUALS

Player—Team	Att.	Yds.	Avg.	Lng.	TD
B. SANDERS, Det.	280	1470	5.3	34	14
Anderson, Chi.	274	1275	4.7	73	11
Hilliard, N.O.	344	1262	3.7	40	13
Bell, Rams	272	1137	4.2	47	15
Craig, S.F.	271	1054	3.9	27	6
Anderson, Giants	325	1023	3.1	t36	14
Walker, Dall.-Minn.	250	915	3.7	47	7
Riggs, Wash.	201	834	4.1	58	4
Fullwood, G.B.	204	821	4.0	38	5
Settle, Atl.	179	689	3.8	20	3
Cunningham, Phil.	104	621	6.0	51	4
Tate, T.B.	167	589	3.5	48	8
Fenney, Minn.	151	588	3.9	25	4
Toney, Phil.	172	582	3.4	44	3
Byner, Wash.	134	580	4.3	24	7
Ferrell, Phoe.	149	502	3.4	t44	6
Byars, Phil.	133	452	3.4	t16	5
Palmer, Dall.	112	446	4.0	t63	2
Delpino, Rams	78	368	4.7	t32	1
Majkowski, G.B.	75	358	4.8	20	5
Howard, T.B.	108	357	3.3	15	1
Morris, Wash.	124	336	2.7	t12	2
Muster, Chi.	82	327	4.0	20	5
Rathman, S.F.	79	305	3.9	13	1
Aikman, Dall.	38	302	7.9	25	0
Tillman, Giants	79	290	3.7	19	0
Harbaugh, Chi.	45	276	6.1	t26	3
Woodside, G.B.	46	273	5.9	t68	1
Wilder, T.B.	70	244	3.5	14	0
Montana, S.F.	49	227	4.6	19	3
Johnston, Dall.	67	212	3.2	13	0
Jordan, Phoe.	83	211	2.5	15	2
Dozier, Minn.	46	207	4.5	38	0
Jones, Atl.	52	202	3.9	19	6
Gagliano, Det.	41	192	4.7	19	4
Anderson, Minn.	52	189	3.6	14	2
Higgs, Phil.	49	184	3.8	13	0
Heyward, N.O.	49	183	3.7	15	1
Jordan, N.O.	38	179	4.7	32	3
Sherman, Phil.	40	177	4.4	37	2
Lang, Atl.	47	176	3.7	22	1
S. Mitchell, Phoe.	43	165	3.8	14	0
Gary, Rams	37	163	4.4	18	1
Carthon, Giants	57	153	2.7	18	0
Peete, Det.	33	148	4.5	t14	4
Sikahema, Phoe.	38	145	3.8	27	0
Simms, Giants	32	141	4.4	15	1
Stamps, T.B.	29	141	4.9	t21	1

Player—Team	Att.	Yds.	Avg.	Lng.	TD
Testaverde, T.B.	25	139	5.6	16	0
Haddix, G.B.	44	135	3.1	10	0
Wilson, Minn.	32	132	4.1	23	1
Flagler, S.F.	33	129	3.9	t29	1
Drummond, Phil.	32	127	4.0	16	0
Sanders, Chi.	41	127	3.1	19	0
Young, S.F.	38	126	3.3	22	2
Meggett, Giants	28	117	4.2	18	0
Frazier, N.O.	25	112	4.5	21	1
Dupard, N.E.-Wash.	37	111	3.0	19	1
Gentry, Chi.	17	106	6.2	29	0
Paige, Det.	30	105	3.5	16	0
Clark, Phoe.-Minn.	20	99	5.0	14	0
McGee, Rams	21	99	4.7	15	1
Fourcade, N.O.	14	91	6.5	14	0
Hogeboom, Phoe.	27	89	3.3	15	1
Hebert, N.O.	25	87	3.5	11	0
Sargent, Dall.	20	87	4.4	43	1
Tupa, Phoe.	15	75	5.0	13	0
Green, Rams	26	73	2.8	9	0
Hostetler, Giants	11	71	6.5	t19	2
Tomczak, Chi.	24	71	3.0	18	1
Fontenot, G.B.	17	69	4.1	19	1
Painter, Det.	15	64	4.3	9	0
Rypien, Wash.	26	56	2.2	15	1
Sydney, S.F.	9	56	6.2	18	0
Rouson, Giants	11	51	4.6	9	0
Suhey, Chi.	20	51	2.6	8	1
Green, Rams	5	46	9.2	t37	1
Kemp, G.B.	5	43	8.6	14	0
Morse, N.O.	2	43	21.5	39	0
Clack, Dall.	14	40	2.9	17	2
R. Johnson, Det.	12	38	3.2	14	0
Jones, Minn.	1	37	37.0	37	0
D. Smith, T.B.	7	37	5.3	17	0
Wolfley, Phoe.	13	36	2.8	t5	1
Haynes, Atl.	4	35	8.8	21	0
Rice, S.F.	5	33	6.6	17	0
Paterra, Atl.	9	32	3.6	8	0
Baker, Phoe.	20	31	1.6	6	0
Everett, Rams	25	31	1.2	t13	1
Dixon, Dall.	3	30	10.0	13	0
Henderson, S.F.	7	30	4.3	t11	1
Reichenbach, Phil.	1	30	30.0	30	0
Adams, Giants	9	29	3.2	8	0
Ro. Brown, Rams	6	27	4.5	12	0
Rosenbach, Phoe.	6	26	4.3	8	0
Rice, Minn.	6	25	4.2	10	0
Sharpe, G.B.	2	25	12.5	26	0
Flowers, Atl.	13	24	1.8	4	1
Teltschik, Phil.	1	23	23.0	23	0
Gray, Det.	3	22	7.3	14	0
J.T. Smith, Phoe.	2	21	10.5	11	0
Miller, Atl.	10	20	2.0	7	0
Clark, Wash.	2	19	9.5	11	0
Sanders, Wash.	4	19	4.8	13	0
Carter, Minn.	3	18	6.0	17	0
Jones, Phoe.	1	18	18.0	18	0
Carter, Phil.	2	16	8.0	11	0
Walsh, Dall.	6	16	2.7	14	0
Tautalatasi, Dall.	6	15	2.5	6	0
Shepard, Dall.	3	12	4.0	12	0
Hipple, Det.	2	11	5.5	10	1
Lewis, Minn.	1	11	11.0	11	0
Turner, Giants	2	11	5.5	14	0
Ellard, Rams	2	10	5.0	6	0
Humphries, Wash.	5	10	2.0	9	0
Kramer, Minn.	12	9	0.8	5	0
Monk, Wash.	3	8	2.7	14	0
Turner, N.O.	2	8	4.0	6	0
Workman, G.B.	4	8	2.0	3	1
Taylor, Chi.	2	7	3.5	7	0
Buford, Chi.	1	6	6.0	6	0
Ferguson, T.B.	4	6	1.5	7	0
Irvin, Dall.	1	6	6.0	6	0
Taylor, S.F.	1	6	6.0	6	0
McKinnon, Chi.	3	5	1.7	3	0
Runager, Phil.	2	5	2.5	5	0
Thornton, Chi.	1	4	4.0	4	0
L. Brown, Det.	1	3	3.0	3	0
Holohan, Rams	1	3	3.0	3	0
Johnson, Phil.	1	3	3.0	3	0
Long, Det.	3	2	0.7	6	0
Reasons, Giants	1	2	2.0	2	0
Ingram, Giants	1	1	1.0	1	0
Saxon, Dall.	1	1	1.0	1	0
Bates, Dall.	1	0	0.0	0	0
Fulhage, Atl.	1	0	0.0	0	0
Hatcher, Rams	1	0	0.0	0	0
Helton, S.F.	1	0	0.0	0	0
Millen, Atl.	1	0	0.0	0	0
Winslow, N.O.	1	0	0.0	0	0
Anderson, Rams	1	−1	−1.0	−1	0
Coleman, Wash.	1	−1	−1.0	−1	0
Herrmann, Rams	2	−1	−0.5	0	0
Reaves, Wash.	1	−1	−1.0	−1	0
McDonald, Det.	1	−2	−2.0	−2	0
Cavanaugh, Phil.	2	−3	−1.5	0	0
Scott, Dall.	2	−4	−2.0	−1	0
Williams, Wash.	1	−4	−4.0	−4	0
Peebles, T.B.	2	−6	−3.0	1	0
Hill, N.O.	1	−7	−7.0	−7	0
Carson, Phil.	1	−9	−9.0	−9	0
Perriman, N.O.	1	−10	−10.0	−10	0
Morris, Chi.	1	−14	−14.0	−14	0
Dixon, Atl.	2	−23	−11.5	0	0

t—Touchdown.
Leader based on most yards gained.

1989 PASSING

HIGHEST RATING
> NFC: 112.4—Joe Montana, San Francisco.
> AFC: 92.1—Boomer Esiason, Cincinnati.

HIGHEST COMPLETION PERCENTAGE
> NFC: 70.2—Joe Montana, San Francisco.
> AFC: 60.5—Steve DeBerg, Kansas City.

MOST ATTEMPTS, SEASON
> NFC: 599—Don Majkowski, Green Bay.
> AFC: 550—Dan Marino, Miami.

MOST COMPLETIONS, SEASON
> NFC: 353—Don Majkowski, Green Bay.
> AFC: 308—Dan Marino, Miami.

MOST YARDS, SEASON
> NFC: 4318—Don Majkowski, Green Bay.
> AFC: 3997—Dan Marino, Miami.

MOST YARDS, GAME
> NFC: 458—Joe Montana, San Fran. at L.A. Rams, December 11 (30-42, 3 TD).
> AFC: 427—Dan Marino, Miami vs. N.Y. Jets, September 24 (33-55, 3 TD).

LONGEST GAIN
> AFC: 97—Bernie Kosar (to Webster Slaughter), Clev. vs. Chi., October 23 (TD).
> NFC: 95—Joe Montana (to John Taylor), S.F. at L.A. Rams, Dec. 11 (TD).

AVERAGE YARDS PER ATTEMPT
> NFC: 9.12—Joe Montana, San Francisco.
> AFC: 8.01—Jim Kelly, Buffalo.

MOST TOUCHDOWN PASSES, SEASON
> NFC: 29—Jim Everett, L.A. Rams.
> AFC: 28—Boomer Esiason, Cincinnati.

MOST TOUCHDOWN PASSES, GAME
> AFC: 5—Jim Kelly, Buffalo at Houston, September 24 (17-29, 363 yards) (OT).
>   Boomer Esiason, Cincinnati vs. T.B., October 29 (17-28, 197 yards.)
> NFC: 5—Randall Cunningham, Phila. at Wash., Sept. 17 (34-46, 447 yards).
>   Joe Montana, San Fran. at Phila., September 24 (25-34, 428 yards).

LOWEST INTERCEPTION PERCENTAGE
> NFC: 1.9—Chris Miller, Atlanta.
> AFC: 2.4—Boomer Esiason, Cincinnati.

TEAM CHAMPION (Net Yards)
> NFC: 4349—Washington.
> AFC: 4216—Miami.

PASSING—TEAM

AMERICAN FOOTBALL CONFERENCE

	Atts.	Com.	Pct. Com.	Gross Yards	Tkd.- Yds. Lost	Net Yards	Avg. Yds. Att.	Avg. Yds. Com.	TD	Lng.	Had Int.
Miami	601	331	55.1	4302	10- 86	4216	7.16	13.00	26	t78	25
New England	610	302	49.5	3972	34-265	3707	6.51	13.15	17	t65	27
Cincinnati	513	288	56.1	3950	41-332	3618	7.70	13.72	32	t74	13
Buffalo	478	281	58.8	3831	35-242	3589	8.01	13.63	32	t78	20
Houston	496	295	59.5	3786	37-287	3499	7.63	12.83	23	55	16
Cleveland	529	309	58.4	3625	34-192	3433	6.85	11.73	20	t97	15
N.Y. Jets	570	338	59.3	3892	62-477	3415	6.83	11.51	14	t63	24
Seattle	559	316	56.5	3583	46-379	3204	6.41	11.34	21	t60	23
Kansas City	435	259	59.5	3220	23-182	3038	7.40	12.43	14	50	23
San Diego	515	270	52.4	3291	39-254	3037	6.39	12.19	15	t69	19
Denver	474	256	54.0	3352	43-351	3001	7.07	13.09	21	69	20
Indianapolis	493	253	51.3	3134	28-174	2960	6.36	12.39	18	t82	17
L.A. Raiders	414	201	48.6	3277	44-326	2951	7.92	16.30	21	t84	22
Pittsburgh	404	210	52.0	2662	51-484	2178	6.59	12.68	10	t79	13
Conf. Total	7091	3909	......	49877	527-4031	45846	......	....	284	t97	277
Conf. Average	506.5	279.2	55.1	3562.6	37.6-287.9	3274.7	7.03	12.76	20.3	....	19.8

NATIONAL FOOTBALL CONFERENCE

	Atts.	Com.	Pct. Com.	Gross Yards	Tkd.- Yds. Lost	Net Yards	Avg. Yds. Att.	Avg. Yds. Com.	TD	Lng.	Had Int.
Washington	581	337	58.0	4476	21-127	4349	7.70	13.28	24	t80	17
San Francisco	483	339	70.2	4584	45-282	4302	9.49	13.52	35	t95	11
L.A. Rams	523	308	58.9	4369	32-236	4133	8.35	14.19	29	t78	18
Green Bay	600	354	59.0	4325	48-277	4048	7.21	12.22	27	t79	20
Atlanta	578	312	54.0	3903	51-389	3514	6.75	12.51	17	t72	12
New Orleans	461	284	61.6	3651	36-271	3380	7.92	12.86	23	t54	19
Tampa Bay	570	302	53.0	3666	43-331	3335	6.43	12.14	23	t78	28
Phoenix	523	279	53.3	3659	56-379	3280	7.00	13.11	17	t77	30
Minnesota	499	272	54.5	3468	40-279	3189	6.95	12.75	17	50	19
Philadelphia	538	294	54.6	3455	45-343	3112	6.42	11.75	23	t66	16
Chicago	484	267	55.2	3262	28-174	3088	6.74	12.22	21	t79	25
N.Y. Giants	444	248	55.9	3355	46-281	3074	7.56	13.53	17	t62	16
Detroit	450	229	50.9	3282	57-343	2939	7.29	14.33	11	t75	24
Dallas	513	266	51.9	3124	30-239	2885	6.09	11.74	14	t75	27
Conf. Total	7247	4091	......	52579	578-3951	48628	......	....	298	t95	282
Conf. Average	517.6	292.2	56.5	3755.6	41.3-282.2	3473.4	7.26	12.85	21.3	....	20.1
League Total	14338	8000	......	102456	1105-7982	94474	......	....	582	t97	559
League Avg.	512.1	285.7	55.8	3659.1	39.5-285.1	3374.1	7.15	12.81	20.8	....	20.0

Leader based on net yards.

TOP TEN PASSING QUALIFIERS

Player—Team	Att.	Cmp.	Pct. Cmp.	Yds.	Avg. Gain	TD	Pct. TD	Lg.	Int.	Pct. Int.	Rating Pts.
MONTANA, JOE, S.F.	386	271	70.2	3521	9.12	26	6.7	t95	8	2.1	112.4
Esiason, Boomer, Cin.	455	258	56.7	3525	7.75	28	6.2	t74	11	2.4	92.1
Everett, Jim, L.A. Rams	518	304	58.7	4310	8.32	29	5.6	t78	17	3.3	90.6
Moon, Warren, Hou.	464	280	60.3	3631	7.83	23	5.0	55	14	3.0	88.9
Rypien, Mark, Wash.	476	280	58.8	3768	7.92	22	4.6	t80	13	2.7	88.1
Kelly, Jim, Buff.	391	228	58.3	3130	8.01	25	6.4	t78	18	4.6	86.2
Hebert, Bobby, N.O.	353	222	62.9	2686	7.61	15	4.2	t54	15	4.2	82.7
Majkowski, Don, G.B.	599	353	58.9	4318	7.21	27	4.5	t79	20	3.3	82.3
Kosar, Bernie, Clev.	513	303	59.1	3533	6.89	18	3.5	t97	14	2.7	80.3
Simms, Phil, N.Y. Giants	405	228	56.3	3061	7.56	14	3.5	t62	14	3.5	77.6

AFC INDIVIDUAL QUALIFIERS

Player—Team	Att.	Cmp.	Pct. Cmp.	Yds.	Avg. Gain	TD	Pct. TD	Lg.	Int.	Pct. Int.	Rating Pts.
ESIASON, Cin.	455	258	56.7	3525	7.75	28	6.2	t74	11	2.4	92.1
Moon, Hou.	464	280	60.3	3631	7.83	23	5.0	55	14	3.0	88.9
Kelly, Buff.	391	228	58.3	3130	8.01	25	6.4	t78	18	4.6	86.2
Kosar, Clev.	513	303	59.1	3533	6.89	18	3.5	t97	14	2.7	80.3
Marino, Mia.	550	308	56.0	3997	7.27	24	4.4	t78	22	4.0	76.9
DeBerg, K.C.	324	196	60.5	2529	7.81	11	3.4	50	16	4.9	75.8
Krieg, Sea.	499	286	57.3	3309	6.63	21	4.2	t60	20	4.0	74.8
O'Brien, Jets	477	288	60.4	3346	70.1	12	2.5	57	18	3.8	74.3
Elway, Den.	416	223	53.6	3051	7.33	18	4.3	69	18	4.3	73.7
McMahon, S.D.	318	176	55.3	2132	6.70	10	3.1	t69	10	3.1	73.5
Brister, Pitt.	342	187	54.7	2365	6.92	9	2.6	t79	10	2.9	73.1
Trudeau, Ind.	362	190	52.5	2317	6.40	15	4.1	71	13	3.6	71.3
Grogan, N.E.	261	133	51.0	1697	6.50	9	3.4	t55	14	5.4	60.8

AFC NON-QUALIFIERS

Player—Team	Att.	Cmp.	Pct. Cmp.	Yds.	Avg. Gain	TD	Pct. TD	Lg.	Int.	Pct. Int.	Rating Pts.
Reich, Buff.	87	53	60.9	701	8.06	7	8.0	t63	2	2.3	103.7
Wilhelm, Cin.	56	30	53.6	425	7.59	4	7.1	t46	2	3.6	87.3
Pelluer, K.C.	47	26	55.3	301	6.40	1	2.1	24	0	0.0	82.0
Beuerlein, Raiders	217	108	49.8	1677	7.73	13	6.0	t67	9	4.1	78.4
Eason, N.E.-Jets	141	79	56.0	1016	7.21	4	2.8	t63	6	4.3	70.5
Kubiak, Den.	55	32	58.2	284	5.16	2	3.6	22	2	3.6	69.1
Wilson, N.E.	150	75	50.0	1006	6.71	3	2.0	t65	5	3.3	64.5
Ramsey, Ind.	50	24	48.0	280	5.60	1	2.0	47	1	2.0	63.8
Chandler, Ind.	80	39	48.8	537	6.71	2	2.5	t82	3	3.8	63.4
Schroeder, Raiders	194	91	46.9	1550	7.99	8	4.1	t84	13	6.7	60.3
Tolliver, S.D.	185	89	48.1	1097	5.93	5	2.7	49	8	4.3	57.9
Jaworski, K.C.	61	36	59.0	385	6.31	2	3.3	32	5	8.2	54.3
Carlson, Hou.	31	15	48.4	155	5.00	0	0.0	23	1	3.2	49.8
Flutie, N.E.	91	36	39.6	493	5.42	2	2.2	36	4	4.4	46.6
Secules, Miami	50	22	44.0	286	5.72	1	2.0	t44	3	6.0	44.3
Pagel, Clev.	14	5	35.7	60	4.29	1	7.1	18	1	7.1	43.8
Mackey, Jets	25	11	44.0	125	5.00	0	0.0	22	1	4.0	42.9
Stouffer, Sea.	59	29	49.2	270	4.58	0	0.0	29	3	5.1	40.9
Blackledge, Pitt.	60	22	36.7	282	4.70	1	1.7	30	3	5.0	36.9
Ryan, Jets	30	15	50.0	153	5.10	1	3.3	25	3	10.0	36.5
Archer, S.D.	12	5	41.7	62	5.17	0	0.0	17	1	8.3	23.6

(Fewer than 10 attempts)

Player—Team	Att.	Cmp.	Pct. Cmp.	Yds.	Avg. Gain	TD	Pct. TD	Lg.	Int.	Pct. Int.	Rating Pts.
Bentley, Ind.	1	0	0.0	0	0.00	0	0.0	0	0	0.0	39.6
Carter, Pitt.	1	1	100.0	15	15.00	0	0.0	15	0	0.0	118.8
Dickerson, Ind.	0	0	......	0	....	0	....	0	0	......	0.0
Elkins, K.C.	2	1	50.0	5	2.50	0	0.0	5	1	50.0	16.7
Evans, Raiders	2	2	100.0	50	25.00	0	0.0	40	0	0.0	118.8
Feagles, N.E.	2	0	0.0	0	0.00	0	0.0	0	0	0.0	39.6
Gossett, Raiders	1	0	0.0	0	0.00	0	0.0	0	0	0.0	39.6
Humphrey, Den.	2	1	50.0	17	8.50	1	50.0	t17	0	0.0	118.8
Jensen, Mia.	1	1	100.0	19	19.00	1	100.0	t19	0	0.0	158.3
Johnson, Buff.	0	0	......	0	....	0	....	0	0	......	0.0
Johnson, Den.	1	0	0.0	0	0.00	0	0.0	0	0	0.0	39.6
Malone, Jets	2	2	100.0	13	6.50	0	0.0	11	0	0.0	93.8
Metcalf, Clev.	2	1	50.0	32	16.00	1	50.0	t32	0	0.0	135.4
Rodriguez, Sea.	1	1	100.0	4	4.00	0	0.0	4	0	0.0	83.3
Saxon, K.C.	1	0	0.0	0	0.00	0	0.0	0	1	100.0	0.0
Schonert, Cin.	2	0	0.0	0	0.00	0	0.0	0	0	0.0	39.6
Strom, Pitt.	1	0	0.0	0	0.00	0	0.0	0	0	0.0	39.6
Tatupu, N.E.	1	1	100.0	15	15.00	0	0.0	15	0	0.0	118.8
Zendejas, Hou.	1	0	0.0	0	0.00	0	0.0	0	1	100.0	0.0

NFC INDIVIDUAL QUALIFIERS

Player—Team	Att.	Cmp.	Pct. Cmp.	Yds.	Avg. Gain	TD	Pct. TD	Lg.	Int.	Pct. Int.	Rating Pts.
MONTANA, S.F.	386	271	70.2	3521	9.12	26	6.7	t95	8	2.1	112.4
Everett, Rams	518	304	58.7	4310	8.32	29	5.6	t78	17	3.3	90.6
Rypien, Wash.	476	280	58.8	3768	7.92	22	4.6	t80	13	2.7	88.1
Hebert, N.O.	353	222	62.9	2686	7.61	15	4.2	t54	15	4.2	82.7
Majkowski, G.B.	599	353	58.9	4318	7.21	27	4.5	t79	20	3.3	82.3
Simms, Giants	405	228	56.3	3061	7.56	14	3.5	t62	14	3.5	77.6
Miller, Atl.	526	280	53.2	3459	6.58	16	3.0	t72	10	1.9	76.1
Cunningham, Phil.	532	290	54.5	3400	6.39	21	3.9	t66	15	2.8	75.5
Wilson, Minn.	362	194	53.6	2543	7.02	9	2.5	50	12	3.3	70.5
Hogeboom, Phoe.	364	204	56.0	2591	7.12	14	3.8	t59	19	5.2	69.5
Testaverde, T.B.	480	258	53.8	3133	6.53	20	4.2	t78	22	4.6	68.9
Tomczak, Chi.	306	156	51.0	2058	6.73	16	5.2	t79	16	5.2	68.2
Gagliano, Det.	232	117	50.4	1671	7.20	6	2.6	t75	12	5.2	61.2
Aikman, Dall.	293	155	52.9	1749	5.97	9	3.1	t75	18	6.1	55.7

NFC NON-QUALIFIERS

Player—Team	Att.	Cmp.	Pct. Cmp.	Yds.	Avg. Gain	TD	Pct. TD	Lg.	Int.	Pct. Int.	Rating Pts.
Young, S.F.	92	64	69.6	1001	10.88	8	8.7	t50	3	3.3	120.8
Fourcade, N.O.	107	61	57.0	930	8.69	7	6.5	t54	4	3.7	92.0
Hostetler, Giants	39	20	51.3	294	7.54	3	7.7	t35	2	5.1	80.5
Millen, Atl.	50	31	62.0	432	8.64	1	2.0	47	2	4.0	79.8
Humphries, Wash.	10	5	50.0	91	9.10	1	10.0	39	1	10.0	75.4
Kramer, Minn.	136	77	56.6	906	6.66	7	5.1	39	7	5.1	72.7
Harbaugh, Chi.	178	111	62.4	1204	6.76	5	2.8	t49	9	5.1	70.5
Peete, Det.	195	103	52.8	1479	7.58	5	2.6	69	9	4.6	67.0
Williams, Wash.	93	51	54.8	585	6.29	1	1.1	46	3	3.2	64.1
Walsh, Dall.	219	110	50.2	1371	6.26	5	2.3	46	9	4.1	60.5
Tupa, Phoe.	134	65	48.5	973	7.26	3	2.2	t77	9	6.7	52.2
Ferguson, T.B.	90	44	48.9	533	5.92	3	3.3	t69	6	6.7	50.8
Rosenbach, Phoe.	22	9	40.9	95	4.32	0	0.0	24	1	4.5	35.2
Hipple, Det.	18	7	38.9	90	5.00	0	0.0	30	3	16.7	15.7

Joe Montana's quarterback rating of 112.4 in 1989 broke the old record of 110.4 set by Milt Plum of the Cleveland Browns in 1960.

	Att	Comp	Pct	Yds	Avg	TD	TD%	Long	Int	Int%	Rating
(Fewer than 10 attempts)											
Awalt, Phoe.	1	0	0.0	0	0.00	0	0.0	0	1	100.0	0.0
Bono, S.F.	5	4	80.0	62	12.40	1	20.0	t45	0	0.0	157.9
Byner, Wash.	1	0	0.0	0	0.00	0	0.0	0	0	0.0	39.6
Camarillo, Phoe.	1	1	100.0	0	0.00	0	0.0	0	0	0.0	79.2
Cavanaugh, Phil.	5	3	60.0	33	6.60	1	20.0	t13	1	20.0	79.6
Dilweg, G.B.	1	1	100.0	7	7.00	0	0.0	7	0	0.0	95.8
Dozier, Minn.	1	1	100.0	19	19.00	1	100.0	t19	0	0.0	158.3
Fontenot, G.B.	0	0	....	0	....	0	....	0	0	......	0.0
Fulhage, Atl.	1	1	100.0	12	12.00	0	0.0	12	0	0.0	116.7
Herrmann, Rams	5	4	80.0	59	11.80	0	0.0	23	1	20.0	76.3
Hill, N.O.	0	0	....	0	....	0	....	0	0	......	0.0
Hilliard, N.O.	1	1	100.0	35	35.00	1	100.0	t35	0	0.0	158.3
Jones, Atl.	1	0	0.0	0	0.00	0	0.0	0	0	0.0	39.6
Long, Det.	5	2	40.0	42	8.40	0	0.0	37	0	0.0	70.4
Rice, Minn.	0	0	....	0	....	0	....	0	0	......	0.0
Ruzek, Phil.	1	1	100.0	22	22.00	1	100.0	t22	0	0.0	158.3
Sanders, Wash.	1	1	100.0	32	32.00	0	0.0	32	0	0.0	118.8
Saxon, Dall.	1	1	100.0	4	4.00	0	0.0	4	0	0.0	83.3
Sikahema, Phoe.	1	0	0.0	0	0.00	0	0.0	0	0	0.0	39.6

t—Touchdown.
Leader based on rating points, minimum 224 attempts.

1989 PASS RECEIVING

MOST RECEPTIONS, SEASON
  NFC: 90—Sterling Sharpe, Green Bay.
  AFC: 88—Andre Reed, Buffalo.

MOST RECEPTIONS, GAME
  NFC: 15—Willie Anderson, L.A. Rams at N.O., November 26 (336 yards).
  AFC: 13—Andre Reed, Buffalo vs. Denver, September 18 (157 yards).

MOST YARDS, SEASON
  NFC: 1483—Jerry Rice, San Francisco.
  AFC: 1312—Andre Reed, Buffalo.

MOST YARDS, GAME
  NFC: 336—Willie Anderson, L.A. Rams at N.O., Nov. 26 (15 receptions, TD).
  AFC: 194—Tim McGee, Cincinnati vs. Det., November 19 (11 receptions, TD).

LONGEST GAIN
  AFC: 97—Webster Slaughter (from Bernie Kosar) Clev. vs. Chi., Oct. 23 (TD).
  NFC: 95—John Taylor (from Joe Montana) S.F. at L.A. Rams, Dec. 11 (TD).

AVERAGE YARDS PER RECEPTION
  NFC: 26.0—Willie Anderson, L.A. Rams.
  AFC: 19.0—Webster Slaughter, Cleveland.

MOST TOUCHDOWNS
  NFC: 17—Jerry Rice, San Francisco.
  AFC: 10—Anthony Miller, San Diego.

TEAM LEADERS
  AFC: BUFFALO: 88, Andre Reed; CINCINNATI: 65, Tim McGee; CLEVE-
        LAND: 65, Webster Slaughter; DENVER: 76, Vance Johnson;
        HOUSTON: 66, Drew Hill; INDIANAPOLIS: 63, Bill Brooks;
        KANSAS CITY: 44, Stephone Paige; L.A. RAIDERS: 57, Mervyn
        Fernandez; MIAMI: 64, Mark Clayton; NEW ENGLAND: 54,
        Eric Sievers; N.Y. JETS: 63, Al Toon; PITTSBURGH: 50, Louis
        Lipps; SAN DIEGO: 75, Anthony Miller; SEATTLE: 77, Brian
        Blades.
  NFC: ATLANTA: 58, Shawn Collins; CHICAGO: 50, Neal Anderson; DALLAS:
        46, Kelvin Martin; DETROIT: 70, Richard Johnson; GREEN
        BAY: 90, Sterling Sharpe; L.A. RAMS: 70, Henry Ellard; MINNE-
        SOTA: 65, Anthony Carter; NEW ORLEANS: 68, Eric Martin;
        N.Y. GIANTS: 38, Odessa Turner; PHILADELPHIA: 68, Keith
        Byars; PHOENIX: 62, J.T. Smith; SAN FRANCISCO: 82, Jerry
        Rice; TAMPA BAY: 86, Mark Carrier; WASHINGTON: 86, Art
        Monk.

TOP TEN PASS RECEIVERS

Player—Team	No.	Yards	Avg.	Long	TDs.
SHARPE, STERLING, Green Bay	90	1423	15.8	t79	12
Reed, Andre, Buffalo	88	1312	14.9	t78	9
Carrier, Mark, Tampa Bay	86	1422	16.5	t78	9
Monk, Art, Washington	86	1186	13.8	t60	8
Rice, Jerry, San Francisco	82	1483	18.1	t68	17
Sanders, Ricky, Washington	80	1138	14.2	68	4
Clark, Gary, Washington	79	1229	15.6	t80	9
Blades, Brian, Seattle	77	1063	13.8	t60	5
Johnson, Vance, Denver	76	1095	14.4	69	7
Williams, John L., Seattle	76	657	8.6	t51	6

TOP TEN PASS RECEIVERS BY YARDS

Player—Team	Yards	No.	Avg.	Long	TDs.
RICE, JERRY, San Francisco	1483	82	18.1	t68	17
Sharpe, Sterling, Green Bay	1423	90	15.8	t79	12
Carrier, Mark, Tampa Bay	1422	86	16.5	t78	9
Ellard, Henry, L.A. Rams	1382	70	19.7	53	8
Reed, Andre, Buffalo	1312	88	14.9	t78	9
Miller, Anthony, San Diego	1252	75	16.7	t69	10
Slaughter, Webster, Cleveland	1236	65	19.0	t97	6
Clark, Gary, Washington	1229	79	15.6	t80	9
McGee, Tim, Cincinnati	1211	65	18.6	t74	8
Monk, Art, Washington	1186	86	13.8	t60	8

AFC—INDIVIDUALS

Player—Team	No.	Yds.	Avg.	Lng.	TD	Player—Team	No.	Yds.	Avg.	Lng.	TD
REED, Buff.	88	1312	14.9	t78	9	Smith, Raiders	19	140	7.4	14	0
Blades, Sea.	77	1063	13.8	t60	5	Mueller, Raiders	18	240	13.3	29	2
Johnson, Den.	76	1095	14.4	69	7	Hayes, K.C.	18	229	12.7	23	2
Williams, Sea.	76	657	8.6	t51	6	Highsmith, Hou.	18	201	11.2	32	2
A. Miller, S.D.	75	1252	16.7	t69	10	Metzelaars, Buff.	18	179	9.9	23	2
Hill, Hou.	66	938	14.2	50	8	Spencer, S.D.	18	112	6.2	23	0
Slaughter, Clev.	65	1236	19.0	t97	6	Beebe, Buff.	17	317	18.6	t63	2
McGee, Cin.	65	1211	18.6	t74	8	Mobley, Den.	17	200	11.8	36	0
Clayton, Mia.	64	1011	15.8	t78	9	Hillary, Cin.	17	162	9.5	17	1
Brooks, Ind.	63	919	14.6	t55	4	Alexander, Raiders	15	295	19.7	61	1
Toon, Jets	63	693	11.0	t37	2	Martin, Cin.	15	160	10.7	21	2
Jensen, Mia.	61	557	9.1	20	6	K. Jones, Clev.	15	126	8.4	36	0
Langhorne, Clev.	60	749	12.5	t62	2	Worley, Pitt.	15	113	7.5	19	0
Thomas, Buff.	60	669	11.2	t74	6	Tyler, Sea.	14	148	10.6	27	0
Fernandez, Raiders	57	1069	18.8	t75	5	Winder, Den.	14	91	6.5	19	0
Givins, Hou.	55	794	14.4	48	3	Beach, Ind.	14	87	6.2	17	2
Sievers, N.E.	54	615	11.4	46	0	Martin, N.E.	13	229	17.6	37	0
Metcalf, Clev.	54	397	7.4	t68	4	Harris, Hou.	13	202	15.5	36	2
Rison, Ind.	52	820	15.8	61	4	T. Brown, Mia.	13	117	9.0	23	0
Brown, Cin.	52	814	15.7	46	6	Dressel, K.C.-Jets	12	191	15.9	t49	1
Bentley, Ind.	52	525	10.1	61	3	Dawson, N.E.	12	101	8.4	17	0
Lipps, Pitt.	50	944	18.9	t79	5	Kattus, Cin.	12	93	7.8	16	0
Holman, Cin.	50	736	14.7	t73	9	Brinson, S.D.	12	71	5.9	11	0
Dykes, N.E.	49	795	16.2	42	5	Early, S.D.	11	126	11.5	21	0
Duper, Mia.	49	717	14.6	41	1	Saxon, K.C.	11	86	7.8	18	0
C. Jones, N.E.	48	670	14.0	t65	6	Boyer, Ind.	11	58	5.3	15	2
Jeffires, Hou.	47	619	13.2	t45	2	Nattiel, Den.	10	183	18.3	43	1
Townsell, Jets	45	787	17.5	t63	5	Smith, Cin.	10	140	14.0	t41	1
Paige, K.C.	44	759	17.3	50	2	Jennings, Cin.	10	119	11.9	t43	1
Duncan, Hou.	43	613	14.3	55	5	McNeil, Clev.	10	114	11.4	32	0
Skansi, Sea.	39	488	12.5	26	5	Caravello, S.D.	10	95	9.5	37	0
Nelson, Minn.-S.D.	38	380	10.0	49	0	Bratton, Den.	10	69	6.9	t17	3
Hector, Jets	38	330	8.7	32	2	Tatupu, N.E.	10	54	5.4	11	0
Carter, Pitt.	38	267	7.0	t22	3	McNeal, Sea.	9	147	16.3	48	0
Brooks, Cin.	37	306	8.3	25	2	Griggs, Jets	9	112	12.4	23	0
Mandley, K.C.	35	476	13.6	44	1	Chadwick, Det.-Sea.	9	104	11.6	19	0
McNair, K.C.	34	372	10.9	24	1	Jackson, Raiders	9	69	7.7	20	0
Hoge, Pitt.	34	271	8.0	22	0	Lofton, Buff.	8	166	20.8	47	3
Vick, Jets	34	241	7.1	21	2	Werner, Jets	8	115	14.4	36	0
Harry, K.C.	33	430	13.0	25	2	Epps, Jets	8	108	13.5	21	0
Edmunds, Mia.	32	382	11.9	30	3	Walker, Jets	8	89	11.1	31	0
McNeil, Jets	31	310	10.0	t25	1	Alexander, Den.	8	84	10.5	28	0
Pinkett, Hou.	31	239	7.7	23	1	R. Thomas, K.C.	8	58	7.3	12	2
Banks, Mia.	30	520	17.3	61	1	Roberts, K.C.	8	55	6.9	25	1
Dickerson, Ind.	30	211	7.0	22	1	Hampton, Mia.	8	25	3.1	12	0
Fryar, N.E.	29	537	18.5	52	3	Schwedes, Mia.	7	174	24.9	t65	1
Harmon, Buff.	29	363	12.5	t42	4	Harper, Jets	7	127	18.1	48	0
Newsome, Clev.	29	324	11.2	31	1	McEwen, S.D.	7	99	14.1	29	0
Shuler, Jets	29	322	11.1	22	0	Kane, Sea.	7	94	13.4	20	0
Perryman, N.E.	29	195	6.7	16	0	Stone, Pitt.	7	92	13.1	16	0
Gault, Raiders	28	690	24.6	t84	4	Smith, Mia.	7	81	11.6	34	0
Morgan, N.E.	28	486	17.4	t55	3	Butts, S.D.	7	21	3.0	8	0
Hill, Pitt.	28	455	16.3	53	1	K. Davis, Buff.	6	92	15.3	29	2
Jackson, Den.	28	446	15.9	49	2	Dupard, N.E.	6	70	11.7	45	0
Largent, Sea.	28	403	14.4	33	3	Tillman, Clev.	6	70	11.7	19	2
Neubert, Jets	28	302	10.8	t35	1	W. Williams, Pitt.	6	48	8.0	16	0
Brennan, Clev.	28	289	10.3	38	0	Ball, Cin.	6	44	7.3	15	0
Dyal, Raiders	27	499	18.5	t67	2	White, Hou.	6	37	6.2	11	0
Manoa, Clev.	27	241	8.9	32	2	Redden, Clev.	6	34	5.7	8	0
Holland, S.D.	26	336	12.9	37	0	Pruitt, Ind.	5	71	14.2	40	1
Sewell, Den.	25	416	16.6	56	3	Worthen, K.C.	5	69	13.8	21	0
Johnson, Buff.	25	303	12.1	36	1	Kinnebrew, Buff.	5	60	12.0	18	0
Clark, Sea.	25	260	10.4	28	1	Logan, Mia.	5	34	6.8	11	0
Heard, K.C.	25	246	9.8	27	1	Riggs, Cin.	5	29	5.8	9	0
Stradford, Mia.	25	233	9.3	32	0	Stock, Pitt.	4	74	18.5	27	0
A. Brown, Mia.	24	410	17.1	t48	5	Thompson, Pitt.	4	74	18.5	28	0
Walker, S.D.	24	395	16.5	49	1	Verhulst, Hou.	4	48	12.0	21	0
Burkett, Buff.-Jets	24	298	12.4	30	1	Horton, Raiders	4	44	11.0	20	1
Weathers, Ind.-K.C.	23	254	11.0	27	0	Taylor, Cin.	4	44	11.0	t18	2
Warner, Sea.	23	153	6.7	24	1	Jackson, Hou.	4	31	7.8	18	0
Young, Den.	22	402	18.3	47	2	Rozier, Hou.	4	28	7.0	8	0
Mularkey, Pitt.	22	326	14.8	34	1	Brown, Jets	4	10	2.5	6	0
Cox, S.D.	22	200	9.1	24	2	Junkin, Raiders	3	32	10.7	28	2
Humphrey, Den.	22	156	7.1	13	1	Mrosko, Hou.	3	28	9.3	14	0
Bernstine, S.D.	21	222	10.6	36	1	Harris, Sea.	3	26	8.7	11	0
Stephens, N.E.	21	207	9.9	37	0	Fenner, Sea.	3	23	7.7	9	0
Kay, Den.	21	197	9.4	t20	2	Oliphant, Clev.	3	22	7.3	9	0
Verdin, Ind.	20	381	19.1	t82	1	Davenport, Mia.	3	19	6.3	9	0
McKeller, Buff.	20	341	17.1	t39	2	Cook, N.E.	3	13	4.3	5	0
Allen, Raiders	20	191	9.6	26	0	Kelly, Den.	3	13	4.3	6	0

Player—Team	No.	Yds.	Avg.	Lng.	TD
Garrett, Cin.	2	29	14.5	18	0
Allen, S.D.	2	19	9.5	11	0
Holifield, Cin.	2	18	9.0	14	0
Dunn, Jets	2	13	6.5	8	0
Okoye, K.C.	2	12	6.0	8	0
Mack, Clev.	2	7	3.5	4	0
Parker, S.D.	2	5	2.5	4	1
Gamble, K.C.	2	2	1.0	6	0
Parker, Cin.	1	45	45.0	45	0
Waiters, Clev.	1	14	14.0	t14	1
Kinchen, Mia.	1	12	12.0	12	0
Bouyer, Sea.	1	9	9.0	9	0
Brown, Raiders	1	8	8.0	8	0
Faaola, Mia.	1	8	8.0	8	0
T. Johnson, Hou.	1	8	8.0	8	0
J. Jones, Sea.	1	8	8.0	8	0
Mueller, Buff.	1	8	8.0	8	0
O'Shea, Pitt.	1	8	8.0	8	0
Floyd, S.D.	1	6	6.0	6	0
Feasel, Sea.	1	5	5.0	5	0
Middleton, Clev.	1	5	5.0	t5	1
Glasgow, Sea.	1	4	4.0	4	0
McMahon, S.D.	1	4	4.0	4	0
Tennell, Clev.	1	4	4.0	t4	1
Carruth, K.C.	1	3	3.0	3	0
Hardy, Mia.	1	2	2.0	2	0
Rolle, Buff.	1	1	1.0	t1	1
Kosar, Clev.	1	−7	−7.0	−7	0
Brister, Pitt.	1	−10	−10.0	−10	0

NFC—INDIVIDUALS

Player—Team	No.	Yds.	Avg.	Lng.	TD
SHARPE, G.B.	90	1423	15.8	t79	12
Carrier, T.B.	86	1422	16.5	t78	9
Monk, Wash.	86	1186	13.8	t60	8
Rice, S.F.	82	1483	18.1	t68	17
Sanders, Wash.	80	1138	14.2	68	4
Clark, Wash.	79	1229	15.6	t80	9
Rathman, S.F.	73	616	8.4	36	1
Ellard, Rams	70	1382	19.7	53	8
R. Johnson, Det.	70	1091	15.6	t75	8
E. Martin, N.O.	68	1090	16.0	t53	8
Byars, Phil.	68	721	10.6	60	0
Carter, Minn.	65	1066	16.4	50	4
Jackson, Phil.	63	648	10.3	33	3
J.T. Smith, Phoe.	62	778	12.5	31	5
Taylor, S.F.	60	1077	18.0	t95	10
Woodside, G.B.	59	527	8.9	33	0
Collins, Atl.	58	862	14.9	47	3
Byner, Wash.	54	458	8.5	27	2
Hilliard, N.O.	52	514	9.9	t54	5
Holohan, Rams	51	510	10.0	31	2
Hill, T.B.	50	673	13.5	53	5
Anderson, Chi.	50	434	8.7	t49	4
Craig, S.F.	49	473	9.7	44	1
Hill, N.O.	48	636	13.3	46	4
Kemp, G.B.	48	611	12.7	39	2
Martin, Dall.	46	644	14.0	46	2
Jones, Phoe.	45	838	18.6	t72	3
Carter, Phil.	45	605	13.4	42	11
Anderson, Rams	44	1146	26.0	t78	5
Green, Phoe.	44	703	16.0	t59	7
Jones, Minn.	42	694	16.5	50	1
Clark, Det.	41	748	18.2	69	2
Jones, Atl.	41	396	9.7	46	0
Haynes, Atl.	40	681	17.0	t72	4
Jones, S.F.	40	500	12.5	t36	4
Walker, Dall.-Minn.	40	423	10.6	52	2
Fontenot, G.B.	40	372	9.3	t38	3
Gentry, Chi.	39	463	11.9	t79	1
Lang, Atl.	39	436	11.2	32	1
Settle, Atl.	39	316	8.1	33	2
Turner, Giants	38	467	12.3	44	4
McGee, Rams	37	303	8.2	25	4
Wilder, T.B.	36	335	9.3	27	3
Jordan, Minn.	35	506	14.5	34	3
Meggett, Giants	34	531	15.6	t62	4
Brenner, N.O.	34	398	11.7	t30	4
Delpino, Rams	34	334	9.8	25	1
Manuel, Giants	33	539	16.3	49	1
Awalt, Phoe.	33	360	10.9	28	1
Heller, Atl.	33	324	9.8	30	1
Muster, Chi.	32	259	8.1	25	3
Morris, Chi.	30	486	16.2	t58	1
Phillips, Det.	30	352	11.7	t55	1
Hall, T.B.	30	331	11.0	32	2
Fenney, Minn.	30	254	8.5	26	2
Howard, T.B.	30	188	6.3	18	1
McKinnon, Chi.	28	418	14.9	41	3
Anderson, Giants	28	268	9.6	26	0
Folsom, Dall.	28	265	9.5	26	2
Mowatt, Giants	27	288	10.7	31	0
Davis, Chi.	26	397	15.3	t52	3
Irvin, Dall.	26	378	14.5	t65	2
Dixon, Atl.	25	357	14.3	t53	2
Johnson, Rams	25	148	5.9	22	5
Dixon, Dall.	24	477	19.9	t75	2
Thornton, Chi.	24	392	16.3	t36	3
Stanley, Det.	24	304	12.7	37	0
B. Sanders, Det.	24	282	11.8	46	0
Query, G.B.	23	350	15.2	45	2
Sikahema, Phoe.	23	245	10.7	37	0
Novacek, Phoe.	23	225	9.8	30	1
Turner, N.O.	22	279	12.7	t54	1
Bavaro, Giants	22	278	12.6	29	3
West, G.B.	22	269	12.2	31	5
Perriman, N.O.	20	356	17.8	47	0
A. Cox, Rams	20	340	17.0	t51	3
Shepard, N.O.-Dall.	20	304	15.2	t37	1
Johnson, Phil.	20	295	14.8	34	1
Anderson, Minn.	20	193	9.7	18	0
Fullwood, G.B.	19	214	11.3	67	0
Toney, Phil.	19	124	6.5	15	0
Bell, Rams	19	85	4.5	14	0
Matthews, G.B.	18	200	11.1	25	0
Ferrell, Phoe.	18	122	6.8	25	0
Ingram, Giants	17	290	17.1	t41	1
Boso, Chi.	17	182	10.7	43	1
Drummond, Phil.	17	180	10.6	21	1
Tautalatasi, Dall.	17	157	9.2	23	0
Burbage, Dall.	17	134	7.9	15	0
Palmer, Dall.	17	93	5.5	13	0
Giles, Phil.	16	225	14.1	t66	2
Johnston, Dall.	16	133	8.3	28	3
Warren, Wash.	15	167	11.1	25	1
Carthon, Giants	15	132	8.8	18	0
Haddix, G.B.	15	111	7.4	23	1
Stamps, T.B.	15	82	5.5	21	0
Drewrey, T.B.	14	157	11.2	18	1
Dozier, Minn.	14	148	10.6	30	0
Gustafson, Minn.	14	144	10.3	22	2
Holmes, Phoe.	13	271	20.8	t77	1
Baker, Giants	13	255	19.6	t39	2
Quick, Phil.	13	228	17.5	40	2
Garrity, Phil.	13	209	16.1	31	2
Mobley, Det.	13	158	12.2	30	0
Heyward, N.O.	13	69	5.3	12	0
Lewis, Minn.	12	148	12.3	t28	1
McDonald, Det.	12	138	11.5	24	0
Peebles, T.B.	11	180	16.4	32	0
Bland, G.B.	11	164	14.9	t46	1
Beckman, Atl.	11	102	9.3	21	1
W. Harris, T.B.	11	102	9.3	21	1
Tate, T.B.	11	75	6.8	19	1
Wilson, S.F.	9	103	11.4	19	1
Tice, N.O.	9	98	10.9	23	1
Suhey, Chi.	9	73	8.1	22	1
Sydney, S.F.	9	71	7.9	13	0
Scott, Dall.	9	63	7.0	12	0
Wilkins, Atl.	8	179	22.4	36	3
Bailey, Atl.	8	170	21.3	41	0
Carson, K.C.-Phil.	8	107	13.4	28	1
Scales, N.O.	8	89	11.1	26	0
Sherman, Phil.	8	85	10.6	17	0
Morris, Wash.	8	65	8.1	17	0
Rouson, Giants	7	121	17.3	39	0
D. Smith, T.B.	7	110	15.7	44	0
Ford, Dall.	7	78	11.1	21	1

Andre Reed's 88 catches in 1989 led the American Football Conference and helped the Buffalo Bills capture the AFC Eastern Division crown.

Player—Team	No.	Yds.	Avg.	Lng.	TD	Player—Team	No.	Yds.	Avg.	Lng.	TD
Didier, G.B.	7	71	10.1	t24	1	Frazier, N.O.	3	25	8.3	22	0
Riggs, Wash.	7	67	9.6	13	0	Higgs, Phil.	3	9	3.0	8	0
Cross, Giants	6	107	17.8	27	1	Edwards, Phil.	2	74	37.0	66	0
Flagler, S.F.	6	51	8.5	30	0	Gray, Det.	2	47	23.5	30	0
Sargent, Dall.	6	50	8.3	21	0	T. Johnson, Det.	2	29	14.5	22	0
Jennings, Dall.	6	47	7.8	14	0	Paige, Det.	2	27	13.5	15	0
Jordan, Phoe.	6	20	3.3	8	0	Baker, Phoe.	2	18	9.0	9	0
Ro. Brown, Rams	5	113	22.6	t39	1	McConkey, Phoe.	2	18	9.0	10	0
Ford, Det.	5	56	11.2	37	0	Clark, Minn.	2	14	7.0	12	0
Green, Chi.	5	48	9.6	21	0	Gary, Rams	2	13	6.5	8	0
Ingram, Minn.	5	47	9.4	21	1	Spagnola, G.B.	2	13	6.5	14	0
Paterra, Atl.	5	42	8.4	20	0	Little, Phil.	2	8	4.0	7	1
Wolfley, Phoe.	5	38	7.6	22	0	Adams, Giants	2	7	3.5	10	0
J. Johnson, Wash.	4	84	21.0	39	0	Greer, S.F.	1	26	26.0	26	0
Clack, Dall.	4	69	17.3	44	0	Banks, Giants	1	22	22.0	t22	1
Jordan, N.O.	4	53	13.3	17	0	Alexander, Dall.	1	16	16.0	16	0
G. Thomas, Atl.	4	46	11.5	16	0	Mitchell, T.B.	1	11	11.0	11	0
Robinson, Giants	4	41	10.3	16	0	S. Mitchell, Phoe.	1	10	10.0	10	0
Williams, Phil.	4	32	8.0	11	0	Tillman, Giants	1	9	9.0	9	0
Rice, Minn.	4	29	7.3	14	0	Cook, N.O.	1	8	8.0	8	0
Walls, S.F.	4	16	4.0	9	1	Usher, Phoe.	1	8	8.0	8	0
Novoselsky, Minn.	4	11	2.8	6	2	Waddle, Chi.	1	8	8.0	8	0
Henderson, S.F.	3	130	43.3	78	0	Reeves, Phoe.	1	5	5.0	5	0
Orr, Wash.	3	80	26.7	48	0	Ruzek, Dall.	1	4	4.0	4	0
Kozlowski, Chi.	3	74	24.7	55	0	Tice, Wash.	1	2	2.0	2	0
Painter, Det.	3	41	13.7	27	0	Green, Rams	1	−5	−5.0	−5	0
Williams, S.F.	3	38	12.7	17	0	Sanders, Atl.	1	−8	−8.0	−8	0
Sanders, Chi.	3	28	9.3	t16	1	Aikman, Dall.	1	−13	−13.0	−13	0

t—Touchdown.
Leader based on most passes caught.

1989 INTERCEPTIONS

MOST INTERCEPTIONS, SEASON
    AFC: 9—Felix Wright, Cleveland.
    NFC: 8—Eric Allen, Philadelphia.

MOST INTERCEPTIONS, GAME
    AFC: 3—David Fulcher, Cincinnati at Kansas City, October 1 (38 yards).
            David Fulcher, Cincinnati vs. Houston, December 17 (22 yards).
    NFC: 2—By 19 players.

MOST YARDS RETURNING INTERCEPTIONS
    AFC: 233—Eddie Anderson, L.A. Raiders.
    NFC: 170—Tim McDonald, Phoenix.

LONGEST INTERCEPTION RETURN
    AFC: 92—Erik McMillan, N.Y. Jets vs. Indianapolis, October 1 (TD).
    NFC: 90—Issiac Holt, Minnesota vs. Detroit, October 8 (TD).

MOST TOUCHDOWNS, SEASON
    AFC: 2—Eddie Anderson, L.A. Raiders.
           Thane Gash, Cleveland.
    NFC: 1—By 20 players.

TEAM LEADERS
    AFC: BUFFALO: 6, Mark Kelso; CINCINNATI: 8, David Fulcher; CLEVE-LAND: 9, Felix Wright; DENVER: 6, Tyrone Braxton; HOUSTON: 5, Steve Brown; INDIANAPOLIS: 7, Keith Taylor; KANSAS CITY: 4, Albert Lewis, Kevin Ross; L.A. RAIDERS: 5, Eddie Anderson; MIAMI: 4, Louis Oliver; NEW ENGLAND: 5, Maurice Hurst; N.Y. JETS: 6, Erik McMillan; PITTSBURGH: 4, Dwayne Woodruff; SAN DIEGO: 7, Gill Byrd; SEATTLE: 5, Eugene Robinson.
    NFC: ATLANTA: 5, Deion Sanders; CHICAGO: 4, Lemuel Stinson; DALLAS: 2, Eugene Lockhart; DETROIT: 6, Jerry Holmes; GREEN BAY: 6, Dave Brown; L.A. RAMS: 6, Jerry Gray; MINNESOTA: 5, Joey Browner; NEW ORLEANS: 6, Dave Waymer; N.Y. GIANTS: 5, Terry Kinard; PHILADELPHIA: 8, Eric Allen; PHOENIX: 7, Tim McDonald; SAN FRANCISCO: 5, Ronnie Lott; TAMPA BAY: 6, Harry Hamilton, Mark Robinson; WASHINGTON: 4, Brian Davis, A.J. Johnson, Alvin Walton.

TEAM CHAMPION
    NFC: 30—Philadelphia.
    AFC: 27—Cleveland.

INTERCEPTIONS—TEAM

AMERICAN FOOTBALL CONFERENCE

Team	No.	Yards	Avg.	Long	TDs.
Cleveland	27	300	11.1	t36	4
San Diego	25	224	9.0	34	0
Buffalo	23	269	11.7	43	1
Indianapolis	21	391	18.6	t80	2
Denver	21	318	15.1	50	2
Houston	21	263	12.5	48	0
Pittsburgh	21	261	12.4	39	0
Cincinnati	21	204	9.7	28	1
L.A. Raiders	18	362	20.1	t87	3
New England	16	118	7.4	28	1
N.Y. Jets	15	261	17.4	t92	2
Kansas City	15	133	8.9	27	0
Miami	15	126	8.4	28	0
Seattle	9	57	6.3	20	0
Conference Total	277	3474	......	t92	16
Conference Average	19.8	248.1	12.5	....	1.1

NATIONAL FOOTBALL CONFERENCE

Team	No.	Yards	Avg.	Long	TDs.
Philadelphia	30	375	12.5	t60	2
Washington	27	284	10.5	t59	3
Chicago	26	268	10.3	43	1
Green Bay	25	232	9.3	53	0
N.Y. Giants	22	330	15.0	t58	2
L.A. Rams	21	372	17.7	t81	3
San Francisco	21	262	12.5	42	0
Tampa Bay	21	234	11.1	t68	2
New Orleans	21	226	10.8	t63	2
Atlanta	20	285	14.3	40	0
Minnesota	18	264	14.7	t90	2
Phoenix	16	275	17.2	t53	2
Detroit	16	107	6.7	36	1
Dallas	7	37	5.3	18	0
Conference Total	282	3364	......	t90	20
Conference Average	20.1	240.3	11.9	....	1.4
League Total	559	6838	......	t92	36
League Average	20.0	244.2	12.2	....	1.3

TOP TEN INTERCEPTORS

Player—Team	No.	Yards	Avg.	Long	TDs.
WRIGHT, FELIX, Cleveland	9	91	10.1	t27	1
Fulcher, David, Cincinnati	8	87	10.9	22	0
Allen, Eric, Philadelphia	8	38	4.8	18	0
Taylor, Keith, Indianapolis	7	225	32.1	t80	1
McDonald, Tim, Phoenix	7	170	24.3	t53	1
Byrd, Gill, San Diego	7	38	5.4	22	0
McMillan, Erik, Jets	6	180	30.0	t92	1
Braxton, Tyrone, Denver	6	103	17.2	t34	1
Kelso, Mark, Buffalo	6	101	16.8	43	0
Prior, Mike, Indianapolis	6	88	14.7	t58	1
Holmes, Jerry, Detroit	6	77	12.8	36	1
Hamilton, Harry, Tampa Bay	6	70	11.7	30	0
Waymer, Dave, New Orleans	6	66	11.0	42	0
Gray, Jerry, Rams	6	48	8.0	t27	1
Robinson, Mark, Tampa Bay	6	44	7.3	16	0
Brown, Dave, Green Bay	6	12	2.0	12	0

AFC—INDIVIDUALS

Player—Team	No.	Yds.	Avg.	Lng.	TD	Player—Team	No.	Yds.	Avg.	Lng.	TD
WRIGHT, Clev.	9	91	10.1	t27	1	Bennett, S.D.	3	4	1.3	4	0
Fulcher, Cin.	8	87	10.9	22	0	McNeal, Mia.	3	—6	—2.0	0	0
Taylor, Ind.	7	225	32.1	t80	1	D. Smith, Den.	2	78	39.0	50	0
Byrd, S.D.	7	38	5.4	22	0	James, N.E.	2	50	25.0	28	0
McMillan, Jets	6	180	30.0	t92	1	L. Smith, Buff.	2	46	23.0	24	0
Braxton, Den.	6	103	17.2	t34	1	Patterson, S.D.	2	44	22.0	34	0
Kelso, Buff.	6	101	16.8	43	0	Jackson, Buff.	2	43	21.5	t40	1
Prior, Ind.	6	88	14.7	t58	1	Williams, Mia.	2	43	21.5	24	0
Anderson, Raiders	5	233	46.6	t87	2	Benson, Raiders	2	36	18.0	19	0
Hasty, Jets	5	62	12.4	t34	1	Judson, Mia.	2	31	15.5	28	0
Brown, Hou.	5	54	10.8	41	0	Lyles, S.D.	2	28	14.0	28	0
Hurst, N.E.	5	31	6.2	t16	1	Cherry, K.C.	2	27	13.5	27	0
Robinson, Sea.	5	24	4.8	20	0	Grayson, Clev.	2	25	12.5	t14	1
Odomes, Buff.	5	20	4.0	13	0	Marion, N.E.	2	19	9.5	18	0
Lyles, Hou.	4	66	16.5	48	0	Robbins, Den.	2	18	9.0	t18	1
McDowell, Hou.	4	65	16.3	21	0	Munford, Den.	2	16	8.0	10	0
Woodruff, Pitt.	4	57	14.3	35	0	Harper, Sea.	2	15	7.5	15	0
Glenn, S.D.	4	52	13.0	31	0	Banks, Ind.	2	13	6.5	11	0
Seale, S.D.	4	47	11.8	25	0	Bennett, Buff.	2	5	2.5	6	0
Lewis, K.C.	4	37	9.3	22	0	Thomas, Mia.	2	4	2.0	4	0
Oliver, Mia.	4	32	8.0	23	0	Young, Ind.	2	2	1.0	6	0
Dishman, Hou.	4	31	7.8	31	0	Harden, Raiders	2	1	0.5	1	0
Ross, K.C.	4	29	7.3	23	0	Billups, Cin.	2	0	0.0	0	0
Thomas, Cin.	4	18	4.5	t18	1	McElroy, Raiders	2	0	0.0	0	0
Everett, Pitt.	3	68	22.7	32	0	Daniel, Ind.	1	34	34.0	34	0
Gash, Clev.	3	65	21.7	t36	2	Drane, Buff.	1	25	25.0	25	0
Henderson, Den.	3	58	19.3	25	0	Kelly, Cin.	1	25	25.0	25	0
Lloyd, Pitt.	3	49	16.3	31	0	Matthews, Clev.	1	25	25.0	25	0
Dixon, Cin.	3	47	15.7	28	0	Robinson, Raiders	1	25	25.0	25	0
Washington, Raiders	3	46	15.3	t32	1	Hobley, Mia.	1	22	22.0	22	0
M. Johnson, Clev.	3	43	14.3	23	0	White, Cin.	1	22	22.0	22	0
Woodson Pitt.	3	39	13.0	39	0	Saleaumua, K.C.	1	21	21.0	21	0
Atwater, Den.	3	34	11.3	30	0	J. Johnson, Sea.	1	18	18.0	18	0
Eaton, Hou.	3	33	11.0	20	0	McSwain, N.E.	1	18	18.0	18	0
Minnifield, Clev.	3	29	9.7	25	0	Plummer, Ind.	1	18	18.0	18	0
Little, Pitt.	3	23	7.7	13	0	Bailey, Buff.	1	16	16.0	16	0
McDaniel, Raiders	3	21	7.0	20	0	Snipes, K.C.	1	16	16.0	16	0
Harper, Clev.	3	8	2.7	8	0	Griffin, Pitt.	1	15	15.0	15	0

Player—Team	No.	Yds.	Avg.	Lng.	TD
Booty, Jets	1	13	13.0	13	0
Kramer, Clev.	1	12	12.0	12	0
Still, Buff.	1	10	10.0	10	0
B.R. Smith, S.D.	1	9	9.0	9	0
Corrington, Den.	1	8	8.0	8	0
Bickett, Ind.	1	6	6.0	6	0
Hall, Pitt.	1	6	6.0	6	0
Ball, Ind.	1	5	5.0	5	0
Carey, Cin.	1	5	5.0	5	0
Feggins, N.E.	1	4	4.0	4	0
Hinkle, Pitt.	1	4	4.0	4	0
Mersereau, Jets	1	4	4.0	4	0
Hill, K.C.	1	3	3.0	3	0
Sutton, Buff.	1	3	3.0	3	0
Carrington, Den.	1	2	2.0	2	0
Dixon, Clev.	1	2	2.0	2	0
Figaro, S.D.	1	2	2.0	2	0
Gordon, Jets	1	2	2.0	2	0
Coleman, N.E.	1	1	1.0	1	0
Dennison, Den.	1	1	1.0	1	0
Ashley, K.C.	1	0	0.0	0	0
Bayless, S.D.	1	0	0.0	0	0
Burruss, K.C.	1	0	0.0	0	0
Bussey, Cin.	1	0	0.0	0	0
Clayborn, N.E.	1	0	0.0	0	0
Comeaux, Sea.	1	0	0.0	0	0
Conlan, Buff.	1	0	0.0	0	0
Glenn, Jets	1	0	0.0	0	0
D. Johnson, Pitt.	1	0	0.0	0	0
R. Johnson, Hou.	1	0	0.0	0	0
Lake, Pitt.	1	0	0.0	0	0
Lankford, Mia.	1	0	0.0	0	0
Lyons, Clev.	1	0	0.0	0	0
Rembert, N.E.	1	0	0.0	0	0
Wright, Buff.	1	0	0.0	0	0
Brown, S.D.	1	−1	−1.0	−1	0
McGrew, N.E.	1	−4	−4.0	−4	0
Donaldson, Hou.	0	14	....	14	0

NFC—INDIVIDUALS

Player—Team	No.	Yds.	Avg.	Lng.	TD
ALLEN, Phil.	8	38	4.8	18	0
McDonald, Phoe.	7	170	24.3	t53	1
Holmes, Det.	6	77	12.8	36	1
Hamilton, T.B.	6	70	11.7	30	0
Waymer, N.O.	6	66	11.0	42	0
Gray, Rams	6	48	8.0	t27	1
Robinson, T.B.	6	44	7.3	16	0
D. Brown, G.B.	6	12	2.0	12	0
Kinard, Giants	5	135	27.0	t58	1
Reynolds, T.B.	5	87	17.4	t68	1
Browner, Minn.	5	70	14.0	34	0
Sanders, Atl.	5	52	10.4	22	0
Lott, S.F.	5	34	6.8	28	0
Massey, N.O.	5	26	5.2	22	0
J. Williams, Det.	5	15	3.0	9	0
A.J. Johnson, Wash.	4	94	23.5	t59	1
Everett, Phil.	4	64	16.0	t30	1
Gordon, Atl.	4	60	15.0	34	0
Stinson, Chi.	4	59	14.8	t29	1
Frizzell, Phil.	4	58	14.5	27	0
Jenkins, Phil.	4	58	14.5	22	0
Walton, Wash.	4	58	14.5	t29	1
Cooper, Atl.	4	54	13.5	38	0
B. Davis, Wash.	4	40	10.0	15	0
Mack, Phoe.	4	15	3.8	9	0
Cook, N.O.	3	81	27.0	t63	1
P. Johnson, Giants	3	60	20.0	t39	1
Lynch, Chi.	3	55	18.3	41	0
Irvin, Rams	3	43	14.3	18	0
Maxie, N.O.	3	41	13.7	t26	1
Gayle, Chi.	3	39	13.0	20	0
Brooks, S.F.	3	31	10.3	19	0
Murphy, G.B.	3	31	10.3	20	0
Merriweather, Minn.	3	29	9.7	t15	1
Bowles, Wash.	3	25	8.3	25	0
Evans, Phil.	3	23	7.7	15	0
Stills, G.B.	3	20	6.7	12	0
P. Williams, Giants	3	14	4.7	14	0
Wilburn, Wash.	3	13	4.3	13	0
Woolford, Chi.	3	0	0.0	0	0
Stewart, Rams	2	76	38.0	t41	1
Dimry, Atl.	2	72	36.0	40	0
Strickland, Rams	2	56	28.0	29	0
Roper, Chi.	2	46	23.0	43	0
Wright, S.F.	2	37	18.5	23	0
Jackson, S.F.	2	35	17.5	19	0
Guyton, Giants	2	27	13.5	14	0
Hicks, Rams	2	27	13.5	27	0
Coleman, Wash.	2	24	12.0	t24	1
Harris, Phil.	2	18	9.0	11	0
S. White, Giants	2	18	9.0	18	0
Jackson, Chi.	2	16	8.0	16	0
Stephen, G.B.	2	16	8.0	8	0
Lockhart, Dall.	2	14	7.0	12	0
Case, Atl.	2	13	6.5	13	0
Collins, Giants	2	12	6.0	12	0
Lee, G.B.	2	10	5.0	10	0
Noble, G.B.	2	10	5.0	10	0
A. White, Giants	2	8	4.0	9	0
Rutland, Minn.	2	7	3.5	7	0
Griffin, S.F.	2	6	3.0	3	0
Rivera, Chi.	2	1	0.5	1	0
Grant, Wash.	2	0	0.0	0	0
Green, Wash.	2	0	0.0	0	0
Lee, Minn.	2	0	0.0	0	0
Mack, N.O.	2	0	0.0	0	0
Morrissey, Chi.	2	0	0.0	0	0
Holt, Minn.	1	90	90.0	t90	1
Newsome, Rams	1	81	81.0	t81	1
Simmons, Phil.	1	60	60.0	t60	1
Dent, G.B.	1	53	53.0	53	0
Millard, Minn.	1	48	48.0	48	0
Turner, S.F.	1	42	42.0	42	0
Reasons, Giants	1	40	40.0	40	0
Downs, Phoe.	1	37	37.0	37	0
Pitts, G.B.	1	37	37.0	37	0
Young, Phoe.	1	32	32.0	32	0
Shelley, Atl.	1	31	31.0	31	0
Dent, Chi.	1	30	30.0	30	0
Holland, G.B.	1	26	26.0	26	0
Golic, Phil.	1	23	23.0	23	0
Holmoe, S.F.	1	23	23.0	23	0
Paul, Chi.	1	20	20.0	20	0
Stams, Rams	1	20	20.0	20	0
Waters, Phil.	1	20	20.0	20	0
O. Harris, T.B.	1	19	19.0	19	0
Bates, Dall.	1	18	18.0	18	0
Edwards, Minn.	1	18	18.0	18	0
Marshall, Wash.	1	18	18.0	18	0
McKyer, S.F.	1	18	18.0	18	0
Cecil, G.B.	1	16	16.0	16	0
Zordich, Phoe.	1	16	16.0	t16	1
Swilling, N.O.	1	14	14.0	14	0
Bell, Phil.	1	13	13.0	13	0
Davis, T.B.	1	13	13.0	t13	1
Romanowski, S.F.	1	13	13.0	13	0
Pollard, S.F.	1	12	12.0	12	0
W. Davis, Wash.	1	11	11.0	11	0
DeOssie, Giants	1	10	10.0	10	0
Gibson, Det.	1	10	10.0	10	0
Henley, Rams	1	10	10.0	10	0
Millen, S.F.	1	10	10.0	10	0
Banks, Giants	1	6	6.0	6	0
Crockett, Det.	1	5	5.0	5	0
Wahler, Phoe.	1	5	5.0	5	0
Owens, Rams	1	4	4.0	4	0
Wilcher, Rams	1	4	4.0	4	0
Albritton, Dall.	1	3	3.0	3	0
Miller, Rams	1	3	3.0	3	0
Zackery, Atl.	1	3	3.0	3	0
Duerson, Chi.	1	2	2.0	2	0
Dusbabek, Minn.	1	2	2.0	2	0
Francis, Dall.	1	2	2.0	2	0
Anderson, G.B.	1	1	1.0	1	0
DeLong, S.F.	1	1	1.0	1	0
Futrell, T.B.	1	1	1.0	1	0
Gouveia, Wash.	1	1	1.0	1	0
Bruce, Atl.	1	0	0.0	0	0

Cincinnati strong safety David Fulcher intercepted three passes in two games in 1989 and finished the season with eight interceptions overall.

Player—Team	No.	Yds.	Avg.	Lng.	TD	Player—Team	No.	Yds.	Avg.	Lng.	TD
Burton, Dall.	1	0	0.0	0	0	Joyner, Phil.	1	0	0.0	0	0
Carter, Phoe.	1	0	0.0	0	0	Noga, Det.	1	0	0.0	0	0
Douglass, Chi.	1	0	0.0	0	0	Studwell, Minn.	1	0	0.0	0	0
Elder, T.B.	1	0	0.0	0	0	Tate, Chi.	1	0	0.0	0	0
Fullington, Minn.	1	0	0.0	0	0	Taylor, Det.	1	0	0.0	0	0
Greene, G.B.	1	0	0.0	0	0	White, Det.	1	0	0.0	0	0
Horton, Dall.	1	0	0.0	0	0	Atkins, N.O.	1	−2	−2.0	−2	0
Jakes, G.B.	1	0	0.0	0	0						

t—Touchdown.
Leader based on most interceptions.

1989 SCORING

MOST POINTS, SEASON
    NFC: 136—Mike Cofer, San Francisco.
    AFC: 120—David Treadwell, Denver.

MOST TOUCHDOWNS
    NFC: 18—Dalton Hilliard, New Orleans.
    AFC: 12—Christian Okoye, Kansas City.
           Thurman Thomas, Buffalo.

MOST EXTRA POINTS
    NFC: 51—Mike Lansford, L.A. Rams.
    AFC: 46—Scott Norwood, Buffalo.

MOST FIELD GOALS
    NFC: 31—Rich Karlis, Minnesota.
    AFC: 27—David Treadwell, Denver.

MOST FIELD GOALS ATTEMPTED
    NFC: 40—Chip Lohmiller, Washington.
    AFC: 37—Tony Zendejas, Houston.

LONGEST FIELD GOAL
    AFC: 59—Pete Stoyanovich, Miami at N.Y. Jets, November 12.
    NFC: 54—Paul McFadden, Atlanta vs. Buffalo, November 5.

MOST POINTS, GAME
    NFC: 21—Rich Karlis, Minnesota vs. L.A. Rams, November 5 (7 FG) (OT).
    AFC: 18—Merril Hoge, Pittsburgh at Miami, November 26 (3 TD).
           Sammie Smith, Miami vs. New England, December 10 (3 TD).

TEAM LEADERS
    AFC: BUFFALO: 115, Scott Norwood; CINCINNATI: 73, Jim Breech; CLEVE-LAND: 88, Matt Bahr; DENVER: 120, David Treadwell; HOUSTON: 115, Tony Zendejas; INDIANAPOLIS: 94, Dean Biasucci; KANSAS CITY: 106, Nick Lowery; L.A. RAIDERS: 103, Jeff Jaeger; MIAMI: 95, Pete Stoyanovich; NEW ENGLAND: 61, Greg Davis; N.Y. JETS: 71, Pat Leahy; PITTSBURGH: 91, Gary Anderson; SAN DIEGO: 80, Chris Bahr; SEATTLE: 72, Norm Johnson.
    NFC: ATLANTA: 63, Paul McFadden; CHICAGO: 90, Neal Anderson; DALLAS: 29, Roger Ruzek; DETROIT: 96, Eddie Murray; GREEN BAY: 108, Chris Jacke; L.A. RAMS: 120, Mike Lansford; MINNESOTA: 120, Rich Karlis; NEW ORLEANS: 108, Dalton Hilliard; N.Y. GIANTS: 84, Ottis Anderson; PHILADELPHIA: 66, Cris Carter; PHOENIX: 82, Al Del Greco; SAN FRANCISCO: 136, Mike Cofer; TAMPA BAY: 99, Donald Igwebuike; WASHINGTON: 128, Chip Lohmiller.

TEAM CHAMPION
    NFC: 442—San Francisco.
    AFC: 409—Buffalo.

SCORING—TEAM

AMERICAN FOOTBALL CONFERENCE

	Tot. Tds.	Tds. R.	Tds. P.	Tds. Misc.	XP	XPA	FG	FGA	Saf.	Tot. Pts.
Buffalo	49	15	32	2	46	48	23	30	0	409
Cincinnati	52	17	32	3	50	52	14	20	0	404
Houston	41	16	23	2	40	41	25	37	2	365
Denver	40	15	21	4	39	40	27	33	1	362
Cleveland	41	14	20	7	40	40	16	24	0	334
Miami	39	10	26	3	38	39	19	26	1	331
Kansas City	35	18	14	3	34	35	24	33	1	318
L.A. Raiders	35	9	21	5	34	35	23	34	1	315
Indianapolis	34	11	18	5	31	33	21	27	0	298
New England	30	12	17	1	27	30	30	40	0	297
San Diego	31	13	15	3	29	31	17	25	0	266
Pittsburgh	29	17	10	2	28	29	21	30	0	265
N.Y. Jets	30	11	14	5	29	30	14	21	1	253
Seattle	28	5	21	2	28	28	15	25	0	241
Conference Total	514	183	284	47	493	511	289	405	7	4458
Conference Avg.	36.7	13.1	20.3	3.4	35.2	36.5	20.6	28.9	0.5	318.4

NATIONAL FOOTBALL CONFERENCE

	Tot. Tds.	Tds. R.	Tds. P.	Tds. Misc.	XP	XPA	FG	FGA	Saf.	Tot. Pts.
San Francisco	51	14	35	2	49	51	29	36	0	442
L.A. Rams	51	19	29	3	51	51	23	30	0	426
New Orleans	46	19	23	4	44	46	20	29	3	386
Washington	42	14	24	4	41	42	29	40	3	386
Green Bay	42	13	27	2	42	42	22	28	1	362
Chicago	45	22	21	2	43	45	15	19	0	358
Minnesota	36	12	17	7	35	36	32	44	2	351
N.Y. Giants	37	17	17	3	35	37	29	38	2	348
Philadelphia	40	14	23	3	40	40	20	33	1	342
Tampa Bay	36	10	23	3	34	36	22	28	2	320
Detroit	36	23	11	2	36	36	20	21	0	312
Atlanta	30	11	17	2	30	30	23	32	0	279
Phoenix	29	10	17	2	28	29	18	26	1	258
Dallas	25	7	14	4	24	25	10	20	0	204
Conference Total	546	205	298	43	532	546	312	424	15	47774
Conference Avg.	39.0	14.6	21.3	3.1	38.0	39.0	22.3	30.3	1.1	3412.4
League Total	1060	388	582	90	1025	1057	601	829	22	9232
League Average	37.9	13.9	20.8	3.2	36.6	37.8	21.5	29.6	0.8	329.7

TOP TEN SCORERS

NON-KICKERS

Player—Team	Total TDs.	Rush TDs.	Pass TDs.	Misc. TDs.	Tot. Pts.
HILLIARD, N.O.	18	13	5	0	108
Rice, S.F.	17	0	17	0	102
Anderson, Chi.	15	11	4	0	90
Bell, Rams	15	15	0	0	90
Anderson, Giants	14	14	0	0	84
B. Sanders, Det.	14	14	0	0	84
Sharpe, G.B.	13	0	12	1	78
Okoye, K.C.	12	12	0	0	72
Thomas, Buff.	12	6	6	0	72
Carter, Phil.	11	0	11	0	66
A. Miller, S.D.	11	0	10	1	66

KICKERS

Player—Team	XP Made	XP Att.	FG. Made	FG. Att.	Tot. Pts.
COFER, S.F.	49	51	29	36	136
Lohmiller, Wash.	41	41	29	40	128
Karlis, Minn.	27	28	31	39	120
Lansford, Rams	51	51	23	30	120
Treadwell, Den.	39	40	27	33	120
Norwood, Buff.	46	47	23	30	115
Zendejas, Hou.	40	40	25	37	115
Jacke, G.B.	42	42	22	28	108
Lowery, K.C.	34	35	24	33	106
Andersen, N.O.	44	45	20	29	104

AFC—INDIVIDUALS

KICKERS

Player—Team	XP Made	XP Att.	FG. Made	FG. Att.	Tot. Pts.	Player—Team	XP Made	XP Att.	FG. Made	FG. Att.	Tot. Pts.
TREADWELL, Den.	39	40	27	33	120	Bahr, Clev.	40	40	16	24	88
Norwood, Buff.	46	47	23	30	115	Bahr, S.D.	29	30	17	25	80
Zendejas, Hou.	40	40	25	37	115	Breech, Cin.	37	38	12	14	73
Lowery, K.C.	34	35	24	33	106	N. Johnson, Sea.	27	27	15	25	72
Jaeger, Raiders	34	34	23	34	103	Leahy, Jets	29	30	14	21	71
Stoyanovich, Mia.	38	39	19	26	95	Staurovsky, N.E.	14	14	14	17	56
Biasucci, Ind.	31	32	21	27	94	Gallery, Cin.	13	13	2	6	19
Anderson, Pitt.	28	28	21	30	91	Johnson, Cin.	0	1	0	0	0

NON-KICKERS

Player—Team	Total TDs.	Rush TDs.	Pass TDs.	Misc. TDs.	Tot. Pts.
OKOYE, K.C.	12	12	0	0	72
Thomas, Buff.	12	6	6	0	72
A. Miller, S.D.	11	0	10	1	66
Metcalf, Clev.	10	6	4	0	60
Brooks, Cin.	9	7	2	0	54
Butts, S.D.	9	9	0	0	54
Clayton, Mia.	9	0	9	0	54
Fernandez, Raiders	9	0	9	0	54
Holman, Cin.	9	0	9	0	54
Reed, Buff.	9	0	9	0	54
Dickerson, Ind.	8	7	1	0	48
Hill, Hou.	8	0	8	0	48
Hoge, Pitt.	8	8	0	0	48
Humphrey, Den.	8	7	1	0	48
McGee, Cin.	8	0	8	0	48
Johnson, Den.	7	0	7	0	42
Stephens, N.E.	7	7	0	0	42
Vick, Jets	7	5	2	0	42
Williams, Sea.	7	1	6	0	42
Brown, Cin.	6	0	6	0	36
Highsmith, Hou.	6	4	2	0	36
Jensen, Mia.	6	0	6	0	36
C. Jones, N.E.	6	0	6	0	36
Kinnebrew, Buff.	6	6	0	0	36
Lipps, Pitt.	6	1	5	0	36
Slaughter, Clev.	6	0	6	0	36
Smith, Mia.	6	6	0	0	36
Bentley, Ind.	5	1	3	1	30
Blades, Sea.	5	0	5	0	30
A. Brown, Mia.	5	0	5	0	30
Duncan, Hou.	5	0	5	0	30
Dykes, N.E.	5	0	5	0	30
Hector, Jets	5	3	2	0	30
Manoa, Clev.	5	3	2	0	30
Skansi, Sea.	5	0	5	0	30
Taylor, Cin.	5	3	2	0	30
Townsell, Jets	5	0	5	0	30
White, Hou.	5	5	0	0	30
Worley, Pitt.	5	5	0	0	30
Bratton, Den.	4	1	3	0	24
Brooks, Ind.	4	0	4	0	24
Carter, Pitt.	4	1	3	0	24
Gault, Raiders	4	0	4	0	24
Harmon, Buff.	4	0	4	0	24
Jackson, Raiders	4	4	0	0	24
Moon, Hou.	4	0	4	0	24
Mueller, Raiders	4	2	2	0	24
Rison, Ind.	4	0	4	0	24
Warner, Sea.	4	3	1	0	24
Largent, Sea.	3	0	3	0	†19
Ball, Cin.	3	3	0	0	18
K. Davis, Buff.	3	1	2	0	18
Edmunds, Mia.	3	0	3	0	18
Elway, Den.	3	3	0	0	18
Fryar, N.E.	3	0	3	0	18
Givins, Hou.	3	0	3	0	18
Jennings, Cin.	3	2	1	0	18
Lofton, Buff.	3	0	3	0	18
McMillan, Jets	3	0	0	3	18
McNeil, Jets	3	2	1	0	18
Morgan, N.E.	3	0	3	0	18
Saxon, K.C.	3	3	0	0	18
Sewell, Den.	3	0	3	0	18
Spencer, S.D.	3	3	0	0	18
Tillman, Clev.	3	0	2	1	18
Alexander, Den.	2	2	0	0	12
Allen, Raiders	2	2	0	0	12
Anderson, Raiders	2	0	0	2	12
Beach, Ind.	2	0	2	0	12
Beebe, Buff.	2	0	2	0	12
Bernstine, S.D.	2	1	1	0	12
Boyer, Ind.	2	0	2	0	12
Cox, S.D.	2	0	2	0	12
Dyal, Raiders	2	0	2	0	12
Gash, Clev.	2	0	0	2	12
Grayson, Clev.	2	0	0	2	12
Harris, Hou.	2	0	2	0	12
Harry, K.C.	2	0	2	0	12
Hayes, K.C.	2	0	2	0	12
Jackson, Den.	2	0	2	0	12
Jeffires, Hou.	2	0	2	0	12
Junkin, Raiders	2	0	2	0	12
Kay, Den.	2	0	2	0	12
Kelly, Buff.	2	2	0	0	12
Langhorne, Clev.	2	0	2	0	12
Logan, Mia.	2	0	0	2	12
Marino, Mia.	2	2	0	0	12
Martin, Cin.	2	0	2	0	12
McKeller, Buff.	2	0	2	0	12
Metzelaars, Buff.	2	0	2	0	12
Paige, K.C.	2	0	2	0	12
Pelluer, K.C.	2	2	0	0	12
Perryman, N.E.	2	2	0	0	12
Pinkett, Hou.	2	1	1	0	12
Rozier, Hou.	2	2	0	0	12
Schwedes, Mia.	2	0	1	1	12
R. Thomas, K.C.	2	0	2	0	12
Toon, Jets	2	0	2	0	12
Trudeau, Ind.	2	2	0	0	12
Verdin, Ind.	2	0	1	1	12
Washington, Raiders	2	0	0	2	12
Winder, Den.	2	2	0	0	12
Woods, Cin.	2	2	0	0	12
Young, Den.	2	0	2	0	12
Alexander, Raiders	1	0	1	0	6
Allen, N.E.	1	1	0	0	6
Banks, Mia.	1	0	1	0	6
Braxton, Den.	1	0	0	1	6
Burkett, Jets	1	0	1	0	6
Bussey, Cin.	1	0	0	1	6
Carson, K.C.	1	0	1	0	6
Chandler, Ind.	1	1	0	0	6
Clark, Sea.	1	0	1	0	6
Davenport, Mia.	1	1	0	0	6
Dishman, Hou.	1	0	0	1	6
R. Dixon, Ind.	1	0	0	1	6
Dressel, K.C.	1	0	1	0	6
Dupard, N.E.	1	1	0	0	6
Duper, Mia.	1	0	1	0	6
Egu, N.E.	1	1	0	0	6
Fenner, Sea.	1	1	0	0	6
Gamble, K.C.	1	1	0	0	6
Glasgow, Sea.	1	0	0	1	6
Glenn, S.D.	1	0	0	1	6
Hasty, Jets	1	0	0	1	6
Heard, K.C.	1	0	1	0	6
Hill, Pitt.	1	0	1	0	6
Hillary, Cin.	1	0	1	0	6
Horton, Raiders	1	0	1	0	6
Hurst, N.E.	1	0	0	1	6
Jackson, Buff.	1	0	0	1	6
Jefferson, Sea.	1	0	0	1	6
Johnson, Buff.	1	0	1	0	6
K. Jones, Clev.	1	1	0	0	6
Kelso, Buff.	1	0	0	1	6
Kosar, Clev.	1	1	0	0	6
L. King, Raiders	1	0	0	1	6
Kragen, Den.	1	0	0	1	6
Maas, K.C.	1	0	0	1	6
Mack, K.C.	1	1	0	0	6
Mandley, K.C.	1	0	1	0	6
Matthews, Clev.	1	0	0	1	6
McNair, K.C.	1	0	1	0	6
Mecklenburg, Den.	1	0	0	1	6
Middleton, Clev.	1	0	1	0	6
Mularkey, Pitt.	1	0	1	0	6
Nattiel, Den.	1	0	1	0	6
Neubert, Jets	1	0	1	0	6
Newsome, Clev.	1	0	1	0	6
Oliphant, Clev.	1	1	0	0	6
Parker, S.D.	1	0	1	0	6
Pearson, K.C.	1	0	0	1	6
Prior, Ind.	1	0	0	1	6
Prokop, Jets	1	1	0	0	6
Pruitt, Ind.	1	0	1	0	6
Radachowsky, Jets	1	0	0	1	6
Redden, Clev.	1	1	0	0	6
Robbins, Den.	1	0	0	1	6

Player—Team	Total TDs.	Rush TDs.	Pass TDs.	Misc. TDs.	Tot. Pts.
Roberts, K.C.	1	0	1	0	6
Rolle, Buff.	1	0	1	0	6
Seale, Hou.	1	0	0	1	6
B.R. Smith, S.D.	1	0	0	1	6
Smith, Cin.	1	0	1	0	6
Smith, K.C.	1	0	0	1	6
Smith, Raiders	1	1	0	0	6
Stradford, Mia.	1	1	0	0	6
Taylor, Ind.	1	0	0	1	6
Tennell, Clev.	1	0	1	0	6
Thomas, Cin.	1	0	0	1	6
Waiters, Clev.	1	0	1	0	6
Walker, S.D.	1	0	1	0	6
Wallace, Pitt.	1	1	0	0	6
White, Cin.	1	0	0	1	6
W. Williams, Pitt.	1	1	0	0	6
Woodruff, Pitt.	1	0	0	1	6
Woodson, Pitt.	1	0	0	1	6
Wright, Clev.	1	0	0	1	6
Adams, Raiders	0	0	0	0	*2
Brooks, Den.	0	0	0	0	*2
McDowell, Hou.	0	0	0	0	*2
McGovern, K.C.	0	0	0	0	*2

NFC—INDIVIDUALS

KICKERS

Player—Team	XP Made	XP Att.	FG. Made	FG. Att.	Tot. Pts.
COFER, S.F.	49	51	29	36	136
Lohmiller, Wash.	41	41	29	40	128
Karlis, Minn.	27	28	31	39	120
Lansford, Rams	51	51	23	30	120
Jacke, G.B.	42	42	22	28	108
Andersen, N.O.	44	45	20	29	104
Igwebuike, T.B.	33	35	22	28	99
Murray, Det.	36	36	20	21	96
Davis, N.E.-Atl.	25	28	23	34	94
Butler, Chi.	43	45	15	19	88
Allegre, Giants	23	24	20	26	83
Del Greco, Phoe.	28	29	18	26	82
Zendejas, Phil.-Dall.	33	33	14	24	75
Ruzek, Dall.-Phil.	28	29	13	22	67
McFadden, Atl.	18	18	15	20	63
Nittmo, Giants	12	13	9	12	39
DeLine, Phil.	3	3	3	7	12
Garcia, Minn.	8	8	1	5	11
Miller, Atl.	0	0	1	1	3
Fontenot, G.B.	4	1	3	0	24
Gagliano, Det.	4	4	0	0	24
Haynes, Atl.	4	0	4	0	24
Hill, N.O.	4	0	4	0	24
Jones, S.F.	4	0	4	0	24
Peete, Det.	4	4	0	0	24
Riggs, Wash.	4	4	0	0	24
Sanders, Wash.	4	0	4	0	24
Turner, Giants	4	0	4	0	24
Bavaro, Giants	3	0	3	0	18
Collins, Atl.	3	0	3	0	18
A. Cox, Rams	3	0	3	0	18
Davis, Chi.	3	0	3	0	18
Dixon, Dall.	3	0	2	1	18
Harbaugh, Chi.	3	3	0	0	18
Jackson, Phil.	3	0	3	0	18
Johnston, Dall.	3	0	3	0	18
Jones, Phoe.	3	0	3	0	18
Jordan, N.O.	3	3	0	0	18
Jordan, Minn.	3	0	3	0	18
McKinnon, Chi.	3	0	3	0	18
Montana, S.F.	3	3	0	0	18
Thornton, Chi.	3	0	3	0	18
Toney, Phil.	3	3	0	0	18
Wilder, T.B.	3	0	3	0	18
Wilkins, Atl.	3	0	3	0	18
Anderson, Minn.	2	2	0	0	12
Baker, Giants	2	0	2	0	12
Bland, G.B.	2	0	1	1	12
Clack, Dall.	2	2	0	0	12
Clark, Det.	2	0	2	0	12
Delpino, Rams	2	1	1	0	12
Dixon, Atl.	2	0	2	0	12
Folsom, Dall.	2	0	2	0	12
Garrity, Phil.	2	0	2	0	12
Giles, Phil.	2	0	2	0	12
Gustafson, Minn.	2	0	2	0	12
Hall, T.B.	2	0	2	0	12
Holohan, Rams	2	0	2	0	12
Hostetler, Giants	2	2	0	0	12
Howard, T.B.	2	1	1	0	12
Irvin, Dall.	2	0	2	0	12
Jordan, Phoe.	2	2	0	0	12
Kemp, G.B.	2	0	2	0	12
Lang, Atl.	2	1	1	0	12
Martin, Dall.	2	0	2	0	12
Morris, Wash.	2	2	0	0	12
Novoselsky, Minn.	2	0	2	0	12
Palmer, Dall.	2	2	0	0	12
Query, G.B.	2	0	2	0	12
Quick, Phil.	2	0	2	0	12
Rathman, S.F.	2	1	1	0	12
Reynolds, T.B.	2	0	0	2	12
Sanders, Chi.	2	0	1	1	12
Shepard, N.O.-Dall.	2	0	1	1	12
Sherman, Phil.	2	2	0	0	12
Suhey, Chi.	2	1	1	0	12
Young, S.F.	2	2	0	0	12
Merriweather, Minn.	1	0	0	1	*8
Banks, Giants	1	0	1	0	6
Beckman, Atl.	1	0	1	0	6
Boso, Chi.	1	0	1	0	6

NON-KICKERS

Player—Team	Total TDs.	Rush TDs.	Pass TDs.	Misc. TDs.	Tot. Pts.
HILLIARD, N.O.	18	13	5	0	108
Rice, S.F.	17	0	17	0	102
Anderson, Chi.	15	11	4	0	90
Bell, Rams	15	15	0	0	90
Anderson, Giants	14	14	0	0	84
B. Sanders, Det.	14	14	0	0	84
Sharpe, G.B.	13	0	12	1	78
Carter, Phil.	11	0	11	0	66
Taylor, S.F.	10	0	10	0	60
Walker, Dall.-Minn.	10	7	2	1	60
Byner, Wash.	9	7	2	0	54
Carrier, T.B.	9	0	9	0	54
Clark, Wash.	9	0	9	0	54
Tate, T.B.	9	8	1	0	54
Ellard, Rams	8	0	8	0	48
R. Johnson, Det.	8	0	8	0	48
E. Martin, N.O.	8	0	8	0	48
Monk, Wash.	8	0	8	0	48
Muster, Chi.	8	5	3	0	48
Craig, S.F.	7	6	1	0	42
Green, Phoe.	7	0	7	0	42
Fenney, Minn.	6	4	2	0	36
Ferrell, Phoe.	6	6	0	0	36
Jones, Atl.	6	6	0	0	36
Anderson, Rams	5	0	5	0	30
Byars, Phil.	5	5	0	0	30
Fullwood, G.B.	5	5	0	0	30
Hill, T.B.	5	0	5	0	30
Johnson, Rams	5	0	5	0	30
Majkowski, G.B.	5	5	0	0	30
McGee, Rams	5	1	4	0	30
Meggett, Giants	5	0	4	1	30
Settle, Atl.	5	3	2	0	30
J.T. Smith, Phoe.	5	0	5	0	30
West, G.B.	5	0	5	0	30
Brenner, N.O.	4	0	4	0	24
Carter, Minn.	4	0	4	0	24
Cunningham, Phil.	4	4	0	0	24

The 49ers' Mike Cofer led the NFL in scoring with 136 points in 1989.

Player—Team	Total TDs.	Rush TDs.	Pass TDs.	Misc. TDs.	Tot. Pts.
Ro. Brown, Rams	1	0	1	0	6
Butler, Atl.	1	0	0	1	6
Coleman, Wash.	1	0	0	1	6
Cook, N.O.	1	0	0	1	6
Cross, Giants	1	0	1	0	6
Davis, T.B.	1	0	0	1	6
Del Rio, Dall.	1	0	0	1	6
Didier, G.B.	1	0	1	0	6
Drewery, T.B.	1	0	1	0	6
Drummond, Phil.	1	0	1	0	6
Everett, Phil.	1	0	0	1	6
Everett, Rams	1	0	1	0	6
Flagler, S.F.	1	1	0	0	6
Flowers, Atl.	1	1	0	0	6
Ford, Dall.	1	0	1	0	6
Fourcade, N.O.	1	1	0	0	6
Frazier, N.O.	1	1	0	0	6
Gary, Rams	1	1	0	0	6
Gentry, Chi.	1	0	1	0	6
Gray, Rams	1	0	0	1	6
Green, Chi.	1	1	0	0	6
Haddix, G.B.	1	0	1	0	6
Haley, S.F.	1	0	0	1	6
W. Harris, T.B.	1	0	1	0	6
Heller, Atl.	1	0	1	0	6
Henderson, S.F.	1	1	0	0	6
Heyward, N.O.	1	1	0	0	6
Hipple, Det.	1	1	0	0	6
Hogeboom, Phoe.	1	1	0	0	6
Holmes, Phoe.	1	0	1	0	6
Holmes, Det.	1	0	0	1	6
Holt, Minn.	1	0	0	1	6
Howard, Wash.	1	0	0	1	6
Ingram, Minn.	1	0	1	0	6
Ingram, Giants	1	0	1	0	6
Jackson, S.F.	1	0	0	1	6
Jeffcoat, Dall.	1	0	0	1	6
A.J. Johnson, Wash.	1	0	0	1	6
P. Johnson, Giants	1	0	0	1	6
Johnson, Phil.	1	0	1	0	6
Jones, Minn.	1	0	1	0	6
Kinard, Giants	1	0	0	1	6
Lewis, Minn.	1	0	1	0	6
Little, Phil.	1	0	1	0	6
Lockhart, Dall.	1	0	0	1	6
Manuel, Giants	1	0	1	0	6
Maxie, N.O.	1	0	0	1	6
McDonald, Phoe.	1	0	0	1	6
Millard, Minn.	1	0	0	1	6
Morris, Chi.	1	0	1	0	6
Morse, N.O.	1	0	0	1	6
Newsome, Rams	1	0	0	1	6
Newton, Minn.	1	0	0	1	6
Novacek, Phoe.	1	0	1	0	6
Phillips, Det.	1	0	1	0	6
Rutland, Minn.	1	0	0	1	6
Rypien, Wash.	1	1	0	0	6
Sanders, Atl.	1	0	0	1	6
Sargent, Dall.	1	1	0	0	6
Simmons, Phil.	1	0	0	1	6
Simms, Giants	1	1	0	0	6
Stamps, T.B.	1	1	0	0	6
Stewart, Rams	1	0	0	1	6
Stinson, Chi.	1	0	0	1	6
Thomas, Minn.	1	0	0	1	6
Tice, N.O.	1	0	1	0	6
Tomczak, Chi.	1	1	0	0	6
Turner, N.O.	1	0	1	0	6
Walls, S.F.	1	0	1	0	6
Walton, Wash.	1	0	0	1	6
Warren, Wash.	1	0	1	0	6
Waters, Phil.	1	0	0	1	6
White, Det.	1	0	0	1	6
Wilson, S.F.	1	0	1	0	6
Wilson, Minn.	1	1	0	0	6
Wolfley, Phoe.	1	1	0	0	6
Woodside, G.B.	1	1	0	0	6
Workman, G.B.	1	1	0	0	6
Zordich, Phoe.	1	0	0	1	6
Berry, Minn.	0	0	0	0	*2
Cocroft, T.B.	0	0	0	0	*2
Forde, N.O.	0	0	0	0	*2
Harris, Phil.	0	0	0	0	*2
Manley, Wash.	0	0	0	0	*2
Marshall, Giants	0	0	0	0	*2
Reasons, Giants	0	0	0	0	*2
S. Smith, T.B.	0	0	0	0	*2
Stokes, Wash.	0	0	0	0	*2
Warren, N.O.	0	0	0	0	*2
Wilson, Phoe.	0	0	0	0	*2
Mohr, T.B.	0	0	0	0	†1

*Safety
†Scored extra point

1989 PUNTING

AVERAGE YARDS PER PUNT
NFC: 43.4—Rich Camarillo, Phoenix.
AFC: 43.3—Greg Montgomery, Houston.

NET AVERAGE YARDS PER PUNT
NFC: 37.8—Sean Landeta, N.Y. Giants.
AFC: 36.1—Greg Montgomery, Houston.

LONGEST PUNT
NFC: 91—Randall Cunningham, Philadelphia at N.Y. Giants, December 3.
AFC: 76—Joe Prokop, N.Y. Jets at New England, November 5.

MOST PUNTS, SEASON
AFC: 97—Bryan Wagner, Cleveland.
NFC: 84—Scott Fulhage, Atlanta.
     Chris Mohr, Tampa Bay.

MOST PUNTS, GAME
AFC: 12—Bryan Wagner, Cleveland vs. Kansas City, November 19 (463 yards).
NFC: 11—Bucky Scribner, Minnesota at Clev., December 17 (378 yards) (OT).

TEAM CHAMPION
NFC: 43.6—Phoenix.
AFC: 42.4—Indianapolis.

PUNTING—TEAM

AMERICAN FOOTBALL CONFERENCE

	Total Punts	Yards	Long	Avg.	TB.	Blk.	Opp. Ret.	Ret. Yds.	In 20	Net Avg.
Indianapolis	80	3392	64	42.4	10	1	51	558	14	32.9
Houston	58	2422	63	41.8	7	2	24	191	15	36.1
Miami	59	2458	58	41.7	6	1	26	256	18	35.3
Pittsburgh	83	3368	57	40.6	9	1	45	361	15	34.1
L.A. Raiders	67	2711	60	40.5	7	0	41	301	12	33.9
Kansas City	67	2688	54	40.1	5	0	40	325	25	33.8
Denver	80	3188	63	39.8	6	0	28	370	25	33.7
San Diego	84	3315	64	39.5	7	0	43	451	11	32.4
Seattle	76	2995	59	39.4	8	1	41	334	17	32.9
N.Y. Jets	87	3426	76	39.4	4	0	34	257	29	35.5
Cleveland	97	3817	60	39.4	6	0	49	418	32	33.8
Cincinnati	65	2504	62	38.5	12	2	33	323	15	29.9
Buffalo	67	2564	60	38.3	9	2	25	227	15	32.2
New England	64	2392	64	37.4	2	1	38	346	13	31.3
Conference Total	1034	41240	76	......	98	11	518	4718	256	......
Conference Average	73.9	2945.7	....	39.9	7.0	0.8	37.0	337.0	18.3	33.4

NATIONAL FOOTBALL CONFERENCE

	Total Punts	Yards	Long	Avg.	TB.	Blk.	Opp. Ret.	Ret. Yds.	In 20	Net Avg.
Phoenix	82	3578	58	43.6	6	0	46	371	23	37.6
N.Y. Giants	70	3019	71	43.1	7	0	29	236	19	37.8
Detroit	83	3538	64	42.6	9	1	46	373	14	36.0
Washington	63	2663	74	42.3	9	1	34	383	21	33.3
Atlanta	85	3472	65	40.8	9	1	43	460	24	33.3
Green Bay	66	2682	63	40.6	11	0	30	416	17	31.0
Minnesota	72	2864	55	39.8	8	0	32	300	16	33.4
Dallas	82	3261	56	39.8	6	2	38	334	19	34.2
San Francisco	56	2226	56	39.8	6	1	35	361	13	31.2
Chicago	72	2844	60	39.5	9	0	30	262	21	33.4
New Orleans	71	2774	56	39.1	5	0	35	244	21	34.2
Philadelphia	87	3389	91	39.0	5	0	37	215	21	35.3
Tampa Bay	86	3311	58	38.5	3	2	54	492	10	32.1
L.A. Rams	74	2834	54	38.3	7	1	34	315	15	32.1
Conference Total	1049	42455	91	......	100	9	523	4762	254	......
Conference Average	74.9	3032.5	....	40.5	7.1	0.6	37.4	340.1	18.1	34.0
League Total	2083	83695	91	......	198	20	1041	9480	510	......
League Average	74.4	2989.1	....	40.2	7.1	0.7	37.2	338.6	18.2	33.7

TOP TEN PUNTERS

Player—Team	Net Punts	Yards	Long	Avg.	Total Punts	TB.	Blk.	Opp. Ret.	Ret. Yds.	In 20	Net Avg.
CAMARILLO, RICH, Phoe.....	76	3298	58	43.4	76	6	0	42	330	21	37.5
Montgomery, Greg, Hou.........	56	2422	63	43.3	58	7	2	24	191	15	36.1
Arnold, Jim, Det.....................	82	3538	64	43.1	83	9	1	46	373	14	36.0
Landeta, Sean, Giants..............	70	3019	71	43.1	70	7	0	29	236	19	37.8
Mojsiejenko, Ralf, Wash.	62	2663	74	43.0	63	9	1	34	383	21	33.3
Stark, Rohn, Ind.....................	79	3392	64	42.9	80	10	1	51	558	14	32.9
Roby, Reggie, Mia.	58	2458	58	42.4	59	6	1	26	256	18	35.3
Fulhage, Scott, Atl.................	84	3472	65	41.3	85	9	1	43	460	24	33.3
Newsome, Harry, Pitt.............	82	3368	57	41.1	83	9	1	45	361	15	34.1
Saxon, Mike, Dall.	79	3233	56	40.9	81	6	2	37	334	19	34.3

AFC—INDIVIDUALS

Player—Team	Net Punts	Yards	Long	Avg.	Total Punts	TB.	Blk.	Opp. Ret.	Ret. Yds.	In 20	Net Avg.
Gr. MONTGOMERY, Hou......	56	2422	63	43.3	58	7	2	24	191	15	36.1
Stark, Ind.	79	3392	64	42.9	80	10	1	51	558	14	32.9
Roby, Mia.	58	2458	58	42.4	59	6	1	26	256	18	35.3
Newsome, Pitt.........................	82	3368	57	41.1	83	9	1	45	361	15	34.1
Gossett, Raiders	67	2711	60	40.5	67	7	0	41	301	12	33.9
Horan, Den.............................	77	3111	63	40.4	77	5	0	28	370	24	34.3
Goodburn, K.C.........................	67	2688	54	40.1	67	5	0	40	325	25	33.8
Ilesic, S.D..............................	76	3049	64	40.1	76	7	0	39	408	11	32.9
Johnson, Cin...........................	61	2446	62	40.1	63	11	2	33	323	14	30.2
Rodriguez, Sea........................	75	2995	59	39.9	76	8	1	41	334	17	32.9
Kidd, Buff..............................	65	2564	60	39.4	67	9	2	25	227	15	32.2
Prokop, Jets............................	87	3426	76	39.4	87	4	0	34	257	29	35.5
Wagner, Clev...........................	97	3817	60	39.4	97	6	0	49	418	32	33.8
Feagles, N.E.	63	2392	64	38.0	64	2	1	38	346	13	31.3

(Non-Qualifiers)

Player—Team	Net Punts	Yards	Long	Avg.	Total Punts	TB.	Blk.	Opp. Ret.	Ret. Yds.	In 20	Net Avg.
Colbert, S.D............................	8	266	46	33.3	8	0	0	4	43	0	27.9
Breech, Cin.............................	2	58	32	29.0	2	1	0	0	0	1	19.0
Kubiak, Den............................	2	43	29	21.5	2	0	0	0	0	1	21.5
Elway, Den..............................	1	34	34	34.0	1	1	0	0	0	0	14.0

NFC—INDIVIDUALS

Player—Team	Net Punts	Yards	Long	Avg.	Total Punts	TB.	Blk.	Opp. Ret.	Ret. Yds.	In 20	Net Avg.
CAMARILLO, Phoe.	76	3298	58	43.4	76	6	0	42	330	21	37.5
Arnold, Det.............................	82	3538	64	43.1	83	9	1	46	373	14	36.0
Landeta, Giants	70	3019	71	43.1	70	7	0	29	236	19	37.8
Mojsiejenko, Wash.	62	2663	74	43.0	63	9	1	34	383	21	33.3
Fulhage, Atl............................	84	3472	65	41.3	85	9	1	43	460	24	33.3
Saxon, Dall.............................	79	3233	56	40.9	81	6	2	37	334	19	34.3
Bracken, G.B.	66	2682	63	40.6	66	11	0	30	416	17	31.0
Helton, S.F.	55	2226	56	40.5	56	6	1	35	361	13	31.2
Scribner, Minn.........................	72	2864	55	39.8	72	8	0	32	300	16	33.4
Barnhardt, N.O.	55	2179	56	39.6	55	4	0	28	174	17	35.0
Buford, Chi.............................	72	2844	60	39.5	72	9	0	30	262	21	33.4
Mohr, T.B.	84	3311	58	39.4	86	3	2	54	492	10	32.1
Teltschik, Phil.	57	2246	58	39.4	57	3	0	29	175	12	35.3
Hatcher, Rams.........................	73	2834	54	38.8	74	7	1	34	315	15	32.1

(Non-Qualifiers)

Player—Team	Net Punts	Yards	Long	Avg.	Total Punts	TB.	Blk.	Opp. Ret.	Ret. Yds.	In 20	Net Avg.
Runager, Phil.	17	568	52	33.4	17	1	0	6	30	5	30.5
Winslow, N.O.	16	595	50	37.2	16	1	0	7	70	4	31.6
Tuten, Phil.	7	256	45	36.6	7	1	0	1	1	1	33.6
Cunningham, Phil.	6	319	91	53.2	6	0	0	1	9	3	51.7
Tupa, Phoe...............................	6	280	51	46.7	6	0	0	4	41	2	39.8
Ruzek, Dall.	1	28	28	28.0	1	0	0	1	0	0	28.0

Leader based on average, minimum 40 punts.

1989 PUNT RETURNS

AVERAGE YARDS PER RETURN
 NFC: 13.8—Walter Stanley, Detroit.
 AFC: 12.9—Clarence Verdin, Indianapolis.

MOST YARDS, SEASON
 NFC: 582—Dave Meggett, N.Y. Giants.
 AFC: 496—Gerald McNeil, Cleveland.

MOST YARDS, GAME
 NFC: 114—Dave Meggett, N.Y. Giants vs. L.A. Raiders, Dec. 24 (5 returns).
 AFC: 103—Gerald McNeil, Clev. at Ind., December 10 (5 returns) (OT).

LONGEST PUNT RETURN
 NFC: 76—Dave Meggett, N.Y. Giants vs. L.A. Raiders, December 24 (TD).
 AFC: 70—Scott Schwedes, Miami at Indianapolis, December 17 (TD).

MOST RETURNS, SEASON
 AFC: 49—Gerald McNeil, Cleveland.
 NFC: 46—Dave Meggett, N.Y. Giants.

MOST RETURNS, GAME
 AFC: 8—Phil McConkey, San Diego at Indianapolis, November 26 (75 yards).
 NFC: 7—Walter Stanley, Detroit vs. New Orleans, December 3 (53 yards).

MOST FAIR CATCHES
 NFC: 27—Leo Lewis, Minnesota.
 AFC: 21—Kenny Johnson, Houston.

TOUCHDOWNS
 AFC: 1—Scott Schwedes, Miami.
         Clarence Verdin, Indianapolis.
 NFC: 1—Dave Meggett, N.Y. Giants.
         Deion Sanders, Atlanta.
         Derrick Shepard, New Orleans.

TEAM CHAMPION
 NFC: 12.7—N.Y. Giants.
 AFC: 12.4—Indianapolis.

PUNT RETURNS—TEAM

AMERICAN FOOTBALL CONFERENCE

	No.	FC	Yards	Avg.	Long	TDs
Indianapolis	26	10	322	12.4	t49	1
Miami	33	11	338	10.2	t70	1
Cleveland	49	15	496	10.1	49	0
L.A. Raiders	40	9	378	9.5	29	0
Buffalo	33	12	301	9.1	26	0
N.Y. Jets	33	12	299	9.1	30	0
New England	45	6	379	8.4	28	0
Seattle	30	17	251	8.4	21	0
Denver	45	9	344	7.6	38	0
Kansas City	44	7	331	7.5	21	0
San Diego	38	20	272	7.2	52	0
Pittsburgh	40	2	278	7.0	20	0
Houston	19	21	122	6.4	19	0
Cincinnati	36	12	209	5.8	17	0
Conference Total	511	163	4320	....	t70	2
Conference Average	36.5	11.6	308.6	8.5	....	0.1

NATIONAL FOOTBALL CONFERENCE

	No.	FC	Yards	Avg.	Long	TDs
N.Y. Giants	46	14	582	12.7	t76	1
Detroit	47	8	572	12.2	74	0
Phoenix	40	13	469	11.7	53	0
San Francisco	39	20	429	11.0	37	0
Atlanta	32	7	341	10.7	t68	1
Minnesota	45	27	448	10.0	65	0
L.A Rams	35	24	332	9.5	25	0
Tampa Bay	32	4	296	9.3	55	0
Philadelphia	37	12	331	8.9	28	0
Washington	26	20	226	8.7	38	0
Green Bay	35	9	289	8.3	17	0
New Orleans	53	9	428	8.1	57	1
Chicago	32	8	220	6.9	24	0
Dallas	31	11	197	6.4	17	0
Conference Total	530	186	5160	....	t76	3
Conference Average	37.9	13.3	368.6	9.7	....	0.2
League Total	1041	349	9480	....	t76	5
League Average	37.2	12.5	338.6	9.1	....	0.2

TOP TEN PUNT RETURNERS

	No.	FC	Yards	Avg.	Long	TDs
STANLEY, WALTER, Detroit	36	5	496	13.8	74	0
Verdin, Clarence, Indianapolis	23	5	296	12.9	t49	1
Meggett, Dave, Giants	46	14	582	12.7	t76	1
Sikahema, Vai, Phoenix	37	13	433	11.7	53	0
Taylor, John, San Francisco	36	20	417	11.6	37	0
Drewrey, Willie, Tampa Bay	20	2	220	11.0	55	0
Sanders, Deion, Atlanta	28	7	307	11.0	t68	1
Lewis, Leo, Minnesota	44	27	446	10.1	65	0
McNeil, Gerald, Cleveland	49	15	496	10.1	49	0
Howard, Joe, Washington	21	18	200	9.5	38	0

AFC—INDIVIDUALS

Player—Team	No.	FC.	Yds.	Avg.	Lng.	TD
VERDIN, Ind.	23	5	296	12.9	t49	1
McNeil, Clev.	49	15	496	10.1	49	0
Townsell, Jets	33	12	299	9.1	30	0
Sutton, G.B.-Buff.	31	10	273	8.8	26	0
Woodson, Pitt.	29	2	207	7.1	20	0
Bell, Den.	21	3	143	6.8	24	0

(Non-Qualifiers)

Player—Team	No.	FC.	Yds.	Avg.	Lng.	TD
Tucker, Buff.-N.E.	19	4	165	8.7	25	0
Martin, N.E.	19	2	164	8.6	28	0
Adams, Raiders	19	5	156	8.2	15	0
Mandley, K.C.	19	2	151	7.9	19	0
Worthen, K.C.	19	5	133	7.0	17	0
K. Johnson, Hou.	19	21	122	6.4	19	0
Schwedes, Mia.	18	3	210	11.7	t70	1
Hollis, Sea.	18	7	164	9.1	21	0
Edmonds, Raiders.	16	4	168	10.5	20	0
McConkey, Pho-SD	15	15	124	8.3	20	0
Martin, Cin.	15	4	107	7.1	17	0
Stradford, Mia.	14	5	129	9.2	19	0
Johnson, Den.	12	6	118	9.8	34	0
Fryar, N.E	12	1	107	8.9	20	0

Player—Team	No.	FC.	Yds.	Avg.	Lng.	TD
Jefferson, Sea.	12	10	87	7.3	19	0
Smith, Cin.	12	2	54	4.5	15	0
Brinson, S.D.	11	0	112	10.2	52	0
Nattiel, Den.	9	0	77	8.6	38	0
Walker, S.D.	6	4	31	5.2	13	0
Hillary, Cin.	6	4	19	3.2	10	0
Hill, Pitt.	5	0	22	4.4	12	0
Brown, Raiders	4	0	43	10.8	29	0
Lipps, Pitt.	4	0	27	6.8	9	0
Carey, Cin.	3	2	29	9.7	13	0
Barnes, K.C.	2	0	41	20.5	21	0
J. Johnson, Pitt.	2	0	22	11.0	13	0
Rison, Ind.	2	2	20	10.0	12	0
Harry, K.C.	2	0	6	3.0	7	0
Woods, Den.	2	0	6	3.0	11	0
Allen, S.D.	2	0	3	1.5	3	0
Ross, K.C.	2	0	0	0.0	0	0
Harden, Raiders	1	0	11	11.0	11	0
Johnson, Buff.	1	0	7	7.0	7	0
Hurst, N.E.	1	0	6	6.0	6	0
C. Washington, Ind.	1	0	6	6.0	6	0
Carrington, Den.	1	0	0	0.0	0	0

Giants rookie Dave Meggett returned five punts for an NFL-season high 114 yards in a December 24 game against the Los Angeles Raiders.

Player—Team	No.	FC.	Yds.	Avg.	Lng.	TD
Figaro, S.D.	1	0	0	0.0	0	0
Lyles, S.D.	1	0	0	0.0	0	0
Gibson, Mia.	1	0	−1	−1.0	−1	0
Byrd, S.D.	0	1	0	......	0	0
Prior, Ind.	0	3	0	......	0	0
Taylor, N.E.	0	2	0	......	0	0
Williams, Mia.	0	3	0	......	0	0

NFC—INDIVIDUALS

Player—Team	No.	FC.	Yds.	Avg.	Lng.	TD
STANLEY, Det.	36	5	496	13.8	74	0
Meggett, Giants	46	14	582	12.7	t76	1
Sikahema, Phoe.	37	13	433	11.7	53	0
Taylor, S.F.	36	20	417	11.6	37	0
Drewrey, T.B.	20	2	220	11.0	55	0
Sanders, Atl.	28	7	307	11.0	t68	1
Lewis, Minn.	44	27	446	10.1	65	0
Howard, Wash.	21	18	200	9.5	38	0
Henley, Rams.	28	19	266	9.5	25	0
Williams, Phil.	30	7	267	8.9	24	0
Query, G.B.	30	7	247	8.2	15	0
Shepard, N.O.-Dall.	31	2	251	8.1	t56	1
Harris, N.O.	27	7	196	7.3	20	0
Jordan, Atl.	4	0	34	8.5	15	0
Martin, Dall.	4	5	32	8.0	12	0
Usher, S.D.-Phoe.	4	0	25	6.3	11	0
Kozlowski, Chi.	4	0	−2	−0.5	4	0
Burbage, Dall.	3	5	5	1.7	5	0
Ellard, Rams.	2	0	20	10.0	10	0
Sanders, Wash.	2	2	12	6.0	7	0
Jones, Phoe.	1	0	13	13.0	13	0
Woolford, Chi.	1	0	12	12.0	12	0
Green, Wash.	1	0	11	11.0	11	0
Perriman, N.O.	1	0	10	10.0	10	0
Griffin, S.F.	1	0	9	9.0	9	0
Irvin, Rams.	1	2	7	7.0	7	0
Turner, N.O.	1	0	7	7.0	7	0
B. Davis, Wash.	1	0	3	3.0	3	0
Greer, S.F.	1	0	3	3.0	3	0
Carter, Minn.	1	0	2	2.0	2	0
Waddle, Chi.	1	0	2	2.0	2	0
Mayhew, Wash.	1	0	0	0.0	0	0
Romanowski, S.F.	1	0	0	0.0	0	0
Massey, N.O.	0	0	54	......	54	0
Pitts, G.B.	0	1	0	......	0	0
Woods, Det.	0	1	0	......	0	0

(Non-Qualifiers)

Player—Team	No.	FC.	Yds.	Avg.	Lng.	TD
Green, Chi.	16	5	141	8.8	24	0
Futrell, T.B.	12	2	76	6.3	15	0
Gray, Det.	11	2	76	6.9	15	0
McKinnon, Chi.	10	3	67	6.7	17	0
Morse, N.O.	10	1	29	2.9	16	0
Edwards, Phil.	7	5	64	9.1	28	0
Hill, N.O.	7	0	41	5.9	13	0
Hicks, Rams.	4	3	39	9.8	15	0

t—Touchdown.
Leader based on average return, minimum 20.

1989 KICKOFF RETURNS

YARDS PER RETURN
AFC: 27.3—Rod Woodson, Pittsburgh.
NFC: 26.7—Mel Gray, Detroit.

MOST YARDS, SEASON
NFC: 1181—James Dixon, Dallas.
AFC: 982—Rod Woodson, Pittsburgh.

MOST YARDS, GAME
NFC: 186—James Dixon, Dallas at Green Bay, October 8 (5 returns).
AFC: 168—James Jefferson, Seattle vs. Kansas City, October 8 (5 returns).

LONGEST KICKOFF RETURN
NFC: 99—Joe Howard, Washington at L.A. Raiders, October 29 (TD).
Bobby Morse, New Orleans at Detroit, December 3 (TD).
AFC: 97—Marc Logan, Miami at Houston, October 1 (TD).
James Jefferson, Seattle vs. Kansas City, October 8 (TD).

MOST RETURNS, SEASON
NFC: 47—Ron Brown, L.A. Rams.
James Dixon, Dallas.
AFC: 36—Rod Woodson, Pittsburgh.

MOST RETURNS, GAME
NFC: 7—Darryl Usher, Phoenix at L.A. Rams, November 19 (145 yards).
AFC: 6—Leonard Harris, Houston at Minnesota, September 10 (142 yards).
Erroll Tucker, New England at Miami, December 10 (118 yards).
Albert Bentley, Indianapolis at New Orleans, December 24 (110 yards).

TOUCHDOWNS
AFC: 1—Marc Logan, Miami.
James Jefferson, Seattle.
Anthony Miller, San Diego.
Rod Woodson, Pittsburgh.
NFC: 1—James Dixon, Dallas.
Joe Howard, Washington.
Bobby Morse, New Orleans.
Thomas Sanders, Chicago.
Herschel Walker, Minnesota.

TEAM CHAMPION
AFC: 23.3—Pittsburgh.
NFC: 22.2—Dallas.

KICKOFF RETURNS—TEAM

AMERICAN FOOTBALL CONFERENCE

Team	No.	Yards	Avg.	Long	TDs.
Pittsburgh	56	1304	23.3	t84	1
New England	69	1462	21.2	47	0
Denver	43	876	20.4	68	0
Buffalo	53	1058	20.0	85	0
Indianapolis	60	1164	19.4	49	0
San Diego	64	1235	19.3	t91	1
Seattle	65	1246	19.2	t97	1
Miami	61	1153	18.9	t97	1
Cleveland	50	932	18.6	49	0
L.A. Raiders	54	1002	18.6	49	0
Kansas City	52	915	17.6	37	0
N.Y. Jets	75	1309	17.5	69	0
Cincinnati	54	941	17.4	33	0
Houston	74	1285	17.4	63	0
Conference Total	830	15882	......	t97	4
Conference Average	59.3	1134.4	19.1	....	0.3

NATIONAL FOOTBALL CONFERENCE

Team	No.	Yards	Avg.	Long	TDs.
Dallas	77	1709	22.2	t97	1
Minnesota	51	1122	22.0	t93	1
Chicago	73	1539	21.1	t96	1
Detroit	61	1272	20.9	62	0
New Orleans	63	1284	20.4	t99	1
Washington	58	1176	20.3	t99	1
Phoenix	83	1650	19.9	52	0
L.A. Rams	67	1328	19.8	74	0
Atlanta	80	1509	18.9	72	0
San Francisco	51	954	18.7	60	0
N.Y. Giants	51	926	18.2	43	0
Green Bay	69	1239	18.0	46	0
Tampa Bay	62	1055	17.0	36	0
Philadelphia	49	828	16.9	45	0
Conference Total	895	17591	......	t99	5
Conference Average	63.0	1256.5	19.7	....	0.4
League Total	1725	33473	......	t99	9
League Average	61.6	1195.5	19.4	....	0.3

TOP TEN KICKOFF RETURNERS

Player—Team	No.	Yards	Avg.	Long	TDs.
WOODSON, ROD, Pittsburgh	36	982	27.3	t84	1
Gray, Mel, Detroit	24	640	26.7	57	0
Logan, Marc, Miami	24	613	25.5	t97	1
Miller, Anthony, San Diego	21	533	25.4	t91	1
Dixon, James, Dallas	47	1181	25.1	t97	1
Howard, Joe, Washington	21	522	24.9	t99	1
Martin, Sammy, New England	24	584	24.3	38	0
Gentry, Dennis, Chicago	28	667	23.8	63	0
Jefferson, James, Seattle	22	511	23.2	t97	1
Metcalf, Eric, Cleveland	31	718	23.2	49	0

AFC—INDIVIDUALS

Player—Team	No.	Yds.	Avg.	Lng.	TD		Player—Team	No.	Yds.	Avg.	Lng.	TD
WOODSON, Pitt.	36	982	27.3	t84	1		Humphrey, Den.	4	86	21.5	29	0
Logan, Mia.	24	613	25.5	t97	1		Ware, Raiders	4	86	21.5	29	0
A. Miller, S.D.	21	533	25.4	t91	1		Dixon, Jets	4	67	16.8	21	0
Martin, N.E.	24	584	24.3	38	0		McNeil, Clev.	4	61	15.3	21	0
Jefferson, Sea.	22	511	23.2	t97	1		Hunter, Ind.	4	58	14.5	19	0
Metcalf, Clev.	31	718	23.2	49	0		K. Jones, Clev.	4	42	10.5	25	0
Jennings, Cin.	26	525	20.2	33	0		Thompson, Pitt.	4	41	10.3	15	0
Bell, Den.	30	602	20.1	33	0		J. Williams, Pitt.	4	31	7.8	22	0
Adams, Raiders	22	425	19.3	37	0		Wonsley, N.E.	3	69	23.0	40	0
Townsell, Jets	34	653	19.2	69	0		Brown, Raiders	3	63	21.0	25	0
Tucker, Buff.-N.E.	23	436	19.0	37	0		Gamble, K.C.	3	55	18.3	23	0
Copeland, K.C.	26	466	17.9	36	0		K. Davis, Buff.	3	52	17.3	20	0
K. Johnson, Hou.	21	372	17.7	39	0		Taylor, N.E.	3	52	17.3	22	0
Holland, S.D.	29	510	17.6	34	0		Mrosko, Hou.	3	46	15.3	19	0
Humphery, Jets	24	414	17.3	52	0		J. Johnson, Pitt.	3	43	14.3	19	0
							Schwedes, Mia.	3	24	8.0	13	0
(Non-Qualifiers)							Saxon, K.C.	3	16	5.3	14	0
Verdin, Ind.	19	371	19.5	29	0		Floyd, S.D.	3	12	4.0	12	0
Harmon, Buff.	18	409	22.7	49	0		Tasker, Buff.	2	39	19.5	20	0
Harris, Sea.	18	334	18.6	25	0		Faaola, Mia.	2	30	15.0	17	0
Bentley, Ind.	17	328	19.3	29	0		Egu, N.E.	2	26	13.0	22	0
Hampton, Mia.	17	303	17.8	34	0		Kinchen, Mia.	2	26	13.0	17	0
White, Hou.	17	303	17.8	29	0		Braggs, Clev.	2	20	10.0	18	0
Beebe, Buff.	16	353	22.1	85	0		Rolle, Buff.	2	20	10.0	14	0
Hollis, Sea.	15	247	16.5	30	0		Bratton, Den.	2	19	9.5	10	0
Harris, Hou.	14	331	23.6	63	0		Hodge, N.E.	2	19	9.5	11	0
Edmonds, Raiders	14	271	19.4	43	0		Smith, Raiders	2	19	9.5	15	0
Hillary, Cin.	14	223	15.9	29	0		Timpson, N.E.	2	13	6.5	13	0
McNair, K.C.	13	257	19.8	37	0		A. Brown, Mia.	2	9	4.5	9	0
T. Johnson, Hou.	13	224	17.2	27	0		Nichols, Jets	2	9	4.5	7	0
Pruitt, Ind.	12	257	21.4	49	0		Williams, Hou.	2	8	4.0	8	0
Rice, N.E.	11	242	22.0	46	0		Redden, Clev.	2	2	1.0	2	0
Epps, Jets	9	154	17.1	43	0		Fryar, N.E.	1	47	47.0	47	0
Rison, Ind.	8	150	18.8	30	0		Clark, Sea.	1	31	31.0	31	0
Stone, Pitt.	7	173	24.7	73	0		Figaro, S.D.	1	21	21.0	21	0
Carrington, Den.	6	152	25.3	68	0		Griffin, Pitt.	1	21	21.0	21	0
Allen, N.E.	6	124	20.7	29	0		Williams, Mia.	1	21	21.0	21	0
Carey, Cin.	6	104	17.3	23	0		Ball, Cin.	1	19	19.0	19	0
Harmon, Sea.	6	84	14.0	19	0		Davenport, Mia.	1	19	19.0	19	0
Reaves, Mia.	6	84	14.0	22	0		Mueller, Buff.	1	19	19.0	19	0
Mueller, Raiders	5	120	24.0	49	0		McNeal, Sea.	f1	17	17.0	17	0
Worthen, K.C.	5	113	22.6	27	0		Woods, Den.	1	17	17.0	17	0
Oliphant, Clev.	5	69	13.8	28	0		Gault, Raiders	1	16	16.0	16	0
Smith, Cin.	5	65	13.0	19	0		Rehder, N.E.	1	14	14.0	14	0

Player—Team	No.	Yds.	Avg.	Lng.	TD	Player—Team	No.	Yds.	Avg.	Lng.	TD
Hinnant, Pitt.	1	13	13.0	13	0	Turk, Raiders	1	2	2.0	2	0
Woods, Sea.	1	13	13.0	13	0	Byrd, Jets	1	1	1.0	1	0
Joines, Clev.	1	12	12.0	12	0	Fairs, Hou.	1	1	1.0	1	0
Washington, Jets	1	11	11.0	11	0	Holifield, Cin.	1	0	0.0	0	0
Ahrens, Mia.	1	10	10.0	10	0	Jackson, Buff.	1	0	0.0	0	0
Comeaux, Sea.	1	9	9.0	9	0	Junkin, Raiders	1	0	0.0	0	0
Goode, Mia.	1	8	8.0	8	0	Lee, Raiders	1	0	0.0	0	0
E. Johnson, Clev.	1	8	8.0	8	0	Lyles, Hou.	1	0	0.0	0	0
Saleaumua, K.C.	1	8	8.0	8	0	Mandley, K.C.	1	0	0.0	0	0
Brudzinski, Mia.	1	6	6.0	6	0	Gl. Montgomery, Hou. ..	1	0	0.0	0	0
Taylor, Cin.	1	5	5.0	5	0	Verhulst, Hou.	1	0	0.0	0	0
Tatupu, N.E.	1	2	2.0	2	0	Jackson, Cin.	f0	0	....	0	0

NFC—INDIVIDUALS

Player—Team	No.	Yds.	Avg.	Lng.	TD	Player—Team	No.	Yds.	Avg.	Lng.	TD
GRAY, Det.	24	640	26.7	57	0	Taylor, S.F.	2	51	25.5	27	0
Dixon, Dall.	47	1181	25.1	t97	1	Wilder, T.B.	2	42	21.0	23	0
Howard, Wash.	21	522	24.9	t99	1	McConkey, Phoe.	2	40	20.0	21	0
Gentry, Chi.	28	667	23.8	63	0	Woodside, G.B.	2	38	19.0	23	0
Meggett, Giants	27	577	21.4	43	0	V. Johnson, N.O.	2	34	17.0	19	1
Sanders, Chi.	23	491	21.3	t96	1	Fontenot, G.B.	2	30	15.0	20	0
A.J. Johnson, Wash.	24	504	21.0	38	0	Lewis, Minn.	2	30	15.0	15	0
Sanders, Atl.	35	725	20.7	72	0	Woods, Det.	2	28	14.0	15	0
Ro. Brown, Rams	47	968	20.6	74	0	McDonald, Rams	2	22	11.0	12	0
Sikahema, Phoe.	43	874	20.3	52	0	Henderson, S.F.	2	21	10.5	13	0
Flagler, S.F.	32	643	20.1	41	0	Pruitt, Chi.	2	17	8.5	11	0
Shepard, N.O.-Dall.	27	529	19.6	32	0	Beckman, Atl.	2	15	7.5	15	0
Jones, Atl.	23	440	19.1	29	0	Little, Phil.	2	14	7.0	12	0
Usher, S.D.-Phoe.	27	506	18.7	33	0	Dallafior, Det.	2	13	6.5	13	0
Elder, T.B.	40	685	17.1	30	0	Ankrom, Dall.	2	6	3.0	5	0
Workman, G.B.	33	547	16.6	46	0	Clark, Phoe.-Minn.	2	6	3.0	6	0
Ingram, Giants	22	332	15.1	29	0	Byars, Phil.	1	27	27.0	27	0
						Drewrey, T.B.	1	26	26.0	26	0
(Non-Qualifiers)						Phillips, N.O.	1	24	24.0	24	0
Harris, N.O.	19	378	19.9	39	0	Hilliard, N.O.	1	20	20.0	20	0
Delpino, Rams	17	334	19.6	30	0	Carter, Minn.	1	19	19.0	19	0
Higgs, Phil.	16	293	18.3	30	0	Curtis, Minn.	1	18	18.0	18	0
Nelson, Minn.	14	317	22.6	32	0	Greer, S.F.	1	17	17.0	17	0
Williams, Phil.	14	249	17.8	28	0	Pillow, T.B.	1	17	17.0	17	0
Walker, Minn.	13	374	28.8	t93	1	Rouson, Giants	1	17	17.0	17	0
Bland, G.B.	13	256	19.7	37	0	Primus, Atl.	1	16	16.0	16	0
Sherman, Phil.	13	222	17.1	45	0	Bruce, Atl.	1	15	15.0	15	0
Dozier, Minn.	12	258	21.5	63	0	Carr, Phoe.	1	15	15.0	15	0
Atkins, N.O.	12	245	20.4	32	0	Painter, Det.	1	14	14.0	14	0
Palmer, Det.	11	255	23.2	62	0	Hill, N.O.	1	13	13.0	13	0
Baker, Phoe.	11	245	22.3	33	0	Rice, Minn.	1	13	13.0	13	0
Fullwood, G.B.	11	243	22.1	35	0	Fenney, Minn.	1	12	12.0	12	0
Green, Chi.	11	239	21.7	37	0	Kozlowski, Chi.	1	12	12.0	12	0
Morse, N.O.	10	278	27.8	t99	1	Tate, Chi.	1	12	12.0	12	0
Tillman, S.F.	10	206	20.6	60	0	Mandeville, Wash.	1	10	10.0	10	0
Stamps, T.B.	9	145	16.1	36	0	Tautalatasi, Dall.	1	9	9.0	9	0
Sanders, Wash.	9	134	14.9	29	0	Chandler, Dall.	1	8	8.0	8	0
Stanley, Det.	9	95	10.6	19	0	Chapura, Chi.	1	8	8.0	8	0
Frazier, N.O.	8	157	19.6	29	0	Crockett, Det.	1	8	8.0	8	0
Paterra, Atl.	8	129	16.1	31	0	Branch, Wash.	1	6	6.0	6	0
G. Thomas, Atl.	7	142	20.3	28	0	Reeves, Phoe.	1	5	5.0	5	0
Jones, Phoe.	7	124	17.7	27	0	Gary, Rams	1	4	4.0	4	0
Query, G.B.	6	125	20.8	28	0	Griffin, Det.	1	1	1.0	1	0
Suhey, Chi.	6	93	15.5	21	0	Collins, Giants	1	0	0.0	0	0
B. Sanders, Det.	5	118	23.6	43	0	Didier, G.B.	1	0	0.0	0	0
Alexander, Det.	5	100	20.0	25	0	Gouveia, Wash.	1	0	0.0	0	0
Howard, T.B.	5	82	16.4	19	0	Jackson, S.F.	1	0	0.0	0	0
Anderson, Minn.	5	75	15.0	36	0	Mandarich, G.B.	1	0	0.0	0	0
Futrell, T.B.	4	58	14.5	22	0	Orr, Wash.	1	0	0.0	0	0
Clack, Dall.	3	56	18.7	24	0	Sargent, Dall.	1	0	0.0	0	0
Burbage, Dall.	3	55	18.3	22	0	Scales, N.O.	1	0	0.0	0	0
Jordan, Atl.	3	27	9.0	13	0	Miller, Det.	f0	0	....	0	0
Edwards, Phil.	3	23	7.7	11	0	Stephen, G.B.	f0	0	....	0	0
Sydney, S.F.	3	16	5.3	16	0						

t—Touchdown.
f—Fair Catch (Stephen, G.B., 2; Miller, Det., 1).
Leader based on average return, minimum 20.

1989 SACKS

MOST SACKS, SEASON
NFC: 21.0—Chris Doleman, Minnesota.
AFC: 14.0—Lee Williams, San Diego.

MOST SACKS, GAME
NFC: 4.0—Tim Harris, Green Bay vs. Atlanta, October 1.
Keith Millard, Minnesota vs. Green Bay, October 15.
Pierce Holt, San Francisco vs. N.Y. Giants, November 27.
Chris Doleman, Minnesota vs. Cincinnati, December 25.
AFC: 3.5—Greg Townsend, L.A. Raiders vs. Washington, October 29.
Leslie O'Neal, San Diego vs. Philadelphia, November 5.

TEAM CHAMPION
NFC: 71—Minnesota.
AFC: 48—San Diego.

TOP TEN IN SACKS

Player—Team	Sacks	Player—Team	Sacks
DOLEMAN, CHRIS, Minnesota	21.0	Simmons, Clyde, Philadelphia	15.5
Harris, Tim, Green Bay	19.5	Taylor, Lawrence, N.Y. Giants	15.0
Millard, Keith, Minnesota	18.0	Williams, Lee, San Diego	14.0
Greene, Kevin, L.A. Rams	16.5	Smith, Bruce, Buffalo	13.0
Swilling, Pat, New Orleans	16.5	O'Neal, Leslie, San Diego	12.5

AFC—TEAM

	Sacks	Yds.
San Diego	48	360
Denver	47	374
Indianapolis	46	384
Cleveland	45	359
Miami	39	268
Buffalo	38	289
Houston	36	277
Kansas City	36	294
L.A. Raiders	35	248
Cincinnati	33	248
Seattle	32	235
New England	31	239
Pittsburgh	31	180
N.Y. Jets	28	177
Conference Total	525	3932
Conference Average	37.5	280.9

NFC—TEAM

	Sacks	Yds.
Minnesota	71	502
Philadelphia	62	424
New Orleans	47	362
San Francisco	43	333
L.A. Rams	42	278
Detroit	40	277
Washington	40	304
Chicago	39	247
N.Y. Giants	39	302
Green Bay	34	214
Tampa Bay	33	222
Atlanta	31	183
Phoenix	30	219
Dallas	29	183
Conference Total	580	4050
Conference Average	41.4	289.3
League Total	1105	7982
League Average	39.5	285.1

AFC—INDIVIDUALS

Player—Team	Sacks	Player—Team	Sacks
WILLIAMS, S.D.	14.0	Smith, K.C.	6.5
B. Smith, Buff.	13.0	Willis, Pitt.	6.5
O'Neal, S.D.	12.5	Buck, Cin.	6.0
Fletcher, Den.	12.0	Jones, Hou.	6.0
Porter, Sea.	10.5	Talley, Buff.	6.0
Townsend, Raiders	10.5	Bennett, Buff.	5.5
Cross, Mia.	10.0	Carreker, Den.	5.5
Grossman, S.D.	10.0	Davis, Raiders	5.5
Hand, Ind.	10.0	Long, Raiders	5.0
D. Thomas, K.C.	10.0	Sochia, Mia.	5.0
Holmes, Den.	9.0	T. Johnson, Pitt.	4.5
Childress, Hou.	8.5	Lageman, Jets	4.5
E. Johnson, Ind.	8.5	McGrew, N.E.	4.5
Bickett, Ind.	8.0	Skow, Cin.	4.5
Nash, Sea.	8.0	Banks, Clev.	4.0
Williams, N.E.	8.0	Blaylock, Clev.	4.0
Baker, Clev.	7.5	Brown, N.E.	4.0
Green, Mia.	7.5	Martin, K.C.	4.0
Mecklenburg, Den.	7.5	Matthews, Clev.	4.0
Byrd, Jets	7.0	Meads, Hou.	4.0
Jeter, N.E.	7.0	Nichols, Jets	4.0
Lloyd, Pitt.	7.0	Seals, Buff.	4.0
Perry, Clev.	7.0	Bryant, Sea.	3.5
Thompson, Ind.	7.0	Golic, Raiders	3.5
Fuller, Hou.	6.5	Williams, Cin.	3.5
Griffin, K.C.	6.5	Wise, Raiders	3.5
Hairston, Clev.	6.5	Brown, Hou.	3.0

Player—Team	Sacks	Player—Team	Sacks
Green, Sea.	3.0	Brooks, Den.	1.0
Krumrie, Cin.	3.0	Burroughs, Buff.	1.0
Pickel, Raiders	3.0	Charlton, Clev.	1.0
Powers, Den.	3.0	Cherry, K.C.	1.0
Sims, N.E.	3.0	Cline, Mia.	1.0
Stewart, Clev.	3.0	Cofield, Buff.	1.0
G. Williams, Pitt.	3.0	Conlan, Buff.	1.0
J. Williams, Pitt.	3.0	Cooper, K.C.	1.0
Woods, Sea.	3.0	Dennison, Den.	1.0
Wright, Buff.	3.0	Frye, Mia.	1.0
Bussey, Cin.	2.5	Glenn, S.D.	1.0
Fairs, Hou.	2.5	Goad, N.E.	1.0
Hinkle, S.D.	2.5	Gordon, Jets	1.0
L. Miller, S.D.	2.5	Graf, Mia.	1.0
Rembert, N.E.	2.5	Grayson, Clev.	1.0
B.R. Smith, S.D.	2.5	Harper, Clev.	1.0
Tuatagaloa, Cin.	2.5	Hobley, Mia.	1.0
Benson, Raiders	2.0	Hunter, Sea.	1.0
Bosa, Mia.	2.0	M. Johnson, Clev.	1.0
Clifton, Jets	2.0	Junior, Mia.	1.0
Frase, Jets	2.0	Kelly, Cin.	1.0
Gash, Clev.	2.0	Krauss, Mia.	1.0
Gibson, Clev.	2.0	Lake, Pitt.	1.0
Hart, Sea.	2.0	Lankford, Mia.	1.0
Herrod, Ind.	2.0	Larson, Ind.	1.0
Jones, Pitt.	2.0	Lewis, K.C.	1.0
Kragen, Den.	2.0	Lyles, S.D.	1.0
Kumerow, Mia.	2.0	Lyons, Jets	1.0
Little, Pitt.	2.0	McDaniel, Raiders	1.0
Lucas, Den.	2.0	McDowell, Hou.	1.0
Lyles, Hou.	2.0	Mitz, Sea.	1.0
McDonald, Ind.	2.0	Munford, Den.	1.0
McMillan, Jets	2.0	Nickerson, Pitt.	1.0
Saleaumua, K.C.	2.0	Odomes, Buff.	1.0
Stallworth, Jets	2.0	Olsavsky, Pitt.	1.0
Thomas, Cin.	2.0	Pearson, K.C.	1.0
Townsend, Den.	2.0	Phillips, S.D.	1.0
White, Cin.	2.0	Pike, Clev.	1.0
Young, Ind.	2.0	Plummer, Ind.	1.0
Hammerstein, Cin.	1.5	Smerlas, Buff.	1.0
McClendon, Cin.	1.5	D. Smith, Hou.	1.0
Gl. Montgomery, Hou.	1.5	Thomas, Mia.	1.0
Offerdahl, Mia.	1.5	Wilcots, Cin.	1.0
Radecic, Buff.	1.5	Williams, Mia.	1.0
Washington, Jets	1.5	Clancy, Ind.	0.5
Zander, Cin.	1.5	Glenn, Jets	0.5
Ahrens, Mia.	1.0	Grant, Cin.	0.5
Alston, Ind.	1.0	Meisner, K.C.	0.5
Armstrong, Ind.	1.0	Mersereau, Jets	0.5
Banks, Ind.	1.0	Mraz, Raiders	0.5
Bayless, S.D.	1.0	Petry, K.C.	0.5
Bell, K.C.	1.0	Robinson, Raiders	0.5

NFC—INDIVIDUALS

Player—Team	Sacks	Player—Team	Sacks
DOLEMAN, Minn.	21.0	Harvey, Phoe.	7.0
Harris, G.B.	19.5	Pitts, Phil.	7.0
Millard, Minn.	18.0	Bruce, Atl.	6.0
Greene, Rams	16.5	Murphy, T.B.	6.0
Swilling, N.O.	16.5	Galloway, Phoe.	5.5
Simmons, Phil.	15.5	Howard, Giants	5.5
Taylor, Giants	15.0	Moss, T.B.	5.5
Jeffcoat, Dall.	11.5	E. Williams, Det.	5.5
Noga, Minn.	11.5	Armstrong, Chi.	5.0
White, Phil.	11.0	Green, Atl.	5.0
Brown, Phil.	10.5	Nunn, Phoe.	5.0
Haley, S.F.	10.5	Spielman, Det.	5.0
Holt, S.F.	10.5	Wilcher, Rams	5.0
Mann, Wash.	9.5	Joyner, Phil.	4.5
Marshall, Giants	9.5	Roper, Chi.	4.5
Warren, N.O.	9.5	Stubbs, S.F.	4.5
Ball, Det.	9.0	Banks, Giants	4.0
Cofer, Det.	9.0	Coleman, Wash.	4.0
Cotton, Atl.	9.0	Goff, T.B.	4.0
Dent, Chi.	9.0	Marshall, Wash.	4.0
Manley, Wash.	9.0	Perry, Chi.	4.0
Thomas, Minn.	9.0	Piel, Rams	4.0
Jackson, N.O.	7.5	Wilks, N.O.	4.0
McMichael, Chi.	7.5	J. Williams, Det.	4.0
Fagan, S.F.	7.0	Caldwell, Wash.	3.5

Player—Team	Sacks	Player—Team	Sacks
Grant, Wash.	3.5	Cannon, T.B.	1.0
Hamel, Dall.	3.5	Case, Atl.	1.0
Hopkins, Phil.	3.5	Collins, Giants	1.0
Merriweather, Minn.	3.5	Cook, N.O.	1.0
Roberts, S.F.	3.5	Cooks, Giants	1.0
Saddler, Phoe.	3.5	Cox, Giants	1.0
Berry, Minn.	3.0	Dimry, Atl.	1.0
Broughton, Dall.	3.0	Geathers, N.O.	1.0
R. Brown, G.B.	3.0	Hall, G.B.	1.0
Chapura, Chi.	3.0	Hill, Phoe.	1.0
Davis, T.B.	3.0	Horton, Dall.	1.0
Faryniarz, Rams	3.0	P. Johnson, Giants	1.0
Golic, Phil.	3.0	V. Johnson, N.O.	1.0
Jarvis, T.B.	3.0	Jones, Dall.	1.0
Kugler, S.F.	3.0	Lee, T.B.	1.0
Mills, N.O.	3.0	Mack, Phoe.	1.0
Reed, Rams	3.0	Mack, N.O.	1.0
Stokes, Wash.	3.0	McNorton, Det.	1.0
Wright, Rams	3.0	Miller, Rams	1.0
Harris, Phil.	2.5	Murphy, G.B.	1.0
W. Martin, N.O.	2.5	Nelson, G.B.	1.0
Norton, Dall.	2.5	Noonan, Dall.	1.0
Robinson, T.B.	2.5	Pete, Det.	1.0
Bell, Phoe.	2.0	Randle, T.B.	1.0
Bethune, Rams	2.0	Reasons, Giants	1.0
Brooks, Det.	2.0	Reid, Atl.	1.0
Casillas, Atl.	2.0	Romanowski, S.F.	1.0
Clarke, Minn.	2.0	Seals, T.B.	1.0
Clasby, Phoe.	2.0	Singletary, Chi.	1.0
Evans, Phil.	2.0	S. Smith, T.B.	1.0
Gann, Atl.	2.0	Stephen, G.B.	1.0
Greene, G.B.	2.0	Strauthers, Minn.	1.0
Hampton, Chi.	2.0	Studwell, Minn.	1.0
Jamison, Det.	2.0	Taylor, Atl.	1.0
Koch, Wash.	2.0	B. Thomas, Atl.	1.0
Lockhart, Dall.	2.0	Tuggle, Atl.	1.0
Noble, G.B.	2.0	Wahler, Phoe.	1.0
Rivera, Chi.	2.0	Walter, S.F.	1.0
B. Smith, Rams	2.0	Waters, Phil.	1.0
Strickland, Rams	2.0	Weddington, G.B.	1.0
Thomas, T.B.	2.0	White, Det.	1.0
Tolbert, Dall.	2.0	Wilson, Phoe.	1.0
Weston, T.B.	2.0	Woods, Chi.	1.0
Winter, G.B.	2.0	Zordich, Phoe.	1.0
Frizzell, Phil.	1.5	Griffin, Det.	0.5
Bowles, Wash.	1.0	Hendrix, Dall.	0.5
Brooks, S.F.	1.0	Jerue, Rams	0.5
Browner, Minn.	1.0	Patterson, G.B.	0.5
Bryan, Atl.	1.0		

1989 FUMBLES

MOST FUMBLES, SEASON
    AFC: 18—Dave Krieg, Seattle.
    NFC: 17—Randall Cunningham, Philadelphia.

MOST FUMBLES, GAME
    AFC: 6—Dave Krieg, Seattle at Kansas City, November 5.
    NFC: 4—Mark Rypien, Washington at L.A. Raiders, October 29.

MOST OWN FUMBLES RECOVERED, SEASON
    AFC: 9—Dave Krieg, Seattle.
    NFC: 6—Don Majkowski, Green Bay.

MOST OWN FUMBLES RECOVERED, GAME
    AFC: 3—Dave Krieg, Seattle at Kansas City, November 5.
    NFC: 2—William Howard, Tampa Bay vs. San Francisco, September 17.
           Steve Walsh, Dallas vs. San Francisco, October 15.
           Earnest Byner, Washington at L.A. Raiders, October 29.
           Chris Miller, Atlanta vs. San Francisco, December 3.
           Dave Meggett, N.Y. Giants vs. L.A. Raiders, December 24.
           Jim Everett, L.A. Rams at New England, December 24.

MOST OPPONENTS' FUMBLES RECOVERED, SEASON
    AFC: 5—Nesby Glasgow, Seattle.
           Carnell Lake, Pittsburgh.
           Dan Saleamua, Kansas City.
    NFC: 5—Chris Doleman, Minnesota.
           James Geathers, New Orleans.

MOST OPPONENTS' FUMBLES RECOVERED, GAME
    AFC: 2—Dave Grayson, Cleveland at Pittsburgh, September 10.
           Billy Ray Smith, San Diego at Phoenix, October 1.
           Carnell Lake, Pittsburgh vs. San Diego, November 19.
           Joe Kelly, Cincinnati vs. Detroit, November 19.
           Dan Saleamua, Kansas City vs. Miami, December 3.
    NFC: 2—James Geathers, New Orleans vs. N.Y. Jets, October 15.
           Michael Stewart, L.A. Rams at Buffalo, October 16.
           Bill Romanowski, San Francisco at N.Y. Jets, October 29.
           Brett Faryniarz, L.A. Rams vs. N.Y. Jets, December 17.

MOST YARDS RETURNING FUMBLES
    AFC: 119—Erik McMillan, N.Y. Jets.
    NFC: 77—Wes Hopkins, Philadelphia.
           Jim Jeffcoat, Dallas.

LONGEST FUMBLE RETURN
    AFC: 81—Vencie Glenn, San Diego vs. N.Y. Giants, October 22 (TD).
    NFC: 77—Al Harris (0) to Wes Hopkins (77), Phila., at Wash., Sept. 17.
           Jim Jeffcoat, Dallas vs. Washington, September 24 (TD).

FUMBLES—TEAM

AMERICAN FOOTBALL CONFERENCE

	Fum.	Own Rec.	Fum. *O.B.	TDs.	Opp. Rec.	Yds.	TDs.	Tot. Rec.
Cleveland	23	7	1	0	11	42	2	18
San Diego	24	6	1	0	12	79	2	18
Denver	26	13	1	0	22	92	2	35
New England	26	12	2	0	12	40	0	24
L.A. Raiders	28	13	3	0	18	65	2	31
Cincinnati	29	10	0	0	16	75	1	26
Buffalo	30	7	2	0	13	13	0	20
Miami	30	12	2	0	8	−1	0	20
N.Y. Jets	32	15	0	0	8	113	2	23
Kansas City	32	12	2	0	18	−26	2	30
Pittsburgh	32	13	1	0	21	17	1	34
Indianapolis	33	21	2	1	15	1	0	36
Houston	39	19	3	0	16	−57	0	35
Seattle	43	24	5	0	13	−6	1	37
Conference Total	427	184	25	1	203	447	15	387
Conference Average	30.5	13.1	1.8	0.1	14.5	31.9	1.1	27.6

NATIONAL FOOTBALL CONFERENCE

	Fum.	Own Rec.	Fum. *O.B.	TDs.	Opp. Rec.	Yds.	TDs.	Tot. Rec.
Tampa Bay	21	10	2	0	18	4	0	28
Chicago	23	5	1	0	12	16	0	17
Phoenix	24	10	0	0	11	−3	0	21
Atlanta	26	15	0	0	12	23	1	27
L.A. Rams	26	11	4	0	15	2	0	26
Minnesota	28	12	2	0	18	93	4	30
New Orleans	28	15	1	0	18	−38	0	33
Dallas	29	13	1	0	10	161	3	23
N.Y. Giants	30	16	0	0	15	15	0	31
San Francisco	32	13	5	0	16	1	1	29
Washington	32	12	0	0	15	12	0	27
Green Bay	35	19	3	2	15	72	0	34
Detroit	37	10	3	1	16	84	0	26
Philadelphia	43	23	4	0	26	161	1	49
Conference Total	414	184	26	3	217	603	10	401
Conference Average	29.6	13.1	1.9	0.2	15.5	43.1	0.7	28.6
League Total	841	368	51	4	420	1050	25	788
League Average	30.0	13.1	1.8	0.1	15.0	37.5	0.9	28.1

*Fumbled out of bounds.

Total yards include all fumble yardage (aborted plays, own and opponents recoveries). Fumbled through end zone, ball awarded to opponents: Pittsburgh (ball awarded to San Diego); New Orleans (ball awarded to N.Y. Jets).

AFC—INDIVIDUALS

Player-Team	Fum.	Own Rec.	Opp. Rec.	Yds.	Tot. Rec.
Adams, Raiders	2	1	0	0	1
Adickes, K.C.	0	1	0	0	1
Alexander, Jets	0	1	0	0	1
Allen, Raiders	2	0	0	0	0
Allen, N.E.	0	0	1	0	1
Allen, Hou.	0	1	0	0	1
Atwater, Den.	0	0	1	29	1
Baab, N.E.	0	1	0	0	1
Bahr, S.D.	0	1	0	0	1
Bailey, Sea.	0	1	0	0	1
Baldinger, Ind.	0	1	0	0	1
Ball, Cin.	3	0	0	0	0
Banker, Clev.	0	1	0	−1	1
Banks, Ind.	0	0	1	0	1
Banks, Mia.	1	1	0	0	1
Banks, Clev.	0	0	2	0	2
Bayless, S.D.	0	0	1	0	1
Beach, Sea.	1	0	0	0	0
Beebe, Buff.	1	0	0	0	0
Bell, Den.	5	4	1	0	5
Bennett, Buff.	0	0	2	5	2
Benson, Raiders	0	0	1	0	1
Bentley, Ind.	3	3	0	7	3
Beuerlein, Raiders	6	3	0	−8	3
Bickett, Ind.	0	0	3	2	3
Blackledge, Pitt.	3	0	0	0	0
Blades, Sea.	3	1	0	0	1
Boyer, Ind.	1	1	0	0	1
Braxton, Den.	0	0	2	35	2
Brennan, Clev.	1	1	0	0	1
Brinson, S.D.	3	0	0	0	0
Brister, Pitt.	4	1	0	0	1
Brooks, Ind.	1	0	0	0	0
Brooks, Cin.	9	1	0	0	1
Brooks, Den.	0	0	2	0	2
A. Brown, Mia.	1	1	0	0	1
Brown, Raiders	1	0	0	0	0
T. Brown, Mia.	1	1	0	0	1
Brown, N.E.	0	0	2	0	2
Buck, Cin.	0	0	1	0	1
Burroughs, Buff.	0	0	1	0	1
Butts, S.D.	2	1	0	0	1
Byrd, Hou.	0	0	2	0	2
Call, Ind.	0	1	0	0	1
Caravello, S.D.	0	1	0	0	1
Carey, Cin.	1	1	0	0	1
Carlson, Hou.	1	1	0	−6	1
Carrington, Den.	1	0	0	0	0
Cherry, K.C.	0	0	2	0	2
Childress, Hou.	0	0	1	0	1
Clancy, Ind.	0	0	3	0	3
Clark, Mia.	0	0	1	0	1
Clark, Sea.	1	0	0	0	0
Clayton, Mia.	1	0	0	0	1
Clifton, Jets	0	0	1	0	1
Comeaux, Sea.	0	0	1	0	1
Cooper, K.C.	0	0	1	6	1
Copeland, K.C.	1	1	0	0	1

Player—Team	Fum.	Own Rec.	Opp. Rec.	Yds.	Tot. Rec.	Player—Team	Fum.	Own Rec.	Opp. Rec.	Yds.	Tot. Rec.
Criswell, Jets	0	1	0	0	1	Humphrey, Den.	4	3	0	0	3
Daniel, Ind.	0	0	1	5	1	Hunley, Raiders	0	1	0	0	1
K. Davis, Buff.	2	0	0	0	0	Jackson, Raiders	1	0	0	0	0
Davis, Raiders	0	0	1	0	1	Jackson, Buff.	0	0	1	0	1
DeBerg, K.C.	4	3	0	—26	3	Jackson, Den.	1	0	0	—8	0
Dennison, Den.	0	0	1	0	1	Jackson, Cin.	0	1	0	0	1
Dickerson, Ind.	10	0	0	0	0	James, N.E.	0	0	1	7	1
Dishman, Hou.	0	0	1	0	1	Jaworski, K.C.	2	2	0	—7	2
R. Dixon, Ind.	0	1	0	0	1	Jefferson, Sea.	3	2	1	0	3
Dixon, Jets	1	0	0	0	0	Jenkins, Sea.	0	0	1	0	1
Donaldson, Ind.	1	1	0	—22	1	Jennings, Cin.	1	0	0	0	0
Dressel, K.C.	1	0	0	0	0	E. Johnson, Ind.	0	0	1	0	1
Duncan, Hou.	1	0	0	0	0	J. Johnson, Pitt.	1	1	0	0	1
Dupard, N.E.	1	0	0	0	0	K. Johnson, Hou.	4	1	2	0	3
Dykes, N.E.	3	1	0	0	1	M.L. Johnson, Sea.	0	0	2	0	2
Eason, N.E.-Jets	3	0	0	0	0	T. Johnson, Hou.	1	0	0	0	0
Eatman, K.C.	0	1	0	0	1	C. Jones, N.E.	1	2	0	4	2
Edmunds, Mia.	1	1	0	0	1	K. Jones, Clev.	1	1	0	0	1
Egu, N.E.	1	1	0	0	1	Jones, Hou.	0	0	2	0	2
Elway, Den.	9	2	0	—4	2	T. Jones, Clev.	0	1	0	0	1
Esiason, Cin.	8	2	0	—4	2	Jordan, N.E.	0	0	1	0	1
Evans, Raiders	1	0	0	0	0	Kay, Den.	0	1	0	0	1
Everett, Pitt.	1	0	1	21	1	Kelly, Buff.	6	3	0	—6	3
Fairs, Hou.	0	0	2	0	2	Kelly, Cin.	0	0	3	23	3
Farren, Clev.	0	1	0	0	1	Kelso, Buff.	0	0	2	0	2
Feagles, N.E.	1	1	0	0	1	Kemp, Sea.	1	0	0	—3	0
Feasel, Sea.	0	1	0	0	1	Kinchen, Mia.	2	0	0	—35	0
Fernandez, Raiders	3	0	0	0	0	L. King, Raiders	0	0	3	15	3
Figaro, S.D.	0	0	1	0	1	Kinnebrew, Buff.	3	0	0	0	0
Fletcher, Den.	0	0	1	0	1	Kosar, Clev.	2	2	0	—1	2
Floyd, S.D.	1	0	0	0	0	Kozak, Hou.	0	0	1	0	1
Flutie, N.E.	1	0	0	0	0	Kozerski, Cin.	0	1	0	0	1
Fryar, N.E.	2	0	0	0	0	Kragen, Den.	0	0	4	17	4
Fulcher, Cin.	0	0	4	0	4	Krieg, Sea.	18	9	0	—20	9
Galbreath, Mia.	0	1	0	0	1	Krumrie, Cin.	0	0	1	9	1
Gannon, S.D.	0	0	1	0	1	Kubiak, Den.	2	1	0	0	1
Gash, Clev.	0	0	1	15	1	Lake, Pitt.	0	1	5	2	6
Givins, Hou.	0	0	1	0	1	Langhorne, Clev.	3	0	0	0	0
Glasgow, Sea.	0	0	5	38	5	Largent, Sea.	0	1	0	0	1
Glenn, S.D.	0	0	1	81	1	LeBel, Raiders	1	0	0	—25	0
Gordon, Jets	0	0	1	0	1	Lee, Raiders	1	0	0	0	0
Grayson, Clev.	0	0	2	31	2	Lipps, Pitt.	2	1	0	0	1
Green, Mia.	0	0	2	0	2	Little, Pitt.	0	1	1	0	2
Green, Sea.	0	0	1	0	1	Lloyd, Pitt.	1	0	3	0	3
Griffin, Pitt.	0	0	1	0	1	Logan, Mia.	1	2	0	—1	2
Grimsley, Hou.	0	0	1	3	1	Long, Raiders	0	0	1	0	1
Grogan, N.E.	3	2	0	0	2	Lutz, K.C.	0	1	0	0	1
Hackett, K.C.	0	0	1	0	1	Lyles, S.D.	1	0	1	0	1
Hall, S.D.	1	0	0	—29	0	Maas, K.C.	0	0	2	4	2
Hall, Pitt.	0	0	1	0	1	Mack, Clev.	1	0	0	0	0
Hammerstein, Cin.	0	0	1	0	1	Mackey, Jets	1	0	0	0	0
Hampton, Mia.	1	0	0	0	0	Maggs, Hou.	0	3	0	0	3
Hand, Ind.	0	0	2	7	2	Malone, Jets	1	0	0	—4	0
Harden, Raiders	0	0	3	22	3	Mandley, K.C.	1	0	0	0	0
Harmon, Buff.	2	0	0	0	0	Manoa, Clev.	2	0	0	0	0
Harper, Sea.	0	0	1	0	1	Marino, Mia.	7	0	0	—4	0
Harper, Clev.	0	0	1	0	1	Marion, N.E.	0	0	1	0	1
Harper, Jets	0	0	1	0	1	Martin, K.C.	0	0	3	0	3
Harris, Sea.	1	0	0	0	0	Martin, Cin.	1	1	0	0	1
Harris, Hou.	1	0	0	0	0	Martin, N.E.	1	0	0	0	0
Harry, K.C.	1	0	0	0	0	Matthews, Hou.	2	0	1	—29	1
Hasty, Jets	1	0	2	2	2	Matthews, Clev.	1	0	2	—2	2
Hayes, K.C.	1	0	0	0	0	Maxwell, Sea.	0	0	1	0	1
Heard, K.C.	2	0	0	0	0	McClendon, Cin.	0	0	1	0	1
Heck, Sea.	0	1	0	0	1	McConkey, S.D.	1	0	0	0	0
Hector, Jets	1	0	0	0	0	McDowell, Hou.	1	0	1	0	1
Henderson, Den.	1	0	0	0	0	McGrew, N.E.	0	0	1	0	1
Highsmith, Hou.	6	2	0	0	2	McKeller, Buff.	1	0	0	0	0
Hill, Pitt.	2	0	0	0	0	McMahon, S.D.	3	1	0	0	1
Hill, Hou.	1	1	0	5	1	McMillan, Jets	0	0	2	119	2
Hill, K.C.	0	0	1	0	1	McNair, K.C.	1	0	0	0	0
Hillary, Cin.	1	0	0	0	0	McNeil, Jets	1	0	0	0	0
Hinkle, Pitt.	0	0	1	0	1	Mecklenburg, Den.	0	0	4	23	4
Hinton, Ind.	0	2	0	0	2	Metcalf, Clev.	5	0	0	0	0
Hobley, Mia.	0	0	1	12	1	Millard, Sea.	0	1	0	4	1
Hoge, Pitt.	2	2	0	0	2	A. Miller, S.D.	1	0	0	0	0
Holifield, Cin.	1	0	0	0	0	Miller, Sea.	0	1	0	0	1
Hollis, Sea.	1	0	0	0	0	L. Miller, S.D.	0	0	1	0	1
Howard, S.D.	0	1	0	0	1	Minnifield, Clev.	0	0	1	0	1
Hull, Buff.	0	2	0	0	2	Gr. Montgomery, Hou.	1	0	0	0	0
Humphery, Jets	4	4	0	0	4	Moon, Hou.	11	6	0	—13	6

Player—Team	Fum.	Own Rec.	Opp. Rec.	Yds.	Tot. Rec.	Player—Team	Fum.	Own Rec.	Opp. Rec.	Yds.	Tot. Rec.
Mueller, Buff.	1	0	0	0	0	Spencer, S.D.	3	0	0	0	0
Mueller, Raiders	0	0	1	0	1	Stephens, N.E.	3	1	0	0	1
Munford, Den.	0	0	1	0	1	Stone, Pitt.	2	1	0	0	1
Munoz, Cin.	0	2	0	0	2	Stouffer, Sea.	3	1	0	0	1
Nattiel, Den.	2	0	0	0	0	Stowe, Pitt.	0	0	2	3	2
Nelson, S.D.	1	0	0	0	0	Stradford, Mia.	4	1	0	0	1
Neubert, Jets	2	1	0	0	1	Strom, Pitt.	1	0	0	-18	0
Newsome, Pitt.	1	1	0	-13	1	Sutton, G.B.-Buff.	2	0	1	0	1
O'Brien, Jets	10	4	0	-4	4	D. Thomas, K.C.	0	0	1	0	1
Okoye, K.C.	8	0	0	0	0	Thomas, Cin.	0	0	1	0	1
Oliphant, Clev.	3	0	0	0	0	R. Thomas, K.C.	1	0	0	0	0
O'Neal, S.D.	0	0	2	10	2	Thomas, Mia.	0	0	2	46	2
Paige, K.C.	3	1	0	0	1	Thomas, Buff.	7	2	0	0	2
Patterson, S.D.	0	0	1	0	1	Thompson, Ind.	0	0	2	0	2
Pelluer, K.C.	2	1	0	-8	1	Timpson, N.E.	1	0	0	0	0
Pennison, Hou.	2	1	0	-17	1	Tolliver, S.D.	4	1	0	-6	1
Perry, Den.	0	1	0	0	1	Townsell, Jets	4	3	0	0	3
Perry, Clev.	0	0	2	0	2	Townsend, Den.	0	0	2	0	2
Perryman, N.E.	2	1	0	0	1	Townsend, Raiders	0	0	1	0	1
Pike, Buff.	0	0	1	0	1	Trudeau, Ind.	10	7	0	-5	7
Pinkett, Hou.	1	0	0	0	0	Tucker, N.E.	2	2	0	0	2
Plummer, Ind.	0	0	1	0	1	Turk, Raiders	1	0	0	-8	0
Plummer, S.D.	0	0	1	0	1	Turner, Mia.	0	0	2	0	2
Porter, Raiders	0	0	1	0	1	Tyrrell, Pitt.	0	0	1	0	1
Prior, Ind.	0	0	1	10	1	Uhlenhake, Mia.	1	0	0	-19	0
Pruitt, Ind.	2	0	0	0	0	Usher, S.D.	1	0	0	0	0
Ramsey, Ind.	1	1	0	0	1	Verdin, Ind.	1	2	0	-5	2
Redden, Clev.	2	0	0	0	0	Vick, Jets	4	1	0	0	1
Reed, Buff.	4	0	0	0	0	Walker, Cin.	0	0	1	0	1
Reich, Buff.	2	0	0	0	0	Walker, S.D.	2	0	0	0	0
Rembert, N.E.	0	0	1	27	1	Ware, Raiders	1	0	0	0	0
Reynolds, N.E.	0	0	1	0	1	Warner, Sea.	7	2	0	0	2
Rice, N.E.	0	0	1	0	1	Washington, Raiders	0	0	3	44	3
Rienstra, Pitt.	0	1	0	0	1	Washington, Jets	0	0	1	0	1
Rison, Ind.	1	0	0	0	0	Weathers, Ind.	1	1	0	2	1
Robbins, Den.	0	0	1	0	1	White, Cin.	0	0	2	22	2
Robinson, Sea.	1	1	0	0	1	White, Hou.	2	1	0	0	1
Robinson, Raiders	1	0	0	0	0	Wilhelm, Cin.	2	1	0	0	1
Roby, Mia.	0	2	0	0	2	Wilkerson, Raiders	0	2	0	0	2
Rodriguez, Sea.	0	1	0	0	1	Williams, N.E.	0	0	2	2	2
Ross, K.C.	1	0	0	0	0	G. Williams, Pitt.	0	0	1	0	1
Rozier, Hou.	4	0	0	0	0	Williams, Sea.	2	1	0	0	1
Saleaumua, K.C.	0	0	5	2	5	W. Williams, Pitt.	0	1	0	0	1
Saxon, K.C.	2	0	0	0	0	Wilson, N.E.	2	0	0	0	0
Schroeder, Raiders	6	2	0	0	2	Winder, Den.	1	0	0	0	0
Schwedes, Mia.	3	2	0	0	2	Wise, Raiders	0	0	2	0	2
Seals, Buff.	0	0	1	0	1	Wisniewski, Raiders	0	3	0	0	3
Sievers, N.E.	1	0	0	0	0	Woodruff, Pitt.	0	0	1	21	1
Slaughter, Clev.	2	0	0	0	0	Woods, Cin.	1	0	0	0	0
A. Smith, Hou.	0	0	1	0	1	Woods, Sea.	1	0	0	0	0
B.R. Smith, S.D.	0	0	2	23	2	Woodson, Pitt.	3	1	3	1	4
D. Smith, Den.	0	1	2	0	3	Worley, Pitt.	9	1	0	0	1
Smith, Cin.	1	0	0	0	0	Worthen, K.C.	1	1	0	0	1
L. Smith, Buff.	0	0	2	14	2	Wright, Buff.	0	0	2	0	2
Smith, K.C.	0	0	2	3	2	Yarno, Hou.	0	1	0	0	1
Smith, Mia.	6	0	0	0	0	Zander, Cin.	0	0	1	25	1
Smith, Raiders	2	1	0	0	1	Zendejas, Hou.	0	1	0	0	1

Touchdowns: McMillan, Jets, 2; R. Dixon, Ind.; Glasgow, Sea.; Glenn, S.D.; Grayson, Clev.; L. King, Raiders; Kragen, Den.; Maas, K.C.; Matthews, Clev.; Mecklenburg, Den.; B.R. Smith, S.D.; Smith, K.C.; Washington, Raiders; White, Cin.; Woodruff, Pitt., 1 each.

NFC—INDIVIDUALS

Player—Team	Fum.	Own Rec.	Opp. Rec.	Yds.	Tot. Rec.	Player—Team	Fum.	Own Rec.	Opp. Rec.	Yds.	Tot. Rec.
Aikman, Dall.	6	3	0	0	3	Bell, Phil.	0	0	1	0	1
Albritton, Dall.	0	0	1	0	1	Bethune, Rams	0	0	1	0	1
Alexander, Phil.	1	1	0	-4	1	Blades, Det.	0	0	1	0	1
Allen, Phil.	1	0	0	7	0	Bland, G.B.	0	2	1	4	3
Anderson, Minn.	3	1	0	0	1	Bortz, Chi.	0	1	0	0	1
Anderson, Chi.	5	0	0	0	0	Bowles, Wash.	0	0	1	0	1
Anderson, Giants	2	0	0	0	0	Branch, Wash.	0	0	1	0	1
Ankrom, Dall.	1	1	0	0	1	Brenner, N.O.	1	0	0	0	0
Armstrong, Chi.	0	0	1	0	1	Brock, N.O.	0	1	0	0	1
Atkins, N.O.	1	1	1	0	2	Brooks, S.F.	0	0	1	0	1
Baker, Phoe.	1	0	0	0	0	Brooks, Det.	1	0	1	3	1
Ball, Det.	0	0	3	0	3	Brown, Phil.	0	0	2	17	2
Banks, Giants	0	0	1	0	1	L. Brown, Det.	0	1	0	0	1
Beckman, Atl.	0	0	1	0	1	Ri. Brown, Rams	0	0	2	0	2
Bell, Rams	7	1	0	0	1	Ro. Brown, Rams	3	0	0	0	0

Player—Team	Fum.	Own Rec.	Opp. Rec.	Yds.	Tot. Rec.	Player—Team	Fum.	Own Rec.	Opp. Rec.	Yds.	Tot. Rec.
Buczkowski, Phoe.	0	0	1	0	1	Hager, Phil.	0	0	2	9	2
Bush, G.B.	0	1	0	0	1	Haley, S.F.	0	0	1	3	1
Butler, Atl.	0	0	1	29	1	Hall, T.B.	0	1	0	0	1
Byars, Phil.	4	4	0	6	4	Hamilton, T.B.	0	0	1	0	1
Byner, Wash.	2	2	0	0	2	Harbaugh, Chi.	2	0	0	0	0
Carrier, T.B.	1	0	0	0	0	Harbour, Wash.	0	0	1	0	1
Carter, Minn.	0	1	0	0	1	Harris, Phil.	0	0	2	0	2
Carter, Phil.	1	1	0	0	1	Harris, N.O.	4	1	0	0	1
Carthon, Giants	1	0	0	0	0	Harris, G.B.	0	0	3	0	3
Casillas, Atl.	0	0	3	0	3	Hebert, N.O.	2	0	0	0	0
Cavanaugh, Phil.	1	0	0	0	0	Heller, Atl.	1	0	0	0	0
Clack, Dall.	1	1	0	0	1	Helton, S.F.	1	1	0	−13	1
Clark, Wash.	1	0	0	0	0	Henderson, S.F.	1	0	1	0	1
Clark, Phoe.-Minn.	2	2	0	0	2	Hendrix, Dall.	0	0	1	0	1
Clark, Det.	2	0	0	0	0	Henley, Rams	1	1	0	0	1
Clayton, Atl.	0	1	0	0	1	Herrmann, Rams	2	0	0	−2	0
Cocroft, T.B.	0	0	1	0	1	Heyward, N.O.	2	1	0	0	1
Coleman, Wash.	1	0	1	0	1	Higgs, Phil.	3	1	0	0	1
Collins, Giants	0	0	2	8	2	Hilgenberg, N.O.	1	1	0	−37	1
Cook, N.O.	1	0	0	0	0	Hill, T.B.	2	0	0	0	0
Covert, Chi.	0	1	0	0	1	Hill, Phoe.	0	0	1	0	1
A. Cox, Rams	1	1	1	4	2	Hill, N.O.	1	0	0	0	0
Craig, S.F.	4	1	0	0	1	Hilliard, N.O.	7	2	0	0	2
Crockett, Det.	0	0	1	0	1	Hogeboom, Phoe.	5	1	0	−4	1
Cross, Giants	1	0	0	0	0	Holland, G.B.	0	0	3	0	3
Cunningham, Phil.	17	4	0	−6	4	Holohan, Rams	1	0	0	0	0
Davis, T.B.	0	0	2	0	2	Holt, S.F.	0	0	1	0	1
Del Rio, Dall.	0	0	2	57	2	Hopkins, Phil.	0	0	3	77	3
Delpino, Rams	1	0	0	0	1	Hostetler, Giants	2	1	0	0	1
Dent, Chi.	0	0	2	0	2	Howard, Giants	0	0	1	0	1
Dill, Phoe.	0	1	0	0	1	Howard, Wash.	2	0	0	0	0
Dixon, Dall.	4	1	0	0	1	Howard, T.B.	2	2	0	4	2
Doleman, Minn.	0	0	5	7	5	Humphries, Wash.	1	1	0	0	1
Dombrowski, N.O.	0	1	0	0	1	Ingram, Giants	2	2	0	0	2
Dorsey, Giants	0	0	1	0	1	Irvin, Dall.	0	0	1	0	1
Douglass, Chi.	0	0	1	0	1	Jackson, Giants	0	0	1	0	1
Dozier, Minn.	2	2	0	0	2	Jackson, S.F.	0	0	1	0	1
Drummond, Phil.	0	1	0	0	1	Jackson, Phil.	1	0	0	0	0
Dusbabek, Minn.	0	0	2	0	2	Jackson, Chi.	0	0	1	0	1
Edwards, Phil.	2	1	0	0	1	Jarvis, T.B.	0	0	1	0	1
Elder, T.B.	2	1	0	0	1	Jeffcoat, Dall.	0	0	3	77	3
Evans, Phil.	0	0	3	21	3	Jiles, Giants	0	0	1	0	1
Everett, Rams	4	4	0	−1	4	P. Johnson, Giants	0	0	1	0	1
Fagan, S.F.	0	0	2	0	2	R. Johnson, Det.	3	0	0	0	0
Faryniarz, Rams	0	0	2	0	2	Johnson, Phil.	2	0	0	0	0
Fenney, Minn.	4	1	0	0	1	V. Johnson, N.O.	0	0	1	−1	1
Ferguson, T.B.	1	0	0	0	0	Johnston, Dall.	3	0	0	0	0
Ferrell, Phoe.	2	0	0	0	0	Jones, Phoe.	3	1	0	0	1
Flagler, S.F.	5	1	0	0	1	Jones, Minn.	2	0	0	0	0
Fontenot, G.B.	0	1	1	0	2	Jones, Det.	0	0	2	0	2
Fontenot, Chi.	0	0	1	0	1	Jordan, Atl.	1	1	1	0	2
Forde, N.O.	0	0	1	0	1	Jordan, Minn.	1	0	0	0	0
Fourcade, N.O.	2	2	0	0	2	Jordan, Phoe.	4	0	0	0	0
Frazier, N.O.	1	0	0	0	0	Kelm, Rams	0	0	1	0	1
Frizzell, Phil.	0	0	3	12	3	Kemp, G.B.	3	1	0	0	1
Fulhage, Atl.	1	1	0	−20	1	Kinard, Giants	0	0	1	4	1
Fullwood, G.B.	6	1	0	0	1	Knight, Phoe.	0	0	1	0	1
Futrell, T.B.	1	1	0	0	1	Kozlowski, Chi.	1	0	0	0	0
Gagliano, Det.	3	2	0	−1	2	Kramer, Minn.	1	0	0	−7	0
Gary, Rams	1	0	0	0	0	Lachey, Wash.	0	0	1	0	1
Gayle, Chi.	0	0	2	11	2	Lang, Atl.	1	1	0	0	1
Geathers, N.O.	0	0	5	0	5	Lewis, Minn.	4	2	0	0	2
Gentry, Chi.	1	0	0	0	0	Little, Phil.	1	0	0	−14	0
Gibson, N.O.	1	0	2	0	2	Lockhart, Dall.	0	0	2	40	2
Gibson, Det.	0	0	3	−4	3	Lowdermilk, Minn.	0	1	0	0	1
Giles, Phil.	0	0	1	0	1	Majkowski, G.B.	15	6	0	−13	6
Goff, T.B.	0	0	1	0	1	Mann, Wash.	0	0	2	0	2
Golic, Phil.	0	0	0	8	0	Manuel, Giants	0	1	0	0	1
Goss, S.F.	0	0	1	0	1	Manusky, Wash.	0	0	1	0	1
Grant, Wash.	0	0	1	0	1	Marshall, Wash.	0	0	2	6	2
Gray, Rams	0	0	1	0	1	E. Martin, N.O.	1	1	0	0	1
Green, Wash.	1	1	0	0	1	W. Martin, N.O.	0	0	2	0	2
Green, Rams	1	0	0	0	0	Marve, T.B.	0	0	1	0	1
Green, Phoe.	2	0	0	0	0	Maxie, N.O.	0	0	1	0	1
Green, Atl.	1	1	1	5	2	May, Wash.	0	2	0	0	2
Greene, Rams	0	0	2	0	2	Mayhew, Wash.	1	0	0	0	0
Greene, G.B.	1	0	1	0	1	McDonald, Phoe.	0	0	1	1	1
Greer, S.F.	1	0	0	0	0	McGee, Rams	2	0	0	0	0
Griffin, S.F.	0	0	1	0	1	McGruder, G.B.	0	1	0	0	1
Guyton, Giants	0	0	3	4	3	McKinnon, Chi.	3	1	0	0	1
Haddix, G.B.	2	0	0	0	0	McMichael, Chi.	0	0	1	0	1

Player—Team	Fum.	Own Rec.	Opp. Rec.	Yds.	Tot. Rec.
Meggett, Giants	8	3	0	0	3
Merriweather, Minn.	0	0	1	0	1
Millard, Minn.	0	0	1	31	1
Millen, Atl.	2	1	0	−11	1
Millen, S.F.	0	0	3	2	3
Miller, Atl.	13	5	0	−3	5
Miller, Det.	0	0	1	0	1
Mills, N.O.	0	0	1	0	1
Mojsiejenko, Wash.	0	0	1	0	1
Monk, Wash.	2	0	0	0	0
Montana, S.F.	9	3	0	−3	3
Moore, Giants	0	2	1	0	3
Moore, Atl.	0	0	1	0	1
Moran, G.B.	0	1	0	0	1
Morris, Wash.	3	0	0	0	0
Morris, Chi.	1	0	0	0	0
Morse, N.O.	0	1	0	0	1
Mowatt, Giants	1	1	0	0	1
Murphy, T.B.	0	0	2	0	2
Murphy, G.B.	0	0	1	0	1
Muster, Chi.	2	0	0	0	0
Najarian, T.B.	0	0	1	0	1
Nelson, G.B.	0	0	1	0	1
Newsome, Rams	0	0	1	0	1
Newton, Minn.	0	0	1	5	1
Noble, G.B.	0	0	1	0	1
Noga, Minn.	0	0	1	0	1
Novacek, Phoe.	0	0	1	0	1
Nunn, Phoe.	0	0	1	0	1
Oates, Giants	1	0	0	0	0
Paige, Det.	1	1	0	0	1
Painter, Det.	1	0	0	0	0
Palmer, Dall.	3	0	0	0	0
Pankey, Rams	0	1	0	0	1
Paris, S.F.	0	1	0	0	1
Paterra, Atl.	2	0	0	0	0
Peebles, T.B.	1	1	0	0	1
Peete, Det.	9	3	0	0	3
Perry, Chi.	0	0	2	5	2
Phillips, Det.	1	0	0	0	1
Piel, Rams	0	1	0	0	1
Pitts, Phil.	0	0	2	0	2
Query, G.B.	1	0	1	0	1
Rade, Atl.	1	0	2	14	2
Rathman, S.F.	1	2	0	12	2
Reed, Rams	0	0	1	0	1
Reeves, Phil.	0	1	0	0	1
Reeves, Phoe.	0	0	1	2	1
Reichenbach, Phil.	0	0	1	0	1
Reynolds, T.B.	0	0	2	0	2
Rice, Minn.	0	1	0	0	1
Riesenberg, Giants	0	2	0	0	2
Riggs, Wash.	3	0	0	0	0
Rivera, Chi.	0	0	1	0	1
Roberts, S.F.	0	0	1	0	1
Robinson, G.B.	0	0	3	0	3
Rocker, Wash.	0	0	1	0	1
Rolling, T.B.	0	0	1	0	1
Romanowski, S.F.	1	0	2	0	2
Roper, Chi.	1	0	0	0	0
Rosenbach, Phoe.	2	1	0	0	1
Rouson, Giants	0	1	0	0	1
Ruettgers, G.B.	0	2	0	0	2
Runager, Phil.	0	1	0	0	1
Rutland, Minn.	0	0	2	27	2
Ruzek, Phil.	0	0	1	0	1
Rypien, Wash.	14	2	0	0	2
B. Sanders, Det.	10	0	0	0	0
Sanders, Atl.	2	1	0	0	1
Sanders, Chi.	2	0	0	0	0
Sargent, Dall.	1	0	0	0	0
Schlereth, Wash.	0	1	0	0	1
Settle, Atl.	1	1	0	0	1
Sharpe, Phoe.	0	1	0	3	1
Sharpe, G.B.	1	1	0	5	1
Shepard, N.O.-Dall.	2	0	0	0	0
Sherman, Phil.	4	3	0	0	3
Sikahema, Phoe.	2	3	0	0	3
Simms, Giants	9	3	0	−1	3
D. Smith, T.B.	1	0	0	0	0
L. Smith, Phoe.	0	0	1	0	1
Spielman, Det.	0	0	2	31	2
Stamps, T.B.	2	1	1	0	2
Stanley, Det.	5	1	0	0	1
Stephen, G.B.	0	0	1	76	1
Stepnoski, Dall.	0	3	0	0	3
Stewart, Rams	1	0	3	4	3
Stokes, Wash.	0	1	1	6	2
Streeter, Chi.	0	1	0	0	1
Strickland, Rams	0	1	0	−3	1
Studwell, Minn.	0	0	2	0	2
Suhey, Chi.	1	0	0	0	0
Swilling, N.O.	0	0	1	0	1
Sydney, S.F.	1	0	0	0	0
Tate, T.B.	2	0	0	0	0
Tautalatasi, Dall.	3	2	0	1	2
Taylor, Phoe.	0	0	1	1	1
Taylor, S.F.	3	0	0	0	0
Taylor, Det.	0	0	1	35	1
Testaverde, T.B.	4	2	0	0	2
B. Thomas, Atl.	0	0	1	9	1
Thomas, Minn.	0	0	3	37	3
Thornton, Chi.	2	0	0	0	0
Tice, N.O.	0	1	0	0	1
Tillman, Giants	1	0	0	0	0
Tillman, S.F.	0	1	0	0	1
Tomczak, Chi.	2	0	0	0	0
Toney, Phil.	4	3	0	−3	3
Tuggle, Atl.	0	1	0	0	1
Tupa, Phoe.	2	1	0	−6	1
Turner, N.O.	1	2	1	0	3
Turner, Phoe.	0	0	1	0	1
Turner, Giants	1	0	0	0	0
Van Horne, Chi.	0	1	0	0	1
Vaughn, Wash.	0	0	1	0	1
Wahler, Phoe.	0	0	1	0	1
Walker, Dall.-Minn.	7	0	0	0	0
Walls, S.F.	1	1	0	0	1
Walsh, Dall.	3	2	0	−14	2
Walter, S.F.	0	0	1	0	1
Walton, Wash.	1	1	0	0	1
Warren, Wash.	0	1	0	0	1
Warren, N.O.	0	0	1	0	1
Washington, Rams	0	1	0	0	1
Washington, Giants	0	0	2	0	2
Waters, Phil.	0	0	3	21	3
Waymer, N.O.	0	0	1	0	1
Weddington, G.B.	0	0	1	0	1
Weston, T.B.	0	0	1	0	1
White, Dall.	1	0	0	0	0
White, Phil.	0	0	1	10	1
White, Det.	0	1	0	20	1
Wilcher, Rams	1	0	0	0	0
Wilder, T.B.	2	1	0	0	1
Wilkins, Atl.	0	1	0	0	1
Williams, Phil.	1	2	1	0	3
J. Williams, Det.	0	0	1	0	1
P. Williams, Giants	1	0	0	0	0
Wilson, S.F.	2	1	0	0	1
Wilson, Minn.	5	2	0	−7	2
Winslow, N.O.	1	0	0	0	0
Woods, Det.	1	0	0	0	0
Woodside, G.B.	4	1	0	0	1
Workman, G.B.	1	1	0	0	1
Young, S.F.	2	1	0	0	1
Zackery, Atl.	0	0	1	0	1

Touchdowns: Bland, G.B.; Butler, Atl.; Del Rio, Dall.; Haley, S.F.; Jeffcoat, Dall.; Lockhart, Dall.; Millard, Minn.; Newton, Minn.; Rutland, Minn.; Sharpe, G.B.; Thomas, Minn.; Waters, Phil.; White, Det., 1 each.

1989 FIELD GOALS

HIGHEST FIELD GOAL PERCENTAGE
  NFC: .952—Eddie Murray, Detroit.
  AFC: .824—Jason Staurovsky, New England.

MOST FIELD GOALS
  NFC: 31—Rich Karlis, Minnesota.
  AFC: 27—David Treadwell, Denver.

MOST FIELD GOAL ATTEMPTS
  NFC: 40—Chip Lohmiller, Washington.
  AFC: 37—Tony Zendejas, Houston.

LONGEST FIELD GOAL
  AFC: 59—Pete Stoyanovich, Miami.
  NFC: 54—Paul McFadden, Atlanta.

1989 AFC FIELD GOALS—TEAM

	Made	Att.	Pct.	Long
Denver	27	33	.818	46
Indianapolis	21	27	.778	55
Buffalo	23	30	.767	48
New England	30	40	.750	52
Miami	19	26	.731	59
Kansas City	24	33	.727	50
Cincinnati	14	20	.700	47
Pittsburgh	21	30	.700	49
San Diego	17	25	.680	53
Houston	25	37	.676	52
L.A. Raiders	23	34	.676	50
Cleveland	16	24	.667	50
N.Y. Jets	14	21	.667	46
Seattle	15	25	.600	50
Conference Total	289	405	......	59
Conference Average	20.6	28.9	.714	....

1989 NFC FIELD GOALS—TEAM

	Made	Att.	Pct.	Long
Detroit	20	21	.952	50
San Francisco	29	36	.806	47
Chicago	15	19	.789	46
Green Bay	22	28	.786	52
Tampa Bay	22	28	.786	53
L.A. Rams	23	30	.767	48
N.Y. Giants	29	38	.763	52
Minnesota	32	44	.727	51
Washington	29	40	.725	48
Atlanta	23	32	.719	54
Phoenix	18	26	.692	50
New Orleans	20	29	.690	49
Philadelphia	20	33	.606	49
Dallas	10	20	.500	47
Conference Total	312	424	......	54
Conference Average	22.3	30.3	.736	....
League Total	601	829	......	59
League Average	21.5	29.6	.725	....

1989 AFC FIELD GOALS—INDIVIDUAL

Kicker and Club	1-19	20-29	30-39	40-49	50 & over	Totals	Avg. Yds. Att.	Avg. Yds. Made	Avg. Yds. Miss	Lg.
Staurovsky, Jason	0-0	4-4	5-7	4-5	1-1	14-17	35.9	35.7	37.0	50
New England	......	1.000	.714	.800	1.000	.824				
Treadwell, David	3-3	13-14	8-8	3-7	0-1	27-33	31.8	29.4	43.0	46
Denver	1.000	.929	1.000	.429	.000	.818				
Biasucci, Dean	2-2	6-6	9-10	3-5	1-4	21-27	40.0	32.5	48.2	55
Indianapolis	1.000	1.000	.900	.600	.250	.778				
Norwood, Scott	0-0	5-6	8-9	10-15	0-0	23-30	37.1	36.3	39.6	48
Buffalo	......	.833	.889	.667	......	.767				
Stoyanovich, Pete	1-1	8-8	5-6	4-8	1-3	19-26	35.7	32.2	45.4	59
Miami	1.000	1.000	.833	.500	.333	.731				
Lowery, Nick	1-1	6-6	10-14	6-9	1-3	24-33	35.9	33.9	41.3	50
Kansas City	1.000	1.000	.714	.667	.333	.727				

Kicker and Club	1-19	20-29	30-39	40-49	50 & over	Totals	Avg. Yds. Att.	Avg. Yds. Made	Avg. Yds. Miss	Lg.
Anderson, Gary	2-2	5-5	5-8	9-15	0-0	21-30	37.6	35.3	42.8	49
Pittsburgh	1.000	1.000	.625	.600	......	.700				
Bahr, Chris	0-0	6-6	6-9	4-6	1-4	17-25	37.7	34.9	43.6	53
San Diego	......	1.000	.667	.667	.250	.680				
Jaeger, Jeff	1-1	8-10	8-9	5-12	1-2	23-34	35.9	33.4	41.2	50
L.A. Raiders	1.000	.800	.889	.417	.500	.676				
Zendejas, Tony	1-1	8-9	9-14	5-11	2-2	25-37	35.0	33.0	39.1	52
Houston	1.000	.889	.643	.455	1.000	.676				
Bahr, Matt	0-0	5-5	6-8	4-9	1-2	16-24	37.9	34.9	43.8	50
Cleveland	......	1.000	.750	.444	.500	.667				
Leahy, Pat	1-1	6-7	3-4	4-8	0-1	14-21	34.7	31.4	41.3	46
N.Y. Jets	1.000	.857	.750	.500	.000	.667				
Johnson, Norm	1-1	6-7	3-4	4-8	1-5	15-25	38.6	34.7	44.5	50
Seattle	1.000	.857	.750	.500	.200	.600				

Non-Qualifiers (Fewer than 15 attempts)

Kicker and Club	1-19	20-29	30-39	40-49	50 & over	Totals	Avg. Yds. Att.	Avg. Yds. Made	Avg. Yds. Miss	Lg.
Breech, Jim	0-0	9-9	3-4	0-1	0-0	12-14	28.4	26.3	41.5	38
Cincinnati	......	1.000	.750	.000	......	.857				
Gallery, Jim	0-0	1-1	0-1	1-4	0-0	2-6	40.2	36.5	42.0	47
Cincinnati	......	1.000	.000	.250	......	.333				
Conference Totals	13-13	99-106	94-124	71-132	12-30	289-405	36.0	33.5	42.3	59
	1.000	.934	.758	.538	.400	.714				

1989 NFC FIELD GOALS—INDIVIDUAL

Kicker and Club	1-19	20-29	30-39	40-49	50 & over	Totals	Avg. Yds. Att.	Avg. Yds. Made	Avg. Yds. Miss	Lg.
Murray, Eddie	0-0	3-3	8-9	8-8	1-1	20-21	38.2	38.5	34.0	50
Detroit	......	1.000	.889	1.000	1.000	.952				
Cofer, Mike	3-3	8-8	8-9	10-15	0-1	29-36	35.1	33.0	43.9	47
San Francisco	1.000	1.000	.889	.667	.000	.806				
Karlis, Rich	3-3	14-15	5-6	8-12	1-3	31-39	33.7	31.1	43.6	51
Minnesota	1.000	.933	.833	.667	.333	.795				
Butler, Kevin	0-0	6-6	6-7	3-5	0-1	15-19	34.5	32.1	43.5	46
Chicago	......	1.000	.857	.600	.000	.789				
Igwebuike, Donald	0-0	9-9	6-6	5-10	2-3	22-28	37.3	34.5	47.2	53
Tampa Bay	......	1.000	1.000	.500	.667	.786				
Jacke, Chris	1-1	9-9	4-6	7-9	1-3	22-28	35.6	33.4	43.8	52
Green Bay	1.000	1.000	.667	.778	.333	.786				
Allegre, Raul	0-0	6-6	8-9	5-9	1-2	20-26	37.0	34.6	45.0	52
N.Y. Giants	......	1.000	.889	.556	.500	.769				
Lansford, Mike	1-1	7-8	7-7	8-10	0-4	23-30	36.5	33.9	44.9	48
L.A. Rams	1.000	.875	1.000	.800	.000	.767				
McFadden, Paul	1-1	4-4	6-7	2-6	2-2	15-20	37.0	34.7	43.6	54
Atlanta	1.000	1.000	.857	.333	1.000	.750				
Lohmiller, Chip	2-2	11-11	13-15	3-11	0-1	29-40	34.7	31.3	43.5	48
Washington	1.000	1.000	.867	.273	.000	.725				
Del Greco, Al	0-0	7-7	5-6	5-11	1-2	18-26	37.1	33.8	44.4	50
Phoenix	......	1.000	.833	.455	.500	.692				
Andersen, Morten	0-0	7-8	10-11	3-6	0-4	20-29	36.9	33.2	45.1	49
New Orleans	......	.875	.909	.500	.000	.690				
Davis, Greg	0-0	6-6	8-12	7-14	2-2	23-34	38.1	36.6	41.3	52
N.E.-Atl.	......	1.000	.667	.500	1.000	.676				
Ruzek, Roger	2-2	3-4	6-10	2-5	0-1	13-22	34.3	31.9	37.8	46
Dall.-Phil.	1.000	.750	.600	.400	.000	.591				
Zendejas, Luis	1-1	3-3	4-6	6-12	0-2	14-24	38.3	35.4	42.5	47
Phil.-Dall.	1.000	1.000	.667	.500	.000	.583				

Non-Qualifiers (Fewer than 15 attempts)

Kicker and Club	1-19	20-29	30-39	40-49	50 & over	Totals	Avg. Yds. Att.	Avg. Yds. Made	Avg. Yds. Miss	Lg.
Miller, Chris	0-0	1-1	0-0	0-0	0-0	1-1	25.0	25.0	0.0	25
Atlanta	......	1.000	......	......	......	1.000				
Nittmo, Bjorn	0-0	4-5	5-5	0-2	0-0	9-12	32.7	30.1	40.3	39
N.Y. Giants	......	.800	1.000	.000	......	.750				
DeLine, Steve	0-0	0-0	1-2	2-5	0-0	3-7	42.4	42.0	42.8	49
Philadelphia	......	......	.500	.400	......	.429				
Garcia, Teddy	0-0	0-0	1-4	0-0	0-1	1-5	38.0	35.0	38.8	35
Minnesota	......	......	.250	......	.000	.200				
Conference Totals	14-14	105-110	105-128	79-141	9-31	312-424	36.0	33.5	43.1	54
	1.000	.955	.820	.560	.290	.736				
League Total	27-27	204-216	199-252	150-273	21-61	601-829	36.0	33.5	42.7	59
	1.000	.944	.790	.549	.344	.725				

CLUB RANKINGS BY YARDS

	OFFENSE			DEFENSE		
	Total	Rush	Pass	Total	Rush	Pass
Atlanta	24	28	9	28	28	19
Buffalo	5	3	8	11	14	10
Chicago	10	2	19	25	15	24
Cincinnati	3	*1	7	15	26	8
Cleveland	16	21	11	7	10	9
Dallas	27	24	27	20	18	20
Denver	15	6	23	3	6	3
Detroit	18	8	26	18	8	27
Green Bay	6	20	5	16	†19	13
Houston	9	12	10	13	9	17
Indianapolis	23	17	24	22	22	15
Kansas City	13	4	21	2	12	2
L.A. Raiders	19	9	25	10	16	5
L.A. Rams	4	13	4	21	5	28
Miami	7	27	3	24	25	18
Minnesota	14	7	17	*1	11	*1
New England	8	19	6	23	17	23
New Orleans	11	11	13	12	*1	26
N.Y. Giants	20	15	20	5	4	7
N.Y. Jets	17	22	12	27	24	25
Philadelphia	12	5	18	8	7	12
Phoenix	25	26	15	26	27	22
Pittsburgh	28	18	28	19	†19	16
San Diego	21	16	22	6	13	4
San Francisco	*1	10	2	4	3	11
Seattle	26	25	16	14	23	6
Tampa Bay	22	23	14	17	21	14
Washington	2	14	*1	9	2	21

*—League Leader.
†—Tied for position.

TAKEAWAYS/GIVEAWAYS

AMERICAN FOOTBALL CONFERENCE

	Takeaways			Giveaways			Net
	Int.	Fum.	Total	Int.	Fum.	Total	Diff.
Denver	21	22	43	20	12	32	11
Pittsburgh	21	21	42	13	18	31	11
Indianapolis	21	15	36	17	10	27	9
Cleveland	27	11	38	15	15	30	8
Cincinnati	21	16	37	13	19	32	5
Houston	21	16	37	16	17	33	4
L.A. Raiders	18	18	36	22	12	34	2
San Diego	25	13	38	19	17	36	2
Buffalo	23	13	36	20	21	41	−5
Kansas City	15	18	33	23	18	41	−8
New England	16	12	28	27	12	39	−11
Seattle	9	13	22	23	14	37	−15
N.Y. Jets	15	9	24	24	17	41	−17
Miami	15	8	23	25	16	41	−18

NATIONAL FOOTBALL CONFERENCE

	Takeaways			Giveaways			Net
	Int.	Fum.	Total	Int.	Fum.	Total	Diff.
Philadelphia	30	26	56	16	16	32	24
San Francisco	21	16	37	11	14	25	12
Atlanta	20	12	32	12	11	23	9
New Orleans	21	18	39	19	12	31	8
N.Y. Giants	22	15	37	16	14	30	7
Green Bay	25	15	40	20	13	33	7
L.A. Rams	21	15	36	18	11	29	7
Washington	27	15	42	17	20	37	5
Minnesota	18	18	36	19	14	33	3
Tampa Bay	21	18	39	28	9	37	2
Chicago	26	12	38	25	17	42	−4
Detroit	16	16	32	24	24	48	−16
Phoenix	16	11	27	30	14	44	−17
Dallas	7	10	17	27	15	42	−25

CLUB LEADERS

	Offense	Defense
First Downs	San Francisco 350	Denver 246
Rushing	Chi., Buff., & Cin. 136	Washington 72
Passing	Washington 217	K.C. & Minn. 140
Penalty	New England 34	New England 11
Rushes	Kansas City 559	San Francisco 372
Net Yards Gained	Cincinnati 2483	New Orleans 1326
Average Gain	Detroit 4.9	Washington 3.5
Passes Attempted	New England 610	Atlanta 437
Completed	Green Bay 354	Kansas City 236
Percent Completed	San Francisco 70.2	Philadelphia 48.8
Total Yards Gained	San Francisco 4584	Kansas City 2821
Times Sacked	Miami 10	Minnesota 71
Yards Lost	Miami 86	Minnesota 502
Net Yards Gained	Washington 4349	Minnesota 2501
Net Yards per Pass Play	San Francisco 8.15	Minnesota 4.47
Yards Gained per Completion	Raiders 16.30	Detroit 11.33
Combined Net Yards Gained	San Francisco 6268	Minnesota 4184
Percent Total Yards Rushing	Pittsburgh 45.5	New Orleans 25.6
Percent Total Yards Passing	Miami 76.0	Kansas City 58.9
Ball Control Plays	New England 1129	Houston 940
Average Yards per Play	San Francisco 6.13	Minnesota 4.10
Average Time of Possession	New Orleans 33:43	—
Third Down Efficiency	Miami 48.3	Minnesota 33.5
Interceptions	—	Philadelphia 30
Yards Returned	—	Indianapolis 391
Returned for TD	—	Cleveland 4
Punts	Cleveland 97	—
Yards Punted	Cleveland 3817	—
Average Yards per Punt	Phoenix 43.6	—
Punt Returns	New Orleans 53	Houston 24
Yards Returned	N.Y. Giants 582	Houston 191
Average Yards per Return	N.Y. Giants 12.7	Philadelphia 5.8
Returned for TD	Five with 1	—
Kickoff Returns	Phoenix 83	Seattle 44
Yards Returned	Dallas 1709	Seattle 814
Average Yards per Return	Pittsburgh 23.3	Buffalo 15.8
Returned for TD	Nine with 1	—
Total Points Scored	San Francisco 442	Denver 226
Total TDs	Cincinnati 52	Denver 25
TDs Rushing	Detroit 23	Philadelphia 6
TDs Passing	San Francisco 35	Denver 13
TDs on Returns and Recoveries	Cleveland & Minnesota 7	Five with 1
Extra Points	L.A. Rams 51	Denver 25
Safeties	N.O. & Wash. 3	—
Field Goals Made	Minnesota 32	Minnesota 13
Field Goals Attempted	Minnesota 44	Four with 21
Percent Successful	Detroit 95.2	Cleveland 53.6

1989 NFL TEAM-BY-TEAM STATISTICAL SUMMARY

AMERICAN FOOTBALL CONFERENCE

OFFENSE

	Buff.	Cin.	Clev.	Den.	Hou.	Ind.	K.C.	Raid.	Mia.	N.E.	N.Y.J.	Pitt.	S.D.	Sea.
First Downs	334	348	285	308	327	273	304	259	310	335	292	244	267	290
Rushing	136	136	101	125	112	118	120	93	88	114	91	106	95	86
Passing	177	183	161	163	185	140	165	143	201	187	189	117	149	180
Penalty	21	29	23	20	30	15	19	23	21	34	12	21	23	24
Rushes	532	529	448	554	495	458	559	454	400	485	400	500	432	405
Net Yards Gained	2264	2483	1609	2092	1928	1853	2227	2038	1330	1749	1596	1818	1873	1392
Average Gain	4.3	4.7	3.6	3.8	3.9	4.0	4.0	4.5	3.3	3.6	4.0	3.6	4.3	3.4
Average Yards per Game	141.5	155.2	100.6	130.8	120.5	115.8	139.2	127.4	83.1	109.3	99.8	113.6	117.1	87.0
Passes Attempted	478	513	529	474	496	493	435	414	601	610	570	404	515	559
Completed	281	288	309	256	295	253	259	201	331	302	338	210	270	316
Percent Completed	58.8	56.1	58.4	54.0	59.5	51.3	59.5	48.6	55.1	49.5	59.3	52.0	52.4	56.5
Total Yards Gained	3831	3950	3625	3352	3786	3134	3220	3277	4302	3972	3892	2662	3291	3583
Times Sacked	35	41	34	43	37	28	23	44	10	34	62	51	39	46
Yards Lost	242	332	192	351	287	174	182	326	86	265	477	484	254	379
Net Yards Gained	3589	3618	3433	3001	3499	2960	3038	2951	4216	3707	3415	2178	3037	3204
Average Yards per Game	224.3	226.1	214.6	187.6	218.7	185.0	189.9	184.4	263.5	231.7	213.4	136.1	189.8	200.3
Net Yards per Pass Play	7.00	6.53	6.10	5.80	6.56	5.68	6.63	6.44	6.90	5.76	5.40	4.79	5.48	5.30
Yards Gained per Completion	13.63	13.72	11.73	13.09	12.83	12.39	12.43	16.30	13.00	13.15	11.51	12.68	12.19	11.34
Combined Net Yards Gained	5853	6101	5042	5093	5427	4813	5265	4989	5546	5456	5011	3996	4910	4596
Percent Total Yards Rushing	38.7	40.7	31.9	41.1	35.5	38.5	42.3	40.8	24.0	32.1	31.8	45.5	38.1	30.3
Percent Total Yards Passing	61.3	59.3	68.1	58.9	64.5	61.5	57.7	59.2	76.0	67.9	68.2	54.5	61.9	69.7
Average Yards per Game	365.8	381.3	315.1	318.3	339.2	300.8	329.1	311.8	346.6	341.0	313.2	249.8	306.9	287.3
Ball Control Plays	1045	1083	1011	1071	1028	979	1017	912	1011	1129	1032	955	986	1010
Average Yards per Play	5.6	5.6	5.0	4.8	5.3	4.9	5.2	5.5	5.5	4.8	4.9	4.2	5.0	4.6
Average Time of Possession	30:12	30:51	30:26	32:17	31:59	27:15	32:35	28:24	28:15	30:55	29:16	28:50	28:55	29:20
Third Down Efficiency	42.4	45.5	38.5	46.3	40.9	34.1	42.3	34.0	48.3	38.3	32.4	31.6	36.3	40.3

	Buff.	Cin.	Clev.	Den.	Hou.	Ind.	K.C.	Raid.	Mia.	N.E.	N.Y.J.	Pitt.	S.D.	Sea.
Had Intercepted	20	13	15	20	16	17	23	22	25	27	24	13	19	23
Yards Opponents Returned	364	42	306	194	171	345	269	298	335	338	282	103	179	248
Returned by Opponents for TD	2	0	1	1	0	2	2	0	1	2	2	1	0	2
Punts	67	65	97	80	58	80	67	67	59	64	87	83	84	76
Yards Punted	2564	2504	3817	3188	2422	3392	2688	2711	2458	2392	3426	3368	3315	2995
Average Yards per Punt	38.3	38.5	39.4	39.8	41.8	42.4	40.1	40.5	41.7	37.4	39.4	40.6	39.5	39.4
Punt Returns	33	36	49	45	19	26	44	40	33	45	33	40	38	30
Yards Returned	301	209	496	344	122	322	331	378	338	379	299	278	272	251
Average Yards per Return	9.1	5.8	10.1	7.6	6.4	12.4	7.5	9.5	10.2	8.4	9.1	7.0	7.2	8.4
Returned for TD	0	0	0	0	0	1	0	0	1	0	0	0	0	0
Kickoff Returns	53	54	50	43	74	60	52	54	61	69	75	56	64	65
Yards Returned	1058	941	932	876	1285	1164	915	1002	1153	1462	1309	1304	1235	1246
Average Yards per Return	20.0	17.4	18.6	20.4	17.4	19.4	17.6	18.6	18.9	21.2	17.5	23.3	19.3	19.2
Returned for TD	0	0	0	0	0	0	0	0	1	0	0	1	1	1
Fumbles	30	29	23	26	39	33	32	28	30	26	32	32	24	43
Lost	21	19	15	12	17	10	18	12	16	12	17	18	17	14
Out of Bounds	2	0	1	1	3	2	2	3	2	2	0	1	1	5
Own Recovered for TD	0	0	0	0	0	1	0	0	0	0	0	0	0	0
Opponents Recovered by	13	16	11	22	16	15	18	18	8	12	8	21	12	13
Opponents Recovered for TD	0	1	2	2	0	0	2	2	0	0	2	1	2	1
Penalties	103	85	128	83	149	89	116	132	83	63	116	116	122	79
Yards Penalized	831	637	973	594	1153	704	878	1105	614	509	953	986	906	738
Total Points Scored	409	404	334	362	365	298	318	315	331	297	253	265	266	241
Total TDs	49	52	41	40	41	34	35	35	39	30	30	29	31	28
TDs Rushing	15	17	14	15	16	11	18	9	10	12	11	17	13	5
TDs Passing	32	32	20	21	23	18	14	21	26	17	14	10	15	21
TDs on Returns and Recoveries	2	3	7	4	2	5	3	5	3	1	5	2	3	2
Extra Points	46	50	40	39	40	31	34	34	38	27	29	28	29	28
Safeties	0	0	0	1	2	0	1	1	1	0	1	0	0	0
Field Goals Made	23	14	16	27	25	21	24	23	19	30	14	21	17	15
Field Goals Attempted	30	20	24	33	37	27	33	34	26	40	21	30	25	25
Percent Successful	76.7	70.0	66.7	81.8	67.6	77.8	72.7	67.6	73.1	75.0	66.7	70.0	68.0	60.0

AMERICAN FOOTBALL CONFERENCE

DEFENSE

	Buff.	Cin.	Clev.	Den.	Hou.	Ind.	K.C.	Raid.	Mia.	N.E.	N.Y.J.	Pitt.	S.D.	Sea.
First Downs	299	280	276	246	314	336	252	308	337	297	328	323	295	293
Rushing	117	114	93	90	119	126	92	121	139	110	127	112	102	119
Passing	156	151	161	142	165	192	140	160	180	176	178	177	172	158
Penalty	26	15	22	14	30	18	20	27	18	11	23	34	21	16
Rushes	484	482	446	426	437	507	445	504	493	495	517	498	479	520
Net Yards Gained	1840	2162	1670	1580	1669	2077	1766	1940	2153	1978	2136	2008	1813	2118
Average Gain	3.8	4.5	3.7	3.7	3.8	4.1	4.0	3.8	4.4	4.0	4.1	4.0	3.8	4.1
Average Yards per Game	115.0	135.1	104.4	98.8	104.3	129.8	110.4	121.3	134.6	123.6	133.5	125.5	113.3	132.4
Passes Attempted	508	482	540	504	467	556	471	506	513	449	514	548	513	445
Completed	255	256	269	268	269	322	236	277	315	259	282	290	283	252
Percent Completed	50.2	53.1	49.8	53.2	57.6	57.9	50.1	54.7	61.4	57.7	54.9	52.9	55.2	56.6
Total Yards Gained	3495	3383	3520	3201	3819	3918	2821	3311	3811	3905	4035	3721	3311	3332
Times Sacked	38	33	45	47	36	46	36	35	39	31	28	31	48	32
Yards Lost	289	248	359	374	277	384	294	248	268	239	177	180	360	235
Net Yards Gained	3206	3135	3161	2827	3542	3534	2527	3063	3543	3666	3858	3541	2951	3097
Average Yards per Game	200.4	195.9	197.6	176.7	221.4	220.9	157.9	191.4	221.4	229.1	241.1	221.3	184.4	193.6
Net Yards per Pass Play	5.87	6.09	5.40	5.13	7.04	5.87	4.98	5.66	6.42	7.64	7.12	6.12	5.26	6.49
Yards Gained per Completion	13.71	13.21	13.09	11.94	14.20	12.17	11.95	11.95	12.10	15.08	14.31	12.83	11.70	13.22
Combined Net Yards Gained	5046	5297	4831	4407	5211	5611	4293	5003	5696	5644	5994	5549	4764	5215
Percent Total Yards Rushing	36.5	40.8	34.6	35.9	32.0	37.0	41.1	38.8	37.8	35.0	35.6	36.2	38.1	40.6
Percent Total Yards Passing	63.5	59.2	65.4	64.1	68.0	63.0	58.9	61.2	62.2	65.0	64.4	63.8	61.9	59.4
Average Yards per Game	315.4	331.1	301.9	275.4	325.7	350.7	268.3	312.7	356.0	352.8	374.6	346.8	297.8	325.9
Ball Control Plays	1030	997	1031	977	940	1109	952	1045	1045	975	1059	1077	1040	997
Average Yards per Play	4.9	5.3	4.7	4.5	5.5	5.1	4.5	4.8	5.5	5.8	5.7	5.2	4.6	5.2
Average Time of Possession	29:48	29:09	29:34	27:43	28:01	32:45	27:25	31:36	31:45	29:05	30:44	31:10	31:05	30:40
Third Down Efficiency	35.2	39.2	35.7	33.8	45.5	43.2	38.4	47.6	34.5	36.2	38.5	46.3	35.7	41.8
Intercepted by	23	21	27	21	21	21	15	18	15	16	15	21	25	9
Yards Returned by	269	204	300	318	263	391	133	362	126	118	261	261	224	57
Returned for TD	1	1	4	2	0	2	0	3	0	1	2	0	0	0

AFC DEFENSE—Continued

	Buff.	Cin.	Clev.	Den.	Hou.	Ind.	K.C.	Raid.	Mia.	N.E.	N.Y.J.	Pitt.	S.D.	Sea.
Punts	75	75	94	84	56	65	82	72	62	81	69	69	79	74
Yards Punted	2870	2935	3797	3440	2107	2702	3205	2902	2416	3413	2746	2793	3050	2902
Average Yards per Punt	38.3	39.1	40.4	41.0	37.6	41.6	39.1	40.3	39.0	42.1	39.8	40.5	38.6	39.2
Punt Returns	25	33	49	28	24	51	40	41	26	38	34	45	43	41
Yards Returned	227	323	418	370	191	558	325	301	256	346	257	361	451	334
Average Yards per Return	9.1	9.8	8.5	13.2	8.0	10.9	8.1	7.3	9.8	9.1	7.6	8.0	10.5	8.1
Returned for TD	0	0	0	0	0	1	0	1	0	1	1	0	0	0
Kickoff Returns	75	55	58	72	59	63	55	59	63	61	47	53	57	44
Yards Returned	1187	1203	1175	1256	1024	1208	1156	1001	1215	1199	1029	1096	1249	814
Average Yards per Return	15.8	21.9	20.3	17.4	17.4	19.2	21.0	17.0	19.3	19.7	21.9	20.7	21.9	18.5
Returned for TD	0	0	0	0	1	0	2	2	0	0	0	0	1	0
Fumbles	31	26	32	43	25	34	32	40	19	22	32	40	21	26
Lost	13	16	11	22	16	15	18	18	8	12	9	21	13	13
Out of Bounds	1	1	2	4	1	1	1	0	2	1	4	2	1	4
Own Recovered for TD	1	0	0	0	1	0	0	0	0	0	0	0	0	0
Opponents Recovered by	21	19	15	12	17	10	18	12	16	12	17	17	17	14
Opponents Recovered for TD	0	0	1	1	0	0	3	0	1	0	0	4	0	1
Penalties	87	122	122	102	109	103	102	105	106	111	90	96	93	118
Yards Penalized	616	1060	985	823	903	772	797	867	831	954	675	785	741	809
Total Points Scored	317	285	254	226	412	301	286	297	379	391	411	326	290	327
Total TDs	34	32	30	25	52	29	32	36	43	48	50	38	29	37
TDs Rushing	15	9	8	10	20	10	9	15	19	19	16	16	13	11
TDs Passing	14	22	20	13	28	15	16	18	21	27	31	17	15	23
TDs on Returns and Recoveries	5	1	2	2	4	4	7	3	3	2	3	5	1	3
Extra Points	33	31	29	25	49	29	31	36	42	46	46	37	27	35
Safeties	1	1	0	0	0	1	0	0	2	0	1	2	1	2
Field Goals Made	26	20	15	17	17	32	21	15	25	19	21	19	29	22
Field Goals Attempted	37	27	28	27	21	43	26	21	33	26	31	27	41	32
Percent Successful	70.3	74.1	53.6	63.0	81.0	74.4	80.8	71.4	75.8	73.1	67.7	70.4	70.7	68.8

NATIONAL FOOTBALL CONFERENCE

OFFENSE

	Atl.	Chi.	Dall.	Det.	G.B.	Rams	Minn.	N.O.	N.Y.G.	Phil.	Phoe.	S.F.	T.B.	Wash.
First Downs	261	302	246	274	342	321	326	304	298	321	262	350	288	338
Rushing	75	136	78	117	114	107	126	108	118	120	83	124	84	101
Passing	173	147	145	139	207	197	172	167	157	171	157	209	174	217
Penalty	13	19	23	18	21	17	28	29	23	30	22	17	30	20
Rushes	318	516	355	421	397	472	514	502	556	540	407	493	412	514
Net Yards Gained	1155	2287	1409	2053	1732	1909	2066	1948	1889	2208	1361	1966	1507	1904
Average Gain	3.6	4.4	4.0	4.9	4.4	4.0	4.0	3.9	3.4	4.1	3.3	4.0	3.7	3.7
Average Yards per Game	72.2	142.9	88.1	128.3	108.3	119.3	129.1	121.8	118.1	138.0	85.1	122.9	94.2	119.0
Passes Attempted	578	484	513	450	600	523	499	461	444	538	523	483	570	581
Completed	312	267	266	229	354	308	272	284	248	294	279	339	302	337
Percent Completed	54.0	55.2	51.9	50.9	59.0	58.9	54.5	61.6	55.9	54.6	53.3	70.2	53.0	58.0
Total Yards Gained	3903	3262	3124	3282	4325	4369	3468	3651	3355	3455	3659	4584	3666	4476
Times Sacked	51	28	30	57	48	32	40	36	46	45	56	45	43	21
Yards Lost	389	174	239	343	277	236	279	271	281	343	379	282	331	127
Net Yards Gained	3514	3088	2885	2939	4048	4133	3189	3380	3074	3112	3280	4302	3335	4349
Average Yards per Game	219.6	193.0	180.3	183.7	253.0	258.3	199.3	211.3	192.1	194.5	205.0	268.9	208.4	271.8
Net Yards per Pass Play	5.59	6.03	5.31	5.80	6.25	7.45	5.92	6.80	6.27	5.34	5.66	8.15	5.44	7.22
Yards Gained per Completion	12.51	12.22	11.74	14.33	12.22	14.19	12.75	12.86	13.53	11.75	13.11	13.52	12.14	13.28
Combined Net Yards Gained	4669	5375	4294	4992	5780	6042	5255	5328	4963	5320	4641	6268	4842	6253
Percent Total Yards Rushing	24.7	42.5	32.8	41.1	30.0	31.6	39.3	36.6	38.1	41.5	29.3	31.4	31.1	30.4
Percent Total Yards Passing	75.3	57.5	67.2	58.9	70.0	68.4	60.7	63.4	61.9	58.5	70.7	68.6	68.9	69.6
Average Yards per Game	291.8	335.9	268.4	312.0	361.3	377.6	328.4	333.0	310.2	332.5	290.1	391.8	302.6	390.8
Ball Control Plays	947	1028	898	928	1045	1027	1053	999	1046	1123	986	1021	1025	1116
Average Yards per Play	4.9	5.2	4.8	5.4	5.5	5.9	5.0	5.3	4.7	4.7	4.7	6.1	4.7	5.6
Average Time of Possession	25:58	31:10	25:34	26:14	30:21	30:35	30:40	33:43	32:23	30:43	28:27	31:45	29:55	32:58
Third Down Efficiency	32.5	43.9	33.2	33.3	45.6	40.5	34.0	43.0	44.0	39.4	39.5	42.1	41.3	43.8

NFC OFFENSE—Continued

	Atl.	Chi.	Dall.	Det.	G.B.	Rams	Minn.	N.O.	N.Y.G.	Phil.	Phoe.	S.F.	T.B.	Wash.
Had Intercepted	12	25	27	24	20	18	19	19	16	16	30	11	28	17
Yards Opponents Returned	85	182	396	447	321	207	138	265	240	147	327	140	240	229
Returned by Opponents for TD	0	1	3	3	2	0	2	1	2	0	3	0	2	1
Punts	85	72	82	83	66	74	72	71	70	87	82	56	86	63
Yards Punted	3472	2844	3261	3538	2682	2834	2864	2774	3019	3389	3578	2226	3311	2663
Average Yards per Punt	40.8	39.5	39.8	42.6	40.6	38.3	39.8	39.1	43.1	39.0	43.6	39.8	38.5	42.3
Punt Returns	32	32	31	47	35	35	45	53	46	37	40	39	32	26
Yards Returned	341	220	197	572	289	332	448	428	582	331	469	429	296	226
Average Yards per Return	10.7	6.9	6.4	12.2	8.3	9.5	10.0	8.1	12.7	8.9	11.7	11.0	9.3	8.7
Returned for TD	1	0	0	0	0	0	0	1	1	0	0	0	0	0
Kickoff Returns	80	73	77	61	69	67	51	63	51	49	83	51	62	58
Yards Returned	1509	1539	1709	1272	1239	1328	1122	1284	926	828	1650	954	1055	1176
Average Yards per Return	18.9	21.1	22.2	20.9	18.0	19.8	22.0	20.4	18.2	16.9	19.9	18.7	17.0	20.3
Returned for TD	0	1	1	0	0	0	1	1	0	0	0	0	0	1
Fumbles	26	23	29	37	35	26	28	28	30	43	24	32	21	32
Lost	11	17	15	24	13	11	14	12	14	16	14	14	9	20
Out of Bounds	0	1	1	3	3	4	2	1	0	4	0	5	2	0
Own Recovered for TD	0	0	0	1	2	0	0	0	0	0	0	0	0	0
Opponents Recovered by	12	12	10	16	15	15	18	18	15	26	11	16	18	15
Opponents Recovered for TD	1	0	3	0	0	0	4	0	0	1	0	1	0	0
Penalties	82	95	100	121	81	102	119	90	83	114	113	109	104	105
Yards Penalized	671	846	771	977	666	823	974	676	675	938	856	922	881	881
Total Points Scored	279	358	204	312	362	426	351	386	348	342	258	442	320	386
Total TDs	30	45	25	36	42	51	36	46	37	40	29	51	36	42
TDs Rushing	11	22	7	23	13	19	12	19	17	14	10	14	10	14
TDs Passing	17	21	14	11	27	29	17	23	17	23	17	35	23	24
TDs on Returns and Recoveries	2	2	4	2	2	3	7	4	3	3	2	2	3	4
Extra Points	30	43	24	36	42	51	35	44	35	40	28	49	34	41
Safeties	0	0	0	0	1	0	2	3	2	1	1	0	2	3
Field Goals Made	23	15	10	20	22	23	32	20	29	20	18	29	22	29
Field Goals Attempted	32	19	20	21	28	30	44	29	38	33	26	36	28	40
Percent Successful	71.9	78.9	50.0	95.2	78.6	76.7	72.7	69.0	76.3	60.6	69.2	80.6	78.6	72.5

DEFENSE

	Atl.	Chi.	Dall.	Det.	G.B.	Rams	Minn.	N.O.	N.Y.G.	Phil.	Phoe.	S.F.	T.B.	Wash.
First Downs	336	332	321	314	307	306	266	293	266	281	329	283	317	274
Rushing	156	118	116	98	116	101	100	79	90	81	113	76	115	72
Passing	163	191	183	189	179	181	140	198	159	171	185	178	170	177
Penalty	17	23	22	27	12	24	26	16	17	29	31	29	32	25
Rushes	572	446	543	454	460	404	462	373	421	426	539	372	479	384
Net Yards Gained	2471	1897	1991	1621	2008	1543	1683	1326	1539	1605	2302	1383	2023	1344
Average Gain	4.3	4.3	3.7	3.6	4.4	3.8	3.6	3.6	3.7	3.8	4.3	3.7	4.2	3.5
Average Yards per Game	154.4	118.6	124.4	101.3	125.5	96.4	105.2	82.9	96.2	100.3	143.9	86.4	126.4	84.0
Passes Attempted	437	554	488	570	476	577	488	577	486	529	531	564	515	530
Completed	259	307	301	370	302	345	252	320	273	258	286	316	301	277
Percent Completed	59.3	55.4	61.7	64.9	63.4	59.8	51.6	55.5	56.2	48.8	53.9	56.0	58.4	52.3
Total Yards Gained	3737	4079	3748	4193	3553	4302	3003	4222	3427	3713	3794	3568	3659	3875
Times Sacked	31	39	29	40	34	42	71	47	39	62	30	43	33	40
Yards Lost	183	247	183	277	214	278	502	362	302	424	219	333	222	304
Net Yards Gained	3554	3832	3565	3916	3339	4024	2501	3860	3125	3289	3575	3235	3437	3571
Average Yards per Game	222.1	239.5	222.8	244.8	208.7	251.5	156.3	241.3	195.3	205.6	223.4	202.2	214.8	223.2
Net Yards per Pass Play	7.59	6.46	6.90	6.42	6.55	6.50	4.47	6.19	5.95	5.57	6.37	5.33	6.27	6.26
Yards Gained per Completion	14.43	13.29	12.45	11.33	11.76	12.47	11.92	13.19	12.55	14.39	13.27	11.29	12.16	13.99
Combined Net Yards Gained	6025	5729	5556	5537	5347	5567	4184	5186	4664	4894	5877	4618	5460	4915
Percent Total Yards Rushing	41.0	33.1	35.8	29.3	37.6	27.7	40.2	25.6	33.0	32.8	39.2	29.9	37.1	27.3
Percent Total Yards Passing	59.0	66.9	64.2	70.7	62.4	72.3	59.8	74.4	67.0	67.2	60.8	70.1	62.9	72.7
Average Yards per Game	376.6	358.1	347.3	346.1	334.2	347.9	261.5	324.1	291.5	305.9	367.3	288.6	341.3	307.2
Ball Control Plays	1040	1039	1060	1064	970	1023	1021	997	946	1017	1100	979	1027	954
Average Yards per Play	5.8	5.5	5.2	5.2	5.5	5.4	4.1	5.2	4.9	4.8	5.3	4.7	5.3	5.2
Average Time of Possession	34:02	28:50	34:26	33:46	29:39	29:25	29:20	26:17	27:37	29:17	31:33	28:15	30:05	27:02
Third Down Efficiency	45.0	40.6	46.3	37.7	45.0	37.7	33.5	38.0	38.5	36.4	43.7	36.2	41.8	38.1
Intercepted by	20	26	7	16	25	21	18	21	22	30	16	21	21	27
Yards Returned by	285	268	37	107	232	372	264	226	330	375	275	262	234	284
Returned for TD	0	1	0	1	0	3	2	2	2	2	2	0	2	3

NFC DEFENSE—Continued

	Atl.	Chi.	Dall.	Det.	G.B.	Rams	Minn.	N.O.	N.Y.G.	Phil.	Phoe.	S.F.	T.B.	Wash.
Punts	56	67	73	80	65	81	95	75	74	85	76	74	69	76
Yards Punted	2342	2655	2911	3293	2644	3364	3859	2956	2964	3571	3155	2875	2781	3047
Average Yards per Punt	41.8	39.6	39.9	41.2	40.7	41.5	40.6	39.4	40.1	42.0	41.5	38.9	40.3	40.1
Punt Returns	43	30	38	46	30	34	32	35	29	37	46	35	54	34
Yards Returned	460	262	334	373	416	315	300	244	236	215	371	361	492	383
Average Yards per Return	10.7	8.7	8.8	8.1	13.9	9.3	9.4	7.0	8.1	5.8	8.1	10.3	9.1	11.3
Returned for TD	0	0	1	0	0	1	0	0	0	0	0	0	0	0
Kickoff Returns	60	68	46	65	63	84	68	55	73	60	57	76	55	74
Yards Returned	1188	1375	853	1037	1389	1633	1287	983	1306	1307	1193	1435	1143	1532
Average Yards per Return	19.8	20.2	18.5	16.0	22.0	19.4	18.9	17.9	17.9	21.8	20.9	18.9	20.8	20.7
Returned for TD	0	0	0	1	0	0	0	0	0	1	0	0	0	1
Fumbles	26	24	22	28	28	38	29	35	38	44	18	34	30	24
Lost	12	12	10	16	15	15	18	18	15	26	11	16	18	15
Out of Bounds	2	1	0	1	2	2	3	3	3	2	3	0	3	1
Own Recovered for TD	1	0	0	0	0	0	0	0	0	0	0	0	1	0
Opponents Recovered by	11	17	15	24	13	11	14	11	14	16	14	14	9	20
Opponents Recovered for TD	3	0	1	0	2	0	0	1	2	0	2	1	1	1
Penalties	79	94	102	107	105	93	116	105	109	118	106	75	109	98
Yards Penalized	682	802	723	993	851	798	903	850	800	956	916	581	869	796
Total Points Scored	437	377	393	364	356	344	275	301	252	274	377	253	419	308
Total TDs	49	43	44	42	41	38	34	35	30	33	41	26	51	38
TDs Rushing	26	21	17	18	15	13	14	10	10	6	12	9	18	9
TDs Passing	19	21	21	19	22	24	18	23	16	26	24	15	29	25
TDs on Returns and Recoveries	4	1	6	5	4	1	2	2	4	1	5	2	4	4
Extra Points	48	41	43	41	39	36	32	34	30	30	40	26	51	38
Safeties	1	0	1	1	1	1	0	0	2	2	2	1	1	0
Field Goals Made	31	26	28	23	23	26	13	19	14	14	29	23	20	14
Field Goals Attempted	36	36	35	33	30	29	21	24	21	26	40	31	24	23
Percent Successful	86.1	72.2	80.0	69.7	76.7	89.7	61.9	79.2	66.7	53.8	72.5	74.2	83.3	60.9

1989 AFC, NFC, AND NFL SUMMARY

	AFC Offense Total	AFC Offense Average	AFC Defense Total	AFC Defense Average	NFC Offense Total	NFC Offense Average	NFC Defense Total	NFC Defense Average	NFL Total	NFL Average
First Downs	4176	298.3	4184	298.9	4233	302.4	4225	301.8	8409	300.3
Rushing	1521	108.6	1581	112.9	1491	106.5	1431	102.2	3012	107.6
Passing	2340	167.1	2308	164.9	2432	173.7	2464	176.0	4772	170.4
Penalty	315	22.5	295	21.1	310	22.1	330	23.6	625	22.3
Rushes	6651	475.1	6733	480.9	6417	458.4	6335	452.5	13,068	466.7
Net Yards Gained	26,252	1875.1	26,910	1922.1	25,394	1813.9	24,736	1766.9	51,646	1844.5
Average Gain	......	3.9	......	4.0	......	4.0	......	3.9	......	4.0
Average Yards per Game	......	117.2	......	120.1	......	113.4	......	110.4	......	115.3
Passes Attempted	7091	506.5	7016	501.1	7247	517.6	7322	523.0	14,338	512.1
Completed	3909	279.2	3833	273.8	4091	292.2	4167	297.6	8000	285.7
Percent Completed	......	55.1	......	54.6	......	56.5	......	56.9	......	55.8
Total Yards Gained	49,877	3562.6	49,583	3541.6	52,579	3755.6	52,873	3776.6	102,456	3659.1
Times Sacked	527	37.6	525	37.5	578	41.3	580	41.4	1105	39.5
Yards Lost	4031	287.9	2932	280.9	3951	282.2	4050	289.3	7982	285.1
Net Yards Gained	45,846	3274.7	45,651	3260.8	48,628	3473.4	48,823	3487.4	94,474	3374.1
Average Yards per Game	......	204.7	......	203.8	......	217.1	......	218.0	......	210.9
Net Yards per Pass Play	......	6.02	......	6.05	......	6.21	......	6.18	......	6.12
Yards Gained per Completion	......	12.76	......	12.94	......	12.85	......	12.69	......	12.81
Combined Net Yards Gained	72,098	5149.9	72,561	5182.9	74,022	5287.3	73,559	5254.2	146,120	5218.6
Percent Total Yards Rushing	......	36.4	......	37.1	......	34.3	......	33.6	......	35.3
Percent Total Yards Passing	......	63.6	......	62.9	......	65.7	......	66.4	......	64.7
Average Yards Per Game	......	321.9	......	323.9	......	330.5	......	328.4	......	326.2
Ball Control Plays	14,269	1019.2	14,274	1019.6	14,242	1017.3	14,237	1016.9	28,511	1018.3
Average Yards per Play	......	5.1	......	5.1	......	5.2	......	5.2	......	5.1
Third Down Efficiency	......	39.4	......	39.4	......	39.9	......	39.9	......	39.7
Interceptions	268	19.1	277	19.8	291	20.8	282	20.1	559	20.0
Yards Returned	3287	234.8	3474	248.1	3551	253.6	3364	240.3	6838	244.2
Returned for TD	16	1.1	16	1.1	20	1.4	20	1.4	36	1.3

1989 AFC, NFC, AND NFL SUMMARY—Continued

	AFC Offense Total	AFC Offense Average	AFC Defense Total	AFC Defense Average	NFC Offense Total	NFC Offense Average	NFC Defense Total	NFC Defense Average	NFL Total	NFL Average
Punts	1034	73.9	1037	74.1	1049	74.9	1046	74.7	2083	74.4
Yards Punted	41,240	2945.7	41,278	2948.4	42,455	3032.5	42,417	3029.8	83,695	2989.1
Average Yards per Punt	......	39.9	......	39.8	......	40.5	......	40.6	......	40.2
Punt Returns	511	36.5	518	37.0	530	37.9	523	37.4	1041	37.2
Yards Returned	4320	308.6	4718	337.0	5160	368.6	4762	340.1	9480	338.6
Average Yards per Return	......	8.5	......	9.1	......	9.7	......	9.1	......	9.1
Returned for TD	2	0.1	3	0.2	3	0.2	2	0.1	5	0.2
Kickoff Returns	830	59.3	821	58.6	895	63.9	904	64.6	1725	61.6
Yards Returned	15,882	1134.4	15,812	1129.4	17,591	1256.5	17,661	1261.5	33,473	1195.5
Average Yards per Return	......	19.1	......	19.3	......	19.7	......	19.5	......	19.4
Returned for TD	4	0.3	6	0.4	5	0.4	3	0.2	9	0.3
Fumbles	427	30.5	423	30.2	414	29.6	418	29.9	841	30.0
Lost	218	15.6	205	14.6	204	14.6	217	15.5	422	15.1
Out of Bounds	25	1.8	25	1.8	26	1.9	26	1.9	51	1.8
Own Recovered for TD	1	0.1	2	0.1	3	0.2	2	0.1	4	0.1
Opponents Recovered by	203	14.5	217	15.5	217	15.5	203	14.5	420	15.0
Opponents Recovered for TD	15	1.1	11	0.8	10	0.7	14	1.0	25	0.9
Penalties	1464	104.6	1466	104.7	1418	101.3	1416	101.1	2882	102.9
Yards Penalized	11,581	827.2	11,618	829.9	11,557	825.5	11,520	822.9	23,138	826.4
Total Points Scored	4458	318.4	4502	321.6	4774	341.0	4730	337.9	9232	329.7
Total TDs	514	36.7	515	36.8	546	39.0	545	38.9	1060	37.9
TDs Rushing	183	13.1	190	13.6	205	14.6	198	14.1	388	13.9
TDs Passing	284	20.3	280	20.0	298	21.3	302	21.6	582	20.8
TDs on Returns and Recoveries	47	3.4	45	3.2	43	3.1	45	3.2	90	3.2
Extra Points	493	35.2	496	35.4	532	38.0	529	37.8	1025	36.6
Safeties	7	0.5	11	0.8	15	1.1	11	0.8	22	0.8
Field Goals Made	289	20.6	298	21.3	312	22.3	303	21.6	601	21.5
Field Goals Attempted	405	28.9	420	30.0	424	30.3	409	29.2	829	29.6
Percent Successful	......	71.4	......	71.0	......	73.6	......	74.1	......	72.5

COACHES WITH 100 CAREER VICTORIES
(Ranked according to career wins)

	Yrs.	REGULAR SEASON Won	Lost	Tied	Pct.	POST-SEASON Won	Lost	Pct.	CAREER Won	Lost	Tied	Pct.
George Halas	40	320	148	30	.673	6	3	.667	326	151	30	.673
*Don Shula	27	269	119	6	.690	18	13	.581	287	132	6	.682
Tom Landry	29	250	162	6	.605	21	18	.538	271	180	6	.600
Curly Lambeau	33	231	133	23	.627	3	2	.600	234	135	43	.626
*Chuck Noll	21	177	132	1	.573	16	8	.667	193	140	1	.579
Paul Brown	21	166	100	6	.621	4	9	.308	170	109	6	.607
Bud Grant	18	158	96	5	.620	10	13	.435	168	109	5	.605
*Chuck Knox	17	155	98	1	.612	7	11	.389	162	109	1	.597
Steve Owen	23	151	100	17	.595	3	8	.273	154	108	17	.582
Hank Stram	17	131	97	10	.571	5	3	.625	136	100	10	.573
Weeb Ewbank	20	130	129	7	.502	4	1	.800	134	130	7	.507
Sid Gillman	18	122	99	7	.550	1	5	.167	123	104	7	.541
George Allen	12	116	47	5	.705	4	7	.364	120	54	5	.684
Don Coryell	14	111	83	1	.572	3	6	.333	114	89	1	.561
John Madden	10	103	32	7	.750	9	7	.563	112	39	7	.731
Buddy Parker	15	104	75	9	.577	3	2	.600	107	77	9	.578
Vince Lombardi	10	96	34	6	.728	8	2	.800	104	36	6	.733
*Joe Gibbs	9	91	45	0	.669	11	3	.786	102	48	0	.680
Bill Walsh	10	92	59	1	.609	10	4	.714	102	63	1	.617

*Active NFL coaches in 1990.

ACTIVE COACHES CAREER RECORDS
(Ranked according to career NFL percentages)

	Yrs.	REGULAR SEASON Won	Lost	Tied	Pct.	POST-SEASON Won	Lost	Pct.	CAREER Won	Lost	Tied	Pct.
George Seifert	1	14	2	0	.875	3	0	1.000	17	2	0	.895
Don Shula	27	269	119	6	.690	18	13	.581	287	132	6	.682
Joe Gibbs	9	91	45	0	.669	11	3	.786	102	48	0	.680
Mike Ditka	8	77	41	0	.653	5	4	.556	82	45	0	.646
Dan Reeves	9	85	50	1	.629	6	5	.545	91	55	1	.622
Chuck Knox	17	155	98	1	.612	7	11	.389	162	109	1	.597
Jerry Burns	4	38	25	0	.603	3	3	.500	41	28	0	.594
Jim Mora	4	38	25	0	.603	0	1	.000	38	26	0	.594
USFL Totals	3	41	12	1	.769	7	1	.875	48	13	1	.782
John Robinson	7	67	44	0	.604	4	6	.400	71	50	0	.587
Marty Schottenheimer	6	52	34	1	.603	2	4	.333	54	38	1	.586
Bill Parcells	7	64	46	1	.581	5	3	.625	69	49	1	.584
Bud Carson	1	9	6	1	.594	1	1	.500	10	7	1	.583
Art Shell	1	7	5	0	.583	0	0	.000	7	5	0	.583
Chuck Noll	21	177	132	1	.573	16	8	.667	193	140	1	.579
Ron Meyer	7	47	36	0	.566	0	2	.000	47	38	0	.553
Sam Wyche	6	49	46	0	.516	2	1	.667	51	47	0	.520
Buddy Ryan	4	33	29	1	.532	0	2	.000	33	31	1	.515
Jerry Glanville	5	33	32	0	.508	2	3	.400	35	35	0	.500
Jack Pardee	6	44	46	0	.489	0	1	.000	44	47	0	.484
WFL Totals	1	14	6	0	.700	2	1	.667	16	7	0	.696
USFL Totals	2	23	13	0	.639	0	2	.000	23	15	0	.605
Marv Levy	9	61	66	0	.480	1	2	.333	62	68	0	.477
CFL Totals	5	43	31	4	.577	7	3	.700	50	34	4	.591
USFL Totals	1	5	13	0	.278	0	0	.000	5	13	0	.278
Lindy Infante	2	14	18	0	.438	0	0	.000	14	18	0	.438
USFL Totals	2	15	21	0	.417	0	0	.000	15	21	0	.417
Wayne Fontes	2	9	12	0	.429	0	0	.000	9	12	0	.429
Ray Perkins	7	37	67	0	.356	1	1	.500	38	68	0	.358
Dan Henning	5	28	51	1	.356	0	0	.000	28	51	1	.356
Jimmy Johnson	1	1	15	0	.063	0	0	.000	1	15	0	.063
Joe Bugel	0	0	0	0	.000	0	0	.000	0	0	0	.000
Bruce Coslet	0	0	0	0	.000	0	0	.000	0	0	0	.000
Rod Rust	0	0	0	0	.000	0	0	.000	0	0	0	.000

LEADING NFC ACTIVE PASSERS
(1000 or more attempts)

	Yrs.	Att.	Comp.	Pct.	Yds.	Avg. Gain	TD	Pct. TD	Int.	Pct. Int.	Pts.
Joe Montana, S.F.	10	4059	2593	63.9	31054	7.65	216	5.3	107	2.6	94.1
Jim Everett, L.A.	4	1484	847	57.1	11356	7.65	78	5.3	56	3.8	83.4
Bobby Hebert, N.O.	5	1385	804	58.1	9667	6.98	57	4.1	51	3.7	77.8
Don Majkowski, G.B.	3	1062	586	55.2	7312	6.89	41	3.9	34	3.2	76.5
Phil Simms, N.Y.	10	3658	1980	54.1	26235	7.17	156	4.3	137	3.7	76.0
Randall Cunningham, Phi.	5	1788	959	53.6	11933	6.67	77	4.3	58	3.2	75.6
Wade Wilson, Minn.	9	1397	775	55.5	10155	7.27	54	3.9	57	4.1	74.6
Tommy Kramer	13	3648	2011	55.1	24775	6.79	159	4.4	157	4.3	73.1
Gary Hogeboom, Phoe.	10	1325	743	56.1	9436	7.12	49	3.7	60	4.5	72.1
Joe Ferguson	17	4511	2367	52.5	29796	6.61	196	4.3	207	4.6	68.6
Dave Wilson, N.O.	8	1039	551	53.0	6987	6.72	36	3.5	55	5.3	63.8
Vinny Testaverde, T.B.	3	1111	551	49.6	7454	6.71	38	3.4	63	5.7	59.0

LEADING AFC ACTIVE PASSERS

(1000 or More Attempts)

	Yrs.	Att.	Comp.	Pct.	Yds.	Avg. Gain	TD	Pct. TD	Int.	Pct. Int.	Pts.
Dan Marino, Mia.	7	3650	2174	59.6	27853	7.63	220	6.0	125	3.4	89.4
Boomer Esiason, Cin.	6	2285	1296	56.7	18350	8.03	126	5.5	76	3.3	87.4
Bernie Kosar, Cleve.	5	1940	1134	58.5	13888	7.16	75	3.9	47	2.4	83.7
Dave Krieg, Sea.	10	2843	1644	57.8	20858	7.34	189	5.9	116	4.1	83.4
Ken O'Brien, N.Y.	7	2467	1471	59.6	17589	7.13	96	3.9	68	2.8	82.8
Jim Kelly, Buff.	4	1742	1032	59.2	12901	7.41	81	4.6	63	3.6	82.6
Tony Eason, N.Y	7	1536	898	58.5	10987	7.15	61	4.0	50	3.3	80.2
Jim McMahon,	8	1831	1050	57.3	13335	7.28	77	4.2	66	3.6	79.2
Warren Moon, Hou.	6	2441	1339	54.9	18300	7.50	101	4.1	99	4.1	75.7
John Elway, Den.	7	3070	1665	54.2	21195	6.90	120	3.9	114	3.7	73.6
Ron Jaworski, K.C.	16	4117	2187	53.1	28190	6.85	179	4.3	164	4.0	72.6
Steve DeBerg, K.C.	13	3735	2118	56.7	25046	6.71	143	3.8	171	4.6	70.8
Jay Schroeder, L.A.	6	1467	721	49.1	10834	7.39	60	4.1	63	4.3	69.6
Steve Grogan, N.E.	15	3501	1829	52.2	26271	7.50	178	5.1	205	5.9	69.3
Marc Wilson, N.E.	9	1816	946	52.1	12766	7.03	80	4.4	91	5.0	68.6
Mike Pagel, Cleve.	8	1305	665	51.0	8323	6.38	43	3.3	52	4.0	65.5
Jack Trudeau, Ind.	4	1042	536	51.4	6287	6.03	29	2.8	40	3.8	63.6
Randy Wright, Pitt.	5	1119	602	53.8	7106	6.35	31	2.8	57	5.1	61.5

LEADING NFC ACTIVE SCORERS

(300 or More Points)

	Yrs.	TDs.	FGs.	XPs.	Pts.
Eddie Murray, Detroit	10	0	212	307	943
Rich Karlis, Minnesota	8	0	168	271	775
Morten Andersen, New Orleans	8	0	171	247	760
Mike Lansford, Los Angeles	8	0	143	273	702
Raul Allegre, New York	7	0	128	167	551
Paul McFadden, Atlanta	6	0	120	160	520
Kevin Butler, Chicago	5	0	108	195	519
Ottis Anderson, New York	11	74	0	0	444
Al Del Greco, Phoenix	6	0	84	190	442
Jerry Rice, San Francisco	5	70	0	0	420
Donald Igwebuike, Tampa Bay	5	0	94	134	416
Roger Craig, San Francisco	7	65	0	0	390
Roy Green, Phoenix	11	65	0	0	390
Curt Warner, Los Angeles	7	62	0	0	372
Mike Quick, Philadelphia	8	60	0	0	360
Greg Bell, Los Angeles	6	57	0	0	342
Gerald Riggs, Washington	8	52	0	0	312
Joe Morris, New York	7	50	0	0	300

LEADING AFC ACTIVE SCORERS

(300 or More Points)

	Yrs.	TDs.	FGs.	XPs.	Pts.
Pat Leahy, New York	16	0	255	496	1261
Chris Bahr,	14	0	241	490	1213
Nick Lowery, Kansas City	11	0	225	338	1013
Jim Breech, Cincinnati	12	0	184	418	970
Matt Bahr, Cleveland	11	0	182	349	895
Gary Anderson, Pittsburgh	8	0	186	260	818
Norm Johnson, Seattle	8	0	136	300	708
Scott Norwood, Buffalo	7	0	123	203	572
Eric Dickerson, Indianapolis	7	86	0	0	516
Tony Zendejas, Houston	5	0	110	177	507
Marcus Allen, Los Angeles	8	80	0	0	480
Stanley Morgan, New England	13	68	0	0	408
James Brooks, Cincinnati	9	66	0	0	396
Dean Biasucci, Indianapolis	5	0	86	133	391
Mark Clayton, Miami	7	64	0	0	384
James Lofton, Buffalo	12	58	0	0	348
Fuad Reveiz, San Diego	4	0	53	161	320

LEADING NFC ACTIVE RUSHERS

(2000 or More Yards)

	Yrs.	Att.	Yds.	TDs.		Yrs.	No.	Yds.	TDs.
Ottis Anderson, N.Y.	11	2274	9317	69	Herschel Walker, Minn.	4	971	4057	31
Gerald Riggs, Wash.	8	1788	7465	52	Earnest Byner, Wash.	6	806	3293	30
Curt Warner, L.A.	7	1649	6705	55	Neal Anderson, Chi.	4	687	3113	26
Roger Craig, S.F.	7	1545	6625	49	Dalton Hilliard, N.O.	4	792	3018	30
James Wilder, Wash.	9	1575	5957	37	Rueben Mayes, N.O.	3	699	2898	16
Joe Morris, N.Y.	7	1318	5296	48	R. Cunningham, Phi.	5	368	2495	18
Greg Bell, L.A.	6	1157	4795	50	Alfred Anderson, Minn.	6	541	2049	19
Stump Mitchell, Phoe.	9	986	4649	32					

LEADING AFC ACTIVE RUSHERS

(2000 or More Yards)

	Yrs.	Att.	Yds.	TDs.		Yrs.	No.	Yds.	TDs.
Eric Dickerson, Ind.	7	2450	11226	82	Kevin Mack, Cleve.	5	757	3119	26
Marcus Allen, L.A.	8	1781	7275	63	Larry Kinnebrew, Buf.	6	770	3115	43
Freeman McNeil, N.Y.	9	1605	7146	30	Herman Heard, K.C.	6	651	2694	13
James Brooks, Cin.	9	1320	6343	42	Christian Okoye, K.C.	3	632	2613	18
Sammy Winder, Den.	8	1453	5307	37	John L. Williams, Sea.	4	577	2414	6
Darrin Nelson, S.D.	8	979	4213	16	Mosi Tatupu, N.E.	12	596	2359	18
Johnny Hector, N.Y.	7	874	3491	39	Gary Anderson, S.D.	4	548	2250	11
James Jones, Sea.	7	960	3452	23	Steve Grogan, N.E.	15	441	2181	35
Mike Rozier, Hou.	5	900	3384	27	John Stephens, N.E.	2	541	2001	11

LEADING NFC ACTIVE RECEIVERS

(200 or More Receptions)

	Yrs.	No.	Yds.	TDs.		Yrs.	No.	Yds.	TDs.
Art Monk, Wash.	10	662	9165	47	Eric Martin, N.O.	5	269	4148	31
J.T. Smith, Phoe.	12	526	6749	33	John Spagnola, G.B.	10	263	2886	15
Roger Craig, S.F.	7	483	4241	16	Earnest Byner, Wash.	6	258	2492	10
Roy Green, Phoe.	11	469	7699	62	Anthony Carter, Minn.	5	256	4720	32
James Wilder, Wash.	9	430	3492	9	Mark Bavaro, N.Y.	5	233	3329	23
Mike Quick, Phila.	8	354	6329	60	Herschel Walker, Minn.	4	229	2480	7
Jimmie Giles,	13	350	5084	41	Lionel Manuel, N.Y.	6	221	3772	23
Ottis Anderson, N.Y.	11	347	2882	5	Don Warren, Wash.	11	220	2337	6
Jerry Rice, S.F.	5	346	6364	66	Hoby Brenner, N.O.	9	211	3125	18
Henry Ellard, L.A.	7	345	5743	36	Stump Mitchell, Phoe.	9	209	1955	9
Gary Clark, Wash.	5	340	5378	35	Ricky Sanders, Wash.	4	204	3202	21
Steve Jordan, Minn.	8	309	4074	20	Stacey Bailey, Atl.	8	202	3378	18
Pete Holohan, L.A.	9	281	3223	12					

LEADING AFC ACTIVE RECEIVERS

(200 or More Receptions)

	Yrs.	No.	Yds.	TDs.		Yrs.	No.	Yds.	TDs.
Ozzie Newsome, Cleve.	12	639	7740	45	Darrin Nelson, S.D.	8	263	2388	5
James Lofton, Buff.	12	607	11251	57	Eddie Brown, Cin.	5	260	4601	30
Stanley Morgan, N.E.	13	534	10352	67	Freeman McNeil, N.Y.	9	256	2521	12
Mickey Shuler, N.Y.	12	438	4819	37	Bruce Hardy, Mia.	12	256	2455	25
Mark Clayton, Mia.	7	405	6565	63	Louis Lipps, Pitt.	6	253	4665	34
Marcus Allen, L.A.	8	388	3661	16	Brian Brennan, Cleve.	6	239	3255	16
Drew Hill, Hou.	10	376	6696	48	Matt Bouza, Ind.	9	234	3064	17
Al Toon, N.Y.	5	355	4574	23	Ernest Givins, Hou.	4	229	3765	17
Mark Duper, Mia.	8	345	6212	42	Willie Gault, L.A.	7	228	4732	33
Andre Reed, Buff.	5	317	4408	31	Rodney Holman, Cin.	8	221	3022	25
James Brooks, Cin.	9	315	3005	24	Jeff Chadwick, Sea.	7	214	3454	17
Stephone Paige, K.C.	7	303	5209	44	Eric Sievers, N.E.	9	206	2408	16
Doug Cosbie,	10	300	3728	30	John L. Williams, Sea.	4	205	1947	12
James Jones, Sea.	7	286	2326	10	Eric Dickerson, Ind.	7	202	1633	4
Vance Johnson, Den.	5	268	3759	24	Phillip Epps, N.Y.	8	200	2992	14

LEADING NFC ACTIVE INTERCEPTORS

(20 or More Interceptions)

	Yrs.	No.	Yds.	TDs.		Yrs.	No.	Yds.	TDs.
Dave Brown, G.B.	15	62	698	5	John Anderson, G.B.	12	25	167	1
Ronnie Lott, S.F.	9	48	617	5	William Judson, Det.	8	24	368	2
Everson Walls, N.Y.	9	44	391	0	Bobby Butler, Atl.	9	24	222	1
Dave Waymer, S.F.	10	37	395	0	Johnnie Johnson,	10	22	390	4
LeRoy Irvin,	10	34	654	5	Scott Case, Atl.	6	21	191	0
Mark Lee, G.B.	10	30	249	0	Carl Lee, Minn.	7	21	280	2
Hanford Dixon, S.F.	9	26	225	0	Jerry Holmes, G.B.	8	21	267	2
Joey Browner, Minn.	7	25	265	2	Darrell Green, Wash.	7	20	184	1

LEADING AFC ACTIVE INTERCEPTORS

(20 or More Interceptions)

	Yrs.	No.	Yds.	TDs.		Yrs.	Att.	Yds.	TDs.
Mike Haynes, L.A.	14	46	688	2	Albert Lewis, K.C.	7	26	232	0
Deron Cherry, K.C.	9	43	617	1	Gill Byrd, S.D.	7	25	347	2
R. Clayborn, Cleve.	13	36	555	1	Felix Wright, Cleve.	5	23	413	2
Mike Harden, L.A.	10	35	644	4	Fred Marion, N.E.	8	23	407	1
Dwayne Woodruff, Pitt.	10	34	579	3	Eugene Daniel, Ind.	6	22	201	1
Vann McElroy, L.A.	8	30	296	1	Kevin Ross, K.C.	6	21	306	1
Roland James, N.E.	10	29	383	0	David Fulcher, Cin.	4	20	175	1
Terry Kinard, Hou.	7	27	574	2	Lionel Washington, L.A.	7	20	247	2

TOP 1989 REGULAR-SEASON PERFORMANCES

*Denotes overtime game.

TOP 40 RUSHING PERFORMANCES BY YARDS

Player—Team Opp. Date	Att.	Yds.	TDs.
Gerald Riggs, Washington vs. Philadelphia, September 17	29	221	1
Greg Bell, L.A. Rams vs. Green Bay, September 24	28	221	2
Greg Bell, L.A. Rams at New England, December 24	26	210	1
Barry Sanders, Detroit at Green Bay, October 29	30	184	0
Marion Butts, San Diego at Kansas City, December 17	39	176	0
Christian Okoye, Kansas City vs. Dallas, October 22	33	170	2
Bo Jackson, L.A. Raiders vs. Cincinnati, November 5	13	159	2
Dalton Hilliard, New Orleans at Atlanta, November 19	29	158	1
Barry Sanders, Detroit at Atlanta, December 24	20	158	3
Christian Okoye, Kansas City at Seattle, October 8	30	156	1
Eric Dickerson, Indianapolis at Cincinnati, October 22	31	152	1
Herschel Walker, Minnesota vs. Green Bay, October 15	18	148	0
Thurman Thomas, Buffalo vs. Miami, October 29	27	148	1
Christian Okoye, Kansas City vs. Miami, December 3	32	148	1
Neal Anderson, Chicago vs. Cincinnati, September 10	21	146	0
Barry Sanders, Detroit vs. Cleveland, November 23	28	145	0
Bo Jackson, L.A. Raiders vs. Washington, October 29	19	144	1
James Brooks, Cincinnati at Houston, November 13	19	141	1
Eric Dickerson, Indianapolis vs. Cleveland, December 10	26	137	0
Roger Craig, San Francisco at Indianapolis, September 10	24	131	2
James Brooks, Cincinnati vs. Tampa Bay, October 29	17	131	1
Eric Dickerson, Indianapolis vs. N.Y. Jets, November 19	31	131	1
Christian Okoye, Kansas City at Green Bay, December 10	38	131	1
Greg Bell, L.A. Rams at Atlanta, September 10	26	128	2
Bobby Humphrey, Denver at Phoenix, December 16	23	128	0
James Brooks, Cincinnati at Pittsburgh, October 8	17	127	2
Thurman Thomas, Buffalo vs. Indianapolis, November 12	29	127	0
Barry Sanders, Detroit vs. Chicago, September 24	18	126	1
Christian Okoye, Kansas City vs. Seattle, November 5	37	126	1
John Stephens, New England vs. Buffalo, November 19	23	126	0
Brent Fullwood, Green Bay vs. New Orleans, September 17	18	125	2
Bobby Humphrey, Denver at L.A. Raiders, December 3	31	125	0
John Stephens, New England vs. Indianapolis, December 3	27	124	1
Sammie Smith, Miami vs. Indianapolis, November 5	25	123	0
Larry Kinnebrew, Buffalo vs. Miami, October 29	21	121	1
Barry Sanders, Detroit at Chicago, December 10	26	120	2
Brent Fullwood, Green Bay vs. Dallas, October 8	28	119	0
Neal Anderson, Chicago vs. Green Bay, December 17	12	119	0
Eric Dickerson, Indianapolis at L.A. Rams, September 17	21	116	1
Neal Anderson, Chicago at Detroit, September 24	16	116	1
Keith Woodside, Green Bay at Chicago, December 17	10	116	1

TOP 40 PASSING PERFORMANCES BY YARDS

Player—Team Opp. Date	Att.	Cmp.	Yds.	TDs.	Int.
Joe Montana, San Francisco at L.A. Rams, December 11	42	30	458	3	2
Jim Everett, L.A. Rams at New Orleans, November 26	*51	29	454	1	2
Randall Cunningham, Philadelphia at Washington, September 17	46	34	447	5	1
Joe Montana, San Francisco at Philadelphia, September 24	34	25	428	5	1
Dan Marino, Miami vs. N.Y. Jets, September 24	55	33	427	3	2
Warren Moon, Houston vs. Cleveland, December 23	51	32	414	2	1
Randall Cunningham, Philadelphia at Chicago, October 2	62	32	401	1	4
Mark Rypien, Washington at Chicago, November 26	47	30	401	4	1
Boomer Esiason, Cincinnati vs. Detroit, November 19	39	30	399	3	1
Jim McMahon, San Diego vs. Houston, September 17	45	27	389	2	3
Ken O'Brien, N.Y. Jets at New England, November 5	29	22	386	2	0
Troy Aikman, Dallas at Phoenix, November 12	40	21	379	2	2
Vinny Testaverde, Tampa Bay vs. Cleveland, November 5	50	27	370	2	4
Jim Everett, L.A. Rams at Indianapolis, September 17	35	28	368	3	1
Don Majkowski, Green Bay vs. Detroit, October 29	45	29	367	2	1
Boomer Esiason, Cincinnati at Minnesota, December 25	54	31	367	3	3
Mark Rypien, Washington at L.A. Raiders, October 29	53	27	364	1	3
Jim Kelly, Buffalo at Houston, September 24	*29	17	363	5	1
Dan Marino, Miami at N.Y. Jets, November 12	34	18	359	3	2
Don Majkowski, Green Bay at Detroit, November 12	59	34	357	1	2
Jim Kelly, Buffalo at New England, November 19	41	21	356	1	2
Steve Grogan, New England at Indianapolis, October 29	46	28	355	1	2
Don Majkowski, Green Bay vs. New Orleans, September 17	32	25	354	3	1
Bernie Kosar, Cleveland at Indianapolis, December 10	40	26	353	0	2
Billy Joe Tolliver, San Diego at Washington, December 10	39	24	350	2	0
Mark Rypien, Washington vs. N.Y. Giants, September 11	32	22	349	2	1
Ken O'Brien, N.Y. Jets vs. L.A. Raiders, October 9	49	25	348	0	2
Warren Moon, Houston vs. Detroit, November 5	38	30	345	2	1
Bob Gagliano, Detroit at N.Y. Giants, September 17	31	21	344	1	3
John Elway, Denver at Seattle, October 22	35	18	344	2	0
Tony Eason, New England vs. Miami, September 17	49	25	341	1	1
Jim Everett, L.A. Rams at Dallas, December 3	37	27	341	4	1

— 335 —

Player—Team Opp. Date	Att.	Cmp.	Yds.	TDs.	Int.
Chris Miller, Atlanta at L.A. Rams, October 8	39	28	340	1	1
Dan Marino, Miami vs. Kansas City, December 24	47	28	339	3	1
Warren Moon, Houston vs. Buffalo, September 24	*42	28	338	1	2
Steve DeBerg, Kansas City at Pittsburgh, October 29	36	24	338	1	2
Vinny Testaverde, Tampa Bay at Cincinnati, October 29	39	23	336	3	3
Don Majkowski, Green Bay at L.A. Rams, September 24	43	25	335	2	3
Chris Miller, Atlanta vs. Detroit, December 24	66	37	334	2	1
Mark Rypien, Washington vs. Phoenix, October 8	42	23	333	3	1
Dan Marino, Miami vs. Green Bay, October 22	37	24	333	2	2

TOP 40 RECEIVING PERFORMANCES BY YARDS

Player—Team Opp. Date	Rec.	Yds.	TDs.
Willie Anderson, L.A. Rams at New Orleans, November 26	*15	336	1
John Taylor, San Francisco at L.A. Rams, December 11	11	286	2
Richard Johnson, Detroit vs. New Orleans, December 3	8	248	1
Henry Ellard, L.A. Rams vs. Indianapolis, September 17	12	230	3
James Dixon, Dallas at Phoenix, November 12	6	203	1
Tim McGee, Cincinnati vs. Detroit, November 19	11	194	1
Michael Haynes, Atlanta vs. Washington, December 17	6	190	2
Webster Slaughter, Cleveland vs. Chicago, October 23	8	186	1
Webster Slaughter, Cleveland vs. Houston, October 29	4	184	2
Richard Johnson, Detroit at N.Y. Giants, September 17	9	172	1
Sterling Sharpe, Green Bay at Tampa Bay, December 3	8	169	2
Ricky Sanders, Washington at Atlanta, December 17	7	167	0
Roy Green, Phoenix at Seattle, September 17	8	166	3
Henry Ellard, L.A. Rams vs. Atlanta, October 8	8	165	0
Jerry Rice, San Francisco at Philadelphia, September 24	6	164	1
Sterling Sharpe, Green Bay at L.A. Rams, September 24	8	164	1
Mark Carrier, Tampa Bay at Chicago, November 19	6	164	1
Jerry Rice, San Francisco at Indianapolis, September 10	6	163	1
Stephone Paige, Kansas City at Pittsburgh, October 29	7	163	0
Henry Ellard, L.A. Rams vs. Phoenix, November 19	5	163	2
Anthony Miller, San Diego vs. Houston, September 17	7	162	2
John Taylor, San Francisco at Atlanta, December 3	5	162	1
Al Toon, N.Y. Jets at Miami, September 24	10	159	1
Bill Brooks, Indianapolis at N.Y. Jets, October 1	7	159	1
Ricky Sanders, Washington at L.A. Raiders, October 29	12	158	1
Andre Reed, Buffalo vs. Denver, September 18	13	157	0
Sterling Sharpe, Green Bay vs. Minnesota, November 26	10	157	2
Vance Johnson, Denver vs. Seattle, November 26	6	154	2
Gary Clark, Washington vs. Philadelphia, September 17	4	153	2
Art Monk, Washington vs. Chicago, November 26	9	152	2
Anthony Miller, San Diego at Washington, December 10	8	152	1
Webster Slaughter, Cleveland at Indianapolis, December 10	6	152	0
Jerry Rice, San Francisco at New Orleans, October 8	7	149	1
Gary Clark, Washington at Seattle, December 23	9	149	1
Cedric Jones, New England at N.Y. Jets, September 10	8	148	0
Vance Johnson, Denver vs. Philadelphia, October 29	9	148	1
Willie Gault, L.A. Raiders vs. Cincinnati, November 5	2	147	1
Tim McGee, Cincinnati vs. Houston, December 17	6	147	1
Brian Blades, Seattle vs. Phoenix, September 17	9	146	1
Vance Johnson, Denver at Cleveland, October 1	5	145	1
Gary Clark, Washington at L.A. Raiders, October 29	8	145	1

NATIONAL FOOTBALL CONFERENCE
INDIVIDUAL LEADERS, 1960-89
(National Football League, 1960-69)

RUSHING

Year	Player	Net Yds.	Att.	TD	Year	Player	Net Yds.	Att.	TD
1989	Barry Sanders, Detroit	1,470	280	14	1974	Lawrence McCutcheon, LA	1,109	236	3
1988	Herschel Walker, Dallas	1,514	361	5	1973	John Brockington, GB	1,144	265	3
1987	Charles White, LA	1,374	324	11	1972	Larry Brown, Washington	1,216	285	8
1986	Eric Dickerson, LA	1,821	404	11	1971	John Brockington, GB	1,105	216	4
1985	Gerald Riggs, Atlanta	1,719	397	10	1970	Larry Brown, Washington	1,125	237	5
1984	Eric Dickerson, LA	2,105	379	14	1969	Gale Sayers, Chicago	1,032	236	8
1983	Eric Dickerson, LA	1,808	390	18	1968	Leroy Kelly, Cleveland	1,239	248	16
1982	Tony Dorsett, Dallas	745	177	5	1967	Leroy Kelly, Cleveland	1,205	235	11
1981	George Rogers, NO	1,674	378	13	1966	Gale Sayers, Chicago	1,231	229	8
1980	Walter Payton, Chicago	1,460	317	6	1965	Jim Brown, Cleveland	1,544	289	17
1979	Walter Payton, Chicago	1,610	369	14	1964	Jim Brown, Cleveland	1,446	280	7
1978	Walter Payton, Chicago	1,395	333	11	1963	Jim Brown, Cleveland	1,863	291	12
1977	Walter Payton, Chicago	1,852	339	14	1962	Jim Taylor, Green Bay	1,474	272	19
1976	Walter Payton, Chicago	1,390	311	13	1961	Jim Brown, Cleveland	1,408	305	8
1975	Jim Otis, St. Louis	1,076	269	5	1960	Jim Brown, Cleveland	1,257	215	9

PASSING

Year	Player	Passes	Com.	Yds.	TD	Int.
1989	Joe Montana, San Francisco	386	271	3,521	26	8
1988	Wade Wilson, Minnesota	332	204	2,746	15	9
1987	Joe Montana, San Francisco	398	266	3,054	31	13
1986	Tommy Kramer, Minnesota	372	208	3,000	24	10
1985	Joe Montana, San Francisco	494	303	3,653	27	13
1984	Joe Montana, San Francisco	432	279	3,630	28	10
1983	Steve Bartkowski, Atlanta	432	274	3,167	22	5
1982	Joe Theismann, Washington	252	161	2,033	13	9
1981	Joe Montana, San Francisco	488	311	3,565	19	12
1980	Ron Jaworski, Philadelphia	451	257	3,529	27	12
1979	Roger Staubach, Dallas	461	267	3,586	27	11
1978	Roger Staubach, Dallas	413	231	3,190	25	16
1977	Roger Staubach, Dallas	361	210	2,620	18	9
1976	James Harris, Los Angeles	158	91	1,460	8	6
1975	Fran Tarkenton, Minnesota	425	273	2,994	25	13
1974	Sonny Jurgensen, Washington	167	107	1,185	11	5
1973	Roger Staubach, Dallas	286	179	2,428	23	15
1972	Norm Snead, New York	325	196	2,307	17	12
1971	Roger Staubach, Dallas	211	126	1,882	15	4
1970	John Brodie, San Francisco	378	223	2,941	24	10
1969	Sonny Jurgensen, Washington	442	274	3,102	22	15
1968	Earl Morrall, Baltimore	317	182	2,909	26	17
1967	Sonny Jurgensen, Washington	508	288	3,747	31	16
1966	Bart Starr, Green Bay	251	156	2,257	14	3
1965	Rudy Bukich, Chicago	312	176	2,641	20	9
1964	Bart Starr, Green Bay	272	163	2,144	15	4
1963	Y. A. Tittle, New York	367	221	3,145	36	14
1962	Bart Starr, Green Bay	285	178	2,438	12	9
1961	Milt Plum, Cleveland	302	177	2,416	18	10
1960	Milt Plum, Cleveland	250	151	2,297	21	5

PASS RECEIVING

Year	Player	No.	Yds.	TD	Year	Player	No.	Yds.	TD
1989	Sterling Sharpe, Green Bay	90	1,423	12	1974	Charles Young, Phila.	63	696	3
1988	Henry Ellard, Los Angeles	86	1,414	10	1973	Harold Carmichael, Phila.	67	1,116	9
1987	J. T. Smith, St. Louis	91	1,117	8	1972	Harold Jackson, Phila.	62	1,048	4
1986	Jerry Rice, SF	86	1,570	15	1971	Bob Tucker, New York	59	791	4
1985	Roger Craig, SF	92	1,016	6	1970	Dick Gordon, Chicago	71	1,026	13
1984	Art Monk, Washington	106	1,372	7	1969	Dan Abramowicz, NO	73	1,015	7
1983	Roy Green, St. Louis	78	1,227	14	1968	Clifton McNeil, San Fran.	71	994	7
1982	Dwight Clark, SF	60	913	5	1967	Charley Taylor, Wash.	70	990	9
1981	Dwight Clark, SF	85	1,105	4	1966	Charley Taylor, Wash.	72	1,119	12
1980	Earl Cooper, San Francisco	83	567	4	1965	Dave Parks, San Francisco	80	1,344	12
1979	Ahmad Rashad, Minnesota	80	1,156	9	1964	Johnny Morris, Chicago	93	1,200	10
1978	Rickey Young, Minnesota	88	704	5	1963	Bobby Joe Conrad, St. Louis	73	967	10
1977	Ahmad Rashad, Minnesota	51	681	2	1962	Bobby Mitchell, Wash.	72	1,384	11
1976	Drew Pearson, Dallas	58	806	6	1961	Jim Phillips, Los Angeles	78	1,092	5
1975	Chuck Foreman, Minnesota	73	691	9	1960	Raymond Berry, Baltimore	74	1,298	10

SCORING

Year	Player	TD	PAT	FG	Tot.	Year	Player	TD	PAT	FG	Tot.
1989	Mike Cofer, SF	0	49	29	136	1984	Ray Wersching, SF	0	56	25	131
1988	Mike Cofer, SF	0	40	27	121	1983	Mark Moseley, Wash.	0	62	33	161
1987	Jerry Rice, SF	23	0	0	138	1982	Wendell Tyler, LA	13	0	0	78
1986	Kevin Butler, Chicago	0	36	28	120	1981	Ed Murray, Detroit	0	46	25	121
1985	Kevin Butler, Chicago	0	51	31	144		Rafael Septien, Dallas	0	40	27	121

SCORING

	TD	PAT	FG	Tot.		TD	PAT	FG	Tot.
1980—Ed Murray, Detroit	0	35	27	116	1969—Fred Cox, Minnesota	0	43	26	121
1979—Mark Moseley, Wash.	0	39	25	114	1968—Leroy Kelly, Cleveland	20	0	0	120
1978—Frank Corral, Los Angeles	0	31	29	118	1967—Jim Bakken, St. Louis	0	36	27	117
1977—Walter Payton, Chicago	16	0	0	96	1966—Bruce Gossett, LA	0	29	28	113
1976—Mark Moseley, Wash.	0	31	22	97	1965—Gale Sayers, Chicago	22	0	0	132
1975—Chuck Foreman, Minn.	22	0	0	132	1964—Lenny Moore, Baltimore	20	0	0	120
1974—Chester Marcol, GB	0	19	25	94	1963—Don Chandler, New York	0	52	18	106
1973—David Ray, Los Angeles	0	40	30	130	1962—Jim Taylor, Green Bay	19	0	0	114
1972—Chester Marcol, GB	0	29	33	128	1961—Paul Hornung, GB	10	41	15	146
1971—Curt Knight, Washington	0	27	29	114	1960—Paul Hornung, GB	15	41	15	176
1970—Fred Cox, Minnesota	0	35	30	125					

FIELD GOALS

1989—Rich Karlis, Minnesota	31	1974—Chester Marcol, Green Bay	25
1988—Mike Cofer, San Francisco	27	1973—David Ray, Los Angeles	30
1987—Morten Andersen, New Orleans	28	1972—Chester Marcol, Green Bay	33
1986—Kevin Butler, Chicago	28	1971—Curt Knight, Washington	29
1985—Morten Andersen, New Orleans	31	1970—Fred Cox, Minnesota	30
Kevin Butler, Chicago	31	1969—Fred Cox, Minnesota	26
1984—Paul McFadden, Philadelphia	30	1968—Mac Percival, Chicago	25
1983—Ali Haji-Sheikh, New York	35	1967—Jim Bakken, St. Louis	27
1982—Mark Moseley, Washington	20	1966—Bruce Gossett, Los Angeles	28
1981—Rafael Septien, Dallas	27	1965—Fred Cox, Minnesota	23
1980—Ed Murray, Detroit	27	1964—Jim Bakken, St. Louis	25
1979—Mark Moseley, Washington	25	1963—Jim Martin, Baltimore	24
1978—Frank Corral, Los Angeles	29	1962—Lou Michaels, Pittsburgh	26
1977—Mark Moseley, Washington	21	1961—Steve Myhra, Baltimore	21
1976—Mark Moseley, Washington	22	1960—Tommy Davis, San Francisco	19
1975—Toni Fritsch, Dallas	22		

PASS INTERCEPTIONS

	No.	Yds.		No.	Yds.
1989—Eric Allen, Philadelphia	8	38	1973—Bob Bryant, Minnesota	7	105
1988—Scott Case, Atlanta	10	47	1972—Bill Bradley, Philadelphia	9	73
1987—Barry Wilburn, Washington	9	135	1971—Bill Bradley, Philadelphia	11	248
1986—Ronnie Lott, San Francisco	10	134	1970—Dick Le Beau, Detroit	9	96
1985—Everson Walls, Dallas	9	31	1969—Mel Renfro, Dallas	10	118
1984—Tom Flynn, Green Bay	9	106	1968—Willie Williams, New York	10	103
1983—Mark Murphy, Washington	9	127	1967—Lem Barney, Detroit	10	232
1982—Everson Walls, Dallas	7	61	Dave Whitsell, New Orleans	10	178
1981—Everson Walls, Dallas	11	133	1966—Larry Wilson, St. Louis	10	180
1980—Nolan Cromwell, Los Angeles	8	140	1965—Bobby Boyd, Baltimore	9	78
1979—Lemar Parrish, Washington	9	65	1964—Paul Krause, Washington	12	140
1978—Ken Stone, St. Louis	9	139	1963—Dick Lynch, New York Giants	9	251
Willie Buchanon, Green Bay	9	93	Rosie Taylor, Chicago	9	172
1977—Rolland Lawrence, Atlanta	7	138	1962—Willie Wood, Green Bay	9	132
1976—Monte Jackson, Los Angeles	10	173	1961—Dick Lynch, New York Giants	9	60
1975—Paul Krause, Minnesota	10	201	1960—Dave Baker, San Francisco	10	96
1974—Ray Brown, Atlanta	8	164	Jerry Norton, St. Louis	10	96

PUNTING

	No.	Avg.		No.	Yds.
1989—Rich Camarillo, Phoenix	76	43.4	1974—Tom Blanchard, New Orleans	88	42.1
1988—Jim Arnold, Detroit	97	42.4	1973—Tom Wittum, San Francisco	79	43.7
1987—Rick Donnelly, Atlanta	61	44.0	1972—Dave Chapple, Los Angeles	53	44.2
1986—Sean Landeta, New York	79	44.8	1971—Tom McNeill, Philadelphia	73	42.0
1985—Rick Donnelly, Atlanta	59	43.6	1970—Julian Fagan, New Orleans	77	42.5
1984—Brian Hansen, New Orleans	69	43.8	1969—David Lee, Baltimore	50	45.3
1983—Frank Garcia, Tampa Bay	95	42.2	1968—Billy Lothridge, Atlanta	75	44.3
1982—Carl Birdsong, St. Louis	54	43.8	1967—Billy Lothridge, Atlanta	87	43.7
1981—Tom Skladany, Detroit	64	43.5	1966—David Lee, Baltimore	49	45.6
1980—Dave Jennings, New York	94	44.8	1965—Gary Collins, Cleveland	65	46.7
1979—Dave Jennings, New York	104	42.7	1964—Bobby Walden, Minnesota	72	46.4
1978—Tom Skladany, Detroit	86	42.5	1963—Yale Lary, Detroit	35	48.9
1977—Tom Blanchard, New Orleans	82	42.4	1962—Tommy Davis, San Francisco	48	45.8
1976—John James, Atlanta	101	42.1	1961—Yale Lary, Detroit	52	48.4
1975—Herman Weaver, Detroit	80	42.0	1960—Jerry Norton, St. Louis	39	45.6

PUNT RETURNS

	No.	Yds.	Avg.		No.	Yds.	Avg.
1989—Walter Stanley, Detroit	36	496	13.8	1980—Kenny Johnson, Atlanta	23	281	12.2
1988—John Taylor, San Francisco	44	556	12.6	1979—John Sciarra, Philadelphia	16	182	11.4
1987—Mel Gray, New Orleans	24	352	14.7	1978—Jackie Wallace, Los Angeles	52	618	11.9
1986—Vai Sikahema, St. Louis	43	522	12.1	1977—Larry Marshall, Philadelphia	46	489	10.6
1985—Henry Ellard, Los Angeles	37	501	13.5	1976—Eddie Brown, Washington	48	646	13.5
1984—Henry Ellard, Los Angeles	30	403	13.4	1975—Terry Metcalf, St. Louis	23	285	12.4
1983—Henry Ellard, Los Angeles	16	217	13.6	1974—Dick Jauron, Detroit	17	286	16.8
1982—Billy Johnson, Atlanta	24	273	11.4	1973—Bruce Taylor, San Francisco	15	207	13.8
1981—LeRoy Irvin, Los Angeles	46	615	13.4	1972—Ken Ellis, Green Bay	14	215	15.4

PUNT RETURNS

	No.	Yds.	Avg.		No.	Yds.	Avg.
1971—Les Duncan, Washington	22	233	10.6	1965—Leroy Kelly, Cleveland	17	265	15.6
1970—Bruce Taylor, San Francisco	43	516	12.0	1964—Tommy Watkins, Detroit	16	238	14.9
1969—Alvin Haymond, Los Angeles	33	435	13.2	1963—Dick James, Washington	16	214	13.4
1968—Bob Hayes, Dallas	15	312	20.8	1962—Pat Studstill, Detroit	29	457	15.8
1967—Ben Davis, Cleveland	18	229	12.7	1961—Willie Wood, Green Bay	14	225	16.1
1966—Johnny Roland, St. Louis	20	221	11.1	1960—Abe Woodson, San Francisco	13	174	13.4

KICKOFF RETURNS

	No.	Yds.	Avg.		No.	Yds.	Avg.
1989—Mel Gray, Detroit	24	640	26.7	1974—Terry Metcalf, St. Louis	20	623	31.2
1988—Donnie Elder, Tampa Bay	34	772	22.7	1973—Carl Garrett, Chicago	16	486	30.4
1987—Sylvester Stamps, Atlanta	24	660	27.5	1972—Ron Smith, Chicago	30	924	30.8
1986—Dennis Gentry, Chicago	20	576	28.8	1971—Travis Williams, Los Angeles	25	743	29.7
1985—Ron Brown, Los Angeles	28	918	32.8	1970—Cecil Turner, Chicago	23	752	32.7
1984—Barry Redden, Los Angeles	23	530	23.0	1969—Bobby Williams, Detroit	17	563	33.1
1983—Darrin Nelson, Minnesota	18	445	24.7	1968—Preston Pearson, Baltimore	15	527	35.1
1982—Alvin Hall, Detroit	16	426	26.6	1967—Travis Williams, Green Bay	18	739	41.1
1981—Mike Nelms, Washington	37	1099	29.7	1966—Gale Sayers, Chicago	23	718	31.2
1980—Rich Mauti, New Orleans	31	798	27.6	1965—Tommy Watkins, Detroit	17	584	34.4
1979—Jimmy Edwards, Minnesota	44	1103	25.1	1964—Clarence Childs, NYG	34	987	29.0
1978—Steve Odom, Green Bay	25	677	27.1	1963—Abe Woodson, San Francisco	29	935	32.3
1977—Wilbert Montgomery, Phila.	23	619	26.9	1962—Abe Woodson, San Francisco	37	1157	31.3
1976—Cullen Bryant, Los Angeles	16	459	28.7	1961—Dick Bass, Los Angeles	23	698	30.3
1975—Walter Payton, Chicago	14	444	31.7	1960—Tom Moore, Green Bay	12	397	33.1

SACKS

1989—Chris Doleman, Minnesota	21.0	1985—Richard Dent, Chicago	17.0
1988—Reggie White, Philadelphia	18.0	1984—Richard Dent, Chicago	17.5
1987—Reggie White, Philadelphia	21.0	1983—Fred Dean, San Francisco	17.5
1986—Lawrence Taylor, New York	20.5	1982—Doug Martin, Minnesota	11.5

AMERICAN FOOTBALL CONFERENCE

INDIVIDUAL LEADERS, 1960-89

(American Football League, 1960-69)

RUSHING

	Net Yds.	Att.	TD		Net Yds.	Att.	TD
1989—Christian Okoye, KC	1,480	370	12	1974—Otis Armstrong, Denver	1,407	263	9
1988—Eric Dickerson, Ind.	1,659	388	14	1973—O. J. Simpson, Buffalo	2,003	332	12
1987—Eric Dickerson, Ind.	1,288	283	6	1972—O. J. Simpson, Buffalo	1,251	292	6
1986—Curt Warner, Seattle	1,481	319	13	1971—Floyd Little, Denver	1,133	284	6
1985—Marcus Allen, Los Angeles	1,759	380	11	1970—Floyd Little, Denver	901	209	3
1984—Earnest Jackson, S.D.	1,179	296	8	1969—Dick Post, San Diego	873	182	6
1983—Curt Warner, Seattle	1,449	335	13	1968—Paul Robinson, Cincinnati	1,023	238	8
1982—Freeman McNeil, N.Y.	786	151	6	1967—Jim Nance, Boston	1,216	269	7
1981—Earl Campbell, Houston	1,376	361	10	1966—Jim Nance, Boston	1,458	299	11
1980—Earl Campbell, Houston	1,934	373	13	1965—Paul Lowe, San Diego	1,121	222	7
1979—Earl Campbell, Houston	1,697	368	19	1964—Cookie Gilchrist, Buffalo	981	230	6
1978—Earl Campbell, Houston	1,450	302	13	1963—Clem Daniels, Oakland	1,099	215	3
1977—Mark van Eeghen, Oakland	1,273	324	7	1962—Cookie Gilchrist, Buffalo	1,096	214	13
1976—O. J. Simpson, Buffalo	1,503	290	8	1961—Billy Cannon, Houston	948	200	6
1975—O. J. Simpson, Buffalo	1,817	329	16	1960—Abner Haynes, Dallas	875	156	9

PASSING

	Passes	Com.	Yds.	TD	Int.
1989—Boomer Esiason, Cincinnati	455	258	3,525	28	11
1988—Boomer Esiason, Cincinnati	388	223	3,572	28	14
1987—Bernie Kosar, Cleveland	389	241	3,033	22	9
1986—Dan Marino, Miami	623	378	4,746	44	23
1985—Ken O'Brien, New York	488	297	3,888	25	8
1984—Dan Marino, Miami	564	362	5,084	48	17
1983—Dan Marino, Miami	296	173	2,210	20	6
1982—Ken Anderson, Cincinnati	309	218	2,495	12	9
1981—Ken Anderson, Cincinnati	479	300	3,754	29	10
1980—Brian Sipe, Cleveland	554	337	4,132	30	14
1979—Dan Fouts, San Diego	530	332	4,082	24	24
1978—Terry Bradshaw, Pittsburgh	368	207	2,915	28	20
1977—Bob Griese, Miami	307	180	2,252	22	13
1976—Ken Stabler, Oakland	291	194	2,737	27	17
1975—Ken Anderson, Cincinnati	377	228	3,169	21	11
1974—Ken Anderson, Cincinnati	328	213	2,667	18	10
1973—Ken Stabler, Oakland	260	163	1,997	14	10
1972—Earl Morrall, Miami	150	83	1,360	11	7
1971—Bob Griese, Miami	263	145	2,089	19	9
1970—Daryle Lamonica, Oakland	356	179	2,516	22	15

PASSING

Year	Player	Passes	Com.	Yds.	TD	Int.
1969	Greg Cook, Cincinnati	197	106	1,854	15	11
1968	Len Dawson, Kansas City	224	131	2,109	17	9
1967	Daryle Lamonica, Oakland	425	220	3,228	30	20
1966	Len Dawson, Kansas City	284	159	2,527	26	10
1965	John Hadl, San Diego	348	174	2,798	20	21
1964	Len Dawson, Kansas City	354	199	2,879	30	18
1963	Tobin Rote, San Diego	286	170	2,510	20	17
1962	Len Dawson, Dallas	310	189	2,759	29	17
1961	George Blanda, Houston	362	187	3,330	36	22
1960	Jack Kemp, Los Angeles	406	211	3,018	20	25

PASS RECEIVING

Year	Player	No.	Yds.	TD	Year	Player	No.	Yds.	TD
1989	Andre Reed, Buffalo	88	1,312	9	1974	Lydell Mitchell, Baltimore	72	544	2
1988	Al Toon, New York	93	1,067	5	1973	Fred Willis, Houston	57	371	1
1987	Al Toon, New York	68	976	5	1972	Fred Biletnikoff, Oakland	58	802	7
1986	Todd Christensen, LA	95	1,153	8	1971	Fred Biletnikoff, Oakland	61	929	9
1985	Lionel James, San Diego	86	1,027	6	1970	Marlin Briscoe, Buffalo	57	1,036	8
1984	Ozzie Newsome, Cleveland	89	1,001	5	1969	Lance Alworth, San Diego	64	1,003	4
1983	Todd Christensen, LA	92	1,247	12	1968	Lance Alworth, San Diego	68	1,312	10
1982	Kellen Winslow, San Diego	54	721	6	1967	George Sauer, New York	75	1,189	6
1981	Kellen Winslow, San Diego	88	1,075	10	1966	Lance Alworth, San Diego	73	1,383	13
1980	Kellen Winslow, San Diego	89	1,290	9	1965	Lionel Taylor, Denver	85	1,131	6
1979	Joe Washington, Baltimore	82	750	3	1964	Charley Hennigan, Houston	101	1,546	8
1978	Steve Largent, Seattle	71	1,168	8	1963	Lionel Taylor, Denver	78	1,101	10
1977	Lydell Mitchell, Baltimore	71	620	4	1962	Lionel Taylor, Denver	77	908	4
1976	MacArthur Lane, KC	66	686	1	1961	Lionel Taylor, Denver	100	1,176	4
1975	Reggie Rucker, Cleveland	60	770	3	1960	Lionel Taylor, Denver	92	1,235	12

SCORING

Year	Player	TD	PAT	FG	Tot.	Year	Player	TD	PAT	FG	Tot.
1989	David Treadwell, Denver	0	39	27	120	1974	Roy Gerela, Pittsburgh	0	33	20	93
1988	Scott Norwood, Buffalo	0	33	32	129	1973	Roy Gerela, Pittsburgh	0	36	29	123
1987	Jim Breech, Cincinnati	0	25	24	97	1972	Bobby Howfield, N.Y.	0	40	27	121
1986	Tony Franklin, N.E.	0	44	32	140	1971	Garo Yepremian, Miami	0	33	28	117
1985	Gary Anderson, Pitts.	0	40	33	139	1970	Jan Stenerud, Kansas City	0	26	30	116
1984	Gary Anderson, Pitts.	0	45	24	117	1969	Jim Turner, New York	0	33	32	129
1983	Gary Anderson, Pitts.	0	38	27	119	1968	Jim Turner, New York	0	43	34	145
1982	Marcus Allen, Los Angeles	14	0	0	84	1967	George Blanda, Oakland	0	56	20	116
1981	Jim Breech, Cincinnati	0	49	22	115	1966	Gino Cappelletti, Boston	6	35	16	119
	Nick Lowery, Kansas City	0	37	26	115	1965	Gino Cappelletti, Boston	9	27	17	132
1980	John Smith, New England	0	51	26	129	1964	Gino Cappelletti, Boston	7	36	25	155
1979	John Smith, New England	0	46	23	115	1963	Gino Cappelletti, Boston	2	35	22	113
1978	Pat Leahy, New York	0	41	22	107	1962	Gene Mingo, Denver	4	32	27	137
1977	Errol Mann, Oakland	0	39	20	99	1961	Gino Cappelletti, Boston	8	48	17	147
1975	O. J. Simpson, Buffalo	23	0	0	138	1960	Gene Mingo, Denver	6	33	18	123

FIELD GOALS

Year	Player	FG	Year	Player	FG
1989	David Treadwell, Denver	27	1975	Jan Stenerud, Kansas City	22
1988	Scott Norwood, Buffalo	32	1974	Roy Gerela, Pittsburgh	20
1987	Dean Biasucci, Indianapolis	24	1973	Roy Gerela, Pittsburgh	29
	Jim Breech, Cincinnati	24	1972	Roy Gerela, Pittsburgh	28
1986	Tony Franklin, New England	32	1971	Garo Yepremian, Miami	28
1985	Gary Anderson, Pittsburgh	33	1970	Jan Stenerud, Kansas City	30
1984	Gary Anderson, Pittsburgh	24	1969	Jim Turner, New York	32
	Matt Bahr, Cleveland	24	1968	Jim Turner, New York	34
1983	Raul Allegre, Baltimore	30	1967	Jan Stenerud, Kansas City	21
1982	Nick Lowery, Kansas City	19	1966	Mike Mercer, Oakland-Kansas City	21
1981	Nick Lowery, Kansas City	26	1965	Pete Gogolak, Buffalo	28
1980	John Smith, New England	26	1964	Gino Cappelletti, Boston	25
	Fred Steinfort, Denver	26	1963	Gino Cappelletti, Boston	22
1979	John Smith, New England	23	1962	Gene Mingo, Denver	27
1978	Pat Leahy, New York	22	1961	Gino Cappelletti, Boston	17
1977	Errol Mann, Oakland	20	1960	Gene Mingo, Denver	18

PASS INTERCEPTIONS

Year	Player	No.	Yds.	Year	Player	No.	Yds.
1989	Felix Wright, Cleveland	9	91		Donnie Shell, Pittsburgh	5	27
1988	Erik McMillan, New York	8	168	1981	John Harris, Seattle	10	155
1987	Mike Prior, Indianapolis	6	57	1980	Lester Hayes, Oakland	13	273
	Mark Kelso, Buffalo	6	25	1979	Mike Reinfeldt, Houston	12	205
	Keith Bostic, Houston	6	−14	1978	Thom Darden, Cleveland	10	200
1986	Deron Cherry, Kansas City	9	150	1977	Lyle Blackwood, Baltimore	10	163
1985	Eugene Daniel, Indianapolis	8	53	1976	Ken Riley, Cincinnati	9	141
	Albert Lewis, Kansas City	8	59	1975	Mel Blount, Pittsburgh	11	121
1984	Kenny Easley, Seattle	10	126	1974	Emmitt Thomas, Kansas City	12	214
1983	Ken Riley, Cincinnati	8	89	1973	Dick Anderson, Miami	8	136
	Vann McElroy, Los Angeles	8	68		Mike Wagner, Pittsburgh	8	134
1982	Ken Riley, Cincinnati	5	88	1972	Mike Sensibaugh, Kansas City	8	65
	Bobby Jackson, New York	5	84	1971	Ken Houston, Houston	9	220
	Dwayne Woodruff, Pittsburgh	5	53	1970	Johnny Robinson, Kansas City	10	155

AFC INDIVIDUAL LEADERS, 1960-89—Continued

PASS INTERCEPTIONS

	No.	Yds.		No.	Yds.
1969—Emmitt Thomas, Kansas City.....	9	146	1965—W. K. Hicks, Houston....................	9	156
1968—Dave Grayson, Oakland................	10	195	1964—Dainard Paulson, New York........	12	157
1967—Miller Farr, Houston	10	264	1963—Fred Glick, Houston	12	180
Tom Janik, Buffalo........................	10	222	1962—Lee Riley, New York	11	122
Dick Westmoreland, Miami	10	127	1961—Bill Atkins, Buffalo	10	158
1966—Johnny Robinson, Kansas City....	10	136	1960—Austin Gonsoulin, Denver............	11	98
Bobby Hunt, Kansas City	10	113			

PUNTING

	No.	Avg.		No.	Yds.
1989—Greg Montgomery, Houston........	56	43.3	1974—Ray Guy, Oakland	74	42.2
1988—Harry Newsome, Pittsburgh.......	65	45.4	1973—Jerrel Wilson, Kansas City...........	80	45.5
1987—Ralf Mojsiejenko, San Diego.......	67	42.9	1972—Jerrel Wilson, Kansas City	66	44.8
1986—Rohn Stark, Indianapolis.............	76	45.2	1971—Dave Lewis, Cincinnati.................	72	44.8
1985—Rohn Stark, Indianapolis.............	78	45.9	1970—Dave Lewis, Cincinnati.................	79	46.2
1984—Jim Arnold, Kansas City.............	98	44.9	1969—Dennis Partee, San Diego	71	44.6
1983—Rohn Stark, Baltimore.................	91	45.3	1968—Jerrel Wilson, Kansas City	63	45.1
1982—Luke Prestridge, Denver	45	45.0	1967—Bob Scarpitto, Denver	105	44.9
1981—Pat McInally, Cincinnati.............	72	45.4	1966—Bob Scarpitto, Denver	76	45.8
1980—Luke Prestridge, Denver.............	70	43.9	1965—Jerrel Wilson, Kansas City	69	45.4
1979—Bob Grupp, Kansas City..............	89	43.6	1964—Jim Fraser, Denver	73	44.2
1978—Pat McInally, Cincinnati.............	91	43.1	1963—Jim Fraser, Denver	81	44.4
1977—Ray Guy, Oakland	59	43.4	1962—Jim Fraser, Denver	55	43.6
1976—Marv Bateman, Buffalo................	86	42.8	1961—Bill Atkins, Buffalo	85	44.5
1975—Ray Guy, Oakland	68	43.8	1960—Paul Maguire, Los Angeles...........	43	40.5

PUNT RETURNS

	No.	Yds.	Avg.		No.	Yds.	Avg.
1989—Clarence Verdin, Ind...............	23	296	12.9	1974—Lemar Parrish, Cincinnati.....	18	338	18.8
1988—Jojo Townsell, New York.......	35	409	11.7	1973—Ron Smith, San Diego	27	352	15.0
1987—Bobby Joe Edmonds, Seattle.	20	251	12.6	1972—Chris Farasopolous, NYJ	17	179	10.5
1986—Bobby Joe Edmonds, Seattle.	34	419	12.3	1971—Leroy Kelly, Cleveland...........	30	292	9.7
1985—Irving Fryar, New England..	37	520	14.1	1970—Ed Podolak, Kansas City........	23	311	13.5
1984—Mike Martin, Cincinnati.......	24	376	15.7	1969—Bill Thompson, Denver	25	288	11.5
1983—Kirk Springs, New York	23	287	12.5	1968—Noland Smith, Kansas City....	18	270	15.0
1982—Rick Upchurch, Denver	15	242	16.1	1967—Floyd Little, Denver	16	270	16.9
1981—James Brooks, San Diego	22	290	13.2	1966—Leslie Duncan, San Diego	18	238	13.2
1980—J. T. Smith, Kansas City	40	581	14.5	1965—Leslie Duncan, San Diego......	30	464	15.5
1979—Tony Nathan, Miami..............	28	306	10.9	1964—Bobby Jancik, Houston...........	12	220	18.3
1978—Rick Upchurch, Denver	36	493	13.7	1963—Claude Gibson, Oakland........	26	307	11.8
1977—Billy Johnson, Houston	30	539	15.4	1962—Dick Christy, New York	15	250	16.7
1976—Rick Upchurch, Denver	39	536	13.7	1961—Dick Christy, New York	18	383	21.3
1975—Billy Johnson, Houston	40	612	18.8	1960—Abner Haynes, Dallas.............	14	215	15.4

KICKOFF RETURNS

	No.	Yds.	Avg.		No.	Yds.	Avg.
1989—Rod Woodson, Pittsburgh	36	982	27.3	1974—Greg Pruitt, Cleveland...........	22	606	27.5
1988—Tim Brown, Los Angeles........	41	1,098	26.8	1973—Wallace Francis, Buffalo........	23	687	29.9
1987—Paul Palmer, Kansas City......	38	923	24.3	1972—Bruce Laird, Baltimore...........	29	843	29.1
1986—Lupe Sanchez, Pittsburgh......	25	591	23.6	1971—Mercury Morris, Miami..........	15	423	28.2
1985—Glen Young, Cleveland...........	35	898	25.7	1970—Jim Duncan, Baltimore	20	707	35.4
1984—Bobby Humphery, New York	22	675	30.7	1969—Bill Thompson, Denver	19	594	31.3
1983—Fulton Walker, Miami	36	962	26.7	1968—George Atkinson, Oakland	32	802	25.1
1982—Mike Mosley, Buffalo.............	18	487	27.1	1967—Zeke Moore, Houston..............	14	405	28.9
1981—Carl Roaches, Houston	28	769	27.5	1966—Goldie Sellers, Denver	19	541	28.5
1980—Horace Ivory, New England .	36	992	27.6	1965—Abner Haynes, Denver	34	901	26.5
1979—Larry Brunson, Oakland........	17	441	25.9	1964—Bo Roberson, Oakland............	36	975	27.1
1978—Keith Wright, Cleveland	30	789	26.3	1963—Bobby Jancik, Houston...........	45	1,317	29.3
1977—Raymond Clayborn, NE	28	869	31.0	1962—Bobby Jancik, Houston...........	24	726	30.3
1976—Duriel Harris, Miami	17	559	32.9	1961—Dave Grayson, Dallas	16	453	28.3
1975—Harold Hart, Oakland	17	518	30.5	1960—Ken Hall, Houston...................	19	594	31.3

SACKS

1989—Lee Williams, San Diego	14.0	1985—Andre Tippett, New England	16.5
1988—Greg Townsend, Los Angeles.................	11.5	1984—Mark Gastineau, New York	22.0
1987—Andre Tippett, New England	12.5	1983—Mark Gastineau, New York	19.0
1986—Sean Jones, Los Angeles	15.5	1982—Jesse Baker, Houston.............................	7.5

ALL-TIME PRO FOOTBALL RECORDS

(Through 1989 season)

RUSHING

LEADING LIFETIME RUSHERS

(Courtesy of Pro Football's Hall of Fame, Canton, Ohio)

Player	League	Yrs.	Att.	Yards	Avg.	TD
WALTER PAYTON	NFL	13	3838	16726	4.4	110
TONY DORSETT	NFL	12	2936	12739	4.3	77
JIM BROWN	NFL	9	2359	12312	5.2	106
FRANCO HARRIS	NFL	13	2949	12120	4.1	91
JOHN RIGGINS	NFL	14	2916	11352	3.9	104
O.J. SIMPSON	AFL-NFL	11	2404	11236	4.7	61
ERIC DICKERSON	NFL	7	2450	11226	4.6	82
JOE PERRY	AAFC-NFL	16	1929	9723	5.0	71
EARL CAMPBELL	NFL	8	2187	9407	4.3	74
O.J. ANDERSON	NFL	11	2274	9317	4.1	69
JIM TAYLOR	NFL	10	1941	8597	4.4	83
LARRY CSONKA	AFL-NFL	11	1891	8081	4.3	55
GERALD RIGGS	NFL	8	1788	7465	4.2	52
MIKE PRUITT	NFL	11	1844	7378	4.0	51
MARCUS ALLEN	NFL	8	1781	7275	4.1	63
LEROY KELLY	NFL	10	1727	7274	4.2	74
GEORGE ROGERS	NFL	7	1692	7176	4.2	54
FREEMAN McNEIL	NFL	9	1605	7146	4.5	30
JOHN HENRY JOHNSON	NFL-AFL	13	1571	6803	4.3	48
WILBERT MONTGOMERY	NFL	9	1540	6789	4.4	45

NOTE—Gerald Riggs attained Top Twenty ranking during the 1989 season. He replaced Chuck Muncie (6702 yards). Of those players active in 1989, Curt Warner (6705 yards), Roger Craig (6625) and James Brooks (6343) are closest to a Top Twenty ranking.

AAFC—All-America Football Conference

AFL—American Football League

NFL—National Football League

Most Yards Gained, Season

2,105—Eric Dickerson, Los Angeles Rams, 1984

1,000-Yard Rushing Seasons by First-Year Players
Beattie Feathers, Chicago Bears, 1934, 1,004 yards
Cookie Gilchrist, Buffalo Bills, 1962, 1,096 yards
Paul Robinson, Cincinnati Bengals, 1968, 1,023 yards
John Brockington, Green Bay Packers, 1971, 1,105 yards
Franco Harris, Pittsburgh Steelers, 1972, 1,055 yards
Larry McCutcheon, Los Angeles Rams, 1973, 1,097 yards. (McCutcheon considered a 1973 rookie as he played only 3 games in 1972 and did not carry the ball, playing only on special teams.)
Don Woods, San Diego Chargers, 1974, 1,162 yards
Tony Dorsett, Dallas Cowboys, 1977, 1,007 yards
Earl Campbell, Houston Oilers, 1978, 1,450 yards
Terry Miller, Buffalo Bills, 1978, 1,060 yards
Ottis Anderson, St. Louis Cardinals, 1979, 1,605 yards
William Andrews, Atlanta Falcons, 1979, 1,023 yards
Billy Sims, Detroit Lions, 1980, 1,303 yards
Joe Cribbs, Buffalo Bills, 1980, 1,185 yards
George Rogers, New Orleans Saints, 1981, 1,674 yards
Joe Delaney, Kansas City Chiefs, 1981, 1,121 yards
Eric Dickerson, Los Angeles Rams, 1983, 1,808 yards
Curt Warner, Seattle Seahawks, 1983, 1,449 yards
Greg Bell, Buffalo Bills, 1984, 1,100 yards
Kevin Mack, Cleveland Browns, 1985, 1,104 yards. (Mack played in the United States Football League in 1984.)
Rueben Mayes, New Orleans Saints, 1986, 1,353 yards
John Stephens, New England Patriots, 1988, 1,168 yards
Ickey Woods, Cincinnati Bengals, 1988, 1,066 yards
Barry Sanders, Detroit Lions, 1989, 1,470 yards
Bobby Humphrey, Denver Broncos, 1989, 1,151 yards

Most Seasons, 1,000 or More Yards Rushing

10—Walter Payton, Chicago Bears, 1976-1981, 1983-1986

Most Yards Gained, Game

275—Walter Payton, Chicago Bears vs. Minnesota Vikings, November 20, 1977

Longest Run From Scrimmage

99—Tony Dorsett, Dallas Cowboys vs. Minnesota Vikings, January 3, 1983

Most Games, 100 Yards or More, Season

12—Eric Dickerson, Los Angeles Rams, 1984

Most Games, 100 Yards or More, Career

77—Walter Payton, Chicago Bears, 1975-1987

Most Consecutive Games, 100 Yards or More
11—Marcus Allen, Los Angeles Raiders, October 28, 1985, through September 14, 1986

Most Games, 200 Yards or More, Career
6—O. J. Simpson, Buffalo Bills, 1969-1976

Most Games, 200 Yards or More, Season
4—Earl Campbell, Houston Oilers, 1980

Most Touchdowns Rushing, Career
110—Walter Payton, Chicago Bears, 1975-1987

Most Touchdowns Rushing, Season
24—John Riggins, Washington Redskins, 1983

Most Touchdowns Rushing, Game
6—Ernie Nevers, Chicago Cardinals vs. Chicago Bears, November 28, 1929

Most Rushing Attempts, Season
407—James Wilder, Tampa Bay Buccaneers, 1984

Most Rushing Attempts, Game
45—Jamie Morris, Washington Redskins at Cincinnati Bengals, December 17, 1988 (OT)

PASSING
LEADING LIFETIME PASSERS
Minimum 1500 attempts
(Courtesy of Pro Football's Hall of Fame, Canton, Ohio)

Player	League	Yrs.	Att.	Comp.	Yds.	TD	Int.	Rating Pts.
JOE MONTANA	NFL	11	4059	2593	31054	216	107	94.0
DAN MARINO	NFL	7	3650	2174	27853	220	125	89.3
BOOMER ESIASON	NFL	6	2285	1296	18350	126	76	87.3
OTTO GRAHAM	AAFC-NFL	10	2626	1464	23584	174	135	86.6
DAVE KRIEG	NFL	10	2843	1644	20858	169	116	83.7
BERNIE KOSAR	NFL	5	1940	1134	13888	75	47	83.4
ROGER STAUBACH	NFL	11	2958	1685	22700	153	109	83.4
KEN O'BRIEN	NFL	6	2467	1471	17589	96	68	83.0
JIM KELLY	NFL	4	1742	1032	12901	81	63	82.7
NEIL LOMAX	NFL	8	3153	1817	22771	136	90	82.7
SONNY JURGENSEN	NFL	18	4262	2433	32224	255	189	82.625
LEN DAWSON	NFL-AFL	19	3741	2136	28711	239	183	82.555
KEN ANDERSON	NFL	16	4475	2654	32838	197	160	81.9
DANNY WHITE	NFL	13	2950	1761	21959	155	132	81.7
BART STARR	NFL	16	3149	1808	24718	152	138	80.5
FRAN TARKENTON	NFL	18	6467	3686	47003	342	266	80.354
TONY EASON	NFL	7	1536	898	10987	61	50	80.3
DAN FOUTS	NFL	15	5604	3297	43040	254	242	80.2
JIM McMAHON	NFL	8	1831	1050	13335	77	66	79.2
BERT JONES	NFL	10	2551	1430	18190	124	101	78.214

NOTE—Bernie Kosar, Jim Kelly and Tony Eason entered the Top Twenty during the 1989 season. They displaced Johnny Unitas (78.201), Frank Ryan (77.6) and Joe Theismann (77.4). Of those players active in 1989 who have the 1500 attempts needed to qualify for the career leadership, Warren Moon (76.0), Phil Simms (75.7), Randall Cunningham (75.4) and John Elway (73.6) rank the highest. Another active passer who would be ranked in the Top Twenty if he had the required 1500 attempts is Jim Everett (1484 att., 83.3).

Rating points based on a combination of performances in the following four categories: percentage of completions, percentage of touchdown passes, percentage of interceptions and average gain per pass attempt.

AAFC—All-America Football Conference
AFL—American Football League
NFL—National Football League

Most Yards Gained, Season
5,084—Dan Marino, Miami Dolphins, 1984

Most Yards Gained, Game
554—Norm Van Brocklin, Los Angeles Rams vs. New York Yankees, September 28, 1951 (27 completions in 41 attempts)

Most Games, 300 or More Yards Passing, Season
9—Dan Marino, Miami Dolphins, 1984

Longest Pass Completion (99 Yards; All Touchdowns)
Frank Filchock to Andy Farkas, Washington Redskins vs. Pittsburgh Steelers, October 15, 1939
Otto Graham to Mac Speedie, Cleveland Browns vs. Buffalo Bills, November 2, 1947
George Izo to Bobby Mitchell, Washington Redskins vs. Cleveland Browns, September 15, 1963
Karl Sweetan to Pat Studstill, Detroit Lions vs. Baltimore Colts, October 16, 1966
Sonny Jurgensen to Gerry Allen, Washington Redskins vs. Chicago Bears, September 15, 1968
Jim Plunkett to Cliff Branch, Los Angeles Raiders vs. Washington Redskins, October 2, 1983
Ron Jaworski to Mike Quick, Philadelphia Eagles vs. Atlanta Falcons, November 10, 1985

Most Touchdowns Passing, Career
  342—Fran Tarkenton, Minnesota Vikings, 1961-65; New York Giants 1967-71; Minnesota Vikings, 1972-78

Most Touchdowns Passing, Season
  48—Dan Marino, Miami Dolphins, 1984

Most Touchdowns Passing, Game
  7—Sid Luckman, Chicago Bears vs. New York Giants, November 14, 1943
    Adrian Burk, Philadelphia Eagles vs. Washington Redskins, October 17, 1954
    George Blanda, Houston Oilers vs. New York Titans, November 19, 1961
    Y. A. Tittle, New York Giants vs. Washington Redskins, October 28, 1962
    Joe Kapp, Minnesota Vikings vs. Baltimore Colts, September 28, 1969

Most Consecutive Games, Touchdown Passes
  47—Johnny Unitas, Baltimore Colts, 1956-60

Most Passing Attempts, Season
  623—Dan Marino, Miami Dolphins, 1986

Most Passing Attempts, Game
  68—George Blanda, Houston Oilers vs. Buffalo Bills, November 1, 1964 (37 completions)

Most Passes Completed, Season
  378—Dan Marino, Miami Dolphins, 1986

Most Passes Completed, Game
  42—Richard Todd, New York Jets vs. San Francisco 49ers, September 21, 1980

Most Consecutive Passes Completed
  22—Joe Montana, San Francisco 49ers vs. Cleveland Browns (5), November 29, 1987, and Green Bay Packers (17), December 6, 1987

Highest Completion Percentage, Season (Qualifiers)
  70.55—Ken Anderson, Cincinnati Bengals, 1982 (309-218)

Highest Completion Percentage, Game (20 attempts)
  90.91—Ken Anderson, Cincinnati Bengals vs. Pittsburgh Steelers, November 10, 1974 (22-20)

Most Passes Had Intercepted, Game
  8—Jim Hardy, Chicago Cardinals vs. Philadelphia Eagles, September 24, 1950 (39 attempts)

Most Passes Had Intercepted, Season
  42—George Blanda, Houston Oilers, 1962 (418 attempts)

Most Passes Had Intercepted, Career
  277—George Blanda, Chicago Bears, 1949, 1950-1958; Baltimore Colts 1950; Houston Oilers, 1960-1966; Oakland Raiders, 1967-1975 (4,007 attempts)

Most Consecutive Passes Attempted Without Interception
  294—Bart Starr, Green Bay Packers, 1964-1965

PASS RECEIVING
LEADING LIFETIME RECEIVERS
(Courtesy of Pro Football's Hall of Fame, Canton, Ohio)

Player	League	Yrs.	No.	Yards	Avg.	TD
STEVE LARGENT	NFL	14	819	13089	16.0	100
CHARLIE JOINER	AFL-NFL	18	750	12146	16.2	65
ART MONK	NFL	10	662	9165	13.8	47
CHARLEY TAYLOR	NFL	13	649	9110	14.0	79
OZZIE NEWSOME	NFL	12	639	7740	12.1	45
DON MAYNARD	NFL-AFL	15	633	11834	18.7	88
RAYMOND BERRY	NFL	13	631	9275	14.7	68
JAMES LOFTON	NFL	12	607	11251	18.5	57
HAROLD CARMICHAEL	NFL	14	590	8985	15.2	79
FRED BILETNIKOFF	AFL-NFL	14	589	8974	15.2	76
HAROLD JACKSON	NFL	16	579	10372	17.9	76
LIONEL TAYLOR	NFL-AFL	10	567	7195	12.7	45
WES CHANDLER	NFL	11	559	8966	16.0	56
LANCE ALWORTH	AFL-NFL	11	542	10266	18.9	85
KELLEN WINSLOW	NFL	10	541	6741	12.5	45
JOHN STALLWORTH	NFL	14	537	8723	16.2	63
STANLEY MORGAN	NFL	13	534	10352	19.4	67
J.T. SMITH	NFL	12	526	6749	12.8	33
BOBBY MITCHELL	NFL	11	521	7954	15.3	65
NAT MOORE	NFL	13	510	7546	14.8	74

NOTE—J.T. Smith attained Top Twenty ranking during the 1989 season. He replaced Dwight Clark (506 catches). Of those players active in 1989, Roger Craig (483) and Roy Green (469) are the closest to a Top Twenty ranking.
  AFL—American Football League
  NFL—National Football League

Most Yards Gained, Season
   1,746—Charley Hennigan, Houston Oilers, 1961

Most Yards Gained, Game
   336—Willie Anderson, Los Angeles Rams vs. New Orleans Saints, November 26, 1989 (OT) (15 receptions)

Longest Pass Reception
   (See receivers mentioned under Longest Pass Completion)

Most Pass Receptions, Season
   106—Art Monk, Washington Redskins, 1984

Most Pass Receptions, Game
   18—Tom Fears, Los Angeles Rams vs. Green Bay Packers, December 3, 1950 (189 yards)

Most Consecutive Games, Pass Receptions
   177—Steve Largent, Seattle Seahawks, 1976-1989

Most Touchdown Receptions, Career
   100—Steve Largent, Seattle Seahawks, 1976-1989

Most Touchdown Receptions, Season
   22—Jerry Rice, San Francisco 49ers, 1987

Most Touchdowns Receptions, Game
   5—Bob Shaw, Chicago Cardinals vs. Baltimore Colts, October 2, 1950
      Kellen Winslow, San Diego Chargers vs. Oakland Raiders, November 22, 1981

Most Consecutive Games, Touchdown Receptions
   13—Jerry Rice, San Francisco 49ers, 1986-1987

PASS INTERCEPTIONS

Most Interceptions, Game
   4—Sammy Baugh, Washington Redskins vs. Detroit Lions, November 14, 1943
      Dan Sandifer, Washington Redskins vs. Boston Yanks, October 31, 1948
      Don Doll, Detroit Lions vs. Chicago Cardinals, October 23, 1949
      Bob Nussbaumer, Chicago Cardinals vs. New York Bulldogs, November 13, 1949
      Russ Craft, Philadelphia Eagles vs. Chicago Cardinals, September 24, 1950
      Bob Dillon, Green Bay Packers vs. Detroit Lions, November 26, 1953
      Jack Butler, Pittsburgh Steelers vs. Washington Redskins, December 13, 1953
      Jerry Norton, St. Louis Cardinals vs. Washington Redskins, November 20, 1960; vs. Pittsburgh Steelers, November 26, 1961
      Goose Gonsoulin, Denver Broncos vs. Buffalo Bills, September 18, 1960
      Dave Baker, San Francisco 49ers vs. Los Angeles Rams, December 4, 1960
      Bobby Ply, Dallas Texans vs. San Diego Chargers, December 16, 1962
      Bobby Hunt, Kansas City Chiefs vs. Houston Oilers, October 4, 1964
      Willie Brown, Denver Broncos vs. New York Jets, November 15, 1964
      Dick Anderson, Miami Dolphins vs. Pittsburgh Steelers, December 3, 1973
      Willie Buchanon, Green Bay Packers vs. San Diego Chargers, September 24, 1978
      Deron Cherry, Kansas City Chiefs vs. Seattle Seahawks, September 29, 1985

Most Interceptions, Season
   14—Dick Lane, Los Angeles Rams, 1952

Most Interceptions, Career
   81—Paul Krause, Washington Redskins, 1964-1967; Minnesota Vikings, 1968- 1979

Most Consecutive Games, Passes Intercepted By
   8—Tom Morrow, Oakland Raiders, 1962 (4), 1963 (4)

Most Yardage Gained via Pass Interceptions, Career
   1,282—Emlen Tunnell, New York Giants, 1948-1958; Green Bay Packers, 1959- 1961

Most Yardage Gained via Pass Interceptions, Season
   349—Charley McNeil, San Diego Chargers, 1961

Most Yardage Gained via Pass Interceptions, Game
   177—Charley McNeil, San Diego Chargers vs. Houston Oilers, September 24, 1961

Longest Run With Intercepted Pass (Touchdown)
   103—Vencie Glenn, San Diego Chargers vs. Denver Broncos, November 29, 1987

Most Touchdowns Scored via Pass Interceptions, Lifetime
   9—Ken Houston, Houston Oilers, 1967 (2), 1968 (2), 1969, 1971 (4)

Most Touchdowns Scored via Pass Interceptions, Season
   4—Ken Houston, Houston Oilers, 1971
      Jim Kearney, Kansas City Chiefs, 1972

Most Touchdowns Scored via Pass Interceptions, Game
   2—Bill Blackburn, Chicago Cardinals vs. Boston Yanks, October 24, 1948
      Dan Sandifer, Washington Redskins vs. Boston Yanks, October 31, 1948

Bob Franklin, Cleveland Browns vs. Chicago Bears, December 11, 1960
Bill Stacy, St. Louis Cardinals vs. Dallas Cowboys, November 5, 1961
Jerry Norton, St. Louis Cardinals vs. Pittsburgh Steelers, November 26, 1961
Miller Farr, Houston Oilers vs. Buffalo Bills, December 7, 1968
Ken Houston, Houston Oilers vs. San Diego Chargers, December 19, 1971
Jim Kearney, Kansas City Chiefs vs. Denver Broncos, October 1, 1972
Lemar Parrish, Cincinnati Bengals vs. Houston Oilers, December 17, 1972
Dick Anderson, Miami Dolphins vs. Pittsburgh Steelers, December 3, 1973
Prentice McCray, New England Patriots vs. New York Jets, November 21, 1976
Kenny Johnson, Atlanta Falcons vs. Green Bay Packers, November 27, 1983
Mike Kozlowski, Miami Dolphins vs. New York Jets, December 16, 1983
Dave Brown, Seattle Seahawks vs. Kansas City Chiefs, November 4, 1984
Lloyd Burruss, Kansas City Chiefs vs. San Diego Chargers, October 19, 1986

SCORING

LEADING LIFETIME SCORERS

(Courtesy of Pro Football's Hall of Fame, Canton, Ohio)

Player	League	Yrs.	TD	PAT	FG	Tot.
GEORGE BLANDA	NFL-AFL	26	9	943	335	2002
JAN STENERUD	AFL-NFL	19	0	580	373	1699
LOU GROZA	AAFC-NFL	21	1	810	264	1608
JIM TURNER	AFL-NFL	16	1	521	304	1439
MARK MOSELEY	NFL	16	0	482	300	1382
JIM BAKKEN	NFL	17	0	534	282	1380
FRED COX	NFL	15	0	519	282	1365
PAT LEAHY	NFL	16	0	496	255	1261
CHRIS BAHR	NFL	14	0	490	241	1213
GINO CAPPELLETTI	AFL	11	42	350	176	1130
RAY WERSCHING	NFL	15	0	456	222	1122
DON COCKROFT	NFL	13	0	432	216	1080
GARO YEPREMIAN	NFL-AFL	14	0	444	210	1074
BRUCE GOSSETT	NFL	11	0	374	219	1031
NICK LOWERY	NFL	11	0	338	225	1013
SAM BAKER	NFL	15	2	428	179	977
JIM BREECH	NFL	11	0	418	184	970
RAFAEL SEPTIEN	NFL	10	0	420	180	960
LOU MICHAELS	NFL	13	1	386	187	*955
EDDIE MURRAY	NFL	10	0	307	212	943

NOTE—Eddie Murray entered the Top Twenty in 1989. He replaced Roy Gerela (903 points). Of those players who were active in 1989, Matt Bahr (895) and Gary Anderson (838) stand next in line to enter the Top Twenty.

*Includes safety.

AAFC—All-America Football Conference
AFL—American Football League
NFL—National Football League

Most Consecutive Games Scoring
151—Fred Cox, Minnesota Vikings, 1963-1973

Most Points, Season
176—Paul Hornung, Green Bay Packers, 1960 (15 TDs, 41 PATs, 15 FGs)

Most Points, Game
40—Ernie Nevers, Chicago Cardinals vs. Chicago Bears, November 28, 1929 (6 TDs, 4 PATs)

Most Touchdowns, Career
126—Jim Brown, Cleveland Browns, 1957-1965

Most Consecutive Games, Scoring Touchdowns
18—Lenny Moore, Baltimore Colts, 1963-1965

Most Touchdowns, Season
24—John Riggins, Washington Redskins, 1983 (all rushing)

Most Touchdowns, Game
6—Ernie Nevers, Chicago Cardinals vs. Chicago Bears, November 28, 1929 (6 rushing)
Dub Jones, Cleveland Browns vs. Chicago Bears, November 25, 1951 (4 rushing, 2 pass receptions)
Gale Sayers, Chicago Bears vs. San Francisco 49ers, December 12, 1965 (4 rushing, 1 pass reception, 1 punt return)

Most Points After Touchdown, Game
9—Pat Harder, Chicago Cardinals vs. New York Giants, October 17, 1948
Joe Vetrano, San Francisco 49ers vs. Brooklyn Dodgers, November 21, 1948
Bob Waterfield, Los Angeles Rams vs. Baltimore Colts, October 22, 1950
Charlie Gogolak, Washington Redskins vs. New York Giants, November 27, 1966

Most Points After Touchdown, Season
66—Uwe von Schamann, Miami Dolphins, 1984 (70 attempts)

Most Consecutive Points After Touchdown
234—Tommy Davis, San Francisco 49ers, 1959-1965

Most Points After Touchdown (no misses), Season

56—Danny Villanueva, Dallas Cowboys, 1966
　　Ray Wersching, San Francisco 49ers, 1984

Most Points After Touchdown (no misses), Game

9—Pat Harder, Chicago Cardinals vs. New York Giants, October 17, 1948
　Joe Vetrano, San Francisco 49ers vs. Brooklyn Dodgers, November 21, 1948
　Bob Waterfield, Los Angeles Rams vs. Baltimore Colts, October 22, 1950

Most Points After Touchdown Attempted, Season

70—Uwe von Schamann, Miami Dolphins, 1984 (66 successful)

Most Points After Touchdown Attempted, Game

10—Charlie Gogolak, Washington Redskins vs. New York Giants, November 27, 1966 (9 successful)

Most Field Goals, Game

7—Jim Bakken, St. Louis Cardinals vs. Pittsburgh Steelers, September 24, 1967
　Rich Karlis, Minnesota Vikings vs. Los Angeles Rams, November 5, 1989

Most Field Goals Attempted, Game

9—Jim Bakken, St. Louis Cardinals vs. Pittsburgh Steelers, September 24, 1967 (7 successful)

Most Field Goals, Season

35—Ali Haji-Sheikh, New York Giants, 1983

Most Field Goals Attempted, Season

49—Bruce Gossett, Los Angeles Rams, 1966
　　Curt Knight, Washington Redskins, 1971

Most Consecutive Field Goals

24—Kevin Butler, Chicago Bears, 1988-89

Most Consecutive Games, Field Goal

31—Fred Cox, Minnesota Vikings, 1968-1970

Longest Field Goal

63—Tom Dempsey, New Orleans Saints vs. Detroit Lions, November 8, 1970

Highest Field Goal Completion Percentage, Career (100 attempts)

77.3—Nick Lowery, New England Patriots, 1978; Kansas City Chiefs, 1980-89 (225 FGs in 291 attempts)

Highest Field Goal Completion Percentage, Season (20 attempts)

95.2—Mark Moseley, Washington Redskins, 1982 (20 FGs in 21 attempts)
　　　Eddie Murray, Detroit Lions, 1988 (20 FGs in 21 attempts)
　　　Eddie Murray, Detroit Lions, 1989 (20 FGs in 21 attempts)

Highest Field Goal Percentage, Game (7 attempts)

100—Rich Karlis, Minnesota Vikings vs. Los Angeles Rams, November 5, 1989 (7 FGs in 7 attempts)

Most Safeties, Career

4—Ted Hendricks, Baltimore Colts, 1969-73; Green Bay Packers, 1974; Oakland Raiders, 1975-81; Los Angeles Raiders, 1982-83
　Doug English, Detroit Lions, 1975-79; 1981-85

Most Safeties, Season

2—Tom Nash, Green Bay Packers, 1932
　Roger Brown, Detroit Lions, 1962
　Ron McDole, Buffalo Bills, 1964
　Alan Page, Minnesota Vikings, 1971
　Benny Barnes, Dallas Cowboys, 1973
　Fred Dryer, Los Angeles Rams, 1973
　James Young, Houston Oilers, 1977
　Tom Hannon, Minnesota Vikings, 1981
　Doug English, Detroit Lions, 1983
　Don Blackmon, New England Patriots, 1985
　Tim Harris, Green Bay Packers, 1988

Most Safeties, Game

2—Fred Dryer, Los Angeles Rams vs. Green Bay Packers, October 21, 1973

PUNT RETURNS

Most Yardage Returning Punts, Career

3,317—Billy (White Shoes) Johnson, Houston Oilers, 1974-1980; Atlanta Falcons, 1982-1987; Washington Redskins, 1988

Most Yardage Returning Punts, Season

692—Fulton Walker, Los Angeles Raiders, 1985

Most Yardage Returning Punts, Game

207—LeRoy Irvin, Los Angeles Rams vs. Atlanta Falcons, October 11, 1981

Most Touchdowns Scored via Punt Returns, Career
    8—Jack Christiansen, Detroit Lions, 1951 (4), 1952 (2), 1954, 1956
       Rick Upchurch, Denver Broncos, 1976 (4), 1977 (1), 1978 (1), 1982 (2)

Most Touchdowns Scored via Punt Returns, Season
    4—Jack Christiansen, Detroit Lions, 1951
       Rick Upchurch, Denver Broncos, 1976

Most Touchdowns Scored via Punt Returns, Game
    2—Jack Christiansen, Detroit Lions vs. Los Angeles Rams, October 14, 1951; vs. Green Bay Packers, November 22, 1951
       Dick Christy, New York Titans vs. Denver Broncos, September 24, 1961
       Rick Upchurch, Denver Broncos vs. Cleveland Browns, September 26, 1976
       LeRoy Irvin, Los Angeles Rams vs. Atlanta Falcons, October 11, 1981
       Vai Sikahema, St. Louis Cardinals vs. Tampa Bay Buccaneers, December 21, 1986

Most Punt Returns, Career
    282—Billy (White Shoes) Johnson, Houston Oilers, 1974-1980; Atlanta Falcons, 1982-1987; Washington Redskins, 1988

Most Punt Returns, Season
    70—Danny Reece, Tampa Bay Buccaneers, 1979

Most Punt Returns, Game
    11—Eddie Brown, Washington Redskins vs. Tampa Bay Buccaneers, October 9, 1977

Longest Punt Return (All Touchdowns)
    98—Gil LeFebvre, Cincinnati Reds vs. Brooklyn Dodgers, December 3, 1933
       Charlie West, Minnesota Vikings vs. Washington Redskins, November 3, 1968
       Dennis Morgan, Dallas Cowboys vs. St. Louis Cardinals, October 13, 1974

KICKOFF RETURNS

Most Yardage Returning Kickoffs, Career
    6,922—Ron Smith, Chicago Bears, 1965; Atlanta Falcons, 1966-67; Los Angeles Rams, 1968-1969; Chicago Bears, 1970-1972; San Diego Chargers, 1973; Oakland Raiders, 1974

Most Yardage Returning Kickoffs, Season
    1,345—Buster Rhymes, Minnesota Vikings, 1985

Most Yardage Returning Kickoffs, Game
    294—Wally Triplett, Detroit Lions vs. Los Angeles Rams, October 29, 1950 (4 returns)

Most Touchdowns Scored via Kickoff Returns, Career
    6—Ollie Matson, Chicago Cardinals, 1952 (2), 1954, 1956, 1958 (2)
       Gale Sayers, Chicago Bears, 1965, 1966 (2), 1967 (3)
       Travis Williams, Green Bay Packers, 1967 (4), 1969; Los Angeles Rams, 1971

Most Touchdowns Scored via Kickoff Returns, Season
    4—Travis Williams, Green Bay Packers, 1967
       Cecil Turner, Chicago Bears, 1970

Most Touchdowns Scored via Kickoff Returns, Game
    2—Tim Brown, Philadelphia Eagles vs. Dallas Cowboys, November 6, 1966
       Travis Williams, Green Bay Packers vs. Cleveland Browns, November 12, 1967
       Ron Brown, Los Angeles Rams vs. Green Bay Packers, November 24, 1985

Most Kickoff Returns, Career
    275—Ron Smith, Chicago Bears, 1965; Atlanta Falcons, 1966-67; Los Angeles Rams, 1968-1969; Chicago Bears, 1970-1972; San Diego Chargers, 1973; Oakland Raiders, 1974

Most Kickoff Returns, Season
    60—Drew Hill, Los Angeles Rams, 1981

Most Kickoff Returns, Game
    9—Noland Smith, Kansas City Chiefs vs. Oakland Raiders, November 23, 1967
       Dino Hall, Cleveland Browns vs. Pittsburgh Steelers, October 7, 1979
       Paul Palmer, Kansas City Chiefs vs. Seattle Seahawks, September 20, 1987

Longest Kickoff Return (All Touchdowns)
    106—Al Carmichael, Green Bay Packers vs. Chicago Bears, October 7, 1956
       Noland Smith, Kansas City Chiefs vs. Denver Broncos, December 17, 1967
       Roy Green, St. Louis Cardinals vs. Dallas Cowboys, October 21, 1979

PUNTING

Highest Punting Average, Career (300 Punts)
    45.10—Sammy Baugh, Washington Redskins, 1937-1952 (338 punts)

Highest Punting Average, Season (Qualifiers)
    51.4—Sammy Baugh, Washington Redskins, 1940 (35 punts)

Highest Punting Average, Game (4 Punts)
    61.8—Bob Cifers, Detroit Lions vs. Chicago Bears, November 24, 1946

Seattle quarterback
Dave Krieg set a
dubious record with
18 fumbles in 1989.

Longest Punt
  98—Steve O'Neal, New York Jets vs. Denver Broncos, September 21, 1969

Most Punts, Career
  1,154—Dave Jennings, New York Giants, 1974-1984; New York Jets, 1985-1987

Most Punts, Season
  114—Bob Parsons, Chicago Bears, 1981

Most Punts, Game
  15—John Teltschik, Philadelphia Eagles vs. New York Giants (OT), December 6, 1987

MISCELLANEOUS RECORDS

Most Seasons, Active Player
  26—George Blanda, Chicago Bears, 1949, 1950-1958; Baltimore Colts, 1950; Houston Oilers, 1960-1966; Oakland Raiders, 1967-1975

Most Games Played, Career
  340—George Blanda, Chicago Bears, 1949, 1950-1958; Baltimore Colts, 1950; Houston Oilers, 1960-1966; Oakland Raiders, 1967-1975

Most Consecutive Games Played, Career
  282—Jim Marshall, Cleveland Browns, 1960; Minnesota Vikings, 1961-1979

Most Seasons, Coach
  40—George Halas, Chicago Bears, 1920-1929; 1933-1942; 1946-1955; 1958-1967

Most Fumbles, Career
  105—Roman Gabriel, Los Angeles Rams, 1962-72; Philadelphia Eagles, 1973-77

Most Fumbles, Season
  18—Dave Krieg, Seattle Seahawks, 1989

Most Fumbles, Game
  7—Len Dawson, Kansas City Chiefs vs. San Diego Chargers, November 15, 1964

Longest Run With Recovered Fumble
  104—Jack Tatum, Oakland Raiders vs. Green Bay Packers, September 24, 1972

TEAM YEAR-BY-YEAR STANDINGS

ATLANTA FALCONS (1966-89)

Year	W.	L.	T.	Pct.	Pts.	Opp.	Head Coach
1989	3	13	0	.188	279	437	Marion Campbell, Jim Hanifan
1988	5	11	0	.313	244	315	Marion Campbell
1987	3	12	0	.200	205	436	Marion Campbell
1986	7	8	1	.469	280	280	Dan Henning
1985	4	12	0	.250	282	452	Dan Henning
1984	4	12	0	.250	281	382	Dan Henning
1983	7	9	0	.438	370	389	Dan Henning
1982‡	5	4	0	.556	183	199	Leeman Bennett
1981	7	9	0	.438	426	355	Leeman Bennett
1980†	12	4	0	.750	405	272	Leeman Bennett
1979	6	10	0	.375	300	388	Leeman Bennett
1978*	9	7	0	.563	240	290	Leeman Bennett
1977	7	7	0	.500	179	129	Leeman Bennett
1976	4	10	0	.286	172	312	Marion Campbell, Pat Peppler
1975	4	10	0	.286	240	289	Marion Campbell
1974	3	11	0	.214	111	271	Norm Van Brocklin, Marion Campbell
1973	9	5	0	.643	318	224	Norm Van Brocklin
1972	7	7	0	.500	269	274	Norm Van Brocklin
1971	7	6	1	.538	274	277	Norm Van Brocklin
1970	4	8	2	.333	206	261	Norm Van Brocklin
1969	6	8	0	.429	276	268	Norm Van Brocklin
1968	2	12	0	.143	170	389	Norb Hecker, Norm Van Brocklin
1967	1	12	1	.077	175	422	Norb Hecker
1966	3	11	0	.214	204	437	Norb Hecker

*NFC wild-card team.
†NFC Western Division champion.
‡NFC playoff qualifier.

BUFFALO BILLS (1960-89)

Year	W.	L.	T.	Pct.	Pts.	Opp.	Head Coach
1989§	9	7	0	.563	409	317	Marv Levy
1988§	12	4	0	.750	329	237	Marv Levy
1987	7	8	0	.467	270	305	Marv Levy
1986	4	12	0	.250	287	348	Hank Bullough, Marv Levy
1985	2	14	0	.125	200	381	Kay Stephenson, Hank Bullough
1984	2	14	0	.125	250	454	Kay Stephenson
1983	8	8	0	.500	283	351	Kay Stephenson
1982	4	5	0	.444	150	154	Chuck Knox
1981‡	10	6	0	.625	311	276	Chuck Knox
1980§	11	5	0	.688	320	260	Chuck Knox
1979	7	9	0	.438	268	279	Chuck Knox
1978	5	11	0	.313	302	354	Chuck Knox
1977	3	11	0	.214	160	313	Jim Ringo
1976	2	12	0	.143	245	363	Lou Saban, Jim Ringo
1975	8	6	0	.571	420	355	Lou Saban
1974‡	9	5	0	.643	264	244	Lou Saban
1973	9	5	0	.643	259	230	Lou Saban
1972	4	9	1	.321	257	377	Lou Saban
1971	1	13	0	.071	184	394	Harvey Johnson
1970	3	10	1	.231	204	337	John Rauch
1969	4	10	0	.286	230	359	John Rauch
1968	1	12	1	.077	199	367	Joel Collier, Harvey Johnson
1967	4	10	0	.286	237	285	Joel Collier
1966†	9	4	1	.692	358	255	Joel Collier
1965*	10	3	1	.769	313	226	Lou Saban
1964*	12	2	0	.857	400	242	Lou Saban
1963	7	6	1	.538	304	291	Lou Saban
1962	7	6	1	.538	309	272	Lou Saban
1961	6	8	0	.429	294	342	Garrard Ramsey
1960	5	8	1	.385	296	303	Garrard Ramsey

*AFL champion.
†AFL Eastern Division champion.
‡AFC wild-card team.
§AFC Eastern Division champion.

CHICAGO BEARS (1920-89)

Year	W.	L.	T.	Pct.	Pts.	Opp.	Head Coach
1989	6	10	0	.375	358	377	Mike Ditka
1988x	12	4	0	.750	312	215	Mike Ditka
1987x	11	4	0	.733	356	282	Mike Ditka
1986x	14	2	0	.875	352	187	Mike Ditka
1985y	15	1	0	.938	456	198	Mike Ditka
1984x	10	6	0	.625	325	248	Mike Ditka
1983	8	8	0	.500	311	301	Mike Ditka
1982	3	6	0	.333	141	174	Mike Ditka
1981	6	10	0	.375	253	324	Neill Armstrong
1980	7	9	0	.438	304	264	Neill Armstrong
1979§	10	6	0	.625	306	249	Neill Armstrong
1978	7	9	0	.438	253	274	Neill Armstrong
1977§	9	5	0	.643	255	253	Jack Pardee
1976	7	7	0	.500	253	216	Jack Pardee
1975	4	10	0	.286	191	379	Jack Pardee
1974	4	10	0	.286	152	279	Abe Gibron
1973	3	11	0	.214	195	334	Abe Gibron
1972	4	9	1	.321	225	275	Abe Gibron
1971	6	8	0	.429	185	276	Jim Dooley
1970	6	8	0	.429	256	261	Jim Dooley
1969	1	13	0	.071	210	339	Jim Dooley
1968	7	7	0	.500	250	333	Jim Dooley
1967	7	6	1	.538	239	218	George Halas
1966	5	7	2	.417	234	272	George Halas
1965	9	5	0	.643	409	275	George Halas
1964	5	9	0	.357	260	379	George Halas
1963*	11	1	2	.917	301	144	George Halas
1962	9	5	0	.643	321	287	George Halas
1961	8	6	0	.571	326	302	George Halas
1960	5	6	1	.455	194	299	George Halas
1959	8	4	0	.667	252	196	George Halas
1958	8	4	0	.667	298	230	George Halas
1957	5	7	0	.417	203	211	John (Paddy) Driscoll
1956‡	9	2	1	.818	363	246	John (Paddy) Driscoll
1955	8	4	0	.667	294	251	George Halas
1954	8	4	0	.667	301	279	George Halas
1953	3	8	1	.273	218	262	George Halas
1952	5	7	0	.417	245	326	George Halas
1951	7	5	0	.583	286	282	George Halas
1950	9	3	0	.750	279	207	George Halas
1949	9	3	0	.750	332	218	George Halas
1948	10	2	0	.833	375	151	George Halas
1947	8	4	0	.667	363	241	George Halas
1946*	8	2	1	.800	289	193	George Halas
1945	3	7	0	.300	192	235	Hunk Anderson, Luke Johnsos (co-coaches)
1944	6	3	1	.667	258	172	Hunk Anderson, Luke Johnsos (co-coaches)
1943*	8	1	1	.889	303	157	Hunk Anderson, Luke Johnsos (co-coaches)
1942†	11	0	0	1.000	376	84	George Halas, Hunk Anderson, Luke Johnsos
1941*	10	1	0	.909	396	147	George Halas
1940*	8	3	0	.727	238	152	George Halas
1939	8	3	0	.727	298	157	George Halas
1938	6	5	0	.545	194	148	George Halas
1937†	9	1	1	.900	201	100	George Halas
1936	9	3	0	.750	222	94	George Halas
1935	6	4	2	.600	192	106	George Halas
1934†	13	0	0	1.000	286	86	George Halas
1933*	10	2	1	.833	133	82	George Halas
1932*	7	1	6	.875			Ralph Jones
1931	8	4	0	.667			Ralph Jones
1930	9	4	1	.692			Ralph Jones
1929	4	8	2	.333			George Halas
1928	7	5	1	.583			George Halas
1927	9	3	2	.750			George Halas
1926	12	1	3	.923			George Halas
1925	9	5	3	.643			George Halas
1924	6	1	4	.857			George Halas
1923	9	2	1	.818			George Halas
1922	9	3	0	.750			George Halas

Chicago Staleys

Year	W.	L.	T.	Pct.	Pts.	Opp.	Head Coach
1921*	10	1	1	.909			George Halas

Decatur Staleys

Year	W.	L.	T.	Pct.	Pts.	Opp.	Head Coach
1920	10	1	1	.909			George Halas

*NFL champion.
†NFL Western Division champion.
‡NFL Western Conference champion.
§NFC wild-card team.
xNFC Central Division champion.
ySuper Bowl champion.

CINCINNATI BENGALS (1968-89)

Year	W.	L.	T.	Pct.	Pts.	Opp.	Head Coach
1989	8	8	0	.500	404	285	Sam Wyche
1988‡	12	4	0	.750	448	329	Sam Wyche
1987	4	11	0	.267	285	370	Sam Wyche
1986	10	6	0	.625	409	394	Sam Wyche
1985	7	9	0	.438	441	437	Sam Wyche
1984	8	8	0	.500	339	339	Sam Wyche
1983	7	9	0	.438	346	302	Forrest Gregg
1982§	7	2	0	.778	232	177	Forrest Gregg
1981‡	12	4	0	.750	421	304	Forrest Gregg
1980	6	10	0	.375	244	312	Forrest Gregg
1979	4	12	0	.250	337	421	Homer Rice
1978	4	12	0	.250	252	284	Bill Johnson, Homer Rice
1977	8	6	0	.571	238	235	Bill Johnson
1976	10	4	0	.714	335	210	Bill Johnson
1975†	11	3	0	.786	340	246	Paul Brown
1974	7	7	0	.500	283	259	Paul Brown
1973*	10	4	0	.714	286	231	Paul Brown
1972	8	6	0	.571	299	229	Paul Brown
1971	4	10	0	.286	284	265	Paul Brown
1970*	8	6	0	.571	312	255	Paul Brown
1969	4	9	1	.308	280	367	Paul Brown
1968	3	11	0	.214	215	329	Paul Brown

*AFC Central Division champion.
†AFC wild-card team.
‡AFC champion.
§AFC playoff qualifier.

CLEVELAND BROWNS (1946-89)

Year	W.	L.	T.	Pct.	Pts.	Opp.	Head Coach
1989y	9	6	1	.594	334	254	Bud Carson
1988z	10	6	0	.625	304	288	Marty Schottenheimer
1987y	10	5	0	.667	390	239	Marty Schottenheimer
1986y	12	4	0	.750	391	310	Marty Schottenheimer
1985y	8	8	0	.500	287	294	Marty Schottenheimer
1984	5	11	0	.313	250	297	Sam Rutigliano, Marty Schottenheimer
1983	9	7	0	.562	356	342	Sam Rutigliano
1982a	4	5	0	.444	140	182	Sam Rutigliano
1981	5	11	0	.313	276	375	Sam Rutigliano
1980y	11	5	0	.688	357	310	Sam Rutigliano
1979	9	7	0	.563	359	352	Sam Rutigliano
1978	8	8	0	.500	334	356	Sam Rutigliano
1977	6	8	0	.429	269	267	Forrest Gregg, Dick Modzelewski
1976	9	5	0	.643	267	287	Forrest Gregg
1975	3	11	0	.214	218	372	Forrest Gregg
1974	4	10	0	.286	251	344	Nick Skorich
1973	7	5	2	.571	234	255	Nick Skorich
1972z	10	4	0	.714	268	249	Nick Skorich
1971y	9	5	0	.643	285	273	Nick Skorich
1970	7	7	0	.500	286	265	Blanton Collier
1969‡	10	3	1	.769	351	300	Blanton Collier
1968‡	10	4	0	.714	394	273	Blanton Collier
1967x	9	5	0	.643	334	297	Blanton Collier
1966	9	5	0	.643	403	259	Blanton Collier
1965‡	11	3	0	.786	363	325	Blanton Collier
1964†	10	3	1	.769	415	293	Blanton Collier
1963	10	4	0	.714	343	262	Blanton Collier
1962	7	6	1	.538	291	257	Paul Brown
1961	8	5	1	.615	319	270	Paul Brown
1960	8	3	1	.727	362	217	Paul Brown
1959	7	5	0	.583	270	214	Paul Brown
1958	9	3	0	.750	302	217	Paul Brown
1957‡	9	2	1	.818	269	172	Paul Brown
1956	5	7	0	.417	167	177	Paul Brown
1955†	9	2	1	.818	349	218	Paul Brown
1954†	9	3	0	.750	336	162	Paul Brown
1953‡	11	1	0	.917	348	162	Paul Brown
1952§	8	4	0	.667	310	213	Paul Brown
1951‡	11	1	0	.917	331	152	Paul Brown
1950†	10	2	0	.833	310	144	Paul Brown
1949*	9	1	2	.900	339	171	Paul Brown
1948*	14	0	0	1.000	389	190	Paul Brown
1947*	12	1	1	.923	410	185	Paul Brown
1946*	12	2	0	.857	423	137	Paul Brown

*AAFC champion.
†NFL champion.
‡NFL Eastern Conference champion.
§NFL American Conference champion.
xNFL Century Division champion.
yAFC Central Division champion.
zAFC wild-card team.
aAFC playoff qualifier.

DALLAS COWBOYS (1960-89)

Year	W.	L.	T.	Pct.	Pts.	Opp.	Head Coach
1989	1	15	0	.063	204	393	Jimmy Johnson
1988	3	13	0	.188	265	381	Tom Landry
1987	7	8	0	.467	340	348	Tom Landry
1986	7	9	0	.438	346	337	Tom Landry
1985y	10	6	0	.625	357	333	Tom Landry
1984	9	7	0	.563	308	308	Tom Landry
1983x	12	4	0	.750	479	360	Tom Landry
1982z	6	3	0	.667	226	145	Tom Landry
1981y	12	4	0	.750	367	277	Tom Landry
1980x	12	4	0	.750	454	311	Tom Landry
1979y	11	5	0	.688	371	313	Tom Landry
1978‡	12	4	0	.750	384	208	Tom Landry
1977§	12	2	0	.857	345	212	Tom Landry
1976y	11	3	0	.786	296	194	Tom Landry
1975‡	10	4	0	.714	350	266	Tom Landry
1974	8	6	0	.571	297	235	Tom Landry
1973*	10	4	0	.714	382	203	Tom Landry
1972x	10	4	0	.714	319	240	Tom Landry
1971§	11	3	0	.786	406	222	Tom Landry
1970‡	10	4	0	.714	299	221	Tom Landry
1969†	11	2	1	.846	369	223	Tom Landry
1968†	12	2	0	.857	431	186	Tom Landry
1967*	9	5	0	.643	342	268	Tom Landry
1966*	10	3	1	.769	445	239	Tom Landry
1965	7	7	0	.500	325	280	Tom Landry
1964	5	8	1	.385	250	289	Tom Landry
1963	4	10	0	.286	305	378	Tom Landry
1962	5	8	1	.385	398	402	Tom Landry
1961	4	9	1	.308	236	380	Tom Landry
1960	0	11	1	.000	177	369	Tom Landry

*NFL Eastern Conference champion.
†NFL Capitol Division champion.
‡NFC champion.
§Super Bowl champion.
xNFC wild-card team.
yNFC Eastern Division champion.
zNFC playoff qualifier.

DENVER BRONCOS (1960-89)

Year	W.	L.	T.	Pct.	Pts.	Opp.	Head Coach
1989*	11	5	0	.688	362	226	Dan Reeves
1988	8	8	0	.500	327	352	Dan Reeves
1987*	10	4	1	.700	379	288	Dan Reeves
1986*	11	5	0	.688	378	327	Dan Reeves
1985	11	5	0	.688	380	329	Dan Reeves
1984†	13	3	0	.813	353	241	Dan Reeves
1983‡	9	7	0	.562	302	327	Dan Reeves
1982	2	7	0	.222	148	226	Dan Reeves
1981	10	6	0	.625	321	289	Dan Reeves
1980	8	8	0	.500	310	323	Red Miller
1979‡	10	6	0	.625	289	262	Red Miller
1978†	10	6	0	.625	282	198	Red Miller
1977*	12	2	0	.857	274	148	Red Miller
1976	9	5	0	.643	315	206	John Ralston
1975	6	8	0	.429	254	307	John Ralston
1974	7	6	1	.586	302	294	John Ralston
1973	7	5	2	.571	354	296	John Ralston
1972	5	9	0	.357	325	350	John Ralston
1971	4	9	1	.308	203	275	Lou Saban, Jerry Smith
1970	5	8	1	.385	253	264	Lou Saban
1969	5	8	1	.385	297	344	Lou Saban

Year	W.	L.	T.	Pct.	Pts.	Opp.	Head Coach
1968	5	9	0	.357	255	404	Lou Saban
1967	3	11	0	.214	256	409	Lou Saban
1966	4	10	0	.286	196	381	Mac Speedie, Ray Malavasi
1965	4	10	0	.286	303	392	Mac Speedie
1964	2	11	1	.154	240	438	Jack Faulkner, Mac Speedie
1963	2	11	1	.154	301	473	Jack Faulkner
1962	7	7	0	.500	353	334	Jack Faulkner
1961	3	11	0	.214	251	432	Frank Filchock
1960	4	9	1	.308	309	393	Frank Filchock

*AFC champion.
†AFC Western Division champion.
‡AFC wild-card team.

DETROIT LIONS (1930-89)

Year	W.	L.	T.	Pct.	Pts.	Opp.	Head Coach
1989	7	9	0	.438	312	364	Wayne Fontes
1988	4	12	0	.250	220	313	Darryl Rogers, Wayne Fontes
1987	4	11	0	.267	269	384	Darryl Rogers
1986	5	11	0	.313	277	326	Darryl Rogers
1985	7	9	0	.438	307	366	Darryl Rogers
1984	4	11	1	.281	283	408	Monte Clark
1983x	9	7	0	.562	347	286	Monte Clark
1982§	4	5	0	.444	181	176	Monte Clark
1981	8	8	0	.500	397	322	Monte Clark
1980	9	7	0	.563	334	272	Monte Clark
1979	2	14	0	.125	219	365	Monte Clark
1978	7	9	0	.438	290	300	Monte Clark
1977	6	8	0	.429	183	252	Tommy Hudspeth
1976	6	8	0	.429	262	220	Rick Forzano, Tommy Hudspeth
1975	7	7	0	.500	245	262	Rick Forzano
1974	7	7	0	.500	256	270	Rick Forzano
1973	6	7	1	.464	271	247	Don McCafferty
1972	8	5	1	.607	339	290	Joe Schmidt
1971	7	6	1	.538	341	286	Joe Schmidt
1970‡	10	4	0	.714	347	202	Joe Schmidt
1969	9	4	1	.692	259	188	Joe Schmidt
1968	4	8	2	.333	207	241	Joe Schmidt
1967	5	7	2	.417	260	259	Joe Schmidt
1966	4	9	1	.308	206	317	Harry Gilmer
1965	6	7	1	.462	257	295	Harry Gilmer
1964	7	5	2	.583	280	260	George Wilson
1963	5	8	1	.385	326	265	George Wilson
1962	11	3	0	.786	315	177	George Wilson
1961	8	5	1	.615	270	258	George Wilson
1960	7	5	0	.583	239	212	George Wilson
1959	3	8	1	.273	203	275	George Wilson
1958	4	7	1	.364	261	276	George Wilson
1957*	8	4	0	.667	251	231	George Wilson
1956	9	3	0	.750	300	188	Buddy Parker
1955	3	9	0	.250	230	275	Buddy Parker
1954†	9	2	1	.818	337	189	Buddy Parker
1953*	10	2	0	.833	271	205	Buddy Parker
1952*	9	3	0	.750	344	192	Buddy Parker
1951	7	4	1	.636	336	259	Buddy Parker
1950	6	6	0	.500	321	285	Alvin (Bo) McMillin
1949	4	8	0	.333	237	259	Alvin (Bo) McMillin
1948	2	10	0	.167	200	407	Alvin (Bo) McMillin
1947	3	9	0	.250	231	305	Gus Dorais
1946	1	10	0	.091	142	310	Gus Dorais
1945	7	3	0	.700	195	194	Gus Dorais
1944	6	3	1	.667	216	151	Gus Dorais
1943	3	6	1	.333	178	218	Gus Dorais
1942	0	11	0	.000	38	263	Bill Edwards, John Karcis
1941	4	6	1	.400	121	195	Bill Edwards
1940	5	5	1	.500	138	153	George (Potsy) Clark
1939	6	5	0	.545	145	150	Elmer (Gus) Henderson
1938	7	4	0	.636	119	108	Earl (Dutch) Clark
1937	7	4	0	.636	180	105	Earl (Dutch) Clark
1936	8	4	0	.667	235	102	George (Potsy) Clark
1935*	7	3	2	.700	191	111	George (Potsy) Clark
1934	10	3	0	.769	238	59	George (Potsy) Clark

Portsmouth Spartans

Year	W.	L.	T.	Pct.	Pts.	Opp.	Head Coach
1933	6	5	0	.545	128	87	George (Potsy) Clark
1932	6	2	4	.750			George (Potsy) Clark
1931	11	3	0	.786			George (Potsy) Clark
1930	5	6	3	.455			George (Potsy) Clark

*NFL champion.
†NFL Western Conference champion.
‡NFC wild-card team.
§NFC playoff qualifier.
xNFC Central Division champion.

GREEN BAY PACKERS (1921-89)

Year	W.	L.	T.	Pct.	Pts.	Opp.	Head Coach
1989	10	6	0	.625	362	356	Lindy Infante
1988	4	12	0	.250	240	315	Lindy Infante
1987	5	9	1	.367	255	300	Forrest Gregg
1986	4	12	0	.250	254	418	Forrest Gregg
1985	8	8	0	.500	337	355	Forrest Gregg
1984	8	8	0	.500	390	309	Forrest Gregg
1983	8	8	0	.500	429	439	Bart Starr
1982x	5	3	1	.611	226	169	Bart Starr
1981	8	8	0	.500	324	361	Bart Starr
1980	5	10	1	.333	231	371	Bart Starr
1979	5	11	0	.313	246	316	Bart Starr
1978	8	7	1	.531	249	269	Bart Starr
1977	4	10	0	.286	134	219	Bart Starr
1976	5	9	0	.357	218	299	Bart Starr
1975	4	10	0	.286	226	285	Bart Starr
1974	6	8	0	.429	210	206	Dan Devine
1973	5	7	2	.429	202	259	Dan Devine
1972§	10	4	0	.714	304	226	Dan Devine
1971	4	8	2	.333	274	298	Dan Devine
1970	6	8	0	.429	196	293	Phil Bengtson
1969	8	6	0	.571	269	221	Phil Bengtson
1968	6	7	1	.462	281	227	Phil Bengtson
1967‡	9	4	1	.692	332	209	Vince Lombardi
1966‡	12	2	0	.857	335	163	Vince Lombardi
1965*	10	3	1	.769	316	224	Vince Lombardi
1964	8	5	1	.615	342	245	Vince Lombardi
1963	11	2	1	.846	369	206	Vince Lombardi
1962*	13	1	0	.929	415	148	Vince Lombardi
1961*	11	3	0	.786	391	223	Vince Lombardi
1960†	8	4	0	.667	332	209	Vince Lombardi
1959	7	5	0	.583	248	246	Vince Lombardi
1958	1	10	1	.091	193	382	Ray (Scooter) McLean
1957	3	9	0	.250	218	311	Lisle Blackbourn
1956	4	8	0	.333	264	342	Lisle Blackbourn
1955	6	6	0	.500	258	276	Lisle Blackbourn
1954	4	8	0	.333	234	251	Lisle Blackbourn
1953	2	9	1	.182	200	338	Gene Ronzani
1952	6	6	0	.500	295	312	Gene Ronzani
1951	3	9	0	.250	254	375	Gene Ronzani
1950	3	9	0	.250	244	406	Gene Ronzani
1949	2	10	0	.167	114	329	Earl (Curly) Lambeau
1948	3	9	0	.250	154	290	Earl (Curly) Lambeau
1947	6	5	1	.545	274	210	Earl (Curly) Lambeau
1946	6	5	0	.545	148	158	Earl (Curly) Lambeau
1945	6	4	0	.600	258	173	Earl (Curly) Lambeau
1944*	8	2	0	.800	238	141	Earl (Curly) Lambeau
1943	7	2	1	.778	264	172	Earl (Curly) Lambeau
1942	8	2	1	.800	300	215	Earl (Curly) Lambeau
1941	10	1	0	.909	258	120	Earl (Curly) Lambeau
1940	6	4	1	.600	238	155	Earl (Curly) Lambeau
1939*	9	2	0	.818	233	153	Earl (Curly) Lambeau
1938†	7	4	0	.636	220	122	Earl (Curly) Lambeau
1937	7	4	0	.636	220	122	Earl (Curly) Lambeau
1936*	10	1	1	.909	248	118	Earl (Curly) Lambeau
1935	8	4	0	.667	181	96	Earl (Curly) Lambeau
1934	7	6	0	.538	156	112	Earl (Curly) Lambeau
1933	5	7	1	.417	170	107	Earl (Curly) Lambeau
1932	10	3	1	.769			Earl (Curly) Lambeau
1931*	12	2	0	.857			Earl (Curly) Lambeau
1930*	10	3	1	.769			Earl (Curly) Lambeau
1929*	12	0	1	1.000			Earl (Curly) Lambeau
1928	6	4	3	.600			Earl (Curly) Lambeau
1927	7	2	1	.778			Earl (Curly) Lambeau
1926	7	3	3	.700			Earl (Curly) Lambeau
1925	8	5	0	.615			Earl (Curly) Lambeau
1924	8	4	0	.667			Earl (Curly) Lambeau
1923	7	2	1	.778			Earl (Curly) Lambeau
1922	4	3	3	.571			Earl (Curly) Lambeau
1921	6	2	2	.750			Earl (Curly) Lambeau

*NFL champion.
†NFL Western Conference champion.
‡Super Bowl champion.
§NFC Central Division champion.
xNFC playoff qualifier.

HOUSTON OILERS (1960-89)

Year	W.	L.	T.	Pct.	Pts.	Opp.	Head Coach
1989‡	9	7	0	.563	365	412	Jerry Glanville
1988‡	10	6	0	.625	424	365	Jerry Glanville
1987↓	9	6	0	.600	345	349	Jerry Glanville
1986	5	11	0	.313	274	329	Jerry Glanville
1985	5	11	0	.313	284	412	Hugh Campbell, Jerry Glanville
1984	3	13	0	.188	240	437	Hugh Campbell
1983	2	14	0	.125	288	460	Ed Biles, Chuck Studley
1982	1	8	0	.111	136	245	Ed Biles
1981	7	9	0	.438	281	355	Ed Biles
1980‡	11	5	0	.688	295	251	O.A. (Bum) Phillips
1979‡	11	5	0	.688	362	331	O.A. (Bum) Phillips
1978‡	10	6	0	.625	283	298	O.A. (Bum) Phillips
1977	8	6	0	.571	299	230	O.A. (Bum) Phillips
1976	5	9	0	.357	222	273	O.A. (Bum) Phillips
1975	10	4	0	.714	293	226	O.A. (Bum) Phillips
1974	7	7	0	.500	236	282	Sid Gillman
1973	1	13	0	.071	199	447	Bill Peterson, Sid Gillman
1972	1	13	0	.071	164	380	Bill Peterson
1971	4	9	1	.308	251	330	Ed Hughes
1970	3	10	1	.231	217	352	Wally Lemm
1969	6	6	2	.500	278	279	Wally Lemm
1968	7	7	0	.500	303	248	Wally Lemm
1967†	9	4	1	.692	258	199	Wally Lemm
1966	3	11	0	.214	335	396	Wally Lemm
1965	4	10	0	.286	298	429	Hugh (Bones) Taylor
1964	4	10	0	.286	310	355	Sammy Baugh
1963	6	8	0	.429	302	372	Frank (Pop) Ivy
1962†	11	3	0	.786	387	270	Frank (Pop) Ivy
1961*	10	3	1	.769	513	242	Lou Rymkus, Wally Lemm
1960*	10	4	0	.714	379	285	Lou Rymkus

*AFL champion.
†AFL Eastern Division champion.
‡AFC wild-card team.

INDIANAPOLIS COLTS (1953-89)

Year	W.	L.	T.	Pct.	Pts.	Opp.	Head Coach
1989	8	8	0	.500	298	301	Ron Meyer
1988	9	7	0	.563	354	315	Ron Meyer
1987x	9	6	0	.600	300	238	Ron Meyer
1986	3	13	0	.188	229	400	Rod Dowhower, Ron Meyer
1985	5	11	0	.313	320	386	Rod Dowhower
1984	4	12	0	.250	239	414	Frank Kush, Hal Hunter

Baltimore Colts

Year	W.	L.	T.	Pct.	Pts.	Opp.	Head Coach
1983	7	9	0	.438	264	354	Frank Kush
1982	0	8	1	.056	113	236	Frank Kush
1981	2	14	0	.125	259	533	Mike McCormack
1980	7	9	0	.438	355	387	Mike McCormack
1979	5	11	0	.313	271	351	Ted Marchibroda
1978	5	11	0	.313	239	421	Ted Marchibroda
1977x	10	4	0	.714	295	221	Ted Marchibroda
1976x	11	3	0	.786	417	246	Ted Marchibroda
1975x	10	4	0	.714	395	269	Ted Marchibroda
1974	2	12	0	.143	190	321	Howard Schn'lenberger, Joe Thomas
1973	4	10	0	.286	226	341	Howard Schnellenberger
1972	5	9	0	.357	235	252	Don McCafferty, John Sandusky
1971§	10	4	0	.714	313	140	Don McCafferty
1970‡	11	2	1	.846	321	234	Don McCafferty
1969	8	5	1	.615	279	268	Don Shula
1968*	13	1	0	.929	402	144	Don Shula
1967	11	1	2	.917	398	198	Don Shula
1966	9	5	0	.643	314	226	Don Shula
1965	10	3	1	.769	389	284	Don Shula

Year	W.	L.	T.	Pct.	Pts.	Opp.	Head Coach
1964†	12	2	0	.857	428	225	Don Shula
1963	8	6	0	.571	316	285	Don Shula
1962	7	7	0	.500	293	288	Weeb Ewbank
1961	8	6	0	.571	302	307	Weeb Ewbank
1960	6	6	0	.500	288	234	Weeb Ewbank
1959*	9	3	0	.750	374	251	Weeb Ewbank
1958*	9	3	0	.750	381	203	Weeb Ewbank
1957	7	5	0	.583	303	235	Weeb Ewbank
1956	5	7	0	.417	270	322	Weeb Ewbank
1955	5	6	1	.455	214	239	Weeb Ewbank
1954	3	9	0	.250	131	279	Weeb Ewbank
1953	3	9	0	.250	182	350	Keith Molesworth

*NFL champion.
†Western Conference champion.
‡Super Bowl champion.
§AFC wild-card team.
xAFC Eastern Division champion.

KANSAS CITY CHIEFS (1960-89)

Year	W.	L.	T.	Pct.	Pts.	Opp.	Head Coach
1989	8	7	1	.531	318	286	Marty Schottenheimer
1988	4	11	1	.281	254	320	Frank Gansz
1987	4	11	0	.267	273	388	Frank Gansz
1986x	10	6	0	.625	358	326	John Mackovic
1985	6	10	0	.375	317	360	John Mackovic
1984	8	8	0	.500	314	324	John Mackovic
1983	6	10	0	.375	386	367	John Mackovic
1982	3	6	0	.333	176	184	Marv Levy
1981	9	7	0	.563	343	290	Marv Levy
1980	8	8	0	.500	319	336	Marv Levy
1979	7	9	0	.438	238	262	Marv Levy
1978	4	12	0	.250	243	327	Marv Levy
1977	2	12	0	.143	225	349	Paul Wiggin, Tom Bettis
1976	5	9	0	.357	290	376	Paul Wiggin
1975	5	9	0	.357	282	341	Paul Wiggin
1974	5	9	0	.357	233	293	Hank Stram
1973	7	5	2	.583	231	192	Hank Stram
1972	8	6	0	.571	287	254	Hank Stram
1971§	10	3	1	.769	302	208	Hank Stram
1970	7	5	2	.583	272	244	Hank Stram
1969‡	11	3	0	.786	359	177	Hank Stram
1968†	12	2	0	.857	371	170	Hank Stram
1967	9	5	0	.643	408	254	Hank Stram
1966*	11	2	1	.846	448	276	Hank Stram
1965	7	5	2	.583	322	285	Hank Stram
1964	7	7	0	.500	366	306	Hank Stram
1963	5	7	2	.417	347	263	Hank Stram

Dallas Texans

Year	W.	L.	T.	Pct.	Pts.	Opp.	Head Coach
1962*	11	3	0	.786	389	233	Hank Stram
1961	6	8	0	.429	334	343	Hank Stram
1960	8	6	0	.571	362	253	Hank Stram

*AFL champion.
†AFL Western Division co-champion.
‡Super Bowl champion.
§AFC Western Division champion.
xAFC wild-card team.

LOS ANGELES RAIDERS (1960-89)

Year	W.	L.	T.	Pct.	Pts.	Opp.	Head Coach
1989	8	8	0	.500	315	297	Mike Shanahan, Art Shell
1988	7	9	0	.438	325	369	Mike Shanahan
1987	5	10	0	.333	301	289	Tom Flores
1986	8	8	0	.500	323	346	Tom Flores
1985‡	12	4	0	.750	354	308	Tom Flores
1984x	11	5	0	.688	368	278	Tom Flores
1983§	12	4	0	.750	442	338	Tom Flores
1982y	8	1	0	.889	260	200	Tom Flores

Oakland Raiders

Year	W.	L.	T.	Pct.	Pts.	Opp.	Head Coach
1981	7	9	0	.438	273	343	Tom Flores
1980§	11	5	0	.688	364	306	Tom Flores
1979	9	7	0	.563	365	337	Tom Flores
1978	9	7	0	.563	311	283	John Madden
1977x	11	3	0	.786	351	230	John Madden

Year	W.	L.	T.	Pct.	Pts.	Opp.	Head Coach
1976§	13	1	0	.929	350	237	John Madden
1975‡	11	3	0	.786	375	255	John Madden
1974‡	12	2	0	.857	355	228	John Madden
1973‡	9	4	1	.679	292	175	John Madden
1972‡	10	3	1	.750	365	248	John Madden
1971	8	4	2	.667	344	278	John Madden
1970‡	8	4	2	.667	300	293	John Madden
1969†	12	1	1	.923	377	242	John Madden
1968†	12	2	0	.857	453	233	John Rauch
1967*	13	1	0	.929	468	233	John Rauch
1966	8	5	1	.615	315	288	John Rauch
1965	8	5	1	.615	298	239	Al Davis
1964	5	7	2	.417	303	350	Al Davis
1963	10	4	0	.714	363	288	Al Davis
1962	1	13	0	.071	213	370	Marty Feldman, William Conkright
1961	2	12	0	.143	237	458	Eddie Erdelatz, Marty Feldman
1960	6	8	0	.429	319	399	Eddie Erdelatz

*AFL champion.
†AFL Western Division champion.
‡AFC Western Division champion.
§Super Bowl champion.
xAFC wild-card team.
yAFC playoff qualifier.

LOS ANGELES RAMS (1937-89)

Year	W.	L.	T.	Pct.	Pts.	Opp.	Head Coach
1989y	11	5	0	.688	426	344	John Robinson
1988y	10	6	0	.625	407	293	John Robinson
1987	6	9	0	.400	317	361	John Robinson
1986y	10	6	0	.625	309	267	John Robinson
1985§	11	5	0	.688	340	277	John Robinson
1984y	10	6	0	.625	346	316	John Robinson
1983y	9	7	0	.562	361	344	John Robinson
1982	2	7	0	.222	200	250	Ray Malavasi
1981	6	10	0	.375	303	351	Ray Malavasi
1980y	11	5	0	.688	424	289	Ray Malavasi
1979x	9	7	0	.563	323	309	Ray Malavasi
1978§	12	4	0	.750	316	245	Ray Malavasi
1977§	10	4	0	.714	302	146	Chuck Knox
1976§	10	3	1	.750	351	190	Chuck Knox
1975§	12	2	0	.857	312	135	Chuck Knox
1974§	10	4	0	.714	263	181	Chuck Knox
1973§	12	2	0	.857	388	178	Chuck Knox
1972	6	7	1	.464	291	286	Tommy Prothro
1971	8	5	1	.615	313	260	Tommy Prothro
1970	9	4	1	.692	325	202	George Allen
1969‡	11	3	0	.786	320	243	George Allen
1968	10	3	1	.769	312	200	George Allen
1967‡	11	1	2	.917	398	196	George Allen
1966	8	6	0	.571	289	212	George Allen
1965	4	10	0	.286	269	328	Harland Svare
1964	5	7	2	.417	283	339	Harland Svare
1963	5	9	0	.357	210	350	Harland Svare
1962	1	12	1	.077	220	334	Bob Waterfield, Harland Svare
1961	4	10	0	.286	263	333	Bob Waterfield
1960	4	7	1	.364	265	297	Bob Waterfield
1959	2	10	0	.167	242	315	Sid Gillman
1958	8	4	0	.667	344	278	Sid Gillman
1957	6	6	0	.500	307	278	Sid Gillman
1956	4	8	0	.333	291	307	Sid Gillman
1955†	8	3	1	.727	260	231	Sid Gillman
1954	6	5	1	.545	314	285	Hampton Pool
1953	8	3	1	.727	366	236	Hampton Pool
1952	9	3	0	.750	349	234	Hampton Pool
1951*	8	4	0	.667	392	261	Joe Stydahar
1950†	9	3	0	.750	466	309	Joe Stydahar
1949†	8	2	2	.800	360	239	Clark Shaughnessy
1948	6	5	1	.545	327	269	Clark Shaughnessy
1947	6	6	0	.500	259	214	Bob Snyder
1946	6	4	1	.600	277	257	Adam Walsh

Cleveland Rams

Year	W.	L.	T.	Pct.	Pts.	Opp.	Head Coach
1945*	9	1	0	.900	244	136	Adam Walsh
1944	4	6	0	.400	188	224	Aldo (Buff)Donelli
1943	(Rams did not play in 1943)						

Year	W.	L.	T.	Pct.	Pts.	Opp.	Head Coach
1942	5	6	0	.455	150	207	Earl (Dutch) Clark
1941	2	9	0	.182	116	244	Earl (Dutch) Clark
1940	4	6	1	.400	171	191	Earl (Dutch) Clark
1939	5	5	1	.500	195	164	Earl (Dutch) Clark
1938	4	7	0	.363	131	215	Hugo Bezdek, Art Lewis
1937	1	10	0	.091	75	207	Hugo Bezdek

*NFL champion.
†NFL Western Conference champion.
‡NFL Coastal Division champion.
§NFC Western Division champion.
xNFC champion.
yNFC wild-card team.

MIAMI DOLPHINS (1966-89)

Year	W.	L.	T.	Pct.	Pts.	Opp.	Head Coach
1989	8	8	0	.500	331	379	Don Shula
1988	6	10	0	.375	319	380	Don Shula
1987	8	7	0	.533	362	335	Don Shula
1986	8	8	0	.500	430	405	Don Shula
1985§	12	4	0	.750	428	320	Don Shula
1984†	14	2	0	.875	513	298	Don Shula
1983§	12	4	0	.750	389	250	Don Shula
1982†	7	2	0	.778	198	131	Don Shula
1981§	11	4	1	.719	345	275	Don Shula
1980	8	8	0	.500	266	305	Don Shula
1979§	10	6	0	.625	341	257	Don Shula
1978*	11	5	0	.688	372	254	Don Shula
1977	10	4	0	.714	313	197	Don Shula
1976	6	8	0	.429	263	264	Don Shula
1975	10	4	0	.714	357	222	Don Shula
1974§	11	3	0	.786	327	216	Don Shula
1973‡	12	2	0	.857	343	150	Don Shula
1972‡	14	0	0	1.000	385	171	Don Shula
1971†	10	3	1	.769	315	174	Don Shula
1970*	10	4	0	.714	297	228	Don Shula
1969	3	10	1	.231	233	332	George Wilson
1968	5	8	1	.385	276	355	George Wilson
1967	4	10	0	.286	219	407	George Wilson
1966	3	11	0	.214	213	362	George Wilson

*AFC wild-card team.
†AFC champion.
‡Super Bowl champion.
§AFC Eastern Division champion.

MINNESOTA VIKINGS (1961-89)

Year	W.	L.	T.	Pct.	Pts.	Opp.	Head Coach
1989‡	10	6	0	.625	351	275	Jerry Burns
1988y	11	5	0	.688	406	233	Jerry Burns
1987y	8	7	0	.533	336	335	Jerry Burns
1986	9	7	0	.563	398	273	Jerry Burns
1985	7	9	0	.438	346	359	Harry (Bud) Grant
1984	3	13	0	.188	276	484	Les Steckel
1983	8	8	0	.500	316	348	Harry (Bud) Grant
1982x	5	4	0	.556	187	198	Harry (Bud) Grant
1981	7	9	0	.438	325	369	Harry (Bud) Grant
1980‡	9	7	0	.563	317	308	Harry (Bud) Grant
1979	7	9	0	.438	259	337	Harry (Bud) Grant
1978‡	8	7	1	.531	294	306	Harry (Bud) Grant
1977‡	9	5	0	.643	231	227	Harry (Bud) Grant
1976§	11	2	1	.821	305	176	Harry (Bud) Grant
1975‡	12	2	0	.857	377	180	Harry (Bud) Grant
1974§	10	4	0	.714	310	195	Harry (Bud) Grant
1973§	12	2	0	.857	296	168	Harry (Bud) Grant
1972	7	7	0	.500	301	252	Harry (Bud) Grant
1971‡	11	3	0	.786	245	139	Harry (Bud) Grant
1970‡	12	2	0	.857	335	143	Harry (Bud) Grant
1969†	12	2	0	.857	379	133	Harry (Bud) Grant
1968*	8	6	0	.571	282	242	Harry (Bud) Grant
1967	3	8	3	.273	233	294	Harry (Bud) Grant
1966	4	9	1	.308	292	304	Norm Van Brocklin
1965	7	7	0	.500	383	403	Norm Van Brocklin
1964	8	5	1	.615	355	296	Norm Van Brocklin
1963	5	8	1	.385	309	390	Norm Van Brocklin
1962	2	11	1	.154	254	410	Norm Van Brocklin
1961	3	11	0	.214	285	407	Norm Van Brocklin

*NFL Central Division champion.
†NFL champion.
‡NFC Central Division champion.
§NFC champion.
xNFC playoff qualifier.
yNFC wild-card team.

NEW ENGLAND PATRIOTS
(1960-89)

Year	W.	L.	T.	Pct.	Pts.	Opp.	Head Coach
1989	5	11	0	.313	297	391	Raymond Berry
1988	9	7	0	.563	250	284	Raymond Berry
1987	8	7	0	.533	320	293	Raymond Berry
1986‡	11	5	0	.688	412	307	Raymond Berry
1985x	11	5	0	.688	362	290	Raymond Berry
1984	9	7	0	.563	362	352	Ron Meyer, Raymond Berry
1983	8	8	0	.500	274	289	Ron Meyer
1982§	5	4	0	.556	143	157	Ron Meyer
1981	2	14	0	.125	322	370	Ron Erhardt
1980	10	6	0	.625	441	325	Ron Erhardt
1979	9	7	0	.563	411	326	Ron Erhardt
1978‡	11	5	0	.688	358	286	C. Fairbanks, R. Erhardt, Hank Bullough
1977	9	5	0	.643	278	217	Chuck Fairbanks
1976†	11	3	0	.786	376	236	Chuck Fairbanks
1975	3	11	0	.214	258	358	Chuck Fairbanks
1974	7	7	0	.500	348	289	Chuck Fairbanks
1973	5	9	0	.357	258	300	Chuck Fairbanks
1972	3	11	0	.214	192	446	John Mazur, Phil Bengtson
1971	6	8	0	.429	238	325	John Mazur

Boston Patriots

Year	W.	L.	T.	Pct.	Pts.	Opp.	Head Coach
1970	2	12	0	.143	149	361	Clive Rush, John Mazur
1969	4	10	0	.286	266	316	Clive Rush
1968	4	10	0	.286	229	406	Mike Holovak
1967	3	10	1	.231	280	389	Mike Holovak
1966	8	4	2	.667	315	283	Mike Holovak
1965	4	8	2	.333	244	302	Mike Holovak
1964	10	3	1	.769	365	297	Mike Holovak
1963*	7	6	1	.538	327	257	Mike Holovak
1962	9	4	1	.692	346	295	Mike Holovak
1961	9	4	1	.692	413	313	Lou Saban, Mike Holovak
1960	5	9	0	.357	286	349	Lou Saban

*AFL Eastern Division champion.
†AFC wild-card team.
‡AFC Eastern Division champion.
§AFC playoff qualifier.
xAFC champion.

NEW ORLEANS SAINTS (1967-89)

Year	W.	L.	T.	Pct.	Pts.	Opp.	Head Coach
1989	9	7	0	.563	386	301	Jim Mora
1988	10	6	0	.625	312	283	Jim Mora
1987*	12	3	0	.800	422	283	Jim Mora
1986	7	9	0	.438	288	287	Jim Mora
1985	5	11	0	.313	294	401	O.A. (Bum) Phillips, Wade Phillips
1984	7	9	0	.438	298	361	O.A. (Bum) Phillips
1983	8	8	0	.500	319	337	O.A. (Bum) Phillips
1982	4	5	0	.444	129	160	O.A. (Bum) Phillips
1981	4	12	0	.250	207	378	O.A. (Bum) Phillips
1980	1	15	0	.063	291	487	Dick Nolan, Dick Stanfel
1979	8	8	0	.500	370	360	Dick Nolan
1978	7	9	0	.438	281	298	Dick Nolan
1977	3	11	0	.214	232	336	Hank Stram
1976	4	10	0	.286	253	346	Hank Stram
1975	2	12	0	.143	165	360	John North, Ernie Hefferle
1974	5	9	0	.357	166	263	John North
1973	5	9	0	.357	163	312	John North
1972	2	11	1	.154	215	361	J.D. Roberts
1971	4	8	2	.333	266	347	J.D. Roberts
1970	2	11	1	.154	172	347	Tom Fears, J.D. Roberts
1969	5	9	0	.357	311	393	Tom Fears
1968	4	9	1	.308	246	327	Tom Fears
1967	3	11	0	.214	233	379	Tom Fears

*NFC wild-card team.

NEW YORK GIANTS (1925-89)

Year	W.	L.	T.	Pct.	Pts.	Opp.	Head Coach
1989y	12	4	0	.750	348	252	Bill Parcells
1988	10	6	0	.625	359	304	Bill Parcells
1987	6	9	0	.400	280	312	Bill Parcells
1986x	14	2	0	.875	371	236	Bill Parcells
1985§	10	6	0	.625	399	283	Bill Parcells
1984§	9	7	0	.563	299	301	Bill Parcells
1983	3	12	1	.219	267	347	Bill Parcells
1982	4	5	0	.444	164	160	Ray Perkins
1981§	9	7	0	.563	295	257	Ray Perkins
1980	4	12	0	.250	249	425	Ray Perkins
1979	6	10	0	.375	237	323	Ray Perkins
1978	6	10	0	.375	264	298	John McVay
1977	5	9	0	.357	181	265	John McVay
1976	3	11	0	.214	170	250	Bill Arnsparger, John McVay
1975	5	9	0	.357	216	306	Bill Arnsparger
1974	2	12	0	.143	195	299	Bill Arnsparger
1973	2	11	1	.179	226	362	Alex Webster
1972	8	6	0	.571	331	247	Alex Webster
1971	4	10	0	.286	228	362	Alex Webster
1970	9	5	0	.643	301	270	Alex Webster
1969	6	8	0	.429	264	298	Alex Webster
1968	7	7	0	.500	294	325	Allie Sherman
1967	7	7	0	.500	369	379	Allie Sherman
1966	1	12	1	.077	263	501	Allie Sherman
1965	7	7	0	.500	270	338	Allie Sherman
1964	2	10	2	.167	241	399	Allie Sherman
1963‡	11	3	0	.786	448	280	Allie Sherman
1962‡	12	2	0	.857	398	283	Allie Sherman
1961‡	10	3	1	.769	368	220	Allie Sherman
1960	6	4	2	.600	271	261	Jim Lee Howell
1959‡	10	2	0	.833	284	170	Jim Lee Howell
1958‡	9	3	0	.750	246	183	Jim Lee Howell
1957	7	5	0	.583	254	211	Jim Lee Howell
1956*	8	3	1	.727	264	197	Jim Lee Howell
1955	6	5	1	.545	267	223	Jim Lee Howell
1954	7	5	0	.583	293	184	Jim Lee Howell
1953	3	9	0	.250	179	277	Steve Owen
1952	7	5	0	.583	234	231	Steve Owen
1951	9	2	1	.818	254	161	Steve Owen
1950	10	2	0	.833	268	150	Steve Owen
1949	6	6	0	.500	287	298	Steve Owen
1948	4	8	0	.333	297	388	Steve Owen
1947	2	8	2	.200	190	309	Steve Owen
1946†	7	3	1	.700	236	162	Steve Owen
1945	3	6	1	.333	179	198	Steve Owen
1944†	8	1	1	.889	206	75	Steve Owen
1943	6	3	1	.667	197	170	Steve Owen
1942	5	5	1	.500	155	139	Steve Owen
1941†	8	3	0	.727	238	114	Steve Owen
1940	6	4	1	.600	131	133	Steve Owen
1939†	9	1	1	.900	168	85	Steve Owen
1938*	8	2	1	.800	194	79	Steve Owen
1937	6	3	2	.667	128	109	Steve Owen
1936	5	6	1	.455	115	163	Steve Owen
1935†	9	3	0	.750	180	96	Steve Owen
1934*	8	5	0	.615	147	107	Steve Owen
1933†	11	3	0	.786	244	101	Steve Owen
1932	4	6	2	.400	93	113	Steve Owen
1931	7	6	1	.538	154	100	Steve Owen
1930	13	4	0	.765	308	98	LeRoy Andrews
1929	13	1	1	.929	312	86	LeRoy Andrews
1928	4	7	2	.364	79	136	Earl Potteiger
1927*	11	1	1	.917	197	20	Earl Potteiger
1926	8	4	1	.667	147	51	Joe Alexander
1925	8	4	0	.667	122	67	Robert Folwell

*NFL champion.
†NFL Eastern Division champion.
‡NFL Eastern Conference champion.
§NFC wild-card team.
xSuper Bowl champion.
yNFC Eastern Division champion.

NEW YORK JETS (1960-89)

Year	W.	L.	T.	Pct.	Pts.	Opp.	Head Coach
1989	4	12	0	.250	253	411	Joe Walton
1988	8	7	1	.531	372	354	Joe Walton
1987	6	9	0	.400	334	360	Joe Walton
1986‡	10	6	0	.625	364	386	Joe Walton
1985‡	11	5	0	.688	393	264	Joe Walton
1984	7	9	0	.438	332	364	Joe Walton
1983	7	9	0	.438	313	331	Joe Walton
1982§	6	3	0	.667	245	166	Walt Michaels
1981‡	10	5	1	.656	355	287	Walt Michaels

Year	W.	L.	T.	Pct.	Pts.	Opp.	Head Coach
1980	4	12	0	.250	302	395	Walt Michaels
1979	8	8	0	.500	337	383	Walt Michaels
1978	8	8	0	.500	359	364	Walt Michaels
1977	3	11	0	.214	191	300	Walt Michaels
1976	3	11	0	.214	169	383	Lou Holtz, Mike Holovak
1975	3	11	0	.214	256	433	Charley Winner, Ken Shipp
1974	7	7	0	.500	279	300	Charley Winner
1973	4	10	0	.286	240	306	Weeb Ewbank
1972	7	7	0	.500	367	324	Weeb Ewbank
1971	6	8	0	.429	212	299	Weeb Ewbank
1970	4	10	0	.286	255	286	Weeb Ewbank
1969†	10	4	0	.714	353	269	Weeb Ewbank
1968*	11	3	0	.786	419	280	Weeb Ewbank
1967	8	5	1	.615	371	329	Weeb Ewbank
1966	6	6	2	.500	322	312	Weeb Ewbank
1965	5	8	1	.385	285	303	Weeb Ewbank
1964	5	8	1	.385	278	315	Weeb Ewbank
1963	5	8	1	.385	249	399	Weeb Ewbank

New York Titans

Year	W.	L.	T.	Pct.	Pts.	Opp.	Head Coach
1962	5	9	0	.357	278	423	Clyde (Bulldog) Turner
1961	7	7	0	.500	301	390	Sammy Baugh
1960	7	7	0	.500	382	399	Sammy Baugh

*Super Bowl champion.
†AFL Eastern Division champion.
‡AFC wild-card team.
§AFC playoff qualifier.

PHILADELPHIA EAGLES (1933-89)

Year	W.	L.	T.	Pct.	Pts.	Opp.	Head Coach
1989‡	11	5	0	.688	342	274	Buddy Ryan
1988x	10	6	0	.625	379	319	Buddy Ryan
1987	7	8	0	.467	337	380	Buddy Ryan
1986	5	10	1	.344	256	312	Buddy Ryan
1985	7	9	0	.438	286	310	Marion Campbell, Fred Bruney
1984	6	9	1	.406	278	320	Marion Campbell
1983	5	11	0	.313	233	322	Marion Campbell
1982	3	6	0	.333	191	195	Dick Vermeil
1981‡	10	6	0	.625	368	221	Dick Vermeil
1980§	12	4	0	.750	384	222	Dick Vermeil
1979‡	11	5	0	.688	339	282	Dick Vermeil
1978‡	9	7	0	.563	270	250	Dick Vermeil
1977	5	9	0	.357	220	207	Dick Vermeil
1976	4	10	0	.286	165	286	Dick Vermeil
1975	4	10	0	.286	225	302	Mike McCormack
1974	7	7	0	.500	242	217	Mike McCormack
1973	5	8	1	.393	310	393	Mike McCormack
1972	2	11	1	.179	145	352	Ed Khayat
1971	6	7	1	.462	221	302	Jerry Williams, Ed Khayat
1970	3	10	1	.231	241	332	Jerry Williams
1969	4	9	1	.308	279	377	Jerry Williams
1968	2	12	0	.143	202	351	Joe Kuharich
1967	6	7	1	.462	351	409	Joe Kuharich
1966	9	5	0	.643	326	340	Joe Kuharich
1965	5	9	0	.357	363	359	Joe Kuharich
1964	6	8	0	.429	312	313	Joe Kuharich
1963	2	10	2	.167	242	381	Nick Skorich
1962	3	10	1	.231	282	356	Nick Skorich
1961	10	4	0	.714	361	297	Nick Skorich
1960†	10	2	0	.833	321	246	Lawrence (Buck) Shaw
1959	7	5	0	.583	268	278	Lawrence (Buck) Shaw
1958	2	9	1	.182	235	306	Lawrence (Buck) Shaw
1957	4	8	0	.333	173	230	Hugh Devore
1956	3	8	1	.273	143	215	Hugh Devore
1955	4	7	1	.364	248	231	Jim Trimble
1954	7	4	1	.636	284	230	Jim Trimble
1953	7	4	1	.636	352	215	Jim Trimble
1952	7	5	0	.583	252	271	Jim Trimble
1951	4	8	0	.333	234	264	Alvin (Bo) McMillin, Wayne Millner
1950	6	6	0	.500	254	141	Earle (Greasy) Neale
1949†	11	1	0	.917	364	134	Earle (Greasy) Neale
1948†	9	2	1	.818	376	156	Earle (Greasy) Neale
1947*	8	4	0	.667	308	242	Earle (Greasy) Neale
1946	6	5	0	.545	231	220	Earle (Greasy) Neale
1945	7	3	0	.700	272	133	Earle (Greasy) Neale
1944	7	1	2	.875	267	131	Earle (Greasy) Neale

Phil-Pitt Steagles
(Combined Philadelphia and Pittsburgh squads.)

Year	W.	L.	T.	Pct.	Pts.	Opp.	Head Coach
1943	5	4	1	.556	225	230	Greasy Neale, Walt Kiesling (co-coaches)

Philadelphia Eagles

Year	W.	L.	T.	Pct.	Pts.	Opp.	Head Coach
1942	2	9	0	.182	134	239	Earle (Greasy) Neale
1941	2	8	1	.200	119	218	Earle (Greasy) Neale
1940	1	10	0	.091	111	211	Bert Bell
1939	1	9	1	.100	105	200	Bert Bell
1938	5	6	0	.455	154	164	Bert Bell
1937	2	8	1	.200	86	177	Bert Bell
1936	1	11	0	.083	51	206	Bert Bell
1935	2	9	0	.182	60	179	Lud Wray
1934	4	7	0	.364	127	85	Lud Wray
1933	3	5	1	.375	77	158	Lud Wray

*NFL Eastern Division champion.
†NFL champion.
‡NFC wild-card team.
§NFC champion.
xNFC Eastern Division champion.

PHOENIX CARDINALS (1920-89)

Year	W.	L.	T.	Pct.	Pts.	Opp.	Head Coach
1989	5	11	0	.313	258	377	Gene Stallings, Hank Kuhlmann
1988	7	9	0	.438	344	398	Gene Stallings

St. Louis Cardinals

Year	W.	L.	T.	Pct.	Pts.	Opp.	Head Coach
1987	7	8	0	.467	362	368	Gene Stallings
1986	4	11	1	.281	218	351	Gene Stallings
1985	5	11	0	.313	278	414	Jim Hanifan
1984	9	7	0	.563	423	345	Jim Hanifan
1983	8	7	1	.531	374	428	Jim Hanifan
1982§	5	4	0	.556	135	170	Jim Hanifan
1981	7	9	0	.438	315	408	Jim Hanifan
1980	5	11	0	.313	299	350	Jim Hanifan
1979	5	11	0	.313	307	358	Bud Wilkinson, Larry Wilson
1978	6	10	0	.375	248	296	Bud Wilkinson
1977	7	7	0	.500	272	287	Don Coryell
1976	10	4	0	.714	309	267	Don Coryell
1975‡	11	3	0	.786	356	276	Don Coryell
1974‡	10	4	0	.714	285	218	Don Coryell
1973	4	9	1	.308	286	365	Don Coryell
1972	4	9	1	.308	193	303	Bob Hollway
1971	4	9	1	.308	231	279	Bob Hollway
1970	8	5	1	.615	325	228	Charley Winner
1969	4	9	1	.308	314	389	Charley Winner
1968	9	4	1	.692	325	289	Charley Winner
1967	6	7	1	.462	333	356	Charley Winner
1966	8	5	1	.615	264	265	Charley Winner
1965	5	9	0	.357	296	309	Wally Lemm
1964	9	3	2	.750	357	331	Wally Lemm
1963	9	5	0	.643	341	283	Wally Lemm
1962	4	9	1	.308	287	361	Wally Lemm
1961	7	7	0	.500	279	267	Frank (Pop) Ivy
1960	6	5	1	.545	288	230	Frank (Pop) Ivy

Chicago Cardinals

Year	W.	L.	T.	Pct.	Pts.	Opp.	Head Coach
1959	2	10	0	.167	234	324	Frank (Pop) Ivy
1958	2	9	1	.182	261	356	Frank (Pop) Ivy
1957	3	9	0	.250	200	299	Ray Richards
1956	7	5	0	.583	240	182	Ray Richards
1955	4	7	1	.364	224	252	Ray Richards
1954	2	10	0	.167	183	347	Joe Stydahar
1953	1	10	1	.091	190	337	Joe Stydahar
1952	4	8	0	.333	172	221	Joe Kuharich
1951	3	9	0	.250	210	287	Earl (Curly) Lambeau
1950	5	7	0	.417	233	287	Earl (Curly) Lambeau
1949	6	5	1	.545	360	301	Phil Handler, Buddy Parker (co-coaches)
1948†	11	1	0	.917	395	226	Jimmy Conzelman
1947*	9	3	0	.750	306	231	Jimmy Conzelman
1946	6	5	0	.545	260	198	Jimmy Conzelman
1945	1	9	0	.100	98	228	Phil Handler

Card-Pitt
(Combined Chicago Cardinals and Pittsburgh squads.)

Year	W.	L.	T.	Pct.	Pts.	Opp.	Head Coach
1944	0	10	0	.000	108	328	Phil Handler, Walt Kiesling (co-coaches)

Chicago Cardinals

Year	W.	L.	T.	Pct.	Pts.	Opp.	Head Coach
1943	0	10	0	.000	95	238	Phil Handler
1942	3	8	0	.273	98	209	Jimmy Conzelman
1941	3	7	1	.300	127	197	Jimmy Conzelman
1940	2	7	2	.222	139	222	Jimmy Conzelman
1939	1	10	0	.091	84	254	Ernie Nevers
1938	2	9	0	.182	111	168	Milan Creighton
1937	5	5	1	.500	135	165	Milan Creighton
1936	3	8	1	.273	74	143	Milan Creighton
1935	6	4	2	.600	99	97	Milan Creighton
1934	5	6	0	.455	80	84	Paul Schissler
1933	1	9	1	.100	52	101	Paul Schissler
1932	2	6	2	.250			Jack Chevigny
1931	5	4	0	.556			LeRoy Andrews, Ernie Nevers
1930	5	6	2	.455			Ernie Nevers
1929	6	6	1	.500			Ernie Nevers
1928	1	5	0	.167			Guy Chamberlin
1927	3	7	1	.300			Fred Gillies
1926	5	6	1	.455			Norman Barry
1925*	11	2	1	.846			Norman Barry
1924	5	4	1	.556			Arnold Horween
1923	8	4	0	.667			Arnold Horween
1922	8	3	0	.727			John (Paddy) Driscoll
1921	2	3	2	.400			John (Paddy) Driscoll
1920	5	2	1	.714			Marshall Smith

*NFL champion.
†NFL Western Division champion.
‡NFC Eastern Division champion.
§NFC playoff qualifier.

PITTSBURGH STEELERS (1933-89)

Year	W.	L.	T.	Pct.	Pts.	Opp.	Head Coach
1989†	9	7	0	.563	265	326	Chuck Noll
1988	5	11	0	.313	336	421	Chuck Noll
1987	8	7	0	.533	285	299	Chuck Noll
1986	6	10	0	.375	307	336	Chuck Noll
1985	7	9	0	.438	379	355	Chuck Noll
1984*	9	7	0	.563	387	310	Chuck Noll
1983*	10	6	0	.625	355	303	Chuck Noll
1982§	6	3	0	.667	204	146	Chuck Noll
1981	8	8	0	.500	356	297	Chuck Noll
1980	9	7	0	.563	352	313	Chuck Noll
1979‡	12	4	0	.750	416	262	Chuck Noll
1978‡	14	2	0	.875	356	195	Chuck Noll
1977*	9	5	0	.643	283	243	Chuck Noll
1976*	10	4	0	.714	342	138	Chuck Noll
1975‡	12	2	0	.857	373	162	Chuck Noll
1974‡	10	3	1	.750	305	189	Chuck Noll
1973†	10	4	0	.714	347	210	Chuck Noll
1972*	11	3	0	.786	343	175	Chuck Noll
1971	6	8	0	.429	246	292	Chuck Noll
1970	5	9	0	.357	210	272	Chuck Noll
1969	1	13	0	.071	218	404	Chuck Noll
1968	2	11	1	.154	244	397	Bill Austin
1967	4	9	1	.308	281	320	Bill Austin
1966	5	8	1	.385	316	347	Bill Austin
1965	2	12	0	.143	202	397	Mike Nixon
1964	5	9	0	.357	253	315	Buddy Parker
1963	7	4	3	.636	321	295	Buddy Parker
1962	9	5	0	.643	312	363	Buddy Parker
1961	6	8	0	.429	295	287	Buddy Parker
1960	5	6	1	.455	240	275	Buddy Parker
1959	6	5	1	.545	257	216	Buddy Parker
1958	7	4	1	.636	261	230	Buddy Parker
1957	6	6	0	.500	161	178	Buddy Parker
1956	5	7	0	.417	217	250	Walt Kiesling
1955	4	8	0	.333	195	285	Walt Kiesling
1954	5	7	0	.417	219	263	Walt Kiesling
1953	6	6	0	.500	211	263	Joe Bach
1952	5	7	0	.417	300	273	Joe Bach
1951	4	7	1	.364	183	235	John Michelosen
1950	6	6	0	.500	180	195	John Michelosen
1949	6	5	1	.545	224	214	John Michelosen
1948	4	8	0	.333	200	243	John Michelosen
1947	8	4	0	.667	240	259	Jock Sutherland
1946	5	5	1	.500	136	117	Jock Sutherland
1945	2	8	0	.200	79	220	Jim Leonard

Card-Pitt
(Combined Pittsburgh and Chicago Cardinals squads.)

Year	W.	L.	T.	Pct.	Pts.	Opp.	Head Coach
1944	0	10	0	.000	108	328	Walt Kiesling, Phil Handler (co-coaches)

Phil-Pitt Steagles
(Combined Pittsburgh and Philadelphia squads.)

Year	W.	L.	T.	Pct.	Pts.	Opp.	Head Coach
1943	5	4	1	.556	225	230	Walt Kiesling, Greasy Neale (co-coaches)

Pittsburgh Steelers

Year	W.	L.	T.	Pct.	Pts.	Opp.	Head Coach
1942	7	4	0	.636	167	119	Walt Kiesling
1941	1	9	1	.100	103	276	Bert Bell, Aldo (Buff) Donelli, Walt Kiesling

Pittsburgh Pirates

Year	W.	L.	T.	Pct.	Pts.	Opp.	Head Coach
1940	2	7	2	.222	60	178	Walt Kiesling
1939	1	9	1	.100	114	216	Johnny Blood (McNally), Walt Kiesling
1938	2	9	0	.182	79	169	Johnny Blood (McNally)
1937	4	7	0	.364	122	145	Johnny Blood (McNally)
1936	6	6	0	.500	98	187	Joe Bach
1935	4	8	0	.333	100	209	Joe Bach
1934	2	10	0	.167	51	206	Luby DiMelio
1933	3	6	2	.333	67	208	Forrest Douds

*AFC Central Division champion.
†AFC wild-card team.
‡Super Bowl champion.
§AFC playoff qualifier.

SAN DIEGO CHARGERS (1960-89)

Year	W.	L.	T.	Pct.	Pts.	Opp.	Head Coach
1989	6	10	0	.375	266	290	Dan Henning
1988	6	10	0	.375	231	332	Al Saunders
1987	8	7	0	.533	253	317	Al Saunders
1986	4	12	0	.250	335	396	Don Coryell, Al Saunders
1985	8	8	0	.500	467	435	Don Coryell
1984	7	9	0	.438	394	413	Don Coryell
1983	6	10	0	.375	358	462	Don Coryell
1982§	6	3	0	.667	288	221	Don Coryell
1981‡	10	6	0	.625	478	390	Don Coryell
1980‡	11	5	0	.688	418	327	Don Coryell
1979‡	12	4	0	.750	411	246	Don Coryell
1978	9	7	0	.563	355	309	Tommy Prothro, Don Coryell
1977	7	7	0	.500	222	205	Tommy Prothro
1976	6	8	0	.429	248	285	Tommy Prothro
1975	2	12	0	.143	189	345	Tommy Prothro
1974	5	9	0	.357	212	285	Tommy Prothro
1973	2	11	1	.179	188	386	Harland Svare, Ron Waller
1972	4	9	1	.308	264	344	Harland Svare
1971	6	8	0	.429	311	341	Sid Gillman, Harland Svare
1970	5	6	3	.455	282	278	Charlie Waller
1969	8	6	0	.571	288	276	Sid Gillman, Charlie Waller
1968	9	5	0	.643	382	310	Sid Gillman
1967	8	5	1	.615	360	352	Sid Gillman
1966	7	6	1	.538	335	284	Sid Gillman
1965*	9	2	3	.818	340	227	Sid Gillman
1964*	8	5	1	.615	341	300	Sid Gillman
1963†	11	3	0	.786	399	256	Sid Gillman
1962	4	10	0	.286	314	392	Sid Gillman
1961*	12	2	0	.857	396	219	Sid Gillman

Los Angeles Chargers

Year	W.	L.	T.	Pct.	Pts.	Opp.	Head Coach
1960*	10	4	0	.714	373	336	Sid Gillman

*AFL Western Division champion.
†AFL champion.
‡AFC Western Division champion.
§AFC playoff qualifier.

SAN FRANCISCO 49ers (1946-89)

Year	W.	L.	T.	Pct.	Pts.	Opp.	Head Coach
1989†	14	2	0	.875	442	253	George Seifert
1988†	10	6	0	.625	369	294	Bill Walsh
1987*	13	2	0	.867	459	253	Bill Walsh
1986*	10	5	1	.656	374	247	Bill Walsh
1985‡	10	6	0	.625	411	263	Bill Walsh
1984†	15	1	0	.938	475	227	Bill Walsh
1983*	10	6	0	.625	432	293	Bill Walsh
1982	3	6	0	.333	209	206	Bill Walsh
1981†	13	3	0	.813	357	250	Bill Walsh
1980	6	10	0	.375	320	415	Bill Walsh
1979	2	14	0	.125	308	416	Bill Walsh
1978	2	14	0	.125	219	350	Pete McCulley, Fred O'Connor
1977	5	9	0	.357	220	260	Ken Meyer
1976	8	6	0	.571	270	190	Monte Clark
1975	5	9	0	.357	255	286	Dick Nolan
1974	6	8	0	.429	226	236	Dick Nolan
1973	5	9	0	.357	262	319	Dick Nolan
1972*	8	5	1	.607	353	249	Dick Nolan
1971*	9	5	0	.643	300	216	Dick Nolan
1970*	10	3	1	.769	352	267	Dick Nolan
1969	4	8	2	.333	277	319	Dick Nolan
1968	7	6	1	.538	303	310	Dick Nolan
1967	7	7	0	.500	273	337	Jack Christiansen
1966	6	6	2	.500	320	325	Jack Christiansen
1965	7	6	1	.538	421	402	Jack Christiansen
1964	4	10	0	.286	236	330	Jack Christiansen
1963	2	12	0	.143	198	391	Howard (Red) Hickey, Jack Christiansen
1962	6	8	0	.429	282	331	Howard (Red) Hickey
1961	7	6	1	.538	346	272	Howard (Red) Hickey
1960	7	5	0	.583	208	205	Howard (Red) Hickey
1959	7	5	0	.583	255	237	Howard (Red) Hickey
1958	6	6	0	.500	257	324	Frankie Albert
1957	8	4	0	.667	260	264	Frankie Albert
1956	5	6	1	.455	233	284	Frankie Albert
1955	4	8	0	.333	216	298	Norman (Red) Strader
1954	7	4	1	.636	313	251	Lawrence (Buck) Shaw
1953	9	3	0	.750	372	237	Lawrence (Buck) Shaw
1952	7	5	0	.583	285	221	Lawrence (Buck) Shaw
1951	7	4	1	.636	255	205	Lawrence (Buck) Shaw
1950	3	9	0	.250	213	300	Lawrence (Buck) Shaw
1949	9	3	0	.750	416	227	Lawrence (Buck) Shaw
1948	12	2	0	.857	495	248	Lawrence (Buck) Shaw
1947	8	4	2	.667	327	264	Lawrence (Buck) Shaw
1946	9	5	0	.643	307	189	Lawrence (Buck) Shaw

*NFC Western Division champion.
†Super Bowl champion.
‡NFC wild-card team.

SEATTLE SEAHAWKS (1976-89)

Year	W.	L.	T.	Pct.	Pts.	Opp.	Head Coach
1989	7	9	0	.438	241	327	Chuck Knox
1988†	9	7	0	.563	339	329	Chuck Knox
1987*	9	6	0	.600	371	314	Chuck Knox
1986	10	6	0	.625	366	293	Chuck Knox
1985	8	8	0	.500	349	313	Chuck Knox
1984*	12	4	0	.750	418	282	Chuck Knox
1983*	9	7	0	.562	403	397	Chuck Knox
1982	4	5	0	.444	127	147	Jack Patera, Mike McCormack
1981	6	10	0	.375	322	388	Jack Patera
1980	4	12	0	.250	291	408	Jack Patera
1979	9	7	0	.563	378	372	Jack Patera
1978	9	7	0	.563	345	358	Jack Patera
1977	5	9	0	.357	282	373	Jack Patera
1976	2	12	0	.143	229	429	Jack Patera

*AFC wild-card team.
†AFC Western Division champion.

TAMPA BAY BUCCANEERS (1976-89)

Year	W.	L.	T.	Pct.	Pts.	Opp.	Head Coach
1989	5	11	0	.313	320	419	Ray Perkins
1988	5	11	0	.313	261	350	Ray Perkins
1987	4	11	0	.267	286	360	Ray Perkins
1986	2	14	0	.125	239	473	Leeman Bennett
1985	2	14	0	.125	294	448	Leeman Bennett
1984	6	10	0	.375	335	380	John McKay
1983	2	14	0	.125	241	380	John McKay
1982†	5	4	0	.556	158	178	John McKay
1981*	9	7	0	.563	315	268	John McKay
1980	5	10	1	.344	271	341	John McKay
1979*	10	6	0	.625	273	237	John McKay
1978	5	11	0	.313	241	259	John McKay
1977	2	12	0	.143	103	223	John McKay
1976	0	14	0	.000	125	412	John McKay

*NFC Central Division champion.
†NFC playoff qualifier.

WASHINGTON REDSKINS (1932-89)

Year	W.	L.	T.	Pct.	Pts.	Opp.	Head Coach
1989	10	6	0	.625	386	308	Joe Gibbs
1988	7	9	0	.438	345	387	Joe Gibbs
1987x	11	4	0	.733	379	285	Joe Gibbs
1986‡	12	4	0	.750	368	296	Joe Gibbs
1985	10	6	0	.625	297	312	Joe Gibbs
1984y	11	5	0	.688	426	310	Joe Gibbs
1983§	14	2	0	.875	541	332	Joe Gibbs
1982x	8	1	0	.889	190	128	Joe Gibbs
1981	8	8	0	.500	347	349	Joe Gibbs
1980	6	10	0	.375	261	293	Jack Pardee
1979	10	6	0	.625	348	295	Jack Pardee
1978	8	8	0	.500	273	283	Jack Pardee
1977	9	5	0	.643	196	189	George Allen
1976‡	10	4	0	.714	291	217	George Allen
1975	8	6	0	.571	325	276	George Allen
1974‡	10	4	0	.714	320	196	George Allen
1973‡	10	4	0	.714	325	198	George Allen
1972§	11	3	0	.786	336	218	George Allen
1971‡	9	4	1	.692	276	190	George Allen
1970	6	8	0	.429	297	314	Bill Austin
1969	7	5	2	.583	307	319	Vince Lombardi
1968	5	9	0	.357	249	358	Otto Graham
1967	5	6	3	.455	347	353	Otto Graham
1966	7	7	0	.500	351	355	Otto Graham
1965	6	8	0	.429	257	301	Bill McPeak
1964	6	8	0	.429	307	305	Bill McPeak
1963	3	11	0	.214	279	398	Bill McPeak
1962	5	7	2	.417	305	376	Bill McPeak
1961	1	12	1	.077	174	392	Bill McPeak
1960	1	9	2	.100	178	309	Mike Nixon
1959	3	9	0	.250	185	350	Mike Nixon
1958	4	7	1	.364	214	268	Joe Kuharich
1957	5	6	1	.455	251	230	Joe Kuharich
1956	6	6	0	.500	183	225	Joe Kuharich
1955	8	4	0	.667	246	222	Joe Kuharich
1954	3	9	0	.250	207	432	Joe Kuharich
1953	6	5	1	.545	208	215	Earl (Curly) Lambeau
1952	4	8	0	.333	240	287	Earl (Curly) Lambeau
1951	5	7	0	.417	183	296	Herman Ball, Dick Todd
1950	3	9	0	.250	232	326	Herman Ball
1949	4	7	1	.364	268	339	John Whelchel, Herman Ball
1948	7	5	0	.583	291	287	Glen (Turk) Edwards
1947	4	8	0	.333	295	367	Glen (Turk) Edwards
1946	5	5	1	.500	171	191	Glen (Turk) Edwards
1945*	8	2	0	.800	209	121	Dudley DeGroot
1944	6	3	1	.667	169	180	Dudley DeGroot
1943*	6	3	1	.667	229	137	Arthur Bergman
1942†	10	1	0	.909	227	102	Ray Flaherty
1941	6	5	0	.545	176	174	Ray Flaherty
1940*	9	2	0	.818	245	142	Ray Flaherty
1939	8	2	1	.800	242	94	Ray Flaherty
1938	6	3	2	.667	148	154	Ray Flaherty
1937†	8	3	0	.727	195	120	Ray Flaherty

Coach Mike Ditka's Chicago Bears endured a 6-10 season in 1989 and failed to win the NFC Central Division title for the first time since 1983.

Boston Redskins

Year	W.	L.	T.	Pct.	Pts.	Opp.	Head Coach
1936*	7	5	0	.583	149	110	Ray Flaherty
1935	2	8	1	.200	65	123	Eddie Casey
1934	6	6	0	.500	107	94	William Dietz
1933	5	5	2	.500	103	97	William Dietz

*NFL Eastern Division champion.
†NFL champion.

Boston Braves

Year	W.	L.	T.	Pct.	Pts.	Opp.	Head Coach
1932	4	4	2	.500	55	79	Lud Wray

‡NFC wild-card team.
§NFC champion.
xSuper Bowl champion.
yNFC Eastern Division champion.

ALL-TIME SERIES RECORDS

Listed below are the all-time regular-season series records for all 28 NFL teams. The date to the right indicates the last time the two teams met in regular-season play. Although many current teams have played in different cities (in parentheses) and with different nicknames, for the purpose of this section franchises are recognized to have started in the following years: Atlanta, 1966; Buffalo, 1960; Chicago, 1920 (Decatur); Cincinnati, 1968; Cleveland, 1950; Dallas, 1960; Denver, 1960; Detroit, 1934; Green Bay, 1921; Houston, 1960; Indianapolis, 1953 (Baltimore); Kansas City, 1960 (Dallas); Los Angeles Raiders, 1960 (Oakland); Los Angeles Rams, 1946; Miami, 1966; Minnesota, 1961; New England, 1960 (Boston); New Orleans, 1967; New York Giants, 1925; New York Jets, 1960; Philadelphia, 1933; Phoenix, 1920 (Chicago, St. Louis); Pittsburgh, 1933; San Diego, 1960 (Los Angeles); San Francisco, 1950; Seattle, 1976; Tampa Bay, 1976; Washington, 1937. American Football League results (1960-69) are recognized; All-America Football Conference results (1946-49) are not.

Atlanta vs. Buffalo (1989)
(Atlanta leads series, 3-2)

Atlanta vs. Chicago (1986)
(Atlanta leads series, 9-6)

Atlanta vs. Cincinnati (1987)
(Cincinnati leads series, 5-1)

Atlanta vs. Cleveland (1987)
(Cleveland leads series, 7-1)

Atlanta vs. Dallas (1989)
(Dallas leads series, 7-4)

Atlanta vs. Denver (1988)
(Denver leads series, 4-3)

Atlanta vs. Detroit (1989)
(Detroit leads series, 15-5)

Atlanta vs. Green Bay (1989)
(Green Bay leads series, 9-7)

Atlanta vs. Houston (1987)
(Atlanta leads series, 4-2)

Atlanta vs. Indianapolis (1989)
(Indianapolis leads series, 10-0)

Atlanta vs. Kansas City (1985)
(Kansas City leads series, 2-0)

Atlanta vs. Los Angeles Raiders (1988)
(Raiders leads series, 4-2)

Atlanta vs. Los Angeles Rams (1989)
(Rams lead series, 34-10-2)

Atlanta vs. Miami (1986)
(Miami leads series, 4-1)

Atlanta vs. Minnesota (1989)
(Minnesota leads series, 11-6)

Atlanta vs. New England (1989)
(Series tied, 3-3)

Atlanta vs. New Orleans (1989)
(Atlanta leads series, 24-17)

Atlanta vs. New York Giants (1988)
(Series tied, 6-6)

Atlanta vs. New York Jets (1989)
(Jets lead series, 3-2)

Atlanta vs. Philadelphia (1988)
(Philadelphia leads series, 7-6-1)

Atlanta vs. Phoenix (1989)
(Phoenix leads series, 8-4)

Atlanta vs. Pittsburgh (1987)
(Pittsburgh leads series, 7-1)

Atlanta vs. San Diego (1988)
(Atlanta leads series, 2-1)

Atlanta vs. San Francisco (1989)
(San Francisco leads series, 27-18-1)

Atlanta vs. Seattle (1988)
(Seattle leads series, 4-0)

Atlanta vs. Tampa Bay (1988)
(Series tied, 4-4)

Atlanta vs. Washington (1989)
(Washington leads series, 10-3-1)

Buffalo vs. Chicago (1988)
(Chicago leads series, 3-1)

Buffalo vs. Cincinnati (1989)
(Cincinnati leads series, 10-6)

Buffalo vs. Cleveland (1987)
(Cleveland leads series, 7-2)

Buffalo vs. Dallas (1984)
(Dallas leads series, 3-1)

Buffalo vs. Denver (1989)
(Buffalo leads series, 14-10-1)

Buffalo vs. Detroit (1979)
(Series tied, 1-1-1)

Buffalo vs. Green Bay (1988)
(Buffalo leads series, 3-1)

Buffalo vs. Houston (1989)
(Houston leads series, 18-11)

Buffalo vs. Indianapolis (1989)
(Series tied, 19-19-1)

Buffalo vs. Kansas City (1986)
(Buffalo leads series, 15-11-1)

Buffalo vs. Los Angeles Raiders (1988)
(Raiders lead series, 13-12)

Buffalo vs. Los Angeles Rams (1989)
(Rams lead series, 3-2)

Buffalo vs. Miami (1989)
(Miami leads series, 34-13-1)

Buffalo vs. Minnesota (1988)
(Minnesota leads series, 4-2)

Buffalo vs. New England (1989)
(New England leads series, 33-26-1)

Buffalo vs. New Orleans (1989)
(Series tied, 2-2)

Buffalo vs. New York Giants (1987)
(Series tied, 2-2)

Buffalo vs. New York Jets (1989)
(Buffalo leads series, 31-28)

Buffalo vs. Philadelphia (1987)
(Philadelphia leads series, 4-1)

Buffalo vs. Phoenix (1986)
(Phoenix leads series, 3-2)

Buffalo vs. Pittsburgh (1988)
(Series tied, 5-5)

Buffalo vs. San Diego (1985)
(San Diego leads series, 16-7-2)

Buffalo vs. San Francisco (1989)
(Series tied, 2-2)

Buffalo vs. Seattle (1989)
(Seattle leads series, 3-1)

Buffalo vs. Tampa Bay (1988)
(Tampa Bay leads series, 4-1)

Buffalo vs. Washington (1987)
(Washington leads series, 3-2)

Chicago vs. Cincinnati (1989)
(Series tied, 2-2)

Chicago vs. Cleveland (1989)
(Cleveland leads series, 7-3)

Chicago vs. Dallas (1988)
(Dallas leads series, 7-6)

Chicago vs. Denver (1987)
(Series tied, 4-4)

Chicago vs. Detroit (1989)
(Chicago leads series, 65-43-3)

Chicago vs. Green Bay (1989)
(Chicago leads series, 76-57-6)

Chicago vs. Houston (1989)
(Houston leads series, 3-2)

Chicago vs. Indianapolis (1988)
(Indianapolis leads series, 21-15)

Chicago vs. Kansas City (1987)
(Chicago leads series, 3-1)

Chicago vs. Los Angeles Raiders (1987)
(Series tied, 3-3)

Chicago vs. Los Angeles Rams (1989)
(Chicago leads series, 32-23-3)

Chicago vs. Miami (1988)
(Miami leads series, 4-1)

Chicago vs. Minnesota (1989)
(Minnesota leads series, 29-26-2)

Chicago vs. New England (1988)
(New England leads series, 3-2)

Chicago vs. New Orleans (1987)
(Chicago leads series, 8-4)

Chicago vs. New York Giants (1987)
(Chicago leads series, 23-14-2)

Chicago vs. New York Jets (1985)
(Chicago leads series, 2-1)

Chicago vs. Philadelphia (1989)
(Chicago leads series, 23-3-1)

Chicago vs. Phoenix (1984)
(Chicago leads series, 52-25-6)

Chicago vs. Pittsburgh (1989)
(Chicago leads series, 18-4-1)

Chicago vs. San Diego (1984)
(San Diego leads series, 4-1)

Chicago vs. San Francisco (1989)
(Chicago leads series, 25-24-1)

Chicago vs. Seattle (1987)
(Seattle leads series, 4-1)

Chicago vs. Tampa Bay (1989)
(Chicago leads series, 18-6)

Chicago vs. Washington (1989)
(Chicago leads series, 14-9)

Cincinnati vs. Cleveland (1989)
(Cincinnati leads series, 20-19)

Cincinnati vs. Dallas (1988)
(Series tied, 2-2)

Cincinnati vs. Denver (1986)
(Denver leads series, 9-6)

Cincinnati vs. Detroit (1989)
(Cincinnati leads series, 3-2)

Cincinnati vs. Green Bay (1986)
(Cincinnati leads series, 4-2)

Cincinnati vs. Houston (1989)
(Cincinnati leads series, 23-18-1)

Cincinnati vs. Indianapolis (1989)
(Indianapolis leads series, 6-5)

Cincinnati vs. Kansas City (1989)
(Kansas City leads series, 10-9)

Cincinnati vs. Los Angeles Raiders (1989)
(Raiders lead series, 12-5)

Cincinnati vs. Los Angeles Rams (1984)
(Cincinnati leads series, 3-2)

Cincinnati vs. Miami (1989)
(Miami leads series, 9-3)

Cincinnati vs. Minnesota (1989)
(Series tied, 3-3)

Cincinnati vs. New England (1988)
(New England leads series, 7-4)

Cincinnati vs. New Orleans (1987)
(Series tied, 3-3)

Cincinnati vs. New York Giants (1985)
(Cincinnati leads series, 3-0)

Cincinnati vs. New York Jets (1988)
(Jets lead series, 7-5)

Cincinnati vs. Philadelphia (1988)
(Cincinnati leads series, 5-0)

Cincinnati vs. Phoenix (1988)
(Cincinnati leads series, 3-1)

Cincinnati vs. Pittsburgh (1989)
(Pittsburgh leads series, 20-19)

Cincinnati vs. San Diego (1988)
(San Diego leads series, 11-7)

Cincinnati vs. San Francisco (1987)
(San Francisco leads series, 4-1)

Cincinnati vs. Seattle (1989)
(Cincinnati leads series, 5-3)

Cincinnati vs. Tampa Bay (1989)
(Cincinnati leads series, 3-1)

Cincinnati vs. Washington (1988)
(Washington leads series, 3-2)

Cleveland vs. Dallas (1988)
(Cleveland leads series, 14-8)

Cleveland vs. Denver (1989)
(Denver leads series, 9-4)

Cleveland vs. Detroit (1989)
(Detroit leads series, 10-3)

Cleveland vs. Green Bay (1986)
(Green Bay leads series, 7-5)

Cleveland vs. Houston (1989)
(Cleveland leads series, 26-13)

Cleveland vs. Indianapolis (1989)
(Cleveland leads series, 11-5)

Cleveland vs. Kansas City (1989)
(Cleveland leads series, 6-5-2)

Cleveland vs. Los Angeles Raiders (1987)
(Raiders lead series, 8-2)

Cleveland vs. Los Angeles Rams (1987)
(Cleveland leads series, 7-6)

Cleveland vs. Miami (1989)
(Cleveland leads series, 4-3)

Cleveland vs. Minnesota (1989)
(Minnesota leads series, 6-3)

Cleveland vs. New England (1987)
(Cleveland leads series, 7-2)

Cleveland vs. New Orleans (1987)
(Cleveland leads series, 8-2)

Cleveland vs. New York Giants (1985)
(Cleveland leads series, 25-15-2)

Cleveland vs. New York Jets (1989)
(Cleveland leads series, 8-4)

Cleveland vs. Philadelphia (1988)
(Cleveland leads series, 30-11-1)

Cleveland vs. Phoenix (1988)
(Cleveland leads series, 31-10-3)

Cleveland vs. Pittsburgh (1989)
(Cleveland leads series, 48-32)

Cleveland vs. San Diego (1987)
(San Diego leads series, 6-5-1)

Cleveland vs. San Francisco (1987)
(Cleveland leads series, 8-5)

Cleveland vs. Seattle (1989)
(Seattle leads series, 8-3)

Cleveland vs. Tampa Bay (1989)
(Cleveland leads series, 4-0)

Cleveland vs. Washington (1988)
(Cleveland leads series, 32-8-1)

Dallas vs. Denver (1986)
(Series tied, 2-2)

Dallas vs. Detroit (1987)
(Dallas leads series, 6-4)
Dallas vs. Green Bay (1989)
(Green Bay leads series, 9-3)
Dallas vs. Houston (1988)
(Dallas leads series, 4-2)
Dallas vs. Indianapolis (1984)
(Dallas leads series, 6-2)
Dallas vs. Kansas City (1989)
(Series tied, 2-2)
Dallas vs. Los Angeles Raiders (1987)
(Raiders lead series, 3-1)
Dallas vs. Los Angeles Rams (1989)
(Rams lead series, 8-7)
Dallas vs. Miami (1989)
(Miami leads series, 5-1)
Dallas vs. Minnesota (1988)
(Dallas leads series, 7-6)
Dallas vs. New England (1987)
(Dallas leads series, 6-0)
Dallas vs. New Orleans (1989)
(Dallas leads series, 11-3)
Dallas vs. New York Giants (1989)
(Dallas leads series, 35-18-2)
Dallas vs. New York Jets (1987)
(Dallas leads series, 4-0)
Dallas vs. Philadelphia (1989)
(Dallas leads series, 36-22)
Dallas vs. Phoenix (1989)
(Dallas leads series, 33-21-1)
Dallas vs. Pittsburgh (1988)
(Series tied, 11-11)
Dallas vs. San Diego (1986)
(Dallas leads series, 3-1)
Dallas vs. San Francisco (1989)
(San Francisco leads series, 8-5-1)
Dallas vs. Seattle (1986)
(Dallas leads series, 3-1)
Dallas vs. Tampa Bay (1983)
(Dallas leads series, 4-0)
Dallas vs. Washington (1989)
(Dallas leads series, 33-23-2)

Denver vs. Detroit (1987)
(Denver leads series, 4-2)
Denver vs. Green Bay (1987)
(Denver leads series, 3-1-1)
Denver vs. Houston (1987)
(Houston leads series, 18-10-1)
Denver vs. Indianapolis (1989)
(Denver leads series, 7-2)
Denver vs. Kansas City (1989)
(Kansas City leads series, 35-24)
Denver vs. Los Angeles Raiders (1989)
(Raiders lead series, 39-18-2)
Denver vs. Los Angeles Rams (1988)
(Series tied, 3-3)
Denver vs. Miami (1985)
(Miami leads series, 5-2-1)
Denver vs. Minnesota (1987)
(Minnesota leads series, 3-2)
Denver vs. New England (1988)
(Denver leads series, 14-12)
Denver vs. New Orleans (1988)
(Denver leads series, 4-1)
Denver vs. New York Giants (1989)
(Giants lead series, 3-2)
Denver vs. New York Jets (1986)
(Jets lead series, 11-10-1)
Denver vs. Philadelphia (1989)
(Philadelphia leads series, 4-2)
Denver vs. Phoenix (1989)
(Denver leads series, 2-0-1)

Denver vs. Pittsburgh (1989)
(Denver leads series, 8-4-1)
Denver vs. San Diego (1989)
(Denver leads series, 30-29-1)
Denver vs. San Francisco (1988)
(Denver lead series, 4-2)
Denver vs. Seattle (1989)
(Denver leads series, 15-10)
Denver vs. Tampa Bay (1981)
(Denver leads series, 2-0)
Denver vs. Washington (1989)
(Denver leads series, 3-2)

Detroit vs. Green Bay (1989)
(Green Bay leads series, 57-50-6)
Detroit vs. Houston (1989)
(Houston leads series, 3-2)
Detroit vs. Indianapolis (1985)
(Series tied, 17-17-2)
Detroit vs. Kansas City (1988)
(Series tied, 3-3)
Detroit vs. Los Angeles Raiders (1987)
(Raiders lead series, 4-2)
Detroit vs. Los Angeles Rams (1988)
(Rams lead series, 32-25-1)
Detroit vs. Miami (1985)
(Miami leads series, 2-1)
Detroit vs. Minnesota (1989)
(Minnesota leads series, 37-18-2)
Detroit vs. New England (1985)
(Series tied, 2-2)
Detroit vs. New Orleans (1989)
(Series tied, 5-5-1)
Detroit vs. New York Giants (1989)
(Detroit leads series, 13-11-1)
Detroit vs. New York Jets (1988)
(Jets lead series, 3-2)
Detroit vs. Philadelphia (1985)
(Detroit leads series, 11-9-2)
Detroit vs. Phoenix (1989)
(Detroit leads series, 26-14-3)
Detroit vs. Pittsburgh (1989)
(Detroit leads series, 13-10-1)
Detroit vs. San Diego (1984)
(Detroit leads series, 3-2)
Detroit vs. San Francisco (1988)
(Detroit leads series, 25-23-1)
Detroit vs. Seattle (1987)
(Seattle leads series, 3-1)
Detroit vs. Tampa Bay (1989)
(Detroit leads series, 13-11)
Detroit vs. Washington (1987)
(Washington leads series, 19-3)

Green Bay vs. Houston (1986)
(Houston leads series, 3-2)
Green Bay vs. Indianapolis (1988)
(Indianapolis leads series, 18-17-1)
Green Bay vs. Kansas City (1989)
(Kansas City leads series, 2-1-1)
Green Bay vs. Los Angeles Raiders (1987)
(Raiders lead series, 5-0)
Green Bay vs. Los Angeles Rams (1989)
(Rams lead series, 38-21-1)
Green Bay vs. Miami (1989)
(Miami leads series, 6-0)
Green Bay vs. Minnesota (1989)
(Green Bay leads series, 29-27-1)
Green Bay vs. New England (1988)
(Series tied, 2-2)
Green Bay vs. New Orleans (1989)
(Green Bay leads series, 11-4)

Green Bay vs. New York Giants (1987)
(Green Bay leads series, 21-19-2)
Green Bay vs. New York Jets (1985)
(Jets lead series, 4-1)
Green Bay vs. Philadelphia (1987)
(Green Bay leads series, 18-4)
Green Bay vs. Phoenix (1988)
(Green Bay leads series, 40-21-4)
Green Bay vs. Pittsburgh (1986)
(Green Bay leads series, 19-11)
Green Bay vs. San Diego (1984)
(Green Bay leads series, 3-1)
Green Bay vs. San Francisco (1989)
(San Francisco leads series, 24-21-1)
Green Bay vs. Seattle (1987)
(Green Bay leads series, 3-2)
Green Bay vs. Tampa Bay (1989)
(Green Bay leads series, 11-10-1)
Green Bay vs. Washington (1988)
(Washington leads series, 11-9)

Houston vs. Indianapolis (1988)
(Indianapolis leads series, 6-5)
Houston vs. Kansas City (1989)
(Kansas City leads series, 21-13)
Houston vs. Los Angeles Raiders (1989)
(Raiders lead series, 19-12)
Houston vs. Los Angeles Rams (1987)
(Rams lead series, 3-2)
Houston vs. Miami (1989)
(Series tied, 10-10)
Houston vs. Minnesota (1989)
(Minnesota leads series, 3-2)
Houston vs. New England (1989)
(New England leads series, 16-13-1)
Houston vs. New Orleans (1987)
(New Orleans leads series, 3-2-1)
Houston vs. New York Giants (1985)
(Giants lead series, 3-0)
Houston vs. New York Jets (1988)
(Houston leads series, 15-11-1)
Houston vs. Philadelphia (1988)
(Philadelphia leads series, 4-0)
Houston vs. Phoenix (1988)
(Phoenix leads series, 3-2)
Houston vs. Pittsburgh (1989)
(Pittsburgh leads series, 25-14)
Houston vs. San Diego (1989)
(San Diego leads series, 17-11-1)
Houston vs. San Francisco (1987)
(San Francisco leads series, 4-2)
Houston vs. Seattle (1988)
(Series tied, 3-3)
Houston vs. Tampa Bay (1989)
(Houston leads series, 3-1)
Houston vs. Washington (1988)
(Houston leads series, 3-2)

Indianapolis vs. Kansas City (1985)
(Kansas City leads series, 6-3)
Indianapolis vs. Los Angeles Raiders (1986)
(Raiders lead series, 3-2)
Indianapolis vs. Los Angeles Rams (1989)
(Indianapolis leads series, 20-17-2)
Indianapolis vs. Miami (1989)
(Miami leads series, 27-13)
Indianapolis vs. Minnesota (1988)
(Indianapolis leads series, 11-6-1)
Indianapolis vs. New England (1989)
(New England leads series, 22-17)
Indianapolis vs. New Orleans (1989)
(Indianapolis leads series, 3-2)

Indianapolis vs. New York Giants (1979)
(Indianapolis leads series, 5-3)
Indianapolis vs. New York Jets (1989)
(Indianapolis leads series, 21-18)
Indianapolis vs. Philadelphia (1984)
(Series tied, 5-5)
Indianapolis vs. Phoenix (1984)
(Phoenix leads series, 5-4)
Indianapolis vs. Pittsburgh (1987)
(Pittsburgh leads series, 9-4)
Indianapolis vs. San Diego (1989)
(Indianapolis leads series, 6-5)
Indianapolis vs. San Francisco (1989)
(Indianapolis leads series, 21-16)
Indianapolis vs. Seattle (1978)
(Indianapolis leads series, 2-0)
Indianapolis vs. Tampa Bay (1988)
(Indianapolis leads series, 4-1)
Indianapolis vs. Washington (1984)
(Indianapolis leads series, 15-6)

Kansas City vs. Los Angeles Raiders (1989)
(Raiders lead series, 34-23-2)
Kansas City vs. Los Angeles Rams (1985)
(Rams lead series, 3-0)
Kansas City vs. Miami (1989)
(Kansas City leads series, 9-6)
Kansas City vs. Minnesota (1981)
(Minnesota leads series, 2-1)
Kansas City vs. New England (1981)
(Kansas City leads series, 11-7-3)
Kansas City vs. New Orleans (1985)
(Series tied, 2-2)
Kansas City vs. New York Giants (1988)
(Giants lead series, 5-1)
Kansas City vs. New York Jets (1988)
(Kansas City leads series, 13-12-1)
Kansas City vs. Philadelphia (1972)
(Philadelphia leads series, 1-0)
Kansas City vs. Phoenix (1986)
(Kansas City leads series, 3-1-1)
Kansas City vs. Pittsburgh (1989)
(Pittsburgh leads series, 12-5)
Kansas City vs. San Diego (1989)
(San Diego leads series, 31-27-1)
Kansas City vs. San Francisco (1985)
(San Francisco leads series, 3-1)
Kansas City vs. Seattle (1989)
(Kansas City leads series, 13-10)
Kansas City vs. Tampa Bay (1986)
(Kansas City leads series, 4-2)
Kansas City vs. Washington (1983)
(Kansas City leads series, 2-1)

L. A. Raiders vs. L. A. Rams (1988)
(Raiders lead series, 4-2)
Los Angeles Raiders vs. Miami (1988)
(Raiders lead series, 13-3-1)
Los Angeles Raiders vs. Minnesota (1987)
(Raiders lead series, 4-2)
Los Angeles Raiders vs. New England (1989)
(Series tied, 12-12-1)
Los Angeles Raiders vs. New Orleans (1988)
(Raiders lead series, 3-1-1)
Los Angeles Raiders vs. N. Y. Giants (1989)
(Raiders lead series, 3-2)
Los Angeles Raiders vs. New York Jets (1989)
(Raiders lead series, 13-9-2)
Los Angeles Raiders vs. Philadelphia (1989)
(Philadelphia leads series, 3-2)
Los Angeles Raiders vs. Phoenix (1989)
(Raiders lead series, 2-1)

Los Angeles Raiders vs. Pittsburgh (1984)
(Raiders lead series, 6-3)
Los Angeles Raiders vs. San Diego (1989)
(Raiders lead series, 37-21-2)
Los Angeles Raiders vs. San Francisco (1988)
(Raiders lead series, 4-2)
Los Angeles Raiders vs. Seattle (1989)
(Seattle leads series, 14-10)
Los Angeles Raiders vs. Tampa Bay (1981)
(Raiders lead series, 2-0)
Los Angeles Raiders vs. Washington (1989)
(Raiders lead series, 4-2)

Los Angeles Rams vs. Miami (1986)
(Miami leads series, 4-1)
Los Angeles Rams vs. Minnesota (1989)
(Minnesota leads series, 13-11-2)
Los Angeles Rams vs. New England (1989)
(New England leads series, 3-2)
Los Angeles Rams vs. New Orleans (1989)
(Rams lead series, 26-14)
Los Angeles Rams vs. New York Giants (1989)
(Rams lead series, 16-5)
Los Angeles Rams vs. New York Jets (1989)
(Rams lead series, 4-2)
Los Angeles Rams vs. Philadelphia (1988)
(Rams lead series, 14-10-1)
Los Angeles Rams vs. Phoenix (1989)
(Rams lead series, 15-9-2)
Los Angeles Rams vs. Pittsburgh (1989)
(Rams lead series, 16-4-2)
Los Angeles Rams vs. San Diego (1988)
(Series tied, 2-2)
Los Angeles Rams vs. San Francisco (1988)
(Rams lead series, 46-30-2)
Los Angeles Rams vs. Seattle (1988)
(Rams lead series, 4-0)
Los Angeles Rams vs. Tampa Bay (1987)
(Rams lead series, 6-2)
Los Angeles Rams vs. Washington (1987)
(Washington leads series, 12-5-1)

Miami vs. Minnesota (1988)
(Miami leads series, 4-1)
Miami vs. New England (1989)
(Miami leads series, 26-20)
Miami vs. New Orleans (1989)
(Miami leads series, 5-2)
Miami vs. New York Giants (1972)
(Miami leads series, 1-0)
Miami vs. New York Jets (1988)
(Miami leads series, 23-22-1)
Miami vs. Philadelphia (1987)
(Miami leads series, 4-2)
Miami vs. Phoenix (1984)
(Miami leads series, 5-0)
Miami vs. Pittsburgh (1989)
(Miami leads series, 6-4)
Miami vs. San Diego (1988)
(San Diego leads series, 8-5)
Miami vs. San Francisco (1986)
(Miami leads series, 4-1)
Miami vs. Seattle (1987)
(Miami leads series, 2-1)
Miami vs. Tampa Bay (1988)
(Miami leads series, 3-1)
Miami vs. Washington (1987)
(Miami leads series, 4-1)

Minnesota vs. New England (1988)
(Series tied, 2-2)
Minnesota vs. New Orleans (1988)
(Minnesota leads series, 10-4)

Minnesota vs. New York Giants (1989)
(Minnesota leads series, 6-3)
Minnesota vs. New York Jets (1982)
(Jets lead series, 3-1)
Minnesota vs. Philadelphia (1989)
(Minnesota leads series, 10-4)
Minnesota vs. Phoenix (1983)
(Phoenix leads series, 7-2)
Minnesota vs. Pittsburgh (1989)
(Minnesota leads series, 6-4)
Minnesota vs. San Diego (1985)
(Series tied, 3-3)
Minnesota vs. San Francisco (1988)
(Minnesota leads series, 14-12-1)
Minnesota vs. Seattle (1987)
(Seattle leads series, 3-1)
Minnesota vs. Tampa Bay (1989)
(Minnesota leads series, 18-6)
Minnesota vs. Washington (1987)
(Washington leads series, 5-3)

New England vs. New Orleans (1989)
(New England leads series, 5-1)
New England vs. New York Giants (1987)
(Giants lead series, 2-1)
New England vs. New York Jets (1989)
(Jets lead series, 32-26-1)
New England vs. Philadelphia (1987)
(Philadelphia leads series, 4-2)
New England vs. Phoenix (1984)
(Phoenix leads series, 4-1)
New England vs. Pittsburgh (1989)
(Pittsburgh leads series, 6-3)
New England vs. San Diego (1983)
(New England leads series, 13-11-2)
New England vs. San Francisco (1989)
(San Francisco leads series, 5-1)
New England vs. Seattle (1989)
(New England leads series, 6-3)
New England vs. Tampa Bay (1988)
(New England leads series, 3-0)
New England vs. Washington (1984)
(Washington leads series, 3-1)

New Orleans vs. New York Giants (1988)
(Giants lead series, 8-6)
New Orleans vs. New York Jets (1989)
(Jets lead series, 4-2)
New Orleans vs. Philadelphia (1989)
(Philadelphia leads series, 9-7)
New Orleans vs. Phoenix (1987)
(Phoenix leads series, 10-5)
New Orleans vs. Pittsburgh (1987)
(New Orleans leads series, 5-4)
New Orleans vs. San Diego (1988)
(San Diego leads series, 3-1)
New Orleans vs. San Francisco (1989)
(San Francisco leads series, 28-11-2)
New Orleans vs. Seattle (1988)
(Series tied, 2-2)
New Orleans vs. Tampa Bay (1989)
(New Orleans leads series, 8-4)
New Orleans vs. Washington (1989)
(Washington leads series, 10-4)

New York Giants vs. New York Jets (1988)
(Series tied, 3-3)
New York Giants vs. Philadelphia (1989)
(Giants lead series, 59-49-2)
New York Giants vs. Phoenix (1989)
(Giants lead series, 60-33-2)
New York Giants vs. Pittsburgh (1985)
(Giants lead series, 43-27-3)

New York Giants vs. San Diego (1989)
(Giants lead series, 4-2)
New York Giants vs. San Francisco (1989)
(Giants lead series, 10-8)
New York Giants vs. Seattle (1989)
(Giants lead series, 4-2)
New York Giants vs. Tampa Bay (1985)
(Giants lead series, 6-3)
New York Giants vs. Washington (1989)
(Giants lead series, 57-45-2)

New York Jets vs. Philadelphia (1987)
(Philadelphia leads series, 4-0)
New York Jets vs. Phoenix (1978)
(Phoenix leads series, 2-1)
New York Jets vs. Pittsburgh (1989)
(Pittsburgh leads series, 10-1)
New York Jets vs. San Diego (1989)
(San Diego leads series, 14-8-1)
New York Jets vs. San Francisco (1989)
(San Francisco leads series, 5-1)
New York Jets vs. Seattle (1987)
(Seattle leads series, 7-3)
New York Jets vs. Tampa Bay (1985)
(Jets lead series, 3-1)
New York Jets vs. Washington (1987)
(Washington leads series, 4-0)

Philadelphia vs. Phoenix (1989)
(Phoenix leads series, 41-39-5)
Philadelphia vs. Pittsburgh (1988)
(Philadelphia leads series, 42-25-3)
Philadelphia vs. San Diego (1989)
(San Diego leads series, 3-2)
Philadelphia vs. San Francisco (1989)
(San Francisco leads series, 11-4-1)
Philadelphia vs. Seattle (1989)
(Philadelphia leads series, 3-1)
Philadelphia vs. Tampa Bay (1988)
(Philadelphia leads series, 3-0)
Philadelphia vs. Washington (1989)
(Washington leads series, 59-43-6)

Phoenix vs. Pittsburgh (1988)
(Pittsburgh leads series, 29-21-3)

Phoenix vs. San Diego (1989)
(San Diego leads series, 4-1)
Phoenix vs. San Francisco (1988)
(Series tied, 8-8)
Phoenix vs. Seattle (1989)
(Phoenix leads series, 3-0)
Phoenix vs. Tampa Bay (1989)
(Phoenix leads series, 6-4)
Phoenix vs. Washington (1989)
(Washington leads series, 53-31-1)

Pittsburgh vs. San Diego (1989)
(Pittsburgh leads series, 10-4)
Pittsburgh vs. San Francisco (1987)
(Pittsburgh leads series, 7-6)
Pittsburgh vs. Seattle (1987)
(Pittsburgh leads series, 4-3)
Pittsburgh vs. Tampa Bay (1989)
(Pittsburgh leads series, 4-0)
Pittsburgh vs. Washington (1988)
(Washington leads series, 38-24-4)

San Diego vs. San Francisco (1988)
(San Diego leads series, 3-2)
San Diego vs. Seattle (1989)
(Seattle leads series, 12-10)
San Diego vs. Tampa Bay (1987)
(San Diego leads series, 3-0)
San Diego vs. Washington (1989)
(Washington leads series, 5-0)

San Francisco vs. Seattle (1988)
(San Francisco leads series, 3-1)
San Francisco vs. Tampa Bay (1989)
(San Francisco leads series, 8-1)
San Francisco vs. Washington (1988)
(San Francisco leads series, 8-6-1)

Seattle vs. Tampa Bay (1977)
(Seattle leads series, 2-0)
Seattle vs. Washington (1989)
(Washington leads series, 4-1)

Tampa Bay vs. Washington (1989)
(Washington leads series, 3-0)

NFL ANNUAL SELECTION MEETING
APRIL 22, 1990

FIRST ROUND

Dallas
Choice exercised in 1989 Supplemental Draft
for Steve Walsh, QB, Miami (Fla.)

1. Indianapolis from Atlanta	GEORGE, Jeff (1)	QB	Illinois
2. New York Jets	THOMAS, Blair (2)	RB	Penn State

Phoenix
Choice exercised in 1989 Supplemental Draft
for Timm Rosenbach, QB, Washington State

3. Seattle from New England	KENNEDY, Cortez (3)	DT	Miami (Fla.)
4. Tampa Bay	McCANTS, Keith (4)	LB	Alabama
5. San Diego	SEAU, Junior (5)	LB	Southern Cal
6. Chicago	CARRIER, Mark (6)	DB	Southern Cal
7. Detroit	WARE, Andre (7)	QB	Houston
8. New England from Seattle	SINGLETON, Chris (8)	LB	Arizona
9. Miami	WEBB, Richmond (9)	T	Texas A & M
10. New England from Indianapolis through Seattle	AGNEW, Ray (10)	DE	North Carolina St.
11. Los Angeles Raiders	SMITH, Anthony (11)	DE	Arizona
12. Cincinnati	FRANCIS, James (12)	LB	Baylor
13. Kansas City	SNOW, Percy (13)	LB	Michigan State
14. New Orleans	TURNBULL, Renaldo (14)	DE	West Virginia
15. Houston	LATHON, Lamar (15)	LB	Houston
16. Buffalo	WILLIAMS, James (16)	DB	Fresno State
17. Dallas from Pittsburgh	SMITH, Emmitt (17)	RB	Florida
18. Green Bay from Cleveland	BENNETT, Tony (18)	LB	Mississippi
19. Green Bay	THOMPSON, Darrell (19)	RB	Minnesota
20. Atlanta from Washington	BROUSSARD, Steve (20)	RB	Washington State
21. Pittsburgh from Minnesota through Dallas	GREEN, Eric (21)	TE	Liberty (Va.)
22. Philadelphia	SMITH, Ben (22)	DB	Georgia
23. Los Angeles Rams	BROSTEK, Bern (23)	C	Washington
24. New York Giants	HAMPTON, Rodney (24)	RB	Georgia

Denver
Choice exercised in 1989 Supplemental Draft
for Bobby Humphrey, RB, Alabama

25. San Francisco	CARTER, Dexter (25)	RB	Florida State

End of Round:
3:30 p.m.

Time of Round:
3 hours, 24 minutes

Elapsed Time:
3 hours, 24 minutes

— 366 —

NFL ANNUAL SELECTION MEETING
APRIL 22, 1990

Start of Round:
3:30 p.m.

SECOND ROUND

1. Dallas	WRIGHT, Alexander (26)	WR	Auburn
2. Atlanta	CONNER, Darion (27)	LB	Jackson State
3. New York Jets	REMBERT, Reggie (28)	WR	West Virginia
4. Seattle from New England	WOODEN, Terry (29)	LB	Syracuse
5. Tampa Bay	COBB, Reggie (30)	RB	Tennessee
6. Phoenix	THOMPSON, Anthony (31)	RB	Indiana
7. Chicago	WASHINGTON, Fred (32)	DT	Texas Christian
8. Chicago from San Diego	COX, Ron (33)	LB	Fresno State
9. Seattle	BLACKMON, Robert (34)	DB	Baylor
10. Detroit	OWENS, Dan (35)	DE	Southern Cal
11. Indianapolis	JOHNSON, Anthony (36)	RB	Notre Dame
12. Los Angeles Raiders	WALLACE, Aaron (37)	LB	Texas A & M
13. Cincinnati	GREEN, Harold (38)	RB	South Carolina
14. Miami	SIMS, Keith (39)	G	Iowa State
15. Kansas City	GRUNHARD, Tim (40)	C	Notre Dame
16. Houston	ALM, Jeff (41)	DT	Notre Dame
17. Buffalo	GARDNER, Carwell (42)	RB	Louisville
18. Pittsburgh	DAVIDSON, Kenny (43)	DE	Louisiana State
19. New Orleans	BUCK, Vince (44)	DB	Central State (O.)
20. Cleveland	HOARD, Leroy (45)	RB	Michigan
21. Washington	COLLINS, Andre (46)	LB	Penn State
22. San Francisco from Minnesota through Dallas	BROWN, Dennis (47)	DT	Washington
23. Green Bay	BUTLER, LeRoy (48)	DB	Florida State
24. Los Angeles Rams	TERRELL, Pat (49)	DB	Notre Dame
25. Philadelphia	BELLAMY, Mike (50)	WR	Illinois
26. New York Giants	FOX, Mike (51)	DT	West Virginia
27. Denver	MONTGOMERY, Alton (52)	DB	Houston
28. San Francisco	DAVIS, Eric (53)	DB	Jacksonville State

End of Round:
6:04 p.m.

Time of Round:
2 hours, 34 minutes

Elapsed Time:
5 hours, 58 minutes

NFL ANNUAL SELECTION MEETING
APRIL 22, 1990

Start of Round:
6:04 p.m.

THIRD ROUND

1. Minnesota   JONES, Mike (54)   TE   Texas A & M
   from Dallas
2. Atlanta   BARNETT, Oliver (55)   DE   Kentucky
3. New York Jets   STARGELL, Tony (56)   DB   Tennessee State
4. San Diego   MILLS, Jeff (57)   LB   Nebraska
   from Tampa Bay
5. Phoenix   PROEHL, Ricky (58)   WR   Wake Forest
6. New England   HODSON, Tommy (59)   QB   Louisiana State
7. San Diego   GOEAS, Leo (60)   G   Hawaii
8. Chicago   RYAN, Tim (61)   DT   Southern Cal
9. Detroit   SPINDLER, Marc (62)   DE   Pittsburgh
10. Chicago*   WILLIS, Peter Tom (63)   QB   Florida State
    from Los Angeles Raiders
11. Dallas   JONES, Jimmie (64)   DT   Miami (Fla.)
    from Seattle through New England
12. Cincinnati   CLARK, Bernard (65)   LB   Miami (Fla.)
13. Miami   OGLESBY, Alfred (66)   DT   Houston
14. San Diego   WILSON, Walter (67)   WR   East Carolina
    from Indianapolis
15. San Francisco   LEWIS, Ron (68)   WR   Florida State
    from Kansas City through Dallas
16. Buffalo   PARKER, Glenn (69)   T   Arizona
17. Pittsburgh   O'DONNELL, Neil (70)   QB   Maryland
18. New Orleans   SMEENGE, Joel (71)   DE   Western Michigan
19. Houston   PEGUESE, Willis (72)   DE   Miami (Fla.)
20. Cleveland   PLEASANT, Anthony (73)   DE   Tennessee State
21. Minnesota   HOBBY, Marion (74)   DE   Tennessee
22. Green Bay   HOUSTON, Bobby (75)   LB   North Carolina St.
23. Washington   ELEWONIBI, Mohammed (76)   G   Brigham Young
24. Philadelphia   BARNETT, Fred (77)   WR   Arkansas State
25. Los Angeles Rams   BERRY, Latin (78)   RB   Oregon
26. New York Giants   MARK, Greg (79)   DE   Miami (Fla.)
27. New England   McMURTRY, Greg (80)   WR   Michigan
    from Denver through Dallas
28. Pittsburgh   VEASEY, Craig (81)   DT   Houston
    from San Francisco through Dallas

*Selected ahead of Dallas, which passed.

End of Round:
7:27 p.m.

Time of Round:
1 hour, 23 minutes

Elapsed Time:
7 hours, 21 minutes

NFL ANNUAL SELECTION MEETING

APRIL 22, 1990

Start of Round:
7:27 p.m.

FOURTH ROUND

1. Denver from Dallas	ROBINSON, Jeroy (82)	LB	Texas A & M
2. Indianapolis from Atlanta	SIMMONS, Stacey (83)	WR	Florida
3. New York Jets	TAYLOR, Troy (84)	QB	California
4. Phoenix	DAVIS, Travis (85)	DT	Michigan State
5. Washington from New England	CONKLIN, Cary (86)	QB	Washington
6. Tampa Bay	ANDERSON, Jesse (87)	TE	Mississippi State
7. Chicago	MOSS, Tony (88)	WR	Louisiana State
8. Seattle*	WARREN, Chris (89)	RB	Ferrum (Va.)
9. Detroit*	HINCKLEY, Rob (90)	LB	Stanford
10. Cincinnati*	BRENNAN, Mike (91)	T	Notre Dame
11. San Francisco from San Diego through L.A. Raiders	CALIGUIRE, Dean (92)	C	Pittsburgh
12. Miami	MITCHELL, Scott (93)	QB	Utah
13. Indianapolis	SCHULTZ, Bill (94)	G	Southern Cal
14. Los Angeles Raiders	DORN, Torin (95)	DB	North Carolina
15. Kansas City	JONES, Fred (96)	WR	Grambling
16. Pittsburgh	CALLOWAY, Chris (97)	WR	Michigan
17. New Orleans	WINSTON, DeMond (98)	LB	Vanderbilt
18. Houston	STILL, Eric (99)	G	Tennessee
19. Buffalo	FULLER, Eddie (100)	RB	Louisiana State
20. Cleveland	BARNETT, Harlon (101)	DB	Michigan State
21. Green Bay	HARRIS, Jackie (102)	TE	N.E. Louisiana
22. Indianapolis from Washington	GRANT, Alan (103)	DB	Stanford
23. Minnesota	HAMPTON, Alonzo (104)	DB	Pittsburgh
24. Detroit from Los Angeles Rams	OLDHAM, Chris (105)	DB	Oregon
25. Indianapolis from Philadelphia	CUNNINGHAM, Pat (106)	T	Texas A & M
26. New York Giants	WHITMORE, David (107)	DB	Stephen F. Austin
27. Tampa Bay from Denver	MAYBERRY, Tony (108)	C	Wake Forest
28. Washington from San Francisco through L.A. Raiders	LABBE, Rico (109)	DB	Boston College

*Selected ahead of San Francisco, which passed.

End of Round:
8:42 p.m.

Time of Round:
1 hour, 15 minutes

Elapsed Time:
8 hours, 36 minutes

NFL ANNUAL SELECTION MEETING
APRIL 22, 1990

Start of Round:
8:42 p.m.

FIFTH ROUND

1. New England   ROBINSON, Junior (110)   DB   East Carolina
   from Dallas through Washington
2. Denver   DAVIDSON, Jeff (111)   G   Ohio State
   from Atlanta through Washington and New England
3. New York Jets   SAVAGE, Tony (112)   DT   Washington State
4. New England   MELANDER, Jon (113)   T   Minnesota
5. Tampa Bay   BECKLES, Ian (114)   G   Indiana
6. Phoenix   CENTERS, Larry (115)   RB   Stephen F. Austin
7. Minnesota   THORNTON, Reggie (116)   WR   Bowling Green
   from San Diego through Dallas
8. Chicago   CHAFFEY, Pat (117)   RB   Oregon State
9. Detroit   CAMPBELL, Jeff (118)   WR   Colorado
10. Seattle   HAYES, Eric (119)   DT   Florida State
11. New England   GRAY, James (120)   RB   Texas Tech
    from Miami through Dallas
12. Atlanta   REDDING, Reggie (121)   TE   Cal St.-Fullerton
    from Indianapolis
13. Cincinnati*   JAMES, Lynn (122)   WR   Arizona State
14. Los Angeles Raiders   SMAGALA, Stan (123)   DB   Notre Dame
15. Kansas City   GRAHAM, Derrick (124)   T   Appalachian State
16. New Orleans   ARBUCKLE, Charles (125)   TE   UCLA
17. Houston   NEWBILL, Richard (126)   LB   Miami (Fla.)
18. Kansas City   HACKEMACK, Ken (127)   T   Texas
    from Buffalo
19. Pittsburgh   FOSTER, Barry (128)   RB   Arkansas
20. Cleveland   BURNETT, Rob (129)   DE   Syracuse
21. Washington   MITCHELL, Brian (130)   RB   S.W. Louisiana
22. Minnesota   SMITH, Cedric (131)   RB   Florida
23. Green Bay   WILSON, Charles (132)   WR   Memphis State
24. Philadelphia   WILLIAMS, Calvin (133)   WR   Purdue
25. New York Jets   McWRIGHT, Robert (134)   DB   Texas Christian
    from Los Angeles Rams
26. New York Giants   KUPP, Craig (135)   QB   Pacific Lutheran
27. Denver   LANG, Le-Lo (136)   DB   Washington
28. Miami   HOLT, Leroy (137)   RB   Southern Cal
    from San Francisco through Los Angeles Raiders and Washington

*Selected ahead of Los Angeles Raiders, who passed.

End of Round: Time of Round: Elapsed Time:
10:07 p.m.   1 hour, 25 minutes   10 hours, 1 minute

NFL ANNUAL SELECTION MEETING
APRIL 23, 1990

SIXTH ROUND

1.	San Diego from Dallas	FRIESZ, John (138)	QB	Idaho
2.	Atlanta	PRINGLE, Mike (139)	RB	Cal St.-Fullerton
3.	New York Jets	MATHIS, Terance (140)	WR	New Mexico
4.	Tampa Bay	DOUGLAS, Derrick (141)	RB	Louisiana Tech
5.	Phoenix	SHAVERS, Tyrone (142)	WR	Lamar
6.	San Diego from New England through Dallas	CORNISH, Frank (143)	C	UCLA
7.	Chicago	MANGUM, John (144)	DB	Alabama
8.	San Diego	POOL, David (145)	DB	Carson-Newman
9.	Seattle	BOLCAR, Ned (146)	LB	Notre Dame
10.	Detroit	HENRY, Maurice (147)	LB	Kansas State
11.	Indianapolis	WALKER, Tony (148)	LB	S.E. Missouri
12.	Los Angeles Raiders	WILSON, Marcus (149)	RB	Virginia
13.	Cincinnati	ODEGARD, Don (150)	DB	Nevada-Las Vegas
14.	Miami	VANHORSE, Sean (151)	DB	Howard
15.	Kansas City	SIMS, Tom (152)	DT	Pittsburgh
16.	Houston	JONES, Tony (153)	WR	Texas
17.	Buffalo	NIES, John (154)	P	Arizona
18.	Pittsburgh	HEARD, Ronald (155)	WR	Bowling Green
19.	New Orleans	BUCK, Mike (156)	QB	Maine
20.	Cleveland	HILLIARD, Randy (157)	DB	N.W. Louisiana
21.	New Orleans from Minnesota through Dallas and Los Angeles Raiders	WILLIAMS, James (158)	LB	Mississippi State
22.	Green Bay	PAUP, Bryce (159)	LB	Northern Iowa
23.	Washington	WELLS, Kent (160)	DT	Nebraska
24.	Los Angeles Rams	STALLWORTH, Tim (161)	WR	Washington State
25.	Philadelphia	THOMPSON, Kevin (162)	DB	Oklahoma
26.	San Diego from New York Giants through Dallas	WALKER, Derrick (163)	TE	Michigan
27.	Denver	HALIBURTON, Ronnie (164)	TE	Louisiana State
28.	San Francisco	POLLACK, Frank (165)	T	Northern Arizona

End of Round:
10:49 a.m.

Time of Round:
49 minutes

Elapsed Time:
10 hours, 50 minutes

NFL ANNUAL SELECTION MEETING
APRIL 23, 1990

SEVENTH ROUND

1. Buffalo from Dallas through New England	GRIFFITH, Brent (166)	G	Minnesota-Duluth
2. New York Jets from Atlanta	WHITE, Dwayne (167)	C	Alcorn State
3. New York Jets	PROCTOR, Basil (168)	LB	West Virginia
4. Phoenix	JOHNSON, Johnny (169)	RB	San Jose State
5. Buffalo from New England	COLLINS, Brent (170)	LB	Carson-Newman
6. Tampa Bay	GARDNER, Donnie (171)	DE	Kentucky
7. San Diego	NOVAK, Jeff (172)	G	S.W. Texas State
8. Los Angeles Raiders from Chicago	LEWIS, Garry (173)	DB	Alcorn State
9. Detroit	HAYWORTH, Tracy (174)	LB	Tennessee
10. Seattle	KULA, Bob (175)	T	Michigan State
11. Chicago from Los Angeles Raiders	ANDERSON, Bill (176)	C	Iowa
12. Cincinnati	OGLETREE, Craig (177)	LB	Auburn
13. Cleveland from Miami	GALBRAITH, Scott (178)	TE	Southern Cal
14. Indianapolis	SINGLETARY, James (179)	LB	East Carolina
15. Kansas City	SZOTT, Dave (180)	G	Penn State
16. Buffalo	DeRIGGI, Fred (181)	NT	Syracuse
17. Pittsburgh	GRAYSON, Dan (182)	LB	Washington State
18. New Orleans	HOUGH, Scott (183)	G	Maine
19. Houston	MURRAY, Andy (184)	RB	Kentucky
20. San Diego from Cleveland	STAYSNIAK, Joe (185)	T	Ohio State
21. Green Bay	ARCHAMBEAU, Lester (186)	DE	Stanford
22. San Diego from Washington	LEWIS, Nate (187)	WR	Oregon Tech
23. Minnesota	LEVELIS, John (188)	LB	C.W. Post (N.Y.)
24. Philadelphia	STROUF, Terry (189)	T	Wis.-LaCrosse
25. Los Angeles Rams	ELMORE, Kent (190)	P	Tennessee
26. New York Giants	EMANUEL, Aaron (191)	RB	Southern Cal
27. Denver	SHARPE, Shannon (192)	WR	Savannah State
28. San Diego from San Francisco	COLLINS, Keith (193)	DB	Appalachian State

End of Round:
11:41 a.m.

Time of Round:
52 minutes

Elapsed Time:
11 hours, 42 minutes

NFL ANNUAL SELECTION MEETING

APRIL 23, 1990

Start of Round:
11:41 a.m.

EIGHTH ROUND

1. Detroit   GREEN, Willie (194)   WR   Mississippi
   from Dallas
2. Atlanta   EPPS, Tory (195)   NT   Memphis State
3. New York Jets   DUFFY, Roger (196)   C   Penn State
4. Los Angeles Raiders   JIMERSON, Arthur (197)   LB   Norfolk State
   from New England through Dallas
5. Los Angeles Rams   SAVAGE, Ray (198)   LB   Virginia
   from Tampa Bay
6. Phoenix   WASHINGTON, Mickey (199)   DB   Texas A&M
7. Chicago   ROUSE, James (200)   RB   Arkansas
8. San Diego   FLANNIGAN, J.J. (201)   RB   Colorado
9. Seattle   HITCHCOCK, Bill (202)   T   Purdue
10. Detroit   FORTIN, Roman (203)   G   San Diego State
11. Cincinnati   WELLSANDT, Doug (204)   TE   Washington State
12. Miami   WOODS, Thomas (205)   WR   Tennessee
13. Indianapolis   CLARK, Ken (206)   RB   Nebraska
14. New Orleans   GDOWSKI, Gerry (207)   QB   Nebraska
    from Los Angeles Raiders
15. Buffalo   PATTON, Marvcus (208)   LB   UCLA
    from Kansas City
16. Pittsburgh   DUNBAR, Karl (209)   DT   Louisiana State
17. New Orleans   CARR, Derrick (210)   DE   Bowling Green
18. Houston   TUCKER, Brett (211)   DB   Northern Illinois

    Buffalo
    Choice exercised in 1989 Supplemental Draft
    for Brett Young, DB, Oregon
19. Cleveland   JONES, Jock (212)   LB   Virginia Tech
20. Indianapolis   WILSON, Harvey (213)   DB   Southern U.
    from Washington
21. Minnesota   SCHLICHTING, Craig (214)   DE   Wyoming
22. Green Bay   BROWN, Roger (215)   DB   Virginia Tech
23. Los Angeles Rams   CRAWFORD, Elbert (216)   C   Arkansas
24. Philadelphia   DYKES, Curt (217)   T   Oregon
25. New York Giants   VOORHEES, Barry (218)   T   Cal St.-Northridge
26. Denver   LEGGETT, Brad (219)   C   Southern Cal
27. San Francisco   PICKENS, Dwight (220)   WR   Fresno State

End of Round:
12:41 p.m.

Time of Round:
1 hour

Elapsed Time:
12 hours, 42 minutes

NFL ANNUAL SELECTION MEETING
APRIL 23, 1990

NINTH ROUND

1. Dallas	GANT, Kenneth (221)	DB	Albany State (Ga.)
2. Atlanta	JORDAN, Darrell (222)	LB	Northern Arizona
3. New York Jets	DAWKINS, Dale (223)	WR	Miami (Fla.)
4. Tampa Bay	COOK, Terry (224)	DE	Fresno State
5. Phoenix	BAVARO, David (225)	LB	Syracuse
6. New England	BOUWENS, Shawn (226)	G	Neb. Wesleyan
7. San Diego	GOETZ, Chris (227)	G	Pittsburgh
8. Chicago	BAILEY, Johnny (228)	RB	Texas A&I
9. Detroit	LINN, Jack (229)	T	West Virginia
10. Los Angeles Raiders	PERRY, Leon (230)	RB	Oklahoma
from Seattle through Dallas			
11. Miami	ROSS, Phil (231)	TE	Oregon State
12. Indianapolis	HUFFMAN, Darvell (232)	WR	Boston University
13. New Orleans	GRAVES, Broderick (233)	RB	Winston-Salem
from Los Angeles Raiders			
14. Cincinnati	PRICE, Mitchell (234)	DB	Tulane
15. Kansas City	OWENS, Michael (235)	RB	Syracuse
16. New Orleans	BROCKMAN, Lonnie (236)	LB	West Virginia
17. Houston	COLEMAN, Pat (237)	WR	Mississippi
18. Buffalo	HINES, Clarkston (238)	WR	Duke
19. Pittsburgh	JONES, Gary (239)	DB	Texas A&M
20. Cleveland	ROWELL, Eugene (240)	WR	So. Mississippi
21. Minnesota	ALLEN, Terry (241)	RB	Clemson
22. Green Bay	BAUMGARTNER, Kirk (242)	QB	Wis.-Stevens Point
23. Washington	MOXLEY, Tim (243)	G	Ohio State
24. Philadelphia	GRAY, Cecil (244)	DT	North Carolina
25. Los Angeles Rams	LOMACK, Tony (245)	WR	Florida
26. New York Giants	JAMES, Clint (246)	DE	Louisiana State
27. Denver	ELLIS, Todd (247)	QB	South Carolina
28. San Francisco	HAGGINS, Odell (248)	DT	Florida State

End of Round:
1:44 p.m.

Time of Round:
1 hour, 3 minutes

Elapsed Time:
13 hours, 45 minutes

NFL ANNUAL SELECTION MEETING

APRIL 23, 1990

TENTH ROUND

1.	Minnesota from Dallas	NEWMAN, Pat (249)	WR	Utah State
2.	Atlanta	SALUM, Donnie (250)	LB	Arizona
3.	New York Jets	QUAST, Brad (251)	LB	Iowa
4.	Phoenix	ELLE, Dave (252)	TE	South Dakota
5.	New England	LANDRY, Anthony (253)	RB	Stephen F. Austin
6.	Tampa Bay	BUSCH, Mike (254)	TE	Iowa State
7.	Chicago	PRICE, Terry (255)	DT	Texas A&M
8.	San Diego	BERRY, Kenny (256)	DB	Miami (Fla.)
9.	Seattle	MORRIS, Robert (257)	DE	Valdosta State
10.	Detroit	MILLER, Bill (258)	WR	Illinois State
11.	Denver from Indianapolis through Dallas and Los Angeles Raiders	SZYMANSKI, James (259)	DE	Michigan State
12.	New Orleans from Los Angeles Raiders	COOPER, Gary (260)	WR	Clemson
13.	Cincinnati	CRIGLER, Eric (261)	T	Murray State
14.	Washington from Miami	FRANCISCO, D'Juan (262)	DB	Notre Dame
15.	Kansas City	HUDSON, Craig (263)	TE	Wisconsin
16.	Houston	THOMAS, Dee (264)	DB	Nicholls State
17.	Buffalo	LODISH, Mike (265)	DT	UCLA
18.	Pittsburgh	MILES, Eddie (266)	LB	Minnesota
19.	New Orleans	SPEARS, Ernest (267)	DB	Southern Cal
20.	Cleveland	WALLACE, Michael (268)	DB	Jackson State
21.	Green Bay	MARTIN, Jerome (269)	DB	Western Kentucky
22.	Washington	RAYAM, Thomas (270)	DT	Alabama
23.	Minnesota	SMITH, Donald (271)	DB	Liberty (Va.)
24.	Los Angeles Rams	BATES, Steve (272)	DE	James Madison
25.	Philadelphia	ADAMS, Orlando (273)	DT	Jacksonville State
26.	New York Giants	MOORE, Otis (274)	DT	Clemson
27.	Denver	THOMPSON, Anthony (275)	LB	East Carolina
28.	San Francisco	HARRISON, Martin (276)	DE	Washington

End of Round:	Time of Round:	Elapsed Time:
2:46 p.m.	1 hour, 2 minutes	14 hours, 47 minutes

NFL ANNUAL SELECTION MEETING
APRIL 23, 1990

ELEVENTH ROUND

1. Dallas	HARPER, Dave (277)	LB	Humboldt State
2. Atlanta	ELLISON, Chris (278)	DB	Houston
3. New York Jets	KELSON, Derrick (279)	DB	Purdue
4. New England	SMITH, Sean (280)	DE	Georgia Tech
5. Tampa Bay	ANTHONY, Terry (281)	WR	Florida State
6. Phoenix	NORMAN, Dempsey (282)	WR	St. Francis (Ill.)
7. San Diego	STOWERS, Tommie (283)	TE	Missouri
8. Chicago	WHITE, Brent (284)	DE	Michigan
9. Detroit	WARNSLEY, Reginald (285)	RB	So. Mississippi
10. Seattle	REED, Daryl (286)	DB	Oregon
11. New Orleans	BURNETT, Webbie (287)	NT	Western Kentucky
from Los Angeles Raiders			
12. Cincinnati	O'CONNOR, Tim (288)	T	Virginia
13. San Francisco	SHELTON, Anthony (289)	DB	Tennessee State
from Miami			
14. Indianapolis	SMITH, Carnel (290)	DE	Pittsburgh
15. Kansas City	THOMPSON, Ernest (291)	RB	Georgia Southern
16. Buffalo	EDWARDS, Al (292)	WR	N.W. Louisiana
17. Pittsburgh	STRZELCZYK, Justin (293)	T	Maine
18. Philadelphia	HUDSON, John (294)	C	Auburn
from New Orleans			
19. Houston	BANES, Joey (295)	T	Houston
20. Cleveland	GORDON, Clemente (296)	QB	Grambling
21. Washington	LEVERENZ, Jon (297)	LB	Minnesota
22. Chicago	MATUSZ, Roman (298)	T	Pittsburgh
from Minnesota through L.A. Raiders			
23. Green Bay	JACKSON, Harry (299)	RB	St. Cloud (Minn.)
24. Philadelphia	WATSON, Tyrone (300)	WR	Tennessee State
25. Los Angeles Rams	GOLDBERG, Bill (301)	DT	Georgia
26. New York Giants	DOWNING, Tim (302)	DE	Washington State
27. Los Angeles Raiders	LEWIS, Ron (303)	WR	Jackson State
from Denver			
28. Los Angeles Raiders	JONES, Myron (304)	RB	Fresno State
from San Francisco through Dallas			

End of Round:
3:44 p.m.

Time of Round:
58 minutes

Elapsed Time:
15 hours, 45 minutes

NFL ANNUAL SELECTION MEETING
APRIL 23, 1990

TWELFTH ROUND

Dallas
Choice exercised in 1989 Supplemental Draft
for Mike Lowman, RB, Coffeyville (Kan.) J.C.

1. Atlanta	McCARTHY, Shawn (305)	P	Purdue
2. New York Jets	DAVIS, Darrell (306)	LB	Texas Christian
3. Tampa Bay	HAMMEL, Todd (307)	QB	Stephen F. Austin
4. Phoenix	RILEY, Donnie (308)	RB	Central Michigan
5. New England	DONELSON, Ventson (309)	DB	Michigan State
6. Chicago	COONEY, Anthony (310)	DB	Arkansas
7. Indianapolis	BENHART, Gene (311)	QB	Western Illinois
from San Diego			
8. Seattle	GROMOS, John (312)	QB	Vanderbilt
9. Detroit	CLAIBORNE, Robert (313)	WR	San Diego State
10. Cincinnati	RILEY, Andre (314)	WR	Washington
11. Miami	HARDEN, Bobby (315)	DB	Miami (Fla.)
12. Indianapolis	BROWN, Dean (316)	G	Notre Dame
13. Los Angeles Raiders	HARRIS, Major (317)	QB	West Virginia
14. Kansas City	JEFFERY, Tony (318)	WR	San Jose State
15. Pittsburgh	BELL, Richard (319)	RB	Nebraska
16. New Orleans	PORT, Chris (320)	G	Duke
17. Houston	SLACK, Reggie (321)	QB	Auburn
18. New England	ROSE, Blaine (322)	G	Maryland
from Buffalo			
19. Cleveland	SIMIEN, Kerry (323)	WR	Texas A & I
20. Minnesota	GOETZ, Ron (324)	LB	Minnesota
21. Green Bay	MAGGIO, Kirk (325)	P	UCLA
22. San Diego	SEARCY, Elliott (326)	WR	Southern U.
from Washington			
23. Philadelphia*	GARRETT, Judd (327)	RB	Princeton
24. Los Angeles Rams	LANG, David (328)	RB	Northern Arizona
25. New York Giants	STOVER, Matt (329)	K	Louisiana Tech
26. Phoenix	McMICHEL, Ken (330)	LB	Oklahoma
from Denver			
27. Los Angeles Raiders	DAVIS, Demetrius (331)	TE	Nevada-Reno
from San Francisco			

*Selected ahead of Los Angeles Rams, who passed.

End of Round:	Time of Round:	Elapsed Time:
4:37 p.m.	53 minutes	16 hours, 38 minutes

TEAM-BY-TEAM NO. 1 DRAFT CHOICES

*—Designates first player chosen in draft.

ATLANTA FALCONS

1990—Steve Broussard, RB, Washington State
1989—Deion Sanders, DB, Florida State
      Shawn Collins, WR, N. Arizona
1988—Aundray Bruce, LB, Auburn*
1987—Chris Miller, QB, Oregon
1986—Tony Casillas, DT, Oklahoma
      Tim Green, LB, Syracuse
1985—Bill Fralic, T, Pittsburgh
1984—Rick Bryan, DT, Oklahoma
1983—Mike Pitts, DE, Alabama
1982—Gerald Riggs, RB, Arizona State
1981—Bobby Butler, DB, Florida State
1980—Junior Miller, TE, Nebraska
1979—Don Smith, DE, Miami (Fla.)
1978—Mike Kenn, T, Michigan
1977—Warren Bryant, T, Kentucky
      Wilson Faumuina, DT, San Jose State
1976—Bubba Bean, RB, Texas A&M
1975—Steve Bartkowski, QB, California*
1974—(No Number One Selection)
1973—(No Number One Selection)
1972—Clarence Ellis, DB, Notre Dame
1971—Joe Profit, RB, Northeast Louisiana
1970—John Small, LB, Citadel
1969—George Kunz, T, Notre Dame
1968—Claude Humphrey, DE, Tennessee State
1967—(No Number One Selection)
1966—Tommy Nobis, LB, Texas*
      Randy Johnson, QB, Texas A&I

BUFFALO BILLS

1990—James Williams, DB, Fresno State
1989—(No Number One Selection)
1988—(No Number One Selection)
1987—Shane Conlan, LB, Penn State
1986—Ronnie Harmon, RB, Iowa
      Will Wolford, T, Vanderbilt
1985—Bruce Smith, DT, Virginia Tech*
      Derrick Burroughs, DB, Memphis State
1984—Greg Bell, RB, Notre Dame
1983—Tony Hunter, TE, Notre Dame
      Jim Kelly, QB, Miami (Fla.)
1982—Perry Tuttle, WR, Clemson
1981—Booker Moore, RB, Penn State
1980—Jim Ritcher, C, North Carolina State
1979—Tom Cousineau, LB, Ohio State*
      Jerry Butler, WR, Clemson
1978—Terry Miller, RB, Oklahoma State
1977—Phil Dokes, DT, Oklahoma State
1976—Mario Clark, DB, Oregon
1975—Tom Ruud, LB, Nebraska
1974—Reuben Gant, TE, Oklahoma State
1973—Paul Seymour, T, Michigan
      Joe DeLamielleure, G, Michigan State
1972—Walt Patulski, DE, Notre Dame*
1971—J.D. Hill, WR, Arizona State
1970—Al Cowlings, DE, Southern California
1969—O.J. Simpson, RB, Southern California*
1968—Haven Moses, WR, San Diego State
1967—John Pitts, DB, Arizona State
1966—Mike Dennis, RB, Mississippi
1965—Jim Davidson, T, Ohio State
1964—Carl Eller, DE, Minnesota
1963—Dave Behrman, C, Michigan State
1962—Ernie Davis, RB, Syracuse
1961—Ken Rice, T, Auburn* (AFL)
1960—Richie Lucas, QB, Penn State

CHICAGO BEARS

1990—Mark Carrier, DB, Southern California
1989—Donnell Woolford, DB, Clemson
      Trace Armstrong, DE, Florida
1988—Brad Muster, RB, Stanford
      Wendell Davis, WR, Louisiana State
1987—Jim Harbaugh, QB, Michigan
1986—Neal Anderson, RB, Florida

1985—William Perry, DT, Clemson
1984—Wilber Marshall, LB, Florida
1983—Jimbo Covert, T, Pittsburgh
      Willie Gault, WR, Tennessee
1982—Jim McMahon, QB, Brigham Young
1981—Keith Van Horne, T, Southern California
1980—Otis Wilson, LB, Louisville
1979—Dan Hampton, DT, Arkansas
      Al Harris, DE, Arizona State
1978—(No Number One Selection)
1977—Ted Albrecht, T, California
1976—Dennis Lick, T, Wisconsin
1975—Walter Payton, RB, Jackson State
1974—Waymond Bryant, LB, Tennessee State
      Dave Gallagher, DE, Michigan
1973—Wally Chambers, DE, Eastern Kentucky
1972—Lionel Antoine, T, Southern Illinois
      Craig Clemons, DB, Iowa
1971—Joe Moore, RB, Missouri
1970—(No Number One Selection)
1969—Rufus Mayes, T, Ohio State
1968—Mike Hull, RB, Southern California
1967—Loyd Phillips, DE, Arkansas
1966—George Rice, DT, Louisiana State
1965—Dick Butkus, LB, Illinois
      Gale Sayers, RB, Kansas
      Steve DeLong, DE, Tennessee
1964—Dick Evey, DT, Tennessee
1963—Dave Behrman, C, Michigan State
1962—Ron Bull, RB, Baylor
1961—Mike Ditka, E, Pittsburgh
1960—Roger Davis, G, Syracuse
1959—Don Clark, B, Ohio State
1958—Chuck Howley, LB, West Virginia
1957—Earl Leggett, DT, Louisiana State
1956—Menan (Tex) Schriewer, E, Texas
1955—Ron Drzewiecki, B, Marquette
1954—Stan Wallace, B, Illinois
1953—Billy Anderson, B, Compton (Calif.) JC
1952—Jim Dooley, B, Miami
1951—Bob Williams, B, Notre Dame
      Billy Stone, B, Bradley
1950—Chuck Hunsinger, B, Florida
1949—Dick Harris, C, Texas
1948—Bobby Layne, QB, Texas
      Max Baumgardner, E, Texas
1947—Bob Fenimore, B, Oklahoma A&M*
1946—Johnny Lujack, QB, Notre Dame
1945—Don Lund, B, Michigan
1944—Ray Evans, B, Kansas
1943—Bob Steuber, B, Missouri
1942—Frankie Albert, B, Stanford
1941—Tom Harmon, B, Michigan*
      Norm Standlee, B, Stanford
      Don Scott, B, Ohio State
1940—Clyde Turner, C, Hardin-Simmons
1939—Sid Luckman, B, Columbia
      Bill Osmanski, B, Holy Cross
1938—Joe Gray, B, Oregon State
1937—Les McDonald, E, Nebraska
1936—Joe Stydahar, T, West Virginia

CINCINNATI BENGALS

1990—James Francis, LB, Baylor
1989—(No Number One Selection)
1988—Rickey Dixon, S, Oklahoma
1987—Jason Buck, DT, Brigham Young
1986—Joe Kelly, LB, Washington
      Tim McGee, WR, Tennessee
1985—Eddie Brown, WR, Miami (Fla.)
      Emanuel King, LB, Alabama
1984—Ricky Hunley, LB, Arizona
      Pete Koch, DE, Maryland
      Brian Blados, T, North Carolina
1983—Dave Rimington, C, Nebraska
1982—Glen Collins, DE, Mississippi State
1981—David Verser, WR, Kansas
1980—Anthony Munoz, T, Southern California

1979—Jack Thompson, QB, Washington State
    Charles Alexander, RB, Louisiana State
1978—Ross Browner, DE, Notre Dame
    Blair Bush, C, Washington
1977—Eddie Edwards, DT, Miami
    Wilson Whitley, DT, Houston
    Mike Cobb, TE, Michigan State
1976—Billy Brooks, WR, Oklahoma
    Archie Griffin, RB, Ohio State
1975—Glenn Cameron, LB, Florida
1974—Bill Kollar, DT, Montana State
1973—Issac Curtis, WR, San Diego State
1972—Sherman White, DE, California
1971—Vernon Holland, T, Tennessee State
1970—Mike Reid, DT, Penn State
1969—Greg Cook, QB, Cincinnati
1968—Bob Johnson, C, Tennessee

CLEVELAND BROWNS

1990— (No Number One Selection)
1989—Eric Metcalf, RB, Texas
1988—Clifford Charlton, LB, Florida
1987—Mike Junkin, LB, Duke
1986— (No Number One Selection)
1985— (No Number One Selection)
1984—Don Rogers, DB, UCLA
1983— (No Number One Selection)
1982—Chip Banks, LB, Southern California
1981—Hanford Dixon, CB, Southern Mississippi
1980—Charles White, RB, Southern California
1979—Willis Adams, WR, Houston
1978—Clay Matthews, LB, Southern California
    Ozzie Newsome, WR, Alabama
1977—Robert Jackson, LB, Texas A & M
1976—Mike Pruitt, RB, Purdue
1975—Mack Mitchell, DE, Houston
1974— (No Number One Selection)
1973—Steve Holden, WR, Arizona State
    Pete Adams, G, Southern California
1972—Thom Darden, DB, Michigan
1971—Clarence Scott, DB, Kansas State
1970—Mike Phipps, QB, Purdue
    Bob McKay, T, Texas
1969—Ron Johnson, RB, Michigan
1968—Marvin Upshaw, DE, Trinity (Tex.)
1967—Bob Matheson, LB, Duke
1966—Milt Morin, TE, Massachusetts
1965— (No Number One Selection)
1964—Paul Warfield, WR, Ohio State
1963—Tom Hutchinson, TE, Kentucky
1962—Gary Collins, WR, Maryland
    Leroy Jackson, B, Western Illinois
1961— (No Number One Selection)
1960—Jim Houston, DE, Ohio State
1959—Rich Kreitling, DE, Illinois
1958—Jim Shofner, DB, Texas Christian
1957—Jim Brown, B, Syracuse
1956—Preston Carpenter, B, Arkansas
1955—Kent Burris, C, Oklahoma
1954—Bobby Garrett, QB, Stanford*
    John Bauer, G, Illinois
1953—Doug Atkins, DT, Tennessee
1952—Bert Rechichar, DB, Tennessee
    Harry Agganis, QB, Boston U.
1951—Ken Konz, B, Louisiana State
1950—Ken Carpenter, B, Oregon State

DALLAS COWBOYS

1990—Emmitt Smith, RB, Florida
1989—Troy Aikman, QB, UCLA*
1988—Michael Irvin, WR, Miami (Fla.)
1987—Danny Noonan, DT, Nebraska
1986—Mike Sherrard, WR, UCLA
1985—Kevin Brooks, DE, Michigan
1984—Billy Cannon, Jr., LB, Texas A & M
1983—Jim Jeffcoat, DE, Arizona State
1982—Rod Hill, DB, Kentucky State
1981—Howard Richards, T, Missouri
1980— (No Number One Selection)
1979—Robert Shaw, C, Tennessee
1978—Larry Bethea, DE, Michigan State
1977—Tony Dorsett, RB, Pittsburgh

1976—Aaron Kyle, DB, Wyoming
1975—Randy White, LB, Maryland
    Thomas Henderson, LB, Langston
1974—Ed Jones, DE, Tennessee State*
    Charles Young, RB, North Carolina State
1973—Billy Joe DuPree, TE, Michigan State
1972—Bill Thomas, RB, Boston College
1971—Tody Smith, DE, Southern California
1970—Duane Thomas, RB, West Texas State
1969—Calvin Hill, RB, Yale
1968—Dennis Homan, WR, Alabama
1967— (No Number One Selection)
1966—John Niland, G, Iowa
1965—Craig Morton, QB, California
1964—Scott Appleton, DT, Texas
1963—Lee Roy Jordan, LB, Alabama
1962— (No Number One Selection)
1961—Bob Lilly, DT, Texas Christian

DENVER BRONCOS

1990— (No Number One Selection)
1989—Steve Atwater, DB, Arkansas
1988—Ted Gregory, DT, Syracuse
1987—Ricky Nattiel, WR, Florida
1986— (No Number One Selection)
1985—Steve Sewell, RB, Oklahoma
1984— (No Number One Selection)
1983—Chris Hinton, G, Northwestern
1982—Gerald Willhite, RB, San Jose State
1981—Dennis Smith, DB, Southern California
1980— (No Number One Selection)
1979—Kelvin Clark, T, Nebraska
1978—Don Latimer, DT, Miami (Fla.)
1977—Steve Schindler, G, Boston College
1976—Tom Glassic, G, Virginia
1975—Louis Wright, DB, San Jose State
1974—Randy Gradishar, LB, Ohio State
1973—Otis Armstrong, RB, Purdue
1972—Riley Odoms, TE, Houston
1971—Marv Montgomery, T, Southern California
1970—Bob Anderson, RB, Colorado
1969— (No Number One Selection)
1968— (No Number One Selection)
1967—Floyd Little, RB, Syracuse
1966—Jerry Shay, DT, Purdue
1965— (No Number One Selection)
1964—Bob Brown, T, Nebraska
1963—Kermit Alexander, DB, UCLA
1962—Merlin Olsen, DT, Utah State
1961—Bob Gaiters, RB, New Mexico State
1960—Roger Leclerc, C, Trinity (Conn.)

DETROIT LIONS

1990—Andre Ware, QB, Houston
1989—Barry Sanders, RB, Oklahoma State
1988—Bennie Blades, S, Miami (Fla.)
1987—Reggie Rogers, DE, Washington
1986—Chuck Long, QB, Iowa
1985—Lomas Brown, T, Florida
1984—David Lewis, TE, California
1983—James Jones, RB, Florida
1982—Jimmy Williams, LB, Nebraska
1981—Mark Nichols, WR, San Jose State
1980—Billy Sims, RB, Oklahoma*
1979—Keith Dorney, T, Penn State
1978—Luther Bradley, DB, Notre Dame
1977— (No Number One Selection)
1976—James Hunter, DB, Grambling
    Lawrence Gaines, FB, Wyoming
1975—Lynn Boden, G, South Dakota State
1974—Ed O'Neil, LB, Penn State
1973—Ernie Price, DE, Texas A & I
1972—Herb Orvis, DE, Colorado
1971—Bob Bell, DT, Cincinnati
1970—Steve Owens, RB, Oklahoma
1969— (No Number One Selection)
1968—Greg Landry, QB, Massachusetts
    Earl McCullouch, E. Southern California
1967—Mel Farr, RB, UCLA
1966— (No Number One Selection)
1965—Tom Nowatzke, RB, Indiana
1964—Pete Beathard, QB, Southern California

1963—Daryl Sanders, T, Ohio State
1962—John Hadl, QB, Kansas
1961— (No Number One Selection)
1960—John Robinson, DB, Louisiana State
1959—Nick Pietrosante, B, Notre Dame
1958—Alex Karras, DT, Iowa
1957—Bill Glass, G, Baylor
1956—Howard Cassidy, B, Ohio State
1955—Dave Middleton, B, Auburn
1954—Dick Chapman, T, Rice
1953—Harley Sewell, G, Texas
1952— (No Number One Selection)
1951— (No Number One Selection)
1950—Leon Hart, E, Notre Dame*
1949—John Rauch, B, Georgia
1948—Y.A. Tittle, B, Louisiana State
1947—Glenn Davis, B, Army
1946—Bill Dellastatious, B, Missouri
1945—Frank Szymanski, B, Notre Dame
1944—Otto Graham, B, Northwestern
1943—Frank Sinkwich, B, Georgia*
1942—Bob Westfall, B, Michigan
1941—Jim Thomason, B, Texas A & M
1940—Doyle Nave, B, Southern California
1939—John Pingel, B, Michigan State
1938—Alex Wojciechowicz, C, Fordham
1937—Lloyd Cardwell, B, Nebraska
1936—Sid Wagner, G, Michigan State

GREEN BAY PACKERS

1990—Tony Bennett, LB, Mississippi
　　　Darrell Thompson, RB, Minnesota
1989—Tony Mandarich, T, Michigan State
1988—Sterling Sharpe, WR, South Carolina
1987—Brent Fullwood, RB, Auburn
1986— (No Number One Selection)
1985—Ken Ruettgers, T, Southern California
1984—Alphonso Carreker, DT, Florida State
1983—Tim Lewis, DB, Pittsburgh
1982—Ron Hallstrom, G, Iowa
1981—Rich Campbell, QB, California
1980—Bruce Clark, DT, Penn State
　　　George Cumby, LB, Oklahoma
1979—Eddie Lee Ivery, RB, Georgia Tech
1978—James Lofton, WR, Stanford
　　　John Anderson, LB, Michigan
1977—Mike Butler, DE, Kansas
　　　Ezra Johnson, DE, Morris Brown
1976—Mark Koncar, T, Colorado
1975— (No Number One Selection)
1974—Barty Smith, RB, Richmond
1973—Barry Smith, WR, Florida State
1972—Willie Buchanon, DB, San Diego State
　　　Jerry Tagge, QB, Nebraska
1971—John Brockington, RB, Ohio State
1970—Mike McCoy, DT, Notre Dame
　　　Rich McGeorge, TE, Elon
1969—Rich Moore, DT, Villanova
1968—Fred Carr, LB, Texas-El Paso
　　　Bill Lueck, G, Arizona
1967—Bob Hyland, C, Boston College
　　　Don Horn, QB, San Diego State
1966—Gale Gillingham, G, Minnesota
　　　Jim Grabowski, RB, Illinois
1965—Donny Anderson, RB, Texas Tech
　　　Larry Elkins, E, Baylor
1964—Lloyd Voss, DT, Nebraska
1963—Dave Robinson, LB, Penn State
1962—Earl Gros, RB, Louisiana State
1961—Herb Adderley, DB, Michigan State
1960—Tom Moore, RB, Vanderbilt
1959—Randy Duncan, B, Iowa*
1958—Dan Currie, C, Michigan State
1957—Paul Hornung, B, Notre Dame*
　　　Ron Kramer, E, Michigan
1956—Jack Losch, B, Miami
1955—Tom Bettis, G, Purdue
1954—Art Hunter, T, Notre Dame
1953—Al Carmichael, B, Southern California
1952—Babe Parilli, QB, Kentucky
1951—Bob Gain, T, Kentucky
1950—Clayton Tonnemaker, G, Minnesota

1949—Stan Heath, B, Nevada
1948—Earl Girard, B, Wisconsin
1947—Ernie Case, B, UCLA
1946—Johnny Strzykalski, B, Marquette
1945—Walt Schlinkman, G, Texas Tech
1944—Merv Pregulman, G, Michigan
1943—Dick Wildung, T, Minnesota
1942—Urban Odson, T, Minnesota
1941—George Paskvan, B, Wisconsin
1940—Hal Van Every, B, Marquette
1939—Larry Buhler, B, Minnesota
1938—Cecil Isbell, B, Purdue
1937—Ed Jankowski, B, Wisconsin
1936—Russ Letlow, G, San Francisco

HOUSTON OILERS

1990—Lamar Lathon, LB, Houston
1989—David Williams, T, Florida
1988—Lorenzo White, RB, Michigan State
1987—Alonzo Highsmith, FB, Miami (Fla.)
　　　Haywood Jeffires, WR, N.C. State
1986—Jim Everett, QB, Purdue
1985—Ray Childress, DE, Texas A & M
　　　Richard Johnson, DB, Wisconsin
1984—Dean Steinkuhler, G, Nebraska
1983—Bruce Matthews, G, Southern California
1982—Mike Munchak, G, Penn State
1981— (No Number One Selection)
1980— (No Number One Selection)
1979— (No Number One Selection)
1978—Earl Campbell, RB, Texas*
1977—Morris Towns, T, Missouri
1976— (No Number One Selection)
1975—Robert Brazile, LB, Jackson State
　　　Don Hardeman, RB, Texas A & I
1974— (No Number One Selection)
1973—John Matuszak, DE, Tampa*
　　　George Amundson, RB, Iowa State
1972—Greg Sampson, DE, Stanford
1971—Dan Pastorini, QB, Santa Clara
1970—Doug Wilkerson, G, North Carolina Central
1969—Ron Pritchard, LB, Arizona State
1968— (No Number One Selection)
1967—George Webster, LB, Michigan State
　　　Tom Regner, G, Notre Dame
1966—Tommy Nobis, LB, Texas
1965—Lawrence Elkins, WR, Baylor* (AFL)
1964—Scott Appleton, DT, Texas
1963—Danny Brabham, LB, Arkansas
1962—Ray Jacobs, DT, Howard Payne
1961—Mike Ditka, E, Pittsburgh
1960—Billy Cannon, RB, Louisiana State

INDIANAPOLIS COLTS

1990—Jeff George, QB, Illinois*
1989—Andre Rison, WR, Michigan State
1988— (No Number One Selection)
1987—Cornelius Bennett, LB, Alabama
1986—Jon Hand, DT, Alabama
1985—Duane Bickett, LB, Southern California
1984—Leonard Coleman, DB, Vanderbilt
　　　Ron Solt, G, Maryland
1983—John Elway, QB, Stanford*
1982—Johnie Cooks, LB, Mississippi State
　　　Art Schlichter, QB, Ohio State
1981—Randy McMillan, RB, Pittsburgh
　　　Donnell Thompson, DT, North Carolina
1980—Curtis Dickey, RB, Texas A & M
　　　Derrick Hatchett, DB, Texas
1979—Barry Krauss, LB, Alabama
1978—Reese McCall, TE, Auburn
1977—Randy Burke, WR, Kentucky
1976—Ken Novak, DT, Purdue
1975—Ken Huff, G, North Carolina
1974—John Dutton, DE, Nebraska
　　　Roger Carr, WR, Louisiana Tech
1973—Bert Jones, QB, Louisiana State
　　　Joe Ehrmann, DT, Syracuse
1972—Tom Drougas, T, Oregon
1971—Don McCauley, RB, North Carolina
　　　Leonard Dunlap, DB, North Texas State
1970—Norm Bulaich, RB, Texas Christian

1969—Eddie Hinton, WR, Oklahoma
1968—John Williams, G, Minnesota
1967—Bubba Smith, DT, Michigan State*
      Jim Detwiler, RB, Michigan
1966—Sam Ball, T, Kentucky
1965—Mike Curtis, LB, Duke
1964—Marv Woodson, DB, Indiana
1963—Bob Vogel, T, Ohio State
1962—Wendell Harris, DB, Louisiana State
1961—Tom Matte, RB, Ohio State
1960—Ron Mix, T, Southern California
1959—Jackie Burkett, C, Auburn
1958—Lenny Lyles, B, Louisville
1957—Jim Parker, T, Ohio State
1956—Lenny Moore, B, Penn State
1955—George Shaw, B, Oregon*
      Alan Ameche, B, Wisconsin
1954—Cotton Davidson, B, Baylor
1953—Billy Vessels, B, Oklahoma

KANSAS CITY CHIEFS

1990—Percy Snow, LB, Michigan State
1989—Derrick Thomas, LB, Alabama
1988—Neil Smith, DE, Nebraska
1987—Paul Palmer, RB, Temple
1986—Brian Jozwiak, T, West Virginia
1985—Ethan Horton, RB, North Carolina
1984—Bill Maas, DT, Pittsburgh
      John Alt, T, Iowa
1983—Todd Blackledge, QB, Penn State
1982—Anthony Hancock, WR, Tennessee
1981—Willie Scott, TE, South Carolina
1980—Brad Budde, G, Southern California
1979—Mike Bell, DE, Colorado State
      Steve Fuller, QB, Clemson
1978—Art Still, DE, Kentucky
1977—Gary Green, DB, Baylor
1976—Rod Walters, G, Iowa
1975—(No Number One Selection)
1974—Woody Green, RB, Arizona State
1973—(No Number One Selection)
1972—Jeff Kinney, RB, Nebraska
1971—Elmo Wright, WR, Houston
1970—Sid Smith, T, Southern California
1969—Jim Marsalis, DB, Tennessee State
1968—Mo Moorman, G, Texas A&M
      George Daney, G, Texas-El Paso
1967—Gene Trosch, DE, Miami
1966—Aaron Brown, DE, Minnesota
1965—Gale Sayers, RB, Kansas
1964—Pete Beathard, QB, Southern California
1963—Buck Buchanan, DT, Grambling* (AFL)
      Ed Budde, G, Michigan State
1962—Ronnie Bull, RB, Baylor
1961—E.J. Holub, C, Texas Tech
1960—Don Meredith, QB, Southern Methodist

LOS ANGELES RAIDERS

1990—Anthony Smith, DE, Arizona
1989—(No Number One Selection)
1988—Tim Brown, WR, Notre Dame
      Terry McDaniel, CB, Tennessee
      Scott Davis, DE, Illinois
1987—John Clay, T, Missouri
1986—Bob Buczkowski, DT, Pittsburgh
1985—Jessie Hester, WR, Florida State
1984—(No Number One Selection)
1983—Don Mosebar, T, Southern California
1982—Marcus Allen, RB, Southern California
1981—Ted Watts, DB, Texas Tech
      Curt Marsh, G, Washington
1980—Marc Wilson, QB, Brigham Young
1979—(No Number One Selection)
1978—(No Number One Selection)
1977—(No Number One Selection)
1976—(No Number One Selection)
1975—Neal Colzie, DB, Ohio State
1974—Henry Lawrence, T, Florida A&M
1973—Ray Guy, P, Southern Mississippi
1972—Mike Siani, WR, Villanova
1971—Jack Tatum, DB, Ohio State
1970—Raymond Chester, TE, Morgan State

1969—Art Thoms, DT, Syracuse
1968—Eldridge Dickey, QB, Tennessee State
1967—Gene Upshaw, G, Texas A&I
1966—Rodger Bird, DB, Kentucky
1965—Harry Schuh, T, Memphis State
1964—Tony Lorick, RB, Arizona State
1963—(No Number One Selection)
1962—Roman Gabriel, QB, N.C. State* (AFL)
1961—Joe Rutgens, DT, Illinois
1960—Dale Hackbart, DB, Wisconsin

LOS ANGELES RAMS

1990—Bern Brostek, C, Washington
1989—Bill Hawkins, DE, Miami (Fla.)
      Cleveland Gary, RB, Miami (Fla.)
1988—Gaston Green, RB, UCLA
      Aaron Cox, WR, Arizona State
1987—(No Number One Selection)
1986—Mike Schad, T, Queens College (Ont.)
1985—Jerry Gray, DB, Texas
1984—(No Number One Selection)
1983—Eric Dickerson, RB, Southern Methodist
1982—Barry Redden, RB, Richmond
1981—Mel Owens, LB, Michigan
1980—Johnnie Johnson, DB, Texas
1979—George Andrews, LB, Nebraska
      Kent Hill, G, Georgia Tech
1978—Elvis Peacock, RB, Oklahoma
1977—Bob Brudzinski, LB, Ohio State
1976—Kevin McLain, LB, Colorado State
1975—Mike Fanning, DT, Notre Dame
      Dennis Harrah, G, Miami
      Doug France, T, Ohio State
1974—John Cappelletti, RB, Penn State
1973—(No Number One Selection)
1972—(No Number One Selection)
1971—Isiah Robertson, LB, Southern
      Jack Youngblood, DE, Florida
1970—Jack Reynolds, LB, Tennessee
1969—Larry Smith, RB, Florida
      Jim Seymour, E, Notre Dame
      Bob Klein, TE, Southern California
1968—(No Number One Selection)
1967—(No Number One Selection)
1966—Tom Mack, G, Michigan
1965—Clancy Williams, DB, Washington State
1964—Bill Munson, QB, Utah State
1963—Terry Baker, QB, Oregon State*
      Rufus Guthrie, G, Georgia Tech
1962—Roman Gabriel, QB, North Carolina State
      Merlin Olsen, DT, Utah State
1961—Marlin McKeever, LB, Southern California
1960—Billy Cannon, RB, Louisiana State*
1959—Paul Dickson, G, Baylor
      Dick Bass, B, Pacific
1958—Lou Michaels, T, Kentucky
      Jim Phillips, E, Auburn
1957—Jon Arnett, B, Southern California
      Del Shofner, B, Baylor
1956—Joe Marconi, B, West Virginia
      Charlie Horton, B, Vanderbilt
1955—Larry Morris, C, Georgia Tech
1954—Ed Beatty, C, Cincinnati
1953—Donn Moomaw, C, UCLA
      Ed Barker, E, Washington State
1952—Bill Wade, B, Vanderbilt*
      Bob Carey, E, Michigan State
1951—Bud McFadin, G, Texas
1950—Ralph Pasquariello, B, Villanova
      Stan West, G, Oklahoma
1949—Bobby Thomason, B, Virginia Military
1948—(No Number One Selection)
1947—Herman Wedemeyer, B, St. Mary's (Calif.)
1946—Emil Sitko, B, Notre Dame
1945—Elroy Hirsch, B, Wisconsin
1944—Tony Butkovich, B, Illinois
1943—Mike Holovak, B, Boston College
1942—Jack Wilson, B, Baylor
1941—Rudy Mucha, C, Washington
1940—Ollie Cordill, B, Rice
1939—Parker Hall, B, Mississippi
1938—Corbett Davis, B, Indiana*
1937—Johnny Drake, B, Purdue

MIAMI DOLPHINS

1990—Richmond Webb, T, Texas A & M
1989—Sammie Smith, RB, Florida State
      Louis Oliver, DB, Florida
1988—Eric Kumerow, DE, Ohio State
1987—John Bosa, DE, Boston College
1986—(No Number One Selection)
1985—Lorenzo Hampton, RB, Florida
1984—Jackie Shipp, LB, Oklahoma
1983—Dan Marino, QB, Pittsburgh
1982—Roy Foster, G, Southern California
1981—David Overstreet, RB, Oklahoma
1980—Don McNeal, DB, Alabama
1979—Jon Giesler, T, Michigan
1978—(No Number One Selection)
1977—A.J. Duhe, DE, Louisiana State
1976—Larry Gordon, LB, Arizona State
      Kim Bokamper, LB, San Jose State
1975—Darryl Carlton, T, Tampa
1974—Don Reese, DE, Jackson State
1973—(No Number One Selection)
1972—Mike Kadish, DT, Notre Dame
1971—(No Number One Selection)
1970—(No Number One Selection)
1969—Bill Stanfill, DE, Georgia
1968—Larry Csonka, RB, Syracuse
      Doug Crusan, T, Indiana
1967—Bob Griese, QB, Purdue
1966—Jim Grabowski, RB, Illinois*
      Rick Norton, QB, Kentucky

MINNESOTA VIKINGS

1990—(No Number One Selection)
1989—(No Number One Selection)
1988—Randall McDaniel, G, Arizona State
1987—D.J. Dozier, RB, Penn State
1986—Gerald Robinson, DE, Auburn
1985—Chris Doleman, LB, Pittsburgh
1984—Keith Millard, DE, Washington State
1983—Joey Browner, DB, Southern California
1982—Darrin Nelson, RB, Stanford
1981—(No Number One Selection)
1980—Doug Martin, DT, Washington
1979—Ted Brown, RB, North Carolina State
1978—Randy Holloway, DE, Pittsburgh
1977—Tommy Kramer, QB, Rice
1976—James White, DT, Oklahoma State
1975—Mark Mullaney, DE, Colorado State
1974—Fred McNeill, LB, UCLA
      Steve Riley, T, Southern California
1973—Chuck Foreman, RB, Miami (Fla.)
1972—Jeff Siemon, LB, Stanford
1971—Leo Hayden, RB, Ohio State
1970—John Ward, DT, Oklahoma State
1969—(No Number One Selection)
1968—Ron Yary, T, Southern California*
1967—Clint Jones, RB, Michigan State
      Gene Washington, WR, Michigan State
      Alan Page, DT, Notre Dame
1966—Jerry Shay, DT, Purdue
1965—Jack Snow, WR, Notre Dame
1964—Carl Eller, DE, Minnesota
1963—Jim Dunaway, T, Mississippi
1962—(No Number One Selection)
1961—Tommy Mason, RB, Tulane*

NEW ENGLAND PATRIOTS

1990—Chris Singleton, LB, Arizona
      Ray Agnew, DL, North Carolina State
1989—Hart Lee Dykes, WR, Oklahoma State
1988—John Stephens, RB, Northwestern (La.) St.
1987—Bruce Armstrong, G, Louisville
1986—Reggie Dupard, RB, Southern Methodist
1985—Trevor Matich, C, Brigham Young
1984—Irving Fryar, WR, Nebraska*
1983—Tony Eason, QB, Illinois
1982—Kenneth Sims, DT, Texas*
      Lester Williams, DT, Nebraska
1981—Brian Holloway, T, Stanford
1980—Roland James, DB, Tennessee
      Vagas Ferguson, RB, Notre Dame
1979—Rick Sanford, DB, South Carolina

1978—Bob Cryder, G, Alabama
1977—Raymond Clayborn, DB, Texas
      Stanley Morgan, WR, Tennessee
1976—Mike Haynes, DB, Arizona State
      Pete Brock, C, Colorado
      Tim Fox, DB, Ohio State
1975—Russ Francis, TE, Oregon
1974—(No Number One Selection)
1973—John Hannah, G, Alabama
      Sam Cunningham, RB, Southern California
      Darryl Stingley, WR, Purdue
1972—(No Number One Selection)
1971—Jim Plunkett, QB, Stanford*
1970—Phil Olsen, DT, Utah State
1969—Ron Sellers, WR, Florida State
1968—Dennis Byrd, DE, North Carolina State
1967—John Charles, DB, Purdue
1966—Karl Singer, T, Purdue
      Willie Townes, T, Tulsa
1965—Jerry Rush, DE, Michigan State
      Dave McCormick, T, Louisiana State
1964—Jack Concannon, QB, Boston Col* (AFL)
1963—Art Graham, E, Boston College
1962—Gary Collins, WR, Maryland
1961—Tommy Mason, RB, Tulane
1960—Ron Burton, RB, Northwestern

NEW ORLEANS SAINTS

1990—Reynaldo Turnbull, DE, West Virginia
1989—Wayne Martin, DE, Arkansas
1988—Craig Heyward, RB, Pittsburgh
1987—Shawn Knight, DE, Brigham Young
1986—Jim Dombrowski, T, Virginia
1985—Alvin Toles, LB, Tennessee
1984—(No Number One Selection)
1983—(No Number One Selection)
1982—Lindsay Scott, WR, Georgia
1981—George Rogers, RB, South Carolina*
1980—Stan Brock, T, Colorado
1979—Russell Erxleben, P, Texas
1978—Wes Chandler, WR, Florida
1977—Joe Campbell, DE, Maryland
1976—Chuck Muncie, RB, California
1975—Larry Burton, WR, Purdue
      Kurt Schumacher, G, Ohio State
1974—Rick Middleton, LB, Ohio State
1973—(No Number One Selection)
1972—Royce Smith, G, Georgia
1971—Archie Manning, QB, Mississippi
1970—Ken Burrough, WR, Texas Southern
1969—John Shinners, G, Xavier (Ohio)
1968—Kevin Hardy, DE, Notre Dame
1967—Les Kelley, RB, Alabama

NEW YORK GIANTS

1990—Rodney Hampton, RB, Georgia
1989—Brian Williams, G, Minnesota
1988—Eric Moore, T, Indiana
1987—Mark Ingram, WR, Michigan State
1986—Eric Dorsey, DT, Notre Dame
1985—George Adams, RB, Kentucky
1984—Carl Banks, LB, Michigan State
      Bill Roberts, T, Ohio State
1983—Terry Kinard, DB, Clemson
1982—Butch Woolfolk, RB, Michigan
1981—Lawrence Taylor, LB, North Carolina
1980—Mark Haynes, DB, Colorado
1979—Phil Simms, QB, Morehead State
1978—Gordon King, T, Stanford
1977—Gary Jeter, DT, Southern California
1976—Troy Archer, DE, Colorado
1975—(No Number One Selection)
1974—John Hicks, G, Ohio State
1973—(No Number One Selection)
1972—Eldridge Small, DB, Texas A & I
      Larry Jacobson, DT, Nebraska
1971—Rocky Thompson, RB, West Texas State
1970—Jim Files, LB, Oklahoma
1969—Fred Dryer, DE, San Diego State
1968—(No Number One Selection)
1967—(No Number One Selection)
1966—Francis Peay, T, Missouri

1965—Tucker Frederickson, RB, Auburn*
1964—Joe Don Looney, RB, Oklahoma
1963—(No Number One Selection)
1962—Jerry Hillebrand, LB, Colorado
1961—(No Number One Selection)
1960—Lou Cordileone, G, Clemson
1959—Lee Grosscup, B, Utah
1958—Phil King, B, Vanderbilt
1957—(No Number One Selection)
1956—Henry Moore, B, Arkansas
1955—Joe Heap, B, Notre Dame
1954—(No Number One Selection)
1953—Bobby Marlow, B, Alabama
1952—Frank Gifford, B, Southern California
1951—Kyle Rote, B, Southern Methodist*
1950—Travis Tidwell, B, Auburn
1949—Paul Page, B, Southern Methodist
1948—Tony Minisi, B, Pennsylvania
1947—Vic Schwall, B, Northwestern
1946—George Connor, T, Notre Dame
1945—Elmer Barbour, B, Wake Forest
1944—Billy Hillenbrand, B, Indiana
1943—Steve Filipowicz, B, Fordham
1942—Merle Hapes, B, Mississippi
1941—George Franck, B, Minnesota
1940—Grenville Lansdell, B, Southern California
1939—Walt Nielson, B, Arizona
1938—George Karamatic, B, Gonzaga
1937—Ed Widseth, T, Minnesota
1936—Art Lewis, T, Ohio

NEW YORK JETS

1990—Blair Thomas, RB, Penn State
1989—Jeff Lageman, LB, Virginia
1988—Dave Cadigan, T, Southern California
1987—Roger Vick, FB, Texas A&M
1986—Mike Haight, T, Iowa
1985—Al Toon, WR, Wisconsin
1984—Russell Carter, DB, Southern Methodist
       Ron Faurot, DE, Arkansas
1983—Ken O'Brien, QB, California-Davis
1982—Bob Crable, LB, Notre Dame
1981—Freeman McNeil, RB, UCLA
1980—Lam Jones, WR, Texas
1979—Marty Lyons, DT, Alabama
1978—Chris Ward, T, Ohio State
1977—Marvin Powell, T, Southern California
1976—Richard Todd, QB, Alabama
1975—(No Number One Selection)
1974—Carl Barzilauskas, DT, Indiana
1973—Burgess Owens, DB, Miami
1972—Jerome Barkum, WR, Jackson State
       Mike Taylor, LB, Michigan
1971—John Riggins, RB, Kansas
1970—Steve Tannen, DB, Florida
1969—Dave Foley, T, Ohio State
1968—Lee White, RB, Weber State
1967—Paul Seiler, G, Notre Dame
1966—Bill Yearby, DT, Michigan
1965—Joe Namath, QB, Alabama
       Tom Nowatzke, RB, Indiana
1964—Matt Snell, RB, Ohio State
1963—Jerry Stovall, RB, Louisiana State
1962—Sandy Stephens, QB, Minnesota
1961—Tom Brown, G, Minnesota
1960—George Izo, QB, Notre Dame

PHILADELPHIA EAGLES

1990—Ben Smith, DB, Georgia
1989—(No Number One Selection)
1988—Keith Jackson, TE, Oklahoma
1987—Jerome Brown, DT, Miami (Fla.)
1986—Keith Byars, RB, Ohio State
1985—Kevin Allen, T, Indiana
1984—Kenny Jackson, WR, Penn State
1983—Michael Haddix, RB, Mississippi State
1982—Mike Quick, WR, North Carolina State
1981—Leonard Mitchell, DE, Houston
1980—Roynell Young, DB, Alcorn State
1979—Jerry Robinson, LB, UCLA
1978—(No Number One Selection)
1977—(No Number One Selection)

1976—(No Number One Selection)
1975—(No Number One Selection)
1974—(No Number One Selection)
1973—Jerry Sisemore, T, Texas
       Charle Young, TE, Southern California
1972—John Reaves, QB, Florida
1971—Richard Harris, DE, Grambling
1970—Steve Zabel, E, Oklahoma
1969—Leroy Kcyes, RB, Purdue
1968—Tim Rossovich, DE, Southern California
1967—Harry Jones, RB, Arkansas
1966—Randy Beisler, T, Indiana
1965—(No Number One Selection)
1964—Bob Brown, T, Nebraska
1963—Ed Budde, T, Michigan State
1962—(No Number One Selection)
1961—Art Baker, B, Syracuse
1960—Ron Burton, B, Northwestern
1959—(No Number One Selection)
1958—Walter Kowalczyk, B, Michigan State
1957—Clarence Peaks, B, Michigan State
1956—Bob Pellegrini, C, Maryland
1955—Dick Bielski, B, Maryland
1954—Neil Worden, B, Notre Dame
1953—(No Number One Selection)
1952—John Bright, B, Drake
1951—Ebert Van Buren, B, Louisiana State
1950—Harry Grant, E, Minnesota
1949—Chuck Bednarik, C, Pennsylvania*
       Frank Tripucka, QB, Notre Dame
1948—Clyde Scott, B, Arkansas
1947—Neil Armstrong, E, Oklahoma A&M
1946—Leo Riggs, B, Southern California
1945—John Yonaker, E, Notre Dame
1944—Steve Van Buren, B, Louisiana State
1943—Joe Muha, B, Virginia Military
1942—Pete Kmetovic, B, Stanford
1941—(No Number One Selection)
1940—Wes McAfee, B, Duke
1939—Davey O'Brien, QB, Texas Christian
1938—John McDonald, B, Nebraska
1937—Sam Francis, B, Nebraska*
1936—Jay Berwanger, B, Chicago*

PHOENIX CARDINALS

1990—(No Number One Selection)
1989—Eric Hill, LB, Louisiana State
       Joe Wolf, G, Boston College
1988—Ken Harvey, LB, California
1987—Kelly Stouffer, QB, Colorado State
1986—Anthony Bell, LB, Michigan State
1985—Freddie Joe Nunn, LB, Mississippi
1984—Clyde Duncan, WR, Tennessee
1983—Leonard Smith, DB, McNeese State
1982—Luis Sharpe, T, UCLA
1981—E.J. Junior, LB, Alabama
1980—Curtis Greer, DE, Michigan
1979—Ottis Anderson, RB, Miami (Fla.)
1978—Steve Little, K, Arkansas
       Ken Greene, DB, Washington State
1977—Steve Pisarkiewicz, QB, Missouri
1976—Mike Dawson, DT, Arizona
1975—Tim Gray, DB, Texas A&M
1974—J.V. Cain, TE, Colorado
1973—Dave Butz, DT, Purdue
1972—Bobby Moore, RB, Oregon
1971—Norm Thompson, DB, Utah
1970—Larry Stegent, RB, Texas A&M
1969—Roger Wehrli, DB, Missouri
1968—MacArthur Lane, RB, Utah State
1967—Dave Williams, WR, Washington
1966—Carl McAdams, LB, Oklahoma
1965—Joe Namath, QB, Alabama
1964—Ken Kortas, DT, Louisville
1963—Jerry Stovall, DB, Louisiana State
       Don Brumm, E, Purdue
1962—Fate Echols, DT, Northwestern
       Irv Goode, C, Kentucky
1961—Ken Rice, T, Auburn
1960—George Izo, QB, Notre Dame
1959—Billy Stacy, B, Mississippi State
1958—King Hill, B, Rice*

1957—Jerry Tubbs, C, Oklahoma
1956—Joe Childress, B, Auburn
1955—Max Boydston, E, Oklahoma
1954—Lamar McHan, B, Arkansas
1953—Johnny Olszewski, QB, California
1952—Ollie Matson, B, San Francisco
1951—Jerry Groom, C, Notre Dame
1950—(No Number One Selection)
1949—Bill Fischer, G, Notre Dame
1948—Jim Spavital, B, Oklahoma A & M
1947—DeWitt (Tex) Coulter, T, Army
1946—Dub Jones, B, Louisiana State
1945—Charley Trippi, B, Georgia*
1944—Pat Harder, B, Wisconsin
1943—Glenn Dobbs, B, Tulsa
1942—Steve Lach, B, Duke
1941—John Kimbrough, B, Texas A & M
1940—George Cafego, B, Tennessee*
1939—Charles Aldrich, C, Texas Christian*
1938—Jack Robbins, B, Arkansas
1937—Ray Buivid, B, Marquette
1936—Jim Lawrence, B, Texas Christian

PITTSBURGH STEELERS

1990—Eric Green, TE, Liberty (Va.)
1989—Tim Worley, RB, Georgia
　　　Tom Ricketts, T, Pittsburgh
1988—Aaron Jones, DE, Eastern Kentucky
1987—Rod Woodson, DB, Purdue
1986—John Rienstra, G, Temple
1985—Darryl Sims, DT, Wisconsin
1984—Louis Lipps, WR, Southern Mississippi
1983—Gabriel Rivera, DT, Texas Tech
1982—Walter Abercrombie, RB, Baylor
1981—Keith Gary, DE, Oklahoma
1980—Mark Malone, QB, Arizona State
1979—Greg Hawthorne, RB, Baylor
1978—Ron Johnson, DB, Eastern Michigan
1977—Robin Cole, LB, New Mexico
1976—Bennie Cunningham, TE, Clemson
1975—Dave Brown, DB, Michigan
1974—Lynn Swann, WR, Southern California
1973—James Thomas, DB, Florida State
1972—Franco Harris, RB, Penn State
1971—Frank Lewis, WR, Grambling
1970—Terry Bradshaw, QB, Louisiana Tech*
1969—Joe Greene, DT, North Texas State
1968—Mike Taylor, T, Southern California
1967—(No Number One Selection)
1966—Dick Leftridge, RB, West Virginia
1965—(No Number One Selection)
1964—Paul Martha, RB, Pittsburgh
1963—(No Number One Selection)
1962—Bob Ferguson, RB, Ohio State
1961—(No Number One Selection)
1960—Jack Spikes, B, Texas Christian
1959—(No Number One Selection)
1958—(No Number One Selection)
1957—Len Dawson, QB, Purdue
1956—Gary Glick, B, Colorado State*
　　　Art Davis, B, Mississippi State
1955—Frank Varrichione, T, Notre Dame
1954—John Lattner, B, Notre Dame
1953—Ted Marchibroda, QB, St. Bonaventure
1952—Ed Modzelewski, B, Maryland
1951—Clarence Avinger, B, Alabama
1950—Lynn Chandnois, B, Michigan State
1949—Bobby Gage, B, Clemson
1948—Dan Edwards, E, Georgia
1947—Hub Bechtol, E, Texas
1946—Doc Blanchard, B, Army
1945—Paul Duhart, B, Florida
1944—Johnny Podesto, B, St. Mary's (Calif.)
1943—Bill Daley, B, Minnesota
1942—Bill Dudley, B, Virginia*
1941—Chet Gladchuk, C, Boston College
1940—Kay Eakin, B, Arkansas
1939—(No Number One Selection)
1938—Byron White, B, Colorado
　　　Frank Filchock, B, Indiana
1937—Mike Basrak, C, Duquesne
1936—Bill Shakespeare, B, Notre Dame

SAN DIEGO CHARGERS

1990—Junior Seau, LB, Southern California
1989—Burt Grossman, DE, Pittsburgh
1988—Anthony Miller, WR, Tennessee
1987—Rod Bernstine, TE, Texas A & M
1986—Leslie O'Neal, DE, Oklahoma State
　　　Jim FitzPatrick, T, Southern California
1985—Jim Lachey, G, Ohio State
1984—Mossy Cade, DB, Texas
1983—Billy Ray Smith, LB, Arkansas
　　　Gary Anderson, WR, Arkansas
　　　Gill Byrd, DB, San Jose State
1982—(No Number One Selection)
1981—James Brooks, RB, Auburn
1980—(No Number One Selection)
1979—Kellen Winslow, TE, Missouri
1978—John Jefferson, WR, Arizona State
1977—Bob Rush, C, Memphis State
1976—Joe Washington, RB, Oklahoma
1975—Gary Johnson, DT, Grambling
　　　Mike Williams, DB, Louisiana State
1974—Bo Matthews, RB, Colorado
　　　Don Goode, LB, Kansas
1973—Johnny Rodgers, WR, Nebraska
1972—(No Number One Selection)
1971—Leon Burns, RB, Long Beach State
1970—Walker Gillette, WR, Richmond
1969—Marty Domres, QB, Columbia
　　　Bob Babich, LB, Miami (Ohio)
1968—Russ Washington, T, Missouri
　　　Jim Hill, DB, Texas A & I
1967—Ron Billingsley, DT, Wyoming
1966—Don Davis, T, Los Angeles State
1965—Steve DeLong, DE, Tennessee
1964—Ted Davis, E, Georgia Tech
1963—Walt Sweeney, E, Syracuse
1962—Bob Ferguson, RB, Ohio State
1961—Earl Faison, E, Indiana
1960—Monty Stickles, E, Notre Dame

SAN FRANCISCO 49ers

1990—Dexter Carter, RB, Florida State
1989—Keith DeLong, LB, Tennessee
1988—(No Number One Selection)
1987—Harris Barton, T, North Carolina
　　　Terrence Flager, RB, Clemson
1986—(No Number One Selection)
1985—Jerry Rice, WR, Mississippi Valley
1984—Todd Shell, LB, Brigham Young
1983—(No Number One Selection)
1982—(No Number One Selection)
1981—Ronnie Lott, DB, Southern California
1980—Earl Cooper, RB, Rice
　　　Jim Stuckey, DE, Clemson
1979—(No Number One Selection)
1978—Ken McAfee, TE, Notre Dame
　　　Dan Bunz, LB, Long Beach State
1977—(No Number One Selection)
1976—(No Number One Selection)
1975—Jimmy Webb, DT, Mississippi State
1974—Wilbur Jackson, RB, Alabama
　　　Bill Sandifer, DT, UCLA
1973—Mike Holmes, DB, Texas Southern
1972—Terry Beasley, WR, Auburn
1971—Tim Anderson, DB, Ohio State
1970—Cedrick Hardman, DE, North Texas State
　　　Bruce Taylor, DB, Boston U.
1969—Ted Kwalick, TE, Penn State
　　　Gene Washington, WR, Stanford
1968—Forrest Blue, C, Auburn
1967—Steve Spurrier, QB, Florida
　　　Cas Banaszek, LB, Northwestern
1966—Stan Hindman, DE, Mississippi
1965—Ken Willard, RB, North Carolina
　　　George Donnelly, DB, Illinois
1964—Dave Parks, E, Texas Tech*
1963—Kermit Alexander, RB, UCLA
1962—Lance Alworth, RB, Arkansas
1961—Jim Johnson, RB, UCLA
　　　Bernie Casey, RB, Bowling Green
　　　Bill Kilmer, QB, UCLA

1960—Monty Stickles, E, Notre Dame
1959—Dave Baker, RB, Oklahoma
      Dan James, C, Ohio State
1958—Jim Pace, RB, Michigan
      Charles Krueger, T, Texas A & M
1957—John Brodie, QB, Stanford
1956—Earl Morrall, QB, Michigan State
1955—Dick Moegel, HB, Rice
1954—Bernie Faloney, QB, Maryland
1953—Harry Babcock, E, Georgia*
      Tom Stolhandske, E, Texas
1952—Hugh McElhenny, RB, Washington
1951—Y.A. Tittle, QB, Louisiana State
1950—Leo Nomellini, T, Minnesota

SEATTLE SEAHAWKS

1990—Cortez Kennedy, DT, Miami (Fla.)
1989—Andy Heck, T, Notre Dame
1988— (No Number One Selection)
1987—Tony Woods, LB, Pittsburgh
1986—John L. Williams, RB, Florida
1985— (No Number One Selection)
1984—Terry Taylor, DB, Southern Illinois
1983—Curt Warner, RB, Penn State
1982—Jeff Bryant, DE, Clemson
1981—Kenny Easley, DB, UCLA
1980—Jacob Green, DE, Texas A & M
1979—Manu Tuiasosopo, DT, UCLA
1978—Keith Simpson, DB, Memphis State
1977—Steve August, G, Tulsa
1976—Steve Niehaus, DT, Notre Dame

TAMPA BAY BUCCANEERS

1990—Keith McCants, LB, Alabama
1989—Broderick Thomas, LB, Nebraska
1988—Paul Gruber, T, Wisconsin
1987—Vinny Testaverde, QB, Miami (Fla.) *
1986—Bo Jackson, RB, Auburn*
      Rod Jones, DB, Southern Methodist
1985—Ron Holmes, DE, Washington
1984— (No Number One Selection)
1983— (No Number One Selection)
1982—Sean Farrell, G, Penn State
1981—Hugh Green, LB, Pittsburgh
1980—Ray Snell, T, Wisconsin
1979— (No Number One Selection)
1978—Doug Williams, QB, Grambling
1977—Ricky Bell, RB, Southern California*
1976—Lee Roy Selmon, DE, Oklahoma*

WASHINGTON REDSKINS

1990— (No Number One Selection)
1989— (No Number One Selection)
1988— (No Number One Selection)
1987— (No Number One Selection)
1986— (No Number One Selection)
1985— (No Number One Selection)
1984— (No Number One Selection)
1983—Darrell Green, DB, Texas A & I
1982— (No Number One Selection)
1981—Mark May, T, Pittsburgh
1980—Art Monk, WR, Syracuse
1979— (No Number One Selection)
1978— (No Number One Selection)
1977— (No Number One Selection)
1976— (No Number One Selection)
1975— (No Number One Selection)
1974— (No Number One Selection)
1973— (No Number One Selection)
1972— (No Number One Selection)
1971— (No Number One Selection)
1970— (No Number One Selection)
1969— (No Number One Selection)
1968—Jim Smith, DB, Oregon
1967—Ray McDonald, RB, Idaho
1966—Charlie Gogolak, K, Princeton
1965— (No Number One Selection)
1964—Charley Taylor, RB, Arizona State
1963—Pat Richter, TE, Wisconsin
1962—Ernie Davis, RB, Syracuse*
      Leroy Jackson, RB, Illinois Central

Illinois quarterback Jeff George was selected by Indianapolis with the first pick in the 1990 NFL draft.

1961—Joe Rutgens, T, Illinois
      Norm Snead, QB, Wake Forest
1960—Richie Lucas, QB, Penn State
1959—Don Allard, QB, Boston College
1958— (No Number One Selection)
1957—Don Bosseler, RB, Miami (Fla.)
1956—Ed Vereb, RB, Maryland
1955—Ralph Guglielmi, QB, Notre Dame
1954—Steve Meilinger, TE, Kentucky
1953—Jack Scarbath, QB, Maryland
1952—Larry Isbell, QB, Baylor
1951—Leon Heath, RB, Oklahoma
1950—George Thomas, RB, Oklahoma
1949—Rob Goode, RB, Texas A & M
1948—Harry Gilmer, QB, Alabama*
1947—Cal Rossi, B, UCLA
1946—Cal Rossi, B, UCLA
1945—Jim Hardy, B, Southern California
1944—Mike Micka, B, Colgate
1943—Jack Jenkins, B, Missouri
1942—Orban Sanders, B, Texas
1941—Forrest Evashevski, B, Michigan
1940—Ed Boell, B, New York U.
1939—I.B. Hale, T, Texas Christian
1938—Andy Farkas, B, Detroit
1937—Sammy Baugh, QB, Texas Christian
1936—Riley Smith, QB, Alabama

1989-90 NFL TRADES
(Covering July 1989 through June 1990)

Defensive tackle KEVIN BROOKS and 4th-round choice in 1990 draft from Dallas to Denver for 3rd-round choice in 1990 draft (7/10). Denver subsequently selected linebacker JEROY ROBINSON (Texas A&M). Dallas subsequently traded choice and 5th- and 7th-round choices in 1990 draft to New England for 3rd-, 6th- and 8th-round choices in 1990 draft (4/22).

Tackle DARYLE SMITH from Dallas to Seattle for 9th-round choice in 1990 draft (7/24). Dallas subsequently traded choice and 6th-, 8th-, 10th- and 11th-round choices to Los Angeles Raiders for rights to cornerback STAN SMAGALA (Notre Dame) (4/22).

Tackle CURT SINGER from Detroit to Seattle for conditional draft choice (7/28).

Tackle WINFORD HOOD from Denver to Phoenix for conditional draft choice (8/4).

Tackle KEVIN THOMAS from Seattle to Phoenix for conditional draft choice (8/5).

Quarterback SCOTT SECULES from Dallas to Miami for 5th-round choice in 1990 draft (8/6). Dallas subsequently traded choice and 3rd- and 7th-round choices in 1990 draft to New England for 3rd-, 6th- and 8th-round choices in 1990 draft (4/22).

Wide receiver GARY LEE from Detroit to Denver for conditional draft choice (8/7).

Tackle DARRYL HALEY from Green Bay to Cleveland for conditional draft choice (8/14).

Tight end PAT CARTER from Detroit to Los Angeles Rams for 4th-round choice in 1990 draft (8/18). Detroit subsequently selected defensive back CHRIS OLDHAM (Oregon).

Quarterback JIM McMAHON from Chicago to San Diego for 2nd-round choice in 1990 draft (8/18). Chicago subsequently selected linebacker RON COX (Fresno State).

Tackle BILL CONTZ from Denver to Indianapolis for conditional draft choice (8/21).

Tackle ZEFROSS MOSS from Dallas to Indianapolis for 10th-round choice in 1990 draft (8/22). Dallas subsequently traded choice and 6th-, 8th-, 9th- and 11th-round choices in 1990 draft to Los Angeles Raiders for rights to cornerback STAN SMAGALA (Notre Dame) (4/22). Los Angeles Raiders subsequently traded choice to Denver for 11th-round choice in 1990 draft (4/23).

Nose tackle CHUCK EHIN from Indianapolis to Dallas for conditional draft choice (8/22).

Defensive tackle DEAN HAMEL from Washington to Dallas for 5th-round choice in

1990 draft (8/28). Washington subsequently traded choice and another 5th-round choice in 1990 draft to New England for 4th-round choice in 1990 draft (4/22).

Punter RALF MOJSIEJENKO from San Diego to Washington for 7th-round choice in 1990 draft (8/29). San Diego subsequently selected wide receiver NATE LEWIS (Oregon Tech).

Fullback JAMES JONES from Detroit to Seattle for cornerback TERRY TAYLOR (8/31).

Guard GUY BINGHAM from New York Jets to Atlanta for 7th-round choice in 1990 draft (9/4). Jets subsequently selected guard DWAYNE WHITE (Alcorn State).

Running back BARRY REDDEN from San Diego to Cleveland for 7th-round choice in 1990 draft (9/4). San Diego subsequently selected tackle JOE STAYSNIAK (Ohio State).

Defensive end RON HOLMES from Tampa Bay to Denver for 4th-round choice in 1990 draft (9/5). Tampa Bay subsequently selected center TONY MAYBERRY (Wake Forest).

Running back HERSCHEL WALKER from Dallas to Minnesota for linebackers JESSE SOLOMON and DAVID HOWARD, cornerback ISSIAC HOLT, running back DARRIN NELSON, defensive end ALEX STEWART, 1st-round choice in 1992 draft and six conditional draft choices (10/12). Conditional choices were assigned to traded players depending on status as of 2/1/90 as follows: Solomon—1st in 1990; Stewart—2nd in 1990; Howard—1st in 1991; Nelson—2nd in 1991; Holt—2nd and 3rd in 1992. Stewart was released and Dallas received that pick. Nelson subsequently traded to San Diego with Dallas keeping his assigned pick, 6th-round choice going from Minnesota to Dallas and 5th-round choice from San Diego to Minnesota through Dallas. Dallas and Minnesota subsequently agreed to allow Solomon, Howard and Holt to remain with Dallas and Minnesota received 3rd- and 10th-round choices in 1990 draft and 3rd-round choice in 1991 draft.

Dallas subsequently traded 1st-round choice in 1990 draft (and 3rd-round choice in 1990 draft) to Pittsburgh for 1st-round choice in 1990 draft (4/22) and traded 2nd-round choice in 1990 draft (and 3rd-round choice in 1990 draft) to San Francisco for running back TERRENCE FLAGLER, defensive end DAN STUBBS and 3rd- and 11th-round choices in 1990 draft (4/19). Minnesota subsequently selected tight end MIKE JONES (Texas A&M) and wide receiver PAT NEWMAN (Utah State).

Quarterback STEVE PELLUER from Dallas to Kansas City for 3rd-round choice in 1990 draft (10/17). Dallas subsequently traded choice and 2nd-round choice in 1990 draft to San Francisco for running back TERRENCE FLAGLER, defensive end DAN STUBBS and 3rd- and 11th-round choices in 1990 draft (4/19).

Running back PAUL PALMER from Detroit to Dallas for 8th-round choice in 1990 draft (10/17). Detroit subsequently selected wide receiver WILLIE GREEN (Mississippi).

Linebacker CHIP BANKS from San Diego to Indianapolis for 3rd-round choice in 1990 draft (10/17). San Diego subsequently selected wide receiver WALTER WILSON (East Carolina).

Running back DARRIN NELSON from Dallas to San Diego (10/17). Dallas received 2nd-round choice in 1991 draft from Minnesota as part of original deal and 6th-round choice in 1990 draft. San Diego sent 5th-round choice in 1990 draft to Minnesota through Dallas. Dallas subsequently traded choice and 8th-, 9th-, 10th- and 11th-round choices to Los Angeles Raiders for rights to cornerback STAN SMAGALA (Notre Dame) (4/22). Minnesota subsequently selected wide receiver REGGIE THORNTON (Bowling Green State).

Running back TERRENCE FLAGLER, defensive end DAN STUBBS and 3rd- and 11th-round choices in 1990 draft from San Francisco to Dallas for 2nd- and 3rd-round choices in 1990 draft (4/19). Dallas subsequently traded 3rd-round choice (and 1st-round choice in 1990 draft) to Pittsburgh for 1st-round choice in 1990 draft (4/22) and traded 11th-round choice (and 6th-, 8th-, 9th- and 10th-round choices in 1990 draft) to Los Angeles Raiders for rights to cornerback STAN SMAGALA (Notre Dame) (4/22). San Francisco subsequently selected defensive tackle DENNIS BROWN (Washington State) and wide receiver RON LEWIS (Florida State).

Tackle CHRIS HINTON, wide receiver ANDRE RISON, 5th-round choice in 1990 draft and 1st-round choice in 1991 draft from Indianapolis to Atlanta for 1st- and 4th-round choices in 1990 draft (4/20). Indianapolis subsequently selected quarterback JEFF GEORGE (Illinois) and wide receiver STACEY SIMMONS (Florida). Atlanta subsequently selected tight end REGGIE REDDING (Cal State-Fullerton).

Los Angeles Raiders traded 4th-round choice in 1990 draft to San Francisco for 4th- and 5th-round choices in 1990 draft (4/20). Raiders subsequently sent choices to Washington as part of Jay Schroeder deal on 9/7/89. San Francisco subsequently selected center DEAN CALIGUIRE (Pittsburgh).

Running back GARY ANDERSON from San Diego to Tampa Bay for 3rd-round choice in 1990 draft and conditional choice in 1991 draft (4/21). San Diego subsequently selected linebacker JEFF MILLS (Nebraska).

New England traded 1st- and 2nd-round choices in 1990 draft to Seattle for two 1st-round choices and 3rd-round choice in 1990 draft and 4th-round choice in 1991 draft (4/22). New England subsequently selected linebacker CHRIS SINGLETON (Arizona), defensive end RAY AGNEW (North Carolina State) and traded 3rd-round choice (and 6th- and 8th-round choices in 1990 draft) to Dallas for 3rd-, 5th- and 7th-round choices in 1990 draft (4/22). Seattle subsequently selected defensive tackle CORTEZ KENNEDY (Miami, Fla.) and linebacker TERRY WOODEN (Syracuse).

Pittsburgh traded 1st-round choice in 1990 draft to Dallas for 1st- and 3rd-round choices in 1990 draft (4/22). Pittsburgh subsequently selected tight end ERIC GREEN (Liberty, Va.) and defensive tackle CRAIG VEASEY (Houston). Dallas subsequently selected running back EMMITT SMITH (Florida).

New England traded 3rd-, 6th- and 8th-round choices in 1990 draft to Dallas for 3rd-, 5th- and 7th-round choices in 1990 draft (4/22). New England subsequently selected wide receiver GREG McMURTRY (Michigan), running back JAMES GRAY (Texas Tech) and traded 7th-round choice (and another 7th-round choice in 1990 draft) to Buffalo for 12th-round choice in 1990 draft and 4th-round choice in 1991 draft (4/23). Dallas subsequently selected defensive tackle JIMMIE JONES (Miami, Fla.), traded 6th-round choice (and two other 6th-round choices in 1990 draft) to San Diego for 3rd-round choice in 1991 draft (4/22) and traded 8th-round choice (and 6th-, 9th-, 10th- and 11th-round choices in 1990 draft) to Los Angeles Raiders for rights to cornerback STAN SMAGALA (Notre Dame) (4/22).

New England traded 4th-round choice in 1990 draft to Washington for two 5th-round choices in 1990 draft (4/22). Washington subsequently selected quarterback CARY CONKLIN (Washington). New England subsequently selected defensive back JUNIOR ROBINSON (East Carolina) and traded other 5th-round choice to Denver for 4th-round choice in 1991 draft (4/22).

New England traded 5th-round choice in 1990 draft to Denver for 4th-round choice in 1991 draft (4/22). Denver subsequently selected guard JEFF DAVIDSON (Ohio State).

Cornerback BOBBY HUMPHERY from New York Jets to Los Angeles Rams for 5th-round choice in 1990 draft (4/22). Jets subsequently selected defensive back ROBERT McWRIGHT (Texas Christian).

Rights to cornerback STAN SMAGALA (Notre Dame) from Los Angeles Raiders to Dallas for 6th-, 8th-, 9th-, 10th- and 11th-round choices in 1990 draft (4/22). Raiders subsequently selected linebacker ARTHUR JIMERSON (Norfolk State), running back LEON PERRY (Oklahoma) and running back MYRON JONES (Fresno State) and traded 6th-round choice (and 8th-, 9th, 10th- and 11th-round choices in 1990 draft) to New Orleans for 4th-round choice in 1991 draft (4/22) and traded 10th-round choice to Denver for 11th-round choice in 1990 draft (4/23).

Los Angeles Raiders traded 6th-, 8th-, 9th-, 10th- and 11th-round choices in 1990 draft to New Orleans for 4th-round choice in 1991 draft (4/22). New Orleans subsequently selected linebacker JAMES WILLIAMS (Mississippi State), quarterback GERRY GDOWSKI (Nebraska), running back BRODERICK GRAVES (Winston-Salem State), wide receiver GARY COOPER (Clemson) and nose tackle WEBBIE BURNETT (Western Kentucky).

Dallas traded three 6th-round choices in 1990 draft to San Diego for 3rd-round choice in 1990 draft (4/22). San Diego subsequently selected quarterback JOHN FRIESZ (Idaho), center FRANK CORNISH (UCLA) and tight end DERRICK WALKER (Michigan).

Washington traded 5th-round choice in 1990 draft to Miami for 10th-round choice in 1990 draft and 4th-round choice in 1991 (4/22). Washington subsequently selected defensive back D'JUAN FRANCISCO (Notre Dame). Miami subsequently selected running back LEROY HOLT (Southern California).

New England traded two 7th-round choices in 1990 draft to Buffalo for 12th-round choice in 1990 draft and 4th-round choice in 1991 draft (4/23). New England subsequently selected guard BLAINE ROSE (Maryland). Buffalo subsequently selected guard BRENT GRIFFITH (Minnesota-Duluth) and linebacker BRENT COLLINS (Carson-Newman).

Chicago traded 7th-round choice in 1990 draft to Los Angeles Raiders for 7th- and 11th-round choices in 1990 draft (4/23). Chicago subsequently selected center BILL ANDERSON (Iowa) and tackle ROMAN MATUSZ (Pittsburgh). Raiders subsequently selected defensive back GARRY LEWIS (Alcorn State).

Miami traded 7th-round choice in 1990 draft to Cleveland for 5th-round choice in 1991 draft (4/23). Cleveland subsequently selected tight end SCOTT GALBRAITH (Southern California).

Cornerback TIM McKYER from San Francisco to Miami for 11th-round choice in 1990 draft and 2nd-round choice in 1991 draft (4/23). San Francisco subsequently selected defensive back ANTHONY SHELTON (Tennessee State).

Los Angeles Raiders traded 10th-round choice in 1990 draft to Denver for 11th-round choice in 1990 draft (4/23). Raiders subsequently selected wide receiver RON LEWIS (Jackson State). Denver subsequently selected defensive end JAMES SZYMANSKI (Michigan State).

Running back NAPOLEON McCALLUM from San Diego to Los Angeles Raiders for conditional draft choice (4/26).

Quarterback CHUCK LONG from Detroit to Los Angeles Rams for conditional draft choice (5/2).

Wide receiver JAMIE HOLLAND from San Diego to Los Angeles Raiders for draft choice (5/3).

The Sporting News AWARDS

NFL Coach of the Year (since 1947)

1947—Jimmy Conzelman, Chi. Cardinals
1948—Earle (Greasy) Neale, Philadelphia
1949—Paul Brown, Cleveland (AAFC)
1950—Steve Owen, New York
1951—Paul Brown, Cleveland
1952—J. Hampton Pool, Los Angeles
1953—Paul Brown, Cleveland
1954—no selection
1955—Joe Kuharich, Washington
1956—Jim Lee Howell, New York
1957—no selection
1958—no selection
1959—no selection
1960—no selection
1961—Vince Lombardi, Green Bay
1962—no selection
1963—George Halas, Chicago
1964—Don Shula, Baltimore
1965—George Halas, Chicago
1966—Tom Landry, Dallas
1967—George Allen, Los Angeles
1968—Don Shula, Baltimore

1969—Bud Grant, Minnesota
1970—Don Shula, Miami
1971—George Allen, Washington
1972—Don Shula, Miami
1973—Chuck Knox, Los Angeles
1974—Don Coryell, St. Louis
1975—Ted Marchibroda, Baltimore
1976—Chuck Fairbanks, New England
1977—Red Miller, Denver
1978—Jack Patera, Seattle
1979—Dick Vermeil, Philadelphia
1980—Chuck Knox, Buffalo
1981—Bill Walsh, San Francisco
1982—Joe Gibbs, Washington
1983—Joe Gibbs, Washington
1984—Chuck Knox, Seattle
1985—Mike Ditka, Chicago
1986—Bill Parcells, N.Y. Giants
1987—Jim Mora, New Orleans
1988—Marv Levy, Buffalo
1989—Lindy Infante, Green Bay

Rookie of the Year (since 1955)

1955—Alan Ameche, FB, Baltimore
1956—J.C. Caroline, HB, Chicago
1957—Jim Brown, FB, Cleveland
1958—Bobby Mitchell, HB, Cleveland
1959—Nick Pietrosante, FB, Detroit
1960—Gail Cogdill, E, Detroit
1961—Mike Ditka, E, Chicago
1962—Ronnie Bull, HB, Chicago
1963—Paul Flatley, WR, Minnesota
1964—Charley Taylor, HB, Washington
1965—Gale Sayers, RB, Chicago
1966—Tommy Nobis, LB, Atlanta
1967—Mel Farr, RB, Detroit
1968—Earl McCullouch, WR, Detroit
1969—Calvin Hill, RB, Dallas
1970—NFC: Bruce Taylor, CB, San Francisco
1971—NFC: John Brockington, RB, Green Bay
1972—NFC: Chester Marcol, PK, Green Bay
1973—NFC: Chuck Foreman, RB, Minnesota
1974—NFC: Wilbur Jackson, RB, San Francisco
1975—NFC: Steve Bartkowski, QB, Atlanta
1976—NFC: Sammy White, WR, Minnesota
1977—NFC: Tony Dorsett, RB, Dallas
1978—NFC: Al Baker, DE, Detroit
1979—NFC: Ottis Anderson, RB, St. Louis
1980—Billy Sims, RB, Detroit
1981—George Rogers, RB, New Orleans
1982—Marcus Allen, RB, L.A. Raiders
1983—Dan Marino, QB, Miami
1984—Louis Lipps, WR, Pittsburgh
1985—Eddie Brown, WR, Cincinnati
1986—Rueben Mayes, RB, New Orleans
1987—Robert Awalt, TE, St. Louis
1988—Keith Jackson, TE, Philadelphia
1989—Barry Sanders, RB, Detroit

AFC: Dennis Shaw, QB, Buffalo
AFC: Jim Plunkett, QB, New England
AFC: Franco Harris, RB, Pittsburgh
AFC: Boobie Clark, RB, Cincinnati
AFC: Don Woods, RB, San Diego
AFC: Robert Brazile, LB, Houston
AFC: Mike Haynes, CB, New England
AFC: A.J. Duhe, DT, Miami
AFC: Earl Campbell, RB, Houston
AFC: Jerry Butler, WR, Buffalo

NOTE: In 1980, The Sporting News began selecting one rookie as Rookie of the Year for the entire NFL.

NFL Executive of the Year

1955—Dan Reeves, Los Angeles
1956—George Halas, Chicago
1972—Dan Rooney, Pittsburgh
1973—Jim Finks, Minnesota
1974—Art Rooney, Pittsburgh
1975—Joe Thomas, Baltimore
1976—Al Davis, Oakland
1977—Tex Schramm, Dallas
1978—John Thompson, Seattle
1979—John Sanders, San Diego

1980—Eddie LeBaron, Atlanta
1981—Paul Brown, Cincinnati
1982—Bobby Beathard, Washington
1983—Bobby Beathard, Washington
1984—George Young, N.Y. Giants
1985—Mike McCaskey, Chicago
1986—George Young, N.Y. Giants
1987—Jim Finks, New Orleans
1988—Bill Polian, Buffalo
1989—John McVay, San Francisco

NOTE: The Executive of the Year Award was not given from 1957-71.

Lindy Infante was chosen NFL Coach of the Year in 1989 after leading the Green Bay Packers to their best record (10-6) since 1972.

Player of the Year (since 1954)

1954—Lou Groza, OT/K, Cleveland
1955—Otto Graham, QB, Cleveland
1956—Frank Gifford, HB, New York
1957—Jim Brown, RB, Cleveland
1958—Jim Brown, RB, Cleveland
1959—Johnny Unitas, QB, Baltimore
1960—Norm Van Brocklin, QB, Philadelphia
1961—Paul Hornung, HB, Green Bay
1962—Y.A. Tittle, QB, New York
1963—Y.A. Tittle, QB, New York
1964—Johnny Unitas, QB, Baltimore
1965—Jim Brown, RB, Cleveland
1966—Bart Starr, QB, Green Bay
1967—Johnny Unitas, QB, Baltimore
1968—Earl Morrall, QB, Baltimore
1969—Roman Gabriel, QB, Los Angeles
1970—NFC: John Brodie, QB, San Francisco   AFC: George Blanda, QB-PK, Oakland
1971—NFC: Roger Staubach, QB, Dallas   AFC: Bob Griese, QB, Miami
1972—NFC: Larry Brown, RB, Washington   AFC: Earl Morrall, QB, Miami
1973—NFC: John Hadl, QB, Los Angeles   AFC: O.J. Simpson, RB, Buffalo
1974—NFC: Chuck Foreman, RB, Minnesota   AFC: Ken Stabler, QB, Oakland
1975—NFC: Fran Tarkenton, QB, Minnesota   AFC: O.J. Simpson, RB, Buffalo
1976—NFC: Walter Payton, RB, Chicago   AFC: Ken Stabler, QB, Oakland
1977—NFC: Walter Payton, RB, Chicago   AFC: Craig Morton, QB, Denver
1978—NFC: Archie Manning, QB, New Orleans   AFC: Earl Campbell, RB, Houston
1979—NFC: Ottis Anderson, RB, St. Louis   AFC: Dan Fouts, QB, San Diego
1980—Brian Sipe, QB, Cleveland
1981—Ken Anderson, QB, Cincinnati
1982—Mark Moseley, PK, Washington
1983—Eric Dickerson, RB, L.A. Rams
1984—Dan Marino, QB, Miami
1985—Marcus Allen, RB, L.A. Raiders
1986—Lawrence Taylor, LB, N.Y. Giants
1987—Jerry Rice, WR, San Francisco
1988—Boomer Esiason, QB, Cincinnati
1989—Joe Montana, QB, San Francisco

NOTE: From 1970-79, a player was selected as Player of the Year for both the NFC and AFC. In 1980, The Sporting News reinstated the selection of one player as Player of the Year for the entire NFL.

1989 Pro Bowl Squads

*Denotes starter.

AFC OFFENSE

WR—Andre Reed, Buffalo*
Webster Slaughter, Cleveland*
Anthony Miller, San Diego
Brian Blades, Seattle
TE—Rodney Holman, Cincinnati*
Ferrell Edmunds, Miami
T—Anthony Munoz, Cincinnati*
Chris Hinton, Indianapolis*
Tunch Ilkin, Pittsburgh
G—Mike Munchak, Houston*
Bruce Matthews, Houston*
Max Montoya, Cincinnati
C—Ray Donaldson, Indianapolis*
Kent Hull, Buffalo
QB—Boomer Esiason, Cincinnati*
Warren Moon, Houston
RB—Christian Okoye, Kansas City*
James Brooks, Cincinnati*
Thurman Thomas, Buffalo
Eric Dickerson, Indianapolis
NOTE: QB Esiason replaced due to injury by John Elway, Denver. Elway replaced due to injury by Dave Krieg, Seattle.

AFC DEFENSE

DE—Bruce Smith, Buffalo*
Lee Williams, San Diego*
Howie Long, L.A. Raiders
DT—Michael Dean Perry, Cleveland*
Greg Kragen, Denver
OLB—Derrick Thomas, Kansas City*
Clay Matthews, Cleveland*
Leslie O'Neal, San Diego
ILB—Karl Mecklenburg, Denver*
John Offerdahl, Miami*
Shane Conlan, Buffalo
CB—Albert Lewis, Kansas City*
Frank Minnifield, Cleveland*
Kevin Ross, Kansas City
S—David Fulcher, Cincinnati*
Erik McMillan, N.Y. Jets*
Dennis Smith, Denver
NOTE: ILB Mecklenburg replaced due to injury by Johnny Rembert, New England.

AFC SPECIALISTS

P—Reggie Roby, Miami
PK—David Treadwell, Denver
KR—Rod Woodson, Pittsburgh
ST—Rufus Porter, Seattle

NFC OFFENSE

WR—Jerry Rice, San Francisco*
Sterling Sharpe, Green Bay*
Henry Ellard, L.A. Rams
John Taylor, San Francisco
TE—Keith Jackson, Philadelphia*
Steve Jordan, Minnesota
T—Gary Zimmerman, Minnesota*
Jackie Slater, L.A. Rams*
Luis Sharpe, Phoenix
G—Randall McDaniel, Minnesota*
Bill Fralic, Atlanta*
Guy McIntyre, San Francisco
C—Jay Hilgenberg, Chicago*
Doug Smith, L.A. Rams
QB—Joe Montana, San Francisco*
Don Majkowski, Green Bay
RB—Barry Sanders, Detroit*
Dalton Hilliard, New Orleans*
Roger Craig, San Francisco
Neal Anderson, Chicago
NOTE: WR Taylor replaced due to injury by Mark Carrier, Tampa Bay. QB Montana replaced due to injury by Mark Rypien, Washington. QB Majkowski replaced due to injury by Jim Everett, L.A. Rams. Everett replaced due to injury by Randall Cunningham, Philadelphia. RB Anderson replaced due to injury by Brent Fullwood, Green Bay.

NFC DEFENSE

DE—Chris Doleman, Minnesota*
Reggie White, Philadelphia*
Charles Mann, Washington
DT—Keith Millard, Minnesota*
Jerry Ball, Detroit
OLB—Tim Harris, Green Bay*
Lawrence Taylor, N.Y. Giants*
Kevin Greene, L.A. Rams
ILB—Mike Singletary, Chicago*
Chris Spielman, Detroit*
Vaughan Johnson, New Orleans
CB—Jerry Gray, L.A. Rams*
Carl Lee, Minnesota*
Eric Allen, Philadelphia
S—Joey Browner, Minnesota*
Ronnie Lott, San Francisco*
Tim McDonald, Phoenix

NFC SPECIALISTS

P—Rich Camarillo, Phoenix
PK—Eddie Murray, Detroit
KR—Dave Meggett, N.Y. Giants
ST—Ron Wolfley, Phoenix

1990 NATIONAL FOOTBALL LEAGUE SCHEDULE
(All times local)

FIRST WEEK
SUNDAY, SEPTEMBER 9

Denver at Los Angeles Raiders	1:00
Houston at Atlanta	4:00
Indianapolis at Buffalo	4:00
New York Jets at Cincinnati	4:00
Miami at New England	4:00
Minnesota at Kansas City	12:00
Phoenix at Washington	1:00
Pittsburgh at Cleveland	4:00
Los Angeles Rams at Green Bay	12:00
San Diego at Dallas	3:00
Seattle at Chicago	12:00
Tampa Bay at Detroit	1:00
Philadelphia at New York Giants	8:00

MONDAY, SEPTEMBER 10

San Francisco at New Orleans	8:00

SECOND WEEK
SUNDAY, SEPTEMBER 16

Atlanta at Detroit	1:00
Buffalo at Miami	1:00
Chicago at Green Bay	12:00
Cincinnati at San Diego	1:00
Cleveland at New York Jets	1:00
New England at Indianapolis	12:00
New Orleans at Minnesota	3:00
New York Giants at Dallas	3:00
Los Angeles Raiders at Seattle	1:00
Los Angeles Rams at Tampa Bay	1:00
Phoenix at Philadelphia	1:00
Washington at San Francisco	1:00
Houston at Pittsburgh	8:00

MONDAY, SEPTEMBER 17

Kansas City at Denver	7:00

THIRD WEEK
SUNDAY, SEPTEMBER 23

Atlanta at San Francisco	1:00
Dallas at Washington	1:00
Indianapolis at Houston	12:00
Kansas City at Green Bay	12:00
Miami at New York Giants	1:00
Minnesota at Chicago	12:00
New England at Cincinnati	1:00
Philadelphia at Los Angeles Rams	1:00
Phoenix at New Orleans	12:00
Pittsburgh at Los Angeles Raiders	1:00
San Diego at Cleveland	1:00
Seattle at Denver	2:00
Detroit at Tampa Bay	8:00

MONDAY, SEPTEMBER 24

Buffalo at New York Jets	9:00

FOURTH WEEK
SUNDAY, SEPTEMBER 30

Chicago at Los Angeles Raiders	1:00
Cleveland at Kansas City	3:00
Dallas at New York Giants	1:00
Denver at Buffalo	1:00
Green Bay at Detroit	1:00
Houston at San Diego	1:00
Indianapolis at Philadelphia	1:00
Miami at Pittsburgh	1:00
New York Jets at New England	4:00
Tampa Bay at Minnesota	12:00
Washington at Phoenix	5:00

MONDAY, OCTOBER 1

Cincinnati at Seattle	6:00

Open date: Atlanta, L.A. Rams, New Orleans, San Francisco

FIFTH WEEK
SUNDAY, OCTOBER 7

Cincinnati at Los Angeles Rams	1:00
Detroit at Minnesota	12:00
Green Bay at Chicago	3:00
Kansas City at Indianapolis	12:00
New Orleans at Atlanta	1:00
New York Jets at Miami	1:00
San Diego at Pittsburgh	1:00
San Francisco at Houston	12:00
Seattle at New England	1:00
Tampa Bay at Dallas	12:00
Los Angeles Raiders at Buffalo	7:30

MONDAY, OCTOBER 8

Cleveland at Denver	7:00

Open date: N.Y. Giants, Philadelphia, Phoenix, Washington

SIXTH WEEK
SUNDAY, OCTOBER 14

Cleveland at New Orleans	12:00
Dallas at Phoenix	1:00
Detroit at Kansas City	12:00
Green Bay at Tampa Bay	1:00
Houston at Cincinnati	1:00
New York Giants at Washington	4:00
Pittsburgh at Denver	2:00
San Diego at New York Jets	1:00
San Francisco at Atlanta	1:00
Seattle at Los Angeles Raiders	1:00
Los Angeles Rams at Chicago	6:30

MONDAY, OCTOBER 15

Minnesota at Philadelphia	9:00

Open date: Buffalo, Indianapolis, Miami, New England

SEVENTH WEEK
THURSDAY, OCTOBER 18

New England at Miami	8:00

SUNDAY, OCTOBER 21

Atlanta at Los Angeles Rams	1:00
Dallas at Tampa Bay	1:00
Denver at Indianapolis	12:00
Kansas City at Seattle	1:00
New Orleans at Houston	12:00
New York Jets at Buffalo	1:00
Philadelphia at Washington	1:00
Phoenix at New York Giants	4:00
Pittsburgh at San Francisco	1:00
Los Angeles Raiders at San Diego	1:00

MONDAY, OCTOBER 22

Cincinnati at Cleveland	9:00

Open date: Chicago, Detroit, Green Bay, Minnesota

EIGHTH WEEK
SUNDAY, OCTOBER 28

Buffalo at New England	1:00
Chicago at Phoenix	2:00
Cleveland at San Francisco	1:00
Detroit at New Orleans	12:00
Miami at Indianapolis	1:00
Minnesota vs. Green Bay at Milwaukee	12:00
New York Jets at Houston	12:00
Philadelphia at Dallas	12:00
Tampa Bay at San Diego	1:00
Washington at New York Giants	4:00
Cincinnati at Atlanta	8:00

MONDAY, OCTOBER 29

Los Angeles Rams at Pittsburgh	9:00

Open date: Denver, Kansas City, L.A. Raiders, Seattle

NINTH WEEK

SUNDAY, NOVEMBER 4

Atlanta at Pittsburgh	1:00
Buffalo at Cleveland	1:00
Chicago at Tampa Bay	4:00
Dallas at New York Jets	1:00
Houston at Los Angeles Rams	1:00
New England at Philadelphia	1:00
New Orleans at Cincinnati	1:00
Phoenix at Miami	1:00
Los Angeles Raiders at Kansas City	12:00
San Diego at Seattle	1:00
San Francisco at Green Bay	12:00
Washington at Detroit	1:00
Denver at Minnesota	7:00

MONDAY, NOVEMBER 5
New York Giants at Indianapolis	9:00

TENTH WEEK

SUNDAY, NOVEMBER 11

Atlanta at Chicago	12:00
Denver at San Diego	1:00
Green Bay at Los Angeles Raiders	1:00
Indianapolis at New England	1:00
Miami at New York Jets	1:00
Minnesota at Detroit	1:00
New York Giants at Los Angeles Rams	1:00
Phoenix at Buffalo	1:00
Seattle at Kansas City	12:00
Tampa Bay at New Orleans	12:00
San Francisco at Dallas	7:00

MONDAY, NOVEMBER 12
Washington at Philadelphia	9:00

Open date: Cincinnati, Cleveland, Houston, Pittsburgh

ELEVENTH WEEK

SUNDAY, NOVEMBER 18

Chicago at Denver	2:00
Dallas at Los Angeles Rams	1:00
Detroit at New York Giants	1:00
Green Bay at Phoenix	2:00
Houston at Cleveland	1:00
Minnesota at Seattle	1:00
New England at Buffalo	1:00
New Orleans at Washington	1:00
New York Jets at Indianapolis	4:00
Philadelphia at Atlanta	1:00
San Diego at Kansas City	12:00
Tampa Bay at San Francisco	1:00
Pittsburgh at Cincinnati	8:00

MONDAY, NOVEMBER 19
Los Angeles Raiders at Miami	9:00

TWELFTH WEEK

THURSDAY, NOVEMBER 22

Denver at Detroit	12:30
Washington at Dallas	3:00

SUNDAY, NOVEMBER 25

Atlanta at New Orleans	12:00
Chicago at Minnesota	12:00
Indianapolis at Cincinnati	1:00
Kansas City at Los Angeles Raiders	1:00
Los Angeles Rams at San Francisco	1:00
Miami at Cleveland	1:00
New England at Phoenix	2:00
New York Giants at Philadelphia	1:00
Pittsburgh at New York Jets	4:00
Tampa Bay vs. Green Bay at Milwaukee	12:00
Seattle at San Diego	5:00

MONDAY, NOVEMBER 26
Buffalo at Houston	8:00

THIRTEENTH WEEK

SUNDAY, DECEMBER 2

Atlanta at Tampa Bay	1:00
Cincinnati at Pittsburgh	1:00
Detroit at Chicago	12:00
Houston at Seattle	1:00
Indianapolis at Phoenix	2:00
Kansas City at New England	1:00
Los Angeles Raiders at Denver	2:00
Los Angeles Rams at Cleveland	1:00
Miami at Washington	1:00
New Orleans at Dallas	3:00
New York Jets at San Diego	1:00
Philadelphia at Buffalo	1:00
Green Bay at Minnesota	7:00

MONDAY, DECEMBER 3
New York Giants at San Francisco	6:00

FOURTEENTH WEEK

SUNDAY, DECEMBER 9

Buffalo at Indianapolis	1:00
Chicago at Washington	4:00
Cleveland at Houston	12:00
Denver at Kansas City	3:00
Minnesota at New York Giants	1:00
New Orleans at Los Angeles Rams	1:00
New England at Pittsburgh	1:00
Phoenix at Atlanta	1:00
San Francisco at Cincinnati	1:00
Seattle vs. Green Bay at Milwaukee	12:00
Philadelphia at Miami	8:00

MONDAY, DECEMBER 10
Los Angeles Raiders at Detroit	9:00

Open date: Dallas, New York Jets, San Diego, Tampa Bay

FIFTEENTH WEEK

SATURDAY, DECEMBER 15

Buffalo at New York Giants	12:30
Washington at New England	4:00

SUNDAY, DECEMBER 16

Atlanta at Cleveland	1:00
Cincinnati at Los Angeles Raiders	1:00
Green Bay at Philadelphia	1:00
Houston at Kansas City	12:00
Indianapolis at New York Jets	1:00
Minnesota at Tampa Bay	1:00
Phoenix at Dallas	12:00
Pittsburgh at New Orleans	12:00
San Diego at Denver	2:00
Seattle at Miami	1:00
Chicago at Detroit	8:00

MONDAY, DECEMBER 17
San Francisco at Los Angeles Rams	6:00

SIXTEENTH WEEK

SATURDAY, DECEMBER 22

Detroit at Green Bay	11:30
Los Angeles Raiders at Minnesota	3:00
Washington at Indianapolis	8:00

SUNDAY, DECEMBER 23

Cincinnati at Houston	12:00
Cleveland at Pittsburgh	1:00
Dallas at Philadelphia	1:00
Kansas City at San Diego	1:00
Miami at Buffalo	1:00
New England at New York Jets	1:00
New Orleans at San Francisco	1:00
New York Giants at Phoenix	2:00
Los Angeles Rams at Atlanta	1:00
Tampa Bay at Chicago	12:00
Denver at Seattle	5:00

SEVENTEENTH WEEK

SATURDAY, DECEMBER 29
Kansas City at Chicago 11:30
Philadelphia at Phoenix 2:00

SUNDAY, DECEMBER 30
Buffalo at Washington 1:00
Cleveland at Cincinnati 1:00
Dallas at Atlanta 1:00
Detroit at Seattle 1:00
Green Bay at Denver 2:00
Indianapolis at Miami 1:00
New York Giants at New England 1:00
New York Jets at Tampa Bay 4:00
San Diego at Los Angeles Raiders 1:00
San Francisco at Minnesota 12:00
Pittsburgh at Houston 7:00

MONDAY, DECEMBER 31
Los Angeles Rams at New Orleans 7:00

NFL PRESEASON GAMES

(All times local)

HALL OF FAME GAME

SATURDAY, AUGUST 4
Chicago vs. Cleveland at Canton, O. 12:00
Denver vs. Seattle at Tokyo 7:00

SUNDAY, AUGUST 5
L.A. Raiders vs. New Orleans at London 12:00

FIRST WEEK

THURSDAY, AUGUST 9
Detroit at Houston 7:00
New England vs. Pittsburgh at Montreal 7:30

SATURDAY, AUGUST 11
Atlanta vs. Washington at Chapel Hill, N.C. 7:30
Cincinnati at Tampa Bay 7:00
Cleveland at Green Bay 6:00
Dallas at San Diego 7:00
Denver at Indianapolis 7:30
Kansas City vs. L.A. Rams at Berlin 1:00
Los Angeles Raiders at San Francisco 6:00
Miami at Chicago 6:00
New Orleans at Minnesota 7:00
New York Jets at Philadelphia 7:30
Seattle at Phoenix 7:30

MONDAY, AUGUST 13
New York Giants at Buffalo 8:00

SECOND WEEK

FRIDAY, AUGUST 17
Buffalo at Detroit 7:30
Indianapolis at Seattle 7:30
Pittsburgh at Washington 8:00

SATURDAY, AUGUST 18
Chicago at Phoenix 7:30
Cincinnati at Atlanta 7:00
Dallas at Los Angeles Raiders 7:00
Miami at Philadelphia 7:30
New England vs. Tampa Bay at Jacksonville, Fla. 8:00
New Orleans vs. Green Bay at Madison, Wis. 1:00
New York Giants at Houston 7:00
New York Jets at Kansas City 7:00
San Diego at Los Angeles Rams 7:00

SUNDAY, AUGUST 19
Minnesota at Cleveland 8:00

MONDAY, AUGUST 20
San Francisco at Denver 6:00

THIRD WEEK

FRIDAY, AUGUST 24
Kansas City at Detroit 7:30
Los Angeles Raiders at Chicago 7:00
Tampa Bay at Seattle 6:00

SATURDAY, AUGUST 25
Atlanta vs. Green Bay at Milwaukee 6:00
Buffalo at New Orleans 7:00
Cincinnati at New England 7:00
Denver at Miami 8:00
New York Jets vs. New York Giants 8:00
Phoenix at Los Angeles Rams 7:00
Pittsburgh at Dallas 8:00
San Francisco at San Diego 7:00
Washington at Cleveland 7:00

SUNDAY, AUGUST 26
Houston at Minnesota 12:00

MONDAY, AUGUST 27
Philadelphia at Indianapolis 8:00

FOURTH WEEK

THURSDAY, AUGUST 30
Buffalo vs. Chicago at Columbia, S.C. 7:00
New York Jets at Tampa Bay 7:00

FRIDAY, AUGUST 31
Atlanta at New England 7:30
Detroit at Cincinnati 7:30
Green Bay at Kansas City 7:30
Indianapolis at New Orleans 7:00
Los Angeles Rams at Washington 7:00
Minnesota at Miami 8:00
Phoenix at Denver 7:00
Seattle at San Francisco 6:00

SATURDAY, SEPTEMBER 1
Cleveland at New York Giants 8:00
Houston at Dallas 8:00
Philadelphia at Pittsburgh 9:00
San Diego at Los Angeles Raiders 1:00

1990 NATIONALLY TELEVISED GAMES
REGULAR SEASON

Sunday,   Sept. 9—Denver at Los Angeles Raiders (day, NBC)
                      Philadelphia at New York Giants (night, TNT)
Monday,   Sept. 10—San Francisco at New Orleans (night, ABC)
Sunday,   Sept. 16—Washington at San Francisco (day, CBS)
                      Houston at Pittsburgh (night, TNT)
Monday,   Sept. 17—Kansas City at Denver (night, ABC)
Sunday,   Sept. 23—Philadelphia at Los Angeles Rams (day, CBS)
                      Detroit at Tampa Bay (night, TNT)
Monday,   Sept. 24—Buffalo at New York Jets (night, ABC)
Sunday,   Sept. 30—Cleveland at Kansas City (day, NBC)
                      Washington at Phoenix (night, TNT)
Monday,   Oct. 1—Cincinnati at Seattle (night, ABC)
Sunday,   Oct. 7—Cincinnati at Los Angeles Rams (day, NBC)
                      Los Angeles Raiders at Buffalo (night, TNT)
Monday,   Oct. 8—Cleveland at Denver (night, ABC)
Sunday,   Oct. 14—New York Giants at Washington (day, CBS)
                      Los Angeles Rams at Chicago (night, TNT)
Monday,   Oct. 15—Minnesota at Philadelphia (night, ABC)
Thursday, Oct. 18—New England at Miami (night, TNT)
Sunday,   Oct. 21—Pittsburgh at San Francisco (day, NBC)
Monday,   Oct. 22—Cincinnati at Cleveland (night, ABC)
Sunday,   Oct. 28—Washington at New York Giants (day, CBS)
                      Cincinnati at Atlanta (night, TNT)
Monday,   Oct. 29—Los Angeles Rams at Pittsburgh (night, ABC)
Sunday,   Nov. 4—Houston at Los Angeles Rams (day, NBC)
                      Denver at Minnesota (night, TNT)
Monday,   Nov. 5—New York Giants at Indianapolis (night, ABC)
Sunday,   Nov. 11—New York Giants at Los Angeles Rams (day, CBS)
                      San Francisco at Dallas (night, ESPN)
Monday,   Nov. 12—Washington at Philadelphia (night, ABC)
Sunday,   Nov. 18—Chicago at Denver (day, NBC)
                      Pittsburgh at Cincinnati (night, ESPN)
Monday,   Nov. 19—Los Angeles Raiders at Miami (night, ABC)
Thursday, Nov. 22—Denver at Detroit (day, NBC)
                      Washington at Dallas (night, CBS)
Sunday,   Nov. 25—Kansas City at Los Angeles Raiders (day, NBC)
                      Seattle at San Diego (night, ESPN)
Monday,   Nov. 26—Buffalo at Houston (night, ABC)
Sunday,   Dec. 2—Los Angeles Raiders at Denver (day, NBC)
                      Green Bay at Minnesota (night, ESPN)
Monday,   Dec. 3—New York Giants at San Francisco (night, ABC)
Sunday,   Dec. 9—New Orleans at Los Angeles Rams (day, CBS)
                      Philadelphia at Miami (night, ESPN)
Monday,   Dec. 10—Los Angeles Raiders at Detroit (night, ABC)
Saturday, Dec. 15—Buffalo at New York Giants (day, NBC)
                      Washington at New England (day, CBS)
Sunday,   Dec. 16—Cincinnati at Los Angeles Raiders (day, NBC)
                      Chicago at Detroit (night, ESPN)
Monday,   Dec. 17—San Francisco at Los Angeles Rams (night, ABC)
Saturday, Dec. 22—Detroit at Green Bay (day, CBS)
                      Los Angeles Raiders at Minnesota (day, NBC)
                      Washington at Indianapolis (night, ABC)
Sunday,   Dec. 23—New Orleans at San Francisco (day, CBS)
                      Denver at Seattle (night, ESPN)
Saturday, Dec. 29—Kansas City at Chicago (day, NBC)
                      Philadelphia at Phoenix (day, CBS)
Sunday,   Dec. 30—Green Bay at Denver (day, CBS)
                      Pittsburgh at Houston (night, ESPN)
Monday,   Dec. 31—Los Angeles Rams at New Orleans (night, ABC)

POSTSEASON

Saturday,   Jan. 5—AFC and NFC First Round Playoffs (ABC)
Sunday,   Jan. 6—AFC and NFC First Round Playoffs (NBC and CBS)
Saturday,   Jan. 12—AFC and NFC Second Round Playoffs (NBC and CBS)
Sunday,   Jan. 13—AFC and NFC Second Round Playoffs (NBC and CBS)
Sunday,   Jan. 20—AFC and NFC Championship Games (NBC and CBS)
Sunday,   Jan. 27—Super Bowl XXV at Tampa Stadium, Tampa, Florida (ABC)
Sunday,   Feb. 3—AFC-NFC Pro Bowl at Honolulu, Hawaii (ESPN)

1990 AFC-NFC INTERCONFERENCE GAMES

Sunday,	Sept. 9	Houston at Atlanta	4:00
		Minnesota at Kansas City	12:00
		San Diego at Dallas	3:00
		Seattle at Chicago	12:00
Sunday,	Sept. 23	Kansas City at Green Bay	12:00
		Miami at New York Giants	1:00
Sunday,	Sept. 30	Chicago at Los Angeles Raiders	1:00
		Indianapolis at Philadelphia	1:00
Sunday,	Oct. 7	Cincinnati at Los Angeles Rams	1:00
		San Francisco at Houston	12:00
Sunday,	Oct. 14	Cleveland at New Orleans	12:00
		Detroit at Kansas City	12:00
Sunday,	Oct. 21	New Orleans at Houston	12:00
		Pittsburgh at San Francisco	1:00
Sunday,	Oct. 28	Cleveland at San Francisco	1:00
		Tampa Bay at San Diego	1:00
		Cincinnati at Atlanta	8:00
Monday,	Oct. 29	Los Angeles Rams at Pittsburgh	9:00
Sunday,	Nov. 4	Atlanta at Pittsburgh	1:00
		Dallas at New York Jets	1:00
		Houston at Los Angeles Rams	1:00
		New England at Philadelphia	1:00
		New Orleans at Cincinnati	1:00
		Phoenix at Miami	1:00
		Denver at Minnesota	7:00
Monday,	Nov. 5	New York Giants at Indianapolis	9:00
Sunday,	Nov. 11	Green Bay at Los Angeles Raiders	1:00
		Phoenix at Buffalo	1:00
Sunday,	Nov. 18	Chicago at Denver	2:00
		Minnesota at Seattle	1:00
Thursday,	Nov. 22	Denver at Detroit	12:30
Sunday,	Nov. 25	New England at Phoenix	2:00
Sunday,	Dec. 2	Indianapolis at Phoenix	2:00
		Miami at Washington	1:00
		Los Angeles Rams at Cleveland	1:00
		Philadelphia at Buffalo	1:00
Sunday,	Dec. 9	San Francisco at Cincinnati	1:00
		Seattle vs. Green Bay at Milwaukee	12:00
		Philadelphia at Miami	8:00
Monday,	Dec. 10	Los Angeles Raiders at Detroit	9:00
Saturday,	Dec. 15	Buffalo at New York Giants	12:30
		Washington at New England	4:00
Sunday,	Dec. 16	Atlanta at Cleveland	1:00
		Pittsburgh at New Orleans	12:00
Saturday,	Dec. 22	Washington at Indianapolis	8:00
		Los Angeles Raiders at Minnesota	3:00
Saturday,	Dec. 29	Kansas City at Chicago	11:30
Sunday,	Dec. 30	Buffalo at Washington	1:00
		Detroit at Seattle	1:00
		Green Bay at Denver	2:00
		New York Giants at New England	1:00
		New York Jets at Tampa Bay	4:00

NFL POST-SEASON PLAN,
1990 TIE-BREAKING PROCEDURES

DIVISION TIES

Two Clubs

1. Head-to-head (best won-lost-tied percentage in games between the clubs).
2. Best won-lost-tied percentage in games played within the division.
3. Best won-lost-tied percentage in games played within the conference.
4. Best won-lost-tied percentage in common games, if applicable.
5. Best net points in division games.
6. Best net points in all games.
7. Strength of schedule.
8. Best net touchdowns in all games.
9. Coin toss.

Three or More Clubs

(Note: If two clubs remain tied after other clubs are eliminated during any step, tie-breaker reverts to step 1 of two-club format.)

1. Head-to-head (best won-lost-tied percentage in games among the clubs).
2. Best won-lost-tied percentage in games played within the division.
3. Best won-lost-tied percentage in games played within the conference.
4. Best won-lost-tied percentage in common games.
5. Best net points in division games.
6. Best net points in all games.
7. Strength of schedule.
8. Best net touchdowns in all games.
9. Coin toss.

WILD CARD TIES

If necessary to break ties to determine the two wild card clubs from each conference, the following steps will be taken:
1. If all the tied clubs are from the same division, apply division tie-breaker.
2. If the tied clubs are from different divisions, apply the following steps:

Two Clubs

1. Head-to-head, if applicable.
2. Best won-lost-tied percentage in games played within the conference.
3. Best won-lost-tied percentage in common games, minimum of four.
4. Best net points in conference games.
5. Best net points in all games.
6. Strength of schedule.
7. Best net touchdowns in all games.
8. Coin toss.

Three or More Clubs

(Note: If two clubs remain tied after other clubs are eliminated, tie-breaker reverts to step 1 of applicable two-club format.)

1. Head-to-head sweep (applicable only if one club has defeated each of the others or one club has lost to each of the others).
2. Best won-lost-tied percentage in games within the conference.
3. Best won-lost-tied percentage in common games, minimum of four.
4. Best net points in conference games.
5. Best net points in all games.
6. Strength of schedule.
7. Best net touchdowns in all games.
8. Coin toss.

PAID ATTENDANCE
NATIONAL FOOTBALL LEAGUE

	Regular Season		Average	*Post-Season	
1989	13,625,662	(224 games)	60,829	635,326	(9)
1988	13,539,848	(224 games)	60,446	608,204	(9)
1987‡	10,032,493	(168 games)	59,717	606,864	(9)
1986	13,588,551	(224 games)	60,663	683,901	(9)
1985	13,345,047	(224 games)	59,567	660,667	(9)
1984	13,398,112	(224 games)	59,813	614,809	(9)
1983	13,277,222	(224 games)	59,273	625,068	(9)
1982†	7,367,438	(126 games)	58,472	985,952	(15)
1981	13,606,990	(224 games)	60,745	587,361	(9)
1980	13,392,230	(224 games)	59,787	577,186	(9)
1979	13,182,039	(224 games)	58,848	582,266	(9)
1978	12,771,800	(224 games)	57,017	578,107	(9)
1977	11,018,632	(196 games)	56,218	483,588	(7)
1976	11,070,543	(196 games)	56,482	428,733	(7)
1975	10,213,193	(182 games)	56,116	443,811	(7)
1974	10,236,322	(182 games)	56,224	412,180	(7)
1973	10,730,933	(182 games)	58,961	458,515	(7)
1972	10,445,827	(182 games)	57,395	435,466	(7)
1971	10,076,035	(182 games)	55,368	430,244	(7)
1970	9,533,333	(182 games)	52,381	410,371	(7)
1969	6,096,127	(112 games)	54,430	242,841	(4)
1968	5,882,313	(112 games)	52,521	291,279	(4)
1967	5,938,924	(112 games)	53,026	241,754	(4)
1966	5,337,044	(105 games)	50,829	135,098	(2)
1965	4,634,021	(98 games)	47,296	100,304	(2)
1964	4,563,049	(98 games)	46,562	79,544	(1)
1963	4,163,643	(98 games)	42,486	45,801	(1)
1962	4,003,421	(98 games)	40,851	64,892	(1)
1961	3,986,159	(98 games)	40,675	39,029	(1)
1960	3,128,296	(78 games)	40,106	67,325	(1)
1959	3,140,000	(72 games)	43,617	57,545	(1)
1958	3,006,124	(72 games)	41,752	123,659	(2)
1957	2,836,318	(72 games)	39,393	119,579	(2)
1956	2,551,263	(72 games)	35,434	56,836	(1)
1955	2,521,836	(72 games)	35,026	85,693	(1)
1954	2,190,571	(72 games)	30,425	43,827	(1)
1953	2,164,585	(72 games)	30,064	54,577	(1)
1952	2,052,126	(72 games)	28,502	97,507	(2)
1951	1,913,019	(72 games)	26,570	57,522	(1)
1950	1,977,753	(78 games)	25,356	136,647	(3)
1949	1,391,735	(60 games)	23,196	27,980	(1)
1948	1,525,243	(60 games)	25,421	36,309	(1)
1947	1,837,437	(60 games)	30,624	66,268	(2)
1946	1,732,135	(55 games)	31,493	58,346	(1)
1945	1,270,401	(50 games)	25,408	32,178	(1)
1944	1,019,649	(50 games)	20,393	46,016	(1)
1943	969,128	(50 games)	19,383	71,315	(2)
1942	887,920	(55 games)	16,144	36,006	(1)
1941	1,108,615	(55 games)	20,157	55,870	(2)
1940	1,063,025	(55 games)	19,328	36,034	(1)
1939	1,071,200	(55 games)	19,476	32,279	(1)
1938	937,197	(55 games)	17,040	48,120	(1)
1937	963,039	(55 games)	17,510	15,878	(1)
1936	816,007	(54 games)	15,111	29,545	(1)
1935	638,178	(53 games)	12,041	15,000	(1)
1934	492,684	(60 games)	8,211	35,059	(1)

*Includes conference and league championship and AFL-NFL championship (Super Bowl) games; number of post-season games in parentheses. Pro Bowl not included.

†A 57-day players' strike reduced 224-game schedule to 126 games.

‡A 24-day players' strike reduced 224-game schedule to 168 non-strike games.

AMERICAN FOOTBALL LEAGUE

Season	Attendance	Teams-Games	Avg. per Game	AFL-NFL Championship	AFL Championship
1969***	2,843,373	10 teams—70 games	40,620	80,562	53,564
1968**	2,635,004	10 teams—70 games	37,643	75,377	62,627
1967	2,295,697	9 teams—63 games	36,439	75,546	53,330
1966	2,160,369	9 teams—63 games	34,291	61,946	42,080
1965	1,782,384	8 teams—56 games	31,828		30,361
1964	1,447,875	8 teams—56 games	25,855		40,242
1963*	1,241,741	8 teams—56 games	22,174		30,127
1962	1,147,302	8 teams—56 games	20,487		37,981
1961	1,002,657	8 teams—56 games	17,904		29,556
1960	926,156	8 teams—56 games	16,538		32,183

***Inter-divisional playoffs: Kansas City-New York, 61,832; Houston-Oakland, 51,692.

**Kansas City-Oakland playoff, 51,811.

*Boston-Buffalo playoff, 33,044.

1989 NFL PAID ATTENDANCE OF 17,399,538 IS HIGHEST IN LEAGUE HISTORY

National Football League paid attendance of 17,399,538 in 1989 was the highest total in the league's 70-year history, according to official figures. The previous all-games season record was 17,304,463 in 1986.

NFL teams played 293 games in 1989, including 59 in the preseason, 224 in the regular season, and 10 in the postseason. The 1989 total represents an increase of 375,112 over the 1988 total of 17,024,426.

The regular-season total paid attendance of 13,625,662 and average of 60,829 both were the highest ever, surpassing the previous records of 13,606,990 and 60,745 set in 1981.

A total of 3,088,105 tickets were sold for the 59 preseason games for an average of 52,341. The 10 postseason games produced the sale of 685,771 tickets, including 72,919 for Super Bowl XXIV.

The 1989 regular season included three weekend totals that are among the 10 highest in league history. The total of 915,401 tickets sold on October 29-30 is the second highest ever, surpassed only by the 934,211 sold on October 16-17, 1988. The 888,271 total on October 8-9, 1989, is the seventh highest ever, and the 888,264 total on September 17-18, 1989, is the eighth highest.

The Buffalo Bills led the NFL in home paid attendance during the 1989 regular season with a total of 626,399. Also exceeding the 600,000 total were Cleveland, 625,240; the New York Giants, 607,611; and the New York Jets, 603,520.

Six other teams topped the half-million total at home: Denver, 598,930, New Orleans, 533,609; Chicago, 528,225; Philadelphia, 525,485; San Francisco, 511,854; and Seattle, 508,960.

ACTUAL 1989 REGULAR-SEASON ATTENDANCE

(Unused tickets not included)

HOME GAMES		ROAD GAMES	
1. Buffalo	619,714	1. Denver	542,541
2. Cleveland	613,415	2. L.A. Raiders	529,285
3. N.Y. Giants	596,319	3. Chicago	511,661
4. Denver	588,144	4. Cincinnati	504,593
5. San Francisco	507,113	5. Minnesota	493,423
6. New Orleans	502,341	6. Dallas	490,586
7. Philadelphia	494,552	7. San Francisco	485,697
8. Chicago	488,976	8. Cleveland	483,024
9. Kansas City	486,055	9. Philadelphia	482,636
10. Seattle	481,233	10. N.Y. Jets	479,375
11. L.A. Rams	470,770	11. Miami	479,103
12. Indianapolis	467,346	12. Indianapolis	475,038
13. Minnesota	463,496	13. Seattle	466,073
14. Miami	453,872	14. Washington	458,692
15. Houston	448,617	15. N.Y. Giants	458,658
16. Green Bay	445,335	16. Kansas City	448,002
17. Cincinnati	440,876	17. L.A. Rams	446,609
18. Tampa Bay	439,685	18. Pittsburgh	440,992
19. N.Y. Jets	429,465	19. New England	439,883
20. Dallas	418,346	20. Houston	438,397
21. Washington	417,749	21. New Orleans	427,536
22. L.A. Raiders	396,962	22. Green Bay	427,109
23. Detroit	392,396	23. Atlanta	422,151
24. Pittsburgh	383,494	24. Tampa Bay	412,571
25. San Diego	376,434	25. San Diego	410,692
26. New England	375,779	26. Phoenix	408,935
27. Phoenix	345,198	27. Buffalo	405,396
28. Atlanta	319,851	28. Detroit	394,875
Total	12,863,533	Total	12,863,533

NATIONAL PROFESSIONAL FOOTBALL
HALL OF FAME

The Pro Football Hall of Fame in Canton, Ohio.

SEVEN NEW INDUCTEES IN 1990

Buck Buchanan, Bob Griese, Franco Harris, Ted Hendricks, Jack Lambert, Tom Landry and Bob St. Clair were inducted into Pro Football's Hall of Fame in 1990, expanding the list of former stars honored at Canton, Ohio, to 155.

Pro Football Hall of Fame

The National Professional Football Hall of Fame is located in Canton, Ohio, site of the organizational meeting in 1920 from which the National Football League grew.

The League recognized Canton as the Hall of Fame site on April 27, 1961, and ground was broken for the Hall on August 11, 1962. Dedication ceremonies were held September 7, 1963.

The National Board of Selectors, consisting of representatives from professional football cities, elected 17 charter members to the Hall. The selections were announced on January 29, 1963.

Subsequent selections were announced on February 28, 1964, January 19, 1965, March 23, 1966, February 8, 1967, February 19, 1968, February 6, 1969, February 2, 1970, February 4, 1971, February 8, 1972, February 6, 1973, February 5, 1974, January 20, 1975, January 26, 1976, January 17, 1977, January 23, 1978, January 30, 1979, January 26, 1980, January 31, 1981, January 28, 1982, February 5, 1983, January 28, 1984, January 22, 1985, January 27, 1986, January 27, 1987, February 2, 1988, January 24, 1989 and January 27, 1990.

ROSTER OF MEMBERS (155)

HERB ADDERLEY (Michigan State), 1980, cornerback, Green Bay Packers (1961-69), Dallas Cowboys (1970-72).

LANCE ALWORTH (Arkansas), 1978, wide receiver, San Diego Chargers (1962-70), Dallas Cowboys (1971-72).

DOUG ATKINS (Tennessee), 1982, defensive end, Cleveland Browns (1953-54), Chicago Bears (1955-66), New Orleans Saints (1967-69).

MORRIS (RED) BADGRO (Southern California), 1981, end, New York Yankees (1926), New York Giants (1930-35).

CLIFF BATTLES (West Virginia Wesleyan), 1968, halfback-quarterback, Boston Braves, Boston Redskins, Washington Redskins (1932-37); coach, Brooklyn Dodgers (1946-47).

SAMMY BAUGH (Texas Christian), Charter 1963, quarterback, Washington Redskins (1937-52); coach, New York Titans (1960-61); Houston Oilers (1964).

CHUCK BEDNARIK (Pennsylvania), 1967, center and linebacker, Philadelphia Eagles (1949-62).

BERT BELL (Pennsylvania), Charter 1963, NFL Commissioner (1946-59).

BOBBY BELL (Minnesota), 1983, linebacker, Kansas City Chiefs (1963-74).

RAYMOND BERRY (Southern Methodist), 1973, offensive end, Baltimore Colts (1955-67), coach, New England Patriots, (1984-89).

CHARLES W. BIDWILL (Loyola), 1967, owner, Chicago Cardinals (1933-47).

FRED BILETNIKOFF (Florida State), 1988, wide receiver, Oakland Raiders (1965-78).

GEORGE BLANDA (Kentucky), 1981, quarterback-placekicker, Chicago Bears (1949-58), Baltimore Colts (1950), Houston Oilers (1960-66), Oakland Raiders (1967-73).

MEL BLOUNT (Southern), 1989, cornerback, Pittsburgh Steelers (1970-83).

TERRY BRADSHAW (Louisiana Tech), 1989, quarterback, Pittsburgh Steelers (1970-83).

JIM BROWN (Syracuse), 1971, fullback, Cleveland Browns (1957-65).

PAUL BROWN (Miami, Ohio), 1967, coach, Cleveland Browns (1946-62), Cincinnati Bengals (1968-75).

ROOSEVELT BROWN (Morgan State), 1975, tackle, New York Giants (1953-66).

WILLIE BROWN (Grambling), 1984, defensive back, Denver Broncos (1963-66), Oakland Raiders (1967-78).

BUCK BUCHANAN (Grambling), 1990, defensive tackle, Kansas City Chiefs (1963-75).

DICK BUTKUS (Illinois), 1979, linebacker, Chicago Bears (1965-73).

TONY CANADEO (Gonzaga), 1974, halfback, Green Bay Packers (1941-44, 1946-52).

JOE CARR, Charter 1963, NFL President (1921-39).

Former Miami quarterback Bob Griese (left) and Kansas City defensive tackle Buck Buchanan began their careers in the American Football League and are among the newest inductees in the Pro Football Hall of Fame.

GUY CHAMBERLIN (Nebraska), 1965, player-coach, Canton Bulldogs, Cleveland, Frankford Yellowjackets, Chicago Bears, and Chicago Cardinals (1919-28).

JACK CHRISTIANSEN (Colorado A&M), 1970, defensive back, Detroit Lions (1951-58); coach, San Francisco 49ers (1963-67).

DUTCH CLARK (Colorado College), Charter 1963, quarterback, Portsmouth Spartans and Detroit Lions (1931-38).

GEORGE CONNOR (Notre Dame), 1975, tackle and linebacker, Chicago Bears (1948-55).

JIMMY CONZELMAN (Washington, Mo.), 1964, halfback, coach, executive, Decatur, Rock Island, Milwaukee, Detroit, Providence, Chicago Cardinals (1920-48).

LARRY CSONKA (Syracuse), 1987, running back, Miami Dolphins (1968-74, 79), New York Giants (1976-78).

WILLIE DAVIS (Grambling), 1981, defensive end, Cleveland Browns (1958-59), Green Bay Packers (1960-69).

LEN DAWSON (Purdue), 1987, quarterback, Pittsburgh Steelers (1957-58), Cleveland Browns (1960-61), Dallas Texans (1962), Kansas City Chiefs (1963-75).

MIKE DITKA (Pittsburgh), 1988, tight end, Chicago Bears (1961-66), Philadelphia Eagles (1967-68), Dallas Cowboys (1969-72), coach, Chicago Bears (1982-present).

ART DONOVAN (Boston College), 1968, defensive tackle, Baltimore Colts, New York Yanks, Dallas Texans, Baltimore Colts (1950-61).

PADDY DRISCOLL (Northwestern), 1965, player-coach, Chicago Cardinals and Chicago Bears (1919-31, 1941-68).

BILL DUDLEY (Virginia), 1966, halfback, Pittsburgh Steelers, Detroit Lions and Washington Redskins (1942-53).

TURK EDWARDS (Washington State), 1969, tackle, Boston Braves, Boston Redskins, Washington Redskins (1932-40).

WEEB EWBANK (Miami, O.), 1978, coach, Baltimore Colts (1954-1962) and New York Jets (1963-1973).

TOM FEARS (Santa Clara, UCLA), 1970, end, Los Angeles Rams (1948-56), coach, New Orleans Saints (1967-70).

RAY FLAHERTY (Gonzaga), 1976, player-coach, Los Angeles Wildcats, New York Yankees (AFL), New York Giants, Boston Redskins, Washington Redskins, New York Yankees (AAFC), Chicago Hornets (1926-1949).

LEN FORD (Michigan), 1976, end, Los Angeles Dons and Cleveland Browns (1948-1958).

DANNY FORTMANN (Colgate), 1965, guard, Chicago Bears (1936-43).

FRANK GATSKI (Marshall), 1985, center, Cleveland Browns (1946-56), Detroit Lions (1957).

BILL GEORGE (Wake Forest), 1974, linebacker, Chicago Bears, and Los Angeles Rams (1952-66).

FRANK GIFFORD (Southern California), 1977, halfback and end, New York Giants (1952-60 and 1962-64).

SID GILLMAN (Ohio State), 1983, end, Cleveland Rams (1936); coach, Los Angeles Rams (1955-59), Los Angeles Chargers (1960), San Diego Chargers (1961-69, 71), Houston Oilers (1973-74).

OTTO GRAHAM (Northwestern), 1965, quarterback, Cleveland Browns (1946-55), coach, Washington Redskins (1966-68).

RED GRANGE (Illinois), Charter 1963, halfback, Chicago Bears (1925, 1929-34), New York Yankees (1926-27).

JOE GREENE (North Texas State), 1987, defensive tackle, Pittsburgh Steelers (1969-81).

FORREST GREGG (Southern Methodist), 1977, tackle, Green Bay Packers and Dallas Cowboys (1956; 1958-71); coach, Cleveland Browns (1975-77), Cincinnati Bengals (1980-83) and Green Bay Packers (1984-87).

BOB GRIESE (Purdue), 1990, quarterback, Miami Dolphins (1967-80).

LOU GROZA (Ohio State), 1974, offensive tackle and placekicker, Cleveland Browns (1946-59, 1961-67).

JOE GUYON (Carlisle, Georgia Tech), 1966, halfback, Canton Bulldogs, Cleveland Indians, Oorang Indians, Rock Island Independents, Kansas City Cowboys and New York Giants (1918-27).

GEORGE HALAS (Illinois), Charter 1963, player, coach, founder, Chicago Bears (1920-83).

JACK HAM (Penn State), 1988, linebacker, Pittsburgh Steelers (1971-82).

FRANCO HARRIS (Penn State), 1990, running back, Pittsburgh Steelers (1972-83), Seattle Seahawks (1984).

ED HEALEY (Dartmouth), 1964, tackle, Rock Island and Chicago Bears (1920-27).

MEL HEIN (Washington State), Charter 1963, center, New York Giants (1931-45).

TED HENDRICKS (Miami, Fla.), 1990, linebacker, Baltimore Colts (1969-73), Green Bay Packers (1974), Oakland-Los Angeles Raiders (1975-83).

WILBUR HENRY (Washington & Jefferson), Charter 1963, tackle, Canton Bulldogs, Akron Indians, New York Giants, Pottsville Maroons, Pittsburgh Steelers (1920-30).

ARNIE HERBER (Regis), 1966, halfback, Green Bay Packers and New York Giants (1930-45).

BILL HEWITT (Michigan), 1971, end, Chicago Bears (1932-36), Philadelphia Eagles (1937-39), Philadelphia-Pittsburgh (1943).

CLARKE HINKLE (Bucknell), 1964, fullback, Green Bay Packers (1932-41).

ELROY (CRAZYLEGS) HIRSCH (Wisconsin), 1968, end-halfback, Chicago Rockets, Los Angeles Rams (1946-57).

PAUL HORNUNG (Notre Dame), 1986, running back, Green Bay Packers (1957-62, 64-66).

KEN HOUSTON (Prairie View), 1986, defensive back, Houston Oilers (1967-72), Washington Redskins (1973-80).

CAL HUBBARD (Centenary, Geneva), Charter 1963, tackle and end, New York Giants, Green Bay Packers and Pittsburgh Steelers (1927-36).

SAM HUFF (West Virginia), 1982, linebacker, New York Giants (1956-63), Washington Redskins (1964-67, 69).

Former Pittsburgh Steeler great Franco Harris rushed for 12,120 yards in 13 seasons and played on four Super Bowl championship teams.

LAMAR HUNT (Southern Methodist), 1972, founder, American Football League, 1959; president, Dallas Texans (1960-62), Kansas City Chiefs (1963-present).

DON HUTSON (Alabama), Charter 1963, end, Green Bay Packers (1935-45).

JOHN HENRY JOHNSON (Arizona State), 1987, fullback, San Francisco 49ers (1954-56), Detroit Lions (1957-59), Pittsburgh Steelers (1960-65), Houston Oilers (1966).

DEACON JONES (South Carolina State), 1980, defensive end, Los Angeles Rams (1961-71), San Diego Chargers (1972-73), Washington Redskins (1974).

SONNY JURGENSEN (Duke), 1983, quarterback, Philadelphia Eagles (1957-63), Washington Redskins (1964-74).

WALTER KIESLING (St. Thomas), 1966, player-coach, Duluth Eskimos, Pottsville Maroons, Boston Braves, Chicago Cardinals, Chicago Bears, Green Bay Packers and Pittsburgh Steelers (1926-56).

FRANK (BRUISER) KINARD (Mississippi), 1971, tackle, Brooklyn Dodgers (1938-45) New York Yankees (1946-47).

CURLY LAMBEAU (Notre Dame), Charter 1963, founder, player, coach, Green Bay Packers (1919-49).

JACK LAMBERT (Kent State), 1990, linebacker, Pittsburgh Steelers (1974-84).

TOM LANDRY (Texas), 1990, coach, Dallas Cowboys (1960-88).

DICK (NIGHT TRAIN) LANE (Scottsbluff JC), 1974, defensive back, Los Angeles Rams, Chicago Cardinals, Detroit Lions (1952-65).

JIM LANGER (South Dakota State), 1987, center, Miami Dolphins (1970-79), Minnesota Vikings (1980-81).

WILLIE LANIER (Morgan State), 1986, linebacker, Kansas City Chiefs (1967-77).

YALE LARY (Texas A & M), 1979, defensive back, Detroit Lions (1952-53, 1956-64).

DANTE LAVELLI (Ohio State), 1975, end, Cleveland Browns (1946-56).

BOBBY LAYNE (Texas), 1967, quarterback, Chicago Bears, New York Bulldogs, Detroit Lions, Pittsburgh Steelers (1948-62).

TUFFY LEEMANS (George Washington), 1978, fullback, New York Giants (1936-1943).

BOB LILLY (Texas Christian), 1980, defensive tackle, Dallas Cowboys (1961-1974).

VINCE LOMBARDI (Fordham), 1971, coach, Green Bay Packers (1959-67), Washington Redskins (1969).

SID LUCKMAN (Columbia), 1965, quarterback, Chicago Bears (1939-50).

ROY (LINK) LYMAN, 1964, tackle, Canton Bulldogs, Cleveland, Chicago Bears (1922-34).

TIM MARA, Charter 1963, founder, New York Giants (1925-65).

GINO MARCHETTI (San Francisco), 1972, defensive end, Dallas Texans (1952), Baltimore Colts (1953-66).

GEORGE PRESTON MARSHALL, Charter 1963, founder, Washington Redskins (1932-1965).

OLLIE MATSON (San Francisco), 1972, halfback, Chicago Cardinals (1952, 1954-58), Los Angeles Rams (1959-62), Detroit Lions (1963), Philadelphia Eagles (1964-66).

DON MAYNARD (Texas Western College), 1987, wide receiver, New York Giants (1958), New York Jets (1960-72), St. Louis Cardinals (1973).

GEORGE McAFEE (Duke), 1966, halfback, Chicago Bears (1940-41, 1945-50).

MIKE McCORMACK (Kansas), 1984, tackle, New York Yanks (1951), Cleveland Browns (1954-62).

HUGH McELHENNY (Washington), 1970, halfback, San Francisco 49ers, Minnesota Vikings, New York Giants and Detroit Lions (1952-64).

JOHNNY BLOOD (McNALLY) (St. John's, Minn.), Charter 1963, halfback, Milwaukee Badgers, Duluth Eskimos, Pottsville Maroons, Green Bay Packers, Pittsburgh Steelers (1925-39).

AUGUST (MIKE) MICHALSKE (Penn State), 1964, guard, New York Yankees and Green Bay Packers (1927-37).

WAYNE MILLNER (Notre Dame), 1968, end, Boston Redskins, Washington Redskins (1936-41, 1945).

BOBBY MITCHELL (Illinois), 1983, running back and receiver, Cleveland Browns (1958-61), Washington Redskins (1962-68).

RON MIX (Southern California), 1979, offensive tackle, Los Angeles Chargers (1960), San Diego Chargers (1961-69), Oakland Raiders (1971).

LENNY MOORE (Penn State), 1975, halfback, Baltimore Colts (1956-67).

MARION MOTLEY (Nevada), 1968, fullback-linebacker, Cleveland Browns, Pittsburgh Steelers (1946-1955).

GEORGE MUSSO (Millikin), 1982, offensive guard and defensive tackle, Chicago Bears (1933-44).

BRONKO NAGURSKI (Minnesota), Charter 1963, fullback and tackle, Chicago Bears (1930-37, 1943).

JOE NAMATH (Alabama), 1985, quarterback, New York Jets (1965-76), Los Angeles Rams (1977).

EARLE (GREASY) NEALE (West Virginia Wesleyan), 1969, coach, Philadelphia Eagles (1941-50).

ERNIE NEVERS (Stanford), Charter 1963, fullback, Duluth Eskimos and Chicago Cardinals (1926-37).

RAY NITSCHKE (Illinois), 1978, linebacker, Green Bay Packers (1958-72).

LEO NOMELLINI (Minnesota), 1969, defensive tackle, San Francisco 49ers (1953-63).

MERLIN OLSEN (Utah State), 1982, defensive tackle, Los Angeles Rams (1962-76).

JIM OTTO (Miami, Fla.), 1980, center, Oakland Raiders (1960-1974).

STEVE OWEN (Phillips), 1966, player-coach, Kansas City Cowboys and New York Giants (1924-53).

ALAN PAGE (Notre Dame), 1988, defensive tackle, Minnesota Vikings (1967-78), Chicago Bears (1978-81).

CLARENCE (ACE) PARKER (Duke), 1972, halfback, Brooklyn Dodgers (1937-41), Boston Yanks (1945), New York Yankees (1946).

JIM PARKER (Ohio State), 1973, guard, Baltimore Colts (1957-67).

JOE PERRY (Compton JC), 1969, fullback, San Francisco 49ers, Baltimore Colts (1948-63).

Linebackers Jack Lambert (left) and Ted Hendricks terrorized opposing offenses during the 1970s and will be inducted into the Hall of Fame in 1990.

PETE PIHOS (Indiana), 1970, end, Philadelphia Eagles (1947-55).

HUGH (SHORTY) RAY (Illinois), 1966, NFL technical adviser and supervisor of officials (1938-56).

DANIEL F. REEVES (Georgetown), 1967, founder, Los Angeles Rams (1941-71).

JIM RINGO (Syracuse), 1981, center, Green Bay Packers (1953-63), Philadelphia Eagles (1964-67).

ANDY ROBUSTELLI (Arnold), 1971, defensive end, Los Angeles Rams (1951-55), New York Giants (1956-64).

ARTHUR J. ROONEY (Georgetown), 1964, founder, Pittsburgh Steelers (1933-82).

PETE ROZELLE (San Francisco), 1985, NFL Commissioner (1960-89).

BOB ST. CLAIR (Tulsa), 1990, tackle, San Francisco 49ers (1953-63).

GALE SAYERS (Kansas), 1977, running back, Chicago Bears (1965-71).

JOE SCHMIDT (Pittsburgh), 1973, linebacker, Detroit Lions (1953-65); coach, Detroit Lions (1967-72).

ART SHELL (Maryland-Eastern Shore), 1989, tackle, Oakland-Los Angeles Raiders (1968-82), coach, Los Angeles Raiders (1989-present).

O.J. SIMPSON (Southern California), 1985, running back, Buffalo Bills (1969-77), San Francisco 49ers (1978).

BART STARR (Alabama), 1977, quarterback, Green Bay Packers (1956-71); coach, Green Bay Packers (1975-83).

ROGER STAUBACH (Navy), 1985, quarterback, Dallas Cowboys (1969-79).

ERNIE STAUTNER (West Virginia), 1969, defensive tackle, Pittsburgh Steelers (1950-63).

KEN STRONG (New York U.), 1967, halfback-placekicker, Staten Island Stapletons, New York Yankees and New York Giants (1929-39, 1944-47).

JOE STYDAHAR (West Virginia), 1967, tackle, Chicago Bears (1936-42, 1945-46).

FRAN TARKENTON (Georgia), 1986, quarterback, Minnesota Vikings (1961-66, 72-78), New York Giants (1967-71).

CHARLEY TAYLOR (Arizona State), 1984, wide receiver, Washington Redskins (1964-75, 77).

JIM TAYLOR (Louisiana State), 1976, fullback, Green Bay Packers (1958-1966), New Orleans Saints (1967).

Tom Landry (left) won 271 games and two Super Bowls in 29 years as coach of the Dallas Cowboys while Bob St. Clair was a standout offensive tackle with the San Francisco 49ers from 1953-63.

JIM THORPE (Carlisle), Charter 1963, halfback, Canton Bulldogs, Oorang Indians, Cleveland Indians, Toledo Maroons, Rock Island Independents, New York Giants (1915-26, 1929).

Y.A. TITTLE (Louisiana State), 1971, quarterback, Baltimore Colts (1948-50), San Francisco 49ers (1951-60), New York Giants (1961-64).

GEORGE TRAFTON (Notre Dame), 1964, center, Chicago Bears (1920-32).

CHARLIE TRIPPI (Georgia), 1968, halfback, Chicago Cardinals (1947-55).

EMLEN TUNNELL (Iowa), 1967, defensive back, New York Giants and Green Bay Packers (1948-61).

CLYDE (BULLDOG) TURNER (Hardin-Simmons), 1966, center-linebacker, Chicago Bears (1940-52); coach, New York Titans (1962).

JOHN UNITAS (Louisville), 1979, quarterback, Baltimore Colts (1956-72), San Diego Chargers (1973).

GENE UPSHAW (Texas A&I), 1987, guard, Oakland Raiders (1967-81).

NORM VAN BROCKLIN (Oregon), 1971, quarterback, Los Angeles Rams (1949-57), Philadelphia Eagles (1958-60), coach, Minnesota Vikings (1961-66), Atlanta Falcons (1968-74).

STEVE VAN BUREN (Louisiana State), 1965, halfback, Philadelphia Eagles (1944-51).

DOAK WALKER (Southern Methodist), 1986, running back, Detroit Lions (1950-55).

PAUL WARFIELD (Ohio State), 1983, receiver, Cleveland Browns (1964-69, 76-77), Miami Dolphins (1970-74).

BOB WATERFIELD (UCLA), 1965, quarterback, Cleveland Rams and Los Angeles Rams (1945-52); coach, Los Angeles Rams (1960-62).

ARNIE WEINMEISTER (Washington), 1984, tackle, New York Yankees (1948-49), New York Giants (1950-53).

BILL WILLIS (Ohio State), 1977, guard, Cleveland Browns (1946-53).

LARRY WILSON (Utah), 1978, defensive back, St. Louis Cardinals (1960-72).

ALEX WOJCIECHOWICZ (Fordham), 1968, center-linebacker Detroit Lions, Philadelphia Eagles (1938-50).

WILLIE WOOD (Southern California), 1989, safety, Green Bay Packers (1960-71).

1990 ROSTER OF OFFICIALS

Art McNally, Director of Officiating
Jack Reader, Assistant Supervisor of Officials
Tony Veteri, Assistant Supervisor of Officials

REFEREES

No.	Name	College	Yrs.
14	Gene Barth	St. Louis	20
43	Red Cashion	Texas A & M	19
6	Tom Dooley	Virginia Military	13
23	Johnny Grier	D.C. Teachers	10
40	Pat Haggerty	Colorado State	26
104	Dale Hamer	California St., Pa.	13
105	Dick Hantack	Southeast Missouri	13
60	Dick Jorgensen	Wisconsin	23
9	Jerry Markbreit	Illinois	15
48	Gordon McCarter	Western Reserve	24
95	Bob McElwee	Navy	15
33	Howard Roe	Wichita State	7
70	Jerry Seeman	Winona State	16
32	Jim Tunney	Occidental	31
123	Tom White	Temple	2

LINE JUDGES

No.	Name	College	Yrs.
25	John Alderton	Portland State	2
116	Bob Baker	East Texas St.	4
55	Tom Barnes	Minnesota	5
56	Ron Baynes	Auburn	4
59	Bob Beeks	Lincoln	23
83	Ron Blum	Marin	6
65	Walt Coleman	Arkansas	2
74	Ray Dodez	Wooster	23
12	Ben Dreith	Colorado State	31
15	Bama Glass	Colorado	12
112	Joe Haynes	Alcorn State	7
54	Jack Johnson	Pacific Lutheran	15
41	Dick McKenzie	Ashland	13
51	Dale Orem	Louisville	11
5	Jim Quirk	Delaware	3
53	Bill Reynolds	West Chester State	16
11	Fred Wyant	West Virginia	25

UMPIRES

No.	Name	College	Yrs.
115	Hendi Ancich	Harbor College	9
110	Ron Botchan	Occidental	11
101	Bob Boylston	Alabama	13
27	Al Conway	Army	22
71	Ed Coukart	Northwestern	2
78	Art Demmas	Vanderbilt	23
57	Ed Fiffick	Marquette	12
50	Neil Gereb	California	10
42	Dave Hamilton	Utah	16
67	John Keck	Cornell	19
117	Ben Montgomery	Morehouse	9
30	Dennis Riggs	Bellarmine	3
103	Rex Stuart	Appalachian St.	7
100	Bob Wagner	Penn State	6
89	Gordon Wells	Occidental	19

BACK JUDGES

No.	Name	College	Yrs.
22	Paul Baetz	Heidelberg	13
24	Roy Clymer	New Mexico State	11
75	Jim Daopoulos	Kentucky	2
85	Ed Hochuli	Texas-El Paso	1
106	Al Jury	S. Bernardino Valley	13
107	Jim Kearney	Pennsylvania	13
98	Bill Lovett	Maryland	1
38	Bruce Maurer	Ohio State	4
80	Tim Millis	Millsaps	2
36	Bob Moore	Dayton	7
92	Jim Poole	San Diego State	16
68	Louis Richard	Southwestern La.	5
118	Tom Sifferman	Seattle	5
52	Ben Tompkins	Texas	20
4	Doug Toole	Stanford	3
99	Banks Williams	Houston	13

HEAD LINESMEN

No.	Name	College	Yrs.
81	Dave Anderson	Salem College	7
26	Mark Baltz	Ohio	2
17	Jerry Bergman	Duquesne	25
111	Earnie Frantz	None	10
72	Terry Gierke	Portland State	10
114	Tom Johnson	Miami-Ohio	9
35	Leo Miles	Virginia State	22
10	Ron Phares	Virginia Polytechnic	6
79	Aaron Pointer	Pacific Lutheran	4
121	Sanford Rivers	Youngstown State	2
21	John Schleyer	Millersville	1
109	Sid Semon	Southern California	13
87	Paul Weidner	Cincinnati	5
8	Dale Williams	California State	11

SIDE JUDGES

No.	Name	College	Yrs.
34	Gerald Austin	Western Carolina	9
94	Mike Carey	Santa Clara	1
39	Don Carlsen	Cal State-Chico	2
63	Bill Carollo	Wisconsin	2
61	Dick Creed	Louisville	13
102	Merrill Douglas	Utah	10
47	Tom Fincken	Kansas State	7
97	Nate Jones	Lewis and Clark	14
108	Stan Kemp	Michigan	5
120	Gary Lane	Missouri	9
49	Dean Look	Michigan State	18
20	Larry Nemmers	Upper Iowa	6
29	Howard Slavin	Southern California	4
119	Ron Spitler	Panhandle State	9
28	Don Wedge	Ohio Wesleyan	19

FIELD JUDGES

No.	Name	College	Yrs.
31	Dick Dolack	Ferris State	25
113	Don Dorkowski	Cal St.-Los Angeles	5
96	Don Hakes	Bradley	14
44	Donnie Hampton	Georgia	3
86	Bernie Kukar	St. John's	7
18	Bob Lewis	None	15
82	Pat Mallette	Nebraska	22
76	Ed Merrifield	Missouri	16
77	Don Orr	Vanderbilt	20
46	John Robison	Utah	3
122	Bill Schmitz	Colorado State	2
73	Bob Skelton	Alabama	6
91	Bill Stanley	Redlands	17
93	Jack Vaughn	Mississippi State	15
84	Bob Wortman	Findlay	25